KU-444-098

RELIGION AND THE DECLINE OF MAGIC

Keith Thomas is President of Corpus Christi College, Oxford, and was formerly Professor of Modern History and Fellow of St John's College. He has written extensively on the social and intellectual history of the early modern period. He is the general editor of the Past Masters series (Oxford University Press) and a Fellow of the British Academy. *Religion and the Decline of Magic*, his first book, won one of the two Wolfson Literary Awards for History in 1972. His most recent book is *Man and the Natural World: Changing Attitudes in England 1500–1800*, which is also published in Penguin.

RELIGION AND
THE DECLINE OF MAGIC

STUDIES IN POPULAR BELIEFS IN SIXTEENTH-
AND SEVENTEENTH-CENTURY ENGLAND

KEITH THOMAS

PENGUIN BOOKS

PENGUIN BOOKS

Published by the Penguin Group
27 Wrights Lane, London W8 5TZ, England
Viking Penguin Inc., 40 West 23rd Street, New York, New York 10010, USA
Penguin Books Australia Ltd, Ringwood, Victoria, Australia
Penguin Books Canada Ltd, 2801 John Street, Markham, Ontario, Canada L3R 1B4
Penguin Books (NZ) Ltd, 182–190 Wairau Road, Auckland 10, New Zealand

Penguin Books Ltd, Registered Offices: Harmondsworth, Middlesex, England

First published by Weidenfeld & Nicolson 1971
Published in Penguin University Books 1973
Reissued in Peregrine Books 1978
7 9 10 8

Printed and bound in Great Britain by
Cox & Wyman Ltd, Reading
Set in Monotype Times Roman

To my parents

CONTENTS

FOREWORD

THIS book began as an attempt to make sense of some of the systems of belief which were current in sixteenth- and seventeenth-century England, but which no longer enjoy much recognition today. Astrology, witchcraft, magical healing, divination, ancient prophecies, ghosts and fairies, are now all rightly disdained by intelligent persons. But they were taken seriously by equally intelligent persons in the past, and it is the historian's business to explain why this was so. I have tried to show their importance in the lives of our ancestors and the practical utility which they often possessed. In this task I have been much helped by the studies made by modern social anthropologists of similar beliefs held in Africa and elsewhere.

As my work progressed, I became conscious of the close relationship which many of these beliefs bore to the religious ideas of the period. In offering an explanation for misfortune, and a means of redress at times of adversity, they seemed to be discharging a role very close to that of the established Church and its rivals. Sometimes they were parasitic upon Christian teaching; sometimes they were in sharp rivalry to it. I therefore widened my scope, so as to make room for a fuller consideration of this aspect of contemporary religion. By juxtaposing it to the other, less esteemed, systems of belief, I hope to have thrown more light on both, and to have contributed to our knowledge of the mental climate of early modern England. I have also tried to explore the relationship between this climate and the material environment more generally.

The result, inevitably, is a very long book. Even so, I am well aware of the compressions and over-simplifications which have resulted from handling so many different topics over so long a period of time. But I am anxious to bring out the interrelated nature of these various beliefs and can only do this by treating them together. The book is arranged so that the reader who wishes to skip some of the sections can easily do so, but the whole is meant to be more than the sum of its parts. I also wish to emphasize the essential unity of the period between the Reformation and the dawn of the Enlightenment. This is why the book begins with the collapse of the medieval Church in the early sixteenth century and ends with the change in the intellectual atmosphere which is so striking in the years approaching 1700. The sources also indicate a halt at the end of the seventeeenth century, since the records of both lay and church courts cease around that time to be so informative on the matters with which I am concerned.

Few of the topics under consideration are peculiarly English; indeed most of them form part of the general cultural history of the Western world. But this survey has been strictly limited to England (with occasional excursions into Wales) and I have resisted the temptation to draw parallels with Scotland, Ireland, and the continent of Europe. An exercise in comparative history, however desirable, is not possible until the data for each country have been properly assembled. As it is, I have only skimmed the surface of the English material and have blurred some important regional distinctions.

I particularly regret not having been able to offer more of those exact statistical data upon which the precise analysis of historical change must so often depend. Unfortunately, the sources seldom permit such computation, although it is to be hoped that the information contained in the largely unpublished judicial records of the time will one day be systematically quantified. My visits to these widely scattered archives have been less frequent and less systematic than I should have liked. In my attempt to sketch the main outlines of the subject I have only too often had to fall back upon the historian's traditional method of presentation by example and counter-example. Although this technique has some advantages, the computer has made it the intellectual equivalent of the bow and arrow in a nuclear age. But one cannot use the computer unless one has suitable material with which to supply it, and at present there seems to be no genuinely scientific method of measuring changes in the thinking of past generations. As a result, there are many points in my argument at which the reader can be given no statistical evidence on which to accept or reject the impressions I have formed after my reading in contemporary sources. But I have been pleased to see that, so far as the subject of witchcraft is concerned, my impressions have been abundantly confirmed by the statistical findings of Dr Alan Macfarlane, whose systematic study of witchcraft prosecutions in Essex, one of the counties for which the evidence permits such an operation, has now been published.* My main aim has been to draw attention to a large and relatively neglected area of the past. I shall be well satisfied if future historians succeed in replacing my tentative generalizations by a more adequate version of the truth.

Foreword to the Penguin Edition

For this edition I have corrected some errors, pruned a few extravagances and added a handful of additional references to the footnotes, mainly to take account of recent publications. I am most grateful to friends, correspondents and reviewers for their suggestions.

1 June 1972   K.T.

*Alan Macfarlane, *Witchcraft in Tudor and Stuart England* (1970).

ACKNOWLEDGEMENTS

So many people have supplied me with ideas or information that I cannot hope to list them all here. I have tried to acknowledge specific obligations in the notes and I offer apologies for any which have been unintentionally omitted. My greatest intellectual debts are to my former tutors at Balliol College and to my past and present pupils at St John's. I am particularly grateful to Dr Christopher Hill, who kindled my interest in the seventeenth century and did so much to guide my early ventures into it. I must also thank those of my friends, notably Mr Richard Grassby, Dr Brian Harrison and Dr John Walsh, who have for years sent me stray references to subjects which they thought would interest me. Many stimulating conversations with Dr Alan Macfarlane have helped me to clarify my own ideas. Parts of this book have been read as papers and lectures in this country and abroad, and I have tried to benefit from the resulting criticisms.

The chapters on witchcraft and popular magic include most of the material (and much of the wording) of my two BBC talks on 'Witches' and 'Wizards' (reprinted in the *Listener*, 5 and 12 March 1970), and of my paper to the Association of Social Anthropologists on 'The Relevance of Social Anthropology to the Historical Study of English Witchcraft' (in *Witchcraft Confessions and Accusations*, ed. M. Douglas, ASA Monograph 9, Tavistock Press, 1970). Of those who gave me references and pieces of information I am especially indebted to Dr Philip Tyler, who provided some valuable information relating to the diocese of York; Miss Elizabeth Allen, who gave me some references to the Peterborough diocesan archives; and Mr F. C. Morgan, who both made it possible for me to work in Hereford Cathedral Library and also let me borrow and quote from his transcripts of the Hereford City Records. For permission to quote from their unpublished theses I am grateful to Dr J. Addy, Dr M. Bindoff, Dr Macfarlane, Lady Neale, Dr J. A. F. Thomson and Dr R. B. Walker. I also wish to thank Dr B. S. Capp, Dr R. A. Houlbrooke, Mr J. A. Sharpe and Mr P. A. Slack.

I have received much help from the many archivists and librarians who have enabled me to consult documents in their custody or provided me with photocopies. I must thank those in charge of the County Record Offices of Cheshire, Cornwall, Devon, Dorset, Essex, Glamorgan, Hampshire, Hertfordshire, Ipswich and East Suffolk, Kent, Lancashire, London, Middlesex, Norfolk, Northamptonshire, Somerset and Yorkshire (East Riding). I am also grateful to the City Librarians of Birmingham, Gloucester and Sheffield, the Archivist at the Leicester City Museum, the custodians of the borough archives of Bridport and Lyme Regis, and the staffs of Lambeth Palace Library, Dr Williams's Library, Reading University Library, the Oxford Museum of the History of Science, the Guildhall Library, the British Museum and the Public Record Office. I am particularly indebted to Mrs N. K. Gurney of the Borthwick Institute of Historical Research, Mrs D. M. Owen of the Cambridge University Library, Mr H. L. Douch of the Royal Institution of Cornwall and Mr E. H. Milligan, Librarian at Friends House. Documents quoted from the Public Record Office are Crown Copyright.

In Oxford my work has been greatly eased by Mr Charles Morgenstern of St John's College Library, Mr G. Webb of the Codrington Library, and the endlessly helpful and tolerant staff of the Bodleian, for whose many kindnesses I am deeply grateful. My college has been generous with leave and with help towards the cost of typing the manuscript. My wife has helped me most of all.

St John's College, Oxford   K.T.
1 July 1970

NOTES ON REFERENCES

THE notes are so numerous that I have dispensed with a formal bibliography. The reader who wishes to follow up any aspect of the subject can draw upon the notes themselves, as well as the brief bibliographical notes which introduce each main section. Aesthetically, it would have been better to cut down the volume of documentation, but I could not do so without making it impossible for the reader to identify the sources upon which statements in the text are founded. I have, however, made extensive use of abbreviations. These are listed in the accompanying Table of Abbreviations. Otherwise, the full title and details of publication have been given for every source on its first citation in the notes to each chapter; thereafter a shortened title has been employed. Greek and Hebrew titles have generally been omitted. Unless otherwise stated, the place of publication is London. In most quotations from contemporary sources the spelling and punctuation have been modernized.

ABBREVIATIONS

Add.	Additional
Ady	T. Ady, *A Candle in the Dark* (1656); reprinted, with same pagination, as *A Perfect Discovery of Witches* (1661)
A.P.C.	*Acts of the Privy Council*
Archaeol.	*Archaeological*
Ashm.	Ashmole MSS (Bodleian Library)
Aubrey, *Gentilisme*	J. Aubrey, *Remaines of Gentilisme and Judaisme*, ed. J. Britten (Folk-Lore Soc., 1881)
Aubrey, *Miscellanies*	J. Aubrey, *Miscellanies upon Various Subjects* (4th edn, 1857)
Bacon, *Works*	*The Works of Francis Bacon*, ed. J. Spedding, R. L. Ellis and D. D. Heath (1857–9)
Bernard, *Guide*	R. Bernard, *A Guide to Grand-Iury Men* (1627)
B.M.	British Museum, London
Bodl.	Bodleian Library, Oxford
Borthwick	Borthwick Institute of Historical Research, York
Brand, *Antiquities*	J. Brand, *Observations on the Popular Antiquities of Great Britain*, revised by Sir H. Ellis (Bohn edn, 1849–55)
Bull.	*Bulletin*
Burton, *Anatomy*	R. Burton, *The Anatomy of Melancholy* (1621) (Everyman edn, 1932)
Calvin, *Institutes*	J. Calvin, *Institutes of the Christian Religion,* trans. H. Beveridge (1957)
C.B.	Court Book
C.S.P.D.	*Calendar of State Papers, Domestic Series*
Cooper, *Mystery*	T. Cooper, *The Mystery of Witchcraft* (1617)
C.U.L.	Cambridge University Library
D.N.B.	*Dictionary of National Biography*
D.R.	Diocesan Records:
	Ely D.R. at C.U.L.
	Exeter D.R. at Devon R.O.
	Gloucester D.R.* at Gloucester City Library
	Hereford D.R.* at Hereford R.O.
	London D.R. at Greater London R.O.
	Norwich D.R. at Norfolk and Norwich R.O.
	Peterborough D.R. at Northants R.O.
	Rochester D.R. at Kent R.O.
	Wells D.R.* at Somerset R.O.

Winchester D.R.* at the Castle, Winchester (now
Hampshire R.O.)

* Not all these records were foliated when I consulted them

D.T.C.	*Dictionaire de Théologie Catholique*, ed. A. Vacant *et al.* (3rd edn, Paris, 1930–)
Durham Depositions	*Depositions and other Ecclesiastical Proceedings from the courts of Durham, extending from 1311 to the Reign of Elizabeth*, ed. J. Raine (Surtees Soc., 1845)
Durham High Commission	*The Acts of the High Commission Court within the Diocese of Durham*, ed. W. H. D. Longstaffe (Surtees Soc., 1858)
E.E.T.S.	Early English Text Society
E.H.R.	*English Historical Review*
Ewen, i	C. L. Ewen, *Witch Hunting and Witch Trials. The Indictments for Witchcraft from the records of 1373 Assizes held for the Home Circuit, A.D. 1559–1736* (1929)
Ewen, ii	C. L. Ewen, *Witchcraft and Demonianism. A concise account derived from sworn depositions and confessions obtained in the courts of England and Wales* (1933)
Ewen, *Star Chamber*	C. L. Ewen, *Witchcraft in the Star Chamber* (n.pl., 1938)
Foxe	*The Acts and Monuments of John Foxe* (4th edn, J. Pratt) (n.d. [1877])
Frere and Kennedy, *Articles and Injunctions*	*Visitation Articles and Injunctions of the period of the Reformation*, ed. W. H. Frere and W. M. Kennedy (Alcuin Club, 1910)
Hale, *Precedents*	W. H. Hale, *A Series of Precedents and Proceedings in Criminal Causes, extending from the year 1475 to 1640; extracted from Act-Books of Ecclesiastical Courts in the Diocese of London* (1847)
Hereford City Records	Bound volumes of transcripts of the records of the City of Hereford made by F. C. Morgan, Esq., and in his possession
Heywood, Diaries	*The Rev. Oliver Heywood, B.A., 1630–1702; his Autobiography, Diaries, Anecdote and Event Books*, ed. J. Horsfall Turner (Brighouse and Bingley, 1882–5)
H.M.C.	*Historical Manuscripts Commission, Reports*
Homilies	*The Two Books of Homilies appointed to be read in churches*, ed. J. Griffiths (Oxford, 1859)
Josten, *Ashmole*	*Elias Ashmole (1617–92). His Autobiographical and Historical Notes, his Correspondence, and other Contemporary Sources relating to his Life and Work*, ed. with a biographical introduction, by C. H. Josten (Oxford, 1966)

Journ.	*Journal*
Kittredge, *Witchcraft*	G. L. Kittredge, *Witchcraft in Old and New England* (1929: reprint, New York, 1956)
Kocher, *Science and Religion*	P.H. Kocher, *Science and Religion in Elizabethan England* (San Marino, Calif., 1953)
Lambeth	Lambeth Palace Library
Lea, *Materials*	*Materials towards a History of Witchcraft*, collected by H. C. Lea, ed. A. C. Howland (Philadelphia, 1939)
Lib.	Library
Lilly, *Autobiography*	*William Lilly's History of his Life and Times from the year 1602 to 1681, written by Himself* (1715), reprint, 1822
Lilly, *Christian Astrology*	W. Lilly, *Christian Astrology Modestly Treated of in Three Books* (1647)
L.P.	*Letters and Papers, Foreign and Domestic of the reign of Henry VIII*, ed. J. S. Brewer *et al* (1862–1932)
Malleus	*Malleus Maleficarum*, trans. M. Summers (1948)
Murray, *Erceldoune*	*The Romance and Prophecies of Thomas of Erceldoune*, ed. J. A. H. Murray (E.E.T.S., 1875)
Notestein, *Witchcraft*	W. Notestein, *A History of Witchcraft in England from 1558 to 1718* (1911; reprint, New York, 1965)
O.E.D.	*A New English Dictionary on Historical Principles*, ed. J. A. H. Murray (Oxford, 1888–1933)
Oxf. Univ. Arch.	Oxford University Archives (Bodleian Library)
Perkins, *Discourse*	W. Perkins, *A Discourse of the Damned Art of Witchcraft* (Cambridge, 1608)
Potts	*Potts's Discovery of Witches in the County of Lancaster . . . 1613*, ed. J. Crossley (Chetham Soc., 1845)
Powicke and Cheney, *Councils and Synods*	*Councils and Synods, ii (A.D. 1205–1313)*, ed. F. M. Powicke and C. R. Cheney (Orford, 1964)
P.R.O.	Public Record Office
Procs.	*Proceedings*
P.S.	Parker Society
Rev.	*Review*
R.O.	Record Office (Archives Office in the case of Kent)
Robbins, *Encyclopedia*	R. H. Robbins, *The Encyclopedia of Witchcraft and Demonology* (1960)
Sarum Manual	*Manuale ad Usum Percelebris Ecclesie Sarisburiensis*, ed. A. Jefferies Collins (Henry Bradshaw Soc., 1960)
Scot, *Discoverie*	R. Scot, *The Discoverie of Witchcraft* (1584) (The best modern edition is by B. Nicholson [1886]. The most recent (by H. R. Williamson, [1964]) has been siently abbreviated)
Sloane	Sloane MSS (British Museum)
Soc.	Society

Somers Tracts	*A Collection of Scarce and Valuable Tracts . . . of the late Lord Somers*, 2nd edn, by W. Scott (1809–15)
Southwell Act Books	Transcript of Southwell Minster Act Books by W. A. James (Reading University Library [942.52])
S.T.C.	A. W. Pollard and G. R. Redgrave, *A Short-title Catalogue of Books printed in England, Scotland and Ireland and of English Books printed abroad, 1475–1640* (1926; reprint, 1956)
Taylor, *Mathematical Practitioners*	E. G. R. Taylor, *The Mathematical Practitioners of Tudor and Stuart England* (Cambridge, 1954)
Thiers, *Superstitions*	J.-B. Thiers, *Traité des Superstitions qui regardent les sacremens* (1679; 5th edn, Paris, 1741)
Thomson, *Later Lollards*	J. A. F. Thomson, *The Later Lollards, 1414–1520* (Oxford, 1965)
Thorndike, *Magic and Science*	L. Thorndike, *A History of Magic and Experimental Science* (New York: Morningside Heights, 1923–58)
Trans.	*Transactions*
T.R.H.S.	*Transactions of the Royal Historical Society*
Turner, *Providences*	W. Turner, *A Compleat History of the Most Remarkable Providences, Both of Judgment and Mercy, which have hapned in this Present Age* (1697)
V.C.H.	*Victoria County History*
Wing	D. Wing, *Short-title Catalogue of Books printed in England, Scotland, Ireland, Wales and British America, and of English Books printed in Other Countries, 1641–1700* (New York, 1945–51)
Wood, *Ath. Ox*	A. Wood, *Athenae Oxonienses*, ed. P. Bliss (Oxford 1813–20)
Wood, *Life and Times*	*The Life and Times of Anthony Wood, antiquary, of Oxford, 1632–95*, ed. A. Clark (Oxford Hist. Soc., 1891–1900)
York Depositions	*Depositions from the Castle of York, relating to offences committed in the Northern Counties in the seventeenth century*, ed. J. Raine (Surtees Soc., 1861)
York Manual	*Manuale et Processionale ad Usum Insignis Ecclesiae Eboracensis*, ed. W. G. Henderson (Surtees Soc., 1875)

For this is man's nature, that where he is persuaded that there is the power to bring prosperity and adversity, there will he worship.

George Gifford, *A Discourse of the Subtill Practices of Devilles by Witches and Sorcerers* (1587), sigs.B4^v-C1

PROLOGUE

1.

THE ENVIRONMENT

IN the sixteenth and seventeenth centuries England was still a pre-industrial society, and many of its essential features closely resembled those of the 'under-developed areas' of today. The population was relatively sparse: there were perhaps two and a half million people in England and Wales in 1500, and five and a half million in 1700. Even in the later seventeenth century the economy gave little indication of the industrialization which was to come. It is true that there was now a highly commercialized agriculture, a vigorous textile industry, a substantial production of coal and a growing volume of colonial trade. But the bulk of the population was still engaged in the production of food, and the development of capitalist organization was still rudimentary. There were few 'factories'. The typical unit of production was the small workshop, and cottage industry was still the basis of textile manufacture.

Most of the population lived in the countryside. Gregory King, the pioneer statistician, to whom we owe most of our figures for this period, calculated that in 1688 nearly eighty per cent of the population lived in villages and hamlets. Most of the urban areas were very small; Birmingham, Bristol, Exeter, Newcastle, Norwich and York were the only provincial cities with more than ten thousand inhabitants. Norwich, the largest of these, had about thirty thousand. The one striking exception to this pattern of life in scattered rural communities was the capital city. London's population multiplied tenfold during these centuries; by 1700 it was well over half a

NOTE. This introductory survey is primarily intended for readers lacking any specialized knowledge of English history during this period. More information about the economy and social structure during these years may be found in such works as *The Agrarian History of England and Wales*, iv (1500–1640), ed. J. Thirsk (Cambridge, 1967); C. Wilson, *England's Apprenticeship, 1603–1763* (1965); P. Laslett, *The World We Have Lost* (1965); D. C. Coleman, 'Labour in the English Economy of the Seventeenth Century', *Econ. Hist. Rev.*, 2nd ser., viii (1955–6); D. V. Glass, 'Two Papers on Gregory King', in *Population in History*, ed. D. V. Glass and D. E. C. Eversley (1965); L. Stone, 'Social Mobility in England, 1500–1700', *Past and Present*, xxxiii (1966); A. Everitt, 'Social Mobility in Early Modern England', ibid.; E. Kerridge, *The Agricultural Revolution* (1967).

million and still growing. It has been estimated that perhaps a sixth of the total population spent at least part of their lives in this great metropolis, many of them returning to their rural communities with newly acquired urban habits of living.[1]

Society was highly stratified and the contrast between rich and poor was everywhere conspicuous. Gregory King calculated that in 1688 over half the population were 'decreasing the wealth of the kingdom', that is to say earning less than they consumed. There can be no doubt that between a third and a half of the population lived at subsistence level and were chronically under-employed. These were the 'cottagers, paupers, labouring people and outservants', as King called them. Many of these were copy-holders occupying their own small tenements, but even more were wage labourers, for the decline of the English peasantry was already under way. Above them came the more prosperous classes of farmers, freeholders and trades-men. At the top was the traditional élite of landed gentry and nobility, now strongly challenged by the rising professional groups, lawyers, clergymen, merchants and officials. King estimated that the landowners and professional classes, though only five per cent of the population, enjoyed a larger proportion of the national income than did all the lower classes (over fifty per cent) put together.

Conditions of life varied so much among these different elements of the population that it is hard for the historian not to be struck more by the differences than by the similarities. Tudor and Stuart England may have been an under-developed society, dependent upon the labours of an under-nourished and ignorant population, but it also produced one of the greatest literary cultures ever known and witnessed an unprecedented ferment of scientific and intel-lectual activity. Not every under-developed society has its Shake-speare, Milton, Locke, Wren and Newton. The social élite was highly educated. It has been calculated that by 1660 there was a grammar school for every 4,400 persons, and that two and a half per cent of the relevant age-group of the male population was receiving some form of higher education, at Oxford and Cambridge, or at the Inns of Court. The latter is a higher figure than any attained again until after the First World War.[2] It was an age of immense creative

1. E. A. Wrigley, 'A Simple Model of London's Importance . . . 1650–1750', *Past and Present*, xxxvii (1967) p. 49.

2. W. K. Jordan, *Philanthropy in England, 1480–1660* (1959), p. 291; L. Stone, 'The Educational Revolution in England, 1540–1640', *Past and Present*,

activity in the fields of drama, poetry, prose, architecture, theology, mathematics, physics, chemistry, history, philology and many other learned disciplines. Yet it was also a time when a large, but as yet unknown, proportion of the population (perhaps between half and two thirds of adult males in the mid seventeenth century) was unable to read, or at least signed with a mark.[3]

It is this huge variation in standard of living, educational level and intellectual sensibility which makes this society so diverse, and therefore so hard to generalize about. Not only did conditions change over the two centuries, but at any one point in time there were so many different layers of belief and levels in sophistication. The invention of the printed word, moreover, had made possible the preservation and dissemination of many different systems of thought, deriving from other societies and sometimes dating from the remote classical past. The task of the historian is thus infinitely harder than that of the social anthropologist, studying a small homogeneous community in which all inhabitants share the same beliefs, and where few of those beliefs are borrowed from other societies. This was no simple unified primitive world, but a dynamic and infinitely various society, where social and intellectual change had long been at work and where currents were moving in many different directions.

The beliefs with which this book is concerned had a variety of social and intellectual implications. But one of their central features was a preoccupation with the explanation and relief of human misfortune. There can be no doubt that this concern reflected the hazards of an intensely insecure environment. This is not to suggest that it was these hazards which brought the beliefs into being. On the contrary, most of the latter had been inherited from earlier generations and therefore preceded the society in which they flourished. Nevertheless, there were certain features of the sixteenth- and seventeenth-century environment by which they could hardly fail to be coloured.

Of these the first was the expectation of life. Systematic demo-

xxviii (1964), pp. 68–9, and pp. 44–7, for some important criticisms of Jordan's estimate of the proportion of schools.

3. The limited evidence so far available on this subject is discussed in L. Stone, 'Literacy and Education in England, 1640–1900', *Past and Present*, xlii (1969), and R. S. Schofield, 'The Measurement of Literacy in Pre-industrial England' in *Literacy in Traditional Societies*, ed. J. Goody (Cambridge, 1968).

6 RELIGION AND THE DECLINE OF MAGIC

graphic research upon the history of England during these two centuries has only just begun, and the inadequacies of the evidence probably mean that our knowledge of the health and physical condition of contemporaries will always be incomplete. But it is beyond dispute that Tudor and Stuart Englishmen were, by our standards, exceedingly liable to pain, sickness and premature death. Even among the nobility, whose chances are likely to have been better than those of other classes, the life expectation at birth of boys born in the third quarter of the seventeenth century was 29.6 years. Today it would be around 70. A third of these aristocratic infants died before the age of five, while the level of mortality among those who lived to be adults closely resembled that of India in the last decade of the nineteenth century.[4] In London, conditions were particularly bad. The first English demographer, John Graunt, estimated in 1662 that, of every hundred live children born in the metropolis, thirty-six died in their first six years and a further twenty-four in the following ten years. He calculated the expectation at birth to be less than that which was to be the figure for India during the influenza pandemic of 1911-21.[5] Graunt's estimate may have been unduly pessimistic. In any case he lived at a time when the mortality rate was untypically high. In the mid sixteenth century the expectation at birth may have been as high as 40-45, for country folk anyway.[6] But contemporaries did not need elaborate demographic investigations to tell them that life was short, and that the odds were against any individual living out his full span. 'We shall find more who have died within thirty or thirty-five years of age than passed it,' remarked a writer in 1635.[7] Even those who survived could anticipate a lifetime of intermittent pain. Literary sources suggest that many persons suffered chronically from some ailment or

4. T. H. Hollingsworth, *The Demography of the British Peerage* (Supplement to *Population Studies*, xviii [1964]), pp. 54, 56, 68. Mr Laslett points out that the expectation of life in the 1690s compared unfavourably with that of Egypt in the 1930s; *The World We Have Lost*, pp. 93–4.

5. *The Economic Writings of Sir William Petty*, ed. C. H. Hull (Cambridge, 1899), ii, pp. 386–7; D. V. Glass, 'John Graunt and his *Natural and Political Observations*', *Notes and Records of the Royal Soc.*, xix (1964), p. 75.

6. This is the conclusion arrived at by E. A. Wrigley in his study of mortality in the Devonshire village of Colyton; *Daedalus* (Spring, 1968). Hollingsworth's figures for the sixteenth-century peerage give a life-expectation at birth of only 35–36 (op. cit., p. 56).

7. D. Person, *Varieties* (1635), pp. 157–8.

other, and this impression is confirmed by inferences from what is known of contemporary diet.

The food supply was always precarious and throughout the period the fate of the annual harvest remained crucial. The meagre evidence available suggests that the yield-ratio on seed corn may have doubled between 1500 and 1660, but so did the population. About one harvest in six seems to have been a total failure, and mortality could soar when times of dearth coincided with (or perhaps occasioned) large-scale epidemics.[8] In the seventeenth century, however, it was rare, but certainly not unknown, for men to die in the streets from starvation or exposure.[9] Yet even at times of plenty most people seem to have suffered from a lack of Vitamin A (yellow and green vegetables) and Vitamin D (milk and eggs). The first of these deficiencies accounts for the numerous complaints of 'sore eyes' (xerophthalmia), the second for the widespread incidence of rickets. Scorbutic diseases were also common. The well-known 'green sickness' in young women, to which contemporaries gave a sexual meaning, was chlorosis, anaemia produced by a lack of iron in the diet, stemming from upper-class disdain for fresh vegetables. The well-to-do ate too much meat and were frequently constipated. They did not regard milk as a drink for adults and they frequently suffered from the infection of the urinary tract which produced the notorious Stuart malady of stone in the bladder. The dietary deficiencies of the lower classes, by contrast, reflected not so much ignorance as simple poverty. Not until the nineteenth century did labourers get enough meat and butter. In the seventeenth century they may have escaped the gout and stone which plagued their betters, and may even have had better teeth from eating more vegetables. But they were chronically under-nourished and vulnerable to tuberculosis and gastric upsets ('griping in the guts')

8. B. H. Slicher van Bath, *Yield Ratios, 810–1820* (Wageningen, 1963), pp. 41–2, 47–8; W. G. Hoskins, 'Harvest Fluctuations and English Economic History, 1480–1619', *Agricultural Hist. Rev.*, xii (1964); id. 'Harvest Fluctuations and English Economic History, 1620–1759', ibid., xvi (1968).

9. Some seventeenth-century allusions to such deaths may be found in J. Hull, *Saint Peters Prophesie of these last daies* (1610), p. 525; *The Works of Gerrard Winstanley*, ed. G. H. Sabine (Ithaca, New York, 1941), p. 650; L. H. Berens, *The Digger Movement in the Days of the Commonwealth* (1906), pp. 159–60; C. Bridenbaugh, *Vexed and Troubled Englishmen* (Oxford, 1968), pp. 376–7; J. E. T. Rogers, *A History of Agriculture and Prices in England* (Oxford, 1866–1902), v, p. 621; Lastlett, *The World We Have Lost*, pp. 115–17; C. Creighton, *A History of Epidemics in Britain* (2nd edn, 1965), i, p. 562.

caused by bad food.[10] Rich and poor alike were victims of the infections generated by the lack of hygiene, ignorance of antiseptics and absence of effective sanitation. Epidemics accounted for thirty per cent of reported deaths in seventeenth-century London. There were periodic waves of influenza, typhus, dysentery and, in the seventeenth century, smallpox, a disease which the contemporary physician Thomas Sydenham assumed would sooner or later attack most people. Thirty thousand people died of smallpox in London between 1670 and 1689; and a study of the newspaper advertisements printed in the *London Gazette* between 1667 and 1774 shows that sixteen out of every hundred missing persons whose descriptions were given bore pockmarks on their faces.[11]

Most dreaded of all was the bubonic plague, which was endemic until the last quarter of the seventeenth century. It was a disease of the towns and it particularly affected the poor, who lived in crowded, filthy conditions, thus attracting the black rats, which are nowadays thought to have carried the fleas which spread the disease. (Like the people of India today, the poorer classes in parts of seventeenth-century England still used cow-dung as fuel.[12]) In the hundred and fifty years before the great visitation of 1665 there were only a dozen years when London was free from plague. Some people were thought to have died of it every year and periodically there were massive outbreaks, although many of the deaths which contemporaries attributed to plague probably occurred for other reasons.

10. I have followed J. C. Drummond and A. Wilbraham, *The Englishman's Food* (revd edn, 1957). The diet of labourers is discussed in *The Agrarian History of England*, iv, pp. 450–53. An interesting piece of contemporary comment on their health may be found in A. Ascham, *Of the Confusions and Revolutions of Governments* (1649), p. 25.

11. Creighton, *A History of Epidemics in Britain*, ii, pp. 454–5; D. V. Glass, 'John Graunt . . . ', *Notes and Records of the Royal Soc.*, xix (1964), p. 72; *The Cambridge Economic History of Europe*, iv, ed. E. E. Rich and C. H. Wilson (Cambridge, 1967), p. 54.

12. *The Agrarian History of England and Wales*, iv, p. 453; *Agriculture and Economic Growth in England, 1650–1815*, ed. E. L. Jones (1967), pp. 61–2; Kerridge, *The Agricultural Revolution*, p. 242. At Maidstone in the 1590s the inhabitants of the almshouses kept pigs in their rooms; W. B. Gilbert, *The Accounts of the Corpus Christi Fraternity and Papers relating to the Antiquities of Maidstone* (Maidstone, 1865), p. 92. Some modern medical historians think that plague may also have been transmitted by the human flea. cf. J.-N. Biraben in *Daedalus* (Spring, 1968), p. 544; *Cambridge Economic History of Europe*, iv, p. 7, n. 1.

In 1563 some 20,000 Londoners are thought to have died; in 1593, 15,000; in 1603, 30,000, or over a sixth of the inhabitants; in 1625, 41,000, another sixth; in 1636, 10,000; and, in 1665, at least 68,000. In provincial towns plague deaths sometimes took away an even higher proportion of the population.[13]

The plague terrified by its suddenness, its virulence and its social effects. The upper classes would emigrate temporarily from the afflicted area, leaving the poor to die. Unemployment, food shortage, looting and violence usually resulted. The refugees themselves were liable to receive rough treatment from country folk, frightened they were bringing the disease with them. Further violence accompanied popular resistance to the quarantine regulations and restrictions on movement imposed by the authorities, particularly to the practice of shutting up the infected and their families in their houses. The plague, said a preacher, was of all diseases,

the most dreadful and terrible; . . . then all friends leave us, then a man or woman sit(s) and lie(s) alone and is a stranger to the breath of his own relations. If a man be sick of a fever it is some comfort that he can take a bed-staff and knock, and his servant comes up and helps him with a cordial. But if a man be sick of the plague then he sits and lies all alone.[14]

When a Western traveller visits a pre-industrial society of this kind today he equips himself with all the resources of modern medicine: he takes pills to keep his stomach free from infection and is vaccinated against smallpox, and inoculated against typhus, plague or yellow fever. No such immunity was available to the inhabitants of Tudor and Stuart England, for medical science was helpless before most contemporary hazards to health. There was an organised medical profession, but it had little to offer. In the sixteenth and early seventeenth centuries university-educated physicians were given a purely academic training in the principles of humoral physio-

13. J. F. D. Shrewsbury, *A History of Bubonic Plague in the British Isles* (Cambridge, 1970), is an important recent survey, though the critical review by C. Morris in *The Historical Journal*, xiv (1971), should also be read. Creighton, op. cit., remains indispensable, but account should be taken of the important criticisms of R. S. Roberts, 'Epidemics and Social History', *Medical History*, xii (1968). Also valuable are W. G. Bell, *The Great Plague in London in 1665* (revd edn, 1951); F. P. Wilson, *The Plague in Shakespeare's London* (new edn, Oxford, 1963) and the recent surveys by K. F. Helleiner in *The Cambridge Economic History of Europe*, iv, chap. 1, and R. S. Roberts in *Procs. Royal Soc. Med.*, lix (1966).

14. *The Works of the Rev. William Bridge* (1845), i, pp. 468–9.

logy as set out in the works of Hippocrates, Aristotle and Galen. They were taught that illness sprang from an imbalance between the four humours (blood, phlegm, yellow bile and black bile). Diagnosis consisted in establishing which of these humours was out of line, and therapy in taking steps to restore the balance, either by blood-letting (by venesection, scarification or applying leeches) or by subjecting the patient to a course of purges and emetics. The physician thus followed a dreary round of blood-letting and purging, along with the prescription of plasters, ointments and potions. He focused on what we should regard as the symptoms of disease – fever or dysentery – rather than the disease itself. The patient's urine was taken to be the best guide to his condition, and there were some practitioners who even thought it enough to see the urine without the patient, though the Royal College of Physicians condemned this habit.[15] It was just as well that in strict Galenic theory one of the humours was bound to predominate unnaturally, so that perfect health was almost by definition unattainable.[16]

In the seventeenth century, accordingly, doctors were quite unable to diagnose or treat most contemporary illnesses. 'Many diseases they cannot cure at all,' declared Robert Burton, 'as apoplexy, epilepsy, stone, strangury, gout . . . , quartan agues; a common ague sometimes stumbles them all.'[17] Internal medicine had to wait upon the slow development of physiology and anatomy. There were no X-rays and no stethoscopes, and a physician was usually quite ignorant of what was actually going on inside a sick person's body. There were surgeons who dealt with tumours, ulcers, fractures and venereal disease. But their art was regarded as an inferior one by the physicians. Besides, without anaesthetics or knowledge of antiseptics, there was very little they could do. Operations were largely confined to amputations, trepanning the skull, cutting for stone, bone-setting and incising abscesses. Patients were understandably terrified of undergoing this kind of torture and the mortality rate after such operations was high. Richard Wiseman's standard *Severall Chirurgicall Treatises* (1676) was popularly known as 'Wiseman's Book of Martyrs'.[18]

15. Sir G. Clark, *A History of the Royal College of Physicians of London* (Oxford, 1964–6), i, p. 178.
16. As is pointed out in R. Klibansky, E. Panofsky and F. Saxl, *Saturn and Melancholy* (1964), p. 11 and n. 27.
17. Burton, *Anatomy*, ii, p. 210.
18. R. North, *The Lives of the . . . North*, ed. A. Jessopp (1890), ii, p. 248.

Nowhere was the inadequacy of contemporary medical technique more apparent than in its handling of the threat presented by the plague. A few physicians noticed that rats came out of their holes at times of plague,[19] but they did not associate them with the disease; indeed, by urging that cats and dogs be killed in order to check infection, they may have actually worsened the situation. Contemporaries preferred to attribute plague to a combination of noxious vapours in the air and corrupt humours in the body, though they disagreed about the causes of these phenomena and about whether or not the disease was contagious. As a preacher bluntly said in 1603, 'Whence it cometh, whereof it ariseth and wherefore it is sent . . . they confess their ignorance.'[20] All sorts of amulets and preservatives were recommended – tobacco, arsenic, quicksilver, dried toads. Much energy was also devoted to finding some means of allaying popular panic, on the assumption that the happy man would not get plague. As a further preventive, the physicians prescribed better hygiene, which was sensible enough, and the locking up of infected parties within their own houses, which was less sensible, since by confining other members of the family to the habitat of the rats they must have increased the toll of deaths. No progress had been made in the study of plague by the time of the great visitation of London in 1665. 'It is a mysterious disease,' confessed the current Secretary of the Royal Society, 'and I am afraid will remain so, for all the observations and discourses made of it.'[21]

Yet the failure of contemporary doctors to offer an adequate therapy for this or most other contemporary diseases did not matter very much to most of the population. The attentions of a qualified physician were effectively beyond their reach, because there was a severely limited supply of trained men. The Royal College of Physicians had been set up in 1518 to supervise and license physicians practising in the City of London and within a seven-mile radius. The College seems to have exercised this monopoly in a jealous and restrictive way, for it kept its numbers small, despite an immense subsequent increase in the size of the City. In the first years of its foundation the College had only a dozen members, whereas London's population was perhaps sixty thousand. By 1589 the

19. e.g., T. Lodge, *A Treatise of the Plague* (1603), sig. C2v.
20. H. Holland, *Spirituall Preservatives against the Pestilence* (1603), p. 35.
21. *The Correspondence of Henry Oldenburg*, ed. and trans. A. R. and M. B. Hall (Madison and Milwaukee, 1965–), ii, p. 527.

College's membership had risen to thirty-eight while the population had more than doubled. Thereafter the number of inhabitants continued to rise spectacularly, but the size of the College remained almost stationary until the Civil War period. The number of Fellows was raised to forty in 1663 and the College expanded further in the later Stuart period. But the ratio of the London population to its resident members and licentiates can never have been less than five thousand to one and was usually very much greater.[22]

In the provinces, where the licensing powers exercised by the College were never so important as those of the Church and Universities, the situation was rather better. The number of country physicians rose steadily through the period. One modern student has compiled a list of 814 physicians who are known to have been licensed between 1603 and 1643.[23] It shows that some towns were relatively well supplied with qualified doctors. Norwich had seventeen, Canterbury twenty-two, Exeter thirteen and York ten. Not all these may have actually practised, but the list itself is an under-estimate, since not all the records of the period have survived. By the end of the seventeenth century there can have been few market-towns without a resident physician. Richard Baxter, the nonconformist divine, who tells us he was very seldom without pain, was able as a young man to consult no fewer than thirty-six different physicians.[24]

Physicians, however, were too expensive for the bottom half of the population, even though they often tailored their bills to fit the pockets of their clients. In the seventeenth century a gentleman could expect to be charged about a pound a day for medical attendance, but humbler persons might get off for a few shillings if the doctor was so disposed.[25] Nevertheless, there were many complaints

22. Clark, *History of the Royal College of Physicians*, i, pp. 70, 71, 132, 188, 190, 304, 315, 356; ii, pp. 736–9. The exact number of licentiates before 1673, when there were nine, is obscure.

23. J. H. Raach, *A Directory of English Country Physicians, 1603–43* (1962). For a thorough discussion of this whole subject see R. S. Roberts, 'The Personnel and Practice of Medicine in Tudor and Stuart England', *Medical History*, vi (1962) and viii (1964).

24. *Reliquiae Baxterianae*, ed. M. Sylvester (1696), i, p. 10.

25. Apart from E. A. Hammond, 'Incomes of Medieval English Doctors', *Journal of the History of Medicine*, xv (1960), and a 'twenty-minutes' talk' by Sir D'A. Power, printed in *Procs. Royal Soc. of Medicine*, xiii (1920), there seems to be no modern discussion of medical fees. The pound-a-day principle is well exemplified in the long series of accounts in *H.M.C., Rutland*, iv; *The Autobiography and Correspondence of Sir Simonds D'Ewes*

that it was only the wealthy who could regularly afford a physician. 'Physic,' declared Bishop Latimer in 1552, 'is a remedy prepared only for rich folks and not for poor; for the poor man is not able to wage the physician.' At the end of the seventeenth century Richard Baxter wrote that 'many a thousand lie sick and die that have not money for physicians': even 'frugal freeholders of twenty or thirty pounds a year' had difficulty in finding 'ten shillings to save their lives in cases of danger'.[25] The Royal College of Physicians in 1687 ruled that their members should give free advice to the poor and soon afterwards set up a short-lived Dispensary to sell medicine at cost price. This step angered the apothecaries (grocers-cum-drug-sellers) and did not solve the problem.[27] Parishes were expected to pay medical fees for their paupers and some municipalities appointed town doctors,[28] but the provision of a state medical service was urged only by utopian thinkers. One of them, John Bellers, declared in 1714 that half the people who died annually suffered from curable diseases, for which only their poverty prevented them from finding a remedy.[29]

In lieu of the physicians, patients could turn to the surgeons and apothecaries. Seventy-two surgeons were licensed to practise in London in 1514, while in 1634 the apothecaries were thought to number at least a hundred and fifty. By 1701 there were said to be a thousand in London and a further fifteen hundred apprentices.

(1845), ii, p. 5; and *Diary of Walter Yonge*, ed. G. Roberts (Camden Soc., 1848), p. xxiii. Clark, *History of the Royal College*, ii, p. 436, suggests that 10s. was the usual charge. In the early eighteen century Claver Morris charged poor men half a crown; *The Diary of a West Country Physician*, ed. E. Hobhouse (1934), p. 26. But in 1697 the surgeon, James Yonge, was demanding up to £5 a day for his services; *The Journal of James Yonge*, ed. F. N. L. Poynter (1963), p. 207.

26. *Sermons by Hugh Latimer*, ed. G. E. Corrie (Cambridge, P.S., 1844), p. 541; F. J. Powicke, 'The Reverend Richard Baxter's Last Treatise', *Bull. John Rylands Lib.*, x (1926), p. 187.

27. Clark, *History of the Royal College*, ii, chaps. xx and xxiii.

28. e.g., Newcastle (Clark, op. cit., i, p. 163 n.); Denbigh (A. H. Dodd, *Life in Elizabethan England* (1961), pp. 46–7); Norwich (J. F. Pound in *Univ. of Birmingham Hist. Journ.*, viii (1961–2), p. 147); Barnstaple (J. B. Gribble, *Memorials of Barnstaple* (Barnstaple, 1830), ii, pp. 293–4); Chester (R. H. Morris, *Chester in the Plantagenet and Tudor Reigns* [n.d.], pp. 357–8). See also R. M. S. McConaghey, 'The History of Rural Medical Practice', in *The Evolution of Medical Practice in Britain*, ed. F. N. L. Poynter (1961), p. 126

29. J. Bellers, *An Essay towards the Improvement of Physick* (1714), p. 2.

They outnumbered the physicians by five to one.[30] The apothecaries thus took on the task of diagnosing and prescribing the medicine as well as supplying it. The physicians resisted this incursion into their territory and the seventeenth century witnessed a protracted legal battle which did not end until 1704, when the apothecaries' right to give medical advice (though not to charge for it) was upheld by the House of Lords. But they had long engaged in general practice in the provinces, where distinctions between themselves and the physicians and surgeons had been less rigid, while in London they claimed to be handling ninety-five per cent of medical practice before the end of the seventeenth century.[31] After 1704 their evolution into the modern general practitioner was assured. Nor was their treatment necessarily inferior to that offered by the physicians. On the contrary, the very size of their clientele forced them into prescribing new drugs, of a kind frowned upon by the Royal College, in place of the time-consuming humoral remedies.[32]

But the impact of organized medicine upon the lower reaches of the population was seldom more than superficial. Many of the poor chose to go outside the ranks of the licensed practitioners altogether, and to consult an empiric, herbalist, wise woman, or other member of that 'great multitude of ignorant persons' whose practice of physic and surgery had been denounced by Parliament in 1512. In 1542–3 another Act had allowed anyone with the necessary knowledge to treat external sores and prescribe for the stone. According to a pamphleteer in 1669, there was 'scarce a pissing-place about the City' which was not adorned by posters advertising the services of some medical quack.[33] Some of the nostrums thus peddled reflected genuine country lore about herbs and roots; others did the patient severe or even fatal damage.[34]

But this was above all a time when medicine began at home. Every housewife had her repertoire of private remedies. 'All the nation are

30. R. R. James in *Janus*, xli (1936); C. Wall and H. C. Cameron, *A History of the Worshipful Society of Apothecaries*, i, ed. E. A. Underwood (1963), pp. 77, 289, 394; K. Dewhurst in *St. Barts. Hospital Journ.*, lxvi (1962), p. 261.
31. Wall and Cameron, op. cit., p. 131.
32. See R. S. Roberts in *History of Science*, v (1966).
33. (D. Coxe), *A Discourse wherein the Interest of the Patient in Reference to Physick and Physicians is Soberly Debated* (1669), p. 313; 3 Hen. viii, cap. 11; 34 and 35 Hen. viii, cap. 8.
34. For a woman killed by an Elizabethan gardener's herbal prescription, see *Middlesex County Records*, ed. J. C. Jeaffreson (1886–92), i, p. 276.

already physicians,' remarked Nicholas Culpepper in 1649. 'If you ail anything, every one you meet, whether a man or woman, will prescribe you a medicine for it.' 'None practise physic or professeth midwifery', reported the villagers of Dry Drayton, Cambridgeshire, in 1662, 'but charitably one neighbour helps one another'.[35] In child-birth, indeed, a physician was never employed, save by the very wealthy, or in cases of unusual emergency. There was no shortage of midwives, licensed and unlicensed, but their qualifications were rudimentary. The forceps had been invented by Peter Chamberlen early in the seventeenth century, but he kept it secret and the usual obstetric tools were cruel and inefficient. A midwife estimated in 1687 that two thirds of contemporary abortions, stillbirths, and deaths in child-bed were to be attributed to the lack of care and skill displayed by her colleagues.[36] The wife of one Newark apothe-cary was so afraid of any midwife coming near her that her husband used to lock her alone in her room until the delivery was over.[37]

As for hospitals, St. Bartholomew's and St. Thomas's were the only two for the physically ill in London at the end of the seven-teenth century and there were few elsewhere. They were in any case meant primarily for the poor. No person of social pretensions would dream of entering one as a patient; and if he did he would certainly be increasing his chances of contracting some fatal infection.

Even less could be done for sufferers from mental illness. Contem-porary medical therapy was primarily addressed to the ailments of the body. 'For the diseases of the mind,' wrote Robert Burton, 'we take no notice of them.' Raving psychotics were locked up by their relatives, kept under guard by parish officers, or sent to houses of correction.[38] Less dramatic forms of mental illness were regarded either as cases of melancholy to be treated by purging and blood-letting, or wrongly diagnosed as 'hysteria', stemming from a condi-

35. N. Culpepper, A Physicall Directory (1649), sig. A2; W. M. Palmer, 'Episcopal Visitation Returns, Cambridge (Diocese of Ely), 1638–62', Trans. Cambs. and Hunts. Archaeol. Soc., iv (1915–30), p. 407. cf. Burton, Anatomy, i, p. 210.

36. E. Cellier, A Scheme for the Foundation of a Royal Hospital (1687) (in Somers Tracts, ix), p. 248.

37. P. Willoughby, Observations on Midwifery, ed. H. Blenkinsop (1863; 1972 reprint, East Ardsley), pp. 240–41. This book gives a remarkable account of the activities of seventeenth-century midwives.

38. Burton, Anatomy, i, p. 69; A. Fessler, 'The Management of Lunacy in Seventeenth-century England', Procs. of the Royal Soc. of Medicine (Hist. section), xlix (1956), based on the Quarter Sessions records for Lancashire.

tion of the uterus. The uterine origin of nervous diseases was not successfully challenged in England until the later seventeenth century, when Thomas Willis formulated the theory of the cerebral origin of hysteria and pioneered the science of neurology.[39]

There was thus no orthodox medical agency which offered a satisfactory cure for mental illness. Various low-grade practitioners took out licences as 'curers of mad folks and distracted persons', and some of them maintained private madhouses. Yet even Bethlem Hospital (Bedlam) in London discharged its inmates as incurable if they had not recovered within a year.[40] It is not surprising that supernatural explanations of mental depression were advanced or that the main psychotherapists were the clergy. Physic alone was not enough to cure melancholy, declared the Puritan oracle, William Perkins.[41]

These were the circumstances in which so many unorthodox methods of healing enjoyed prestige. The population at large disliked Galenic physic for its nauseous remedies,[42] and were frightened by the prospect of surgery. Some of the most intelligent laymen of the day expressed total contempt for conventional medicine; and the unorthodox empirics hounded by the Royal College of Physicians often turned out to have influential champions.[43] King James I regarded academic medicine as mere conjecture and therefore useless. Francis Bacon thought that 'empirics and old women' were 'more happy many times in their cures than learned physicians'. Robert Burton, Archbishop Abbot, and many less notable contemporaries, said the same. Some scientists and intellectuals followed the example of Paracelsus and were prepared to learn from herbalists and wise women.[44] Thomas Hobbes, who took a keen interest in the

39. See I. Veith, Hysteria. The History of a Disease (Chicago, 1965); G. Abricossoff, L'Hystérie aux XVIIe et XVIIIe siècles (Paris, 1897); I. Hunter and R. A. Macalpine, Three Hundred Years of Psychiatry (1963), pp. 69, 187.

40. Hunter and Macalpine, op. cit., passim; Clark, History of the Royal College, i, p. 263; R. R. James in Janus, xli (1937), p. 102; E. H. Carter, The Norwich Subscription Books (1937), p. 138; J. Spencer, A Discourse of Divers Petitions (1641); J. J. M., 'A Clerical Mad-Doctor of the Seventeenth Century', The East Anglian, i (new ser.), (1885–6).

41. Cited by Kocher, Science and Religion, pp. 300–1.

42. As was observed by J. Primrose, Popular Errours, trans. R. Wittie (1651), pp. 231-3, 278, 280, although proof is hardly needed.

43. Clark, History of the Royal College, i, pp. 111, 114, 116, 143–7, 195, 262.

44. Sir G. Keynes, The Life of William Harvey (Oxford, 1966), p. 142; Bacon, Works, iv, p. 388; Burton, Anatomy, i, p. 257; Clark op. cit., i, p. 195. See also H.M.C., Rutland, i, p. 163; Yorkshire Diaries, ed. C. Jackson (Sur-

problem of survival, concluded that he would 'rather have the advice or take physic from an experienced old woman that had been at many sick people's bedsides, than from the learnedst but unexperienced physician'.[45] Doctors of physic, thought the sectary, Lodowick Muggleton, were 'the greatest cheats ... in the world. If there were never a doctor of physic in the world, people would live longer and liver better in health.'[46]

Before discounting such lay opinions we should recall that even Thomas Sydenham, the greatest physician of the seventeenth century, thought that it would have been better for many patients if the art of physic had never been invented, remarking that many poor men owed their lives to their inability to afford conventional treatment.[47] Nor was he alone among his colleagues in holding such opinions. 'I have heard the learned and pious Dr. Ridgeley, M.D., say,' recalled John Aubrey, 'that if the world knew the villainy and knavery (beside ignorance) of the physicians and apothecaries, the people would throw stones at 'em as they walked in the streets.'[48]

Helplessness in the face of disease was an essential element in the background to the beliefs with which we shall be concerned. So too was vulnerability to other kinds of misfortune, particularly when it came suddenly. Next to plague, perhaps the greatest single threat to security was fire. This was more of a risk in the sixteenth and seventeenth centuries than it is today and contemporaries were much less well-equipped to deal with it. The towns were particularly vulnerable with their thatched roofs, wooden chimneys and crowded living conditions. Since there were no safety matches, people often chose to fetch a bucket of burning coals from a neighbour rather than waste time struggling with a tinder-box. At night they were dependent on candles, which, when set down in a draughty place, could easily put a house on fire. 'Fear candle, good wife,' warned the agricultural writer, Thomas Tusser, 'Fear candle in hay loft, in barn and in shed.' When the chimney needed cleaning it was common to take a short cut by firing a gun up it or even setting it on fire: this was how the Beccles fire was started in 1586, with eighty houses burned down as

tees Soc., 1877), p. 221; G. Harvey, *The Art of Curing Diseases by Expectation* (1689), p. 6.

45. J. Aubrey, *Brief Lives*, ed. A. Powell (1949), p. 251.

46. L. Muggleton, *The Acts of the Witnesses* (1699), p. 111.

47. K. Dewhurst, *Dr Thomas Sydenham (1624–89)* (1966), pp. 163, 116.

48. Bodl., Aubrey MS 10, f. 113v.

a result.[49] A further risk came from the numerous industrial work-shops, scattered among the houses, and observing the most rudimentary safety precautions. Dyers, brewers and soapboilers were a constant source of danger: the fire which did £200,000-worth of damage at Tiverton in 1612 began when a dyer's furnace was allowed to become overheated.[50]

Some of the biggest conflagrations were the result of carelessness engendered by primitive living conditions. A hundred and fifty buildings were damaged at Woburn in 1595 after an old woman had set her thatched house alight by throwing all her used bed-straw on the fire. Tiverton was heavily damaged in 1598 when a fire was started by some beggar-women who had been pathetically trying to cook pancakes on straw because they could not afford to buy wood. Much of Northampton was destroyed in 1675 when a woman left her pot of washing on the fire for too long. Most of the Palace of Whitehall was burned down in 1698 because a Dutch washerwoman tried to hasten the drying of her linen by lighting a charcoal fire indoors.[51]

Once fire had broken out it seldom encountered much in the way of effective resistance. Fire-fighting techniques were virtually unchanged in England between the Norman Conquest and the death of Elizabeth I.[52] Even the most advanced municipality possessed nothing more in the way of equipment than some leather buckets, a few ladders and iron hooks for pulling down thatch so as to stop the fire spreading. Until the mid seventeenth century there were no engines to project water to a height, and the water supply itself was usually unreliable. Some towns required householders to keep buckets of water outside their doors. Others tried to check the erection of wooden buildings and thatched roofs. This had been the official policy of the City of London since the twelfth century. But

49. T. Tusser, *His Good Points of Husbandry*, ed. D. Hartley (1931), p. 177; *A Collection of Seventy-Nine Black-Letter Ballads and Broadsides* (1867), p. 82.

50. F. J. Snell, *The Chronicles of Twyford* (Tiverton, n.d. [c. 1893]), p. 60.

51. (T. Wilcocks), *A Short, yet a True and Faithfull Narration of the Fearfull Fire that fell in the Towne of Wooburne* (1595), p. 4; *The True Lamentable Discourse of the Burning of Teverton* (1598); *The State of Northampton* (1675); *A Full and True Account of a Most Dreadful ... Fire ... at Whitehall (1698) (The Harleian Miscellany*, ed. T. Park (1808–13), vi, p. 398).

52. The early history of fire-fighting is surveyed in the opening sections of G. V. Blackstone, *A History of the British Fire Service* (1957). Much relevant material may be found in contemporary borough records.

such regulations were easier to make than to enforce, and the fire-fighting equipment usually proved sadly inadequate when the blaze was under way. There were no fire brigades, and the scene at a fire was usually one of unrelieved chaos. The only effective way contemporaries knew of stopping a fire was to blow up all the buildings around it to stop it spreading. When the flames dwindled there was invariably trouble with pilferers.[53]

Unable to prevent the outbreak of fire, and virtually helpless during the actual conflagration, contemporaries showed little more resource when it came to bearing the loss. There was no organised fire insurance until the last two decades of the seventeenth century. All that the victim of fire could do was to apply for a Church brief, authorising a collection to be made on his behalf in places of public worship. These begging letters were issued for a variety of charitable purposes and were as unreliable as modern flag-days. Nor was their prestige enhanced by the numerous petty frauds which grew around them. But they help us to form some estimate of the actual scale of fire damage. They show, for example, that in the last fifty years of the seventeenth century there were eighty-nine separate fires in which the damage incurred was estimated at £1,000 or more: the total cost of this group of large fires was put at £913,416.[54] In assessing this figure we should recall that it excludes the Great Fire of London (1666), which did £10 millions of damage, destroying over 13,000 houses, and leaving perhaps 100,000 people homeless.[55] It also excludes numerous smaller fires, as well as those for which no record has survived, or for which no brief was issued. All this, moreover, took place at a time when fire-fighting methods had begun to improve; in the sixteenth century the situation was worse.

As a purely economic factor, therefore, fire was exceedingly important. But its human consequences are even more obvious, for there was no occurrence which so graphically symbolized the instability of human fortunes. 'He which at one o'clock was worth five thousand pounds and, as the prophet saith, drank his wine in bowls of fine silver plate, had not by two o'clock so much as a wooden dish left

53. See, e.g., G. Atwell, *The Faithfull Surveyour* (Cambridge, 1962), pp. 95–6.

54. I have worked out this total from the list of briefs in W. A. Bewes, *Church Briefs* (1896). For some additional figures see E. L. Jones, 'The Reduction of Fire Damage in Southern England, 1650–1850', *Post-Medieval Archaeology*, ii (1968).

55. W. G. Bell, *The Great Fire of London* (3rd edn, 1923), pp. 174, 224.

to eat his meat in, nor a house to cover his sorrowful head."[56] The briefs which were read aloud in the churches on Sundays served as a constant reminder of how men could be reduced in an instant from wealth to utter penury, and how there was no telling whose turn it might be next. The psychological threat was increased by the capriciousness of the danger. Some towns escaped serious fire; whereas others suffered again and again. Tiverton was burned down three times (1598, 1612, 1731). Marlborough, Blandford, Dorchester and Beaminster all suffered repeatedly. Warwick and Northampton had only one serious fire each, but in both cases it destroyed a large part of the town. In the metropolis fires were so common that when the great fire in 1666 began scarcely anyone outside its immediate vicinity took any notice.[57]

Poverty, sickness, and sudden disaster were thus familiar features of the social environment of this period. But we must not make the anachronistic mistake of assuming that contemporaries were as daunted by them as we should be, were we suddenly pitchforked backwards in time. In Tudor and Stuart England men were fully accustomed to disease and a low expectation of life. Parents were slower to recognise the individuality of their children, for they well knew that they might lose them in their infancy. Husbands and wives were better adjusted to the idea of the surviving partner marrying after the other's death. The attitude of the poor to their lot seems often to have been one of careless stoicism. Many middle-class observers commented on their insensibility in face of the dangers of the plague, and were shocked by the general reluctance to obey regulations designed for their own safety.[58] When starvation threatened, the poor were capable of using violence to secure food for themselves, but they made little contribution to the political radicalism of the time and showed no interest in attempting to change the structure of the society in which they found themselves. Unlike the inhabitants of today's under-developed countries, they knew of no foreign countries where the standard of living was notably higher. Instead of working

56. Snell, *The Chronicles of Twyford*, p. 50.
57. Bell, *Great Fire of London*, pp. 30–31. There is a list of London fires in *Flagellum Dei* (1668).
58. See, e.g., *H.M.C. Gawdy*, p. 163; *C.S.P.D.*, 1665–6, p. 5; W. Kemp, *A Brief Treatise of the Nature ... and Cure of the Pestilence* (1665), pp. 15–16; Wilson, *The Plague in Shakespeare's London*, p. 41.

for social reform they often turned to more direct methods of liberation.

Drink, for example, was built into the fabric of social life. It played a part in nearly every public and private ceremony, every commercial bargain, every craft ritual, every private occasion of mourning or rejoicing. At fairs and markets, which remained exempt until 1874 from ordinary licensing restrictions, the consumption could be enormous. 'Go but to the town's end where a fair is kept,' remarked a preacher in 1638, 'and there they lie, as if some field had been fought; here lies one man, there another.' As a Frenchman observed in 1672, there was no business which could be done in England without pots of beer.[59] Late medieval preachers complained that working-men got drunk at least once a week; while in the reign of Charles II foreign visitors noticed that artisans did not let a day go by without a visit to the alehouse.[60]

The beer was cheap to make. The Elizabethan country clergyman, William Harrison, had 200 gallons brewed every month in his household, for an outlay of only twenty shillings a time.[61] We do not know the size of his household, but the daily consumption was obviously high. At sea and on land the standard allowance of beer per head seems to have been a gallon a day.[62] Beer was a basic ingredient in everyone's diet, children as well as adults. The first available figures for the total national consumption date from the late seventeenth century. They show that in 1684 duty was charged in England and Wales on a total of 6,318,000 barrels of beer (4,384,000 of strong beer, 1,934,000 of small beer), each barrel containing thirty-six gal-

59. (R. Younge), *The Drunkard's Character* (1638), p. 338; R. V. French, *Nineteen Centuries of Drink in England* (2nd edn, n.d.), p. 224. For an informative survey by an early temperance reformer of pre-industrial drinking customs, see J. Dunlop, *The Philosophy of Artificial and Compulsory Drinking Usage in Great Britain and Ireland* (6th edn., 1839).

60. G. R. Owst, *Literature and Pulpit in Medieval England* (2nd edn, Oxford, 1961), p. 364; (L. Magalotti), *Travels of Cosmo the Third, Grand Duke of Tuscany, through England* (1821), p. 398.

61. W. Harrison, *Description of England*, ed. F. J. Furnivall (New Shakespere Soc. (1877–1908)), i, pp. 158–9.

62. E. M. Myatt-Price, 'A Tally of Ale', *Journ. Royal Statistical Soc.*, ser. A, cxxiii (1960); L. Stone, *The Crisis of the Aristocracy, 1558–1641* (Oxford, 1965), p. 558; M. Oppenheim, *A History of the Administration of the Royal Navy*, i (1896), p. 140; F. G. Emmison, *Tudor Secretary. Sir William Petre at Court and at Home* (1961), p. 150; J. D. Chambers, *Nottinghamshire in the Eighteenth Century* (2nd edn, 1966), pp. 290–91.

lons in London, and thirty-four in the provinces. This suggests that each member of the population, man, woman and child, consumed almost forty gallons a year, i.e. nearly a pint a day. But allowance must also be made for the beer brewed privately on which excise was not charged: Gregory King estimated that in 1688 this came to a further seventy per cent of the original total. Even without this addition the *per capita* consumption figure is higher than anything known in modern times.[63] And this is to take no account of the foreign wine imports or the growing volume of spirit consumption.

It may be that the greater quantity of salt meat and fish consumed in the seventeenth century made men thirstier. It is also likely that the listlessness produced by a predominantly cereal diet created a greater demand for a stimulant. The absence of alternative beverages further helped to drive men to alcohol. Tea and coffee were still luxuries. Tea cost twenty shillings a pound at the end of the seventeenth century[64] and did not establish itself as a working-class drink until the last quarter of the eighteenth century. Coffee played an even slighter part in the drinking habits of the population at large, though it became very fashionable among London sophisticates.

Alcohol was thus an essential narcotic which anaesthetized men against the strains of contemporary life. Drunkenness broke down social distinctions, and brought a temporary mood of optimism to the desperate. It was extensive in Elizabethan prisons[65] and among the lower classes. (It was only during the seventeenth century that the lord replaced the beggar as proverbially the drunkest member of the community.)[66] The poor took to drink to blot out some of the horror in their lives. Alcohol flowed freely at times of plague: 'I have myself seen,' recalled a preacher in 1638, 'when the Bills [of Mortality] were at the highest, even bearers who had little respite from carrying dead corpses to their graves and many others of the like rank go reeling in the streets.'[67] At executions drink was always

63. B. R. Mitchell and P. Deane, *Abstract of British Historical Statistics* (Cambridge, 1962), p. 251; G. King, *Natural and Political Observations* (in G. Chalmers, *Estimate of the Comparative Strength of Great Britain* [1802]), pp. 55–6. cf. G. B. Wilson, *Alcohol and the Nation* (1940), table 2.

64. Drummond and Wilbraham, op. cit., p. 117.

65. *Shakespeare in His Own Age*, ed. A. Nicoll (*Shakespeare Survey*, xvii [Cambridge, 1964]), pp. 98–9.

66. A change noted by J. Hart, *The Diet of the Diseased* (1633), p. 135, and H. Moseley, *An Healing Leaf* (1658), p. 4.

67. Younge, *The Drunkard's Character*, p. 248. cf. *The Plague Pamphlets of Thomas Dekker*, ed. F. P. Wilson (Oxford, 1925), pp. 150–51.

offered to the condemned: the witch, Anne Bodenham, who was executed at Salisbury in 1653, kept asking for drink and would have died drunk if her persecutors had allowed her.[68] Ale, wrote a contemporary,

doth comfort the heavy and troubled mind; it will make a weeping widow laugh and forget sorrow for her deceased husband; ... it is the warmest lining of a naked man's coat; it satiates and assuages hunger and cold; with a toast it is the poor man's comfort; the shepherd, mower, ploughman, and blacksmith's most esteemed purchase; it is the tinker's treasure, the pedlar's jewel, the beggar's joy; and the prisoner's loving nurse.[69]

As a means of making life appear momentarily tolerable, drink had few rivals among the very poor. There was more good in a cask of ale than in the four gospels, declared a fifteenth-century heretic; malt, he thought, did more to justify God's ways to man than the Bible.[70]

A newer form of narcotic was tobacco. Smoking was introduced to England early in the reign of Elizabeth I and had become well-established by the time of her death. At first there was an attempt to represent tobacco as being taken only for medicinal purposes, but the pretence soon became unconvincing. In 1597 a contemporary remarked that addicts were consuming it 'for wantonness ... and cannot forbear it, no, not in the middest of their dinner'. Jacobean observers were familiar with the chain smoker who puffed his pipe from morning to night, and even in bed.[71] 'Tis death to some to be barred tobacco,' declared a Member of Parliament in 1621.[72] Yet pipe-smoking was an expensive habit. Tobacco varied widely in price according to the supply, but it seldom sold for less than a pound per pound in the reign of James I, and often cost more. Figures for domestic consumption are spasmodic, but they indicate a steady rise, from an annual average of 140,000 pounds in 1614–21 to 11,300,000 pounds in 1699–1709. This suggests that the consumption per head of population went up from less than an ounce a year at the beginning of the century to nearly two pounds at the end. Not until 1907

68. E. Bower, *Doctor Lamb revived* (1653), pp. 34, 36.
69. John Taylor, the Water Poet, quoted in W. T. Marchant, *In Praise of Ale* (1888), p. 57.
70. Thomson, *Later Lollards*, p. 62.
71. A. Chute, *Tobacco*, ed. F. P. Wilson (Luttrell Soc., 1961), p. xxvii; W. B. Willcox, *Gloucestershire. A Study in Local Government* (New Haven, 1940), p. 158.
72. M. Prestwich, *Cranfield* (Oxford, 1966), p. 313.

did the figures reach this level again.[73] Tobacco must have done something to steady the nerves of Stuart Englishmen. One modern historian has suggested, not entirely frivolously, that it helped to foster the virtues of political compromise which emerged in the later seventeenth century. Holy Communion, thought Christopher Marlowe, would have been 'much better being administered in a tobacco pipe'.[74]

A further escape from reality was gambling. In modern times the prospect of winning a fortune on the football pools attracts millions of people and sustains the optimism of many working-class folk in adverse circumstances. In the seventeenth century gambling diverted the attention of the labouring poor from the possibilities of self-help and political activism, by holding out the prospect that a lucky person would be able to better himself despite the inequities of the social system. Men gambled on cards, dice, horses, foot-races, bear-baiting, cock-fighting, and a host of similar pastimes. Even very poor men engaged heavily in speculative ventures; and the judicial records of the time contain occasional references to labourers who were unable to support their wives and children because they had lost all their money at cards.[75] In 1663 Samuel Pepys was amazed to see ordinary working-folk losing as much as ten or twenty pounds on bear-baiting and cock-fighting.[76]

These were the habits which generations of middle-class reformers attempted to break in their successive campaigns for the Reformation of Manners, by battling against popular pastimes, 'superfluous' alehouses and lower-class tippling. What they were combating was the fatalistic hopelessness of those who saw no alternative but to drown their sorrows. The beliefs to which we must now turn were all concerned to explain misfortune and to mitigate its rigour. But we must not forget that some contemporaries preferred recourse to cruder and more immediate forms of escape.

73. C. M. MacInnes, *The Early English Tobacco Trade* (1926), p. 35; Mitchell and Deane, *Abstract of British Historical Statistics*, pp. 355–7; A. Rive, 'The Consumption of Tobacco since 1600', *Economic History*, i (1926).
74. D. Ogg, *England in the Reign of Charles II* (2nd edn, Oxford, 1955), i, p. 76; P. H. Kocher, *Christopher Marlowe* (Chapel Hill, 1946), pp. 35–6, 60.
75. T. Gataker, *Of the Nature and Use of Lots* (2nd edn, 1627), pp. 288–9; *Quarter Sessions Records*, ed. J. C. Atkinson (North Riding Rec. Soc., 1884–7), i, p. 209; (T. Brasbridge), *The Poore Mans Jewell* (1578), sig. biii^v.
76. S. Pepys, *Diary*, 21 Dec. 1663.

RELIGION

2.

THE MAGIC OF THE
MEDIEVAL CHURCH

Surely, if a man will but take a view of all Popery, he shall easily see
that a great part of it is mere magic.

William Perkins, *A Golden Chaine* (1591)
(in *Workes* [Cambridge, 1616-18], i, p. 40)

NEARLY every primitive religion is regarded by its adherents as a
medium for obtaining supernatural power. This does not prevent it
from functioning as a system of explanation, a source of moral injunctions, a symbol of social order, or a route to immortality; but it
does mean that it also offers the prospect of a supernatural means of
control over man's earthly environment. The history of early Christianity offers no exception to this rule. Conversions to the new
religion, whether in the time of the primitive Church or under the
auspices of the missionaries of more recent times, have frequently
been assisted by the view of converts that they are acquiring not just
a means of other-worldly salvation, but a new and more powerful
magic. Just as the Hebrew priests of the Old Testament endeavoured
to confound the devotees of Baal by challenging them publicly to
perform supernatural acts, so the Apostles of the early Church

BIBLIOGRAPHICAL NOTE. A fundamental source for this aspect of the
medieval Church is A. Franz, *Die kirchlichen Benediktionen im Mittelalter*
(Freiburg-im-Breisgau, 1909), which is based on early medieval liturgical
books. But it does not have much material relating to the later Middle Ages
or to England. In addition to the *York Manual* and *Sarum Manual* I have
drawn upon the liturgical texts contained in W. Maskell, *Monumenta Ritualia
Ecclesiae Anglicanae* (2nd edn, Oxford, 1882). The thirteenth-century *Rationale* of G. Durandus is an invaluable guide to the Church's ritual (French
translation by Ch. Barthélémy [Paris, 1854]), and so are many of the articles
in *D.T.C.* The most comprehensive survey of the superstitions surrounding
the sacraments is still Thiers, *Superstitions*. C. G. Loomis, *White Magic.
An Introduction to the Folklore of Christian Legend* (Cambridge, Mass.,
1948) provides a useful analysis of the miraculous content of the Saints' *Lives*,
and there is a suggestive, though crude, account of Church magic in V.
Rydberg, *The Magic of the Middle Ages*, trans. A. H. Edgren (New York,
1879), chap. 2. See also P. Delaunay, *La Médicine et l'église* (Paris, 1948).

attracted followers by working miracles and performing supernatural cures. Both the New Testament and the literature of the patristic period testify to the importance of these activities in the work of conversion; and the ability to perform miracles soon became an indispensable test of sanctity. The claim to supernatural power was an essential element in the Anglo-Saxon Church's fight against paganism, and missionaries did not fail to stress the superiority of Christian prayers to heathen charms.[1]

The medieval Church thus found itself saddled with the tradition that the working of miracles was the most efficacious means of demonstrating its monopoly of the truth. By the twelfth and thirteenth centuries the *Lives* of the Saints had assumed a stereotyped pattern. They related the miraculous achievements of holy men, and stressed how they could prophesy the future, control the weather, provide protection against fire and flood, magically transport heavy objects, and bring relief to the sick. Many of these stories were retold in *The Golden Legend*, a popular compilation by a thirteenth-century Archbishop of Genoa, which was to be translated by Caxton in 1483 and reissued in England at least seven times before the Reformation.[2]

On the eve of the Reformation the Church did not as an institution claim the power to work miracles. But it reaped prestige from the doings of those of its members to whom God was deemed to have extended miraculous gifts. It stressed that the saints were only intercessors whose entreaties might go unheeded, but it readily countenanced the innumerable prayers offered to them on more optimistic assumptions. The shrines of the saints at Glastonbury, Lindisfarne, Walsingham, Canterbury, Westminster, St Albans and similar holy places had become objects of pilgrimage to which the sick and infirm made long and weary journeys in the confident expectation of obtaining a supernatural cure. Over 500 miracles were associated with Becket and his shrine; and at the Holy Rood of Bromholm in Norfolk

1. See, e.g., B. Colgrave, 'Bede's Miracle Stories', *Bede, His Life, Times and Writings*, ed. A. Hamilton Thompson (Oxford, 1935), and the passages in Bede cited by J. D. Y. Peel, 'Syncretism and Religious Change', *Comparative Studies in Soc. and Hist.*, x (1967–8), p. 134, n. 40.

2. *S.T.C.* lists eight editions between 1483 and 1527. There is a modern reprint edited by F. S. Ellis (Temple Classics, 1900) and a discussion in H. C. White, *Tudor Books of Saints and Martyrs* (Madison, Wisc., 1963), chap. 2. For early instances of ecclesiastical healing see W. Bonser, *The Medical Background of Anglo-Saxon England* (1963), pp. 118–19, and Loomis, *White Magic, passim.*

thirty-nine persons were said to have been raised from the dead and twelve cured of blindness. Holy relics became wonder-working fetishes, believed to have the power to cure illness and to protect against danger; around 1426 the Bishop of Durham's accounts contain a payment for signing sixteen cattle with St Wilfrid's signet to ward off the murrain.[3]

Images were similarly credited with miraculous efficacy. The representation of St Christopher, which so frequently adorned the walls of English village churches, was said to offer a day's preservation from illness or death to all those who looked upon it. St Wilgerfort, better known as St Uncumber, whose statue stood in St Paul's, could eliminate the husbands of those discontented wives who chose to offer her a peck of oats. The large mounted wooden figure of Derfel Gadarn at Llandderfel, near Bala, protected men and cattle, rescued souls from Purgatory, and inflicted disease upon his enemies: Henry VIII's visitors found five or six hundred worshippers at the shrine on the day they went there to pull it down.[4] Saints indeed were believed to have the power to bestow diseases as well as to relieve them. 'We worship saints for fear,' wrote William Tyndale in the early sixteenth century, 'lest they should be displeased and angry with us, and plague us or hurt us; as who is not afraid of St Laurence? Who dare deny St Anthony a fleece of wool for fear of his terrible fire, or lest he send the pox among our sheep?'[5]

The worship of saints was an integral part of the fabric of medieval society and was sustained by important social considerations. Individual churches had their own patron saints, and strong territorial associations could give hagiolatry an almost totemic character: 'Of all Our Ladies,' says a character in one of Thomas More's writings, 'I love best Our Lady of Walsingham', ' "and I", saith the other,

3. P. A. Brown, *The Development of the Legend of Thomas Becket* (Philadelphia, 1930), p. 258; W. Sparrow Simpson, 'On the Pilgrimage to Bromholm in Norfolk', *Journ. Brit. Archaeol. Assoc.*, xxx (1874); Kittredge, *Witchcraft*, pp. 37–8. Examples of resort to miraculous shrines can be found in J. C. Wall, *Shrines of British Saints* (1905), pp. 129, 213.

4. One hundred and eighty-six examples of the painting of St Christopher are cited by M. D. Anderson, *Looking for History in British Churches* (1951), pp. 144–5. For St Uncumber, T. More, *The Dialogue concerning Tyndale*, ed. W. E. Campbell (1931), pp. 166–7, and for Derfel Gadarn, G. Williams, *The Welsh Church from Conquest to Reformation* (Cardiff, 1962), pp. 495, 502.

5. W. Tyndale, *Expositions and Notes*, ed. H. Walter (Cambridge, P.S., 1849), p. 165. cf. D. Erasmus, *Pilgrimages to St Mary of Walsingham and St Thomas of Canterbury*, ed. J. G. Nichols (1849), p. 79.

"Our Lady of Ipswich." " Pilgrims brought money into the community and the inhabitants grew dependent upon them: in Elizabethan times, for example, it was pointed out that St Wistan's church in Leicestershire had previously been maintained by the proceeds of the annual pilgrimage.' Every medieval trade had the patronage of its own especial saint, who was corporately worshipped, and whose holy day had strong occupational affiliations:

Our painters had Luke, our weavers had Steven, our millers had Arnold, our tailors had Goodman, our sowters [cobblers] had Crispin, our potters had S. Gore with a devil on his shoulder and a pot in his hand. Was there a better horseleech . . . than S. Loy? Or a better sowgelder than S. Anthony? Or a better toothdrawer than S. Apolline?

Reginald Scot could thus mock these occupational saints in the years after the Reformation, but his words reveal the depth of the social roots of this form of popular devotion. The patronage of the saints give a sense of identity and of corporate existence to small and otherwise undifferentiated institutions. Hence their enduring popularity as names for colleges and schools even in a Protestant era.

Local loyalties could thus sustain an individual's allegiance to a particular saint. But the worship of saints in general depended upon the belief that the holy men and women of the past had not merely exemplified an ideal code of moral conduct, but could still employ supernatural powers to relieve the adversities of their followers upon earth. Diseases, like occupations and localities, were assigned to the special care of an appropriate saint, for in the popular mind the saints were usually regarded as specialists rather than as general practitioners. 'S. John and S. Valentine excelled at the falling evil,' recalled Scot,

S. Roch was good at the plague, S. Petronill at the ague. As for S. Margaret she passed Lucina for a midwife, ... in which respect S. Marpurge is joined with her in commission. For madmen and such as are possessed with devils, S. Romane was excellent, and friar Ruffine was also prettily skilful in that art. For botches and biles, Cosmus and Damian; S. Clare for the eyes. S. Apolline for teeth, S. Job for the pox. And for sore breasts S. Agatha.[8]

6. More, *Dialogue Concerning Tyndale*, p. 62. On saints and their localities see the statistical summary in F. Arnold-Forster, *Studies in Church Dedications* (1899), iii, and F. Bond, *Dedications and Patron Saints of English Churches* (1914).

7. W. G. Hoskins, *The Midland Peasant* (1957), p. 79.

8. Scot, *Discoverie: A Discourse of Divels*, chap. xxiv. For typical lists of

The saints were always on call to deal with a variety of daily eventualities. Pregnant women could use holy relics – girdles, skirts and coats – kept for the purpose by many religious houses, and they were urged by midwives to call upon St Margaret or the Virgin Mary to reduce the pangs of labour, or to invoke St Felicitas if they wished to ensure that the new child would be a boy. Henry VII's queen paid 6s. 8d. to a monk for a girdle of Our Lady for use in childbirth.[9] The variety of other secular contexts in which saints could also be invoked is indicated by John Aubrey's nostalgic description of the part they had once played in the daily lives of the Wiltshire country folk:

At St Oswaldsdown and Fordedown, &c thereabout, the shepherds prayed at night and at morning to St Oswald (that was martyred there) to preserve their sheep safe in the fold ... When they went to bed they did rake up their fire and make a cross in the ashes and pray to God and St Osyth to deliver them from fire and from water and from all misadventure ... When the bread was put into the oven, they prayed to God and to St Stephen, to send them a just batch and an even.[10]

The impetus behind the worship of saints seems to have slackened considerably during the fifteenth century.[11] But until the Reformation miracles at holy shrines continued to be reported. In 1538 a Sussex parson was still advising his parishioners to cure their sick animals by making offerings to St Loy and St Anthony.

The powers popularly attributed to the saints were, however, only one particular instance of the general power which the medieval Church, in its role as dispenser of divine grace, claimed to be able to exercise. By the early Middle Ages the ecclesiastical authorities had developed a comprehensive range of formulae designed to draw down God's practical blessing upon secular activities. The basic

saints and their appropriate specialisms see T. J. Pettigrew, *On Superstitions connected with the History and Practice of Medicine* (1844), pp. 37–8; Brand, *Antiquities*, i, pp. 363–4; W. G. Black, *Folk-Medicine* (1883), pp. 90–94.

9. *The Whole Works of ... Jeremy Taylor*, ed. R. Heber and revd by C. P. Eden (1847–54), vi, p. 257; C. F. Bühler, 'Prayers and Charms in Certain Middle English Scrolls', *Speculum*, xxxix (1964), p. 274, n. 31. cf. *Later Writings of Bishop Hooper*, ed. C. Nevinson (Cambridge, P.S., 1852), p. 141; Frere and Kennedy, *Articles and Injunctions*, ii, p. 58, n. 2; C. S. L. Linnell, *Norfolk Church Dedications* (York, 1962), pp. 11-12 n.

10. Aubrey, *Gentilisme*, p. 29.

11. See R. M. Clay, *The Mediaeval Hospitals of England* (1909), p. 9, and G. H. Gerould, *Saints' Legends* (Boston, 1916), p. 292.

12. *L.P.*, xiii (1), no. 1199.

ritual was the benediction of salt and water for the health of the body and the expulsion of evil spirits. But the liturgical books of the time also contained rituals devised to bless houses, cattle, crops, ships, tools, armour, wells and kilns. There were formulae for blessing men who were preparing to set off on a journey, to fight a duel, to engage in battle or to move into a new house. There were procedures for blessing the sick and for dealing with sterile animals, for driving away thunder and for making the marriage bed fruitful. Such rituals usually involved the presence of a priest and the employment of holy water and the sign of the cross. Basic to the whole procedure was the idea of exorcism, the formal conjuring of the devil out of some material object by the pronunciation of prayers and the invocation of God's name.[13] Holy water, thus exorcised, could be used to drive away evil spirits and pestilential vapours. It was a remedy against disease and sterility, and an instrument for blessing houses and food; though whether it worked automatically, or only if the officiating priest was of sufficient personal holiness, was a matter of theological dispute.

Theologians did not claim that these procedures made the practical precautions of daily life superfluous, but they did undoubtedly regard them as possessing a power which was more than merely spiritual or symbolic. The formula for consecrating the holy bread, given away to the laity on Sundays in lieu of the eucharist, called on God to bless the bread, 'so that all who consume it shall receive health of body as well as of soul'.[14] It was regarded as a medicine for the sick and a preservative against the plague.

As for holy water, there were some theologians who thought it superstitious to drink it as a remedy for sickness or to scatter it on the fields for fertility; but the orthodox view, firmly based upon the words of the benediction, was that there was nothing improper about such actions, provided they were performed out of genuine Christian faith.[15] Periodically, therefore, the holy water carrier went round the parish so that the pious could sprinkle their homes, their fields and their domestic animals. As late as 1543, when a storm burst over Canterbury, the inhabitants ran to church for holy water to sprinkle in their houses, so as to drive away the evil spirits in the air, and to

13. For these rituals, see the *Bibliographical Note* above. A large collection was translated and published as *The Doctrine of the Masse Booke* by N. Dorcastor in 1554.

14.   *Sarum Manual*, p. 4; Maskell, *Monumenta Ritualia*, i, p. cccxviii, n. 74.

15. Thiers, *Superstitions*, ii, p. 24.

protect their property against lightning. At about the same date the vicar of Bethersden, Kent, could advise a sick parishioner to drink holy water as a help to her recovery.[16] In the seventeenth century Jeremy Taylor lamented of the Irish that 'although not so much as a chicken is nowadays cured of the pip by holy water, yet upon all occasions they use it, and the common people throw it upon children's cradles, and sick cows' horns, and upon them that are blasted, and if they recover by any means, it is imputed to the holy water'.[17] The Devil, it was agreed, was allergic to holy water, and wherever his influence was suspected it was an appropriate remedy. In the reign of Elizabeth I, Widow Wiseman, later a Catholic martyr, threw holy water at her persecutor, Topcliffe, whose horse thereupon flung him to the ground. Topcliffe raged against her, 'calling her an old witch, who by her charms had made his horse to lay him on the ground, but [relates the Catholic source for this episode] she with good reason laughed to see that holy water had given him so fine a fall'.[18] Here, as Protestant commentators were to urge, the distinction between magic and religion was an impossibly fine one.

The same was true of the numerous ecclesiastical talismans and amulets whose use the Church encouraged. As one Protestant versifier wrote:

About these Catholics' necks and hands are always hanging charms,
That serve against all miseries and all unhappy harms.[19]

Theologians held that there was no superstition about wearing a piece of paper or medal inscribed with verses from the gospels or with the sign of the cross, provided no non-Christian symbols were also employed.[20] The most common of these amulets was the agnus dei, a small wax cake, originally made out of paschal candles and blessed by the Pope, bearing the image of the lamb and flag. This was intended to serve as a defence against the assaults of the Devil and as a preservative against thunder, lightning, fire, drowning, death in child-bed and similar dangers. After the Reformation

16. *L.P.*, xviii (2), pp. 296, 300.

17. *The Whole Works ... of Jeremy Taylor*, vi, p. 268.

18. *The Chronicle of the English Augustinian Canonesses Regular of the Lateran, at St Monica's in Louvain*, ed. A. Hamilton (1904), i, p. 84.

19. T. Naogeorgus, *The Popish Kingdome*, trans. B. Googe, ed. R. C. Hope (1880), f. 57ᵛ.

20. See Aquinas, *Summa Theologica*, II.2.96.4; Scot, *Discoverie*, XII.ix; J. L. André, 'Talismans', *The Reliquary*, n.s., vii (1893).

Bishop Hall commented on the survival of the associated belief in the protective power of St John's Gospel, 'printed in a small roundel and sold to the credulous ignorants with this fond warrant, that whosoever carries it about with him shall be free from the dangers of the day's mishaps'.[21] In the seventeenth century rosaries were similarly blessed as a protection against fire, tempest, fever and evil spirits.[22]

The same preservative power was attributed to holy relics: in 1591, for example, John Allyn, an Oxford recusant, was said to possess a quantity of Christ's blood, which he sold at twenty pounds a drop: those who had it about them would be free from bodily harm.[23] The sign of the cross was also employed to ward off evil spirits and other dangers. In North Wales it was reported in 1589 that people still crossed themselves when they shut their windows, when they left their cattle, and when they went out of their houses in the morning. If any misfortune befell them or their animals their common saying was 'You have not crossed yourself well today', or 'You have not made the sign of the rood upon the cattle', on the assumption that this omission had been the cause of their mishap.[24]

Ecclesiastical preservatives of this kind were intended to give protection in a wide variety of contexts. The consecration of church bells made them efficacious against evil spirits and hence enabled them to dispel the thunder and lightning for which demons were believed to be responsible. When a tempest broke out the bells would be rung in an effort to check the storm: this happened at Sandwich, for example, in 'the great thundering' of 1502, and again in 1514.[25] Alternatively, one could invoke St Barbara against thunder, or tie a charm to the building one wished to protect – though an agnus dei failed to save St Albans Abbey from being struck by lightning in

21. *The Works of . . . Joseph Hall*, ed. P. Wynter (Oxford, 1863), vii, p. 329. On the agnus dei see *D.T.C.*, i, cols. 605–13.

22. *H.M.C., Rutland*, i, p. 526.

23. *C.S.P.D., 1591–4*, p. 29. The Venetian practice of flocking to the altars of St Charles Borromeo to seek preservation against sudden death is described in *H.M.C.*, x, appx. i, p. 553.

24. P.R.O., SP 12/224/145ᵛ (also printed in *Archaeologia Cambrensis* [3rd ser.], i [1855], p. 236).

25. D. Gardiner, *Historic Haven. The Story of Sandwich* (Derby, 1954), p. 166. Other examples in Kittredge, *Witchcraft*, p. 158; Aubrey, *Miscellanies*, p. 141; J. C. Cox, *Churchwardens' Accounts* (1913), pp. 212–13; B. Weldon, *Chronological Notes concerning the . . . English Congregation of the Order of St. Benedict* (1881), p. 185. The formula for consecrating bells is in *Sarum Manual*, pp. 175–7.

the thirteenth century.²⁶ As a protection against fire there were 'St Agatha's letters', an inscription placed on tiles, bells or amulets. Fasting on St Mark's day was another means of gaining protection; or one could appeal to St Clement or to the Irish saint Columbkille.²⁷ In 1180 the holy shrine of St Werberga was carried round Chester and miraculously preserved the city from destruction by fire.²⁸ In addition, there were exorcisms to make the fields fertile; holy candles to protect farm animals; and formal curses to drive away caterpillars and rats and to kill weeds. At the dissolution of the Abbey of Bury St Edmunds there were discovered 'relics for rain, and certain other superstitious usages for avoiding of weeds growing in corn'.²⁹

The medieval Church thus acted as a repository of supernatural power which could be dispensed to the faithful to help them in their daily problems. It was inevitable that the priests, set apart from the rest of the community by their celibacy and ritual consecration, should have derived an extra *cachet* from their position as mediators between man and God. It was also inevitable that around the Church, the clergy and their holy apparatus there clustered a horde of popular superstitions, which endowed religious objects with a magical power to which theologians themselves had never laid claim. A scapular, or friar's coat, for example, was a coveted object to be worn as a preservative against pestilence or the ague, and even to be buried in as a short cut to salvation: Bishop Hugh Latimer confessed that he used to think that if he became a friar it would be impossible for him to be damned.³⁰ The church and churchyard also enjoyed a special power in popular estimation, primarily because of

26. T. Walsingham, *Gesta Abbatum monasterii Sancti Albani*, ed. H. T. Riley (Rolls Series, 1867–9), i, p. 313.

27. *Homilies*, p. 62, n. 20; V. Alford, 'The Cat Saint', *Folk-Lore*, lii (1941); P. B. G. Binnall in ibid., liii (1943), p. 77; W. Tyndale, *An Answer to Sir Thomas More's Dialogue*, ed. H. Walter (Cambridge, P.S., 1850), p. 61; G. R. Owst, *Literature and Pulpit in Medieval England* (2nd edn, Oxford, 1961), p. 147; C. Singer, 'Early English Magic and Medicine', *Procs. Brit. Acad.*, ix (1919–20), p. 362.

28. Wall, *Shrines of British Saints*, p. 61.

29. B. Willis, *An History of the Mitred Parliamentary Abbies and Conventual Cathedral Churches* (1718), i, appx., p. 58; G. Storms, *Anglo-Saxon Magic* (The Hague, 1948), pp. 313–14; Scot, *Discoverie*, XII.xxi (holy candles); B. L. Manning, *The People's Faith in the Time of Wyclif* (Cambridge, 1919), p. 94; G. G. Coulton, *The Medieval Village* (Cambridge, 1925), p. 268; id., 'The Excommunication of Caterpillars', *History Teachers Miscellany*, iii (1925); G. R. Elton, *Star Chamber Stories* (1958), p. 206.

30. Foxe, vii, p. 489; *Homilies*, p. 59. For the origin of the notion, H. C,

the ritual consecration of the site with salt and water. The key of the church door was said to be an efficacious remedy against a mad dog;[31] the soil from the churchyard was credited with special magical power; and any crime committed on holy ground became an altogether more heinous affair, simply because of the place where it had occurred. This was recognised by a statute of the reign of Edward VI imposing special penalties for such offences; if the consecrated area were polluted by some crime of violence a special act of reconciliation was necessary before it could be used again for religious purposes.[32] Even the coins in the offertory were accredited with magical value; there were numerous popular superstitions about the magical value of communion silver as a cure for illness or a lucky charm against danger.

But it was above all in connection with the sacraments of the Church that such beliefs arose. The Mass, in particular, was associated with magical power and for this, it must be said, the teaching of the Church was at least indirectly responsible. During the long history of the Christian Church the sacrament of the altar had undergone a process of theological reinterpretation. By the later Middle Ages the general effect had been to shift the emphasis away from the communion of the faithful, and to place it upon the formal consecration of the elements by the priest. The ceremony thus acquired in the popular mind a mechanical efficacy in which the operative factor was not the participation of the congregation, who had become virtual spectators, but the special power of the priest. Hence the doctrine that the laity could benefit from being present at the celebration even though they could not understand the proceedings. If too ignorant to follow a private mass book, they were encouraged to recite whatever prayers they knew; so that during the Mass the priest and people in fact pursued different modes of devotion. The ritual was said, in a notorious phrase, to work 'like a charm upon an adder'.[33] In the actual miracle of transubstantiation the 'instru-

---

Lea, *A History of Auricular Confession and Indulgences* (1896), iii, pp. 263, 496–500, and H. Thurston, 'Scapulars', *The Month*, cxlix–cl (1927).

31. Thiers, *Superstitions*, ii, p. 499.

32. A Watkin, *Dean Cosyn and Wells Cathedral Miscellanea* (Somerset Rec. Soc., 1941), p. 158; 5 and 6 Edward VI cap. 4 (1551–2).

33. For this expression, G. G. Coulton, *Medieval Studies*, 14 (2nd edn, 1921), pp. 24–5. For this controversial subject I have drawn on both C. W. Dugmore, *The Mass and the English Reformers* (1958), and F. Clark, *Eucharistic Sacrifice and the Reformation* (1960).

mental cause' was the formula of consecration. Theologians refined this doctrine considerably, but their subtleties were too complicated to be understood by ordinary men.[34] What stood out was the magical notion that the mere pronunciation of words in a ritual manner could effect a change in the character of material objects.

The reservation of the sacrament at the altar as an object of devotion had become customary in England by the thirteenth century and the element of mystery attaching to it was enhanced by the construction in the later Middle Ages of enclosed sanctuaries to protect the elements from the gaze of the public. Literalism generated anecdotes of how the Host had turned into flesh and blood, even into a child.[35] The notion spread that temporal benefits might be expected from its mere contemplation, and the belief was enhanced by the readiness of the Church to multiply the secular occasions for which masses might be performed as a means of propitiation. There were masses for the sick and for women in labour, masses for good weather and for safe journeys, masses against the plague and other epidemics. The *Sarum Missal* of 1532 contained a special mass for the avoidance of sudden death.[36] In 1516 the Priory of Holy Cross at Colchester received a grant of land, in return for the celebration of a solemn mass 'for the further prosperity of the town'.[37] It was common to attach special value to the performance of a certain number of masses in succession – five, seven, nine or thirty (a trental). The ceremony could even be perverted into a maleficent act by causing masses for the dead to be celebrated for persons still alive, in order to hasten their demise. The fifteenth-century treatise *Dives and Pauper* inveighed against those

that for hate or wrath that they bear against any man or woman take away the clothes of the altar, and clothe the altar with doleful clothing, or beset the altar or the cross about with thorns, and withdraw light out

34. C. W. Dugmore, in *Journ. of Theol. Studs.*, n.s., xiv (1963), p. 229.

35. C. N. L. Brooke, 'Religious Sentiment and Church Design in the Later Middle Ages', *Bull. of the John Rylands Lib.*, l (1967). For a good example of popular literalism see E. Peacock, 'Extracts from Lincoln Episcopal Visitations', *Archaeologia*, xlviii (1885), pp. 251–3.

36. G. G. Coulton, *Five Centuries of Religion* (Cambridge, 1923–50), i, pp. 117–18. For lists of such purposes, Delaunay, *La Médicine et l'église*, pp. 10–11; Maskell, *Monumenta Ritualia*, i, pp. lxxx–lxxxi; Dugmore, *The Mass and the English Reformers*, pp. 64–5. The fullest account (for Germany) is A. Franz, *Die Messe im deutschen Mittelalter* (Freiburg-im-Breisgau, 1902).

37. *Essex Review*, xlvi (1937), pp. 85–6.

of the church or ... do sing mass of requiem for them that be alive, in hope that they should fare the worse and the sooner die.[38]

The clear implication was that the clergy themselves were sometimes involved in these perversions.

A plethora of sub-superstitions thus accumulated around the sacrament of the altar. The clergy's anxiety that none of the consecrated elements should be wasted or accidentally dropped on the floor encouraged the idea that the Host was an object of super-natural potency. The officiating priest was required to swallow the remaining contents of the chalice, flies and all if need be, and to ensure that not a crumb of the consecrated wafer was left behind.[39] The communicant who did not swallow the bread, but carried it away from the church in his mouth, was widely believed to be in possession of an impressive source of magical power. He could use it to cure the blind or the feverish; he could carry it around with him as a general protection against ill fortune, or he could beat it up into a powder and sprinkle it over his garden as a charm against caterpillars. Medieval stories relate how the Host was profanely employed to put out fires, to cure swine fever, to fertilize the fields and to encourage bees to make honey. The thief could also convert it into a love-charm or use it for some maleficent purpose. Some believed that a criminal who swallowed the Host would be immune from discovery; others held that by simultaneously communicating with a woman one could gain her affections.[40] In the sixteenth century John Bale complained that the Mass had become a remedy for the diseases of man and beast. It was employed by 'witches . . . sorcerers, charmers, enchanters, dreamers, soothsayers, necromancers, conjurers, cross-diggers, devil-raisers, miracle-doers, dog-leeches and bawds'. The first Edwardian Prayer Book accordingly insisted that the bread should be placed by the officiating minister

38. *Dives and Pauper* (1536), f. 51. cf. Kittredge, *Witchcraft*, p. 75; Thiers, *Superstitions*, iii, 5, chaps. vii–viii, xi; G. R. Owst, '*Sortilegium* in English Homiletic Literature of the Fourteenth Century', in *Studies Presented to Sir Hilary Jenkinson*, ed. J. C. Davies (1957), p. 281.

39. A doctrine well illustrated by the nauseous anecdote in Weldon, *Chronological Notes*, pp. 234–5.

40. Coulton, *Five Centuries of Religion*, i, cap. 7; Thiers, *Superstitions*, ii, 3, chap. xi; P. Browe, *Die eucharistischen Wunder des Mittelalters* (Breslau, 1938); *Mirk's Festial*, ed. T. Erbe (E.E.T.S.), i (1905), pp. 173–4; *The Works of John Jewel*, ed. J. Ayre (Cambridge, P.S., 1845–50), i, p. 6; Scot, *Discoverie*, XII.ix.

direct in the communicant's mouth, because in past times people had often carried the sacrament away and 'kept it with them and diversely abused it, to superstition and wickedness'.[41]

It was because of this magical power thought to reside in consecrated objects that ecclesiastical authorities had long found it necessary to take elaborate precautions against theft. The Lateran Council of 1215 had ruled that the eucharist and the holy oil should be kept under lock and key, and the later medieval English Church showed a keen interest in enforcing this stipulation. As late as 1557, for example, Cardinal Pole, in his Injunctions for Cambridge University, insisted that the font should be locked up, so as to prevent the theft of holy water.[42] Thefts of the Host are known to have occurred periodically – three were reported in London in 1532 – and communion bread continued to be employed illegitimately for magical purposes in the post-Reformation era: James Device, one of the Lancashire witches of 1612, was told by his grandmother, Old Demdike, to present himself for communion and bring home the bread.[43]

Many of these superstitions, however, did not require anything so dramatic as the theft of the Host from the altar. Mere attendance at Mass might secure temporal benefits. In his *Instructions for Parish Priests* John Myrc, the fourteenth-century Austin Canon of Lilleshall, claimed the authority of St Augustine for the view that anyone who saw a priest bearing the Host would not lack meat or drink for the rest of that day, nor be in any danger of sudden death or blindness.[44] 'Thousands,' wrote William Tyndale in the early sixteenth century, believed that, if they crossed themselves when the priest was reading St John's Gospel, no mischance would happen to them that day.[45] The Mass could also be a means of prognosticating the future or of gaining success in some projected venture. The clergy disseminated stories of the miraculous benefits which had been known to spring from communicating, and of the disastrous

41. *Select Works of John Bale*, ed. H. Christmas (Cambridge, P.S., 1849), p. 236; *The Two Liturgies . . . in the Reign of King Edward VI*, ed. J. Ketley (Cambridge, P.S., 1844), p. 99. For a case in point, A. G. Dickens, *Lollards and Protestants in the Diocese of York, 1509–1558* (1959), p. 16.

42. Powicke and Cheney, *Councils and Synods, passim*; Kittredge, *Witchcraft*, p. 470; Frere and Kennedy, *Articles and Injunctions*, ii, p. 416.

43. Kittredge, *Witchcraft*, p. 150; Potts, sig. H3.

44. J. Myrc, *Instructions for Parish Priests*, ed. E. Peacock (E.E.T.S., 1868), p. 10. cf. W. Harrington, *In this Boke are Conteyned the Comendacions of Matrymony* (1528), sig. Eiii^v.

45. Tyndale, *An Answer to Sir Thomas More's Dialogue*, p. 61.

consequences which participation in the ceremony might have for the unworthy communicant.[46] In the Communion Service in the Prayer Book of 1549 the curate was required to warn the congregation that anyone who received unworthily did so to his own damnation, both spiritual and temporal, for in this way 'we kindle God's wrath over us; we provoke him to plague us with divers diseases and sundry kinds of death'. In the seventeenth century the Catholic Church was noted by an intelligent observer to teach that the Mass might still be efficacious for 'safe-journeying by sea or land, on horseback or on foot; for women that are barren, big, or bringing forth; for fevers and toothaches; for hogs and hens; for recovery of lost goods and the like'.[47]

Like the Mass, the other Christian sacraments all generated a corpus of parasitic beliefs, which attributed to each ceremony a material significance which the leaders of the Church had never claimed. By the eve of the Reformation most of these rituals had become crucial 'rites of passage', designed to ease an individual's transition from one social state to another, to emphasise his new status and to secure divine blessing for it. Baptism, which signified the entry of the new-born child into membership of the Church, was necessary to turn the infant into a full human being, and by the thirteenth century was expected to take place within the first week of birth. The Church taught that the ceremony was absolutely necessary for salvation and that children who died unbaptized were usually consigned to limbo, where they would be perpetually denied sight of the vision of God and even, according to some theologians, subjected to the torments of the damned.[48] At the baptismal ceremony the child was, therefore, exorcised (with the obvious implication that it had previously been possessed by the Devil), anointed

46. Thiers, *Superstitions*, iii, v, chap. xii; Manning, *The People's Faith in the Time of Wyclif*, p. 79; J. A. Herbert, *Catalogue of Romances in the Department of Manuscripts in the British Museum*, iii (1910), *passim*.

47. H. More, *A Modest Enquiry into the Mystery of Iniquity* (1664), p. 76.

48. A. van Gennep has a brief discussion of baptism in his pioneering work, *The Rites of Passage*, trans. M. B. Vizedom and G. L. Caffee (1960), pp. 93–6. For medieval teaching on the subject, G. G. Coulton, *Infant Perdition in the Middle Ages* (*Medieval Studies*, 16, 1922) and G. W. Bromiley, *Baptism and the Anglican Reformers* (1953), pp. 48–52. The meaning of the rites of passage is further discussed by M. Gluckman in *Essays on the Ritual of Social Relations*, ed. Gluckman (Manchester, 1962) and R. Horton, 'Ritual Man in Africa', *Africa*, xxxiv (1964).

with chrism (consecrated oil and balsam) and signed with the cross in holy water. Around its head was bound a white cloth (chrisom), in which it would be buried if it should die in infancy.

The social significance of the baptismal ceremony as the formal reception of the child into the community is obvious enough, and it is not surprising that greater meaning should have been attached to the ceremony than the Church allowed. Even in the early twentieth century it was believed in some rural communities that children 'came on better' after being christened. In the later Middle Ages it was common to regard baptism as an essential rite if the child were physically to survive at all, and there were stories about blind children whose sight had been restored by baptism. Sundry superstitions related to the day on which the ceremony should take place, the sort of water which should be used, and the qualifications of the godparents. There were also attempts to apply the rite in inappropriate contexts, for example, by baptising the caul in which the infant was born, or by exorcising the mother when she was in labour.⁴⁹ Particularly common was the idea that animals might benefit from the ceremony. It is possible that some of the numerous cases recorded in the sixteenth and seventeenth centuries of attempts to baptize dogs, cats, sheep and horses⁵⁰ may not have arisen from drunkenness or Puritan mockery of Anglican ceremonies, but have reflected the old superstition that the ritual had about it a physical efficacy which could be directed to any living creature.

Very similar ideas surrounded the ceremony of confirmation. This rite had originally been combined with that of baptism as one integrated ceremony of Christian initiation. But by the early Middle Ages the two rituals had drawn apart, though confirmation was still expected to take place when the child was very young. Various maximum ages, ranging from one year to seven, were prescribed by English bishops in the thirteenth century; and, although a minimum age of seven came to be thought appropriate, the custom was slow

49. On these notions, Thiers, *Superstitions*, ii, i, *passim*; Brand, *Popular Antiquities*, ii, pp. 374–5; F. A. Gasquet, *Parish Life in Mediaeval England* (1906), pp. 189–90; Delaunay, *La Médicine et l'église*, p. 10; W. M. Williams, *The Sociology of an English Village: Gosforth* (1956), pp. 59–60; W. Henderson, *Notes on the Folk-Lore of the Northern Counties* (new edn, 1879), p. 15; *County Folk-Lore*, v, ed. Mrs Gutch and M. Peacock (Folk-Lore Soc., 1908), pp. 228–9; R. F(arnworth), *The Heart Opened by Christ* (1654), p. 5.

50. e.g., *V.C.H., Oxon*, ii, p. 42; *Sussex Archaeol. Collns.*, xlix (1960), pp. 53–4; *C.S.P.D., 1611–18*, p. 540; *1631–3*, p. 256; *Southwell Act Books*, xxii, p. 213; *H.M.C., Hatfield*, x, p. 450; Lilly, *Autobiography*, p. 97.

to establish itself: Elizabeth, daughter of Henry VIII, was baptized and confirmed at the age of three days. Only in the mid sixteenth century did the Council of Trent require the child to be approaching years of discretion and capable of rehearsing the elements of his belief.[51] At the confirmation ceremony the bishop would lay his hands on the child and tie around its forehead a linen band which he was required to wear for three days afterwards. This was believed to strengthen him against the assaults of the fiend, and the notion became current that it was extremely bad luck to untie the band under any circumstances. Here too physical effects were vulgarly attributed to the ceremony: a belief which survived until the nineteenth century, as evidenced by the case of the old Norfolk woman who claimed to have been 'bishopped' seven times, because she found it helped her rheumatism.[52]

Another ecclesiastical ritual with a strong social significance was the churching, or purification, of women after childbirth, representing as it did society's recognition of the woman's new role as mother, and her resumption of sexual relations with her husband after a period of ritual seclusion and avoidance. Extreme Protestant reformers were later to regard it as one of the most obnoxious Popish survivals in the Anglican Church, but medieval churchmen had also devoted a good deal of energy to refuting such popular superstitions as the belief that it was improper for the mother to emerge from her house, or to look at the sky or the earth before she had been purified. The Church chose to treat the ceremony as one of thanksgiving for a safe deliverance, and was reluctant to countenance any prescribed interval after birth before it could take place. Nor did it accept that the woman should stay indoors until she had been churched. Like the *Sarum Manual*, *Dives and Pauper* stressed that unpurified women might enter church whenever they wished, and that 'they that call them heathen women for the time that they lie in be fools

51. Powicke and Cheney, *Councils and Synods*, pp. 32, 71, 298, 369, 441, 591, 703, 989; J. D. C. Fisher, *Christian Initiation* (Alcuin Club, 1965), pp. 122–3; W. A. Pantin, *The English Church in the Fourteenth Century* (Cambridge, 1955), p. 199; Maskell, *Monumenta Ritualia*, i, pp. cclx–cclxiii, 42, n. 9; Tyndale, *Answer to More's Dialogue*, p. 72; Harrington, *In this Boke are conteyned the Cōmendacions of Matrymony*, sig. Eii.

52. R. Forby, *The Vocabulary of East Anglia* (1830), ii, pp. 406–7. cf. Thiers, *Superstitions*, ii, 2, chap. iii; W. Tyndale, *Doctrinal Treatises*, ed. H. Walter (Cambridge, P.S., 1848), p. 225; *County Folk-Lore*, v. ed. Gutch and Peacock, p. 108; *Folk-Lore Journ.*, ii (1884), p. 348.

and sin . . . full grievously'. But for people at large churching was indubitably a ritual of purification closely linked to its Jewish predecessor.[53]

Radical Protestants were later to blame the ceremony itself, which 'breedeth and nourisheth many superstitious opinions in the simple people's hearts; as that the woman which hath born a child is unclean and unholy'.[54] But a fairer view would have been to regard the ritual as the result of such opinions, rather than the cause. Virginity, or at least abstinence from sexual intercourse, was still a generally accepted condition of holiness; and there were many medieval precedents for the attitude of the Laudian Vicar of Great Totham, Essex, who refused communion to menstruating women and those who had had sexual intercourse on the previous night.[55] Such prejudices may have been reinforced by the all-male character of the Church and its insistence on celibacy, but they are too universal in primitive societies to be regarded as the mere creation of medieval religion. The ceremony of the churching of women took on a semi-magical significance in popular estimation; hence the belief, which the Church vainly attempted to scotch, that a woman who died in child-bed before being churched should be refused Christian burial.[56] The idea of purification survived the Reformation; even at the end of the seventeenth century it was reported from parts of Wales that 'the ordinary women are hardly brought to look upon churching otherwise than as a charm to prevent witchcraft, and think that grass will hardly ever grow where they tread before they are churched'.[57]

It is hardly necessary to detail the allied superstitions which attached themselves to the ceremony of marriage. Most of them

53. *Dives and Pauper* (1536), f. 229; *Sarum Manual*, p. 44; Harrington, *In this Boke are Conteyned the Cōmendacions of Matrymony*, sig. Div; T. Comber, *The Occasional Offices . . . Explained* (1679), pp. 506, 507, 510.

54. J. Canne, *A Necessitie of Separation* (1634), ed. C. Stovel (Hanserd Knollys Soc., 1849), p. 109 n.

55. J. White, *The First Century of Scandalous, Malignant Priests* (1643), p. 50. The Catholic Church regarded abstinence as desirable but not essential; Thiers, *Superstitions*, iv, pp. 563–4.

56. J. Toussaert, *Le Sentiment religieux en Flandre à la fin du Moyen-Âge* (Paris, 1963), p. 101. cf. *Sermons and Remains of Hugh Latimer*, ed. G. E. Corrie (Cambridge, P.S., 1845), p. xiv.

57. Kittredge, *Witchcraft*, p. 145. cf. the nineteenth-century survivals recorded in J. E. Vaux, *Church Folk-Lore* (2nd edn, 1902), pp. 112–13; *County Folk-Lore*, v, p. 228.

taught that the fate of the alliance could be adversely affected by the breach of a large number of ritual requirements relating to the time and place of the ceremony, the dress of the bride, and so forth. Typical was the notion that the wedding ring would constitute an effective recipe against unkindness and discord, so long as the bride continued to wear it.[58] Such notions provide a further demonstration of how every sacrament of the Church tended to generate its attendant sub-superstitions which endowed the spiritual formulae of the theologians with a crudely material efficacy.

This tendency was perhaps less apparent in the various rituals accompanying the burial of the dead, such as the convention that the corpse should face East or that the funeral should be accompanied by doles to the poor. Important though such observances were in popular estimation, they related primarily to the spiritual welfare of the soul of the deceased, and were seldom credited with any direct impact upon the welfare of the living, save in so far as a ghost who could not rest quietly might return to trouble the dead man's survivors.[59] Funeral customs are worth studying for the manner in which they helped to ease the social adjustments necessary to accommodate the fact of death, but by their very nature they do not testify in the same way as the other rites of passage to the extent of popular belief in the material effects of ecclesiastical ritual.

Before a man died, however, he was extended the last of the seven sacraments, extreme unction, whereby the recipient was anointed with holy oil and tendered the viaticum. In the eyes of everyone this was a dreadful ritual, and from Anglo-Saxon times there had been a deep conviction that to receive the viaticum was a virtual death sentence which would make subsequent recovery impossible. The medieval Church found it necessary to denounce the superstition that recipients of extreme unction who subsequently got better should refrain from eating meat, going barefoot, or having intercourse with their wives.[60] It may have been in an attempt to counter this fear that the leaders of the Church chose to stress the possibility that extreme unction might positively assist the patient's recovery, provided he had sufficient faith. The Council of Trent emphasized that the

58. W. Taswell, *The Church of England not Superstitious* (1714), p. 36; Thiers, *Superstitions*, iv, 10.

59. See below, pp. 701–17.

60. *Sarum Manual*, p. 113; Powicke and Cheney, *Councils and Synods*, pp. 305–6, 596, 707, 996; Thiers, *Superstitions*, iv, 8, chap 7.

ceremony could boost the recipient's will to live, and Bishop Bonner wrote in 1555 that:

Although in our wicked time small is the number of them that do escape death, having received this sacrament . . . yet that is not to be ascribed unto the lack or fault of this sacrament, but rather unto the want and lack of steadfast and constant faith, which ought to be in those that shall have this sacrament ministered unto them; by which strong faith the power of almighty God in the primitive church did work mightily and effectually in sick persons anointed.[61]

This was to link unction to the Church's other rites of blessing and anointing the sick to which it was closely related, and in which the intentions had been curative rather than merely symbolic.[62] As such it represents a final manifestation of the physical significance which the sacraments of the Church were so widely believed to possess.

Next to the sacraments as a means of access to divine assistance came the prayers of the faithful. Such prayer took many forms, but the kind most directly related to temporal problems was that of intercession, whereby God was called upon to provide both guidance along the path to salvation, and help with more material difficulties. In times of disaster it was appropriate for the clergy and people to invoke supernatural assistance. Private men made their solitary appeals to God, while communities offered a corporate supplication, most characteristically in large processions arranged by the Church. Such processions were common in medieval England as a response to plague, bad harvests and foul weather; and it was confidently believed that they could induce God to show his mercy by diverting the course of nature in response to the community's repentance. In 1289 the Bishop of Chichester ruled that it was the duty of every priest to order processions and prayers when he saw a storm was imminent, without waiting for orders from above.[63]

61. E. Bonner, *A Profitable and Necessarye Doctryne, with Certayne Homelies Adioyned Therunto* (1555), sig. Ddiii; Council of Trent, Session xiv, Doctrine on the Sacrament of Extreme Unction, chap. ii.

62. R. M. Woolley, *Exorcism and the Healing of the Sick* (1932); B. Poschmann, *Penance and the Anointing of the Sick*, trans. F. Courtney (Freiburg, 1964), pp. 233–57. A 'blessing for sore eyes' is reproduced on pp. 6–7 of the appendix to W. Beckett, *A Free and Impartial Enquiry into . . . Touching for the Cure of the King's Evil* (1722).

63. Powicke and Cheney, *Councils and Synods*, p. 1086, and index under 'processions'.

This belief that earthly events could be influenced by supernatural intervention was not in itself a magical one. For the essential difference between the prayers of a churchman and the spells of a magician was that only the latter claimed to work automatically; a prayer had no certainty of success and would not be granted if God chose not to concede it. A spell, on the other hand, need never go wrong, unless some detail of ritual observance had been omitted or a rival magician had been practising stronger counter-magic. A prayer, in other words, was a form of supplication: a spell was a mechanical means of manipulation. Magic postulated occult forces of nature which the magician learned to control, whereas religion assumed the direction of the world by a conscious agent who could only be deflected from his purpose by prayer and supplication. This distinction was popular with nineteenth-century anthropologists, but has been rejected by their modern successors, on the ground that it fails to consider the role which the appeal to spirits can play in a magician's ritual and which magic has occupied in some forms of primitive religion.[64] But it is useful in so far as it emphasizes the non-coercive character of Christian prayers. The Church's teaching was usually unambiguous on this point: prayers might bring practical results, but they could not be guaranteed to do so.

In practice, however, the distinction was repeatedly blurred in the popular mind. The Church itself recommended the use of prayers when healing the sick or gathering medicinal herbs. Confessors required penitents to repeat a stated number of Paternosters, Aves and Creeds, thereby fostering the notion that the recitation of prayers in a foreign tongue had a mechanical efficacy. The chantries of the later Middle Ages were built upon the belief that the regular offering of prayers would have a beneficial effect upon the founder's soul: they presupposed the quantitative value of masses, and gave, as their most recent historian puts it, 'almost a magical value to mere repetition of formulae'.[65] Salvation itself could be attained, it seemed, by mechanical means, and the more numerous the prayers the more likely their success. It therefore became worthwhile to secure other people to offer up prayers on one's own behalf. In the reign of Henry VIII the Marchioness of Exeter paid twenty shillings to Eliza-

64. For the distinction, see, e.g., J. G. Frazer, *The Magic Art* (3rd edn, 1911), i, chap. 4; and for criticism G. and M. Wilson, *The Analysis of Social Change* (Cambridge, 1945), p. 72, and below, pp. 318–25, 765–8.

65. K. L. Wood-Legh, *Perpetual Chantries in Britain* (Cambridge, 1965), pp. 308, 312.

beth Barton, the Nun of Kent, to pray that she would not lose her next child in childbirth, and that her husband would come home safely from the wars.[66] Sir Thomas More told of a friar in Coventry who declared that anyone who said his rosary once a day would be saved. The Enchiridion of Salisbury Cathedral contained a formula with the rubric: 'Whosoever sayeth this prayer following in the worship of God and St Rock shall not die of the pestilence by the grace of God.' The Catholics, said Jeremy Taylor, taught 'that prayers themselves *ex opere operato* ... do prevail', and 'like the words of a charmer they prevail even when they are not understood'.[67]

The medieval Church thus did a great deal to weaken the fundamental distinction between a prayer and a charm, and to encourage the idea that there was virtue in the mere repetition of holy words. It was the legacy of Catholic teaching, thought two Elizabethan pamphleteers, that 'the ignorant sort, beholding a man affected but only with melancholy, are so strongly conceited that it is no physical means, but only the good words and prayers of learned men that must restore them again to their perfect health'.[68] Because medieval theologians encouraged the use of prayers as an accompaniment to the gathering of herbs, the notion survived that these plants were useless unless plucked in a highly ritual manner. The distinguishing feature of the village wizards of the sixteenth and seventeenth centuries was their assumption that the ritual and unaccompanied pronunciation of special prayers could secure the patient's recovery.[69] This had not been the teaching of the medieval Church, for prayers, though necessary, were not intended to be effective without medical treatment. But the clergy had claimed that the recitation of prayers could afford protection against vermin or fiends;[70] and without the Church's encouragement of the formal repetition of set forms of prayer the magical faith in the healing power of Aves and Pater-

66. *L.P.*, vi, p. 589; A. D. Cheney, 'The Holy Maid of Kent', *T.R.H.S.*, n.s. xviii (1904), p. 117, n. 2.

67. H. M. Smith, *Pre-Reformation England* (1938), pp. 161–2; *Private Prayers Put forth by Authority during the Reign of Queen Elizabeth*, ed. W. K. Clay (Cambridge, P.S., 1851), p. 392, n. 1; *Whole Works of ... Jeremy Taylor*, vi, p. 251.

68. J. Deacon and J. Walker, *A Summarie Answere to ... Master Darel his Bookes* (1601), pp. 211–12.

69. See below, pp. 210–16, 318.

70. Manning, *The People's Faith in the Time of Wyclif*, pp. 93–4.

nosters could never have arisen. The rural magicians of Tudor England did not invent their own charms: they inherited them from the
medieval Church, and their formulae and rituals were largely derivative products of centuries of Catholic teaching. For, in addition
to the prayers officially countenanced, there was a large undergrowth
of semi-Christian charms which drew heavily on ecclesiastical
formulae. The following extract from the commonplace-book of
Robert Reynys, a fifteenth-century church reeve at Acle, Norfolk,
is typical:

> Pope Innocent hath granted to any man that beareth the length of the
> three nails of Our Lord Jesus Christ upon him and worship them daily
> with five Paternosters and five Aves and a psalter, he shall have seven
> gifts granted to him. The first, he shall not be slain with sword nor knife.
> The second, he shall not die no sudden death. The third, his enemies
> shall not overcome him. The fourth, he shall have sufficient good and
> honest living. The fifth, that poisons nor fever nor false witness shall
> grieve him. The sixth, he shall not die without the sacraments of the
> Church. The seventh, he shall be defended from all wicked spirits, from
> pestilence and all evil things.[71]

Charms of this kind were to be a common feature of popular
magic in the century after the Reformation; and so were the old
Catholic prayers ritually recited: the repetition for fifteen days,
for example, of the prayers known as St Bridget's Oes (because they
all began with the invocation 'O') was thought to be a means of
divining the date of one's own death.[72] Prayers could also be used
for maleficent purposes, for example, by being recited backwards.[73]
Dives and Pauper asserts that 'it hath oft been known that witches,
with saying of their Paternoster and dropping of the holy candle in
a man's steps that they hated, hath done his feet rotten of'. This was
apparently no exaggeration: in 1543 Joanna Meriwether of Canterbury, 'for the displeasure that she bore towards a young maid named
Elizabeth Celsay and her mother, made a fire upon the dung of the
said Elizabeth; and took a holy candle and dropt upon the said

71. C. L. S. Linnell, 'The Commonplace Book of Robert Reynys', *Norfolk
Archaeology*, xxxii (1958–61), p. 125.
72. Deacon and Walker, *A Summarie Answere*, p. 211. The same prayers
could also be used to deliver one's ancestors from Purgatory, H. C. White,
The Tudor Books of Private Devotion (Madison, Wisc., 1951), pp. 216–17
(their text is in Maskell, *Monumenta Ritualia*, iii, pp. 275–82).
73. Thomson, *Later Lollards*, p. 83. A Cambridgeshire woman was slander-
ously accused of doing this in 1619; Ely D.R., B 2/37, f. 78.

dung. And she told the neighbours that the said enchantment would make the cule [buttocks] of the said maid to divide into two parts.'[74]

Another way of coercing God into granting the suppliant's requests was to increase the incentive by making a vow of some reciprocal service, conditional upon the success of the prayer. God and man would thus be united by a bond of mutual self-interest. A sailor in peril of shipwreck might vow candles to a shrine or assert his readiness to undertake an arduous pilgrimage should he escape his present danger.[75] In the seventeenth century women could still emulate the example of Hannah by solemnly vowing to dedicate their children to a religious career if only their barrenness could be terminated.[76] The ritual condition of fasting was also thought efficacious. By the fifteenth century the belief had arisen that one could avoid sudden death by fasting all the year round on the day of the week on which the Feast of the Annunciation happened to occur. Conversely, there were the 'black-fasts', designed to secure the death of an enemy.[77]

A further example of the supernatural power thought to be at the disposal of the medieval Church is provided by the religious sanctions employed in the administration of justice. The standard method of inducing a witness to give honest testimony was to require him to swear a solemn oath as to the truth of his evidence. The assumption behind this procedure was that perjury would call forth the vengeance of God, certainly in the next world and quite possibly in this one. Hence the slowness of the lay authorities to treat perjury as a civil offence. The force of such an oath might be further enhanced by requiring that it be taken on some sacred object – a Bible, or a relic. The holy taper of Cardigan Priory, for example, was 'used of men to swear by in difficult and hard matters', and it proved a useful source of revenue to the monks. A note on the eleventh-century Red Book of Derby asserts that 'it was commonly believed that who should swear untruly upon this book should run mad'. The

74. Dives and Pauper, f. 53; Ewen, ii, p. 447.

75. The Colloquies of Erasmus, trans. N. Bailey and ed. E. Johnson (1878), i, pp. 278–9; L.P., i, no. 1786. For a similar attitude in a modern South Italian village, E. C. Banfield, The Moral Basis of a Backward Society (Glencoe, Ill., 1958), pp. 131–2.

76. Aubrey, Gentilisme, p. 97; R. H. Whitelocke, Memoirs of Bulstrode Whitelocke (1860), p. 288.

77. Dives and Pauper, ff. 60ᵛ–61ᵛ; below, pp. 611–12.

sixteenth-century Irish made similar use of St Patrick's staff, believing that to perjure oneself on this holy object would provoke an even worse punishment than if the oath had been sworn on the gospels. In the same way Anglo-Saxon charters had been kept on an altar or copied into a gospel or holy book in order to stiffen the sanction against any party who subsequently broke faith.[78] The effectiveness of such deterrents is another matter: the historians of early medieval law declare that 'our ancestors perjured themselves with impunity', and the frequency of perjury in the courts had become a matter of general complaint by the later Middle Ages.[79] But the reality of the divine sanction never ceased to be upheld by the Church.

An alternative device for supporting testimony and making agreements binding was the unofficial use of the Mass as a form of poison ordeal. The suspected party would be required to communicate, on the assumption that he would be damned if guilty or dishonest. His willingness to undergo the test would thus constitute proof of his innocence. In the Tudor period men sometimes took communion as a means of clearing themselves of some notorious slander.[80] The same principle gave rise to the convention, which Archbishop Laud attempted to make obligatory, that newly married persons should take the sacrament together immediately after the marriage service as a means of confirming their promises. In modern times the Christian sacraments have been similarly employed as a poison ordeal by newly converted African peoples.[81] In the Middle Ages holy relics

78. *Three Chapters of Letters relating to the Suppression of Monasteries,* ed. T. Wright (Camden Soc., 1843), p. 186; *York Manual,* p. xx; E. Campion, *Two bokes of the histories of Ireland,* ed. A. F. Vossen (Assen, 1963), p. [22]; P. Chaplais, 'The Origin and Authenticity of the Royal Anglo-Saxon Diploma', *Journ. of the Soc. of Archivists,* iii (1965), p. 53. cf. *Whole Works of ... Jeremy Taylor,* vi, p. 175. On oaths in general see J. E. Tyler, *Oaths, their Origins, Nature and History* (1834); H. C. Lea, *Superstition and Force* (3rd edn, Philadelphia, 1878), pp. 323–7; *Dives and Pauper,* ff. 93v–94; Aubrey, *Gentilisme,* p. 128; C. Hill, *Society and Puritanism in Pre-Revolutionary England* (1964), chap. 11.

79. Sir F. Pollock and F. W. Maitland, *The History of English Law* (2nd edn, Cambridge, 1952), ii, p. 543; D. Wilkins, *Concilia* (1737), iii, p. 534; *Sermons by Hugh Latimer,* ed. G. E. Corrie (Cambridge, P.S., 1844), p. 301.

80. *The Works of John Jewel,* i, p. 6; C. Chardon, *Histoire des Sacremens* (Paris, 1745), ii, p. 239; Thiers, *Superstitions,* ii, pp. 320–24; Coulton, *Five Centuries of Religion,* i, p. 114.

81. *C.S.P.D., 1640,* p. 279; Aubrey, *Gentilisme,* p. 130; cf. M. G. Marwick, *Sorcery in its Social Setting* (Manchester, 1965), p. 90.

were also used for this purpose. Bishop Latimer commented on how people flocked to see Christ's Blood at Hailes Abbey, Gloucestershire, believing 'that the sight of it with their bodily eye doth certify them and putteth them out of doubt that they be in clean life, and in state of salvation without spot of sin'.[82]

There were also supernatural remedies to check theft, especially the theft of holy objects. The lives of the saints abounded in stories of the miraculous retribution which had overtaken those who tried to raid ecclesiastical treasure-houses or to penetrate some holy shrine. The thief was unable to get out once he had got in, or the stolen object had stuck to his hands. The man who stole pyxes from a London church in 1467 was unable to see the Host until he had confessed and been absolved.[83] There were also sundry popular methods of thief-detection in which Christian prayers or holy books played a key role; a Suffolk witch advised her clients in 1499 to give their horses holy bread and water to prevent them being stolen.[84]

The medieval Church thus appeared as a vast reservoir of magical power, capable of being deployed for a variety of secular purposes. Indeed it is difficult to think of any human aspiration for which it could not cater. Almost any object associated with ecclesiastical ritual could assume a special aura in the eyes of the people. Any prayer or piece of the Scriptures might have a mystical power waiting to be tapped. The Bible could be an instrument of divination, which opened at random would reveal one's fate. The gospels could be read aloud to women in child-bed to guarantee them a safe delivery. A Bible could be laid on a restless child's head so as to send it to sleep. *Dives and Pauper* declared that it was not wrong to try to charm snakes or birds by reciting holy words, provided the operation was done with reverence.[85]

82. *Sermons and Remains of Hugh Latimer*, ed. Corrie, p. 364.

83. Smith, *Pre-Reformation England*, p. 156. cf. Loomis, *White Magic*, pp. 55, 85, 97–8, 194; L. F. Salzman, 'Some Sussex Miracles', *Sussex Notes and Queries*, i (1926–7), p. 215.

84. C. Jenkins, 'Cardinal Morton's Register', *Tudor Studies*, ed. R. W. Seton-Watson (1924), p. 72. Other ecclesiastical remedies for lost goods occur in Owst, *Literature and Pulpit*, pp. 147–8; Scot, *Discoverie*, XII.ix, xvii; Deacon and Walker, *A Summarie Answere*, p. 210. cf. below, p. 254.

85. Tyndale, *An Answer to Sir Thomas More's Dialogue*, pp. 61–2; B. Holyday, *Motives to a Good Life* (Oxford, 1657), p. 129; *Dives and Pauper*, f. 59.

The widely dispersed nature of such notions is eloquent testimony to the power with which many Englishmen credited the apparatus of the Church. Comparable assumptions are to be found among many newly converted African peoples today. Many of the Cewa of Zambia and Malawi believe that Christians use the Bible as a powerful means of divination, and assume that conversion is a likely prelude to worldly success; indeed the prophets of the native Pentecostal Churches have tended to usurp the role of the traditional diviners. The Makah Indians of North America similarly regarded Christianity as a new means of divination and healing. In Sekhukuniland the Pedi were attracted to the new religion by the hope of gaining additional protection against sickness and for the Bantu the healing message of Christianity was the central pivot of evangelization.[86] In medieval England the same connection between religion and material prosperity was given vivid expression in 1465, when a man who had been excommunicated at the suit of another party retorted defiantly that the excommunication could not have been valid, for his wheat crop had been no smaller than that of his neighbours, which it would have been if God had upheld the decree.[87]

It would, of course, be a gross travesty to suggest that the medieval Chuch deliberately held out to the laity an organized system of magic designed to bring supernatural remedies to bear upon earthly problems. The Church was other-worldly in its main preoccupations. Most of the magical claims made for religion were parasitic to its teaching, and were more or less vigorously refuted by ecclesiastical leaders. Indeed our very knowledge of many of these superstitions is due to the medieval theologians and Church Councils who denounced them. It would be wrong to infer the attitude

86. Marwick, *Sorcery in its Social Setting*, p. 90; J. R. Crawford, *Witchcraft and Sorcery in Rhodesia* (1967), pp. 41, 221 ff.; P. Tyler, 'The Pattern of Christian Belief in Sekhukuniland', *Church Qtly Rev.*, clxvii (1966), pp. 335–6; B. G. M. Sundkler, *Bantu Prophets in South Africa* (2nd edn, 1961), pp. 220, 254–5; B. A. Pauw, *Religion in a Tswana Chiefdom* (1960), chaps. 2 and 6; E. Colson, *The Makah Indians* (Manchester, 1953), p. 277. cf. M. J. Field, *Search for Security* (1960), pp. 51–2; M. Wilson, *Communal Rituals of the Nyakyusa* (1959), p. 184; R. W. Lieban, *Cebuano Sorcery* (Berkeley and Los Angeles, 1967), pp. 32–3; J. D. Y. Peel, 'Understanding Alien Belief Systems', *Brit. Journ. Sociology*, xx (1969), p. 76.

87. *Parliamentary Papers*, 1883, xxiv (*Report of the Commissioners Appointed to Inquire into the Constitution and Working of the Ecclesiastical Courts*, i), p. 162. For similar beliefs in modern Ireland, K. H. Connell, *Irish Peasant Society* (Oxford, 1968), p. 155.

of medieval Church leaders from the indictments of the Protestant reformers. Medieval ecclesiastics usually stressed the primarily intercéssionary nature of the Church's rites. The recitation of prayers, the worship of saints, the use of holy water and the sign of the cross were all propitiatory, not constraining. As the perpetual extension of Christ's incarnation, the Church claimed to be the mediator between Man and God, and the dispenser of God's grace through prescribed channels (the *opus operatum*). The sacraments worked automatically (*ex opere operato*), regardless of the moral worth of the officiating priest, and thus gave medieval Christianity an apparently magical character.[88] But most other ecclesiastical operations could only be accomplished by a good priest and a pious laity (*ex opere operantis*). They were dependent upon the spiritual condition of those participating: the agnus dei, for example, might fail to protect its wearer if he was weak in faith.

It was only at a popular level that such agencies were credited with an inexorable and compelling power. Many later medieval theologians were strongly 'rationalist' in temperament, and preferred to stress the importance of human self-help. They had inherited rites from a more primitive era and they viewed them cautiously. They regarded the sacraments as symbolic representations rather than as instruments of physical efficacy. As an institution, the Church was zealous to check the 'excesses' of devotion, to vet more closely any claims to new miracles, to restrain popular 'superstition'.[89] Moreover, the late medieval Catholic laity were not all ignorant peasants; they included educated urban dwellers who were intellectually more sophisticated than many of the clergy. The vernacular literature of the fifteenth century testifies to their realistic social outlook.[90]

Nevertheless, there were several circumstances which helped to consolidate the notion that the Church was a magical agency, no less than a devotional one. The first was the legacy of the original conversion. It was not just that the leaders of the Anglo-Saxon Church

88. cf. Pauw, *Religion in a Tswana Chiefdom*, pp. 147–8, 195.

89. Franz, *Die kirchlichen Benediktionen*, ii, pp. 120–3; Manning, *The People's Faith in the Time of Wyclif*, pp. 83–5; E. Delcambre, *Le Concept de la sorcellerie dans le Duché de Lorraine* (Nancy, 1948–51), pp. 132–3; A. B. Ferguson, 'Reginald Pecock and the Renaissance Sense of History', *Studies in the Renaissance*, xiii (1966), p. 150.

90. A. B. Ferguson, *The Articulate Citizen and the English Renaissance* (Durham, N.C., 1965), chaps. 1–5.

had laid so much stress upon the miracle-working power of their
saints, and had disseminated anecdotes illustrating their superiority
to any magic the pagans had to offer; though this in itself made
difficult the later efforts to purge religious teaching of any 'grossness'. The real difficulty stemmed from the notorious readiness of
the early Christian leaders to assimilate elements of the old paganism into their own religious practice, rather than pose too direct a
conflict of loyalties in the minds of the new converts. The ancient
worship of wells, trees and stones was not so much abolished as
modified, by turning pagan sites into Christian ones and associating
them with a saint rather than a heathen divinity. The pagan festivals
were similarly incorporated into the Church year. New Year's Day
became the feast of the Circumcision; May Day was SS. Philip and
James; Midsummer Eve the Nativity of St John the Baptist. Fertility rites were converted into Christian processions and the Yule
Log was introduced into celebrations of the birth of Christ.[91]

This well-known process of assimilation was not achieved without some cost, for it meant that many of the purposes served by
the older paganism were now looked for from nominally Christian
institutions. The hundreds of magical springs which dotted the
country became 'holy wells', associated with a saint, but they were
still employed for magical healing and for divining the future. Their
water was sometimes even believed to be peculiarly suitable for use
in baptism.[92] Observance of the festivals of the Christian year was
thought to encourage fertility and the welfare of the crops. An
eclectic range of ritual activities was conducted under the auspices
of the Church: 'leading of the plough about the fire' on Plough
Monday, 'for good beginning of the year, that they should fare the
better all the year following';[93] the annual fires kindled on the hillsides on May Day, St John Baptist Eve and other occasions;[94] the

91. On this large subject see especially E. K. Chambers, *The Mediaeval
Stage*, i (Oxford, 1903), chap. 6, and C. R. Baskervill, 'Dramatic Aspects of
Medieval Folk-Festivals in England', *Studies in Philology*, xvii (1920).

92. Brand, *Antiquities*, ii, pp. 374–5; and for some examples, ibid., pp. 369,
385; R. C. Hope, *The Legendary Lore of the Holy Wells of England* (1893);
Kittredge, *Witchcraft*, p. 34; *V.C.H., Oxon.*, ii, p. 17. A case of ecclesiastical
action against excessive well-worship is in *Diocese of Hereford. Extracts from
the Cathedral Registers, A.D. 1275–1535*, trans. E. N. Dew (Hereford, 1932),
p. 97.

93. *Dives and Pauper*, f. 50.

94. *Mirk's Festial*, p. 182; Sir J. G. Frazer, *Balder the Beautiful* (1913),
i, pp. 196–7; below, p. 82.

flowers draped by the villagers around holy wells; the offerings of oats, cheese and other commodities at the shrines of saints.[95] Some were customary calendar rituals whose pagan origins had long been forgotten, whereas others retained a frankly magical purpose. Material prosperity was assumed to be integrally connected with their observance; and their annual recurrence gave men confidence in face of their daily problems. The consolations afforded by such practices were too considerable for the Church to ignore; if the people were going to resort to magic anyway it was far better that it should be a magic over which the Church maintained some control.

The Church's magical claims were also reinforced by its own propaganda. Although theologians drew a firm line between religion and superstition their concept of 'superstition' always had a certain elasticity about it. It was 'superstitious' to use consecrated objects for purposes other than those for which they were intended. It was 'superstitious' to attempt to achieve effects, other than those which might have natural causes, by any operation which had not been authorized by the Church. But in these, as in other definitions, the last word always lay with the Church. In general, the ceremonies of which it disapproved were 'superstitious'; those which it accepted were not. As the Council of Malines ruled in 1607: 'It is superstitious to expect any effect from anything, when such an effect cannot be produced by natural causes, by divine institution, or by the ordination or approval of the Church.'[96] There was, therefore, no superstition in believing that the elements could change their nature after the formula of consecration had been pronounced over them: this was not magic, but an operation worked by God and the Church; whereas magic involved the aid of the Devil. The authors of a fifteenth-century treatise against witchcraft stressed that only natural operations could achieve natural effects; but they exempted from this rule such approved practices as carrying around the Host in an attempt to allay a thunderstorm.[97] As Catholic theologians never ceased to emphasize, it was the presence or absence of the Church's authority which determined the propriety of any action.

95. Frere and Kennedy, *Articles and Injunctions*, ii, p. 57; Bodl., Oxford Dioc. Papers c. 22 (Depositions, 1590–3), f. 76.
96. Thiers, *Superstitions*, ii, p. 8. cf. *Malleus*, II.2.7; R. Whytforde, *A Werke for Housholders* (n.d., copy in Bodl., Ashm. 1215), sig. Cii^v. On the relativity of the notion, cf. H. Thurston, *Superstition* (1933), pp. 15–19.
97. *Malleus*, II.2.7.

The difference between churchmen and magicians lay less in the effects they claimed to achieve than in their social position, and in the authority on which their respective claims rested. As the Elizabethan Reginald Scot wrote sardonically of the Pope: 'He canonizeth the rich for saints and banneth the poor for witches.'[98]

Theologians further enhanced popular belief in the existence of the Church's magical powers by stressing the mystical powers available to the faithful as a means of preservation against the assault of evil spirits. They did not deny that devils could do material damage by bringing thunderstorms or by tormenting men and animals with occult diseases. But they drew attention to the counter-magic at the Church's disposal. If a cow was bewitched it should have holy water poured down its throat. If a man thought he saw a devil he should make the sign of the cross. If evil spirits brought storms then consecrated bells could be rung to repel them. And if the Devil took possession of a human being the Church could ritually exorcize him.[99] So long as certain physical misfortunes were explained in spiritual terms they could be countered with spiritual weapons; and here the Church claimed a monopoly.

The leaders of the Church thus abandoned the struggle against superstition whenever it seemed in their interest to do so. Throughout the Middle Ages their attitude to the credulities of their simpler followers was fundamentally ambivalent. They disliked them as gross and superstitious, but they had no wish to discourage attitudes which might foster popular devotion. If a belief in the magical efficacy of the Host served to enhance respect for the clergy and to make the laity more regular church-goers, then why should it not be tacitly tolerated? Such practices as the worship of relics, the recitation of prayers, or the wearing of talismans and amulets, could all be taken to excess, but what did it matter so long as their effect was to bind the people closer to the true Church and the true God? It was the intention of the worshipper, not the means employed, which counted. Chaucer's Parson commented that 'charms for wounds or malady of men or of beasts, if they take any effect, it may be peradventure that God suffereth it, for folk should give the more faith and reverence to his name'. Provided such techniques reflected a genuine trust in God and his saints, no serious harm could come from them.

98. Scot, *Discoverie: A Discourse of Divels,* chap. xxiv.
99. See below, pp. 570, 588.

So at least most churchmen reasoned.[100] In doing so they made the medieval Church into a more flexible institution than they perhaps intended. For they were condoning a situation in which a belief in the potency of Church magic was often fundamental to popular devotion. Medieval theologians and modern historians alike have tended to regard such an attitude as merely parasitic to the main corpus of medieval Catholicism, an accretion which could have been shorn off without affecting the essential core of belief. So, from the point of view of the theologians, it was. But it is doubtful whether this austere distinction between true religion and parasitic superstition could have been upheld at a popular level. The magical aspects of the Church's function were often inseparable from the devotional ones. Many of the parochial clergy themselves drew no distinction: the suggestion made to a child at Rye in 1538 that he should drink three times from the chalice to cure his whooping cough did not emanate from some ignorant parishioner; it was made by the curate himself.[101] The line between magic and religion is one which it is impossible to draw in many primitive societies; it is equally difficult to recognize in medieval England.

100. Chaucer, *Parson's Tale*, 1.606; Aquinas, *Summa Theologica*, II.2.96.4; Owst, *Literature and Pulpit*, pp. 141, 148; Lea, *Materials*, p. 135; Manning, *The People's Faith in the Time of Wyclif*, pp. 78–83.

101. *L.P.*, xiii (1), p. 430. For the same formula, Scot, *Discoverie*, XII.xvii, and for the role of the clergy in popular magic, below, pp. 326–7.

3.

THE IMPACT OF THE REFORMATION

IF the distinction between magic and religion had been blurred by the medieval Church, it was strongly reasserted by the propagandists of the Protestant Reformation. From the very start, the enemies of Roman Catholicism fastened upon the magical implications which they saw to be inherent in some fundamental aspects of the Church's ritual. The ultra-Protestant position was firmly stated as early as 1395 by the Lollards in their Twelve Conclusions:

> That exorcisms and hallowings, made in the Church, of wine, bread, and wax, water, salt and oil and incense, the stone of the altar, upon vestments, mitre, cross, and pilgrims' staves, be the very practice of necromancy, rather than of the holy theology. This conclusion is proved thus. For by such exorcisms creatures be charged to be of higher virtue than their own kind, and we see nothing of change in no such creature that is so charmed, but by false belief, the which is the principle of the devil's craft.[1]

As an example of this principle, the Lollards cited the case of holy water. If the Church's exorcisms and blessing could really work material effects, they argued, then holy water would be the best medicine for any sickness. That this was not the case showed that it was unreasonable and impious to expect God to assist at a ceremony designed to give ordinary water the power to bring health of mind and body, to expel spirits, or drive away pestilence. Holy water, in fact, had no more virtue than well-water or river-water.[2]

NOTE: The aspect of the English Reformation considered in this chapter is only briefly discussed in the admirable recent survey, A. G. Dickens, *The English Reformation* (1964). Representative Lollard and Protestant opinion can be found in Foxe and in the volumes of the Parker Society, but much additional material is contained in other contemporary writings and in the largely unpublished records of the ecclesiastical courts. In this chapter the word 'Protestant' has been used to characterize the principles of the sixteenth-century reformers; I am not concerned with their subsequent dilution or re-interpretation.

1. H. S. Cronin, 'The Twelve Conclusions of the Lollards', *E.H.R.*, xxii (1907), p. 298.
2. Foxe, iii, pp. 179–80, 590, 596; iv, p. 230; E. Welch, 'Some Suffolk

Neither did holy bread possess any new quality merely because an incantation had been pronounced over it.[3] Similar objections were made to the consecration of church bells against tempests, and the wearing of words of scripture as a protection against danger.[4] Such operations were sheer necromancy, a spurious attribution of effective virtue to the mere enunciation of words, a hopeless attempt to endow objects with a power and strength exceeding their natural qualities. The very procedures of the priests were modelled on those of the magicians, observed the Lollard Walter Brute. Both thought their spells more effective when pronounced in one place and at one time rather than another; both turned to the East to say them; and both thought that mere words could possess a magical virtue.[5]

This attitude, which was common to most of the differing opinions usually bracketed together as 'Lollardy', thus involved a sweeping denial of the Church's claim to manipulate any aspects of God's supernatural power. Ecclesiastical blessings, exorcisms, conjurations and hallowings had no effect. Neither did the curses which the clergy chose to call down upon lay offenders. Either such delinquents had broken God's law, in which case God had already cursed them himself; or they had not, in which case the Church's curse could be of no avail.[6] Early Protestantism thus denied the magic of the *opus operatum*, the claim that the Church had instrumental power and had been endowed by Christ with an active share in his work and office. For a human authority to claim the power to work miracles was blasphemy – a challenge to God's omnipotence. 'For, if ye may make at your pleasure such things to drive devils away and to heal both body and soul, what need have ye of Christ?'[7]

Lollards', *Procs. Suffolk Inst. Archaeology*, xxix (1962), p. 164; Thomson, *Later Lollards*, p. 248.

3. Foxe, iii, p. 596; iv, p. 230; *Lincoln Diocese Documents, 1450–1544*, ed. A. Clark (E.E.T.S., 1914), p. 91. The extreme Lollard view that holy bread and water were not just ineffective, but positively the worse for having been conjured (*V.C.H., Cambs.*, ii, p. 164; Foxe, iii, p. 598) may have underlain the curious observation of a Kentish Lollard that one could obtain riches by abstaining from blessed bread and water on three Sundays in the year (Thomson, *Later Lollards*, p. 185).

4. Foxe, iii, pp. 590, 596, 581; *An Apology for Lollard Doctrines*, ed. J. H. Todd (Camden Soc., 1842), pp. 90–92.

5. Foxe, iii, pp. 179–80.

6. Foxe, iii, p. 107. See also below, p. 600.

7. N. Dorcastor, *The Doctrine of the Masse Booke* (1554), sig. Aiii.

This theme was taken up with some relish during the Tudor Reformation, when the denial of the efficacy of the Catholic rituals of consecration and exorcism became central to the Protestant attack. Who were 'the vilest witches and sorcerers of the earth', demanded James Calfhill, if not 'the priests that consecrate crosses and ashes, water and salt, oil and cream, boughs and bones, stocks and stones; that christen bells that hang in the steeple; that conjure worms that creep in the field; that give St John's Gospel to hang about men's necks?' How could the 'conjuration' of the agnus dei, asked Bishop Jewel, endow it with the power to preserve its wearer from lightning and tempest? Of what avail was a mere piece of wax against a storm sent by God? As for St Agatha's letters, the holy remedy against burning houses, they were, declared Bishop Pilkington, sheer sorcery, and the use of consecrated bells in a thunder-storm mere 'witchcrafts'.[8] In a similar manner were dismissed the sign of the cross,[9] the relics of the saints, and the whole apparatus of Catholic magic. The Edwardian Injunctions of 1547 forbade the Christian to observe such practices as

casting holy water upon his bed, ... bearing about him holy bread, or St John's Gospel, ... ringing of holy bells; or blessing with the holy candle, to the intent thereby to be discharged of the burden of sin, or to drive away devils, or to put away dreams and fantasies; or ... putting trust and confidence of health and salvation in the same ceremonies.

In the reign of Elizabeth the import of the agnus dei or similar tokens was made into a serious offence.[10]

All this was but a preliminary to the onslaught on the central Catholic doctrine of the Mass. For if conjurations and exorcisms were ineffective, then what was transubstantiation but a spurious piece of legerdemain – 'the pretence of a power, plainly magical, of changing the elements in such a sort as all the magicians of Pharaoh could never do, nor had the face to attempt the like, it being so beyond all credibility'. The Papists, wrote Calvin, 'pretend there is a magical force in the sacraments, independent of efficacious faith'.

8. J. Calfhill, *An Answer to John Martiall's Treatise of the Cross*, ed. R. Gibbings (Cambridge, P.S., 1846), p. 17; *The Works of John Jewel*, ed. J. Ayre (Cambridge, P.S., 1845–50), ii, p. 1045; *The Works of James Pilkington*, ed. J. Scholefield (Cambridge, P.S., 1842), pp. 177, 536, 563.

9. Notably in Calfhill's lengthy *Answer to Martiall*.

10. *Documents Illustrative of English Church History*, ed. H. Gee and W. J. Hardy (1896), p. 428n; 13 Eliz., cap. 2.

For Bishop Hooper the Roman Mass was 'nothing better to be esteemed than the verses of the sorcerer or enchanter ... – holy words murmured and spoken in secret'.[11] In place of the miraculous transubstantiation of the consecrated elements was substituted a simple commemorative rite, and the reservation of the sacrament was discontinued. It went without saying that none of the Protestant reformers would countenance any of the old notions concerning the temporal benefits which might spring from communicating or from contemplating the consecrated elements. Instead, their prescriptions for the communion service were specially designed to eliminate any ground for the ancient superstitions. The 1552 Prayer Book specified that ordinary bread should be used for the communion service, in place of the special unleavened wafers of the Catholic past. There were even objections to the old precaution of consecrating no more bread and wine than was needed by the communicants, because it implied that the elements changed their quality during the rite. In such ways the Edwardian reformers violently repudiated Catholic ritual, and what Bishop Bale called 'their masses and other sorcerous witchcrafts'.[12]

In the reign of Elizabeth I the Kentish squire, Reginald Scot, further developed this line of argument in his *Discoverie of Witchcraft* (1584). This brilliant work is chiefly remembered today for its protest against the persecution of harmless old women, but it is also important as a thorough-going demonstration of the magical elements in medieval Catholicism and their affiliation with other contemporary kinds of magical activity. As far as Scot was concerned, the power of exorcism was a special gift to the Apostles, which had long ceased to be operative. The error of the Catholic Church was to have preserved the ritual into a time when miracles could no longer be expected. Its formulae were as vain and superstitious as those of the back-street conjurers of Elizabethan London. Indeed, declared Scot, 'I see no difference between these and Popish conjurations: for they agree on order, words and matter, differing in no circumstances, but that the Papists do it without shame openly, the

11. H. More, *A Modest Enquiry into the Mystery of Iniquity* (1664), p. 428; F. Clark, *Eucharistic Sacrifice and the Reformation* (1960), p. 359; Frere and Kennedy, *Articles and Injunctions*, ii, p. 274.

12. F. Procter and W. H. Frere, *A New History of the Book of Common Prayer* (1901), p. 74; C. W. Dugmore, *The Mass and the English Reformers* (1958), p. 120; *The Labororyouse Journey and Serche of John Leylande ... enlarged by Johan Bale*, ed. W. A. Copinger (1895), p. 10.

other do it in hugger mugger secretly.' A Popish consecration, agreed a contemporary, was but 'a magical incantation'.[13]

A century of Protestant teaching was summed up in the incisive prose of Thomas Hobbes. In *Leviathan* (1651) he denounced the Roman Catholics for 'the turning of consecration into conjuration, or enchantment'. As he carefully explained,

> to *consecrate* is, in Scripture, to offer, give or dedicate, in pious and decent language and gesture, a man, or any other thing to God, by separating of it from common use; that is to say to sanctify or make it God's ... and thereby to change not the thing consecrated, but only the use of it, from being profane and common, to be holy and peculiar to God's service. But when, by such words, the nature or quality of the thing itself, is pretended to be changed, it is not consecration, but either an extraordinary work of God, or a vain and impious conjuration. But seeing, for the frequency of pretending the change of nature in their consecrations, it cannot be esteemed a work extraordinary, it is no other than a *conjuration* or *incantation*, whereby they would have men to believe an alteration of nature that is not, contrary to the testimony of man's sight, and of all the rest of his senses.

The supreme example of such conjuration, declared Hobbes, was the Roman sacrament of the Mass, in which the mere pronunciation of the appropriate formula was said to change the nature of the bread and wine, even though no visible change was apparent to the human senses. A similar incantation was used in baptism, 'where the abuse of God's name in each several person, and in the whole Trinity, with the sign of the cross at each name, maketh up the charm'. For did not the Catholic priest conjure the devil out of the holy water, salt and oil, and then proceed to make the infant himself 'subject to many charms'? And 'at the church door the priest blows thrice in the child's face, and says: *Go out of him unclean spirit and give place to the Holy Ghost the comforter*': after which came exorcisms and 'some other incantations'. Similarly, 'other rites, as of marriage, of extreme unction, of visitation of the sick, of consecrating churches and churchyards, and the like', were not 'exempt from charms; inasmuch as there is in them the use of enchanted oil and water, with the abuse of the cross, and of the holy word of David, *asperges me Domine hyssopo*, as things of efficacy to drive away phantasms, and imaginary spirits'.[14]

13. Scot, *Discoverie*, XV, xxii; E. Bulkeley, *A Sermon* (1586), sig. B4ᵛ.
14. T. Hobbes, *Leviathan* (1651), chap. 44.

It was in accordance with this attitude that all the sacraments of the Church had been scrutinized by the early Protestants for any magical affiliations they might possess. Baptism, which some of the Lollards had declared to be unnecessary for salvation,[15] was purged of its more dramatic features. The exorcism was dropped from the second Edwardian Prayer Book, because of its implication that unbaptised infants were demoniacs, and so were the anointing and the chrisom. Nevertheless, the rite retained a status which was more than merely symbolic. The fate of infants who died before baptism was still controversial. The first Prayer Book stressed the need for baptism within the first days of life and its Elizabethan successor emphasised the urgency of the matter by permitting it on days other than Sundays and holidays in cases of 'necessity'. Most Elizabethan theologians denied the Tridentine doctrine that baptism was *absolutely* necessary for salvation, but they still regarded it as 'formally' necessary. Anxiety on this score led some clergy to defend baptism in an emergency by a midwife or a layman and provoked others into such outspoken assertions as that of the Vicar of Ashford, Kent, who declared in 1569 that children who died without baptism were the firebrands of Hell. The issue long remained controversial.[16]

It is not surprising that for many Puritans the rite still had 'superstitious' aspects. They denied that the font-water had any special virtue; they objected to the sign of the cross; and they disliked the office of godparent. The Presbyterian *Directory of Public Worship* (1644) omitted the sign of the cross, along with the requirement that the font should be placed in a special position near the church door. The minister was further required to remind the congregation that baptism was not so necessary that an infant might be damned for want of it. Such stipulations did something to play down the impor-

15. Thomson, *Later Lollards*, pp. 76, 106, 127; Welch in *Procs. Suffolk Inst. Archaeology*, xxix (1962), p. 163.

16. A. Hussey, 'Archbishop Parker's Visitation, 1569', *Home Counties Magazine*, v (1903), p. 286. cf. *Proceedings Principally in the County of Kent*, ed. L. B. Larking (Camden Soc., 1862), p. 118. For arguments on the subject, see G. W. Bromiley, *Baptism and the Anglican Reformers* (1953), pp. 48–64, and W. H(ubbocke), *An Apologie of Infants in a Sermon* (1595). For talk on the subject at Archbishop Neile's dinner-table see *Associated Architectural Societies, Reports and Papers*, xvi (1881), p. 48. For a Puritan view, W. Perkins, '*A Discourse of Conscience*' ..., ed. T. F. Merrill (Nieuwkoop, 1966), pp. 130–34; and for a Baptist one, T. Grantham, *The Infants Advocate, against the Cruel Doctrine of those Presbyterians, who hold that the Greatest Part of Dying Infants shall be Damned* (1688).

tance of the ceremony as a rite of passage; a tendency which the sectarian demand for the abolition of infant baptism was to take to its logical conclusion. Yet some of the early separatists who had rejected infant baptism returned to the Church of England when they became parents, lest their children should die before they were christened;[17] and in nineteenth-century Dorset some country-folk had their children speedily baptized, because 'they understood that if a child died without a name he did flit about in the woods and waste places and could get no rest'. In modern Britain there are many otherwise non-religious people who think it unlucky not to be baptized.[18]

Confirmation, which had already been attacked by the Lollards, was even more sweepingly dismissed by some reformers as nothing 'but plain sorcery, devilry, witchcraft, juggling, legerdemain, and all that naught is. The bishop mumbleth a few Latin words over the child, charmeth him, crosseth him, smeareth him with stinking popish oil, and tieth a linen band about the child's neck and sendeth him home.'[19] The Church of England denied the sacramental character of the ceremony and discarded the holy oil and linen band. It also made concessions to those who thought that the medieval Church had confirmed children too young, by requiring that no one be admitted to the rite until he had learned to say the Creed, the Lord's Prayer and the Decalogue, and to answer questions in the Catechism. It thus laid its emphasis on the catechetical preparation rather than on the ceremony itself. But these changes did not satisfy Puritan opinion. The laying-on of hands was thought to reinforce the old Catholic superstition that the bishop could give the child strength against the Devil; in any case the rite of baptism was deemed to make the ceremony superfluous. The Millenary Petition of 1604 accordingly requested its abolition.[20] In fact, of course, the Church

17. P. Collinson, *The Elizabethan Puritan Movement* (1967), p. 369; Procter and Frere, *A New History of the Book of Common Prayer*, pp. 159–60; *The Writings of Henry Barrow, 1590–1*, ed. L. H. Carlson (1966), p. 92; (A. Gilby), *A pleasant dialogue* (1581), sig. M5; A. G. Matthews, *Calamy Revised* (Oxford, 1934), p. 521; A. C. Carter, *The English Reformed Church in Amsterdam in the Seventeenth Century* (Amsterdam, 1964), p. 56.

18. *Kilvert's Diary*, ed. W. Plomer (new edn, 1960), ii, pp. 442–3; B. R. Wilson, *Religion in Secular Society* (1966), pp. 10–12.

19. T. Becon, *Prayers and other Pieces*, ed. J. Ayre (Cambridge, P.S., 1844), p. 234. cf. Thomson, *Later Lollards*, p. 127; Welch in *Procs. Suffolk Inst. Archaeology*, xxix (1962), pp. 159, 163.

20. Gee and Hardy, *Documents Illustrative of English Church History*, p. 509; *The Seconde Parte of a Register*, ed. A. Peel (Cambridge, 1915), i,

of England kept the rite. Indeed the subsequent raising of the age at which children are expected to undergo it to fourteen or so has given it a more pronounced role as a rite of passage marking the arrival of 'social' puberty.[21]

Nevertheless the Protestant attack on sacramental magic had severely eroded the ritual of the established Church. Of the seven sacraments of the Catholic Church (baptism, confirmation, marriage, the Mass, ordination, penance, extreme unction), only baptism and the eucharist retained their undoubted sacramental character, and even these had been considerably reduced in significance. The Lollard view that marriage in a church was unnecessary[22] reappeared in the sectarian concept of civil marriage as a private contract, though it did not gain full legal recognition until 1833. Extreme unction and the sacrament of penance were abandoned.[23] Between 1547 and 1549 the Church also discarded holy water, holy oil and holy bread. The anointing of the invalid was omitted in the ritual for the Visitation of the Sick prescribed by the second Edwardian Prayer Book; and the belief that consecrated bells could drive away devils was given up, along with faith in the wonder-working power of holy candles and the sign of the cross. By the end of the sixteenth century there was substantial acceptance for the extreme Protestant view that no mere ceremony could have any material efficacy, and that divine grace could not be conjured or coerced by any human formula. 'The sacraments,' said the separatist John Canne, 'were not ordained of God to be used . . . as charms and sorceries.'[24]

Another delicate subject was the consecration of churches. The whole notion of consecrated ground had been violently attacked by the Lollards[25] and there can be no doubt that it would have been

pp. 200, 259. For lay resistance see, e.g., *Wiltshire County Records. Minutes of Proceedings in Sessions, 1563 and 1574 to 1592*, ed. H. C. Johnson (Wilts. Archaeol. and Nat. Hist. Soc., 1949), p. 123.

21. For the post-Reformation history of confirmation, S. L. Ollard, 'Confirmation in the Anglican communion', *Confirmation and the Laying on of Hands, by Various Writers*, i (1926), pp. 60–245. The distinction between 'social' and physiological puberty is drawn by A. van Gennep, *The Rites of Passage*, trans. M. B. Vizedom and G. L. Caffee (1960), pp. 65, 67.

22. Thomson, *Later Lollards*, pp. 41, 127.

23. On confession see below, pp. 183–7.

24. J. Canne, *A Necessitie of Separation* (1634), ed. C. Stovel (Hanserd Knollys Soc., 1849), pp. 116–17.

25. B. L. Woodcock, *Medieval Ecclesiastical Courts in the Diocese of Canterbury* (1952), p. 80; Thomson, *Later Lollards*, pp. 40, 78, 183.

abandoned if the Edwardian reformers had had their way. John Scory, preaching at Faversham in 1542, denounced the dedication of the churches as a superstitious ceremony, invented for the profit of the bishops. If it were really necessary to conjure the devil out of bricks and mortar, he argued, it was surprising that any man's house was fit to live in. Most of his Protestant contemporaries would have agreed that a church was 'made a holy place, not by superstitious words of magical enchantment; not by making of signs and characters in stone; but by the will of God and ... godly use'.²⁶ Bishop Ridley accordingly forbade the hallowing of altars; and no ceremony for the consecration of churches was included in the Elizabethan Prayer Book. Only at the end of the sixteenth century did such formulae creep back. They were a prominent feature of the Laudian revival, and came to be accepted even by moderate Anglicans.²⁷

Meanwhile, the Elizabethan separatist Henry Barrow pointed out the magical notions implicit in the whole structure of existing church buildings. At their foundation, he observed,

the first stone must be laid by the hands of the bishop or his suffragan, with certain magical prayers, and holy water, and many other idolatrous rites ... They have at the west end their hallowed bells, which are also baptised, sprinkled, etc. ... They have in the body of their church their hallowed font, to keep the holy water wherewith they baptise ... They have also their holiest of all, or chancel, which peculiarly belongeth to the priest ... They have their roodloft as a partition between their holy and holiest of all. The priest also hath a peculiar door unto his chancel, through which none might pass but himself ... This church, thus reared up, is also thoroughly hallowed with their sprinkling water, and dedicated and baptised into the name of some especial saint or angel, as to the patron and defender thereof, against all enemies, spirits, storms, tempests, etc. Yet hath it within also the holy army of saints and angels in their windows and walls, to keep it. Thus I think can be no doubt made, but that the very erections of these synagogues (whether they were by heathens or papists) were idolatrous.

The sectarian conclusion, therefore, was that the arrangement of the very stones of church buildings was so inherently superstitious that there was nothing for it but to level the whole lot to the ground

26. *L.P.*, xviii (2), p. 305; Calfhill, *An Answer to John Martiall's Treatise*, p. 131.

27. Introduction by J. W. Legg to *English Orders for Consecrating Churches in the Seventeenth Century* (Henry Bradshaw Soc., 1911), esp. pp. xvii-xix.

and begin again. It was no answer to say that the churches had been purged of their idolatry by the Reformation, for

how then do they still stand in their old idolatrous shapes with their ancient appurtenances with their courts, cells, aisles, chancel, bells, etc.? Can these remain and all idolatrous shapes and relics be purged from them; which are so inseparably inherent unto the whole building, as it can never be cleansed of this fretting leprosy, until it be desolate, laid on heaps, as their younger sisters, the abbeys and monasteries are ... The idolatrous shape so cleaveth to every stone, as it by no means can be severed from them whiles there is a stone left standing upon a stone.[28]

It thus became a commonplace for religious nonconformists to declare their indifference or contempt for consecrated places. Like their Lollard predecessors, the separatists boggled at the idea of burying the dead on consecrated soil, and denied that prayers offered up on holy ground were any more likely to prevail. In 1582 Elizabeth Jones of Cheltenham declared that she could serve God in the fields as well as in church. In 1613 an Essex woman justified her absence from church by defiantly asserting that she could say her prayers as effectively at home. On the eve of the Civil War a man at Portsmouth was presented for saying that the church and churchyard were no holier than the common field.[29] This attitude reached its aggressive culmination in 1640, when the Root and Branch petition condemned the bishops for 'the christening and consecrating of churches and chapels, the consecrating fonts, tables, pulpits, chalices, churchyards, and many other things, and putting holiness in them; yea, reconsecrating upon pretended pollution, as though everything were unclean without their consecrating'.[30] Soon afterwards the sects resumed the demand for pulling down superstitious church buildings. It was wrong to worship in consecrated surroundings: a barn, stable

28. *The Writings of Henry Barrow, 1587–90*, ed. L. H. Carlson (1962), pp. 466–8, 478. Similar views in C. Burrage, *The Early English Dissenters* (Cambridge, 1912), i, pp. 89, 240.

29. Thomson, *Later Lollards*, pp. 132, 183; Foxe, v, p. 34; B. Hanbury, *Historical Memorials relating to the Independents* (1839–44), ii, p. 88; Gloucester D.R., Vol. 50; Essex R.O., D/AEA 27, f. 35 (kindly shown me by Dr Alan Macfarlane); *Extracts from Records ... of the Borough of Portsmouth*, ed. R. J. Murrell and R. East (Portsmouth, 1884), p. 124. For an extreme statement of the alternative viewpoint, N. Wallington, *Historical Notices*, ed. R. Webb (1869), i, pp. 189–90.

30. Gee and Hardy, *Documents Illustrative of English Church History*, p. 541.

or pigsty would do as well." The plain and functional Quaker meeting-house was the ultimate achievement of this school of thought.

Another semi-magical ceremony which the Anglican Church seemed reluctant to discard was the churching of women. In its prescription for this rite the Elizabethan Prayer Book followed medieval practice in laying its emphasis on the element of thanksgiving for a safe deliverance. But to Puritan observers it seemed that too many remnants of the old idea of ritual purification had been retained. They took offence at the stylized accompaniments of childbirth – lying-in 'with a white sheet upon her bed', coming forth 'covered with a veil, as ashamed of some folly'. The rubric of the Prayer Book did not require the woman to wear a white veil, but orthodox clergy insisted upon it and it was upheld in a legal judgement in the reign of James I." Many churches had a special seat for the new mother, with her midwife at a discreet distance behind her. All this seemed to the Puritans to imply that a woman was unclean after childbirth until she had been magically purified; and it was true that some of the bishops regarded 'purifying' as the *mot juste*. The need for such purification, declared one preacher, speaking of sexual intercourse, was clear proof 'that some stain or other doth creep into this action which had need to be repented'." Puritan suspicions were not allayed by the recitation at the ceremony itself of Psalm 121, with its strange incantation: 'The sun shall not smite thee by day, nor the moon by night' – as if, snorted John Milton, the woman 'had been travailing not in her bed, but in the deserts of Arabia'."

The taboo elements in the whole ritual were sardonically analysed by Henry Barrow:

After they have been safely delivered of childbirth, and have lain in, and been shut up, their month of days accomplished; then are they to

31. T. Edwards, *Gangraena* (2nd edn, 1646), i, p. 30; ii, p. 5; iii, p. 62. cf. *C.S.P.D., 1635*, p. 40; *1637*, p. 508; C. Hill in *Historical Essays 1600–1750 presented to David Ogg*, ed. H. E. Bell and R. L. Ollard (1963), p. 51.

32. *The Puritan Manifestoes*, ed. W. H. Frere and C. E. Douglas (1907), pp. 28–9; R. Burn, *Ecclesiastical Law* (2nd edn, 1767), i, p. 290.

33. *The Works of Henry Smith*, ed. T. Smith (1866–7), i, p. 12. cf. W. P. M. Kennedy, *The 'Interpretations' of the Bishops* (Alcuin Club, 1908), p. 36.

34. *Complete Prose Works of John Milton* (New Haven, 1953–), i, p. 939. cf. Gilby, *A Pleasant Dialogue*, sig. M5; K. Chidley, *The Justification of the Independant Churches of Christ* (1641), p. 57.

repair to church and to kneel down in some place nigh the communion table (not to speak how she cometh wimpled and muffled, accompanied with her wives, and dare not look upon the sun nor sky, until the priest have put her in possession again of them) unto whom (thus placed in the church) cometh Sir Priest; straight ways standeth by her, and readeth over her a certain psalm, viz. 121, and assureth her that the sun shall not burn her by day, nor the moon by night, [and] sayeth his Pater Noster, with the prescribed versicles and response, with his collect. And then, she having offered her accustomed offerings unto him for his labour, God speed her well, she is a woman on foot again, as holy as ever she was; she may now put off her veiling kerchief, and look her husband and neighbours in the face again ... What can be a more apish imitation, or rather a more reviving of the Jewish purification than this?

For Barrow the surest proof of the magical element in the ceremony was the ritual period of isolation which preceded it:

If she be not defiled by childbirth, why do they separate her? Why do they cleanse her? Why may she not return to Church (having recovered strength) before her month be expired? Why may she not come after her accustomed manner, and give God thanks? ... Why is she enjoined to come, and the priest to receive her in this prescript manner? Why are the women held in a superstitious opinion that this action is necesary?[35]

Resistance to churching or to wearing the veil thus became one of the surest signs of Puritan feeling among clergy or laity in the century before the Civil War.[36] But the Anglican Church hung on to the ceremony, though dropping Psalm 121 after the Restoration, and quietly abandoning the emphasis upon the obligatory character of the rite.

The same aversion to anything smacking of magic governed the Protestant attitude to prayer. Indeed the conventional distinction between a prayer and a spell seems to have been first hammered out, not by the nineteenth-century anthropologists, with whom it is usually associated, but by sixteenth-century Protestant theologians. It was well expressed by the Puritan Richard Greenham when he explained that parishioners should not assume that their ministers could give them immediate relief when their consciences were troubled.

35. *The Writings of Henry Barrow, 1587–90*, pp. 462–3.
36. For some examples, Hale, *Precedents*, pp. 167, 169, 225, 230, 237; A. Gibbons, *Ely Episcopal Records* (1890), p. 84; *The State of the Church in the Reigns of Elizabeth and James I*, ed. C. W. Foster (Lincoln Rec. Soc., 1926), pp. xxxix, lxxix, lxxxi; *V.C.H. Beds.*, i, p. 336n. 3; *V.C.H., Wilts.*, iii, p. 36; *C.S.P.D., 1637–8*, pp. 382–3.

This [he wrote] is a coming rather as it were to a magician (who, by an incantation of words, makes silly souls look for health) rather than to the minister of God, whose words being most angelical comfort, not until, and so much as, it pleaseth the Lord to give a blessing unto them; which sometime he doth deny, because we come to them with too great an opinion of them; as they were wise men [i.e. wizards], not unto such, as using their means, yet do look and stay for our comfort wholly from God himself.

Words and prayers, in other words, had no power in themselves, unless God chose to heed them; whereas the working of charms followed automatically upon their pronunciation. This same distinction lay behind William Tyndale's denunciation of the Roman Catholics for what he called

a false kind of praying, wherein the tongue and lips labour, ... but the heart talketh not, ... nor hath any confidence in the promises of God; but trusteth in the multitude of words, and in the pain and tediousness of the length of the prayer; as a conjurer doth in his circles, characters, and superstitious words of his conjuration.

A prayer 'repeated without understanding', said another Protestant, was not 'any better than a charm'.[37]

In an effort to remove the incantatory aspects of formal prayer the Anglican Church went over from Latin to the vernacular. Steps were also taken to eliminate any prayers which seemd to imply that supernatural power lay anywhere other than with God. Relics were no longer to be adored for their supposedly miraculous properties, and the idea of praying to saints was regarded as reprehensible; the Lollards had dismissed one of the most famous objects of pilgrimage as 'the witch of Walsingham'.[38] Most of the great shrines were systematically dismantled during the early Tudor Reformation.[39] The Church also abandoned those other Popish rituals which, like the hymns sung on the feast of the Invention of the Cross, it thought to have been 'conceived in the character of magic spells'.[40] The Puritans would have liked to have gone further, and to have reformed or abolished

37. *The Workes of ... Richard Greenham*, ed. H. H(olland) (3rd edn, 1601), p. 5; W. Tyndale, *Expositions and Notes*, ed. H. Walter (Cambridge, P.S., 1849), p. 80; Cooper, *Mystery*, p. 351.
38. J. C. Dickinson, *The Shrine of our Lady of Walsingham* (Cambridge, 1956), p. 27.
39. See the account in J. C. Wall, *Shrines of British Saints* (1905), chap. 6.
40. T. Jackson, *A Treatise containing the Originall of Unbelief* (1625), p. 236.

the Litany, whose numerous petitions they regarded as 'nothing but an impure mass of conjuring and charming battologies'. At the Hampton Court Conference an effort was made to delete the prayer for delivery from violent death, on the grounds that it was a particularly obnoxious 'conjuring of God'.[41]

But the incantatory character of many prayers was not so easily eliminated. John Rogers, the seventeenth-century Fifth Monarchy Man, tells us that as a child he used to reel off his prayers in the hope that they would act as charms to keep him safe at night, when he was afraid 'the devils would tear [him] to pieces'; sometimes frantically repeating them twice over, for fear he might have made some slip in pronunciation the first time. In the same way men had become habituated to reciting set prayers when planting and grafting, or even when looking for things they had lost.[42]

The Anglican Church clung on to the principle of set prayer, but it did at least take steps to remove rituals which appeared to be attempts to coerce the deity rather than to entreat him. In 1547 the Royal Injunctions put a stop to the religious processions traditionally held at times of special need. This step was said at first to have been taken because of the strife for precedence and general disorder which marked these occasions. But ultimately processions were admitted to be superfluous: prayer was just as effective if offered up, less ostentatiously, within the church building.

One procession alone was retained: the annual perambulation of the parish in Rogation week. This was the sole survivor of the many medieval ceremonies which had been conducted in the open to secure fertility and good weather: blessing the trees on the Twelfth Day after Christmas, reading gospels to the springs to make their water purer, and the blessing of the corn by the young men and maids after they had received the sacrament on Palm Sunday.[43] The medieval Litanies or Rogations (major on St Mark's Day (25 April), and minor on the three days before Ascension Day) derived from earlier pagan ceremonies, and had been designed to combat war, illness, violent death and other non-agricultural terrors. But they also in-

41. Procter and Frere, *A New History of the Book of Common Prayer*, pp. 137–8, 129–30. cf. *The Writings of Henry Barrow, 1590-1*, p. 94.

42. E. Rogers, *Some Account of the Life and Opinions of a Fifth-Monarchy Man* (1867), pp. 8, 11; *The Country-man's Recreation* (1654), p. 60; J. Dod and R. Cleaver, *A Plaine and Familiar Exposition of the Ten Commandements* (18th edn, 1632), p. 95.

43. Aubrey, *Gentilisme*, pp. 40, 58, 59.

volved processing across the fields with cross, banners and bells to
drive away evil spirits and bless the crops. Under the reformed procedure, laid down in the Royal Injunctions of 1559 and amplified in
subsequent instructions, there was to be an annual perambulation of
the parish boundaries at the accustomed time, i.e. Monday, Tuesday
or Wednesday of Ascension week, carried out by the curate and substantial men of the parish. At convenient places the curate was to
admonish the people of the need to give thanks for the fruits of the
earth, and to warn them of the curse which fell upon those who removed their neighbour's landmarks. Two psalms and the Litany
were to be sung, and a sermon or homily preached. Every effort was
made to purge these occasions of any popish associations. The
curate was not to wear a surplice and there was to be no carrying of
banners or stopping at wayside crosses. The ceremony, as Bishop
Grindal stressed, was 'not a procession but a perambulation'.[44]

The perambulation was thus intended to make sure that the parish
boundaries had not been encroached upon during the course of the
year; and also to offer prayers for good weather and a successful
harvest. But many contemporaries attributed a mechanical efficacy
to the ceremony; it was too closely linked to its medieval antecedents: what Tyndale called 'saying of gospels to the corn in the
field in the procession week, that it should the better grow'.[45] The
meaning of such procedures had been emphasized as late as 1540
in the *Postils* of Richard Taverner, the Erasmian associate of Thomas
Cromwell. Observing how pestilence was caused by the evil spirits
which infected the air, Taverner explained that

for this cause be certain gospels read in the wide field amongst the corn
and grass, that by the virtue and operation of God's word, the power of
the wicked spirits which keep in the air may be laid down, and the air
made pure and clean, to the intent the corn may remain unharmed and
not infected of the said hurtful spirits, but serve us for our use and bodily
sustenance.

Provided that the processions were made with due reverence, thought
Taverner, there was no doubt 'but that God's word will utter and
execute his virtue and strength upon the corn and air, that those

44. Frere and Kennedy, *Articles and Injunctions*, iii, pp. 160, 164, 177,
208, 264, 290, 308–9, 334, 378; *The Remains of Edmund Grindal*, ed. W.
Nicholson (Cambridge, P.S., 1843), pp. 240–41.
45. W. Tyndale, *An Answer to Sir Thomas More's Dialogue*, ed. H.
Walter (Cambridge, P.S., 1850), p. 62.

noisome spirits of the air shall do no hurt at all to our corn and cattle'.[46]

The notion that the appropriate religious ritual could bring material benefit thus lingered on. The clergy had to be coerced into leaving behind their surplices and banners; and they were reluctant to give up reading prayers at the spots where the wayside crosses had once stood. Crosses were sometimes cut on tree trunks to mark where the gospel used to be read. At Standlake, Oxfordshire, the parson used to read it at the barrel's head in the cellar of the Chequers Inn, allegedly the site of the original cross. Indeed the medieval practice of reading the gospels in the corn fields survived in some areas until the Civil War, even though the perambulation was supposed to limit itself to the parochial boundaries. Most parishes had their idiosyncratic customs about refreshment and entertainment on the route: at Great Gransden, Huntingdonshire, it was the practice to hold the vicar upside down with his head in a waterhole.[47]

The Puritans accordingly displayed hostility towards the whole business. 'Is there an idol here to be worshipped that you have a drinking?', demanded an Essex perambulator in 1565. 'Charming the fields', Henry Barrow called it.[48] At Deddington, Oxfordshire, typical scruples were displayed in 1631 by the Puritan incumbent, William Brudenell, who refused to wear his surplice on the outing, much to his parishioners' dismay, and jibbed at reading a gospel at the customary spot where a cross had been carved in the earth. He demanded 'to what end he should read one, and said he would not stand bare to a hole, which any shepherd or boy might make for ought he knew, and said it was Popery to observe old customs; and he went further on and stood in a ditch under an elder tree, and then read in a book a homily'. On another occasion he refused to go around the boundaries, demanding what purpose it served, and (sig-

46. R. Taverner, *Postils on the Epistles and Gospels*, ed. E. Cardwell (Oxford, 1841), p. 280. The passage suggests that the rationalism of contemporary 'Erasmianism' can be exaggerated.
47 T. S. Maskelyne, 'Perambulation of Burton, 1733', *Wilts. Archaeol. and Nat. Hist. Mag.*, xl (1918); R. P(lot), *The Natural History of Oxford-Shire* (Oxford, 1677), p. 203; Aubrey, *Gentilisme*, pp. 32–4, 40; M. W. Beresford and J. K. S. St Joseph, *Medieval England; an Aerial Survey* (1958), p. 77.
48. F. G. Emmison, *An Introduction to Archives* (1964), plate 12; *The Writings of Henry Barrow, 1587–90*, p. 543. cf. *The Puritan Manifestoes*, p. 33; *A short dialogue* (1605), p. 12; Canne, *A Necessitie of Separation*, p. 123.

nificantly) 'whether it would be any benefit or profit to the poor'. The only answer he received was that the ritual was a customary one; this failed to satisfy him, and he abstained from the perambulation.[49]

These Rogation ceremonies, 'gang days', or 'cross days', as they were called, were, of course, not primarily regarded as a magical method for making the crops grow. Basically, they were the corporate manifestation of the village community, an occasion for eating and drinking, and the reconciliation of disputes. They fell into desuetude, less from any growth of rationalism, than because of the social changes which broke up the old community, and physically impeded anything so cumbersome as a perambulation around parochial boundaries. The ritual was well designed for open-field country, but enclosure and cultivation led to the destruction of old landmarks and blocking of rights of way. The decline of corporate feeling showed itself in the increasing reluctance of wealthy householders to pay for the riff-raff of the village to drink themselves into a frenzy. At Goring in the 1620s a definite stand was taken when several inhabitants declared themselves ready to go to law rather than foot the bill for drink.[50] Meanwhile the spread of better methods of surveying and map-making were making much of the procedure obsolete. The Laudian bishops tried to keep it alive as a means of intercession at time of threatened scarcity,[51] and some parishes retained it for convivial reasons until the nineteenth century. But after the sixteenth century there were few men who suggested that the ceremony had any material efficacy.

Protestantism also launched a new campaign against the relics of paganism with which the early Church had done so much to compromise. Popery was portrayed as the great repository of 'ethnic superstitions', and most Catholic rites were regarded as thinly concealed mutations of earlier pagan ceremonies. Much energy was

49. Bodl., Oxford Diocesan Papers, c 26, ff. 182–184. Other examples of non-cooperation by ministers occur in Ely D.R., B 2/15, f. 4ᵛ; Wells D.R., A 102.

50. Bodl., Oxford Diocesan Papers, d 11, f. 226ᵛ. For other instances of drink being refused, Hale, *Precedents*, p. 243; W. H. Turner, in *Procs. of the Oxford Architectural and Hist. Soc.*, n.s., iii (1872–80), p. 137; Ely D.R., B 2/21, f. 83ᵛ (1601); *V.C.H. Wilts.*, iii, p. 46; and for obstructions caused by enclosure and cultivation, M. Bowker, *The Secular Clergy in the Diocese of Lincoln, 1495–1520* (Cambridge, 1968), pp. 113–14; Hale, *Precedents,* pp. 162, 237, 243; Heywood, *Diaries*, ii, p. 291.

51. e.g., *Articles to be enquired of ... in the trienniall visitation of ... Lancelot Lord Bishop of Winton ... 1625*, sig. B1.

spent in demonstrating that holy water was the Roman *aqua lustralis*, that wakes were the *Bacchanalia*, Shrove Tuesday celebrations *Saturnalia*, Rogation processions *ambarvalia*, and so forth.[52] The early reformers also set out to stop such traditional calendar customs as the Plough Monday procession (banned in 1548), and the saints' days associated with special trades and occupations (prohibited in 1547). By the dissolution of the religious gilds they put an end to such village institutions as plough gilds, hobby-horses and collections for plough lights. The annual feast of the parish church's dedication was compulsorily moved to the first Sunday in October, and all other wakes forbidden. Later ecclesiastical injunctions prohibited the entry into the church or churchyard of Rush-bearing processions, Lords of Misrule and Summer Lords and Ladies.[53]

On these matters, as on so many others, later Protestant opinion was divided. The leaders of the Church in the early seventeenth century allowed May-games, Whitsun Ales, Morris dancing and maypoles, whereas the Puritans wanted the abolition of all remaining holy days, a ban on maypoles and Sunday dancing, and the purge of all secular accompaniments of religious ceremony.[54] They objected to the bagpipes and fiddlers who accompanied the bridal couple to the church and to the throwing of corn (the sixteenth-century equivalent of confetti). They repudiated such ritual appurtenances of funerals as the tolling bell, the mourning garments, and the distribution of doles to the poor, as 'superstitious and heathenical'. They rejected the custom of giving New Year's gifts for the same reason.[55] No doubtful practice escaped their eye. At Oxford the initia-

52. This is the theme of such works as T. Moresinus, *Papatus, seu depravatae religionis Origo et Incrementum* (Edinburgh, 1594), and J. Stopford, *Pagano-Papismus: or, an exact parallel between Rome-Pagan and Rome-Christian in their Doctrines and Ceremonies* (1675). It culminated in Conyers Middleton's *A Letter from Rome* (1729). cf. W. Lambarde, *A Perambulation of Kent* (1596), p. 335; S. Harsnet, *A Declaration of Egregious Popish Impostures* (1603), p. 88; Hobbes, *Leviathan*, chap. 45.

53. Frere and Kennedy, *Articles and Injunctions*, ii, pp. 126, 175; iii, p. 271; *Journal of the English Folk Dance and Song Soc.*, viii (1957), p. 76, n. 65; (A. Sparrow), *A Collection of Articles* (1684), p. 167.

54. See C. Hill, *Society and Puritanism in Pre-Revolutionary England* (1964), chap. 5.

55. On weddings: *Puritan Manifestoes*, p. 27; *Chetham Miscellanies*, v (1875), p. 7; see also, below, pp. 740–41. On funerals: *Puritan Manifestoes*, p. 28; Canne, *A Necessitie of Separation*, p. 113; *The Writings of Henry Barrow, 1590–1*, pp. 82–3; W. M. Palmer, in *Procs. Cambs. Antiq. Soc.*, xvi (1912), pp. 147–8; and below, pp. 721–2. On New Year's gifts: Brand,

tion rites for freshmen were discontinued under the Commonwealth and Protectorate; and in 1644 the Westminster Assembly even resolved to ask Parliament 'to review the superstitions that may be in the order of knighthood'.[56] The custom of drinking healths was also seen as a heathen survival, an oblation to some half-forgotten pagan deity. When the Cheshire Puritan John Bruen attended a High Sheriff's feast he refused to drink to the King, but said that he would pray for him instead.[57] To contemporaries it was ideological scrupulosity of this kind which seemed the Puritan's distinguishing characteristic, and Sir John Harington could satirize the godly brother whose reaction, when someone exclaimed 'Christ help!' after sneezing, was to say ' 'twas witchcraft and deserved damnation'.[58] By obsessive attention to trivia of this kind the Puritans signified their desire to eliminate all ceremonies, superstitions and observances which had non-Christian or magical overtones.

Extreme Protestants also diminished the role of supernatural sanctions in daily life by a new attitude to oath-taking. Although the courts of law after the Reformation continued to regard the oath as a guarantee of testimony, the Lollards' objections to the practice were revived by the Tudor separatists and their successors. Apart from the Anabaptists, the Reformers did not explicitly reject the use of oaths altogether. They merely repudiated the practice of swearing by God's creatures (such as the saints or holy objects) rather than by God himself.[59] But the Protestant emphasis upon the individual conscience inevitably shifted the ultimate sanction for truthfulness from the external fear of divine punishment to the godly man's internal

Antiquities, i, pp. 16, 18–19; *The Workes of ... William Perkins* (Cambridge, 1616–18), ii, p. 676.

56. Wood, *Life and Times*, i, p. 140 (for earlier resistance, W. D. Christie, *A Life of Anthony Ashley Cooper, 1st Earl of Shaftesbury* (1871), i, appx., pp. xii–xiii); *Minutes of the Sessions of the Westminster Assembly*, ed. A. F. Mitchell and J. Struthers (1874), p. 24.

57. W. Hinde, *A Faithfull Remonstrance of the Holy Life ... of John Bruen* (1641), pp. 192–3. cf. M. Scrivener, *A Treatise against Drunkennesse* (1685), pp. 120–21; J. Geree, *A Divine Potion* (1648), p. 5; A. Hildersham, *CVIII. Lectures upon the Fourth of John* (4th edn, 1656), p. 123; T. Vincent, *Words of Advice to Young Men* (1668), p. 96.

58. *The Letters and Epigrams of Sir John Harington*, ed. N. E. McClure (Philadelphia, 1930), p. 180. Sneezing was sometimes regarded as an omen; W. Shelton, *A Discourse of Superstition* (1678), p. 25.

59. A distinction pointed out by H. G. Russell, 'Lollard opposition to oaths by creatures', *American Hist. Rev.*, li (1946).

sense of responsibility. A man should keep his word simply because he had given it, Thomas Hobbes declared: 'The oath adds nothing to the obligation.' The Quakers accordingly refused to take oaths because of their unacceptable implication that an affirmation un-accompanied by an oath was less likely to be sincere; and in univer-sity ceremonies at Oxford during the Commonwealth oaths were replaced by promises.[60]

For less conscientious men, however, the oath became less im-portant because the terrors of supernatural vengeance had steadily receded. Complaints of perjury multiplied in the sixteenth and seven-teenth centuries and successive statutes on the subject testify to the lack of any adequate secular sanction against the offence. The godly took oaths seriously, but the attitude of most people was less scrupu-lous, if the complaint of an early seventeenth-century Puritan is to be believed:

How many oaths are ministered daily to churchwardens, constables, jurors and witnesses, at every assize and sessions, in every court, baron and leet, in every commission, . . . and no man regardeth them any more than the taking up of a straw; they think it is no more than the laying on the hand and kissing of the book. 'Tush', thinks every man, 'the taking of these oaths is a matter of nothing; all my neighbours have taken them before me, and made no reckoning of them.'

In the later seventeenth century Sir William Petty agreed that 'the sacred esteem of oaths is much lessened'.[61] In New England the colonists devised severe laws against perjury because they could no longer trust in miraculous punishments.[62] At home the law was slower to be reformed. But in the business world self-interest had begun to supersede divine vengeance as the sanction for truthfulness. The oath was gradually replaced by the promise, which no successful trader could afford to break: as one Tudor merchant remarked: 'If

60. Hobbes, *Leviathan*, chap. 14; Wood, *Life and Times*, i, pp. 165, 207. For a fuller discussion of the whole subject of oaths, Hill, *Society and Puritanism*, chap. 11.

61. A. Hildersham, *CLII Lectures upon Psalm LI* (1635), p. 184; *The Petty Papers*, ed. Marquis of Lansdowne (1927), i, p. 275. cf. T. Comber, *The Nature and Usefulness of Solemn Judicial Swearing* (1682), p. 22; Sir J. F. Stephen, *A History of the Criminal Law of England* (1883), iii, pp. 244–8.

62. B. C. Steiner, *Maryland during the English Civil Wars* (Baltimore, 1906–7), ii, pp. 92, 98; G. L. Haskins, *Law and Authority in Early Massa-chusetts* (New York, 1960), p. 125.

goods were lost much were lost; if time were lost more were lost; but if credit were lost all were lost."⁶³ So long as honesty was the best policy the decline of supernatural sanctions mattered less.

In all these different ways the Protestant reformers rejected the magical powers and supernatural sanctions which had been so plentifully invoked by the medieval Church. In Protestant mythology the Middle Ages became notorious as the time of darkness, when spells and charms had masqueraded as religion and when the lead in magical activity had been taken by the clergy themselves. Scholastic learning was said to have included the arts of divination, and numerous English clerics, from Dunstan to Cardinals Morton and Wolsey, were portrayed as sorcerers who had dabbled in diabolic arts. An enormous list of Popes who had been conjurers, sorcerers or enchanters was put in circulation; and it included all eighteen pontiffs between Sylvester II and Gregory VII.⁶⁴ Such legends may have been reinforced by the way in which some of the Renaissance Popes had indeed compromised with hermetic magic and Neoplatonism.⁶⁵ But it was not the rediscovery of classical magic which underlay the complaints of the reformers: it was the basic ritual of the Catholic Church.

In the reign of Elizabeth I, therefore, the term 'conjurer' came to be a synonym for recusant priest.⁶⁶ Bishop Richard Davies reminded the Welsh people of the 'superstition, charms and incantations' which had formed the religion of popish times, and a Puritan manifesto described the Church of Rome as the source of 'all wicked sorcery'. A Yorkshire Protestant, shown a batch of Roman indulgences in 1586, could recognize them immediately as 'witchcrafts, and papistry'. Catholic miracles were confidently attributed to witchcraft. Popery, in the words of Daniel Defoe, was 'one entire system

63. *John Isham, Mercer and Merchant Adventurer*, ed. G. D. Ramsay (Northants. Rec. Soc., 1962), p. 172.
64. A. G. Dickens, *Lollards and Protestants in the Diocese of York* (1959), p. 124; Tyndale, *Expositions and Notes*, p. 308; F. Coxe, *A Short Treatise* (1561), sig. Biiijᵛ; J. Geree, *Astrologo-Mastix* (1646), p. 19; T. Rogers, *The Catholic Doctrine of the Church of England*, ed. J. J. S. Perowne (Cambridge, P.S., 1854), p. 180.
65. As is suggested by F. A. Yates, *Giordano Bruno and the Hermetic Tradition* (1964), p. 143.
66. e.g., J. Strype, *Annals* (1725), ii, pp. 181–2; S. Haynes, *A Collection of State Papers* (1740), p. 603.

of anti-Christian magic', and the Pope for the Elizabethan lawyer William Lambarde was the 'witch of the world'.[67]

For Anglicans, however, this type of polemic could be embarrassing. The attack launched by the early reformers generated more radical variants; so that ultimately almost any kind of formal prayer or ceremony came to be denounced by its opponents as 'witchcraft' or 'sorcery'. As Leslie Stephen was to remark, Protestantism inevitably became a screen for rationalism.[68] The Church of England, which had kept what Bishop Jewel called its 'scenic apparatus', was duly criticised by radical Protestants for its 'magical ceremonial rites'; and the sectary Henry Barrow described the Elizabethan clergy as 'Egyptian enchanters'.[69] This terminology became so much part of the rhetoric of Puritanism that nonconformists could speak of the Prayer Book as 'witchcraft' and even interrupt the service by calling on the minister to 'leave off his witchery, conjuration and sorcery'. Sir John Eliot thought that Parliament should stand firm against Laudian innovations 'by restricting their ceremonies, by abolishing their sorceries'.[70] By 1645 the reaction against formal

67. G. Williams, *The Welsh Church from Conquest to Reformation* (Cardiff, 1962), p. 461; *The Seconde Parte of a Register*, i, p. 50; Borthwick, R.VI.G 2456; H. Foley, *Records of the English Province of the Society of Jesus* (1877–84), iv, p. 131; (D. Defoe), *A System of Magick* (1727), p. 352; *William Lambarde and Local Government*, ed. C. Read (Ithaca, N.Y., 1962), p. 101. For other examples of the extensive tradition linking Popery with magic see E. Worsop, *A Discoverie of Sundry Errours* (1582), sig. E4; H. Holland, *A Treatise against Witchcraft* (Cambridge, 1590), sig. B1; A. Roberts, *A Treatise of Witchcraft* (1616), p. 3; Bernard, *Guide*, pp. 16–17; J. Gaule, *Select Cases of Conscience touching Witches and Witchcrafts* (1646), pp. 16–17; R. Bovet, *Pandaemonium* (1684), ed. M. Summers (Aldington, Kent, 1951), pp. 71–3; Brand, *Antiquities*, iii, pp. 255–6; R. T. Davies, *Four Centuries of Witch-Beliefs* (1947), pp. 120–22.

68. L. Stephen, *History of English Thought in the Eighteenth Century* (3rd edn, 1902), i, p. 79.

69. *The Zurich Letters*, trans. and ed. H. Robinson (Cambridge, P.S., 1842), p. 23; *The Writings of Henry Barrow, 1587–90*, pp. 346, 353, 381.

70. F. W. X. Fincham, 'Notes from the ecclesiastical court records at Somerset House', *T.R.H.S.*, 4th ser., iv (1921), p. 121; T. Richards, *Religious Developments in Wales (1654–62)* (1923), p. 399 and n. 11; *The Diary of Abraham de la Pryme*, ed. C. Jackson (Surtees Soc., 1870), p. 293; S. R. Gardiner, *History of England from the Accession of James I to the Outbreak of the Civil War* (1904–5), vi, p. 234. Davies, *Four Centuries of Witch-Beliefs*, pp. 122–4, gives a good illustration of how Laudian ceremonies could be genuinely mistaken for ritual magic, but his suggestion that Eliot's speech implied that the Laudians had attempted to interfere with the 1604 witchcraft statute seems fanciful.

prayer had gone so far that an Essex Anabaptist could declare that
'none but witches and sorcerers use to say the Lord's Prayer'.[71] Extreme sectarians regarded the very idea of a professional clergyman
as magical. John Webster asserted that all who were ordained by
men, or who preached for hire, were 'magicians, sorcerers, enchanters, soothsayers, necromancers, and consulters with familiar spirits'.
The Quakers, having dispensed with the priesthood, did not hesitate
to denounce clergymen as 'conjurers'; and in Gerrard Winstanley's
Digger utopia anyone who professed the trade of preaching and
prayer was to be put to death 'as a witch'.[72]

Of course, this new Protestant attitude to ecclesiastical magic did
not win an immediate victory; and some of the traditions of the
Catholic past lingered on. Many of the old holy wells, for example,
retained their semi-magical associations, even though Protestants
preferred to regard them as medicinal springs working by natural
means. In some areas the practice of bringing New Year's Day water
or the 'flower of the well' into the church and placing it on the altar
survived into the seventeenth century; and the dressing and decoration of such shrines long continued.[73] Pilgrimages, sometimes very
large ones, were made to the famous well of St Winifred at Holywell
throughout the seventeenth century, and it was not only recusants
who went there in search of a cure. When a man was found dead at
the well in 1630 after having made scoffing remarks about its sup-

71. Essex R.O., Q/SBa 2/58 (a reference kindly supplied by Dr Alan
Macfarlane).
72. Introduction by J. Crossley to *Potts* (for Webster); *A Brief Relation
of the Irreligion of the Northern Quakers* (1653), p. 74; *The Works of
Gerrard Winstanley*, ed. G. H. Sabine (Ithaca, N.Y., 1941), p. 597. The
Quaker leader, George Whitehead, was said to have declared that 'he who
asserts there be three persons in the blessed Trinity is a dreamer and a conjuror', R.B., *Questions propounded to George Whitehead and George Fox*
(1659), p. 1.
73. Plot, *Natural History of Oxford-Shire*, pp. 49–50; R. Lennard, 'The
Watering-Places', *Englishmen at Rest and Play*, ed. R. Lennard (Oxford,
1931), p. 10; Aubrey, *Gentilisme*, pp. 33, 223–4; Brand, *Antiquities*, ii, pp.
374, 377–8; R. C. Hope, *The Legendary Lore of the Holy Wells of England*
(1893), pp. 159, 170; *The Diary of Thomas Crosfield*, ed. F. S. Boas (1935),
p. 93; D. Edmondes Owen, 'Pre-Reformation Survivals in Radnorshire',
Trans. of the Hon. Soc. of Cymmrodorion, 1912; A. R. Wright,
British Calendar Customs, ed. T. E. Lones (Folk-Lore Soc., 1936–40), ii,
pp. 21–2.

posed powers a local jury brought in a verdict of death by divine judgement."

The wells also helped to keep alive the names of the saints, as did the holy days in the church year, and the dedications of ecclesiastical buildings. In 1589 in the Caernarvonshire parish of Clynnog, it was still customary to drive bullocks into the churchyard to dedicate them to the local patron, St Beuno, in the belief that the market price of the animals would rise accordingly. Each parish church in the Clynnog area had a saint who was held, according to an informant, 'in such estimation as that in their extremities they do pray unto him for help ... when some sudden danger do befall them' – only remembering to couple the name of God after more deliberation, when 'they say, "God and Beuno, God and Ianwg, or God and Mary and Michael help us" '. In the later seventeenth century it was still believed that a sick person laid on St Beuno's tomb on a Friday would either recover or die for certain within three weeks."⁵ John Aubrey retails the story of old Simon Brunsdon, the parish clerk of Winterbourne Bassett in Wiltshire, who had been appointed under Mary Tudor, but lived on into the reign of James I with his faith in the local patron saint unimpaired: 'When the gad-fly had happened to sting his oxen, or cows, and made them run away in that champaign country, he would run after them, crying out, praying, "Good St Katharine of Winterbourne, stay my oxen. Good St Katharine of Winterbourne, stay my Oxen." ' Even in modern times gratings from the statues of saints on Exeter Cathedral have been employed in rural Devonshire to keep away disease from cattle and pigs."⁶

Some of the old calendar rituals proved equally difficult to eradicate. Plough Monday remained a date in the agricultural year despite the Reformation, and gild ploughs were kept in some village churches

74. For the extensive sixteenth- and seventeenth-century history of the well, see *Analecta Bollandiana*, vi (Paris, 1887), pp. 305–52; *The Life and Miracles of S. Wenefride* (1712) (reissued with hostile commentary by W. Fleetwood in 1713); Foley, *Records of the English Province of the Society of Jesus*, iv, pp. 534–7. For a similar list of cures at St. Vincent's Well, Bristol, but without the same religious implications, see Sloane 640, ff. 340–51; 79, ff. 110–11.

75. P.R.O., SP 12/224, f. 145 (also in *Archaeologia Cambrensis*, 3rd ser., i (1855), pp. 235–7); *Memorials of John Ray*, ed. E. Lankester (1846), p. 171.

76. Aubrey, *Gentilisme*, pp. 28–9; *Trans. Devonshire Assoc.*, lxxxiii (1951), p. 74; ibid., lxxxvi (1954), p. 299; T. Brown, 'Some Examples of Post-Reformation Folklore in Devon', *Folk-Lore*, lxxii (1961), pp. 391–2.

until the late seventeenth century. Straw images or corn 'dollies' were made at harvest homes." In his *Characters* (1615) Sir Thomas Overbury wrote of *The Franklin* that 'Rock Monday, and the wake in summer, Shrovings, the wakeful ketches [i.e. catches or songs] on Christmas Eve, the holy or seed cake, these he yearly keeps, yet holds them no relics of Popery.' Such calendar customs were convenient ways of dividing up the agrarian year, and provided a welcome source of entertainment. But they were also still credited with a preventive or prophylactic power against evil spirits, or, more vaguely, bad luck. The rules about the special games or food-stuffs associated with these customs had to be strictly observed. Hot cross buns on Good Friday could bring good fortune and protect the house from fire; a Michaelmas goose meant luck for those who ate it; giving gifts at the New Year brought good fortune to the givers. The same sanctions were thought to attach to the wassail bowl at Christmas, or the wearing of new clothes at Easter.[78]

It is hard to tell how clearly this aspect of such ritual observances was appreciated by those who took part; and often the 'play' element must have predominated. But there is no doubt that such rites survived, though sometimes in an attenuated form, until the nineteenth century in many parts of the country. The fires on the hillsides continued to be lit on St John Baptist or St Peter's Eve;[79] and the maypole and morris dance returned after their temporary banishment during the Commonwealth. Such activities could still retain a ritual solemnity. Between the two world wars an anthropologically-minded German professor asked an elderly member of a party of country mummers who had come to perform at an Oxford garden party whether

77. Ely D.R., B 2/34, ff. 4ᵛ–5; W. Saltonstall, *Picturae Loquentes* (Luttrell Soc., 1946), p. 28; Wright, *British Calendar Customs*, ii, p. 101; Brand, *Antiquities*, ii, pp. 16–33; M. W. Barley, 'Plough Plays in the East Midlands', *Journ. of the Eng. Folk Dance and Song Soc.*, vii (1953); W. M. Palmer, 'Episcopal visitation returns', *Trans. Cambs. and Hunts. Archaeol. Soc.*, v (1930–7), p. 32 (ploughs to be removed from Willingham and Comberton, 1665).

78. Brand, *Antiquities*, i, pp. 63, 156, 370, and *passim*; Wright, *British Calendar Customs*, i, pp. 69–73, 83; *County Folk-Lore*, ii, ed. Mrs Gutch (Folk-Lore Soc., 1901), p. 243. Rock Monday (i.e. Distaff Monday) was the Monday after Twelfth Day, when spinning restarted: *O.E.D.*

79. *Durham Depositions*, p. 235; *Kilvert's Diary*, iii, p. 344; Brand, *Antiquities*, i, pp. 299–311; A. Hussey, 'Archbishop Parker's Visitation, 1569', *Home Counties Magazine*, v (1903), p. 208; Wright, *British Calendar Customs*, iii, pp. 6–12, 24–5.

women were ever allowed to take part. The reply was significant: 'Nay sir, mumming don't be for the likes of them. There be plenty else for them that be flirty-like, but this here mumming be more like parson's work'.[80]

There is also evidence to suggest that the old Catholic protective formulae could sometimes survive in otherwise Protestant *milieux*. In Lollard eyes the sign of the cross could 'avail to nothing else but to scare away flies', yet as late as 1604 the people of Lancashire were said to be in the habit of crossing themselves 'in all their actions, even when they gape'.[81] Elizabethans still swore 'by our Lady', and a stylized version of the agnus dei was a common merchant's mark. Bishop Hall later assumed that a superstitious man would wear 'a little hallowed wax' as 'his antidote for all evils'.[82] Some Elizabethan Protestants thought that relics gave protection against the Devil; they were kept in York Minster as late as 1695.[83] A few Anglican clergy even carried round holy water and made the sign of the cross over their parishioners or anointed them with holy oil when they were sick.[84] Parasitic superstitions about the curative value of communion bread and offertory money survived into modern times; and there were many allied beliefs concerning the protective value of Bibles and other religious objects.[85]

80. R. R. Marett, in *Journ. of the Eng. Folk Dance and Song Soc.*, i (1933), p. 75. For the morris see Brand, *Antiquities*, i, pp. 247–70; B. Lowe, 'Early Records of the Morris in England', *Journ. of the Eng. Folk Dance and Song Soc.*, viii (1957); E. C. Cawte, 'The Morris Dance in Herefordshire, Shropshire and Worcestershire', ibid., ix (1963).

81. Welch in *Procs. Suffolk Inst. Archaeology*, xxix (1962), p. 158; *H.M.C., Montagu of Beaulieu*, p. 40. See also *Shropshire Folklore*, ed. C. S. Burne (1883–6), p. 167.

82. Gilby, *A Pleasaunt Dialogue*, sig. M3ᵛ; F. A. Girling, *English Merchants' Marks* (1964), pp. 14, 17; *The Works of ... Joseph Hall*, ed. P. Wynter (Oxford, 1863), vi, p. 110. See also J. Deacon and J. Walker, *A Summarie Answere* (1601), p. 210.

83. S. Harsnet, *A Discovery of the Fraudulent Practices of John Darrel* (1599), p. 60; N. Sykes, *From Sheldon to Secker* (Cambridge, 1959), p. 186.

84. J. S. Purvis, *Tudor Parish Documents* (Cambridge, 1948), p. 177; J. White, *The First Century of Scandalous, Malignant Priests* (1643), p. 40; *The Private Diary of Dr John Dee*, ed. J. O. Halliwell (Camden Soc., 1842), p. 35; *D.N.B.*, 'Whiston, William'; and see below, p. 590.

85. Kittredge, *Witchcraft*, p. 145; *County Folk-Lore*, v, ed. Mrs Gutch and M. Peacock (Folk-Lore Soc., 1908), pp. 94, 107–8; *A Frenchman in England, 1784*, ed. S. C. Roberts (Cambridge, 1933), p. 86; *Kilvert's Diary*, ii, p. 414, Fox, viii, pp. 148–9. cf. *The Wonderful Preservation of Gregory Crow* [1679].

All this merely goes to show that fundamental changes are not accomplished overnight. 'Three parts at least' of the people' were 'wedded to their old superstition still', declared a Puritan document in 1584. This was not a reference to formal recusancy: the number of actively committed Catholics is uncertain, but the figure for Yorkshire in 1604 has been estimated at only one and a half per cent.[86] It is, however, a reminder that the devotional attitudes of the Catholic Middle Ages still lingered. The implications of the Protestant rejection of magic were slow to affect those areas where a preaching ministry had not yet been established. Sir Benjamin Rudyerd reminded the House of Commons in 1628 of 'the utmost skirts of the North, where the prayers of the common people are more like spells and charms than devotions'. He did not have self-conscious Catholic recusants in mind, but a semi-literate population who, in his opinion, knew little more about the central dogmas of Christianity than did the North American Indians.[87] In such *milieux* the primitive idea of religion as a direct source of supernatural power could still survive.

It was also kept alive by the teachings of the Catholic Church on the Continent, for the Papists preserved their trust in relics, pilgrimages and the agnus dei; and the Catholic martyrs swelled the number of holy objects and places. Recusant midwives produced holy girdles for their patients to wear in labour or encouraged them to call upon the Virgin for relief. Catholic missionaries prepared for the journey to England with special masses designed to secure protection from plague and other dangers;[88] and recusant propagandists made great play with the numerous healing miracles still accomplished by Catholic clergy in England or at Catholic shrines on the Continent.[89] It is true that the official spokesmen of post-Tridentine Catholicism endeavoured to restrain the excesses of popular devotion by carefully investigating miracles, prohibiting the attempt to cure diseases by

86. *The Seconde Parte of a Register*, i, p. 254; A. G. Dickens, 'The Extent and Character of Recusancy in Yorkshire, 1604', *Yorks. Arch. Journ.*, xxxvii (1948), p. 33 (cf. id. and J. Newton in *ibid.*, xxxviii (1955)). In Hampshire it was much the same, J. E. Paul, 'Hampshire Recusants in the time of Elizabeth I', *Procs. of the Hants. Field Club*, xxi (1959), p. 81, n. 151.

87. *Memoirs of Sir Benjamin Rudyerd*, ed. J. A. Manning (1841), p. 136.

88. *H.M.C., Hatfield*, xv, p. 387.

89. e.g., *Miracles lately wrought by the intercession of the glorious Virgin Marie, at Montaigu, nere unto Siche in Brabant*, trans. R. Chambers (Antwerp, 1606). Instances of miraculous cures and deliverances in English recusant literature are too many to be worth enumerating. But see below, pp. 147 n. 51, 583.

mere prayers or holy symbols, reducing the more obviously superstitious masses, and curbing the more licentious aspects of fertility
rituals; Cardinal Bellarmine even questioned the utility of holy bells
as a remedy against thunder.[90] But such a change of attitude was less
discernible at the popular level, and it was the 'superstitious' character of popular devotion which most attracted the attention of English
visitors to the Continent. The Catholic Church continued to provide
a friendly environment for a variety of semi-magical practices. In
South Germany peasants flocked to get water blessed by the image of
St Francis Xavier as a preservative against the plague. In Rome it
was the image of the Virgin Mary which drove away the pestilence.
In Venice the inhabitants turned to St Rock. So long as it was possible for a Catholic prelate, like the Bishop of Quimper in 1620, to
throw an agnus dei into a dangerous fire in the hope of putting it out,
the Roman Church could hardly fail to retain the reputation of laying claim to special supernatural remedies for daily problems.[91] In
their campaign to re-establish the faith some of the recusant clergy
did not fail to stress this aspect of their religion; and it is small
wonder that those Englishmen who still trusted in the healing power
of communion wine should have thought it particularly efficacious
when received from the hands of a Catholic priest.[92]

But despite these Catholic survivals there is no denying the remarkable speed with which the distaste for any religious rite smacking of magic had spread among some of the common people. It had
started with the Lollards, who had been mostly men of humble means
and little learning. In the fifteenth century pilgrimages and hagio-
graphy were on the decline; and Reginald Pecock was already com-
plaining that some of the sacraments were by 'some of the lay people
holden to be points of witchcraft and blindings'.[93] By the time of the

90. R. Dingley, *Vox Coeli* (1658), pp. 134–5. On this neglected aspect of
the Counter-Reformation, see M. Grosso and M. F. Mellano, *La Controri-
forma nella Arcidiocesi di Torino (1558–1610)* (Rome, 1957), ii, pp. 209,
250, 257; iii, p. 227 (cited by J. Bossy in his paper, 'Regimentation and
Initiative in the Popular Catholicism of the Counter Reformation', prepared
for the *Past and Present* Conference on Popular Religion, 1966); A. Franz,
Die Messe im deutschen Mittelalter (Freiburg-im-Breisgau, 1902), chap. 10.
    91.   V. L. Tapié, *The Age of Grandeur*, trans. A. R. Williamson (1960)
pp. 154–5; R. Crawfurd, *Plague and Pestilence in Literature and Art* (Oxford, 1914); *D.T.C.*, i, col. 612; and Thiers, *Superstitions, passim*.
    92. Kittredge, *Witchcraft*, p. 148; and see below, pp. 586–8.
    93. R. Pecock, *The Repressor of Over Much Blaming of the Clergy*, ed. C.

Henrician Reformation there was a vigorous foundation of popular
Protestantism. The vehemence of this attitude is reflected in the
coarseness of the language with which the more outspoken Protestants rejected the conjurations and exorcisms of the Roman Church.
Holy water, it was said, was 'more savoury to make sauce . . . because
it is mixed with salt' and 'a very good medicine for a horse with a
galled back; yea, if there be put an onion thereunto it is a good sauce
for a giblet of mutton'.⁹⁴ In the diocese of Gloucester in 1548 two inhabitants of Slimbridge were presented for saying that holy oil was
'of no virtue but meet to grease sheep'. At Downhead in Somerset a
man was reported to have remarked that 'his mare will make as good
holy water as any priest can', and that his hands were 'as good to
deliver the sacrament of the altar to any man as well as the priest's
hands'. When summoned to explain himself, he told the court that,
since water was made holy by being blessed, the blessing might be
bestowed upon his mare's water to the same effect. Small wonder
that a statute was passed in the first year of Edward VI to restrain
irreverent speaking of the sacrament.⁹⁵

Yet, crude as this language was, it conveyed an essential point.
Many men were now unwilling to believe that physical objects could
change their nature by a ritual of exorcism and consecration. The
Edwardian Reformation saw much iconoclasm and deliberate foul-
ing of holy objects. Mass books, vestments, roods, images and crosses
were summarily destroyed. Altar-stones were turned into paving
stones, bridges, fireplaces, or even kitchen sinks. Dean Whittingham
of Durham used two ex-holy-water stoups for salting beef and fish in
his kitchen, and his wife burned St Cuthbert's banner.⁹⁶ Common
people sardonically demanded chrisom clothes for their new-born
foals, or ostentatiously fed holy bread to their dogs. Images were
taken away and given to children to play with as dolls. In Norfolk
an advanced Protestant declared that he could 'honour God as well

Babington (Rolls Series, 1860), p. 563; and the references cited above, p. 31,
n.11.
  94. D. Wilkins, *Concilia* (1737), iii, pp. 804–7.
  95. Gloucester D.R., Vol. 4, p. 34; Wells D.R., A 22 (no foliation); 1
Edw. VI cap 1.
  96. *English Church Furniture*, ed. E. Peacock (1866), *passim*; F. G. Lee,
The Church under Queen Elizabeth (new edn, 1896), pp. 134–7; 'The Life
of Mr William Whittingham', ed. M. A. E. Green (*Camden Miscellany*, vi,
1871), p. 32, n. 3; *A Description . . . of all the Ancient . . . Rites . . . within
the Monastical Church of Durham* (1593), ed. J. Raine (Surtees Soc, 1842),
p. 23.

with a fork full of muck as with a wax candle'. In Lincoln a shoe-maker's wife claimed that her urine was as good holy water 'as [that] the priest now makes and casteth upon us'. An early seven-teenth-century diarist recorded how 'four drunken fellows' in Derby-shire drove a recently calved cow into church 'and that which is appointed for churching a woman they read . . . for the cow, and led her about the font: a wicked and horrible fact'. When the Civil War broke out Parliamentary troops resumed the work of iconoclasm, and even chopped down the Glastonbury thorn.[98] Distasteful though all this violence and invective was intended to be, it exemplified a thoroughly changed attitude to the apparatus of the medieval Church. The decline of old Catholic beliefs was not the result of persecution; it reflected a change in the popular conception of religion.[99]

Protestantism thus presented itself as a deliberate attempt to take the magical elements out of religion, to eliminate the idea that the rituals of the Church had about them a mechanical efficacy, and to abandon the effort to endow physical objects with supernatural quali-ties by special formulae of consecration and exorcism. Above all, it diminished the institutional role of the Church as the dispenser of divine grace. The individual stood in a direct relationship to God and was solely dependent upon his omnipotence. He could no longer rely upon the intercession of intermediaries, whether saints or clergy; neither could he trust in an imposing apparatus of ceremonial in the hope of prevailing upon God to grant his desires. The reformers set out to eliminate theatricality from church ritual and decoration, and to depreciate the status of the priesthood. The priest was no longer set apart from the laity by the ritual condition of celibacy, and he was no longer capable of working the miracle of the Mass. Extreme Protestants reacted against the surviving popish traditions which seemed to attach holy qualities to material things – days of the week, patches of ground, parts of the church. They denied that miracles

97. Gloucester D.R., Vol. 20, p. 25 (1563); Hale, *Precedents*, p. 124; J. W. Blench, *Preaching in England in the Late Fifteenth and Sixteenth Centuries* (Oxford, 1964), p. 122; *L.P.*, xii(i), no. 1316; R. B. Walker, *A History of the Reformation in the Archdeaconries of Lincoln and Stow, 1534–94* (Ph.D. thesis, Univ. of Liverpool, 1959), p. 238.

98. Sloane 1457, f. 19ᵛ; Hanbury, *Historical Memorials Relating to the Independents*, iii, p. 343.

99. cf. J. Bossy, Introduction to A. O. Meyer, *England and the Catholic Church under Queen Elizabeth* (1967 edn), p. xxiv.

were any longer an attribute of the true Church, and they dismissed
the miracles of the papists as frauds, delusions or the work of the
Devil; the Evesham recusant who scoffed at the Anglican clergy in
1624, declaring that they were but Parliamentary ministers and
could do no miracles, was echoing a standard Catholic reproach.[100]
The Protestants were helping to make a distinction in kind between
magic and religion, the one a coercive ritual, the other an intercessionary one. Magic was no longer to be seen as a false religion,
which was how medieval theologians had regarded it; it was a
different sort of activity altogether.

By depreciating the miracle-working aspects of religion and elevat-
ing the importance of the individual's faith in God, the Protestant
Reformation helped to form a new concept of religion itself. Today
we think of religion as a belief, rather than a practice, as definable
in terms of creeds rather than in modes of behaviour.[101] But such a
description would have fitted the popular Catholicism of the Middle
Ages little better than it fits many other primitive religions. A medieval peasant's knowledge of Biblical history or Church doctrine was,
so far as one can tell, usually extremely slight. The Church was important to him not because of its formalized code of belief, but because its rites were an essential accompaniment to the important
events in his own life – birth, marriage and death. It solemnized these
occasions by providing appropriate rites of passage to emphasize
their social significance. Religion was a ritual method of living, not
a set of dogmas. In the seventeenth century Jeremy Taylor wrote of
the Irish peasantry that they could

give no account of their religion what it is: only they believe as their
priest bids them, and go to mass which they understand not, and reckon
their beads to tell the number and the tale of their prayers, and abstain
from eggs and flesh in Lent, and visit St Patrick's well, and leave pins
and ribbons, yarn or thread in their holy wells, and pray to God, S. Mary
and S. Patrick, S. Columbanus and S. Bridget, and desire to be buried
with S. Francis cord about them, and to fast on Saturdays in honour
of our Lady.[102]

100. *C.S.P.D., 1623–5*, p. 187. cf. Yates, *Giordano Bruno and the Hermetic Tradition*, p. 208; Foley, *Records of the English Province of the
Society of Jesus*, vii, p. 1058.
101. A. R. Radcliffe-Brown, *Structure and Function in Primitive Society*
(1952), pp. 155, 177.
102. *The Whole Works of ... Jeremy Taylor*, ed. R. Heber and revd by
C. P. Eden (1847–54), vi, p. 175.

To Catholics the Church was also important as a limitless source of supernatural aid, applicable to most of the problems likely to arise in daily life. It offered blessings to accompany important secular activities, and exorcisms and protective rituals to secure them from molestation by evil spirits or adverse forces of nature. It never aimed to make human industry and self-help superfluous but it did seek to give them ecclesiastical reinforcement.

At first sight the Reformation appeared to have dispensed with this whole apparatus of supernatural assistance. It denied the value of the Church's rituals and referred the believer back to the unpredictable mercies of God. If religion continued to be regarded by its adherents as a source of power, then it was a power which was patently much diminished. Yet the problems for which the magical remedies of the past had provided some sort of solution were still there – the fluctuations of nature, the hazards of fire, the threat of plague and disease, the fear of evil spirits, and all the uncertainties of daily life. How was it that men were able to renounce the magical solutions offered by the medieval Church before they had devised any technical remedies to put in their place? Were they now mentally prepared to face up to such problems by sole reliance upon their own resources and techniques? Did they have to turn to other kinds of magical control in order to replace the remedies offered by medieval religion? Or was Protestantism itself forced against its own premises to devise a magic of its own? It is to these and associated questions that we must now turn.

4.

PROVIDENCE

The Country Parson considering the great aptness country people
have to think that all things come by a kind of natural course, and
that if they sow and soil their grounds they must have corn; if they
keep and fodder well their cattle, they must have milk and calves;
labours to reduce them to see God's hand in all things, and to believe that things are not set in such an inevitable order but that God
often changeth it according as he sees fit, either for reward or
punishment.

George Herbert,
A Priest to the Temple, chap. xxx

Let us look into providences: surely they mean somewhat.
Oliver Cromwell to Col.
Robert Hammond, 25 November 1648

This is much like as at Beverley, late, when much of the people
being at a bear-baiting, the church fell suddenly down at evensong
time and overwhelmed some that then were in it. A good fellow that
after heard the tale told: Lo, quod he, now may you see what it is
to be at evensong when you should be at the bear-baiting.

Thomas More,
The Dialogue concerning Tyndale, iii. 2

1. *The divine origin of misfortune*

As we have seen, Protestants denied the claim of the medieval
Church to be able to manipulate God's grace for earthly purposes.
Instead of holding out the prospect of supernatural aid they preferred to remind the faithful that the hardships of this life would be
made tolerable by the blessings of the next, and that the hope
of immortal bliss was more than sufficient compensation for the
pains and sorrows of human existence. But this distant hope was not
all that now remained of the power formerly attributed . to the
Christian God. Divine omnipotence was still believed to be reflected
in daily happenings, and the world provided abundant testimony to
the continuous manifestation of God's purpose.

All post-Reformation theologians taught that nothing could
happen in this world without God's permission. If there was a com-

mon theme which ran through their writings it was the denial of the
very possibility of chance or accident. 'That which we call fortune,'
wrote the Elizabethan bishop, Thomas Cooper, 'is nothing but the
hand of God, working by causes and for causes that we know not.
Chance or fortune are gods devised by man and made by our ignorance of the true, almighty and everlasting God.' 'Fortune and adventure,' declared John Knox, 'are the words of Paynims, the significa-
tion whereof ought in no wise to enter into the heart of the faithful.
... That which ye scoffingly call Destiny and Stoical necessity ... we
call God's eternal election and purpose immutable."[1]

Knox was echoing the words of St Basil, for the denial of the
heathen concept of Fortune or Destiny had always been a popular
Christian theme. Yet there is some reason for thinking that the Reformation period saw a new insistence upon God's sovereignty.
Whereas Aquinas had stressed that the notion of Divine Providence
did not exclude the operation of chance or luck, a sixteenth-century
writer like Bishop Pilkington could declare categorically that there
was no such thing as chance.[2] Medieval Christians from Boethius to
Dante had maintained the pagan tradition of the goddess Fortuna
side by side with a belief in God's omnipotence, but for Tudor theologians the very idea of Fortune was an insult to God's sovereignty.
To make Fortune into a goddess was a heathen error, declared the
Anglican *Homilies*. As the Marian martyr John Bradford assured his
interrogators, 'Things are not by fortune to God at any time, though
to man they seem so sometimes."[3]

Every Christian thus had the consolation of knowing that life was
not a lottery, but reflected the working-out of God's purposes. If
things went wrong he did not have to blame his luck but could be
assured that God's hand was at work: the events of this world were
not random but ordered. 'Whensoever misery or plague happeneth to
man,' wrote Bishop Cooper, 'it cometh not by chance or fortune, or
by a course of nature, as vain worldly men imagine, but by the
assured providence of God.' 'Nature, Fortune, Destiny,' wrote a

1. T. Cooper, *Certaine Sermons* (1580), p. 164; *The Works of John Knox*,
ed. D. Laing (Edinburgh, 1846–64), v, pp. 32, 119 (echoing Calvin,
Institutes, I.xvi.8).
2. Aquinas, *Summa contra Gentiles*, III, lxxiv; *The Works of James
Pilkington*, ed. J. Scholefield (Cambridge, P.S., 1842), p. 309.
3. H. R. Patch *The Goddess Fortuna in Medieval Literature* (Cambridge,
Mass., 1927); *Homilies*, p. 478; *The Writings of John Bradford*, ed. A.
Townsend (Cambridge, P.S., 1848–53), i, p. 491.

Nottinghamshire clergyman in his journal. 'These three I hold to be the inevitable will of God.' One should not speak of 'fate', declared Oliver Cromwell to the first Protectorate Parliament; it was 'too paganish a word'. Life's ship was never without a steersman; whether the passengers woke or slept, God was always at the helm.'

It is doubtful whether many laymen spent a great deal of time worrying about the precise mechanism by which this divine providence operated. Theologians gave much attention to the problem of primary and secondary causes, and debated whether God worked through nature or above it. Most agreed with Cooper when he said that what we call nature 'is nothing but the very finger of God working in his creatures'. God's sovereignty was thought to be exercised through regular channels, and the natural world was fully susceptible of study by scientists seeking causes and regularities. Many early-seventeenth-century theologians taught that God had bound himself to keep the laws of nature which he had laid down.' Yet no one dared to assert that divine control was only remote. Calvin had declared that supernatural events happened daily,' and no Elizabethan scientist ruled out their possibility. The Bible showed that God had been able to make the sun stand still and could interrupt the course of nature. By the sixteenth century the general opinion was that such miracles had ceased, but that since the world was entirely governed by divine providence God could still produce earthquakes, floods and similar disasters whenever he chose. By the concurrent operation of separate chains of cause and effect he could also bring about striking accidents or coincidences – 'special providences'. His hand could underlie the most trivial occurrence.'

4. Cooper, *Certaine Sermons*, p. 176; T. M. Blagg and K. S. S. Train, 'Extracts from the Paper Book of Robert Leband, Vicar of Rolleston, 1583–1625', *A Second Miscellany of Nottinghamshire Records*, ed. K. S. S. Train (Thoroton Soc., 1951), p. 19; T. Carlyle, *The Letters and Speeches of Oliver Cromwell*, ed. S. C. Lomas (1904), ii, p. 424. When in 1578 the University of Cambridge offered to stage before Queen Elizabeth a disputation *de fortuna et fato* Burghley objected that the subject 'might yield many reasons impertinent for Christian ears, if it were not circumspectly used'; C. H. Cooper, *Annals of Cambridge*, ii (Cambridge, 1843), p. 362.

5. Cooper, *Certaine Sermons*, p. 163; P. Miller, *Errand into the Wilderness* (Cambridge, Mass., 1956), pp. 66–7.

6. Calvin, *Institutes*, I.v.11.

7. J. Preston, *Life Eternall* (1631), p. 154 (2nd pagination); T. Browne, *Religio Medici* (1643), I, xvii; R. C. Winthrop, *Life and Letters of John Winthrop* (Boston, 1864), p. 316; W. Sherlock, *A Discourse Concerning the*

The mechanical philosophy of the later seventeenth century was to subject this doctrine of special providences to a great deal of strain. Under its influence many writers tended to speak as if God's providence consisted solely in the original act of creation and that thereafter the world had been left to be governed mechanically by the wheels which the Creator had set in motion. Yet most of those who conceived of the universe as a great clock were in practice slow to face up to the full implications of their analogy. Both Boyle and Newton showed some diffidence about renouncing the miracles of the Bible and the role of providence in daily life.[8] In the eighteenth century there were ingenious attempts to argue that natural disasters were not effected by God in immediate response to some piece of human evil-doing, but had been inserted by him in the original scheme of creation because he had foreseen the moral choices which men would make and the occasions when they would need to be tried or punished. In this way fluctuations in human conduct could still be matched by fluctuations in the natural order, and a theory of rewards and punishments reconciled with new mechanical science.[9] But before 1700 such elaborate rationalization was seldom necessary. The world was generally agreed to be a purposive one, responsive to the wishes of its Creator; the idea of a *deus absconditus* who had abandoned his creation to its own devices was reprehensible.[10] The possibility of the occasional miracle was not to be ruled out, but the immediacy of God's power was sufficiently demonstrated by the ordinary working of natural events. 'We must not ... expect miracles,' declared William Sherlock, 'He who has the absolute government of the natural and moral world can do what he pleases without miracles.'[11]

The victim of misfortune could thus draw some stoical consolation from the knowledge that God was controlling his fate, even if the respective roles of God, man and nature were sometimes a matter

Divine Providence (1694), p. 42. There are excellent discussions of this large subject in Kocher, *Science and Religion*, chap. 5, and P. Miller, *The New England Mind. The Seventeenth Century* (1939), pp. 227–31. See also H. Baker, *The Wars of Truth* (1952), pp. 12–25.

8. See for this R. S. Westfall, *Science and Religion in Seventeenth-century England* (New Haven, 1958), esp. pp. 75, 86–9, 95, 203–4, and D. Kubrin, 'Newton and the Cyclical Cosmos: Providence and the Mechanical Philosophy', *Journ. Hist. Ideas*, xxviii (1967).

9. See T. D. Kendrick, *The Lisbon Earthquake* (1956), pp. 15–19.

10. For examples of such heretics, see below, pp. 127, 202.

11. Sherlock, *A Discourse concerning the Divine Providence*, p. 389.

for delicate computation. This can be seen from the reflections of the Berkshire farmer, Robert Loder, when entering up his account for 1616:

> This year in sowing too early I lost (the Lord being the cause thereof, but that the instrument wherewith it pleased him to work) ... the sum of £10 at least, so exceeding full was my barley with charlock, in all likelihood by means of that instrumental cause, the Lord my God ... being without doubt the efficient cause thereof.[12]

As Calvin had pointed out, the perils of daily existence would have made life intolerable for men who believed that everything happened by chance and that they were subject to every caprice of arbitrary fortune. The Christian could submit himself to God, secure in the knowledge that no harm could befall him unless the Almighty permitted it, and that if adversities still came his way, they were at least intended for his own good. Anyone who fully grasped the doctrine of predestination, thought Bishop Davenant, 'patiently endureth whatsoever misfortunes can befall him'.[13] The twin themes of patience in adversity ('sanctified affliction') and the felicity of a pious mind dominate the religious literature of sixteenth- and seventeenth-century England. The very titles of the devotional works of the period reveal their consoling purpose: *The Sicke Man's Salve, wherein all faithful Christians may learne ... howe to behave themselves patiently and thankfully in the time of sicknesse; Advice and support to the Godly under the loss of dear relations; Comfort for parents mourning over their hopeful children that dye young.*[14]

There is no doubt of the reality of the consolation afforded by such works. The old woman who told a visitor that she would have gone distracted after the loss of her husband but for the *Sayings* of the Puritan pastor, John Dod, which hung in her house,[15] may stand as the representative of the countless numbers of bereaved persons for whom religion was the only alternative to utter despair. As the preachers wryly noted, the experience of trouble and adversity did

12. *Robert Loder's Farm Accounts, 1610–20*, ed. G. E. Fussell (Camden Ser., 1936), p. 124.

13. Calvin, *Institutes*, I.xvii.11; J. D(avenant), *Animadversions* (1641), p 403.

14. By T. Becon (1561), J. Flavel (in *A Token for Mourners* [1674]), and T. Whitaker (1693). On the universality of religious belief in the sanctifying power of sorrow, cf. E. Durkheim, *The Elementary Forms of the Religious Life*, trans. J. W. Swain (New York, 1961), p. 354.

15. W. Haller, *The Rise of Puritanism* (New York, 1938), p. 59.

more than anything else to direct men's minds to religion, and there was no greater enemy of piety than worldly success.[16] To sufferers religion could bring comfort and even elation; and there is no reason to discount the truth of the edifying stories, reproduced in the Puritan biographies of the seventeenth century, of the men and women who went serenely to their deaths, singing psalms and rejoicing in their maker. The doctrine of divine providence consoled men for the death of their close relatives, comforted them in their worldly misfortunes, and held out the prospect of eternal felicity as compensation for the short-lived sorrows of earthly existence. In the Scriptures the devout could find immediate analogies with their own experience and they drew reassurance from the knowledge that the worst of their tribulations had been undergone by Job, Jeremiah or some other Biblical hero.

At the same time it can hardly escape notice that the doctrine of divine providence had about it a self-confirming quality. For there was no way in which the theory once accepted could be faulted. If the wicked man encountered adversity this was clearly a punishment from God; if a godly man was smitten then he was being tested and tried. The pious Christian for whom events went well could thank God for his good fortune without being worried by the equal prosperity of his reprobate neighbour, since he knew that the absence of worldly afflictions could sometimes be a dreadful sign of God's lost love. Indeed some suffering was almost essential as proof that God retained an interest in the person concerned. In this way religion was positively reinforced by the hardships of life. Temporal afflictions were usually signs of God's affection, thought the Puritan divine John Downame. It was the very fact that he had no such outward afflictions or troubles of conscience which temporarily convinced the fifteen-year-old James Ussher, the future Archbishop, that God no longer loved him.[17] The belief in providence was thus extraordinarily elastic. In a good year Robert Loder praised the Lord for his assistance; in a bad one he reflected stoically that God distributed his mercies as he pleased.

But all this could be unpalatable doctrine for the man of uncertain faith, and much of the pastoral energy of the clergy was given over

16. *The Workes of ... Richard Greenham*, ed. H. H(olland) (3rd edn, 1601), p. 1; T. Tymme, *The Chariot of Devotion* (1618), p. 29. cf. Bacon, *Works*, vi, p. 414.

17. J. Downame, *The Christian Warfare* (3rd edn, 1612), pp. 204–5; N. Bernard, *The Life and Death of ... Dr James Usher* (1656), p. 28.

to explaining to their flock why even the most tragic misfortune should be patiently accepted as the will of God. A man whose son had been drowned came to the Puritan Richard Greenham in the deepest anguish, demanding to know what terrible sin he could have committed to deserve so dreadful a punishment. Greenham replied by citing the case of Job, as evidence that no sin was necessary to explain the event: any of a number of possible reasons could lead God to act harshly. In this particular instance he might have been correcting the father for his over-great sense of security, his immoderate love of his son, his unthankfulness for his son's spiritual development, or his failure to pray often enough on his behalf; or perhaps the Lord had taken away the youth so that the father might have more time to devote himself to God.[18]

The correct reaction on the part of a believer stricken by ill fortune was therefore to search himself in order to discover the moral defect which had provoked God's wrath, or to eliminate the complacency which had led the Almighty to try him. When the infant son of Ralph Josselin, vicar of Earl's Colne, Essex, died of diphtheria in 1648 his bereaved father sought to know which of his faults God was punishing, and concluded that the judgement must have partly been provoked by his vain thoughts and unseasonable playing at chess. When physicians failed to cure Sir Lewis Mansel of his vertigo, he wrote to Vicar Rees Prichard to know why God had laid this affliction upon him. He received a reply exhorting patience and urging the necessity of being chastened and afflicted. When the sister of Adam Martindale, the Presbyterian minister, died of smallpox her face swelled up; Martindale took it as a sure sign of God's anger at the pride she had taken in her physical appearance.[19]

It was also customary for national disasters to be regarded as God's response to the sins of the people. The *Homilies* taught that penury, dearth and famine were caused by God's anger at the vices of the community. The Bible showed that plagues and misfortunes

18. *The Workes of ... Richard Greenham*, p. 35. For a list of reasons why God sometimes brought his people into extremity, see T. Mocket, *The Churches Troubles and Deliverance* (1642), pp. 5–17.

19. *The Diary of the Rev. Ralph Josselin, 1616–83*, ed. E. Hockcliffe (Camden Ser., 1908), pp. 46–7; R. Prichard, *The Welshman's Candle*, trans. W. Evans (Carmarthen, 1771), pp. 358–65; *The Life of Adam Martindale, written by himself*, ed. R. Parkinson (Chetham Soc., 1845), p. 18. For the general principle, Calvin, *Institutes*, III.iv.11, and J. Dod (and R. Cleaver), *Ten Sermons* (1632), pp. 25–6.

were usually a punishment for some notorious sin, and that divine vengeance was as likely in this world as the next.[20] *A View of the Threats and Punishments recorded in the Scriptures, alphabetically composed*, by Zachary Bogan (Oxford, 1653), comprised over 600 pages carefully tabulating the appropriate punishments for every sin from *Adultery* to *Worship of God neglected*.

So, whenever disaster struck, the preachers and pamphleteers were quick to indicate its direct origin in the moral delinquencies of the people. From the earthquake of 1580 to the great storm of 1703 every spectacular natural occurrence brought with it a flood of homiletic literature and moralizing commentary.[21] Famine, plague flood and fire were acts of God, directly provoked by the moral condition of those upon whom they fell. When thirty west country towns were flooded in 1607 a pamphleteer could remind his readers that 'God ... can as well now drown all mankind as he did at the first'. And when the Jamaican town of Port Royal was destroyed by the great earthquake of 1692 the immediate reaction of the Non-conformist clergyman Edmund Calamy was to reflect that 'it might have been the like with us here in England, had not God in his merciful providence been pleased to make a difference'.[22] Thunderstorms seemed another manifestation of divine displeasure; indeed death by lightning was often taken as a direct act of God.[23] When a man and his son were killed at the plough by lightning at Cookham, Berkshire, in 1680, the coroner's jury returned the verdict that death had been caused by the 'immediate providence of Almighty God'.[24]

20. *Homilies*, pp. 85–6, 158, 166, 299, 497. For an analysis of God's instruments of wrath, R. Bernard, *The Bibles Abstract and Epitome* (attached to *Thesaurus Biblicus* [1644]), pp. 87–92.

21. A list of pamphlets occasioned by the earthquake of 6 April 1580 is given in *Thomas Twyne's Discourse on the earthquake of 1580*, ed. R. E. Ockenden (Oxford, 1936), pp. 7–14. *S.T.C.* and Wing provide the best guides to subsequent literature.

22. *1607. A True Report of Certaine Wonderfull Overflowings of Waters*, sig. A3; E. Calamy, *An Historical Account of My Own Life* (1830), i, p. 326.

23. See, e.g., S. Harward, *A Discourse of the Severall Kinds and Causes of Lightnings* (1607); J. Hilliard, *Fire from Heaven* (1613); R. Fludd, *Mosaicall Philosophy* (1659), pp. 115–9; *Dreadful News from Southwark* (1679?).

24. *A Full and True Relation of the Death and Slaughter of a Man and His Son at Plough* (1680). For a legal definition of 'an act of God', C. Durnford and E. H. East, *Reports of Cases ... in the Court of King's Bench* (1787–1800), i, p. 33 (*Forward v. Pittard*, 1785).

The fires which were the terror of seventeenth-century towns were similarly regarded. 'Newport, sin no more, lest a worse punishment befall thee,' wrote the incumbent of the Shropshire town in the parish register, when recording details of the fire of 1665, which had left 162 families homeless and caused £30,000's worth of damage.[25]

The explanatory function of this belief in an immediate divine providence was particularly evident when the element of coincidence or chance seemed unusually prominent. Lewis Bayly in his widely influential devotional guide, *The Practice of Piety* (3rd edn, 1613), had no hesitation in blaming the first two of Tiverton's three fires on the inhabitants' practice of allowing preparations for market-day to profane the Sabbath.[26] This readiness to identify the cause of God's wrath contrasted with the tactful observation by the Council of State on the fire at Marlborough in 1653 that God's judgements were unsearchable and past finding out.[27]

The incidence of sickness was particularly liable to be viewed theologically. The Elizabethan Prayer Book required the clergy when visiting a sick parishioner to begin by reminding him that whatever form the sickness might take he must realize that it was God's visitation. Of course a doctor should try to cure the patient by natural means. But such remedies were to be employed cautiously, with the recognition that they could only work if God permitted. It was lawful to take physic, but unlawful to trust in it too much. One clerical writer warned his readers in 1637 that they should not 'ascribe too much to physical means: but . . . carefully look and pray to God for a blessing by the warrantable use of them'.[28] Health came from God, not from doctors. Surgeons should pray before carrying out their operations, and their patients should be careful not to employ ungodly physicians, no matter how learned.[29]

25. *Shropshire Parish Documents* (Shrewsbury [1903]), p. 248. cf. O. Stockton, *Counsel to the Afflicted; or Instruction and Consolation for such as have suffered Loss by Fire* (1667).

26. 1708 edn, p. 247. When Tiverton was burned down for the third time the charge was resurrected. A collector on behalf of the destitute inhabitants rebutted the slander, declaring, 'There was no truth in it and the Practice of Piety had done them much wrong – which words bearing a double sense occasioned much laughter' (*Anecdotes and Traditions*, ed. W. J. Thoms [Camden Soc., 1839], p. 60).

27. W. A. Bewes, *Church Briefs* (1896), p. 365.

28. J. Sym, *Lifes Preservative against Self-Killing* (1637), p. 14.

29. *Early Writings of John Hooper*, ed. S. Carr (Cambridge, P.S., 1843), p. 308; *Sermons by Hugh Latimer*, ed. G. E. Corrie (Cambridge, P.S., 1844),

This was the teaching of most theologians and moralists, at least until the later seventeenth century. Yet we know that in practice both doctors and laymen often regarded disease as a purely natural phenomenon. Some physicians continued to pay lip-service to the idea that sin was the most frequent cause of sickness, but the readiness of medical men to ignore the spiritual side of illness had long gained them a reputation for atheism. Most of the clergy seem to have assumed that God worked through the normal courses of nature, though they laid more stress on the divine initiation of natural processes than did the doctors. Some theologians even declared that under certain circumstances God might strike a man down without employing natural causes at all. He would do this, though infrequently, thought William Turner in 1555, 'for the revenging and punishing of some open sin or offence'. Archbishop Grindal similarly believed that a particularly sudden death could be recognized as a specific judgement of God. Calvin had stressed that if the Almighty had marked out the moment of a man's death then no medicine could avert it.[30]

This fatalistic view of disease seems to have been most commonly invoked with reference either to venereal disease, where the element of moral retribution seemed obvious, or to epidemics, particularly of plague, when the scale of the visitation cried out for explanation in terms of the sins of the whole community, or particular sections of it. Puritans, for example, attributed the epidemics to the toleration of the Catholics, to the theatres, to sabbath-breaking, or to the Laudian innovations. 'The plague of God is in the land for the new mixture of religion that is commanded in the Church,' declared John Dod in 1635. Others blamed it upon covetousness or impiety or some other conspicuous sin.[31]

p. 542; J. Halle, *An Historiall Expostulation*, ed. T. J. Pettigrew (Percy Soc., 1844), pp. 46, 47; M. Fotherby, *Atheomastix* (1622), p. 235. Kocher, *Science and Religion*, chap. 13, is an excellent survey of the whole subject.

30. W. Turner, *A New Booke of Spirituall Physik* (1555), f. 57ᵛ; *The Remains of Edmund Grindal*, ed. W. Nicholson (Cambridge, P.S., 1843), p. 9; Calvin, *Institutes*, I.xvii.3.

31. *C.S.P.D., 1636-7*, p. 514 (for Dod). Other examples in H. Holland, *Spiritual Preservatives against the Pestilence* (1603), sig. A5ᵛ; (H. Burton), *A Divine Tragedie lately acted* (1636), p. 30; R. Kingston, *Pillulae pestilentiales* (1665), pp. 30-32; A. F. Herr, *The Elizabethan Sermon* (Philadelphia, 1940), pp. 42-3; M. Maclure, *The Paul's Cross Sermons, 1534-1642* (Toronto, 1958), p. 228; P. Morgan, in *Bodleian Library Record*, vii (1967), pp. 305-7.

At the local level the clergy did not hesitate to identify the scapegoat responsible for the community's sufferings. When 190 persons died of the plague at Cranbrook, Kent, in 1597–8, the vicar of St Dunstan's church entered his diagnosis in the parish register : it was a divine judgement for the town's sins, and in particular for 'that vice of drunkeness which did abound here'. Had it not begun 'in the house of one Brightlinge, out of which much thieving was committed', and did it not end in that of 'one Henry Grymocke, who was a pot companion, and his wife noted for much incontinency'? Moreover, 'the infection was got almost into all the inns and victualling-houses of the town, places then of great disorder, so that God did seem to punish that himself which others did neglect and not regard'. At Hitchin the minister blamed the plague of 1665 on the local prostitute.[32]

Most of those who saw plague as the product of divine wrath assumed that God worked through natural causes, bringing the epidemic by contagion or by the putrefaction of the air, according to whichever theory they favoured. But all theologians agreed that there was little to be hoped from natural remedies until the patient had repented of his ways. 'It is not the clean keeping and sweeping of our houses and streets that can drive away this fearful messenger of God's wrath,' declared Laurence Chaderton in 1578, 'but the purging and sweeping of our consciences from ... sin.' Richard Greenham similarly considered that repentance was the only remedy for strange diseases which did not respond to medical treatment. He therefore took the opportunity of condemning the naturalistic views of the Family of Love, the contemporary religious sect, whose members apparently attributed all troubles to outward causes, and had expelled a member for regarding a chill he had caught as a divine visitation.[33]

From making recovery depend upon repentance it was but a short step to suggesting that religious conformity would provide immunity against disease. The fifteenth-century author of *Dives and Pauper*

32. C. E. Woodruff, *An Inventory of the Parish Registers and Other Records in the Diocese of Canterbury* (Canterbury, 1922), pp. 59–60; R. L. Hine, *Relics of an Un-common Attorney* (1951), p. 71.

33. Chaderton is quoted in J. O. W. Haweis, *Sketches of the Reformation* (1844), p. 262 (for another expression of the same opinion, F. Hering, *Certaine Rules, Directions, or Advertisments for this time of Pestilentiall Contagion* [1625], sig. A3); *The Workes of ... Richard Greenham*, pp. 362, 419–20.

had conceded that individual good men might sometimes suffer misfortune without having done anything to deserve it. But he was confident that the misfortunes of a whole community were invariably
the product of sin.[34] In the sixteenth century this position was taken
further. Bishop Hooper was confident that no sickness could harm
the man who truly feared God; only disobedience to his precepts
made men subject to disease. The putrefaction of the air would not
therefore affect the man whose conscience was clear, for no one died
of the plague save by God's appointment.[35] Others argued that it was
pointless to run away from a plague-stricken area, since God's judgement could not be so easily evaded.[36] Some even thought that a
minority of plague deaths were completely supernatural, being produced by the direct stroke of a ministering angel.[37]

The idea was also put about that, since the victims of plague were
foredoomed by God's decree, the disease was not in itself contagious;
there should be no ban on visiting the sick and any protective measures were useless. Although the majority of clergy and physicians
rejected this notion, it was said in 1603 to be 'maintained not only by
the rude multitude, but by too many of the better sort'.[38] A later
writer attributed the badness of contemporary medicine to the widely
held belief that there was a certain span of life allotted to every man
which nothing could prolong.[39] From 1588 onwards the government's
Plague Orders required the clergy to refute the idea that it was unnecessary to refrain from visiting infected houses. Henoch Clapham,
a prominent preacher, was imprisoned in 1603 for reasserting this
position. He had maintained in a published work that the plague
only struck sinful men and that no believer would die of it unless he

34. *Dives and Pauper* (1536), f. 337.

35. *Early Writings of John Hooper*, pp. 308, 333. cf. W. Cupper, *Certaine
Sermons concerning Gods late visitation* (1592), p. 100; *The Workes of ...
William Perkins* (Cambridge, 1616–18), iii, pp. 476–7.

36. *Early Writings of John Hooper*, p. 333; Hering, *Certaine Rules, Directions, or Advertisments*, sig. A3^v; J. Primrose, *Popular Errours, or the
Errours of the People in Physick*, trans. R. Wittie (1651), p. 101. This was
a common medieval attitude. cf. J. F. Royster, 'A Middle English Treatise
on the Ten Commandments', *Studies in Philology*, vi (1910–11), p. 16.

37. S. Forman, 'Of the Plague generally and of his sortes' (1607) (Ashm.
1436), f. 105^v; S. Bradwell, *Physick for the Sicknesse, commonly called the
Plague* (1636), p. 2; R. Kephale, *Medela Pestilentiae* (1665), pp. 49 ff;
Kocher, *Science and Religion*, pp. 273 ff.

38. J. Balmford, *A Short Dialogue* (1603), sig. A2^v, quoted by Kocher,
Science and Religion, p. 274.

39. Primrose, *Popular Errours*, p. 108.

was lacking in faith. Fatalism of this kind was actively combated by the authorities.[40]

Nevertheless, some persons continued to assume that true believers were immune from the plague and that precautions were therefore unnecessary. 'Pestilence is above all other diseases catching,' declared Thomas Jackson in the reign of Charles I, 'And such as have been most observant of its course tell us men of covetous minds or unseasonably greedy of gain are usually soonest caught by it, though exposed to no greater or more apparent visible danger than others are.'[41] In keeping with this attitude 'some foolish people' were said in 1637 to believe that death in the plague was evidence of a man's reprobation.[42] In an age of Biblical literalism it was hard to ignore the message of Psalm 91: 'There shall no evil befall thee, neither shall any plague come nigh thy dwelling.' This was not a promise of total immunity, thought William Bridge, 'but the drift and scope of the Psalm is to hold forth a *speciality of protection* for believers in the time of a plague'.[43]

There was thus a strong tendency to assume that obedience to God's commandments could conduce to prosperity and safety. No guarantees were given, for the ways of the Lord were inscrutable, and it was not only the sinful who were chastized. But the Biblical commentators, Dod and Cleaver, were sure that the godly would never need to beg; and the meteorologist, Robert Dingley, declared that it was relatively unusual for lightning to strike one of God's chosen. The freer from sin, wrote the Puritan Richard Rogers, the freer from trouble. A female sectary confessed during the Inter-

40. Clapham's views were set out in *An Epistle Discoursing upon the Present Pestilence* (1603), and retracted from the Clink in *Henoch Clapham, his Demaundes and Answeres touching the Pestilence* (1604). The same line was taken by W. T., *A Casting up of Accounts of Certain Errors* (1603).

41. T. Jackson, *Diverse Sermons* (1637), p. 47 (2nd pagination).

42. T.S., *Sermons, Meditations, and Prayers upon the Plague* (1637), p. 53. This view had been expressed in 1603 by John Lowe, a Puritan cleric in Norwich; *The Registrum Vagum of Anthony Harrison*, ed. T. F. Barton (Norfolk Rec. Soc., 1963–4), i, p. 163.

43. *The Works of the Rev. William Bridge* (1845), i, p. 475 (and 491). For a more literal use of this text by the separatists, R. Boye, *A Iust Defence of the Importunate Beggers Importunity* (1636), sig. C1v; E. Norice, *The True Gospel* (1638), pp. 50–51; C. F. Mullett, *The Bubonic Plague and England* (Lexington, 1956), p. 97. Most commentators were more cautious; see, e.g., (T. Wilcox), *A Right Godly and Learned Exposition upon the whole Book of Psalmes* (1586), p. 294.

regnum that she fell into a religious depression when she saw her neighbours prosper in the world more than she did; for it could only mean that they prayed at home more than she did. It is not surprising that Max Weber concluded that no religion did as much as Puritanism to identify economic achievement with spiritual success.[44]

This is a difficult subject and it would be easy to exaggerate. A Protestant clergyman did not set out to promise health and worldly success to those who followed the word of God; he tried to bring spiritual consolation, not the hope of material prosperity. But until the end of the seventeenth century, and in many cases long afterwards, the overwhelming majority of clerical writers and pious laymen sincerely believed that there was a link between man's moral behaviour and his fortune in this world, whether in bodily health or professional success. It was impossible to reiterate the view that sin was the most probable cause of misfortune without conveying the implication that godliness was somehow linked with prosperity. Of course, the preachers would have explained that it was only spiritual prosperity with which they were concerned, and that God's promises related solely to the life to come. But their flock only too often took a cruder view, and so on occasions did the clergy themselves.

2. Cautionary tales

The course of worldly events could thus be seen as the working-out of God's judgements. This was but a refinement of the more basic assumption that the material environment responded to man's moral behaviour. It was also reflected in the belief that unusual happenings in the natural world ('prodigies') were likely indications ('portents') of judgements to come. This latter belief is not universal in primitive societies; indeed their inhabitants are sometimes quite uninterested in impressive natural phenomena. A certain amount of scientific awareness may be required before any irregularities can attract attention.[45] But in England the belief in natural portents had always been widespread; in the later seventeenth century Bishop

44. Dod and Cleaver, *Ten Sermons*, pp. 100–1 (cf. J. Bentham, *The Societie of Saints* (1630), p. 70); R. Dingley, *Vox Coeli* (1658), p. 159; R. Rogers, *Seven Treatises* (1603), p. 530; V. Powell, *Spirituall Experiences of Sundry Beleevers* (2nd edn, 1653), p. 79; M. Weber, *The Sociology of Religion*, trans. E. Fischoff (1965), p. 205.

45. E. E. Evans-Pritchard, *Theories of Primitive Religion* (Oxford, 1965), p. 54 and n. 1.

Sprat thought that vulnerability to supposed prodigies and providences was a weakness to which his countrymen were peculiarly subject.[46]

It was not just that contemporaries attached moral importance to such natural occurrences as thunder and lightning, earthquakes, eclipses or comets; even more striking was their capacity for seeing apparitions in the sky of a kind denied to us – galloping horses, dragons or armies in battle. These counterparts of our flying saucers might assume bizarre forms: for example, the vision seen by two country women shortly before sunset on 16 April 1651 of a battle in the sky, followed by angels of 'a blueish colour and about the bigness of a capon, having faces (as they thought) like owls'.[47] But usually they illustrate that in hallucination, no less than in ordinary vision, human perception is governed by stereotypes inherited from the particular society in which men live. Until the end of the seventeenth century there was no shortage of pamphlet literature describing the birds which fluttered over death-beds, the apparitions which wrecked ships at sea, and the armies which battled in the sky.[48]

Of course many of these accounts were propagandist in intention and designed for an unsophisticated audience. But it would be wrong to assume that men of education necessarily despised them. Very often they were publicly upheld by the leaders of Church and State. John Foxe believed that special prodigies had heralded the Reformation. Bishop Jewel was worried by stories of monstrous births. Everyone took the earthquake of 1580 as a portent, though it was agreed that such prodigies were only warnings and that it was an Anabaptist error to regard the arrival of subsequent calamities as inevitable. 'God doth premonish before he doth punish,' declared William Greenhill, the Puritan divine.[49] Throughout the seventeenth century preachers reiterated that comets, floods and monstrous births were sent by God to draw men to repentance. An army of

46. T. Sprat, *History of the Royal Society*, ed. J. I. Cope and H. W. Jones (St Louis, 1959), p. 362. cf. W. J. Brandt, *The Shape of Medieval History* (New Haven, 1966), pp. 52–9.

47. Ashm. 423, f. 182.

48. As can be seen by a perusal of *S.T.C.* and Wing. For some discussion, see L. H. Buell, 'Elizabethan Portents: Superstition or Doctrine?' *Essays Critical and Historical dedicated to Lily B. Campbell* (Berkeley, 1950); R. A. Fraser, *Shakespeare's Poetics* (1962), pp. 18–24.

49. Foxe, iv, p. 257; *The Works of John Jewel*, ed. J. Ayre (Cambridge, P.S., 1845–50), iv, p. 1253; Jackson, *Diverse Sermons*, sig. V1; W. Greenhill, *The Axe at the Root* (1643), p. 13.

horse seen in the sky at Blackheath in 1643 was carefully noted down by so scrupulous a contemporary as the mathematician William Oughtred. The belief that trivial occurrences might be omens sent by God to presage success or failure was deeply held by Archbishop Laud, who was badly shaken when he found one day in 1640 that his portrait on his study wall had fallen to the floor. Catholic recusants looked hopefully for supernatural indications of their coming deliverance, while some of the Dissenters systematically exploited the contemporary belief in portents in an effort to overthrow the Restoration settlement.[50] From the Dissolution of the Monasteries to the Revolution of 1688 there was scarcely any important public event which educated men did not believe to have been presaged by some occurrence in the natural world.[51] The deaths and misfortunes of ordinary people were also sometimes thought to have been thus foretold, and there were many stories about the omens thought to presage disaster for a particular family.[52]

Modern historians like to believe that the tough and self-reliant men of Stuart England, the pioneers of modern science and the founders of the British Empire, were too much like ourselves to be really worried by battles in the sky or tales of monstrous births. Yet there is no reason why we should feel embarrassed when confronted by such primitive survivals. For the disposition to see prodigies, omens and portents, sprang from a coherent view of the world as a moral order reflecting God's purposes and physically sensitive to the moral conduct of human beings. Such an attitude was not necessarily 'unscientific'. The search for correlations between disparate events is a valid form of inquiry and the analysis of God's

50. Josten, *Ashmole*, pp. 344–5; *The Works of . . . William Laud*, ed. W. Scott and J. Bliss (Oxford, 1847–60), iii, p. 237; *C.S.P.D., 1619–23*, p. 29. For the Dissenters, below, pp. 111–12.

51. M. Chauncy, *The Passion and Martyrdom of the Holy English Carthusian Fathers*, trans. A. F. Radcliffe and ed. G. W. S. Curtis (1935), pp. 57–9 (Dissolution); Brand, *Popular Antiquities*, iii, p. 112 (1688); *Yorkshire Diaries*, ed. C. Jackson (Surtees Soc., 1877), pp. 363–4 (Civil War); Josten, *Ashmole*, pp. 485–6 (execution of Charles I).

52. W. Sikes, *British Goblins* (1880), book II, chap. vii; N. Wanley, *The Wonders of the little World* (1678), pp. 549–54; Josten, *Ashmole*, p. 241; R. Gough, *Antiquities and Memoirs of the Parish of Myddle* (Shrewsbury, 1875), pp. 47–8; A. Malloch, *Finch and Baines* (Cambridge, 1917), p. 72; R. Plot, *The Natural History of Oxford-Shire* (Oxford, 1677), pp. 204–6.

portents was often conducted in a highly meticulous manner.[53] The belief that natural events had moral import was quite consistent with some awareness of the laws governing meteorological phenomena, just as the knowledge that a man had been killed by a fall was consistent with the view that his death was a punishment by God. Comets did not cease to be seen as divine warnings when in the later seventeenth century it came to be appreciated that they had natural causes and could be predicted. 'I am not ignorant that such meteors proceed from natural causes,' confided the antiquarian Ralph Thoresby to his diary in 1682, 'yet [they] are frequently also the presages of imminent calamities.'[54] When in the eighteenth century many clergy argued that God had in his original scheme of creation included a variety of natural occurrences, scheduled to go off at intervals down the course of human history as portentous warnings of trouble in store, there was no scientific way of questioning this assumption. It sprang not from ignorance about the workings of nature, but from the ancient belief that there was an intimate relationship between man's moral behaviour and the apparent caprices of his environment.

The same belief underlay the providential view of history, in which the rise and fall of nations appeared as the expression of God's unsearchable purposes. This type of history was usually written by those who felt they knew what these purposes were. A good example was the influential myth, popularized by John Foxe, according to which the English were a people singled out by God for a special purpose, an elect nation called upon to play a particular part in the designs of providence. This was a powerful element in Protestant mythology and animated much historical writing in the century after the Reformation.[55] It taught that England's lucky escapes, from the Armada or the Gunpowder Plot, were direct manifestations of the hand of God, and that the fortunes of her kings varied directly

53. cf. the comments of B. de Jouvenel, *The Art of Conjecture*, trans. N. Lary (1967), pp. 89–90. For a list of possible types of portent, T. Jackson, *Signs of the Times*, in his *Diverse Sermons*, sig. V2. Jackson compiled a large work on the subject (ibid., sig. Ee2ᵛ), but I have not discovered if it was ever published.

54. *The Diary of Ralph Thoresby*, ed. J. Hunter (1830), i, p. 132. For comets, below, pp. 396, 415.

55. Discussed by W. Haller, *Foxe's Book of Martyrs and the Elect Nation* (1963). For its appropriation by New England, Miller, *The New England Mind*, chap. 16, and by Scotland, S. A. Burrell, 'The Apocalyptic Vision of the Early Covenanters', *Scottish Hist. Rev.*, xliii (1964).

with the godliness of their policies. When the Calvinist bishop, George Carleton, wrote a history of England it was natural that he should entitle it *A Thankfull Remembrance of Gods Mercy, in a historicall collection of the great and merciful deliverances of the Church and State of England, since the Gospell began here to flourish.*[56] The *Homilies* declared that God was the only giver of victory in battle, and most clerics held that it was the moral behaviour of nations which determined their rise and fall. The conquest of England by Danes and Normans, for example, had been a punishment for the successive perjury of her rulers; the Wars of the Roses and military defeats in France had been the result of the persecution of the Lollards; and it was the sins of the land which had shortened the life of James I's son, Prince Henry.[57] The general assumption that virtue and vice would gain their true deserts acted as a powerful sanction for the morality of the day. Puritan zeal for the Reformation of Manners was animated by the conviction that, if men did not reform, God's wrath would fall upon the land in a direct and recognizable manner. The story of Jonah was used by Bishop Hooper to show that sinners should be punished in order to prevent judgements falling upon the whole community; and in 1637 the crew of the *Tenth Whelp* refused to sail again under their captain for fear that his blasphemous swearing would sink the ship.[58] Many of the more blatant examples of Puritan intolerance are to be explained by the firm conviction of the godly that everyone would suffer if action was not taken on God's behalf against Catholics, Laudians, Quakers, or whoever his enemies might be.[59] The torrent

56. 1624, and three later editions. For other examples of 'providential' history see F. S. Fussner, *The Historical Revolution* (1962), chap 7; F. J. Levy, *Tudor Historical Thought* (San Marino, Calif., 1967), index, *s.v.* 'Providence'; M. Fixler, *Milton and the Kingdoms of God* (1964), p. 38; R. M. Benbow, 'The Providential Theory ... in *Holinshed's Chronicles*', *Texas Studies in Literature and Language*, i (1959).

57. *Homilies*, p. 10; *Dives and Pauper*, f. 105; *A Proper Dyalogue betwene a Gentillman and a Husbandman* (1530), sigs. Bii^v-iii; T. Gataker, *A Discours Apologetical* (1654), p. 36.

58. J. W. Blench, *Preaching in England in the Late Fifteenth and Sixteenth Centuries* (Oxford, 1964), p. 94; *C.S.P.D., 1636–7*, p. 339.

59. For this belief, C. Richardson, *A Sermon concerning the Punishment of Malefactors* (1616), sig. B3; C. Russell, 'Arguments for Religious Unity in England, 1530–1650', *Journ. of Ecclesiastical Hist.*, xviii (1967), p. 222; Heywood, *Diaries*, i, p. 146; iii, p. 18; and for some practical instances, *Proceedings Principally in the County of Kent*, ed. L. B. Larking

of homiletic literature which accompanied the major calamities of plague and fire emphasized this link between moral reform and material self-interest. The search for a scapegoat sprang from the conviction that every natural disaster must necessarily have a moral cause.

Contemporaries showed little hesitation about recognizing God's judgements on their neighbours or identifying the particular sin which had provoked them. They happily collected stories of the judgements which had fallen upon blasphemers, cursers, perjurers, murderers, adulterers and sabbath-breakers, and they were confident that the Lord would avenge himself upon their political opponents. It is not surprising that, as a leading divine noted, many people prayed regularly, out of fear that if they failed to do so, 'they should be seized upon with some remarkable judgement in their own persons, families or goods, by fire, robbery, tempest, ill success, death . . . or other fearful accident'.[60]

In the Middle Ages preachers had enlivened their sermons with *exempla* – edifying tales of judgements upon sinners and mercies shown to the pious. In the sixteenth and seventeenth centuries the accumulation of such stories became a religious duty for everyone. The Puritan layman was expected to keep a record of the mercies bestowed upon him by Providence. Hence the vogue of diaries and autobiographies chronicling the notable happenings in the writer's life – 'accidents', as the astrologers called them. The godly writer would solemnly detail all his childhood illnesses and his preservation from a variety of mishaps. He would also be on the look-out for notable judgements which had befallen others. Any fortunate coincidence could be recognized as a 'providence' and any lucky escape might be seen as a 'deliverance': the casual visitor who arrived at the moment when some unhappy man was about to commit suicide; the horse which stumbled when its rider was on the way to make an unsatisfactory marriage; the sudden death which overtook some persecutor of God's people – such was the stuff of the anecdotes which the pious collected and recorded in their journals.[61]

(Camden Soc., 1862), pp. 20–22, and *Diary of Thomas Burton*, ed. J. T. Rutt (1828), i, pp. 26, 110.

60. R. Bolton, *Some Generall Directions for a Comfortable Walking with God* (5th edn, 1638), p. 45.

61. Examples of this extensive genre may be found in virtually any Puritan biography or autobiography, e.g., *Reliquiae Baxterianae*, ed. M. Sylvester (1696), i, pp. 11–12, 21; *Memoirs of the Life of Mr Ambrose Barnes*, ed. W. H. D. Longstaffe (Surtees Soc., 1867), pp. 237–8; W. Hinde,

Indeed the readiness of the Puritan diarists to detect the hand of God in daily events is for modern readers the most striking feature of their journals; and the sense of being God's especial preoccupation has been rightly noted as an essential feature of Puritanism.[62]

Out of such private records were gathered great published compilations of judgements and providences. The genre had its roots in such didactic historical works as John Lydgate's *Fall of Princes* (written in the 1430s) and the mid-Tudor *Mirror for Magistrates*, with their stories of the fate which overtook evil rulers. Like other early Tudor writings, the *Mirror* was a transitional work in which the pagan notion of Fortune's mutability was combined with the Christian conception of a purposive providence.[63] In the later sixteenth and early seventeenth centuries these writings multiplied. They no longer related solely to the fate of the great and they were more exclusively Christian in their assumptions. John Foxe initiated the fashion of recording the fate of persecutors, while such Elizabethan Puritans as Anthony Munday, John Field and Philip Stubbes compiled lists of the judgements which had befallen sabbath-breakers, drunkards and other sinners.[64] In *The Doome warning all men to the Iudgemente* (1581) the clergyman, Stephen Batman, produced an extensive chronicle of every prodigy and monstrous birth recorded in every book he had read. The most influential of these writers was Thomas Beard, Oliver Cromwell's schoolmaster, and author of *The Theatre of Gods Iudgments* (1597), which drew upon the Scriptures and the classics for its examples of the punishments which had overtaken evil-doers, as well as upon the writings of contemporaries.

A Faithfull Remonstrance of the Holy Life and Happy Death of Iohn Bruen (1641), chap. 46; J. Beadle, *The Journal or Diary of a Thankful Christian* (1656); *The Life and Death of Mr Vavasor Powell* (1671), pp. 124–6; Heywood, *Diaries*, iii, pp. 179 ff.; Sir W. Waller, *Recollections* (in *The Poetry of Anna Matilda* [1788]).

62. Miller, *The New England Mind*, pp. 33–4.

63. W. Farnham, *The Medieval Heritage of Elizabethan Tragedy* (Oxford, 1956), pp. 279–80; Levy, *Tudor Historical Thought*, pp. 28, 222. See in general H. A. Kelly, *Divine Providence in the England of Shakespeare's Histories* (Cambridge, Mass., 1970).

64. Foxe, esp. viii, pp. 628–71 (on his inaccuracies in this connection, Wood, *Ath. Ox.*, ii, cols. 789–90); A. Munday, *A view of sundry examples* (1580) (reprinted in A. Munday, *John a Kent and John a Cumber*, ed. J. P. Collier [Shakespeare Soc., 1851], pp. 67–98); J. Field, *A Godly Exhortation* (1583); P. Stubbes, *The Anatomie of Abuses*, ed. F. J. Furnivall (New Shakespere Soc., 1877–82), i, pp. 94–6, 111–3.

Beard's work was several times reissued and augmented, and it provided a rich fund of material for subsequent preachers and moralists. An abridgement, *The Thunderbolt of Gods wrath*, was published by Edmund Rudierd in 1618.

Once established, this genre had many imitators. In 1621 John Reynolds, an Exeter merchant, put out *The Triumph of God's Revenge against the crying and execrable sinne of murther*, and it was many times reissued before the end of the seventeenth century. In *A Divine Tragedie lately acted* (1636) Henry Burton provided fifty-six examples of judgements which had overtaken sabbath-breakers in the previous two years, and his book was clandestinely disseminated as part of the Puritan campaign against the Book of Sports; a similar compilation by Nehemiah Wallington, a London turner, remained in manuscript.[65] Prominent among other collectors of God's judgements and mercies was the Nonconformist clergyman, Samuel Clarke, whose *Mirror or Looking-Glasse both for saints and sinners* (1646) had by 1671 swollen into a fourth edition in two large folio volumes.

Towards the end of the Cromwellian Protectorate an even more elaborate 'Design for registring of Illustrious Providences' was initiated by the Presbyterian Minister, Matthew Poole, in collaboration with other divines at home and in New England. The idea was that a complete list of fully documented providences should be compiled as a cooperative venture which would cross denominational barriers. Every county should have a secretary who would gather together the material sent in to him and forward it on to Syon College, to be analysed by Poole. The close parallel with the methods used by the scientists of the Royal Society for collecting and classifying natural phenomena is obvious enough, and it is worth recalling that Francis Bacon had himself urged the desirability of compiling a definitive history of the workings of providence.[66] Poole's scheme, however, seems to have foundered, although it was later to be the

---

65. *H.M.C.*, iii, p. 191. Wallington's collection, mostly out of contemporary pamphlets, is in Sloane 1457 (extracts in N. Wallington, *Historical Notices of Events*, ed. R. Webb [1869]). Another sizeable collection was (S. Hammond), *Gods Judgements upon Drunkards, Swearers and Sabbath-breakers, in a Collection of the Most Remarkable Examples* (1659).

66. Bacon, *Works*, iii, pp. 341–2. Poole's scheme is briefly explained in the preface to I. Mather, *An Essay for the Recording of Illustrious Providences* (Boston, 1684). Copies of relevant letters from the period 1657–61 are in C.U.L., MS Dd.iii.64, ff. 136–141v.

inspiration for Increase Mather's *Essay for the Recording of Illustrious Providences* (Boston, 1684), a similar project which arose out of a meeting of Massachusetts ministers in 1681, but drew upon a manuscript left by Poole.

Meanwhile the radical wing of the Dissenting cause busied itself in compiling a sensational and partly fictitious collection of anti-Royalist prodigies, issued in three parts in 1661-2 as *Mirabilis Annus*. This work was a continuation of Henry Jessey's *The Lords Loud Call to England* (1660), which enumerated 'judgments or handiworks of God, by earthquake, lightning, whirlwind, great multitude of toads and flies, and also the strikings of divers persons with sudden death', all in the first two months after the Restoration of Charles II. The first instalment of *Mirabilis Annus* continued the story with a list of fifty-four signs in the heavens, twenty-three on earth, ten on water, and twenty-seven judgements on particular persons. All of these were cited as divine testimony against the Crown and the Anglican Church. Godly ministers might have been removed from their parishes, commented the editor, 'yet the defect of their ministry hath been eminently supplied by the Lord's immediate preaching to us from heaven'. Further prodigies were recorded in the second and third parts, much to the government's disgust. The tracts were seized, but, despite extensive inquiries, their authorship remained uncertain. As propaganda they were very crude; indeed Richard Baxter, who thought them the work of Fifth Monarchists, believed they did the cause more harm than good.[67] Nevertheless, they showed that an appeal to prodigies, manufactured if necessary, was still thought likely to influence public opinion. The learned minister, Philip Henry, was sufficiently impressed by *Mirabilis Annus* to think it worth copying out long extracts into his journal, while the Presbyterian John Flavell commented on the way in which God's people had been vindicated by 'a sensible suspension and stop put to the course of nature'. As Matthew Poole had ob-

---

67. *Reliquiae Baxterianae*, i, pp. 432-3. The three parts are *Mirabilis Annus, or the Year of Prodigies and Wonders* (1661); *Mirabilis Annus Secundus, or the Second Year of Prodigies* (1662), and *Mirabilis Annus Secundus, or the Second Part of the Second Years Prodigies* (1662). A selection with hostile commentary was published in 1707 as *The Oracles of the Dissenters*. For their authorship, see Wood. *Ath. Ox.*, iv, col. 408; Josten, *Ashmole*, p. 838; C. E. Whiting. *Studies in English Puritanism* (1931), pp. 547-51; and for government inquiries, *C.S.P.D., 1661-2*, pp. 23, 54, 87, 104, 106, 107, 128, 173, 184, 426, and *1663-4*, pp. 180, 257, 297.

served, most men were 'more easily drawn by examples than arguments'. It was only the government's Licensing Act which prevented *Mirabilis Annus* from going into further instalments.[68]

A didactic purpose also underlay the last of these seventeenth-century compilations: *A Compleat History of the most remarkable Providences, both of Judgment and Mercy, which have hapned in this present age,* published by William Turner, vicar of Walberton, Sussex, in 1697. But its intention was to justify the claims, not of one sect, but of religion as a whole. 'To record providences,' Turner declared, 'seems to be one of the best methods that can be pursued against the abounding atheism of this age.' It was for the same reason that William Whiston, scientist and divine, was to urge fifty years later that yet another attempt be made to compile a definitive History of Judgements.[69]

3. *Sacrilege*

The Puritans had undoubtedly been the readiest to spot God at work in daily occurrences; indeed much of the earliest news-reporting took the form of Puritan-inspired pamphlets relating accidents and disasters of moral importance. But the principle of divine retribution for evil-doing was upheld by men of every religious opinion. Many of the Puritan anecdotes about the sudden judgements which overtook blasphemers, perjurers and sabbath-breakers were derived from the *exempla* retailed by the medieval Church. After the Reformation, Catholic supporters did not hesitate to blame plagues and other misfortunes upon the new religious changes, or to see as judgements the misfortunes which sometimes fell upon their persecutors.[70]

68. *Diaries and Letters of Philip Henry,* ed. M. H. Lee (1882), pp. 101, 104–7; J. Flavell, *Divine Conduct: or, the Mysterie of Providence* (1678), p. 15; *H.M.C., Rawdon Hastings,* iv, p. 121; *C.S.P.D., 1664–5,* p. 344; C.U.L., MS. Dd.iii.64, f. 136ᵛ; *Bishop Parker's History of his own Time,* trans T. Newlin (1727), pp. 23–6.

69. Turner, *Providences,* sig. b1ᵛ; D. P. Walker, *The Decline of Hell* (1964), pp. 101–2.

70. Examples in F. W. X. Fincham, 'Notes from the Ecclesiastical Court Records at Somerset House', *T.R.H.S.,* 4th ser., iv (1921), p. 117; F. G. Lee, *The Church under Queen Elizabeth* (new edn, 1896), pp. 38–9; *The Troubles of Our Catholic Forefathers,* ed. J. Morris (1872–7), iii, pp. 56, 57–9; *L.P.,* viii, no. 949; Blench, *Preaching in England,* p. 280; R. Challoner, *Memoirs of Missionary Priests* (1741–2), i, pp. 7–9; ii, p. 404; H. Foley, *Records of the English Province of the Society of Jesus* (1877–84), iv, pp. 494–6; v, pp. 74–5, 208; vii, pp. 1072, 1073, 1139.

Catholic influence also lay behind the widely disseminated tradition that the monastic estates confiscated by Henry VIII carried with them a divine curse upon their new owners for appropriating to secular uses property once dedicated to God. Several different elements went to make up this idea. The first was the ancient assumption that sacrilege of any kind brought its own penalty. Nothing prospered when alienated from God. Hence the numerous medieval stories of the terrible fate which had overtaken those who attempted to rob holy shrines or to violate the goods of the church. As John Aubrey pointed out, the iconoclast Henry Sherfield in 1630 broke not only a window depicting God the Father in St Edmund's, Salisbury, but also his own leg while standing on a pew to do it. Many of Aubrey's contemporaries shared the belief that those who profaned or robbed churches infallibly came to a bad end.[71]

To this perennial sanction was joined another less strictly ecclesiastical notion embodied in the common English proverb that ill-gotten goods never prospered. This was extant in many versions: 'Evil-gotten goods lightly come and lightly go'; 'Ill-gotten goods will not last three crops'; or, most commonly, that ill-gotten goods would not last to the third heir. 'We be taught by experience,' declared the Homilies, 'how Almighty God never suffereth the third heir to enjoy his father's wrong possessions.'[72] This traditional belief was well-designed to deter acquisitive behaviour of many kinds. It was said, for example, that the disinheriting of the eldest son always brought bad luck, and that the families of notorious enclosers always died out in three generations: no depopulating landlord in Northamptonshire or Buckinghamshire had subsequently thrived, thought John Aubrey.[73] It also presupposed the idea that guilt could be inherited,

71. Aubrey, Gentilisme, p. 105. cf. H. Peacham, The Complete Gentleman, ed. V. B. Heltzel (Ithaca, N.Y., 1962), p. 181.

72. Homilies, p. 497. For other versions, see M. P. Tilley, A Dictionary of the Proverbs in England (Ann Arbor, 1950), p. 267; R. Whytforde, A Werke for Householders (n.d., copy in Ashm. 1215), sig. Eiv; A. Dent, The Plaine Mans Pathway to Heaven (16th edn, 1617), pp. 156–8; Gough, Antiquities and Memoirs of the parish of Myddle, p. 84.

73. Bodl., Aubrey MS 10, f. 133; Aubrey, Gentilisme, p. 107; R. H. Tawney, The Agrarian Problem in the Sixteenth Century (1912), p. 148, n. 1; Gough, op. cit, p. 49; Bacon, Works, vi, p. 391. For superstitions about enclosers, see W. H. Hosford, 'An Eye-Witness's Account of a Seventeenth-century Enclosure', Econ. Hist. Rev., 2nd ser., iv (1951–2), p. 216; E. Kerridge, Agrarian Problems in the Sixteenth Century (1969), p. 102.

and that the corporate responsibility of the family continued after the death of the original evil-doer.

Such beliefs in the reality of divine retribution were readily applied in obvious cases of sacrilege. In 1686, for example, when the communion cup was stolen from the church of St Peter's in Thanet, the event was solemnly recorded in the parish register along with a brief discourse on the sin of sacrilege, emphasizing God's readiness to punish both the guilty party and his posterity, if necessary rooting out whole families. 'Read the annals of all ages,' demanded a pamphleteer in 1649, 'Show me but one church-robber's heir that prospered upon the third generation.'[74]

The belief that a curse lay upon the purchasers of monastic lands did not clearly develop until the early seventeenth century, but it germinated from notions about sacrilege which had been current much earlier. Some of the monks themselves had prophesied that God would take vengeance upon the destroyers of the abbeys, and many general warnings about the fate of the sacrilegious had been issued during the general spoliation of Church property which had accompanied the religious changes of the mid sixteenth century.[75] Even so, the specific notion that the families of those who acquired monastic lands were likely to die out, probably after the third generation, does not seem to have been put about until at least the later years of Queen Elizabeth. It was not fully present in Everard Digby's *Dissuasive from taking away the Lyvings and Goods of the Church* (1590), which justified the dissolution of the monasteries, but held, as had many Protestants at the time, that their goods should not have been converted to lay uses. Digby cited the judgement which had overtaken William Rufus for a smaller act of spoliation in the eleventh century, but offered no contemporary applications. In 1593 the author of a memorandum on concealed lands belonging to the Church remarked that God's curse (*Malachi*, iii, 9) lay on those who misappropriated lands dedicated to his use.[76] It was also about this time that the Yorkshire clergyman Michael Sherbrook wrote in an

74. Woodruff, *An Inventory of the Parish Registers and Other Records in the Diocese of Canterbury*, pp. 162–3; H. Brown, *The Ox Muzzled and Ox-Ford dried* (1649), p. 6. For a list of judgements on sacrilegious persons, *The Cheshire Sheaf*, lvi (1961), pp. 48–9.

75. See, e.g., J. E. Oxley, *The Reformation in Essex* (Manchester, 1965), pp. 126–7. The Marian abbot of Westminster, John Feckenham, wrote *Caveat Emptor* on this subject, but I have not traced a copy.

76. *C.S.P.D., 1591–4*, p. 325.

unpublished treatise of the punishments which had overtaken Wolsey, Cromwell, Edward VI and other principal authors of the spoliation of the Church.[77]

The more sweeping assertion that all holders of monastic lands were involved in a corporate guilt for which they or their families would infallibly suffer is hard to trace back further than the reign of James I. In 1613 it was fully expressed by the Cambridge preacher, Foulke Robartes:

If we should make a catalogue of all those courtiers and others who in the dissolution of the abbeys were much enriched by the spoil of the Church, how few of so great estates are not already ruinated? It is true that there is an interchange of things in this world, and that it is a vain thing for men to think that their names, lands and houses shall continue for ever; but yet that in so short a space so great a change should be of so many families, so likely to have continued for longer space, must needs make men see . . . that the fact was displeasing unto almighty God, and that *It is destruction for a man to devour that which is holy*, Prov. xx, 25.[78]

The man who did most to disseminate this opinion was Sir Henry Spelman. His first work, published in 1613 and issued four times during the century, was *De non temerandis ecclesiis*, which attacked the impropriation of tithes by laymen and emphasized the divine punishments customarily inflicted upon the sacrilegious. His *Larger Treatise concerning tithes* was published posthumously in 1647 by the clergyman Jeremiah Stephens in a book entitled *Tithes too Hot to be Touched*. But Spelman's most sensational work was *The History and Fate of Sacrilege*. This had been prompted by his own misfortunes in connection with two monastic sites in Norfolk, which had involved him in protracted litigation until he came to see 'the infelicity of meddling with consecrated places'. The book was incomplete at his death and, although continued by Stephens, was not published until 1698. Some of its conclusions, however, had been advertised in 1646 by the author's son Clement Spelman in his admonitory Preface to the third edition of *De non temerandis ecclesiis*. The great bulk of the book was a laborious history of the punishments which God had bestowed for sacrilege from the time of the

77. *Tudor Treatises*, ed. A. G. Dickens (Yorks. Archaeol. Soc., 1959), p. 142.
78. F. Robartes, *The Revenue of the Gospel is Tythes* (Cambridge, 1613), p. 79.

Old Testament onwards, but the most influential part related to the purchasers of the monastic lands in England. Spelman systematically analysed the fate of the owners of all the ex-monastic estates in Norfolk within a twelve-mile radius of Rougham, the seat of the Yelvertons. The result was the discovery that in less than a century 'the monasteries had flung out their owners with their names and families (all of them save two) thrice at least, and some of them four or five or six times, not only by fail of issue, or ordinary sale, but very often by grievous accidents or misfortunes'. Furthermore no one had dared to build upon the otherwise attractive sites of the monasteries themselves 'for dread of infelicity that pursueth them'.[79]

This was the most precise demonstration of the thesis which had yet been made. A slightly less elaborate exercise of the same kind was performed by Sir Simon Degge's *Observations upon the possessors of monastery-lands in Staffordshire*, an essay written in 1669 to convey the author's reflections on reading the draft of a history of the county. It showed that in the previous sixty years no less than half the lands of Staffordshire had changed hands, and attributed this fact primarily, though not exclusively, to the sacrilege of the Dissolution. Degge's conclusions were, like Spelman's, regarded as too dangerous to be published at the time, and only appeared in print in 1717.[80] In the following year the legend was further reinforced by Browne Willis in his *History of the Mitred Parliamentary Abbies and Conventual Cathedral Churches* (1718). Like most antiquarians, Willis lamented the desecration of buildings and manuscripts which had accompanied the dissolution and did not fail to point the moral. The descendants of the man who pulled down Battle Abbey now lived near the site 'in a mean capacity', while a series of disasters had overtaken the lay owners of Biddlesden Abbey, Bucks. Willis declined to enumerate 'other particulars of this nature, which might be equally invidious', but the general tendency of his researches was clear enough. His fellow antiquary Thomas Hearne

---

79. *The History and Fate of Sacrilege* (4th edn., 1895) by 'two priests of the Church of England' (J. M. Neale and J. Haskoll, with appendix by C. F. S. Warren), pp. i, 136. The authors of this edition brought Spelman up to date by calculating that the families of over 600 of the original 630 grantees had paid for their sacrilege by the nineteenth century.

80. As an appendage to S. Erdeswicke, *A Survey of Staffordshire* (1717). For the taboo on such inquiries, see *The English Works of Sir Henry Spelman* (1723), sig. b3; J. Blaxton, 'The English appropriator or sacrilege condemned' (n.d., [after 1634]), Bodl. MS Add. A 40, f. 131.

PROVIDENCE 117

shared his views, but was equally guarded about expressing them.[81]

Historical research of this kind was long frowned upon as offensive to those nobility and gentry whose fortunes rested upon the acquisition of ecclesiastical property. But the belief in the curse upon sacrilegious landowners was widespread. In the early seventeenth century the most explicit statements about the misfortunes pursuing the owners of the abbey lands were made by Catholic controversialists.[82] But warnings of the punishments certain to overtake the sacrilegious and their posterity were issued by many leading Anglican clergy, including John Whitgift, Francis Godwin, Lancelot Andrewes, Jeremy Taylor, Joseph Mede, Isaac Basire and Robert South.[83] Thomas Bayly, the Royalist rector of Brasted, Kent, was expelled during the Civil War for declaring that 'the curse of God was on them that kept the abbey lands and therefore they did not prosper'.[84]

The same idea can be found in the writings of many contemporary historians and antiquarians. It had a useful explanatory function, for it appeared to account for the unprecedented mobility of land during the sixteenth and seventeenth centuries, and the remarkable number of noblemen who had come to an untimely end on the scaffold.[85] Laymen were impressed by stories of the bad luck which dogged the families of those who had pulled down churches or despoiled them at the Reformation.[86] Osmund, the eleventh-century Bishop of

81. B. Willis, *An History of the Mitred Parliamentary Abbies and Conventual Cathedral Churches* (1718), i. p. 33; ii, pp. 14–15; *Reliquiae Hearnianae*, ed. P. Bliss (2nd edn, 1869), ii, pp. 106, 127; J. Leland, *De Rebus Britannicis Collectanea*, ed. T. Hearne (1774), vi, p. 84. cf. W. Dugdale, *Monasticon Anglicanum*, ed. J. Stephens (1718), p. xi.

82. e.g., C. Reyner, *Apostolatus Benedictinorum in Anglia* (Douai, 1626), pp. 225–31. cf. N. Strange's Preface (p. [22]) to *A Missive to His Majesty of Great Britain, King James. Written divers yeers since by Doctor Carier* (Paris, 1649).

83. F. G(odwin), *Annales of England*, trans. M. Godwyn (1630), p. 175; *The Works of ... Joseph Mede* (1677), p. 123; and citations in Spelman, *Sacrilege* (1895 edn), pp. lxxiii-lxxxvi.

84. J. White, *The First Century of Scandalous, Malignant Priests* (1643), p. 40.

85. Clement Spelman asserted that more peers had been attainted or executed in the twenty years after the Dissolution than in the whole period since the Norman Conquest (Preface to H. Spelman, *De Non Temerandis Ecclesiis* [1646], sig. d2).

86. J. Harington, *Nugae Antiquae*, ed. T. Park (1804), ii, p. 147; G. Holles, *Memorials of the Holles family*, ed. A. C. Wood (Camden Ser., 1937), pp. 63, 214.

Salisbury, was known to have put a curse on anyone who alienated the manor of Sherborne from the bishopric; in the reign of James I it was pointed out that recent lay owners of the property included Prince Henry, who had died young, Sir Walter Raleigh, who had been executed, and the Earl of Somerset, who had fallen from his position as the King's premier favourite.[87] Among those who warned their children against purchasing church lands or otherwise hinted at the fate in store for the sacrilegious were William Cecil, Lord Burghley, Thomas Wentworth, Earl of Strafford, Edward Hyde, Earl of Clarendon, and even the calculating General George Monk, who, according to his clerical biographer 'would never make a purchase of that which had been once dedicated to God'.[88]

The warning about the consequences of sacrilege was not uttered only by Catholic sympathizers, lamenting the disappearance of the abbeys and romanticizing the medieval past. It also made sense to those who were concerned about the fate of the lands belonging to the Anglican Church and the monastic tithes which the laity had impropriated at the Reformation. The vigorous Jacobean preacher, Thomas Adams, for example, had no love for monks, but he bitterly regretted the system of lay impropriations because it starved the ministry of their due; and he regarded it as a form of sacrilege which carried the certainty of divine punishment; church-robbers never thrived, he told his congregation in 1612: 'I am persuaded many a house of blood in England had stood at this hour, had not the forced springs of impropriations turned their foundation to a quagmire. In all your knowledge, think but on a church-robber's heir that ever thrived to the third generation.'[89] Most clergy agreed that the im-

87. *C.P.S.D., 1623–5*, p. 548. Later versions of this story can be found in *March 2. Matters of Great Note and Consequence* (1641), and R. Boreman, *The Country-Mans Catechisme* (1652), p. 32.

88. In addition to citations on pp. lxxv–lxxviii of Spelman, *Sacrilege* (1895 edn) see *Calendar of the Clarendon State Papers*, ed. O. Ogle and W. H. Bliss, i (Oxford, 1872) p. 371; T. Gumble, *The Life of General Monck* (1671), p. 472; *Reliquiae Hearnianae*, ii. p. 106 n. Other instances of the belief occur in W. Dugdale, *The Antiquities of Warwickshire* (1656), p. 148; *The Diary of Abraham de la Pryme*, ed. C. Jackson (Surtees Soc., 1870), pp. 159, 174; Aubrey, *Miscellanies*, p. 28; T. Fuller, *The Church History of Britain* (1837), ii, p. 202; *Crosby Records. A Cavalier's Notebook*, ed. T. E. Gibson (1880), p. 210; Wood, *Ath. Ox.*, ii, col. 742; L. Atterbury, *The Grand Charter of Christian Feasts* (1686), p. 23.

89. *The Works of Thomas Adams*, ed. J. Angus (Edinburgh, 1861–2), ii, p. 245. cf. G. Hakewill, *An Answere to a Treatise written by Dr Carier* (1616), pp. 148–9, 252–3.

PROVIDENCE   119

propriations had been improperly acquired by the monks and should
have been returned to the Church at the Dissolution. Such possessions brought a curse upon their lay owners, declared a preacher at
St Paul's in 1628.[90]

The same threat of divine vengeance was later invoked by Anglicans in their efforts to repel the Puritan attack upon episcopal lands.
In 1642 Ephraim Udall, a Puritan divine turned Royalist, pointed
out in his warning pamphlet, *Noli me tangere* (1642), that Henry
VIII's posterity had been punished for the Dissolution by childlessness, and that many lay impropriators had also come to a bad end.

It is a thing to be thought on [he remarked] that many ancient families (as some intelligent men have observed) who inherited the lands of
their ancestors, . . . when they took in some of the spoils made in tithes
and glebe by the statute of Dissolution, their possessions quickly spewed
out the old possessors of them as a loathsome thing.

Gentry who wished to preserve their inheritances without ruin to
their posterity were accordingly advised to take no spoils from the
Church 'lest they be spoiled by them'. Other writers agreed that the
estates of those who engaged in the Edwardian spoliation of church
goods and chantry lands had withered away 'by the secret curses of
God'.[91]

Such arguments failed, of course, to check the confiscation and
sale of Church lands during the Interregnum, although Cornelius
Burges found it necessary to publish three editions of his *No Sacrilege nor Sinne to aliene or purchase the lands of bishops* (1659). But a
Royalist opponent was able to point out with some satisfaction that
the impious Burges, who had been personally involved in heavy
transactions in land belonging to the diocese of Bath and Wells, had
been reduced to poverty and consumed by cancer of the neck. It was
notable, however, that not even Burges denied that God's curse fell
upon the sacrilegious; he merely redefined sacrilege to mean robbery
of what was God's by divine right; since the Scriptures said nothing

90. W. Walker, *A Sermon Preached in St. Pauls-Church* (1629), p. 44.
Blaxton, 'The English appropriator . . .', is an eclectic treatise which reveals
how many others had written on this theme.

91. Udall, op. cit., pp. 26–7 (misprinted as 18–19); S. Clarke, *A Mirror or
Looking-Glass both for Saints and Sinners* (4th edn, 1671), ii, p. 643, and i,
p. 575. Two Anglican tracts citing the fate of the sacrilegious are *An Answer
to a Letter Written at Oxford, and superscribed to Dr Samuel Turner* (1647),
esp. pp. 44–5, and (J. Warner), *Church-lands not to be sold* (1648).

about bishop's lands, he argued, no such sanction could be claimed on their behalf.[92]

Nevertheless, the brisk transactions in monastic lands after the Dissolution and in Church lands during the Interregnum showed that the fear of sacrilege could not effectively deter men for long. For most people it was a case of *video meliora proboque, deteriora sequor*. But at least ten individuals are known to have restored impropriations or augmented vicarages under the direct influence of Sir Henry Spelman or his books, and many others came to consult him on the subject. King Charles I himself made a solemn vow in 1646 to restore all monastic lands and impropriations held by the Crown should he ever regain his throne.[93] There are also a few stories which suggest that scruples were sometimes felt by would-be purchasers of monastic lands or destroyers of abbey or church buildings; for example, when the work of destruction was halted after an ominous series of accidents had befallen the workmen involved. High-principled clergymen also had doubts about inheriting portions of abbey land.[94] The nineteenth-century continuators of Spelman were able to cite numerous local traditions relating to the bad luck which surrounded monastic ruins and dogged the progress of those whose ancestors had dabbled in monastic lands.[95] But all the evidence suggests that such scruples existed only to be overcome. When the English were fighting the French in Scotland in 1560 they hesitated to bombard the churches in which the enemy had prudently taken refuge, on the ground that it would be sacrilege to destroy the holy buildings. But it did not take them long to renew the attack after formulating the excuse that the French, by fortifying the churches, had robbed them of their sacred character.[96] In the same way the

92. I. Basire, *Deo & Ecclesiae sacrum* (2nd edn., 1668), sig. c2. Burges's transactions are discussed by D. Underdown in *E.H.R.*, lxxviii (1963).

93. V. Staley, *The Life and Times of Gilbert Sheldon* (n.d.), pp. 40–6. A list of converts is given by Jeremiah Stephens in his Preface to Spelman's *Larger treatise concerning tithes* (1647 edn) (in *The English Works of Sir Henry Spelman* [1723], pp. lxii–lxiv). For others see R. Bolton, *Last and Learned Worke* (1632), pp. 178–9; *A Certificate from Northamptonshire* (1641), pp. 9–10; Boreman, *The Country-Mans Catechisme*, pp. 30–31.

94. Spelman, *Sacrilege* (1895 edn), pp. 142–3, 151; T. Sharp, *The Life of John Sharp*, ed. T. Newcome (1825), ii. pp. 113–16.

95. Spelman, *Sacrilege* (1895 edn), pp. xxvii, chap. vii; F. G. Lee, *Glimpses in the Twilight* (1885), p. 412; G. Baskerville, *English Monks and the Dissolution of the Monasteries* (1937), p. 275.

96. Sir J. Hayward, *Annals of the First Four Years of the Reign of Queen Elizabeth*, ed. J. Bruce (Camden Soc., 1840), pp. 58–60.

attractive power of the monastic lands was too strong to be easily diminished by scruples of conscience.

In any case the notion was not accepted by everyone. Strenuous Protestants, like Thomas Fuller or John Milton, hotly denied that there was any element of sacrilege about the dispersal of monkish cells. 'When the founders of abbeys laid a curse upon those that should take away those lands', snorted the Erastian John Selden, 'I would fain know what power they had to curse me.'[97] By 1685 a preacher could declare that sacrilege was 'grown rife and of so potent an interest that he had need be a man of courage that dares arraign it for a sin'. Two years later another contemporary pointed out that 'all that Sir Henry Spelman hath writ in his book [De non temerandis ecclesiis] . . . hath hitherto made no very great converts, though it hath been reprinted five times'. Nor, as Bishop Burnet remarked, did anyone ever regard the Crown's appropriations of First-Fruits and Tenths in 1534 as sacrilegious, though 'sacrilege was charged on other things, on very slight grounds'.[98] The myth that a curse attached to the owners of monastic lands is interesting for its testimony to the survival of the belief that God's judgements could take earthly forms. But its relative ineffectiveness is proof of the failure of such convictions to move many in a direction opposite to that dictated by their material interests.

4. The doctrine and its uses

Most anecdotes about God's judgements were intended to reinforce some existing moral code. To the Puritan there was no more powerful argument for sabbath observance than the case-histories of the disasters which had overtaken individual sabbath-breakers. An immediate didactic purpose was served by these tales of men drowned while bathing in sermon-time or of towns burned down after shops had been allowed to stay open on Sunday.[99] The same was true of the

97. J. Selden, Table-Talk (Temple Classics, n.d.), p. 1. cf. T. Fuller, The Historie of the Holy Warre (1651), p. 240; id., Church History, ii, pp. 295–6; Complete Prose Works of John Milton (New Haven, 1953–), iii, p. 469.

98. Atterbury, The Grand Charter of Christian Feasts, p. 22; N. Johnston, The Assurance of Abby and other Church-Lands (1687), p. 113; Bishop Burnet's History of His Own Time (Oxford, 1823), v, p. 118.

99. Examples of such anecdotes are too numerous to list. Their complete continuity with medieval stories about the fate of sabbath-breakers can be seen from the contributions of A. S. Napier and R. Priebsch to An English Miscellany Presented to Dr Furnivall (Oxford, 1901).

carefully preserved stories relating to the fate of such notorious perjurers as Elizabeth Earwacker of Meonstoke, who 'fell dead on
appealing to God in confirmation of a lie',[100] or the vengeance which
had overtaken those who had the temerity to persecute God's people.
Political attitudes could also be reinforced in this way. In the sixteenth century official histories specialized in retailing the disasters
which infallibly overtook rebels and disobedient children.[101] During
the Civil War the Royalists were no less ready than the Parliamentarians to see God's judgement behind the defeats of their enemies;
and the misfortunes of republicans and sequestrators were retailed
in the same way as had been those of sabbath-breakers and blasphemers.[102]

As a means of influencing opinion, however, such stories were of
limited value. No doubt the occasional godly youth owed his conversion to the sudden fate which overtook some notorious reprobate
with whom he had previously associated.[103] But the seed could only
grow in favourable soil and an accident was unlikely to be recognized
as a 'judgement' at all unless the appropriate moral attitude was
already held by the eye-witness. For what was an obvious providence
to one man might be only a case of bad luck to another. On 26
October 1623 nearly a hundred persons were killed or injured when
the floor collapsed under the weight of a Roman Catholic congregation at Blackfriars, London, assembled to hear a Jesuit preacher.
For Protestants this was a manifest judgement, but the Papists
stressed the accidental nature of the tragedy and drew attention to
the rotten state of the floorboards.[104] The Great Fire of London was

100. W. A. Fearon and J. F. Williams, *The Parish Registers and Parochial
Documents in the Archdeaconry of Winchester* (1909), p. 34.

101. W. H. Greenleaf, *Order, Empiricism and Politics* (1964), pp. 110–14;
W. Notestein, *The English People on the Eve of Colonization* (1954), p. 49;
P. Laslett, *The World We Have Lost* (1965), p. 178.

102. e.g., J. Taylor, *The Noble Cavalier caracterised* (Oxford, 1643); *The
Visible Vengeance: or, a True Relation of the Suddaine, Miserable End, of
one White, late Mayor of Exceter* (1648); Woodruff, *An Inventory of the
Parish Registers and other Records in the Diocese of Canterbury*, p. 81;
Crosby Records. A Cavalier's Notebook, pp. 211, 292–3.

103. For an example, Mather, *An Essay for the Recording of Illustrious
Providences*, Preface.

104. (T.G.), *The Dolefull Even-Song* (1623); *Something Written by Occa-
sion of that Fatall and Memorable Accident in the Blacke Friers* (1623);
S. R. Gardiner, *History of England ... 1603–1642* (1904–5), v, pp. 142–3.
This accident was frequently cited in later Protestant literature along with

hailed by clergy of all denominations as a punishment for the sins of the inhabitants. But the sins they had in mind varied according to sectarian taste; the Dutch regarded the Fire as a divine judgement upon the country with whom they were at war, while a Spanish account noted that a Catholic chapel in the Strand had been miraculously spared: sure evidence that God's intention was to rebuke the Protestants for their heresy.[105] The decline of old landed families appeared to some High Churchmen as a judgement for their sacrilegious appropriation of monastic lands, but to the Dissenter Oliver Heywood it was a punishment for their idleness and self-indulgent style of life; the fact of social mobility impressed everyone, but it was interpreted in different ways.[106]

It was, therefore, the observer's point of view which determined whether, and by whom, an event was held as a judgement or a deliverance. Contemporary Royalists were unlikely to be impressed by the tales of Parliamentary soldiers whose lives were saved by the pocket Bibles which preserved them from a passing bullet.[107] Neither were Catholics much worried by such stories as that of Elizabeth Middleton, who in 1679 wished a judgement upon herself if there was any truth in the talk of a Popish Plot, only to be mysteriously deprived of her sight two days later.[108] 'Everyone that seems to prevail over another', observed Gerrard Winstanley, 'says God gave him the victory.'[109] When Oliver Cromwell saw the defeat of his naval expedition to Hispaniola as a divine judgement against him he was displaying a magnanimity which was unusual in such circumstances.[110] Normally men saw only those judgements and providences which appeared to reinforce their own prejudices.

But the very subjectivity of the belief gave it its power. By unconsciously selecting only those episodes which were capable of a favourable interpretation a man could powerfully fortify his conviction that

the 'deliverances' of 1588 and 1605, e.g., S. Clarke, *Englands Remembrancer* (1657), pp. 87–100.

105. W. G. Bell, *The Great Fire of London* (3rd edn, 1923), pp. 99, 314–15, 321.

106. Heywood, *Diaries*, iii, p. 194. cf. Calvin, *Institutes*, I.xvi.6, and below, pp. 279, 644.

107. In *Reliquiae Baxterianae*, i, p. 46; *Memoirs of the life of Mr Ambrose Barnes*, p. 107.

108. *A Full and True Narrative of one Elizabeth Middleton* (1679).

109. *The Works of Gerrard Winstanley*, ed. G. H. Sabine (Ithaca, N.Y., 1941), p. 297.

110. Carlyle, *Letters and Speeches of Oliver Cromwell*, ii, p. 471.

the Lord was on his side. So long as some casuists taught that every lucky chance was to be seen as a God-given opportunity which it was a man's duty to exploit to the full,[111] the doctrine of providences became a morale-booster of some consequence: when the Dissenter Colonel Blood attempted to steal the Crown Jewels in 1671, he carried with him a book containing the record of sixty notable deliverances from situations of great danger.[112] The tendency of the Puritans to see the hand of God behind their individual choices was peculiarly irritating to their opponents, although the habit was sometimes so guileless as to be inoffensive: when the godly John Bruen was attending a religious exercise, his eye was caught by an unusually attractive young woman. The immediate thought arose in his mind: 'Lo! this may be the woman that the Lord hath intended for my wife.' And so she turned out to be, though neither Bruen nor his biographer saw any irony in regarding his courtship as the solemn pursuit of the Lord's purposes. Less self-indulgent was John Winthrop, who, finding that he was a bad shot, took this to be an indication of the sinfulness of wildfowl shooting (which he very much liked).[113]

But sometimes the doctrine took more savage forms. In 1658 John Beverley, minister of Rothwell, Northamptonshire, complacently recorded the death of the child of one of his parishioners, 'by God's stroke; for ... a little before he had scornfully objected to me that I had no children, nor never would, when I reproved him for no better educating his'.[114] Only too often the belief in providence degenerated into a crude justification of any successful policy. Preachers warned their flocks against making providence 'a warrant of our actions', insisting that although God might sometimes make the meaning of his judgements clear they were normally unsearchable.[115] The relish with which the Puritans recorded any monstrous births or comparable misfortunes which befell their opponents led one Anglican clergyman to wish that those who preached so much

111. G. L. Mosse, *The Holy Pretence* (Oxford, 1957), pp. 100–1, 124–5, 135. For the doctrine in action, *H.M.C., Portland*, i, p. 421.

112. *H.M.C.*, vi, p. 370.

113. R. Halley, *Lancashire: Its Puritanism and Nonconformity* (2nd edn, Manchester, 1872), p. 107; *D.N.B.*, 'Winthrop, John'.

114. N. Glass, *The Early History of the Independent Church at Rothwell* (1871) pp. 7–8.

115. W. Lyford, *The Plain Mans Senses Exercised* (1655), p. 32; *The Works of William Bridge*, i, p. 433; *The Works of ... Isaac Barrow*, ed. J. Tillotson (3rd edn, 1700), iii, pp. 228–38.

about judgements might have their tongues clipped, since God was after all the God of mercy.[116] No one laid more weight upon 'extraordinary dispensations' than did Oliver Cromwell; as a member of one of his Parliaments remarked, the doctrine of Providence and Necessity was a two-edged sword; a thief might lay as good a title to every purse he took upon the highway.[117]

Such a link between virtue and success is taken for granted in many primitive societies. Modern, post-Kantian moralists assume that duty and inclination are likely to conflict. But the older assumption, common, for example, among the Greeks, is that virtue and material prosperity are closely connected. In a primitive society the first reaction to a misfortune is to identify its moral origin by taking stock of the previous conduct of the individuals involved.[118]

In Tudor and Stuart England the same assumptions were widely held, by scientists as well as by theologians. They were reflected, for example, in the microcosm theory, whereby physical disorders in the heavens were believed to presage or reflect moral and social disorders upon earth. They also permeated the science of embryology. Moralists had always taught that incest, adultery and other forms of sexual immorality were punished by ill-health and monstrous births; this belief was taken over by doctors and midwives, who as late as the eighteenth century held that deformed children might well result from indecent sexual relations – on the faintly rationalized ground that the state of mind of the copulating parties helped to give the embryo its distinctive shape.[119]

Behind such ideas lay the universal reluctance to recognize that the rewards and punishments of this world did not always go to those who deserved them. The doctrine of providences was a conscientious attempt to impose order on the apparent randomness of the human fortunes by proving that, in the long run, virtue was rewarded and

116. A. G. Matthews, *Walker Revised* (Oxford, 1948), p. 215.
117. *Diary of Thomas Burton*, i, p. lxix. For an earlier version of this analogy, J. M. Wallace, *Destiny his Choice: the Loyalism of Andrew Marvell* (Cambridge, 1968), p. 62. cf. G. F. Nuttall, *The Holy Spirit in Puritan Faith and Experience* (Oxford, 1946), pp. 124–6.
118. A Macintyre, *A Short History of Ethics* (1967), pp. 59, 84–5, 114; D. Forde, in *African Worlds* (1954), p. xii. But for a primitive universe devoid of moral purpose, S. F. Nadel, *Nupe Religion* (1954), pp. 33, 37.
119. *Dives and Pauper*, f. 35; I.R., *A Most Strange and True Discourse of the Wonderfull Iudgement of God* (1600); J. Maubray, *The Female Physician* (1724), p. 54.

vice did not go unpunished. In place of unacceptable moral chaos was erected the edifice of God's omnipotent sovereignty. But as a fully explanatory system the device was only moderately persuasive. Despite the attempts of the covenant theologians to bind God to keep his promises, it was impossible for even the most optimistic exponent of the doctrine of providence to maintain that virtue was *always* rewarded; instead he was forced to concede that it was only the justice of the next world which would fully compensate for the apparent capriciousness of this one. All he could do was to argue that there were many instances in which the link between morality and material success was too close to be ignored.

But by the later seventeenth century even this proposition seemed unconvincing. It had never been clear by what mechanism God's rewards and punishments in this world had been distributed. Miracles as such had been relegated by most Protestants to the days of the early Church. Under the influence of the mechanical philosophy even the Biblical miracles began to evaporate. In his pamphlet, *Miracles no violations of the Laws of Nature* (1683), an anonymous author, probably the deist Charles Blount, drew on the writings of Hobbes and Spinoza to support the view that there never had been a miracle which went against the laws of nature. The botanist Nehemiah Grew denied that the Biblical miracles had supernatural causes and the astronomer Halley argued that even the Flood could be explained scientifically. In the eighteenth century such writers as Thomas Woolston, Conyers Middleton and David Hume were to press these arguments home to their logical conclusion.[121] Portents and prodigies were similarly rejected by scientists who specialized in devising the most ingenious 'natural' causes for bizarre events. For Bishop Sprat its was quite sufficient that God governed by natural causes and effects: Christianity did not require the acceptance of vulgar prodigies.[122]

Meanwhile stricter standards of proof were employed to challenge the doctrine of immediate providences. New emphasis was laid on

120. Westfall, *Science and Religion in Seventeenth-century England*, pp. 99–101. For Protestant opinion on miracles see also below, 146–7, 585.

121. Sir L. Stephen, *History of English Thought in the Eighteenth Century* (3rd edn, 1902), i, gives a general account of these and similar controversialists. See also W. E. H. Lecky, *History of the Rise and Influence of the Spirit of Rationalism* (1910 edn), i, pp. 149–58.

122. Sprat, *History of the Royal Society*, p. 360. cf. J. Spencer, *A Discourse concerning Prodigies* (2nd edn, 1665).

the original Calvinist principle that God's secrets were inscrutable. 'We cannot tell what is a judgement of God,' declared John Selden, ' 'tis presumption to take upon us to know.' The eighteenth-century physician, Richard Mead, similarly refuted the view that sickness might come direct from God by pointing out that the supreme lawgiver could hardly achieve his object this way, 'unless a sure rule was given whereby his vengeance might be distinguished from common events, in as much as the innocent may be equal sharers in such calamities with the guilty'.[123]

In historical writing it became increasingly unfashionable after the mid seventeenth century to explain events in terms of God's providence. The Earl of Clarendon did not deny that God's finger could be perceived in the Great Rebellion; but he nevertheless chose to concentrate on the 'natural causes' which had brought it about.[124] Most men reacted against enthusiasts who readily identified the judgements of God in daily life; and even the Dissenting sects came to lay less emphasis upon providences than they had once done. No religious group had given more publicity to such 'judgements' than the Society of Friends, but when the Quaker Thomas Ellwood brought out his edition of George Fox's Journal in 1692–4 he tactfully omitted some of the 'judgements' on persecutors which it had originally contained. In 1701 the Quakers put a stop to their practice of requiring every Friends' Meeting to make an annual return of the judgements which had come upon persecutors during the previous twelve months.[125]

Fashionable infidelity worked in the same direction. At Christ Church, Oxford, in 1666, there had been 'wits' who publicly disputed 'whether there be any such a thing as the providence of God'. In 1682 John Oldham wrote:

> There are, who disavow all Providence
> And think the world is only steered by chance;
> Make God at best an idle looker-on.
> A lazy monarch lolling on his throne.[126]

123. J. Selden, *Table-Talk*, p. 62; R. Mead, *Medica Sacra*, trans. T. Stack (1755), p. 31.

124. *The History of the Great Rebellion*, ed. W. D. Macray (Oxford, 1888), i, pp. 1–2. cf. Fussner, *The Historical Revolution*, pp. 25, 245, 283.

125. *The Journal of George Fox*, ed. N. Penney (Cambridge, 1911), i, pp. xvi-xvii, 394.

126 *H.M.C. Finch*, i, p. 443; C. Hill, 'Newton and His Society', *The Texas Quarterly*, 1967, p. 38.

Without reverting to Epicurean scepticism of this kind the Anglican clergy were nevertheless changing their views on the way in which divine providence could be expected to work. If temporal felicity infallibly attended all good actions, remarked John Wilkins in his *Principles and Duties of Natural Religion* (published posthumously in 1678), virtue would lose its merit.[127] The world for most eighteenth-century clergymen was to be a place of probation, not of retribution. This did not mean that virtue could no longer be expected to pay. On the contrary, there was a close correlation between the vices castigated by moralists and the imprudent habits which precipitated the downfall of the economically unwary. Drinking, wenching, idleness; all brought a speedy retribution. The sanctification of the economic virtues during the years after the Restoration made honesty literally the best policy. It also reduced the old need for supernatural intervention to justify the righteous and punish the sinner. Ungodly conduct would bring its own punishment. 'When persons are very sinful and profane,' wrote Oliver Heywood, 'God leads them into such ways ... as ... may form and hasten their own ruin.' Even when vice was not brought to book, there still remained the horrors of a disturbed conscience. The less they spoke of divine judgements the more did Protestant moralists elaborate upon the pangs of a troubled mind.[128]

Of course the belief in God's immediate providences did not wither away altogether. 'The vicissitudes of the seventeenth century enhanced rather than weakened the providential view of politics', says a recent writer. Many intelligent contemporaries found it impossible to believe that catastrophic events like the Great Plague of 1665 had only natural causes.[129] In the later seventeenth century it was still necessary for the Marquis of Halifax to warn against 'that common error of applying God's judgements upon particular occasions'. In the 1680s and 1690s many clergymen waged a last-ditch defence of the doctrine of special providences against the new mechanical philosophy.[130]

127. J. Wilkins, *Of the Principles and Duties of Natural Religion* (5th edn, 1704), p. 87.

128. Heywood, *Diaries*, i, p. 221. For this theme. Q. D. Leavis, *Fiction and the Reading Public* (1932), pp. 104, 296–7. cf. Kendrick, *The Lisbon Earthquake*, p. 156; Weber, *The Sociology of Religion*, p. 43.

129. Wallace, *Destiny his choice*, p. 257; *C.S.P.D.*, *1665–6*, p. 344.

130. *The Complete Works of George Savile, First Marquess of Halifax*, ed. W. Raleigh (Oxford, 1912), p. 7; Miller, *The New England Mind*, p. 229.

In fact the belief in God's immediate providence proved remarkably tenacious. Eighteenth-century epidemics, fires and earthquakes continued to be hailed as acts of God. Methodists and Evangelicals saw 'providences' and 'deliverances' as frequently as their Puritan predecessors. Victorian clergymen could regard venereal disease as a punishment for fornication, and recognize in the cattle plague a retribution for the ill-treatment of farm labourers. The ninety-first psalm continued to be cited to prove that the godly would not be touched by epidemics, and smallpox inoculation was seen by some as a 'doubting of providence'.[131] In many respects nineteenth-century Evangelicals and sectarians had as literal a faith in the doctrine of divine providence as any to be found in the age of Cromwell or Baxter. Here, as with so many other beliefs, the distinction between its status in earlier and later times seems to be only one of degree. But there is a difference none the less. In the sixteenth and early seventeenth centuries we are confronted by a coherent theory to which most educated members of the community subscribed. In the nineteenth we meet only the survival of earlier assumptions, no longer fully compatible with the scientific principles of the day, and no longer accepted by many of the clergy themselves.

But even in the sixteenth and seventeenth centuries there had been limits to the doctrine's influence. The post-Reformation emphasis on God's sovereignty had itself been something of an innovation, designed to supersede the notion of a capricious Fortune, Fate or Chance, inherited from classical times, and still enjoying a good deal of literary esteem during the Middle Ages. It is possible that the notion of a random distribution of worldly rewards and punishments enjoyed far greater currency before the Reformation than it did for some time afterwards. In ordinary life medieval people were fully acquainted with the idea of chance, and felt no need to ascribe every event to the workings of divine providence. There was undoubtedly greater credulity extended to tales of miraculous prodigies: most seventeenth-century Englishmen, for example, would have had little time for the fourteenth-century story that the corn crop in Norfolk had been destroyed by a plague of flies bearing the words *Ira* on

131. Kendrick, *The Lisbon Earthquake*, p. 160, and *passim*; F. K. Brown, *Fathers of the Victorians* (Cambridge, 1961); W. L. Burn, *The Age of Equipoise* (1964), p. 45; J. Hart, in *Past and Present*, xxxi (1965), p. 56; W. Daniell, *Warminster Common* (1850), p. 376; E. Gosse, *Father and Son* (Harmondsworth, 1949), pp. 39, 202, 221; *Life and Struggles of William Lovett* (1920), i, p. 5.

one wing and *Dei* on the other.[132] But when confronted by routine misfortunes our medieval ancestors did not necessarily invoke a supernatural explanation. 'Death by misadventure' was a common verdict at inquests, both in the Middle Ages and thereafter; and the concept of 'chance' as a lucky accident was also current by the thirteenth century. There were plenty of proverbs about good and bad luck in circulation by Tudor times.[133] In his *Institutes* (1536) Calvin remarked that the opinion 'almost universally prevailing in our own day' was that all things happened fortuitously. 'The true doctrine of Providence has not only been obscured, but almost buried.'

If one falls among robbers, or ravenous beasts; if a sudden gust of wind at sea causes shipwreck; if one is struck by the fall of a house or a tree; if another, when wandering through desert paths, meets with deliverance; or, after being tossed by the waves, arrives in port, and makes some wondrous hairbreadth escape from death – all these occurrences, prosperous as well as adverse, carnal sense will attribute to fortune.[134]

The theologians of the post-Reformation period were thus imposing the doctrine of God's omnipotence upon a populace long accustomed to a variety of other types of explanation. They had been able to explain misfortune in terms of the working of good and evil spirits; or they could see it as the result of the neglect of sundry omens and observances relating to good or bad luck; or they could regard it as random and capricious. The doctrine of providence was meant to override these other theories. It also drew a more direct connection between misfortune and guilt by suggesting that there was an element of punishment for past offences in many of God's judgements.

The appeal of an explanatory theory based on guilt may have been assisted by new methods of child-rearing, based on the small, nuclear family, and designed to instil a strong sense of personal responsibility in the growing child. Certainly there is some reason for thinking that in other societies different types of adult reaction to misfortune are linked with the different ways in which children are brought up.[135]

132. G. R. Owst, *The Destructorium Viciorum of Alexander Carpenter* (1952), p. 18.

133. R. F. Hunnisett, *The Medieval Coroner* (Cambridge, 1961), pp. 20–21; *O.E.D., s.v.* 'chance'; Tilley, *A Dictionary of the Proverbs*, index, *s.v.* 'luck'.

134. Calvin, *Institutes*, I.xvi.2.

135. See J. W. M. Whiting and I. L. Child, *Child Training and Personality: a Cross-cultural Study* (New Haven, 1953).

But too little is known at present about child-training in Tudor and Stuart England for it to be worth speculating along these lines. Instead it may be pointed out that the doctrine of providence was always less likely to appeal to those at the bottom end of the social scale than the rival doctrine of luck. For the believer in luck can account for misfortune without jeopardizing his self-esteem. The concept of luck explains any apparent discrepancy between merit and reward and thus helps to reconcile men to the environment in which they live. 'The best seed ground for superstition,' wrote Gilbert Murray, 'is a society in which the fortunes of men seem to bear practically no relation to their merits and efforts.'[136] The worship of the goddess of Fortune began in the classical world, where the social system gave little opportunity for hard work to reap its own reward. In modern times the gambling complex – seeing life in terms of 'the lucky break' – remains the philosophy of the unsuccessful.

The belief that men usually got their just deserts inevitably made its greatest appeal to those with the opportunity to better themselves. The merchant, the shopkeeper and the aspiring artisan might all hope to see their virtue gain its own reward. Indeed the paradox was that those who did most to proclaim God's sovereignty were also those most active in helping themselves. They combined a faith in providence with an active reliance upon self-help, though the alliance was sometimes subject to strain. Even in Tudor England the *Homilies* complained that men were often reluctant to admit that all their success came from God : they might allow this to be true of spiritual goods, but as for 'such things which we call goods of fortune, as riches, authority, promotion and honour, some men ... think that they ... come of our industry and diligence, of our labour and travail rather than supernaturally'. This was the attitude which the fashionable clergyman Robert South, preaching in 1685, could safely challenge, stressing that it was chance not merit which did most to determine human fortunes; and that chance was controlled by God.[137]

But lower down the social scale the problem was different, for

136. G. Murray, *Five Stages of Greek Religion* (Oxford, 1925), p. 164. I owe this reference, and some of these reflections, to R. K. Merton, *Social Theory and Social Structure* (revd edn, Glencoe, Ill., 1957), pp. 147–9, and V. Aubert, 'Chance in Social Affairs', *Inquiry*, ii (1959).

137. *Homilies*, p. 478; R. South, *Twelve Sermons* (6th edn, 1727), p. 327. cf. E. Bonner, *A Profitable and Necessarye Doctryne* (1555), sig. ZZi; G. A. Starr, *Defoe and Spiritual Autobiography* (Princeton, N.J., 1965), p. 192; and the passage from George Herbert printed as epigraph to this chapter.

there was no risk that the poor would overrate the potentialities of self-help. In the seventeenth century most economic writers were happy to teach that the poor had only themselves to blame; it was their idleness and improvidence which had landed them where they were.[138] This was comfortable doctrine for the well-to-do, but it can hardly have appealed to that sizeable proportion of the population which never had any hope of dragging itself above subsistence level. The clergy therefore endeavoured to console these unfortunates with the doctrine of divine providence, stressing that there was a purpose behind everything, even if an unknown one. It was a gloomy philosophy, teaching men how to suffer, and stressing the impenetrability of God's will. At its most optimistic it promised that those who bore patiently with the evils of this world would have a chance of being rewarded in the next. But, as a contemporary remarked, 'the poor man lies under a great temptation to doubt of God's providence and care'.[139] It is not surprising that many should have turned away to non-religious modes of thought which offered a more direct prospect of relief and a more immediate explanation of why it was that some men prospered while others literally perished by the wayside.

138. See, e.g., E. S. Furniss, *The Position of the Laborer in a System of Nationalism* (Boston, 1920), pp. 99–104.
139. R. Kidder, *Charity Directed: or the Way to give Alms to the Greatest Advantage* (1676), p. 23.

5.

PRAYER AND PROPHECY

Verily, verily, I say unto you,
Whatsoever ye shall ask the Father
in my name he will give it you.
John, xvi, 23

1. *Prayer*

THEIR teachings on the subject of divine providence show that the Protestant reformers believed that God might of his own volition intervene in earthly affairs so as to help his people. They also maintained that there was no benefit which the pious Christian might not obtain by praying for it. 'Whensoever we need or lack anything pertaining either to the body or the soul,' declared the *Homily* on Prayer, 'it behoveth us to run only unto God, who is the only giver of all good things.'' The Church did not only allow such requests; it positively commanded them. It was a Christian duty to ask each day for one's daily bread, as a reminder that even in the most material context man could not hope to be sustained by his own efforts alone. In their visitation articles the officers of the Church called upon the parochial clergy to remind their flock that they should give thanks to God in time of plenty and call upon his mercy whenever scarcity threatened. Petitionary prayer was to be regularly offered up, no less for the maintenance of one's normal health and estate than for guidance and relief in conditions of unusual difficulty.

Of course not all such requests were to be for material goods; the godly man should pray first for such spiritual blessings as faith and the forgiveness of sins. But after he had asked for the goods of the soul it was entirely proper to add petitions relating to the goods of the body. Health, prosperity, good harvests, a safe delivery in childbirth, a comfortable and unmolested journey, professional success, advice on personal problems; all these were in the Lord's power to bestow. And bestow them he often did: 'If I should go through all the stories which show us the efficacy of prayers,' declared Bishop

1. *Homilies*, p. 324.

Latimer, 'I should never have done. For no doubt faithful prayer faileth never; it hath ever remedied all matters."

In accordance with this principle, the Litany in the Book of Common Prayer contained special intercessions for every material blessing, from good weather to preservation from sudden death. At times of threatened calamity additional prayers were circulated, in a collective attempt to ward off famine, pestilence, war or foul weather. Such forms of prayer were frequently issued throughout the seventeenth century, and beyond.³ Prayers of this type were not controversial. Puritans and Anglicans, Catholics and Dissenters offered them with equal conviction.

Some individuals, however, objected to certain types of petitionary prayer. The Henrician martyr, Thomas Bilney, thought it wrong to pray for the relief of any bodily infirmity.⁴ Similarly, the Elizabethan Puritan Thomas Cartwright protested against the prayer in the Litany for preservation from thunder and lightning. But his point was simply that there would be no end to the formal begging of such deliverances if this relatively trivial hazard was to be specifically mentioned: 'You might as well bring in a prayer that men may not have falls from their horses, may not fall into the hands of robbers, may not fall into waters; and a number such more sudden deaths, wherewith a greater number are taken away than by thunderings or lightnings.' Whitgift replied that the danger might be infrequent, but it was more terrible than many commoner hazards because, unlike them, it was 'not by any help of man to be repelled'. To this Cartwright had no answer, though his objection was often reiterated by his Puritan colleagues.⁵

Otherwise, the only discernible difference between Puritans and others in their attitude to petitionary prayer was that the Puritans laid greater emphasis on the need for it to be accompanied by fasting and personal austerity. There was nothing peculiarly Puritanical about fasting as such, for the Elizabethan Church often ordered Fast Days at times of plague. But it was among the Puritans that this

    2. *Sermons by Hugh Latimer*, ed. G. E. Corrie (Cambridge, P.S., 1844), pp. 508–9.

    3. Lists of the Anglican special prayers can be found in *S.T.C.* ('Liturgies: State Services' and 'Special Forms of Prayer on Various Occasions') and Wing ('Church of England').   4. Foxe, iv, p. 629.

    5. *The Works of John Whitgift*, ed. J. Ayre (Cambridge, P.S., 1851–3), ii, pp. 477, 482–3; (A. Gilby), *A Pleasaunt Dialogue* (1581), sig. M4ᵛ; *The Writings of Henry Barrow, 1590–1*, ed. L. H. Carlson (1966), pp. 94–5.

primitive rite was most extensively employed. The strict doctrine of the fast required participants to forego meat and drink, to refrain from their daily labour, to take less than their usual amount of sleep, to wear sober clothes, and to abstain from sexual activity. In this ritual condition, they were to pass the day reading the Word, singing psalms and offering prayers.[6] The Anglican Canons of 1604 forbade special meetings for fasting and prayer unless specifically authorized by the diocesan bishop.[7] But this provision was widely flouted, even before the Civil War, and afterwards it became common for sectarian congregations to hold fasts to bring favourable weather or to cure sick members. Fasts and Days of Humiliation were frequently ordered during the Interregnum at times of political crisis. Indeed the public fast remained a familiar method of turning away God's judgements upon the community until the end of the eighteenth century.

Petitionary prayer was thus a routine procedure, for which divines were very ready to suggest appropriate formulae. In *A Method of Prayer* (1710) the Dissenter, Matthew Henry, offered a comprehensive repertory, typical of many such productions. In addition to catering for the usual exigencies of birth, marriage and death, he provided a suitable form of words for those seeking relief from such hazards as fire, tempest or infectious disease, as well as for those Christians who were embarking on journeys or other potentially risky ventures.[8] Prayer could thus be adapted to serve on every occasion. Indeed some men were said to employ it in the pursuit of wildly inappropriate goals. Sir Thomas More observed that among the Welsh and the Irish it was common for thieves to pray for success before going out to steal; a case is recorded of a seventeenth-century Presbyterian who prayed for two hours before engaging in highway robbery.[9] ' 'Tis not a ridiculous devotion to say a prayer before a game at tables', thought Sir Thomas Browne.[10]

6. *Cartwrightiana*, ed. A. Peel and L. H. Carlson (1951), pp. 127–52; H. Mason, *Christian Humiliation, or a Treatise of Fasting* (1625); A. Hildersham, *The Doctrine of Fasting and Praier* (1633).

7. See below, pp. 579–80.

8. For an earlier list of occasions for petitionary prayer, W. Perkins, *A Golden Chaine* (1591), sig. H6.

9. T. More, *The Dialogue concerning Tyndale*, ed. W. E. Campbell (1931) p. 168; *Diary of Dr Edward Lake*, ed. G. P. Elliott (*Camden Miscellany*, i, 1847), p. 31.

10. *Religio Medici* (1643), I, xviii. cf. T. Jackson, *A Treatise containing the Originall of Unbeliefe* (1625), p. 354.

To the orthodox divine such activities were reprehensible. One should pray, but one's requests should always be of a seemly nature, and·one should never ask for some private advantage against the public interest.[11] Subject to this limitation, godly men could pray abundantly, and their efforts did not go unrewarded. In Puritan and Dissenting circles it became as fashionable to keep records of 'signal returns to prayer' as it was to record other manifestations of divine providence. Numerous instances·of successful prayer are recorded in the journals and biographies of seventeenth-century divines.[12] Indeed one of the purposes of the spiritual biographers was to demonstrate the efficacy of prayer. They illustrated how bad weather or apparently fatal sickness could be arrested by the sustained prayer of godly persons, or the fasting and prayer of a whole congregation. The *Life* of Dr Samuel Winter (1603–66), for example, enumerated eleven separate instances of efficacious prayer. They ranged from the prayer which had helped Winter to choose a tranquil day for his sea-crossing to Ireland, to the intercessions which had enabled him to save the lives of Colonel Jones's wife in Kilkenny, who was thought to be dying of jaundice; of his nephew, who was suspected to have the plague; of his sister-in-law, who suffered a serious haemorrhage; of a merchant's wife, who nearly died in childbed; and his own daughter, who was critically ill with 'the twisting of her guts'. Other instances of Winter's 'power and prevalency in prayer' might have been cited, remarked his biographer, but these were more than sufficient to demonstrate that the Lord was 'a prayer-hearing God'.[13]

But no one claimed that prayer was automatically efficacious in every context. Many Christians prayed for material benefits and were granted them. But there were even more whose petitions were denied. This apparent uncertainty did not worry the defenders of petitionary prayer, for they were never short of explanations as to why any particular request had not been granted. It might be that the petitioner was insufficiently contrite for his previous sins. Wicked men could not expect to have their prayers conceded. Neither could

11. T. Becon, *The Early Works*, ed. J. Ayre (Cambridge, P.S., 1843), p. 167.
12. e.g., Heywood, *Diaries*, i, pp. 47, 63, 285; iii, pp. 151 ff.; iv, pp. 67, 73, 78, 107, 157, 158; *The Diary of the Rev. Ralph Josselin, 1616–83*, ed. E. Hockliffe (Camden Ser., 1908), pp. 15, 68; Sir W. Waller, *Recollections* (in *The Poetry of Anna Matilda* [1788]), pp. 126 ff.; Aubrey, *Miscellanies*, pp. 163–4; Turner, *Providences*, ii, pp. 90–93.   .
13. S. Clarke, *The Lives of Sundry Eminent Persons* (1683), i, pp. 103–9.

godly men if their requests were unsuitable. (There was, of course, no telling what *was* suitable or unsuitable, for circumstances varied in different cases and God was the sole judge: 'God doth know better what is expedient for us than we ourselves.') God might deny a request in order to try the petitioner's faith: 'If a man beg of God riches, honour, health, liberty and such like, and he receiveth them not, but instead thereof hath God's grace and providence to sustain him, he receiveth therein from God much more than he asked.' Everyone who prayed could be sure that he would get what was good for him, though it might not be what he was hoping for. The less material the request the more likely was it to be granted: 'If thou ask no earthly or worldly thing, but such things as are spiritual and heavenly, then thou shalt be sure to obtain.'[14]

The belief in petitionary prayer was thus a self-confirming system. Once the petitioner had accepted the doctrine, his faith need never slacken, however unsuccessful his own requests for material aid. When the Elizabethan Church offered prayers for relief from plague or tempest it was always careful to add that God, for reasons best known to himself, might see fit to deny the people deliverance, and that these reasons were, by definition, good ones. Churchmen asked for divine judgements to be lifted, but they added that they had, of course, deserved everything which the Lord chose to inflict upon them. The widespread faith in the possibility of material relief by divine means was thus sustained by the knowledge that there was no failure which could not be satisfactorily explained away.

Other types of prayer could serve their purpose without drawing on this simple explanatory device. There was non-petitionary prayer, when the Christian worshipped and gave thanks, strengthening his own piety and devotion in the process. There was also the kind of prayer which helped men to take decisions in difficult situations. Many diaries and autobiographies of the period show how devout men were able by praying to focus their minds upon a problem, and so to hit upon a solution. Thus when Margaret Roper, the daughter of Sir Thomas More, fell ill with the sweating sickness, the doctors despaired of her life. Her father began to pray, whereupon 'incontinent [it] came into his mind that a clyster should be the only way to

14. T. Tymme, *The Chariot of Devotion* (1618), pp. 19–20, a work which admirably sums up arguments to be found in many other writers. cf. Becon, *Early Works*, pp. 141–3, 257–8; G. Webbe, *Augurs Prayer* (1621), pp. 44–9; A. Hildersham, *CLII. Lectures upon Psalme LI* (1635), pp. 70–71, 81–3; id., *CVIII. Lectures upon the Fourth of John* (4th edn, 1656), pp. 361–4.

help her'; and so it proved to be. In the same way the mathematician Dr Pell told John Aubrey that he believed that it was God who had helped him solve some of his more difficult problems.[15]

Prayer was also employed as a means of divination, that is to say of seeking supernatural guidance when the petitioner was confronted by a choice of possible actions. The Yorkshire yeoman Adam Eyre asked God to decide whether or not he should cast off his unsatisfactory wife. The Essex clergyman Ralph Josselin sought divine advice as to where in the county he should live. The godly layman Gervase Disney turned to prayer to know whether or not he should leave Nottingham.[16] In 1681 a religious youth at Warley, Yorkshire, resorted to prayer in an attempt to discover the identity of the thieves who had stolen his father's corn; he saw three men in a vision and asked for a warrant to arrest them. Here the function of prayer becomes comparable to that of the thief-magic of contemporary village wizards, who employed mirrors and polished stones in which their clients might discern the features of those who had stolen their goods.[17]

A graphic example of such divinatory prayer is provided by the Dissenting clergyman, Oliver Heywood, who records in his journal how he and his wife were contemplating a journey to York in 1673:

> There were several reasons that might induce us to take that season and some that contradicted. I was long *in aequilibrio*, doubted much what course to take, went to God in prayer, as I have done many times ... and presently I found a strong inclination to stay at home. And in a little time my thoughts were established that way, according to *Proverbs*, xvi, 3 ['Commit thy works unto the Lord and thy thoughts shall be established'].[18]

The psychological processes underlying such a procedure must be left for the reader to determine. But it is obvious that prayer, used in this way, could discharge a role much like that of other divining agencies. It helped the client to know his own mind and gave him the resolution to act accordingly. Behind his own unconscious inclinations he saw the hand of God.

15. W. Roper, *The Life of Sir Thomas Moore*, ed. E. V. Hitchcock (E.E.T.S., 1935), pp. 28–9; Aubrey, *Miscellanies*, pp. 115–16.

16. *Yorkshire Diaries*, ed. C. Jackson (Surtees Soc., 1877), p. 53; *Diary of Ralph Josselin*, pp. 9, 57–8; *Some Remarkable Passages in the Holy Life and Death of Gervase Disney* (1692), p. 64.

17. Heywood, *Diaries*, iv, pp. 31–2. cf. below, pp. 252–9.

18. Heywood, *Diaries*, iii, pp. 155–6.

Orthodox believers had no objection to praying for divine guidance in this way. But they were less happy about using sortilege to coerce God into taking decisions on their behalf. Many members of the early Christian Church had attempted to invoke divine aid by recourse to lots. In the style of the *sortes Virgilianae* of the classical world they prayed for guidance and then opened a Bible or Psalter, on the assumption that the verse on which their eyes alighted would give the answer to their problem. The medieval Church consistently deplored the habit of taking decisions in this way, on the grounds that it constituted a superstitious tempting of God. But its prohibitions were only moderately effective. 'From the fourth to the fourteenth century,' wrote Gibbon, 'these *sortes sanctorum*, as they are styled, were repeatedly condemned by the decrees of councils and repeatedly practised by kings, bishops and saints.' By the later Middle Ages the leaders of the Church did not publicly resort to such devices in the way that some of them had done at earlier periods. But at a popular level the divinatory recourse to holy books was a well established practice.[19]

The Reformation seems to have made little difference in this respect. The Bible and Psalter continued to play an important part in popular divination,[20] while recourse to scriptural *sortes* is recorded in the lives of many Protestant divines and public figures of the sixteenth and seventeenth centuries. When Edwin Sandys was Vice-Chancellor of Cambridge University he was assigned the delicate task of preaching before the Duke of Northumberland during the political uncertainties following the death of Edward VI; he chose a text by praying for guidance and then opening his Bible at random. The religious enthusiast Andrew Humphrey consulted his Bible in 1632 before sending off an account of his revelations to the Secretary of State. The same technique was employed around 1636 by the tailor John Dane, when deciding whether or not to emigrate, and by Christopher Monk, the master of a Bermudian ship, when captured by Algerian corsairs in 1681.[21] Similar stories are told about

19. E. Gibbon, *The Decline and Fall of the Roman Empire*, ed. J. B. Bury (1900–2), iv, p. 115; Abbé du Resnel, 'Recherches historiques sur les sorts appelés communément par les payens *sortes Homericae*', *Mémoires de littérature tirés des registres de l'Académie Royale des Inscriptions et Belles-Lettres*, xix (Paris, 1753); J. T. McNeill and H. M. Gamer, *Medieval Hand-books of Penance* (New York, 1938), p. 229; *Dives and Pauper* (1536), f. 50ᵛ; Kittredge, *Witchcraft*, p. 384.   20. Below, p. 254.
21. S. Clarke, *A Generall Martyrologie* (2nd edn, 1660), ii, p. 7; *C.S.P.D.*,

many other contemporaries, including Charles I and Archbishop Laud.[22] Some are true, others undoubtedly spurious. Either way, they illustrate the general disposition to believe in the possibility of supernatural guidance in times of difficulty. As the Independent preacher, William Bridge, put it, there was no telling when God might 'please to open a place of Scripture to the Soul'.[23]

In fact, society as a whole had long been accustomed to referring potentially contentious decisions to lot. Tacitus records that this was the practice of the ancient Germans; and in the twelfth century pilgrims had cast lots to determine which shrine they should visit. In the sixteenth century borough officers were sometimes chosen by lot; in 1583 the Chapter of Wells Cathedral even apportioned patronage in this manner.[24] Lotteries were often used to allocate goods to which there was more than one claimant: in early seventeenth-century Reading three maid-servants annually cast lots on Good Friday for money left by a benefactor.[25] Church pews were sometimes allocated in the same way.[26] On a national level lotteries were regularly used to raise funds for government purposes from the reign of Elizabeth onwards.[27] The practice of forcing condemned men to choose by lot which of their number should die was a common feature of military discipline, and much employed during the Civil War.[28] When Queen

---

1631-3, p. 344; C. Bridenbaugh, *Vexed and Troubled Englishmen* (Oxford, 1968), p. 462; C. Mather, *Wonders of the Invisible World*, in R. Baxter, *The Certainty of the World of Spirits* (1834), p. 138.

22. Brand, *Popular Antiquities*, iii, pp. 336–8; *The Works of ... William Laud*, ed. W. Scott and J. Bliss (Oxford, 1847–60), iii, p. 146; H. Jessey, *A Looking-Glass for Children*, ed. H.P. (3rd edn, 1673), p. 19; Clarke, *The Lives of Sundry Eminent Persons*, p. 113; Aubrey, *Gentilisme*, pp. 90–91, 232; C. Doe, *A Collection of Experience of the Work of Grace* (1700), p. 23; Turner, *Providences*, i, p. 123.

23. *The Works of the Rev. William Bridge* (1845), i, p. 425.

24. Tacitus, *Germania*, x; D. J. Hall, *English Mediaeval Pilgrimage* (1965), p. 97; C. Gross, 'The Early History of the Ballot in England', *American Hist. Rev.*, iii (1897–8), p. 456; W. H. Turner, *Selections from the Records of the City of Oxford* (1880), pp. 290–91; *H.M.C., Wells Cathedral*, p. 243.

25. *Reading Records*, ed. J. M. Guilding (1892–6), ii, p. 48. R. Howell, *Newcastle upon Tyne and the Puritan Revolution* (Oxford, 1967), p. 315, for another instance.

26. e.g., Hertfordshire R.O., A.S.A. 7/17.

27. C. L. Ewen, *Lotteries and Sweepstakes* (1932); J. Cohen, 'The Element of Lottery in British Government Bonds', *Economica*, n.s. xx (1953).

28. e.g., *C.S.P.D., 1640*, p. 189; *H.M.C. Egmont*, i, p. 285; Wood, *Life*

Anne's Bounty was set up in 1704 to augment the livings of poor clergy the choice of the particular livings to be augmented was made by lot. A decision of 1665 even allowed juries to cast lots to resolve their differences as an alternative to a retrial when agreement could not be reached. (This concession was set aside eleven years later, however, and by the eighteenth century it had become a serious misdemeanour for juries to reach their decision in this way.)[29]

For many persons the extensive use of lotteries was simply a convenient device, a way of getting a clear answer by which all the contestants would abide. But others regarded it as having a greater significance. In 1653 a London congregation proposed that a new Parliament should be selected from nominees chosen by each religious congregation 'by lot after solemn prayer (a way much used and owned by God in the scriptures)'.[30] The clear implication here was that a choice made in this way would have received some sort of divine approval. The same belief may have underlain the use of lots by medieval rustics to choose appropriate times for sowing corn or cutting trees.[31] It certainly played a part in the choice of condemned men for execution, for the lucky ticket was sometimes labelled 'life given by God'.[32] It was also present in the minds of the godly when they used lots for decision-making; as when the itinerant preacher Laurence Clarkson, on the road out of Colchester, 'set up my cane upright upon the ground; and which way it fell that way would I go'. In 1649 the Council of the Army sought God by prayer and then cast lots to determine which regiments should be sent to Ireland.[33] The Scottish leader, Archibald Johnston, Lord Wariston, took many of his decisions this way, and so did some of the early Methodists.

---

and Times, i, p. 93; C. H. Firth, *Cromwell's Army* (1905), pp. 287–8, 295; R. Gough, *Antiquities and Memoirs of the Parish of Myddle* (1875), p. 42; R. E. Scouller, *The Armies of Queen Anne* (Oxford, 1966), p. 267, n. 4.

29. P. H. Winfield, *The History of Conspiracy and Abuse of Legal Procedure* (Cambridge, 1921), p. 190.

30. J. Nickolls, *Original Letters and Papers of State Addressed to Oliver Cromwell* (1743), p. 122. A similar scheme for choosing M.P.s by lot was proposed in 'Theophilus P.', *Salus Populi, Desperately Ill of a Languishing Consumption* (1648), p. 10 (kindly shown me by Mr Blair Worden).

31. B.M., Royal MS 13 A VII, f. 5 (quoted in *A Contemporary Narrative of the Proceedings against Dame Alice Kyteler*, ed. T. Wright [Camden Soc., 1843], p. xxxi).

32. B. Whitelock, *Memorials* (Oxford, 1853), iii, p. 20.

33. L. Claxton, *The Lost Sheep Found* (1660), p. 21; Whitelock, *Memorials*, iii, p. 19.

After John Wesley's death the Methodist conference resolved the important question of whether or not Methodist preachers had spiritual authority to administer Communion, by recourse to prayer, followed by the drawing of lots.[34]

Until the beginning of the seventeenth century the lot was generally regarded as a direct appeal to divine providence. It was, as William Perkins put it, 'an act of religion in which we refer unto God the determination of things of moment that can no other way be determined'. As such its use was to be both solemn and infrequent. 'We are not to use lots,' continued Perkins, 'but with great reverence, in that the disposition of them immediately cometh from the Lord, and their proper use is to decide great controversies.' Lots should not be employed to resolve trivialities; nor were they to be used if some alternative way of reaching a decision was available. 'When a man hath other means to try by,' wrote John Weemse, 'then it is a tempting of God to use lots.' This was the position which had been taken by the theologians and canon lawyers of the medieval Church and it was now reiterated by the Puritan divines.[35] On a strict interpretation it meant that games of chance – 'lusory lots' as the casuists called them – were totally forbidden since they involved recourse to divine providence for unworthy reasons. All games depending upon hazard or chance were to be strictly eschewed, not just because they encouraged bad habits of idleness or improvidence, but because they were inherently disrespectful to God. 'The lot is cast into the lap,' said the *Proverbs*, 'but the whole disposing thereof is of the Lord.' It was 'the very ordinance of God'.[36]

34. *Diary of Sir Archibald Johnston of Wariston*, ii (1650–54), ed. D. H. Fleming (Scottish Hist. Soc., 1919), pp. 64–5, 77, 125, 126, 157, 202, 296–7 ('after some conjuring ejaculations I drew the lot'); ibid., iii (1655–60), ed. J. D. Ogilvie (Scottish Hist. Soc., 1940), pp. 45, 52–3, 74–5, 110–11, 132, 169; (S. Gott), *Nova Solyma*, ed. W. Begley (1902), ii, pp. 114–15. cf. *Procs. of the Wesley Hist. Soc.*, xiii (1922), pp. 189–90; xiv (1924), pp. 15, 18, 144; R. Southey, *The Life of Wesley*, ed. M. H. Fitzgerald (Oxford, 1925), i, pp. 95, 132, 154, 170, 246; R. A. Knox, *Enthusiasm* (Oxford, 1950), pp. 452–3.

35. *The Workes of ... William Perkins* (Cambridge, 1616–18), ii, pp. 141–2; Perkins, *A Golden Chaine*, sig. H2; J. Weemse, *A Treatise of the Foure Degenerate Sonnes* (1636), p. 79; B. Hanbury, *Historical Memorials* (1839–44), i, p. 444; W. Ames, *Conscience with the Power and Cases thereof* (1639), IV, xxiii. cf. Aquinas, *Summa Theologica*, II.2.95.8; G. R. Owst, in *Studies presented to Sir Hilary Jenkinson*, ed. J. C. Davies (1957), pp. 279–80; Thiers, *Superstitions*, I, 3, chap. vi; W. Tyndale, *Doctrinal Treatises*, ed. H. Walter (Cambridge, P.S., 1848), p. 456; Scot, *Discoverie*, XI.x.

36. D. Fenner, *A Short and Profitable Treatise of Lawfull and Unlawfull*

For the same reason some theologians condemned the employment of lotteries for many other routine purposes. They allowed their use in certain circumstances for dividing property or ending controversies ('divisory lots'). But lotteries were strictly forbidden as a means of taking everyday decisions, choosing ecclesiastical officers, or raising money. They were also reprehensible if employed for the detection or trial of suspected criminals. The old judicial ordeal had been condemned by the medieval Church as a tempting of the Lord and had accordingly been abandoned since the early thirteenth century. But some survivals, such as the right to trial by battle in certain circumstances, had lingered on; while the ordeal principle was to be extensively employed in the thief-magic practised by the wizards and cunning folk of the countryside. Such 'divinatory lots' were condemned by theologians as highly improper.[37] When in 1635 Richard Lilburne proposed to exercise his right to resolve a lawsuit by trial by battle, King Charles I disliked the idea 'as not agreeable to religion'.[38]

There were thus three types of attitude to the use of lots. The first was to regard them as a readily available instrument for settling daily problems with God's aid; hence the extensive use of ordeals in medieval times. The second was the growing conviction that it was irreverent and sinful to invoke God's aid on every trivial occasion; hence the prohibitions of medieval canonists and such sweeping Tudor condemnations of 'lusory' lots as Dudley Fenner's *Treatise of lawfull and unlawfull recreations* (1587, reissued 1592), and James Balmford's *Short and plaine dialogue concerning the unlawfulness of playing at cards* (1593, reissued 1623). The third stage brings us into the modern world, for it involved the denial that a lot was a divine providence at all; or rather the denial that it was any more providential than any other event.

The first systematic exponent of this view was the Puritan divine, Thomas Gataker, in his treatise *Of the nature and use of lots* (1619; second edition, 1627). Gataker's object was to eliminate unnecessary scruples about the use of lotteries and to justify their employment in

---

Recreations (Middleburgh, 1587), sigs. A6ᵛ–A7; (E. Topsell), *Times Lamentation* (1599), p. 384; J. Balmford, *A Modest Reply to Certaine Answeres* (1623). For the use made of *Prov.* xvi, 33, Calvin, *Institutes*, I.xvi.6.

37. See, in addition to works cited in note 35 above, G. A(lley), *The Poore Mans Librarie* (1571), f. 38; Cooper, *Mystery*, pp. 149–50.

38. *C.S.P.D., 1634–5*, p. 464. cf. Aquinas, *Summa Theologica*, II.2.95.8; *The Reformation of the Ecclesiastical Laws*, ed. E. Cardwell (Oxford, 1850), pp. 79–80. For the ordeal see below, pp. 259–61.

routine secular contexts. For him a lot was 'a casualty or casual event purposely applied to the deciding of some doubt', or in other words a result obtained by chance. For most divines, of course, the very idea of chance was a heathenish concept; they preferred to see God's immediate hand behind the most casual occurrence. But Gataker emphatically rejected such an assumption: God determined all events, he said, but only in the most general sense. The fall of dice was no more an immediate providence than the daily rising of the sun: God's role was no greater in events that were accidental than those which were contingent or inevitable. By taking the divinity out of chance occurrences Gataker was able to free the secular use of lots from any hint of impiety. Divisory lots then became as good a way of dividing up property as any other, provided no one regarded the result as a special decree by God. Games of chance also became acceptable. Divinatory lots, however, were absurd, for there was no reason to credit them with any special prognosticatory power. The idea that chance itself might be subject to law was to follow from Gataker's work.[39]

But although his book carried a laudatory preface by another well-known divine, Daniel Featley, it was a long time before his ideas were fully accepted: as late as 1687 Increase Mather could dismiss his arguments as unrepresentative of the main body of theological opinion.[40] The French jurist Barbeyrac developed Gataker's position in the early eighteenth century, pointing out that many Greeks and Romans had used lots extensively without endowing them with any superstitious meaning.[41] But his views were hotly contested. The objection to games of chance lingered; and it remained a relatively advanced position to regard the result of lots and ordeals as purely random.[42]

39. See below, pp. 784–5. W. E. H. Lecky first drew attention to the importance of Gataker's book; *History of the Rise and Influence of the Spirit of Rationalism in Europe* (1865) (1910 edn, i, p. 280, n. 1).

40. I. Mather, *A Testimony against Several Prophane and Superstitious Customs* (1687), pp. 13–15.

41. J. Barbeyrac, *Discours sur la nature du sort*, in his translation of G. Noodt, *Du Pouvoir des souverains* (2nd edn, Amsterdam, 1714), pp. 82–207. It is notable that his opponent, P. de Joncourt, had based himself on the authority of Perkins (*Quatre Lettres sur les jeux de hazard* [La Haye, 1713], pp. 202–5).

42. But for examples of those who held it in seventeenth-century England, Burton, *Anatomy*, ii, p. 82; Gott, *Nova Solyma*, ii, p. 114. For later uncertainty see, e.g., *A Narrative of the Life of Mr Richard Lyde* (1731), p. 66.

Meanwhile, the seventeenth century had witnessed some striking examples of the use of lots by pious individuals seeking God's opinion on some specific matter. Sir William Waller, the Parliamentary general, used Biblical *sortes* to divine whether his wife would come safely out of her labour.[43] Many writers retold the story of Mrs Honywood, the Tudor gentlewoman, who, despairing of her salvation, hurled a glass to the floor, declaring that it was as certain that she was damned as that the glass would break; miraculously it remained intact, and she recovered her confidence.[44] A hundred years later a hysterical girl, Sarah Wight, threw down an earthenware cup, saying that as sure as the cup would break there was no Hell. On this occasion also the cup remained unbroken. A similar tale concerned Mrs Joan Drake of Amersham, who in her periods of great temptation had a habit of opening the Bible and putting her fingers suddenly on a verse at random, declaring, 'Now whatsoever my finger is upon is just my case, whatsoever it be, and my doom.' 'But the Lord did so order it,' we are told, 'that looking upon the verse it was always found encouraging and comfortable.'[45]

Other contemporaries made God's intervention on their behalf a test of his existence. 'Christ, my Christ,' the Essex witch, Elizabeth Lowys, was alleged to have exclaimed in 1564, 'if thou be a saviour come down and avenge me of my enemies, or else thou shalt not be a saviour.'[46] Another Elizabethan sceptic, David Baker, was reclaimed for religion after surviving a nasty moment when his horse stuck on a narrow bridge over a dangerous river: he declared that if he got back safely he would believe there was a God. The Quaker James Nayler told of a young man who was tempted to put his hand in a boiling kettle to see whether God would preserve him from the consequences. His co-religionist Solomon Eccles challenged the Baptists to do without food and sleep for seven days as proof of their religion. Another eccentric, wandering through the North of England

43. Waller, *Recollections* (in *The Poetry of Anna Matilda*), pp. 126–7.
44. For versions of this anecdote, Aubrey, *Miscellanies*, pp. 126–7; J. F. Mozley, *John Foxe and His Book* (1940), pp. 106–7; P. Collinson, *A Mirror of Elizabethan Puritanism* (1964), p. 30; S. Clarke, *A Mirrour or Looking-Glasse both for Saints and Sinners* (1646), pp. 10–11; R. Younge, *A Sovereign Antidote*, p. 189 *(in A Christian Library* [1660]); J. Flavell, *Divine Conduct* (1678), p. 73.
45. H. Jessey, *The Exceeding Riches of Grace advanced* ... *in* ... *Mrs Sarah Wight* (2nd edn, 1647), p. 11; Turner, *Providences*, i, p. 123.
46. Essex R.O., D/AEA 2 (reference kindly supplied by Dr Alan Macfarlane).

in the 1670s, dealt with his adversaries by inviting them to pray that
God might immediately strike whichever of them was in error.⁴⁷ In
their sermons and homiletic writings, many moralists held out such
sanctions as evidence for religion. They retailed stories of persons
who falsely invoked God on their behalf with dire consequences, and
of justified curses which took effect.⁴⁸ The possibility of divine intervention was thus widely upheld in a variety of popular beliefs and
anecdotes, some of which were systematically disseminated by the
clergy. Among the people the lot retained its appeal for divination
and decision-taking. 'Among the ignorant and superstitious sort,'
thought William Perkins, 'such practices are common and in great
account.' Even the judicial ordeal survived informally; in the
seventeenth-century witch-trials the suspect's failure to pronounce
the Lord's Prayer correctly, or to sink when immersed in water, was
taken by educated observers as certain proof of guilt.⁴⁹

2. Healing

Although most post-Reformation theologians upheld the efficacy of
petitionary prayer, they usually stressed that it was intended to supplement natural remedies rather than to supersede them. For a
man to rely solely on divine aid in a context where he was perfectly
capable of helping himself was both impertinent and superstitious.
'It is not a praying of God, but a tempting of God,' said one Elizabethan bishop, 'to beg his blessing without doing also our own endeavour'; it was as if a husbandman were to pray for a good harvest,
but let his plough stand still. Only after all natural aids had been
exhausted should the petitioner throw himself upon God's mercy,
and even then he should not tempt providence by asking for the
impossible.⁵⁰ Catholics might continue to rely on unaccompanied

47. Wood, *Ath. Ox.*, iii, cols. 8–9; H. Barbour, *The Quakers in Puritan
England* (New Haven, 1964), p. 115; C. E. Whiting, *Studies in English
Puritanism* (1931), pp. 165, 193; Heywood, *Diaries*, i, p. 361.

48. For curses, below, pp. 602–5.

49. *The Workes of ... William Perkins*, iii, p. 625; below, p. 658.

50. Wm Day, later Bishop of Winchester (quoted in Sir J. Harington,
Nugae Antiquae, ed. T. Park [1804], ii, p. 97); *The Life of Mr Robert Blair*,
ed. T. M'Crie (Wodrow Soc., 1848), p. 63; Burton, *Anatomy*, ii, p. 9; Cooper,
Mystery, p. 46; Hildersham, *CVIII. Lectures upon the Fourth of John*, p.
232; G. A. Starr, *Defoe and Spiritual Autobiography* (Princeton, 1965),
pp. 189–90. cf. G. Lienhardt, *Divinity and Experience. The Religion of the
Dinka* (Oxford, 1961), pp. 283, 291.

prayer and even achieve miracles in this way[51], but Protestants were not to look for miraculous aid of any kind. Miracles were the swaddling-bands of the early Church, necessary for the initial conversion of unbelievers, but redundant once the faith had securely established itself. The Catholics were wrong to maintain that the power to work miracles was an essential feature of the true Church.[52]

This idea took some time to establish itself. Early Protestants had not always managed to renounce the notion that the true religion carried with it a superior magic. Miraculous cures were said to have been effected at the grave of the Lollard martyr Richard Wyche, and John Foxe had no hesitation in publicising the story that a conjuror was unable to do his diabolical tricks so long as he remained in the godly presence of William Tyndale.[53] Faith in the power of unaccompanied petitionary prayer lingered on. In 1617 a writer complained of the vulgar belief that prayers were enough to cure disease: 'Hence that speech of theirs; God hath sent it, and he can take it away.' In Northern Ireland a preacher met a man who thought 'that there was need of no other mean to be used but prayer, whatever ailed, soul or body, young or old, corn or cattle'.[54] During the century before the Civil War isolated religious enthusiasts bragged of their power to use prayer to work supernatural effects. The Elizabethan fanatic, William Hacket, boasted that if he pronounced the appropriate word it would not rain even though all the divines in England prayed for it to do so; similar claims were made by two London weavers in 1636. The separatist, Rice Boye, published several treatises in defence of the view that God would grant the means of subsistence to anyone who devoutly prayed for it.[55]

51. See the anecdotes in R. Challoner, *Memoirs of Missionary Priests* (1741–2); *The Troubles of our Catholic Forefathers*, ed. J. Morris (1872–7); H. Foley, *Records of the English Province of the Society of Jesus* (1875–83), *passim*. The principle that one should not tempt God when ordinary remedies were available had been laid down by St Augustine.

52. T. Fuller, *The Holy State* (3rd edn, 1652), p. 39, and *The Church History of Britain* (1837), ii, p. 239; *An Apology for Lollard Doctrines*, ed. J. H. Todd (Camden Soc., 1842), p. 92; Calvin, *Institutes*, IV.xix.19; J. White, *The Way to the True Church* (2nd edn, 1610), pp. 301–2, 453–5.

53. C. Barron, review of Thomson, *Later Lollards*, in *Journ. of the Soc. of Archivists*, iii (1967), pp. 258–9; Foxe, iii, pp. 702–3; v, p. 129.

54. Cooper, *Mystery*, p. 264; *The Life of Mr Robert Blair*, ed. M'Crie, p. 63.

55. (R. Cosin), *Conspiracie, for Pretended Reformation* (1592), p. 22; and below, p. 158; R. B(oye), *The Importunate Begger* (1635), and *A Iust Defence of the Importunate Beggers Importunity* (1636).

There was, however, no precedent for the scale of enthusiastic activity following the meeting of the Long Parliament in 1640 and the collapse of the ecclesiastical and prerogative courts. There are various ways of explaining why the sects should have multiplied so remarkably during these years. One can point to the disintegrative tendencies of the unchecked Protestant conscience, and the extent to which the new religious groups expressed the social and political aspirations of the poorer members of society for whom the Anglican Church had never adequately catered. But one should also recognize the importance of the claim made by many sectarians to provide that supernatural solution to earthly problems which the makers of the Protestant Reformation had so sternly rejected. The sects revived the miracle-working aspect of medieval Catholicism without its Roman and hierarchical features. They practised prophesying and faith-healing; they generated a widespread faith in the possibilities of un-accompanied prayer for healing the sick and for accomplishing other miraculous feats; they even claimed to raise persons from the dead. Such pretensions were condemned and despised by most educated persons, but they appealed powerfully to others less fortunate.

For, despite a hundred years of Protestantism, the problems to which the magic of the medieval Church had attempted to provide an answer still lacked any alternative solution. The helplessness of the poorer classes in the face of disease and the physical hazards of their environment had not noticeably lessened. When the Church collapsed in 1640 it was the sects who came forward to fill the gap. Sectarian leaders sometimes attempted to perform marvels as proof of their credentials: the clergy should not be heeded unless they could work miracles, said the Ranter, Thomas Webbe.[56] The prospect of supernatural relief helped to give the sects their drawing power; just as in modern times an emphasis upon religious healing, divina-tion and prophecy has brought recruits to the Pentecostal Churches of the Bantu and similar African separatist groups.[57]

Not that all the miracles claimed by the English sectaries had any very obvious practical value. Some embarked upon marathon fasts, abstaining from food of any kind for forty days or more, as a demon-stration of their spiritual virtuosity.[58] Spectacular abstinence of this

56. E. Stokes, *The Wiltshire Rant* (1652), p. 55.
57. B. A. Pauw, *Religion in a Tswana Chiefdom* (1960), esp. chap. 6; J. D. Y. Peel, 'Syncretism and Religious Change', *Comparative Studies in Society and History*, x (1967–8), pp. 130–4.
58. Examples in J. Reynolds, *A Discourse upon Prodigious Abstinence*

kind, particularly at a time of high food prices, may have helped to drive home the message that with spiritual aid it was possible to triumph over the difficulties of this world. But it cannot be seriously argued that it did much to help anyone's material problems. On the other hand the claim to heal disease by the mere pronunciation of prayers had an obvious attraction. The Baptists based their healing upon James, v, 14 ('Is any sick among you? Let him call for the elders of the church; and let them pray over him, anointing him with oil in the name of the Lord'). Hanserd Knollys resolved to take no more medicine, but to be anointed and prayed over by his colleagues. With William Kiffin he attempted to restore sight to the blind by prayer and holy oil.[59] Henry Denne claimed to cure women by dipping them. A Sandwich tailor was encouraged by a vision in 1647 to attempt the miraculous healing of the sick and the blind.[60] Another enthusiast, Matthew Coker of Lincoln's Inn, announced in 1654 that God had given him the gift of healing by touch, and that he had already put it to use to relieve a leper, a blind person and a cripple.[61] In 1659 the ministers of Stamford resolved that a wonderful cure had been accomplished by the personal intervention of an angel.[62]

For the performance of spectacular miracles there was no sect to rival the Quakers. Over 150 cures were attributed to their leader George Fox alone,[63] and many other Friends boasted similar healing powers. Several emulated the Ranter John Robins, who had been

(1669); *George Fox's 'Book of Miracles'*, ed. H. J. Cadbury (Cambridge, 1948), pp. 32–6; G. F. Nuttall, *James Nayler. A Fresh Approach* (Supplement 26 to *Journ. of the Friends' Hist. Soc.*, 1954), pp. 9–10, 13.

59. R. Barclay, *The Inner Life of the Religious Societies of the Commonwealth* (3rd edn, 1879), p. 219 n.; *George Fox's 'Book of Miracles'*, pp. 2–3; For other instances of recourse to holy oil, *Mr Tillam's account examined* (1657), p. 31; *The Life and Death of Mr Vavasor Powell* (1671), p. 15; *Narrative of the Miraculous Cure of Anne Munnings of Colchester ... 1705* (Totham, 1848) (copy in Bodl., MS Rawlinson B 243, f. 5).

60. T. Edwards, *Gangraena* (2nd edn, 1646), i, p. 213; *The Divell in Kent* (1647).

61. *A Short and Plain Narrative of Matthew Coker* (1654); *A Prophetical Revelation given from God himself unto Matthew Coker* (1654); M. Coker, *A Whip of Small Cords to Scourge AntiChrist* (1654); *Conway Letters*, ed. M. H. Nicolson (1930), pp. 99–103; *The Faithful Scout*, 189 (21–28 July, 1654), p. 1508.

62. *The Good Angel of Stamford* (1659).

63. *George Fox's 'Book of Miracles'*, p. ix. cf. Fox's *Journal*, ed. N. Penney (Cambridge, 1911), i, pp. 108, 140–41, 420–21, 433; ii, pp. 234, 310, 342.

credited with the power to raise the dead. James Nayler was said in 1656 to have claimed to have resurrected the widow Dorcas Erbury in Exeter gaol. In 1657 Susanna Pearson attempted to raise the corpse of William Pool, a Quaker suicide, but the result was a fiasco.[64] At his death Fox left a 'Book of Miracles' to be published for the edification of his followers. The early days of Quakerism had been marked by healing miracles on a scale comparable to those of the early Church; they helped to make the Friends numerically the most successful of the sects.

There is scope for argument about the exact status of these feats in Fox's own eyes. He did not neglect natural remedies and he seems to have been fully aware of the possibility of healing the body by addressing himself to the mind. 'Many of Fox's cures,' says a modern authority, 'must be treated as the normal control of strong personality over physical or mental illness.' But it would be wrong to see him as a psychiatrist born before his time. He carried out many of his cures in a state of high religious excitement. He was convinced of their miraculous character; and he did not hesitate to reject medicines when he felt that such 'carnal' means were spiritually inappropriate. He also claimed dramatic telepathic powers: his enemies understandably regarded him as a witch, and he was believed by some to bring the rain with him.[65]

The cult of miraculous healing was not totally extinguished in sectarian circles by the Restoration. Quaker miracles continued, and Baptists long maintained their ritual of anointing the sick with oil. Fasting and prayer were frequently resorted to by Dissenters in cases of sickness. In early eighteenth-century England the refugee French Camisard prophets, working in an atmosphere of intense religious excitement, cured Sir Richard Bulkeley of a rupture and endeavoured (unsuccessfully) to raise one of their dead members from the grave.[66] Healing and exorcising of this kind involved a reversion to

64. George Fox's 'Book of Miracles', pp. 6, 13–15; J. Taylor, Ranters of Both Sexes (1651), p. 2; A List of some of the Grand Blasphemers (1654).

65. Fox, Journal, i, pp. 50, 273; ii, pp. 5, 110; and the admirable discussion by H. J. Cadbury in his introduction to George Fox's 'Book of Miracles'.

66. For the Baptists see, e.g., R. Davis, Truth and Innocency Vindicated (1692), p. 86, and T. W. W. Smart in Sussex Archaeol. Collections, xiii (1861), pp. 67–8, and for the Camisards, J. Douglas, The Criterion (1807), pp. 234–6. Accounts of other miraculous cures may be found in George Fox's 'Book of Miracles', pp. 79–83; H.M.C., v. p. 384; A True Relation of the Wonderful Cure of Mary Maillard (1694); A Relation of the Miraculous Cure of Mrs Lydia Hills (2nd edn, 1696); T. A(ldridge), The Prevalency

the very type of religion which the Reformation had endeavoured to overthrow. The sectaries, observed William Prynne, made recruits by 'working miracles and casting devils out of men possessed, by their exorcisms, as the Jesuits and Papists do'.[67]

3. Prophecy

Although most orthodox members of the Church of England assumed that the Reformation had brought an end to miracles, they were less certain about the status of religious prophecy. Some took the view that Christians now had all the revelation they needed, but others felt that the possibility of further messages from God could not be entirely ruled out. The primitive belief in the supernatural significance of vivid and repetitive dreams had been kept alive by the early Church: even the pagan practice of seeking foreknowledge by ritual incubation at the shrine of Asclepius had been replaced for a time by nocturnal vigils at the shrine of Christian saints.[68] In the sixteenth century importance was still attached to dreams. Theologians taught that most of them had purely physical causes and were not to be heeded. But they admitted that some might be supernatural in inspiration, though as likely to be diabolical as divine. Many post-Reformation writers busied themselves establishing the criteria by which one might distinguish a divine intimation from a diabolical imposture or the effects of indigestion. Some severe Protestants paid little attention to dreams: Archbishop Cranmer thought them deceptive, and when James I refused to allow an inauspicious dream of his wife's to deter him from a proposed journey to Scotland his subjects were impressed by his strong-mindedness.[69] Gervase Holles tells us in a revealing anecdote how in 1635 he dreamed, correctly as it turned out, that he would lose his wife and infant in childbirth; but when he told his parents-in-law, 'they, being rigid Puritans, made light of it'.[70]

Nevertheless, the generally accepted view was that divine dreams,

of Prayer (1717); M. Pratt, A List of a Few Cures performed by Mr and Mrs De Loutherbourg ([1789]).

67. Quoted in George Fox's 'Book of Miracles', p. 1.

68. E. R. Dodds, Pagan and Christian in an Age of Anxiety (Cambridge, 1956), pp. 46–53.

69. T. Cranmer, Miscellaneous Writings and Letters, ed. J. E. Cox (Cambridge, P.S., 1846), pp. 43–4; C.S.P.D., 1611–18, p. 438; H.M.C., iii, p. 38.

70. Memorials of the Holles Family, 1493–1656, ed. A. C. Wood (Camden Ser., 1937), p. 231.

though unlikely, were still possible.[71] Those who are known to have taken at least some dreams seriously include such diverse individuals as John Foxe, Nicholas Wotton, Francis Bacon, Richard Greenham, William Laud, Peter Heylyn, William Sancroft, as well as many lesser figures.[72] The Puritan Colonel Hutchinson was not normally superstitious, but when one particular dream stuck in his mind both he and his wife agreed that it might have been of divine origin. The Suffolk minister, Francis Tilney, felt a little sheepish about the 'night visions' of public events which came to him during the opening months of the Civil War, but he nevertheless thought it worth sending an account of them to his M.P., Sir Harbottle Grimstone, on the grounds that they were almost certainly premonitory.[73] Anthony Gilby, the Puritan minister at Ashby-de-la-Zouch, persuaded the mother of Joseph Hall, the future bishop, that a dream promising an end to her chronic illness was of divine origin. Mrs Alice Thornton, the pious seventeenth-century Yorkshirewoman, was told by her husband and her aunt to forget about her dreams, but they turned out to be 'ominous'.[74] For the collectors of illustrious providences and the biographers of Puritan saints, dreams were a staple ingredient, and through their compilations they entered Protestant mythology in general. 'Such dreams as these are not to be slighted,' thought the Cheshire minister, Edward Burghall.[75]

71. For representative opinions: F. Seafield, *The Literature and Curiosities of Dreams* (2nd edn, 1869), pp. 113–15; Cooper, *Mystery*, pp. 144 ff.; M. Fotherby, *Atheomastix* (1622), p. 127; D. Person, *Varieties* (1635), pp. 252–3; R. Bernard, *Thesaurus Biblicus* (1644), appendix, pp. 159–60; P. Goodwin, *The Mystery of Dreames, historically discoursed* (1658), esp. pp. 268, 318–19; M. Amyraldus, *A Discourse concerning the Divine Dreams mention'd in Scripture*, trans. J. Lowde (1676), esp. pp. 126–7.

72. Foxe, vii, pp. 146–7; viii, pp. 454, 456–7; I. Walton, *Lives* (World's Classics, 1927), p. 102; *The Workes of . . . Richard Greenham*, ed. H. H(olland) (3rd edn, 1601), p. 10; Bacon, *Works*, ii, pp. 666–7; *The Works of William Laud*, iii, *passim*; J. Barnard, *Theologo-Historicus* (1683), 280–81; Bodl., MS Sancroft 51, pp. 1–6, 37. A list of aristocratic ladies who had divine dreams is given by J. Heydon, *Theomagia, or the Temple of Wisdome* (1664), iii, pp. 228–9.

73. *Memoirs of the Life of Colonel Hutchinson Written by His Wife Lucy* (Everyman Lib., n.d.), pp. 340–1; Hertfordshire R.O., VIII, B.153 (partly summarized in *H.M.C., Verulam*, p. 35).

74. *The Works of Joseph Hall*, ed. P. Wynter (Oxford, 1863), i, p. xxi; *The Autobiography of Mrs Alice Thornton*, ed. C. Jackson (Surtees Soc., 1875), pp. 123, 169.

75. E. Burghall, *Providence Improved*, ed. J. Hall (Lancs. and Cheshire Rec. Soc., 1889), p. 4.

Religion thus reinforced the ancient belief in the divinatory power
of dreams. The manuscript guides to dream-interpretation which
had circulated in medieval England[76] were replaced by such printed
works as *The Most Pleasaunte Art of the Interpretacion of Dreames*
by the Elizabethan Thomas Hill. Another popular handbook was
The Judgment of Dreams by the Greek physician Artemidorus of
Ephesus; translated into English in 1518, it had reached its twentieth
edition by 1722. Dream-interpretation was one of the services performed by wizards and astrologers for their clients,[77] and there were
sundry magical formulae for procuring divinatory dreams, for example, by placing objects under a young girl's pillow so that she
might see her future husband in her sleep.[78] Dreams helped men to
take decisions, and gave expression to their hopes and fears. In 1559
Nicholas Colman, citizen of Norwich, announced that a band of
foreigners dressed in beggars' cloaks, but with silk doublets underneath, would go through the realm, setting fire to market-towns and
villages, and burning down Norwich itself; he knew this because he
had foreseen it in his sleep. Other nocturnal visionaries bombarded
Elizabeth's ministers with similar warnings.[79] In the mid seventeenth
century John Aubrey thought that 'many' of his contemporaries took
careful note of their dreams.[80] The belief in their supernatural possibilities was much exploited by the sectaries.[81] Most of the 'visions'
and 'revelations' which were so common during the Interregnum
were probably what we should call dreams.

The possibility of religious prophecy was also admitted in more

76. On medieval dream-lore see W. C. Curry, *Chaucer and the Medieval
Sciences* (2nd edn, 1960), chaps. 8 and 9; M. Förster, in *Archiv für das
Studium der neueren Sprachen*, cxxv (1910), cxxvii (1911) and cxxxiv (1916);
G. R. Owst, *The Destructorium Viciorum of Alexander Carpenter* (1952),
p. 35; notes by Hélin to his facsimile edn of *La Clef des songes* (Paris, 1925).
77. Thorndike, *Magic and Science*, vi, p. 476; Josten, *Ashmole*, p. 31;
Ashm. 420, ff. 344, 346ᵛ.
78. A typical dream-inducing charm is in Bodl., MS e Mus 243, f. 31ᵛ.
79. *Depositions Taken before the Mayor and Aldermen of Norwich,
1549–67*, ed. W. Rye (Norfk & Norwich Archaeol. Soc., 1905), pp. 61–2;
H.M.C., Hatfield, xi, pp. 132–3; xiii, pp. 215–16.
80. Aubrey, *Gentilisme*, p. 57.
81. Examples in W. Y. Tindall, *John Bunyan, Mechanick Preacher* (New
York, 1964 reprint), pp. 19, 228; E. Rogers, *Some Account of the Life and
Opinions of a Fifth-Monarchy Man* (1867), pp. 11–12, 21–2; Jessey, *The
Exceeding Riches of Grace Advanced*, pp. 148 ff.; *Mr Evans and Mr Pen-
ningtons Prophesie* (1655); *A Narration of the Life of Mr Henry Burton*
(1643), pp. 9–10, 17–18.

orthodox circles. 'It was our bishop's opinion,' wrote the biographer of John Hacket, the Restoration Bishop of Coventry and Lichfield, 'that the spirit of prophecy was not quite dried up, but sometimes *pro hic et nunc* God gave mankind still a knowledge of future events.' Richard Baxter criticized the sects for placing too much reliance upon revelations as opposed to scripture, but he did not dismiss the possibility of revelation altogether.[82] Neither indeed did Bishop Sprat, though he thought it highly unlikely.[83]

In the later Middle Ages, when mystical activity was common, such revelations had been familiar enough. Hermits sometimes functioned as prophets and counsellors, and religious persons were often credited with special access to knowledge of the future.[84] The Duke of Buckingham's execution in 1521 came after his consultations with the Carthusian monk, Nicholas Hopkins, who foretold by divine revelation that Henry VIII would have no male issue and that Buckingham would succeed him. The Nun of Kent, Elizabeth Barton, who had long claimed divine prophetic powers, employed them to predict that the King would lose his throne if he persisted in his intention to marry Anne Boleyn.[85] Visions were a standard attribute of sanctity and Catholic martyrs like Sir Thomas More and the Carthusian fathers were said by their hagiographers to have enjoyed prophetic gifts. In the 1530s the Catholic cause drew some support from the visions and prophecies of contemporary hermits; and in the reign of Elizabeth there were many attempts to exploit the revelations of hysterical women to make propaganda on behalf of Mary Queen of Scots or for the return of the Mass.[86]

82. T. Plume, *An Account of the Life ... of ... John Hacket*, ed. M. E. C. Walcott (1865), p. 42; *Reliquiae Baxterianae*, ed. M. Sylvester (1696), i, p. 387; G. F. Nuttall, *The Holy Spirit in Puritan Faith and Experience* (Oxford, 1946), p. 56.

83. T. Sprat, *History of the Royal Society*, ed. J. I. Cope and H. W. Jones (1959), p. 359.

84. R. M. Clay, *The Hermits and Anchorites of England* (1914), chap. xii; C. J. Holdsworth, 'Visions and Visionaries in the Middle Ages', *History*, xlviii (1963); A. G. Dickens, *The English Reformation* (1964), p. 18.

85. *3rd Report of the Deputy Keeper of the Public Records* (1842), appx. ii, pp. 231–2; A. D. Cheney, 'The Holy Maid of Kent', *T.R.H.S.*, n.s., xviii (1904); L. E. Whatmore, 'The Sermon against the Holy Maid of Kent', *E.H.R.*, lviii (1943); *Three Chapters of Letters relating to the Suppression of Monasteries*, ed. T. Wright (Camden Soc., 1843), pp. 34 ff.

86. H. C. White, *Tudor Books of Saints and Martyrs* (Madison, Wisc., 1963), pp. 120–21, 125; M. Chauncy, *The Passion and Martyrdom of the Holy English Carthusian Fathers*, trans. A. F. Radcliffe and ed. G. W. S. Cur-

It is less well known that similar prophetic power was attributed to the heroes of early English Protestantism. The Marian persecution was said to have been predicted by Hooper, Bradford, Latimer and other Protestant martyrs. The pages of John Foxe's *Acts and Monuments* abound in stories of the martyrs who foretold their own deaths or kept up the hopes of their supporters by correctly prognosticating Queen Mary's death and the end of persecution.[87] These predictions were not regarded as the result of political sagacity but as proof of direct inspiration. 'God hath revealed unto me secrets unknown to the world,' declared John Knox in 1565.[88] Through Foxe's great book the tradition that a godly man might have supernatural knowledge of the future was widely disseminated among English Protestants. The martyrologist himself was said to have preached a sermon in exile in which he announced, by miraculous prescience, that the time had at last come for the return to England, though the news of Queen Mary's death on the previous day had not yet reached him. In 1634 Foxe's granddaughter claimed that there was an old man still alive who had been present on that notable occasion. Stories of this kind were to be an important source of inspiration to the Civil War sectaries.[89]

It was thus quite common for the biographers of Tudor and Stuart divines to attach a prophetic significance to some casual remark on their subject's part. The Civil War was said to have been predicted by Richard Hooker, Lancelot Andrewes, George Abbot, Thomas Jackson, Nicholas Ferrar, James Ussher, Robert Catlin and others.[90]

tis (1935), pp. 59, 117, 159–61; *The Letters and Despatches of Richard Verstegan*, ed. A. G. Petti (Catholic Rec. Soc., 1959), pp. 177, 180; B. Riche, *The True Report of a Late Practice enterprised by a Papist, with a Yong Maiden in Wales* (1582), and F. Peck, *Desiderata Curiosa* (1779), pp. 105, 113 (Elizabeth Orton); Kent R.O., High Commission Act Book (PRC 44/3), pp. 161–3 (Marie Taylor, 1588). A 'messenger of Christ' who supported Anne Boleyn appears in *L.P.*, vi, p. 655.

87. Foxe, iii, pp. 543, 702; vi, pp. 608–9, 638; vii, pp. 146–7, 313, 463; viii, pp. 456–7.

88. Quoted by S. R. Maitland, *Notes on the Contributions of the Rev. George Townsend* (1841–2), ii, p. 116.

89. G. Atwell, *An apology* (1660), pp. 32–3. cf. Mozley, *John Foxe*, pp. 105–7. For Civil War citations of Foxe: *Yorkshire Diaries*, ed. Jackson, p. 364; B. Hubbard, *Sermo Secularis* (1648), p. 50; *Works of William Bridge*, i, p. 417; Jessey, *The Exceeding Riches of Grace Advanced*, p. 140.

90. Most of these traditions are collected in Plume, *Life of Hacket*, pp. 41–2, and *A Practical Discourse on the Late Earthquakes*, by 'a reverend

A jocular remark by the Puritan Edward Dering was converted by posterity into a solemn prophecy concerning the fall of the bishops; Richard Baxter predicted the great fire at Bridgnorth; John Hampden foresaw Oliver Cromwell's later career; Thomas Goodwin had a misleading revelation that the Protector's final illness would not be fatal and subsequently complained that God had deceived him; inspiration from Heaven enabled John Welsh at Ayr to discern the plague in a pack of clothes.[91] Many godly men were thought to have had divine presages of the date of their own deaths; and the same privilege was enjoyed by those miniature Puritan heroes, the children who were too good to live.[92] These stories became an essential feature of the spiritual biographies of the seventeenth century. They reflected the popular assumption that a man who was holier than his contemporaries was likely to be endowed with a special gift of foreknowledge.

Casual *obiter dicta* by men of accepted godliness belonged to a different category from the ecstatic claims to immediate revelation made by obscure persons who thrust themselves into the limelight to enjoy a brief moment of glory, before society descended upon them with condign punishment for their pretensions. It was the Civil War period which saw most enthusiastic activity of this kind, but there had been a steady procession of would-be prophets during the previous century, some of them even claiming to be Christ in person or his appointed representative: a pretension which had been familiar in medieval England and which was well known to Tudor writers

divine' (1692). For others, B. Oley's *Life of George Herbert* (1652: 1836 reprint), pp. ci-civ; J. E. B. Mayor in *Cambs. Antiqn. Soc., Commns.*, i (1859) p. 263; W. Haller, *The Rise of Puritanism* (New York, 1957), p. 208; *Autobiography of Mrs Alice Thornton*, p. 24; C. S. R. Russell in *Bull. Institute Hist. Research*, xli (1968), p. 235.

91. Collinson, *A Mirror of Elizabethan Puritanism*, pp. 26–7; Barclay, *Inner Life*, p. 208; Sir R. Bulstrode, *Memoirs and Reflections* (1721), p. 193; *Bishop Burnet's History of his Own Time* (1823), i, p. 141; Clarke, *The lives of sundry eminent persons*, i, p. 213.

92. Plume, *Life of Hacket*, pp. 137–8; Clarke, *A Generall Martyrologie*, ii, p. 12; Wood, *Ath. Ox.*, ii, col. 434; Barnard, *Theologo-Historicus*, pp. 280–281; R. Ward, *The Life of ... Henry More*, ed. M. F. Howard (1911), pp. 152–3; *Diaries and Letters of Philip Henry*, ed. M. H. Lee (1882), pp. 160, 377; Turner, *Providences*, i, pp. 71 ff.; J. Janeway, *A Token for Children* (1676), pp. 47, 68. For stories of 'wise children' see *The Wonderful Child*, ed. W. E. A. Axon (*Chetham Miscellanies*, n.s., i [1902]).

on mental illness.[93] Others cast themselves and their associates for the role of the Two Witnesses promised by Revelation, xi, 3–11, with their prophetic power, and their capacity to control the weather, to bring down plague, to kill their enemies and to rise from the grave. The Bible also hinted at the existence of other prophets who might be expected to make a personal appearance before Judgement Day: a Newbury Lollard had looked forward to the coming of Enoch and Elijah in 1491,[94] and similar hopes of an Elias or Elijah, as foretold in Malachi, iv, 5, were entertained by many of his Protestant successors.

The reign of Elizabeth produced a small army of pseudo-Messiahs. In London in April 1561 John Moore was whipped and imprisoned for saying he was Christ; the same treatment was meted out to his companion, William Jeffrey, who declared that he was Peter who followed Christ. A month later a 'stranger' was set in the stocks for claiming to be the Lord of Lords and King of Kings. In the following year Elizeus Hall, a draper, was arrested and interrogated by the Bishop of London for assuming the title of Eli, the carpenter's son. He confessed to having had visions in which he had been selected as a messenger from God to the Queen and privileged with a two-day visit to Heaven and Hell. He abstained from flesh, fish and wine, and appears to have worn a special costume, of which the details unfortunately do not survive. He was sent to Bridewell, and Bishop Pilkington preached a special sermon against him before the Queen.[95] In 1586 John White, shoemaker of Rayleigh, Essex, claimed to be John the Baptist, while Ralph Durden, a minister from the same county, announced himself as the King of Kings and Lord of Lords who would lead the saints to Jerusalem. In the following year Miles Fry, alias Emmanuel Plantagenet, informed Burghley that he was the son of Queen Elizabeth by God the Father and that his authority

93. F. W. Maitland, *Roman Canon Law in the Church of England* (1898), chap. 6; A. Boorde, *The Breviary of Healthe* (1557), f. lxxviii; P. Barrough, *The Method of Phisick* (3rd edn, 1596), p. 46; R. A. Hunter and I. Macalpine, *Three Hundred Years of Psychiatry, 1535–1860* (1963), pp. 103–5.

94. Thomson, *Later Lollards*, p. 76. cf. Sir J. Harington, *A Discourse showing that Elias must personally come before the Day of Judgment* (*Nugae Antiquae*, ed. Park, ii).

95. J. Strype, *Annals of the Reformation* (Oxford, 1824), i(1), pp. 400, 433–5; *Holinshed's Chronicles* (1807–8), iv, p. 202; P.R.O., SP 12/23, ff. 91–2. Further information about Hall is contained in a document offered for sale by Bernard Quaritch Ltd. (London) in 1972; *Catalogue*, no. 914, item 4.

was greater than Gabriel's.[96] Usually the government dismissed such prophets as 'brainsick' or 'frantic'.[97] But when the enthusiast's activities threatened to have political consequences the authorities were quick to act, and in 1591 the case of William Hacket moved rapidly to a grisly conclusion.

Hacket was an illiterate and bankrupt ex-serving-man, who had persuaded himself that he was the Messiah and had come to judge the world on God's behalf. He laid claims to gifts of prophecy and miracle-working; and he threatened a series of plagues upon England unless immediate reformation took place. He was a fierce man,' who was said to have bitten off and eaten an antagonist's nose; 'his manner of praying' was observed to be 'as it were speaking God face to face'. Hacket had already been roughly treated in various English provincial towns, and his prominence in 1591 sprang from his association with two Puritan gentlemen, Edmund Copinger and Henry Arthington, whom he persuaded of his claims and appointed his prophets, one of mercy and one of judgement. Those of whom Hacket approved were to be sealed on the forehead as elect persons by Copinger; those whom he disliked were to be handed over to Arthington for consignment to eternal vengeance. Copinger, it should be noted, was a younger brother, and Arthington had fallen into debt; it may be that both saw Hacket's cause as a possible solution to their difficulties. Arthington subsequently attributed Hacket's influence over him to witchcraft, but Copinger was a whole-hearted disciple who had convinced himself that anything Hacket prayed for would automatically be granted. Hacket, he believed, was both King of Europe and the Angel who would come before the Last Judgement to separate the sheep from the goats; if he were imprisoned, the bolts would miraculously fall off his heels.

On 16 July 1591 Hacket and his companions announced their claims on a cart in Cheapside. A crowd gathered, and heard Hacket declare that the Privy Council should be reconstituted and that the Queen had forfeited her crown. The trio was arrested; and Hacket was charged with impugning the Queen's authority and treasonably defacing the royal arms. He was executed, despite his hopes that a miracle would save him at the last moment. Copinger starved himself to death in gaol, while Arthington recanted and, with the aid of

96. Strype, *Annals*, iii (1), pp. 637–9, 693–5; iii (2), pp. 479–87; C. H. Cooper, *Annals of Cambridge*, ii (Cambridge, 1843), pp. 446–7.

97. *H.M.C. Hatfield*, vii, pp. 259–60; xi, p. 219; xiii, p. 519; Ewen, ii, p. 175.

a pension from the Earl of Cumberland, gave himself over to the composition of pious works.[98]

The episode was probably inflated by the bishops in an effort to discredit the Puritan movement as a whole. The official account of the affair stressed Hacket's links with Penry, Udall, Egerton, Paul Wentworth and other prominent Puritans; and the event certainly contributed to the general setback which the Puritan party were experiencing at the time. But there was no real link between Hacket and orthodox Puritanism; instead the incident gave a lively foretaste of the enthusiastic activities of some of the Civil War sects. In the seventeenth century an old man was to tell Richard Baxter that Arthington and Copinger had been possessed with the spirit of the Grindletonians, the Yorkshire Antinomian sect which preceded the Seekers and Quakers.[99] Hacket's formal handing-over of sinners to judgement also anticipated the ceremonial cursing which was to be employed in the 1650s by Lodowick Muggleton.

These exploits were closely paralleled by two weavers, Richard Farnham and John Bull, who attracted a good deal of public attention in London in 1636. They too claimed to be divine prophets, armed with the power to inflict plagues upon mankind and the knowledge of all things to come. 'I am one of the two witnesses that are spoken of in the 11[th chapter] of Revelation,' declared Farnham. 'The Lord hath given me power for the opening and shutting of the heavens.' Both men were imprisoned by the High Commission and died in 1642, but not before they had promised to rise again and reign for ever. They left a small sect of female disciples who remained confident that the two prophets had risen from the dead and gone to convert the ten tribes of Israel; in due course they would return to rule the kingdom. Their supporters were 'esteemed by understanding men to be women of good parts, honest of conversation and very ready in the Scriptures'.[100] The claim to be the Two Witnesses in

98. Cosin, *Conspiracie for Pretended Reformation*; *C.S.P.D., 1591–4*, pp. 75–6; *H.M.C. Hatfield*, xi, p. 154; J. Stow, *The Annales of England* (1592), pp. 1288–90; R. Bancroft, *Daungerous Positions and Proceedings* (1593), pp. 144–83; H. Arthington, *The Seduction of Arthington by Hacket* (1592); P. Collinson, *The Elizabethan Puritan Movement* (1967), pp. 424–5; H. A(rthington), *The exhortation of Salomon* (1594).

99. R. Gilpin, *Daemonologia Sacra* (1677), ed. A. B. Grosart (1867), p. 145; Nuttall, *The Holy Spirit*, appx. i; Whiting, *Studies in English Puritanism*, pp. 290–91.

100. T. H(eywood), *A True Discourse of the Two Infamous Upstart*

Revelation was later revived by the two tailors, John Reeve and
Lodowick Muggleton, who established a sect during the Commonwealth, after announcing themselves to be the forerunners of Christ,
armed with the keys of Heaven and Hell.

Yet another pre-Civil War Messiah was the Anabaptist and Arian,
Edward Wightman, who in 1612 became the last Englishman to be
burned for heresy. He claimed to be the Elias or Elijah foretold in
Malachi, iv, 5; the Prophet who Moses had said would be raised up
from among his brethren (Deuteronomy, xviii, 18; Acts, iii, 22; vii,
37), and the Comforter predicted in John, xv, 26; those who denied
his claims would meet the fate of the children who had mocked
Elijah.[101] These threats did not save Wightman from his terrible
death, but neither did his fate deter others from emulating his pretensions. The Seeker, John Wilkinson, announced himself in 1623
as a new prophet sent by God; John Traske, the Jacobean Judaist,
thought himself a second Elias, and, believing himself able to do
miracles, offered to cure King James's gout. In 1628, a separatist
claimed to be one of the Apostles.[102]

With the outbreak of the Civil War such figures multiplied. Roland
(or Reynold) Bateman, a day-labourer, was imprisoned in London
in the summer of 1644 after declaring that he was Abel the Righteous, who would be slain and rise again. A few months later he was
examined at Essex Assizes after running away from the Parliamentary army into which he had been impressed. Questioned as to his
reasons, he stated that 'they that did press him did compel God to
go against God. And that the young child that is conceived in King
Charles and himself, both united in one, is the King of Heaven and
. . . that when he shall be put to death then King Charles will come
home and not before.' Furthermore, no one had 'knowledge of the

Prophets (1636); *False Prophets Discovered* (1642); *C.S.P.D.*, *1636–7*, pp.
459–60, 487–8; *1637–8*, p. 66.

101. C. Burrage, *The Early English Dissenters* (Cambridge, 1912), i, pp.
218–19; Ashm. 1521 (vii).

102. Burrage, op. cit., i, p. 194 and n.; E. Norice, *The New Gospel, not
the True Gospel* (1638), pp. 7–8; Whiting, *Studies in English Puritanism*,
pp. 314–16; *The Diary of Thomas Crosfield*, ed. F. S. Boas (1935), p. 20. In
the reign of James I the three Legate brothers, Walter, Thomas and Bartholomew, who were active Socinians, were said to have 'had a conceit that their
name did (as it were) foreshew and entitle them to be the new Apostles
that must do this new work'. Walter was drowned, Thomas died in Newgate,
and Bartholomew was burned at Smithfield. E. Jessop, *A Discovery of the
Errors of the English Anabaptists* (1623), p. 77.

Scripture, but King Charles and himself and three Lords. And ...
when he ... is put to death after three days he shall rise again and
then whom he will he will save and whom he will he will damn.'[103]

This was an unusual case of a Royalist Messiah. Such pretensions
were more commonly found among the radical wing of the Parliamentary party, particularly after the spread of perfectionist ideas.
An army captain, accused of saying he was Christ, explained that he
meant that anyone with faith was in Christ and had Christ in him.
Such doctrines confused observers and perfectionists alike. 'Some
poor creatures call themselves Christ,' admitted the Fifth Monarchist
prophetess, Hannah Trapnel: 'because of this oneness with Christ
they will have no distinguishing.' This failure to distinguish between
the inner spirit and its earthly vessel underlay the messianic delusions
of the Quaker James Nayler.[104] It made possible the career of the
Ranter, John Robins, who was deified by his followers; they also
cast his wife as the Virgin Mary and his son as the infant Jesus.
Robins himself disclaimed any such divinity, but had no hesitation
about claiming a direct revelation from the Holy Ghost and a divine
instruction to carry out the conversion of the Jews and the re-
conquest of Jerusalem.[105]

A similar figure was William Franklin, the London ropemaker
whose claim to be the Messiah resulted in a crestfallen recantation
before Winchester assizes in 1650. He had appointed disciples to
perform the roles of destroying angel, healing angel, and John the
Baptist, and his activities attracted 'multitudes of persons'. In 1666
William Woodward, Rector of Trottescliffe, Kent, was deprived of
his living for declaring that Franklin, who had become his lodger,
was Christ and Saviour. He had lost a Hampshire living for the
identical offence in 1650.[106] Other episodes in the same tradition include the unsuccessful attempt of three Newbury Anabaptists to
ascend to Heaven in 1647; the claim by Thomas Tany to be God's

103. *Beware of False Prophets* (1644); Essex R.O., transcript of P.R.O.,
Assizes 35/85/T/34 (examination of 6 Sept. 1644), kindly sent me by Mr
Arthur Searle.

104. Capt. F. Freeman, *Light vanquishing Darknesse* (1650), pp. 12–13,
35, 48 ff.; (A. Trapnel), *The Cry of a Stone* (1654), p. 66; Nuttall, *The Holy
Spirit*, p. 182.

105. G.H., *The Declaration of John Robins* (1651); L. Muggleton, *The
Acts of the Witnesses* (1699), p. 21; *All the Proceedings at the Sessions of the
Peace holden at Westminster, on the 20 day of June 1651* (1651).

106. H. Ellis, *Pseudochristus* (1650); *Return of all appeals made to High
Court of Delegates, 1533–1832* (*Parl. Papers*, 1867–8, lvii), pp. 20–21.

high priest, sent to gather in the Jews; the boast by the Ranter, Mary
Adams, that she had conceived a child by the Holy Ghost; the appearance of several other would-be Messiahs; and the crucifixion of
an elderly woman at Pocklington by a couple who were said to have
persuaded her that she would rise again on the third day.[107]

There were also many persons who, without making any Messianic
claims, nevertheless boasted of direct revelation from Heaven. 'All
saints have in measure a spirit of prophecy', said the Fifth Monarchist, Mary Cary.[108] Much the best-known such prophet before the
Civil War was Lady Eleanor Davis (or Douglas), the daughter of the
Earl of Castlehaven, who married first Sir John Davis and then
Sir Archibald Douglas.[109] In 1625 she 'heard early in the morning a
Voice from Heaven, speaking as through a trumpet these words:
"There is nineteen years and a half to the Judgment Day" '. From
then until her death in 1652 she had a continuous career of prophetic
utterance, interrupted only by consequential periods of imprison-
ment. Contemporaries believed her to have predicted the deaths of
Charles I, Laud and Buckingham, as well as that of her first husband.
Her ecstatic and utterly obscure pronouncements were frequently
printed, and as frequently suppressed. In 1633 she was imprisoned
and heavily fined by the High Commission for illegally printing at
Amsterdam a commentary on Daniel in which she made dark predictions about the fate awaiting Laud and Charles I. A few years
later she went beserk in Lichfield Cathedral, defiling the altar hang-
ings and occupying the episcopal throne, declaring she was the Pri-
mate of all England. This led to a further period of restraint.

Nevertheless she had her supporters. A leading politician like Sir
Edward Dering could fully accept the idea that she had genuine fore-

107. *A Looking-Glas for Sectaryes* (1647); *D.N.B.*, 'Tany, Thomas'; *The
Ranters monster* (1652); *Hell broke Loose* (1646), p. 6; *Perfect Proceedings*,
290 (1655); *D.N.B.*, 'Evans, Arise'; Middlesex R.O., Calendar of Sessions
Records, 1644–52 (typescript), p. 83 (Nicholas Nelson, 1647, 'the Lord's
anointed for this Kingdom'); Ewen, ii, p. 454; Gilpin, *Daemonologia Sacra*,
p. 395. Others are enumerated in *A List of Some of the Grand Blasphemers*
(1654).

108. M. Cary, *The Little Horns Doom and Downfall* (1651), p. 106.

109. See S. G. W(right), 'Dougle fooleries', *Bodl. Qtly Record*, viii
(1932); C. J. Hindle, *A Bibliography of the Printed Pamphlets and Broadsides of Lady Eleanor Douglas* (Edinburgh Bibliog. Soc., revd edn, 1936);
T. Spencer, 'The history of an unfortunate lady', *Harvard Studies and Notes
in Philol. and Litre.*, xx (1938); and the list of her works in *H.M.C.*, *Rawdon
Hastings*, iv, pp. 343–6.

knowledge, and her champions included the refugee Queen of Bohemia, and the Anglican divine Peter du Moulin.[110] Her enemies either thought her a dangerous sectary or accepted the contemporary anagram of her name 'Dame Eleanor Davis: (never so mad a ladie)'. The modern reader, to whom most of her effusions appear incomprehensible, may well be tempted to agree that she was insane. Yet, though undoubtedly linked to a hysterical temperament, her eccentricity is probably best regarded as a response to the social obstacles with which she had to contend. Both her husbands disapproved of her interest in public affairs and succeeded in burning some of her books; to the High Commission her great offence was that 'she took upon her (which much unbeseemed her sex) not only to interpret the Scriptures ... but also to be a prophetess'. Women at this time were denied access to any of the normal means of expression afforded by Church, State or University; and those who tried to break into these male preserves were very liable to develop a bizarre exterior, if only as a form of self-defence: the eccentric blue-stocking, Margaret Cavendish, Duchess of Newcastle, was another case in point.[111]

Indeed the prominence of women among the religious prophets of this period is partly explained by the fact that the best hope of gaining an ear for female utterances was to represent them as the result of divine revelation. Women were forced into such postures because the more conventional vehicles of pulpit and printed sermon were denied them, although the collapse of the censorship during the Civil War years gave more opportunities for self-expression: Lady Eleanor Douglas published at least thirty-seven tracts between 1641 and her death eleven years later. But, before the Civil War, recourse to prophecy was the only means by which most women could hope to disseminate their opinions on public events.

Thus in 1629 a Huntingdonshire woman, Jane Hawkins, had ecstatic visions of the downfall of the bishops and the Anglican Church. She preached in verse on the subject before a large congregation while the local curate took notes; only prompt intervention by Bishop Williams prevented the matter from going further.[112] Another prophetess, Grace Cary, a Bristol widow, had a vision in 1639 which

110. *Proceedings, Principally in the County of Kent*, ed. L. B. Larking (Camden Soc., 1862), p. xii; *C.S.P.D., 1625–49*, p. 458; G. Ballard, *Memoirs of British Ladies* (1775), p. 197.
111. See D. Grant, *Margaret the First* (1957).
112. J. Hacket, *Scrinia Reserata* (1693), ii, pp. 47–8; *C.S.P.D., 1628–9*, pp. 530–31, 537.

was subsequently taken to have foreshadowed the Civil War. She followed the King around, urging him to reform before it was too late, by giving liberty to the Puritans, taking action against Papists and doing something about Henrietta Maria's blatant Catholicism.[113] Several male prophets were making similar requests during these years;[114] doubtless they too found it easier to represent their demands as the result of heavenly visions than to risk putting them forward as their private opinions.

During the Civil War period it became common for prophets to lobby the King or the Army leaders with accounts of the visions in which God had declared his political preferences. Their political or social objectives were usually transparent, and so were the attractions of this method of proceeding; for a private person, however obscure, could, by claiming a divine sanction for his particular panacea, be sure of gaining an audience which would be at least temporarily respectful. On at least half a dozen occasions between 1647 and 1654 the deliberations of Oliver Cromwell and his colleagues were interrupted, so that some obscure prophet, often a woman, could be admitted to deliver her message.[115] The fasting and trances which were a common preliminary to such utterances helped to draw attention to the prophetess; properly publicised, they could ensure that her pronouncements would be scrutinized by an altogether larger audience than she might otherwise have ever hoped to command.

113. C.U.L., MS Add. 32; *H.M.C.*, vii, p. 514; Theophilus Philalethes Toxander, *Vox Coeli to England* (1646).

114. e.g., Andrew Humphrey (*C.S.P.D.*, *1631–3*, pp. 291, 344, 413; *1633–4*, pp. 146, 204–5; *1634–5*, p. 279); Robert Seale (*C.S.P.D.*, *1634–5*, p. 186). For Jacobean prophets, see *C.S.P.D.*, *Addenda, 1580–1625*, p. 552; *Ben Jonson*, ed. C. H. Herford, P. Simpson and E. Simpson (Oxford, 1925–52), x, p. 276.

115. (1) John Saltmarsh (*D.N.B.*); (2) The 'Dutch prophet' (*The Moderate Intelligencer*, 134 [7–14 Oct. 1647]; B. Whitelocke, *Memorials* [1682], p. 284); he may possibly be identified with the 'German' who thought himself appointed by God to be Fifth Monarch and rule as David II (H. More, *Enthusiasmus Triumphatus* [1656], pp. 30–31) and with the Dutch prophet whose predictions of English victory in the Second Dutch War were published in the *Gazette* in Jan. 1666 (Josten, *Ashmole*, p. 1049); (3) Elizabeth Poole (*The Clarke Papers*, ed. C. H. Firth [Camden Soc., 1891–1901], ii, pp. 150–54, 163–70; Sir W. Dugdale, *A Short View of the Late Troubles* [Oxford, 1681], p. 367; E. Poole, *An Alarum of War* [1649]; *A Vision* [1649]; Whitelocke, *Memorials*, p. 360); (4) Henry Pinnell (H. Pinnell, *A Word of Prophesy* [1648], pp. 6–7, 9–10); (5) Mary Pope ([M. Pope], *Heare, heare, heare, heare. A Word or Message from Heaven* [1648], p. 38); (6) Katherine Johnson (J. Price, *The Mystery and Method of his Majesty's Happy Restauration* [1680],

Moreover, so long as theories of divine right were invoked in support of the status quo, it remained important for any reformer to prove that God was on his side. He could do this by extracting moral and political recommendations from those parts of the Bible which appeared to justify his point of view: this had long been a staple form of political argument, and no one found it cramping to have to quote scripture in support of his position. But a much wider range of possibilities was opened by revelation. For prophecy claimed to supersede the mere written law of God, and there was no way of refuting it, save by recourse to counter-prophecy. The sectary who asserted in 1646 that she knew it was wrong to baptize infants, because Christ had personally appeared to tell her so, ran no risk of being outwitted in a battle of Biblical texts.[116]

Such considerations help to explain why visions and revelations were so prominent during the troubled years of the Interregnum. The claim to divine inspiration was an accompaniment to radical politics with which only such uncharacteristically sophisticated figures as the Leveller leaders could afford to dispense. Of course, not all the visionary literature of these years had a political aim, and some which had was conservative rather than radical.[117] But the overwhelming majority of those who claimed divine authority for their utterances were seeking authority for a political or social programme.

This association of prophecy with radicalism was not new. Earlier separatist polemic had often taken the form of revelation, predicting woe to the bishops and the Church of Rome; while 'Captain Pouch' (John Reynolds), the leader of the Midland peasants' revolt of 1607, had boasted a divine commission to throw down enclosures.[118] But the tendency was taken furthest during the Interregnum, when every kind of prophecy was ventilated. There were predictions by young

p. 39); (7) Eleanor Channel (W. Gostelo, *The coming of God* [1658], sig. A3; A. Evans, *A Message from God . . . by E. Channel* [1653]). George Foster failed to gain admission (G. Foster, *The Sounding of the Last Trumpet* [1650], sig. A3).

116. Edwards, *Gangraena*, i, p. 88.

117. e.g., Arise Evans *(D.N.B.)*; Eleanor Channel (n. 115, above); Walter Gostelo *(Charls Stuart and Oliver Cromwell united* [1655]; *C.S.P.D., 1663–4*, p. 214); Gilbert Anderson *(C.S.P.D., 1660–1*, p. 14). Several Royalist infants prophesied the Restoration; *Vox Infantis or, the Propheticall Child* (1649); *The Age of Wonders* (1660).

118. Burrage, *The Early English Dissenters*, p. 240; E. F. Gay, 'The Midland Revolt and the Inquisitions of Depopulation of 1607', *T.R.H.S.*, n.s., xviii (1904), i, p. 217, n. 1.

children, and by old men on their death-beds. There were sectaries who claimed to have been personally visited by Christ and others who had been entrusted with revelations, by angels. There were sermons which contemporaries chose to regard as 'almost prophetical', and many bold claims to foreknowledge. George Fox had no hesitation about declaring that he had predicted the death of Cromwell, the collapse of the Protectorate, the second Dutch War and the Plague of London. Many of his Quaker colleagues made similar claims. Since they made a habit of foretelling the destruction of the wicked by fire and plague, it was not difficult to provide some evidence in support of these boasts.[119]

Many of the prophets who made themselves prominent in the century before the Civil War had either predicted the imminence of the Last Judgement or seen themselves as playing a personal role in the dramatic events which, according to Revelation, were to precede it. Their activities reflected the widespread belief that, in one form or another, the Kingdom of God was at hand. There was nothing new about such a conviction. Messianic prophecies inherited from the ancient world had exerted much influence in Europe during the Middle Ages, particularly upon minority groups to whom the prospect of future bliss seemed compensation for their present afflictions. Periodically waves of expectancy had swept Europe and the idea that it was necessary to prepare for the reign of God on earth by destroying the representatives of Anti-Christ had long been familiar.[120] In England some of the Lollards had also reflected these tendencies. The destruction of Babylon, predicted in Revelation, xviii, seemed an obvious reference to Rome; verbal glosses on this and similar passages of the Apocalypse circulated extensively on the eve of the Reformation. Foxe's *Acts and Monuments* made it an article of faith to hold that the Protestant reform of the Church had

119. *Journal of George Fox*, i. pp. 107, 281, 302–3, 327, 342, 346; ii, pp. 89–90, 315; Barbour, *The Quakers in Puritan England*, p. 153; F. Wilde, *Prophecy Maintain'd* (1654); *The Vision of Humphrey Smith* (1660); E. Biddle, *A Warning from the Lord God* (1660), and *The Trumpet of the Lord* (1662); D. Baker, *A Certaine Warning* (1659), and *Yet one Warning more, to thee O England* (1660); (T. Reeve), *Mr Reeves his Alarm to London* (1678).
120. N. Cohn, *The Pursuit of the Millennium* (Mercury Books, 1962) is an admirable survey. A comprehensive anthology of the interpretation of Biblical prophecy is contained in the Seventh-Day-Adventist publication of L. E. Froom, *The Prophetic Faith of Our Fathers* (Washington, D.C., 1950–4).

been predicted by a long line of medieval prophets, while the 1,260 days (or years) of Anti-Christ (Revelation, xi, 3) could easily be recognized as those of Popish darkness.[121]

By making the Scriptures generally accessible, the Reformation increased the attention given to the prophetic parts of Daniel and Revelation. It also made popular a more literal interpretation than that favoured by medieval schoolmen. In the reign of Elizabeth many learned men agreed that the world was in its dotage and that the end could not be far off. There was widespread speculation about its timing: in 1589 the courtier, Anthony Marten, testified to 'the number of prophets that God doth daily send to admonish all people of the latter day, and to give them warning to be in a readiness'.[122] Theologians regarded it as highly improper to attempt to calculate the date of Doomsday, but, as Bishop Jewel observed in 1583, men had been doing so for the last two hundred years, though without success.[123] Linked to this older belief in the imminence of Doomsday, moreover, was the more distinctively millenarian view that, when it happened, the end of the world would be heralded by a series of spectacular and symbolic events, including the Conversion of the Jews, the Defeat of the Turk, the Fall of Rome, and the personal rule of Christ with his saints, either for a thousand years (Revelation, xx, 4) or for ever (Daniel, vii, 18, 27).

According to most commentators, this millennium had already begun. But in the seventeenth century various authors began to suggest that it was still to come. Of the many dates canvassed, 1666 was particularly popular, since the number of the Beast who had first to be overthrown was 666 (Revelation, xiii, 18).[124] An alternative date

121. Foxe, iii, pp. 105–6; iv, pp. 93 ff., 109–14, 115–16, 230, 237, 240, 253–9; v, p. 655; vii, pp. 664, 689; viii, p. 441; Thomson, *Later Lollards*, pp. 36, 76, 115, 240–1, 242, 243; C. Welch in *Procs. Suffolk Inst. Archaeol.*, xxix (1962), p. 158; M. Fixler, *Milton and the Kingdoms of God* (1964), p. 16. For an admirable treatment of this whole subject, see now C. Hill, *Antichrist in Seventeenth-century England* (1971).

122. A. Marten, *A Second Sound, or Warning of the Trumpet unto Judgement* (1589), f. 21ᵛ. W. B. Stone, 'Shakespeare and the Sad Augurs', *Journ. Eng. & Germanic Philol.*, lii (1953), provides an excellent account of Elizabethan eschatology.

123. *The Works of John Jewel*, ed. J. Ayre (Cambridge, P.S., 1845–50), ii, pp. 872–3. cf. E. Coke, *Institutes*, iii, chap. 55; Kocher, *Science and Religion*, pp. 64, 79; V. Harris, *All Coherence Gone* (Chicago, 1949), p. 115; C. Hill, *Intellectual Origins of the English Revolution* (Oxford, 1965), pp. 269–70.

124. For a few examples of the interest in 1666: *A Prophesie that huth lyen hid above these 2000 yeares* (1610), p. 45; *C.S.P.D., 1629–31*, p. 327;

was 1656, since this was the number of years which were supposed to have elapsed between the Creation and the Flood.[125] But a good case could be made for various other years, particularly around the end of the seventeenth century.[126]

These speculations had long been taken seriously by scholars and theologians; by 1649 there were said to have been some eighty books published in England on the subject.[127] Millennial expectations, in the sense of a belief in the imminent collapse of Anti-Christ, were now very widely diffused among the orthodox religious groups.[128] But under the pressure of the Civil War and its aftermath the calculation of the Second Coming ceased to be a donnish hobby and became a matter of intense concern to the uneducated. As early as May 1643 Parliamentary troops in the Wallingford area were discussing a report that Christ was coming to destroy Charles I, and that the Earl of Essex was John the Baptist. Four years later William Sedgwick, preacher at Ely Cathedral, set out for London with the news 'that the world will be at an end within fourteen days, Christ then coming to judgment, and that Christ appeared to him in his study the

---

1663–4, pp. 468, 652; *1665–6*, p. 184; Brand, *Antiquities*, iii, pp. 267–8; *Diary of Thomas Burton*, ed. J. T. Rutt (1828), i, p. cxlvii, n.; Heywood, *Diaries*, iii, p. 93; J. B. Williams, *Memoirs of ... Sir Matthew Hale* (1835), p. 224; *The Last Letters to the London-Merchants and Faithful Ministers* (1666); W. Lilly, *Merlini Anglici Ephemeris* (1667), sigs. A3–4ᵛ; E. N. Hooker, 'The Purpose of Dryden's *Annus Mirabilis*', *Huntington Lib. Qtly.*, x (1946–7).

125. e.g., R. Saunders, *Apollo Anglicus* (1656), sig. C7; Nuttall, *The Holy Spirit*, p. 109; id., *Visible Saints* (Oxford, 1957), p. 146; J. Swan, *Speculum Mundi* (Cambridge, 1635), p. 20; *The Records of a Church of Christ, Meeting in Broadmead, Bristol, 1640–87*, ed. E. B. Underhill (Hanserd Knollys Soc., 1847), p. 60.

126. Some favourite dates are assembled in Swan, *Speculum Mundi*, pp. 9–27, and *Memoirs of the Life of Mr Ambrose Barnes*, ed. W. H. D. Longstaffe (Surtees Soc., 1867), pp. 246–7. See also L. F. Brown, *The Political Activities of the Baptists and Fifth Monarchy Men* (New York, 1911,) pp. 23–4; C. Hill, 'Newton and His Society', *Texas Quarterly*, 1967, pp. 41–3, and *Antichrist in Seventeenth-century England*, p. 111.

127. Nuttall, *Visible Saints*, p. 157. See Froom, *The Prophetic Faith of Our Fathers*, ii, pp. 512–18, 524–5, 535–97. For the trial of a Catholic, who predicted on the basis of Daniel that James I would die in 1621, see *Cobbett's Complete Collection of State Trials*, ii (1809), cols. 1085–8.

128. As has been recently emphasized by W. M. Lamont, *Godly Rule* (1969), and J. F. Wilson, *Pulpit in Parliament* (Princeton, N.J., 1969), chap. vii. See B. S. Capp, '*Godly Rule* and English Millenarianism', *Past and Present*, lii (1971).

last week at Ely and told him so'.[129] The active millenarianism of the
Parliamentarians thus co-existed with the older belief in an imminent
Doomsday.

For the most part the feeling was one of excited but passive expectation. But the prospect that the Four Monarchies (Babylon, Persia,
Greece and Rome) might now be followed by the rule of the Saints
brought forth an activist group: the Fifth Monarchy Men, who
played a prominent part in English politics from 1651 onwards. To
attain the millennium, this association of preachers, soldiers and
urban lower classes was prepared to resort to political action and, in
the case of a minority, even violence. The forthcoming utopia was an
obvious projection of their own social ideals. The rule of the Saints
was to be marked by the abolition of tithes, the reform of the law, the
raising of the humble, and the pulling down of the great. There would
be no painful labour, no premature death, no famine: 'there is no
creature comfort, no outward blessing, which the Saints shall then
want'.[130] But their impact on events was pathetically slight. After the
collapse of the Barebones Parliament in December 1653 they maintained a vociferous but ineffective opposition to the Protectorate. The
end came with the failure of armed risings led by the wine-cooper,
Thomas Venner, in 1657 and 1661, although traces of Fifth Monarchist sentiment lingered on for some years. After the Restoration
millenarianism relapsed into its more passive intellectual mood again;
the prospects for 1666 or 1697 were keenly discussed, but there was
never again to be so active an attempt to give history a push.

It is hard to say for certain just why this brief but notable shift
from passive to active millenarianism should have occurred during
the Interregnum. Probably more important than the effects of the
high prices and other economic hardships of the later 1640s was the
apocalyptic sense generated by an awareness of living in a time of
unprecedented political change. The realization that the Civil War
and the execution of the King had no parallel in earlier English history exerted a decisive influence. It explains why radicals like the

129. *Journal of Sir Samuel Luke*, ed. I. G. Philip (Oxfordshire Rec. Soc.,
1950), p. 76; A. G. Matthews, *Calamy Revised* (Oxford, 1934), p. 432; *Clarke
Papers*, i, p. 4. The millenarianism of the 1640s is surveyed in B. S. Capp,
*The Fifth Monarchy Men. A Study in Seventeenth-century English
Millenarianism* (1972), chap. 2.

130. Cary, *The Little Horns Doom*, p. 302. Dr Capp's book is a comprehensive study.

Levellers were able to break away from the idea that a precedent had always to be cited in defence of any political proposal, and could self-consciously reject the past as irrelevant.[131] It also accounts for the conviction held by so many of the Civil War sects that the period in which they lived was somehow the climax of human history, the era for which all previous events had been a mere preparation. For the Fifth Monarchy Men it was above all the execution of King Charles which left the way open for King Jesus. When after so signal a deliverance the Rump and Cromwell in turn failed to inaugurate the new era it seemed necessary for the Saints to act for themselves.

The social anthropologist can recognize in the millenarian sentiment of the Interregnum a parallel phenomenon to the chiliastic movements which still occur in the underdeveloped countries of today. The 'cargo' cults of Melanesia involve ritual practices designed to secure European riches ('cargo') from a supernatural source. They display the same note of expectancy and waiting for an imminent deliverance. Such movements are normally said to be produced by a sense of blockage and deprivation, experienced by those unintegrated and disorientated members of society to whom ordinary political action seems to offer no hope of relief.[132] To some extent the Fifth Monarchy Men also fit this description. But their economic hardships had been long endured; it was not their social situation which gave them their new hope of deliverance, but the striking series of events set in motion by the execution of the King. Certain local ingredients also gave them a distinctive flavour: the belief that the English were an Elect Nation, specially chosen for the accomplishment of God's purposes; the long tradition of Biblical exegesis; and the widespread faith in the prophetic potentialities open to the Biblical commentator, particularly when he claimed to be divinely inspired.

Even so, active millenarianism could never have got under way but for the breakdown of the censorship during the Interregnum and the collapse of many traditional social controls. Conversely, it was

131. See below, pp. 512–13.
132. *Millennial Dreams in Action*, ed. S. L. Thrupp (Supplement ii to *Comparative Studies in Society and History* [The Hague, 1962]); P. Lawrence, *Road Belong Cargo* (Manchester, 1964). There is a stimulating discussion of the political function of millenarianism in P. Worsley, *The Trumpet Shall Sound* (1957).

only the firm maintenance of social order during the previous century which had prevented some of the pre-Civil War prophets and pseudo-Messiahs from attracting a substantial following. As it was, Traske, Farnham and Bull had founded sects, while Hacket had been followed by 'a great multitude of lads and young persons of the meaner sort'.[133] But for prompt government intervention, any one of them might have triggered off a millenarian explosion. Chiliastic sentiment had been endemic in English society since at least the fifteenth century, and it was primarily the absence of the normal restraints which made the Civil War period so remarkable for the extent and variety of its millenarian activity.

The spate of prophecy was sharply checked by the Restoration, the return of the Anglican Church, and the persecution of the Dissenting sects. The governing classes were determined to prevent any recurrence of the social anarchy of the Interregnum years and most of the sectarians themselves were anxious to demonstrate their law-abiding character. There were still some visionaries who claimed direct revelations from God or who uttered prophecies of imminent doom,[134] but after the 1660s they became less common. The Fifth Monarchists melted away; and when another would-be Elias, John Mason, Rector of Water Stratford, Buckinghamshire, assembled with his small group of followers in 1694 to await the millennium, they aroused contemporary amusement rather than indignation.[135] But many Anglican clergy remained passive millenarians and the break with the prophetic past was only gradual. From 1697 the distinctly middle-class Society of Philadelphians began to publish testimonies concerning the imminence of the millennium. In 1707 three of the Camisard prophets, who had come from France after their persecution by Louis XIV, were put in the pillory in Lon-

133. Cosin, *Conspiracie for pretended reformation*, sig. I4.
134. Examples (excluding numerous Quaker prophets) in *The Revelation ... unto ... Anne Wentworth* (1679); Josten, *Ashmole*, p. 1498; *C.S.P.D.*, *1661–2*, p. 81; *1663–4*, p. 161, *1680–1*, p. 151; N. Glass, *The Early History of the Independent Church at Rothwell* (1871), p. 57; N. Luttrell, *A Brief Historical Relation* (Oxford, 1857), i, p. 86; G. D. Nokes, *A History of the Crime of Blasphemy* (1928), pp. 47–8.
135. C. Hill, *Puritanism and Revolution* (1958), chap. 12, for an entertaining account. The contemporary correspondence in B.M., Add. MS 34,274, ff. 142–4, adds a few details. Like many of his predecessors, Mason saw himself as Elijah and appointed two followers as Witnesses (F. Hutchinson, *A Short View of the Pretended Spirit of Prophecy* [1708], p. 45).

don for announcing that the Last Days had begun; in that year over four hundred persons were said to be prophesying in different parts of the country.[136] As late as 1746 William Whiston, Isaac Newton's successor as Lucasian Professor at Cambridge, could assume that the millennium was only twenty years off.[137]

Changes in public opinion are always difficult to chart. In the nineteenth century the English countryside periodically threw up village Messiahs as bizarre as any to be found during the Interregnum, and the calculation of the number of the Beast long remained an indoor sport for eccentric clergymen. During the French Revolutionary and Napoleonic period prophetic preaching and writing in England were extensive.[138] But such survivals should not blind us to the change which had occurred. Even in the Middle Ages some sophisticated observers had regarded the activities of so-called religious prophets as a form of mental illness.[139] In the seventeenth century this attitude became increasingly common. Bacon and Hobbes explored the physical and psychological explanations for vivid dreams and premonitions. Bishop Sprat stressed that sickness could masquerade as inspiration. Others pointed to the physical connection between the fasting and austerity of the sects and their readiness to prophesy and see visions. Many would-be religious enthusiasts were locked up as insane. By 1655 Meric Casaubon could go so far as to declare that every case of religious ecstasy was no more than 'a degree and species of epilepsy'.[140] In the later seventeenth century it became orthodox to declare that the gift of prophecy had ceased; God had sent all the revelation that was needed and the books of

136. Whiting, *Studies in English Puritanism*, pp. 298–308; D. P. Walker, *The Decline of Hell* (1964), chaps. xiii-xv; *D.N.B.*, 'Lacy, John'; J. Sutherland, *Background for Queen Anne* (1939), pp. 225–6.

137. *D.N.B.*, 'Whiston, W.'

138. See, e.g., Froom, *The Prophetic Faith of Our Fathers*, ii, pp. 640–95; E. P. Thompson, *The Making of the English Working Class* (1963), pp. 116–19, 382–8; R. Matthews, *English Messiahs* (1936); P. G. Rogers, *Battle in Bossenden Wood* (1961). The prophetic literature of the 1790s would repay analysis.

139. R. Klibansky *et al.*, *Saturn and Melancholy* (1964), p. 94.

140. Bacon, *Works*, ii, pp. 666–7; iv, pp. 376–7; Hobbes, *Leviathan*, chaps. 27, 32, 33; Sprat, *History of the Royal Society*, p. 359; Hill, *Puritanism and Revolution*, p. 335; id., *Intellectual Origins of the English Revolution*, p. 121; Hunter and Macalpine, *Three Hundred years of Psychiatry, 1535–1860*, pp. 103–5; M. Casaubon, *A Treatise concerning Enthusiasme* (1655), p. 95; (J. Twysden), *A Short Discourse of the Truth and Reasonableness of the Religion delivered by Jesus Christ* (1662), pp. 240–1.

Daniel and Revelation were to be understood metaphorically, not literally. 'If a man pretend to me that God hath spoken to him supernaturally and immediately and I make doubt of it', remarked Hobbes, 'I cannot easily perceive what argument he can produce to oblige me to believe it.'[141] By 1700 even the Qakers had come to regard prophecy as distinctly odd.[142] The common lawyers consolidated the movement of opinion by ruling that it was an offence to pretend to extraordinary commissions from God or to terrify the people with threatened judgements.[143] The change may be best expressed by saying that in the sixteenth century the claims of a would-be prophet would always be seriously investigated, even if ultimately exposed as groundless, but by the eighteenth century the majority of educated men concurred in dismissing them *a priori* as inherently ridiculous.[144]

4. *Conclusion*

Religion, therefore, did not immediately lose all its wonder-working qualities as a result of the Reformation. It is true that the most extravagant claims for its material efficacy were made by the sects of the Civil War period, and they may fairly be regarded as untypical, both by virtue of their relatively small numbers (the Quakers, the most numerous, had only between thirty and forty thousand members by 1660), and because of the unusually chaotic circumstances of the Interregnum years. But it has been seen that the possibility of prophecy, miracle-working and successful prayer was also maintained in more conventional circles.

It should, however, be emphasized that some of these activities were prized for their side-effects as much as for their overt purpose. They would be misunderstood if they were taken only at face value. The Elizabethans who gathered together to pray for the ending of the plague were not simply engaging in a form of magic intended to

141. Hobbes, *Leviathan*, chap. 32. cf. John Wildman at Putney in 1647; *The Clarke Papers*, ed. Firth, i, p. 384.

142. Barbour, *The Quakers in Puritan England*, p. 234; R. S. Mortimer, 'Warnings and Prophecies', *Journ. of the Friends' Hist. Soc.*, xliv (1952); W.C. Braithwaite, *The Second Period of Quakerism* (119), p. 603.

143. W. Hawkins, *A Treatise of the Pleas of the Crown* (2nd edn, 1724), i, p. 7.

144. But for a Shropshire prophet who claimed in 1741 to be in regular communication with Sir Robert Walpole and the Archbishop of Canterbury, see *H.M.C., Egmont Diary*, iii, pp. 178–9, 226.

be materially efficacious. They asked God for relief, it is true, though without any certainty that it would be granted. But they were also testifying publicly to the concern aroused in the whole community by the threat which confronted it. By assembling together . they demonstrated their social solidarity in face of the epidemic; and, by confessing the sins which they thought might have occasioned it, they reaffirmed the ethical standards of their society. Such corporate manifestations were a valuable means of checking panic and dis-order. Even today at times of national emergency people will pack the churches without necessarily believing that in so doing they are increasing their prospects of material relief. They turn to religious ritual because they gain comfort from participating in this manifes-tation of the community's unity in face of crisis. In this sense prayer can never be in vain. The rite has what sociologists call a latent function, no less than a manifest one. As an anthropologist has re-marked of the religious ceremonies employed by the Dinka of the Sudan, 'instrumental efficacy is not the only kind of efficacy to be derived from their symbolic action. The other kind is achieved in the action itself.'[145]

Such considerations must be borne in mind if we are to discern the full meaning of the special prayers of the Elizabethans or the General Fasts and Days of Humiliation celebrated in the mid seventeenth century. Nor should we forget the numerous political purposes which such occasions could serve. An Elizabethan Puritan would zealously attend an organized fast in order to meet fellow members of the godly party; the occasion was a manifestation of collective solidarity. The leaders of the Long Parliament used Fast Day sermons as a means of rallying members and signalling changes in the party line.[146] The New Model Army also proclaimed fasts as a preliminary to some new effort : an Army fast, observed a Royalist contemporary, usually heralded some new act of mischief, for Crom-well's soldiers never sought the Lord until the time was ripe.[147]

A comparable symbolic function was discharged by the petition-ary prayer of individuals at moments of intense personal difficulty.

145. M. Douglas, *Purity and Danger* (1966), p. 68 (expounding Lienhardt, *Divinity and Experience*, which affords an excellent statement of this view [see, e.g., pp. 234, 240, 289, 291–2]).

146. Collinson, *The Elizabethan Puritan Movement*, pp. 214–15; H. R. Trevor-Roper, *Religion, the Reformation and Social Change* (1967), chap. 6.

147. Price, *The Mystery and Method of his Majesty's Happy Restaura-tion*, pp. 87–8.

The ritual helped men to focus their attention and to take stock of their situation. It also allayed anxiety by mitigating their feelings of helplessness. The moral strength to be derived from this procedure is not to be underrated. The psalms which Cromwell's troops sang on the eve of battle or the prayers which the Marian martyrs uttered to sustain them in their agonies were not superfluous irrelevancies; they made such achievements possible.[148]

Public prayers could also help members of society to suspend the pursuit of their own private interests and to concentrate on problems common to the whole community. The decline of special days of national prayer and supplication bears some relation to the uninhibited growth of class-consciousness and sectional interests. In 1853 the Presbytery of Edinburgh petitioned Queen Victoria for a national fast against the cholera. Lord Palmerston brushed the request aside with the suggestion that scrubbing brushes and chloride of lime would be more to the point.[149] He is normally commended for the 'rationalism' displayed in this action; but it may well be thought that his was a shallow view when compared with that of those social conservatives who saw church-going and national intercession as a means of patching over the divisive interests of class and of diverting attention from social causes of popular misfortunes.

Some weight should also be given to the therapeutic possibilities of prayer when used as a means of faith-healing. When we learn that one of George Fox's patients, John Banks, had visions that Fox alone would be able to cure him, we are not surprised to discover that he turned out to be one of the Quaker leader's successful cases; on the other hand, when Fox met a cripple at Kendal and told him to throw away his crutches, it is no wonder that, although the man did so, he still remained a cripple.[150]

The social functions of religious prophecy will be better under-

148. For a striking example, see the account by a late-seventeenth-century sailor of how God came to his aid at every stage of a fight with a Frenchman, quoted in full by W. James, *The Varieties of Religious Experience* (32nd imp., 1920), p. 471 n. cf. R. R. Willoughby, 'Magic and Cognate Phenomena: an Hypothesis', in *A Handbook of Social Psychology*, ed. C. Murchison (Worcester, Mass., 1935), p. 489; M. Spiro, 'Religion: Problems of Definition', *Anthropological Approaches to the Study of Religion*, ed. M. Banton (1966), pp. 113–14.

149. E. Ashley, *The Life and Correspondence of . . . Viscount Palmerston* (1879), ii, pp. 265–6.

150. Fox, *Journal*, ii, pp. 466–7; *George Fox's 'Book of Miracles'*, p. 21. For a fuller discussion of faith-healing, see below, pp. 246–51.

stood when compared with the various kinds of non-religious prophecy with which it competed. But certain conclusions suggest themselves even at this stage. One is the role of prophecy as a validating myth. Men drew upon visions and revelations in order to persuade others of the rightness of the course upon which they had embarked. Dreams, for example, could serve as an external sanction for policies which were otherwise difficult to recommend. The Lincolnshire knight who informed King Henry II that the voices of St Peter and the Archangel Gabriel had told him to present a number of demands foreshadowing Magna Carta was perhaps the first of many English radicals who thought it safer to claim a supernatural sanction for their political programme. The Digger prophet, William Everard, who in 1649 pleaded a divine vision as authority for his communist ideas, was in the same tradition. Indeed it was the agency of a dream which led the Diggers to choose St George's Hill as the site for their experiment.[151] Dreams provided men with the authority to take decisions, identify thieves and engage in controversial activity. The case of Maria Marten of the Red Barn (1828) is only the most famous of the murder mysteries resolved by denunciation on the alleged basis of a dream.[152] Conversely, it was possible to commit murder under the influence of the spirit: in 1633 Enoch ap Evan, a farmer's son from Clun, Shropshire, killed his mother and brother, after quarrelling with them over whether communion should be received kneeling, a topic on which he had recently received divine inspiration.[153]

One should, therefore, hesitate before dismissing all these prophets and healers as psychotics, the victims of hallucination brought on by

151. W. L. Warren, *King John* (1961), p. 179; Whitelocke, *Memorials*, iii, p. 18; *The Works of Gerrard Winstanley*, ed. G. H. Sabine (Ithaca, N.Y., 1941). pp. 15, 260.

152. D. Gibbs and H. Maltby, *The True Story of Maria Marten* (Ipswich, 1949), pp. 32–3. For earlier cases, J. Cotta, *The Infallible True and Assured Witch* (1624), pp. 149–50; F. Nicholson and E. Axon, *The Older Nonconformity in Kendal* (Kendal, 1915), pp. 250–6; J. Beaumont, *An Historical, Physiological and Theological Treatise of Spirits* (1705), pp. 240–4; Seafield, *Literature and Curiosities of Dreams*, pp. 386–8.

153. *C.S.P.D.*, 1633–4, pp. 133, 162, 183; P. Studley, *The Looking-Glasse of Schisme* (1635); the Puritans, however, disowned responsibility for this episode (R. More, *A True Relation of the Murders committed in the Parish of Clunne* [1641]); *Proceedings, Principally in the County of Kent*, ed. Larking, pp. 86–7). For a similar case, Collinson, *The Elizabethan Puritan Movement*, p. 150.

fasting or of hysteria induced by sexual repression.[154] It is not enough to describe such men as lunatics. One has to explain why their lunacy took this particular form. One cannot disregard the fact that religious prophecy and inspiration were potentially open to everyone. Only the qualified could teach, remarked a mid-seventeenth-century writer, but anyone might be inspired to prophesy.[155] Biblical exegesis or political philosophy were activities calling for a certain amount of education, and therefore largely restricted to the upper classes. Many of the prophets, by contrast, were persons of no education at all: Hacket and Farnham were illiterate, most of the sectarians were drawn from the ranks of artisans and petty tradesmen. For them prophecy was an easy way of gaining attention. As one enthusiast confessed, 'Sometimes the flesh . . . would put me forward with motives of pride, vain-glory, singularity, popular applause, getting a name, becoming famous, eminent and be[ing] taken notice of, as Mr Sedgwick, [and] Mr Saltmarsh were; and why should not I say something as well as they?'[156]

Naturally, this gave uncontrolled prophecy an anarchic character. As Thomas Cromwell wrote of the Nun of Kent: 'If credence should be given to every such lewd person as would affirm himself to have revelations from God, what readier way were there to subvert all commonwealths and good order in the world?'[157] The association between religious enthusiasm and social radicalism, always close, was strengthened during the Interregnum, when God, 'that mighty Leveller', as one contemporary called him,[158] was invoked as authority for every kind of revolutionary scheme. A typical example of popular aspirations cast in religious form was the divine vision attributed to John Brayne, a Winchester minister, in a broadside published in 1649:

Monarchy shall fall, first in England, then in France, then in Spain; and after in all Christendom; and when Christ hath put down this

154. N. Walker, *Crime and Insanity in England*, i (Edinburgh, 1968), p. 38, Cohn, *The Pursuit of the Millennium*, p. 336, and E. Le Roy Ladurie, *Les Paysans de Languedoc* (Paris, 1966), p. 644, n. 4, represent different versions of this approach.

155. E. Drapes, *Gospel-Glory Proclaimed* (1649), p. 10.

156. Pinnell, *A Word of Prophesy*, pp. 4–5.

157. *Three Chapters of Letters relating to the Suppression of Monasteries,* ed. Wright, p. 29.

158. G. Foster, *The Pouring Forth of the Seventh and Last Viall* (1659). sig. A3.

power, he himself will begin to reign, and first in England, where the meanest people that are now despised shall have first the revelation of truth, and it shall pass from them to other nations.[159]

It was to be a long time before sentiments of this kind could be safely expressed in non-religious form. Meanwhile religious prophecy provided an admirable vehicle for radical propaganda. As a Roman Catholic pointed out,

there is no reformer so forgetful or stupid, but his spirit pretends Scripture, the glory of the Lord, the light and liberty of the Gospel, the planting of saving truth, etc.; and whosoever is opposite to his Spirit is Anti-Christ, the Whore of Babylon, the Beast of the Apocalypse, and therefore must be pulled down, whosoever he be.[160]

The belief that God was on their side brought lower-class radicals self-confidence and revolutionary dynamism. It was correspondingly resented by the men of property, who were naturally offended, as one Fifth Monarchist put it, 'that a company of illiterate men and silly women should pretend to any skill in dark prophecies, and to a foresight of future events, which the most learned Rabbis, and the most knowing politicians have not presumed to hope for'.[161] After the Restoration religious enthusiasm and levelling were bracketed together in the minds of the ruling classes. They saw them as joint aspects of what Bishop Atterbury was to call the 'desperate contrivance of the needy to bring all things into common'; [162] and they did not tire of insisting that the voice of the people should never again be confused with the voice of God.

159. *A Vision which one Mr Brayne (one of the ministers of Winchester) had in September, 1647* (brs., 1649).
160. Preface by N. Strange to *A Missive to his Majesty of Great Britain, King James, written divers yeers since by Doctor Carier* (Paris, 1649), p. 24.
161. Preface by C. Feake to Cary, *The Little Horns Doom*, sig. A6.
162. Quoted by U. Lee, *The Historical Backgrounds of Early Methodist Enthusiasm* (New York, 1931), p. 106.

6.

RELIGION AND THE PEOPLE

On Nov 4 1681 as I travel'd towards Wakefield about Hardger moor I met with a boy, who would needs be talking. I begun to ask him some questions about the principles of religion; he could not tell me how many gods there be, nor persons in the godhead, nor who made the world nor anything about Jesus Christ, nor heaven or hell, or eternity after this life, nor for what end he came into the world, nor what condition he was born in – I askt him whether he thought he was a sinner; he told me he hop't not; yet this was a witty boy and could talk of any worldly things skilfully enough ... he is 10 yeares of age, cannot read and scarce ever goes to church.

Oliver Heywood, *Diaries,* iv, p. 24

It was never merry England since we were impressed to come to the church.

Browne, the lighterman at Ramsgate, 1581
(*Archaeologia Cantiana,* xxvi [1904], p. 32)

1. *The Church and society*

EVEN after the Reformation, therefore, organized religion continued to help men cope with the practical problems of daily life by providing an explanation for misfortune and a source of guidance in times of uncertainty. There were also attempts to use it for divination and supernatural healing. Why then did some find it necessary to have recourse to magic, astrology and other non-religious systems of belief? This is the problem with which much of the rest of this book will be concerned.

The strength of the challenge presented by these less orthodox beliefs is at first glance very surprising, in view of the apparently impregnable position occupied by the official religion of the post-Reformation period. For the Anglican Church was nothing less than society itself in one of its most important manifestations.[1] Every

1. Further information on this subject may be found in S. L. Ware, *The Elizabethan Parish in Its Ecclesiastical and Financial Aspects* (Baltimore, 1908); A. Heales, *The History and Law of Church Seats or Pews. I. History* (1872); and in Dr Christopher Hill's discussions of the social role of religion in *Economic Problems of the Church from Archbishop Whitgift to the Long Parliament* (Oxford, 1956) and *Society and Puritanism in Pre-revolutionary England* (1964).

child was deemed to be born into it. He was expected to be baptized by the local clergyman and sent by his parents or employer to be catechized in the rudiments of the faith. It was a criminal offence for a man to stay away from church on Sundays, and the very mode of worship there symbolized the society in which he lived. Like the carefully arranged processions of the medieval Church, the Anglican seating arrangements reflected the social gradations among the parishioners; the women were separated from the men and the young women from the matrons; the rich sat in front and the poor at the back. Sometimes the humbler members of the congregation stood up and bowed out of respect when the gentry came in.[2] The 'better sort' might communicate on a separate day; and in some parishes even the quality of the communion wine varied with the social quality of the recipients.[3]

Men's attitude to God himself reflected the same social conventions. In church they took off their hats and knelt down, just as they uncovered their heads and knelt before their social superiors. God was 'the great landlord', as some preachers called him;[4] or he was an authoritarian father whose attributes were those of the fathers men themselves knew. His ordinances were those of society itself. A Kentish parson taught in 1543 that there was not one Heaven but three: one for very poor men; the second for men of a mean estate and condition; and the third for great men.[5]

But religious worship emphasized the unity of society as well as its social divisions. It was a collective act – 'common prayer' – an affirmation of social solidarity. As such, religious worship emphasized the common concerns which all members of society shared. In addition to superintending the rites of passage which gave meaning and social recognition to the stages of a man's life, the Church also provided the moral teaching upon which society rested. Homilies, sermons and catechizings played a crucial part in the

2. *Anecdotes and Traditions*, ed. W. J. Thoms (Camden Soc., 1839), p. 59; *Documents relating to Cambridgeshire Villages*, ed. W. M. Palmer and H. W. Saunders (Cambridge, 1925–6), iv, p. 73.

3. Hill, *Society and Puritanism*, p. 427; Norfolk R.O., MSC 9 (articles against James Buck, no. 28); Ware, *The Elizabethan Parish*, p. 79; H. N. Brailsford, *The Levellers and the English Revolution*, ed. C. Hill (1961), p. 45; *Elizabethan Churchwardens' Accounts*, ed. J. E. Farmiloe and R. Nixseaman (Pubs. Beds. Hist. Rec. Soc., 1953), p. xxviii.

4. R. Bernard, *The Ready Way to Good Works* (1635), p. 7; N. Homes, *Plain Dealing* (1652), p. 33.

5. *L.P.*, xviii (2), p. 294.

formation of every citizen; most observers agreed that society would have been impossible without them, or the supernatural sanctions on which they rested.

The Church was also a huge landowner, and its leaders, the bishops and archbishops, sat in the House of Lords and played a prominent part in politics and government. It also controlled public opinion. Clerics played a dominant part in the censorship of the press, the licensing of school-masters and doctors, and the government of the universities. In an age without radio, television or (until the mid seventeenth century) newspapers, the pulpit was the most important means of direct communication with the people. Contemporary sermons discussed not just theology, but morals, politics, economics and current affairs generally. The Church's tentacles stretched out through the ecclesiastical courts, which exercised a wide jurisdiction over marriage and divorce, defamation, the probate of wills and every conceivable aspect of private morality. If a man quarrelled with his wife, committed adultery with his housemaid, gossiped maliciously about his neighbours, worked on a saint's day or lent money at interest, it was before the ecclesiastical court that he was likely to come. There he might be compelled to undergo some humiliating form of public penance or even be excommunicated, that is to say expelled from the sacraments of the Church and, in its more severe form, subjected to total social and economic ostracism by the rest of the community; a punishment which reflected the assumed identity of Church and society.

This great social and administrative structure was not financed simply from its own endowments, but from the tithes, church rates and miscellaneous fees which the parishioners were required to pay to the clergy. Neither were its functions purely ecclesiastical. The parish was the lowest administrative unit in the country, used for a variety of secular purposes. The church building itself was an important meeting-place where men did business.

The religious groups which came to exist outside the Anglican Church provided the same all-embracing framework. The Dissenters re-created the values of the shared community by exercising a close supervision over the personal lives of their members, providing machinery for the adjudication of their internal disputes, and regulating intimate matters with which even the church courts might have hesitated to interfere. 'Brother Smith . . . for having no conjugal affection . . . Brother Campion for proffering love to one sister whilst engaged to another': these items from the agenda of an Independent congregation in Northamptonshire indicate the extent to which the sects tried to guide the lives of their members.[6] It is not surprising that they were particularly successful in London, where they may well have functioned as a home-from-home for first-generation immigrants, just as in modern South Africa separatist churches have helped to fill the gap created by decaying tribal loyalties.[7]

Religion, therefore, had a multi-dimensional character which gave it an importance which contemporary magical beliefs could never rival. They lacked its institutional framework, its systematic theology, its moral code and its wide range of social functions. Nevertheless, orthodox religion did not enjoy a monopoly of popular loyalty, and in several respects it was highly vulnerable to competition from outside.

2. *The need for advice*

The parish clergyman did not merely preside over the formal occasion of religious worship. He was also expected to be a guide and mentor to his parishioners. When disputes broke out between the laity it was to him they were ideally referred. It was often claimed that there were fewer lawsuits in Catholic countries because their priests acted as arbiters for their flocks.[8] But the same ideal of clerical counselling was to be found in a Protestant environment. George Herbert expected the model parson to be a lawyer as well as a pastor: 'He endures not that any of his flock should go to law; but in any controversy that they should resort to him as their judge.' Bishop Williams of Lincoln was praised by his biographer for arbitrating in contentious matters so as to avoid litigation; while Samuel Fairclough was only one of many Puritan ministers who were famous for making up quarrels between their parishioners.[9] Peace-making was

6. N. Glass, *The Early History of the Independent Church at Rothwell* (Northampton, 1871), pp. 77, 75. cf. the comments of C. Hill, *Reformation to Industrial Revolution* (1967), p. 166, and B. R. Wilson, *Sects and Society* (1961), p. 354.

7. B. G. M. Sundkler, *Bantu Prophets in South Africa* (2nd end, 1961), and B. A. Pauw, *Religion in a Tswana Chiefdom* (1960).

8. A. O. Meyer, *England and the Catholic Church under Elizabeth*, trans. J. R. McKee (1916), p. 209. cf. Aubrey, *Miscellanies*, p. 220.

9. G. Herbert, *A Priest to the Temple* (1652), chap. xxiii; J. Hacket, *Scrinia Reserata* (1693), ii, p. 61; S. Clarke, *The Lives of Sundry Eminent Persons* (1683), i, p. 175; ii, pp. 120–1; id., *The Lives of Two and Twenty*

a duty incumbent upon all brands of clergy. During the Civil War the lawyers in Parliament were said to have fallen out with their Presbyterian allies, 'not so much upon conscience, as upon fear that the Presbytery spoil their market, and take up most of the country pleas without law'.[10] It is notable, moreover, that the method which George Herbert prescribed for the clerical reconciliation of disputes made the parson the medium through whom the collective sentiments of the whole community were expressed. For when faced by a controversy, the priest 'never decides it alone; but sends for three or four of the ablest of the parish to hear the cause with him, whom he makes to deliver their opinion first; out of which he gathers, in case he be ignorant himself, what to hold'.[11]

The clerical performance of these tasks, however, had been much weakened by the abolition of the confessional at the Reformation. It is impossible to assess the full nature and working of auricular confession in the Middle Ages, for the evidence simply does not exist; and it would be very easy to exaggerate the sacrament's importance in the life of the Catholic laity. An annual appearance at confession was thought adequate by some clergy, and the layman was seldom required to confess more than three times a year unless he felt himself in deadly sin or imminent danger of death.[12] Confession was thus a relatively infrequent occurrence in the lives of most men, though it was no doubt possible to save up important matters to be ventilated on such occasions. It is hard to tell exactly what passed between the priest and the penitent, though the many extant manuals for medieval confessors make it fairly clear what was supposed to happen: the layman was to confess the sins he had committed since last being shriven, to be examined in the articles of his faith, and to be interrogated about other possible sins of which he had also been guilty but which he had not confessed. The priest then pronounced absolution and imposed some appropriate penance,

---

English Divines (appended to *A General Martyrologie* (1660)), p. 210. On the Church's peace-making role, see also below, p. 628.

10. *The Letters and Journals of Robert Baillie*, ed. D. Laing (Edinburgh, 1841–2), ii, p. 360.

11. Herbert, op. cit.

12. B. L. Manning, *The People's Faith in the Time of Wyclif* (Cambridge, 1919), p. 32; W. Lyndwood, *Provinciale* (Oxford, 1679), p. 343; (W. Harrington), *In this Boke are Conteyned the Comendacions of Matrymony* (1528), sig. Eiii. The English *Prymer* (Rouen, 1538), however, urged weekly shriving; F. A. Gasquet, *The Eve of the Reformation* (1900), p. 287.

usually the recitation of prayers. All this, moreover, took place with a relative lack of privacy, for the modern box confessional was an innovation of the sixteenth century.

This procedure was well designed to secure the enforcement of religious morality, and its disappearance at the Reformation was generally thought to have left a vacuum which even the increasingly active ecclesiastical courts were unable to fill. The personal confession and interrogation of every single layman was potentially an altogether more comprehensive system of social discipline than the isolated prosecution of relatively notorious offenders. The medieval priest, for example, had been able to act as an agent for the detection of theft; there are known cases in which stolen money was handed back as a result of his interrogations.[13] Some Protestants accordingly looked back to the Middle Ages as a time when the clergy had been able to enforce the standards they taught. 'Then were the consciences of the people kept in so great awe by confession,' wrote John Aubrey, 'that just dealing and virtue was habitual.'[14] Sir Edwin Sandys tells us that before he set out upon his European travels he had always assumed that the confessional was an effective means of discipline and 'a very great restraint to wickedness' (in fact he was to be disappointed, for he found that it operated in a very perfunctory way).[15] The theme was taken up by many Catholic propagandists. The abolition of the confessional had weakened the fabric of society, declared the Catholic émigré, Benjamin Carier:

> The servants have great liberty against their masters by this means, the children against their parents, the people against their prelates, the subjects against their King ... for without the use of this sacrament neither can inferiors be kept in awe, but by the gallows, ... nor superiors be ever told of their errors but by rebellion.[16]

Modern population studies suggest that the rate of illegitimacy and pre-nuptial pregnancy may have been higher in seventeenth-century England than in seventeenth-century France.[17] If this con-

13. C. T. Martin in *Archaeologia*, lx(2) (1907), pp. 361–3. cf. below, pp. 599–601.   14. Aubrey, *Miscellanies*, p. 218.

15. (Sir E. Sandys), *Europae Speculum* (Hague, 1629), p. 10.

16. *A Missive to His Majesty of Great Britain, King James, written Divers Yeers since by Doctor Carier* (Paris, 1649), p. 48.

17. cf. P. Goubert, *Beauvais et le Beauvaisis de 1600 à 1730* (Paris, 1960), pp. 31, 69; id. in *Population in History*, ed. D. V. Glass and D. E. C. Eversley (1965), p. 468; and in *Daedalus* (Spring, 1968), p. 594; L. Pérouas, *Le Diocèse*

jecture turns out to be true, it will be tempting to see the presence or
absence of the confessional as the decisive factor, just as Victorian
commentators attributed the superior chastity of Irish girls to the
same circumstance.[18] Indeed the notable correlation between high
illegitimacy rates and Protestantism which so impressed nineteenth-
century demographers did not go unnoticed in the seventeenth century. George Hickes, the future Non-Juror and philologist, observed
in a remarkable attack upon the Scottish Presbyterians in 1677 that

> as for adulteries and fornications, those common failings of these
> Pharisees, there are more of them committed, and more bastards born
> within their country, the Western Holy-land, than in all our nation
> besides. This is evident from comparing the parish registers and the
> registers of the presbyteries or rural deaneries of those shires with the
> rest of the parish and presbytery registers in every diocese of the
> Church.[19]

This must have been one of the earliest recorded exercises in the
use of parish registers for sociological purposes, and it testifies to
the widespread conviction that the unaided Protestant conscience
was an inadequate sanction for morality, particularly sexual
morality.

In the Middle Ages the confessional had made it easier for the
layman to take his problems to the local parson. It had been a rule
that confessors should listen patiently to everything the penitent said,
regardless of its immediate relevance.[20] It may be reasonably surmised that a conscientious priest could find himself being asked for
advice on a wide variety of matters, not all of them necessarily spiritual. It was notoriously common for the person confessing to ex-
patiate upon the sins of his neighbours as well as his own. Only in
the eighteenth century was the practice of asking for names of
accomplices prohibited; every Protestant polemicist knew that the

de la Rochelle de 1648 à 1724 (Paris, 1964), p. 171; P. Laslett, The World
We Have Lost (1965), pp. 134, 140; E. A. Wrigley in Econ. Hist. Rev., 2nd
ser., xix (1966), p. 86.
  18. F. W. Newman, Miscellanies, iii (1889), p. 273; H. C. Lea, A History
of Auricular Confession, and Indulgences in the Latin Church (1896), ii,
pp. 433–5. But, as J.-L. Flandrin points out, figures about illegitimacy tell one
little about actual sexual behaviour unless one makes the (probably in-
correct) assumption that fornicating couples employed no form of contraception; Annales (économies, sociétés, civilisations), 24e année (1969).
  19. (G. Hickes), Ravillac Redivivus (1678), p. 73 ('53').
  20. Lyndwood, Provinciale, p. 328.

Roman priest was acquainted with the most intimate secrets of husbands and wives, masters and servants.[21] It was customary for a Catholic to enlist the aid of the priest when taking decisions about which he felt uncertain. In the seventeenth century a notorious example was Walter Whitford, who in 1649 organized the murder of Isaac Dorislaus, the Commonwealth envoy to the Netherlands, after consulting a popish confessor as to the propriety of the action.[22] The primary purpose of private confession, said a Laudian bishop, was 'to inform, instruct and counsel Christian people in their particular actions'.[23]

The Church of England had discarded regular auricular confession, but the clergy still wished to keep their role as counsellors and advisers to their flock. The Prayer Book required the curate when administering the Lord's Supper to exhort all those troubled in conscience or needing guidance to repair to him privately for 'ghostly counsel, advice and comfort'. Many bishops made a point of asking in their visitation articles whether this exhortation was being made and whether the secrecy of all resulting confessions was preserved, as required by the Canons of 1604.[24] Similar confessions were invited in the Order for the Visitation of the Sick. The Laudians were consequently accused of attempting to revive the practice of compulsory auricular confession;[25] and from time to time individual ministers got into trouble for privately ordering their parishioners to do penance without any warrant from the ecclesiastical courts.[26]

The fact was that most of the clergy felt wistful about the dis-

21. Lea, *A History of Auricular Confession*, i, pp. 394–5; W. Tyndale, *Doctrinal Treatises*, ed. H. Walter (Cambridge, P.S., 1848), p. 337.

22. *H.M.C., Portland*, i, pp. 591–2. cf. Lea, op. cit., ii, p. 440.

23. Francis White, Bishop of Ely, cited in C. Wordsworth, *Appendix to a Sermon on Evangelical Repentance* (1842), p. 77.

24. E. B. Pusey, *Preface to Abbé Gaume's Manual for Confessors* (2nd edn, Oxford, 1878), pp. xli–xliii.

25. *A Large Supplement of the Canterburian Self-Conviction* (1641), p. 61; J. White, *The First Century of Scandalous, Malignant Priests* (1643), pp. 29, 40, 43; *Walker Revised*, ed. A. G. Matthews (Oxford, 1948), p. 331; *H.M.C., House of Lords, addenda, 1514–1714*, p. 434; J. Rushworth, *Historical Collections* (1721), ii(2), pp. 1378–80; H. Foley, *Records of the English Province of the Society of Jesus* (1877–84), ii, p. 565.

26. P. Collinson, *The Elizabethan Puritan Movement* (1967), p. 347; Wells D.R., A 77 (Walter Rawlins, Vicar of Middlezoy, 1587–8). Questions were sometimes asked about this practice in contemporary visitation articles.

appearance of the confessional. The practice of confessing to a minister, on special occasions at least, was defended by Latimer, Ridley, Jewel, Ussher, and many other pillars of the Anglican Church.[27] The Presbyterian, Thomas Cartwright, recommended that those in doubt should 'hunt and seek out some discreet and learned minister of God's Word', for information, counsel and comfort about such matters as vows, marriage, restitution of goods and reconciliation with enemies.[28] The Puritan, Arthur Hildersham, agreed that private confession to the minister had certain advantages; Richard Greenham was quite certain that more had been lost than gained by abandoning the old system.[29] 'For want of auricular confession,' declared one Laudian clergyman, 'some have been brought to confess at the gallows.' 'It will never be well with the Church of England,' said another, 'until confession be set up in it.'[30] Everyone agreed that recourse to a minister at times of trouble might be, as Jeremy Taylor put it, 'of great use and benefit'.[31]

In place of the confessional the clergy tried to develop new means (in addition to preaching and exhortation) of influencing the laity in the making of their decisions. Casuistry, that is the resolution of moral dilemmas by skilled theologians, had been a feature of medieval handbooks for confessors; and in the seventeenth century Protestant divines turned out many volumes of 'cases of conscience', in which the educated reader might find the resolution of some hypothetical problem close to his own.[32] It was also possible for the godly layman to turn inwards, entrusting his doubts and uncertainties to a spiritual diary, and resolving his problems by recourse to prayer; the psychological function of the Puritan diary or autobio-

27. Many of these expressions of opinion were collected for partisan purposes in such nineteenth-century works as Wordsworth, *Appendix to a Sermon on Evangelical Repentance*, and Pusey's preface to *Abbé Gaume's Manual for Confessors*. cf. T. W. Drury, *Confession and Absolution* (1903).
28. *Cartwrightiana*, ed. A. Peel and L. H. Carlson (1951), pp. 92–7.
29. A. Hildersham, *CLII Lectures upon Psalm LI* (1635), pp. 164–6; *The Workes of ... Richard Greenham*, ed. H. H(olland) (5th edn, 1612), p. 359. cf. R. A. Marchant, *The Puritans and the Church Courts in the Diocese of York, 1560–1642* (1960), pp. 226–7.
30. White, *The First Century of Scandalous, Malignant Priests*, p. 39; N. Wallington, *Historical Notices of Events*, ed. R. Webb (1869), i, p. 192.
31. Quoted by Pusey in preface to *Abbé Gaume's Manual*, p. cxiii.
32. Some of this writing is discussed in T. Wood, *English Casuistical Divinity during the Seventeenth Century* (1952); G. L. Mosse, *The Holy Pretence* (Oxford, 1957); K. Kelly, *Conscience: Dictator or Guide?* (1967).

graphy was, as has often been pointed out, closely parallel to that of the Catholic confessional. But for most people there was no substitute for personal advice; as Jeremy Taylor remarked, 'men will for ever need a living guide'.[33] Godly figures like John Foxe had a charisma which attracted clients with troubled consciences from far and wide; and it has been justly remarked that many Puritan ladies tended to lean on a preacher for regular advice and guidance, just as devout Catholics had looked to their confessor.[34] Clerical counselling was an important form of psychotherapy, and the melancholic or would-be suicide was regularly referred to the clergy for help and comfort. Even the magician, John Dee, handed over cases of hysterical illness to the ministrations of godly preachers.[35] A skilled casuist, like the Biblical translator, John Rainolds, could thus become 'an oracle', resolving the doubts of all comers; the same term was applied to many of his colleagues.[36]

But this activity was too informal and uncoordinated to be capable of filling the gap left by the confessional. In any case, it took all sorts of clergy to make the Church; and they still included the ignorant, the non-resident, and the indifferent. In 1603 at least a sixth of all livings were held in plurality.[37] Even the best-intentioned minister could set a parish by the ears, for single-minded insistence on the elimination of vice could make him a figure of terror rather than an approachable counsellor; and, however great his devotion to duty, he had lost that faintly magical aura which could lurk behind even the least impressive medieval clerk. Besides, he could no longer compel men to seek his advice. It is not surprising that some of the laity should have turned for guidance to those who were less hesitant about claiming supernatural gifts or special access to some occult source of wisdom.

33. Quoted in Wood, op. cit., p. xiii.
34. J. F. Mozley, *John Foxe and his Book* (1940), p. 96; P. Collinson in *Studies in Church History*, ii, ed. G. J. Cuming (1965), p. 260.
35. R. Hunter and I. Macalpine, *Three Hundred Years of Psychiatry* (1963), p. 240; Ewen, ii, p. 186. cf. J. Sym, *Lifes Preservative against Self-Killing* (1637), p. 324.
36. Wood, *Life and Times,* i, p. 460; Heywood, *Diaries,* i, p. 43; Hunter and Macalpine, op. cit., p. 113; S. Clarke, *The Marrow of Ecclesiastical History* (2nd edn, 1654), pp. 851, 926, 931; id., *The Lives of Two and Twenty Divines,* pp. 210–11; *Memoirs of . . . Ambrose Barnes,* ed. W. H. D. Longstaffe (Surtees Soc., 1867), p. 422; Hacket, *Scrinia Reserata,* ii, pp. 61–2; *Samuel Hartlib and the Advancement of Learning,* ed. C. Webster (Cambridge, 1970), p. 76.   37. Hill, *Economic Problems of the Church,* p. 226.

3. *Ignorance and indifference*[38]

The attraction of non-religious systems of belief was enhanced by
the fact that the hold of orthodox religion upon the English people
had never been complete. Indeed it is problematical as to whether
certain sections of the population at this time had any religion at all.
Although complete statistics will never be obtainable, it can be
confidently said that not all Tudor or Stuart Englishmen went to
some kind of church, that many of those who did went with considerable reluctance, and that a certain proportion remained
throughout their lives utterly ignorant of the elementary tenets of
Christian dogma.

The extent of actual church attendance is impossible to assess,
though research currently being done on the few surviving contemporary censuses of communicants will tell us something about the
number of persons who made their annual Easter communion: results so far suggest that, although there was a wide variation between
parishes, the ninety-nine per cent performance of Easter duties
achieved by the Counter-Reformation Church in late seventeenth-
century France was almost never attained in England.[39] There is also
enough circumstantial evidence to show decisively that the actual extent of church-going never approached the legal ideal. Owing to the
constant shift of population, for example, some parish churches
were too small to hold even half of their potential congregation.[40]
Others were too far away.[41] Many of the recusants and Dissenters
who stayed away for reasons of conscience had their own form of
religious activity. But there was another class of absentee without
any such alibi. For below a certain social level the efforts of the
authorities to enforce the duty of church attendance appear to have
flagged. Archbishop Grindal's Injunctions for the Province of York

38. Much additional evidence relating to this and the following section
may be found in C. Hill, 'Plebeian Irreligion in England', in *Studien über
die Revolution*, ed M. Kossok (Berlin, 1969), which I missed when writing
this book.
    39. Laslett, *The World We Have Lost*, pp. 71–3. For France, see G. Le
Bras, *Études de sociologie religieuse* (Paris, 1955), i, pp. 276–7; Pérouas, *Le
Diocèse de la Rochelle de 1648 à 1724*, p. 162.
    40. Comments on their physical inadequacy may be found in *C.S.P.D.,
1625–6*, p. 525; *1637*, p. 125; (E. Chamberlayne), *Englands Wants* (1667),
pp. 6–7; N. G. Brett-James, *The Growth of Stuart London* (1935), p. 201;
R. Nelson, *An Address to Persons of Quality and Estate* (1715), p. 105.
    41. W. Vaughan, *The Spirit of Detraction* (1611), p. 94.

in 1571, for example, said that all lay people should come to church, 'especially householders': servants and the poor were another matter.[42]

Although few avoided participation in the rites of baptism, matrimony and holy burial, there is a good deal of evidence to suggest that many of the poorest classes never became regular church-goers. This was true in the Elizabethan age, when a writer listed among the many sins of the poor, 'their seldom repairing to their parish churches to hear and learn their duties better'; and it was still true in the early eighteenth century when an Oxfordshire minister excused the low attendance in his parish church on holy days by explaining that 'they are all poor labouring people, and I cannot expect them without a breach of charity'.[43] In between there was a steady flow of complaints that the poor stayed away out of indifference, hostility or some other reason. Some pleaded that they lacked suitable clothes;[44] others were deliberately excluded, for fear that they carried the plague on their persons.[45]

More substantial members of the community also offered excuses for their absence: they were sick, they had work to do, or they were afraid of venturing abroad for fear of being arrested for debt.[46] Many stayed away because they had been excommunicated by the church courts for some offence; in some dioceses in the early seventeenth century the hardened excommunicates and their families may have accounted for as much as fifteen per cent of the population.[47] In 1540-42 it was said that not half the communicants in the parish of St Giles, Colchester, went to church on Sundays and holi-

42. *The Remains of Edmund Grindal*, ed. W. Nicholson (Cambridge, P.S., 1843), p. 138.

43. H. Arth(ington), *Provision for the Poore* (1597), sig. C2; *Articles of Enquiry . . . at the Primary Visitation of Dr Thomas Secker, 1738*, ed. H. A. Lloyd Jukes (Oxon. Rec. Soc., 1957), p. 6. Much other evidence is cited by Hill, *Society and Puritanism*, pp. 472-4.

44. *The Churchwardens' Presentments in the Oxfordshire Peculiars of Dorchester, Thame and Banbury*, ed. S. A. Peyton (Oxon. Rec. Soc., 1928), p. 68; *Barlow's Journal*, ed. B. Lubbock (1934), i, pp. 15-16; F. J. Powicke, 'The Reverend Richard Baxter's Last Treatise', *Bull. John Rylands Lib.*, x (1926), p. 215.

45. C. Creighton, *A History of Epidemics in Britain* (2nd edn, 1965), i, p. 314.

46. Examples of the last of these excuses may be found in Ely D.R., B 2/12, f.20v; Wells D.R., A 91 (at least six instances); Bodl., Oxford Archdeaconry papers, c. 13, f. 174; Bodl., Oxford Dioc. papers, d. 11, f. 189.

47. R. A. Marchant, *The Church under the Law* (Cambridge, 1969), p. 227.

days; in 1633 there were twelve hundred absentees at Easter communion in Great Yarmouth. Many contemporaries echoed the complaint of the Jacobean preacher who said that there were 'sometimes not half the people in a parish present at holy exercises upon the Sabbath day, so hard a thing is it to draw them to the means of their salvation'.[48] It really was a case of two or three persons gathered together in God's name, wrote a pamphleteer in 1635; sometimes there were more pillars in church than people.[49] In Winchester in 1656 the almsmen had to be forced into church by the threat of being denied poor relief if they stayed away.[50]

Even when they did put in a reluctant appearance, the conduct of many church-goers left so much to be desired as to turn the service into a travesty of what was intended. Presentments made before the ecclesiastical courts show that virtually every kind of irreverent (and irrelevant) activity took place during divine worship. Members of the congregation jostled for pews, nudged their neighbours, hawked and spat, knitted, made coarse remarks, told jokes, fell asleep, and even let off guns.[51] Preaching was popular with the educated classes but aroused the irritation of the others. Stephen Gardiner told in 1547 of one parish in Cambridge where, 'when the vicar goeth into the pulpit to read that [he] himself hath written, then the multitude of the parish goeth straight out of the church, home to drink'; it is clear that the alehouse could compete effectively with a sermon.[52] Once he mounted the pulpit, moreover, the incumbent ran the risk of being humiliated by frivolous or insulting asides from his audience. When Mr Evans, rector of Holland Magna, Essex, preached in 1630 about Adam and Eve making themselves

48. J. E. Oxley, *The Reformation in Essex* (Manchester, 1965), p. 145; *C.S.P.D., 1634–5*, p. 538; W. Warde, *Gods Arrowes, or, Two Sermons* (1607), f. 23v.

49. W. Scott, *An Essay of Drapery* (1635), pp. 109–10. cf. *The Letters of Stephen Gardiner*, ed. J. A. Muller (Cambridge, 1933), p. 356; S. Hammond, *Gods Judgements upon Drunkards, Swearers, and Sabbath-Breakers* (1659), sig. C1; *A Representation of the State of Christianity in England* (1674), p. 5.

50. C. Bailey, *Transcripts from the Municipal Archives of Winchester* (Winchester, 1856), p. 73.

51. Bodl., MS Gough Eccl. Top. 3, f. 101, for knitting, and Ely D.R., B 2/20, f. 79v, for discharging a fowling-piece. Complaints about jostling and sleeping are innumerable.

52. *The Letters of Stephen Gardiner*, p. 314; Ware, *The Elizabethan Parish*, p. 24 n; *The Works of Thomas Adams*, ed. J. Angus (Edinburgh, 1861–2), i, p. 298; Winchester D.R., C.B. 60 (1588).

coats of fig-leaves, one loud-mouthed parishioner demanded to know where they got the thread to sew them with.[53] When another contemporary preacher attempted to explain that Heaven was so high that a millstone would take hundreds of years to come down from it, one of his hearers asked how long in that case it would take a man to get up there.[54] When the Elizabethan curate of Stogursey, Somerset, went on too long, a member of the congregation bawled out that it was time for him to come down so that the maids might go milking.[55]

Such disrespect was frequently punished in the church courts, but it could arouse sympathy among the congregation. A Cambridgeshire man was charged with indecent behaviour in church in 1598 after his 'most loathsome farting, striking, and scoffing speeches' had occasioned 'the great offence of the good and the great rejoicing of the bad'.[56] The tone of many Elizabethan congregations seems to have been that of a tiresome class of schoolboys. When they poured out of church into the tavern a stream of blasphemous jokes signified their release from unwelcome restraint. At Westbury, Gloucestershire, in 1610 a gang of youths, after being catechized by the minister, 'fell to dancing, quaffing and rioting', and composed a blasphemous and irreverent catechism of their own.[57] A tailor of Wisbech was presented in 1601 for a characteristic piece of third-form humour: after a sermon by the vicar on the text, *Thou art Peter and upon this rock I will build my church.*

he in an alehouse taking a full pot in his hand in jesting manner pronounced these words: 'Upon this rock I will build my faith'. And there being in the company one whose name was Peter he applied the matter unto him, saying, 'Thou art Peter', and then, taking the pot he said, 'But upon this rock I will build my church.'[58]

In 1623 a Bromsgrove butcher got into trouble after he had 'reverently' offered a crooked pin to an acquaintance, declaring, 'Take thee this in remembrance that Parkins of Wedgebury died for thee and be thankful.'[59]

53. S. C. Powell, *Puritan Village* (New York, 1965), p. 89.
54. R. Coppin, *Truth's Testimony* (1655), p. 42.
55. Wells D.R., A 98 (1593–4).
56. Ely D.R., B 2/14, f. 137.
57. Gloucester D.R., Vol. 111.
58. Ely D.R., B 2/20, f. 59.
59. *Worcester County Records. The Quarter Sessions Rolls*, ii, ed. J. W. Willis Bund (Worcs. Hist. Soc., 1900), p. 360 (and cf. p. 362).

It is small wonder that in the seventeenth century the godly came to see themselves as a tiny minority in an unregenerate world, and regarded the lower ranks of the people as the greatest enemies of true religion. 'If any would raise an army to extirpate knowledge and religion,' declared Richard Baxter in 1691, 'the tinkers and sow-gelders and crate-carriers and beggars and bargemen and all the rabble that cannot read . . . will be the forwardest to come into such a malitia.' The 'far greater part of the people', he thought, hated practical godliness.[60] The young people were as bad as the poor: not one young person in a thousand enjoyed prayer or preaching, thought Edward Topsell in 1596. As for beggars, they were 'for the most part utterly void of all fear of God'.[61]

The inculcation of religious doctrine was thus a difficult business. The clergy often pitched their discourse far above the capacity of most of their listeners. Those interested in preferment sought to secure it by publishing learned sermons which would attract the eye of an influential patron. In the process they tended to forget that the majority of their local congregation lacked the intellectual sophistication of an educated schoolboy. 'Most ministers in England usually shoot over the heads of their hearers', thought John Dod; and John Locke agreed: 'You . . . may as well talk Arabic to a poor day-labourer as the notions and languages that the books and disputes of religion are filled with; and as soon you will be understood.'[62] 'There are now extant in English sundry books very profitable, which few of the common people do make use of,' remarked a writer in 1631, 'for that their style and words for the most or a great part are for scholars' reading only.'[63]

The inadequacies of popular education meant that the efforts of many godly preachers were in vain. Sir Simonds D'Ewes tells us how he learned to take notes on sermons and became a 'rational hearer, . . . whereas before I differed little from the brute creatures that

60. Powicke, 'The Reverend Richard Baxter's Last Treatise', *Bull, John Rylands Lib.*, x (1926), p. 182; R. B. Schlatter, *Richard Baxter and Puritan Politics* (New Brunswick, N.J., 1957), p. 63.

61. (E. Topsell), *The Reward of Religion* (1596), pp. 239, 119.

62. Clarke, *The Lives of Two and Twenty English Divines*, p. 209; *The Works of John Locke* (12th edn, 1824), vi, pp. 157–8. The Jacobean incumbent of Much Dewchurch, Herefordshire, who used to quote the Fathers in Latin before translating them for the benefit of his hearers, provoked one of them to comment that he would rather 'hear a horse fart than the vicar preach in Latin'; Hereford D.R., C.B. 71 (1616–17).

63. E. Reeve, *The Christian Divinitie* (1631), sig. A5ᵛ.

were in the church with me, never regarding or observing any part of divine service'.[64] William Pemble records the salutary story of the man of sixty who had all his life attended sermons, twice on Sundays, and frequently on other occasions in the week. Yet the answers he gave the minister who questioned him on his death-bed spoke for themselves:

Being demanded what he thought of God, he answers that he was a good old man; and what of Christ, that he was a towardly young youth; and of his soul, that it was a great bone in his body; and what should become of his soul after he was dead, that if he had done well he should be put into a pleasant green meadow.

This, says Pemble, was a man who had heard at least two or three thousand sermons in his lifetime:

But, my brethren, be assured this man is not alone; there be many a hundred in his case who come to church and hear much, haply a hundred and fifty sermons in a year; yet at year's end are as much the better for all, as the pillars of the church against which they lean, or the pews wherein they sit.[65]

The impression of popular religious ignorance was initially enhanced by the difficulties of the transition from Latin prayers to a vernacular religion. When in 1551 the new Protestant Bishop of Gloucester carried out a survey of the diocesan clergy he found that of 311 there were 171 who could not repeat the Ten Commandments, twenty-seven who did not know the author of the Lord's Prayer, and ten who could not repeat it.[66] A few years later a petition for services in English complained that before the Reformation none of the laity who knew no Latin could say the Lord's Prayer in English, or knew any article of the Creed, or could recite the Ten Commandments.[67] An Essex minister reported in 1598 that the religious knowledge of half the population would disgrace a ten-year-old

64. *The Autobiography and Correspondence of Sir Simonds D'Ewes*, ed. J. O. Halliwell (1845), i, p. 95.

65. *The Workes of ... Mr William Pemble* (3rd edn, 1635), p. 559. For similar anecdotes see G. Firmin, *The Real Christian, or a Treatise of Effectual Calling* (1670), pp. 162, 229.

66. J. Gairdner in *E.H.R.*, xix (1904), pp. 98–9. Some good reasons for not taking these results at their face value are, however, offered by P. Heath, *The English Parish Clergy on the Eve of the Reformation* (1969), pp. 74–5.

67. Foxe, viii, p. 123.

child. 'The poor people do not understand as much as the Lord's Prayer.'[68] Three years later another minister observed that in places where there was no preaching the people were ignorant of God as Turks or pagans: in one parish of four hundred he had found only ten per cent who had any knowledge of the basic Christian dogmas.[69] Hugh Latimer remarked that many people preferred tales of Robin Hood to a sermon: in 1606 Nicholas Bownd observed that they certainly knew more about Robin Hood than they did about the stories in the Bible, which were 'as strange unto them as any news that you can tell them'. 'Many are so ignorant,' Bishop Jewel had said, '[that] they know not what the Scriptures are; they know not that there *are* any Scriptures.'[70]

Many different circumstances helped to determine the extent of religious knowledge in any individual parish: the zeal of the incumbent, the occupations of the parishioners, the availability of schools, the attitude of the local gentry. Religious ignorance was probably particularly common in the heath and forest areas, where society was less rigid and disciplined than in the stable, nucleated villages of the fielden communities. There dwelt the squatters, whose heathenlike ignorance of Christianity was mentioned by William Harrison in the reign of Elizabeth, and by the topographer, John Norden, in 1607:

In some parts where I have travelled, where great and spacious wastes, mountains and heaths are, ... many ... cottages are set up, the people given to little or no kind of labour, living very hardly with oaten bread, sour whey, and goats' milk, dwelling far from any church or chapel, and are as ignorant of God or of any civil course of life as the very savages amongst the infidels.[71]

In the north at this time there were said to be heathens everywhere. On the borders of Cumberland the inhabitants could not say the Lord's Prayer; in Northumberland men died without ever learning

68. G. Gifford, *A Brief Discourse of Certaine Points of the Religion, which is among the Common Sort of Christians* (1598), f. 43.

69. J. Nicholls, *The Plea of the Innocent* (1602), pp. 218–19.

70. *Sermons by Hugh Latimer*, ed. G. E. Corrie (Cambridge, P.S., 1844), p. 208; N. Bownd, *Sabbathum Veteris et Novi Testamenti* (2nd edn, 1606), p. 339; *The Works of John Jewel*, ed. J. Ayre (Cambridge, P.S., 1845–50), ii, p. 1014.

71. J. N(orden), *The Surveyors Dialogue* (1607), p. 107. cf. *The Agrarian History of England and Wales*, iv, ed. J. Thirsk (Cambridge, 1967), pp. 409–11.

it.⁷² In Elizabethan Wales John Penry reported there were thousands of people who knew nothing of Christ – 'yea almost that never heard of him'.⁷³

But this state of affairs was not confined to the dark corners of the land. In Essex in 1656 there were said to be people as ignorant of Christianity as the Red Indians; in the Isle of Axholme the inhabitants had been virtual heathens until the drainage of the Fens; in parts of Wiltshire there was total ignorance of religion; in Hampshire there were 'ignorant heathenish people'.⁷⁴ When thirteen criminals were executed after the London sessions in 1679 the prison chaplain found them 'lamentably ignorant of the principles of religion, as if they had been born in Affrick and bred up amongst the savages of America'.⁷⁵

In the Middle Ages it had been well known that many of the rural population were innocent of religious dogma. The fourteenth-century preacher, John Bromyard, used to tell the story of the shepherd who, asked if he knew who the Father, Son and Holy Ghost were, replied, 'The father and the son I know well for I tend their sheep, but I know not that third fellow; there is none of that name in our village.'⁷⁶ Medieval religion had laid its emphasis upon the regular performance of ritual duties, rather than on the memorizing of theological beliefs.⁷⁷ After the Reformation it was assumed that popular ignorance was merely a hangover from Popery; later it was attributed by the Puritans to the lack of a preaching ministry; ultimately it was accepted as a fact of life. Periodic waves of evangelization made their impact on many parishes, but the problem remained. Everyone knows that George Whitefield found the miners of Kingswood – significantly a forest area – 'little

72. C.S.P.D., 1629–31, p. 473; 1598–1601, p. 362; Calendar of Border Papers, ii, p. 494.

73. J. Penry, Three Treatises concerning Wales, ed. D. Williams (Cardiff, 1960), p. 32. Religious ignorance in Wales and the North is discussed by J. E. C. Hill, 'Puritans and the Dark Corners of the Land', T.R.H.S., 5th ser., xiii (1963).

74. G. F. Nuttall, Visible Saints (Oxford, 1957), p. 136; The Diary of Abraham de la Pryme, ed. C. Jackson (Surtees Soc., 1870), p. 173; Clarke, The Lives of Sundry Eminent Persons, i, p. 19.

75. The Execution . . . of . . . Thirteen Prisoners (1679), p. 2.

76. Quoted by G. G. Coulton, The Medieval Village (Cambridge, 1925), pp. 265–6. cf. the same author's Ten Medieval Studies (3rd edn, Cambridge, 1930), chap. 7.

77. cf. above, p. 88.

better than heathens'; and in the nineteenth century the impact of organized religion upon the population of the industrial towns was often negligible.[78] But it was not the pressure of industrialization which created the problem: it had always been there. The Reverend Francis Kilvert recorded in his diary how the vicar of Fordington, Dorset, found total ignorance in his rural parish when he arrived there in the early nineteenth century. At one church in the area there were only two male communicants. When the cup was given to the first he touched his forelock and said, 'Here's your good health, sir.' The second, better informed, said, 'Here's the good health of our Lord Jesus Christ.' At Chippenham a poor man took the chalice from the vicar and wished him a Happy New Year.[79]

Of course, some allowance must be made for the exacting standards of severe divines, quick to denounce as 'heathens' those whom they had merely caught out in a mild state of theological confusion. Richard Hooker may have been right when he observed that there were very few persons by whom God was 'altogether unapprehended' and that they were of such 'grossness of wit' as scarcely to deserve the name of human being.[80] But a concept of God as vague as this was compatible with all sorts of beliefs of which the Church strongly disapproved. Even the ordinary ecclesiastical rites of passage were sometimes evaded. Confirmation was a formality in many areas, and there were dioceses, like Oxford and Ely in the reign of Elizabeth, where a protracted episcopal vacancy meant that the ceremony lapsed for several decades. When White Kennett visited Rutland as Bishop of Peterborough in 1722 he found there had been no confirmation there for forty years.[81] Some even escaped being christened: in the mid eighteenth century a writer commented on the 'perhaps no inconsiderable number among the lowest class of the people who never are brought to be baptised at all'.[82]

78. L. Tyerman, *The Life of the Rev. George Whitefield* (1876), i, p. 182; K. S. Inglis, *Churches and the Working Classes in Victorian England* (1963).

79. *Kilvert's Diary*, ed. W. Plomer (new edn, 1960), ii, p. 442; iii, p. 133.

80. R. Hooker, *Of the Laws of Ecclesiastical Polity*, v. ii.

81. *Reliquiae Baxterianae*, ed. M. Sylvester (1696), i, p. 250; J. Strype, *The Life and Acts of John Whitgift* (Oxford, 1822), iii, pp. 288–90; G. V. Bennett, *White Kennett, 1660–1728* (1957), p. 227. For a similar situation in the thirteenth century, see Coulton, *Ten Medieval Studies*, p. 119.

82. *A Collection of the Yearly Bills of Mortality from 1657 to 1758* (1759), p. 4.

4. *Scepticism*

So despite theoretical uniformity there was plenty of scope in six-
teenth- and seventeenth-century England for a wide degree of religious heterodoxy. The many Elizabethan and Jacobean writers who
lamented the growth of 'atheism' used the word loosely and pejora-
tively to cover any kind of immorality or non-conformity. In so far as
they were concerned with actual scepticism they usually had in mind
the little group of aristocratic intellectuals who were influenced by
classical writings and Paduan Averroism into taking up a deistical
posture from which they denied the immortality of the soul, the
reality of Heaven and Hell, and sometimes even the divinity of
Christ. It is doubtful whether many of these were atheists in the
strict sense of the word. They were the counterparts and imitators
of the Italian humanists and French *libertins*. But some endorsed
the Machiavellian view of religion as a useful device for instilling
good behaviour into the common people and denied many orthodox Christian tenets: Christopher Marlowe indeed expressed the
view that the New Testament was 'filthily written', that Christ was
a bastard and the apostles 'base fellows'. He also anticipated some
modern theologians by suggesting that Jesus was a homosexual.[83]
Sir Walter Raleigh and his friends were said to have denied the
reality of Heaven and Hell, declaring that 'we die like beasts and
when we are gone there is no more remembrance of us'.[84] A similar
type of outrageous iconoclastic atheism was charged against Thomas
Hariot, George Gascoigne, John Caius, Nicholas Bacon, the earl
of Oxford and other leading Elizabethan intellectuals. In 1617 the
Spanish ambassador estimated the number of English atheists at
900,000.[85] This figure may be confidently disregarded, but it is
clear that under humanist influence some contemporary intellec-

83. P. H. Kocher, *Christopher Marlowe* (Chapel Hill, 1946), chaps. 2 and 3.
84. P. Lefranc, *Sir Walter Raleigh écrivain* (Paris, 1968), p. 381 (and chap.
12 for a thorough discussion of Raleigh's religion).
85. *Correspondence of Matthew Parker*, ed. J. Bruce and T. T. Perowne
(Cambridge, P.S., 1853), pp. 251–2; E. A. Strathmann, *Sir Walter Ralegh*
(Morningside Heights, 1951), chap. 2; Lefranc, op. cit., p. 341; *C.S.P.D.,
1547–80*, p. 444; M. J. Havran, *The Catholics in Caroline England* (Stanford,
1962), p. 83. On this subject in general, see F. Brie, 'Deismus und Atheismus
in der Englischen Renaissance', *Anglia*, xlviii (1924); G. T. Buckley, *Atheism
in the English Renaissance* (Chicago, 1932); D. C. Allen, *Doubt's Boundless
Sea. Skepticism and Faith in the Renaissance* (Baltimore, 1964).

tuals had devised a form of religion which was very different from orthodox Christianity. During the seventeenth century the writings of Hobbes and Spinoza gave this type of scepticism some reinforcement.

Aristocratic infidelity of this kind is well known to historians. But they have paid less attention to the evidence of scepticism among humbler members of the population. One of the most striking features of the spiritual biographies of the time is their revelation that atheistical thoughts could trouble even 'persons of eminent and singular holiness'.[86] Many future Puritan saints seem to have temporarily doubted the existence of God and the Devil, the reality of Heaven and Hell, and the truthfulness of the Scriptures. This was the case with John Bunyan, Richard Baxter and many other notable believers whose difficulties are only known to us because they were recorded and published so as to help others.[87] But incidental evidence suggests that such doubts were widely shared. Lady Monson, for example, wife of the well-known Jacobean admiral, was forced to consult an astrologer in 1597, because 'she cannot sleep; she hath many ill thoughts and cogitations; ... she thinks the Devil doth tempt her to do evil to herself and she doubteth whether there is a God'.[88]

There was nothing new about this tendency to doubt the basic tenets of the Christian faith. Many medieval clergy and laity had been beset by overwhelming temptations to blasphemy and atheism,[89] and a wide range of popular scepticism was uncovered by the fifteenth century church courts. Much of it has been wrongly

86. R. Gilpin, *Daemonologia Sacra*, ed. A. B. Grosart (Edinburgh, 1867), p. 243.

87. J. Bunyan, *Grace Abounding*, ed. R. Sharrock (Oxford, 1962), p. 31; G. F. Nuttall, *Richard Baxter* (1965), p. 28; *Autobiography and Correspondence of Sir Simonds D'Ewes*, i, pp. 251–2; *Nicholas Ferrar. Two Lives*, ed. J. E. B. Mayor (Cambridge, 1855), p. 5; H. Jessey, *The Exceeding Riches of Grace Advanced ... in ... Mrs Sarah Wight* (2nd edn, 1647), pp. 7, 11–12, 78, 128; T. Taylor, *The Pilgrims Profession* (in *Three Treatises* [1633]), pp. 165–6, 168; Clarke, *The Lives of Sundry Eminent Persons*, i, pp. 70–1; W. Haller, *The Rise of Puritanism* (New York, 1957), p. 99; L. Muggleton, *The Acts of the Witnesses* (1699), p. 18; *Satan his Methods and Malice baffled. A Narrative of God's Gracious Dealings with that Choice Christian Mrs Hannah Allen* (1683), pp. 3, 15, 58.

88. Ashm. 226, f. 233. For similar temptations, below, pp. 565–6.

89. See, e.g., G. G. Coulton, *The Plain Man's Religion in the Middle Ages (Medieval Studies*, no. 13, 1916), pp. 6–8.

bracketed by historians under the general title of 'Lollardy'. But it was not Wycliffite or proto-Protestant theology which underlay this reluctance to accept some of the most elementary doctrines of Christianity. Several of these heretics denied the immortality of the soul and the possibility of a future resurrection. One challenged the Biblical account of creation. Some denied the resurrection of Christ.[90] Others professed a frank indifference, like a London woman accused of practising magic in 1493, who declared that because she had a heaven in this earth she did not care about any heaven in the next world.[91] There were bizarre survivals: a man at Bexley in 1313 made images of wood and stone in his garden and worshipped them as gods, before proceeding to kill his maidservant.[92] And there were bemused heretics, like the Rutland woman who confessed in 1518 that she had given up going to church and betaken herself to the Devil, as a result of a sudden impulse which she was unable to explain.[93]

It is impossible to know how representative were the sceptics who appeared before the church courts. The high proportion of aliens and strangers to the district suggests that those most likely to be denounced for religious heterodoxy were the outsiders not fully accepted by the community; like those later accused of witchcraft, they were the persons whose position in society was ambiguous or insecure. If this is true, then the actual volume of disbelief may have been much greater than that which the surviving evidence indicates.

The Reformation did not break the continuity of popular scepticism. Heretics who denied the immortality of the soul, and therefore the existence of Heaven and Hell, were well known in the reign of Edward VI. Both Anabaptists and Familists sympathized with the 'mortalist' doctrine that the soul slept until the Day of Judgement; in 1573 a group of sectaries in the diocese of Ely held that the notion of Hell was purely allegorical.[94] Doubts were also expressed about the Incarnation. In 1542 an inhabitant of Dartford

90. Thomson, *Later Lollards*, pp. 27, 36–7, 76, 80, 82, 160, 186, 248; id., in *Studies in Church History*, ii, ed. Cuming, p. 255. Thomson's valuable work is marred by a tendency to dismiss unconventional sceptics as 'drunk' or 'of unsound mind', thus missing the tradition to which many of their utterances belonged.   91. Hale, *Precedents*, p. 36.
92. F. R. H. Du Boulay, *The Lordship of Canterbury* (1966), p. 312.
93. *An Episcopal Court Book for the Diocese of Lincoln, 1514–20*, ed. M. Bowker (Lincoln Rec. Soc., 1967), pp. 84–5.
94. Buckley, *Atheism in the English Renaissance*, pp. 29–30, 48–50; *The*

was cited for saying that 'the body of Christ which he received in the womb of the Virgin Mary did not ascend into Heaven nor is not in Heaven'.[95] Fourteen years later another Kentishman, this time the parson of Tunstall, was accused of saying that whoever believed that Christ sat on the right hand of the Lord was a fool.[96] In 1576 a 'desperate fellow' in Norfolk went so far as to affirm that there were 'divers Christs'.[97] Another was presented at Wootton, Gloucestershire, in 1582 for holding repugnant opinions about the manner of Christ's Incarnation.[98] It was shortly after this time that John Dee's associate, Edward Kelly, was tempted to deny Christ's divinity. Another doubter appeared before Star Chamber in 1596 after declaring that 'Christ was no saviour and the gospel a fable'.[99]

Religious unorthodoxy of this kind could shade off into out-and-out scepticism. At Woodchurch, Kent, in 1573 one Robert Master was charged with erroneous opinions, 'for that he denieth that God made the sun, the moon, the earth, the water, and that he denieth the resurrection of the dead'.[100] The Bishop of Exeter complained in 1600 that in his diocese it was 'a matter very common to dispute whether there be a God or not'; Bancroft encountered similar doubters in the diocese of London.[101] In Essex a husband-

---

Two Liturgies ... Set Forth ... in the Reign of King Edward VI, ed. J. Ketley (Cambridge, P.S., 1844), p. 537; J. Strype, *Annals of the Reformation* (Oxford, 1824), ii(i), p. 563; L. Einstein, *Tudor Ideals* (1921), p. 226; C. Hill, 'William Harvey and the Idea of Monarchy', *Past and Present*, xxvii (1964), pp. 62–4; J. Strype, *The Life and Acts of Matthew Parker* (1711), p. 437.

95. Rochester D.R., DRb/Jd 1 (Deposition Books, 1541–71), f. 7.

96. Kent R.O., PRC 39/2, f. 23ᵛ. In 1563 Thomas Lovell of Hevingham, Norfolk, was accused of asking why 'we do believe in God the Son, considering we pray to God the Father and not to God the Son; and that God the Son was not believed upon [in] his own country, but driven out; and they [did] better than we do'; Norfolk and Norwich R.O., Norfolk Archdeaconry General Books, 2A (1563). (I owe this reference to Dr R. A. Houlbrooke.)

97. *H.M.C., Hatfield*, ii, p. 136.

98. Gloucester D.R., Vol. 50.

99. M. Casaubon, *A True and Faithful Relation of what passed ... between Dr John Dee ... and Some Spirits* (1659), p. 240; J. Hawarde, *Les Reportes del Cases in Camera Stellata, 1593 to 1609*, ed. W. P. Baildon (1894), pp. 41–2.

100. C. Jenkins, 'An Unpublished Record of Archbishop Parker's Visitation in 1573', *Archaeologia Cantiana*, xxix (1911), p. 314.

101. *H.M.C., Hatfield*, x, p. 450; J. Swan, *A True and Breife Report of Mary Glovers Vexation* (1603), p. 68.

man of Bradwell-near-the-Sea was said to 'hold his opinion that all things cometh by nature, and does affirm this as an atheist'.[102] In Worcestershire in 1616 Thomas Aston of Ribsford-with-Bewdley was said to have remarked that 'stage plays were made by the Holy Ghost and the word of God was but man's invention'.[103] At Wing, Rutland, in 1633 Richard Sharpe was accused of saying 'there is no God and that he hath no soul to save'.[104] From Durham in 1635 came the case of Brian Walker who, when asked if he did not fear God, retorted that, 'I do not believe there is either God or Devil; neither will I believe anything but what I see': as an alternative to the Bible he commended 'the book called Chaucer'.[105] Many less assertive sceptics had doubts about the existence of divine providence: William Gardiner, a prominent Elizabethan Surrey J.P., was accused in 1582 of saying 'that God hath nothing to do with the world since he created it, and that the world was not governed by him'.[106]

The relative freedom of the Interregnum brought much of this endemic scepticism into the open.[107] In 1648 the authors of the Blasphemy Ordinance of that year found it necessary to prescribe punishments for those who denied immortality, cast doubt on the Scriptures, rejected Christ and the Holy Ghost, and even denied that there was a God or that he was almighty.[108] Some of these heresies found a refuge among the sects. The Socinians denied the divinity of Christ. The Ranters denied the immortality of the soul, the literalness of the Resurrection, the overriding authority of the Scriptures, and the physical existence of Heaven and Hell. Like the Familists, they still used such concepts, but chose to treat them symbolically: Heaven was when men laughed, ran one version, Hell when they were in pain. There was no Hell, save in man's imagina-

102. Cited by Sister Mary Catherine in *Essex Recusant*, viii (1966), p. 92 (no date given).

103. Hereford D.R., Court Book 70.

104. Peterborough D.R., Correction Book 65 (1633–5), f. 75ᵛ.

105. *Durham High Commission*, pp. 115–16.

106. L. Hotson, *Shakespeare versus Shallow* (1931), pp. 55, 198, 202. cf. W. R. Elton, *King Lear and the Gods* (San Marino, Calif., 1966), p. 19; Wood, *Ath. Ox.*, iii, cols. 8–9; J. Flavell, *Divine Conduct: or, the Mysterie of Providence* (1678), sig. A5.

107. On this whole subject, see now C. Hill, *The World Turned Upside Down* (1972) and A. L. Morton, *The World of the Ranters* (1970).

108. *Acts and Ordinances of the Interregnum, 1642–60*, ed. C. H. Firth and R. S. Rait (1911), i, pp. 1133–6.

tion, Richard Coppin was alleged to have said: 'Whilst we live in the fear of Hell we have it.'[109] The Digger Gerrard Winstanley scoffed at the notion of an 'outward heaven, which is a fancy your false teachers put into your heads to please you with while they pick your purses'. In the later seventeenth century many intellectuals were to reject the doctrine that the wicked suffered perpetual torment, but it was the mystical sects of the Interregnum who had done most to publicize such scepticism.[110]

Ultimately, such heresies could lead to the formal rejection of all religion. The Ranter Laurence Clarkson came to believe that there was no god but nature; so did one of the followers of the prophet William Franklin. Lodowick Muggleton said he had met many persons who held this view.[111] In 1656 two Lacock weavers were charged with a variety of heretical beliefs ranging from star-worship to the assertion that, 'if the Scriptures were a-making again, Tom Lampire of Melksham would make as good Scripture as the Bible'. They also said that 'there was neither Heaven nor Hell but in a man's own conscience; for if he had a good fortune and did live well in the world that was Heaven; and if he lived poor and miserable that was Hell and death itself, for then he would die like a cow or a horse'. One of them combined the Antinomian doctrine 'that God was in all things and that whatever sins or wickedness he did commit, God was the author of them all and acted them in him', with the reflection that he would sell all religions for a jug of beer.[112]

When assessing such utterances it must be remembered that for most of this period religious unorthodoxy was still regarded as an extremely serious offence, not least because a belief in Heaven and Hell was thought an indispensable sanction for good behaviour by the lower classes. Between 1548 and 1612 at least eight persons were burned at the stake for holding anti-Trinitarian beliefs. Of these the ploughwright Matthew Hamont, who was burned at Norwich in 1578, combined his denial of Christ's divinity and resurrection with the reflection that the New Testament was 'but mere

109. *C.S.P.D., 1648–9*, p. 425; Coppin, *Truth's Testimony*, pp. 40–41. For Ranter doctrine, see Morton, *The World of the Ranters*, and Hill, *The World Turned Upside Down*.

110. D. W. Petegorsky, *Left-wing Democracy in the English Civil War* (1940), p. 144; D. P. Walker, *The Decline of Hell* (1964).

111. H. Ellis, *Pseudochristus* (1650), pp. 32, 37; Muggleton, *The Acts of the Witnesses*, p. 19. For Clarkson, below, p. 567.

112. *H.M.C., Various Collections*, i, pp. 132–3. cf. below, pp. 457–8.

foolishness, a story of men, or rather a mere fable'.[113] Those who gave vent to such sentiments ran serious risks, even after 1612, for some of the Laudian bishops regretted the cessation of such executions: Archbishop Neile wanted to burn a heretic as late as 1639;[114] and Hobbes feared that he might undergo this fate after the Restoration.[115] Only in 1677 was the punishment for heresy reduced from death by burning to mere excommunication. Against this background the evidence of widespread religious scepticism is not to be underrated, for it may be reasonably surmised that many thought what they dared not say aloud. It is not surprising that in the reign of Charles II, Dudley, the fourth Lord North, came to the view that the number of contemporaries who believed in life after death was very small, 'especially among the vulgar'.[116]

To this self-conscious rejection of religious dogma must be added the incalculable forces of worldliness and apathy. One historian has called the Elizabethan period 'the age of greatest religious indifference before the twentieth century',[117] and although this may seem an exaggeration it is certain that a substantial proportion of the population regarded organized religion with an attitude which varied from cold indifference to frank hostility. The church courts uncovered only the more blatant offenders: like the two inhabitants of Cheshire in 1598 who said that they would give money to pull the parish church down, but none to build it up; the butcher in the diocese of Ely in 1608 who set his dog on the people as they went to church; the London actor who said that a man might learn more good at one of his plays that at twenty sermons.[118] But there were

113. H. J. MacLachan, *Socinianism in Seventeenth-century England* (Oxford, 1951), p. 31; J. Stow, *The Annales of England* (1592), pp. 1173–4; Buckley, *Atheism in the English Renaissance*, pp. 56–8.
114. L. O. Pike, *A History of Crime in England* (1873–6), ii, p. 125; *C.S.P.D., 1639*, pp. 455–6. A heretic was condemned but subsequently reprieved in 1618; *C.S.P.D., 1611–18*, pp. 522, 525, 526, 527.
115. J. Aubrey, *Brief Lives*, ed. A. Powell (1949), p. 245.
116. *D.N.B.*, 'North, Dudley, 4th Baron North'.
117. L. Stone in *E.H.R.*, lxxvii (1962), p. 328. Similar opinions may be found in R. G. Usher, *The Reconstruction of the English Church* (New York, 1910), i, p. 281; M. M. Knappen, *Tudor Puritanism* (Gloucester, Mass., 1963), p. 380.
118. 'The Bishop of Chester's Visitation for the year 1598', *The Cheshire Sheaf*, 3rd ser., i (1896), p. 69; Ely D.R., B 2/26, f. 133; F. W. X. Fincham, 'Notes from the Ecclesiastical Court Records at Somerset House', *T.R.H.S.*, 4th ser., iv (1921), p. 138.

innumerable men and women who chose to concentrate on the business of living and to let spiritual matters look after themselves; like the Hereford money-lender, who, when urged to give over 'his lewd life and detestable usury for his soul's sake', replied: 'What pass I for my soul? Let me have money enough [and] I care not whether God or the Devil have my soul.'[119]

The growth of secularism is not a topic which has received much systematic historical investigation.[120] These authorities who have considered it have tended to pursue the analysis of the sociologist, Emile Durkheim, to its logical conclusion. If it is by religious ritual that society affirms its collective unity, they argue, then the decline of that ritual reflects the disappearance of that unity. The break-up of shared values, consequent upon the growth of urbanism and industrialism, makes such collective affirmations increasingly difficult. This disintegration became apparent with the formation of rival religious groups after the Reformation. It was completed when the Industrial Revolution further dissolved the moral unity of English society. Norms which had previously seemed God-given henceforth appeared as mere rules of utility needing adaptation in the face of changing circumstances. In the country villages, where some moral unity survived, it was possible for organized religion to retain some social meaning. But in the cities religious indifference became most marked, because it was there that society's moral unity had most obviously been broken.[121]

This conventional interpretation undoubtedly exaggerates the moral unity of medieval society. Durkheim himself romanticized the Middle Ages as a time when men were cosily bound to each other in little units of manor, village and gild; and similar idealization has affected the work of unhistorically minded sociologists. Indeed the whole problem may be wrongly posed. We do not know enough about the religious beliefs and practices of our remote ancestors to be certain of the extent to which religious faith and

119. *Hereford City Records*, ix, f. 3438.
120. cf. C. Geertz in *Anthropological Approaches to the Study of Religion*, ed. M. Banton (1966), p. 43: 'If the anthropological study of religious commitment is underdeveloped, the anthropological study of religious non-commitment is non-existent.'
121. For a consideration of such arguments, see B. R. Wilson, *Religion in Secular Society* (1966), part 1, and A. Macintyre, *Secularization and Moral Change* (1967).

practice have actually declined. Not enough justice has been done
to the volume of apathy, heterodoxy and agnosticism which existed
long before the onset of industrialism. Even the most primitive
societies have their religious sceptics.[122] It may be that social changes
increased the volume of scepticism in sixteenth- and seventeenth-
century England. What is clear is that the hold of organized religion
upon the people was never so complete as to leave no room for rival
systems of belief.

122. cf. P. Radin, *Primitive Man as Philosopher* (New York, 1927), chap.
xix.

MAGIC

7.

MAGICAL HEALING

> Sorcerers are too common; cunning men, wizards, and white witches, as they call them, in every village, which, if they be sought unto, will help almost all infirmities of body and mind.
>
> Robert Burton, *Anatomy of Melancholy*
> (1621) II, i, 1

> Charming is in as great request as physic, and charmers more sought unto than physicians in time of need.
>
> William Perkins, *A Discourse of the Damned Art of Witchcraft* (Cambridge, 1608), p. 153

> I kneele for help; O! lay that hand on me,
> Adored Caesar! and my Faith is such,
> I shall be heal'd, if that my KING but touch.
> The Evill is not Yours: my sorrow sings,
> Mine is the Evill, but the Cure, the KINGS.
>
> Robert Herrick, *Hesperides* (1648)

> If this principle of believing nothing whereof we do not see a cause were admitted, we may come to doubt whether the curing of the King's Evil by the touch of a monarch may not be likewise called charming.
>
> Sir George Mackenzie, *Pleadings in Some Remarkable Cases* (Edinburgh, 1672), p. 186

1. *Charmers and cunning men*

'A GREAT many of us,' said Bishop Latimer in 1552, 'when we be in trouble, or sickness, or lose anything, we run hither and thither to witches, or sorcerers, whom we call wise men ... seeking aid and comfort at their hands.' Over a hundred years later the Puritan divine, Anthony Burgess, used almost the same words: 'If men have

BIBLIOGRAPHICAL NOTE: A great deal of information about the healing activities of the cunning men is contained in Kittredge, *Witchcraft*. I have supplemented it by drawing on some of the unpublished records of the ecclesiastical courts before which such persons periodically appeared. E. Delcambre, *Le Concept de la sorcellerie dans le Duché de Lorraine, III: Les Devins-Guérisseurs* (Nancy, 1951) is an excellent account of some of their continental counterparts. W. G. Black, *Folk-Medicine* (1883) and T. J. Petti-

lost anything, if they be in any pain or disease, then they presently run to such as they call wise men." Many other observers testified to the deep-rooted appeal held for contemporaries by the traditional dispenser of magical remedies – the village wizard, or 'wise man' (the term is the same as in the three 'Wise men', or Magi, from the East). During the sixteenth and seventeenth centuries these popular magicians went under a variety of names – 'cunning men', 'wise women', 'charmers', 'blessers', 'conjurers', 'sorcerers', 'witches' – and they offered a variety of services, which ranged from healing the sick and finding lost goods to fortune-telling and divination of all kinds. This chapter will be concerned only with their medical activities, but these usually formed only one branch of a very diverse repertoire.

It has already been seen how the inadequacies of orthodox medical services left a large proportion of the population of Tudor and Stuart England dependent upon traditional folk medicine. This was essentially a mixture of common-sensical remedies, based on the accumulated experience of nursing and midwifery, combined with inherited lore about the healing properties of plants and minerals. But it also included certain types of ritual healing, in which prayers, charms or spells accompanied the medicine, or even formed the sole means of treatment. Magical healing of this kind might sometimes be attempted by the patient himself or a member of his family. More often it was the business of the cunning man, to whom the sufferer would have recourse and to whom he would normally be expected to make some form of payment. Sometimes these wizards specialized in particular ailments; others claimed to be able to deal with them all.[2]

Much of this magical healing reflected the old belief in the curative power of the medieval Church. A typical practitioner was

grew, *On Superstitions connected with the History and Practice of Medicine and Surgery* (1844) are both useful. So is W. Bonser, *The Medical Background of Anglo-Saxon England* (1963).

The history of the ritual treatment of the King's Evil was outlined by T. J. Pettigrew, op. cit., pp. 117–54, expanded by R. Crawfurd, *The King's Evil* (Oxford, 1911), and given magisterial treatment in M. Bloch, *Les Rois thaumaturges* (Paris, 1925: reprinted 1961).

1. *Sermons by Hugh Latimer*, ed. G. E. Corrie (Cambridge, P.S., 1844), p. 534; A. Burgess, *CXLV Expository Sermons upon the Whole 17th Chapter of the Gospel according to St John* (1656), p. 95.

2. J. Mason, *The Anatomie of Sorcerie* (Cambridge, 1612), p. 37.

Margaret Hunt, who in 1528 described her methods before the Commissary of London. First, she ascertained the names of the sick persons. Then she knelt and prayed to the Blessed Trinity to heal them from all their wicked enemies. Then she told them to say for nine consecutive nights five Paternosters, five Aves and a Creed, followed by three more Paternosters, three Aves and three Creeds 'in the worship of Saint Spirit'. At bedtime they were to repeat one Paternoster, one Ave and one Creed in worship of St. Ive, to save them from all envy. For the ague she prescribed various herbs. For sores she also recommended herbs, but taken with a little holy water and some prayers. The formulae she had learned from a Welsh woman, Mother Elmet.[3]

The pronunciation of Catholic prayers in Latin long remained a common ingredient in the magical treatment of illness. In 1557 one Cowdale of Maidstone, allegedly a centenarian, confessed to healing people by such prayers alone, regardless of the type of sickness involved. He simply prescribed five Paternosters, five Aves and a Creed, to be said in honour of the Holy Ghost and Our Lady. Henry Matthew of Guisley confessed before the Archbishop of York's court in 1590 that he had sixteen years previously washed a woman's sore eyes and then said three Paternosters and a Creed, but that he had now given up such practices because he had been regarded as 'a charmer' for using them.[4] It was common for those accused of charming or sorcery to deny the charge by asserting indignantly that they had done nothing by magic, but had merely helped people by their prayers. Thus in 1607 Isabella Beckett of Owston, Yorkshire, informed the local vicar that his sick cow had been healed by God and her own good prayers.[5]

Such formulae were often not so much supplications as admonitory formulae couched in religious language. This can be seen in the case of Goodwife Veazy, an expert in the cure of 'ringworm, tetter-worm and canker-worm', whose services were recommended to Robert Cecil in 1604. Her method was to say three times, 'In the name of God I begin and in the name of God I do end. Thou tetter-worm (or thou canker-worm) begone from hence in the name of the Father, of the Son, and of the Holy Ghost'; after which she applied

3. Hale, *Precedents*, pp. 107–8.
4. *Archdeacon Harpsfield's Visitation, 1557*, ed. L. E. Whatmore (Catholic Rec. Soc., 1950–1), p. 216; Borthwick, R. VI. A 10, f. 61.
5. Borthwick, R. VI. B 3, f. 66. below, p. 318.

a little honey and pepper to the afflicted part.[6] Such was the mechanical efficacy attributed to prayers of this type that they were sometimes not even pronounced aloud, but merely written down on a piece of paper, and hung round the patient's neck. James Sykes of Guiseley, for example, confessed in 1590 to curing horses by writing prayers on paper and hanging them in their manes.[7]

Some of the other charms employed by the wise men had a more tangled pedigree. These were debased versions of Christian prayers or barely intelligible bits of semi-religious verse, describing supposed episodes in the life of Christ or the saints. They reflected the ancient belief that mythical events could be a timeless source of supernatural power.[8] A typical narrative charm was the following, used at Hawkshead in the early eighteenth century as a remedy against bleeding:

There was a man born in Bethlem of Judaea whose name was called Christ. Baptised in the River Jordan in the water of the flood; and the Child also was meek and good; and as the water stood so I desire thee the blood of [such a person or beast] to stand in their body, in the name of the Father, Son and Holy Ghost.

For a scald there was this from Devonshire in the mid seventeenth century:

Two angels came from the West.
The one brought fire, the other brought frost.
Out fire! In frost!
In the name of the Father, Son and Holy Ghost.

For toothache an even simpler formula was recorded by the astrologer, William Lilly. The patient had to write three times on a piece of paper the verse:

Jesus Christ for mercy sake
Take away this toothache.

He then repeated it aloud and burned the paper.[9]

6. *H.M.C., Hatfield*, xvi, pp. 280–81.
7. Borthwick, R. VI. A 10, f. 61.
8. See A. A. Barb, 'The Survival of Magic Arts', in *The Conflict between Paganism and Christianity in the Fourth Century*, ed. A. Momigliano (Oxford, 1963), pp. 122–3.
9. *Trans. Cumbs. and Westmorland Antiqn and Archaeol. Soc.*, xiv (1897), p. 372; F. G(lanvile) *et al., The Tavistocke Naboth proved Nabal* (1658), pp. 40–41; Ashm. 364, p. 119 (another version in Aubrey, *Miscellanies,* p. 135).

Sometimes Hebrew words for the divinity were employed, like Sabaoth, Adonay, or Yhvh (the four-letter word, Tetragrammaton). Originally they had reflected a belief in the magical power of holy names. But by the sixteenth century they often meant as little to the wizard as to his clients. Conjurers, remarked a contemporary, used hybrid names like Ravarone, Hur, Asmobias, Mebarke, Geballa; they were not English, Latin, Hebrew, Greek, Arabic, Syriac or anything else.[10] Thus one Elizabethan wizard had an elaborate remedy for the toothache:

First he must know your name, then your age, which in a little paper he sets down. On the top are these words, *In verbis et in herbis, et in lapidibus sunt virtutes.* Underneath he writes in capital letters, AAB ILLA, HYRS GIBELLA, which he swears is pure Chaldee, and the names of the three spirits that enter into the blood and cause rheums, and so consequently the toothache. This paper must be likewise burned, which being thrice used is of power to expel the spirits, purify the blood, and ease the pain.[11]

Other formulae reflected memories of the magical squares and acrostics of antiquity, like this prescription for the ague:

Write these words: 'Arataly, Rataly, Ataly, taly, aly, ly,' and bind these words about the sick man's arm nine days, and every day say three *Pater Nosters* in worship of St Peter and St Paul, and then take off that and burn it and the sick shall be whole.[12]

Hundreds of such charms have survived, preserved in contemporary notebooks, or disclosed during the course of court proceedings against their users. Some were well known to everyone, like the so-called White Paternoster, of which a version survives in the children's prayer: 'Matthew, Mark, Luke and John, Bless the bed that I lie on'; others were closely guarded secrets. There were charms for women in labour, mad dogs, sick horses, and every conceivable ache and pain: as a contemporary put it, for 'the stinging of serpents, bleeding at the nose, blastings, inflammations, burnings with fire, scalding with water, agues, toothache, cramps, stitches, prickings, ragings, achings, swellings, heart burnings, flowings of the head, &c'.[13] Others were used when ritually gathering medical herbs.

10. E. Digby, *Theoria Analytica* (1579), p. 384.
11. H. Chettle, *Kind-Heart's Dream* (1592), ed. E. F. Rimbault (Percy Soc., 1841), pp. 29–30.   12. Sloane 3846, f. 14ᵛ.
13. E. P(oeton), 'The Winnowing of White Witchcraft' (Sloane, 1954), f. 173ᵛ. For versions of the White Paternoster, see W. J. Thoms, 'Chaucer's

Vervain, which was thought to have special protective qualities, had to be crossed and blessed when gathered:

> Hallowed be thou Vervain, as thou growest on the ground
> For in the mount of Calvary there thou was first found.
> Thou healedst our Saviour, Jesus Christ, and staunchedst
> his bleeding wound,
> In the name of the Father, the Son, and the Holy Ghost,
> I take thee from the ground.[14]

Much erudition would be needed to trace the genealogy of the obscure and meaningless formulae into which many classical and early Christian charms had degenerated by the sixteenth and seventeenth centuries. Some afford striking testimony to the survival of classical influences through the Dark Ages. Others reveal a direct line of descent from Anglo-Saxon to Tudor times. Many are almost identical with magical formulae used in continental Europe.[15] But by this period their original meaning was often hidden from those who used them. Indeed the people who wore them round their necks were often illiterate. The very impenetrability of the formula helped to give it its power.

Certain assumptions underlying these charms can, however, be

Night-Spell', *Folk-Lore Record*, i (1878), and W. D. Macray, 'Lancashire Superstitions in the Sixteenth and Seventeenth Centuries', *Local Gleanings relating to Lancs. and Cheshire*, i (1875–6).

14. J. White, *The Way to the True Church* (2nd impn, 1610), sig. C2ᵛ. For some of the many MS collections of charms compiled during the sixteenth and seventeenth centuries see Bodl., MS e Mus. 243 and MS Add. B. 1; Sloane 3846; W. Rye, 'A Note Book of Sir Miles Branthwayt in 1605', *Norfolk Archaeology*, xiv (1900), pp. 131–2. For more detail and discussion, see, in addition to the works of Kittredge, Pettigrew, Black, and Bonser cited in the *Bibliographical Note* above, Scot, *Discoverie*, XII.xiv; W. Sparrow Simpson, 'On a Seventeenth-century Roll Containing Prayers and Magical Signs', *Journ. of Brit. Archaeol. Assoc.*, xl (1884); G. Storms, *Anglo-Saxon Magic* (The Hague, 1948); T. Davidson, 'Animal Charm Cures and Amulets', *Amateur Historian*, iii (1956–8); C. F. Bühler, 'Prayers and Charms in Certain Middle English Scrolls', *Speculum*, xxxix (1964); T. R. Forbes, *The Midwife and the Witch* (New Haven, 1966), pp. 80–93.

15. Many interesting parallels are afforded by the numerous charms contained in *Leechdoms, Wortcunning, and Starcraft of Early England*, ed. O. Cockayne (Rolls Series, 1864–6), and analysed by F. Grendon, 'The Anglo-Saxon Charms', *Journ. of American Folk-Lore*, xxii (1909). For their miscellaneous pedigree, see C. Singer, 'Early English Magic and Medicine', *Procs. of Brit. Acad.*, ix (1919–20). cf. the curative formulae in Delcambre, *Le Concept de la sorcellerie*, iii, pp. 229–38.

detected. There was the idea that disease was a foreign presence in the body needing to be conjured or exorcised out. There was also the belief that religious language possessed a mystical power which could be deployed for practical purposes. Such charms could be efficacious regardless of the moral value of the operator; others depended upon the special qualities of the healer: the Lancashire charmer, Thomas Hope, explained in 1638 that he owed his powers to having been washed in special water at Rome, which he had visited with his uncle as a small boy.[16]

All three constituents of primitive healing were thus present at one time or another: the spell, the medicine and the special condition of the performer.[17] But no coherent theory underlay the visits of the clients to the cunning men. Indeed the patient was often kept in ignorance of the formula employed, which, like the details of much modern medicine, might be deemed too secret to be entrusted to laymen.

There is one Alice Prabury in our parish [reported the churchwardens of Barnsley, Gloucestershire, in 1563] that useth herself suspiciously in the likelihood of a witch, taking upon her not only to help Christian people of diseases strangely happened, but also horses and all other beasts. She taketh upon her to help by the way of charming, and in such ways that she will have nobody privy of her sayings.[18]

Similar precautions had been taken in the reign of Mary Tudor by another charmer, Elizabeth Page. According to the Somerset mother who had called her in to treat her sick child, she

looked on it lying in a cradle; . . . and kneeling by the cradle, crossing the forehead of the said child, and demanding the name of it, . . . she spoke certain words over the said child; but what they were this deponent cannot tell. And then rose and bade this deponent to be of good comfort and her child should do well.

Two days later the infant had recovered.[19] Such secrecy was always important, and, although many contemporary charm-books survive, they were never printed and published, save by those who wished to expose them as fraudulent or diabolical. Unquestioning trust was displayed by the patients who wore the prescribed charms

16. Lancashire R.O., QSB/1/202/89.
17. cf. C. Geertz, *The Religion of Java* (Glencoe, Ill., 1960), p. 94.
18. Gloucester D.R., Vol. 20, p. 58.
19. Wells D.R., D 7 (Depositions, 1554–6).

on their body. When in 1623 John Walter of Felpham visited one Sowton of Sompting, a Sussex charmer, on behalf of a neighbour, he was given a bottle of water for her to take, and a paper with crosses and characters on it for her to wear.[20] The procedure was as matter-of-fact as the issuing of a modern doctor's prescription.

Yet like modern drugs, the formulae employed were often credited with highly dramatic effects. In 1617, for example, Edmund Langdon, who practised medicine in the Bedminster area of Somerset, gave one of his patients a piece of paper to be worn on his body for protection, which, he said, was so powerful, that 'if it were hanged about a cock's neck no man should have the power to kill the ... cock'.[21] Such prescriptions were often given to animals. In Cambridgeshire in 1601 Oliver Den was accused of practising sorcery

by using to write certain words in a piece of bread which he giveth to dogs bitten with a mad dog, thereby to keep them from it; and ... one, Walter Ward, having certain hogs who had been bitten with a mad dog, the said Den did take apples and cut them into halves and did take the half parts of these apples and wrote certain letters on them, and gave the same to the said hogs, by which he said he would keep the said hogs from running mad or ... dying.

Feeding mad dogs or those bitten by them with charms written on paper was a common procedure.[22]

In most cases, therefore, the wizard was simply a 'blesser' or 'charmer' who mumbled a few words over the afflicted part of the body, or wrote down the curative formulae on a piece of paper. When Elizabeth Cracklow, the wise woman of Adderbury, Oxfordshire, was consulted in 1546 by one Gibbons, whose arm was 'out of joint', she caused her husband to 'hold forth and preach over the said Gibbon's arm, and then she crossed his arm in sundry places and bid [her] husband say one "God's forbade" '. She enjoyed a considerable reputation, and had been 'sent for to divers places for the curing of people'.[23] Such practitioners deemed the cure to lie in

20. *Churchwardens' Presentments (17th Century). Part I: Archdeaconry of Chichester*, ed. H. Johnstone (Sussex Rec. Soc. [1949]), pp. 82, 92.

21. *Records of the County of Wilts*, ed. B. H. Cunnington (Devizes, 1932), pp. 61–2.

22. Ely D.R., B 2/20, f. 48. Other examples in Aubrey, *Miscellanies*, p. 135, and *Gentilisme*, p. 125; J. Hewitt, 'Medical Recipes of the Seventeenth Century', *Archaeol. Journ.*, xxix (1872), pp. 75–6.

23. Bodl., Oxford Diocesan Papers, d. 14, f. 86.

the correct pronunciation of the appropriate formulae. But a few technical aids might also be employed. Thus in Northumberland in 1604 Katherine Thompson and Anne Nevelson were presented as 'common charmers of sick folks and their goods'; their method was to put the bill of a white duck to the sick person's mouth and then mumble charms. Another wise woman from the North East, Ann Green, admitted in 1654 to charming 'heart-ache' by crossing a garter over the patient's ears and saying nine times, 'Boate [i.e. help], a God's name.' She also cured pains in the head by taking a lock of the victim's hair, boiling it in his urine, and then throwing the mixture into the fire.[24]

A further common method of magical diagnosis was to examine some item of the patient's clothing, preferably his belt or girdle, on the assumption that it would sympathetically reflect the wearer's state of health by fluctuating in size. In Cambridgeshire Elizabeth Mortlock described this procedure in 1566. She would begin with

five Paternosters in the worship of the five Wounds of our Lord, five Aves in the worship of the five Joys of our Lady, and one Creed in the worship of the blessed Father, the Son and the Holy Ghost ... and the holy Apostles, in the vulgar tongue. Which done, she measureth the girdle or band of any such persons being sick or haunted, from her elbow to her thumb, craving God for Saint Charity's sake that if [they] be haunted with a fairy, yea or no, she may know, and saith that if it be so the band will be shorter and her cubit will reach further than commonly it doth.

In this way she claimed she had been able to cure several children troubled by the 'fairy'.[25] The highly traditional nature of this method is shown by the fact that her account almost exactly reproduces the confession of Agnes Hancock, made in another county, Somerset, over a century earlier, in 1438. She too professed to treat children afflicted with the 'feyry' by inspecting the invalid's girdle or shoe.[26]

Girdle-measuring of this kind was an ancient procedure, widely dispersed throughout Europe. The assumption behind it was that the presence of an evil spirit ('fairy') would reflect itself in the inconstancy of the measured length. It was still practised at the end of the

24. *York Depositions*, pp. 127 n., 64–5.
25. Ely D.R., B 2/5, f. 273.
26. *The Register of John Stafford ... 1425–43*, ed. T. S. Holmes (Somerset Rec. Soc., 1915–16), ii, pp. 225–7.

sixteenth century. Matilda Allin of Dullingham, Cambridgeshire, was charged in 1592 with carrying 'kerchiefs, fillets, girdles and partlets from divers sick persons, and measuring of sick swine, and carrying these things unto such as are suspected to use sorcery and witchcraft'. Two years previously the wife of Thomas Bolton of Hickleton, Yorkshire, was said to have 'made a girdle about a thing and told one that she would not die at that time'. (On this occasion the Archbishop of York's Court was 'doubtful whether the same be a charmer or no'.) A variant method of magical cure, also based on the sympathetic qualities of the girdle, was revealed by Joan Sergeant of Minehead, who confessed in 1532 that when her child was sick, she was advised by a wandering beggar to 'cut her ... child's girdle in five pieces and then to go to the church and say five Paternosters and five Aves and then to take the same pieces of the girdle and hide it in five sundry grounds'.[27]

Other techniques included burning or burying an animal alive to help the sick party recover,[28] dipping him in south-flowing water, dragging him through trees or bushes,[29] and touching him with a special staff; in 1523 John Thornton of Sapcote, Leicestershire, claimed to have been curing animals with a 'Moses rod' for thirty years.[30] Other wizards advised their clients to dig holes in churchyards, boil eggs in urine, and tie staves, salt and herbs in cows' tails.[31]

27. Ely D.R., B 2/12, f. 11; Borthwick, R. VI. A 10, f. 224; Wells D.R., A 7. cf. A. D. Rees, 'The Measuring Rod', *Folk-Lore*, lxvi (1955). For examples outside England see Thorndike, *Magic and Science*, i, p. 512; Delcambre, *Le Concept de la sorcellerie*, iii, pp. 31–5; J. Grimm, *Teutonic Mythology*, trans. J. S. Stallybrass (4th edn, 1883), pp. 1163–5; P. Kemp, *Healing Ritual. Studies in the Technique and Tradition of the Southern Slavs* (1935), pp. 120–26; Lea, *Materials*, p. 619.

28. e.g., Kittredge, *Witchcraft*, pp. 93–7; C. M. L. Bouch, *Prelates and People of the Lake Counties* (Kendal, 1948), p. 216; *Notes and Queries*, i (1849–50), p. 294.

29. Ewen, ii, p. 447; *Durham Depositions* pp. 99–100; Brand, *Popular Antiquities*, iii, pp. 287–93; T. Jackson, *A Treatise containing the Originall of Unbeliefe* (1625), p. 179; A. Hussey, 'Archbishop Parker's Visitation, 1569', *Home Counties Magazine*, v (1903), p. 115.

30. A. P. Moore, 'Proceedings of the ecclesiastical courts in the Archdeaconry of Leicester, 1516–35', *Assocd Architectl Socs., Reports and Papers*, xxviii (1905–6), p. 613. Similar cases in Hale, *Precedents*, p. 108; *The Fabric Rolls of York Minster*, ed. J. Raine (Surtees Soc., 1859), p. 266. On the Moses Rod, see below, pp. 280–81.

31. W. Drage, *Daimonomageia* (1665), p. 39; Bouch, *Prelates and People*

In Kent Alice Bowreman used red nettles, blue cloth and certain words. In Northumberland Margaret Stothard put her lips to the sick child's mouth, 'and made such chirping and sucking that the mother of the said child thought that she had sucked the heart of it out, and was sore affrighted'." It would be possible to draw up a long list of such methods of magical cure. But the meaning of the primitive symbolism from which these techniques had originally sprung is very largely lost to view. In the sixteenth century these practices did not reflect a single coherent cosmology or scheme of classification, but were made up out of the debris of many different systems of thought.

Perhaps the most distinctive feature of the cunning man's medical dealings was his readiness to diagnose a supernatural cause for the patient's malady by saying that he was haunted by an evil spirit, a ghost, or 'fairy', or that he had been 'overlooked', 'forspoken', or, in plainer language, bewitched. Indeed his authority in this domain gave him much of his reputation. Thus if any inhabitant of mid-sixteenth-century Maidstone suspected that he had been forspoken, he would go off for advice to one Kiterell, a sorcerer who lived at Bethersden, and specialised in such things: and when James Hop-kinne of Hornchurch, Essex, in 1576 thought that his master's cattle had been bewitched, it was to the cunning woman, Mother Persore, that he naturally turned for help. In Yorkshire in 1598 William Taylor was charged with sending to two wise women, Widow Haigh and Widow Carr, to know a remedy for his sickness; their resolution was that he had been bewitched." Many other cunning folk specialized in this area.

The methods by which the wizard purported to diagnose the witchcraft were diverse. He might use a technique familiar to the lay public, such as boiling the victim's urine, or burning a piece of thatch from the suspected witch's house to see whether this brought her running to the scene. He might alternatively have recourse to a mirror, a crystal ball, a sieve and shears, a familiar spirit, or some

---

of the Lake Counties, p. 216; Hertfordshire R.O., HAT/SR 2/100 (more briefly in Hertford County Records, i, ed. W. J. Hardy [Hertford, 1905], pp. 3–4).

32. Archdeacon Harpsfield's Visitation, 1557, i, p. 109; E. Mackenzie, An Historical, Topographical, and Descriptive View of the County of Northumberland (2nd edn, Newcastle, 1825), ii, p. 34.

33. J. Halle, An Historiall Expostulation, ed. T. J. Pettigrew (Percy Soc., 1844), pp. 28–9; Hale, Precedents, p. 163; Borthwick, R. VI. E. 1a, f. 64.

other method of divination.[34] When Joan Tyrry, who had been quick to identify witches among her Taunton neighbours, was called upon in 1555 to explain how she did it, she answered simply that she could tell because the fairies told her.[35] In York in 1594 Cuthbert Williamson claimed to possess a kind of extra-sensory perception by which he could always tell whether a client had been forspoken, for his own eyes would run with tears if he had. Other wizards taught that the patient was bewitched if he could not see his reflection in the wise man's eyes, or if he could not say his prayers.[36]

Having pronounced that the patient had been bewitched, the cunning man had various remedies. Some of them reflected the idea that the resources of the Christian religion, if properly mobilized, were sufficient to deal with the powers of darkness. When in 1622 the London empiric, Robert Booker, informed a patient that he had been bewitched, he anointed him with oil and pronounced a charm: 'Three biters have bit him – heart, tongue and eye; three better shall help him presently – God the Father, God the Son, and God the Holy Spirit.' This was a standard formula, and many examples of its use survive.[37] It indicated the three supposed sources of witchcraft – concealed malevolence ('heart'), bitter words ('tongue'), and ocular fascination ('eye') – and it emphasized that the forces of religion were strong enough to deal with them. This was not a view held in orthodox Protestant circles, and when found among the cunning men its Catholic affiliations were usually obvious. Thus Joan Bettyson of Nottinghamshire used to effect the recovery of forspoken cattle in the early 1590s by reciting fifteen Paternosters, fifteen Aves and three Creeds – a recipè she had learned from her

34. On these techniques see below, chap. 8. Representative examples of their use may be found in Lambeth, V/Di/III/3 (sieve and shears 'in the name of God and St Stephen', 1558); Ewen, ii, pp. 190, 230 (mirror and crystal), 234 (spirit).

35. Wells D.R., A 21 and A 22. cf. below, pp. 296, 317.

36. J. S. Purvis, *Tudor Parish Documents* (Cambridge, 1948), pp. 199–200; Bodl., MS e Mus. 173, f. 63ᵛ; Bernard, *Guide*, p. 138.

37. C. Goodall, *The Royal College of Physicians* (1684), pp. 403–4, and Sir G. Keynes, *The Life of William Harvey* (Oxford, 1966), p. 65 (for Booker). Other examples in Kittredge, *Witchcraft*, p. 39; Lancashire R. O., QSB/1/139 (81) (Henry Baggilie, 1634); A. Watkin, *Dean Cosyn and Wells Cathedral Miscellanea* (Somerset Rec. Soc., 1941), p. 157. Other versions in B.M., Egerton MS 825, f. 109ᵛ; Bodl., MS e Mus. 173, f. 63; Bodl., Douce MS 116, pp. 145, 148; Bodl., Add. MS B. 1, f. 45ᵛ; K. M. Briggs, *Pale Hecate's Team* (1962), pp. 262–3.

grandfather. Another Nottingham sorcerer named Groves in the early seventeenth century used to sell his clients copies of St John's Gospel as a preservative against witchcraft. The fairies' confidant, Joan Tyrry, prescribed herbs for bewitched persons, to be gathered to the accompaniment of five Paternosters, five Aves and a Creed. In Carmarthenshire Margaret David effected her cures with water and earth 'from Jerusalem'.[38]

Sometimes, however, the action taken bore no obvious relationship to religious beliefs at all. Witness the dramatic procedure followed by Elizabeth Page in Blagdon, Somerset, in 1555. Elizabeth Wryte had asked her to cure her sick daughter, but when the wise woman first came to see the child she departed without offering any comment. A few days later the anxious mother went to her again to ask 'if she could help her child if it were overlooked or bewitched; who answered, "Yea" ', explaining that to cure her

she must cause herself to be in as ill a case as the said child then was (who was then likely to die) ere that she could help her, but said that it would be midnight before her husband would be fast or sound asleep and then she would take pains to rise and help the child by her means, willing this deponent [the mother] to take the said child into her bed that night and about midnight her child should recover. And even so she did. And at one of the clock after midnight the same child, lying by this deponent all the night (being as it were in a trance) recovered and took sustenance. And ... afterwards, when it should happen the said Elizabeth [Page] [came] at any time to see the said child she would openly say in the presence of people, 'This is my child, for she had been dead, and [i.e. if] I had not been.'[39]

The whole episode is eloquent testimony to the survival of the concept of disease as a foreign element which, by the appropriate procedure, could be transferred from one carrier to another. The same notion underlay the practice of the Lancashire charmer, Henry Baggilie, who confessed in 1634 to using a formula which his father. had been taught by 'a Dutchman', adding that 'during all the time of his blessing he ... hath always been suddenly taken with sickness

38. R. F. B. Hodgkinson, 'Extracts from the Act Books of the Archdeacons of Nottingham', *Trans. Thoroton Soc.*, xxx (1926), p. 51; *Records of the Borough of Nottingham* (Nottingham, 1882–1956), iv, p. 275; Wells D.R., A 21; Ewen, ii, p. 331. For a fuller discussion of the role of Catholic prayers in the treatment of the bewitched, see below, chap. 15.

39. Wells D.R., D 7.

or lameness, and that always in the same manner that the man or beast that he blessed was troubled withal'.[40]

Closely affiliated to the magical treatment of disease were the various practices designed to safeguard the woman in child-bed. The invocation of the Virgin Mary and the use of sanctified objects at difficult stages of labour had been encouraged by the medieval Church and often survived the Reformation. But other techniques had never carried any ecclesiastical blessing. The use of girdles and measures to relieve labour pains, the opening of chests and doors, and the pronunciation of charms and prayers, were all common features of the country midwife's repertoire.[41] Along with them went the belief that the infant's expectation of life could be divined from scrutiny of the after-birth, or that good fortune would accompany the child born with the caul (or 'sillyhow') over its head. Even in the mid seventeenth century a country gentleman might regard his caul as a treasure to be preserved with great care, and bequeathed to his descendants.[42]

There are also occasional indications of magical attempts to control the conception of children or determine their sex. There were plenty of equivalents to the powder which the sorceress, Mary Woods, admitted in 1613 to having given the Countess of Essex to wear round her neck when she wished to conceive.[43] Less common was the claim made in 1533 by Edith Hooker of New Alresford, Hampshire, that she could enable women to conceive 'sine virili semine'; a witness said she 'gave medicine to a certain woman to bring her with child, and the medicine was made of the spawn of a trotter'. This may have been a folk version of the alchemical attempt to create homunculi, reflected in the supposed desire of the Rosicrucians to beget descendants without what Sir Thomas Browne

40. Lancashire R.O., QSB/1/139(81) (other examples of the same principle in Ewen, ii, pp. 175, 323, 448; Drage, *Diamonomageia*, p. 43). For the other remedies against witchcraft, see below, pp. 648–50.

41. Kittredge, *Witchcraft*, pp. 114–15; Brand, *Popular Antiquities*, ii, pp. 67–72; Scot, *Discoverie*, XI.xv; below, p. 308. For typical charms, B.M., Harley MS 1735, f. 40; Sloane 1311, f. 33ᵛ.

42. Brand, *Popular Antiquities*, iii, pp. 114–19; A. Roberts, *A Treatise of Witchcraft* (1616), pp. 65–6; Aubrey, *Gentilisme*, p. 113; *The Memoirs of Sir Daniel Fleming*, ed. R. E. Porter and W. G. Collingwood (Kendal, 1928), p. 69; T. F. Thiselton-Dyer, *Old English Social Life* (1898), pp. 120–21.

43. *C.S.P.D.*, 1611–18, p. 187 (cf. p. 183). Similar formulae in Sloane 3846, f. 15ᵛ; Bodl., MS e Mus. 243, f. 13.

called 'this trivial and vulgar way of coition'.⁴⁴ A parallel case comes
from South Leigh, Oxfordshire, in 1520, where John Phipps and
his wife were presented by the churchwardens for keeping a cradle
beside their bed at night and treating it 'as if a child was in it'.⁴⁵
This was thought by the authorities at the time to be a case of
idolatry, but it is more likely to have been an example of sympathetic
magic in which the desired effect was to be produced by imitation;
presumably the couple wanted a child. The relative rarity of charms
to prevent conception, however, suggests that as a means of birth-
control they were less popular than the well-known, if unobtrusive,
practice of *coitus interruptus*, and the numerous potions and medicines to procure abortion.⁴⁶

As for the prior determination of sex, various traditions had been
inherited from classical medicine concerning the right side of the
bed to lie on to conceive a child of the desired kind. They were
widely disseminated in such handbooks as the popular *Aristotle's
Masterpiece* (1684, and often reissued),⁴⁷ but it is difficult to find
evidence as to whether they were taken seriously. Wizards were
occasionally asked to predict the sex of an unborn child, and they
did this by one of their routine methods of divination, in some of
which classical influence was again apparent. Few potential mothers
however, attained the virtuosity of Mrs Parish, mistress of the late-
seventeenth-century Whig politician, Goodwin Wharton, whose
magical skill was such that she knew instantaneously when she had
conceived, confidently identifying the child's sex on every occasion.
She was, of course, a fraud, but her lover took her claims seriously.⁴⁸

44. Winchester D.R., C.B. 6, pp. 71, 75; Sir T. Browne, *Religio Medici*
(1643), ii. 9.
45. *Oxfordshire Archaeol. Soc. Report*, lxx (1925), p. 95.
46. For magical abortion and contraception, Ewen, i, p. 318; Aubrey,
Gentilisme, p. 118; Borthwick, R. VI A 13, ff. 64ᵛ–5 (1594); W. W(illiams),
Occult Physick (1660), p. 135; J. T. Noonan, Jr., *Contraception* (New York,
1967); below, pp. 759–60. cf. the graphic early sixtenth-century description of
coitus interruptus in *Three Chapters of Letters relating to the Dissolution of
Monasteries*, ed. T. Wright (Camden Soc., 1843), p. 97.
47. cf. (T. Lupton), *A Thousand Notable things* (1660), pp. 13, 24. For
Galen's teaching on this subject, Thorndike, *Magic and Science*, i, p. 175.
Similar methods were occasionally employed in stock-breeding (see below,
p. 776.
48. See Wharton's autobiography (B.M., Add. MSS 20,006–7), i, ff. 45,
68ᵛ, 83ᵛ, 84ᵛ, 106ᵛ, 107, etc. The midwife in Ben Jonson's *An Entertainment
at the Blackfriars* (1620) could foretell sex. Dr Alan Macfarlane has found a
case in which sieve and shears were used for sex divination in 1589 (Essex

In this whole field there was often no clear distinction between the use of natural remedies and supernatural or symbolic ones. Many seventeenth-century prescriptions which seem magical to us were in fact based on obsolescent assumptions about the physical properties of natural substances. When Sir Christopher Hatton sent Queen Elizabeth a ring to protect her against the plague or when Elias Ashmole wore three spiders to counteract the ague, they were not resorting to magic, but employing a purely physical form of treatment.[49] No student of the period can fail to notice the recourse to such objects at every level of society. There was the rattling eagle-stone (aetites) which the Countess of Newcastle was invited to wear in 1633 to ease her labour pains; the hare-foot which Samuel Pepys, F.R.S., slung round his neck as a cure for the colic; the moss from a dead man's skull by which the eminent Nonconformist John Allin set such store; and the gold bullet which Richard Baxter swallowed to cure his chronic illness, but was unable to get out again, until its passage was assisted by the prayers of his despairing congregation.[50] The belief in the utility of such objects ultimately stemmed from ancient systems of classification which implied the existence of correspondences and analogies between different parts of creation. Even in this period there were still many believers in the doctrine of signatures, according to which every herb was stamped with a more or less clear sign of its uses; so that, for example, a yellow blossom indicated a likely cure for jaundice, or a root shaped like a foot became a remedy for gout.[51] On such analogous reasoning it is not difficult to see why the aetites stone, with another rattling inside it, should have been thought helpful to a pregnant woman. But by the seventeenth century most of this symbolism had been lost.

R.O., D/ACA 18, f. 80). See in general, Forbes, *The Midwife and the Witch*, pp. 50–63.

49. B. M., Harley MS 416, f. 200; Josten, *Ashmole*, p. 1680.

50. *H.M.C., Portland*, ii, p. 123; W. G. Bell, *The Great Plague in London* (revd edn, 1951), pp. 163–4, 259–60; R. Baxter, *The Certainty of the World of Spirits* (1691 : 1834 edn), p. 70. For some evidence on this large subject, Scot, *Discoverie*, XIII.vi; Aubrey, *Gentilisme*, index, *s.v.* 'amulets'; Burton, *Anatomy*, ii, p. 250; Forbes, *The Midwife and the Witch*, pp. 64–79; G. F., Still, *The History of Paediatrics* (1931), p. 122; N. Hodges, *Loimologia*, ed. J. Quincy (1720), pp. 218–22; J. Evans, *Magical Jewels of the Middle Ages and the Renaissance* (Oxford, 1922), chaps. 7 and 8; C. N. Bromehead, 'Aetites or the Eagle-Stone', *Antiquity*, xxi (1947); A. A. Barb, 'Birds and Medical Magic. 1. The Eagle-Stone', *Journ. Warburg and Courtauld Institutes*, xiii (1950).

51. cf. below, p. 265.

Instead, the medicinal use of toads, pigeons, gold-rings or snake-skins had come to be justified by reference to their supposedly inherent natural properties.

A similar ambiguity surrounded the wizards' practice of making both diagnosis and prognostication on the basis of the patient's urine. A handbook of 1631 assured its readers that one could tell whether a sick man would live or die by immersing a nettle in his water for twenty-four hours. If the plant dried up as a result he would die; if it remained fresh and green he would live.[52] Yet learned physicians also made extensive use of urine, and it is hard to indicate the point at which the practice ceased to be natural. For that matter, there were many contemporary Neoplatonist intellectuals who were even prepared to attribute a purely natural effect to the incantation of words and charms.

The supreme example of a magical cure justified by the Neoplatonist belief in occult influences and sympathies was the weapon-salve, around which a fierce controversy raged in the 1630s. The idea that one could cure a wound by anointing the weapon which had caused it may strike us as absurd, but the intention was not in any way magical. By plunging the weapon into a special ointment, it was argued, one could assist the vital spirits of the congealed blood to reunite with the victim's body, and thus heal the wound even at a distance of thirty miles. Sir Kenelm Digby's book, in which he explained how the weapon-salve cure could be accomplished 'naturally and without any magic', went into twenty-nine editions. Nearly every country barber-surgeon knew the formula, he claimed in 1658. But at a popular level it is doubtful whether the use of sympathetic cures was justified on this rarified intellectual basis; and they continued to be prominent in folk medicine until the nineteenth century, when such rationalization had long been forgotten.[53]

52. G. Simotta, *A Theater of the Planetary Houres* (1631), pp. 30–1. Similar lore in *The Iudycyall of Uryns* (n.d., ? 1527); *The Key to Unknowne Knowledge* (1599); J. Hart, *The Anatomie of Urines* (1625); T. Brian, *The Pisse-Prophet, or Certaine Pisse-Pot Lectures* (1637); E. P(oeton), 'The urinall crackt in the carriage' (Sloane 1954, ff. 143–60). For urine and pregnancy tests, Forbes, *The Midwife and the Witch*, pp. 34, ff.

53. W. Foster, *Hoplocrisma-Spongus* (1631); (R. Fludd), *Doctor Fludds answer unto M. Foster* (1631) (claiming over a thousand cures, some among the nobility), p. 124; id., *Mosaicall Philosophy* (1659), pp. 221–34, 236–92 (citing many examples of cures); Sir K. Digby, *A Late Discourse . . . touching the Cure of Wounds by the Powder of Sympathy*, trans. R. White (1658), pp. 3, 14; N. Highmore, *The History of Generation* (1651), appx; J. Prim-

From the patient's point of view, indeed, all medical prescriptions beyond his comprehension were in a sense magical, since they worked by occult means. Hence the deep-rooted association of poison with sorcery.[54] Laymen have always been baffled by professional medicine and do not expect to understand the rationale behind every kind of treatment. In the late seventeenth century Samuel Butler could write of 'A Medicine-Taker' that 'he believes a doctor is a kind of conjurer that can do strange things and he is as willing to have him think so'. Another contemporary observed that 'some people . . . send for a physician as for one that deals in charms and can remove all their afflictions, while they are wholly passive'. According to the resident physician in 1697, even the pool at Bath was regarded by many as one 'that cures by miracle'.[55]

Men did not thus discriminate very much between the status of different types of cure. John Grave admitted going to the Essex wizard, Father Parfoothe, in 1592 for medicine for sick cattle, but declared that he had never thought of him as a witch; Paul Rigden confessed before the Archdeacon of Canterbury in 1598 that when his wife fell sick he sent to one Mother Chambers because she was known to have done good to many other sick persons, and not because he wanted to consult a sorceress as such.[56] Very often the accused wizard protested that he had only employed conventional remedies. Joan Warden of Stapleford, Cambridgeshire, when charged in 1592 with being a cunning woman, declared that 'she doth not use any charms, but that she doth use ointments and herbs to cure many diseases'. The same plea was made by a Yorkshire woman, Alice Marton, in 1590, when she admitted to curing cattle

---

rose, *Popular Errours*, trans. R. Wittie (1651), pp. 400–34; B.M., Add. MS 28,273, f. 141 (recipe belonging to John Locke's father); R. T. Petersson, *Sir Kenelm Digby* (1956), pp. 264–74; S. Boulton, *Medicina Magica* (1656); [C. Irvine], *Medicina Magnetica* (1656); H. More, *The Immortality of the Soul* (1659), pp. 453–7; Pettigrew, *On Superstitions connected with the History and Practice of Medicine*, pp. 157–67; Sir J. G. Frazer *Aftermath* (1936), pp. 60–2; and see below, pp. 266, 649.

54. cf. below, p. 520.

55. S. Butler, *Characters and Passages from Note-Books*, ed. A. R. Waller (Cambridge, 1908), p. 143; R. Hunter and I. Macalpine, *Three Hundred Years of Psychiatry, 1535–1860* (1963), p. 292; R. Peirce, *Bath Memoirs* (Bristol, 1697), p. 7. See also below, p. 800.

56 *Lincoln Diocese Documents, 1450–1544*, ed. A. Clark (E.E.T.S., 1914), p. 109; A. Hussey, 'Visitations of the Archdeacon of Canterbury', *Archaeologia Cantiana*, xxvi (1904), p. 21.

diseases by medicine and drinks, but not by charming.[57] As the very name reminds us, a *cunning* woman was simply a woman who knew more than other people; it did not necessarily mean that she used supernatural remedies.

In practice the presence or absence of charms as an accompaniment to the medicine became the test of whether magic was involved; to this extent, contemporaries, however simple, knew the difference between a doctor and a charmer. But even here there were difficulties, for it was notoriously wrong to rely on natural remedies without God's aid, and a prayer was always appropriate. In the last resort the only means of telling whether a cure was magical or not was to refer it to the authorities – the Church, the Law, and the Royal College of Physicians. If they permitted its employment, then no scruples need be felt by laymen.

2. *Healing by touch*

The one kind of magical healing to which official indulgence was liberally extended was the cure by the royal touch. At a special religious service conducted by leading Anglican clergy the monarch laid his hands upon each member of the long queue of sufferers. The patients approached one by one and knelt before the monarch, who lightly touched them on the face, while a chaplain read aloud the verse from St Mark: 'They shall lay hands on the sick and they recover.' They then retired and came forward again so that the King might hang round their necks a gold coin strung from a white silk ribbon.

This was the healing ritual for the King's Evil, the name given to scrofula or struma, the tubercular inflammation of the lymph glands of the neck. In practice the term was employed more loosely to comprehend a wide variety of complaints affecting the head, neck, and eyes, particularly swollen lips, tumours, sores and blisters. Scrofula itself was probably caused by infected milk, and a steady stream of deaths from the Evil was recorded in the seventeenth-century London Bills of Mortality.[58] Quite apart from this ultimate risk, the pain and unsightliness of the malady were such that sufferers under-

57. Ely D.R., B 2/12, f. 10ᵛ; Borthwick, R. VI. A. 11, f. 13.

58. John Graunt calculated that of the 229,250 deaths between 1629–36 and 1647–58 there were 537 from the King's Evil; *The Economic Writings of Sir William Petty*, ed. C. H. Hull (Cambridge, 1899), ii, p. 406. There were 86 in 1665; *Guildhall Miscellany*, ii (1965), p. 317. Bloch's judgement (*Les Rois thaumaturges*, p. 28) needs modification on this point, but on few others.

standably went to some trouble in their attempts to secure a cure. All over the country parish authorities raised funds to make it possible for the affected to travel to London to be healed. Some of the King's clients even came from overseas.

Despite its primitive affiliations, the belief in the healing power of the royal hand did not go back to time immemorial. The procedure was initiated by Edward the Confessor and the full ceremonial was laid down in the reign of Henry VII. Its popularity mounted with usage. Edward I is known to have touched over a thousand sufferers *per annum* at the end of the thirteenth century, but, so far as can be told from rather inadequate sources, the healing activities of the Plantagenet sovereigns never reached anything like the dimensions of those of the later Stuarts. Charles II is known to have ministered to over 90,000 persons in the twenty years, 1660– 64 and 1667–83. The peak was reached between May 1682 and April 1683, when 8,577 entries appear in the King's Register of Healing. The numbers were swelled by patients returning for a second time, but the figures are impressive testimony to the rite's appeal. One contemporary declared that Charles II had touched 'near half the nation'.[59]

Adequate figures do not survive for the therapeutic activities of the previous Tudor and Stuart monarchs, but there is no shortage of evidence to indicate the steady prestige of the royal touch throughout the two centuries. James I had scruples about taking part in what he thought a superstitious ceremony, but he was ultimately persuaded to conform to the practice of his predecessors. From 1634 the ritual of royal healing was included in the Book of Common Prayer, where it remained until nearly the middle of the eighteenth century.[60] Only in the years after the 1688 Revolution did the ceremony decline, partly as a reaction to the Roman Catholic character which James II had given it by reviving the pre-Reformation liturgy. William III would have nothing to do with it; and, although the rite was employed by Queen Anne (whose best-known patient was the infant Samuel Johnson), she was the last English sovereign to do so. Johnson had been sent to the Queen on the advice of the famous

59. Cited in Bloch, op. cit., p. 377 n. For the figures and problems relating to them see ibid., pp. 97–105, 378, n. 1. A good example of the 'recidivistes' to whom Bloch draws attention was William Vickers, who was touched twice by Charles II and three times by James II; W. Vickers, *An Easie and Safe Method for Curing the King's Evil* (9th edn, 1713), p. 5.

60. Until 1728 in the English version; 1744 in the Latin.

physician, Sir John Floyer, but in the eighteenth century doctors ceased to recommend the cure by royal touch.

This did not mean, however, that there was a total cessation in popular demand. Some people now went abroad in search of a cure from the exiled Stuarts, who were glad to fill the vacuum created by the scruples of the Hanoverians and their advisers. At home there was still a brisk traffic in the touch-pieces given to the sufferer at the royal ceremony, and subsequently worn round the neck as a souvenir or a protective amulet. An eighteenth-century cunning man in Yorkshire is known to have prescribed as a cure for the King's Evil a glass of water in which thirteen King Charles I farthings had been previously boiled. At Ashburnham, Kent, a relic of Charles I was preserved in the church and visited by sufferers from scrofula as late as 1860. In Scotland some people attributed the healing power to Queen Victoria.[61]

The exact status of the cure achieved by the monarch's touch was a matter of opinion. As Reginald Scot noticed, 'Some refer [it] to the property of their persons, some to the peculiar gift of God, some to the efficacy of words.'[62] It was never claimed that the King's Evil could not be cured by natural means. Contemporary doctors prescribed for it, as for any other complaint, and surgeons often operated upon the affected part. Cures were also believed to have been effected by traditional charms.[63] It was only as a last resort that the patient was advised to seek the King's aid. Even then it was much disputed whether the King had any healing power in his own person or whether his role was confined to religious intercession on the patient's behalf. 'Her Majesty,' wrote Scot, 'only useth godly and divine prayer, with some alms, and referreth the cure to God and the physicians.'[64]

61. Bloch, op. cit., p. 396; W. H. Dawson, 'An Old Yorkshire Astrologer and Magician, 1694–1760', *The Reliquary*, xxiii (1882–3), p. 200; C. J. S. Thompson, *Magic and Healing* (1947), p. 49.

62. Scot, *Discoverie*, XIII.ix.

63. cf. *The Autobiography and Personal Diary of Dr Simon Forman*, ed. J. O. Halliwell (1849), p. 15; R. C. Hope, *The Legendary Lore of the Holy Wells of England* (1893), p. 157; F. N. L. Poynter and W. J. Bishop, *A Seventeenth-century Doctor and his Patients* (Beds. Hist. Rec. Soc., 1951), pp. 4, 100–1; J. Hall, *Select Observations*, trans. J. Cooke (1657), pp. 309–11; R. Wiseman, *Severall Chirurgicall Treatises* (1676), pp. 245–335; T. Fern, *A Perfect Cure for the King's Evil* (1709) (claiming 400 cures); J. Gibbs, *Observations of Various Eminent Cures of Scrophulous Distempers* (1712).

64. Scot, *Discoverie*, XII.ix. This view was taken by James I, a copy of

But popular belief was often less moderate. The proclamations regulating the ceremony spoke of the King's power to heal by his sacred touch and the invocation of God's name, but in the reign of Charles I the reference to the invocation of God was on several occasions omitted.[65] Many contemporaries clearly thought that the cure was efficacious without any religious ceremony at all. John Aubrey tells of the religious visionary, Arise Evans, who 'had a fungous nose and said it was revealed to him that the King's hand would cure him, and at the first coming of King Charles II into St. James's Park he kissed the King's hand and rubbed his nose with it; which disturbed the King, but cured him'.[66]

Even the sufferers who took their turn at the official healings noticed that the atmosphere was not particularly religious in character. ' 'Tis true (indeed) there are prayers read at the touching,' said John Aubrey, 'but neither the King minds them nor the chaplains.' Most of the energies of the participants were spent trying to avoid being trampled in the crush.[67]

Some argued that the miraculous power sprang from the monarch's consecration with holy oil at his coronation, a rite which had survived the scruples of the early reformers.[68] Thus in 1650 when Mary Eure was thought to have scrofula, she was sent to be touched by the young Louis XIV in Paris, only to learn on arrival that his touch would have no effect because he had not yet been formally consecrated.[69] But in fact the English kings of the seventeenth century usually began to touch from the day of their accession, without waiting for any such consecration. Most people thus regarded the power to cure the Evil as an intrinsic quality pertaining to the sacred person of the monarch. By emphasizing the holy oil at the coronation and invoking God at the healing rite, theologians tried to bring the ceremony into line with orthodox religious beliefs. But so far as the public was concerned, the monarch's healing power

whose 'extempore speech at the first touching of a diseased child of the King's Evil' is in B.M., Add. MS 22,587, f. 4.

65. Crawfurd, *The King's Evil*, pp. 165, 175, 176.

66. Aubrey, *Miscellanies*, p. 128 (and J. Browne, *Adenochoiradelogia* [1684], iii, pp. 162-4).

67. Aubrey, *Gentilisme*, p. 241; Crawfurd, op. cit., p. 107.

68. P. E. Schramm, *A History of the English Coronation*, trans. L. G. W. Legg (Oxford, 1937), pp. 99-100, 102, 139; Crawfurd, op. cit., p. 70; Browne, *Adenochoiradelogia*, iii, p. 3.

69. M. M. Verney, *Memoirs of the Verney Family* (2nd edn, 1904), i, p. 499. She was ultimately touched by Charles II in 1653 (i, p. 509).

was an innate, mystical quality attaching to his office. As a Royalist supporter told Charles I in 1643, it was a 'supernatural means of cure which is inherent in your sacred majesty'. The same belief in the protective mystique of kingship was reflected in the contemporary passion for wearing royal rings and portraits as personal talismans.[70]

The ability to cure the Evil therefore became a touchstone for any claimant to the English throne, on the assumption that only the legitimate king could heal the scrofulous. Elizabeth I's healings were cited as proof that the Papal Bull of Excommunication had failed to take effect; and were even claimed as justification for giving her ambassadors diplomatic precedence over those of Spain.[71] Charles I's sacred touch made Royalist propaganda during the aftermath of the Civil War, when people flocked to be touched by the captive monarch at Holmby House, thoughtfully bringing their pieces of gold along with them, in view of his impoverished condition. His cures were cited, along with the miraculous handkerchiefs dipped in his blood, as irrefutable testimony to the injustice and impiety of his execution.[72] Charles II began touching while still in exile and lost no time in exploiting the political possibilities of the healing power after the Restoration. Only a few days after landing in England he touched 600 persons in one sitting; the enormous figures of sufferers touched subsequently during his reign, and particularly during the Royalist reaction after 1681, reflect the efforts of the Stuart dynasty to consolidate itself after the upheavals of the Interregnum. The Duke of Monmouth predictably felt it necessary to touch the scrofulous as part of his bid for the throne in 1680, and again in 1685; just as the healing power of the exiled dynasty became an indispensable element in Jacobite propaganda after 1688.[73] The

70. *To the Kings most excellent majesty. The Humble Petition of divers hundreds of the Kings poore subjects afflicted with . . . the King's Evill* (1643), p. 6 (almost certainly a piece of Royalist propaganda); R. C. Strong, *Portraits of Queen Elizabeth* (Oxford, 1963), p. 39.

71. *H.M.C., Hatfield*, x, pp. 166–7; Bloch, *Les Rois thaumaturges*, p. 335, n. 3. cf. M. del Rio, *Disquisitionum Magicarum Libri Sex* (Leyden, 1608), pp. 14, 63.

72. Crawfurd, *The King's Evil*, pp. 98–101; Bloch, op. cit., pp. 373–5; F. Peck, *Desiderata Curiosa* (1779 edn), p. 392; T.A., *The Excellency or Handy-Work of the Royal Hand* (1665), pp. 8–9; Josten, *Ashmole*, pp. 485–6; Wiseman, *Severall chirurgicall treatises*, pp. 246–7; Browne, *Adenochoiradelogia*, iii, pp. 150–5; D. H. Atkinson, *Ralph Thoresby the Topographer* (Leeds, 1885–7), ii, p. 237.

73. Crawfurd, op. cit., pp. 138–9, 154–5; T. B. Howell, *A Complete Collec-*

supposedly personal gift of God to Edward the Confessor had thus
become a lasting symbol of legitimacy and dynastic continuity. The
anointing at the coronation and the prayers at the healing ceremony
were subordinate in the popular mind to considerations of blood and
status.[74]

Magical power was also widely attributed to the piece of gold
which the King hung round the sufferer's neck. By the time of
Charles I this had developed from a mere coin given as alms into
a touch-piece minted specially for the occasion. Not every commentator considered it to be an essential part of the ceremony, but it
was widely regarded as a talisman in which the curative power was
deposited. Mary Tudor had urged her patients never to part with it,
and many believed that the cure would cease if they did. The parish
register of West Worldham, Hampshire, records the death in 1657
of one Mary Boyes, who had recovered from Evil after being
touched by Charles I at Hampton Court in 1647, but 'leaving from
about her neck the money given her at the time of her being touched,
the disease broke out again and proved irrecoverable'.[75] The talis-
manic character attributed to the touch-piece was an effective answer
to the eighteenth-century cynic[76] who suggested that the main attraction of the ceremony for the patient was the prospect of the piece of
gold. Undoubtedly some sufferers were quick to cash in their medals,
for they were often to be found in the shops. But many others
treated the object as a precious heirloom.[77]

---

tion of State Trials, xi (1811), col. 1059; His Grace the Duke of Monmouth
honoured (1680); Bloch, op. cit., pp. 392–5; H. Farquhar, 'Royal Charities',
Brit. Numismatic Journ., xv (1921), pp. 161 ff.; D.N.B., 'Carte, Thomas'. Healing miracles occurred at James II's grave in 1703, H.M.C. Stuart, i, pp. 186–7.

74. The need for the king to be legitimate is stressed by Browne, Adenochoiradelogia, iii, pp. 80–82.

75. W. A. Fearon and J. F. Williams, The Parish Registers and Parochial
Documents in the Archdeaconry of Winchester (Winchester, 1909), p. 83. cf.
Bloch, op. cit., pp. 320–21; Crawfurd, op. cit., p. 67; Browne, op. cit., iii,
pp. 148–9.

76. D. Barrington, Observations on the More Ancient Statutes (4th edn,
1775), p. 107.

77. Browne, Adenochoiradelogia, iii, p. 93, for their presence in the shops.
For their appearance in legacies see, e.g., Bloch, Les Rois thaumaturges, p.
396; H. Aveling, Northern Catholics (1966), p. 404; Kent R.O., Shoreham
Box 28; Bedfordshire R.O., AB P/W 1731/20 (bequest by a Luton tinplate
worker in 1731 of 'two pieces of gold, with the chain which I generally wear
by way of prevention of the King's Evil').

Other parasitic superstitions inevitably attached themselves to the ceremony, such as the belief that it was only effective on a Good Friday. When the coffin of Edward the Confessor was discovered in February 1685 many bystanders took away little bits, under the impression that they would have the power to cure the Evil. During the Interregnum one surgeon even explained that he would be unable to cure the King's Evil until he possessed some of the late King's lands, on the grounds that the healing power went along with them.[78] The truth was that the religious ceremonies which surrounded the royal power of healing were merely a protective framework for a more primitive piece of magic.

Inevitably there was a steady undercurrent of Protestant scepticism which regarded the whole ritual as superstitious humbug. A ceremony whose authenticity was said to derive from the miracles of Edward the Confessor could hardly commend itself to those who, like the Puritan Mrs Hutchinson, regarded that monarch as 'the superstitious prince, who was sainted for his ungodly chastity'.[79] Puritan hostility to the ceremony found open expression during the Civil War, when the republican Henry Marten excited scandalized comment by cheerfully remarking that, in the absence of Charles I, the Great Seal of Parliament might be used instead to heal the scrofulous.[80] The resort of sufferers to the captive King in 1647 led Parliament to set up a committee to prepare a declaration 'concerning the superstition of being touched for the healing of the King's Evil', and the soldiers who guarded Charles I irreverently gave him the pet name of 'Stroker'.[81] The public execution of the King marked, among so many other things, the formal repudiation of the belief that any magical power attached to his person. In the freer atmosphere of the Protectorate, Francis Osborne could openly assert in his popular, though iconoclastic, *Advice to a Son* that the cure by the

78. Browne, *Adenochoiradelogia*, iii, pp. 106–7; *Revolution Politicks* (1733), i, p. 9; T.A., *The Excellency or Handy-Work of the Royal Hand*, p. 20.
79. *Memoirs of the Life of Colonel Hutchinson by his Wife Lucy* (Everyman, n.d.), p. 3.
80. S. R. Gardiner, *History of the Great Civil War, 1642–49* (new edn, 1893), iii. p. 242. On Puritan and Dissenting dislike of the rite, W. Tooker, *Charisma sive Donum Sanationis* (1597), p. 109; Browne, op. cit., *passim*; (D. Lloyd), *Wonders no Miracles* (1666), p. 13; H. Stubbe, *The Miraculous Conformist* (1666), p. 9.
81. *Commons Journals*, v, p. 151 (but no trace of any resulting declaration); H. N. Brailsford, *The Levellers and the English Revolution*, ed. C. Hill (1961), p. 336.

royal touch was 'altogether . . . improbable to sense'. In the following century the Quaker, William Stout, whose sister had been touched by Charles II, saw it as 'but the remains of a popish ceremony', which, he wrongly supposed, had gone out with James II.[82]

Political considerations, however, always limited the public expression of scepticism. It had been all very well for James I to remark privately that, since miracles had ceased, the whole ritual must be superstitious. But free thought on the part of an ordinary citizen could be a dangerous luxury. The Presbyterian minister, Thomas Rosewell, found himself on trial for treasonable utterances in 1684 after (*inter alia*) allegedly casting aspersions on the reality of the royal healing power.[83] But the relative absence of explicit scepticism of this kind in contemporary literature suggests that self-conscious disbelief in the royal cure may have always been confined to an educated or anti-Royalist minority. Certainly the execution of Charles I created an undoubted vacuum which many rival healers thought it worth rushing to fill. A blacksmith in Cromhall, Gloucestershire, claimed to have performed some successful cures of the Evil and was recommended in 1648 to sufferers in other parts of the country. Another healer functioned at Newgate in London.[84] In Yorkshire Dr Robert Ashton claimed 'a revelation since the late King's decease to heal the Evil', and carried out a monthly healing ceremony, clad in a long white garment, laying his hands on the sufferers and pronouncing 'some form of prayers like a charm'.[85] Of the sectarians who claimed a divine gift to heal the Evil the most notable was George Fox, who was said in 1659 to have cured a scrofula victim by touch; but, when William III allowed the ceremony to lapse, the Hertfordshire Baptists claimed that a shepherd had been cured of the Evil, merely by attending one of their services.[86] In normal times, indeed, many Puritans and Dissenters were

82. F. Osborne, *Advice to a Son*, ed. E. A. Parry (1896), p. 126; *The Autobiography of William Stout of Lancaster, 1665–1752*, ed. J. D. Marshall (Manchester, 1967), p. 69.

83. *Reliquiae Baxterianae*, ed. M. Sylvester (1696), ii, pp. 199–200; *Notes and Queries*, clv (1928), p. 112; A. G. Matthews, *Calamy Revised* (Oxford, 1934), p. 418.

84. Glamorgan R.O., DI/DF F/249; *Perfect Occurrences of Every Daie Journall in Parliament* (30 April–7 May 1647), p. 144.

85. *York Depositions*, pp. 36–8. This may be the same case as that of 1651 in *Quarter Sessions Records*, ed. J. C. Atkinson (North Riding Rec. Soc., 1884–92), v, p. 85.

86. *The Journal of George Fox*, ed. N. Penney (Cambridge, 1911), ii, p.

ready to submit themselves to the royal ministrations. The Quakers formally acknowledged the efficacy of the King's touch in an address to James II in 1687.[87]

The touch for scrofula was not the only form of royal healing. Until the accession of Elizabeth I, the monarch had also participated in a ceremony designed to bring relief to sufferers from epilepsy and associated diseases. At first the money offered by the King at his devotions on Good Friday was redeemed by a sum of the same amount so that the original coins might be converted into rings to be worn by epileptics. In due course the pretence of giving money was abandoned and the rings were simply hallowed by the King at a special ceremony in which they were rubbed between his fingers and then distributed to the sufferers. These 'cramp-rings', as they were called, were not the only type of ring worn by patients seeking a magical cure for the falling sickness, but they were the ones to which most prestige attached. They were employed not only against epilepsy, but also to ward off convulsions, rheumatism and muscular spasms. Their hallowing was well established by the reign of Edward II and continued without a break until the death of Mary Tudor. They were very popular in the early sixteenth century and some were even exported to the continent of Europe.[88]

The ceremony reflected the old idea that any money retrieved from the church offertory had a magical value; there had been many medieval recipes for making magic rings out of church offerings. What happened between the fourteenth and sixteenth centuries was that the monarchy deliberately commandeered the older belief in order to build up the supernatural status of kingship. The monarch, whose participation had originally been superfluous, was given

310; *George Fox's 'Book of Miracles'*, ed. H. J. Cadbury (Cambridge, 1948), pp. 98, 117; *A True Copy of a Letter of the Miraculous Cure of David Wright* (1694).

87. H. Farquhar, 'Royal Charities', *Brit. Numismatic Journ.*, xiv (1920), p. 100. For examples of sectarian believers, *Yorkshire Diaries*, ed. C. Jackson (Surtees Soc., 1877), p. 62; Browne, *Adenochoiradelogia*, iii, pp. 141, 172–3.

88. For this and the following paragraph see the full account by R. Crawfurd, 'The Blessing of Cramp-Rings: a Chapter in the History of the Treatment of Epilepsy', *Studies in the History and Method of Science*, ed. C. Singer (Oxford, 1917), and discussion in Bloch, *Les Rois thaumaturges*, pp. 159–83, 323–7, 332–4, 445–8. Another example of the export of cramp-rings is in P.R.O., SP 46/162/174 (in 1556).

first a secondary role in the ceremony and then a primary one. In the final, Marian, version of the ritual the efficacy of the cramp-rings was explicity stated to come from being rubbed by royal hands, sanctified by the unction of holy oil. Their power was thus derived ultimately from God, but in practice all the prestige attached itself to his representative on earth, the rings being produced ready-made to be implanted with a supernatural quality by the monarch. A clergyman like Stephen Gardiner could point out that they had to be sprinkled with holy water and that the curative gift possessed by the royal hands was 'not of their own strength, but by invocation of the name of God'.[89] But in popular estimation their essential virtue derived from the personal *mana* of the sovereign.

The blessing of cramp-rings was abandoned immediately and without comment upon the accession of Elizabeth I. Protestant scruples presumably lay behind the change, though there is little direct evidence on this point,[90] and it is noticeable that the pious young Edward VI had shown no such inhibition once the ceremony had been shorn of its Roman appurtenances. In Catholic circles some nostalgia for the old rite lingered. In the mid seventeenth century a Hereford goldsmith was brought consecrated shillings by Papists who wanted him to make cramp-rings out of them. James II may even have planned the reintroduction of the ceremony, for in his reign the old order of service was resurrected and issued in print, as a *ballon d'essai*, though the Revolution prevented matters being taken any further.[91]

The claim to heal by touch was not unique to kings. Touching or stroking was a common part of the curative ritual followed by cunning men and women. Yet they were harried by the church courts and accused of magic and witchcraft. There was, as John Donne remarked, a certain irony about this situation, when the King of England was publicly practising the same methods. Indeed a debate between two controversialists on the propriety of the weapon-salve was only ended, it was said, when 'authority (to vindicate the usual cure of the King's Evil from being an operation of the Devil) did

89. *The Works of Nicholas Ridley*, ed. H. Christmas (Cambridge, P.S., 1841), p. 500.

90. *Pace* Bloch, op. cit., pp. 332–4, where more is read into Gardiner's letter to Ridley (*Works of Nicholas Ridley*, pp. 495–504) than the text will support.

91. *A Narrative of the Life of Mr Richard Lyde of Hereford* (1731), p. 8; Bloch, op. cit., p. 388, n. 1.

step in betwixt them'.[92] Like the King, the cunning folk usually accompanied the touch with the pronunciation of a prayer or charm. But sometimes they expected it to work unaccompanied. In 1624 a healer offered to cure the deranged Lord Purbeck, brother of James I's Duke of Buckingham, by merely touching the patient's head. A decade later the Royal College of Physicians apprehended a weaver, Christopher Barton, who professed to cure diseased scalps by laying on hands. In 1647 a letter-writer reported the activities of Anne Jefferies, a young girl in Cornwall who could cure sufferers from broken bones or epilepsy by the mere touch of her hand.[93]

These healers by touch usually fell into one of two categories. There were those who were presumed to have been personally endowed with miraculous power by God or some other mystical source, and there were those who owed their gifts to their peculiar social position. Of these latter the most obvious were the so-called seventh sons, or, better still, seventh sons of seventh sons. The origin of the peculiar aura attached to these genealogical freaks is difficult to uncover. Although widely disseminated over Europe in modern times, the idea was not to be found before the sixteenth century and in England was rare before the beginning of the seventeenth.[94] But by 1700 a number of such healers had achieved prominence, and there must have been many more who left no record behind them.

Usually their activities only came to light because the authorities saw them as a threat to the royal monopoly of the power to heal the King's Evil by touch alone. The government of Charles I was particularly sensitive on this score and several times intervened to check the *lèse-majesté* of rival healers. In 1632 a Frenchman, Boisgaudre, prisoner in the King's Bench, was examined before the Lord Chief

92. J. Donne, *Biathanatos* (1646), pp. 216–17; F. Osborne, *A Miscellany of Sundry Essays*, p. 28 (in *Miscellaneous Works of ... Francis Osborn* [11th edn, 1722],i). For the prosecution of wizards see below, pp. 292–3, 307–13.

93. (T. Longueville), *The Curious Case of Lady Purbeck* (1909), p. 99; *Privy Council Registers preserved in the P.R.O.*, viii (1968), p. 190; C. Goodall, *The Royal College of Physicians of London* (1684), pp. 467–8; *Devon and Cornwall Notes and Queries*, xiii (1924), pp. 312–14 (and below, p. 727.)

94. See Bloch, *Les Rois thaumaturges*, pp. 293–8, 498–9. The first known reference in England occurs in T. Lupton, *A Thousand Notable Things* (1579, and often reprinted).

Justice for taking it upon himself to cure the Evil. His method was to spit on his hands and rub the patient's sores, making the sign of the cross, and giving the sufferer a paper to hang round his neck on which was inscribed *In nomine Jesu Christi, ipse sanetur*. He was said to have been dealing with up to 140 cases a day, and to have been paid twenty-five shillings by one client, just for a glass of water. No doubt Boisgaudre, who had been imprisoned for debt, was taking practical steps to improve his fortunes. But he claimed to have cured 200 people, and attributed his success to being the youngest of seven sons.[95]

Five years later the Royal College of Physicians was ordered by the Privy Council to investigate the case of James Leverett, another alleged seventh son (actually a fourth), who healed the Evil and other ailments by touching his patients and declaring, in obvious imitation of the royal ceremony, 'God bless; I touch; God heals.' He was also said to have made disparaging references to the healing sessions of his rival Charles I, and to have boasted that the very sheets in which he slept would subsequently have the power to cure diseases. The Privy Council had him whipped and sent to Bride-well.[96] Another case in 1637 was that of Richard Gilbert, seventh son of a Somerset husbandman, who had established a record by beginning his career as a 'stroker' when one day old. Now aged five, he was holding healing sessions every Monday at his home, where he touched sufferers from wens, swellings and the Evil, declaring sanctimoniously, 'I touch; God heals.' In this case the child's grandmother seems to have been responsible for initiating the procedure. But her motives were honest enough. No fees were charged, and the only profit went to the local inns, which were crowded with persons of quality who came to witness the healing.[97]

All these cases were concerned with the King's Evil. But there were other seventh sons whose healing gifts were less specialised.

95. *C.S.P.D.*, *1631–3*, pp. 252, 347–8.
96. Goodall, *The Royal College of Physicians*, pp. 446–63; *C.S.P.D.*, *1636–7*, p. 328; *Privy Council Registers preserved in the P.R.O.*, i–ii (1637–8) (1967), pp. 220, 309, 437, 515; Keynes, *The Life of William Harvey*, pp. 264–8. For other instances of Royalist hostility to the competing claims of seventh sons see T.A., *The Excellency or Handy-Work of the Royal Hand*, pp. 1, 3; J. Bird, *Ostenta Carolina* (1661), p. 78.
97. *C.S.P.D.*, *1631*, pp. xl–xlii, 450, 548–9. Bloch argued (pp. 296–7) that this episode reflected the direct influence of Lupton's *A Thousand Notable Things*, but failed to note that the infant had already touched a sufferer before the book's authority was invoked.

In 1607 a seventh son who healed the deaf, blind and lame was investigated and found incompetent by the Bishop of London. In 1623 sixteen persons were dealt with by the Archdeacon of Nottingham for going to be stroked by 'the wise boy at Wisall'. Probably soon afterwards 'the boy of Godlyman' (Godalming), the seventh son of a fiddler, embarked on a similar career of stroking the sick; both he and his patients were required to fast during the healing process, a common procedure among miraculous healers. At the end of the century a little boy at Brinkley, Cambridgeshire, also a seventh son, was performing cures upon the blind, lame and deaf.[98] Such healing powers were thought to extend to seventh daughters as well as sons, and to include powers of foresight. The belief retained its vigour in rural areas as late as the nineteenth century.[99]

The seventh sons derived their healing power from the accident of birth, as did the royal healers and those who imitated them; for example, James Middleton, a wandering north-countryman, apprehended at Lichfield in 1587, who declared himself to be a Stuart, sprung from a line of Scottish kings, and endowed with a special power to heal the falling sickness.[100] But others claimed, regardless of their genealogical origins, to have been directly empowered by God to effect wonderful cures, sometimes of a particular disease, more commonly of all kinds of malady. Such claimants were particularly prominent among the sects of the Interregnum, as we have seen.[101] But the Catholics also had their miraculous healers. A man

98. *Diary of Walter Yonge,* ed. G. Roberts (Camden Soc., 1848), p. 13; R. F. B. Hodgkinson, 'Extracts from the Act Books of the Archdeacons of Nottingham', *Trans. of the Thoroton Soc.*, xxx (1926), p. 57; E. P(oeton), 'The Winnowing of White Witchcraft' (Sloane 1954), ff. 190–2; E. L. Cutts, 'Curious Extracts from a MS Diary, of the Time of James II and William and Mary', *Trans. Essex Archaeol. Soc.*, i (1858), p. 124. For others see W. H. Dawson in *The Reliquary*, xxiii (1882–3), p 200; Ashm. 1730, f. 162; Sir T. Matthew, *The Life of Lady Lucy Knatchbull* (1931), p. 35.

99. Brand, *Popular Antiquities*, iii, pp. 265–6; *Folk-Lore*, vi (1895), p. 205; ibid., vii (1896), pp. 295–6; G. A. Cranfield, *The Development of the Provincial Newspaper, 1700–60* (Oxford, 1962), p. 221; Thiselton-Dyer, *Old English Social Life*, p. 77; C. J. S. Thompson, *The Quacks of Old London* (1928), pp. 71–2, 189; *Trans. Cumbs. and Westmorland Antiqn. and Archaeol. Soc.*, xiii (1895), p. 362; ibid., xiv (1896), p. 373. But in J. Quincy, *Dr Carr's Medicinal Epistles* (1714), p. 132, seventh sons are said to have lost their popular prestige.

100. His methods, however, involved recourse to conventional prayers, exorcisms and charms, P.R.O., SP 12/206/54–53 (ii); SP 12/208/2.

101. Above, pp. 148–51.

named Blake, believed to be a priest or Jesuit, arrived at the Mitre Hotel, Oxford, in July 1663 and attempted to cure the sick and lame by pronouncing Latin words and making the sign of the cross over them. At Chester in the following month he drew large crowds and claimed to have cast a devil out of a possessed woman. Earlier he had performed at a public ceremony (tickets only) in the Queen's chapel in St James's, where, to the accompaniment of Catholic ritual, he tied ribbons round his patients' necks.[102] The resemblance to the royal healing ceremony must have been embarrassingly close; and it formed a suitable prologue to the subsequent arrival of Blake's fellow-countryman, Valentine Greatrakes, the most famous occult healer of the seventeenth century.

Greatrakes was an Irish gentleman who had served in Cromwell's army. Shortly after the Restoration he was informed by a mysterious impulse that he had the gift to cure the King's Evil by touching. Responding to this divine injunction, he found to his surprise that his stroking worked, and he embarked upon a career as a healer, later extending his operations to the ague and other diseases. After building up a reputation in Ireland, where his patients included the astronomer Flamsteed, he was brought over in 1666 to Ragley, Warwickshire, to try his hand at curing the chronic headaches of Anne, Viscountess Conway. This proved beyond his power (although he had been able to cure his own), but his reputation attracted hundreds of miscellaneous sufferers upon whom he performed a number of successful cures. Championed by many of the leading intellectuals of the day, including the Cambridge Platonists, More, Cudworth and Whichcote, and the scientists Robert Boyle and John Wilkins, he was brought in triumph to London, where he healed many members of the crowd who besieged his lodgings. But he failed in a demonstration before Charles II and his court, and in May 1666, only five months after his arrival, returned to Ireland to resume his life as a J.P. and country squire.[103]

102. Wood, *Life and Times*, i, p. 486; J. Barrow, *The Lord's Arm stretched out in an answer of Prayer: or, a True Relation of the Wonderful Deliverance of James Barrow* (1664), sig. BI; *C.S.P.D., 1663–4*, p. 243 (I have assumed that all these references are to Blake, but several other Irishmen and Jesuits were engaged in magical healing around this time: see, e.g., Hunter and Macalpine, *Three Hundred Years of Psychiatry, 1535–1860*, p. 151; Sloane 1926, f. 4; J. Heydon, *Theomagia, or the Temple of Wisdome* [1664], iii, p. 224).

103. His career can be elicited from a series of contemporary pamphlets:

This brief episode attracted enormous public attention, for, despite his many failures, Greatrakes appeared to have cured a sizeable proportion of his clientele. He had, moreover, no financial motive for imposture, since he made no charge for his services, other than travel expenses. As far as he was concerned, his was a miraculous power directly bestowed by God. This interpretation was unattractive to those Protestant divines whose habit it was to maintain that all miracles had ceased. They preferred to seek the explanation in the healer's physiology, looking for some inherent quirk which gave his body a natural 'sanative contagion', as Henry More put it. Pursuing this line of inquiry, George Rust, Dean of Connor, convinced himself that Greatrake's urine smelled of violets.[104] But others threw doubt upon the efficacy of his cures, or regarded him as a conjuror, dependent upon diabolical assistance. 'However it looks at London, it was laughed at in the University,' recalled a Cambridge correspondent in 1676.[105]

Greatrakes's own motives are unfathomable. He almost certainly believed what he said about divine impulses and seems to have had a genuinely obsessive impulse to cure. It is highly probable that his healing career, which had after all begun with touching for the King's Evil, was a veiled sectarian protest against the Restoration and the miraculous powers claimed by Charles II. Although he declared his loyalty to the Church of England, Greatrakes had been actively associated with the Cromwellian régime in Ireland, and an admirer of Boehme.[106] A contemporary who claimed to have know him well said afterwards that he was a strange fellow, full of talk of devils and witches.[107] Those who linked his activities with the numerous other anti-monarchical prodigies manufactured by

Wonders if not Miracles (1665); (D. Lloyd), Wonders no Miracles (1666); H. Stubbe, The Miraculous Conformist (Oxford, 1666); A Brief Account of Mr Valentine Greatraks (1666), and 'A Detection of the Imposture of Mr V.G.' (Sloane 1926, ff. 1–10). See also Conway Letters, ed. M. H. Nicolson (1930) and D.N.B. There is suggestive discussion of his cures by R. A. Hunter and I. Macalpine in St. Bartholomew's Hospital Journ., lx (1956).

104. Stubbe, The Miraculous Conformist, p. 11; J. Glanvill, Saducismus Triumphatus (1681), i, pp. 90–92. Herbert Croft, Bishop of Hereford, however, regarded his cures as supernatural; Correspondence of the Family of Hatton, ed. E. M. Thompson (Camden Soc., 1878), i. p. 49.

105. C.U.L., Add. MS 1, no. 26.

106. Sloane 1926, f. 4v.

107. The Diary of Abraham de la Pryme, ed. C. Jackson (Surtees Soc., 1870), pp. 90–91.

the Dissenters in the years immediately after the Restoration were probably right.

'Stroking', as such, was not necessarily a 'superstitious' form of cure. It could be rationalized to fit Galenic medical theory according to which the excess humours needed to be evacuated in order to restore the body to equilibrium. The conventional methods of re-establishing this balance were purging, vomiting and blood-letting. But stroking could be represented as a magnetic means of easing the evil humours down through the limbs and out through the extremities. This is what Greatrakes claimed to do, and the same theory may have underlain the activities of some of the other 'strokers' of the period. It was also exemplified in the ghastly habit of lifting up sufferers from goitre and other diseases to be touched by the dead hand of a freshly hanged man, a remedy which even Robert Boyle thought useful.[108] James Leverett, the seventh son who healed the Evil in 1637, asserted that he could feel the strength going out of his body every time he performed a cure, and had to take to his bed after a heavy day's stroking.[109] But in most cases there was no attempt made by the healer or his followers to postu-late any such physiological mechanism. His power was deemed to spring from an innate quality, sometimes conventionally described as a gift of God, but essentially an inherent capacity, pertaining either to the healer's office (as in the case of the King), to his genea-logical status (as with the seventh sons), or to his inexplicable *mana* (as with Greatrakes and many of the cunning men).

3. *The efficacy of magical healing*

It can thus be seen that a wide variety of methods of mystical heal-ing were available in Tudor and Stuart England. But how effective were they, and why was it that so many patients were prepared to submit themselves to their ministrations?

Great claims were made for the healing value of the royal touch. The surgeon, Richard Wiseman, testified to having witnessed hun-dreds of cures, and asserted that Charles II healed more sufferers in one year 'than all the surgeons of London had done in an age'.[110]

---

108. Quincy, *Dr Carr's Medicinal Epistles*, p. 132. For an attempt in 1687 to use a corpse's head to cure the King's Evil, see *Local Population Studies*, v (1970), p. 62.   109. Keynes, *The Life of William Harvey*, p. 265.

110. Wiseman, *Severall Chirurgicall Treatises*, pp. 246, 247; also Browne, *Adenochoiradelogia*, iii, p. 81.

But allowance must be made for the obsequious royalism behind such remarks. Most contemporary claims for the success of the royal miracle evaporate upon closer inspection. Its official defenders never suggested that the royal hand was infallible or that its effects were instantaneous. Most of the 'cures' seem to have occurred after an interval of time, and may be reasonably attributed to the tendency of some kinds of glandular tuberculosis to heal spontaneously.[111] Others involved one of the superficial maladies which were customarily included under the label of the King's Evil: nearly all instances of 'sore eyes', for example, were deemed suitable for admission to the royal ceremony.

The minority of apparent cures of the scrofula were put down by rationalist contemporaries to the effects of the imagination. 'Physicians,' wrote a pamphleteer, 'do attribute the cause more to the parties' imagination than to the virtue of the touch.'[112] In the case of scrofula this diagnosis seems implausible. But many of the associated conditions may well have been hysterical in origin and hence open to the possibility of spectacular cure. The uplifting effects of the religious ceremony, the nervous excitement felt in the presence of the King, upon whom they had perhaps never previously set eyes, the washing of their limbs by the surgeons before they were admitted to the royal presence – all these factors, acting individually or in combination, may well have been sufficient to effect a cure upon those sufferers whose condition did not spring from any real organic disorder. Moreover, scrofula tended to be periodic in its manifestations and thus to give a temporary appearance of being cured; the subsequent return of the symptoms would be deemed a 'relapse', for which the patient's failure to go on wearing his touch-piece might often constitute an acceptable explanation.

In such ways a reputation of the royal touch could be sustained in the face of repeated failure. The example of Lourdes reminds us that one apparent cure will efface the memory of a hundred failures. Faith in the royal touch did not arise from a systematic examination of the medical histories of all those who had submitted to its ministrations. It lay rather in the public's disposition to believe in the possibility of such a miracle, a disposition which sprang from a mystical view of kingship and of the monarch's place in society. It

111. Keynes, *The Life of William Harvey*, p. 269; Primrose, *Popular Errours*, p. 442.
112. *An Answer to a Scoffing and Lying Lybell* (1681), p. 2.

was this attitude which produced the reputed healings, not the healings which inculcated the attitude. In the words of the great French
historian of the King's Evil:

> What created faith in the miracle was the idea that there should be a
> miracle. It was this idea too which allowed it to survive, plus, as the
> centuries passed, the accumulated testimony of generations who had
> believed and whose evidence, founded it seemed upon experience,
> one could not doubt. As for the cases, numerous enough by all ac-
> counts, in which the Evil resisted the touch of these august fingers,
> they were soon forgotten. Such is the happy optimism of believing
> souls.[113]

Faith in the royal miracle, thought Marc Bloch, was the result of
a collective error, arising from a belief in the supernatural character
of kingship. This belief had its social advantages, for it prevented
the monarch from being too closely identified with any one section
of his subjects, by raising him to a mystical plane from which he
might symbolise the unity of them all.[114] In seventeenth-century
England this mystique was diminishing. Patriarchal adoration of
the sovereign was challenged by a frank republican scepticism,
exemplified in the increasingly common assertion that 'kings were
but men as other men'.[115] Faith in the royal healing power was thus
linked to a decaying political attitude: the belief that royal blood
had its unique characteristics, and a special genealogy extending
back to Noah. Kings were not as other mortals, but were account-
able to God alone. But the decline of the doctrine of Divine Right
and the triumph of the Hanoverian dynasty meant the end of royal
miracles. Men did not look for them, and therefore they did not
happen.

The special status of the monarch helps to explain the prestige of
his healing power. But no such consideration will account for the
appeal of the village wizard. The chief factor here, no doubt, was the
shortage of able physicians, particularly for the poorer classes.
Wizards' fees varied considerably, but they usually compared
favourably with those charged by contemporary doctors. 'Their

113. Bloch, *Les Rois thaumaturges*, p. 429 (freely rendered). I have drawn
heavily on his penetrating discussion on pp. 409–29.
114. cf. E. E. Evans-Pritchard, *Essays in Social Anthropology* (1962),
p. 84.
115. Words used by a prisoner at Tangier in 1664; H. A. Kaufman, *Conscientious Cavalier* (1962), p. 193.

reward,' said one authority, 'is . . . what people commonly will give them; some take more, some take but little, often nothing, and some may not take any thing at all, as some have professed that if they should take anything they could do no good.' There may have been many 'blessers' like Mary Shaw, a Lancashire tailor's wife, who took no money, 'but what they would give her of goodwill', or Henry Baggilie, who only 'received meal or cheese or commodities of the like nature, but never did take silver or any other reward'.[116] Charms and prayers, moreover, compared favourably with the attentions of most contemporary doctors. A painless remedy seemed attractive beside the prospect of surgery or a routine of purges and vomits. The royal touch had similarly been far preferable to the painful cauterization which physicians recommended for the Evil.

The stubborn reluctance of the lower sections of the seventeenth-century population to forgo their charmers and wise men resembles the unwillingness of some primitive peoples today to rely exclusively upon the newly introduced Western medicine. They notice that men die, even in hospitals, and that the Europeans have virtually no remedy for such complaints as sterility and impotence. They therefore stick to their traditional remedies, some of which afford a degree of psychological release and reassurance not to be found in Western medicine. They cherish the dramatic side of magical healing, the ritual acting-out of sickness, and the symbolic treatment of disease in its social context. Primitive psychotherapy, in particular, can compare favourably with its modern rivals.[117] If this is true today, when medical technique has made such striking advances, we can hardly wonder at the attitude of seventeenth-century villagers, when medical therapy still proceeded along its traditional paths of purging and blood-letting. There is little more reason for asking why the wizards were able to retain their prestige than for inquiring how it was that the pretensions of Galenic physicians remained so long unchallenged.

Nevertheless, the reputation enjoyed by the cunning men is at first sight remarkable. 'There are divers and sundry kinds of maladies,' it was said, 'which though a man do go to all the physicians

116. Bernard, *Guide*, pp. 131–2; Lancashire R.O., QSB/1/78/49, and QSB/1/139(81). For more on fees, see below, pp. 295–8.
117. See, e.g., S. F. Nadel, *Nupe Religion* (1954), pp. 161–2; R. Firth, 'Ritual and Drama in Malay Spirit Mediumship', *Compve. Studs. in Soc. and Hist.*, ix (1966–7), p. 207; R. W. Lieban, *Cebuano Sorcery* (Berkeley, 1967), chap. 5; and *Magic, Faith and Healing, Studies in Primitive Psychiatry Today*, ed. A. Kiev (1964), *passim.*

that can be heard of, yet he shall find no remedy; whereas sometimes they are cured by those which are called cunning folks.' Anne Bodenham, the old Wiltshire witch, declared outright that her remedies 'could cure such diseases as the best doctors could not do'.[118] We cannot now test the veracity of such stories as that of the wizard in Wells who cured over a hundred people of the ague, merely by giving them a paper to wear, with 'abracadabra' written on it in the form of an acrostic,[119] but we do know that many intelligent contemporaries believed that such remedies really worked. 'We see commonly the toothache, gout, falling sickness, biting of a mad dog and many such maladies cured by spells, words, characters and charms,' remarked Robert Burton, the Anatomist.[120] It was not only the ignorant who were clients of the cunning men, and they were often protected by men in high places.[121] Indeed the best testimony to their success was provided by some of the very persons who were most anxious to harry them out of the land. Many theologians stressed the wickedness of magical cures, but not their futility. 'Not only cankers,' admitted William Fulke, 'but also fistulas, toothache, and many other diseases have been healed by charms.'[122]

In accounting for this reputation, some weight should be given to the practical remedies which were sometimes combined with magical ones. Cunning men could identify ordinary maladies and prescribe medicine for them.[123] They could draw upon the extensive and sometimes genuine herb-lore which had been accumulated over the centuries. Their sympathetic cures kept the wound free from harmful ointment and allowed it to make a natural recovery.[124]

118. Mason, *The Anatomie of Sorcerie*, p. 69; E. Bower, *Doctor Lamb revived* (1653), p. 25.   119. Aubrey, *Miscellanies*, pp. 134–5.

120. Burton, *Anatomy*, i, p. 256.

121. For examples, Scot, *Discoverie*, XV.xli; *C.S.P.D., 1625–6*, p. 367; Thompson, *The Quacks of Old London*, p. 30; above, p. 16.

122. W. Fulke, *Answers to Stapleton, Martiall and Sanders* (Cambridge, P.S., 1848), p. 157. Thomas Lodge (*Complete Works* [1963 reprint], iv, p. 35), Gervase Babington (*Workes* [1622], iii, p. 27), and James Cotta (*Cotta contra Antonium* [Oxford, 1623], p. 39) agreed. cf. below, p. 305.

123. Scot, *Discoverie*, XVI.v, comments on their simultaneous use of medicine. cf. Bernard, *Guide*, p. 149. For a 'charmer' who diagnosed jaundice, see A. Hussey, 'Visitations of the Archdeacon of Canterbury', *Archaeologia Cantiana*, xxvi (1904), p. 21.

124. As Pettigrew points out, *On Superstitions connected with the History and Practice of Medicine*, pp. 163–4; and see Petersson, *Sir Kenelm Digby*, p. 274.

Greatrakes even went in for a certain amount of amateur surgery, lancing tumours and squeezing out the matter. As so often among primitive peoples, magic and technique were simultaneously employed. Fraud might also help, as in the case of the Venetian physician in London in the reign of Edward VI who was confronted with an unconscious patient; well aware that the man was in no real danger he declared he would perform a miracle by raising him from the dead, and duly did so.[125]

Weight should also be attached to the natural tendency of the human body to rid itself of trivial maladies without outside help. Many of the complaints miraculously 'cured' by the cunning men were of the kind which time alone could heal – fevers, earache, warts, open wounds. Apparent success in such spheres undoubtedly helped to conceal failures in the face of more deadly infections to which the body could offer no resistance. Significantly, there was seldom any suggestion that a cunning man could cure a victim of the plague, though he might be able to give him a charm or amulet which would prevent him from catching it.

When failure was unavoidable the belief in witchcraft provided a ready excuse. By informing their clients that they had been 'overlooked' or 'forspoken', the cunning men could imply that if only the disease had been natural they would have been able to cure it. Even the Catholic who held charming sessions at St James's in 1664 was prepared to fall back on this.[126] In this way the wizard's procedure could be virtually foolproof. For if the patient recovered it was a tribute to the cunning man's perception, and if he died then the witch was to blame. By submitting himself to the cunning man's ministrations the patient was forging bonds from which there was no escape. As Richard Bernard remarked of wizards, 'it is found by daily experience that those which most use them most need them'.[127]

But of all the factors sustaining the cunning man's reputation the greatest was the appeal of his remedies to his client's mind. Many amateur healers can achieve a reasonable degree of success when dealing with patients whose symptoms are somatic, yet without any organic pathology. Two modern doctors have shrewdly pointed

125. A. A. Ruddock, 'The Earliest Records of the High Court of Admiralty (1515–58)', Bull. of Institute of Hist. Research, xxii (1949), p. 145.
126. Barrow, The Lord's Arm Stretched Out, sig. B2.
127. Bernard, Guide, p. 143.

out that 'what Greatrakes did was to realise intuitively that various somatic aches, pains, dysfunctions or pareses occur in the absence of organic disease'. He healed his patients through their minds rather than through their bodies, and his methods anticipated the practice of Mesmer, Charcot and subsequent students of psychosomatic illness.[128] The cunning man's greatest asset was his client's imagination; and, in view of what is known today about the potentialities of any cure in which both doctor and patient have complete faith, its power cannot be disregarded.

The scientific study of the role of suggestion in healing has only recently begun, but the results are already sufficiently startling to make historians chary about discounting the genuine potency of seventeenth-century healers who worked only with spells and charms. The role of what is now called the 'placebo effect' in modern medicine has been fully demonstrated, although its causes are not yet clear and the matter remains controversial. The pill in which both patient and doctor have faith may achieve remarkable results, however trivial its pharmacological content. Experiments have revealed that placebos, i.e. inert substances administered as if they were real drugs, can sometimes have a high rate of success in dissipating such complaints as headaches, seasickness or postoperative pain. They can be effective tranquillizers, alleviating tension and stress. Indeed the success rate of the placebo is in some cases demonstrably as great as that of the genuine drug.[129]

This raises the importance of faith in therapy to a point which can only shock the layman, accustomed to thinking of medicine as something directed to the body rather than the mind. Its relevance to primitive medicine is all the greater in view of experiments which suggest that the placebo has a higher success rate with the regular churchgoer than with the agnostic, and with the person who has had to pay than with the patient who has received it free through

128. Hunter and Macalpine in *St Bartholomew's Hospital Journ.*, lx (1956), p. 368.

129. A key article on this subject is L. Lasagna *et al.*, ' A Study of the Placebo Response', *American Journ. of Medicine*, xvi (1954), and there is a useful survey of the literature in J. D. Frank, *Persuasion and Healing* (1961), chap. 4. See also B. Inglis, *Fringe Medicine* (1964), and id., *Drugs, Doctors and Diseases* (1965). A stimulating paper delivered by Dr David Surridge at the St John's College Essay Society first made me aware of the importance of this topic. Its relevance for primitive medicine is pointed out by J. Jahn, *Muntu. An Outline of Neo-African Culture*, trans. M. Grene (1961), pp. 127–9.

the Health Service. It is also more effective when the treatment is accompanied by a certain amount of impressive ritual. Just as the wizards sometimes had recourse to bizarre effects, so the manufacturer of placebos is careful to see that his pills are very large or very small, highly coloured and in appearance as unlike such familiar drugs as aspirin as possible. The seventeenth-century charmer, operating in a Christian environment, believing personally in his methods, and accompanying them by an intimidating ritual, was thus ideally equipped to achieve results. In the light of modern research into the medical role of faith and imagination it seems that his claim to effect healing by touch, by command, by incantation, or even by action at a distance, must be taken seriously.

Intelligent contemporaries were well aware of this therapeutic power of the imagination and its importance for the sorcerer. They noticed that the cunning man required willing cooperation from his patients: 'These witches profess that they cannot heal such as do not believe in them,' said Richard Bernard;[130] and they keenly explored the evidence suggesting that therapy directed to the mind could heal the body. 'As some are ... molested by fantasy,' wrote Robert Burton, 'so some again by fancy alone and a good conceit are as easily recovered ... there is no virtue in charms or cures, but a strong conceit and opinion.' Francis Bacon also accepted the healing power of 'miracle-working faith', while Dr Edward Jorden, one of the most perceptive contemporary writers on witchcraft, observed, when discussing the medical value of such remedies as charms, amulets and holy water, that any success they might have was to be attributed, not to inherent supernatural virtue, but to 'the confident persuasion which melancholic and passionate people may have in them'.[131] Opinions of this kind were supported by some devastating anecdotes, of which one retold by Denis Granville, who was Dean of Durham, 1684–91, was typical: a French doctor had a patient who was convinced that he was possessed by the Devil. The doctor called in a priest and a surgeon, meanwhile equipping himself with a bag containing a live bat. The patient was told that it would take a small operation to cure him. The priest offered up prayer, and the surgeon made a slight incision in the man's side. Just as the cut

130. Bernard, *Guide*, p. 139; and also Cooper, *Mystery*, pp. 219, 245. cf. V. W. Turner in *Magic, Faith and Healing*, ed. Kiev, p. 263.
131. Burton, *Anatomy*, i, p. 256; Bacon, *Works*, ii, p. 641; iv. p. 400; E. Jorden, *A Briefe Discourse of a Disease called the Suffocation of the Mother* (1603), p. 25.

was given, the doctor let the bat fly into the room, crying, 'Behold, there the devil is gone!' The man believed it and was cured.[132]

If anything, the concept of psychosomatic disease was wider in the seventeenth century than it is now, for contemporary intellectuals tended to exaggerate the powers of the imagination. They thought that epidemics were more likely to strike the fearful, and they believed that a pregnant woman could shape the unborn foetus by her thoughts.[133] Such notions were reinforced by contemporary Neoplatonism, but they also drew strength from the numerous instances of psychosomatic healing in an age when the potentialities open to purely physical remedies were very limited.

Sometimes, however, the charmer could cure the sceptic as well as the credulous. Arthur Wilson, a well-educated writer, records how, when stricken with the ague while travelling in France in the early seventeenth century, he consulted a Gascon miller, who cured him with a charm, as he had cured many others. Wilson's account of this episode reveals his genuine perplexity. His imagination was not responsible, for he did not believe beforehand in the miller's powers. Could it be that the man's eyes had some mystic power, or that mere characters written on a paper could have some occult virtue? Satan could hardly have been responsible, for the miller was a devout Huguenot. The result left him baffled.[134] There are many such cases in which the client is known to have approached the cunning man without any particular confidence in his methods, but rather in the spirit of try-anything-once. The most plausible explanation for their outcome is that, in a credulous age, even the sceptic may have a repressed will to believe, which under propitious circumstances can break out of captivity; just as the normally reasonable man may sometimes be overcome by the overwhelming influence of a crowded revivalist meeting. But Arthur Wilson's ague, no doubt, would have cleared up whether or not he had visited the miller.

132. Cited by Kittredge, *Witchcraft*, p. 135. For similar stories, G. Gifford, *A Dialogue concerning Witches and Witchcrafts* (1593) (Shakespeare Assoc., 1931), sig. G4; J. Selden, *Table-Talk* (Temple classics, n.d.), pp. 40–41; Turner, *Providences*, ii, p. 135; Ewen, ii, p. 129.

133. Hunter and Macalpine, *Three Hundred Years of Psychiatry*, p. 230; W. Pagel, *Paracelsus* (Basel, 1958), pp. 121–5; Still, *History of Paediatrics*, p. 342; M. Underwood, *A Treatise on the Disorders of Childhood* (1797), ii, pp. 199–209. The role of the imagination is emphasized in most contemporary plague tracts.   134. Peck, *Desiderata Curiosa*, p. 461.

The historian who attempts to investigate the working of the magical healers of an earlier age is thus led into the paths of speculative psychology in which his competence must necessarily fail him. But it is clear that these healing agencies were not necessarily ineffective or fraudulent. Of course, it would be wrong to move from a position of complete scepticism to the opposite pole of indulgent belief. More than ten years ago the British Medical Association listed no less than six factors to account for most magical 'cures': (1) mistaken diagnosis; (2) mistaken prognosis; (3) alleviation of the illness; (4) remission; (5) spontaneous cure; (6) simultaneous use of other remedies.[135] All these we have seen to be present in the cures of this period. Even if we recognize that some of these factors also account for many of the successes claimed by the medical profession itself, it is nevertheless true that primitive medicine was ill-equipped to deal with organic disorders by drugs or surgery. Many men undoubtedly died from incompetent diagnosis or treatment whose lives would have been saved today. Magic cannot counter infection and is no substitute for hygiene, or X-rays and other modern aids to diagnosis. But it may have provided as effective a therapy for the diseases of the mind as anything available today.

135. *Divine Healing and Co-operation between Doctors and Clergy* (B.M.A., 1956), p. 10.

8.

CUNNING MEN AND
POPULAR MAGIC

> You have heard of Mother Nottingham, who for her time was
> prettily well skilled in casting of waters, and after her, Mother
> Bomby; and then there is one Hatfield in Pepper Alley, he doth
> pretty well for a thing that's lost. There's another in Coleharbour
> that's skilled in the planets. Mother Sturton in Golden Lane is for
> fore-speaking; Mother Phillips, of the Bankside, for the weakness
> of the back; and then there's a very reverend matron on Clerken-
> well Green good at many things. Mistress Mary on the Bankside is
> for erecting a figure; and one (what do you call her?) in West-
> minster, that practiseth the book and the key, and the sieve and
> the shears: and all do well according to their talent.
>
> T. Heywood, *The Wise-woman of Hogsdon*
> (1638), III, i

> Undoubtedly if this necromancy did exist, as is believed by shallow
> minds, there is nothing on earth that would have so much power
> either to harm or to benefit man.
>
> *The Notebooks of Leonardo da Vinci*,
> ed. E. MacCurdy (1938), i, p. 87

> The fortune-tellers are the moralists, as well as the consolers of
> the lower classes. They supply a want that society either cannot
> or will not do.
>
> *The Book of Days*, ed. R. Chambers
> (1863), i, p. 284

1. *Lost property*

HEALING was only one of the magical functions performed by
cunning men and wise women. Of the others the most common

BIBLIOGRAPHICAL NOTE: The largest compilation of material relating to
popular magic in England before the seventeenth century is still Kittredge,
Witchcraft, although the author did little to interpret the evidence he so
diligently collected. An excellent account of the activities of a seventeenth-
century wizard, seen through the eyes of a contemporary medical practitioner, remains unpublished: E. P(oeton), *The Winnowing of White Witchcraft* (Sloane 1954, ff. 161–93). Further information may be gleaned from
such other contemporary writers on witchcraft as Règinald Scot, William
Perkins, Thomas Cooper and Richard Bernard. But the best sources for the

seems to have been the detection of theft and the recovery of stolen goods, a matter for which society made very little alternative provision. In such cases the wizard would proceed by employing one of the several possible methods of divination to determine who it was had stolen the missing goods.

A common formula was that of the sieve and the shears:

Stick a pair of shears in the rind of a sieve and let two persons set the top of each of their forefingers upon the upper part of the shears holding it with the sieve up from the ground steadily; and ask Peter and Paul whether A, B, or C hath stolen the thing lost; and at the nomination of the guilty person the sieve will turn round.[1]

This procedure did not call for any special qualities on the part of the persons operating it, and was not the sole prerogative of the cunning men, but available to anyone who happened to know the technique. Thus in 1554 William Hasylwoode, a cleric, confessed before the Commissary's Court of London that

having ... lost a purse with fourteen groats in the same, and thereupon remembering that he being a child did hear his mother declare that when any man had lost anything then they would use a sieve and a pair of shears to bring to knowledge who had the things lost, ... so [he took] a sieve and a pair of shears and hanged the sieve by the point of the shears and said these words, 'By Peter and Paul, he hath it', naming the person whom he in that behalf suspected.

---

activities of the cunning folk are the largely unpublished depositions made in connection with their prosecution before the secular and ecclesiastical courts. A valuable analysis of this material so far as it relates to Essex is contained in Alan Macfarlane, *Witchcraft in Tudor and Stuart England* (1970). Many accounts of the doings of nineteenth-century wizards can be found in the numerous regional studies of English folklore. A useful guide to some of these is W. Bonser, *A Bibliography of Folklore as Contained in the First Eighty Years of the Publications of the Folklore Society* (Folklore Soc., 1961). The description of 'the wise man' in J. C. Atkinson, *Forty Years in a Moorland Parish* (1907 edn), pp. 103–25, is particularly revealing.

On the more intellectual aspects of the magical tradition much can be learned from Thorndike, *Magic and Science;* D. P. Walker, *Spiritual and Demonic Magic from Ficino to Campanella* (1958), and F. A. Yates, *Giordano Bruno and the Hermetic Tradition* (1964), *Theatre of the World* (1969), and 'The Hermetic Tradition in Renaissance Science', in *Art, Science and History in the Renaissance*, ed. C. S. Singleton (Baltimore, 1967).

1. Bodl., MS Add. B 1, f. 25 (later sixteenth century). Other versions may be found in Scot, *Discoverie*, XII, xvii, and Aubrey, *Gentilisme*, p. 25.

Similarly in 1598 John Casson admitted to the Archdeacon of Nottingham that

about three quarters of a year since, a wether being lost in their parish there was a device used to know what was become of the said wether by taking a sieve and a pair of shears and saying, 'In the name of the Father and of the Son and of the Holy Ghost', after which words the sieve would turn about – which device he and his sister . . . once without any ill intent tried.

In 1641 a labourer's wife appeared before Lancashire Quarter Sessions for using the sieve and shears to find out who had stolen a sheep and a hen, and to ascertain whether two local women were with child.[2] The technique was simple to grasp, required nothing out of the ordinary in the way of equipment, and was widely employed.[3]

Another version of the same principle was divination by a key and book (the latter usually being a psalter or Bible). Again a very simple procedure was followed. A key was placed at a chosen point in the book. The names of possible suspects were then written on separate pieces of paper and inserted one after another in the hollow end of the key. When the paper bearing the name of the thief was put in, the book would 'wag' and fall out of the fingers of those who held it.[4] A version of this technique was employed by William Newport, vicar of St Owen's, Gloucester, in 1551. According to witnesses, the clergyman inserted the key and tied the book up with string. He then invoked the Father, Son and Holy Ghost, bidding the key to turn when he reached the name of the guilty party. It turned when he pronounced the name of Margaret Greenhill; and the participants then left the chancel of the church, where the ritual had been carried out, to search the suspect's bed-straw for the miss-

2. Hale, *Precedents*, p. 139; R. F. B. Hodgkinson, 'Extracts from the Act Books of the Archdeacons of Nottingham', *Trans. Thoroton Soc.*, xxx (1926), p. 51; Lancashire R.O., QSB 1/255/38, 70–1.

3. To the instances of its use cited by Kittredge, *Witchcraft*, pp. 198–200, 511–13, may be added those in Borthwick, R. VI. A. 18, f. 195 (1615), and R. VI. E1a, f. 60ᵛ (1598); Peterborough D.R., Correction Book 62, f. 35 (1629); *H.M.C., Various Collections*, i, pp. 283, 307 (1633); T. F. Thiselton-Dyer, *Old English Social Life* (1898), p. 77 (1715); and above, p. 220 n.34. For a photograph of a similar technique (scissors and winnower) used in the Philippines today see R. W. Lieban, *Cebuano Sorcery* (Berkeley, 1967), facing p. 85.

4. Scot, *Discoverie*, XVI, v. The psalm at which the key was inserted seems to have varied.

ing objects.[5] This divination by key and book had been well known in the Middle Ages and was still current in many rural areas in the nineteenth century.[6]

A third way of isolating the guilty party from a list of suspects was to wrap up the pieces of paper bearing their names inside little clay balls, and put them into a bucket of water to see which would unroll first. This too had many variants.[7] The cunning men, however, were often equipped with more sophisticated techniques. Some purported to operate by astrology and would produce a description of the thief after setting a figure. Others engaged in geomancy – interpreting the meaning of the pattern of dots produced by the random doodlings of the wizard in a state of semi-trance. Yet others used mirrors or crystal balls in which the client would be asked if he could perceive the features of the guilty party. John Dee had a crystal for this purpose, 'as big as an egg: most bright, clear and glorious'.[8] A small boy's thumbnail, polished up, might be similarly employed; or even a bucket of water.[9]

Elaborate rituals of a semi-religious kind might accompany such divination. One wizard explained in 1631 that 'any man going about to find out stolen goods doth it with great difficulty, with fasting and praying three days together and great pains taken therein'.[10] Aubrey

5. *H.M.C., Various Collections*, vii, p. 53; F. D. Price, 'Gloucester Diocese under Bishop Hooper, 1551–53', *Trans. Bristol and Glos. Archaeol. Soc.*, lx (1938), pp. 120–21.

6. For many examples see Kittredge, *Witchcraft*, pp. 196–8, 509–10, and W. E. A. Axon, 'Divination by Books', *The Manchester Qtly*, ci (1907), p. 32. Others may be found in A. H. Thompson, *The English Clergy and their Organization in the Later Middle Ages* (Oxford, 1947), p. 222 (1448); J. E. Oxley, *The Reformation in Essex* (Manchester, 1965), pp. 102–3 (1530s); Hereford D.R., Office Court Book 64 (1582); *The Book of Examinations and Depositions, 1622–44, ii (1627–34)*, ed. R. C. Anderson (Southampton Rec. Soc., 1931), p. 108; *Kilvert's Diary*, ed. W. Plomer (1960), i, pp. 300–1; *Trans. Devonshire Assoc.*, lxxxiv (1952), p. 300.

7. Different recipes occur in Sloane 3846, ff. 43–4; Bodl., MS e Mus. 173, f. 20ᵛ; Bodl., MS Add. B.1, ff. 11ᵛ–12. For their use, see Kittredge, *Witchcraft*, pp. 192–2; *Kilvert's Diary*, i, pp. 300–1. For other allied techniques, see B.M., Egerton MS 825, f. 109ᵛ, and Sloane 3846, f. 27ᵛ.

8. T. Besterman, *Crystal-Gazing* (1924), p. 18. cf. H. Syer Cuming, 'On Crystals of Augury', *Journ. of Brit. Archaeol. Assoc.*, v (1850).

9. Kittredge, *Witchcraft*, p. 187; M. R. James, 'Twelve Medieval Ghost-Stories', *E.H.R.*, xxvii (1922), pp. 420–21; B.M., Egerton MS 2618, ff. 159–60ᵛ.

10. *The Book of Examinations and Depositions, 1622–44*, ii, p. 104.

tells of a Herefordshire clothier who, after enduring many thefts of cloth from his racks, went out about midnight with his crystal, taking a little boy or girl with him as a scryer ('for they say it must be a pure virgin') to look into the crystal and see the likeness of the thief.[11] Crystal-gazing of this kind was, of course, only one stage removed from the deliberate invocation of spirits. A west country cunning man, John Walsh, confessed in 1566 that in order to discover lost goods he employed a familiar who would appear sometimes in the shape of a pigeon, sometimes in that of a dog, sometimes in that of a man with cloven feet. When William Lawse, clerk, of Halden, Kent, found his cattle injured and corn stolen in 1610, he repaired to William Childes, a weaver at Bethersden, to find out who was responsible. Following the directions in a conjuring book, they drew a large chalk circle on the floor in which they wrote certain Latin words. A third member of the party was required to read aloud from the Psalms, while Childes declaimed 'I exorcise and conjure thee.' Despite this intimidating procedure no spirit appeared. But when a servant was blamed in 1662 for the theft of goods from the Greyhound Inn, Blandford, Dorset, he went off to a conjurer, who with the aid of an evil spirit identified the real thief and miraculously produced him from fifty miles away.[12]

Once the identity of the thief had been thus revealed the clients showed no hesitation about pursuing the matter.

I pray you, good man Fakques [said an aggrieved Londoner in 1510] let me have my money, for ye have my money, the which I lost, and that was taken from and conveyed out of my bowchett [purse], for ye have it as it is shewed me by a soothsayer. For he shews me that there was a man in our company that hath a blemish in his face which he saith has it, and there was none but you that hath any such token, and therefore I pray you let me have it, for you be he that has it.[13]

The public's faith was not always as ingenuous as this, and there were clients who prudently deferred their payment of the wizard's fee until his identification proved to be correct.[14] But until at least the later seventeenth century the verdict of a village wizard on questions

11. Aubrey, *Miscellanies*, p. 157.

12. *The Examination of John Walsh* (1566), sig. Av^v; *Records of Maidstone* (Maidstone, 1926), pp. 266–7; *Mirabilis Annus Secundus* (1662), p. 41.

13. London D.R., DL/C/206, f. 21^v.

14. e.g., E. Peacock, 'Extracts from Lincoln Episcopal Visitations', *Archaeologia*, xlviii (1885), p. 262.

of theft or similar crimes was a matter of some consequence. Officers of the law are known to have apprehended the supposed culprit on the basis of such identifications; indeed it was sometimes thought worth bribing a cunning man so as to secure an arrest.[15]

Such methods of thief-detection were by no means as futile as they may look. It was common to most of them that the search for the thief did not begin in a void, but took the form of scrutinizing a list of suspects supplied by the client. All the cunning man had to do was to isolate the guilty one. It is more than likely that he saw his main task as that of discovering the identity of the party whom the the client himself most strongly suspected. This is certainly the practice of the modern African diviner, whose activities, as observed by social anthropologists, seem to bear a strong resemblance to those of the English cunning man. Almost all African divining methods, it has been pointed out, are open to manipulation on the part of the diviner, who 'is successful because he reveals what his inquirer hopes he will reveal'.[16] However intricate the divinatory procedure, it always leaves room for subjective judgement and interpretation on the part of the wizard. During the séance he 'smells out' the answer to the problem, with the aid of leading questions and a clear series of indications from his audience as to whether or not he is on the right track. Almost invariably the client has a definite suspect in mind, but one for whose guilt conventional evidence is lacking. The diviner's task is to confirm these suspicions and thus enable the client to act upon a view he had already reached before the consultation began.[17]

On this analogy with African diviners it seems probable that the

15. Ewen, *Star Chamber*, p. 16. For arrests after magical detection, see Kittredge, *Witchcraft*, pp. 188, 195–6; *Archaeologia*, lx(2) (1907), pp. 377–8; Thompson, *The English Clergy and their Organization*, p. 221; *A.P.C.*, xvii, pp. 31–2; J. Brinley, *A Discovery of the Impostures of Witches and Astrologers* (1680), p. 20.

16. E. E. Evans-Pritchard, *Witchcraft, Oracles and Magic among the Azande* (Oxford, 1937), p. 173. cf. B. Reynolds, *Magic, Divination and Witchcraft among the Barotse of Northern Rhodesia* (1963), p. 126.

17. M. Hunter, *Reaction to Conquest* (1936), pp. 308–9, 336, 346; B. A. Marwick, *The Swazi* (Cambridge, 1940), p. 246; E. J. and J. D. Krige, *The Realm of a Rain-Queen* (1943), pp. 227–8, 260–62; H. Kuper, *An African Aristocracy* (1947), p. 168; J. Middleton, *Lugbara Religion* (1960), pp. 81, 137; G. Lienhardt, *Divinity and Experience* (Oxford, 1961), p. 69; M. Gelfand, *Witch Doctor* (1964); M. G. Marwick, *Sorcery in Its Social Setting* (Manchester, 1965), pp. 91–2; W. Bascom, *Ifa Divination* (Bloomington, 1969), p. 69.

cunning man, sensitive to the reactions of the audience, was very likely to find the sieve or key turning when he pronounced the name of the party whom his clients mostly strongly suspected. If, as often happened, the injured person, trembling with excitement and indignation, carried out the procedure himself, a similar result was even more probable. That this is not mere conjecture is shown by the observations of Thomas Gataker, the seventeenth-century preacher, who remarked how,

when using the sieve and shears, and naming many whom they think good to question, but among those many strongly suspecting some one, the strong imagination of those, or one of those, that hold it between them (though no wilful sleight otherwise be interposed by either of them) may be a means sufficient to work an insensible motion in the hand of the holder so strongly possessed for the turning of the sieve and shears upon the naming of the parties by him or them formerly suspected.

The prose is clumsy, but the diagnosis goes to the heart of the matter.[18]

On this interpretation, therefore, the object of the divining *séance* was not so much to establish the identity of the thief, for that was often known already, as to stiffen the client's determination to accuse him. What the wizard did was to provide an apparently independent confirmation of the original suspicions. This is well illustrated by the ingenuous admission of a witness in 1590 that he had come to realise that the Hertfordshire cunning man, Thomas Harding, was a fraud, because he had refused to accuse any of the persons he suspected of firing his house, even after he had pointed them out to him.[19] The crystal ball was equally capable of confirming existing suspicions. The client was invited to inspect the glass to see if he could recognize the features of the man revealed there, and usually did.[20] Alternatively, the cunning man described the vision as it took shape and waited for the customer's reactions. In either case the operation performed the same function. The solemnity with which the experiment was conducted did not so much provide the client with new evidence as help him to know his own mind.

18. T. Gataker, *Of the Nature and Use of Lots* (2nd edn, 1627), p. 403. Both Reginald Scot and Francis Bacon had made the same point, *Discoverie*, XII, xvii; *Works*, ii, p. 660.   19. Hertfordshire R.O., HAT/SR/2/100.

20. A good example is in *H.M.C., 10th Report*, appx, pt iv, p. 476 (full text in *Essex R.O., Transcript no. 49*).

As a reconstruction of the actual consultations held by the magical thief-detectors of our period this picture may seem hypothetical. But the analogy with the practice of the African diviners is consistent with what evidence has survived. Thus when Thomas Nottingham, a fifteenth-century priest-magician, was called in by a Norwich citizen to identify Agnes Watts as a thief he made the mistake of accusing another woman altogether, until his client whispered in his ear that Agnes was the guilty one, whereupon the book and key confirmed the accusation.[21] Such divination was notoriously open to manipulation: there was, for example, a way of wrapping the clay around the paper bearing the name of the guilty party so as to ensure that it would be the first to open when put in water.[22] It would be wrong to imply that all diviners were disingenuous or that all clients had a definite suspect in mind. But the ability of these procedures to confirm suspicions already formed did much to sustain their prestige.

A second feature of this thief-magic was its tendency to intimidate the guilty. This too is a common aspect of divination among primitive peoples. An ordeal is devised which all suspects must undergo on the assumption that, whereas the innocent parties will remain unharmed, the guilty will suffer excruciating torment. This had been a feature of the judicial ordeal, familiar in England until 1215, when the Church refused to continue its sanction of the procedure. Of the many types of ordeal the four most common had been the hot iron, which the victim was required to carry; the boiling water, into which he plunged his hand; the 'holy morsel' of consecrated bread and cheese, which he was expected to swallow if innocent and choke on if guilty; and the cold water in which he was immersed and would sink, if innocent. Such procedures were doubtless inefficient methods of detection, but it would be wrong to conclude with one well-known legal historian that they 'can only be described as irrational'.[23] The experience of many primitive societies shows that the ordeal is not usually invoked until the suspect has already been identified. It is merely an additional test of his guilt, not the initial means of discovering the criminal. Its employment reflects the

21. L. F. Salzman, *More Medieval Byways* (1926), p. 172.
22. Gataker, *Of the Nature and Use of Lots*, pp. 402–3.
23. T. F. T. Plucknett, *Edward I and Criminal Law* (Cambridge, 1960), p. 69. For a survey of the main types of ordeal current in medieval Europe, see F. Patetta, *Le Ordalie* (Turin, 1890), chap. 7.

weakness of a central authority unable to enforce penalities without the additional sanction of supernatural assent.[24] But the ordeal also serves a psychological purpose. As often as not, the guilty party will break down before undergoing the test. His nerve will crack and he confesses. Alternatively, the terror produced by his belief in the infallibility of the procedure may lead him to fail so simple a test as that of having to swallow some food or drink. The innocent man, on the other hand, may welcome the challenge as a means of vindicating himself.[25]

In the medieval judicial ordeal, accordingly, any faltering or mistake in the ritual was seen as evidence of guilt. Refusals to take the ordeal were common, and it seems that the system worked to some extent by sheer intimidation. It also appears that, whereas some ordeals were very difficult to get through – notably the hot iron – others, like the cold water test, were almost impossible to fail. It does not seem improbable that the choice of method was often determined according to whether or not the accused was already believed to be guilty. The function of the ordeal would then be to reinforce a verdict which had already been reached.

Such speculations are best left to be investigated by the medieval historian.[26] But it is indisputable that, so long as all participants believed in the supernatural efficacy of these primitive rituals, they could on occasion function as effectively as any more sophisticated methods of crime-detection. In the sixteenth and seventeenth centuries traces of the ordeal still survived. Persons accused on appeal of treason or felony (that is, formally accused by the injured person or his heir) could, if they wished, demand trial by battle as an alter-

24. J. M. Roberts, 'Oaths, Autonomic Ordeals and Power', *American Anthropologist*, lxvii (2) (1965), pp. 208–9.

25. Roberts, art. cit., p. 207; Reynolds, *Magic, Divination and Witchcraft among the Barotse*, pp. 121–7.

26. For some suggestive insights see E. B. Tylor, 'Ordeals and Oaths', *Macmillan's Magazine*, xxxiv (1876), p. 4; H. C. Lea, *Superstition and Force* (3rd edn, Philadelphia, 1878), p. 274; P. Vinogradoff, 'Ordeal (Christian)', in *Encyclopaedia of Religion and Ethics*, ed. J. Hastings (Edinburgh, 1908–26), ix; T. P. Oakley, *English Penitential Discipline and Anglo-Saxon Law* (New York, 1923), pp. 159–60; H. Nottarp, *Gottesurteile. Ein Phase im Rechtsleben der Völker* (Bamberg, 1949), pp. 12 ff.; A. L. Poole, *Obligations of Society in the XII and XIII Centuries* (Oxford, 1946), pp. 79–80, 82–3; E. Bentz, 'Ordeal by Fire', in *Myths and Symbols*, ed. J. M. Kitagawa and C. H. Long (Chicago, 1969). Dr. P. R. Hyams of Pembroke College, Oxford, is at present working on this subject.

native to a jury. In civil actions, however, the judicial duel was confined to questions about ownership on writ of right and even then the
defendant or tenant could refuse the duel if he chose and submit the
matter to a jury. Otherwise, the right to trial by battle remained
technically intact until its abolition in 1819, all earlier attempts to
get rid of it having proved unsuccessful. On several occasions in the
sixteenth and seventeenth centuries a duel between champions was
actually arranged, though the encounter was always called off at
the last moment, much to the relief of the lawyers.[27] At an informal
level the old ordeal of cold water reappeared in the practice of
'swimming' suspected witches.[28]

Another associated practice was that of compelling a person suspected of murder to touch the victim's corpse, on the assumption
that, if he were guilty, the body would gush forth anew with blood.
Contemporary scientists who believed in doctrines of sympathy and
antipathy had no difficulty in accepting the validity of this procedure; and it is known to have been formally employed by judges and
coroners on a number of ocasions during the sixteenth and seventeenth centuries. Both Reginald Scot and Francis Bacon were prepared to believe that it worked.[29] Its main role, however, seems to
have been to deter the potential murderer from committing the
otherwise perfect crime for fear of being supernaturally detected.
The suspect's reluctance to undergo the ordeal might also be taken
as proof of his guilt. At Ormskirk in 1636 it was urged that Joan
Elderson, a suspected witch, had stayed away from the funeral of
two children she was supposed to have killed, for fear that she

27. G. Neilson, *Trial by Combat* (Glasgow, 1890), pp. 158–60, 323–31;
Notes and Queries, 7th ser., iv (1887), pp. 461–2.

28. Below, p. 658.

29. Scot, *Discoverie*, XIII, ix; Bacon, *Works*, ii, p. 660. Examples of its
use occur in G. D. Owen, *Elizabethan Wales* (Cardiff, 1962), p. 181 (by a
coroner in 1574); Potts, sig. Y3 (1612); Brand, *Popular Antiquities*, iii, p. 231
(Hertford Assize, 4 Car. I); *H.M.C. Finch*, i, p. 62 (1620s); *Diary of Walter
Yonge*, ed. G. Roberts (Camden Soc., 1848), p. xxiii (by a J.P. in 1613);
J. Webster, *The Displaying of Supposed Witchcraft* (1677), pp. 305–6 (1661);
York Depositions, p. 172 (possibility raised in 1669); W. A. Fearon and
J. F. Williams, *The Parish Registers and Parochial Documents in the Arch-
deaconry of Winchester* (Winchester, 1909), p. 83 (1681); *The Weekly
Miscellany*, 171 (27 March 1736), p. 3 (by a jury in 1736); *County Folk-Lore*,
v, ed. Mrs Gutch and M. Peacock (1908), p. 142 (1832); *Bye-gones relating
to Wales and the Border Counties*, 2nd ser., v (1897–8), p. 424 (1796).
cf. Lea, *Superstition and Force*, pp. 315–23.

would have been made to touch their corpses; and in Somerset in 1613 a murderer fled, rather than touch his victim's body.[30]

Similar considerations underlay the magical thief-detection practised by the wizards. The act of divination could be a very alarming business when conducted before all the parties concerned. In spirit, it was much like the last chapter in the modern thriller where the detective reconstructs the crime before the assembled suspects, while strong men 'wait to prevent the guilty party from bolting for the door. Undoubtedly an element of bluff was involved. When Jane Bulkeley of Caernarvon was sent for in 1618 to detect a thief, she cut a cheese into ten portions, wrote a charm on each of them, and gave a piece to every suspect to eat. Her procedure was identical with that used for the 'holy morsel' administered to clergy suspected of crime in the early Middle Ages; the feelings of the guilty party confronted by this sinister lump of cheese may be imagined.[31] An alternative was to prescribe dry powder, which would be likely to stick in the dry throat of the guilty party. Or one could draw a large eye upon the wall and invite the suspects to look at it; the guilty man's eyes would water when he did so.[32] Even the ritual of key and book could be converted into a form of ordeal. The pious eighteenth-century lady Joanna Turner recalls how when she stole a shilling at her genteel boarding-school in the 1740s she was, along with the other girls, 'tried with the Bible and key, as was the custom, *to see whose hand shook most*'.[33]

A basic principle of magical thief-detection was therefore to induce fear into the mind of the thief so that he would be forced to reveal himself or to restore the stolen goods. This was fully appreciated, both by contemporary writers on magic, and by some of the lay public, who would deliberately give out that they had visited a cunning man, or were intending to visit one. 'When they return home', wrote an almanac-maker in 1609,

they report (yet most falsely) as followeth. 'I have been you know', saith she (for you must understand that the greatest part of such are

30. Lancashire R.O., QSB. 1/170/59; *The Autobiography and Correspondence of Sir Simonds D'Ewes*, ed. J. O. Halliwell (1845), i, pp. 59–60.

31. Ewen, *Star Chamber*, p. 16. Similar instances in L. F. Salzman, *Medieval Byways* (1913), p. 14; M. Aston, *Thomas Arundel* (Oxford, 1967), p. 63, n. 3.

32. Sloane 3846, f. 41; Bodl., Add. MS B 1, f. 11; K. M. Briggs, *Pale Hecate's Team* (1962), p. 261.

33. *The Triumph of Faith ... exemplified in the life ... of ... Mrs Joanna Turner* (Bristol, 1787), p. 22 (my italics).

women), 'with such a man who is exceeding learned, and he did shew
me in a glass the party that had my ring, and he told me where it is,
and that if it be not brought me again before tomorrow morning that
I shall go to him again, and he will make it come again to the cost of
the party that hath it', etc. Now this is spoken where all the household
shall hear it (yet seeming to be said in secret). He or she who hath it
(through fear) is moved to convey it to some place where it may soon
be found; and then flyeth out a report that such a cunning man hath
caused it to be brought again.[34]

So when a fifteenth-century London housewife mysteriously pronounced that she could choose a time to hang out clothes in her
garden, so that 'all the thieves in England' should not steal them,
there may have been some method in her madness.[35] In 1788 a
Sheffield workman got his stolen savings back after the town crier
had announced that he had gone to a conjurer to find the thief. In the
late eighteenth century a servant even murdered his employer to
prevent him from visiting a wizard and so discovering the theft he
had committed.[36] Cunning men were known to have magical recipes
which could inflict physical injury upon the culprit, or paralyse him
so that he would be unable to make off with the goods.[37] Their deterrent effect was much like that of modern devices to shower burglars
with indelible paint. When his brother's money had been stolen, one
Jacobean landowner went to see a cunning man near Ringwood.
Soon afterwards the thief was caught in a storm, which he naturally
attributed to the witch's machinations; his guilty conscience did the
rest, forcing him to return the cash.[38]

In a society which accepted the possibility of magic, the cunning

34. *Pond. 1609. A President for Prognosticators. MDCIX. A New
Almanacke* (1609), sigs. C6ᵛ–7.

35. J. A. F. Thomson, *Clergy and Laity in London, 1376–1531* (Oxford,
D.Phil. thesis, 1960), p. 69. A similar boast, made in 1493, is in Bodl., Tanner
MS 100, f. 57 (Visitation of Norwich, 1494) (kindly shown me by Dr R. A.
Houlbrooke).

36. *The Gentleman's Magazine Library: Popular Superstitions,* ed. G. L.
Gomme (1884), p. 291; Brand, *Popular Antiquities,* iii, p. 64.

37. Typical formulae in Ashm. 421 ff. 231–2; Bodl. MS Add. B 1, ff. 11,
24ᵛ; MS Ballard 66, pp. 55–6; Scot, *Discoverie,* XII, xxii; Kittredge, *Witchcraft,* pp. 190–91, 200–2; Briggs, *Pale Hecate's Team,* p. 260; Sloane 3846,
ff. 17ᵛ, 20, 26–27ᵛ. A carrier who was robbed in 1505 was told by a London
wizard that he could have the thief's arm, eye or leg, if he wished, *Select
Cases in the Council of Henry VII,* ed. C. G. Bayne and W. H. Dunham
(Selden Soc., 1958), p. 165.

38. *The Oglander Memoirs,* ed. W. H. Long (1888), pp. 134–5.

man could thus provide both a deterrent, and a means of detection. In a small community – a village, a monastery, a school – his technique was particularly efficacious, but it had some value everywhere. For even if the magician made a false accusation, the person who had been wrongly accused would then have an interest in detecting the real thief. He might have recourse to another conjurer to get a second opinion which would clear him and direct suspicions elsewhere; or he would bring an action against his accuser for defamation.[39] Either way, the process would go on until the full resources of the community were enlisted in the detection of the criminal. Ill-considered accusations could, of course, arouse dissension,[40] but at its best the system of magical detection had an undoubted utility. The mathematician, William Oughtred, Rector of Albury, Surrey, was regarded by the country folk as a conjurer, and, according to John Aubrey, was well content to have them think so. 'There was never a merry world since the fairies left dancing and the parson left conjuring,' thought John Selden. 'The opinion of the latter kept thieves in awe and did as much good in a country as a Justice of the Peace.'[41]

2. *Conjuring and the magical tradition*

Until the later seventeenth century the work of the practising wizard was sustained by the parallel activities of many contemporary intellectuals. Indeed the possibility of certain types of magic was a fundamental presupposition for most scientists and philosophers. Traditional cosmology portrayed an inanimate Earth or elemental world upon which played the influence of the heavenly bodies. This in itself was sufficient to encourage speculation about the astral reasons for earthly phenomena, and to give rise to much lore about the astrologically derived properties of plants and minerals. It also suggested the possibility that the magician might find some means of

39. Examples in Hale, *Precedents*, pp. 63, 84; *Archaeologia*, lx(2) (1907), pp. 377–8; Kittredge, *Witchcraft*, pp. 192–5; Thompson, *The English Clergy and their Organization*, p. 221; *York Depositions*, pp. 101–2; Ashm. 175, f. 131ᵛ.

40. See, e.g., G. R. Owst, in *Studies presented to Sir Hilary Jenkinson*, ed. J. C. Davies (1957), p. 291; Kittredge, *Witchcraft*, p. 192; *Gentleman's Magazine*, xxiv (1754), p. 290.

41. J. Aubrey, *Brief Lives*, ed. A. Clark (Oxford, 1898), ii, p. 109; J. Selden, *Table-Talk* (Temple Classics, n.d.), p. 97. cf. Atkinson, *Forty Years in a Moorland Parish*, pp. 122–3.

tapping the influence of the stars and diverting it to other purposes. Throughout the Middle Ages there had been a continuous stream of magical speculation along these lines.

But the potentialities open to human ingenuity were greatly enhanced by the tide of Neoplatonism which swept through Renaissance Europe. The revival of this, the last school of ancient pagan philosophy, fostered a disposition to blur the difference between matter and spirit. Instead of being regarded as an inanimate mass, the Earth itself was deemed to be alive. The universe was peopled by a hierarchy of spirits, and thought to manifest all kinds of occult influences and sympathies. The cosmos was an organic unity in which every part bore a sympathetic relationship to the rest. Even colours, letters and numbers were endowed with magical properties. The investigation of such phenomena was the primary task of the natural philosopher, and their employment for his own purposes was the distinguishing mark of the magician. Three main types of magical activity thus lay open: natural magic, concerned to exploit the occult properties of the elemental world; celestial magic, involving the influence of the stars; and ceremonial magic, an appeal for aid to spiritual beings.

In this general intellectual climate it was easy for many magical activities to gain a plausibility which they no longer possess today. The doctrine of correspondences, or relationships between each part of the physical world, made possible the belief in systems of divination like palmistry and physiognomy; for, just as an individual man was believed to mirror the world in miniature, so the hand or the face mirrored the man. Such systems worked by what the German, Cornelius Agrippa, called 'the harmoniacal correspondency of all the parts of the body'.[42] From the disposition of the part one could infer that of the whole. In the same way one could accept the doctrine of signatures, according to which every herb bore a visible indication of its medical role. The work of the astrologers was similarly reinforced, for the influence of the celestial bodies upon the constitution of earthly ones could not be doubted. Even geomancy could be justified as the prophetic message of the soul communicated in a state of rapture.[43]

42. H. C. Agrippa, *Three Books of Occult Philosophy*, trans. J. F(reake?) (1651), p. 107.
43. On signatures, see, e.g., H. More, *An Antidote against Atheisme* (1653), II. 6 (and above, p. 224), and on geomancy, C. H. Josten, 'Robert Fludd's Theory of Geomancy and His Experiences at Avignon in the Winter

Further support for this kind of reasoning came from the doctrine of the magnet, set out by William Gilbert, himself a convinced believer in the theory that the world was alive. The magnet seemed to open the possibility of telepathy, magical healing and action at a distance.⁴⁴ Sympathetic healing by the weapon-salve was easily acceptable, for it exploited the invisible effluvia and influences with which the world vibrated. It made sense to apply the ointment to the weapon rather than the wound because then the vital spirits in the blood congealed on the weapon would be drawn along in the air to rejoin the body. The technique, said Robert Fludd, was not 'cacomagical, but only naturally magical'. The Royal Society accordingly showed considerable interest in such 'magnetical cures' during its early years.⁴⁵ The use of the divining-rod was also stimulated by magnetic theory, for the instrument could be seen as a kind of lodestone, 'drawing iron to it by a secret virtue, inbred by nature, and not by any conjuration as some have fondly imagined'. It too was taken seriously by the Royal Society.⁴⁶ 'If we should consider the operations of this magnet,' wrote the virtuoso Elias Ashmole, 'there is no other mystery, celestial, elemental or earthly, which can be too hard for our belief.'⁴⁷

Neoplatonic theory also emphasized the influence of the imagination upon the body, of the mind upon matter, and of words, incantations and written charms upon physical objects. By the exercise of his imagination, and the use of magic, symbols and incantations, the operator could transform either himself or his victim. Since the world was a pulsating mass of vital influences and invisible spirits, it was only necessary that the magician should devise the appropriate technique to capture them. He could then do wonders.

The intellectual study of magic was a European phenomenon

---

of 1601 to 1602', *Journ. of the Warburg and Courtauld Institutes*, xxvii (1964).

44. W. Gilbert, *On the Magnet*, ed. D. J. Price (New York, 1958), V. xii; Kocher, *Science and Religion*, pp. 181–2. There is a valuable discussion of the prospects raised by Gilbert's work in A. G. Debus, 'Robert Fludd and the Use of Gilbert's *De Magnete* in the Weapon-Salve Controversy', *Journ. of the Hist. of Medicine*, xix (1964).

45. R. Fludd, *Mosaicall Philosophy* (1659), p. 289; T. Birch, *The History of the Royal Society of London* (1756–7), i, pp. 25, 29, 31, 33; *Philosophical Trans.*, xix (1697), pp. 518–21. See above, p. 225.

46. (G. Plattes), *A Discovery of Subterraneall Treasure.* (1639), p. 13; Birch, op. cit., i, pp. 231–2, 234, 270.

47. E. Ashmole, *Theatrum Chemicum Britannicum* (1652), p. 464.

emerging in the Florentine Renaissance with the Platonism of such writers as Ficino and Pico della Mirandola, and spreading to Northern Europe through the works of Paracelsus and Cornelius Agrippa. A key role in the movement was played by Ficino's Latin translation of the *Corpus Hermeticum*, the supposed teachings of the ancient Egyptian god Thoth, or 'Hermes Trismegistus'. This compilation had been put together during the first few centuries after Christ, but was generally believed by Renaissance intellectuals to be pre-Christian, pre-Platonic and possibly even pre-Mosaic. It taught that by mystical regeneration it was possible for man to regain domination over nature which he had lost at the Fall. Its astrological and alchemical lore helped to create an intellectual environment sympathetic to every kind of mystical and magical activity.[48]

In England esoteric magical speculation was largely a derivative affair, stimulated by continental writings, but adding little of its own. It found no place in conventional Protestant education. Dee, Gilbert and Raleigh were deeply influenced, but Bacon was sceptical of the doctrines of sympathy and antipathy, which he thought 'but idle and most slothful conjectures', and he regarded talk of secret hidden virtues as an arrogant substitute for painstaking thought and investigation.[49] The most elaborate English hermeticist was Robert Fludd (1574–1637), whose misfortune it was to have been born at a time when the intellectual presuppositions of the system had already come under attack. Yet although Isaac Casaubon's scholarship deprived the Hermetic books of their claim to be pre-Christian as early as 1614, the cult of Hermes Trismegistus had its English adherents throughout the seventeenth century, partly no doubt because Casaubon's discovery was tucked away in his polemic against the Counter Reformation historian, Baronius. Fludd wrote prolifically during the following decades, untroubled by Casaubon's findings,

48. For modern editions see *Hermetica*, ed. W. Scott (Oxford, 1924–36), and *Corpus Hermeticum*, ed. A. D. Nock and A.-J. Festugière (Paris, 1945–54). For a full account of the hermetic tradition see the works of Miss Yates cited in the Bibliographical Note above.

49. Bacon, *Works*, ii, p. 671–2; iv, pp. 84, 167, 255, 355, 366–8, 376 (views which were already held in 1601 by William Barlow, later Archdeacon of Salisbury, *H.M.C., Hatfield*, xi, p. 4); and see Walker, *Spiritual and Demonic Magic*, pp. 199–202; P. M. Rattansi in *Ambix*, xiii (1966), pp. 133–5; P. Lefranc, *Sir Walter Raleigh écrivain* (Paris, 1968), pp. 434–67; and Yates, 'The Hermetic Tradition in Renaissance Science', pp. 265–70. On Dee, see Peter J. French, *John Dee. The World of an Elizabethan Magus* (1972).

and John Everard's translation of the hermetic *Pymander* (1649) disseminated the tradition more widely. The preface unrepentantly asserted that the work had been written 'some hundreds of years before Moses'. In the latter half of the century astrologers and occult physicians continued to assert its antiquity and near-divinity: 'Hermes Trismegistus' even appears as a Christian name in a Hampshire parish register.[50]

But by the time this magical tradition had begun to make any substantial impact upon the population at large it was beginning to lose its intellectual repute. Around the middle of the century most serious scientists were moving over from an animistic universe to a mechanistic one. Those virtuosi who continued to search for occult virtues and correspondences were essentially outside the mainstream of scientific thinking which was to culminate with Isaac Newton; though even Newton subscribed to the hermetic notion that the true knowledge of the universe had been earlier revealed by God to the ancients, the *prisci theologi*.[51] Natural science owed much to the stimulus of hermetic thinking but its emancipation from that tradition was accomplished in the later seventeenth century.[52]

For much of the period, therefore, magical inquiry possessed some intellectual respectability. At the universities many Jacobean students were interested in magic; both in the natural variety, and in the conjuration of spirits, which seems to have been the equivalent

50. Fearon and Williams, *The Parish Registers ... in the Archdeaconry of Winchester*, p. 24. For some seventeenth-century English hermeticists see C. L. Marks, 'Thomas Traherne and Hermes Trismegistus', *Renaissance News*, xix (1966); J. Maxwell, *A New Eight-fold Probation of the Church of Englands Divine Constitution* (1617), sig. B1; C. R. Markham, *A Life of the great Lord Fairfax* (1870), p. 368; H. C. Agrippa, *His Fourth Book of Occult Philosophy*, trans. R. Turner (1655), sig. A3^v; E. Maynwaring, *Medicus Absolutus* (1668), p. 25; Webster, *The Displaying of Supposed Witchcraft*, p. 314; H. More, *Tetractys Anti-Astrologica* (1681), p. 18; W. Salmon, *Medicina Practica: or, Practical Physick* (1692), sig. A2; T. Tryon, *A Treatise of Dreams and Visions* (2nd edn, n.d.), p. 239; J. Case, *The Angelical Guide* (1697), sigs. b5^v–6; and W. Shumaker, *The Occult Sciences in the Renaissance* (Berkeley and Los Angeles, 1972), pp. 236–48. There are recent discussions of Fludd by S. Hutin, *Robert Fludd (1574–1637* (Paris, 1971)), by A. G. Debus, *The English Paracelsians* (1965), chap. 3, and by Yates in *Theatre of the World*.
51. J. E. McGuire and P. M. Rattansi, 'Newton and the "Pipes of Pan"', *Notes and Recs. of the Royal Soc.*, xxi (1966). cf. below , pp. 511–12.
52. Yates, 'The Hermetic Tradition in Renaissance Science'; P. M. Rattansi, 'The Intellectual Origins of the Royal Society', *Notes and Recs. of the Royal Soc.*, xxiii (1968).

of drug-taking today as the fashionable temptation for under-graduates. There were quite a few confessions of youthful participation in conjuring séances,[53] and many known examples of university-based magicians.[54] The potentialities of love philtres were publicly debated at Oxford in 1620, 1637, 1652 and 1669;[55] and, although it was maintained in 1605 that spells could not cure diseases, the reality of cures by sympathy was confidently upheld in 1653.[56] Other disputations concerned the potentialities of natural magic, the existence of occult qualities, and the power of incantation. In 1657 it was reported to be the recreation of Oxford students of optics to practise 'delusions of the sight' of a kind which former generations would have regarded as magical.[57] Small wonder that for the populace learning still meant magic: 'Thou art a scholar; speak to it, Horatio.' What was learning for if not to deal with spirits? 'Nowadays among the common people,' it was said in 1600, 'he is not adjudged any scholar at all, unless he can tell men's horoscopes, cast out devils, or hath some skill in soothsaying.'[58]

The democratization of this magical tradition came during the

53. See *H.M.C., Various Collections,* v. p. 246; Cooper, *Mystery,* pp. 9–13; Sloane 1926, f. 7ᵛ, and 1954, ff. 179–82ᵛ; Bodl., Rawlinson MS D 253, pp. 50, 63–4; Heywood, *Diaries,* i, p. 340; *The Diary of Abraham de la Pryme,* ed. C. Jackson (Surtees Soc., 1870), pp. xviii, 22, 26, 27; *The Cheats of London Exposed* (n.d.: copy in Bodl., Douce Adds f. 4), p. 55.

54. e.g. John Fletcher of Caius (B.M., Add. MS 36,674, ff. 23–46ᵛ); John Waller and William Cobbie of King's (Wood, *Ath. Ox.,* i, cols. 188–9); John Bowckeley of New Inn, Oxford (*Archaeologia,* xl (1866), pp. 391–4); Richard Johns of Oxford (1532; *L.P.,* v, p. 695); and others referred to in Wood, *Ath. Ox.,* ii, col. 275; Bodl., Rawlinson MS D 253, p. 50, and *The Life and Death of Gamaliel Ratsey* (Shakespeare Assoc. facsimiles, 1935), sig. B4ᵛ. There were magical books at All Souls (R. T. Gunther, *Early Science in Oxford* (1923–67), xi, p. 331); and in 1655 Robert Turner's translation of the *Fourth Book of Occult Philosophy,* the magical work spuriously attributed to H. C. Agrippa, was prefaced by commendatory verses by six members of Cambridge University.

55. *Register of the University of Oxford, II* (1571–1622), i, ed. A. Clark (Oxford Hist. Soc., 1887), p. 179; Oxf. Univ. Arch., Q 16 f. 179ᵛ; Qa 17, f. 151; Qb 18, f. 177ᵛ.

56. *Register of the University of Oxford, II* (1571–1622), i, p. 191; Oxf. Univ. Arch., Qa 17, f. 151ᵛ.

57. Oxf. Univ. Arch., Qb 18 ff. 174, 175ᵛ; Bd 19, f. 204ᵛ; *Register of the University of Oxford, II* (1571–1622), i, p. 171; W. E. Houghton, 'The English Virtuoso in the Seventeenth Century', *Journ. of the Hist. of Ideas,* iii (1942), p. 203.

58. W. Vaughan, *The Golden-Grove* (1600), sig. Y8ᵛ. For another instance of the magical association of the word 'scholar' see J. Fletcher, *The Chances* (1647), V. i.

Civil War and Interregnum, a period which saw the fall of so many other aristocratic citadels. There was a spate of translations into English of the major continental works on magic, hitherto couched in the learned obscurity of Latin or a foreign language. They included the writings of Agrippa, della Porta, 'Hermes', Naudé and Paracelsus; and they coincided with the publication or republication of the native compositions of Roger Bacon, John Dee, Elias Ashmole and Thomas Vaughan. More books on alchemy were published in England between 1650 and 1680 than before or afterwards.[59] Magic may have been unfashionable with the scientists whose meetings in London and Oxford gave rise to the Royal Society, but it gained new converts among the radical sects thrown up by the Civil War, many of whose members pressed for the introduction of the occult sciences into the educational curriculum.[60] At the time of the Restoration the Polish émigré, Samuel Hartlib, was at the centre of a flourishing hermetical movement.[61] Magic's very success during the Interregnum may have helped to accelerate its rejection afterwards by scientists, anxious to shake off overtones of sectarian radicalism.[62]

How far can the activities of the village wizard be regarded as a popular application of the magical theories current in intellectual circles? There is an obvious parallel to be seen between his pursuits and the doctrines of the Neoplatonic philosophers. Belief in the power of sympathy underlay the attention paid by the magical healer to the patient's girdle or other clothing. Faith in the occult virtues of precious stones justified the use of amulets and preservatives. The enunciation of charms and incantations was believed to set up rhythms and emanations in the air which might exert an occult influence upon the sufferer. Natural magic of the kind made popular by the Neapolitan, della Porta, showed an obsessive fascination with the production of marvellous effects by natural means; it

59. According to J. Ferguson in *Journ. of the Alchemical Soc.*, 1914 (cited by D. Geoghegan in *Ambix.*, x [1962], p. 97 n. 5). cf. R. S. Wilkinson in *Ambix*, xv (1968); p. 56. W. Cooper, *A Catalogue of Chymicall Books* (1675), gives an idea of the volume of alchemical literature which had become available.

60. P. M. Rattansi, 'Paracelsus and the Puritan Revolution', *Ambix*, xi (1963); and below, p. 446.

61. C. Webster, 'English Medical Reformers of the Puritan Revolution', *Ambix*, xiv (1967), pp. 29–35. For Hartlib's belief in magical sigils, Josten, *Ashmole*, p. 72.

62. P. M. Rattansi, 'The Intellectual Origins of the Royal Society', *Notes and Recs. of the Royal Soc.*, xxiii (1968), pp. 136–7.

encouraged all kinds of trickery with mirrors and disguises. Astrology, geomancy, palmistry and similar methods of divination had a recognized intellectual basis. Even the attempts to procure conception by magical means were echoed in the widely held belief that life might spring from the putrefaction of matter. Alchemy was equally consistent with the popular theory that metals were living organisms which could grow like plants. Since the unity of matter was presupposed, it followed that all substances might be reducible to their perfect form. The transmutation of metals was only one of a wide range of Utopian objectives which it was hoped the discovery of the stone would achieve. With Paracelsus alchemy had shifted from a search for gold to a quest for a better pharmacopoeia. Gold in its liquid form (*aurum potabile*) would be a remedy for all diseases and help to produce the elixir of long life. The creation of *homunculi* and the power to see at a distance would be other incidental achievements.

It would thus be tempting to explain the practice of popular magic as the reflection of the intellectual interests of contemporary scientists and philosophers. But such a chain of reasoning would almost certainly be mistaken. By this period popular magic and intellectual magic were essentially two different activities, overlapping at certain points, but to a large extent carried on in virtual independence of each other. Most of the magical techniques of the village wizard had been inherited from the Middle Ages, and had direct links with Anglo-Saxon and classical practice. Many can be paralleled in other primitive societies. They were only slightly affected by the Renaissance revival of magical inquiry or by the learned volumes which were its most characteristic product. Both John Dee (in his Preface to Henry Billingsley's *Euclid* [1570]) and Reginald Scot (in Book XII of his *Discoverie of Witchcraft* [1584]) did something to publish knowledge of natural magic in the vernacular; but few of the continental writings on magic had been translated into English before the mid seventeenth century. England's leading contributor to this field, Robert Fludd, wrote nearly all his books in Latin and had them published abroad.

So although virtuosi and university-based magicians can be shown to have been much influenced by Renaissance speculations on magic,[63] the same is not true of the village wizards. It was relatively

63. For instances involving reference to Porta, Agrippa and Paracelsus, see, e.g., *L.P.*, v, p. 69 (Richard Johns, 1532); P.R.O., SP 12/71, f. 160ᵛ (John Bowckeley, 1570); Josten, *Ashmole*, p. 536 (Ashmole, 1650).

uncommon for such persons to possess books, or for their activities to rest upon a body of self-conscious theory. Of course a wizard might possess a printed guide to fortune-telling or some recipes from Agrippa or della Porta. But usually his technique was learned verbally from some relative or neighbour.[64] Such theory as underlay it was derived either from medieval religion or from modes of thought which were ancient by the time of the Renaissance. Healing, counter-witchcraft and thief-magic were almost totally unaffected by the speculations of contemporary intellectuals. Even when the cunning man's procedures are recognizable as debased reflections of Neoplatonic or hermetic theories there is usually little to suggest that he was aware of this descent. His was a stereotyped ritual, not an application of previously worked-out theory.

Indeed in the sixteenth century the influence was as much the other way around. Instead of the village sorcerer putting into practice the doctrines of Agrippa or Paracelsus, it was the intellectual magician who was stimulated by the activities of the cunning man into a search for the occult influences which he believed must have underlain them. The period saw a serious attempt to study long-established folk procedures with a view to discovering the principles on which they rested. In the process the adherents of natural magic were led into attempting to rationalize magical recipes which had no intellectual basis at all. Even the weapon-salve traced its descent from folk practice. Here, as in so many other fields, existing technique was the stimulus to theoretical science, not a consequence of it.

But for some kinds of popular magic books were essential, and in them the direct influence of contemporary intellectual speculation can be seen. The most obvious was the conjuring of spirits. Since classical times, it had been believed that, by following the appropriate ritual, it was possible to get in touch with supernatural beings so as to employ their superior resources for earthly purposes. Many such rituals were extant during the Middle Ages, and their numbers multiplied under the stimulus of Renaissance Neoplatonism. It would be a long and separate task to trace the evolution of these different formulae and to establish the precise genealogy linking the many different essays in the 'notory art' – the *Key of Solomon*, the *Constitution of Honorius*, the *Liber Spirituum*, and the others.

64. For typical data on this point, see Hale, *Precedents*, pp. 108, 139; Hodgkinson, in *Trans. Thoroton Soc.*, xxx (1926), p. 51; *The Examination of John Walsh*, sig. Av; E. Bower, *Doctor Lamb revived* (1653), pp. 26–7; Webster, *The Displaying of Supposed Witchcraft*, p. 35.

Usually they circulated in manuscript and were guarded with the utmost secrecy by their owners; which was hardly surprising, since for much of the period the conjuration of spirits was a capital offence. From time to time, however, the arcana were rudely exposed in print, most notably in the expanded third edition of Scot's *Discoverie of Witchcraft* (1665) where much of Book XV was devoted to an exposition of such formulae, but also in Robert Turner's translations of the spurious *Fourth Book of Agrippa* (1655) and the *Notory Art of Solomon* (1656). These works opened up to the reader the possibility of invoking the whole hierarchy of angels and demons, each with their own names and attributes. The rituals for such spirit-raising varied, but usually involved such procedures as drawing chalk circles on the ground, pronouncing incantations, observing ritual conditions of fasting and prayer, and employing such apparatus as holy water, candles, sceptres, swords, wands and metal lamina.[65]

There is no doubt whatsoever that these rituals were extensively practised, both by contemporary intellectuals and by less educated would-be magicians. The so-called 'Books of Magic' often found in manuscript collections of the period contain quite explicit formulae for invoking spirits, and there is no shortage of evidence for such séances in the manuscript 'Books of Experiments' which have survived. (Something of the attitude of the participants can be deduced from the early use of the word 'experiment' in this context.) The records of the most famous of these séances, held by John Dee and his confidant Edward Kelly, were published *in extenso* in 1659 to demonstrate the spiritual dangers of such activities. But they were in no way unique.[66] There is enough objective evidence relating to

65. For a general account of the main texts, see E. M. Butler, *Ritual Magic* (Cambridge, 1949). *The Key of Solomon the King (Clavicula Salomonis)* is trans. and ed. by S. L. M. Mathers (1909). (The art was 'notory' because it involved marks and signs.)

66. M. Casaubon, *A True and Faithful Relation of what passed for many yeers between Dr John Dee ... and some Spirits* (1659). For other magical books and experiments, see K. M. Briggs, 'Some Seventeenth-century Books of Magic', *Folk-Lore*, lxiv (1953), and *Pale Hecate's Team*, appx. iv; Bodl. Ballard MS 66; Bodl., MSS e Mus. 238, 243 and 245; Bodl., MS Add. B 1; Bodl., Douce MS 116; Sloane 3714, ff. 16–17; 3846; 3851; 3853; B.M., Add. MS 36, 674; Thorndike, *Magic and Science*, ii, p. 284. Bodl., Rawlinson MS D253 is a book which passed through the hands of four successive wizards. A detailed description of the equipment left behind by conjurers interrupted during a séance in 1590 is in *Archaeologia*, xl (1866), p. 397, and a typical

the manufacture of conjuring apparatus and the holding of conjuring sessions to show that spirit-raising was a standard magical activity. Spiritual beings were thought to offer a short cut to riches, love, knowledge and power of all kinds; and the Faustian legend had a literal meaning for its Elizabethan and Jacobean audiences.

It is best left to the psychologist to determine just what happened at these spirit-raising sessions. Very often the venture was frustrated and there was no sign of a spirit, although a high wind would be taken as evidence that supernatural beings were around. But sometimes a spirit was really believed to have appeared, in a crystal ball, in a disembodied voice (with an Irish accent, according to William Lilly),[67] or even in human shape. Sometimes he was visible only to the scryer, conventionally a young boy or girl, whose imagination was doubtless adequate for the purpose. Sometimes he made himself felt through a suggestible or fraudulent intermediary, like Kelly, who made it possible for Dee to carry on numerous conversations with spirits on a wide variety of topics. Sometimes the magician may have been the victim of self-induced hallucination.

A closely allied activity was necromancy, that is to say magic with the aid of a dead person. This was an ancient form of sorcery. A celebrated case before the Court of King's Bench in 1371 concerned a magician who was found carrying a bag containing a Saracen's head which he had bought in Toledo, within which he proposed to enclose a spirit which would answer his questions. In 1440 a person involved in a conspiracy case confessed to having been told that a man who carried a dead person's arm holding a candle could escape arrest.[68] In the sixteenth and seventeenth centuries skulls, corpses and graveyard earth make occasional appearances in magical formulae, and there were attempts to use the ghosts of dead persons for magical purposes.[69] But the connection between these activities and the theories of contemporary intellectuals was very slight.

conjurer's confession in J. Hawarde, *Les Reportes del Cases in Camera Stellata*, ed. W. P. Baildon (1894), p. 251.

67. Lilly, *Autobiography*, p. 199.

68. *Select Cases in the Court of King's Bench under Edward III*, vi, ed. G. O. Sayles (Selden Soc., 1965), pp. 162–3; M. Aston, 'A Kent Approver of 1440', *Bull. Institute of Hist. Research*, xxxvi (1963), pp. 86–7.

69. Ewen, i. pp. 91, 209; C. M. L. Bouch, *Prelates and People of the Lake Counties* (Kendal, 1948), p. 216; Kittredge, *Witchcraft*, pp. 142–5, 312–4; Bodl., Ballard MS 66, p. 35; *The Examination of John Walsh*, sig. Avij; *The Autobiography and Personal Diary of Dr Simon Forman*, ed. J. O. Halliwell (1849), p. 19; below, p. 281.

3. *Popular magic and divination*

By tapping the resources of the spirit world, the magicians were able to open up an infinite range of possibilities. Charms of obvious Christian origin were used side by side with metal sigils cast at astrologically propitious moments and familiar spirits locked up in rings and stones. There was magic to win at cards,[70] to defeat one's opponents in a lawsuit,[71] or to escape arrest. The cunning woman, Anne Bodenham, sent a customer a charm, telling him that once he put it on 'he need not fear what money he owed, for no bailiff could take hold or meddle with him'. Conversely, the conjurers, Bubb and Bostock, had a client in 1621 who wanted them to help him recover money owed by a kinsman.[72] Adam Squire, Master of Balliol College, Oxford, 1571–80, nearly lost his job for allegedly selling gamblers a 'fly' (or familiar spirit) which would guarantee success at dice.[73] Dr Elkes, an Elizabethan conjurer, was also asked to supply a client with a ring for use at the gambling table; it had a spirit enclosed within it and bore a Hebrew inscription.[74]

Other sigils brought immunity in battle, made their wearer invisible, kept off vermin and gave protection against lightning;[75] and there was magic to put out fires, make children sleep and avoid drunkenness.[76] A conjurer promised Lord Neville in 1544 that with the help of the spirit Orpheus he would be able to 'play as well on the lute and virginals as any man in England'. William Barckseale assured six potential burglars of a ship riding at anchor in Southampton harbour in 1631 that his magical art would enable him to put the crew to sleep whenever they wished. The vagrant, William Wake, confessed in 1586 that wherever he went he persuaded people 'that if they hanged such papers as he gave them about their neck they should always have good fortune'.[77]

70. Kittredge, *Witchcraft*, p. 229; Sloane 3846, f. 33v; 3851, ff. 144v–145; Bodl., MS e Mus 243, ff. 15v–16v.   71. Kittredge, *Witchcraft*, pp. 55, 406.
72. Bower, *Doctor Lamb revived*, p. 4; B.M., Royal MS 17 B XXIV, f. 3.
73. *Ben Jonson*, ed. C. H. Herford, P. and E. Simpson (Oxford, 1925–52), x, pp. 62–3.   74. P.R.O., SP 12/186/92.
75. Sloane 2628, ff. 8v, 9, 38v–39; Aubrey, *Gentilisme*, p. 181; Kittredge, *Witchcraft*, p. 176.
76. Bodl., Rawlinson MS D 253, p. 176, and Aubrey, *Gentilisme*, p. 136 (fires); Bodl. MS e Mus. 243, f. 13v (children); *The Works of . . . Joseph Hall*, ed. P. Wynter (Oxford, 1863), vii, p. 330; Bodl., MS e Mus. 243, f. 17 (drunkenness).
77. Kittredge, *Witchcraft*, p. 67; *The Book of Examinations and Depositions*, ii, p. 105; P.R.O., SP 12/192, f. 49.

Protective amulets of this kind were numerous. The inscription, *Jesus autem transiens per medium eorum ibat*, on the noble coined by Edward III, was taken by some to constitute immunity against both theft of the coin and harm to its owner. Queen Elizabeth sent one to the Earl of Essex to guard him on the 1597 expedition to the Azores.[78] The 'siege pieces' cast at Newark during the Civil War also became talismans: Anthony Ascham, the Commonwealth ambassador to Spain, was wearing one at the time of his assassination in 1650.[79]

Those engaged in hazardous political enterprises were indeed particularly likely to have recourse to some magical aid. Just as the King's healing power had been taken as evidence of his legitimacy, so rebels often fortified their efforts by rumoured claims to supernatural assistance. Jack Cade was accused of raising the Devil and using magical books to promote his rebellion in 1450.[80] Sir Anthony Fortescue and the two Pole brothers employed wizards to conjure spirits during their plot against Queen Elizabeth in 1562.[81] The third Earl of Gowrie was supposed to have used magical aids in his conspiracy against James VI of Scotland.[82] The leader of the 1607 agrarian rising in the Midlands, John Reynolds *alias* 'Captain Pouch', claimed to carry a magical preservative against all comers.[83] In 1639 one John Hammond boasted that he had the magical power to take away the monarch's life at one hour's notice and give the crown to someone else. In 1660 a witch in Worcestershire declared that she would have prevented the Restoration, had she not been arrested in advance.[84] Even the Duke of Monmouth carried manu-

78. E. Le Blant, 'Notes sur quelques anciens talismans de bataille', *Mémoires de l'Institut national de France. Acad. des Inscriptions et Belles-Lettres*, xxxiv (1895); J. S. Corbett, *The Successors of Drake* (1900), pp. 167–8.

79. Royal Cssn on Historical Monuments (England), *Newark on Trent. The Civil War Siegeworks* (1964), p. 73; Josten, *Ashmole*, p. 428, n. 1. See in general Aubrey, *Gentilisme*, pp. 76, 153–4, 238; Kittredge, *Witchcraft*, pp. 53–5, 405–6; and the splendidly illustrated survey by L. Hansmann and L. Kriss-Rettenbeck, *Amulett und Talisman. Erscheinungsform und Geschichte* (Munich, 1966).   80. *H.M.C.*, v, p. 455.

81. Kittredge, *Witchcraft*, pp. 260–61.

82. J. Chamber, 'A confutation of astrologicall demonologie' (1604) (Bodl., Savile MS 42), f. 198; D. Calderwood, *The History of the Kirk of Scotland*, ed. T. Thomson (Wodrow Soc., 1842–9), vi, p. 44.

83. E. F. Gay, 'The Midland Revolt and the Inquisitions of Depopulation of 1607', *T.R.H.S.*, n.s., xviii (1904), p. 217, n. 1.

84. *C.S.P.D., 1639–40*, p. 269; *Diary of Henry Townshend*, ed. J. W. Willis-Bund (Worcestershire Hist. Soc., 1920), i, pp. 40–41.

script spells and conjurations during his bid for the throne, although
he affected not to take them seriously.[85]

Closely allied* was the magic designed to bring the operator into
favour with persons in high places. Both Wolsey and Thomas Cromwell were alleged to have used magic rings in order to secure the
favour of Henry VIII, and there is no doubt that such methods were
employed by lesser figures; for example by William Neville in 1532.[86]
In 1620 a schoolmaster named Peacock was examined and tortured
for practising magic to infatuate James I's judgement in the *cause
célèbre* arising from the charges of defamation brought by Lady
Exeter against Sir Thomas Lake and his family.[87]

At a popular level the making of love charms and aphrodisiacs
was a standard item in the repertoire of the village wizard. In 1492
Richard Lawkiston appeared before the Commissary of London
for offering, for a fee, to provide a poor widow with a husband
worth a thousand pounds. His wife, he had assured her, knew
a 'cunning man that by his cunning can cause a woman to have any
man that she hath favour to'. In 1561 Leonard Bilson, Prebendary
of Winchester, procured a Catholic priest to 'hallow conjurations'
to enable him to obtain the love of Lady Cotton, widow of Sir
Richard Cotton.[88] Charms for 'the accomplishment of the pleasure
of the flesh' or the removal of marital impotence were a common
feature of contemporary magical books. Goodwife Swan of Margate
claimed in 1582 to be able to make a drink 'which, she saith, if she
give it to any young man that she liketh well of, he shall be in love
with her'.[89] In the same year Alexander Atherton, a Lancashire yeoman, complained to the Star Chamber that there had been a conspiracy to use magic to make him in love with Elizabeth Winstanley,

85. *H.M.C.*, iii, p. 41.

86. Kittredge, *Witchcraft*, pp. 63–4, 109–10; G. R. Elton, *Policy and
Police* (Cambridge, 1972), pp. 50–56.

87. J. Spedding, *The Letters and the Life of Francis Bacon* (1861–74), vii,
pp. 76, 70–80; *C.S.P.D., 1619–23*, p. 125. Details of this squalid case are given
by S. R. Gardiner, *History of England 1603–42* (1904–5), iii, pp. 189–94.

88. Hale, *Precedents*, p. 32; G. L. Kittredge, in *Harvard Studies and Notes
in Philol. and Litre.*, xvi (1934), p. 99.

89. A. Hussey, 'Visitations of the Archdeacon of Canterbury', *Archaeologia Cantiana*, xxvi (1904), p. 19. For such formulae see Sloane 3851, f. 58ᵛ;
3846, f. 15; Bodl., MS e Mus. 173, ff. 73ᵛ–75; T. Lupton, *A Thousand
Notable Things* (1660), p. 20; M. Gaster, 'English Charms of the Seventeenth
Century', *Folk-Lore*, xxi (1910), p. 376.

and that he was pining away because she refused to marry him.[90]

The opportunities open to the pedlar of recipes for love were revealed by the wandering quack, Thomas Fansome, who was apprehended by the High Commission in the Diocese of Canterbury in 1590. He confessed to issuing one woman with a charm to make her husband love her, for which he was paid six and eightpence plus two half-kirtles and a gold ring, and to supplying another with a charm to enable her to procure 'my Lord of Dover's' goodwill towards her husband (for which he also received six and eight). He had also supplied three men with magical writings to secure them the love of maids, and advised a fourth about a propitious time at which to make a proposal of marriage.[91]

It was not only the common people who had recourse to such recipes. In 1559 Lady Frances Throgmorton, daughter of Lord Chandos, turned out to have been conferring with wizards in an effort 'to obtain her husband's entire and perfect love'. In 1613 during the scandal following the murder of Sir Thomas Overbury, it emerged that Frances, Countess of Essex, and her confidante, Mrs Turner, had visited the astrologer and magician, Simon Forman, with a view to procuring the love respectively of the Earl of Somerset and Sir Christopher Maynwaring. Later in the reign of James I, Frances Shute, mistress of the Earl of Sussex, paid an annual retainer for a magician to gain her the sympathies of the royal favourite, Buckingham.[92] Such practices recall the recurring allegations in late medieval court circles of attempts to infatuate the King by magical means.[93]

Love magic could also involve the cunning man in attempts to find missing persons in the same way as he traced missing goods. It was reported in 1617 of John Redman of Sutton, Cambridgeshire, that when his wife left him he 'went from wizard to wizard, or, as they term them, "wise men", to have them bring her again'. Similarly in 1712 Joan Stevens, on meeting Elizabeth Watkins of Church Withington, Hertfordshire, and 'hearing she was in love with one Samuel Smyth, who had gone from her, told her that she could

90. W. W. Longford, 'An Accusation of Witchcraft, 1582', *Trans. Hist. Soc. of Lancs. and Cheshire*, xcii (1941).

91. Kent R.O., PRC 44/3, pp. 167–8.

92. P.R.O., SP 12/7, ff. 76–7ᵛ; *Cobbett's Complete Collection of State Trials*, ii (1809), pp. 932–3; C. L. Ewen, 'Robert Radcliffe, Fifth Earl of Sussex; Witchcraft Accusations', *Trans. Essex Archaeol. Soc.*, n.s., xxii (1936–40).   93. cf. Kittredge, *Witchcraft*, pp. 84–5, 105–7.

fetch him back again'. As payment in advance she obtained a silver necklace, a gold ring worth ten shillings, and three and sixpence in money.[94] When some prisoners escaped from Reading Gaol in 1635 the Deputy Gaoler, William Turner, 'would have gone to a cunning woman ... but his dame was not willing he should do so'. At Ormskirk Sessions in 1634 the wizard John Garnett was said to have told some clients that a missing friend had been murdered and thrown into the local marl-pits; two innocent labourers were temporarily arrested on the basis of this denunciation.[95]

The search for missing persons is intelligible enough, but magicians were also associated with a less obviously reasonable request: the hunt for buried treasure. The assumption that the country was riddled with caches of treasure may appear one of the more bizarre of contemporary illusions, but it should be remembered that in the absence of an alternative system of deposit banking the possibility of coming across hidden treasure was by no means a chimera. It was still common for rich men to keep their valuables in a box under the bed or to bury them in the ground.[96] Such savings were often turned up accidentally, and, along with the ancient coin-hoards of the Middle Ages, provided some justification for the would-be treasure seeker. Whole families were rumoured to owe their rise to lucky finds with the ploughshare or spade. These stories served to account for otherwise puzzling instances of social mobility; they are common in many static societies where it is assumed that only luck can change a man's fortunes.[97] Contemporaries were impressed, and the search for treasure engaged the energies of many whose tastes in a later age would have led them into speculation on the Stock Exchange.

In popular mythology the treasure was likely to be in one of certain conventional hiding-places, for example, the ruins of a monastery or castle. Primitive mounds or barrows were particularly favoured; by the early Tudor period their excavation in the hope of

94. Ely D.R., B 2/35, f. 205ᵛ; *Hereford City Records*, v, p. 99 (6 June 1712).

95. *Reading Records*, ed. J. M. Guilding (1892–6), iii, p. 261; Lancashire R.O., QSB/1/138/59.

96. See, e.g., L. Stone, *The Crisis of the Aristocracy, 1558–1641* (Oxford, 1965), pp. 509–10; S. Pepys, *Diary*, 19 June and 10–11 Oct. 1667; A. G. Matthews, *Walker Revised* (Oxford, 1948), p. 341.

97. cf. G. M. Foster, 'Peasant Society and the Image of the Limited Good', *American Anthropologist*, lxvii (1965), pp. 307–8.

quick riches was so common that 'hill-digger' had become a recognized term of abuse for a man on the make.[98] An associated title was
'cross-digger', arising from the belief that treasure was to be found
under wayside crosses, an assumption which animated such treasure-
seeking expeditions as that of Lord Neville, the Earl of Westmorland's son, in 1546. It was the search for treasure, as much as any
Protestant iconoclasm, which lay behind the hostile reference in the
preamble of the witchcraft statute of 1542 to persons who had
'digged up and pulled down an infinite number of crosses within this
realm – for despite of Christ, or for love of money'.[99] At Brackley,
in Northamptonshire, the antiquary John Leland found that one of
the three stone crosses had been 'thrown down a-late by thieves that
sought for treasure'. As late as 1615 three men were in trouble at
Chester for pulling down crosses for this purpose.[100]

There was not necessarily anything magical about the search for
treasure as such, but in practice the assistance of a conjurer or
wizard was very frequently invoked. This was partly because it was
thought that special divining tools might help, such as the 'Mosaical
Rods' for which many contemporary formulae survive; John Dee
believed that he could discover hidden treasure by exploiting the
laws of sympathy and antipathy.[101] But a magician was also needed
when the treasure had been found to exorcize the demon or evil
spirit who was likely to be mounting guard over it. Directions for
dealing with treasure are to be found in many contemporary magical
books,[102] and there was a long series of clandestine treasure-seeking

98. e.g., *Norwich Consistory Court Depositions, 1499–1512, and 1518–30*,
ed. E. D. Stone and B. Cozens-Hardy (Norwich Rec. Soc., 1938), no. 6;
and D. Turner in *Norfolk Archaeology*, i (1847), p. 51. For early barrow-
digging, see L. V. Grinsell, *The Ancient Burial-Mounds of England* (2nd
edn, 1953), pp. 110–11.
99. Kittredge, *Witchcraft*, pp. 67–8, 205, 209–10. John Bale listed
'cross-diggers' with other kinds of sorcerers, *Select Works*, ed. H. Christmas
(Cambridge, P.S., 1849), p. 236.
100. *The Itinerary of John Leland*, ed. L. T. Smith (1964), ii, p. 36;
Ewen, ii, p. 415. A case in 1519 is in *An Episcopal Book for the Diocese
of Lincoln, 1514–20*, ed. M. Bowker (Lincoln Rec. Soc., 1967), pp. 111–2.
101. *A Collection of Letters Illustrative of the Progress of Science*, ed.
J. O. Halliwell (1965 reprint), pp. 15–16 (Dee). For divining-rods, see Aubrey,
Gentilisme, p. 115; J. Childrey, *Britannia Baconica* (1661), pp. 44–5; Bodl.,
Douce MS 116, p. 77; Lilly, *Autobiography*, p. 79, and below, p. 796.
102. e.g., Scot, *Discoverie*, XV, x; *The Key of Solomon*, ed. Mathers,
pp. 57–8; Sloane 3846, ff. 27ᵛ–29; 3824, f. 5ᵛ; Bodl., MS e Mus. 173, ff. 29,
40ᵛ–41, 64.

expeditions, operating with magical assistance and sometimes involving persons of high rank.[103] In 1589, for instance, a prisoner in the Tower informed Burghley that there was treasure hidden in Skenfrith Castle, Monmouthshire, guarded by a devil and his wife. In 1634 the Dean of Westminster allowed an expedition, equipped with Mosaical rods and led by the King's clock-master, Davy Ramesey, to search for treasure in the Abbey. Around 1652 Anne Bodenham was offering a magic charm to find £1,000 which, she claimed, had been buried in Wilton garden by the late Earl of Pembroke. In 1680 there was an attempt at Bridgwater, guided by the local cunning man, to find treasure by spirit-raising and the use of divining-rods. At the Wiltshire Quarter Sessions in 1692 a woman was presented for fortune-telling and professing to be able to discover hidden treasure.[104]

But of all such episodes there was none more remarkable than that involving the Whig politician, Goodwin Wharton (1653–1704), who for the last twenty-five years of the seventeenth century was almost continuously engaged in a treasure quest, for which he enlisted spirits, fairies and the latest resources of contemporary technology. He was joined in 1685 by the ex-Leveller, John Wildman, currently a supporter of the Duke of Monmouth and anxious to lay his hands on money for the cause. With the aid of 'George', the disembodied spirit of an executed felon, Wharton and Wildman looked for treasure at Somerset House, exorcized four devils (Wildman heard one of them 'hiss'), and embarked on a quest for the Urim and Thummim from the breastplate of the High Priest of the Temple (Wildman calculated that the jewels alone would be worth £25,000). A house in Holborn was thought to contain treasure guarded by spirits, so Wildman infiltrated himself as a lodger, but this move was of no

103. There are general accounts in Kittredge, *Witchcraft*, chap. 12; W. J. Andrew, 'Buried Treasure', *Journ. of Brit. Archaeol. Assoc.*, n.s., ix (1903); and C. R. Beard, *The Romance of Treasure Trove* (1933). For other instances, see, e.g., Ewen, i, p. 186; Ewen, ii, p. 428; C. Jenkins in *Tudor Studies*, ed. R. W. Seton-Watson (1924), pp. 72–3; Ashm. 200, f. 239ᵛ; Sloane 3677, ff. 180–81ᵛ; S. Harsnet, *A Declaration of Egregious Popish Impostures* (1603), pp. 13–14; A. Clark, 'Buried Treasure at Beeleigh Abbey', *Essex Review*, xvi (1907); L. A. Vidler, *A New History of Rye* (Hove, 1934), p. 70.
104. Owen, *Elizabethan Wales*, p. 65; Lilly, *Autobiography*, pp. 78–81; Bower, *Doctor Lamb revived*, p. 26; E. E. Trotman, 'Seventeenth-century Treasure-Seeking at Bridgwater', *Somerset and Dorset Notes and Queries*, xxvii (1961), pp. 220–21; *H.M.C., Various Collections*, i, p. 160.

more avail than were the fifty guineas which he was subsequently persuaded to leave as a tip for the fairies. When the ex-Leveller grumbled that 'God could not be the author of disappointments and delays: and it could not come from Him if they were thus deceived', the angels retorted that his lack of faith was hindering the operation. The issue of a warrant for Wildman's arrest as a rebel terminated his interest in the proceedings, but Wharton continued the quest, egged on by his unscrupulous medium and mistress, Mrs Parish. In 1691, with the aid of diving-equipment invented by the angels, he examined a Spanish galleon wrecked off the north coast of Scotland. Meanwhile he grew increasingly important in the House of Commons, and was in 1697 appointed a Lord of the Admiralty – a striking example of how secret magical interests could be combined with external respectability.[105]

The remaining branch of the magician's art was fortune-telling. This was usually only an application of one of the many schemes of prediction available to contemporaries, whether professional wizards or not. It must, however, be distinguished from attempts to foretell the course of future events by a rational assessment of probabilities, for example by weather forecasting on the basis of observed natural regularities, a type of prognostication which was already well-known, and which can be seen in such compilations as the rules attributed to John Claridge, 'the Shepherd of Banbury', printed in 1670 and often reissued.[106] For the magician characteristically made his forecast on the basis of evidence which would today be regarded as irrelevant.

Some of these divining systems had a respectable learned origin. There was some basis for the activities of the vagrant magicians denounced in sundry sixteenth-century statutes for 'feigning themselves to have foreknowledge in Physiognomy, Palmistry, or other abused sciences, whereby they bear the people in hand they can tell

105. Autobiography of Goodwin Wharton (B.M., Add. MSS 20,006–07), esp. at I, ff. 59–120. For references to his special diving equipment, see B. Woodcraft, *Titles of Patents of Invention* (1854), p. 37; *H.M.C.*, v, p. 381.

106. *The Shepheards Legacy: or, John Clearidge, his forty years' experience of the weather* (1670); J. Claridge, *The Shepherd of Banbury's rules to judge of the changes of the weather* (1744, etc.). For an earlier effort see *Perpetuall and Naturall Prognostications of the Change of Weather*, trans. from Italian by I.F. (1598).

their destinies, deaths and fortunes, and other such like fantastical imaginations'.[107] These elaborate systems of divination, with their subdivisions, such as divination by moles on the face, or lines on the forehead (metopomancy), had been set out in many medieval treatises and from Elizabethan times were widely disseminated in printed handbooks, often illustrated with crude diagrams of sample hands and faces.[108] Lore of this kind was taken seriously by many Renaissance intellectuals, however debased its practice at the village level may have been. Bacon accepted the potentialities of physiognomy and John Aubrey thought it could be an infallible guide to character.[109] The Jacobean sectary, John Traske, even claimed to be able to determine whether a man was saved or damned by examining his face.[110] The obvious lineal descendant of this type of thought was phrenology, divination by the shape of the skull, so popular with the Victorians.

Other divinatory handbooks had a less discernible intellectual basis. There was *Arcandam*, 'teaching the fatal destiny of every man', translated from the French by William Warde, subsequently Professor of Physic at Cambridge, which went into seven editions between 1562 and 1637, and several more before the end of the seventeenth century.[111] Based on an elaborate calculation of the

107. On these Acts, see below, p. 292.
108. For medieval writings in this *genre*, see H. Craig's introduction to *The Works of John Metham* (E.E.T.S., 1916), pp. xix–xxxi, and *An Old Palmistry*, ed. D. J. Price (Cambridge, 1953). Later guides included J. ab Indagine (von Hagen), *Briefe introductions ... unto the Art of Chiromancy ... and Phisiognomy*, trans. F. Withers (1558), and later edns; B. Cocles, *A Brief and Most Pleasaunt Epitomye of the whole Art of Phisiognomie*, trans. T. Hill (1556); G. Wharton, *Chiromantia* (1652), a translation of J. Rothmann's standard work (Erfurt, 1595); R. Saunders, *Physiognomie and Chiromancie* (1653), and *Palmistry* (1663). There were sections on both arts in *The Compost of Ptolomeus* (below, p. 350), and on physiognomy in *Arcandam* (see below), as well as in such works as *The True Fortune-Teller* (2nd edn, 1686), *Aristotle's Masterpiece* (1684, etc.), etc. For some discussion, see W. C. Curry, *Chaucer and the Medieval Sciences* (2nd edn, 1960), pp. 56–90; Brand, *Popular Antiquities*, iii, pp. 348–51, 355–6; L. B. Wright, *Middle-Class Culture in Elizabethan England* (Chapel Hill, 1935), pp. 565–7; C. Camden, 'The Mind's Construction in the Face', *Philological Qtly*, xx (1941), and 'Elizabethan Chiromancy', *Modern Language Notes*, lxii (1947).
109. Bacon, *Works*, iii, p. 368; Bodl., Aubrey MS 10, f. 85.
110. (J. Falconer), *A Briefe Refutation of John Traskes Iudaical and Novel Fancyes* (1618), p. 7.
111. See *S.T.C.* and Wing. I see no reason to accept the view of W. D. Smith (*Shakespeare Qtly*, ix [1958], p. 168) that the work was a satire. It was

numerical value of the letters in a person's name, it was derived
from the Spheres of Life and Death, a genre which went back to the
ancient world. These Spheres or 'wheels' were usually attributed to
Plato or Pythagoras or some early Christian saint. Normally they
consisted of a circle divided up into compartments containing different fortunes, from which one was selected by calculating the
numerical value of the client's name, adding the day of the month
and dividing by some other figure. They survive plentifully in medieval manuscripts and appeared in print in the later sixteenth
century.[112] Their arbitrariness resembled that of the medieval Books
of Fate, from which the reader chose his fortune by throwing dice.[113]
This type of fortune-telling was also included in the printed guides
which have continued to be issued, with minor variations, from the
seventeenth century to the present day.

Finally, there were the numerous weather and harvest prognostications based upon occurrences on certain key dates in the year, the
weather, perhaps, or the day of the week on which they fell. Thus
if Christmas Day was a Sunday it would be a good year; or if
St Paul's Day was wet, corn would be dear.[114] There were many such
formulae, concerning the twelve days of Christmas, the saints' days
and the days of the moon. Predictions based on St Swithin's Day
have survived as a lone example of this once extensive genre. On the
same principle one could tell an individual's fortune, according to
the day of the week or the month on which he was born – 'Monday's

---

used in 1584 by a Shoreditch wizard, John Perkins (London D.R., D/LC
301, f. 28, a reference kindly supplied by Dr Alan Macfarlane).
    112. See Thorndike, *Magic and Science*, i, pp. 682–4, and C. Singer in
Procs. British Acad., ix (1919–20), pp. 348–51. There are many copies in
the Harley, Sloane and other B.M. MSS. Printed versions in *A Brefe and
Plesaunte Worke, and Sience of the Phelosopher, Pictagoras* (1560?); *The
Geomancie of Maister Christopher Cattan*, trans. F. Sparry (1591), pp.
236–40; S. Strangehopes, *A Book of Knowledge* (1663); *The True Fortune-
Teller* (2nd edn, 1686). For some instances of their employment, *Dives and
Pauper* (1534), f. 50ᵛ; Sloane 1926, f. 7ᵛ; J. S. Purvis, *Tudor Parish Docu-
ments* (Cambridge, 1948), p. 198; London, D.R. D/LC 301, f. 28; *C.S.P.D.*,
1666–7, p. 134.
    113. See T. C. Skeat, 'An Early Mediaeval Book of Fate ... with a Note
on Books of Fate in General', *Medieval and Renaissance Studies*, iii (1954).
For fortune-telling with dice see Sloane 513, ff. 98ᵛ–99ᵛ, and *The Dutch
Fortune-teller* (1650), apocryphally attributed to John Booker.
    114. G. Markham, *The English Husbandman* (1635 edn), pp. 14–17;
Brand, *Popular Antiquities*, i, pp. 39–42.

child is fair of face'. The symbolism which such adages reflected was largely lost by the seventeenth century, but the slogans themselves lived on.[115]

Printed literature of this kind was used by many cunning men or wandering fortune-tellers. A wise woman claimed as early as 1493 to have a book which told her everything about the future.[116] Robert Harris, who startled the people of Maidstone in 1556 by great feats of divination, worked by staring at his clients' faces. The principles of physiognomy also underlay the activities of Valentine Staplehurst, who arrived at the same town four years later, claiming, despite his illiteracy, to be able to tell both past and future.[117] Others used private divining systems of their own: Joan Mores of East Langdon, Kent, was said in 1525 to tell the future from the croaking of frogs; seventeenth-century farmers predicted the price of corn by watching the behaviour of grains placed on a hot hearth; in the eighteenth century wizards claimed to divine by 'casting coffee-grounds', presumably an anticipation of the more modern practice of 'reading the tea-leaves'.[118] Some cunning women claimed second sight because they were seventh children.[119] Others have left no indication of how it was they were able to predict the future.

The layman could also get a glimpse of the future without ever

115. The types of prognostication are discussed by M. Förster, 'Die Kleinliteratur des Aberglaubens im Altenglischen', *Archiv, für das Studium der neueren Sprachen*, cx (1903), and 'Beiträge zur mittelalterlichen Volkskunde', ibid., cxx–cxxix (1908–12). See also *The Works of John Metham*, pp. xxxii–xlii, 146–58; C. Swainson, *A Handbook of Weather Folk-Lore* (1873); Thorndike, *Magic and Science*, i, chap. 29; R. H. Robbins, 'English Almanacks of the Fifteenth Century', *Philological Qtly*, xviii (1939); C. F. Bühler, 'Astrological Prognostications in MS 775 of the Pierpont Morgan Library', *Modern Language Notes*, lvi (1941); M. A. Denham, *A Collection of Proverbs and Popular Sayings relating to the Seasons, the Weather, and Agricultural Pursuits* (Percy Soc., 1846); A. Taylor, *The Proverb* (1931), pp. 109–21. Two early printed examples, spuriously attributed to Aristotle, are *De Cursione Lune* (1530?) and *Here begynneth the nature, and dysposycyon of the dayes in the weke* (1535?). Many others exist in manuscript.

116. Hale, *Precedents*, p. 37.

117. J. Halle, *An Historiall Expostulation*, ed. T. J. Pettigrew (Percy Soc., 1844), pp. 6, 11.

118. B. L. Woodcock, *Medieval Ecclesiastical Courts in the Diocese of Canterbury* (Oxford, 1952), p. 81; Markham, *The English Husbandman*, pp. 16–17; *Anti-Canidia: or Superstition Detected* (n.d., ?1754), p. 42.

119. e.g., the 'gentlewoman, the daughter of a seventh daughter', whose (late seventeenth-century) advertisement is preserved in B. M. Harley 5946, no. 6.

going near the cunning man. In addition to the wide range of divinatory techniques diffused throughout the community there were numerous unsought-for omens, whether dreams, cloud formations or chance encounters with birds or animals. Any of these might have portentous significance.[120] More spectacular were the all-night vigils kept at certain times of the year. John Aubrey records the practice of sitting up on Midsummer Eve in the church porch in order to watch the apparitions of those who were to die during the ensuing twelve months – 'mostly used by women; I have heard 'em tell strange stories of it'. That this was no mere fiction is demonstrated by the presentment of Katherine Foxgale of Walesby before the Archdeacon of Nottingham on 1608 for being a scold and curser of her neighbours, and 'for watching upon St Mark's Eve at night last in the church porch to presage by devilish demonstration the death of some neighbours within the year'.[121] Stories circulated freely of the terrible revelations made to those who took part in these curious vigils. In 1634 two inhabitants of Burton, Lincolnshire, saw the spectre of the minister of their parish reading the burial service over five of their neighbours, all of whom duly died in the following year. And when Robert Halywell, a tailor of Axholme, Lincolnshire, tried the experiment about the same period he was horrified to see the phantom shapes of numbers of his fellow-parishioners. The sight made him so aghast that he was reported to have looked 'like a ghost ever since'. When all the persons he had seen died in the ensuing twelve months, the tailor was summoned by Lord Sheffield to give an account of his experience. 'The fellow, fearing my lord would cause him to watch [in] the church porch again, hid himself in the Carrs [i.e. fens] till he was almost starved.' These vigils survived until the nineteenth century.[122]

120. See below, pp. 745–8.
121. Aubrey, *Gentilisme*, pp. 26, 97;. Hodgkinson in *Trans. Thoroton Soc.*, xxx (1926), p. 52.
122. Both stories recorded by Gervase Holles, B.M., Lansdowne MS 207(c), ff. 193ᵛ–95; partly printed in *County Folk-Lore*, v, ed. Gutch and Peacock (Folk-Lore Soc., 1908), pp. 132–5. cf. *Life in the Middle Ages*, ed. G. G. Coulton, i (Cambridge, 1930), p. 34; A. Watkin, *Dean Cosyn and Wells Cathedral Miscellanea* (Somerset Rec. Soc., 1941), p. 157; R. Bovet, *Pandaemonium* (1684), ed. M. Summers (Aldington, 1951), pp. 126–9; Brand, *Popular Antiquities*, i, pp. 192–3; *The Autobiography of Samuel Bamford*, ed. W. H. Chaloner (1967), i, p. 161; *Folk-Lore Journ.*, iii (1885), p. 279; A. R. Wright, *British Calendar Customs*, ed. T. E. Lones (Folk-Lore Soc., 1936–40), ii, pp. 189–92; iii, pp. 19–20.

The nature of the surviving evidence makes it easier to reconstruct the range of popular beliefs about divination and fortune-telling than to ascertain the contexts in which particular individuals had recourse to them. The cunning men were too prudent and usually too ill-educated to keep records of their consultations, and such information about their activities as survives is seldom adequate for any detailed reconstruction of their relationship with their clients. In any explanation of the social role of divination, therefore, speculation and analogy with the practice of diviners elsewhere must play a large part.

It does, however, seem clear that recourse to a fortune-teller was not normally a frivolous affair, but usually occurred when the client had some matter weighing on his mind. The wife of Gilbert Wright, Master of the Salters' Company in 1624, frequently consulted cunning men in order to find out whether she would outlive her husband, and there is some evidence to suggest that this was a common type of inquiry.[23] In many cases it seems that the wish was father to the thought, and that the question directly reflected the tensions of an unhappy marriage. Thus when Dr Suckling's wife visited Mary Woods, the Norwich palmist, in 1613, to find out when her husband would die, she followed up her inquiry by offering the wise woman money if she would poison him. Indeed this particular fortune-teller used to conceal her magical activities from the authorities by threatening her clients that if they denounced her she would accuse them of trying to do away with their husbands, an accusation which must have had some plausibility before it could have been made.[24]

The mere ventilation of the client's worries could in itself have a cathartic effect, but the fortune-teller might also be expected to offer some personal advice. The oracles of classical antiquity were customarily asked to pronounce upon the merits of two alternative courses of action, or to indicate the best way of attaining an already chosen goal.[25] It is likely that the cunning men of this period often

123. Lilly, *Autobiography*, pp. 28–9. cf. J. Hall, *The Court of Virtue* (1565), ed. R. A. Fraser (1961), p. 298; E. Worsop, *A Discoverie of Sundry Errours* (1582), sig. F4; *The Knowledge of Things Unknown ... Godfridus* (1649), p. 167; *The Severall Notorious and Lewd Cousnages of John West, and Alice West* (1613), sigs. B2v, B3; J. Heydon, *Theomagia* (1664), iii, pp. 80–81; below, pp. 375, 454.

124. Ewen, ii, p. 451; *C.S.P.D., 1611–18*, p. 134.

125. P. Amandry, *La Mantique apollinienne à Delphes* (Paris, 1950), pp. 171, 174 (kindly shown me by Mr D. A. Russell).

performed the same task. Nicholas Gretton, who operated in the Lichfield area in 1654, is known to have been asked such questions as where a client should go to buy certain commodities, or whether he would be well advised to ask his family for a loan; and the Earl of Somerset, James I's ex-favourite, is said to have consulted a wizard about how to reinstate himself.[126] Divination could also resolve disagreement by providing a firm answer to a specific question. As far back as the year 785 the Church had banned the use of sorcery as a means of resolving controversies. In the Middle Ages the people who visited the miraculous well of St Margaret at Binsey, near Oxford, are said to have gone 'to ease their burdened souls and obtain resolution of their doubts, as they would to an oracle'.[127] Used in this way, divination could help men to take decisions when other agencies failed them. Its basic function was to shift the responsibility away from the actor, to provide him with a justification for taking a leap in the dark, and to screw him up into making a decision whose outcome was unpredictable by normal means.

The diviner's predictions, therefore, did not deflect his clients from their original intentions; on the contrary, it was the process of consultation which forced them to know their own minds. Divination could set the imagination free.[128] There was an element of hypnotic self-suggestion in crystal-gazing and similar subjective activities. It is this which explains why conspirators so frequently found it necessary to enhance their determination by getting a magician to predict that their cause would prevail. For there is no evidence that would-be rebels were ever deterred from making their attempts by an unfavourable prognostication. On the contrary they seem to have clutched at every straw which might seem to justify them in pursuing the path upon which they were already set. The man who has to toss a coin to gain support for some desired plan is unlikely to be deterred by an unfavourable result. He will toss again, or look for some other method of confirming his original purpose.[129] Omens bear a similar

126. R. F(arnworth), *Witchcraft Cast Out* (1655), pp. 13–14; Sir A. Weldon, *The Court and Character of King James*, in *Secret History of the Court of James the First* (Edinburgh, 1811), i, 425–6.

127. J. Johnson, *A Collection of the Laws and Canons of the Church of England* (Oxford, 1850–51), i, p. 280; R. C. Hope, *The Legendary Lore of the Holy Wells of England* (1893), p. 125.

128. cf. M. Douglas, 'Nommo and the Fox', *Listener*, 12 September 1968.

129. cf. O. Fenichel, 'The Misapprehended Oracle', *Collected Papers*, ed. H. Fenichel and D. Rapaport (1954–5), ii, chap. 16.

relationship to human intentions. We dream many dreams, but those which we remember are the ones which harmonize with our existing hopes and fears. The utterances of the three weird sisters were treated with suspicion by Banquo. But they struck an answering chord in the heart of Macbeth.

Diviners thus existed to strengthen their clients' resolution and to sustain their optimism. When Anne Boleyn was pregnant, it was no accident that all the contemporary wizards predicted that the child she bore Henry VIII would be a son.[130] Like other kinds of magic, divination could stiffen morale. 'It may be speciously pretended,' observed Bacon, 'that ceremonies and characters, charms, gesticulations, amulets, and the like, do not derive their power from any tacit or sacramental contact with evil spirits, but serve only to strengthen and exalt the imagination of him who uses them.' Carrying a magical ring or sigil could make a man 'more active and industrious and again more confident and persisting than otherwise he would be. Now the great effects that may come of industry and perseverance (especially in civil business) who knoweth not?'[131]

But if divination could strengthen the determination of the man who half-knew what he should do, it also helped the person who had no idea. It legitimized random behaviour by enabling men to make a choice between different courses of action when on rational grounds there was nothing to choose between them. Today the person who allows his faith in a 'lucky number' to influence his choice of a raffle ticket at least knows that there is no superior method of making a selection. In the seventeenth century the miner who sought ore with a divining-rod was also without any more rational alternative. Divination allowed men to follow their fancy; it countenanced departures from the norm in an otherwise traditional society.[132]

Diviners thus offered a method of decision-making which many found indispensable. Like their African counterparts, they maintained their prestige by a combination of fraud and good psychology. They might have their clients ushered into a waiting-room where their conversation could be overheard by the wizard, who would then appear, armed with an apparently miraculous knowledge of their problems and personal circumstances. Or they might in some

130. *L.P.*, vi, p. 465.
131. Bacon, *Works*, iv, p. 400; ii, p. 642.
132. cf. J. Cohen, *Behaviour in Uncertainty and Its Social Implications* (1964), esp. pp. 11–12; and G. K. Park, 'Divination and Its Social Contexts', *Journ. Roy. Anth. Inst.*, xciii (1963).

other way acquire advance information about their customers which would make a great impression when casually let drop during the interview.[133] Sometimes their activities, especially in love matters, took the form of attempts to arrange the future rather than predict it;[134] many of them acquired an unsavoury reputation as pimps and panders. Even without any conscious deceit they might pick up a good deal of local knowledge, and adapt their recommendations accordingly. In such ways an established wizard could maintain his reputation among a regular clientele, while others who led a more vagrant existence could at least pass muster for the short period of time they would spend in any one community. Like the ancient Greek oracle, they probably tended to give firm advice but only vague predictions, incapable of proof or disproof. Besides, an occasional success could sustain a great deal of failure. 'If they hit once,' wrote a contemporary, 'it is cried up and told everywhere; but if they err an hundred times, it is soon buried in silence and oblivion.'[135]

But they were not necessarily popular. They knew too much about the conflicts and suspicions latent within a small community. Ellen Spink was reported by the churchwardens of Buttercrambe, Yorkshire, in 1575 to be 'an evil woman amongst her neighbours who takes on hand to declare their destinies'. In Somerset, Nicholas Butler, who purported to be able to recover stolen goods and identify the thieves, was accused in 1557 of 'deceiving divers persons, and causing great dissension between man and man'. The same charge of sowing discord amongst her neighbours was brought in 1588 against the sorceress and palmist, Joan Corfe of Norwell in Nottinghamshire.[136] Some magicians like John Dee had a reputation for peace-making,[137] but only too often so-called fortune-telling meant

133. For examples of such techniques, *Dives and Pauper*, f. 46ᵛ; *The Brideling, Sadling and Ryding, of a Riche Churle in Hampshire* (1595); *The Severall Notorious and Lewd Cousnages of Iohn West*, sig. C1; *H.M.C., Hatfield*, v, 81–3; T. Brian, *The Pisse-Prophet* (1637); J. Wilson, *The Cheats*, ed. M. C. Nahm (Oxford, 1935), p. 193; R. Gough, *Antiquities and Memoirs of the Parish of Myddle* (1875), p. 61.

134. (D. Defoe), *A System of Magick* (1727), pp. 360–77, provides a typical example.

135. M. R. Nilsson, *Cults, Myths, Oracles, and Politics in Ancient Greece* (Lund, 1951), p. 125; Webster, *The Displaying of Supposed Witchcraft*, p. 29 (probably echoing Scot, *Discoverie*, XI.xxii).

136. Borthwick, R. VI. A 5, f. 44; Wells, D.R., A 27; *Southwell Act Books*, xxii, p. 292.   137. Josten, *Ashmole*, pp. 1333–4.

wild predictions of sudden death or bastard children for one's enemies. Sometimes the diviner brought the client's own tensions to the surface, but on other occasions he could insert new worries quite independent of those which had originally led the patient to seek his aid. The Jacobean wizard, John Lambe, was said to have caused many dissensions between married people.[138] In the courts charges of sorcery were sometimes accompanied by allegations of anti-social offences like contentiousness and scolding; in extreme cases the cunning woman might find herself faced with the more deadly charge of maleficent witchcraft.[139] The practice of magic of any brand set the sorcerer a little apart from the rest of the community, and although the wise woman might have hundreds of clients she was always perched precariously on the brink of social isolation.

4. The magical profession

Contemporary homilists had no doubt that the cunning men were both numerous and active. In 1590, for example, Henry Holland, a Cambridge preacher, lamented 'the continual traffic and market which the rude people have with witches'; and in 1621 Robert Sanderson, the future Bishop of Lincoln, speaking of 'charmers and fortune-tellers and wizards', declared that it was 'scarce credible how generally and miserably our common ignorants are besotted with the opinion of their skill; and how pitifully they are gulled by their damnable impostures, through their own foolish credulity'.[140] But such numerical estimates as were offered are very imprecise. In 1549 William Wycherley, an apprehended sorcerer, stated that 'there be within England above five hundred conjurers as he thinketh . . . and specially in Norfolk, Hertfordshire, and Worcestershire and Gloucestershire'.[141] Thirty-five years later Reginald Scot wrote that every parish had its miracle-worker, and that some had seventeen or eighteen. Robert Burton repeated the assertion that there was a

138. *A Briefe Description of the Notorious Life of John Lambe* ('Amsterdam', 1628), p. 2; *H.M.C.; Finch*, i, p. 62. cf. J. Beattie, 'Divination in Bunyoro, Uganda', *Sociologus*, xiv (1964), p. 50.

139. See below, p. 677.

140. (H. Holland), *A Treatise against Witchcraft* (Cambridge, 1590), sig. B1; *The Works of Robert Sanderson*, ed. W. Jacobson (Oxford, 1854), iii, p. 117.

141. *Narratives of the Days of the Reformation*, ed. J. G. Nichols (Camden Soc., 1859), p. 335.

cunning man in every village.[142] At the turn of the sixteenth century well-informed contemporaries thus thought the wizards roughly comparable in numbers to the parochial clergy.

This assessment is difficult to confirm, for if he were lucky the cunning man left no records behind him, and his consultations were always more or less furtive affairs. Apart from the liability of all concerned to punishment in the ecclesiastical courts, there were three parliamentary statutes which imposed secular penalties for some of the most common forms of popular magic. In 1542 it was made a felony, i.e. a capital offence, to use magic for treasure-seeking, for the recovery of stolen goods, or 'to provoke any person to unlawful love'. This Act, repealed in 1547, was followed by the statute of 1563, which proscribed the same activities, though reducing the penalty to a year's imprisonment and four appearances in the pillory for the first offence, and life imprisonment and forfeiture of goods for the second. This measure was in turn superseded in 1604 by a more stringent Act imposing the death penalty on second offenders. Conjuring of spirits was a felony in all three Acts.[143] There were also numerous statutes against itinerant fortune-tellers,[144] and a total prohibition of alchemy, the transmutation of metals remaining a felony until 1689. For most of the period, therefore, the main activities of the cunning men were blatantly illegal. Even the use of charms for healing was proscribed by the Church and banned by the various authorities responsible for licensing doctors.

In practice, however, the attitude of the authorities may have been more lenient. Prosecutions of black witches suspected of doing harm to other people were numerous enough. But the records of assizes and quarter sessions suggest that their white counterparts were unlikely to find themselves in the courts unless their activities had been fraudulent or otherwise harmful. Every kind of magic was prosecuted at one time or another; fortune-telling, divining for lost goods, healing by charms, or conjuring for treasure.[145] But the number of

142. Scot, Discoverie, I.ii; Burton, Anatomy, ii. p. 6. cf. Cooper, Mystery, p. 315 ('these good witches ... are rife almost in every parish').

143. With the difference that the 1542 Act forbade conjuration of any spirits for an unlawful purpose, whereas the later two concerned the conjuration of evil spirits for any purpose. See Ewen, i, pp. 13–21.

144. 22 Hen. VIII, c. 12; 14 Eliz., c. 5; 39 Eliz., c. 4; 1 Jac. I, c. 7.

145. e.g., fortune-telling: Ewen, ii, pp. 393, 451; Kittredge, Witchcraft, p. 230; Quarter Sessions Records, ed. J. C. Atkinson (North Riding Rec. Soc., 1884–92), vi, p. 133; C.S.P.D., 1611–18, pp. 348, 565; 1667, p. 30; H.M.C., Various Collections, i, p. 160; Hertford County Records, i, pp.

extant cases seems disproportionately small beside that of the prosecutions for maleficent witchcraft, especially in view of what can be inferred about the number of cunning men and extent of their activities.[146] It may be reasonably surmised that the wizard was normally respected by his customers, and that only when one of them fell out with him was the matter taken up at a higher level. Moreover, no secular legal action lay against the charmer who succeeded in curing his patients and took no money. Widespread popular tolerance of white magic thus helped to mitigate the rigours of the law. Even less frequent were prosecutions of the wizard's customers, perhaps because the section in the witchcraft statutes concerning 'aiders, abettors and counsellors' seems to have related only to those who went to cunning men for purposes of conjuration or black witchcraft: it was unclear whether the client of the white witch was committing an offence or not, and he very seldom made an appearance in the law courts. As a Puritan writer indignantly commented, 'the blesser escapes and the silly people that run to this white Devil are let alone'.[147]

Nevertheless, the risk of prosecution was great enough to deter the cunning man from courting unnecessary publicity, and this makes it all the more difficult to determine just how common a figure he was. No useful statistics can be derived from the records of the secular courts, where his appearance was only desultory. The church

267–8, 275. Lost goods: Ewen, i, p. 285; Ewen, ii, pp. 280, 414, 424, 436; *Quarter Sessions Records*, ed. Atkinson, iv, p. 20; Owen, *Elizabethan Wales*, pp. 62–3; B.M., Harley MS 1026, f. 68^v; Lancashire R.O., QSB 1/255 (38), (70–71); *Norfolk Archaeology*, iv (1885), pp. 250–51. Healing: Ewen, ii, p. 415; H. H. Copnall, *Nottinghamshire County Records* (Nottingham, 1915), p. 45; J. Stow, *The Annales of England* (1592), p. 1021; Lancashire R.O., QSB 1/78/49; 1/202/33, 38, 39; 1/139/81. Treasure: Ewen, i, p. 186; *C.S.P.D., 1611–18*, p. 29.

146. Dr Macfarlane found that in Essex white magic accounted for 13 out of 48 witch cases at Quarter Sessions and only 11 out of 503 at Assizes *(Witchcraft Prosecutions in Essex, 1560–1680* (Oxford D.Phil. thesis, 1967), pp. 42, 44).

147. Cooper, *Mystery*, p. 200. The only printed cases known to me in which clients were prosecuted in secular courts are in Ewen, i, p. 220; Ewen, ii, p. 418; *Records of the Borough of Nottingham* (Nottingham, 1882–1956), iv, p. 275; *Middlesex County Records*, ed. J. C. Jeaffreson (1886–92), iii, p. 252; and *Hertfordshire County Records*, v (1928), p. 131. The Rump's committee on law reform would have removed the ambiguity by making it an offence to visit cunning men (below, p. 309). James I had wanted such clients to be put to death (*Daemonologie* [Edinburgh, 1597], III. vi).

courts, however, unearthed wizards with great regularity. No one can say how many of their names are contained in the voluminous and almost entirely unpublished court books and visitation records which survive, often in their hundreds, for virtually every diocese in England. It would be the work of a lifetime for an individual to produce even an approximate answer to the question.[148] The excerpts in print are too brief and selective to offer many statistics, though it is worth noting that in 1597 an episcopal visitation of the diocese of Norwich unearthed fourteen cunning men and women, while some thirty names are yielded for the diocese of Canterbury in the later sixteenth century by the published extracts from visitation records, supplemented by the unpublished Act Books.[149] Where deeper shafts have been sunk the results are abundant. There are well over a hundred cases of popular magic between 1560 and 1640 in the records of the diocese of York.[150] In Essex, where the records are perhaps uniquely extensive and where the only really systematic inquiry has been made, sixty-one cunning folk have been identified, of whom at least forty-one practised within the county boundary. In Elizabethan Essex no one lived more than ten miles from a known cunning man.[151] If allowance is made for the numerous wizards who must have succeeded in keeping their names out of the law courts we get an even more striking impression of their ubiquity.

The visitation records in a wide range of other dioceses yield the general impression, for what it is worth, that it was unusual for any single visitation by bishop or archdeacon in the late sixteenth century not to uncover at least one white witch, and quite common for there to be more. If we recall that there were twenty-one dioceses in England we may form some idea of the possible annual average of sorcerers who were detected, bearing in mind that these represent an

148. The late B. L. Woodcock thought that 'all modern scholars will be dead before a thousandth part of the *Acta* of English ecclesiastical courts can be printed, so vast is their bulk'; *Medieval Ecclesiastical Courts*, p. 140.

149. *Diocese of Norwich. Bishop Redman's visitation, 1597*, ed. J. F. Williams (Norfolk Rec. Soc., 1946), p. 26. *Archdeacon Harpsfield's Visitation, 1557*, ed. L. E. Whatmore (Catholic Rec. Soc., 1950–51); *Home Counties Magazine*, iii–xiii (1901–11); *Archaeologia Cantiana*, xxvi–xxix (1904–11); Lambeth Lib., V/Di/III/3–5.

150. Total based on my own researches in Borthwick, combined with evidence from the same source kindly supplied by Dr Philip Tyler. cf. P. Tyler, 'The Church Courts at York and Witchcraft Prosecutions, 1567–1640', *Northern History*, iv (1969), p. 93.

151. Macfarlane, *Witchcraft in Tudor and Stuart England, passim.*

unknown but probably small proportion of the total number at work.

As for the chronology of these cases, the records of the ecclesiastical courts indicate that they were at their peak in the reign of Elizabeth I, steadily dwindled under the early Stuarts, and virtually disappeared after the Restoration. Almost certainly this graph tells us more about the changing interests and efficiency of the church courts than it does about the history of the cunning men. Ecclesiastical prosecutions of every kind declined in the later seventeenth century, and it became less common for bishops to inquire in their visitation articles about wise men or cunning women.[152] It would be rash to conclude from the ecclesiastical court records of this period that the village wizard was disappearing. On the contrary, modern students of folklore have assembled plenty of evidence to show that the white witch was a conspicuous feature of nineteenth-century rural life. 'A cunning-man, or a cunning-woman, as they are termed, is to be found near every town,' wrote Robert Southey in 1807, 'and though the laws are occasionally put in force against them, still it is a gainful trade.'[153]

It would be tempting to explain this long survival of magical practices by pointing out that they helped to provide many professional wizards with a respectable livelihood. The example of the legal profession is a reminder that it is always possible for a substantial social group to support itself by proffering solutions to problems which they themselves have helped to manufacture. The cunning men and wise women had an undoubted interest in upholding the prestige of magical diagnosis and may by their mere existence have helped to prolong a mode of thinking which was already obsolescent. By the seventeenth century sorcery no longer constituted the route to power and influence which it may have been in primitive times; wizards, as Sir Thomas Browne rightly observed, were 'commonly men of inferior rank'.[154] But the fees derived from giving advice did at least help many persons to supplement an otherwise meagre income. As is the case with his modern African counterpart, it was relatively unusual for a wizard to subsist entirely upon the proceeds of his magical activities. Usually he followed some artisan's occupation – as a miller perhaps, or a shoemaker, or cordwainer, and

152. Below, pp. 309–10.
153. R. Southey, *Letters from England*, ed. J. Simmons (1951), p. 295. cf. the publications of the Folk-Lore Society, *passim*.
154. Sir T. Browne, *Pseudodoxia epidemica* (1646), I.iii.

practised sorcery only as a sideline. Magical practitioners might be of either sex and could be found at various levels of society. The nine persons arrested in one swoop by the Council in 1561 for various magical offences comprised a merchant, an ironmonger, a salter, a goldsmith, a miller, a yeoman and three clerics.[155] But those who plied for hire in the country villages were usually of very humble status. Some, particularly the women, were virtually dependent upon the fees paid by their clients. As the Somerset wise woman, Joan Tyrry, admitted in 1555: the fairies 'taught her such knowledge that she getteth her living by it'.[156]

The fees themselves seem to have varied enormously. Magicians had no professional organisation and consequently no recognised scale of charges. Moreover, payment was frequently conditional upon success, as was sometimes the case with the fees paid to orthodox medical practitioners. Etheldreda Nixon, who practised magic in Suffolk at the end of the fifteenth century, took a regular twenty-five per cent of the value of the stolen goods she succeeded in restoring;[157] but charges can seldom have been as systematic as this. A great deal of information exists concerning the fees paid to individual wizards for particular transactions since the sum involved was usually quoted in any subsequent litigation. But no clear pattern is to be discerned. The most that can be safely said is that the sum claimed by the village wizard was normally under a pound, and usually only a few shillings. Thus Joan Betyson, who in 1595 admitted to treating forspoken cattle, charged only a penny per animal, and did it for nothing if her client was very poor. A penny was also the sum offered to Margaret Stothard as 'charmer's dues' in 1653. In fact she settled for a fleece of wool, for it was common for payments to be made in kind. Thomas Harding, who was active in Hertfordshire around 1590, took money, bacon and pigeons to the value of five shillings when searching for lost goods on one occasion. His other known fees range from sixpence for treating a sick child to a promise of twenty pounds (of which two pounds was payable in advance) for identifying an arsonist.[158]

The rewards could thus be substantial. Copies of St John's Gospel

155. (Sir E. Coke), *A Booke of Entries* (1614), f. 1.   156. Wells D.R., A 22.
157. Jenkins in *Tudor Studies*, ed. Seton-Watson, p. 72.
158. Hodgkinson in *Trans. Thoroton Soc.*, xxx (1926), p. 51; E. Mackenzie, *An Historical ... View of the County of Northumberland* (2nd edn, Newcastle, 1825), ii, p. 36 (corrected date in Ewen, ii, p. 323); Hertfordshire R.O., HAT/SR 2/100.

were sold as preservatives against witchcraft in early seventeenth-century Nottingham at ten shillings each. Christiana Weekes of Clyffe Pypard, Wiltshire, received four guineas in 1651 for charming an evil spirit from a client's leg. Edward Ashmore got five pounds a few decades later for tracking down a debtor who had fled to Ireland. A Derbyshire webster who proposed to cure a lunatic with a paper charm in the reign of Charles I demanded three pounds down, and three more when the patient was cured.[159] An early Tudor wizard was promised a ten pound annuity for making a magic ring for Henry, Lord Neville, while John Lambe, the Duke of Buckingham's protégé, demanded forty or fifty pounds for some individual cures. The Jacobean wizard and astrologer, Mathias Evans, was offered a retainer of fifty pounds *per annum* by Frances Shute, mistress of the fifth Earl of Sussex. The conjurers Bubb and Ripton proposed to claim thirty-five pounds plus expenses for restoring the money owed to one of their clients. Another Jacobean practitioner, Alice West, was said to have extracted sixty pounds from a gentleman who was anxious to know whether he would outlive his wife.[160]

A practitioner's annual income could thus be considerable, especially if his business was as brisk as that of the wise woman mentioned by George Gifford who had as many as forty customers in a week. A sawyer named Kiterell, of Bethersden, Kent, who inspected urine and prescribed for witchcraft, was said in 1565 to have made enough money to buy land and build a house. A Cambridge magician told Richard Bernard in the early seventeenth century that if he had persisted with his art of finding stolen goods with a mirror it would have brought him an annual income of two hundred pounds. At the end of the century a low-grade fortune-teller in Lincolnshire is known to have been earning between thirty and forty pounds *per annum*. He was probably as typical of his profession as was the itinerant wizard Joseph Heynes, who in 1676 reckoned his takings after telling fortunes at Ware, Hertfordshire, at 'five pounds . . . three maidenheads, and a broken shin'.[161]

159. *Records of the Borough of Nottingham*, iv, p. 275; *H.M.C., Various Collections*, i. p. 120; F. J. Pope, ' "A Conjuror or Cunning Man" of the Seventeenth Century', *British Archivist*, i (1914); J. C. Cox, *Three Centuries of Derbyshire Annals* (1890), ii, p. 88.

160. Kittredge, *Witchcraft*, p. 67; C. Goodall, *The Royal College of Physicians* (1684), p. 397; Ewen in *Trans. Essex Archaeol. Soc.*, xxii (1936–40), p. 236; B.M., Royal MS 17 B XXIV, f. 3; *The Severall Notorious and Lewd Cousnages of Iohn West*, sig. B2ᵛ.

161. G. Gifford, *A Dialogue concerning Witches (1593)* (Shakespeare

When it is remembered that a late-seventeenth-century labourer in husbandry could seldom hope to earn more than a shilling a day, and that nearly half of the benefices of the Church of England were worth less than fifty pounds *per annum* in 1704,[162] it can be seen that the financial rewards open to the magicians were not contemptible. It is easy to understand why some were frauds who practised for the sake of the cash, and privately lacked any faith in their own procedures. So far as one can tell, self-confessed impostors were only a minority among the large fraternity of practising wizards, but even bona-fide magicians had an obvious financial interest in their art. Their advertisements by word of mouth or printed bill must have drawn in clients who had not previously been interested in magic, just as the fortune-tellers who wandered through the countryside were able to offer advice to people who might never have ventured outside their own village to find a diviner for themselves.

But an explanation for the sustained recourse to magic which laid its stress upon the vested interests of the professional magician would be hopelessly misleading. Charmers and blessers sometimes performed their services without making any formal charge; as with some of their modern African counterparts the prestige was sufficient reward.[163] Besides, if anything is clear in the history of this difficult subject it is that sorcery arose to meet a need. Far from having to advertise his services, a professional wizard was likely to be overwhelmed by the demand. William Wycherley, an expert in the use of the psalter and key, complained in 1549 that 'people are so importunate upon him daily for this purpose that he is not able to avoid them, but keepeth himself within his doors'. It was said to be nothing for 'rude people' to travel twenty or forty miles to consult a witch if they had a problem they particularly wanted to put to her.[164] The traffic in popular magic continued despite the prohibitions of the Church, the invective of the clergy, and the severity of the witchcraft

Assoc., 1931), sig. H1; Halle, *An Historiall Expostulation*, pp. 28–9; Bernard, *Guide*, p. 138; *Diary of Abraham de la Pryme*, pp. 56–7; *Hertford County Records*, i, p. 268.

162. J. E. T. Rogers, *Six Centuries of Work and Wages* (10th edn, 1909), pp. 392–6; A. Savidge, *The Foundation and Early Years of Queen Anne's Bounty* (1955), p. 9.

163. B. G. M. Sundkler, *Bantu Prophets in South Africa* (2nd edn, 1961), p. 22; J. R. Crawford, *Witchcraft and Sorcery in Rhodesia* (1967), p. 203. cf. above, pp. 244–5.

164. *Narratives of the Period of the Reformation*, p. 332; Holland, *A Treatise against Witchcraft*, sig. B1.

statutes. Men took risks when they went to wizards, for there was always the danger of getting involved in conjurations which would carry the death penalty. Moreover, a visit to the cunning man could be a frightening experience in itself. The wizard might be imposingly dressed – the charlatan, Alexander Hart, was said to have 'sat like an alderman in his gown' – and was often ready to frighten his client by boasting of his ability to raise spirits.[165] The Archbishop of York's Court was told in 1633 how William Dowe set out on a cunning man's advice beyond Malton in search of a lost cow: 'at which time, as he after reported, his hat was torn off his head, and [he] was glad he so 'scaped'.[166]

But for all their nervousness clients were not deterred. 'If the loss of a little worldly pelf come to us,' lamented the preacher, Richard Greenham, 'we are straight void of all fear . . . we are unquiet until we have consulted with wizards and witches, not standing in awe of God's threatenings against that sin.'[167] The defiance of established authority implicit in this continued intercourse with sorcerers was well expressed by one John Shonnke, charged in 1585 with having consulted the Essex wizard, Father Parfoothe. The accusation was true, Shonnke confessed, but Father Parfoothe was a 'good witch' and 'for the help of his wife he went to him; and if it were again he would do the like to help his wife'.[168]

The cunning men thus attracted a plentiful supply of unsolicited custom. As the churchwardens of Aldeburgh said of the wise woman, Margaret Neale, in 1597, 'She taketh upon her to cure diseases by prayer, and *therefore* hath recourse of people to her far and wide.' Similarly when an old woman in Stowmarket claimed, a few decades previously, to be able to heal all diseases by 'words of conjuration', it was a predictable consequence that 'people . . . resorted [to her] out of all parts in great numbers'.[169] The process was much the same as that which had in the Middle Ages enabled the shrines of saints to attract great concourses of people, once they had

165. Lilly, *Autobiography*, p. 62. cf. Kittredge, *Witchcraft*, pp. 107–8; *C.S.P.D., 1581–90*, pp. 246–7; *The Journal of George Fox*, ed. N. Penney (Cambridge, 1911), i, p. 10; Borthwick, R. VII.I.660.

166. Borthwick, R. VI. B4, f. 427ᵛ.

167. *The Workes of . . . Richard Greenham*, ed. H. H(olland) (3rd edn, 1601), p. 662.

168. Hale, *Precedents*, pp. 185–6.

169. *Bishop Redman's Visitation*, p. 133 (my italics); C.U.L., MS Ee. 2. 34, no. 129, f. 112ᵛ.

obtained their initial reputation for healing. In their own communities the cunning folk were often feared and respected. If a wise woman fell under suspicion from the authorities her neighbours might rally to her defence, providing compurgators in the ecclesiastical court, or drawing up certificates testifying to her innocence. Even if she was gaoled, they still thronged to her ministrations.[170] William Perkins summed up the whole process, 'Let a man's child, friend, or cattle be taken with some sore sickness, or strangely tormented with some rare and unknown disease, the first thing he doth is to bethink himself and inquire after some wise man or wise woman, and thither he sends and goes for help.' And when as a result of his charms the sick party recovers, 'the conclusion of all is the usual acclamation: "Oh, happy is the day that ever I met with such a man or woman to help me!" '[171]

170. For resort to witches in prison, *The Chronicle of the English Augustinian Canonesses Regular of the Lateran, at St Monica's in Louvain*, ed. A. Hamilton (1904–6), i, p. 83, and Ewen, i, p. 37. For certificates by neighbours on their behalf, *H.M.C., Kenyon*, i, p. 36, and *Somerset and Dorset Notes and Queries*, v (1896–7), pp. 308–9. For compurgation, below, p. 312.

171. Perkins, *Discourse*, p. 175.

9.

MAGIC AND RELIGION

This radical conflict of principle between magic and religion sufficiently explains the relentless hostility with which in history the priest has often pursued the magician. The haughty self-sufficiency of the magician, his arrogant demeanour towards the higher powers, and his unabashed claim to exercise a sway like theirs could not but revolt the priest, to whom, with his awful sense of the divine majesty, and his humble prostration in presence of it, such claims and such a demeanour must have appeared an impious and blasphemous usurpation of prerogatives that belong to God alone. And sometimes, we may suspect, lower motives concurred to whet the edge of the priest's hostility. He professed to be the proper medium, the true intercessor between God and man, and no doubt his interests as well as his feelings were often injured by a rival practitioner, who preached a surer and smoother road to fortune than the rugged and slippery path of divine favour.

Sir J. G. Frazer, *The Golden Bough*
(3rd edn, 1932), i, p. 226

Some professors of this black art, though their work be devilish, yet they pretend to do it in the name of Jesus.

Joseph Hall, *Works*, ed. P. Wynter
(Oxford, 1863), ii, p. 383

There are many who hearing in the Word of the wonderful creation, redemption, and preservation of man, and of the matter of the Sacraments, cannot believe them, yet afterwards go to witches.

Richard Greenham, *Workes* (3rd edn, 1601), p. 554

1. *Ecclesiastical opposition to magic*

EVER since its arrival in England, the Christian Church had campaigned against the resort of the laity to magic and magicians. The Anglo-Saxon clergy forbade soothsaying, charming and love philtres, along with such survivals of paganism as the worship of wells and trees, and the making of sacrifices to heathen divinities. This proscription of sorcery and divination was continued after the Norman Conquest and was frequently reiterated in the councils and synods of the medieval Church. By the thirteenth century it had become customary for the clergy to pronounce an annual excommunication of all sorcerers *in genere*, and parish priests were expected to use the confessional as a means of coercing their flock into abandoning their time-honoured recourse to magic. The various magical practices which were current in the sixteenth and seventeenth centuries had all been listed in such earlier mandates as that of Ralph Baldock, Bishop of London, who in 1311 ordered his archdeacon to proceed against those who practised sorcery for recovering lost goods and foretelling the future, and who conjured spirits or made use of stones and mirrors. In the later Middle Ages preachers inveighed against the practice of magic by the laity, while the ecclesiastical courts regularly proceeded against wizards and those who had recourse to them.[1]

The theory underlying such a prohibition was coherent enough.[2] There was no objection to attempts to heal the sick or foretell the

1. For ecclesiastical action against magic before the sixteenth century, see Kittredge, *Witchcraft*, chap. ii; Ewen, i, pp. 2–10; J. Johnson, *A Collection of the Laws and Canons of the Church of England* (Oxford, 1850–51), i, pp. 219, 230, 244, 267, 280; ii, pp. 15, 36, 355; Powicke and Cheney, *Councils and Synods*, pp. 214, 222, 230, 303, 434, 444, 457, 496, 632, 644, 820, 1062, 1073, 1089, 1349–50. An inquiry about sorcerers occurs in the earliest extant set of episcopal visitation articles (*Annales Monastici*, ed. H. R. Luard [Rolls Series, 1864–9], i, p. 297 [Lichfield, 1252]). For general excommunication see below, p. 599; the use of the confessional is illustrated in J. Myrc, *Instructions for Parish Priests*, ed. E. Peacock (E.E.T.S., 1868), p. 27. Many examples of prosecutions are cited in Kittredge, *Witchcraft*, chap. ii, and pp. 85, 107, 113, 114, 130, 187–8, 191–2, 207–8, 209, 228; and above, pp. 217–8, 278. For others see *Archaeologia Cantiana*, xxxii (1917), p. 169; *The Register of John de Grandisson, Bishop of Exeter (A.D. 1327–69)*, ii, ed. F. C. Hingeston-Randolph (1894–9), pp. 1044–5; M. Aston, *Thomas Arundel* (Oxford, 1967), pp. 63 and n., 404; *E.H.R.*, xlv (1930), p. 97; ibid., li (1936), p. 4, n. 3; Thomson, *Later Lollards*, pp. 63, 179, 241; *T.R.H.S.*, 3rd ser., viii (1914), p. 117; *The Register of Bishop Philip Repingdon, 1404–19*, ed. M. Archer (Lincoln Rec. Soc., 1963), p. xxxiii; A. H. Thompson, *The English Clergy and their Organization* (Oxford, 1947), pp. 220–22; *V.C.H., Oxon.*, ii, p. 19; *Lincoln Diocese Documents, 1450–1544*, ed. A. Clark (E.E.T.S., 1914), p. 111; B. L. Woodcock, *Medieval Ecclesiastical Courts in the Diocese of Canterbury* (Oxford, 1952), p. 81; *Journ. Soc. Archivists*, iii (1968), p. 339; Bodl., Tanner MS 100, f. 57 (Visitation of Norwich diocese, 1494).

2. For representative statements see John of Salisbury, *Policraticus* (relevant sections translated by J. B. Pike as *Frivolities of Courtiers* [Minneapolis, 1938]); *Corpus Iuris Canonici*, ed. A. L. Richter and E. Friedberg (Leipzig, 1879), i, cols. 1020–36, 1045; Aquinas, *Summa Theologica*, II.ii.95–6; G. R. Owst, '*Sortilegium* in English Homiletic Literature of the Fourteenth Century', *Studies presented to Sir Hilary Jenkinson*, ed. J. C. Davies (1957); *Dives and Pauper* (1536), 1st commandment, chaps. 30–36, 39–40, 47–8.

future by purely natural means. The Church never discouraged the use of medicine, for example, or the attempt to predict the weather on the basis of observable natural phenomena. But any claim to have achieved some effect greater than that which could be shown to have arisen from known natural causes was immediately suspect. If a healing power was claimed for charms or written words, or if the weather was foretold by reference to such unconnected data as the day of the week on which Christmas had fallen, then the matter needed to be closely scrutinized. The Church did not deny that supernatural action was possible, but it stressed that it could emanate from only two possible sources: God or the Devil. Certain supernatural effects could be confidently expected by faithful men who followed the rituals prescribed by God and the Church, for example those pertaining to the Mass or the power of holy water. Others might occur miraculously, as with the healing activities of the saints. But the remainder were diabolical and to be abhorred. Any magician, therefore, who sought to achieve a marvellous result by means which were neither purely natural nor commanded by God was guilty of allying himself, either tacitly or expressly, with Satan. This was the offence of those who superstitiously attributed a healing power to words or rituals unauthorized by the Church, or who attempted by some system of divination to penetrate those secrets of the future which only God could know. In Dante's *Inferno* such prognosticators were discovered with their heads twisted backwards as a penalty for their impious curiosity.[3]

Two aspects of this attitude are immediately obvious. The first is that the legitimacy of any magical ritual depended upon the official view taken of it by the Church. So long as theologians permitted the use of, say, holy water or consecrated bells in order to dispel storms, there was nothing 'superstitious' about such activity; the Church, as we have already seen, had no compunction about licensing its own brand of magical remedies. The second feature is that the Church's view of any other technique would depend upon its prior assumptions about what was or was not 'natural'. Those sixteenth- and seventeenth-century clergymen influenced by Neoplatonism, for example, were disposed to attribute much more to natural causes than

3. *Inferno*, xx, 13–15. Perhaps it is too fanciful to discern an echo of this tradition in the report by a Suffolk countrywoman in 1499 that after she had talked with 'les elvys' her head was temporarily twisted backwards (C. Jenkins, 'Cardinal Morton's Register', *Tudor Studies*, ed. R. W. Seton-Watson [1924], p. 73).

their conservative brethren who subscribed to the less flexible Aristotelian view of matter. For Robert Fludd, the weapon-salve was an entirely commendable attempt to harness the invisible forces he believed to be pulsating through the natural world; but for his clerical opponent, William Foster, the parson of Hedgerley, Buckinghamshire, the procedure was diabolical and its original inventor, Paracelsus, a monstrous conjuror working outside the bounds of nature. Had not Aristotle shown that nothing could work at a distance?[4] What was at issue here was not any difference of religious principle; it was a view of the natural world. If the clergy tended to be quicker than some laymen in detecting the hand of the Devil, it was as much because of their university training in Aristotelianism as because of their religion. At every stage in the progress of science there were to be discoveries so marvellous that conservatives, unable to accept that such effects could spring from mere nature, fell back on the view that they must have stemmed from the Devil.

The boundaries of 'magical' activity were thus determined by the attitude of the Church to its own formulae and to the potentialities of nature. The Reformation in England saw a spectacular reduction in the power attributed to holy words and objects, so that the more extreme Protestants virtually denied the existence of any Church magic at all. At the same time their attitude to the practice of non-ecclesiastical magic remained as hostile as ever. Divination, charming, fortune-telling, and all the other activities of the village wizard were still reprehensible. Any device which seemed to produce miraculous effects for no discernible natural reason was immediately suspect. Even the tricks performed for entertainment by conjurers and jugglers were sometimes suspected to involve diabolical aid.[5] For those Protestants who believed that the age of Christian miracles was over, all supernatural effects necessarily sprang from either fraudulent illusion or the workings of the Devil. Satan, it was believed, was well acquainted with the secrets of nature and might counterfeit an effect when he could not reproduce it directly. Those

4. W. Foster, *Hoplocrisma-Spongus: or, a Sponge to wipe away the Weapon-Salve* (1631), and Kocher, *Science and Religion*, pp. 70–71. For others who thought the salve diabolical see Sloane 1954, f. 189 (E. Poeton); Bernard, *Guide*, pp. 97, 125–6; J. Stearne, *A Confirmation and Discovery of Witch-craft* (1648), p. 51.

5. e.g., Foxe, v, p. 129; J. Webster, *The Displaying of Supposed Witchcraft* (1677), p. 61. The suspicion must have been enhanced by a popular manual of conjuring tricks which asserted that some of the profession did indeed use familiar spirits; *Hocus Pocus Junior* (3rd edn, 1638), sig. H3ᵛ.

persons who sought to use objects for purposes which nature could not justify were guilty of idolatry, superstition, and at least implicitly of soliciting the aid of the Devil.

This was not a very different position from that which had been assumed by the medieval Church. The main change was that the Protestants now attacked not only folk magic, but also large parts of the old ecclesiastical magic as well. They therefore looked less indulgently upon some of the parasitic vagaries of popular devotion. Village wizards who used Christian prayers to heal or to divine the future now seemed as diabolical as those whose techniques were blatantly derived from pagan tradition. By using such prayers, thought Thomas Cooper, the 'blessers' and 'good witches' merely advanced 'lip-labour and formal devotion, the very life of Popery'.[6]

The cunning man was therefore guilty of blatant *lèse-majesté*, by seeking to achieve supernatural results without God's aid. But it was his *claim* to perform such miracles rather than any actual success which excited religious opinion; for, on the question of the actual efficacy of the wizard's charms, the theologians were divided between those who regarded them as entirely illusory – 'they have not power to hurt nor to help us', wrote the Puritan, Richard Greenham – and those who conceded their effectiveness, but chose to attribute it to the tacit assistance of the Devil, who had forwarded the sorcerer's project in order to capture both his soul and those of his clients.[7] Some thought that a sick man cured by a witch would soon relapse again;[8] others held that he would be healed in this world, but damned in the life to come.

Seen from this point of view, the cunning man was an even more deadly menace than the black witch, for the latter's acts of malevolence made him unpopular with the community at large, whereas the remedies offered by the white witch were positively seductive. 'The most horrible and detestable monster,' resolved William Perkins accordingly, 'is the *good* witch.' The black witch might do harm to his neighbour's body, but the cunning man struck a mortal blow at his soul.[9] Many theological writers thus chose to blur the difference

6. Cooper, *Mystery*, pp. 4–5.
7. *The Workes of ... Richard Greenham,* ed H. H(olland) (5th edn, 1612), pp. 821–2. The leading continental authorities on either side are cited in Burton, *Anatomy*, ii, pp. 5–6. See also above, p. 246.
8. e.g., I. Basire, *Deo et Ecclesiae Sacrum. Sacriledge Arraigned* (1668), p. 150.
9. Perkins, *Discourse*, p. 174. Similar statements in Cooper, *Mystery*,

between different kinds of magical activity, on the grounds that they all involved diabolical aid and were all equally likely to draw away the allegiance of God's people. In the ecclesiastical courts such terms as 'witch', 'sorcerer', 'charmer' and 'blesser' were used almost interchangeably.

But in fact the white witches were never heavily punished. It was always theoretically open to ecclesiastical judges to commit extreme heretics to the secular arm for burning, but this never seems to have been done in cases of magic, for which more moderate penalties were in practice inflicted. Those post-Reformation writers who would like to have seen the cunning men and women put to death[10] were thus unable to achieve their objective through the agency of the church courts. The plan for a reformed canon law drawn up by a commission in the reign of Edward VI had recommended the imposition of the heaviest penalties (*poenas gravissimas*) upon both cunning men and their clients, but the scheme never came into effect. Neither did the proposal of William Alley, Bishop of Exeter, to Convocation in 1563, that 'penal, sharp, yea, capital pains' be inflicted upon 'witches, charmers, sorcerers, enchanters and such like'.[11] Only the secular law, in the form of the Tudor statutes against witchcraft, ever prescribed genuinely heavy penalties for magical activity, and even then those cunning men who were not accused of doing anyone any physical damage were treated with relative leniency. Popular magic was treated by the church courts as neither more or less serious than such other routine offences as sabbath-breaking, defamation and fornication. It was not singled out as peculiarly diabolical. The writers who continued to agitate for severer treatment of the village wizard seem, with a few exceptions, to have belonged to the more aggressively Protestant section of the Anglican Church and, as time

---

pp. 232, 294; Bernard, *Guide*, sigs. A5ᵛ–A6; J. Gaule, *Select Cases of Conscience touching Witches* (1646), pp. 30–31.

10. For examples: Kittredge, *Witchcraft*, p. 70 (Hooper); *The Sermons of Edwin Sandys*, ed. J. Ayre (Cambridge, P.S., 1841), p. 129; G. Gifford, *A Dialogue concerning Witches* (Shakespeare Assoc., 1931), sig. H2; H. Howard, Earl of Northampton, *A Defensative against the Poyson of Supposed Prophecies* (1620), f. 44; Perkins, *Discourse*, p. 256; C. Richardson *A Sermon concerning the Punishing of Malefactors* (1616), pp. 15–16; Bernard, *Guide*, pp. 254, 256–8; T. Gataker, *Of the Nature and Use of Lots* (2nd edn, 1627), pp. 373–5, 379–80; Stearne, *A Confirmation and Discovery*, sig. A3.

11. *The Reformation of Ecclesiastical Laws*, ed. E. Cardwell (Oxford, 1850), pp. 33–5; Kittredge, *Witchcraft*, p. 263.

went on, to have been increasingly unrepresented at the top of the ecclesiastical hierarchy. None of the clergy would have denied that a tacit compact with Satan was implicit in the practice of magic, but very few seem to have taken the implications of this as seriously as might have been expected.

Nevertheless, Protestants and Catholics in the mid sixteenth century were equally vehement in their hostility to popular magic, and both denounced it in terms which would have been approved by their medieval predecessors. The Royal Injunctions of 1547 fulminated against charmers, sorcerers, enchanters, witches and soothsayers in language which was closely echoed seven years later by Edmund Bonner, the Marian Bishop of London. Indeed Bonner wrote at length against magic, asserting that 'witches, conjurers, enchanters, and all such like, do work by the operation and aid of the Devil' and that 'all such commit so high offence and treason to God, that there can be no greater'.[12] The Elizabethan Injunctions of 1559 similarly forbade the laity to employ 'charms, sorcery, enchantments, invocations, circles, witchcrafts, soothsaying or any such like crafts or imaginations invented by the devil', and banned their resort to magicians 'for counsel and help'. These offences were subsequently inquired after by the bishops and archdeacons in their visitation articles, so that those guilty of them might be hauled up before the eclesiastical courts. The types of magic most commonly mentioned included the detection of stolen goods, the use of charms to heal men and animals, the prediction of men's destinies, and the use of unlawful prayers or invocations. A full list was given by Edwin Sandys, Bishop of Worcester, in 1569: 'charms to cure men or beast; invocations of wicked spirits; telling where things lost or stolen are become by key, book, tables, shears, sieves; looking into crystals or other casting of figures'.[13] Any individual known to have employed such techniques, or reputed to have dabbled in any other kind of magical activity, was supposed to be reported to the bishop or archdeacon by the incumbent and churchwardens of the parish in which he

12. Frere and Kennedy, *Articles and Injunctions*, ii, pp. 111 (1547), 353 (Bonner), and others at pp. 301, 388, 425. Bonner's views are set out in his *A Profitable and Necessarye·Doctryne* (1555), sig. Hhii.

13. Frere and Kennedy, *Articles and Injunctions*, iii, pp. 5 (1559), 227–8 (Sandys); and others at pp. 92, 106, 214, 270, 313, 343; W. P. M. Kennedy, *Elizabethan Episcopal Administration* (1924), ii, pp. 15, 60, 121–2, 131; iii, pp. 166, 230, 263, 328; J. S. Purvis, *Tudor Parish Documents* (Cambridge, 1948), p. 14.

lived; and so was anyone who could be proved to have been one of the wizards' customers. In the Church's eyes it was as much an offence to take one's problems to a sorcerer as to be one.

Ecclesiastical anxiety to repress popular magic may also have been one of the chief reasons for the assumption by the early sixteenth-century Church of control over the licensing of doctors and mid-wives. The statute of 1512 giving the bishops authority to license medical practice cited the superstitious activities of contemporary quacks and empirics as justification for the step,[14] while the concern to repress the use of magic in childbirth clearly lay behind the intro-duction of a licensing system for midwives during the reign of Henry VIII. It is sometimes said that it was the changes brought by the Reformation which led the Church to take an interest in the religious orthodoxy of all midwives, since these women had the authority to baptize any newly-born infant thought likely to die before a priest could be fetched. But the *Malleus Maleficarum* (1486) had already urged that midwives should take an oath in order to eliminate any possibility of their resort to witchcraft. The fifteenth-century Church in England had prosecuted superstitious midwives, and the licensing system is known to have been employed by Bishop Fitz-James of London (1506–22) before the Reformation began. Midwives had always been 'the occasion of much superstition and dishonour of God', as Bishop Latimer put it.[15] The earliest surviving example of the midwife's oath dates from 1567, and it includes a promise to refrain from the use of any kind of sorcery or enchantment during the period of labour. This stipulation was retained until the second half of the eighteenth century; and in addition the bishops inquired in their visitation articles about the use of girdles, invocations and charms by pregnant women.[16]

14. 3 Hen. VIII, c. 11.
15. *Malleus*, iii.34; *The Fabric Rolls of York Minster*, ed. J. Raine (Sur-tees Soc., 1859), p. 260; J. H. Bloom and R. R. James, *Medical Practitioners in the Diocese of London* (Cambridge, 1935), pp. 84–5; *Sermons and Remains of Hugh Latimer*, ed. G. E. Corrie (Cambridge, P.S., 1845), p. 114; above, p. 222. T. R. Forbes, *The Midwife and the Witch* (New Haven, 1966) is a recent compilation. This aspect of the subject is not mentioned by Sir G. Clark in his rather inconclusive 'Note on the Licensing of Midwives' (*A History of the Royal College of Physicians* (Oxford, 1964–6), i, pp. 66–7).
16. The 1567 oath is printed in *Registrum Matthei Parker*, ed. E. M. Thompson and W. H. Frere (Canterbury and York Soc., 1928), p. 472. Later examples in *Bull. of the Hist. of Medicine*, xli (1967), pp. 75–6 (1588); Ely D.R., F 5/34, f. 142 (c. 1636–8); *The Book of Oaths* (1649); *T.R.H.S.*,

During the first half of the seventeenth century the Church continued its campaign against the cunning man, although questions
about popular magic were possibly a less frequent feature of visitation inquiries than they had been in the Tudor period. The erratic
survival of these articles makes exact comparison difficult. But there
is no reason for thinking that the Anglican Church's attitude to
sorcery on the eve of the Civil War was very different from that of
its medieval predecessor." Nor did the Interregnum constitute much
of a break in this respect. The Presbyterians showed strong hostility
to popular magic, and an ordinance of 1648 imposed the penalty of
suspension from the Lord's Supper upon all those who repaired for
advice to witches or fortune-tellers. Independents, Huguenots, Baptists and Quakers took the same attitude.[18] Under the Rump the
committee set up to reform the law proposed to make it a criminal
offence to repair to a cunning man 'for finding out any goods lost
or stolen, or to know who shall be their husbands or wives, or any
other such like future contingencies'.[19] This provision would have
filled the gap left by the temporary disappearance of the church
courts, but like so many other would-be law reforms it never came
into effect.

The real change in attitude seems to have come with the Restoration of the Anglican Church after 1660. The inquiries after charmers
and sorcerers which had been so prominent a feature of visitation
articles before the Civil War now silently disappeared from the list
of matters on which the bishops and archdeacons normally sought
information from their flock. Cases of magical activity were still
sporadically prosecuted in the ecclesiastical courts, and there were
occasional inquiries about sorcerers at visitations – the latest example

---

4th ser., iv (1921), p. 138 (1673); *Sussex Archaeol. Collections*, iv (1851),
p. 249 (1675); *Journ. Derbyshire Archaeol. and Nat. Hist. Soc.*, xix (1897),
pp. 46–8 (1686); R. Burn, *Ecclesiastical Law* (2nd edn, 1767), ii, p. 440.
Visitation articles in Frere and Kennedy, *Articles and Injunctions*, ii, pp.
58–9, 292, 356, 372; iii, pp. 270, 383, and Kennedy, *Elizabethan Episcopal
Administration*, ii, pp. 166, 230.

17. See below, pp. 596–7.

18. *Acts and Ordinances of the Interregnum*, ed. C. H. Firth and R. S.
Rait (1911), i. p. 1206. cf. A. M. Gummere, *Witchcraft and Quakerism*
(1908), pp. 27–8; Bedfordshire R.O., x 239/1, p. 29 (Stevington Baptist Church
Book, 14 April 1693); *Actes du consistoire de l'église française de Thread-
needle St, Londres, i (1560–65)*, ed. E. Johnston (Pubs. Huguenot Soc., 1937),
p. 34; *Colloques et synodes, 1581–1654*, ed. A. C. Chamier (ibid., 1890), p. 10.

19. *Somers Tracts*, vi, p. 237 (kindly pointed out to me by Dr W. R. Prest).

so far traced is in the Bishop of Norwich's articles for 1716.[20] But their occurrence had been rare during the previous fifty years and any attempt at an organised campaign was clearly over. The sermon literature of the later seventeenth century reflects the same indifference to what had once been regarded as a problem of pressing urgency. It appears that the Church no longer thought popular magic worth taking seriously. So far had old fears been forgotten, that in 1710 the Barber-Surgeon's Company, when petitioning against the Archbishop of Canterbury's power to license surgical practitioners, could assume that the intention to repress magical healing asserted by the 1512 statute, which gave the bishops their licensing powers, had been a mere blind: 'an artificial motion set up by the Popish clergy in those times to draw within their own verge the inspection and approbation of all such persons as attended the beds of dying men'.[21]

Even while it lasted, the Church's campaign against magic had been of doubtful efficacy. So long as the records of the ecclesiastical courts remain largely unpublished, its precise impact is impossible to assess; especially as the irritating tendency of ecclesiastical judges to postpone cases repeatedly before reaching a final decision often makes it very difficult to discover what the result of an individual prosecution may have been. But certain conclusions may be fairly confidently reached.[22]

In the first place, it must be appreciated that the ultimate success of any campaign waged through the church courts depended upon the extent of the cooperation it received from the local incumbent and his churchwardens, upon whom fell the onus of presenting sus-

20. *Articles to be enquired of and answered unto ... in the Ordinary Visitation of ... Charles [Trimnell] Lord Bishop of Norwich, 1716*, p. 6. Other post-Restoration examples occur in the articles of the Bishops of Lichfield and Coventry (John Hacket, 1662, 1664, 1668); Chichester (Peter Gunning, 1670); Ely (Peter Gunning, 1679, 1682); Rochester (John Warner, 1662; John Dolben, 1668); St Asaph (Isaac Barrow, 1671, 1678); the Deans of Lichfield (William Paul, 1662) and York (Henry Finch, 1705); and the Archdeacon of York (Knightley Chetwood, 1705). There is no mention of magic in the remaining 132 extant visitation articles for the period 1660–1720 which I have been able to examine.

21. S. Young, *The Annals of the Barber-Surgeons of London* (1890), pp. 347–8.

22. They do not, I think, conflict with Dr R.A. Marchant's valuable assessment of the efficacy of the disciplinary side of the eccelesiastical courts (*The Church under the Law* [Cambridge, 1969], chap. 6), which I was unable to see until this chapter was in proof.

pects in response to the inquiries of the bishop or his deputy. The extent of this cooperation varied greatly. In the later seventeenth century, for example, it seems to have been common in some areas for *nil* returns to be regularly made by way of reply to a comprehensive set of inquiries relating to all aspects of the spiritual state of the parish. Indeed as early as 1622 all but one of the fifty-four extant churchwardens' presentments for the diocese of Ely were blank.[23] Such declarations of *omnia bene* are valueless as evidence of the actual state of any parish, however useful the incidental light they may shed upon the declining effectiveness of the whole system of episcopal visitation. As the seventeenth century wore on, these blank returns became increasingly common. In the later Stuart period parishes maintained a keen interest in reporting cases of bastardy, presumably because of their consequences for the rates, but they tended to pass over other ecclesiastical offences which must have been committed no less frequently. Even in the Elizabethan period, when returns were usually much fuller, replies to questions about such matters as sabbath-breaking or clerical nonconformity had tended to reflect the state of religious opinion in the parish as much as the extent to which such ecclesiastical crimes had actually been committed. The presentation of sorcerers, therefore, may be reasonably presumed to have fluctuated according to the attitude taken to them by the leading parishioners. A wise woman who was popular with her neighbours might escape delation; whereas one who had fallen out with them might find herself accused not just of charming, but even of black witchcraft. Sometimes, moreover, the culprit might be too powerful for the churchwardens to risk denouncing her. In 1619 the parish officers of King's Sutton, Northamptonshire, stated darkly that some unnamed persons had resorted to sorcerers for things lost, but that they hesitated to present the guilty parties, because the latter 'profess that they have ten pounds and such large sums of money to spend to ride the minister out of town for so joining in the presentment'.[24]

Even if a cunning man did fall into the hands of the ecclesiastical courts – and thousands must have done so – his ultimate fate still

23. C. Hill, *Society and Puritanism in Pre-revolutionary England* (1964), p. 392, n. 2. A similar set of returns for the Archdeaconry of Leicester, 1640, is in Leicester City Museum, 1 D 41/21.

24. *The Churchwardens' Presentments in the Oxfordshire Peculiars of Dorchester, Thame and Banbury*, ed. S. A. Peyton (Oxfordshire Rec. Soc., 1928), p. 294. At the next visitation they were still prevaricating (p. 299).

depended considerably upon his relations with the people of his own neighbourhood. If he denied the charge, the normal procedure was for the ecclesiastical judge to order him to bring compurgators from his own parish to testify to his innocence. If he succeeded in producing the required number (usually between four and eight), he could count on being let off with a caution. The wizard's ability to muster compurgators was thus the crucial factor in the whole proceedings. Primarily, of course, his success or failure here was an index of his popularity. The court itself might be held miles away from the parish concerned and the compurgators would be put to trouble and expense, which the accused party might be expected to refund. Without money or influence, he could have difficulty in persuading any supporters to turn up. Agnes More in 1583 denied the charge of witchcraft for which she had been brought before the court of the collegiate church of Southwell, but was released without punishment, because 'she is a poor woman and not of ability to bring in any of her neighbours to purge her'.[25] But such indulgence could not be relied upon.

Even so, the opportunity of summoning compurgators, and the reluctance of his friends to testify against him, gave the accused magician a good chance of getting off altogether: in the diocese of York in the later sixteenth century about half of the sorcery cases were ultimately dismissed, with or without purgation.[26] Even if the wizard was convicted, his penalty was light, when compared with the imprisonment, pillory, or even death, to which he would have been liable in a common law court. After the Reformation the church courts had abandoned the practice of inflicting corporal punishment.[27] This left them with greater or lesser excommunication, or, in less serious cases, penance. Excommunication was normally reserved for those who did not turn up, or otherwise proved recalcitrant. The wizard who stood his trial and was convicted was most

25. *Southwell Act Books*, xxii, p. 121.

26. Purvis, *Tudor Parish Documents*, p. 197. Dr P. Tyler found a record of a punishment being imposed in only 25 out of 117 cases in `the York Act Books between 1567 and 1640; 'The Church Courts at York and Witchcraft Prosecutions, 1567–1640', *Northern History*, iv (1969), p. 98.

27. There are a few isolated post-Reformation instances in Purvis, op. cit., p. 86; *Southwell Act Books*, xxi, pp. 83–4 (1566); S. L. Ware, *The Elizabethan Parish* (Baltimore, 1908), p. 56, n. 189. Dr. Tyler has encountered several others in the Act Books of the Northern High Commission. But I know of no instances of flogging being imposed for sorcery as it had been earlier (e.g. Thompson, *The English Clergy and their Organization*, p. 221).

likely to be sentenced to perform penance with a varying degree of publicity, usually in church before the parishioners at service-time, sometimes in the market-place of a neighbouring town. Clad in a white sheet, carrying a wand, and placarded with the details of his offence, the hapless sorcerer was undoubtedly subjected to a great deal of public humiliation, a penalty which was felt even more keenly in the tightly knit society of those days than it would be now. But in the process he was getting a good deal of free advertisement, and when it was all over he might well resume his practice.[28]

In this manner the church courts proceeded in their battle against the cunning man until the later seventeenth century, when the whole system of ecclesiastical jurisdiction slipped into a rapid decline. Even in its heyday, the achievement of the courts had been limited. Many sorcerers, like other offenders, flouted the whole procedure by refusing to turn up at all. Although such recalcitrants were usually excommunicated, there is little evidence to suggest that they were consigned forty days later to a secular prison, as strict legal theory demanded. The general situation was thus much the same as it had been in the days before the Reformation. The agencies of clerical repression were not in themselves strong enough to cut off popular magic from its social roots.

2. Similarities and differences

The battle against popular magic was fought in the pulpit as well as in the courts. Generations of clergy harangued their flocks with the warning that all traffic with white witches could only work towards their ultimate spiritual destruction. 'In time of need it is better to call upon Christ in prayer than to have recourse to a wizard and a diviner for help.' The words are those of Wulfstan, the Anglo-Saxon homilist,[29] but they might have been uttered by any cleric in Tudor and Stuart England. If prayer was of no avail it was wicked to turn to spells and charms as a substitute, for if Satan healed the body he would certainly capture the soul. Besides, 'if the faithful and devout prayer of holy men . . . hath no such assurance or suc-

28. Elizabeth Cracklow, the wise woman of Adderbury (above, p. 216), ignored the command of the Official of the Bishop of Oxford to desist from using charms (Bodl., Oxford Dioc. Papers d 14, f. 86); and in 1573 the Bishop of Norwich complained of an old woman in Stowmarket who repeatedly flouted his orders to give up curing diseases by conjuration (J. Strype, *The Life and Acts of Matthew Parker* [1711], p. 369).

29. Cited by Kittredge, *Witchcraft*, p. 30.

cess . . . without laborious industry and the use of good means, how can . . . senseless mumbling of idle words, contrary to reason?'[30]

This advice might have been more effective if it had not so obviously coincided with the interests of the clergy as a professional class. In the cunning man the godly minister could hardly fail to recognise a powerful rival to his own pastoral dominion. 'In such wise witches,' lamented Sir Thomas More, 'have many fools more faith a great deal than in God.' 'Hath not the blesser more proselytes and patients than the physician,' asked a Jacobean minister, 'yea than the conscionable preacher?' As late as 1680 a Staffordshire gentleman echoed the complaint: white witches had 'as many followers as the greatest divines'.[31]

In trouble, sickness or loss, men flew not to God, but to witches. This was the burden of the clergy's complaint, and it was but another way of saying that the cunning man threatened to usurp some of their own most important functions. 'As the ministers of God do give resolution to the conscience in matters doubtful and difficult,' wrote the Reverend Thomas Pickering in 1608, 'so the ministers of Satan, under the name of wise men and wise women, are at hand by his appointment to resolve, direct and help ignorant and unsettled persons in cases of distraction, loss or other outward calamities.'[32] The laity went to sorcerers for help and advice, and whether their trouble was physical or psychological they gained comfort and assistance. 'This is a common thing and well tried by experience', wrote George Gifford, 'that many in great distress have been relieved and recovered by sending unto such wise men or wise women, when they could not tell what should else become of them and of all that they had.' William Lilly tells us that his mistress could only keep her first husband from suicide by means of a sigil made by Simon Forman.[33]

It is small wonder that the sorcerer's claim to produce practical results should have so often proved more attractive than stern clerical insistence that all must be left to God's inscrutable mercies;

30. J. Cotta, *A Short Discoverie of the Unobserved Dangers of Severall Sorts of Ignorant and Unconsiderate Practisers of Physicke* (1612), p. 49.

31. T. More, *A Dialogue of Cumfort* (Antwerp, 1573), f. 43ᵛ; Cooper, *Mystery*, p. 19; J. Brinley, *A Discovery of the Impostures of Witches and Astrologers* (1680), p. 4. Similar testimony in *Homilies*, pp. 480–81.

32. Epistle dedicatory to Perkins, *Discourse*, sig. 93ᵛ.

33. G. Gifford, *A Discourse of the Subtill Practises of Devilles by Witches and Sorcerers* (1587), sig. H1ᵛ; Lilly, *Autobiography*, pp. 33–4.

and that it was better to lose a thing utterly than to recover it by
diabolical means. The lawfulness of an action was not to be judged
by its mere effectiveness, wrote Richard Bernard. 'Better lose clothes
or coin, than recover either by Satan,' declared Thomas Gataker.³⁴
Inevitably the advice of these fierce Puritan clergy proved repellent
to many of those in trouble or danger. Stories were disseminated of
men who had died because their ministers had forced them to burn
the protective charms the cunning men had given them. Such interfering clergy seemed regardless of the people's material welfare. In
1570 the very keeper of Canterbury gaol frankly admitted to having
allowed liberty of egress to an imprisoned wise woman, on the
grounds that 'the witch did more good by her physic than Mr Pun-
dall and Mr Wood, being preachers of God's word'; and a character
in George Gifford's *Dialogue concerning Witches* (1593) declared of
the local wise woman that 'she doth more good in one year than all
these scripture men will do so long as they live'.³⁵

Similar issues were posed by the cunning man's claim to diagnose
and treat the effects of malevolent witchcraft. Many lay folk would
never have contemplated resorting to magical aids, had they not
suspected that magic had already been used against them. But here
the clash between the rival therapies of magic and religion was at its
sharpest. For although most of the clergy accepted the possibility
of maleficent witchcraft, they were unable to compete effectively
with the remedies offered by the cunning man or with the various
traditional folk procedures. The Anglican Church had rejected holy
water, the sign of the cross, and all the paraphernalia of the Roman
Catholic exorcists, but they had nothing to put in their place, save
a general injunction to prayer and repentance. The Church thus
maintained the traditional view of the potency of witchcraft,
although it had abandoned the ecclesiastical counter-magic which
made such a notion tolerable. The sufferer who invoked a magical
remedy against witchcraft ran the risk of finding himself prosecuted
before the ecclesiastical courts.³⁶ Better that a bewitched child should

34. Bernard, *Guide*, p. 152; Gataker, *Of the Use and Nature of Lots*, p. 388.
The same view had been stated by Aquinas, *Summa Theologica*, II, ii. 95. 4,
cf. below, p. 434.
35. Aubrey, *Miscellanies*, pp. 135–6; Ewen, i, p. 37; Gifford, *Dialogue*,
sig. M3ᵛ.
36. e.g., W. J. Pressey, 'The Records of the Archdeaconries of Essex and
Colchester', *Trans Essex Archaeol. Soc.*, xix (1927–30), p. 18; Peterborough
D.R., Correction Book 43, f. 110; 46, f. 97ᵛ.

die, thought the clergy, than that his life should be saved by a cunning man.³⁷ In such circumstances it was only to be expected that the
remedies of the sorcerer should have appeared increasingly attractive. As Reginald Scot sagely observed, the place left empty by the
saints of the medieval Church was filled by the wise women of the
Tudor countryside. Devout Catholics could pray to St Vincent or St
Anthony of Padua for the recovery of goods which had been lost
or stolen; the Protestants only had the cunning man. At the end of
the sixteenth century 'the more ignorant sort' were regretfully observed by Perkins to be better acquainted with charms and spells
than with the word of God.³⁸

Against this state of affairs the clergy struggled vainly. Through
the ecclesiastical courts, they did their best to curb their rivals, by
punishing the customers of the cunning men, forcing them to confess
publicly to being 'heartily sorry for seeking man's help, and refusing
the help of God'.³⁹ But the trouble was that such clients did not
regard the wizards as ordinary men, and could not see that there
was anything wrong about having recourse to their remedies. 'Men
rather uphold them,' wrote John Stearne, 'and say why should any
man be questioned for doing good.' 'I have heard them say full often
myself,' wrote the Bridgettine monk, Richard Whytforde, of 'the
simple people' in the early sixteenth century, ' "Sir, we mean well
and we do believe well and we think it a good and charitable deed
to heal a sick person or a sick beast".'⁴⁰ The attempt by the theologians to wipe out the distinction between black and white witches
by branding them both as diabolical never got through to the people
to whom these witches ministered. On the contrary, they were more

37. Perkins, *Discourse*, p. 156; Bernard, *Guide*, pp. 153–4; Gaule, *Select
Cases of Conscience*, p. 167; and see below, pp. 591–2.

38. Scot, *Discoverie: A Discourse of Divels and Spirits*, chap, xxiv; *The
Whole Works of . . . Jeremy Taylor*, ed. R. Heber and revd. by C. P. Eden
(1847–54), vi, p. 257; *Miracles lately wrought by the Intercession of the
glorious Virgin Marie*, trans. R. Chambers (Antwerp, 1606), sig. B4; Perkins,
Discourse, p. 131.

39. Hale, *Precedents*, pp. 185–6. Other examples of such prosecutions in
ibid., p. 219; *A Miscellany of Notts. Records*, ed. T. M. Blagg (Thoroton
Soc., 1945), p. 36; Ely D.R., B 2/17, f. 124; K. Major, 'The Lincoln Diocesan Records', *T.R.H.S.*, 4th ser., xxii (1940), p. 59; Peterborough D.R.,
Correction Book 36, ff. 78, 101; 41, p. 475; 43, f. 214ᵛ; 47, ff. 11ᵛ, 63; A. D. J.
Macfarlane, *Witchcraft Prosecutions in Essex, 1560–1680* (Oxford D.Phil.
thesis, 1967), p. 65 (38 cases).

40. Stearne, *A Confirmation and Discovery*, p. 11; R. Whytforde, *A Werke
for Housholders* (n.d., copy in Ashm. 1215), sig. Cii.

likely to believe that the cunning folk were taught by God, or that they were helped by angels, or even that they possessed some divinity of their own. The common people, wrote Thomas Cooper, assumed that the power of these wizards came by 'some extraordinary gift of God'. They honoured cunning men, wrote another, 'no less than demi-gods'. They followed the London poulterer, Grig, who cured patients by his prayers, 'as if he had been a god', and they gave the Tudor conjurer, Robert Allen, the sobriquet of 'the god of Norfolk'.[41]

The cunning folk themselves sometimes encouraged these assumptions. In Somerset in 1555 Joan Tyrry protested that 'her doings in healing of man and beast, by the power of God taught to her by the ... fairies, be both godly and good'; and in Flintshire in 1657 Anne Ellis declared that she had done good in blessing children and animals, 'for ... God's blessing must do good, given by those that have the power and grace to speak it'. When Agnes Clerk's daughter was presented by the fairies in 1499 with a holly stick, her mother in her simplicity brought it to the curate of Ashfield, Suffolk, asking him to bless it so that it could then be used in order to find hidden treasure.[42] Many folk may well have believed that cunning men were somehow specially marked out by God. But usually the precise source of the wizard's skill seems to have been left conveniently undefined. He owed his reputation to his technique and knowledge ('his cunning'), rather than to any special holiness of life. He could 'do a thing or two', as he would modestly put it.[43] In rare cases he might purport to employ a familiar spirit, who could be charitably regarded as a good angel, but he did not usually have any other spiritual pretensions. It was the clergy who forced him into the posture of the divine healer by their refusal to allow that magical powers might have a theologically neutral status. The cunning man who acquired a reputa-

41. Cooper, Mystery, p. 37 (and cf. pp. 205, 232); E. Poeton in Sloane 1954, f. 164ᵛ. C. Wriothesley, A Chronicle of England, ed. W. D. Hamilton, ii (Camden Soc., 1877), p. 42: Narratives of the Days of the Reformation, ed. J. G. Nichols (Camden Soc., 1859), p. 330. Similar testimony in Gifford, Dialogue, sigs. F1ᵛ, M3ᵛ; Bernard, Guide, p. 150; Gaule, Select Cases of Conscience, p. 125. In Lorraine the Catholic Church similarly failed to break down the popular distinction between good and bad witches, E. Delcambre, Le Concept de la sorcellerie dans le Duché de Lorraine (Nancy, 1948–51), iii, chap. 16.
42. Wells D.R., A 21; Ewen, ii, p. 334; C. Jenkins in Tudor Studies, p. 73.
43. For a tailor's wife in 1630 who blessed animals and boasted 'she could do some little thing', Lancashire R.O., QSB/1/78/49.

tion as a demi-god sometimes did so in order to throw off the label
of devil-worshipper.

But even in the years after the Reformation it would be wrong to
regard magic and religion as two opposed and incompatible systems
of belief. There were magical elements surviving in religion, and
there were religious facets to the practice of magic. This could make
it difficult for the clerical opponents of magic to know where to draw
the line. Charmers and blessers often sought to heal their patients
by reciting standard religious prayers. So long as the Protestant
Church admitted that disease might be divinely imposed, and therefore divinely withdrawn, it was in no position to disparage the invocation of God as such. It could, of course, distinguish between legitimate and illegitimate forms of prayer, by prohibiting the use of such
Roman Catholic formulae as Latin Paternosters and Creeds, or the
invocation of the Virgin Mary and the saints. Equally prohibited
were the charms in which Christian terminology was jumbled up
with meaningless bits of abracadabra. But there still remained the
problem of the cunning woman who cured the diseases of her neighbour by reciting perfectly acceptable Protestant prayers. How could
the church courts justify taking action against such women as
Bridget, alias Goldenbeard, who claimed in 1576 to have helped
many of the people of Gloucester 'with her good prayers', or Margery Skelton in Essex, who was accused in 1566 of witchcraft and
sorcery, but simply retorted that 'with praying of her prayers' she
had healed six persons?⁴⁴ The answer, of course, was that the Church
regarded it as improper to expect God to perform a miraculous cure
without first attempting a natural one. The use of prayer was not
meant to impede the use of medicine but to accompany it. It was as
superstitious to rely upon prayer alone, as it was impious to trust
solely to physic. But the distinction was a subtle one. When even
some of the clergy thought that some diseases might be directly inflicted by God without any natural cause, it is not surprising that
some of the laity were confused.⁴⁵

If religion still retained some of its magical aspects, then magic
was in turn affected by contemporary religion. For just as the use
of Christian charms by the cunning men sprang from a presumed
association between holiness and occult power, so the spirits which

44. Gloucester D.R., Vol. 40, f. 5; Hale, *Precedents*, p. 148.
45. cf. above, pp. 99, 101.

the more ambitious magicians attempted to conjure were either
Christian angels, or members of an intermediary body half way
between angels and devils.[46] The conjurer's ritual, moreover, with
its hallowings, fumigations and consecrations, was strongly reminiscent of the Roman Mass, as many commentators pointed out.[47] Of
course most clergy strongly frowned upon such conjuration, maintaining that there were no theologically neutral spirits, but only
good or bad ones; the good ones were unlikely to answer so peremp-
tory a summons, while the bad ones were only too eager to seize the
chance of capturing the souls of such reckless men. Most clergy either
declared these familiar spirits to be malignant demons, or asserted
the futility of the notory art, on the grounds that it was impossible
for men to make contact with the spiritual world.[48] Much depended,
however, upon the intellectual tradition in which the clergyman
concerned had been reared, for those influenced by Neoplatonic
speculation were much more prepared to recognize the theoretical
possibility of such activity. But Neoplatonists were rare among the
English clergy, despite Robert Fludd's claim to have the patronage
of three bishops. As his opponent, William Foster, observed, 'Our
Universities and our reverend bishops, God be thanked, are more
cautelous than to allow the printing of magical books here.' Hermetic magic was not without its clerical supporters, in England as in
Italy, but for the most part the tone of the Anglican Church was pro-
foundly hostile to any kind of conjuration or spirit-raising.[49]

Yet for the magicians themselves the summoning of celestial

46. K. M. Briggs, *The Anatomy of Puck* (1959), pp. 169–71. A scrupulous
attempt to practise thief-magic with the aid of a guardian angel is recorded
in Ashm. 421, ff. 231–2.

47. e.g., J. Melton, *Astrologaster* (1620), pp. 16–17. cf. the form of consecration preserved by the wizard Arthur Gauntlett in Sloane 3851, f. 11ᵛ.

48. Aquinas, *Summa Theologica*, II.ii.96.1; Kocher, *Science and Religion*,
pp. 119–20; G. Alley, *The Poore Mans Librarie* (1571), f. 54; R. H. West,
The Invisible World. A Study of Pneumatology in Elizabethan Drama
(Athens, Ga., 1939), p. 230; Thorndike, *Magic and Science*, i, p. 506; H.
Hallywell, *Melampronoea: or, a Discourse of the Polity and Kingdom of
Darkness* (1681), p. 50; H. More, *A Modest Enquiry into the Mystery of
Iniquity* (1664), p. 66.

49. *Doctor Fludds Answer unto M. Foster* (1631), p. 22; Foster,
Hoplocrisma-Spongus, p. 37; F. A. Yates, *Theatre of the World* (1969). pp.
64, 68, 70. Hooper's opposition to the printing of the works of Trithemius
and Agrippa (*Early Writings*, ed. S. Carr [Cambridge, P.S., 1843], p. 327)
contrasts with Fell's intention to publish Roger Bacon (*Reliquiae Hearnianae*, ed. P. Bliss [2nd edn, 1869], ii, p. 153).

beings was a religious rite, in which prayer played an essential part, and where piety and purity of life were deemed essential. 'When a spirit is raised,'- said a Southampton wizard in 1631, 'none hath power to see it but children of eleven and twelve years of age, or such as are true maids.'[50] Fludd himself took a vow of chastity, and regarded the flesh as the root of all evil.[51] Spiritual magic or theurgy was based on the idea that one could reach God in an ascent up the scale of creation made possible by a rigorous course of prayer, fasting and devotional preparation. For many, this was no mechanical manipulation of set formulae, but a humble supplication that God should extend to them the privilege of a unique view of his mysteries. 'The art of magic,' wrote Sir Walter Raleigh, 'is the art of worshipping God.'[52] At Prague John Dee told the Emperor Rudolph II that for forty years he had sought knowledge, only to find that no book or living man could tell him what he wanted. He had therefore determined, with the aid of a special stone and holy angels, to make intercession to God to reveal to him the nature of his creation. In his dealings with angels he was always careful to ensure that the spirits which came to him were good, and not demons. At no point in his occult wanderings did he consider himself to have passed the bounds of Christianity.[53]

At this level the practice of magic became a holy quest; the search for knowledge, not by study and research, but by revelation. The notion that purity of life was an essential preliminary to scientific discovery ran through the long history of alchemy and shaped the Rosicrucianism of the seventeenth century. It remains uncertain whether the Fraternity of the Rosy Cross ever had more than a symbolic existence, but its values were familiar; they went back to

50. *The Book of Examinations and Depositions, 1622–44*, ii (1627–34), ed. R. C. Anderson (Southampton Rec. Soc., 1931), pp. 104–5. cf. Kittredge, *Witchcraft*, pp. 51, 185–7, 190; Bodl., Aubrey MS 10, f. 114. cf. above, p. 256.

51. S. Hutin, 'Robert Fludd, le Rosicrucien', *Revue Métapsychique*, xx (1953), pp. 7, 9 n.

52. Quoted by K. M. Briggs, *Pale Hecate's Team* (1962), p. 44. The same sentiment (derived from Plato) is expressed in R. Turner's translation of the *Fourth Book of Occult Philosophy* attributed to Agrippa (1655), sig. A2v.

53. M. Casaubon, *A True and Faithful Relation of . . . Dr John Dee . . . and Some Spirits* (1659), p. 231; C. H. Josten, 'An Unknown Chapter in the Life of John Dee', *Journ. Warburg and Courtauld Institutes*, xxviii (1965), p. 235. Dee, however, persisted in treasure-seeking, despite the warning that wicked angels had to be invoked for this operation, as they were lords of this world; Casaubon, op. cit., p. 171, sig. *43.

the ancient tradition of *gnosis*: the seeking of knowledge by revelation, through prayer, fasting and communion with God. From this point of view religion and magic were not rivals, but travelling companions along the path to one identical and comprehensive truth. Religious perfection would bring magical power.

Most of the leading alchemists accordingly thought of themselves as pursuing an exacting spiritual discipline, rather than a crude quest for gold. The transmutation of metals was secondary to the main aim, which was the spiritual transformation of the adept. Alchemy was associated with asceticism and contempt for the world. It was no accident that, despite various prohibitions, many medieval alchemists had been monks,[54] and that the monasteries retained a reputation for occult learning of this kind in the century after the Reformation. The numerous stories about the pots of miraculous tincture found in monastic ruins helped to create a widespread mythology about the link between magic and holiness.[55] Of course such tales were not usually countenanced by the established Church: indeed the attitude of most orthodox Calvinist clergy to alchemy was distinctly hostile. They distrusted it for the same reason that they were suspicious of all kinds of magic: it was an arrogant attempt to transform nature which could only play into the Devil's hands. The alchemists, thought Thomas Jackson, displayed 'some spice of that spirit of pride which first sublimated physic into magic'. Most seventeenth-century Puritans condemned alchemy as diabolical.[56]

Yet the old tradition of the spiritual quest, reinforced by the influence of Renaissance hermeticism, could still capture the imagina-

54. The best-known was George Ripley, an Augustinian canon. For others *Visitations of Religious Houses in the Diocese of Lincoln*, ed. A. H. Thompson (Lincoln Rec. Soc., 1914–23), ii, pp. 208–12; *Visitations of the Diocese of Norwich*, ed. A. Jessopp (Camden Soc., 1888), p. 267; G. G. Coulton, *A Medieval Garner* (1910), pp. 518–21; W. C. Waller, 'An Essex Alchemist', *Essex Rev.*, xiii (1904).

55. Josten, *Ashmole*, pp. 78–9, 564, 588; E. J. Holmyard, *Alchemy* (Harmondsworth, 1957), p. 204; Bodl., Wood MS F 39, f. 354.

56. T. Jackson, *A Treatise containing the Originall of Unbeliefe* (1625), p. 184; W. Fulke, *A most pleasant Prospect into the Garden of Naturall Contemplation* (3rd edn, 1640), ff. 65ᵛ, 66; *The Private Diary of Dr John Dee*, ed. J. O. Halliwell (Camden Soc., 1842), p. 47; *The Workes of ... William Perkins* (Cambridge, 1616–18), ii, p. 227; Bernard, *Guide*, p. 57; *The Complete Works of Stephen Charnock*, ed. J. M'Cosh (Edinburgh, 1864–5), i, p. 518; Kocher, *Science and Religion*, p. 66 and n. cf. *Dives and Pauper*, 1st commandment, chap. 49.

tion of highly religious persons. The Anglican clergyman, Meric Casaubon, was prepared to concede in 1659 that many chemical secrets had been learned through the revelation of spirits. Other Anglican clergy with alchemical interests included John Thornborough, Bishop of Worcester, and patron of Fludd, Richard Swayne, a Dorset vicar, and William Oughtred, the mathematician.⁵⁷ The two leading mid-seventeenth-century hermeticists, Thomas Vaughan and John Everard, had both been Anglican clergymen. But Everard became a Familist and it was among the mystical sects that alchemy struck some of its deepest roots. The Interregnum was an important period in the translation and publication of standard alchemical and Rosicrucian texts, and alchemy was closely linked with religious enthusiasm. As early as 1601 a clergyman could associate Cabalism with the Familists, and long before the Civil War the preachers had begun to attack the 'rosycross wolves which turn divinity into fancies'. The sectarians were as great 'enthusiasts in physick' as they had been in divinity, thought one contemporary.⁵⁸ Both alchemists and sectaries had a coterie aspect, and laid great stress on the need for potential entrants to be in a suitable spiritual condition. Sectarians like John Webster, John Allin and Thomas Tryon kept alive the hermetic tradition of divine magic until the end of the seventeenth century.⁵⁹ Several leading Quakers were interested in 'Hermes'; and for the Familists or Behmenists, alchemy was an outward symbol of internal regeneration.⁶⁰ As late as 1784 a Cornish

57. Casaubon, *A True and Faithful Relation*, sig. E4; *D.N.B.*, 'Thornborough, John'; R. Fludd, *Mosaicall Philosophy* (1659), p. 118; C. F. Richardson, *English Preachers and Preaching, 1640–70* (1928), p. 152.

58. H. Clapham, *Aelohim-triune, displayed by his Workes* (1601), sig. A3ᵛ; S. Denison, *The White Wolfe* (1627), p. 38; W. Ramesey, *Some Physical Considerations of the Matter, Origination, and Several Species of Wormes* (1668), p. 3. For the association of alchemy with religious enthusiasm: T. Sprat, *History of the Royal Society*, ed. J. I. Cope and H. W. Jones (St Louis, 1959), pp. 37–8; C. Hill, *Intellectual Origins of the English Revolution* (Oxford, 1965), pp. 122–3.

59. Webster, *The Displaying of Supposed Witchcraft*, pp. 5, 7, 9; T. W. W. Smart, 'A Notice of Rev. John Allin', *Sussex Archaeol. Colls.*, xxxi (1881); *Some Memoirs of the Life of Mr Tho. Tryon* (1705), sig. C7. Other sectarian adepts included John Canne (C. Burrage, *The Early English Dissenters* [Cambridge, 1912], i, p. 181); John Winthrop, Jr. (R. S. Wilkinson in *Ambix*, xi [1963]); Charles Hotham (*D.N.B.*); Israel Tongue (Wood, *Ath. Ox.*, iii, cols. 1262, 1264). Alchemists of various religious brands are cited in Richardson, *English Preachers and Preaching, 1640–70*, pp. 152–4.

60. H. J. Cadbury, 'Early Quakerism and Uncanonical lore', *Harvard*

physician commended the discipline of alchemy as 'a study which brings a man nearer to the Creator'.[61]

The influence of this presumed connection between magic and holiness can be seen at many levels. It underlay the conduct of a Puritan like Sir Thomas Myddelton, who could commission the manufacture of astrologically-based magic sigils, but felt it necessary to pronounce a special prayer before putting them on.[62] It explains why William Barckseale, the low-grade Southampton wizard, used to fast and pray three days before engaging in the detection of stolen goods; and why an inhabitant of Norfolk could claim in 1605 to have gained access by prayer to an angelic spirit which would tell him the truth about all matters.[63] It can also be seen in the popular tradition that the great Biblical heroes had themselves been magicians, an idea stimulated by the hermetic theory that Adam's knowledge of all natural things, though lost at the Fall, had been transmitted downward through Noah, Solomon and other select adepts. Moses, 'learned in all the wisdom of the Egyptians' (Acts vii, 22), was especially famous for his magical powers. He had been portrayed as a sorcerer in some of the medieval mystery plays, and Calvin had had to reject the aspersion that the patriarch was a mere wizard. Christopher Marlowe was one of several 'atheists' to be accused of contemptuously declaring that 'Moses was but a juggler'.[64] Contemporary magicians aspired to the powers which they believed had once been possessed by the holy men of antiquity, and sought to reconstruct the fabulous instruments with which they imagined their successes had been accomplished – Moses's rod, Elisha's ring, Solomon's ring. Books of ritual magic were attributed to Enoch or Solomon, and a medieval guide to dream-interpretation was known as the *Book of Daniel*. It was, as Bishop Jewel remarked,

---

Theol. Rev., xl (1947), pp. 191–5; M. L. Bailey, *Milton and Jakob Boehme* (New York, 1914), pp. 77–82, 107; *Some memoirs of ... Tho. Tryon*, sigs. C8, ff. cf. below, pp. 446–7.

61. J. W. Etheridge, *The Life of ... Adam Clarke* (1858), p. 81 (kindly shown me by Dr J. D. Walsh).

62. Ashm. 431, f. 152; Sloane 3822, f. 35.

63. Above, p. 275; *H.M.C., Hatfield*, xvii, p. 25. On the role of fasting in magic see H. Holland, *The Christian Exercise of Fasting* (1596), sig. A1ᵛ.

64. Calvin, *Institutes*, I.viii.6; L. B. Wright, in *Modern Philology*, xxiv (1927), pp. 271–2. P. H. Kocher, *Christopher Marlowe* (Chapel Hill, 1946), pp. 45–9, discusses Marlowe and gives references for the Moses tradition. Another instance is in *C.S.P.D., 1611–18*, p. 527. See also E. M. Butler, *The Myth of the Magus* (Cambridge, 1948), part 1, chap. 2.

common for the most ignorant wizards to boast that their cunning was derived from Adam and Abel, Moses and Athanasius, or the Archangel Raphael. Even the most disreputable conjurer might regard fasting and prayer as part of his technique.[65]

So although the Church in its official capacity protested against the practice of magic there is some evidence that at the popular level the heinousness of the sin was simply not appreciated. The case of the churchwardens of Thatcham, Berkshire, who in 1583–4 sent to a cunning woman to find out who had stolen the cloth from their communion table, illustrates how the minor officials of the Anglican Church did not always see any conflict between their religion and a little practical magic. It was but one of several recorded sixteenth-century instances in which the search for stolen communion plate or other church property was entrusted to the local wizard.[66] Miles Blomfield, a prominent Essex alchemist and cunning man, was himself chosen churchwarden at Chelmsford in 1582. 'Seeking to witches and sorcerers,' said a minister, 'was a common sin, even of hearers of the word.'[67] Indeed the very clergy themselves were not above having recourse to magicians. Several medieval abbots and priors consulted sorcerers for the recovery of missing objects,[68] while Thomas Becket and Bishop Odo of Bayeux are but two examples of leading clergy who are known to have been influenced by fortune-tellers.[69] Instances

65. *The Works of John Jewel*, ed. J. Ayre (Cambridge, P.S., 1845–50), i, p. 23; ii, p. 991; J. Hall, *A Poesie in Forme of a Vision* (1563), sig. Biiii; Scot, *Discoverie*, XV.xxxi; Josten, *Ashmole*, pp. 85, 88. For Abel as the inventor of magic, L. Thorndike in *Mélanges Auguste Pelzer* (Louvain, 1947), p. 241. For Solomon, G. Naudé, *The History of Magick*, trans. J. Davies (1657), pp. 279–82, and G. R. Owst in *Studies presented to Sir Hilary Jenkinson*, p. 286; Thomas Cromwell was believed to have a Solomon's ring (*L.P.*, v, p. 696). On the Book of Enoch, Thorndike, *Magic and Science*, i, chap. 13, and on Moses's rod, above, p. 280. For the Book of Daniel, C. du F. Ducange, *Glossarium* (1884–7), s.v., 'somnialia'.

66. Kittredge, *Witchcraft*, pp. 197–8; C. H. Poole, *The Customs, Superstitions and Legends of the County of Stafford* (1883), p. 72. In the mid seventeenth century a cunning man was asked to recover a missing Bible, *The Hartford-shire Wonder* (1669), p. 2.

67. I. Gray, 'Footnote to an Alchemist', *Cambridge Review*, lxviii (1946), pp. 172–4; T. Taylor, *Christs Victorie over the Dragon* (1633), p. 506.

68. Kittredge, *Witchcraft*, p. 48 (Abbot of Selby, 1280); *Visitations of Religious Houses*, ed. Thompson, ii, 209–11 (Abbot of Leicester, 1440); iii, p. 233 (Prior of Newnham, 1440); *H.M.C.*, viii, p. 265 (Abbot of Westminster, c. 1450–60).

69. John of Salisbury, *Frivolities of Courtiers*, pp. 127–8; *D.N.B.*, 'Odo'.

of such consultation can also be found after the Reformation, whether involving high ecclesiastics, like Patrick Adamson, Archbishop of St Andrews, who had recourse in 1579 to the ministrations of a wise woman, or mere parochial clergy, like Edmund Curteis, Vicar of Cuckfield, Sussex, and brother of the Bishop of Chichester, who was deprived of his living in 1579 as a 'seeker to witches'. As late as 1640 a violent storm which occurred at Esher was popularly thought to be the consequence of a visit made by the local Laudian clergyman to a conjurer to find out who had pulled down his altar rails.[70]

It would be easy to regard these associations between magic and religion as a temporary survival from pre-Reformation times. The old Latin prayers were particularly popular for use as charms, and Catholic symbolism figured prominently in magical rites, both in the séances of the ritual magicians and in popular divinatory techniques. Among Protestant contemporaries it was certainly a platitude to declare that the practice of magic was an inheritance from the Popish past, when such goings-on were believed to have been infinitely more extensive.[71] But the accuracy of this presumed association between Catholicism and magic is difficult to evaluate. It is clear that the English Church was battling against popular sorcery before the Reformation, no less than afterwards. On this matter the methods and attitude of the church courts were, as we have seen, substantially unchanged between the later Middle Ages and the seventeenth century. Of the charmers and blessers uncovered before the Reformation, moreover, several are known to have had Lollard sympathies.[72] The Counter-Reformation Church, which proceeded strongly against magic, sometimes explicitly associated sorcery with the rise of Protestantism.[73] Neoplatonic influences did not really make themselves much felt in England until Protestant times. Magic

70. *D.N.B.*, 'Adamson, P.'; H. N. Birt, *The Elizabethan Religious Settlement* (1907), pp. 431–2; *C.S.P.D., 1640*, p. 486. For other clerical consultations see Kittredge, *Witchcraft*, p. 188; Thompson, *The English Clergy and their Organization*, p. 221; Scot, *Discoverie*, I.ii; J. Heydon, *Theomagia, or the Temple of Wisdome* (1664), iii, pp. 97–107.

71. See above, p. 78. For a spirited denial of the association between Catholicism and popular magic, see A.D., *A Reply made unto Mr Anthony Wotton and Mr Iohn White ministers* (1612), pp. 35–9.

72. Thomson, *Later Lollards*, pp. 179, 241; *V.C.H.*, Bucks., i, p. 297.

73. D. P. Walker, *Spiritual and Demonic Magic from Ficino to Campanella* (1958), p. 178; R. Mandrou, *Magistrats et sorciers en France au XVIIᵉ siècle* (Paris, 1968), p. 144. For Counter-Reformation action against magic,

in the exalted sense intended by Dee (himself a beneficed Anglican clergyman) was not a medieval survival but a Renaissance discovery of a classical tradition. At a humbler level there is no reason to believe that the number of village wizards and charmers unearthed by an Elizabethan episcopal visitation necessarily differed from an average haul in the fifteenth century. Only towards the mid seventeenth century did the numbers fall off, and this, as we have seen, was probably as much a symptom of the declining efficiency of the ecclesiastical courts as of any disappearance of popular magic.

In its attitude to sorcery the medieval Church did not differ greatly from its Protestant successor. What did distinguish it was the much wider range of its own magical remedies. In the Mass, the healing power of saints and relics, and the exorcism of the possessed, the Catholic Church had a magical repertoire with which the English Church of the sixteenth and seventeenth centuries could not hope to compete. But this did not make Catholicism more sympathetic towards the activities of the village wizard; on the contrary it was precisely because the Church had its own magic that it frowned on that of others. Yet even though the medieval Church prohibited popular magic and made sorcery a disqualification for the priesthood,[74] the roles of priest and magician were by no means clearly distinguished in the popular mind. This was partly because the local clergyman was often the best educated man in the community, and therefore the most capable of reading and understanding the books of spells and formulae of conjuration which were employed in the invocation of spirits. But it also reflected the magical aura which a priest could assume in the eyes of illiterate laity by virtue of his consecration, and his decisive role in the miracle of the Mass. Set apart by his learning, his unique ritual power, and his official virginity, the priest was admirably qualified to be a key figure in the practice of popular magic.

The late medieval clergy were thus often regarded as the possessors of knowledge relating to all the curious arts of divination and invocation. Friars and chaplains were invariably involved in the political conspiracies of the fifteenth century which made any use of

---

see, e.g., E. Brouette, in *Satan* [*Études carmélitaines*, 1948], pp. 366–7; *The Canons and Decrees of the Council of Trent*, ed. T. A. Buckley (1851), p. 287.

74. *Corpus Iuris Canonici*, ed. Friedberg, i, col. 1045; W. Lyndwood, *Provinciale* (Oxford, 1679), I.iv.2; *Dives and Pauper*, f. 51.

magical aids.[75] It is a striking feature of the sorcery cases recorded in the early sixteenth century that the participants so often included a priest. This was particularly true of treasure-seeking expeditions or other operations requiring the conjuration of spirits, for which the participation of a cleric was deemed essential by some magical writers.[76] Other clergy appear to have circulated magical treatises among themselves and to have practised magic among their parishioners. Villagers in late medieval England, no less than the peasantry of modern Catholic countries, seem to have often assumed that their local curate possessed special powers of healing or divination, and consulted him accordingly.[77]

The Reformation by contrast is justly commemorated for having robbed the priest of most of his magical functions. His powers of exorcism were taken away, and his formulae of benediction and consecration much reduced. The end of the belief in transubstantiation, the discarding of Catholic vestments, and the abolition of clerical celibacy, cumulatively diminished the mystique of the clergyman within his parish. At the same time the growth of facilities for lay education weakened the clergy's monopoly of learning, which, even

75. Kittredge, *Witchcraft*, pp. 50, 79–84.

76. For such expeditions, A. G. Dickens, *Lollards and Protestants in the Diocese of York* (1959), p. 16; D. Turner in *Norfolk Archaeology*, i (1847), pp. 46–64; *L.P.*, iv, pp. 2221–2; xii (2), p. 387; G. R. Elton, *Policy and Police* (Cambridge, 1972), p. 48; Kittredge, *Witchcraft*, pp. 207–10. cf. the treasure-seeking instructions in Bodl., MS Add. B 1, ff. 3–10ᵛ.

77. For examples of pre-Elizabethan monks, friars and clergy who practised conjuring, thief-magic, divination and magical healing, see Kittredge, *Witchcraft*, pp. 38, 56, 58, 62, 65, 71, 80, 187, 198–9; Ewen, ii, pp. 36–7; Aston, *Thomas Arundel*, p. 63; Foxe, iv, pp. 233, 656; A. Watkin, *Dean Cosyn and Wells Cathedral Miscellanea* (Somerset Rec. Soc., 1941), p. 158; *Journ. Soc. Archivists*, iii (1968), p. 339; Thomson, *Later Lollards*, p. 179; *E.H.R.*, xxxvii (1922), pp. 420–21; ibid., xliv (1929), p. 287; A. F. Pollard, *The Reign of Henry VII* (1913–14), i, p. 205; J. E. Oxley, *The Reformation in Essex* (Manchester, 1965), pp. 102–3; Elton, *Policy and Police*, pp. 47–8; *Narratives of the Days of the Reformation*, pp. 333–4; Thompson, *The English Clergy and their Organization*, p. 222; Sloane 513 (magical tracts belonging to a fifteenth-century monk); Bodl., MS e Mus. 238 (sixteenth-century copies of magical tracts of friarly origin); *Visitations in the Diocese of Lincoln*, ed. A. H. Thompson (Lincoln Rec. Soc., 1940–7), ii, p. 122; *Original Letters Illustrative of English History*, ed. Sir H. Ellis (3rd ser., 1846), iii, pp. 41–2; W. Hone, *The Year Book* (1832), cols. 425–7; G. R. Owst, *The Destructorium Viciorum of Alexander Carpenter* (1952), p. 18; *The Examination of John Walsh* (1566), sigs, Aij, Aiijᵛ. cf. *Cistercian Statutes, A.D. 1256–7*, ed. J. T. Fowler (1890), p. 56.

before the Reformation, had been crumbling away. To such changes the apparent diminution in the extent of clerical participation in popular magic must be attributed. But the change was a gradual one, and the association in the popular mind between magic and the priesthood was only slowly eradicated.

In many country parishes after the Reformation the minister combined his religious functions with the practice of medicine, and his methods sometimes differed little from those employed by the folk healers of the day. 'Many poor country vicars,' wrote Robert Burton, 'for want of other means, are given to ... turn mountebanks, quacksalvers, empirics.'[78] A successful medical practitioner, like Hugh Atwell, parson of Calverleigh, Devon, and rector of St Ewe, Cornwall (1599–1615), could easily gain the reputation of being a magician, simply because his cures actually worked.[79] But there were often good grounds for such suspicions. In urging the clergy to act as healers to their flock, George Herbert stressed than 'in curing of any, the parson and his family use to premise prayers, for this is to cure like a parson'.[80] But such a use of prayers could easily degenerate into a superstitious reliance upon their unaccompanied efficacy. In 1606 the Royal College of Physicians had to step in to prevent the Reverend John Bell from continuing to treat fevers by writing words on a piece of paper. In 1632 the Court of High Commission dealt sharply with another cleric, Joseph Harrison, for ill-living and suspected 'charming of pigs'. Five years later, the vicar of Fleckney, Leicestershire, was charged with making charms to cure toothache. The curate of Capel, Surrey, John Allen, sequestrated in 1645, was also said to have written a charm for toothache, remarking sensibly enough that if the sufferer would believe in it it could help him. When a woman was conscience-striken after hearing the warning in the Communion service against profane livers, the minister of Hope, Derbyshire, a Mr Jones, 'gave her an amulet, viz. some verses of *John i* written in a paper to hang about her neck, as also certain

78. Burton, *Anatomy*, i, p. 36. James Hart complained in 1625 that medical parsons were to be found 'in most corners of the country', *The Anatomie of Urines* (1625), p. 113; and Sir George Clark thought this state of affairs more marked in the seventeenth century than the sixteenth, *History of the Royal College of Physicans*, i, p. 248.

79. On his reputation as a cunning man, T. Brian, *The Pisse-Prophet, or, Certaine Pisse-Pot Lectures* (1637), p. 95. For other instances, cf. J. Cotta, *The Infallible True and Assured Witch* (1624), p. 75.

80. *A Priest to the Temple* (1652), chap. xxiii.

herbs to drive the devil out of her'. As late as 1804 the Reverend William Ettrick, vicar of Alfpuddle and Toner's Puddle, Dorset, cured his supposedly bewitched child, by the application of 'a phylactery inscribed with sacred words in the original character'.[81] Nonconformist clergy were sometimes accused of similar practices. Nicholas Gretton, cunning man and astrologer, was leader of an Independent congregation near Lichfield in the 1650s. Defoe claims to have known a Baptist preacher in Bedfordshire who cured the ague by reciting words and giving the patient a piece of paper to carry around in his pocket.[82]

Instances of petty sorcery by the parochial clergy were sometimes uncovered by the ecclesiastical courts. John Betson was ordered in 1564 by the Northern Court of High Commission to hand in his copies of *Plato's Sphere* and *Pythagoras's Sphere*, which he had used to recover stolen goods for his clients. John Garsett, a Lincolnshire minister, was deprived for conjuring and incontinency in 1601.[83] In Cambridgeshire John Knightley, vicar of Gilden Morden, protested in 1599 that he had been acquitted of sorcery by the Official of the Archdeacon of Ely, but his parishioners continued to levy the accusation for years afterwards.[84] In the Puritan *Survey of the Ministry* (1586) no less than three Norfolk incumbents were accused of conjuring. Similar accusations reappeared during the attack on the Anglican clergy in the 1640s.[85] Sometimes the clergy concerned had Catholic tendencies. Leonard Bilson, Prebendary of

81. Clark, *History of the Royal College*, i, pp. 198–9; *Reports of Cases in the Courts of Star Chamber and High Commission*, ed. S. R. Gardiner (Camden Soc., 1886), p. 272 (kindly shown me by Mr John Bowle); *Assocd Architectl Socs., Reports and Papers*, xxix (1908), p. 524; A. G. Matthews, *Walker Revised* (Oxford, 1948), p. 348; *Diaries and Letters of Philip Henry*, ed. M. H. Lee (1882), p. 194; *Witchcraft at Toner's Puddle*, ed. C. Hole (Dorset Rec. Soc., 1964).

82. R. F(arnworth), *Witchcraft cast out* (1655); *Journal of George Fox*, ed. N. Penney (Cambridge, 1911), i, pp. 180–81; (D. Defoe), *A System of Magick* (1727), p. 155.

83. Purvis, *Tudor Parish Documents*, p. 198; *H.M.C., Hatfield*, xi, pp. 565, 586.

84. Ely D.R., B 2/17, f. 124^v; W. M. Palmer, 'The Archdeaconry of Cambridge and Ely, 1599', *Trans. Cambridgeshire and Hunts. Archaeol. Soc.*, vi (1947), p. 4. He was also accused of not wearing a surplice, Ely D.R., B 2/11, ff. 62^v, 93.

85. A. Peel, *The Seconde Parte of a Register* (Cambridge, 1915), ii, pp. 147, 151, 154 (and one in Warwickshire, p. 169); Matthews, *Walker Revised*, p. 237.

Winchester, whose magical activities were exposed in 1561, seems to have been one of a Catholic group; it may have been his case which led Bishop Jewel to inquire in his visitation articles for Salisbury Cathedral in 1568 as to whether any prebend there was in the habit of invoking the Devil or engaging in divination or similar arts[86]

A few Anglican clergy were even accused of maleficent witchcraft; and one of them, John Lowes, vicar of Brandeston, Suffolk, was executed for it in 1645, the culmination of a series of accusations of charming and magical practices which had been brought against him during the previous three decades. Lowes was no Catholic, but as a young man had shown Puritan tendencies. His highly untypical case reflected the unusually antipathetic relationship which had developed between his parishioners and himself.[87] Normally the sorcerer-parson worked with his flock, not against them. The species was not extinguished by the Reformation, for as late as the nineteenth century there were some parish clergy who enjoyed a magical reputation among their parishioners.[88]

It is doubtful whether the Church's official campaign against magic did much to reduce its popular appeal. Both before and after

86. G. L. Kittredge, in *Harvard Studies and Notes in Philology and Litre.*, xvi (1934), pp. 98–9; P.R.O., SP 12/16, f. 120; *Essex Recusant*, iii (1961), pp. 3 ff.; Frere and Kennedy, *Articles and Injunctions*, iii, p. 204. Other examples of Catholic clergy involved in magic are in J. Strype, *Annals of the Reformation* (2nd edn, 1725–8), ii, pp. 181–2; S. Harsnet, *A Declaration of Egregious Popish Impostures* (1603), p. 13; B.M., Royal MS 17 B XXIV, f. 4; Ewen, ii, p. 66; *A.P.C.*, xvii, pp. 31–2; *H.M.C., Hatfield*, xi, p. 135; ibid, xvi, p. 248; Kittredge, *Witchcraft*, p. 261.

87. See Ewen, *Star Chamber*, pp. 44–54. For other accusations against clergymen, Kittredge, *Witchcraft*, p. 88; Ewen, ii, p. 425.

88. Examples in *County Folk-Lore*, v, ed. Mrs Gutch and M. Peacock (1908), p. 76; J. E. Vaux, *Church Folk Lore* (2nd edn, 1902), p. 401; *Folk-lore*, lxv (1954), pp. 110–11. Other sixteenth- and seventeenth-century clergy involved in magic can be found in Purvis, *Tudor Parish Documents*, p. 196; P. Tyler, 'The Church Courts at York and Witchcraft Prosecutions, 1567–1640', *Northern History*, iv (1969), pp. 93–4; W. R. Dawson, 'A Norfolk Vicar's Charm against Ague', *Norfolk Archaeology*, xxiv (1930–2); *H.M.C., Hatfield*, xvii, p. 22; xxi, p. 128; *A.P.C.*, xii, pp. 23, 26–7; J. Aubrey, *Brief Lives*, ed. A. Clark (Oxford, 1898), ii, pp. 108–11; F. Coxe, *A Short Treatise* (1561), sig. Aviij; R. Bovet, *Pandaemonium*, ed. M. Summers (Aldington, 1951), p. 54; above, pp. 253–4, and below, p. 450. For parish clerks with magical interests, see *Lincolnshire Archives Committee. Archivists' Report* (1954–5), p. 51; Borthwick, R. VI. A20, f. 101ᵛ (clerk of Methley, Yorks., 1623); above, p. 256.

the Reformation the ecclesiastical courts had harried the sorcerer, and so helped to give his activities the clandestine character which the witchcraft statutes of the sixteenth and seventeenth centuries further reinforced. But the courts had their deficiencies at the best of times, and during the seventeenth century they grew increasingly ineffective. They only worked well so long as they were enforcing standards to which the local communities themselves subscribed. It is difficult to believe that they could have eliminated popular magic while the popular demand for it lasted. The growth of Puritanism is testimony to the ultimate ineffectiveness of clerical resources in the face of any movement with genuine popular roots. If they had had only the church courts to fear, the wizards need never have disappeared.

But there was another way in which religion contributed to the declining prestige of magical remedies, and it was ultimately a more effective one. The appeal of magic could only be decisively eclipsed when people found a more attractive alternative to the practical aids which the cunning man provided for his clients. It was here that post-Reformation religion made its great contribution. The medieval Church had tried to counter popular magic by providing a rival system of ecclesiastical magic to take its place. The Protestants' solution was fundamentally different. Instead of proffering a rival panacea, they disparaged the whole notion of a magical solution as such. In this they were only partly successful, for as we have seen, magic could creep back into religion, even in a Protestant environment. But the Reformation had initiated advance in a fundamentally new direction. For the people were now taught that their practical difficulties could only be solved by a combination of self-help and prayer to God. The substitute action involved in the practice of magic was condemned as both impious and useless. The strong emphasis upon the virtues of hard work and application which was to become so pronounced a feature of the religious teaching of the sixteenth and seventeenth centuries, Catholic as well as Protestant, both reflected and helped to create a frame of mind which spurned the cheap solutions offered by magic, not just because they were wicked, but because they were too easy. Man was to earn his bread by the sweat of his brow. This was why Francis Bacon objected to magical remedies which 'propound those noble effects which God hath set forth unto man to be bought at the price of labour, to be attained by a few easy and slothful observances'. The

Northamptonshire physician, John Cotta, employed almost *ipsissima verba* a few years later:

> God hath give nothing unto man but for his travail and pain; and according to his studious industry, care, prudence, providence, assiduity and diligence, he dispenseth unto him every good thing. He hath not ordained wonders and miracles to give supply unto our common needs, nor to answer the ordinary occasions or uses of our life.

It was this affirmation of the potentialities of human labour which was to encourage men to seek a technological solution to their problems rather than a magical one.[89]

But until such sturdy self-reliance was more generally diffused no religion could hope to drive out popular magic. The wizards discharged too many useful functions. They retained their appeal in post-Reformation England, just as witch-doctors have preserved their influence upon many nominal Christian converts in modern Africa.[90] In a sermon preached in 1552, Bernard Gilpin, the 'Apostle of the North', commented on the extent to which magic had survived the religious changes of the early Tudor period. 'What gross superstition and blindness remaineth still among the people only through lack of faithful preachers,' he exclaimed, 'infidelity, idolatry, sorcery, charming, witchcrafts, conjuring, trusting in figures, with such other trumpery ... lurk in corners and began of late to come abroad, only for lack of preaching.'[91] 'Faithful preachers' were indeed the deadly enemies of such practices, but Gilpin was wrong to imply that the clergy could ever hope to triumph by mere exhortation. It took a combination of social and intellectual forces to destroy popular magic. In this revolution the dogmas of Protestantism played some part. But the Reformation could never have killed magic without the changes in the mental and physical environment which accompanied it.

89. Bacon, *Works*, iii, p. 381; Cotta, *A Short Discoverie*, p. 35. cf. below, chap. 22.

90. See, e.g., P. Tyler, 'The Pattern of Christian Belief in Sekhukuniland', *Church Qtly Rev.*, clxvii (1966), p. 230.

91. B. Gilpin, *A Sermon preached in the Court at Greenwitch* (1552) (1630), p. 21.

ASTROLOGY

10.

ASTROLOGY:
ITS PRACTICE AND EXTENT

I resolve these ensuing astrological questions: the sick whether
they shall recover or not; the party absent whether living or dead;
how many husbands or children a woman shall have; whether you
shall marry the desired party or whom else, whether she has her
maidenhead or no, or shall be honest to you after marriage, or her
portion well paid; if a man be wise or a fool; whether it be good
to put on new clothes, or turn courtier this year or the next;
if dreams are for good or evil; whether a child be the reputed
father's or not, or shall be fortunate or otherwise; ships at sea,
whether safe or not; whether it be good to remove your dwelling
or not; of law-suits which side shall have the better; and generally
all astrological questions whatsoever.

John Wilson, The Cheats (1662), ii, 2

1. Introduction

OF the various systems of belief to be considered in this book
astrology was much the most intellectually demanding. Its principles
rested upon an ancient body of learning initiated by the Babylonians,
developed by the Greeks and Romans, and further extended by the

BIBLIOGRAPHICAL NOTE: The earlier history of astrology can be fol-
lowed in A. Bouché-Leclercq, L'Astrologie grecque (Paris, 1899), A. J.
Festugière, La Révélation d'Hermès trismégiste, I. L'Astrologie et les sciences
occultes (2nd edn, Paris, 1950), F. H. Cramer, Astrology in Roman Law and
Politics (Philadelphia, 1954), and F. Boll and C. Bezold, Sternglaube und
Sterndeutung. Die Geschichte und das Wesen der Astrologie, ed. W. Gundel
(Leipzig, 1926). Thorndike, Magic and Science, provides a reliable historical
account of the books and manuscripts relating to astrology, but has little
to say about its actual practice or social significance. A useful supplement
is F. J. Carmody, Arabic Astronomical and Astrological Sciences in Latin
Translation. A Critical Bibliography (Berkeley and Los Angeles, 1956).
Much information of a primarily iconographic kind is contained in R.
Klibansky, E. Panofsky and F. Saxl, Saturn and Melancholy (1964). A simple
guide to astrological medicine is C. A. Mercier, Astrology in Medicine
(1914), while much relevant learning is contained in H. Bober, 'The Zodiacal
Miniature of the Très Riches Heures of the Duke of Berry – its Sources and
Meaning', Journ. of the Warburg and Courtauld Institutes, xi (1948).
For England the best starting-points are T. O. Wedel, The Mediaeval

Arab astrologers of the early Middle Ages. Despite refinements in detail, the astrology known to sixteenth- and seventeenth-century Englishmen was recognizably the same subject as that expounded by the Egyptian Ptolemy in his *Tetrabilos* in the second century A.D. In the seventeenth century the English astrologers were to popularize the doctrines of the science in a vernacular literature which laid every detail of the subject open to public inspection, but the doctrines they enunciated were essentially traditional. Indeed, several of the English treatises on astrology were little more than translations of earlier Latin writings.¹ Like Christianity, astrology proved strikingly

---

Attitude toward Astrology, Particularly in England (Yale Studies in English, 1920), and D. C. Allen, *The Star-Crossed Renaissance. The Quarrel about Astrology and Its Influence in England* (Durham, N. Carolina, 1941). An excellent account of the polemical writing against the astrologers is to be found in the introduction by H. G. Dick to his edition of Thomas Tomkis, *Albumazar* (Berkeley and Los Angeles, 1944). For the intellectual background, M. H. Nicolson, *The Breaking of the Circle* (revd edn, New York, 1962), H. Craig, *The Enchanted Glass* (Oxford, 1960), and Kocher, *Science and Religion*, chap. 10, are all useful. Other helpful guides are C. Camden, 'Elizabethan Astrological Medicine', *Annals of Medical History*, new ser., ii (1930), id., 'Astrology in Shakespeare's Day', *Isis*, xix (1933), and M. Sondheim, 'Shakespeare and the Astrology of His Time', *Journ. of the Warburg Institute*, ii (1939). The best survey of sixteenth-century astrological publication is the appendix on 'Sources of the Renaissance Englishman's Knowledge of Astrology' to J. Parr, *Tamburlaine's Malady, and Other Essays on Astrology in Elizabethan Drama* (Alabama, 1953). There is no comparable bibliography for the seventeenth century, though many relevant titles are contained in F. Leigh Gardner, *A Catalogue Raisonné of Works on the Occult Sciences, II, Astrological Books* (1911).

Historians have devoted very little attention to studying the actual practice of astrology, as opposed to its intellectual content, but some information is contained in C. J. S. Thompson, *The Quacks of Old London* (1928), Josten, *Ashmole*, and H. G. Dick, ' "Students of Physic and Astrology" ', *Journ. of Hist. of Medicine*, i (1946). My account is based upon the ephemeral astrological literature of the period, and the unpublished letters and casebooks of contemporary astrologers. Much of this material is described in the *Index to the Sloane Manuscripts in the British Museum* by E. J. L. Scott (1904) and the excellent catalogue of the Ashmolean manuscripts in the Bodleian Library by W. H. Black (Oxford, 1845).

1. Thus William Lilly's *Christian Astrology* (1647), the most influential vernacular treatise of the seventeenth century, was said to be little more than a translation of the medieval Arab astrologer, Albohazen Haly filius Abenragel (J. Gadbury, *Dies Novissimus* [1664], p. 47). Lilly, though claiming that the first part of the book at least was original (*Autobiography*, p. 129), appended an impressive bibliography which gave some indication of his dependence upon his predecessors.

adaptable to the needs of a social environment which was very different from that in which it had originated.

The basic astrological assumptions are not difficult to grasp. For if astronomy is the study of the movements of the heavenly bodies, then astrology is the study of the effects of those movements. The astronomers of the ancient world had been impressed by the regular behaviour of the heavens, in contrast with the flux and mutation of life upon earth. They accordingly assumed a division of the universe whereby the superior, immutable bodies of the celestial world ruled over the terrestrial or sublunary sphere, where all was mortality and change. It was assumed that the stars had special qualities and influences which were transmitted downwards upon the passive earth, and which varied in their effects, according to the changing relationship of the heavenly bodies to each other. Owing to their inadequate techniques of astronomical observation, the early scientists had no conception of the infinite number of existing solar systems nor of the vast distances which separate the visible stars from each other. They were thus led to postulate a single system in which the seven moving stars or planets – Sun, Moon, Saturn, Jupiter, Mars, Venus and Mercury – shifted their position in relation to the earth and each other, against a fixed backcloth of the twelve signs of the zodiac. The nature of the influence exerted by the heavens at any one moment thus depended upon the situation of the various celestial bodies. By drawing a map of the heavens, or horoscope, the astrologer could analyse this situation and assess its implications. By an extension of the same principle, he could, given the necessary astronomical knowledge, construct a horoscope for some future point of time, and thus predict the influence which the heavens would exert on that occasion.

There was nothing esoteric about these general assumptions. At the beginning of the sixteenth century astrological doctrines were part of the educated man's picture of the universe and its workings. It was generally accepted that the four elements constituting the sublunary region – earth, air, fire and water – were kept in their state of ceaseless permutation by the movement of the heavenly bodies. The various planets transmitted different quantities of the four physiological qualities of heat and cold, dryness and moisture. In the resulting interaction was comprised all physical change. This relationship between earthly events and the movements of the heavens was but one example of the many links and correspondences which were thought to bind the physical universe together. Astrology was thus less a separate discipline than an aspect of a generally accepted world picture. It was necessary for the understanding of physiology and therefore of medicine. It taught of the influence of the stars upon the plants and minerals, and therefore shaped botany and metallurgy. Psychology and ethnography also presupposed a good deal of astrological dogma. During the Renaissance, even more than in the Middle Ages, astrology pervaded all aspects of scientific thought. It was not a coterie doctrine, but an essential aspect of the intellectual framework in which men were educated.

Nevertheless, the subject had a life and independent momentum of its own, especially when the prestige of the Ptolemaic picture of the universe began to crumble under the pressure of the astronomical discoveries of the century and a half between Copernicus and Newton. During this period astrology gradually lost its role as a universal symbolism, and ossified into a separate, and ultimately obsolete, system of belief. This change was still in the future when the sixteenth century opened. Although there had been many sceptics about particular details of astrological dogma, especially as regards the possibility of making definite predictions concerning the behaviour of specific human beings, there were not yet any real heretics, so far as the basic principles of the subject were concerned. No one denied the influence of the heavens upon the weather or disputed the relevance of astrology to medicine or agriculture. Before the seventeenth century, total scepticism about astrological doctrine was highly exceptional, whether in England or elsewhere.

During the sixteenth and seventeenth centuries there were four main branches to the practice of judicial astrology (to give it its full title, for the term 'astrology' by itself was often used as synonymous with 'astronomy'). First, there were the *general predictions*, based on the future movements of the heavens, and taking note of such impending events as eclipses of the sun and moon, or the conjunction of the major planets in one sign of the zodiac. These forecasts related to the weather, the state of the crops, mortality and epidemics, politics and war. They indicated the fate of society as a whole, but not that of particular individuals. Secondly, there were *nativities*, maps of the sky at the moment of a person's birth, either made on the spot at the request of the infant's parents, or reconstructed for individuals of mature years who could supply the details of their time of birth. If the date of the birth had been lost; the astrologer could try to work it out by inference from the relationship between the 'accidents', or notable events in his client's life, and the state of the heavens at the time. The horoscope at birth could subsequently be followed up by 'annual revolutions', in which the astrologer calculated the individual's prospects for the coming year.

The details of the client's nativity were also needed before he could avail himself of the astrologer's third main service, that of making *elections,* or choosing the right moment for the right action. By comparing the relationship between the tendencies indicated by the client's horoscope with what was known about the future movement of the heavens, certain times could be identified as more propitious than others for embarking upon any potentially risky undertaking, such as going on a journey or choosing a wife. The election of a proper time was also a desirable procedure for routine operations, like cutting one's hair and nails, or having a bath. Finally, there were *horary questions,* the most controversial part of the astrologer's art, and one which had only been developed after the days of Ptolemy by the Arabs. Its optimistic assumption was that the astrologer could resolve any question put to him by considering the state of the heavens at the exact moment when it was asked – on the principle that 'as the nativity is the time of the birth of the body, the horary question is the time of the birth of the mind'.[2] If the question was a medical one the patient might accompany it with a sample of his urine; the astrologer then based his answer upon his interpretation of the sky at the moment when the urine had been voided, or when it had arrived at his consulting-room. But every kind of personal problem could be dealt with as an horary question.

These four spheres of activity–general predictions, nativities, elections and horary questions – formed the sum of the astrologer's art. An individual practitioner might specialise in one rather than another, but he was expected to be a master of them all. He might also possess a certain amount of medical learning. Different signs of the zodiac were thought to rule over different parts of the body, and a proper election of times had to be made for administering medicine, letting blood, or carrying out surgical operations. This was generally recognized by all sixteenth-century physicians. But there had also developed a more idiosyncratic system of astrological medicine which linked every stage of treatment to the disposition of the heavens. By casting a figure for the *decumbiture,* or moment

2. J. Gadbury, *The Doctrine of Nativities* (1658), ii, p. 235.

when the patient felt ill, and by resolving a question on sight of his urine, the astrological doctor claimed to be able to diagnose the disease, prescribe the treatment, foretell when the sickness would reach its crisis, and prognosticate its eventual outcome.

Such were the main branches of English (and indeed European) astrology during the sixteenth and seventeenth centuries. Although purporting to be an objective science, the system was highly flexible, since it left room for infinite possibilities of disagreement, both over general principles, and over the interpretation of any particular problem. Every astrological prognosis involved a figure of the heavens, in which the sky was divided up into twelve sections or 'houses', each relating to different aspects of human life. Lack of precision in time-recording made the construction of this figure difficult enough in itself, and there was plenty of scope for mathematical error in the intricate astronomical calculations required. But even when the horoscope had been drawn and agreed upon, the problem of its interpretation remained. The planets were deemed to have colours, sexes, physical qualities, and so forth. But the elaborate mythologies which proliferated along these lines were not always consistent. The planets, moreover, were only one variable in a densely crowded mosaic of fluctuating constituents – elements, humours, qualities, houses and signs of the zodiac. The client's own horoscope might also need to be compared with that of the country in which he lived, or those of the other persons with whom he had dealings. The astrologer thus found himself involved in a welter of combinations and permutations which greatly complicated the task of interpretation. It was generally agreed that to pick his way through them he needed not mere technical skill, but judgement. In other words any interpretation was in the last resort bound to be subjective. Different practitioners might give different answers to the same question, and the more specific the prediction the less likely was it to command unanimous assent.

Astrology was probably the most ambitious attempt ever made to reduce the baffling diversity of human affairs to some sort of intelligible order, but as the vocabulary and techniques swelled to reflect the richness and variability of the material with which it was concerned the problem of reaching a definite answer became increasingly intractable. The more subtle the astrologer's terminology, the greater the number of factors he took into account, the more certainly did the prospect of objective pronouncement elude his grasp.

His efforts to sharpen his conceptual tools only meant that he came nearer to reproducing on paper the chaotic diversity which he saw in the world around him.

Such difficulties were only dimly apprehended in England at the beginning of the sixteenth century, when astrological activity seems to have been at a relatively low ebb. In the Middle Ages there had been many prominent English astrological authors, but their numbers fell off sharply during the fifteenth century and did not revive for over a hundred and fifty years.[3] The prognostications in circulation during the early sixteenth century were therefore largely of foreign origin. There was, for example, no English contribution to the large literature produced by the conjunction in 1524 of all seven planets in the water sign of Pisces, even though rumours of the impending deluge in that year are said to have induced Prior Bolton of St Bartholomew's, Smithfield, to build himself a house on Harrow Hill and stock it with provisions to withstand the threat of inundation.[4] The lack of English astrological writings during this period reflected the general torpor of English science. Interest revived with the mathematical renaissance pioneered by John Dee and the Digges family during the reign of Elizabeth I, and was more or less sustained until the end of the seventeenth century. If the prestige of astrology is to be measured by the publication of astrological works, then the story is one of a peak reached at around the end of the sixteenth century, followed by a discernible lull in the twenty years before the Civil War, and thereafter an unprecedented torrent of publication, which began with the War, but went on until the end of the seventeenth century.

In terms of popular accessibility, therefore, the crucial period of English astrological publication was the last sixty years of the seventeenth century, and particularly the Interregnum. In the age of Edward VI the bulk of astrological learning was still locked up in the obscurity of a learned language, whereas by the time of Charles II there was no branch of the subject which could not be studied by the English reader. During the Elizabethan period a few original works

3. Thorndike, *Magic and Science*, iii, pp. 104–18, 143–5, 325–46; iv, pp. 98, 145–6; R. T. Gunther, *Early Science in Oxford*, ii (Oxford, 1923), pp. 42–67; G. Hellmann, 'Versuch einer Geschichte der Wettervorhersage im XVI. Jahrhundert', *Abhandlungen der Preussischen Akademie der Wissenschaften, Physikalisch-Mathematische Klasse*, 1924, p. 18.

4. *Hall's Chronicle* (1809 edn), p. 675. cf. Thorndike, *Magic and Science*, v, chap. xi.

and foreign translations were published, but the most elaborate native piece of astrological learning, Thomas Allen's commentary on Ptolemy, remained in manuscript.[5] As has already been seen, Robert Fludd's voluminous works were written in Latin and published abroad. Only during the Interregnum, that period when so many other *arcana* were exposed to public gaze, did the first vernacular guides to the subject pour off the English presses. The popular writings of William Lilly, Nicholas Culpepper, William Ramesey and John Gadbury were followed after the Restoration by the similar vulgarizations of Richard Saunders, John Partridge, William Salmon and John Case. Designed for a mainly non-learned audience, they constituted a comprehensive summary of astrological beliefs, issued, ironically, at the very period when the whole system was ceasing to command respect in intellectually more pretentious *milieux*. Ptolemy's astrology was not published in English until 1701.[6]

The availability of English treatises on astrology is thus a poor barometer for the actual prestige of the subject. Despite the lack of a vernacular literature, most Tudor monarchs and their advisers encouraged astrologers and drew upon their advice. Both Henry VII and those engaged in plotting against him maintained relations with the Italian astrologer William Parron.[7] Henry VIII patronized the German, Nicholas Kratzer, prevented his bishops from censuring astrology, and received astrological advice from John Robins, the only contemporary English writer on the subject of any importance.[8] Cardinal Wolsey's interest in astrology was notorious. He was rumoured to have calculated Henry VIII's nativity in order to be able to pander to the King's whims; and he timed the departure of his French embassy in 1527 to coincide with an astrologically propitious moment.[9] The Protector Somerset seems to have been personally sceptical of the predictive powers of astrology,[10] but after

5. There is a copy in Ashm. 388.
6. *Ptolemy's Quadripartite*, trans. J. Whalley (1701).
7. C. A. J. Armstrong, 'An Italian Astrologer at the Court of Henry VII', in *Italian Renaissance Studies*, ed. E. F. Jacob (1960); A. F. Pollard, *The Reign of Henry VII* (1913–14), i, pp. 117–22.
8. Taylor, *Mathematical Practitioners*, pp. 12, 165; J. J. Scarisbrick, *Henry VIII* (1968), p. 406; Thorndike, *Magic and Science*, v, pp. 320–21.
9. W. Tyndale, *Expositions and Notes*, ed. H. Walter (Cambridge, P.S., 1849), p. 308; *H.M.C., MSS in the Welsh Language*, i, p. vi (I owe this reference to Dr P. T. J. Morgan).
10. *Narratives of the Days of the Reformation*, ed. J. G. Nichols (Camden Soc., 1859), p. 173.

his fall the Italian savant, Jerome Cardan, came to England to cast the horoscopes of the young Edward VI and his tutor, John Cheke, a well-known addict.[11] Another leading administrator who shared this interest was the Secretary of State, Sir William Paget, to whom the Basle edition of the Italian astrologer, Guido Bonatus, was dedicated in 1550.[12] His colleague, Sir William Paulet, supported the almanac-maker George Hartgill,[13] while for Sir Thomas Smith, the ambassador and future Secretary of State, the practice of astrology was no casual interest, but so consuming a passion that he could 'scarcely sleep at night from thinking of it'.[14]

Similar enthusiasm was displayed by the courtiers of Elizabeth I. The Earl of Leicester employed Richard Forster as his astrological physician and commissioned Thomas Allen to set horoscopes. He also offered Allen a bishopric.[15] It was at Leicester's invitation that John Dee chose an astrologically propitious day for the coronation of Elizabeth I. Dee maintained relations with many of the leading nobility of his day and was called in by the Queen to offer his views on the comet of 1577.[16] Burghley made notes on astrological matters,[17] and the Earl of Essex is known to have possessed an

11. H. Morley, *Jerome Cardan* (1854), ii, chap. vi. Payments made around 1552 to royal 'astronomers' are recorded in *C.S.P.D., 1601–3, and Addenda*, p. 420. For Cheke's astrological interests see Foxe, viii, p. 257; Taylor, *Mathematical Practitioners*, pp. 314, 168, 170; J. Strype, *The Life of the learned Sir John Cheke* (1705), p. 221.

12. G. Bonatus, *De Astronomia Tractatus* (Basle, 1550). The editor, Nicholas Prukner, dedicated an edition of the fourth-century astrologer, Firmicus Maternus, to Edward VI in the following year.

13. Taylor, *Mathematical Practitioners*, p. 332.

14. J. G. Nichols in *Archaeologia*, xxxviii (1860), p. 103; M. Dewar, *Sir Thomas Smith* (1964), pp. 65, 78, 131, 181–3. Smith's calculations are in Sloane 325, and there is a list of his astrological books in J. Strype, *The Life of ... Sir Thomas Smith* (Oxford, 1820), p. 279. A contemporary witness says that Smith did not accept the truth of astrology (ibid., p. 163), but even Roger Ascham, who was normally a sceptic, asked him for astrological advice; L. V. Ryan, *Roger Ascham* (1963), p. 242.

15. Taylor, *Mathematical Practitioners*, pp. 170, 320; J. Aubrey, *Brief Lives*, ed. A. Clark (Oxford, 1898), i, p. 27; Wood, *Ath. Ox.*, ii, col. 542. Robert Greene dedicated *Planetomachia*, containing a defence of astrology, to Leicester in 1585.

16. *Autobiographical Tracts of Dr John Dee*, ed. J. Crossley (in *Chetham Miscellanies*, i [Chetham Soc., 1851]), p. 21. An astrological astrolabe bearing the Queen's arms is described by G. H. Gabb in *Archaeologia*, lxxxvi (1936).

17. J. Strype, *Annals of the Reformation* (2nd edn, Oxford, 1725–31), ii, appx., iv (on which see Nichols in *Archaeologia*, xxxviii [1860], p. 110).

elaborate fifteenth-century treatise on astrology and geomancy.[18] Sir Christopher Hatton, Elizabeth's future Lord Chancellor, received the dedication of John Maplet's *The Diall of Destiny* (1581), an astrological text-book. The evidence for Sir Philip Sidney's attitude to astrology is conflicting,[19] but the Earl of Oxford certainly studied the subject.[20] Small wonder that the Puritan Laurence Humphrey complained in 1563 that among the nobility the science of astrology was 'ravened, embraced, and devoured of many'.[21] It was customary for aristocratic families to have horoscopes cast at the birth of their children,[22] and more or less unavoidable for them to have recourse to doctors who used semi-astrological methods.[23]

During the seventeenth century this situation changed only slowly. Many of the leading nobility and politicians retained astrological leanings. The Earl of Arundel employed the almanac-maker, Humphrey Llwyd, as his personal physician. Lord Scrope, President of the Council of the North (1619–28), was a patient of the astrological doctor, Richard Napier. Charles I's Treasurer, Lord Weston, appointed the astrologer, Nicholas Fiske, as tutor to his son. The second Earl of Bristol was himself a highly skilled astrologer. The Marquis of Huntly, executed in 1649, was thought to have been ruined by bad astrological advice. 'He believed the stars,' wrote Burnet, 'and they deceived him.' Another aristocratic victim of the Civil Wars, the Marquis of Montrose, had as a young man travelled overseas with the Earl of Denbigh; together 'they consulted all the astrologers they could hear of'.[24]

18. *H.M.C.*, iii, pp. 112–13. But an early attack on astrology, W. C(ovell), *Polimanteia* (Cambridge, 1595), was dedicated to him.

19. M. S. Goldman, 'Sidney and Harington as Opponents of Superstition', *Journ. English and Germanic Philology*, liv (1955); R. Howell, *Sir Philip Sidney* (1968), pp. 222–3; J. M. Osborn, 'Mica Mica Parva Stella: Sidney's Horoscope', *Times Lit. Supp.*, 1 July 1971; P. J. French, *John Dee* (1972), chap. 6.

20. B. M. Ward, *The Seventeenth Earl of Oxford* (1928), p. 50.

21. L. Humfrey, *The Nobles: or, of Nobilitye* (1563), sig. y vi^v.

22. For some examples, see N. Williams, *Thomas Howard, Fourth Duke of Norfolk* (1964), p. 1 (1538); C. D. Bowen, *The Lion and the Throne* (1957), p. 64 (1584); *H.M.C.*, ix (2), p. 375 (1584); *Trans. Anglesey Antiqn Soc. and Field Club* (1937), p. 28 (1632); F. H. Sunderland, *Marmaduke Lord Langdale* (1926,) pp. 36–8 (1627–39).

23. e.g., *H.M.C.*, *Hatfield*, xvi, p. 310 (1604); *C.S.P.D., 1629–31*, p. 210; below, pp. 420-22.

24. Taylor, *Mathematical Practitioners*, p. 319; Ashm. 421, ff. 162^v–4;

During the Royalist exile Sir Edward Dering, later a prominent
London merchant, had attempted to keep up the spirits of his colleagues by assuring them that the stars were on their side. After
the Restoration he became a great patron of contemporary astrologers.[25] Charles II himself took astrological advice upon occasions,
as we shall see.[26] Indeed in 1669 Louis XIV thought it worth appoint-
ing a French astrologer, the Abbé Pregnani, as a special diplomatic
agent to England, after the Duke of Monmouth, one of the Abbé's
clients, had told him of the monarch's faith in the art. The venture
miscarried after a trip to Newmarket races, where the Abbé unfortunately failed to provide the King with any winners, thus provoking a diplomatic incident which led to his recall.[27] Even after the
Revolution of 1688 astrological interests were to be found in high
places. Sir John Trenchard, Secretary of State to William III, had
his horoscope cast, and confessed on his death-bed that everything
the astrologer had predicted for him had come true.[28]

For intellectuals astrology remained a topic of consuming interest.
A random list of sympathizers could include such celebrated names
as those of Sir Walter Raleigh,[29] Robert Burton, the Anatomist,[30]

Lilly, *Autobiography*, p. 73; Edward, Earl of Clarendon, *The History of the
Rebellion*, ed. W. D. Macray (Oxford, 1888), vi, p. 49; *Bishop Burnet's
History of His Own Time* (Oxford, 1823), i, pp. 64–5, 51.

25. Josten, *Ashmole*, pp. 241–2; J. Gadbury, *Cardines Coeli* (1684), p. 17;
Autobiography and Anecdotes by William Taswell, ed. G. P. Elliott, in
Camden Miscellany, ii (1853), pp. 30–31; J. Partridge, *Merlinus Liberatus*
(1697), dedication. For the interest of the exiled Royalists in astrological
prognostications see *C.S.P.D., 1657–8*, pp. 304, 327, and J. Price, *The Mystery
and Method of His Majesty's happy Restauration* (1680), pp. 40–41.
26. Below, p. 371.
27. M. Mignet, *Négociations relatives à la succession d'Espagne sous
Louis XIV* (Paris, 1835–42), iii, pp. 73–80; C. H. Hartmann, *Charles II and
Madame* (1934), pp. 239–41. For another attempt to exploit the king's belief
in astrology, see W. Harris, *An Historical and Critical Account of . . . Charles
II* (1814), v, p. 374.
28. Wood, *Ath. Ox.*, iv, cols. 405–6. His horoscope (in the Trenchard
Papers in the Dorset R.O.) shows his date of birth was 30 March 1649, not
1640, as in *D.N.B.*
29. Allen, *The Star-Crossed Renaissance*, p. 153.
30. ibid., p. 153; Wood, *Ath. Ox.*, ii, cols. 652–3; *Oxford Bibliogl Soc.*,
Procs. and Papers, i (1922–6), p. 186. It was a passage in Burton which was
to kindle John Gadbury's interest in astrology; Gadbury, *Cardines Coeli*,
p. 59.

Lord Herbert of Cherbury,[31] Sir Kenelm Digby[32] and Sir Thomas Browne.[33] Among seventeenth-century scientists, the mathematician Edmund Gunter is known to have cast horoscopes, while belief in the possibilities of astrology, in part or whole, was shared by such notables as Napier of Merchiston, Samuel Hartlib, William Harvey and Henry Oldenburg.[34] As a young man Isaac Newton bought a book on judicial astrology at Stourbridge Fair.[35] Among the papers of John Aubrey is the nativity of Walter Charleton, sometime President of the Royal College of Physicians, set by Lord Brouncker, the first President of the Royal Society.[36] John Dryden remained an astrological devotee throughout his life.[37]

These miscellaneous names testify to the sympathetic attitude in which astrology was held in the sixteenth and seventeenth centuries by many men of rank and intellectual importance. Of course it is not always easy to say just how seriously they took it. Many no doubt had horoscopes cast out of mere amusement or curiosity,[38] whereas others based important decisions on their outcome. But it is certain that until the mid seventeenth century astrology was no private fad but a form of divination to which many educated people had recourse.

What is more remarkable, however, is that astrological interests were not confined to court circles, or to the entourage of the great, as they had largely been in the Middle Ages, but were widely dis-

31. Although he thought it worked only for general predictions, not particular ones; *The Autobiography of Edward, Lord Herbert of Cherbury*, ed. S. Lee (2nd edn, n.d.), p. 27 and n.

32. R. T. Petersson, *Sir Kenelm Digby* (1956), pp. 15–16, 72–3, 98, 328; Ashm. 174, no. 4; Ashm. 243, f. 124.

33. Below, p. 417.

34. Aubrey, *Miscellanies*, p. 62; Lilly, *Autobiography*, p. 237; Josten, *Ashmole*, p. 565; F. N. L. Poynter in *Journ. of the Hist. of Medicine*, xvii (1962), p. 157; *The Correspondence of Henry Oldenburg*, ed. A. R. and M. B. Hall (Madison, Milwaukee, 1965–), i, pp. 281, 308. The astrologer, John Bishop, claimed Robert Boyle as a patron; R. Kirby and J. Bishop, *The Marrow of Astrology* (1687), ii, dedication.

35. L. T. More, *Isaac Newton* (1934), p. 32; there is some slight evidence to suggest that it was an interest in astrology which led him on to astronomy; F. E. Manuel, *Isaac Newton, Historian* (Cambridge, 1963), pp. 263, 274.

36. Bodl., Aubrey MS 23, f. 54.

37. *The Works of John Dryden*, ed. Sir W. Scott and G. Saintsbury, xviii (1893), p. 134; Aubrey, *Brief Lives*, ed. Clark, i, p. 241. For more on the attitude of seventeenth-century scientists, see below, pp. 416–20.

38. As was suggested by J. Fage, *Speculum Aegrotorum. The Sicke Mens Glasse* (1606), sig. A3.

seminated throughout the people. For this the invention of printing was chiefly responsible. By its means, astrology was made available to an infinitely wider audience than that enjoyed by the court-based astrologers of the medieval world. The lead in this dissemination was taken by the most widespread form of fugitive literature in early modern England – the almanac.

2. Almanacs and prognostications

Strictly speaking, the almanac comprised three quite separate items.[39] There was the Almanac proper, which indicated the astronomical events of the coming year, eclipses, conjunctions and movable feasts. There was the Kalendar, which showed the days of the week and the months, and the fixed Church festivals. Finally, there was the Prognostication, or astrological forecast of the notable events of the year. Usually they were all sold together as one piece, interlarded with the sort of miscellaneous information which diaries still carry today – a list of markets and fairs, a guide to highways and distances by road, a brief chronology of notable historical events since the Creation, medical recipes, legal formulae, hints on gardening. By the mid seventeenth century they also carried advertisements for books, patent medicines, or teachers of mathematics. These little pocket-books were quite distinct from the broadside sheet almanac, the ancestor of the modern calendar. They contained more information, and were less ephemeral. Contemporaries found them invaluable as diaries, note-books, and vade-mecums generally. As a consequence large collections still survive in the Bodleian, British Museum and other large libraries.

The most obvious difference between the pocket almanac and the modern diary is the strong astrological emphasis of the former. The more elaborate almanacs included Ephemerides, or tables showing the daily position of the heavenly bodies throughout the year.

39. The starting-point for this subject is the pioneer work of E. F. Bosanquet: *English printed Almanacks and Prognostications. A Bibliographical History to the year 1600* (1917) (with additions and *corrigenda* in *The Library*, 4th ser., viii [1927–8] and 4th ser., xviii [1937–8]); and 'English Seventeenth-Century Almanacks', *The Library*, 4th ser., x (1930). See also C. Camden, 'Elizabethan Almanacs and Prognostications', ibid., 4th ser., xii (1932), and C. Blagden, 'The Distribution of Almanacks in the Second Half of the Seventeenth Century', *Studies in Bibliography. Papers of the Bibliogl Soc. of the Univ. of Va.*, ed. F. Bowers, xi (1958). Lists of extant almanacs of the period may be found in *S.T.C.* and Wing.

With their aid the reader could predict the movement of the planets through the signs of the zodiac, and foresee the various conjunctions and oppositions. Thus armed, he was in a position to set about casting his own horoscopes. In addition he could consult the almanac's diagram of the Anatomical Man indicating the dominion of the different signs of the zodiac over the different parts of the human body. From this he could work out the appropriate time for taking medicine or medical treatment. Above all, there was the prognostication, in which the author of the almanac demonstrated his virtuosity by detailed forecasts of politics, the weather, the state of the crops, and the health of the population in the year to come.

Medieval almanacs had circulated in manuscript, but they seem to have been intended primarily for students and physicians. It was only in the Tudor period that the printed English almanac rose to a position of enormous popular success. During the early sixteenth century various translations of continental prognostications were issued, some of which sold very briskly.[40] But not until 1545 is an Englishman known to have composed his own forecast for publication. He was Andrew Boorde, an ex-Carthusian, and his prognostication was the first of many. Foreign prognostications still circulated, but their place was steadily usurped by domestic products. By 1600 there had been probably over 600 different almanacs published in England, and they were still on the increase. The number of separate almanacs issued in the seventeenth century has been estimated at more than 2,000, and well over 200 authors must have been concerned in their publication. The size of a typical edition is unknown. But it is significant that almanacs, like Bibles, were exempt from the original limit of 1,250 to 1,500 copies imposed by the Stationers' Company on single editions of other publications. William Lilly's annual almanac and prognostication, *Merlinus Anglicus,* printed 13,500 copies in 1646, 17,000 in 1647, and 18,500 in 1648. By 1649 it was said to be selling nearly 30,000 a year.[41] This particular almanac was unusually popular, but it is clear that the figure of 3,000,000 to 4,000,000, which is sometimes suggested as the total production of almanacs in the seventeenth century, is a

40. As is revealed by the accounts of the Oxford bookseller, John Dorne (ed. F. Madan in *Collectanea*, i, ed. C. R. L. Fletcher [Oxford Hist. Soc., 1885]).

41. H. R. Plomer, 'A Printer's Bill in the Seventeenth Century', *The Library,* new ser., vii (1906), p. 35; J. A(llen), *Judicial Astrologers totally routed* (1659), p. 15. In 1635 the normal limit for other publications was raised to 2000 or, on special application, 3000.

distinct under-estimate; the ten years after November 1663 alone nearly reached that total. Not even the Bible sold at this rate.[42]

It is easy to see why the almanacs were commercially so successful. They were issued to fit the varying astronomical meridians of different parts of the country, special almanacs being published for particular towns, even relatively small ones like Aylesbury or Saffron Walden. The information they contained was carefully selected according to the type of readership aimed at. Thus there might be legal terms for the Justice of the Peace, advice on land measurement for the surveyor, or nautical hints for the seaman. By the mid seventeenth century the almanacs even catered for different varieties of political taste. They were also cheap. In the seventeenth century the standard price seems to have been twopence, although more elaborate productions cost more.[43]

Astrological forecasts, however, were by no means an invariable feature of the almanac, and even when included might relate only to the weather. Highly political prognostications, of the kind common during the Civil War, had been relatively infrequent during the previous century. By the 1630s the so-called Prognostication was often merely an additional calendar of secular occurrences during the year. It was only the subsequent breakdown in censorship which made political forecasting commonplace.

Yet even without a prognostication, the almanac provided a guide to daily action. It indicated astrologically favourable days for blood-letting, purging and bathing; and it showed right and wrong times for engaging in most kinds of agricultural operation, planting, sowing, mowing or gelding animals. Armed with his pocket almanac for the year, or perhaps a more durable guide, like Leonard Digges's *Prognostication ... for ever* (1555, and frequently reissued),[44] the countryman was well equipped to carry out his recurring tasks, while the sick man, whose relatives were responsible for giving him medi-

42. Blagden in *Studies in Bibliography*, xi (1958), pp. 115–16. For figures of Bible-printing, see C. Bridenbaugh, *Vexed and Troubled Englishmen* (Oxford, 1968), p. 278 & n.

43. Bosanquet, in *The Library*, 4th ser., x (1930), p. 366; *Robert Loder's Farm Accounts, 1610–20*, ed. G. E. Fussell (Camden Ser., 1936), p. 71; *Durham High Commission*, p. 40. A representative collection of almanacs for 1659 (Bodl., Rawl. Alm. 11) cost 2d. each, save for the larger productions of Blagrave, Lilly and Wharton, which were 6d.

44. Most recently as an *Old Ashmolean Reprint* (Oxford, 1926). On its popularity see E. F. Bosanquet in *Oxford Bibliogl Soc., Procs. and Papers*, i (1922–6).

cine or letting his blood, knew that they were operating according to well-established formulae.

In practice, however, the genuine astrological almanac had to compete for popular favour with some much lower-grade products. Chief among these was the prognostication of *Erra Pater*, allegedly 'a Jew out of Jewry'. ('If one affirm he learned it of a Jew,' ran a contemporary jingle, 'The silly people think it must be true'.) *Erra Pater* was in fact derived from the perpetual prognostication of *Esdras*, which had circulated extensively in the Middle Ages.[45] Like Digges's almanac it gave a table forecasting the weather according to the day of the week on which New Year began. It also included a list of unlucky days, 'on which if any man or woman be let blood of wound or vein they shall die within twenty-one days following; or who so falleth into sickness on any of these days they shall never 'scape till dead'. (These were not astrological at all, but were a version of the so-called 'Egyptian days', which Englishmen had regarded as unlucky since Anglo-Saxon times.) This crude brochure was reissued at least a dozen times between 1536 and 1640. By the eighteenth century it was being advertised as the work of William Lilly. Henry Peacham wrote of the early Stuart husbandman that '*Erra Pater*, and this year's almanac (if he can read) are the only two books he spends his time in', while Bishop Hall said in his 'Character' of *The Superstitious Man*, that he would never go out 'without an *Erra Pater* in his pocket'.[46]

Closely allied to *Erra Pater* were other crude works of prognostication, vaguely astrological in character, but lacking the rigour of the astrological almanac proper. There was *The Kalender of Shepherdes*, translated from the French in 1503, and reissued at least seventeen times during the ensuing century and a half, despite its distinctly Roman Catholic character. It offered a guide to the influence of the planets upon the human body and a semi-astrological method of telling fortunes.[47] Its astrological portions were subsequently pirated under the title of *The Compost of Ptolomeus* (1532?), which enjoyed an independent life for at least four editions

45. E. Worsop, *A Discoverie of Sundrie Errours* (1582), sig. F4ᵛ; *The Works of John Metham*, ed. H. Craig (E.E.T.S., 1916), pp. xxxii–xxxvii.

46. H. Peacham, *The Truth of our Times* (1638), p. 119; *The Works of . . . Joseph Hall*, ed. P. Wynter (Oxford, 1863), vi, p. 110. A similar production was *Verus Pater, or a bundell of truths* (1611 and 1622). On the 'Egyptian days' see below, pp. 735–6.

47. There is a modern edition by H. O. Sommer (1892).

thereafter. A similar handbook was *Godfridus*, to which was attached *The Husbandman's Practice, or a Prognostication for Ever*. It included a system of long-range weather forecasting, based on the day of the week on which Christmas fell, and a prediction of the fate of persons born on different days of the week or phases of the moon. There were at least twelve editions of this work in the second half of the seventeenth century.[48] These were in addition to *Arcandam*, the *Sphere of Pythagoras*, and other non-astrological handbooks of divination.[49] 'These be their great masters and in this manner their whole library, with some old parchment rolls, tables and instruments,' wrote Gabriel Harvey of the Elizabethan wizards: '*Erra Pater*, their hornbook; the *Shepherd's Kalendar*, their primer; the *Compost of Ptolomeus*, their Bible; *Arcandam*, their New Testament'.[50] The astrological almanac was thus but one of a whole *genre* of publications which told readers how to make predictions about the future, and to choose days which would be particularly favourable for any given course of action. The astrological kind differed from the others only in its intellectual rigour. At the level of popular readership it is doubtful whether the distinction can have been so clear.

The appeal of the almanac was closely related to the belief in the significance of the changing phases of the moon which was extensively held in rural areas and still lingers on today.[51] Most primitive people attribute to the moon an influence upon the weather and upon conception and growth, whether of vegetation, animals or human beings. In medieval theory the balance of humours in the human body was believed to fluctuate with the phases of the moon. The moon was thought to control the amount of moisture in the human body, and the brain, as the moistest part of the body, was believed to be particularly subject to its influence. Hence the notion

48. There are ten editions in Wing and I have noticed two others (for 1660 and 1679) in recent catalogues issued by antiquarian booksellers.

49. Above, pp. 283–4.

50. *Gabriel Harvey's Marginalia*, ed. G. C. Moore Smith (Stratford-on-Avon, 1913), p. 163.

51. For this subject: E. B. Tylor, *Researches into the Early History of Mankind* (2nd edn, 1870), pp. 134–5; H. Webster, *Rest Days* (New York, 1916), chap. 5; P. Saintyves [E. Nourry], *L'Astrologie populaire étudiée spécialement dans les doctrines et les traditions relatives à l'influence de la lune* (Paris, 1937); J. G. Frazer, *Adonis, Attis, Osiris* (2nd edn, 1907), iii, chap. 9; Brand, *Popular Antiquities*, iii, pp. 141–53; W. Farnham, 'The Days of the Mone', *Studies in Philology*, xx (1923).

of the insane as 'lunatic' or 'moonstruck'.[52] A child born at full moon, declared an astrologer in 1660, would never be healthy.[53]

Many people accordingly allowed the phases of the moon to determine their timing of various activities. The medieval Church had inveighed against the practice of only celebrating marriages or moving to a new house when the moon was waxing. In the sixteenth and seventeenth centuries the rising moon was still thought of as the time for putting on new clothes or embarking upon some new course of action.[54] Thomas Tusser and other agricultural writers advised farmers to cut crops when the moon was in the wane and to sow when it was on the increase.[55] In the later seventeenth century, hair-cutting and nail-paring were said to be 'commonly done according to the increase of the moon'.[56] Some of the popular handbooks of prognostication took the principle further by decreeing that specific activities should be timed to coincide with specific days of the month. They laid down appropriate days for blood-letting, purging, going on journeys, buying and selling, even for starting school. Hardly any of their recommendations would have been endorsed by serious astrologers, and they provide a further reminder of the large gulf between would-be scientific astrology on the one hand, and popular beliefs of a vaguely astrological character on the other.

Published astrological forecasts were always in demand. When Thomas Gataker, the Puritan divine, wanted to compose a refutation of one of Lilly's prognostications in 1653, he had great difficulty in finding a copy, so rapidly had it sold out.[57] But readers could be scep-

52. W. C. Curry, *Chaucer and the Mediaeval Sciences* (2nd edn, 1960), pp. 13–14; D. Person, *Varieties* (1635), p. 12; W. Drage, *A Physical Nosonomy* (1665), pp. 12–13.   53. G. Atwell, *An Apology, or Defence* (1660), pp. 6–7.

54. Powicke and Cheney, *Councils and Synods*, p. 179; G. R. Owst in *Studies Presented to Sir Hilary Jenkinson*, ed. J. C. Davies (1957), p. 291; Brand, *Popular Antiquities*, iii, pp. 151–2; T. Harley, *Moon Lore* (1885), p. 210; Aubrey, *Gentilisme*, p. 85.

55. *Thomas Tusser. His Good Points of Husbandry*, ed. D. Hartley (1931), pp. 59, 96; (T. Hill), *The Profitable Arte of Gardening* (3rd edn, 1574), sig. Eiij^v, p. 18; C. Lucar, *A Treatise named Lucarsolace* (1590), p. 152; [W.L.], *A New Orchard and Garden* (1623), pp. 18, 19; J. B(lagrave?), *The Epitome of the Whole Art of Husbandry* (1669), pp. 62 ff.

56. R.H., 'Astrologia Siderata, or a whip for divining Soothsayers' (Sloane 412), f. 47^v. cf. J. Primrose, *Popular Errours*, trans. R. Wittie (1651), pp. 247–8.

57. T. Gataker, *His Vindication of the Annotations by him published* (1653), p. 2.

ASTROLOGY: ITS PRACTICE AND EXTENT 353

tics. Weather forecasts in particular were received with a good deal of scorn;[58] and the almanac met with a stream of satire and burlesque. From the anonymous *A Mery Prognostication* in 1544 to Swift's pitiless mockery of John Partridge in 1708, there was an unbroken barrage of anti-astrological squibs. In 1569 Nicholas Allen in in his pamphlet, *The Astronomer's Game,* made effective capital out of a side-by-side comparison of the predictions of three contemporary almanac-makers, and this became a standard method of attack.[59]

But the very frequency with which Elizabethan and Jacobean wits found it necessary to denounce the almanacs and prognostications is in itself testimony to the influence which they exerted. 'Who is there,' asked one writer in 1612, 'that maketh not great account of his almanac to observe both days, times and seasons, to follow his affairs for his best profit and use?'[60] In 1561 Frances Coxe complained of the common people that 'scant would they ride or go any journey unless they consulted, either with these blind prophets, or at least with their prophecies'. William Perkins declared that men bought almanacs so as to profit by knowing in advance the state of the crops and the price of commodities. A later writer also noticed that 'the common people in reading ... almanacs are very cautelous in observing them'. In 1652 John Gaule observed that it was notorious that the people at large preferred 'to look into and commune of their almanacs, before the Bible'.[61] In March 1642, on the eve of the Civil War, a responsible observer reported from Westminster that 'the best sort even of Parliament men' were much agitated by some passages in John Booker's almanac which forecast 'that cruel and bloody counsels shall be put in execution the latter end of this month'.[62] Unusually dramatic testimony to the almanac's supposed influence was provided in 1666, when the *London Gazette* revealed

58. As is remarked by *Gilden, 1619. A new Almanacke and Prognostication,* sig. B2.
59. Allen, *The Star-Crossed Renaissance,* chap. 5; F. P. Wilson, 'Some English Mock-Prognostications', *The Library,* 4th ser., xix (1939).
60. J.M., *A Christian Almanacke* (1612), sig. A3.
61. F. Coxe, *A short treatise* [1561], sig. Avj; W. P(erkins), *Foure great lyers* [1585], sig. B2 (for authorship, see H. G. Dick in *The Library,* 4th ser., xix [1938–9]); Primrose, *Popular Errours,* p. 242; J. Gaule, *The Mag-Astro-Mancer, or the Magicall-Astrologicall Diviner posed, and puzzled* (1652), sig. A3.
62. D. Gardiner, *Historic Haven. The Story of Sandwich* (Derby, 1954), pp. 253–4.

that six ex-Parliamentary soldiers involved in a republican plot had chosen the third of September for their attempt, after consulting Lilly's almanac and making an astrological calculation.[63] As late as 1708 Jonathan Swift observed that many country gentlemen spent time 'poring in Partridge's almanac to find out the events of the year, at home and abroad; not daring to propose a hunting match till Gadbury or he have fixed the weather'.[64]

In addition to the routine prognostication attached to the almanac, there was a fugitive literature devoted to such unusual celestial occurrences as comets, eclipses and conjunctions of the major planets, all of which were thought to portend comparable upheavals upon earth. 'There was never any great change in the world,' wrote the Tudor mathematician Robert Recorde, 'neither translations of empires, neither scarce any fall of famous princes, no dearth and penury, no death and mortality, but God by the signs of heaven did premonish men thereof, to repent and beware betimes.'[65] The 'new star' which appeared in the constellation of Cassiopeia in 1572, the comet of 1577, the conjunctions of Jupiter and Saturn in 1583,[66] 1603 and 1623, the solar eclipse of 1652, the comet of 1680 – all excited extensive discussion and prognostication. Elizabeth I gained great prestige by manifesting her indifference to the comet of 1577. When her courtiers tried to deter her from looking at the dreaded object, she advanced boldly to the window, declaring *Iacta est alea* – 'The dice is thrown'.[67] James I was reported (after his death) to have summoned Cambridge mathematicians to explain the comet of 1618, and then prophesied both the Thirty Years War, and the fall of the Stuarts.[68]

The reaction which such heavenly portents could produce is well illustrated by 'Black Monday' – the solar eclipse of 29 March 1652. Over a quarter of the publications collected by the bookseller Thomason for the month of March related to the eclipse and its sig-

63. *The London Gazette*, 48 (26–30 April 1666). There is, however, nothing relevant in Lilly's almanac for that year.

64. *Predictions for the year 1708*.

65. (R. Recorde), *The Castle of Knowledge* (1556), sig. av. For general discussion see S. K. Heninger, Jr, *A Handbook of Renaissance Meteorology* (Durham, N. Carolina, 1960); Parr, *Tamburlaine's Malady*, pp. 74–9.

66. On which see M. E. Aston, 'The Fiery Trigon Conjunction: an Elizabethan Astrological Prediction', *Isis*, lxi (1970).

67. H. Howard, Earl of Northampton, *A Defensative against the Poyson of Supposed Prophecies* (1620), f. 77.

68. *The Most True and Wonderfull Relation of a Starre* (1658), pp. 2–3; retold in *The Worlds Wonder* (1659).

nificance.[69] Even the Lord Mayor and Aldermen of London heard a
sermon on the subject on the 28th.[70] The alarm among the people
was such, recalled John Evelyn, that 'hardly any would work, none
stir out of their houses, so ridiculously were they abused by knavish
and ignorant star-gazers'.[71] The rich loaded up their coaches and fled
from London, while mountebanks did a thriving trade in cordials
which purported to allay the effects of the eclipse. At Dalkeith the
poor were said to have thrown away their possessions, 'casting themselves on their backs, and their eyes towards heaven and praying
most passionately that Christ would let them see the sun again, and
save them'.[72] One contemporary diarist considered that the ultimate
effect of the eclipse was to discredit the prognosticators. No terrible
effects followed; indeed it seems to have been a fine day, 'so that the
astrologers lost their reputation exceedingly'.[73] But the forecasts of
the astrologers had been political. Lilly predicted the fall of Presbyterianism, the reform of the law and the setting up of a new representative. Culpepper forecast the onset of democracy and the Fifth
Monarchy. Other radicals predicted the fall of Rome and the universal end of monarchy.[74] They were probably aiming to counter the
original *Black Monday* tract, a veiled piece of Royalist propaganda
issued in December 1651. At a popular level the damage had been
done by anonymous pamphleteers predicting darkness, sudden death
and 'great madness, raging and terrifying thousands of the people'.
In the end the Council of State put out a paper explaining that
eclipses were natural events which could have no political effects.[75]

69. *Catalogue of the Pamphlets ... collected by George Thomason, 1640–
61*, ed. G. K. Fortescue (1908), i, pp. 863–6. Lilly estimated that the eclipse
provoked a total of twenty-four pamphlets (*Merlini Anglici Ephemeris* [1653],
sig. A2).

70. F. Bellers, *Jesus Christ the Mysticall or Gospell Sun ... or Eclipses
Spiritualized* (1652).   71 *Diary*, ed. E. S. de Beer (Oxford, 1955), iii, p. 63.

72. *On Bugbear Black-Monday, March 29 1652* (brs., BM. 669 f. 16 [42]); J.
G(adbury), *Philostragus Knavery epitomized* (1652), p. 14; Gataker, *His
Vindication of the Annotations*, p. 114; W. Lilly, *Merlini Anglici Ephemeris*
(1653), sigs. A2–A4. For other reverberations see T. F. Thiselton-Dyer, *Old
English Social Life* (1898), p. 372; *H.M.C., De Lisle and Dudley*, vi. p. 613.

73. 'The Diary of John Greene (1635–57),' *E.H.R.*, xliv (1929), p. 112.

74. W. Lilly, *Annus Tenebrosus* (1652), pp. 28, 54; N. Culpepper, *Catastrophe Magnatum* (1652); *The Levellers Almanack: for the Year of Wonders, 1652* (1651) (copy in Library of Christ Church, Oxford); S. Thurston, *Angelus Anglicanus* [1651]; N.R., *Strange Newes of the Sad Effects of
the Fatall Eclipse* (1652); *The Year of Wonders* (1652).

75. L.P., *The Shepherds Prognostication* (1652); ·F. A. Inderwick, *The
Interregnum* (1891), p. 132 (though I cannot trace his reference).

Printed publication was thus one of the main methods by which the astrologers made their impact upon the life and thought of the period. Some almanacs were so popular that they took on a life of their own and continued to appear long after the death of their original founders. The year 1655, for example, saw the publication of almanacs attributed to Allestree, Pond, Dade, Vaux and Woodhouse, all of whom were dead. But despite their enormous sales, the almanacs did not usually bring their authors much in the way of remuneration: Sir Thomas Overbury assumed in 1615 that an almanac-maker earned 40 shillings a year; and this was probably the normal rate in the seventeenth century.[76] But the almanac enabled the practising astrologer to draw attention to the facilities he had to offer by way of private consultation. For it was private practice which gave the professional astrologer his regular means of subsistence; and it was also the way in which he made his greatest impact upon the lives of other human beings.

3. *Astrological practitioners*

By the reign of Elizabeth I astrology had become, as one contemporary put it, 'a very handicraft, so that many lived thereby'.[77] Astrological practice was carried on by men (and in a few cases women) of very different degrees of learning and honesty. Sometimes it was only a sideline to some other occupation. In 1560 William Fulke thought that most astrologers were doctors.[78] Many physicians cast horoscopes in connection with their practice, and some gave astrological advice on non-medical matters as well. Astrological procedures were also advertised by village wizards who purported to be able to set figures for fortune-telling or the recovery of stolen goods. At the other end of the scale there were professionals, with extensive London practices, and high-class virtuosi, who cast horoscopes for themselves or their friends, out of curiosity or intellectual interest.

How long this situation had existed is hard to tell, for the origins of regular astrological practice in England are lost in obscurity. Astrological knowledge seems to have been a rare accomplishment in

76. Sir T. Overbury, 'An Almanack-maker', in *New and Choise Characters* (1615); (R. Braithwaite), *Whimzies: or, a new cast of Characters* (1631), p. 3; Blagden in *Studies in Bibliography*, xi (1958), p. 111.

77. Coxe, *A Short Treatise*, sig. Avj.

78. W. Fulke, *Antiprognosticon* (1560), sig. D7ᵛ. cf. J. Cotta, *The Infallible, True and Assured Witch* (1624), p. 75.

Anglo-Saxon England (although King Edwin of Northumbria is said to have had an *astrologus* called Pellitus who gave him advice on military matters).[79] It probably only became familiar in court circles with the scientific revival of the twelfth century and the diffusion of Arabic astrological writing. Previously there would have been few men capable of making the observations necessary to set a horoscope. Thereafter it was not uncommon for medieval kings to receive astrological advice or for interest to be aroused by some astrological prognostication. What was much less common was the existence of professional astrologers catering for a wide clientele. Astrology was primarily the concern of Court, nobility and Church. Peter of Blois in the twelfth century thought it worth issuing warnings against astrological consultations, but there is no apparent evidence for the existence in medieval England of anything like the consulting facilities which were available in some contemporary Mediterranean countries.[80]

The first unambiguous testimony to the existence of private astrological practice in England dates from the fifteenth century.[81] A lawsuit of 1505 reveals that the immediate reaction of a carrier, who had money stolen from his pack while lodging at an inn in St Ives, Huntingdonshire, was to look for an astrologer to help him identify the thief. He failed to find one among the clerks of Cambridge and was

79. W. Bonser, *The Medical Background of Anglo-Saxon England* (1963), pp. 155–6.

80. C. H. Haskins, *Studies in the History of Mediaeval Science* (Cambridge, Mass., 1924), p. 128; Kittredge, *Witchcraft*, p. 45. Geoffrey of Monmouth endowed many of the monarchs in his *Historia* with astrologers (J. S. P. Tatlock, *The Legendary History of Britain* [Berkeley and Los Angeles, 1950], p. 368), and a number of medieval English court astrologers are listed in the fifteenth-century compilation of Symon de Phares, *Receuil des plus célèbres astrologues et quelques hommes doctes*, ed. E. Wickersheimer (Paris, 1929), e.g., pp. 195, 231, 232–3, 240, 241–2, 244, 252, 261. There are various royal nativities in B.M., Royal MS 12 F XVII, ff. 153ᵛ, 180, and R. T. Gunther, *Early Science in Cambridge* (Oxford, 1937), p. 139. But there is nothing comparable to the record of Gherardo da Sabbionetta's astrological practice in Italy in the 1250s (see B. Concampagni in *Atti dell' Accademia Pontificia de' Nuovi Lincei*, i [1851], pp. 458–60).

81. The notebook of Richard Trewythian, who practised in London (1442–58), shows him to have answered horary questions for his clients; Sloane 428. For John Crophill, an Essex practitioner of astrological medicine, see E. W. Talbert, 'The Notebook of a Fifteenth-century Practicing Physician', *Studies in English* (Univ. of Texas), 1942. For others, see *The Paston Letters, AD 1422–1509*, ed. J. Gairdner (1904), ii, p. 147; Kittredge, *Witchcraft*, pp. 82, 227–8.

forced to go on to London to get a horoscope cast.[82] But he clearly assumed that facilities would be available. (The astrologer he found was described as a 'necromancer' and it may be that some of the 'necromancers' of the late Middle Ages had also operated by astrological means; it was common for them to be described as 'calculating' the whereabouts of lost goods.)[83] Yet sixteenth-century astrology still retained aristocratic associations. The most famous Elizabethan practitioner, John Dee, was no back-alley quack, but the confidant of the Queen and her ministers, though he also gave advice to humbler persons. As late as 1603, Sir Christopher Heydon, the astrological writer, declared that astrology had not 'much conversed at any time with the mean and vulgar sort, but . . . hath been ever most familiar with great personages, princes, kings and emperors'. But by this date there was a large, though indeterminate, number of low-level consultants scattered through the country, claiming to operate by astrological methods, and substantially patronized by a popular and unsophisticated clientele.[84]

In practice many of these were indistinguishable from the village wizards. Astrological treatises in English were uncommon before the mid seventeenth century, so it is doubtful if the learning of earlier would-be astrologers can have amounted to very much. Many, when apprehended by the authorities, proved to be utterly ignorant of the principles of the art which they claimed to practise. Others operated on the basis of a small collection of tattered magical recipes and astrological figures bequeathed by some earlier practitioner. Stephen Trefulacke, for example, who was imprisoned in 1591, proved to be carrying an extensive reference library: two Ephemerides, *Arcandam*, a translation of the *Judgment of Nativities* by the Frenchman, Ogier Ferrier, and a variety of such miscellaneous formulae as

figures to know how long one shall live and whether they shall obtain the treasures hoped for; figures to know things lost; a book of conjuration for divers things, . . . sundry conjurations of raising spirits and binding them and loosing them . . . figures to know whether a man be

82. *Select Cases in the Council of Henry VII*, ed. C. G. Bayne and W. H. Dunham (Selden Soc., 1958), pp. 151–69.

83. e.g., C. T. Martin in *Archaeologia*, lx (2) (1907), p. 372.

84. Sir C. Heydon, *A Defence of Iudiciall Astrologie* (Cambridge, 1603), sig. qq1. John Chamber, Heydon's literary antagonist, observed in 1604 that astrological questions were being posed daily throughout the land; Bodl., Savile MS 42, f. 112. For similar testimony, see *The Workes of . . . William Perkins* (Cambridge, 1616–18), iii, p. 471.

dead or alive or whether he has another wife; to obtain the love of any woman and other like matters.

This was an imposing if heterogeneous armoury.[85] By contrast, there were cheerful impostors who knew no astrology at all, like John Steward, an ex-schoolmaster, living at Knaresborough in 1510, and frequently consulted in cases of theft. He readily confessed that he tried to impress clients by pretending to consult a book of astronomy, but that in fact 'he could nothing do', although by good luck things did sometimes turn out as he predicted.[86] Astrology was similarly claimed as the basis of his procedures by Thomas Lufkyn, to whom women flocked in Maidstone in 1558, 'as it were to a God to know all secrets, past and to come'. He was in fact quite innocent of any astrological knowledge, despite his readiness to predict the number of husbands and children his clients would have, and to prophesy death in the coming month for others.[87] Even the notorious 'Doctor' John Lambe. Buckingham's confidant, when examined by the Royal College of Physicians in 1627 proved to be ignorant of the astrological science he professed.[88]

Pretenders of this sort continued to be common, even in the later seventeenth century, when the dissemination of astrological guides in English made it easy enough for those with only a modest education to take up the art. Elias Ashmole complained in 1652 that astrology was being debased by the existence of 'divers illiterate professors' who gave the subject an undeserved bad name;[89] and similar protests continued to be made by many serious practitioners. They had in mind such charlatans as the wandering fortune-teller who caused havoc in a Lincolnshire town in 1695 by informing some of his clients that they were in imminent danger of death, and assuring others that they were undoubtedly bewitched. His equipment comprised some mouldy old almanacs, astrological schemes, and a copy of Wingate's *Arithmetic*.[90]

85. P.R.O., SP 12/243, f. 354. For his trial, see Ewen, ii, p. 431.

86. J. Raine, in *Archaeol. Journ.*, xvi (1859), p. 80.

87. J. Halle, *An Historiall Expostulation*, ed. T. J. Pettigrew (Percy Soc., 1844), p. 9.

88. Sir G. Clark, *A History of the Royal College of Physicians* (Oxford, 1964–6), i, p. 259; Sir G. Keynes, *The Life of William Harvey* (Oxford, 1966), pp. 152–3.

89. E. Ashmole, *Theatrum Chemicum Britannicum* (1652), p. 453. cf. the comments by Worsop, *A Discoverie of Sundrie Errours*, sig. F4.

90. *The Diary of Abraham de la Pryme*, ed. C. Jackson (Surtees Soc., 1870), pp. 56–7.

But apart from the score or so of prominent practitioners who wrote books on the subject and conducted large-scale London practices, there were many provincial figures who were genuinely acquainted with the basic principles of judicial astrology. Edward Banbury, a Glastonbury apothecary, for example, was asked in 1653 to help in a case of stolen goods. He looked in a book, and wrote out a note, for which he charged two shillings. Accused before the quarter sessiōns of practising magic, he protested that he worked 'according to the rules of astrology and not by a diabolical art'. He may in fact have been a pupil of William Lilly. Not far away was Jasper Bale of Cheddon Fitzpaine, near Taunton, who also purported to find stolen goods by 'rules of astrology', though with a uniform lack of success.[91] Such people could be found in most parts of England. William Ramesey, physician to Charles II, thought there were astrologers 'in every town and country'.[92] There were after all several hundred almanac-makers in the seventeenth century and many of these were practising astrologers. But there must have been far more practitioners at a humbler level. So often it is only an accident which makes us aware of their existence at all. Edward Ashmore, for example, a Nottingham cordwainer in the 1680s, is only known because he happened to be involved in a Chancery suit, during which his astrological activities were exposed in an effort to discredit him as a witness. The resulting depositions reveal that Ashmore had given hundreds of consultations during the course of his career.[93]

The elite of the astrological profession, however, was to be found in London, and it was the mid seventeenth century which saw it at the peak of its influence. How far the activities of William Lilly and his associates constituted a genuine astrological revival, how far the Interregnum merely brought into the open what had long been practised underground, is difficult to determine. Lilly himself disparaged the achievements of his predecessors and was happy to see himself as the chief restorer of 'this art which was almost lost, not only here but almost all Europe over'.[94] Other contemporary testimony sup-

91. *Quarter Sessions Records for the County of Somerset*, iii (*Commonwealth, 1646–60*), ed. E. H. Bates Harbin (Somerset Rec. Soc., 1912), pp. lv–lvi, 331–2. A *Thomas* Banbury of Glastonbury was one of Lilly's west country disciples; Ashm. 423, f. 207.

92. W. Ramesey, *Some Physical Considerations of the Matter, Origination, and Severall Species of Wormes* (1668), p. 81.

93. F. J. Pope, ' "A Conjuror or Cunning Man" of the Seventeenth Century', *The British Archivist*, i (1914).

94. H. Warren, *Magick and Astrology vindicated* (1651), p. 16. cf. Ashm.

ports the view that astrology attained an unprecedented vogue during the Interregnum. Judicial astrology, thought Nathanael Homes in 1652, had been 'heeded more of late with us than ever was (to our shame let it be spoken) in any Christian Commonwealth since the Creation'. It was, agreed Thomas Gataker in the following year, 'a practice grown of late with us into great esteem'. And, looking back from the next century, Daniel Defoe asserted that in the years immediately before the Great Plague of 1665 'the people ... were more addicted to prophecies and astrological conjurations ... than ever they were before or since'.[95]

It is hard to assess such claims. Where earlier evidence survives, as in the elaborate case-books of the late Elizabethan astrologer Simon Forman,[96] it suggests that the demand for astrological advice was as great then as it ever was during the Interregnum. The literature of prognostication had an unbroken history throughout the sixteenth century, while the sales of the almanacs testify to the Tudor taste for astrological forecasts. But the mid seventeenth century saw a new departure in two respects: first, in the extensive publication of astrological handbooks in English, and second, in the publicity and relative freedom which the astrologers enjoyed. A formal Society of Astrologers was constituted, and is known to have had annual dinners in London most years between 1649 and 1658, and to have been temporarily revived in 1682. It appointed stewards, arranged an annual sermon, and banned the discussion of politics. In 1649 it had a membership of over forty. It thus constituted a notable would-be scientific organization, a full decade before the formation of the Royal Society.[97] The leading astrological masters had pupils who came to study with them, and admirers who corresponded from all parts of the country. Lilly, in particular, built up a large personal following. By 1647 he could claim to have 'made more scholars in this

423, ff. 168, 197; Lilly, *Autobiography*, p. 61; id., *Christian Astrology*, sig. B4ᵛ.

95. N. Homes, *Plain Dealing* (1652), p. 57; Gataker, *His Vindication of the Annotations*, p. 188; D. Defoe, *A Journal of the Plague Year* (New York, 1960), p. 29. cf. W. Ramesey, *Lux Veritatis* (1651), sig. A4.

96. Below, pp. 362–3.

97. Information relating to the Society may be found in Josten, *Ashmole*, Index, *s.v.*, 'Astrologers: Club'; W. Lilly, *Merlinus Anglicus* (1649), sig. B1; Ashm. 423, ff. 168–9. Sermons preached before it include R. Gell, *Stella Nova* (1649); id., *A Sermon touching God's Government* (1650); E. Reeve, *The New Jerusalem* (1652); J. Swan, *Signa Coeli* (1652); R. Carpenter, *Astrology proved harmless, useful, pious* (1657).

profession than all that profess this art in England'.[98] A list survives
of his west country 'scholars' and he had other admirers and disciples
in Cambridge, Lancashire, Northamptonshire, Norwich, Rutland
and Wiltshire, and many other parts of England. Clients and inquiries came to him from as far afield as Naples, Madrid and Barbados.[99] William Hills, a miller at Birden, Essex, confessed in 1651
to having helped people to recover stolen goods 'by the art of astrology which he learned of Mr Lilly'. Thirty years later Anne Kings-
bury told the Mayor of Bridgwater that it was Lilly who had taught
her to use divining rods to find treasure.[100]

Lilly was thus at the centre of the charmed circle of astrologers,
and it is fortunate that these are the members of the profession about
whom most evidence has survived. The nature of their business can
be broadly inferred from their published handbooks, which outline
the method of setting a horoscope and explain how to resolve the
type of questions most likely to be asked. But a much more revealing
source of information is to be found in the remarkable series of
case-books, subsequently acquired by the virtuoso Elias Ashmole,
and now part of his collection of books and manuscripts in the Bodleian Library. With the aid of these unique documents it is possible
to reconstruct in detail the working of a seventeenth-century astrological practice, and it is to them that we must now turn.

4. *In the consulting-room*

The astrologers whose activities are best illustrated by the Ashmolean manuscripts are Simon Forman, William Lilly and John
Booker, all of whom practised in London. There is also a long run
of case-books kept by Richard Napier, who as rector of Great Linford, Buckinghamshire, practised a combination of astrology and
medicine for over forty years until his death in 1634. Of the four the
earliest was Forman (1552–1611), a Wiltshireman who gave up
schoolmastering to practise medicine in London on and off from
1583 until his death. During his career he acquired a good deal of
notoriety as magician, alchemist and astrologer. He was persecuted
as an unlicensed practitioner by both Church and Royal College of
Physicians, and underwent several brief periods of imprisonment.

98. Lilly, *Christian Astrology*, sig. B2.
99. Ashm. 423, *passim*.
100. *H.M.C., 10th rept.*, appx., iv, p. 511; E. E. Trotman, in *Somerset and
Dorset Notes and Queries*, xxvii (1961), pp. 220–21.

His posthumous reputation took a further downward step in 1615, when the investigation into the poisoning of Sir Thomas Overbury revealed his association with the Countess of Essex and other court ladies. The brisk account of his secret life contained in his private papers shows that his sexual reputation was not unjustified (in the mid nineteenth century the Camden Society projected an edition of his personal diary, but according to the *Dictionary of National Biography*, 'the astrologer's frank confession of his immoral habits led the committee to cancel the publication after a few sheets had passed through the press'). Although the College of Physicians considered Forman to be ignorant of astrology, the University of Cambridge gave him a licence to practise medicine. His personal papers show him to have been a meticulous practitioner, who kept records of his cases in considerable detail.[101]

John Booker (1603–67) was a more respected figure. He was born in Manchester and had been both haberdasher's apprentice and writing-master before taking up astrology in 1630. He published almanacs from 1631 and the records of his extensive practice as an astrological consultant survive from 1648. During the Civil War he was appointed licenser of mathematical books, an ironical case of poacher turned gamekeeper, since he had himself been in trouble with the High Commission for putting out unlicensed almanacs during the previous decade. Booker's records are also meticulously kept, but in shorthand.[102]

Lilly (1602–81) had also come to London as a young man to make a career. His father was a poor Leicestershire yeoman and Lilly began as a domestic servant, but made good by marrying his master's widow. He learned astrology in seven or eight weeks in 1632 and began to practise seriously in 1641. His first almanac came out in 1644 and was followed by a spate of publications. He enjoyed a great deal of political influence and was the acknowledged leader of his profession. His case-books throw light upon his consulting-practice, but

101. *D.N.B.*; C. Goodall, *The Royal College of Physicians* (1684), pp. 337–9; *H.M.C. Hatfield*, xii, pp. 290, 551–3; J. Strype, *The Life and Acts of John Whitgift* (Oxford, 1822), ii, pp. 457–8; *A Companion to Arber*, ed. W. W. Greg (Oxford, 1967), pp. 146–7; A. L. Rowse, *The Elizabethan Renaissance* (1971), pp. 144–52. A somewhat bowdlerized edition of Forman's autobiography was privately published by J. O. Halliwell in 1849 as *The Autobiography and Personal Diary of Dr Simon Forman*.

102. *D.N.B.*; Josten, *Ashmole*, p. 21n; *C.S.P.D., 1634–5*, p. 378; I have not succeeded in adequately deciphering his shorthand.

he himself remains a devious character, and his *Autobiography* leaves many questions unanswered.[103]

All three sets of case-books contain the same type of material – astrological figures, accompanied, usually but not always, by the name or description of the client who had occasioned them, and the nature of his or her problem. The client normally consulted the astrologer in person, but sometimes might do so by letter or messenger. On receipt of the question the astrologer recorded the precise time at which it had been asked, drew up his horoscope, pondered over it and then announced his findings. The whole operation might take less than a quarter of an hour.[104] Unfortunately the notebooks usually leave us ignorant of what the client was ultimately told.

The immediate impression made by the notebooks is that of the enormous volume of business these men handled. Between 1597 and 1601 Forman set an average of over 1,000 figures a year, and the inquiries received from his patients were well in excess of this number. Lilly's case-books, which survive intermittently between 1644 and 1666, reveal a rapidly rising practice which, at its peak, was approaching 2,000 cases a year. John Booker, for whom the most complete records have survived, averaged roughly 1,000 cases a year from 1648 to 1665; he dealt with approximately 16,500 inquiries over the whole period.[105] When it is recalled that these four were not necessarily the busiest[106] of the 200 and upward astrologers who are known for certain to have flourished between the accession of Elizabeth I and the death of Anne, some impression can be gained of the remarkable extent to which the English people had recourse to astrological divination during the period.

The registers are too erratic to lend themselves to statistical summary, but they show the main types of cases with which the astrologers dealt. Like the wizards they offered a procedure for the recovery of lost property. Most of the clients under this heading seem to have been housewives in search of mislaid bits of crockery

103. The original text of the *Autobiography* is in Ashm. 421, ff. 178ᵛ–224. The run of Lilly's case-books in the Ashmolean MSS is not complete. One of the missing volumes was seen in a bookshop early this century; L. F. Salzman, *Mediaeval Byways* (1913), pp. 18–19.

104. Josten, *Ashmole*, p. 469, estimates that Ashmole took between seven and fifteen minutes.

105. Calculations based on the relevant case-books in Ashm.

106. Culpepper, for instance, who practised *c.* 1640–54, is said to have averaged forty clients in a morning; F. N. L. Poynter, 'Nicholas Culpeper and His Books', *Journ. of the Hist. of Medicine*, xvii (1962), p. 156.

and stolen washing, or servants from great households who came to inquire after missing silver or other valuables. In 1646–7, for example, Lilly was asked by various clients about plate lost in Gray's Inn; about £150 missing from a ship belonging to a Spanish merchant; about a robbery at a public house called the 'Cardinal Wolsey' and about £20 stolen from 'a fat woman in Southwark'.[107] When in the winter of 1569–70 the stationer William Bedo wanted to trace money which had been stolen from a friend's house in Kent, he inquired in Oxford for someone to help him, and was referred to John Bowckeley, scholar of New Inn, who cast an astrological figure for him, though without success.[108] At St John's College, Oxford, in the 1590's Robert Fludd was asked by his tutor to use astrology to find out who had robbed him. Similarly in 1637 John Rogers, an apothecary, had immediate recourse to a London astrologer when his copy of Gerard's *Herball* was stolen from his shop.[109] Usually the astrologer gave a physical description of the culprit rather than putting a name to him. The carrier who was robbed at an inn in St Ives in 1505 secured a description of the thief from a London astrologer, on the basis of which he arrested the innkeeper's son. Unfortunately he had omitted to check in advance whether the youth had the discoloured teeth mentioned in the description. When the boy was made to open his mouth, he revealed a set of impeccable molars, thus discomfiting the carrier and provoking a counter-action for unlawful arrest.[110]

To the problem of missing goods was allied that of missing persons. In an age of desperately slow communications there were many distraught wives who had had no news of their husbands after long absence on business or at sea. The astrologers specialized in locating the whereabouts of the missing persons and had rules to determine every conceivable detail relating to their health and general condition.[111] They catered for clients like Anna Overbury, who came in 1595 to Simon Forman about her husband, who had been at sea in a man-of-war for eighteen weeks, or Alice White of Grub Street, who

107. Ashm. 185, ff. 68ᵛ, 233, 236, 225ᵛ.
108. W. H. Hart, 'Observations on Some Documents relating to Magic in the Reign of Queen Elizabeth', *Archaeologia*, xl (1866), pp. 391–4.
109. F. A. Yates, *Theatre of the World* (1969), pp. 61–2; G. Le Neve, 'Vindicta Astrologiae Judiciariae' (Ashm. 418), p. 430.
110. *Select Cases in the Council of Henry VII*, ed. Bayne and Dunham, pp. 151–69. There is an account of the procedure followed in theft cases in Parr, *Tamburlaine's Malady*, chap. 11.
111. e.g., Forman's rules to know 'Whether the absent be dead or alive' and 'What state the absent is in' (Ashm. 240, ff. 1–7).

consulted another astrologer in 1617 'for the return of her husband, being 366 miles from London'.[112] Lilly's case-books are full of wives seeking to know whether their husbands are dead or alive; indeed it is hard to think of a source which gives a more vivid indication of the human suffering caused by the Civil War than do these neatly-kept registers. Long after the fighting had stopped the inquiries still kept coming in. When in July 1649 a baker's wife asked after her husband, who had gone to be a soldier in 1643, Lilly informed her that he had died five years previously.[113] Perhaps she was relieved by the news.

The naval adventures of the 1650s similarly took their toll in human anxiety. During a few weeks in the summer of 1645 Lilly was asked by one client whether her husband, a ship's carpenter captured by Prince Rupert, was still alive; by another what had happened to her spouse, a surgeon who had gone in the ship *Charity* to Virginia, and by a third about a trooper who had been sent to Ireland three years previously.[114] In the following year he was consulted by relatives of men serving in the fleets of Blake and Penn or trading in Spain at the time of the commercial embargo imposed by the Spanish government in retaliation for Cromwell's attack on the West Indies.[115]

The astrologers also gave advice to employers about runaway servants, and assisted such worried men as Thomas Pitches, under-keeper at the Ludgate gaol, who in 1640 had managed to lose a prisoner committed to his charge.[116] In 1528, when the Lutheran heretic, Thomas Garret, fled from Oxford to avoid arrest, the Warden of New College and the Bishop's Commissary employed an astrologer to work out the direction he had taken.[117] Similarly in 1652, when the Royalist, Lieutenant-General John Middleton, escaped from the Tower, it was not long before John Booker was dealing with an anxious inquiry as to his whereabouts.[118] Later in the century John Whalley, a Dublin astrologer, was asked by the authorities to work out where the Duke of Monmouth was hiding.[119]

Missing ships could also be located by astrological means. Many shipowners seem to have gone straight to the astrologer if their ves-

112. Ashm. 363, f. 252ᵛ; Ashm. 330, f. 152ᵛ.   113. Ashm. 210, f. 100.
114. Ashm. 427, ff. 21, 9ᵛ, 20.   115. Ashm. 427, ff. 98, 107ᵛ, 140, 141ᵛ, 162.
116. Ashm. 418, p. 449.
117. J. A. Froude, *History of England from the Fall of Wolsey to the Defeat of the Spanish Armada* (n.d.), i, pp. 539–41.
118. Ashm. 387, p. 320.   119. *D.N.B.*, 'Whalley, J.'

sels were unaccountably delayed. Indeed the seafaring community may have formed as much as a sixth of Lilly's clientele.[120] In the later Elizabethan period the great sea captain Sir William Monson did not hesitate to consult Simon Forman about the prospects for an impending voyage; and in 1603 Forman was asked by Mr Leate (probably the merchant Nicholas Leate) to determine whether or not there was a northern passage to Cathay. Forman's relationship with Monson was intimate, and involved frequent advice on legal and money matters; he was also consulted by Lady Monson during her husband's absence at sea.[121] In 1602 he was in Plymouth making calculations about the prospects for the Queen's ships.[122]

After Forman's day astrologers continued to deal with the otherwise intractable problem of missing ships. The notebooks of Lilly and his colleagues contain the names of scores of ships inquired after by their owners, or by relatives of the crew. The astrologers chose appropriate days for launching a ship or beginning a voyage, and gave advice to many sailors pondering the dangers of an ocean voyage to Barbados, Virginia or Morocco.[123] They offered reassurance to nervous passengers, worried about the risk of drowning, and to businessmen wondering whether to take shares out in a particular ship, or uneasy about the reasons for its delay. During the Civil War period, they dealt with questions about the risk of pirates or of interception by the enemy at sea.[124] At the end of the seventeenth century the inhabitants of Jamaica were said to be reluctant to go to sea without first consulting an astrologer; and even in the middle of the eighteenth century it was customary in North America for a horoscope to be cast to determine sailing-dates.[125]

120. See p. 379, note 192 below.
121. For Monson, see E. G. R. Taylor, 'Sir William Monson Consults the Stars', *The Mariner's Mirror*, xix (1933); Ashm. 226, ff. 103, 107. For Lady Monson, ibid., ff. 37, 233. For Leate, Ashm. 236, f. 1ᵛ; Ashm. 802, ff. 234 ff.; Ashm. 411, f. 148; Ashm. 219, ff. 5ᵛ, 16ᵛ, 20ᵛ, 31ᵛ, 71.
122. *H.M.C., Hatfield*, xii, p. 290.
123. e.g., R. Saunders, *Apollo Anglicus* (1656), sigs. C7ᵛ–8; id., *Palmistry* (1663), ii, pp. 159–60.
124. For examples of these various types of inquiry, see Ashm. 427, ff. 254ᵛ, 274; Ashm. 184, f. 9; Ashm. 420, f. 3; Ashm. 178, f. 41. For a naval officer's astrological explanation of the course of his ship's fortunes during the Second Dutch War see *Three Sea Journals of Stuart Times*, ed. B. S. Ingram (1936), pp. 27–87.
125. F. Crow, *The Vanity and Impiety of Judicial Astrology* (1690), sig. A2ᵛ; G. L. Kittredge, *The Old Farmer and his Almanack* (Boston, 1904), pp. 39–40.

A sceptic observed that, if the astrologers really knew so much about the fate of ships at sea, they could have made their fortunes by dabbling in marine insurance, and advising the insurers how to collect easy profits.[126] In fact astrologers *were* frequently consulted on insurance problems during these early days of marine insurance. Lilly's case-books contain several entries relating to clients who came to ask him whether or not to insure a ship.[127] Indeed he made advertising copy out of the fact that he had correctly confirmed the safety of a ship reported lost *en route* to Spain in 1644, even though the insurers were so convinced of its loss that they had refused to accept a premium of sixty per cent.[128] John Gadbury, in his elaborate guide to astrological lore for seamen, gave several examples of cases in which he claimed to have saved shipowners thousands of pounds in insurance premiums. He had also advised such well-known contemporary sea captains as Sir Frescheville Holles, and Owen Cox.[129]

On other business problems the astrologers were equally forthcoming. The prognostications in their almanacs were intended to predict 'every year what things shall be dear and what good cheap', as one guide put it.[130] In the sixteenth century the great Antwerp merchants had employed astrologers to forecast market fluctuations,[131] and in seventeenth-century England there were many businessmen who turned to them in an effort to reduce the uncertainties inherent in their occupation. There were inquiries about the advisability of buying houses, horses, ships, copyholds, and every other

126. J.S., *The Starr-prophet Anatomiz'd and Dissected* (1675), p. 6.

127. Ashm. 178, f. 74; Ashm. 427, ff. 84, 170, 221ᵛ; Ashm. 184, f. 65; Ashm. 420, ff. 297, 333.

128. Lilly, *Christian Astrology*, p. 162. At this time it was customary to take out marine insurance only when the ship was already overdue. See below, p. 780.

129. J. Gadbury, *Nauticum Astrologicum* (1691, but completed twelve years previously), pp. 95–6, 105. Cox was a client of Lilly and it was he who brought back from Sweden Charles X's gift to the astrologer of a gold chain; Lilly, *Autobiography*, p. 171; Ashm. 427, f. 59ᵛ.

130. *The Rules and ryght ample Documentes, touching the Use and Practise of the Common Almanackes*, trans. H. Baker [1558], sig. Giiiᵛ. Typical rules for such computations can be found in W. Ramesey, *Astrologia Restaurata* (1653), pp. 285–87; Ashm. 177, f. 130 (price of corn); Sloane 1312, f. 38 ('Questions of dearth and plenty'); Sloane 2535, f. 78 ('To know the price of wheat every year'); J. Middleton, *Practical Astrology* (1679), pp. 146 ff. (price of land).

131. R. Ehrenberg, *Capital and Finance in the Age of the Renaissance*, trans H. M. Lucas (1928), pp. 240–42.

commodity. Women asked how they should invest their annuities or whether to set up a shop. Margaret Crew in 1616 wanted 'to know what profit will come by twisting of silver'. A more ambitious speculator asked about the prospects of a project to transport men into Italy.[132] There was scarcely any form of business speculation upon which the astrologers were not asked to pronounce. When the great wood-carver, Grinling Gibbons, embarked in 1682 upon 'a concern of great consequence' which involved sending a factor overseas, he felt it necessary to seek Ashmole's astrological advice as to whether or not the venture was likely to be a success.[133]

When all went wrong the astrologer could conduct the inquest. Preserved in the case-books are many inquiries from victims of business failure, seeking an explanation 'An old man at Aldgate – what to do? – the cause of his not thriving?': this terse entry in Lilly's dossier for 1644–5 is typical of many.[134] One client wrote from Coggeshall in 1651 to ask John Booker if he could explain why he had lost £800 in trade in only four years. 'What have been the causes of this great decay?' he demanded. Had anyone spoiled his credit by malice: and (by the way) when would his father die, and to whom would his estate be left?[135]

In such ways an inquiry about the past subtly turned into speculation about the future. On a number of occasions Lilly was asked to predict the result of a particular legal action, presumably so that the client would know whether it was worth continuing to fight it.[136] One customer asked despairingly in September 1649 if he would 'ever have justice'.[137] Others showed anxiety about the plight of the condemned. One woman wanted to know if her husband would be executed for stealing thirty bullocks; another 'if her friend in Newgate should be hanged'.[138] In 1592 the suspected Catholic, Mrs Shelley, asked John Fletcher, the Cambridge astrologer, whether her condemned husband had a chance of escaping execution.[139] It was probably because so many of his clients were on the wrong side of the

132. Ashm. 330, f. 143ᵛ; Ashm. 185, f. 256. Similar inquiries in Ashm. 210, f. 111ᵛ; Ashm. 427, ff. 10ᵛ, 36ᵛ, 147, 149; Josten, *Ashmole*, p. 193; J. Russel, *Astrological Predictions* (1659), p. 15.

133. Josten, *Ashmole*, p. 1711.

134. Ashm. 184, f. 47. cf. Ashm. 420, ff. 96, 108ᵛ, 303ᵛ; Ashm. 210, f. 118.

135. Ashm. 225, f. 308.

136. e.g., Ashm. 210, f. 126ᵛ; Ashm. 427, ff. 83ᵛ, 162.

137. Ashm. 210, f. 135ᵛ.

138. Ashm. 427, ff. 122ᵛ, 121.

139. J. Venn, in *The Caian*, vi (1896), pp. 30–33.

law that Simon Forman devised rules to reveal 'whether a man's house hath been searched or not by officers'.[140] Pinned inside one of Booker's case-books is an illiterate missive from one Thomas Wilson:

Ser my desier is you would be pleased to anser me thes queareyes I am indetted and am in danger of aresting. My desier is to know wether the setey or the conterey will (be) best for me, if the setey whatt part thearof if the contery what partt therof, and whatt tim will be most dangeros unto me, and when best to agree with my creditores I pray doe youer best.[141]

Demands for fortune-telling, however, could come from a higher social level. Matthew Andrews asked Lilly in 1670 whether he should proceed to deal with Lord St Albans for the purchase of the Register's place in Chancery and a commissioner's place in the Navy.[142] Dr Thomas Wharton inquired of Ashmole in 1650 whether he would ever be elected a Fellow of the Royal College of Physicians.[143] Such questions throw light upon the querent's aspirations, though not all are as crude as that put to Forman by a gentlewoman in 1597, whose husband had gone to sea with the Earl of Essex and who 'demanded in his absence whether she should be a Lady or not'.[144] At times the astrologer may appear to have been little more than a high-grade tipster. Richard Napier was asked who would win the cup at Stamford races. John Booker was asked questions about the results of cock-fights. Lilly was invited in 1646 to pick out the winner of a horse-race from 'the chestnut, the dapple grey and the iron grey'. He tipped the chestnut.[145]

But not all inquiries were so frivolous. Throughout the period the astrologers were consulted on matters of high policy and asked to predict the outcome of important political events. Forman was asked

140. Ashm. 389, p. 134.
141. Ashm. 183, f. 305. cf. Ashm. 210, f. 133; Ashm. 420, p. 197.
142. Ashm. 240, f. 212. On Andrews, see Josten, *Ashmole*, p. 1181, n. 3.
143. Josten, *Ashmole*, p. 559.
144. Ashm. 354, f. 296. It was during Essex's lavish distribution of knighthoods (on which see L. Stone, *The Crisis of the Aristocracy, 1558–1641* [Oxford, 1965], pp. 72–3) that the astrological writer, Sir Christopher Heydon, obtained his title.
145. Ashm. 240, f. 135; Ashm. 386, pp. 123, 122; Ashm. 178, f. 93. John Vaux also gave racing tips (*Durham High Commission*, p. 37). In the mid sixteenth century Robert Allen had astrological rules for success at cards and dice (*Narratives of the Reformation*, ed. Nichols, pp. 326–7).

about such matters as the 1597 session of Parliament, the siege of Ostend, the Irish adventures of the Earl of Essex, and the search for Thomas Percy, one of the Gunpowder Plotters.[146] Ashmole was plied by Sir Robert Howard with questions about the likely course of relations between Charles II and the Cavalier Parliament. Howard was Secretary to the Treasury Commissioners between 1671 and 1673, and by all accounts a very bad one. It is touching that one of his questions was whether Parliament would 'proceed to the removing of great men who may appear not to have managed things or counsels so regularly and well as might be wished'.[147] More striking is the revelation that Ashmole was consulted by Charles II himself, who wanted astrological advice about his future relations with Parliament, and an astrologically propitious moment for delivering the speech which he made to Parliament on 27 October 1673.[148] When so skilful a politician as the King himself felt it worth seeking aid from such a quarter it is not surprising that so many lesser men did the same. Another notable consultation was that of Mrs Cellier, 'the Popish midwife', with John Gadbury, to determine whether Thomas Dangerfield would be a suitable accomplice in the so-called Meal Tub Plot of 1680 to murder Charles II.[149]

The case-books illustrate many problems of conduct and allegiance generated by the Civil War. Lilly was only once asked the most basic of contemporary questions – 'whether best to adhere to King or Parliament?'[150] – but he had plenty of clients seeking to know whether they should enlist and how they would be expected to fare if they did. 'If good for the son to go to war, and if return safe?' – Mr Whitby's question of March 1644 echoed the fears of many less courageous Parliamentary supporters. (A Roundhead himself, Lilly judged he would return safely, 'and with reputation').[151] There were

146. Ashm. 354, pp. 96, 256; Ashm. 219, f. 23; Ashm. 363, f. 241.

147. Josten, *Ashmole*, pp. 189–90, 1340–41. cf. S. B. Baxter, *The Development of the Treasury, 1660–1702* (1957), pp. 181, 258.

148. This was discovered by Dr. Josten (*Ashmole*, pp. 189, 1347–8, 1350–51, 1362), who has deciphered the shorthand in which many of Ashmole's jottings are concealed. The King may possibly have consulted Ashmole again in 1679 (ibid., p. 234). For his speech on 27 October 1673, see *The Parliamentary Diary of Sir Edward Dering, 1670–73*, ed. B. D. Henning (New Haven, 1940), p. 151.

149. *Mr Tho. Dangerfeilds Particular Narrative* (1679), pp. 25–6; J. Partridge, *Mene Tekel* (1688), p. 3 (2nd pagination).

150. Ashm. 184, f. 3.

151. Ashm. 184, f. 1ᵛ.

many clients like Captain Willoughby, who wanted to know whether he would prosper in the war, and Mr Robinson, who asked whether he would do better to seek civil or military preferment.[152] On the Royalist side was Lady Holborne, who asked Lilly in the autumn of 1645 whether her husband, Sir Robert, should make terms with Parliament.[153] But the most remarkable of all these appeals for advice was that of Richard Overton, one of the leaders of the Leveller party, who in April 1648 sent a note to Lilly asking 'whether, by joining with the agents of the private soldiery of the Army for the redemption of common right and freedom to the land and removal of oppressions from the people, my endeavours shall be prosperous or no'. Overton, a modern historian has remarked, was 'a rationalist over whom dogma had all but lost its hold'. There is no stronger testimony to the appeal of astrological advice in the mid seventeenth century than this request by one of the most sophisticated and 'rationalist' of contemporary political thinkers.[154]

In addition to helping with personal decisions, Lilly was also asked to resolve a variety of military and political issues. Would Basing-House be taken? When would Pontefract surrender? Was it true that the King had taken Cambridge? Would he bring troops over from Ireland?[155] In 1645 Lilly told Bulstrode Whitelocke that, if the Parliamentary forces could avoid a fight before the 11th of June, they would win their greatest victory. He was duly gratified by the result at Naseby on the 14th.[156] When the war was over Lilly set figures on the quarrel between Parliament and the Army, and was invited by Sir Thomas Myddleton of Chirk to calculate how long

152. Ashm. 184, f. 40; Ashm. 178, f. 163.

153. Ashm. 178, f. 24. Holborne's estate was sequestrated (*H.M.C.*, vi, p. 87), and on 3 Dec. 1646 he asked to compound (*Calendar of the Committee for Compounding*, ii, p. 1586).

154. Ashm. 420, attached to f. 267; P. Zagorin, *A History of Political Thought in the English Revolution* (1954), p. 21. Overton's uncertainty presumably arose from the decision of the Agitators at St Albans on 24 April, on the eve of the Second Civil War, to resume their demands for reform, even though the unity of the Army might be jeopardized as a result. See S. R. Gardiner, *History of the Great Civil War* (new edn, 1894), iv, pp. 116–17. The key to his interest in astrology may be the influence of Robert Fludd; S. Hutin, *Les Disciples anglais de Jacob Boehme aux XVIIe et XVIIIe siècles* (Paris, 1960), pp. 62, 215.

155. Ashm. 184, ff. 160, 62v; Lilly, *Christian Astrology*, pp. 199, 455–6.

156. (B. Whitelocke), *Memorials of the English Affairs* (1732), p. 144.

Presbyterianism might be expected to last.[157] The confiscations of the lands belonging to Crown, Church and Royalists are reflected in the many questions posed by speculators, anxious to know whether their purchases were a safe investment, or delinquents, still hoping to recover their property.[158] The Parliamentary Visitation of the University of Oxford led one hopeful aspirant to ask in February 1648, 'If purging of the University will succeed', and 'if the querent's son will come in [as a] Fellow'.[159] During the Commonwealth and Protectorate Lilly set figures on the outcome of Parliamentary elections and on the business before the Protector and his Council.[160] There was virtually no contemporary political problem which did not sooner or later turn up in his consulting-room.

But if one question stands out from all the others by the frequency with which it was asked, it is *'Quid agendum?'*, as Lilly used to note it down in his dog Latin – 'what is to be done?'. For it was the need to make decisions which brought men and women to the astrologer's studio. These decisions were as various as could be. Some related to the choice of a career, for, since the astrologers held that the time of a man's birth determined his general aptitudes, they felt well qualified to advise on this matter. Forman, for example, had a set of rules showing 'in what trade or science a man shall best ... live by'.[161] In 1664 John Cocke, a twenty-year-old student at the Middle Temple, presented Booker with a comprehensive questionnaire, ranging from the suitability of the Law as a career, to his prospects of marriage and future estate.[162] Richard Hunt wrote from Cambridge in 1649 to ask Lilly which subject he should read, Oriental Languages or Divinity.[163] Apprentices asked whether or not they should stay with their present masters.[164]

As might have been expected, there was an incessant stream of servant girls asking about their future husbands, or wanting to know how to handle their current boy-friends. 'If have the man now wooing? If not, what kind of man?' Or, as one maiden put it, 'Of two

157. Ashm. 420, f. 47; Ashm. 185, f. 211 (cf. Lilly, *Christian Astrology*, pp. 439–42); Lilly, *Autobiography*, p. 189.
158. Ashm. 210, ff. 101, 125ᵛ, 133, 148; Ashm. 420, f. 188; Ashm. 185, f. 69; Lilly, *Christian Astrology*, pp. 448–9.
159. Ashm. 420, f. 201ᵛ.
160. Ashm. 427, ff. 6ᵛ, 33, 36ᵛ.
161. Ashm. 389, p. 647.
162. Ashm. 180, f. 122 (the reply is at f. 125).
163. Ashm. 423, f. 165.
164. e.g., Ashm. 385, p. 128; Ashm. 178, f. 8.

propounded which to accept?[165] These enquiries to Lilly are typical
of hundreds. A female weaver wanted to know 'if her friend loved
her as he should love her'. Joan Jones of the Strand asked whether
John Fuller was likely to marry her. (It may have been the information that she was 'no maid' which led the astrologer to pronounce
that he would not. A similar entry is in Lilly's case-book for 1646:
'One got with child; if the man would marry her?') Another girl
asked Forman whether the man offering her marriage did so in good
faith.[166] There were sensitive clients, like the anonymous querent
who was worried whether a gentleman 'were vexed at receipt of a
letter', and lofty ones, like the lady who asked Lilly 'if good to marry
the little man'. It says something for the astrologer's common sense
that the answer to the latter was a firm negative.[167]

In addition to the plethora of maidservants asking if their masters
loved them, and widows wondering whether or not to remarry, there
were male clients with similar problems. For these Forman had
drawn up a comprehensive set of astrological rules. How rich was
the proposed bride? Was she really in love? Was she not really a
whore? Was the wife an adultress? Whatever the question, 'Oracle
Forman', as Ben Jonson called him, had an answer.[168] Delicate family
problems were meat and drink to the astrologers. They catered for
husbands worried about the legitimacy of their children, employers
like Napier's client who wanted to know 'whether his servant's child
were his' and the bastard who wanted Lilly to tell him who his
father was.[169] A lady who had quarrelled with her lover asked if he
would carry out his threat to publish her letters; a young gentleman
wanted to know 'if some gentlewoman intended not to put a trick
upon him'; a wife asked if she would 'have the better of her husband'; a maidservant inquired 'if her mother-in-law would do her
prejudice'; a young man sought to know 'what his father will do for
him'; a worried couple asked for the horoscope of their son, 'ever
running away from his parents'.[170] Sooner or later every kind of

165. Ashm. 185, ff. 173, 11ᵛ.
166. Ashm. 427, f. 45ᵛ; Ashm. 336, f. 135; Ashm. 178, f. 156; Ashm. 354,
p. 128.
167. Ashm. 185, ff. 6ᵛ, 234.
168. Ashm. 390, ff. 2–36ᵛ; B. Jonson, *The Devil is an Ass* (acted 1616),
II.iii.
169. Ashm. 390, ff. 161–5; Ashm. 182, f. 86; Ashm. 427, f. 201ᵛ.
170. Ashm. 178, ff. 143ᵛ, 125; Ashm. 184, f. 113ᵛ; Ashm. 185, f. 172;
Ashm. 330, f. 144ᵛ; Ashm. 210, f. 112ᵛ.

domestic entanglement was ventilated in the astrologer's consulting-room.

Particularly revealing was the frequent inquiry about the life-expectation of close relatives. In 1615 Mary Worship of Coleman Street made tactful inquiries of an astrologer about the size of her husband's estate,[171] and there were many of Lilly's female clients who wanted to know when they would enjoy their jointures. Astrologers, like cunning men, were often asked by husbands or wives whether they would outlive their partners. It was a stock question for Forman, and Lilly was presented with it on at least thirteen separate occasions in 1644–5.[172] In the *Character of a Quack Astrologer* (1673) a satirist spoke truly enough of how 'the young gallant bribes him with a guinea to know when his miserable father will have the civility to go to heaven'. Lilly advised his colleagues to be wary about prognosticating the exact time of anyone's death, explaining that he personally tried to avoid giving firm answers. The trouble was, he admitted, that there was a great demand for such information, since 'the knowledge hereof is of excellent use for such as would purchase any lease or office, or thing for life or lives'.[173]

The remaining major department of the astrologers' art was medicine. The thorough-going astrological doctor proceeded entirely by the stars and did not even demand to see the patient. Simon Forman, for example, assured the Royal College of Physicians in 1593 that he used no help to know diseases, other than an Ephemeris, and that by celestial signs, aspects and constellations he could tell at once what the cause of the illness might be.[174] Richard Napier was similarly said to treat his patients' illness as straight horary questions.[175] There was no false modesty about such practitioners. 'It hath been many times experimented and proved,' declared one textbook, 'that that

171. Ashm. 330, f. 130ᵛ.

172. A Weldon, *The Court and Character of King James* (1651), in *Secret History of the Court of James the First* (Edinburgh, 1811), i, p. 417: Ashm. 184, *passim*. Other examples in Ashm. 420, ff. 334, 336ᵛ; Ashm. 427, ff. 7, 110ᵛ, 194. Rules for the inquiry can be found in R. Ball, *Astrology Improv'd* (2nd edn, 1723), pp. 189, 191–2.

173. *Character of a Quack Astrologer* (1673), sig. C1ᵛ; Lilly, *Christian Astrology*, p. 132. But Richard Saunders claimed to have told people when they would die; *The Astrological Judgment and Practice of Physick* (1677), p. 79. cf. Russel, *Astrological Predictions*, p. 17 ('In questions of life and death I never speak positively').

174. *H.M.C.*, viii (I), p. 228.

175. Atwell, *An Apology*, pp. 26–7 (Atwell had been one of his patients).

which many physicians could not cure or remedy with their greatest and strongest medicines, the astronomer hath brought to pass with one simple herb, by observing the moving of the stars.'[176] These 'students of physic and astrology', as they liked to style themselves, 'piss-prophets' as their enemies preferred to call them, sometimes wrote quite elaborate treatises on the astrological diagnosis of disease.[177] But it is significant that Forman also made calculations to show 'what profit and commodity the physician shall have by the sick person, and whether the sick will pay him well or no'.[178]

The astrologers were further expected to diagnose pregnancy, estimate how the mother would fare when her labour started, and prognosticate the sex of the unborn child.[179] Their consulting-rooms were full of women made desperate by prolonged and unaccountable childlessness, in an age when childbearing was regarded as their prime social duty and when so much could depend upon inheritance and the perpetuation of the family line. Were they capable of having children, and, above all, would they have a son? This was the burden of numerous inquiries by well-to-do women, and it presented many problems. When Lady Ersfield came in December 1635 to ask Richard Napier whether she was pregnant, the answer seemed easy. 'With child, and did look it', he entered in his case-book. But a few weeks later she was back again, and this time there was a new diagnosis: 'Not with child; stomach ill; body swelled.' Another of Napier's patients had ceased to have her menstrual periods after an accident in a fire. Did this mean that she was now pregnant?[180] Lilly, who had devised astrological rules telling him 'how the mother shall do in travail', must have used them in December 1646 to answer a client who wanted to know if he would 'lose his wife in travail of childbirth'.[181] Even professional midwives had recourse to astrologers, though it is to be hoped that not many found themselves in the position of the midwife Mrs Nicholson, who rushed for an astrologer's aid in 1614 'on an accident happening to a gentlewoman'.[182]

176. J. Indagine, *Briefe Introductions ... unto the Art of Chiromancy, or Manuel Divination, and Phisiognomy*, trans. F. Withers (1575), sig. Jv.

177. e.g., Ashm. 355; Ashm. 1495, ff. 45–454.

178. Ashm. 389, p. 174.

179. This type of case constituted the bulk of the unidentified London astrologer's practice (1614–19) recorded in Ashm. 330.

180. Ashm. 340, ff. 151, 174; Ashm. 412, f. 296^v.

181. Ashm. 364, p. 55; Ashm., 185, f. 110.

182. Ashm. 330, f. 5^v.

The general impression given by the case-books is that Lilly dealt with his patients sensibly enough, and his remedies, so far as they are recorded, were not necessarily particularly astrological in character. He was prepared to prescribe medicine, and, on at least one occasion, chose to refer his client to a doctor. On another he was merely asked to recommend whether the patient should consult a young doctor or an old one.[183] But, like all the astrologers, he was prepared to admit the possibility of witchcraft and had rules to determine whether or not it was the cause of his patients' sufferings. Many suspicions of this kind came his way.[184]

The case-books also illustrate the contemporary fascination with hidden treasure. Forman, Napier, Culpepper, Gadbury and others drew up astrological rules for calculating the whereabouts of buried treasure.[185] Forman was asked in 1597 to determine whether there was treasure hidden in a house formerly inhabited by Sir Francis Drake.[186] Lilly's clients included 'two who digged for treasure'. His correspondence included a letter from Limerick, where in 1654 there was rumoured to be 'abundance of ... treasure', offering him fifty per cent of the proceeds if he could find it. Ashmole also set figures about hidden treasure; and as late as 1697 an astrologer was reported to have succeeded in finding treasure hidden by Jesuits at the Savoy.[187]

The astrologers were also consulted by seekers after the philosopher's stone. Forman ruled that 'the science of alchemy belongeth to the ninth house', and endeavoured by astrology and geomancy to divine both his own prospects and those of interested clients.[188] Lilly and Booker were occasionally asked to assess a client's chances of alchemical success. In his textbook Lilly reports having told a client that he would only ruin his health if he persisted in the quest, though

183. Ashm. 427, ff. 184, 160; Ashm. 185, f. 1.
184. For this see below, pp. 756–7.
185. Ashm. 392, ff. 1–39; Ashm. 205, ff. 124–35ᵛ; Ashm. 177, f. 160; Ashm. 175, f. 20; N. Culpepper, *Opus Astrologicum* (1654), sigs. F4ᵛ–F6ᵛ; J. Gadbury, *The Doctrine of Nativities* (1658), ii, pp. 260–2; J. Middleton, *Practical Astrology* (1679), pp. 157–61; H. Coley, *Clavis Astrologiae Elimata* (2nd edn, 1676), pp. 170–2; Ball, *Astrology Improv'd* (2nd edn), pp. 116–18, 272.
186. Ashm. 354, p. 280.
187. Ashm. 427, ff. 35, 64ᵛ, 69, 104ᵛ, 111ᵛ, 201; Ashm. 240, f. 119; Josten, *Ashmole*, pp. 55, 468; *The Portledge Papers*, ed. R. J. Kerr and I. C. Duncan (1928), p. 252.
188. Ashm. 354, pp. 176–7; Ashm. 219, ff. 30ᵛ, 122ᵛ.

he had every confidence that the philosopher's stone could be attained. 'But as it is a blessing beyond all blessings upon earth,' he wrote, 'I hold that it is given but to very few, and to those few rather by revelation of the good angels of God than the proper industry of man.'[189]

The incomplete nature of the annotations in the case-books makes it impossible to produce exact figures for each type of inquiry. Too many of Lilly's pages give an inadequate indication of the topic under investigation. Some are mere calculations without any word of explanation; others have only vague notes, usually in dog Latin, about the type of client or problem; *'Generosa de viro'* (a well-born lady about a man) or *'de servo'* (about a servant) are typical. But the main topics of inquiry are clear. Personal relationships, business and journey prospects, sickness, lost property, and missing persons account (roughly in that order) for the overwhelming bulk of the astrologer's business.

From this it may be inferred that there were two predicaments which most commonly drove the client to the astrologer. The first was the need for information which no other agency would provide – the whereabouts of some lost goods, a missing ship or an absent person; the diagnosis of a disease which ordinary doctors could not identify. The second was the need, not for information but for advice – although this need might well be disguised as a request for information. The very wording of their questions reveals the uncertainties in the clients' minds. 'What course to take?' 'To whom to apply?' 'If good to go on?' 'If good to be bound surety?' 'If have the better of her husband?' 'If she were well dealt with in her business?' 'If a trick was put upon her or no?' 'If suffer infamy from a friend?' 'If friend faithful in adversity?' These formulae all come from Lilly's case-book for 1644–5.[190] They show how his clients, by consulting the astrologer, hoped to lessen their own anxiety. They would leave it to Lilly to choose a propitious day for their undertakings and to diagnose the thoughts and motives of others. The astrologer's essential task was to help the client make up his own mind and to give him confidence in his relations with other people.

The clients themselves were drawn from every walk of life, though here again the lack of systematic recording in the notebooks makes

189. Ashm. 420, f. 25; Ashm. 427, f. 200; Ashm. 225, f. 328ᵛ; Lilly, *Christian Astrology*, pp. 442–4.
190. Ashm. 184, *passim.*

any statistical analysis misleading. The astrologers' enemies liked to dismiss their customers as 'the silly sort of ignorant and profane people',[191] and there is no denying that domestic servants, seamen and other members of the lower classes were prominent among Lilly's clientele. So were the many foreigners and rootless sojourners in the ever-growing metropolis. Over a third of Lilly's clients in one sample are simply labelled *ancilla* (female servant). But men and women were almost equally represented, and many customers were members of the nobility or persons of social distinction. The gentry and their wives may have formed over a sixth of Lilly's clientele.[192] He received encouragement from James, Lord Galloway, and gave advice to Lord Gerard (later Earl of Macclesfield), Lady Kensington, and a host of other aristocrats. On the eve of the Restoration he was consulted by Anthony Ashley Cooper, later first Earl of Shaftesbury, to whose astrological interests the historian Burnet makes an unfriendly reference.[193] Another client was Philip, fourth Earl of Pembroke, whose predecessor in the earldom died on the very day prognosticated by his astrologically-minded tutor.[194]

Forman also catered for the nobility. After Frances Pranell had made a clandestine marriage with Edward Seymour, Earl of Hertford, in 1600, it was to him that she went, to know whether she was

191. Gataker, *His Vindication of the Annotations*, p. 180.

192. Between June 1654 and September 1656 Lilly set 4,403 figures (Ashm. 427). In only 683 cases (i.e. about 15 per cent) did he record clear indications of the client's occupation or status. These were made up as follows

Gentry and above	124
Professional	36
Trades, crafts and other employments (59 different occupations)	128
Seafarers	104
Military	32
Female servants	254
Paupers	4

Of Booker's 2,003 clients in 1656–7, 990 can be identified as men and 957 as women (Ashm. 183).

193. Lilly's *Autobiography*, pp. 89–90; Ashm. 178, f. 185ᵛ; Ashm. 243, f. 198; *Bishop Burnet's History*, i, p. 164 (but cf. *H.M.C.*, Egmont, ii, pp. 508–9). Among his more persistent clients were Lady Slingsby, Lady Diana Porter (daughter of Lord Goring and wife of George, son of Endymion Porter), Lady Abergavenny and Lady Wildgoose (perhaps the wife of Sir Robert Wildgoose).

194. Ashm. 185, f. 18; Clarendon, *History of the Rebellion*, i, p. 73.

pregnant and, if not, when she would be.[195] Another of his clients was
the Countess of Essex, whose advisers included the woman astrologer, Anne Taylor of Southwark.[196] The notebook of Patrick Saunders,
another practitioner, shows that he dealt with a case of theft from
Sir John Underhill in 1629 and was consulted by Sir Walter Cope,
Master of the Court of Wards.[197] Nicholas Fiske cast a horoscope for
Sir Robert Holborne, Hampden's counsel in the Ship-Money case,
and subsequently Lilly's client and 'singular friend'.[198] Richard
Napier catered for many gentry and lesser nobility. John Booker
was consulted by Lord Berkeley, Earl Rivers, Sir Edward Harington,
and a number of titled ladies.[199] Another of his clients was Oliver
Cromwell's son-in-law, John Claypole.[200] Ashmole's clients, apart
from Charles II, Sir Robert Howard and Lord Treasurer Clifford,
included Martha Beale, the painter, Sir John Hoskins, President of
the Royal Society, and John Ogilby, the future translator of Homer
and Virgil (who asked for a propitious time to start learning
Greek).[201] Two other notables who appear to have furnished details
of their lives to astrologers were the demographer, Gregory King,
and the politician, Henry St John, Viscount Bolingbroke.[202]

Any astrological notebook is thus likely to contain the name of
some celebrated contemporary, and it is obvious that the financial
rewards of the successful practitioner could be considerable. Lilly
used to give medical advice to the poor for nothing, or for a shilling
to half a crown if they chose to offer it. But although he urged his

195. Ashm. 411, f. 161ᵛ; G. E. C(okayne), *The Complete Peerage*, ed.
V. Gibbs (1910–59), vi, p. 506.
196. *C.S.P.D., 1611–18*, p. 339.
197. Ashm. 419, ii, ff. 49, 19.
198. Ashm. 394, ff. 2 ff.; Josten, *Ashmole*, p. 471, n. 1; Ashm. 420, f. 304;
Lilly, *Autobiography*, p. 231; W. Lilly, *Monarchy or no Monarchy* (1651),
p. 49.
199. Ashm. 426, ff. 120, 133, 184; Ashm. 387, p. 432; Ashm. 385, ff. 37,
404, 465. For Napier's clients, see the names cited in the *Catalogue* of
Ashmolean MSS.
200. Ashm. 419, i, f. 144ᵛ; Ashm. 426, f. 295ᵛ (which gives his date of
birth as 21 Aug. 1625, a fact unrecorded in the *D.N.B.*).
201. Above, p. 371; Josten, *Ashmole*, pp. 188–9, 1296 (Clifford), 659
(Ogilby), 520 (Beale), 1477 (Hoskins). Clifford also consulted Gadbury and
took his horoscope seriously (Ashm. 179, 1; Evelyn, *Diary*, ed. de Beer, iv,
p. 22; C. H. Hartmann, *Clifford of the Cabal* [1937], pp. 9 n., 305–7), though,
like many others, he affected to despise astrology (Hartmann, op. cit., pp.
301–2).
202. B.M., Add. MS 27,986, f. 27*; Egerton MS 2378, f. 37ᵛ.

colleagues to 'give freely to the poor, both money and judgement', he frankly admitted that he set up practice in London because he saw 'there was money to be got'.[203] For routine astrological consultations half a crown was probably his standard charge.[204] But he got much more for providing confidential advice to high ranking politicians. In 1647 he received twenty pieces of gold for recommending to a Royalist intermediary that Charles I should make for Essex if he succeeded in escaping frcm Hampton Court. In 1649 he entered the employment of the Commonwealth Council of State, at the rate of £50 down, and an annual pension of £100.[205] He also earned money from pupils. In 1640 John Humphrey paid him £40 for tuition and would gladly have given him £200 for some additional secrets, which the master, however, preferred to keep to himself.[206] A growing practice and a voluminous range of publications gave him a respectable competence. In 1662 he was said to have been earning £500 a year.[207] Some of his colleagues also did well. Simon Forman left £1,200 and Richard Delahay £2,000 to £3,000. John Partridge was worth over £2,000 at his death.[208] Another successful astrologer was John Case, who hung out as his sign the doggerel verse

Within this place
Lives Dr Case.

'He is said to have got more by this distich,' remarked Addison, 'than Mr Dryden did by all his works.'[209] On the other hand William Poole, Nicholas Fiske and William Ramesey all died extremely poor, while John Dee was in his later days forced to sell books to pay for his meals.[210] Astrological fees fluctuated with the standing of the astrologer and the resources of the client. Booker usually expected

203. Lilly, *Autobiography*, pp. 241–2; Lilly, *Christian Astrology*, sig. B1.

204. Ashm. 185, f. 146; Lilly, *Autobiography*, p. 168.

205. Lilly, *Autobiography*, pp. 140, 145 (and below, p. 442). The pension, which was only paid for two years, was for providing foreign intelligence.

206. Lilly, *Autobiography*, pp. 85–6. cf. ibid., p. 231.

207. J. Heydon, *The Harmony of the World* (1662), sig. c6. Other information in *The late Storie of Mr William Lilly* (1648), p. 6; C. Blagden, in *Studies in Bibliography*, xi (1958), p. 111. Anthony Wood estimated Lilly's income from his practice at £200 p.a.; Wood, *Life and Times*, ii, p. 543.

208. Lilly, *Autobiography*, pp. 44, 68; *D.N.B.*, 'Partridge, John'. cf. *London Inhabitants within the Walls* (London Record Soc., 1966), p. 224.

209. *Tatler*, no. 240 (21 Oct. 1710).

210. Lilly, *Autobiography*, pp. 68, 75, 227; J. Gadbury, *Ephemeris* (1697), sig. A7; (J. Younge), *Sidrophel Vapulans* (1699), p. 31.

to be paid at least 2s. 6d.,[211] while Nicholas Fiske was said to have got £100 for casting the nativity of Sir Robert Holborne.[212] Probably a typical scale of early seventeenth-century charges was that of John Vaux, the clerk of St Helen's, Auckland, who used to sell his almanacs at the communion-table. For finding a stolen mare he charged 1s; for a horse and mare, 4s., plus 8d. in drink; for other stolen goods 5s. – the same, he commented, 'as ... was due to any lawyer for his fee'.[213]

Enough has been said to demonstrate that, until at least the later seventeenth century, a cross-section of the English people took the astrologers very seriously. Their almanacs and prognostications were snapped up as soon as they appeared, while their consulting-rooms can seldom have been empty. Some contemporaries attributed their success to 'the blockish stupidity of many of our ignorant country people',[214] but the astrological practices for which most evidence has survived were metropolitan in character. The clients who flocked to Forman, Lilly and Booker included aristocrats, merchants and persons of oustanding intellectual and artistic distinction. The problem now is to explain why this was so.

211. Ashm. 225, f. 295.
212. J. Gadbury, *Collectio Geniturarum* (1662), p. 124.
213. *Durham High Commission*, pp. 34–40.
214. J. Hart, *The Diet of the Diseased* (1633), p. 22.

11.

ASTROLOGY:
ITS SOCIAL AND INTELLECTUAL ROLE

The true use of Astrology consisteth in these ten following: first, it sheweth us the causes of the admirable dissimilitude, not only as concerning regions, but touching the wits of men and their manners, under diverse climates. Secondly, it remonstrateth what is the cause, that so great diversity ariseth. Thirdly, what destinies or events at certain times are like to fall upon countries, being called Judicial Astrology. Fourthly, it foretelleth the variable state of the air, and other elements at every moment. Fifthly, it telleth us the happy or unhappy increase of fruits, be it corn, wine, oil, or whatsoever else the earth bringeth forth: which was experimented by Thales; who, foreknowing a dearth to come, kept in his fruits, and sold them at an high rate. Sixthly, wars, famine, unusual drought, inundations, death of cattle, changes of kingdoms, destruction of princes, and so forth. Seventhly, what times are fit to sow, plant, or to do any other thing appertaining to the art of husbandry. Eighthly, it giveth much light to those who profess physic, take upon them to be pilots, discoverers of countries and kingdoms, or will gain them any knowledge in the art apodemical. Ninthly, from this science are made prognostications and ephemerides, needful for all sorts of men. Last of all, it sheweth us the temperature of all kind of individuous, all kind of hourly, daily, weekly, monthly, yearly dispositures, alterations and inclinations.

William Ingpen,
The Secrets of Numbers (1624), pp. 68–9

Now something was done but nothing to what I pretended; however, monies I gained.

Laurence Clarkson on his career as
a practising astrologer
(*The Lost Sheep Found* [1660], p. 32)

1. *Aspirations*

NOTHING did more to make astrology seductive than the ambitious scale of its intellectual pretensions. It offered a systematic scheme of explanation for all the vagaries of human and natural behaviour, and there was in principle no question which it could not answer. 'Who that knew well astronomy,' wrote a medieval authority, 'there is nothing in the world of which he could enquire by reason but he should have knowledge thereof.'¹ Every earthly occurrence was capable of astrological explanation. As Lilly pointed out in his *Christian Astrology* (1647), there was 'nothing appertaining to the life of man in this world which in one way or another hath not relation to one of the twelve houses of heaven'.² It was this comprehensiveness which made the art so compelling. In the absence of any rival system of scientific explanation, and in particular of the social sciences – sociology, social anthropology, social psychology – there was no other existing body of thought, religion apart, which even began to offer so all-embracing an explanation for the baffling variousness of human affairs. Nor had the sciences of medicine, biology and meteorology developed enough to offer a convincing and complete understanding of the world of nature. This was the intellectual vacuum which astrology moved in to fill, bringing with it the earliest attempts at a universal natural law. For a long time the alternative was stark; either one accepted astrological teachings, or, as John Gadbury put it in 1674, one had to admit one's ignorance of the true causes of events, and 'be content to rank them among the occult qualities of nature of which no certain reason can be given'.³

As a starting-point, the astrologers set out to explain why it was that individual human being differed from each other. It was the influence of the heavens at the moment of birth which accounted for men's physical characteristics, aptitudes and temperament. Not that other factors were irrelevant. The astrologers would not have agreed with George Herbert that the manners of infants were 'moulded more by the example of parents than by stars at their nativities',⁴ but they did recognize that heredity, environment and education all played their part in the formation of character. The nativity, however, was the basic determinant. Not only did it explain human differences; it also helped to provide a useful vocabulary with which to describe them. Astrology, it has been justly said, was the 'first known attempt at a complete system of human typology'.⁵ So persuasive and plausible was it that such astrologically-derived epithets

1. *Caxton's Mirrour of the World*, ed. O. H. Prior (E.E.T.S., 1913), p. 160.
2. Lilly, *Christian Astrology*, p. 50.
3. J. Gadbury, *Ephemeris* (1674), sig. A5ᵛ.
4. *Jacula Prudentum* (1640), in *The Remains of ... George Herbert* (1836), p. 184.
5. L. MacNeice, *Astrology* (1964), p. 258.

as 'jovial', 'mercurial', and 'saturnine' have retained a permanent place in our language.

The disadvantage of the system was its rigidity. Since there was a limited number of planets, houses and signs of the zodiac, the astrologers tended to reduce human potentialities to a set of fixed types and to postulate only a limited number of possible variations. Its more intelligent adherents were well aware of this danger and attempted to devise a more refined technique. John Aubrey, for example, was convinced that 'we are governed by the planets, as the wheels and weights move the hands of a clock', but he fully appreciated the infinite vagaries of human personality, and the need for an astrological vocabulary which would do them justice. Accordingly, when gathering the biographical data which were to become famous as the *Brief Lives,* he was careful, as befitted a Fellow of the Royal Society, to note the exact nativity of his subjects whenever it could be discovered; in this way he hoped to make possible a scientific comparison of the course of human life with the astrological circumstances of its inception, and thus to arrive at a more exact astrology.[6] As the Baconian Joshua Childrey observed, 'the way to go forward in this excellent art is to look back and compare the accidents of men and states with the influences of heaven, and this will not only try the truth of the old principles, but add new ones: such (it is very likely) as the sons of art do not yet dream of'.[7]

From the differences between human beings, the astrologer moved on to the wider issues presented by the course of history. The political history of a nation could to some extent be explained in terms of the individual psychology of its rulers. In an age of near-absolute monarchy the attention paid to the horoscopes of royal princes was fully justified. William Camden suggested that astrological factors explained Queen Elizabeth I's infatuation with the Earl of Leicester.[8] John Gadbury asserted that the whole career of Charles I was

6. Bodl., Wood MS F 39, f. 206; J. Aubrey, *Brief Lives,* ed. A. Clark (Oxford, 1898), i, p. 9. Aubrey included much unpublished astrological detail in his *Collectio Geniturarum* (1677) (Bodl., Aubrey MS 23), and was closely in touch with the astrologer, Henry Coley (ibid., ff. 4, 7, 104–7, 110, ff.).

7. J. Childrey, *Britannia Baconica* (1661), sig. B6.

8. W. Camden, *The History of the most renowned and victorious Princess Elizabeth* (3rd edn, 1675), p. 419. For Camden's favourable opinion of astrology see T. Smith, *V.Cl. Gulielmi Camdeni, et illustrium virorum ad G. Camdenum Epistolae* (1691), p. 130. These passages are cited by F. S. Fussner,

implicit in the astrological circumstances of his nativity.[9] Others declared that Gustavus Adolphus of Sweden would never have been killed at Lützen had he not chosen an astrologically unpropitious moment for the battle.[10] The movement of the planets could account for every type of historical occurrence. Jerome Cardan attributed Henry VIII's breach with Rome to the conjunction of Mars, Mercury and Jupiter in Aries in 1533.[11] Henry Coley observed that 'Harvey found out the circulation of the blood upon a conjunction of Saturn and Jupiter in the fiery trigon'.[12] William Lilly offered an interpretation of the whole of sixteenth-century English history based on contemporary planetary movements. This was an extension of the common practice of linking the deaths of kings and great persons to the chronology of comet appearances.[13]

Such exercises in astrological history may strike us today as fundamentally unrewarding, but their intellectual importance was considerable. During the Italian Renaissance astrological doctrines about the recurrence of planetary conjunctions and their influence upon the course of affairs had helped to form the concept of a historical 'period'. The lesser conjunctions (every twenty years), the middling conjunctions (every 240 years) and the great conjunctions (every 960 years) gave unity to segments of the otherwise infinite and indistinguishable flow of human events.[14] Such astrological doctrines influenced English historiography during the sixteenth and seventeenth centuries. The historical speculations of men like Lilly

---

The Historical Revolution (1962), p. 243, n. 2, and seem to support the interpretation he places upon them. Camden also attributed the Oswestry fires of 1542 and 1567 to eclipses of the Sun in Aries (*Britannia,* ed. R. Gough [2nd edn, 1806], iii, p. 8) and blamed the sweating sicknesses of 1485, 1518 and 1551 upon conjunctions or oppositions of the superior planets (ibid., p. 7). As a young man he had spent much time working on astrological problems; F. J. Levy, *Tudor Historical Thought* (San Marino, Calif., 1967), p. 5. cf. *Original Letters of Eminent Literary Men.,* ed. Sir H. Ellis (Camden Soc., 1843), p. 128.

9. J. Gadbury, *The Nativity of the late King Charls* (1659), sig. A4.

10. R. Saunders, *Palmistry* (1663), ii, pp. 18–21.

11. D. C. Allen, *Doubt's Boundless Sea* (Baltimore, 1964), pp. 50–51.

12. Sloane 2281, f. 57ᵛ.

13. W. Lilly, *Englands Propheticall Merline* (1644), pp. 10–20. cf. J. Gadbury, *De Cometis* (1665), pp. 38–44. For studies by Bodin and his imitators of the link between eclipses and political change, see F. E. Manuel, *Shapes of Philosophical History* (1965), pp. 61–62.

14. N. Rubinstein in *Fritz Saxl. A Memorial Volume,* ed. D. J. Gordon (1957), p. 179; Thorndike, *Magic and Science,* i, p. 648.

and Gadbury were usually outside the main stream of contemporary historical writing, but the currents sometimes converged. Sir Isaac Newton's well-known attempt to use astronomical data to reconstruct the otherwise lost chronology of the ancient world (*The Chronology of Ancient Kingdoms amended* [1728]), was the product of an intellectual *milieu* in which a relationship between the history of stars and of nations had long been assumed.[15]

Like the ancient climatic theory, which attributed differences between nations to their geography, astrological speculation was an attempt to explain the otherwise inexplicable. Its great merit, thought John Booker, was that 'it can yield reasons which other arts cannot', such as the answer to the problem of 'why customs, rites, manners, laws and temperaments be divers [i.e. different] in people inhabiting in several climates'.[16] As Auguste Comte was to recognize,[17] the astrologers were pioneering a genuine system of historical explanation. In their confident assumption that the principles underlying the development of human society were capable of human explanation, we can detect the germ of modern sociology.

If any one attitude united the astrologers of the seventeenth century it was an overwhelming intellectual curiosity – a desire to reduce things to order, and a conviction that they had the tools with which to do so. It is exemplified in *Astro-Meteorologica* (1686), the *magnum opus* of John Goad, the crypto-Catholic headmaster of Merchant Taylors' School. This bulky treatise, dedicated to James II, was an elaborate attempt to ascertain the influence of the planets upon the weather, and upon human epidemics and misfortunes. It was based upon a diary of relevant occurrences kept by the author for some thirty years, and augmented by other records of events in England and abroad from the year 1500. It aimed to further knowledge by discovering a coincidence in time between particular happenings and certain planetary dispositions. Goad's book was published, ironically enough, in the year in which Newton's *Principia* was presented to the Royal Society, and it would be easy for us to dismiss it as the jetsam of an obsolescent system of thought. Yet anyone who reads this forgotten work cannot fail to be impressed by its conscientious and empirical approach, and its occasional flashes of

15. As is pointed out by F. E. Manuel, *Isaac Newton, Historian* (Cambridge, 1963), pp. 68–70, 274.

16. J. Booker, *A Bloody Irish Almanack* (1646), p. 47.

17. W. E. H. Lecky, *History of the Rise and Influence of the Spirit of Rationalism in Europe* (1910), i, p. 277.

genuine prescience. Goad, for example, must have been one of the earliest writers to notice that suicide rates vary according to the time of the year. He explained this by invoking the conjunction of Saturn and Jupiter, a solution which must strike us as absurd; but it must be remembered that modern investigators have also been better at noticing variations in suicide rates than at explaining them.[18] What is impressive is Goad's pioneering readiness to find patterns in what had always been thought of as random behaviour.

It was this willingness of the astrologers to proffer an answer when no other explanation was forthcoming which helps to account for their popular appeal. In 1664 Francis Bernard wrote to Lilly, outlining a new theory about the causes of the many contemporary outbreaks of fire. He had, he explained, long entertained the hypothesis that horoscopes could be cast for cities, just as for men. The difficulty hitherto had been that, whereas the exact moment of a man's birth could usually be ascertained, it was virtually impossible to identify the nativity of a town, 'most cities having increased insensibly and the dates of their first rising being either disputed or forgotten'. But Bernard had hit upon a substitute method. This was to treat fires as if they were analogous to fevers in men. A city's nativity could then be reconstructed from its 'accidents'. By ascertaining the astrological circumstances of London fires, from the burning of London Bridge in 1212 onwards, Bernard had convinced himself that he had hit upon London's horoscope, and to his great delight was now frequently able to predict the exact weeks in which future London fires could be expected. Encouraged by his success for London, he proposed to do the same for Amsterdam. 'Time only will show us whether we may direct the fate of cities as of men.'[19]

The absence of any alternative also left the way open for an astrological explanation of plague. As Gadbury rightly claimed, 'no other art, whatsoever, is capable of predictions of this kind'.[20] An astrological interpretation had been the one most favoured by intellectuals at the time of the Black Death,[21] and it remained widely

18. J. Goad, *Astro-Meteorologica, or Aphorisms and Discourses of the Bodies Coelestial* (1686), pp. 506–7. cf. A. Leffingwell, *Illegitimacy, and the Influence of Seasons upon Conduct* (2nd edn, 1892), pp. 92–8.

19. Ashm. 242, ff. 83–4, 75, 85. Bernard has other notes on the subject in Sloane 1707, ff. 35–8. For other examples of the calculation of horoscopes for cities, see J. Gadbury, *Cardines Coeli* (1684), pp. 45–50.

20. J. Gadbury, *London's Deliverance predicted* (1665), p. 40.

21. Thorndike, *Magic and Science*, iii, chaps 20 and 21.

current until the epidemics ceased in the later seventeenth century. It fitted in well with the fashionable miasma theory, for the changing state of the heavens offered a plausible explanation for the putre-faction of the air: when the stars brought heat and moisture it was natural that decay should set in.[22]

The theory was tested in a way which was by no means unscien-tific. The astrologers listed all the great plagues of the past. They compared them with what was known about the positions of the heavenly bodies at the time, and they arrived at a correlation between the two.[23] Thereafter they felt able to predict both the incidence and the duration of any serious outbreak. Forman had rules to forecast the weekly number of deaths.[24] Gadbury boasted that the Great Plague of 1665 had been foretold both by himself and by four of his colleagues.[25] Astrologers could thus refute the notion that plagues re-curred every twenty years,[26] or the theory, made plausible by the great plagues of 1603 and 1625, that the cause of the epidemics was the death of the reigning monarch.[27] Other sicknesses were also ac-counted for astrologically. John Caius invoked planetary conjunc-tions as a partial explanation for the 'sweat'.[28] John Goad did the same in 1679 in a letter to Ashmole 'concerning our coughs, and the increase of the Mortality Bill'. Such events, he declared, could not be understood 'without the astrologer, who gives the wonderful cause of the inequalities of the air, and the strange secret powers of planets'. He recalled how in 1675 Charles II had asked him what the cause of the coughs might be. 'I knew not then,' he confessed, 'but now I think . . .'[29]

22. For examples of such arguments: T.S., *Sermons, Meditations, and Prayers upon the Plague* (1637), pp. 157–8; S. Bradwell, *Physick for the Sickness, commonly called the Plague* (1636), p. 3; G. Thomson, *Loimologia* (1665), pp. 4–5; N. Hodges, *Loimologia* (1720), pp. 3–4. Edward Gresham wrote a treatise in 1603 to allay the rúmour of a falling planet, which 'even . . . the better sort' feared would increase the plague (Ashm. 192, ii, f. 1).

23. Gadbury, *London's Deliverance predicted*, pp. 6–8, is a good example of this procedure.

24. Ashm. 384, f. 30. cf. his treatise on the plague of 1607 in Ashm. 1436.

25. *London's Deliverance predicted*, pp. 34–5; *The Prophecies and Predic-tions, for London's Deliverance* (1665), p. 6.

26. For this idea, see T.S., *Sermons*, p. 157, and Hodges, *Loimologia*, p. 3.

27. For this theory: J. Brayne, *The New Earth* (1653), pp. 52–3; W. Lilly, *Merlini Anglici Ephemeris* (1658), sig. B3ᵛ; J. Graunt, *Natural and Political Observations* (3rd edn, 1665), pp. 79–80.

28. R. S. Roberts in *Medical History*, ix (1965), p. 386.

29. Ashm. 368, f. 62.

It is not necessary to follow Goad along the path taken by his *esprit d'escalier* to see how sheer intellectual pleasure was the driving-force behind such efforts. 'The world understands not how noble our contemplation is,' he wrote, 'and what satisfaction we take when we see the heavens obey our prediction.'[30] It is no coincidence that a high proportion of the pamphlets attacking astrology were by authors who had themselves been temporarily enmeshed in its spells.[31] But the trouble was that the subject was ill-fitted to become a real experimental science. The careful correlation of past events with the movement of the heavens was the key to the whole endeavour, but life moved too slowly for quick results. If the great conjunction of Saturn and Jupiter only occurred once every 800 years, observed John Selden, it was going to be difficult to verify or refute any theories relating to it.[32]

Such obstacles notwithstanding, the astrological explanation of personal misfortune seems to have appealed to clients. When William Bredon's two daughters died in successive months, their bereaved father wrote to Richard Napier to discuss 'the astrological cause' for the tragedy.[33] Many of the clients who entered an astrologer's consulting-room were seeking an explanation for the sundry misfortunes which had beset them – illness, sterility, miscarriage, political failure, bankruptcy. No doubt it was more comforting to learn that one had been crossed at birth than to be told that one had no one to blame for one's misfortunes but oneself. John Aubrey was able to console himself for his sundry worldly failures with Henry Coley's opinion that he had since birth been 'labouring under a crowd of ill directions'.[34] The Elizabethan herald and historian, Francis Thynne, wrote to Burghley in 1588 attributing his lack of of worldly success to the froward influence of the heavenly

30. Ashm. 368, f. 304.
31. For example, William Fulke (*Antiprognosticon* [1560], sig. Dvii^v); W[illiam] P[erkins] (*Foure Great Lyers* [1585], sig. B1); Francis Coxe (D. C. Allen, *The Star-Crossed Renaissance* [Durham, N. Carolina, 1941], p. 112); John Raunce (*Astrologia Accusata* [1650], sig. A2); John Brayne (*Astrologie proved to be the Old Doctrine of Demons* [1653], p 1); John Allen (*Judicial Astrologers totally routed* [1659]), sig. A2^v).
32. *Table-Talk* (Temple Classics, n.d.), p. 33. He develops the point in *God made Man* (1661), pp. 49–51.
33. Ashm. 240, f. 97. For other fathers who sought astrological reasons for their children's death see R. Kirby and J. Bishop, *The Marrow of Astrology* (1687), ii, pp. 69–70, 72–3.
34. Aubrey, *Brief Lives*, ed. Clark, i, p. 35.

bodies.[35] Such instances give point to Edmund's sardonic reflections in *King Lear*:

> This is the excellent foppery of the world, that when we are sick in fortune – often the surfeit of our own behaviour – we make guilty of our disasters the sun, the moon, and the stars: as if we were villains by necessity, fools by heavenly compulsion, knaves, thieves and treachers by spherical predominance; drunkards, liars and adulterers by an enforced obedience of planetary influence; and all that we are evil in, by a divine thrusting on: an admirable evasion of whoremaster man, to lay his goatish disposition to the charge of a star![36]

Astrology could thus appeal as a means of evading responsibility, removing guilt from both sufferer and society at large.[37] Like religion, it also combated the notion that misfortune was purely random in its incidence. There really was no such thing as *chance* in nature, declared the astrologer John Butler.[38] Astrological hypotheses explained everything, from the compatibility of two persons in love[39] to the unexpected failure of a surgical operation.[40] Those who rejected them, said Sir Christopher Heydon, were left with a choice between two equally unattractive doctrines, the rule of blind chance, or the sovereignty of a capricious deity.[41] In the place of such unpalatable concepts, astrology played the role of intellectual long-stop.

The primary reason for the appeal of astrological explanation was thus an intellectual one: its provision of a coherent and comprehensive system of thought. The second was more practical. For by offering men a realistic assessment of their dispositions the astrologer held out the prospect of that greater freedom which comes from self-knowledge. After establishing the client's nativity, explained Lilly, 'I judge upon the general good or ill [which] may befall that party in a natural course of life during his days, as also of his temperament, constitution, qualities, person, etc. Then I direct the advantageous years and discommodious, either for health, loss of

35. P.R.O., SP 12/218, f. 49. He became Lancaster Herald in 1602.
36. *King Lear*, I.ii. cf. *All's Well that Ends Well*, I.i; *Julius Caesar*, I.ii.
37. cf. M. Fortes, *Oedipus and Job in West African Religion* (Cambridge, 1959), p. 40.
38. J. Butler, *The Most Sacred and Divine Science of Astrology* (1680), p. 23.
39. Burton, *Anatomy*, iii, p. 310.
40. C. H. Talbot and E. A. Hammond, *The Medical Practitioners in Medieval England* (1965), pp. 61, 175.
41. Sir C. Heydon, *A Defence of Iudiciall Astrologie* (Cambridge, 1603), sig. ¶4ᵛ.

estate, preferment, etc.'[42] The attraction of having one's horoscope cast was not unlike that of undergoing psychoanalysis today. The reward would be a penetrating analysis of the individual's innermost attributes, the qualities which he should develop, and the limitations against which he should be on his guard. Of course the astrologers insisted that the figure cast at a person's nativity could never be more than a guide to the possibilities open to him; it did not mean that he was in the clutch of an ineluctable destiny. But if there were future hazards in store it was as well to be apprised of them in advance. 'An expert and prudent astrologer,' wrote Richard Napier, 'may through his cunning skill show us how to prevent many evils proceeding from the influence of the stars.'[43] Or, as another practitioner put it: 'The use and end of astrology is to discover and make manifest the causes of those mutations and accidents that happen in general, as war or peace, dearth or plenty, etc., and particularly to man, as health or sickness, riches, poverty, etc., to the end that, such accidents being foreseen, we may as wise men augment the good, and divert the evil.'[44]

All the possibilities inherent in a scientific system of divination thus appeared to unfold. According to John Aubrey, astrology was 'the best guide to direct us to what professions (or callings) children are by nature most fit or most inclined to';[45] and even one of the Tudor clergymen who denounced astrology for its impiety conceded that 'an astronomer may tell by the observation of the stars to what occupation, to what estate of life, every man is most ... apt by nature'.[46] John Gadbury went so far as to propose that entry to the Universities of Oxford and Cambridge should be restricted to those 'whose genitures render them capable of learning what they ... teach'.[47]

The astrologers also claimed to predict the course of political events. 'I believe,' wrote Gadbury, 'that much of the mischief this nation (during its Civil Wars) underwent might (by such knowledge) have been prevented.'[48] If the Scots had read Lilly's almanac, thought

42. W. Lilly, *Englands Propheticall Merline* (1644), sig. b2.

43. Ashm. 242, f. 190.

44. R. Edlyn, *Observationes Astrologicae* (1659), p. 5.

45. Bodl., Aubrey MS 10, f. 144. cf above, p. 373.

46. *The Works of Roger Hutchinson*, ed. J. Bruce (P.S., Cambridge, 1842), pp. 87–8.

47. (J. Gadbury), *A Brief Relation of the Life and Death of ... Vincent Wing* (1670), p. 4.

48. J. Gadbury, *Ephemeris* (1664), sig. A1^v.

William Paine, they would have known in advance that their invasion of England was doomed to defeat.[49] In 1663 Richard Saunders pointedly drew attention to the recommendation of his French colleague, J.-B. Morin, that the King should have at least three astrologers in his private council.[50]

Like other forms of divination astrology helped men to take decisions for which there was no rational basis. A typical section in Joseph Blagrave's *Introduction to Astrology* (1682) told the reader 'how to choose a fit time to visit any kinsman, brother or neighbour, so as to obtain any thing desired from them'. Other parts gave rules for knowing when to engage in a lawsuit, fight a duel, or propose marriage.[51] By observing the masculine signs in the heavens it was even possible to choose the appropriate moment for begetting a male child. John Case's instructions were attractively simple: 'If thou want'st an heir, or man-child to inherit thy land, observe a time when the masculine planets and signs ascend, and [are] in full power and force, then take thy female, and cast in thy seed, and thou shalt have a man-child.' *Mutatis mutandis*, the same instructions were to be followed for a daughter.[52] Blagrave prescribed various herbal medicines to accompany this formula, which, he declared, had in his experience worked very well, 'always provided the persons were capable thereof'.[53] Astrology, though beginning as a system of explanation, thus ended as one which held out the prospect of control. Like other kinds of magic, the astrological election was a formula to which men might resort at moments of impotence and uncertainty, when all other human agencies had failed.

2. *Successes and failures*

It is not difficult therefore to appreciate the psychological appeal of astrological diagnosis, once the premises of the system had been accepted. But the problem still remains: why should anyone have believed in it in the first place? To our eyes the notion that the daily

49. Ashm. 423, f. 142.

50. Saunders, *Palmistry*, ii, pp. 14–15.

51. J. Blagrave, *Blagrave's Introduction to Astrology* (1682), p. 194, and part ii, *passim*.

52. J. Case, *The Angelical Guide* (1697), p. 61.

53. *Blagrave's Introduction to Astrology*, p. 200. Other instances in W. Ramesey, *Astrologia Restaurata* (1653), pp. 152–3; Saunders, *Palmistry*, ii, pp. 99–100.

life of human beings should be determined by the motions of the
heavenly bodies seems so fantastic that it is difficult to understand
how men of intelligence and perspicacity could ever have accepted
it. Even some of the modern historians who write most sympathetically about the gropings of early scientists have tended to become
facetious or patronizing when confronted by the history of astrology
and its devotees.

At one level it is sufficient to point out that astrological doctrines
followed from the accepted Ptolemaic world-picture and were
strongly reinforced by Renaissance doctrines of macrocosm and
microcosm. As Nicholas Culpepper put it:

> If you do but consider the whole universe as one united body, and
> man an epitome of this body, it will seem strange to none but mad-
> men and fools that the stars should have influence upon the body of
> man, considering he, be[ing] an epitome of the Creation, must needs
> have a celestial world within himself ... Every inferior world is
> governed by its superior, and receives influence from it.[54]

This type of thinking was to be made unfashionable by the new
science, but it remained respectable in all but the most rarified
milieux until at least the middle of the seventeenth century.[55]

But at a popular level the appeal of astrology was not just a
reflection of prevailing scientific theories. It was rooted in the conditions of social life. Ordinary people were much more aware of the
heavenly bodies than they are today. It is artificial lighting, in street
and house, which has made us less conscious of their endless mutations. Few dwellers in large cities now know what the current phase
of the moon may be, and an eclipse will pass unnoticed by all save
professional astronomers. But in the pre-industrial world men carried torches to light their way and arranged their journeys to coincide
with a full moon. In Elizabethan England the working day was
longer in the summer than the winter because there was more daylight. The artificial hour – a twelfth of the daylight period – still
survived in popular usage.[56] Contemporaries still used the sun to

54. N. Culpepper, *Pharmocopoeia Londinensis: or the London Dispen-
satory* (1654), sigs. A3ᵛ–A4. The *Epistle to the Reader* contains an excellent
exposition of the macrocosm theory.

55. M. H. Nicolson, *The Breaking of the Circle* (New York, 1962), pp.
133, 143, 155; V. Harris, *All Coherence Gone* (Chicago, 1949), pp. 199, 232.
For survivals, see, e.g., J. Russel, *Astrological Predictions* (1659), and Case,
The Angelical Guide.

56. For an example, G. Langenfelt, *The Historic Origin of the Eight
Hours Day* (Stockholm, 1954), p. 12.

tell the time; indeed the seventeenth century was the great age of sundialling.

So long as men were intimately acquainted with the movement of the heavenly bodies it is not very surprising that there should have been some attempt to relate their changes to those of terrestrial phenomena. In Sir Walter Raleigh's words:

> If we cannot deny but that God hath given virtue to springs and fountains, to cold earth, to plants and stones, minerals and to the excremental parts of the basest living creatures, why should we rob the beautiful stars of their working powers? For, seeing they are many in number and of eminent beauty and magnitude, we may not think that in the treasury of his wisdom who is infinite there can be wanting, even for every star, a peculiar virtue and operation; as every herb, plant, fruit, flower, adorning the face of the earth hath the like.[57]

There was much plausibility in this view. It was known that the movement of the heavens produced the recurrence of day and night, and the course of the seasons. The moon controlled the tides. Flowers opened to reflect the appearance of the sun. Since prevailing medical theory taught that all diseases were caused by a superabundance or a deficiency of heat, cold, dryness or moisture, and since any fluctuation in these qualities could be plausibly regarded as the result of the weather, it was not too much to believe that diseases were determined by the stars. (The influence of the sky upon the human body seemed all the greater, remarked Goad, 'when our age hath been taught that our blood circulates in our body every twenty-four hours'.[58]) The extensive lore about the impact of the moon upon vegetation and the weather lingered on in the nineteenth-century countryside, unaffected by two centuries of science. Francis Kilvert recorded in his diary for 1878 how he visited an old lady in his parish who was very ill. ' " 'Tis the dog star," she said. "I shall not be better till Saturday when the dog days end. 'Tis an evil star." ' She was echoing a doctrine which went back *via* the popular literature of the seventeenth century to the writings of Hippocrates.[59] It was not unlike the ancient belief that dying men went out with the tide; the state of the tide at the death of a parishioner is actually

57. Quoted by E. M. W. Tillyard, *The Elizabethan World Picture* (1948), p. 51.

58. Goad, *Astro-meteorologica*, p. 17.

59. *Kilvert's Diary*, ed. W. Plomer (new edn, 1960), iii, p. 410. cf. Hippocrates, *Aphorisms*, iv, 5; J. Primrose, *Popular Errours*, trans. R. Wittie (1651), pp. 243, 254–61.

recorded in one Elizabethan parish register.[60] Such notions were not
so much survivals of intellectual doctrines about sympathy and correspondence as the direct product of life in a primitive world where
human dependence on tides and the weather was fundamental, and
where it seemed natural to postulate a sympathetic relationship between man and his environment.

Even in the eighteenth century most sections of the English
economy were dependent upon the weather.[61] It was this which gave
astrological predictions their plausibility. To predict the weather was
to predict the harvest; and to predict the harvest was to predict the
discontent which would follow a food shortage, and the rebellion
which might follow the discontent. It was precisely along these lines
that the Danish astronomer, Tycho Brahe, constructed his defence
of astrology.[62] It was equally plausible for an astrologer to prognosticate disease and mortality since it was generally accepted that the
people's health was affected by the state of the air and that the air
was influenced by the heavens. So long as comets were believed to
be sublunar exhalations of a hot, dry character, it was not absurd to
predict that they might scorch up the earth and bring famine, just
as by drying men's blood they could produce choler and hence
quarrels and warfare.[63] Even today we are ready to attribute an
improvement in our health and disposition to 'a change of air'.

In brief, in a society which was dependent upon the weather for
its efficient functioning, and had fewer means of guarding itself
against the depredations of storm or drought, it was not possible for
a weather forecast to remain simply a weather forecast. Inexorably,
it carried with it a chain of far-reaching consequences of a social and
political character. The prognostications which the astrologers issued
annually in their almanacs were therefore highly plausible. As even
Calvin conceded, the most insidious feature of astrology was that it
started out from a series of undeniable truths.[64]

60. At Hesleden, near Hartlepool, 1595; W. Henderson, *Notes on the
Folk-lore of the Northern Counties* (1879), p. 58. cf. J. Lucas, *History of
Warton Parish* (c. 1710–40), ed. J. R. Ford and J. A. Fuller-Maitland
(Kendal, 1931), p. 44.
61. T. S. Ashton, *Economic Fluctuations in England, 1700–1800* (Oxford,
1959), chaps. 1 and 2.
62. J. L. E. Dreyer, *Tycho Brahe* (New York, 1963 edn), pp. 75–6.
63. Aristotle, *Meteorologica*, i, 7; Kocher, *Science and Religion*, pp. 166–7;
Bacon, *Works*, iv,p. 131; J. Swan, *Speculum Mundi* (Cambridge, 1635), p. 103.
64. J. Calvin, *An Admonicion against Astrology Iudiciall*, trans. G.
G(ylby) [1561], sig. Dii.

But mere plausibility was hardly sufficient to sustain the system against the repeated failures in prediction to which it was inevitably doomed. How was astrology able to retain the allegiance of intelligent men, when it was utterly incapable of providing the accurate prognostications they wanted? During the seventeen years for which we have a continuous record, John Booker's astrological practice showed no signs of slackening. On the contrary, the same clients returned again and again, and brought their friends as well. How was he able to keep their custom? And why was the demand for the almanacs and prognostications not slackened by their massive and repeated errors?

When approaching this problem one must bear in mind that the astrologers, or at least the reputable ones, did not claim for their predictions a binding and inexorable character. All they said was that they were very likely to be fulfilled. From Ptolemy to Partridge, it was a platitude of astrological writing to assert that the stars inclined, but did not compel. The portrait which Lilly made the frontispiece to his annual almanac showed the astrologer bearing a book on which was inscribed the significant motto – *non cogunt*. It was always possible for a man to overcome the tendencies indicated in his horoscope by exercising free-will and self-determination. In this way two men born under the same star might well have a different destiny. Astrologers, a practitioner asserted, did not make definite predictions, but only 'a probable conjecture by natural causes [of] what may possibly happen if the influence of those celestial bodies be not restrained'.[65] Once this essential limitation was recognised, it became easy enough to explain why astrological predictions did not always turn out to be correct. The astrologer only claimed to identify tendencies in his client's disposition; he could not tell whether or not he would succumb to them. He could also remind his client that the horoscope of an individual might be out-trumped by that of the country in which he lived. For did not Ptolemy rule that the fate of a kingdom overruled that of individual men? There was thus a conflict between the precise forecast the client wanted and the conditional answer which the astrologer preferred to give.[66]

It therefore became customary for prognostications to be phased ambiguously, and shrouded with 'ifs' and 'buts'. This meant that,

65. Nathaniel Sparke in Ashm. 356, f. 4ᵛ.
66. Ptolemy, *Tetrabilos*, i, 2–3; Russel, *Astrological Predictions*, p. 21; Kocher, *Science and Religion*, p. 207.

whatever happened, it was hard to say that the almanac-maker had been wrong. Thus one almanac in 1607 hinted that an eclipse might occasion 'much private enmity, malice and secret grudges, death of great beasts, many imprisonments, and the death of some ecclesiastical persons'. Another in 1614 forecast 'loss and hindrance of divers husbandmen in their beasts and cattle'.[67] The trick was promptly spotted by the satirists. *Poor Robin*, a mock almanac which enjoyed almost as much commercial success as the real thing, predicted for February 1664 that, 'We may expect some showers or rain either this month or the next, or the next after that, or else we shall have a very dry spring'.[68] Jonathan Swift delivered an even more crushing indictment:

For their observations and predictions, they are such as will equally suit any age or country in the world. 'This month a certain great person will be threatened with death or sickness'. This the newspapers will tell them; for there we find at the end of the year, that no month passes without the death of some person of note; and it would be hard if it should be otherwise, when there are at least two thousand persons of note in this kingdom, many of them old, and the almanac-maker has the liberty of choosing the sickliest season of the year, where he may fix his prediction. Again, 'this month an eminent clergyman will be preferred'; of which there may be many hundreds, half of them with one foot in the grave. Then, 'such a planet in such house shows great machinations, plots, conspiracies that may in time be brought to light', after which, if we hear of any discovery, the astrologer gets the honour; if not, his predictions still stand good. And at last, 'God preserve King William from all his open and secret enemies. Amen.' When, if the king should happen to have died, the astrologer plainly foretold it; otherwise it passes but for the pious ejaculation of a loyal subject.[69]

The extent of the exaggeration here is remarkably slight. Ambiguity was an essential feature of these prognostications, which were usually contrived 'so cunningly and equivocatingly that, be the event what it will, still the words shall be capable of intimating it'.[70] Moreover, as Reginald Scot pointed out, one truth gave credit to all their lies; so 'that ever after we believe whatsoever they say'.[71] Even more irritatingly, the astrologer could fall back on the excuse of divine

67. *Gresham. 1607*, sig. C1; *Upcot. 1614*, sig. C3ᵛ.
68. *Poor Robin* (1664), sig. A6.
69. (J. Swift), *Predictions for the year 1708 . . . by Isaac Bickerstaff, Esq.*
70. J.S., *The Starr-Prophet anatomiz'd and dissected* (1675), p. 29.
71. Scot, *Discoverie*, XI.xxii.

intervention. Judicial astrology, held Lilly, was confined to the analysis of natural causes; it did not pretend to be able to explain God's miracles. There were, for example, no astrological causes for Noah's Flood, which had been the Almighty's sole handiwork.[72] The confused events of the Interregnum forced Lilly to have repeated recourse to the concept of the unpredictable miracle in order to vindicate erroneous prognostications. In 1652 he explained that the manner of Charles I's death was something which no astrologer could have been expected to foresee; in this case 'Providence rather acted by Miracle than Nature'. For 1659 he forecast that in May the Protector Richard Cromwell would 'manifest himself unto the whole world that he hath abilities to govern'. When May turned out to be the month of the Protector's abdication, the astrologer assured his readers that such political fluctuations could never have been found out by astrology for they were obviously a direct manifestation of the hand of God. He also hinted that even if he had foreseen them it would have been impolitic to have said so. The Restoration forced Lilly back yet again on to the notion of divine intervention. How could he have been expected to predict such a miracle? These were acts above nature, impenetrable by any human inquirer.[73]

All this may strike us as the crudest subterfuge, but there is no reason to believe that Lilly was not sincere or that his readers rejected his explanation. George Wharton also attributed the defeat of the Royalists in the Civil War to a supernatural cause which could not be discerned in advance.[74] Vincent Wing concluded his prognostication for 1647 with the pious reminder that 'the Almighty [might] dispose otherwise and so frustrate the portents of Heaven'.[75] Samuel Tucker assumed that the 'starry influences operated inevitably ... unless the Almighty suspend nature and work immediately of himself, and that I suppose hath the term of a miracle'.[76]

Equally persuasive were the quiet hints of censorship. There undoubtedly were occasions when almanacs had been so censored,[77]

72. W. Lilly, *Merlini Anglici Ephemeris* (1656), sig. A3^v.

73. W. Lilly, *Merlini Anglici Ephemeris* (1652), sig. F7^v; ibid (1659); ibid. (1660), sigs. A2, A3; ibid (1661), sig. A1.

74. *The Works of ... Sir George Wharton*, ed. J. Gadbury (1683), p. 277.

75. *Wing, 1647. An Almanack and Prognostication*, sig. C4^v.

76. Ashm. 244, f. 149. Miracles were similarly excluded by William Ramesey *(Lux Veritatis* [1651], sig. A5^v), John Gadbury *(Natura Prodigiorum* [1660], sig. A4), and Richard Saunders *(Apollo Anglicanus* [1656], sig. C5).

77. See below, pp. 408–9.

and the reader could never tell whether the licenser had not inter-vened to prevent the astrologer from telling the real truth. This remained a plausible excuse for astrologers until the end of govern-ment censorship in 1695. Timothy Gadbury, whose prediction of Charles II's return appeared only a fortnight before the event itself, explained that he had, of course, known about it long before, but had refrained from making the news public, because of the censor-ship, and also because he had no wish to prejudice the King's chances by forewarning his enemies.[78] As always, repression, un-accompanied by intellectual refutation, did more to foster belief than to end it. A curious piece of contemporary testimony to the myth of the almanac-makers' infallibility is to be found in the note-book of John Ward, vicar of Stratford-upon-Avon, who solemnly records the report that most of the astrologers had predicted the Great Fire of London in 1666, but that this part of their forecast had been struck out by the licenser, Sir Roger L'Estrange.[79]

In the last resort the astrologer would concede that a mistake had occurred in the calculations. Blagrave reminded his readers that things might go wrong if his clock was slow, or if the messenger bearing the inquiry was delayed *en route*.[80] A client might also wreck the calculation by failing to supply all the relevant facts. There was in any case plenty of room for argument about the proper procedure to be followed. As one contemporary observed, 'there are no less than six ways of erecting a scheme, in each of which the prediction of events shall be different'.[81]

An individual astrologer who had got the wrong result might therefore go back over his calculations to see where he had gone wrong. The most celebrated example of such wisdom after the event was provided by the Italian astrologer, Jerome Cardan, who came to England in the mid sixteenth century and predicted that the boy-king Edward VI would live to be at least fifty-five. Unabashed by the death of his client shortly afterwards, Cardan published the horo-scope, together with an apologia entitled 'What I thought after-wards on the subject'. In it he explained that his error arose from

78. T. Gadbury, *A Health to the King* (1660).
79. *Diary of the Rev. John Ward*, ed. C. Severn (1839), p. 94.
80. Quoted by H. G. Dick, *Journ. Hist. Medicine*, i (1946), p. 420.
81. J. Glanvill, *Saducismus Triumphatus* (1681), i, p. 68. There were four ways according to Joseph Moxon (*A Tutor to Astronomie and Geographie* [1659], p. 123), five according to Henry More (*Tetractys· Anti-Astrologica* [1681], pp. 46–7).

having shirked some extra calculations which would have taken him at least a hundred more hours; he had been lazy and the calculated risk had not come off. At the same time he confessed to some relief, since to have predicted the imminent demise of the reigning monarch would have been an infallible way of getting into serious trouble.[82]

Most other astrologers were equally undaunted by failure. No human science was perfect, they reminded themselves, and astrology was certainly no worse than medicine. If different astrologers produced different results, then so did different theologians and lawyers.[83] Everyone knew that some practitioners were better than others and that the profession was infested by charlatans and quacks. The number of good astrologers was very few, and even the best astrologers made mistakes.[84] The paradox was that the mistakes of any one astrologer only served to buttress the status of the system as a whole, since the client's reaction was to turn to another practitioner to get better advice, while the astrologer himself went back over his calculations to see where he had slipped up. The notorious internal disputes among the astrological fraternity, the bitter quarrels between Lilly and Wharton, Gadbury and Partridge, did not discredit astrology as such, any more than did religious controversy make men atheists. They merely stimulated the public desire to know which side was right. By concentrating on each other's particular errors the astrologers thus diverted attention from their art as a whole.

But to understand fully why it was that the public did not tire sooner of the astrologers and their pronouncements it must be remembered that many of their rulings were not predictions at all. A large part of the astrological practitioner's business consisted in giving advice and in helping men to resolve personal problems and to take their own decisions. This was not an activity which it was easy to discredit. If the astrologer chose an unpropitious day for some action he could hardly be rebuked, for there was no telling whether

82. *Hieronymi Cardani, in Cl. Ptolemaei de Astrorum Iudiciis ... Commentaria* (Basel, 1578), pp. 603–13 (summarized by H. Morley, *Jerome Cardan* [1854], ii, pp. 138–42). In his autobiography, however, the boastful Cardan cited his horoscope of Edward VI as proof of his professional acumen; *The Book of My Life*, trans. J. Stoner (New York, 1962 edn), p. 200.
83. Ashm., 240, f. 128ᵛ; *Bowker, 1634*, sig. C8; Sloane 2279, f. 37ᵛ (William Drage's vindication of astrology); J. Butler, *A Brief (but true) Account of the Certain Year, Moneth, Day and Minute of the Birth of Jesus Christ* (1671), p. 300; J. Gadbury, *Cardines Coeli* (1684), pp. 4–5.
84. J. Partridge, *Prodromus* (1679), p. 9.

some other day might not have proved even worse. In fact his advice was probably often based on sound common sense and a real acquaintance with the facts at issue. It has already been seen how modern African diviners can be vehicles for the expression of fears and suspicions already present in their clients' minds. The wizard equips himself with a good grasp of local gossip before embarking on his consultation and is quick to follow any lead given him by his customers. His final verdict is strongly influenced by the situation as it emerges during the interview. Conversely, the client who does not receive the answer he wants will try another practitioner in the hope of getting it. Professor Evans-Pritchard concluded from his study of oracles among the Azande that the client would take advantage of any loophole allowing him to do what he originally wanted to do.[85]

The evidence is insufficient to make possible a detailed comparison between the workings of the seventeenth-century astrologer and those of the African diviner. For although the records of tens of thousands of astrological consultations are extant – a figure which must surely dwarf the corresponding total of divining *séances* which have been observed by anthropologists – the essential information is usually missing. The case-books seldom reveal what the astrologer told his client and they contain no record of the conversation which accompanied the construction of the horoscope. This makes it impossible to provide the sort of analysis open to the anthropologist who has been an eye-witness to the *séance* itself.

There is, however, some *prima facie* evidence to suggest that much astrological consultation was a less 'loaded' process than that of the African diviner. For much of the astrologers' business was done by post and many of the letters they received were from complete strangers. They included straight requests for information about stolen goods or sickness, which gave no clue whatsoever to the desired answer, or even any intimation that one answer was desired more than another. Indeed clients were sometimes extremely anxious to secure perfect laboratory conditions for the question and to avoid predisposing the astrologer either way.[86] Besides, astrology was supposed to be a science. There were strict rules to be followed when

85. E. E. Evans-Pritchard, *Witchcraft, Oracles and Magic among the Azande* (Oxford, 1937), p. 350. See in general pp. 257–8 above.

86. See, e.g., the account by one of Booker's clients of his elaborate use of lots to determine a perfect moment for putting to the astrologer a question about his chances of recovering arrears of rent from a tenant (Ashm. 385, p. 636 [19 Oct. 1654]).

giving a judgement. The result was not meant to be faked, so as to fit in with some clue let slip by the client during the course of the interview. Indeed under certain circumstances it was the astrologer's duty to rule that the party suspected by the client was in fact innocent.[87]

Yet, for all its apparent objectivity, astrology left everything in the last resort to the judgement and common sense of the practitioner, and the system, far from being exact, was highly flexible.[88] As with many kinds of African divination, there were rules to be followed, but their interpretation was ultimately subjective. 'The most striking feature of Nupe sand-divining', writes one anthropologist, 'is the contrast between its pretentious theoretical framework and its primitive and slipshod application in practice.'[89] The same must have been true of much English astrological consultation. The rules themselves allowed weight to be given to the client's suspicions. Lilly, for example, taught that witchcraft should never be diagnosed unless it was already suspected.[90] Like African diviners, the astrologers seldom named names, but simply issued physical descriptions – 'A female servant with a wart under her ear and another on her body'.[91] This practice made it easier for the client to fasten his suspicions where he chose. When Mrs. Jane Shelley asked the Elizabethan astrologer-don, John Fletcher of Caius College, Cambridge, to discover what had become of her jointure she got the Delphic answer that 'knaves be knaves'.[92]

The less scrupulous practitioners were ready enough to provide the judgements their customers wanted. Lilly professed to be shocked when his tutor in astrology, the ex-clergyman, Evans, gave a client a prognostication which was the reverse of what the horoscope indicated; his master admitted the deception, but pleaded that 'had he not so judged to please the woman, she would have given him nothing; and he had a wife and family to provide for'. An astrologer,

87. e.g., Sloane 1312, f. 46 (rules of a seventeenth-century practitioner).
88. Above, pp. 340, 400.
89. S. F. Nadel, *Nupe Religion* (1954), p. 63. cf. E. J. and J. D. Krige, *The Realm of a Rain-Queen* (1943), p. 227 ('Despite intricate rules, divination is in the last resort not an exact science, but an interpretation in which the diviner's ingenuity, his knowledge of human nature and his estimate of the interplay of motives in the society play an important part').
90. Lilly, *Christian Astrology*, p. 263.
91. *Quarter Sessions Records for the County of Somerset*, ed. E. H. Bates Harbin, iii (Somerset Rec. Soc., 1912), pp. 331–2. cf. above, pp. 256, 365.
92. P.R.O., SP 12/244, f. 112.

thought Lilly, should never give a judgement against his rules, however much he was paid. But Booker later told Pepys that Lilly was equally pliable.[93] 'Tell him whom you suspect, and he'll guess shrewdly', says a character in a Jacobean play of a false astrologer.[94] The 'Quack Astrologer' described in one contemporary pamphlet always prefaced his calculation in cases of theft by asking his client whether there were any suspicious characters who frequented the house. After that the erection of a figure was a pure formality.[95]

The astrologer could also rely upon a certain proportion of his predictions to fulfil themselves simply because they had been predicted. As a contemporary put it, 'if one were to fight a duel, the astrologer tells him he shall have the victory; and hereupon the consulter hath his courage heightened, and so prevails'.[96] 'Doth not all the virtue of their art', asked another, 'consist more in the inferior's confidence than in the superior's influence?'[97] It was notorious that to predict a famine was to make its arrival more probable. 'What a dearth of victuals you cause in the commonwealth,' said William Fulke to the astrologers in 1560, 'while the farmers of the country . . . believing your oracles of the intemperance of weathers do so craftily dispose their wares that in abundance of all things the common people suffer a great and grievous scarcity'.[98] The same point was repeated by the Earl of Northampton: 'Pamphlets which prognosticated famine have been causes of the same; not by the malice of the planets, . . . but by the greediness of husbandmen, who, being put in fear of such a storm, . . . by forestalment, and . . . by the secret hoarding up of grain, enhance the prices in respect of scarcity'.[99] It was common to attribute dearth to hoarding; and there must have been many corn-engrossers who, as the preacher Thomas Adams said, made the almanac their Bible. The 'farmer who hang'd himself on expectation of plenty', mentioned by the porter in *Macbeth*, had

93. Lilly, *Autobiography*, pp. 55, 60; *The Late Storie of Mr William Lilly* (1648), p. 8; *Diary of Samuel Pepys*, 24 Oct. 1660.

94. [J. Fletcher?],*The Bloody Brother* (?1st performed 1617), IV.ii.

95. *Character of a Quack Astrologer* (1673), sig. B4ᵛ. Local knowledge was thought in the fifteenth century to be an essential part of the astrologer's equipment; B. L. Manning, *The People's Faith in the Time of Wyclif* (Cambridge, 1919), p. 90.

96. 'A Learned Divine', *The Late Eclipse Unclasped* (1652), p. 9.

97. J.S., *The Starr-Prophet Anatomiz'd*, p. 25.

98. Fulke *Antiprognosticon*, sig. Aviijᵛ.

99. H. Howard, Earl of Northampton, *A Defensative against the Poyson of Supposed Prophecies* (1620; 1st pubd 1583), f. 113ᵛ.

presumably been studying the latest prognostication. Sordido in Jonson's *Every Man out of his Humour* resolves to hoard his corn because the almanac predicts a bad summer.[100] 'That silly reverence which vulgar persons give to these predictions,' wrote John Allen in 1609, 'sets them upon the fulfilling of them because they esteem them unavoidable.'[101]

This was why political predictions were taken so seriously by the governments of the day. At the accession of Elizabeth I they seemed to threaten the very establishment of the Anglican Church. One contemporary records that the people did

so waver, the whole realm was so troubled and so moved with blind enigmatical and devilish prophecies of that heaven-gazer Nostradamus ... that even those which in their hearts could have wished the glory of God and his Word most flourishing to be established were brought into such an extreme coldness of faith that they doubted God had forgotten his promise.[102]

Nostradamus was the French astrologer and prophet, a protégé of Catherine de Medici, whose semi-astrological prognostication for 1559 had been translated into English, with its gloomy predictions of 'divers calamities, weepings and mournings' and 'civil sedition and mutination of the lowest against the highest'. Archbishop Parker dismissed these maunderings as a 'fantastical hotch-potch', and the government took legal action against the booksellers who sold them.[103] But their influence was indisputable. Fulke recalled that

none almost of them that gave any credit to prognostications durst be bold to open their faith and religion ... Without the good luck of his prophecies it was thought that nothing could be brought to effect ... Except the true preachers of God's Word had sharply rebuked the

100. *The Workes of Tho. Adams* (1629), p. 836; *Macbeth*, II.iii; B. Jonson, *Every Man out of His Humour*, I.i; and other literary examples cited in *Ben Jonson*, ed. C. H. Herford, P. and E. Simpson, ix (Oxford, 1950), pp. 429–30.

101. *Judicial Astrologers totally routed*, p. 16. For a ludicrous example of this process at work, see Lilly, *Autobiography*, pp. 117–18.

102. F. Coxe, *A Short Treatise declaringe the Detestable Wickednesse of Magicall Sciences* [1561], sig. Av.

103. *Correspondence of Matthew Parker*, ed. J. Bruce and T. T. Perowne (Cambridge, P.S., 1853), pp. 59–60. For published versions of Nostradamus's prognostications for 1559 and 1566 see *S.T.C.* A MS copy, which belonged to Lord Lumley, of the prognostication for 1560 is in B.M., Royal MS 17 B xxxviii.

people for crediting such vain prophecies, there should have been none end of fear and expectation.[104]

It was during the Civil War, however, that the political potentialities of astrological forecasts were most systematically exploited. From 1642 the newspapers printed astrological predictions,[105] and the astrologers were taken up by both sides in the conflict, with Lilly and Booker prominent among the supporters of Parliament, and George Wharton writing on behalf of the King.[106] When Cromwell's army was in Scotland, Lilly records, a soldier stood with his almanac in his hand, crying out as the troops passed by, 'Lo, hear what Lilly saith; you are in this month promised victory; fight it out, brave boys!'[107] During the siege of Colchester in 1648 Lilly and Booker were sent for to encourage the soldiers, 'assuring them the town would very shortly be surrendered, as indeed it was'. While inside the beleaguered garrison the Royalist astrologer, John Humphrey, endeavoured to keep up the spirits of the Governor, Sir Charles Lucas, with delusory prognostications of relief.[108] It was said that if the King could have bought over Lilly he would have been worth more than half a dozen regiments.[109] During the early years of the Interregnum Lilly's almanacs were prefaced by miniature leading articles, justifying the new régime, announcing the permanent downfall of monarchy, and urging his readers to buy confiscated lands.[110] Nicholas Culpepper also wrote with an avowedly political purpose, cheerfully admitting that there might be no astrological basis for his prediction that the eclipse of 1652 would bring republicanism to Europe: 'What harm will it do princes to prepare for the loss of a kingdom, though it never come,' he retorted. 'Is it not the way to teach them humility?'[111]

104. Fulke, *Antiprognosticon*, sig. Aviij. On this period see also S. V. Larkey, 'Astrology and Politics in the First Years of Elizabeth's Reign', *Bull. Institute of the Hist. of Medicine*, iii (1935).

105. J. Frank, *The Beginnings of the English Newspaper, 1620–60* (Cambridge, Mass., 1961), pp. 177, 212, 215, 222, 227, 247, 259, 326, n. 36.

106. An account of the main pamphlet exchanges between this trio is given by H. Rusche, '*Merlini Anglici*: Astrology and Propaganda from 1644 to 1651', *E.H.R.*, lxxx (1965).

107. Lilly, *Autobiography*, p. 189.

108. ibid., pp. 153–4; Wood, *Ath. Ox.*, iv, cols. 747–9.

109. *The Late Storie of Mr William Lilly*, p. 7.

110. And were consequently denounced at the Restoration: *A Declaration of the Several Treasons ... by ... William Lilly* (1660); W. Prynne, *A True and Perfect Narrative* (1659), p. 60.

111. N. Culpepper, *Catastrophe Magnatum* (1652), p. 75.

Until nearly the end of the century it remained conventional for most political issues to be given some form of astrological expression. The last years of the Interregnum, for example, saw a fierce conflict over foreign policy, in which Lilly championed the alliance with Sweden (and was sent a gold chain by Charles X as a reward), while John Gadbury put the case for Denmark, correctly predicting the death of the Swedish monarch in 1660.[112] After the Restoration there was astrological propaganda in support of the Dutch wars,[113] and in connection with the Exclusion Crisis, when John Partridge and John Holwell led the 'Protestant' attack against the Catholic, John Merrifield, and the future Jacobite, George Parker. After 1688 Partridge's predictions were triumphantly reprinted by a publisher who affirmed his disbelief in astrology but his conviction of its political value.[114]

Astrological prediction had long been associated with conspiracy and rebellion. Thomas Nashe wrote of the astrologer that 'all malcontents intending any invasive violence against their prince and country run headlong to his oracle'. Almanacs had done more harm than all the writings of Milton and the regicides, declared a later critic.[115] The astrologer's most common contribution was to calculate the reigning monarch's life expectation. In popular estimation this was not far removed from malevolent conjuration to take away the ruler's life. Several fifteenth-century astrologers were executed for this type of offence.[116] Some of the conspiracies against Henry VII drew on astrological advice,[117] and all the Tudor monarchs were

112. F. Dahl, 'King Charles Gustavus of Sweden and the English Astrologers, William Lilly and John Gadbury', *Lychnos* (Annual of the Swedish History of Science Soc.) (1937), a useful, though not always reliable, survey of this affair.

113. e.g., T. Trigge, *The Fiery Trigon Revived* (1672); *The Dangerous Condition of the United Provinces Prognosticated and Plainly Demonstrated by Mr William Lilly* (1672).

114. *Annus Mirabilis, or Strange and Wonderful Predictions gathered out of Mr John Partridge's Almanack* (1689). For Partridge, Holwell, Parker and Merrifield, see *D.N.B.* (corrected in the case of Partridge by G. P. Mayhew in *Studies in English Literature*, i [1961]).

115. T. Nashe, *Works*, ed. R. B. McKerrow (1904–8), i, p. 367; (J. Younge), *Sidrophel Vapulans: or, the Quack-Astrologer toss'd in a Blanket* (1699), sig. a3ᵛ. cf. ibid., pp. 21–2.

116. Kittredge, *Witchcraft*, pp. 81–2, 138–9.

117. T. O. Wedel, *The Mediaeval Attitude toward Astrology* (Yale Studies in English, 1920), pp. 28–9; C. A. J. Armstrong, 'An Italian Astrologer at the Court of Henry VII', in *Italian Renaissance Studies*, ed. E. F. Jacob (1960), p. 436.

made the subject of astrological calculation by dissident groups.[118] In 1581 Parliament made it a statutory felony to erect figures, cast nativities, or calculate by prophecy how long the Queen would live or who would succeed her.[119] Elizabethan recusants and Gunpowder plotters were both fortified by such calculations.[120] Robert Cecil had a Scottish astrologer banished for predicting the death of Prince Henry, and there were rumours that similar calculations had been made concerning James I.[121] One of the charges brought against the Duke of Buckingham in 1667 was that he had engaged John Heydon to calculate Charles II's horoscope;[122] Heydon was earlier said to have been imprisoned under the Protectorate for predicting Cromwell's death.[123] During the Popish Plot period John Gadbury confessed that Mrs Cellier, 'the Popish Midwife', had asked him to cast the King's nativity, although the astrologer claimed to have refused to do so.[124]

In such circumstances governments displayed keen interest in the activities of contemporary astrologers, and did not hesitate to censor their texts, prohibit their publications, and call them to account for their activities. Tudor printers, booksellers and almanac-makers were frequently in trouble when their forecasts were thought to have

118. Examples in *L.P.*, xv, p. 216; *A.P.C.*, iii, pp. 279, 300; *Narratives of the Days of the Reformation*, ed. J. G. Nichols (Camden Soc., 1859), pp. 172-3; *C.S.P.D.*, *1547–80*, p. 67; *1595–7*, p. 42; Foxe, vii, p. 85; *D.N.B.*, 'Fortescue, Sir Anthony'; *C.S.P. Spanish, 1558–67*, p. 208; P.R.O., SP 12/244, f. 112; *H.M.C.*, *Hatfield*, iv, p. 403.

119. 23 Eliz. c. 2. It was said to have been previously 'punishable by fine and imprisonment' (Sir E. Coke, *Institutes*, iii, chap. 1).

120. Sir W. Churchill, *Divi Britannici* (1675), p. 313; J. Hawarde, *Les Reportes del Cases in Camera Stellata, 1593 to 1609*, ed. W. P. Baildon (1894), p. 297; *H.M.C.*, *Hatfield*, v, p. 25; xvii, p. 530; *C.S.P.D.*, *1603–10*, p. 263.

121. *Secret History of the Court of James the First* (Edinburgh, 1811), i, p. 393; *C.S.P.D.*, *1611–18*, p. 303; E. Bower, *Doctor Lamb revived* (1653), pp. 26-7. The alleged resort of 300 Catholic plotters to an astrologer in 1641 was doubtless fictitious; *A Plot lately discovered for the Taking of the Tower by Negromancie* (1641).

122. *D.N.B.*; J. Heydon, *Theomagia* (1664), iii, p. 132; Pepys, *Diary*, 3 Mar. 1667; *C.S.P.D.*, *1666–7*, pp. 490, 541 (presumably John Heydon, not Peter); *1667–8*, pp. 286, 298, 343, 542-3; A. Browning, *Thomas Osborne, Earl of Danby* (Glasgow, 1944–51), i, pp. 45-6.

123. T. Carte, *The Life of James, Duke of Ormond* (Oxford, 1851), iv, p. 293.

124. *Diary of the Times of Charles the Second by the Honourable Henry Sidney*, ed. R. W. Blencowe (1843), i, pp. 253-5.

over-stepped the mark.[125] It was commonplace for the astrological writers of the Interregnum to contrast their new freedom with the strict control to which they had been subjected under the Laudian licensers. John Booker complained that before the Civil War the episcopal licensers had cut out half of his almanacs.[126] Nicholas Fiske attributed his failure to publish anything before 1650 to the long-prevailing ban on astrological writing, and the Gloucestershire astrologer, John Pool, explained that it was the censorship, in his case by the Presbyterians in the 1640s, which had delayed the publication of his *Country Astrology* until 1650.[127] The aftermath of the Civil War was, correspondingly a bad time for Royalist astrologers. The Parliamentarians were bent on the execution of George Wharton, and it was only the intercession of Lilly with his patron Bulstrode Whitelocke that secured his release.[128] After the Restoration a measure of state licensing was resumed. Lilly's almanac for 1674 was censored, and Partridge was denied liberty of the press at the beginning of the Exclusion Crisis.[129] John Gadbury, who was suspected of being a crypto-Catholic, was imprisoned in 1679 and again in 1690 for alleged implication in seditious activities.[130]

The political role of astrology arose from its self-fulfilling character. Any forecast once made had to be taken seriously. In the detection of stolen goods the astrologer could also be effective, and it was

125. For examples of such incidents, see *L.P.*, viii, p. 2; Sheffield City Archives, Bacon-Frank collection 2/17, f. 137; C. D. Shanahan in *Essex Recusant*, iii (1961), pp. 121–2; *H.M.C., Hatfield*, i, p. 576; ibid., xvii, pp. 22–3, 25, 33, 36; *C.S.P.D., 1598–1601*, p. 585. cf. the comments of Robert Ryece in a letter to John Winthrop in 1636; *Mass. Hist. Soc. Collectns.*, 4th ser., vi (Boston, 1863), p. 410.

126. Lilly, *Autobiography*, p. 104; Booker, *A Bloody Irish Almanack* (1664), sig. A3; id., *MDCXLIII Almanack et Prognosticon*, sigs. A4ᵛ–A5; Ashm. 190, f. 109 (plea for liberty of the press, undated). Booker had been imprisoned by High Commission for printing unlicensed almanacs in 1634 (*C.S.P.D., 1634–5*, p. 378). He presumably owed his appointment in 1643 as Parliamentary licenser of mathematical books to his office of Reader at Gresham College; *Acts and Ordinances of the Interregnum*, ed. C. H. Firth and R. S. Rait (1911), i, p. 187.

127. N. Fiske, preface to Sir C. Heydon, *An Astrological Discourse* (1650), sigs. A4–5; J. Pool, *Country Astrology* (1650), sig. A2.

128. *D.N.B.*, 'Wharton, Sir G.'; *Commons Journals*, v, p. 316.

129. Josten, *Ashmole*, p. 1377, n. 1; J. Partridge, *Vox Lunaris* (1679), p. 2.

130. *D.N.B.*, 'Gadbury, J.'.

not unknown for arrests to be made on the basis of astrological diagnosis alone. It would be interesting to know how many village Dog-
berries there were like Thomas Law, the constable of Quendon,
Essex, whose reaction in 1651 on being informed of a robbery was to
call on the astrologer, William Hills, 'with an intent to hear what he
might say, that so he might make his search accordingly'.[131] Like the
thief-magic of the cunning men, astrology could be a useful deterrent. Readers of Stendhal will recall that the Italian priest, Father
Blanès, practised astrology in order to keep the peasants from
stealing.[132]

But questions relating to theft were a notoriously tricky branch
of the astrologer's art. As John Pool concluded after twenty years'
practical experience in Gloucestershire:

It's a most difficult and laborious task ... for though we describe the
party or thief never so exactly, yet if the goods be not presently retaken
with the thief, or if the party so accused or described by us do complain
to an ignorant Justice of the Peace ... and pretend themselves injured,
either the simplicity of the master or [the] covetousness of the Clerk,
will causelessly bind over the artist to answer the fact at the next
Sessions ... which silly act of some Justices is no other than an encouragement unto thieves.[133]

John Partridge told the same story: 'In matters of theft people are
never satisfied and they do expect more from the art than that or
the artist is able to perform; and ... an unhappy judgement may
bring his person into scandal.'[134] In a large city the task was especially
difficult, because a physical description of the thief might easily fit
more than one person. Small wonder that Henry Coley despairingly
asserted in 1676 that 'no man ever yet could force back stolen goods
by the help of astrology only'.[135] There had been too many embarrassing failures. Simon Forman recorded in his diary for 1584 that
'certain brawls and slanders fell out against me about the detecting
of one that had stolen certain things, whereby I was like to have been

131. Essex R.O., Q/SBa 2/76 (Deposition of Thomas Law, 21 April 1651).
For an arrest on the sole basis of astrological calculation, see above,
p. 365.
132. *La Chartreuse de Parme*, chap. 2.
133. Pool, *Country Astrology*, sig. A3.
134. J. Partridge, *An Astrological Vade Mecum* (1679), pp. 69–70.
135. H. Coley, *Clavis Astrologiae Elimata* (2nd edn, 1676), p. 209. cf. Lilly,
Englands Propheticall Merline (1644), sig. bl^v.

spoiled'. Captain Bubb was put in the pillory for a wrong identification in the reign of James I; while Lilly was sent an anonymous letter in 1650, warning him that any further attempt on his part to accuse the physician, Dr. Luke Ridgeley, would result in his being 'wonderfully beaten'.[136] John Booker was said to have temporarily broken up a Wakefield mercer's marriage by implying that it was the wife who was responsible for the theft of some money about which her husband had consulted him.[137]

Astrologers could easily gain a reputation for trouble-making. John Lambe caused many divisions between husband and wife by diagnosing infidelity; and Lilly was accused of starting family quarrels, by pronouncing 'elder brothers childless and younger brothers certain heirs of their estates'.[138] We have seen enough of the questions brought to the practitioners to appreciate that it was with the client himself that these suspicions usually originated, the astrologer being merely invited to adjudicate upon them. But it was difficult to handle such matters without getting personally involved. Astrologers were accused of upsetting projected marriages in aristocratic families and persuading unsuitable clients to marry each other. Lilly, for example, incurred a great deal of odium for allegedly assisting John Howe of Langar, Nottinghamshire, to secure the hand of Annabella Scrope, natural daughter of the Earl of Sunderland, who was worth £2,500 per annum. What he had done was to give an affirmative answer to Howe's question as to whether he would ever enjoy the lady.[139] Isabel Williams, an unmarried maidservant from Whitechapel, was informed by Simon Forman that she was pregnant; affronted by this aspersion on her honour, she rushed home to fetch her mistress, but

136. *The Autobiography and Private Diary of Dr Simon Forman*, ed. J. O. Halliwell (1849), p. 17; Lilly, *Autobiography*, p. 64; Ashm. 240, f. 350.

137. 'G. Naworth' (G. Wharton), *Mercurio-Coelico-Mastix* (1644), sig. B3.

138. *A Briefe Description of the Notorious Life of Iohn Lambe* ('Amsterdam', 1628), p. 2; *Mercurius Elenticus* (2–9 Feb. 1648), p. 79; Ashm. 240, f. 350.

139. *Mercurius Elenticus* (12–19 Nov. 1647), pp. 22–3, for the charge, and for Lilly's defence, *Monarchy or no Monarchy* (1651), p. 49; *Mr William Lilly's True History of King James the First, and King Charles the First* (1715), pp. 102–4. For Lilly's involvement in another matrimonial case, see *Alimony Arraign'd; or the Remonstrance and Humble Appeal of Thomas Ivie, Esq.* (1654), p. 22; and for similar allegations (W. Rowland), *Judiciall Astrologie judicially Condemned* (1652), p. 7; *Character of a Quack Astrologer* (1673), sig. C2.

the astrologer proved right enough in the end.[140] The astrologer who displayed too detailed a knowledge of his neighbour's doings could thus incur a corresponding degree of odium. When John Dee left for Poland in 1583 his house at Mortlake was pillaged by an angry mob, while John Lambe, despite the patronage of the Duke of Buckingham and the protection of a bodyguard, was stoned to death in a London street.[141]

Since the astrologers had no certain legal basis for their activities they could ill afford to alienate public opinion. Astrology was not specifically banned in the statutes against witchcraft, but so long as its technicalities remained abracadabra to the lay public there was always a risk that the practitioner might find himself arrested for sorcery. The first English almanac-maker, Andrew Boorde, clearly assumed that the 1542 Witchcraft Act was intended to curtail the activities of men like himself, just as Robert Allen protested in the reign of Edward VI that his art was lawful because the 1542 Act had been repealed.[142] When witchcraft became a statutory offence again in 1563, astrologers reincurred the risk of prosecution, although the astrologer, Richard Harvey, asserted in 1583 that there was no law against astrology as such.[143] The repeated Tudor enactments against vagrant fortune-tellers provided another stick with which to beat the lesser members of the profession. In addition, the Royal College of Physicians of London took proceedings against unlicensed practitioners of astrological physic,[144] while the Anglican Church required its incumbents and church-wardens to denounce those parishioners who practised medicine without permission, or engaged in fortune-telling and divination. When one recalls that, on top of all these deterrents, there was the Act against calculating the the Queen's nativity, and a series of statutes and proclamations designed to curb the publication of false prophecies and punish their authors, the full range of the hazards besetting the astrological profession becomes apparent.

140. Ashm. 363, f. 199.
141. T. Smith, *The Life of John Dee*, trans. W. A. Ayton (1908), p. 52; *A Briefe Description of the Notorious Life of Iohn Lambe*, pp. 20–21; *The Court and Times of Charles the First* (1848), i, pp. 364–5.
142. E. F. Bosanquet, *English Printed Almanacks and Prognostications* (1917), p. 5; *Narratives of the Days of the Reformation*, ed. Nichols, p. 173.
143. R. Harvey, *An Astrological Discourse* (1583), sigs. qv^v–qvi.
144. e.g., Sir G. Clark, *A History of The Royal College of Physicians* (Oxford, 1964–6), i, pp. 232, 259.

In the reign of Edward VI there were several prosecutions, the lapse of the 1542 Act notwithstanding.[145] Under Elizabeth, Simon Forman incurred repeated persecution,[146] and in the seventeenth century there were many arrests.[147] Of the better-known practitioners, Nicholas Culpepper may have been the person of that name who was tried for his life in 1643 on a charge of bewitching a woman to death,[148] while Lilly, after surviving several political investigations, was indicted before Middlesex Sessions under the witchcraft statute in 1654, on a charge of deceitfully taking money for locating lost goods. He got off after being defended by the Recorder, who declared that astrology was a lawful art.[149] Lilly's Royalist rival, George Wharton, issued his works under the anagrammatic pseudonym of 'Naworth' to avoid identification. Almanac-makers, he declared, were only too often regarded by the public as 'wise men' and badgered with silly questions and therefore 'branded as conjurers, [and] wizards', so that they continually ran the risk of prosecution under the witchcraft statute before a judge with a bias against astrology.[150]

But when one considers practitioners like John Booker, who conducted his huge business in the heart of London for over thirty years, it seems clear that the astrologer could usually count on a good deal of public tolerance. The machinery for his prosecution was there, but it was only occasionally invoked. In many cases the practitioner was positively encouraged. Apart from the wealthy clientele which might flow into his consulting-room and the prospect of

145. Kittredge, *Witchcraft*, p. 229.
146. *D.N.B.*
147. Examples in B. H. Cunnington, *Records of the County of Wilts.* (Devizes, 1932), pp. 61–2 (Edmond Langdon, 1617); *County of Middlesex. Calendar to the Sessions Records,* new ser., ed. W. Le Hardy (1935–41), i, pp. 199, 372 (John Wheeler, 1613); ibid., iv, p. 309, Ewen, ii, p. 433, Wood, *Ath. Ox.,* ii, col. 555, and Ashm. 421, f. 170 (Mathias Evans, 1617–18); W. Drage, *Daimonomageia* (1665), pp. 39–40 (Redman of Amersham); Pool, *Country Astrology,* sig. A3 (unnamed astrologer, c. 1650); *C.S.P.D., 1654,* p. 146 (unnamed); F. W. Jessup, *Sir Roger Twysden, 1597–1672* (1965), p. 154 (John Higgs, 1662); *Middlesex County Records,* ed. J. C. Jeaffreson (1886–92), iv, pp. 212–13 (John Holwell, 1683, for publishing *Catastrophe Mundi*).
148. Ewen, ii, p. 434 (though described as from St. Leonard's, Shoreditch, whereas Culpepper lived in Spitalfields). This may have been one of the 'other cross transactions of his life' which his contemporary biographer chose to omit; *Culpeper's School of Physick* (1659), sig. C6.
149. Ewen, ii, p. 456; Lilly, *Autobiography,* pp. 167–71, 253–6.
150. *The Works of ... Sir George Wharton,* pp. 275–6.

government encouragement at moments of political crisis, there was also a chance of gaining formal respectability. Lambe, Lilly, William Salmon and several other astrologers obtained episcopal licences to practise medicine.[151] And there is no telling how many humbler itinerant operators there were like William Taylor, 'student in astrology', who on 17 November 1683 was formally given leave by the City of Norwich 'to use his art in that science for a week from this day'.[152]

3. *Decline*

If astrology was discharging so many useful functions, why did it nevertheless rapidly decline in status towards the end of the seventeenth century? There are only two possible ways of answering this question. One is to say that the problems which astrologers claimed to solve became less acute. This possibility will be discussed in the conclusion to this book. The other is to say that the solutions which they offered came to appear less convincing. This is the more conventional answer and it needs little in the way of explanation. The intellectual pretensions of astrological theory were irreparably shattered by the astronomical revolution initiated by Copernicus and consummated by Newton. The assumption that the heavens were immutable was upset by the appearance of previouly unobserved nebulae, like the 'new stars' of 1572 and 1604; if the sky was changing, how could its influence be predicted? Galileo's discovery of the four satellites of Jupiter made men aware that the heavens were full of unseen stars whose influence was unaccountable. The telescope, by uncovering new celestial bodies, confirmed the hypothesis of a plurality of worlds. The cosy, man-centred universe of Ptolemy was no more. Yet none of these changes – not even the revelation that the heavens were infinite – made astrology impossible, though they did make astrological calculation much more difficult. Heliocentrism was consistent with astrology. If the earth was constantly changing its position then certain calculations would have to be made all over again, but the task was not impossible. 'Whether (as Copernicus saith) the sun be the centre of the world,' declared Sir Christopher Heydon in 1603, 'the astrologer careth not.'[153]

151. Below, p. 435, n. 44.
152. *Extracts from the Court Books of the City of Norwich, 1666–88*, ed. W. Rye (Norfolk and Norwich Archaeol. Soc., 1903), p. 173.
153. Heydon, *A Defence of Iudiciall Astrologie*, p. 371.

What really destroyed the possibility of scientific astrology was the undermining of the Aristotelian distinction between terrestrial and celestial bodies, what Bacon called 'the imaginary divorce between superlunary and sublunary things'.[154] On the one hand the earth was revealed as a planet of the same quality as any other and subject to the same laws of motion; on the other, the heavens were robbed of their former perfection. Galileo observed spots on the sun and an irregular surface on the moon. Tycho Brahe demonstrated that comets were above the moon, not below, and that the heavens were therefore subject to corruption and change. Moreover, once comets were seen to be so far away it became implausible to argue that they were capable of scorching the earth and producing droughts. By the beginning of the eighteenth century Edmond Halley had computed the orbits of twenty-four comets, proved that the comets of 1531, 1607 and 1682 were all the same one, and correctly predicted its next appearance in 1758. It became harder to regard a comet in the sky as a heaven-sent warning of a particular disaster.[155]

The old dichotomy between things sublunar and things celestial, which had been the very foundation of astrological theory, thus became increasingly untenable. Once abandoned, it became impossible to define the nature of that one-way astrological influence which the stars had been supposed to exert upon the earth. Given time, astrology could have adapted itself to any number of new discoveries about the landscape of the universe, for these merely meant that the calculation of the manner in which the celestial bodies exerted their influence became more complicated. But the removal of the very idea of such an influence made the task impossible. The world could no longer be envisaged as a compact interlocking organism; it was now a mechanism of infinite dimensions, from which the old hierarchical subordination of earth to heavens had irretrievably disappeared.[156]

154. Bacon, *Works*, iv, p. 349.
155. See, e.g., J. H. Robinson, *The Great Comet of 1680. A Study in the History of Rationalism* (Northfield, Minnesota, 1916), chap. 8; C. D. Hellman, *The Comet of 1577: its Place in the History of Astronomy* (New York, 1944), and 'The Role of Measurement in the Downfall of a System: Some Examples from Sixteenth-century Comet and Nova Observations', in *Vistas in Astronomy*, ed. A. Beer, ix (1967).
156. For some discussion of the impact of astronomical discovery on astrology, see M. Graubard, 'Astrology's Demise and Its Bearing on the

But the new ideas were slow to permeate downwards. Indeed the astronomers themselves were slow to recognize their implications. For a time they clung to their faith in astrology, even as their own discoveries were undermining it. They struggled unsuccessfully to define the nature of the astrological force which emanated from the stars because they were reluctant to give up the emotional satisfaction provided by a coherent and interrelated universe. Usually they compromised by allowing general predictions but rejecting specific ones. Both Galileo and Kepler hesitated to face up to the full import of their discoveries and it took Gassendi and Bayle to deliver the *coup de grâce* to astrological claims. In England the same hesitation and inconsistencies were to be seen. The earliest converts to Copernicanism had included such active astrologers as Leonard Digges, John Field, and the almanac-makers Edward Gresham and Thomas Bretnor.[157] Sir Henry Wootton could cheerfully assume that Galileo had 'overthrown ... all astrology', but many of his contemporaries were not so sure. Astrology, thought Bacon, needed to be reformed, but not abolished.[158] William Gilbert scoffed at astrologers who thought that metals were ruled by the planets, but he did not doubt that children were influenced by the stars at birth.[159] John Bainbridge, first Savilian Professor of Astronomy at Oxford, knew that comets were above the moon, but could not forbear an interpretative gloss on the moral significance of the comet of 1618; though he affected to base it upon 'celestial hieroglyphics' rather than 'vulgar astrology'.[160] In his inaugural lecture as Gresham Professor of Astronomy in 1657 Christopher Wren declared that there was 'a true astrology to be found by the inquiring philosopher, which would be

Decline and Death of Beliefs', *Osiris*, xiii (1958); T. S. Kuhn, *The Copernican Revolution* (Cambridge, Mass., 1957), esp. pp. 93, 221–2; Nicolson, *The Breaking of the Circle*; Thorndike, *Magic and Science*, vi, pp. 69–71 (Brahe); vii, pp. 17–28 (Kepler), 35–6 (Galileo), 446–51 (Gassendi).

157. Bosanquet, *English Printed Almanacks and Prognostications*, pp. 33–4; Thorndike, *Magic and Science*, v. pp. 417, 419, 422; vi, pp. 15, 30–1, 39; F. R. Johnson, *Astronomical Thought in Renaissance England* (Baltimore, 1937), p. 250.

158. *The Life and Letters of Sir Henry Wotton*, ed. L. P. Smith (Oxford, 1907), i, p. 486; Bacon, *Works*, iv, pp. 349–55.

159. W. Gilbert, *On the Magnet*, ed. D. J. Price (New York, 1958), I.vii; III.xii.

160. J. Bainbridge, *An Astronomicall Description of the Late Comet* (1619), p. 32.

of admirable use to physick'.[161] A 'sober and regulated astrology' was the ideal of Sir Thomas Browne.[162]

The mid seventeenth century saw a determined effort to bring the subject up to date, fired by such taunts as George Herbert's remark that 'astrology is true, but the astrologers cannot find it'.[163] The Frenchman J.-B. Morin attempted a thoroughgoing reform, and his ideas had some influence in England.[164] The Baconian Joshua Childrey urged his colleagues to adapt their calculations to fit the new astronomical facts, in full confidence that all would be well once the necessary adjustments had been effected. Astrology's achievements so far might be small, he admitted, but 'that there is such a science ... there is no question to be made'.[165] Jeremy Shakerley, the second man to observe the transit of Mercury, was well aware that most contemporary astrologers, 'being ignorant of the astronomical part of their art, [were] not be trusted', yet he resolved not to abandon the subject, but 'from philosophical principles [to] seek a foundation for a more refined astrology'.[166] Despite the new knowledge about comets, a welter of tracts on their prophetic significance was published in the 1680s. Most of the almanac-makers had gone over to Copernicanism by this time,[167] but it made no difference to their prognosticatory activities.

This last phase, in which an attempt was made to reconcile astrology with the new science, was of only brief duration. Serious astronomers had ceased to make any contributions to astrology, even if they were reluctant to abandon it. For Seth Ward astrology was a 'ridiculous cheat'. Robert Hooke, once a believer, gradually came to see that the activity was 'vain'. Ralph Cudworth saw it as resting upon ' a very weak and tottering, if not impossible foundation'. Henry More thought it 'a fanciful study built upon very slight grounds'. Meric Casaubon said it was 'founded upon mere imaginary suppositions and poetical fictions, words and names which have no ground

161. C. Wren, *Parentalia* (1750), p. 203.

162. *Pseudodoxia Epidemica* (1646), IV.xiii.

163. *The Remains of ... George Herbert* (1836), p. 166.

164. Thorndike, *Magic and Science*, vii, chap. 16. cf. R. Saunders, *The Astrological Judgment and Practice of Physick* (1677), p. 10; *The Works of ... Sir George Wharton*, pp. 105–10, 184–208.

165. J. Childrey, *Indago Astrologica* (1652); id., *Britannia Baconica* (1661), sig. B5.

166. *H.M.C., Various Collections*, viii, p. 61.

167. M. Nicolson, 'English Almanacs and the "New Astronomy"', *Annals of Science*, iv (1939–40), p. 24.

at all in nature'. The astronomer, Abraham Sharp, frankly despised it. Hobbes coolly omitted it from his list of demonstrable spheres of knowledge. Sprat made a hostile reference to it in his history of of the Royal Society, a body which was distinctly hostile to astrological pretensions.[168] Yet, curiously enough, scarcely anyone attempted a serious refutation of astrology in the light of the new principles, although Gassendi's polemic was translated into English in 1659. Bayle's devastating refutation of the idea that comets could be presages was published in Holland in 1682, but it did not appear in English until 1708.[169] For the most part the subject was left to die a natural death. The clergy and the satirists chased it into its grave, but the scientists were unrepresented at the funeral.

By the end of the seventeenth century, therefore, astrology had lost its scientific prestige. Some individual scientists may have felt reluctant to see it go, but the Newtonian system could not accommodate the concept of celestial influences. The gigantic structure of astrological explanation accordingly collapsed. Centuries of intellectual speculation had merely led further and further up a blind alley.

Of course, many of astrology's defects had been pointed out before the coming of the new science. Astrology, it was observed, was rigid and arbitrary. The zodiac and twelve houses had no reality. Nor was mere coincidence in time between an event and a celestial occurrence any proof that a causal relationship between the two existed. Astrology lacked the essential quality of a science – the capacity for demonstration. 'The rules of this art have no foundation in experience,' wrote Thomas Cooper.[170] Such objections were more fundamental than the time-honoured quibbles about twins, born under

168. (S. Ward), *Vindiciae Academiarum* (1654), pp. 30–32; M. 'Espinasse, *Robert Hooke* (1956), p. 119; R. Cudworth, *The True Intellectual System of the Universe*, trans. J. Harrison (1845), i, p. 7; H. More, *Enthusiasmus Triumphatus* (1656), p. 41; M. Casaubon, *Of Credulity and Incredulity in things Natural, Civil, and Divine* (1668), p. 141; W. Cudworth, *Life and Correspondence of Abraham Sharp* (1889), p. 152; T. Hobbes, *English Works*, ed. Sir W. Molesworth (1839–45), i, p. 11; Sprat, *History of the Royal Society*, ed. J. I. Cope and H. W. Jones (St Louis, 1959), p. 97. cf. J. Gadbury, *Obsequium Rationale* (1675), p. 32.

169. P. Gassendus, *The Vanity of Judiciary Astrology*, trans. by 'a Person of Quality' (1659); P. Bayle, *Miscellaneous Reflections occasion'd by the Comet which appear'd in December 1680* (1708).

170. Cooper, *Mystery*, p. 141. For the same argument, see Fulke, *Antiprognosticon*, sig. Bii.

the same star, but having different destinies, or armies of men, killed in the same battle, but having different nativities. But once the old cosmology collapsed they became equally unanswerable.

The change in opinion could be seen in the two Universities. In Tudor times many dons had been keenly interested in astrology and some, like their medieval predecessor, Chaucer's clerk Nicholas, turned an honest penny by setting figures for clients. As late as the 1650s Lilly claimed to have many admirers in both Universities, while the Quaker Henry Clark denounced Oxford and Cambridge for turning out so many astrologers to cheat the people.[171] But from the reign of Elizabeth there is evidence of scepticism. The young Fellow of St. John's, Edmund Campion, could greet the Queen on her arrival at Oxford in 1566 with a disputation on the theme that the inferior bodies were ruled by higher ones,[172] but most of the theses subsequently maintained by M.A.s at their inception reveal an increasing hostility to the pretensions of astrology.[173] John Chamber lectured against it at Oxford in the 1570s, while Robert Greene thought in 1585 that the learned laughed at its practitioners as charlatans.[174] In the early years of the Commonwealth Seth Ward maintained the thesis that prognosticatory astrology was both *inanis* and *illicita*. Thereafter it became usual for participants in these disputations to deny the influence of the heavens upon disease or human

171. Ashm. 423, f. 173; Lilly, *Autobiography*, p. 169; H. Clark, *A Rod Discovered* (1657), pp. 38–9. Well-known sixteenth-century university astrologers included John Robins of All Souls (above, p. 342); John Fletcher of Caius (J. Venn in *The Caian*, vi [1896]); John Bowckeley of New Inn (W. H. Hart in *Archaeologia*, xl (1866), pp. 391–4); John Maplet of Catharine Hall (author of *The Diall of Destiny* [1581]). For the astrological interests of an early seventeenth-century don, see W. C. Costin, 'The Inventory of John English, B.C.L., Fellow of St John's College', *Oxoniensia*, xi–xii (1946–7), pp. 113–14. See also *Visitations in the Diocese of Lincoln, 1517–31*, ed. A. H. Thompson (Lincoln Rec. Soc., 1940–7), iii, p. 73; H. Rashdall, *The Universities of Europe in the Middle Ages*, ed. F. M. Powicke and A. B. Emden (Oxford, 1936), iii, p. 161; *The Works of ... Joseph Mede* (1664), i, pp. viii–ix.

172. F. Peck, *Desiderata Curiosa* (new edn, 1779), p. 276.

173. *Register of the University of Oxford, ii (1571–1622)*, ed. A. Clark (Oxford Hist. Soc., 1887), i, pp. 170 (1581), 172 (1590), 178 (1618), 199 (1596); Oxf. Univ. Arch., P 15, ff. 247 (1630), 277ᵛ (1633); Q 16, f. 178ᵛ (1635); Qa 17, ff. 150 (1651), 152 (1653).

174. J. Chamber, *Astronomiae Encomium* (1601), pp. 38–40 (appended to *A Treatise against Iudicial Astrologie* [1601]); *The Life and Complete Works ... of Robert Greene*, ed. A. B. Grosart (1881–6), v, pp. 17–18.

affairs, and to reject the possibility of prediction from comets or other alleged portents.[175] Similarly in Cambridge it was maintained in 1603 that judicial astrology was a mere imposture.[176] In 1659 John Gadbury complained that 'your freshmen and junior sophists at Oxford and Cambridge . . . bawl aloud in the Schools *astrologia non est scientia*'. 'Do you hear the news from Alma Mater?' wrote John Butler to Ashmole in 1680, 'All astrology must be banished.'[177] In fact the statutes establishing the Savilian chair of Astronomy in 1619 had long ago banned its holders from teaching judicial astrology or the doctrine of nativities, even if less formal astrological studies had continued.[178]

Astrology was also disappearing from orthodox medicine. In the mid seventeenth century all but a few sceptics[179] had accepted its value, so far as the choice of days for blood-letting or administering medicine was concerned. But during the ensuing hundred years astrological medicine was quietly discarded, although the evidence for medical practice is as yet too slight for the historian to chart the change with much confidence. A writer claimed in 1617 that learned physicians had abandoned astrology; and when Burton published his *Anatomy of Melancholy* four years later the place of astrology in medicine was undoubtedly controversial. Writing in 1633, the physi-

175. Oxf. Univ. Arch., Qa 17, f. 152ᵛ (Ward); Qb 18, f. 178 (1669); Be 20, f. 202 (1681); Bd 19, ff. 205 (1674), 206 (1675), 209 (1680). But for some exceptions to this trend see *Register of the University*, ed. Clark, p. 179 (1621); R. South, *Opera Posthuma Latina* (1717), pp. 24–8 (1657); Oxf. Univ. Arch., Bd 19 f. 207 (1676).

176. J. Chamber, 'A Confutation of Astrologicall Demonology' (Bodl., Savile MS 42), ff. 99ᵛ–100. For other instances, see W. T. Costello, *The Scholastic Curriculum at Early Seventeenth-century Cambridge* (Cambridge, Mass., 1958), p. 91.

177. J. Gadbury, *The Nativity of the late King Charls* (1659), sig. A5ᵛ; J. B(utler), *The Most Sacred and Divine Science of Astrology* (1680), ii, ep. ded.

178. P. Allen, 'Scientific Studies in the English Universities of the Seventeenth Century', *Journ. Hist. Ideas*, x (1949), p. 226. John Preston had studied astrology as a Fellow of Queens', Cambridge (*c.* 1609), as did Ashmole at Oxford (*c.* 1644–5) (T. Ball *The Life of the Renowned Dr Preston*, ed. E. W. Harcourt [Oxford, 1885], pp. 14–16; Josten, *Ashmole*, p. 353).

179. e.g., Fulke, *Antiprognosticon*, sig. Dviiᵛ (following P. Daquet, *Almanack novum et perpetuum* [1556], a treatise arguing that all medical operations should be timed with reference to the state of the patient's body, not the stars).

cian James Hart rejected it altogether.[180] The Royal College of Physicians had for some time been censuring astrological doctors and prohibiting the practice of making diagnoses on the basis of the patient's urine alone. Yet Richard Forster, an astrological almanacmaker, was elected the College's President in 1601–4 and again in 1615–16, and there were astrological touches in the College's official Pharmacopoeia. Sir Richard Napier, though an astrologer, became an Honorary Fellow in 1664.[181]

Thorough-going astrological medicine had probably always been exceptional. Even in the reign of Elizabeth it was said that not one in a hundred physicians knew the proper rules.[182] But the old belief in the influence of the moon upon the human body continued to be accepted by many of those who, like Francis Bacon and Henry More, rejected most other parts of astrological theory. Both Nehemiah Grew and Robert Boyle believed that the moon affected the brain.[183] Richard Mead, the leading physician in early eighteenth-century London, and Vice-President of the Royal Society in 1717, wrote *A Treatise concerning the Influence of the Sun and Moon upon Human Bodies*, to preserve this element of truth which he thought underlay the hotch-potch of judicial astrology. Mead argued that the sun and moon produced changes in atmospheric pressure which determined the amount of nervous fluid in the human body. The incidence of epilepsy, vertigo, hysteria and asthma, as well as of menstruation and childbirth,[184] was in his opinion to be attributed to the phases of the moon. The survival of such beliefs in such a

180. Cooper, *Mystery*, p. 144; Burton, *Anatomy*, ii, pp. 15–16; J. Hart, *The Diet of the Diseased* (1633), pp. 256 ff. cf. Primrose, *Popular Errours*, pp. 246–7.

181. Clark, *A History of the Royal College of Physicians*, i, pp. 168, 316. A number of well-known contemporary physicians who observed astrological principles are cited by *Bretnor. 1619. A New Almanacke and Prognostication*, sig. C3.

182. J. Indagine, *Brief Introductions*, trans. F. Withers (1575), sig. Jiiij.

183. Bacon, *Works*, ii, pp. 635–7; iv, p. 354; Scot, *Discoverie*, IX.ii; *Conway Letters*, ed. M. H. Nicolson (1930), p. 132; R. Hunter and I. Macalpine, *Three Hundred Years of Psychiatry* (1963), p. 285; *The Works of the Hon. Robert Boyle* (1744), v, p. 96.

184. R. Mead, *A Treatise concerning the Influence of the Sun and Moon upon Human Bodies*, trans. T. Stack (1748). There is a similar *Mechanical Account of the Natural Causes of the Influence of the Moon upon Human Bodies* in (J.) Gibbs, *Observations of Various Eminent Cures of Scrophulous Distempers* (1712), pp. 54–64.

quarter makes one chary about putting a firm date to the end of astrological medicine in its wider sense. Some late-seventeenth-century doctors of note, like Francis Bernard, physician to James II, set horoscopes in the traditional manner.[185] In 1680 John Butler thought that astrological physicians were still 'famous and . . . greatly sought after'. Even John Locke believed in the astrological choice of times for picking medicinal herbs.[186]

Among the population at large the movement of opinion on astrology is impossible to chart with any accuracy. The general impression left by the literary evidence is that the current of scepticism, already well-established in the reign of Elizabeth, had swept most educated opinion along with it by the end of the seventeenth century. Throughout the period the astrologers themselves never ceased to lament the opposition they had to endure. Most people despised 'astronomers', said the almanac-maker, John Securis, in 1568. They saw astrology as an entertaining recreation rather than a genuine science, agreed John Fage in 1606.[187] Despite his thriving practice, Lilly complained of 'the small conceit and opprobrious judgement the English nation have of astrology'. 'The citizens of London make small reckoning of astrology', he grumbled.[188] Like others, he had suffered from the sceptics who penetrated into his consulting-room, bringing misleading samples of horses' urine, and ready to try any deception which would expose the unwary astrologer.[189]

After the Restoration it became obvious that changes in intellectual fashion were leaving the astrologers behind. Gadbury complained that most people neglected or condemned the subject, and in John Wilson's play, *The Cheats* (1662), the astrologer Mopus (based on John Heydon) laments the decline of his trade.[190] In Reading Joseph Blagrave grumbled that his practice was falling off

185. W. Munk, *The Roll of the Royal College of Physicians* (2nd edn, 1878), i, p. 499; A. Malloch, *Finch and Baines* (Cambridge, 1917), pp. 66–7. Some of his astrological figures are in Sloane 1707.

186. Butler, *The Most Sacred and Divine Science of Astrology*, ii, p. 27; M. Cranston, *John Locke* (1957), p. 91.

187. J. Securis, *A New Almanacke and Prognostication . . . MDLXVIII* sig. Aii; J. Fage, *Speculum Aegrotorum, the Sicke-Mens Glasse* (1606), 'To the Reader'.

188. W. Lilly, *Anglicus* (1645), sig. A3v; id., *Christian Astrology*, 'To the Reader'.

189. Ashm. 363, f. 2v; 185, f. 154v.

190. J. Gadbury, *Britains Royal Star* (1661), p. 12; J. Wilson, *The Cheats*, ed. M. C. Nahm (Oxford, 1935), p. 145. Defoe thought that the

because clients had scruples about the legality of their consultations and (significantly) feared loss of reputation, should the neighbours discover where they had been.[191] The vulgar treated astrological predictions as mere fables, bemoaned Richard Saunders in 1677; in the same year John Webster, himself a sympathiser, lamely admitted that astrology was 'a general cheat as it is commonly used'.[192] In 1679 John Middleton lamented that the science was 'much despised and . . . slightly looked on', while Gadbury confessed that even the vulgar regarded the almanacs as contemptible.[193] Most readers, it was said, could not even remember what the picture of the Anatomical Man was for. As the astrologer William Hunt sadly concluded in 1696, there were now 'but few students or lovers of this art'.[194]

The truth seems- to be that astrology had ceased, in all but the most unsophisticated circles, to be regarded as either a science or a crime: it had become simply a joke. In *Hudibras* Samuel Butler had mocked Lilly and Booker under the sobriquets of Sidrophel and Whackham, and he continued the attack in his other writings. The astrologer, Foresight, in Congreve's *Love for Love* (1695) is a mere figure of fun. Any dignity the profession might still have retained was finally lost after Swift's comic assault on the wretched astrologer, Partridge, in his *Predictions of Isaac Bickerstaff for 1708* and ensuing squibs.[195] This brought an end to the transitional period, when intellectuals paid lip-service to astrology without believing in it very deeply, like Ben Jonson, who cast horoscopes, but 'trust[ed] not in them', or Lord Treasurer Clifford, who consulted astrologers, but

astrologers who infested the metropolis before the Great Plague never returned afterwards; *A Journal of the Plague Year* (1722) (New York, 1960), pp. 176–7.

191. J. Blagrave, *Blagraves Astrological Practice of Physick* (1671), Ep. ded.

192. Saunders, *The Astrological Judgment and Practice of Physick*, ii, p. 172; J. Webster, *The Displaying of Supposed Witchcraft* (1677), p. 25.

193. J. Middleton, *Practical Astrology* (1679), sig. A1ᵛ; (J. Gadbury), *Magna Verĭtas: or John Gadbury . . . not a Papist* (1680), p. 10.

194. G. L. Kittredge, *The Old Farmer and his Almanack* (Boston, 1904), p. 58; W. Hunt, *Demonstration of Astrology* (1696), sig. A3.

195. S. Butler, *Characters and Passages from the Note-Books*, ed. A. R. Waller (Cambridge, 1908), pp. 71, 416, 457. A list of the satires directed against Partridge is given by W. A. Eddy in *Studies in Philology*, xxix (1932), pp. 38–40. Swift's attack had been anticipated by Tom Brown in the 1690s.

also disparaged them.[196] After 1700 the volume of astrological writing appears to have fallen off sharply. The almanacs continued, although their prognostications were vaguer and emptier than ever, and they were issued under the names of their seventeenth-century founders – Saunders, Partridge, *et al.* No new generation of astrologers had arisen to put their name to such forecasts. 'Astrology suffers great calumny in these days,' lamented the editor of Coley's almanac in 1733.[197] There were still practising astrologers who made predictions, gave advice to clients, and went through all the motions of their predecessors, but they were less likely to draw notables to their consulting-rooms. In the nineteenth century, and after, astrology was to undergo several revivals, but the intellectual vitality the subject had once possessed was gone for ever.

196. B. Jonson, *Conversations with William Drummond of Hawthornden*, xiii; above, p. 380.
197. *Merlinus Anglicus Junior* (1733), sig. C4ᵛ. For some account of astrological publication after 1700, see E. Howe, *Urania's Children* (1967).

12.

ASTROLOGY AND RELIGION

> This wicked art is everywhere practised and run after by most
> men and women, but especially of some who would needs be
> taken to be professors of the Gospel of the Lord Christ.
>
> John Raunce, *A Brief Declaration against
> Judicial Astrologie* (1650), p. 1

1. Conflict

THE relations between astrology and religion had been coloured by
mutual suspicion since the early Christian era. During the century
after the Reformation the two systems of belief came into sharp conflict. Many of the English clergy denounced judicial astrology as an
impious art whose teachings were fundamentally incompatible with
some of the basic tenets of Christianity. Most of the arguments they
employed in their sermons and pamphlets were derived from earlier
European writers, but they deployed them with unmistakable vehemence.

The first line of attack was to point out that religion and astrology
frequently offered conflicting explanations for the same phenomena.
Whereas the Christian was taught to regard storms, famines or earthquakes as the manifestations of God's secret purposes, the astrologer made them subject to the movement of the celestial bodies and
therefore predictable by his art. This attribution of good or bad luck
to the stars was a direct threat to Christian dogma: as Calvin said,
it 'put ... clouds before our eyes to drive us away from the providence of God'. Bishop Hooper similarly warned h's hearers that 'it
is neither Sun, neither Moon, Jupiter nor Mars, that is the occasion
of wealth or woe, plenty or scarcity, of war or peace': it was God
himself. Long life was the reward for godliness, not the legacy of
the planets.[1] Much of the war against astrology was fought at this
basic level of causation. As the Presbyterian Thomas Gataker de-

---

1. J. Calvin, *An Admonicion against Astrology Iudiciall*, trans. G. G(ylby)
[1561], sig. Cvi[v]; *Early Writings of John Hooper*, ed. S. Carr (Cambridge,
P.S., 1843), p. 333.

clared in 1653, it was essential that Christians should regard all events, 'not with an astrological, but a theological eye'.[2]

The astrologers caused the deepest offence by offering a secular explanation for some of the most delicate matters in religious history. They did not hesitate to proffer astral reasons for the dominance of different religions in different parts of the world; some practitioners even continued the notorious medieval attempts to cast the nativity of Christ himself.[3] It was a horrified reaction against blasphemy of this kind which led so many clerics to cast their polemic against astrology in what must seem to us fundamentally antiscientific language. Foreknowledge, whether of religious history or of human behaviour in general, was a perquisite of God alone, and it was presumptuous to usurp such a prerogative. 'If a man shall undertake by the stars to foretell future events, which are accidental, dependent on the wills of and actions of men,' declared the Independent divine, William Bridge, 'he doth plainly step into the chair of God.'[4] 'God,' said John Gaule, 'hath resumed the foreknowledge and foreshewing of things future to himself; and hath discharged . . . man from all such curiosities and presumptions; and hath expressly forbidden us . . . both the consulting with and assenting to them.'[5] This prohibition was doubtless meant less literally than it sounds, for its author had no objection to natural science as such, and did not deny the usefulness of astronomy for navigation, medicine and agriculture. But his distaste for judicial astrology drove him to enunciate principles which would have constituted an effective block against many forms of scientific endeavour. 'Heaven is God's book, which we must leave to him,' said another cleric; 'To what end has God placed us so far from the stars, if with astrolabes, staves and quadrants we can do all things as if we were nearer?'[6] This was as anti-

2. T. Gataker, *His Vindication of the Annotations by him published* (1653), p. 153.

3. Calvin, *An Admonicion against Astrology Iudiciall*, sig. Dvj; W. E. Peuckert, *L'Astrologie*, trans. R. Jouan and L. Jospin (Paris, 1965), p. 151; Scot, *Discoverie*, XI.xxii; Ashm. 1730, f. 170; J. G(regory), *Notes and Observations upon Some Passages of Scripture* (1646), p. 152; J. Butler, *A Brief (but true) Account of the Certain Year, Moneth, Day and Minute of the Birth of Jesus Christ* (1671); H. More, *Tetractys Anti-Astrologica* (1681), p. vi.

4. *The Works of the Rev. William Bridge* (1845), i, p. 438.

5. J. Gaule, *The Mag-Astro-Mancer, or the Magicall-Astrologicall-Diviner Posed and Puzzled* (1652), p. 48.

6. J. Chamber, *A Treatist against Iudicial Astrologie* (1601), p. 102.

scientific as the associated argument that astrology should be condemned because it made men forget the role of God in human affairs. 'While we are detained in the view of natural causes,' wrote John Geree, 'we shall not look to supernatural ends or uses, or not so much as we should, and otherways would." Science could only be tolerated so long as it was never allowed to get out of hand. 'We must make philosophy wait and submit to divinity,' said Thomas Hall. 'Every science must keep its proper bounds." The attack upon judicial astrology thus posed the basic issue of whether human curiosity should be allowed to play freely upon the works of creation.

But if this had been all there was to the conflict between the two systems of belief, it could have been fairly easily resolved. Religion was to prove itself adaptable in the face of the scientific revolution, and there was no difficulty about formulating theological arguments to justify and even to stimulate the study of natural science. The stars and the planets had been set in the heavens by God himself, it was urged. Their workings were to be observed as an exemplification of his majesty and power. They could never be more than secondary causes of earthly events, but there was no reason why God should not achieve his purposes by working through them if he pleased. Knowledge of their operation could only redound to his greater glory. These were the lines along which most later seventeenth-century theologians justified the study of natural science; and if there had been no other objections to astrology it too might have become as compatible with piety as any other form of natural knowledge. Of course, there were some awkward Biblical passages to be explained away, notably the hostile reference in Isaiah, xlvii, 13, to 'the astrologers, the stargazers, the monthly prognosticators'. But against this could be set the reminder in Genesis, i, 14, that God had placed the stars in the firmament as signs to men; even better, there was the example of the star in the East leading the Magi to Bethlehem. The resources of the Authorised Version and the ingenuity of its commentators made the task of assimilating the new science a simple one.

It was not therefore because astrology claimed to be a natural science that it incurred so much theological opposition. Nor was it because of its intellectual weaknesses. In their campaign the theologians naturally drew upon the armoury of debating points against

7. J. Geree, *Astrologo-Mastix* (1646), p. 5.
8. T. Hall, *Vindiciae Literarum* (1655), p. 51.

astrology accumulated by earlier writers, from Cicero to Pico della Mirandola. But intellectual objections to the subject did not lie at the root of their hostility. Neither did the fact that astrology had begun as a heathen form of learning, in texts written by Muslims, pagans, and what Gataker called 'the ancient Egyptian wizards'.[9] It is true that some sectaries condemned astrology along with the writings of the pagan Aristotle,[10] just as the more extreme Protestants revived the early Christian campaign to rebaptize the days and the months with names which were not derived from pagan divinities.[11] But such scrupulosity was only found on the extreme fringe of Puritanism. Most conventional brands of religion were able enough to absorb Plato and Aristotle, along with classical literature, Arab science, and other forms of pagan learning.

The real origin of the theological attack on astrology was the conviction that the astrologers taught an astral determinism which was incompatible with Christian doctrines of free will and moral autonomy. This was the point at which the spokesmen of the medieval Church had parted company with the astrologers. They had readily conceded the claims of the *natural* part of the subject – the influence of the heavens upon climate, vegetation and physiology – and had recognized astrology as an essential part of agriculture or medicine. What they found intolerable was the *judicial* side of the art – the exact prediction, not just of the weather, but of human behaviour, whether of people in the mass or as individuals. The more specific the prediction the more did it offend against the belief in free will. Theologians could not accept that men were so much the victims of their own inherited dispositions as to be unable to break out of this astral bondage, and exercise independent moral choice. The stars, they conceded, might influence the body, but they could not touch the soul. The astrologer could never infallibly tell how any particular man would behave because the will and the intellect remained free. A practitioner who claimed certainty for his predictions was no more

9. Gataker, *His Vindication of the Annotations*, p. 175. cf. *The Works of John Jewel*, ed. J. Ayre (Cambridge, P.S., 1845–50), ii, p. 872.

10. J. Brayne, *Astrologie proved to be the old Doctrine of Demons* (1653), pp. 12–13, 25.

11. e.g., J. W. Blench, *Preaching in England* (Oxford, 1964), p. 267; G. F. Nuttall, *The Holy Spirit* (Oxford, 1946), p. 153; J. B(rinsley), *Calendar Reformation* (1648); [E.W.], *The Life and Death of Mr Henry Jessey* (1671), pp. 63–4; J.W., *A Mite* (1653), p. 17; J. Brayne, *The New Earth* (1653), p. 19; G. F(ox), *To the Parliament . . . Fifty Nine Particulars* (1659), pp. 9–10.

than a heretic. This fundamental objection to the very possibility of prognostications *pro certo* had been stated by St Augustine, and reformulated by Aquinas.[12] During the sixteenth and seventeenth centuries it was constantly reaffirmed. The theologians, in other words, saw greater danger in an exact *social* science than they did in a natural one. Modern apologists have been able to show that Protestant theology seldom hindered the progress of natural science during this period. But to the scientific study of human behaviour it provided much greater resistance, for it was this which seemed to present the greater threat to faith and morality.

Yet even here the conflict was often more apparent than real. For the astrologers, as we have seen, were the first to admit that their forecasts of human behaviour were only provisional guesses. A horoscope indicated a tendency not a certainty. The stars inclined, but did not force. The whole point of astrological diagnosis was to widen human freedom of choice by making the client aware of just what possibilities were open to him.

The trouble was that these qualifications were not always remembered by the clients themselves. At a popular level, astrology may well have helped to slacken moral responsibility in the way the theologians predicted, for even educated men were quick to attribute their own personal weaknesses and misfortunes to the crippling influence of the planets. 'Think not to fasten thy imperfections on the stars, and so despairingly conceive thyself under a fatality of being evil.' We have seen how there were many of his contemporaries to whom Sir Thomas Browne's warning could have been appropriately directed.[13] In strict theory the astrologers were perfectly correct to maintain that their doctrines were compatible with a belief in free will, just as modern psychoanalysts can refute the vulgar objection that their tenets put an end to all notions of moral responsibility. But in practice men were not always capable of appreciating such sophisticated distinctions, and the clergy were right to be worried about astrology's implications. The Church simply could not afford to concede that human autonomy might not exist, for to do so would

12. Augustine, *De Civitate Dei*, V, i–ix (and Thorndike, *Magic and Science*, i, pp. 513–21); Aquinas, *Summa Theologica*, II.xcv. 3–5, and *Summa Contra Gentiles*, III.lxxxii, lxxxv–lxxxvi. See in general T. O. Wedel, *The Mediaeval Attitude toward Astrology* (Yale Studies in English, 1920), and R. C. Dales, 'Robert Grosseteste's Views on Astrology', *Mediaeval Studies*, xxix (1967).

13. T. Browne, *Christian Morals*, iii.7. cf. above, pp. 390–91.

be to wreck the whole doctrine of rewards and punishments on which
its religion was based.

Committed to the belief that the will was necessarily free, the
clergy therefore reasoned that it was impossible to predict future
human behaviour. If the astrologers did so, it could only mean that
they were in league with the Devil. Charms and spells, said Bishop
Carleton, were the Devil's rudiments, but judicial astrology was the
Devil's university. Astrologers in tacit league with Satan deserved
the fate prescribed for every other kind of witch.[14] They were also
suspect because of their mathematical calculations. The memory of
Roger Bacon had been much besmirched by the assumption that
mathematics was part of the black art,[15] and it was notorious that
the Edwardian reformers had destroyed mathematical manuscripts
at Oxford under the delusion that they were conjuring books. 'Where
a red letter or a mathematical diagram appeared, they were sufficient
to entitle the book to be Popish or diabolical.' (This may account
for the disappearance at this period of nearly all the works of the
fourteenth-century Merton College school of astronomers.)[16] Modern
historians tend to think that few genuine Elizabethan scientists were
liable to be accused of witchcraft. Yet both John Dee and Thomas
Hariot suffered from such suspicions and in the seventeenth century
John Aubrey recalled how the Elizabethan astrologer, Thomas
Allen, was maligned by the belief, 'in those dark times', that astrologer, mathematician and conjurer were all the same thing.[17] During
the reign of Mary, a clergyman, William Living, was arrested by an
ignorant constable who found among his books a copy of the astronomical textbook, John de Sacrobosco's *Sphere*, exclaiming, 'It is
no marvel the Queen be sick, seeing there be such conjurers in privy

14. G. C(arleton), *The Madnesse of Astrologers* (1624), sig. A4ᵛ. Works
urging the death penalty for astrologers included John Chamber, *A Treatise
against Iudicial Astrologie*, pp. 78–9; J. H(arvey), *A Discoursive Probleme
concerning Prophesies* (1588), p. 72; J. M(elton), *Astrologaster, or, the
Figure-Caster* (1620), p. 78; Geree, *Astrologo-Mastix*, p. 19.

15. Taylor, *Mathematical Practitioners*, p. 8.

16. E. Ashmole, *Theatrum Chemicum Britannicum* (1652), sig. A2ᵛ; Bodl.,
Wood MS F 39, f. 282 ('If the Greek Professor had not accidentally come
along, the Greek Testament had been thrown into the fire for a conjuring
book too'). On the Merton MSS, see R. T. Gunther, *Early Science in Oxford*,
ii (Oxford, 1923), pp. 42–3.

17. Kocher, *Science and Religion*, pp. 140, 153; J. Aubrey, *Brief Lives*, ed.
A. Clark (Oxford, 1898), i, p. 27. Allen's servant-girl threw away his watch,
thinking it a devil (ibid., p. 28).

corners; but now, I trust, he shall conjure no more."[18] The Elizabethan surveyor, Edward Worsop, also commented on the popular
assumption that books with crosses, figures, circles and Greek geo-
metrical terms were likely to be works of conjuration.[19]

Such prejudices lasted well into the seventeenth century, and were
fanned by the widespread conviction that anything mysterious might
have a diabolical origin. 'A very lode-stone in some scholar's hand
before a silly townsman's eye is enough to make the former a conjuror,' wrote Thomas Fuller.[20] The sequestrators who seized the
papers of the mathematician Walter Warner in 1644 were reported
to be 'much troubled at the sight of so many crosses and circles in
the superstitious algebra and that black art of geometry'.[21] 'Let a
man know more than a common student,' lamented the astrologer
Henry Harflete, 'then he is accounted a conjurer; he deals with the
devil."[22] In 1651 John Rowley reported sadly to Lilly that when he
used his instruments to measure the height of the church steeple the
local parson had accused him of conjuring.[23] A contemporary pamphlet referred to Lilly as the 'glory of the black art', while his pupil
and successor, Henry Coley, was deeply offended by Anthony
Wood's description of astrologers as 'conjurers'.[24]

Although such aspersions often sprang from simple convictions
honestly held, it is difficult to resist the conclusion that one of the
clergy's objections to astrologers was that they saw them as professional rivals. For, whatever the theoretical compatibilities of astrology and religion, there was little doubt that in practice they were
competing agencies, offering rival methods of divination. The godly
man might be able to prophesy by prayer and revelation, just as the
astrologer made predictions after studying the movement of the

18. Foxe, viii, p. 528.
19. E. Worsop, *A Discoverie of Sundry Errours* (1582), sig. C1.
20. T. Fuller, *Abel Redevivus* (1651), p. 432.
21. *A Collection of Letters Illustrative of the Progress of Science in England*, ed. J. O. Halliwell (1965 reprint), p. 80.
22. H. Harflete, *Vox Coelorum* (1645), p. 26.
23. Taylor, *Mathematical Practitioners*, p. 238. cf. J. Dee, Preface to *The
Elements of Geometrie of* . . . *Euclide*, (trans.) H. Billingsley [1570], sigs.
Aj^v–Aiij; F. Osborne, *Advice to a Son*, ed. E. A. Parry (1896), p. 14. In
Presbyterian Scotland the idea 'that nothing was taught at Oxford but the
black arts' lingered into the eighteenth century; J. Hogg, *The Private Memoirs and Confessions of a Justified Sinner* (1824: 1947 edn), p. 208.
24. *The Devil seen at St Albans* (1648), p. 6; A. Powell, *John Aubrey and
His Friends* (1948), p. 230.

heavenly bodies. But was there room for both? 'If a man can foretell future things by the stars,' asked William Bridge, 'then what need of prophecy?'[25] The conflict was emphasized by the readiness of astrologers like John Gadbury to mock sectarian claims to visions and revelations, sneer at the delusions of the Fifth Monarchy Men, and generally reject the claims of any non-astrological type of prophecy whatsoever.[26] They boasted of the scientific character of their mathematically-based forecasts, as opposed to the inspirational and subjective nature of religious revelations. 'I look upon prophecies and predictions astrological to be different,' declared Thomas Trigge. 'The prophet speaks by inspiration; the astrologer from a known and physical ground, considering the mundane effects as they lie embodied in their proper causes.'[27] Correspondingly, the Quakers thought Lilly's predictions worthless, because they sprang from the stars, not from the Light within.[28]

Another delicate problem was the relationship between astrology and prayer. The astrologers of classical antiquity had emphasized the futility of seeking divine relief from the influence of the stars; and in the sixteenth and seventeenth centuries English Protestant writers were quick to point out that prayer would be useless if such doctrines of astral destiny were accepted.[29] The doctrine of astrological elections, moreover, seemed to imply that no prayer could be effective unless offered at an astrologically propitious moment. This Arab idea was said to have been taught by some English astrologers.[30] It had close affiliations with magical beliefs about the need to time operations to fit phases of the moon or sun. The Elizabethan conjurer, Thomas Allen, told a client that if he waited for the sun to come to the 'quick of noon', and then struck an anvil three times, he would have the answer to any question he chose to ask.[31] The

25. *The Works of the Rev. William Bridge*, i, p. 437.

26. J. Gadbury, *Coelestis Legatus* (1656), p. 13; *Natura Prodigiorum* (1660), pp. 187 ff.; *Britains Royal Star* (1661), p. 33; *Dies Novissimus* (1664), pp. 20 ff.   27. T. Trigge, *The Fiery Trigon Revived* (1672), p. 26.

28. F. E(llington), *Christian Information concerning these Last Times* (1664), pp. 5–6. cf. below, p. 448 n. 117.

29. S. Bradwell, *Physick for the Sicknesse, commonly called the Plague* (1636), p. 4; Geree, *Astrologo-Mastix*, p. 6. cf. E. R. Dodds, *The Greeks and the Irrational* (Berkeley, 1963), p. 262, n. 61.

30. Scot, *Discoverie*, IX.iii; XI.xxii; A. Willet, *Hexapla in Genesin* (1632), p. 9; J. Swan, *Speculum Mundi* (Cambridge, 1635), p. 352; Ady, p. 24.

31. B.M., Harley MS 6998, f. 250 (articles against William Bassett, 34 Eliz.). cf. R. Turner, *Ars Notoria* (1657), p. 11.

Royalist visionary, Arise Evans, as a fourteen-year-old boy, heard 'some say that whatsoever one did ask of God upon Whitsunday morning, at the instant when the Sun arose and played, God would grant it him'.[32]

But on the question of prayer, as of that of free will, most astrologers tried to paper over the cracks, so as to prevent the gap between astrology and religion from becoming too obvious. They were quick to echo the opinion of Archbishop Laud that fervent prayer could overcome even the dire effects of a conjunction of Saturn and Mars, since God could hinder malign aspects and overrule conjunctions.[33] Planetary influences, a preacher told the Society of Astrologers, might always be countered by genuine religious belief. As a later writer put it, 'Prayers and endeavours frustrate the stars.'[34] In the same spirit, Cardinal Pole had declared that, whatever the astrological significance of his nativity, it was cancelled out by the grace of his second birth, or spiritual regeneration.[35]

But the potential rivalry of the two systems could not always be so easily concealed. For the godly drew their keenest sense of pain from an awareness that men and women took to the astrologers the very problems which the clergy themselves might normally have expected to resolve. Although it also offered an abstract system of explanation, astrology was first and foremost a practical agency, providing advice on a wide range of personal difficulties. Its clients wanted help in dealing with their wives, servants, business colleagues; or they needed guidance on some perplexing issue of conduct or allegiance. That they should turn to star-gazers in their hour of need, rather than to the traditional pastoral agencies of the Church, seemed a direct

32. Quoted by J. Crofts, 'Wordsworth and the Seventeenth Century', *Procs. Brit. Acad.*, xxvi (1940), p. 188. cf. the widespread folk belief that the sun danced on Easter Day; *County Folk-Lore*, v, ed. Mrs Gutch and M. Peacock (Folk-Lore Soc., 1908), p. 13; A. R. Wright, *British Calendar Customs*, ed. T. E. Lones (Folk-Lore Soc., 1936/40), i, pp. 96–8; T. M. Owen, *Welsh Folk Customs* (Cardiff, 1959), p. 84.

33. *The Works of William Laud*, ed. W. Scott and J. Bliss (Oxford, 1847–60), i, p. 169. cf. W. Ramesey, *Astrologia Restaurata* (1653), p. 5; J. B(utler), *The Most Sacred and Divine Science of Astrology* (1680), pp. 23–4; W. Kemp, *A Brief Treatise of the Nature . . . and Cure of the Pestilence* (1665), p. 13.

34. R. Gell, *Stella Nova* (1649), p. 19; *Cometomantia. A Discourse of Comets* (1684), p. 217.

35. G. Hakewill, *An Apologie* (2nd edn, 1630), p. 106. In the same way it was said that spiritual regeneration could offset the effect of a man's physiognomy; C. Camden, in *Philological Qtly*, xx (1941), p. 403.

threat to the moral supremacy of the clergy, whose privilege it had always been to resolve disputes and to give advice. The man who regulated his life by the almanac was thus showing a fundamental distrust of God.[36] 'Hearkening unto these diviners,' protested the Reverend Francis Crow, 'is opposed to our hearkening unto Christ.'[37] But the complaints poured in. Astrological prophecies were 'studied more than the Bible'. Many looked 'more to the fulfilling of what such prognostics and almanacs say than to the Scriptures'. Some gave 'more credit to judiciary astrologers than to God's word', and 'put more confidence in Lilly than they did in God'.[38]

At this point no compromise was possible. On an intellectual level astrological doctrine could somehow be fitted into a theological framework. But when the astrologers began to develop a consulting agency which in scope and comprehensiveness threatened to eclipse the pastoral role of the clergy, then drastic action had to be taken. The great Puritan preacher, William Perkins, declared that it was better that a man should lose his goods irrecoverably rather than retrieve them by astrological help.[39] But this severe view could not be expected to capture the enthusiasm of a materially-minded populace. The only remedy was repression, and this the church courts struggled to provide. As late as 1716 the Bishop of Norwich was seeking to know whether there were any of his flock who 'by sorcery, charms, *or astrology,* pretend to tell fortunes and discover lost goods, or any that consult with such persons'.[40]

In this respect the post-Reformation Church maintained complete continuity with the attitude taken by its medieval predecessor. The canon law had always prohibited the observance of astrologically chosen times.[41] When his clerical contemporaries had recovered from the shock of discovering a book on astrology under the pillow on which Archbishop Gerard of York had died in 1108 they resolved

36. *The Workes of . . . William Perkins* (Cambridge, 1616–18), iii, p. 654.
37. F. Crow, *The Vanity and Impiety of Judicial Astrology* (1690), p. 16.
38. J. Spencer, *A Discourse concerning Vulgar Prophecies* (1665), p. 29; A. Burgess, *CXLV Expository Sermons* (1665), p. 396; 'A Learned Divine near London', *The Late Eclipse Unclasped* (1652), p. 7; L.P., *The Astrologers Bugg-Beare* (1652), sig. A3ᵛ. cf. Brand, *Popular Antiquities*, iii, p. 344, and *Dives and Pauper* (1536), f. 43ᵛ ('Nowadays men take none heed to God's dooms, but to the dooms of astronomers and to the course of the planets.')   39. Perkins, *Discourse*, p. 88; cf. above, pp. 314-15.
40. *Articles to be enquired of . . . in the Ordinary Visitation of . . . Charles, Lord Bishop of Norwich, 1716* (Norwich, 1716), p. 6.
41. *Corpus Iuris Canonici*, ed. E. Friedberg (Leipzig, 1879–81), i, col. 1046.

that it was unfit that his body should be buried in the cathedral.[42] From the later Middle Ages onwards a figure-caster discovered plying his trade among the people could expect to be brought before a church court for correction. In 1577 one of them, Simon Pembroke, caused a sensation by dropping dead before the tribunal which was trying him.[43] But astrologers seem to have appeared before the ecclesiastical courts very much less frequently than did the cunning men and wise women; and it is doubtful whether ecclesiasical action constituted a very effective check to their activities, especially after several leading astrologers had been given episcopal licences authorizing them to practise medicine like any orthodox practitioner.[44] Ecclesiastical censorship apart, the preventive action taken by the Anglican Church seems to have been largely ineffective. Even the paper war against astrology may have defeated its own purpose. As one astrologer, Joseph Blagrave, confessed in 1671, 'The truth is, after the ministers had preached against me and my art, I had twice so much custom as I had before, for they could not have done me better service; for many which before had not heard of me made much inquiring after me, hearing what great cures I had done.'[45]

Although clergymen of all brands were suspicious of astrology, there can be no doubt that in post-Reformation England the most sustained opposition to it came from the Puritans, that is those Protestants who were most anxious to purge the Anglican Church of its remaining 'Popish' elements. Following their Continental masters,

42. Sir F. Pollock and F. W. Maitland, *The History of English Law* (2nd edn, Cambridge, 1952), ii, p. 553. The book was that of Julius Firmicus Maternus, who ultimately became a Christian.

43. *A Most Strange and Rare Example of the Just Judgment of God executed upon a Lewde and Wicked Conjuror* (1577). Other examples in Kittredge, *Witchcraft*, p. 228; J. S. Purvis, *Tudor Parish Documents* (Cambridge, 1948), p. 198; *Durham High Commission*, pp. 34–42; *Essex Recusant*, iii (1961), pp. 121–2.

44. John Lambe was licensed by the Bishop of Durham (H. G. Dick in *Journ. of Hist. of Medicine*, i [1946], p. 309); Lilly by the Archbishop of Canterbury (R. R. James in *Janus*, xli [1937], p. 103); Richard Napier by the Archdeacon of Buckingham, and his nephew, Sir Richard, by the Bishop of Lincoln (*D.N.B.*); Robert Le Neve, William Williams (author of *Occult Physick* [1660]), and Thomas Saffold by the Bishop of London (J. H. Bloom and R. R. James, *Medical Practitioners in the Diocese of London* [Cambridge, 1935], pp. 59, 74, 67–8); and William Salmon by the Bishop of Norwich (E. H. Carter, *The Norwich Subscription Books* [1937], p. 145).

45. J. Blagrave, *Blagraves Astrological Practice of Physick* (1671), p. 117.

Calvin, Beza, Bullinger and Peter Martyr, the Edwardian Protestants wrote strongly against astrology, particularly Miles Coverdale, John Hooper, John Foxe and Roger Hutchinson. Calvin's treatise on the subject was translated by the Puritan George Gylby in 1561. Thereafter the attack was continued by writers who were Calvinist in theology and strongly anti-Roman in their general outlook. They included John Jewel, the Marian exile; William Fulke, the Puritan divine; Philip Stubbes, moralist and social reformer; John Chamber, canon of Windsor, and admirer of Ramus and Calvin; William Perkins, the godly preacher, and George Carleton, the Calvinist Bishop of Chichester. Other participants included Puritan divines like Laurence Humphrey and Thomas Cooper, and theologians like Andrew Willet and George Hakewill.[46] Of those who wrote at length against astrology before the Civil War only a tiny minority did not have affiliations with this school of religious thought.[47] In the 1640s, when the controversy over astrology mounted to a crescendo of preaching and pamphleteering, the opposition was dominated by Presbyterians, – Thomas Gataker, John Geree, Thomas Hall, John Vicars – with the subsequent assistance of some of the Independent clergy (though not laymen), like John Goodwin, John Owen, William Bridge and Philip Nye. It was a group of the latter who in February 1652 petitioned Parliament to suppress the practice of judicial astrology altogether.[48]

How is the marked antipathy of Puritanism for astrology to be

46. For reference to most of these writings, see the index to this book and the general surveys in D. C. Allen, *The Star-Crossed Renaissance* (Durham, N. Carolina, 1941), esp. chap. 3; Kocher, *Science and Religion,* chap. 10; H. Schultz, *Milton and Forbidden Knowledge* (New York, 1955), pp. 52–7. Coverdale's rejection of astrology comes in the preface to his translation of *A Faythfull and True Pronosticatiō upon the Yere MCCCCCXLVIII* (1547?) (reissued with only slight changes and without acknowledgement by J.M. as *A Christian Almanacke* [1612]). For the others see J. H. Smith, 'John Foxe on Astrology', *English Literary Renaissance,* i (1971); *The Works of John Jewel,* ed. Ayre, ii, pp. 872–3; Cooper, *Mystery,* pp. 137–44; Hakewill, *An Apologie,* pp. 107–8; Willet, *Hexapla in Genesin,* pp. 9–10.

47. The most prominent exceptions were the crypto-Catholic, Henry Howard, Earl of Northampton, author of *A Defensative against the Poyson of Supposed Prophecies* (1583), and the future Straffordian, John Melton, who published *Astrologaster* in 1620.

48. *The Humble Proposals of Mr Owen, Mr Tho. Goodwin, Mr Nye, Mr Sympson, and other ministers* (1652), p. 6; *Severall Proceedings in Parliament,* 131 (25 Mar.–1 Apr. 1652); W. Lilly, *Merlini Anglici Ephemeris* (1653), sig. A2. Notable anti-astrological writings of the Interregnum period,

accounted for? It would be tempting to hail it as further proof of the frequently postulated link between Puritanism and the rise of modern science, by suggesting that 'rationally-minded' Puritans were quicker to spot the intellectual deficiencies of astrological method. But this does not seem to have been the case. The spuriousness of astrological procedures was not normally the basis of the Puritans' objection. Indeed they often conceded that the astrologers might be correct in their prognostications, but cited this very success as further evidence for the diabolical nature of their art. 'Do astrologers foretell right sometimes?' sneered John Geree, 'So do witches'. Geree quoted the opinion of the Puritan mathematician, Henry Briggs, who had abandoned the study of astrology, partly because he found no certainty in its rules, but also because he feared that 'to those who addicted themselves to the practice of divining astrology, the Devil did at first secretly lend his assistance, and at length *gradatim* (unless God graciously prevented) entice them into contract'.[49] So the astrologers lost either way. If their predictions were wrong, this proved they were charlatans; if they were right, then they were in league with the Devil.[50]

There was nothing new about this view, for it had been inherited from the medieval schoolmen. Indeed the Puritan clergy often came very near to endorsing the old Catholic view that ignorance was the mother of devotion.[51] 'Solicit not thy thoughts with matters hid'; Raphael's advice to Milton's Adam[52] summed up a century of hesitation. The Puritans may also have been particularly sensitive about astrology because they felt that there was a 'Popish' character about many of its practitioners' activities. The consultation was reminiscent of the confessional, while the election of times appeared an

---

not cited elsewhere in this book or in Allen, *The Star-Crossed Renaissance,* pp. 144–5, include Gataker's diatribe in his contribution to the cooperative work, *Annotations upon all the Books of the Old and New Testament* (2nd edn, 1651), *s.v. Jeremiah,* x, 2; J. Vicars, *Against William Li-Lie (alias) Lillie* (1652), and John Goodwin's sermon against judicial astrology (partly extant in Ashm. 436, ff. 47–8).

49. Geree, *Astrologo-Mastix,* pp. 11, 14–15. Briggs nevertheless maintained a friendly correspondence with the astrologer, Sir Christopher Heydon, whose letters to him are in Ashm. 242, ff. 164–71.

50. Carleton, *The Madnesse of Astrologers,* p. 27; J. Raunce, *Astrologia Accusata pariter et Condemnata* (1650), p. 19; Gaule, *The Mag-Astro-Mancer,* pp. 165 ff.; *The Works of William Bridge,* i, p. 440.

51. See Kocher, *Science and Religion,* pp. 16–17.

52. *Paradise Lost,* viii.167.

obvious cousin of the red-letter and black-letter days in the Church calendar. Astrological images and sigils paralleled the charms worn by the Catholic laity, and the notion that a separate sign of the zodiac ruled each part of the body recalled the Popish belief that there was a saint for every disease.[53] Efforts to brand judicial astrology as a 'Popish' practice were, of course, unlikely to carry much weight with the well-informed, who knew that it was the medieval clergy who had first formulated the objections to astrology, and that the Counter-Reformation Church on the Continent was proceeding against the science with considerable vigour.[54] But the smear was superficially plausible.

The Puritans were also very sensitive to any apparent threat to the notion of God's omnipotence, and intolerant of any attempt to penetrate his mysteries. At the core of their thinking lay a fundamental belief in man's abject predicament, compared with the Almighty's irresistible power. Some other clergy, by contrast, took a more optimistic view of the potentialities open to unaided human reason.[55] They were, therefore, less easily roused by the pretensions of the astrologers. Astrology accordingly found a good deal of sympathy among the leaders of the Church, particularly the Laudians. Peter Baro, who introduced Arminianism to Cambridge, was an astrologer.[56] Laud himself was keenly interested.[57] So was Robert Sanderson, future Bishop of Lincoln.[58] Peter Heylyn, Laud's biographer, also took the subject seriously;[59] while other Laudian sympathizers in-

53. Melton, *Astrologaster*, pp. 19, 59 ff.; Gaule, *The Mag-Astro-Mancer*, pp. 128, 177; Allen, *Judicial Astrologers totally routed*, p. 15.

54. The attitude of the Counter-Reformation Church was expressed in the Tridentine decrees and the Papal Bulls of 1586 and 1631; see D. P. Walker, *Spiritual and Demonic Magic from Ficino to Campanella* (1958), pp. 205–6, 219–20, and Thorndike, *Magic and Science*, vi, chap. 34. The most prominent English Catholic opponent of judicial astrology was Christopher Davenport ('Francis a Sancta Clara'); J. B. Dockery, *Christopher Davenport* (1960), p. 95. But for astrological calculations by Jesuits in England in 1635, see *The Memoirs of Gregorio Panzani*, trans. J. Berington (1793), p. 175.

55. See J. F. H. New, *Anglican and Puritan* (1964), esp. pp. 19–21.

56. R. Harvey, *An Astrological Discourse* (1583), sig. Aij. cf. H. C. Porter, *Reformation and Reaction in Tudor Cambridge* (Cambridge, 1958), pp. 376–90.

57. *The Works of ... William Laud*, ed. W. Scott and J. Bliss (Oxford, 1847–60), i, p. 169; iii, pp. 140, 157. cf. John Gadbury's admiring comments in his *Cardines Coeli* (1684), sig. a2.   58. Gadbury, op. cit., sig. a1v.

59. J. Barnard, *Theologo-Historicus, or the True Life of ... Peter Heylyn* (1683), p. 149.

cluded the Royalist, Thomas Swadlin, who was commissioned to preach before the Society of Astrologers in 1653,[60] and Edmund Reeve, a keen defender of the Book of Sports, who had preached to them in the previous year.[61] Another of Lilly's confidants was the time-server, John Gauden, who was distinctly anti-Laudian in outlook, but who nevertheless became Bishop of Worcester at the Restoration.[62]

This apparent sympathy of the Arminians towards astrological activity does not seem to have attracted any particular comment at the time, and, it must be admitted, did not result in any greater freedom for astrological writers during the 1630s. But during the decade of the Civil War it became apparent to everyone that the most deadly enemies of judicial astrology were the Calvinists, and especially the Presbyterians. This antipathy may well be explained by doctrinal considerations. For, as the astrologers wryly observed, it was the very writers who came closest in their own beliefs to the notion of implacable destiny who were most easily offended by the fatalism of astrology. Who was the chief opponent of astral science, asked John Gadbury, if not 'the supercilious man in black' – 'the angry *presbyter*, who of all men most emulates astrology, and yet hugs an opinion an hundred times more ridiculous than any one principle thereof ... viz., that of predestination in the most terrifying sense?'[63] It was precisely because the doctrines of the astrologers were so close in form to their own, and yet so opposed in content, that the Puritans were aroused. Rival systems of explanation, each purporting to account for the mutations of human life in terms of a fixed and omnipotent providence, each offering some general prediction of the likely course of future events, Calvinism and astrology were enemies from the start. As a contemporary wrote of the Puritans, 'our supercilious Precisians ... unwarrantably pretend to judge of any man's future state and salvation by more secret symptoms and ... signs than the astronomers can find signs in Heaven'.[64] In fact, most Calvinist thinkers stressed that the mystery of predestination was not one for men to inquire into.

60. *D.N.B.*; Laud, *Works*, iii, pp. 193–4. His sermon, *Divinity no Enemy to Astrology* (1653), was not delivered because of illness.
61. *The New Jerusalem* (1652); *D.N.B.*
62. Lilly, *Autobiography*, p. 187.
63. J. G(adbury), *A Brief Relation of the Life ... of ... Vincent Wing* (1670), sig. A2.
64. R.H., 'Astrologia Siderata, or a Whip for Divining Soothsayers' (Sloane 412), f. 62.

Let it ... be our first principle [Calvin himself had written] that to desire any other knowledge of predestination than that which is expounded by the word of God, is no less infatuated than to walk where there is no path, or to seek light in darkness. Let us not be ashamed to be ignorant in a matter in which ignorance is learning. Rather let us willingly abstain from the search after knowledge, to which it is both foolish as well as perilous and even fatal to aspire.[65]

In deference to this warning, every attempt to identify the elect had been frowned upon as an insidious heresy. Yet to penetrate this mystery was precisely what the astrologers seemed to be attempting to do. Not only did they predict an individual's expectation of life and his fortune in the world. Their textbooks even taught that the stars could indicate a client's prospects of getting to Heaven. It was the final insult, thought Bishop Carleton, that 'we must repair to the astrologer to know who are regenerate in the Church and who are not'.[66]

Astrology was thus a mode of thought which, though bearing many resemblances to predestination, yet managed to cut right across it. It seemed that the star-gazers had taken the Calvinist dogmas and twisted them into a new and secular form, 'turning ... eternal predestination into fatal destiny; and the election of grace into sidereal elections'.[67] Astrology, wrote William Perkins, 'teaching by the casting of nativities what men will be, is ridiculous and impious, because it determineth that such shall be very like in life and conversation whom God in his predestination hath made unlike'.[68]

2. Assimilation

But on the issue of astrology's legitimacy, as on many others, English Protestantism was to demonstrate strongly fissiparous tendencies. For although the Puritans and Presbyterians provided the focus of opposition, the Independents and radical sects of the Civil War period were to furnish the astrologers with many active enthusiasts and supporters. Symbolic of this association was the close link between William Lilly and the political leaders of the Independent

65. Calvin, *Institutes*, III.xxi.2.
66. Carleton, *The Madnesse of Astrologers*, pp. 25–6; Scot, *Discoverie*, XI.xxiii; Willet, *Hexapla in Genesin*, p. 9.
67. Gaul, *The Mag-Astro-Mancer*, sigs. *1ᵛ–*2.
68. W. Perkins, *A Golden Chaine* (1591), sig. V8ᵛ.

party.[69] At the outset of the Civil War Lilly, despite a Puritan upbringing, was, if anything, Royalist in sympathy. He had a Cavalier patron in William Pennington of Muncaster, and his first published works maintained a pose of studied neutrality.[70] But his London practice brought him into touch with the Parliamentary leaders. When John Pym lay dying in 1643 a friend took a sample of his urine to the astrologer, who correctly prognosticated his imminent decease. This transaction took place without Pym's knowledge,[71] but in the same year Mrs Lisle, wife of the regicide John Lisle (and best known as the Alice Lisle who was condemned by Judge Jeffreys after Monmouth's rebellion), brought him the urine of Bulstrode Whitelocke, soon to be a highly influential figure in the counsels of the Independent party. Lilly successfully predicted the patient's recovery, thereby earning Whitelocke's permanent confidence and support.

Through his new patron the astrologer forged close ties with other Parliamentary leaders, including Denzil Holles, Sir Philip Stapleton, Sir Christoper Wray, Robert Reynolds and Sir Robert Pye. These men differed considerably in their political sympathies, but Lilly's position, and that of astrology in general, gradually came to be identified with the fortunes of the lay Independents and the Army, as against the clerical Presbyterians.

Many of the soldiers were wholly for it [he wrote], and many of the Independent party; and I had abundance of worthy men in the House of Commons, my assured friends, no lovers of Presbytery, which were then in great esteem and able to protect the art. For should the Presbyterian party have prevailed . . . I knew well that they would have silenced my pen annually.

In the autumn of 1647 Lilly and Booker went in state to visit the Army at Windsor, where they were welcomed by General Fairfax, who confessed that he did not understand astrology, but expressed the hope that 'it was lawful and agreeable to God's word'. Lilly

69. The following paragraphs are based on Lilly's *Autobiography*. Historians are chary these days about speaking of 'Independents' and 'Presbyterians' *tout court*, but I have followed Lilly's own usage.

70. e.g., *Englands Propheticall Merlin* (1644), 'To the Reader'. cf. *Autobiography*, p. 107.

71. Lilly, *Englands Propheticall Merlin* (1644), p. 130. No reference is made to it in the official *A Narrative of the Disease and death of . . . John Pym* (1643).

reassured him on this point and went off to discuss secret matters with Hugh Peter, the Army chaplain.

Ironically enough, the astrologer at this very same period was being consulted by one of Charles I's female supporters as to how the King could escape from his captivity at Hampton Court. He supplied further advice (together with hack-saws and acid) in the autumn of 1648, when he was simultaneously raising the morale of the Parliamentary besiegers of Colchester.[72] Lilly in fact had a sharp eye for the main chance, as his comfortable survival after the Restoration was to demonstrate. In his textbook on astrology he characteristically advised would-be practitioners to 'be sparing in delivering judgment against the commonwealth in which you live'[73] —a precept which he was always careful to observe.

More important than the obscure but trivial question of Lilly's personal loyalties is the striking eagerness of some Independents to take him up. He became a powerful propagandist and an influential figure behind the scenes. When he got into trouble he could count upon assistance and protection from his new friends. They came to his aid in 1645 when he fell foul of the Committee of Examinations after his almanac had cast aspersions on the Excise Commissioners.[74] They rescued him again in 1652, when he foretold the dissolution of the Rump by a combination of Army and people.[75] On this latter occasion he claims to have been abetted by Speaker Lenthall ('ever my friend') and championed by Sir Arthur Haselrig, Walter Strickland, Richard Salway, Hugh Peter, and Oliver Cromwell himself. During his temporary imprisonment he was visited by the secretary of the Army, John Rushworth. The fall of the Rump in 1653 heralded his period of greatest influence. He repaid his debt to Whitelocke by successfully recommending through his client, John Claypole, Cromwell's son-in-law, that his patron should be

72. The intermediary was Jane Whorwood (on whom see *D.N.B.*). Her last consultation was in Sept. 1648, when Lilly advised that the King should agree to the Treaty of Newport; see Wood, *Life and Times*, i, pp. 227–8.

73. Lilly, *Christian Astrology*, sig. B1.

74. 'If eleven shillings out of twenty go to the officers, the excise will do us little good,' ran the December prognostication of *Anglicus* (1645). A MS note on Lilly's copy of the almanac (Ashm. 121) reads: 'For these words a black ass (Miles Corbet) like a Jew questioned me, but I was delivered by a willing friend, Mr Robert Reynolds.'

75. In his *Annus Tenebrosus* (1652), p. 54; *Commons Journals*, vii, p. 195; Josten, *Ashmole*, p. 628.

appointed Ambassador to Sweden. When Cromwell became Protector, Lilly could regard 'all the soldiery' as his friends.

All this can be learned from Lilly's *Autobiography*. But his unpublished case books and papers throw an even more intimate light upon the connection between astrology and the Independents, Army radicals and sectaries. The nature of these dealings amply disproves any notion that the politicians simply used Lilly as a convenient means of propaganda without believing in the truth of astrology itself. We have already seen how Lilly was consulted by Richard Overton at a crucial stage of his career as a Leveller leader.[76] It may now be added that the other Levellers, or Army radicals, who had recourse to astrological advice, usually from Lilly or John Booker, included Major Rainsborough,[77] Lieutenant-Colonel Read,[78] Adjutant-General Allen,[79] Cornet Joyce,[80] Roger Crab,[81] Owen Cox, the Fifth Monarchist sea captain,[82] and several unidentifiable 'Agitators', i.e. elected Army representatives.[83] John Booker dealt with various questions about the Levellers in 1649, while Mrs Lilburne, wife of Freeborn John, remained a regular client from

76. Above, p. 372.

77. A Leveller and later a Ranter; brother of the better known Col. Thomas Rainsborough (C. Hill, *Intellectual Origins of the English Revolution* [Oxford, 1965], p. 275; N. Cohn, *The Pursuit of the Millennium* [1962 edn], p. 352). His (and his wife's) astrological consultations with Booker are in Ashm. 387, ff. 86, 217, and Ashm. 385, f. 120.

78. A passionate republican and learned in Hebrew. Removed from the Governorship of Poole in 1651 after being accused of sheltering Ranters and Levellers; B.M., Stowe MS 189, ff. 52–3ᵛ, 74. His astrological consultations are in Ashm. 420, ff. 76ᵛ–7, and Ashm. 243, f. 173ᵛ.

79. Leading agitator and convinced republican; C. H. Firth and G. Davies, *The Regimental History of Cromwell's Army* (Oxford, 1940), ii, p. 614; P. H. Hardacre in *Baptist Qtly.*, xix (1961–2). Said to have championed Lilly before Charles I (Lilly, *Autobiography*, pp. 144–5). His consultation with the astrologer (Ashm. 210, f. 134ᵛ) reveals his date of birth to have been 9 Feb. 1616.

80. His nativity by Francis Bernard is in Sloane 1707, f. 11ᵛ.

81. Famous as radical, teetotaller and vegetarian (see C. Hill, *Puritanism and Revolution* [1958], pp. 314–22). Twice consulted Lilly (Ashm. 210, ff. 107ᵛ, and Ashm. 427, f. 51ᵛ), although publicly expressing hostility to astrology and preferring to foretell the future by the daily behaviour of the birds of the air sent him by God (*Harleian Miscellany*, 1808–11), vi, p. 402.

82. On whom see J. R. Powell, *The Navy in the English Civil War* (1962), pp. 209, 215, 217–18; *C.S.P.D., 1661–2*, pp. 128, 188; *1664–5*, pp. 234. Above, p. 368.

83. Ashm. 420, ff, 177, 184.

1653 until the astrologer's death in 1667.[84] Lilly may also have been consulted in 1648 by the commonalty of the Silk-Weavers Company, who were then engaged in democratic agitation.[85] The case books further reveal that, on different occasions, Lilly or Booker gave consultations to Hugh Peter,[86] and to the two prominent Cromwellian soldiers, Sir John Reynolds,[87] and Colonel Thomas Morgan.[88] The list is completed by the name of Major-General John Lambert, who was chosen as patron by the astrologer, Jeremy Shakerley, and became one of Lilly's clients. In 1661 he was reported to have consulted the astrologer as to whether he should attempt to escape from the Tower, where he had been imprisoned since the Restoration.[89]

In addition to these celebrities, a number of lesser figures with astrological interests are known to have had sectarian or radical associations. Between April 1647 and September 1648, Lilly had at least five clients who were Anabaptists. In 1645 a 'widow separatist' wanted to know whether she would 'have the man desired', and in later years the astrologer gave advice to a Ranter, a Quaker, and the wife of a 'Shaker'.[90] The Puritan origins of many of Booker's clients are indicated by such names as Sobriety Bollsby, Discipline Whiting and Wisdom Hampson (though none of these equals the felicity of one of Geoffrey le Neve's customers – Contented Bird).[91]

84. Ashm. 419, I, ff. 82^v, 83^v; Ashm. 385, f. 240; Ashm. 428, ff. 192^v, 200, 214^v, 222^v, 241^v, 254^v, 259, 260^v, 261, 268^v, 269^v; Ashm. 347, ff. 71^v, 75^v, 77.

85. Ashm. 420, f. 188.

86. Ashm. 430, f. 11^v. cf. Lilly, *Autobiography*, pp. 134, 148; R. P. Stearns, *The Strenuous Puritan* (Urbana, 1954), p. 332, n. 35.

87. Associated with the army agitators in 1647 (*The Clarke Papers*, ed. C. H. Firth [Camden Soc., 1891–1901], i, p. 426), but subsequently an apostate to the radical cause. Said to have been unwilling to go as commander of the Cromwellian army in Flanders in 1657 until having first consulted Lilly, but, as John Gadbury scornfully pointed out (*Collectio Geniturarum* [1662], pp. 147–8), he was nevertheless drowned on the return voyage. See also Ashm. 240, ff. 205–6^v, and Sloane 1707, f. 11.

88. Ashm. 241, f. 30^v. He was 2nd-in-command to Reynolds in 1657.

89. Ashm. 423, ff. 117, 119; J. Shakerley, *The Anatomy of Urania Practica* (1649), dedication; Ashm. 174, f. 153; Ashm. 427, f. 52; Josten, *Ashmole*, p. 814. Lambert saw an early draft of Webster's *Academiarum Examen* (1654), which urged the introduction of astrology to the universities. See Preface to the book, and below, p. 446.

90. Ashm. 420, ff. 253, 259^v, 298, 310; Ashm. 184, f. 143^v; Ashm. 427, ff. 107, 131^v, 239.

91. Ashm. 428, ff. 66^v, 74, 87^v; Ashm. 418, p. 99.

There is much additional evidence for this link between astrology and sectarianism. Nicholas Gretton was both astrologer and leader of a sectarian group.[92] The Fifth Monarchist, John Spittlehouse, praised astrology as the princess of the sciences, and Lilly as 'the prince of astrologers'.[93] The Ranter and ex-Leveller, Laurence Clarkson, took up the practice of astrology in 1650; and the Digger, Gerrard Winstanley, recommended that the subject be taught in his Utopia.[94] Some of the leading practitioners were men of advanced beliefs. Simon Forman had been very radical in his political opinions;[95] John Pool was a strong republican;[96] Nicholas Culpepper was another radical with a chequered sectarian history.[97] John Heydon was arrested in 1663 for writing a book saying that Charles II was a tyrant.[98] Lilly himself became an Anglican church-warden, but his second wife, who was buried in 1654 'without bells, without ceremony, and priest, etc., she so desiring it before her death', was very probably a Quaker.[99] So was the astrologer George Parker at one stage.[100] Even John Gadbury, who ultimately became a Royalist and crypto-Catholic, had been a Ranter and a convert of Abiezer Coppe at the beginning of his astrological career.[101]

The Interregnum saw an influx into the astrological profession which closely resembled the storming of the pulpit by the tub-preachers. 'The late years of the tyranny,' recalled John Heydon in 1664, 'admitted stocking-weavers, shoemakers, millers, masons, carpenters, bricklayers, gunsmiths, porters, butlers, etc. to write

92. Ashm. 423, ff. 218–9; above, p. 329.

93. J. Spittlehouse, *Rome Ruin'd by Whitehall* (1650), sigs. b3–4ᵛ.

94. L. Claxton, *The Lost Sheep Found* (1660), p. 32 (though he subsequently came to think it a 'great cheat' [p. 33]); *The Works of Gerrard Winstanley*, ed. G. H. Sabine (Ithaca, New York, 1941), p. 578.

95. See Ashm. 195, f. 151.

96. J. Pool, *Country Astrology* (1650), sig. A3ᵛ.

97. N. Culpepper, *Catastrophe Magnatum* (1652), p. 11; *Mr Culpepper's Ghost* in *Two Books of Physick* (1656); *Mercurius Pragmaticus*, 21 (4–11 Sept. 1649).

98. *C.S.P.D., 1663–4*, p. 230. cf. above, p. 408. Heydon, however, professed abhorrence of the Levellers and Fifth Monarchists; *Advice to a Daughter* (2nd edn, 1659), p. 161.

99. Ashm. 698, f. 9ᵛ; Ellington, *Christian Information concerning these Last Times*, p. 6; *Merlinus Phanaticus*, no. 1 (23 May 1660), p. 4; Josten, *Ashmole*, p. 1232. He thought Calvin 'an ass'; Ashm. 551 (2), sig. *2.

100. *Reliquiae Hearnianae*, ed. P. Bliss (2nd edn, 1869), ii, pp. 166n.–7n.

101. *D.N.B.*; Ashm. 250, f. 187.

and teach astrology and physic.'[102] The radical sects set out to revive
all the occult sciences. John Webster attacked the universities of
Oxford and Cambridge for their failure to provide adequate instruction in natural magic – 'that sublime knowledge whereby the
wonderful gifts of the Creator are discovered, and innumerable
benefits produced'.[103] This was a field which the reformers thought
more likely to produce immediate practical results than the mechanical philosophy which was becoming the dominant scientific
idiom of the day. Webster accordingly chided the Universities for
despising astrology – 'so noble and beneficial a science' – and warmly
commended the efforts of Ashmole, Lilly, Saunders and Culpepper.[104] With astrology were linked the companion studies of
alchemy, cryptography, magnetism, dreams and Paracelsian
medicine.

Astrology was thus particularly associated with what the Presbyterian Thomas Hall called the 'Familistical-Levelling-Magical
temper'.[105] The sects admired it for its practical utility, and for its
congeniality with the Familist, Theosophist or Behmenist doctrines
of illumination, which were enjoying a considerable vogue at this
time. Between 1644 and 1662 the whole of the writings of the
German mystic Jacob Boehme were translated into English, and
the sect of 'Behmenists' was picked up by Richard Baxter as one
of the significant religious groups of the Interregnum period. The
Familists, who held that Christ was 'a Type, and but a Type',
believed that it was possible for man 'totally to be inhabited by
Christ'. That is to say, they were perfectionists, envisaging that man
could attain a holy state in this existence.[106] They were a powerful

102. J. Heydon, The Wise-Mans Crown: or, the Glory of the Rosie-Cross
(1664), sig. C3ᵛ.
103. Webster, Academiarum Examen (1654), pp. 69–70. For this subject
see P. M. Rattansi, 'Paracelsus and the Puritan Revolution', Ambix, xi
(1963), and Schultz, Milton and Forbidden Knowledge, p. 52.
104. Webster, op. cit., p. 51. His reforming ally, Noah Biggs, however,
took a slightly less sympathetic view of astrology; see his Mataeotechnica
Medicinae Praxeos (1651), pp. 37–40.
105. T. Hall, Histrio-Mastix (1654), appended to Vindiciae Literarum
(1655), p. 199. A contemporary Jesuit spoke of 'Magi-Calvinists'; W. Foster,
Hoplocrisma-Spongus (1631), sig. A2. For sectarians and alchemy, cf. above,
p. 322.
106. Reliquiae Baxterianae, ed. M. Sylvester (1696), pp. 77–8; G. F. Nuttall, James Nayler. A Fresh Approach, supplement no. 26 to Journ. Friends'
Histl Soc., 1954. cf. above, p. 161. The translations of Boehme are listed in
S. Hutin, Les Disciples anglais de Jacob Boehme (Paris, 1960), pp. 39–9.

influence upon the Quakers, and barely distinguishable from some of the Ranters. The appeal of Boehme's intolerably obscure writings is difficult to appreciate today, but his mysticism was founded upon the old doctrines of microcosm and macrocosm, and his thought, like that of Swedenborg after him, preserved important elements of the hermetic tradition. He therefore regarded astrology as at least a partial road to the truth.[107]

According to his leading English interpreter, John Sparrow, Boehme took the view that the way to God and to the understanding of the universe lay through the scrutiny of the human soul, for man, as microcosm, contained within himself the epitome of nature. This fundamental kinship of man with the universe was the basis for mystical union with God.[108] As a later English disciple, Thomas Tryon, put it, 'There is an astrology within Man as well as without him. A microcosmical sun and moon and all the rest of the planets we carry about us.' Another of Boehme's followers, the Welshman Morgan Llwyd, also believed that the seven planets could be found within man.[109] The mystical aim of the Behmenists was to theologize this internal astrology, and to convert it into a spiritual force. A work attributed to Valentine Weigel, an earlier German writer of the same school, was translated in 1649 with the title *Astrologie Theologized*. For many of the Familists, however, Behmenism was a more practical affair, holding out the prospect of special power from occult knowledge. 'The Familists are very confident,' wrote a contemporary, 'that by knowledge of astrology and the strength of reason they shall be able to conquer over the whole world.'[110] As William Law subsequently remarked, Boehme's seventeenth-century readers wished to steal from him certain mysteries of nature and to run away with the philosopher's stone.[111]

Whatever their motivation, it seems clear that a keen interest in astrological speculation united the leading English Behmenists. Dr

107 See, e.g., J. Boehme, *Aurora*, trans. J. Sparrow (1656), pp. 583–4; A. Koyré, *La Philosophie de Jacob Boehme* (Paris, 1929), pp. 83–5, 91, and *passim;* D. Hirst, *Hidden Riches* (1964), p. 87.

108. J. Boehme, *Forty Questions of the Soul*, trans. J. Sparrow (1665), sigs. a11–12.

109. *Some Memoirs of the Life of Mr Tho. Tryon ... by himself* (1705), p. 24; A. N. Palmer, *A History of the Older Nonconformity of Wrexham and its Neighbourhood* (Wrexham, n.d. [1888?]), p. 16.

110. B. Bourne, *The Description and Confutation of Mysticall Anti-Christ* (1646), sig. T1.

111. Quoted by Hirst, *Hidden Riches*, p. 246.

John Pordage, rector of Bradfield, practised astrology and was temporarily ejected in 1655 for his occult activities. His son Samuel was a regular client of John Booker. Another student of astrology was Charles Hotham, who introduced Behmenism to Cambridge in 1646.[112] Other prominent Familists included Roger Crab, whom we have already encountered in Lilly's consulting-room,[113] Thomas Tryon, famous as a teetotaller, and keenly interested in astrology,[114] and Robert Gell, who preached before the Society of Astrologers on several occasions.[115] Comfort Everard, described in Booker's notebook as 'the young woman that practiseth astrology', may have been related to the Everard who was one of Pordage's followers, while John Gadbury is known for certain to have had a Familist phase. Even Lilly, who professed to abhor the Ranters, was an admirer of Boehme, whom he regarded as a godly man, and not the 'Dutch wizard' the Presbyterians made him out to be.[116]

But, although individual members of the sects flirted with astrology, the attitude of the main sectarian bodies was usually hostile. There were individual Quaker astrologers, but the Quakers regarded the practice as ungodly and violently attacked it.[117] Some of the Fifth

112. Josten, *Ashmole*, p. 527; Ashm. 428, ff. 125ᵛ, 180, 258, 271ᵛ (Samuel Pordage); Hutin, *Les Disciples anglais de Jacob Boehme*, p. 42; A. G. Walker, *Calamy Revised* (Oxford, 1934), p. 279; Ashm. 240, f. 256 (Hotham).

113. Above, p. 443. For his Familism, see Nuttall, *James Nayler, A. Fresh Approach*, p. 9 n.

114. On his closeness to Familism, see A. Gordon, *A Pythagorean of the Seventeenth Century* (1871), p. 41. His daughter's nativity is in Gadbury, *Collectio Geniturarum*, p. 195. The astrologer John Case dedicated his *Angelical Guide* to him in 1697. His faith in astrology ('a science too rashly decried by some') began, however, when he was an Anabaptist (*Some Memoirs of the Life of Mr Tho. Tryon*, p. 21).

115. Above, p. 361, n. 97. See also his *An Essay toward the Amendment of the Last English-Translation of the Bible* (1659), pp. 136 ff. Gell's social radicalism is revealed in his attack upon 'the empty name of gentility' (*Gell's Remaines* [1676], i, p. 626).

116. Ashm. 419, I, f. 110ᵛ (Comfort Everard); above, p. 445 (Gadbury). Lilly's opinion of Boehme is in his *Merlini Anglici Ephemeris* (1654), sig. B6ᵛ, and ibid. (1655), sig. A4ᵛ. cf. his *Autobiography*, p. 156. Other astrologically minded Familists and Ranters included James Barker (L. Muggleton, *The Acts of the Witnesses* [1699], pp. 53–6); Laurence Clarkson (above, p. 445); and Edward Howes, Rector of Goldhanger, Essex, an evident Perfectionist, who refers in his commonplace-book (1643–7) to 'the inferior astrology of, or in man' (Sloane 979, f. 56ᵛ).

117. For Quaker astrologers: *The Journal of George Fox*, ed. N. Penney (Cambridge, 1911), i, pp. 292–3, 451; A. M. Gummere, *Witchcraft and Quakerism* (Philadelphia, 1908), pp. 27, 40–7, 52; Sloane 2280, f. 36, and for

Monarchists thought it a wicked and inferior form of prophecy.[118] The Baptists displayed similar scruples, though their attitude was at first more hesitant. A meeting of ministers at Bridgwater in 1655 discussed the question of 'Whether astrology in physic be lawful?' To this they resolved:

We cannot at present determine this question, but desire to wait upon the Lord for light in this matter. Nevertheless, we desire brethren may be very cautious how they meddle with the practice of it, because if prosecuted to the utmost it leads to an ear to that which is evil and such evil work as it is judged the Scripture most eminently condemneth.
2nd. Because several brethren [who] have known and practised the same formerly have left the practice thereof upon the account of evil work they saw in the same.
3rd. Because it is very hard to practise any part thereof without bringing damage to the profession of the Gospel by an evil report.[119]

A more forthright answer was delivered by Lodowick Muggleton, who confidently pronounced that the sun, moon and stars were, like men, mere parts of God's creation, and could hardly be of importance since 'the compass of their bodies are not much bigger than they appear to our natural sight'.[120] The organized Nonconformist bodies ultimately proved to be as unfriendly to the practice of astrology as the earlier Puritans.

Quaker clients of astrologers: Sloane 2282, f. 26; BM., Add. MS 27,986, f. 59; above, p. 444. Examples of Quaker attacks on astrology are E. Burrough, *A Trumpet of the Lord sounded out of Sion* (1656), pp. 5–6; (G. Fox), *Here are Several Queries* (1657); H. Clark, *A Rod Discovered* (1657), pp. 38–9; G. F(ox), *A Declaration of the Ground of Error* (1657), p. 35; S. Eccles, *The Quakers Challenge* (1668), p. 5. John Raunce, author of several works against astrology, was a Quaker schismatic; R. T. Vann in *Past and Present*, xliii (1969), pp. 80–81.

118. e.g., M. Cary, *The Resurrection of the Witnesses* (2nd edn, 1653), sig. B2; *A Collection of the State Papers of John Thurloe*, ed. T. Birch (1754), iv, p. 650. John Brayne, who wrote an attack on astrology (above, p. 428, n. 10), was a millenarian minister.

119. G. Roberts, *The History and Antiquities of the Borough of Lyme Regis and Charmouth* (1834), p. 279. A generation later the Baptists were less ambiguous in their disapproval; B. S. Capp, *The Fifth Monarchy Men* (1972), p. 188.

120. (L. Muggleton), *A Divine Looking Glass* (1656; 1760 edn), p. 37 (in *The Works of John Reeve and Lodowicke Muggleton* [1832]). cf. R. Bolton, *Some Generall Directions for a Comfortable Walking with God* (5th edn, 1638), p. 324 ('The common people generally conceive of the sun's magnitude that it is not past a foot round'.)

Outside the sects it was not unknown for more orthodox clergymen to flirt with astrology. The wealth of astrological books and manuscripts in the monastic libraries reflected the leading part which the clergy had played in medieval astrological learning,[121] and the clerical practitioner continued to be a familiar figure. As John Gadbury rightly said, 'many of our best authors in astrology have been divines'. When in 1656 he drew up a list of leading English astrologers he included a number of clergy, remarking that he could have added 'many reverend divines in most counties in England, that at this present are very great proficients in astrology', but that he had magnanimously not done so, so as to avoid getting them into trouble.[122] Some of these 'reverend divines' must have been renegades, like the Welshman, John Evans, who first taught Lilly how to set a figure, and whom some scandal had forced to flee from his living in Staffordshire (although he still wore his surplice when conjuring).[123] Another eccentric was William Bredon, vicar of Thornton, Bucks., one-time chaplain to Sir Christopher Heydon, whose *Defence of Judicial Astrologie* (1603) he had helped him to compose. Noted for his habit of smoking bell-ropes when out of tobacco, Bredon was said to be an able astrologer, 'strictly adhering to Ptolemy, which he well understood', and reluctant to set figures on a Sunday.[124]

Best known of all was Richard Napier, rector of Great Linford, Bucks. (1590–1634)), pupil of Simon Forman, and one of the most fashionable practitioners of astrology and physic of the seventeenth century. According to Lilly, he instructed many other ministers in astrology, and 'would lend them whole cloak-bags of books'. Although he employed a curate to preach in his place, Napier was famous as a man of exemplary piety. He said prayers before setting a figure, and prayed over every patient. His knees, says John Aubrey, were 'horny with praying'. His voluminous papers show how closely his religion was intertwined with his medicine and astrology and, for that matter, magic and conjuring. Most of his activities

121. *Medieval Libraries of Great Britain,* ed. N. R. Ker (2nd edn, 1964), pp. 46, 47, 84, 141, 214.

122. J. Gadbury, *Cardines Coeli* (1684), ep. ded.; id., *Coelestis Legatus* (1656), sig. cc2ᵛ.

123. He was said to have practised as a conjurer and figure-setter while curate of Enville, Staffs; see P.R.O., St Ch. 8/255/24.

124. Lilly, *Autobiography,* pp. 54–9, 75; Ashm. 240, f. 98. Bredon seems to have had no inhibitions about making predictions *pro certo* and informed Richard Napier, the younger, that he would marry in 1629 (ibid., f. 87).

were reprehensible by the standards of orthodox religious opinion, yet Napier held on to his Anglican living and preceded every magical operation with prayer to the Almighty.[125]

Another clerical astrologer was Anthony Ascham, rector of Methley, Yorkshire, brother of Roger Ascham the Tudor humanist, and one of the earliest almanac-makers. Other sixteenth-century clergy who published prognostications or astrological guides included Richard Harvey, Thomas Buckminster, John Maplet, Stephen Batman and George Hartgill.[126] They had their counterparts in the following century, even though the ecclesiastical attitude to judicial astrology had hardened in the meantime. Joshua Childrey, notable for his attempt to reconstruct astrology on a Copernican foundation, was chaplain to Lord Herbert, and became a beneficed clergyman after the Restoration. Nathaniel Sparke, who in 1653 brought out a new edition of the French astrological guide by Claude Dariot, was a Kentish minister who married the step-daughter of the astrologer, George Atwell.[127] Some of the Nonconformists ejected at the Restoration had astrological interests,[128] while within the Church John Butler, chaplain to the Duke of Ormonde, rector of Litchborough, Northamptonshire, and a future Non-Juror, published an important work in defence of judicial astrology as late as 1680, though he admitted that this was an unusual thing for a clergyman to do.[129] Other clergymen who defended or practised astrology included Edmund Chilmead, chaplain of Christ Church, Oxford;

125. Above, p. 362; Lilly, *Autobiography*, p. 126; Aubrey, *Miscellanies*, pp. 159–61; G. Atwell, *An Apology* (1660), pp. 26–7.

126. In addition to *D.N.B.* and *S.T.C.* see, for Ascham, A. G. Dickens in *T.R.H.S.*, 5th ser., xii (1963), pp. 65–6, and for Hartgill, Gadbury, *Coelestis Legatus*, sig. Ccl, and P. Morgan, 'George Hartgill: an Elizabethan Parson-Astronomer and His Library', *Annals of Science*, xxiv (1968). I have not seen a complete copy of Ascham's almanac, but it is clear from W. Fulke, *Anti-Prognosticon* (1560), sig. B1, that it included a prognostication. There is a weather forecast in the surviving fragment of his 1551 almanac (Bodl., Vet. A 1 f. 150).

127. *D.N.B.*, 'Childrey, J.'; Taylor, *Mathematical Practitioners*, p. 80; Wing; N. S(parke), *Dariotus Redivivus* (1653); Ashm. 186, ff. 185^v ff.; Ashm. 356, ff. 1 ff., 47–8^v.

128. e.g., John Allin, an active alchemist and astrologer (*Archaeologia*, xxxvii [1857], pp. 17–18; *Sussex Archaeol. Collns*, xxxi [1881], pp. 139–40, 149–50, 154); Charles Hotham (above, p. 448).

129. Butler, *The Most Sacred and Divine Science of Astrology*, p. 1. On him see G. Baker, *The History and Antiquities of the County of Northampton* (1822–30), i, pp. 409–10.

Richard Carpenter, author of *Astrology proved Harmless, Useful and Pious* (1657); and Charles Atkinson, minister of Kirk Hammerton, Yorkshire, who issued an annual almanac between 1670 and 1673 and advertised his readiness to deal with nativities, lost goods and horary questions.[130] This sort of thing was rare, but at a less ostentatious level there were a few clergymen like William Locke, rector of Askerswell in rural Dorset (1674–86), who not only calculated the nativities of his two children, but copied their horoscopes into the parish register.[131] Many ministers made notes on almanacs and prognostications.[132]

Any remaining doubt concerning the divided loyalties of the clergy is resolved by the evidence of the astrologers' case-books, where the names of individual divines recur with some frequency. In the fifteenth century Bishop Pecock had observed that priests, no less than laymen, were subject to the influence of the stars. John Gadbury made the same point in 1658: 'It is notoriously known that the clergy are not more sanctimonious than other persons, but subject to the same passions, etc. and therefore may be benefited by the art of astrology even as others.'[133] Lilly included clergymen

130. Chilmead translated J. Gaffarel, *Unheard of Curiosities* (1650), which contained a defence of astrology and astrological magic. For Carpenter, see *D.N.B.* Atkinson was an ex-Royalist soldier; he gives some account of himself in his almanac, *Panterpe* (1670), sigs. B7ᵛ–B8.

131. Dorset R. O., Askerswell RE 1, pp. 98, 113. For other examples of this practice see T. F. Thiselton-Dyer, *Old English Social Life* (1898), pp. 121–2; J. C. Cox, *The Parish Registers of England* (1910), p. 41; *The Registers of the Church of St. Mary, Dymock, 1538–1790*, ed. I. Gray and J. E. Gethyn-Jones (Bristol and Glos. Archaeol. Soc., 1960), p. 51, and *Yorks. Archaeol. Journ.*, xxxvi (1944–7), p. 121. Other seventeenth-century clerical astrologers or active sympathizers included Robert Burton (above, p. 345); William Oughtred (*A Collection of Letters*, ed. Halliwell, p. 93; Aubrey, *Brief Lives*, ed. Clark, ii, pp. 105, 108; Taylor, *Mathematical Practitioners*, p. 357); William Milburne (Taylor, ibid., p. 207); Thomas Gouge (E. Calamy, *An Historical Account of My Own Life*, ed. J. T. Rutt [1830], i, p. 181); William Crafts (Gadbury, *Coelestis Legatus*, sig. cc2); Parson Smith of Swethland, Leics. (ibid.); W.G., 'minister of the gospel', (who published *Memento's to the World* [1680]); William Bedwell (Lilly, *Autobiography*, pp. 59–60, where he is confused with William Bedell).

132. e.g., *The Diary of the Rev. Ralph Josselin, 1616–83*, ed. E. Hockliffe (Camden Ser., 1908), p. 108; *Diaries and Letters of Philip Henry*, ed. M. H. Lee (1882), pp. 319–20; Turner, *Providences*, i, p. 61.

133. R. Pecock, *The Repressor of over much blaming of the Clergy*, ed. C. Babington (Rolls Ser., 1860), ii, p. 450; J. Gadbury, *The Doctrine of Nativities* (1658), ii, p. 287.

among his clients, most of them chiefly concerned with their future preferment. One Dr Humphries asked whether he could secure a living; a sea chaplain inquired about his prospects of future employment; and an anonymous querent confessed his interest in 'preferment to a fat benefice'.[134] Another minister, Mr Devorax, frequently commissioned the astrologer to resolve his personal problems,[135] and there were many other inquiries about benefices.[136] Lilly's correspondents included several country clergy, one of whom, Robert Sterrell, parson of Little Wigborough, Essex, asked him to calculate whether he had any chance of becoming skilful in astrology himself.[137] John Booker's customers included two London clergymen, John Mackerness, curate of St Botolph without Aldgate, and William Harrison, of St James, Duke's Place.[138] One client even asked Lilly in 1647 to resolve astrologically whether his brother should go into the Church.[139] In their published text-books the astrologers pointedly included rules for determining a client's prospects of ecclesiastical preferment.[140]

Godly laymen might also succumb to this most seductive of arts. Edward Gresham, the Jacobean prognosticator, was also the author of *Sabbath Day's Exercises* and *Positions in Divinitie*.[141] Samuel Jeake, father and son, prominent Rye Nonconformists in the later seventeenth century, were both active astrologers.[142] Sir Thomas

134. Ashm. 184, f. 27; Ashm. 327, ff. 197ᵛ, 241ᵛ.

135. Ashm. 178, f. 205; Ashm. 420, ff. 208ᵛ, 214ᵛ: he is perhaps to be identified with Jonathan Devereux, who was intruded into St Andrew Holborn in 1646 (G. Hennessy, *Novum Repertorium ecclesiasticum parochiale Londinense* [1898], p. 463).

136. e.g., Ashm. 420, ff. 166, 223ᵛ, 236; Ashm. 427, ff. 91ᵛ, 127ᵛ, 232ᵛ, 243, 269ᵛ.

137. Ashm. 423, f. 147. cf. f. 142 (Rev Wm Paine, intruded rector of Grafton Regis, Northants).

138. Ashm. 180, ff. 52, 54; Ashm. 428, f. 272; Gadbury, *Collectio Geniturarum*, pp. 115–16; Hennessy, *Novum Repertorium*, p. 106.

139. Ashm. 420, f. 13.

140. e.g., H. Coley, *Clavis Astrologiae Elimata* (2nd edn, 1676), pp. 225, 259; J. Middleton, *Practical Astrology* (1679), pp. 254–5; J. Partridge, *An Astrological Vade Mecum* (1679), sig. A10. Other evidence of clerical consultations may be found in Ashm. 337, f. 43; Ashm. 427, ff. 4, 197; 420, ff. 32, 85; Gadbury, *Collectio Geniturarum*, pp. 110–13, 117; Matthews, *Calamy Revised*, p. 119; A. L. Rowse, *The Elizabethan Renaissance* (1971), pp. 147–9.

141. Gresham. *A Prognostication for this present yeare of our Lord, 1607* (1606), sig. B2ᵛ.

142. T. W. W. Smart, 'A Biographical Sketch of Samuel Jeake, Snr, of Rye', *Sussex Archaeol. Collns.*, xiii (1861).

Myddelton, father of the Parliamentary general, employed Richard Napier to make astrological sigils without any apparent scruple about their propriety.[143] But some clients had prickings of conscience. One informed Booker that he had only decided to consult him after reading Sir Christopher Heydon's *Defence of Judicial Astrologie*; another told Lilly that he would like to learn about astrology, having at last satisfied himself that it was in accord with the word of God.[144]

Many people resort unto us [remarked a Jacobean astrologer], offering great sums of money or other gifts to tell them of a silver spoon, a ring, or a jewel stolen from them, cattle strayed, and such like, protesting (if they find us unwilling to hear them) that they will keep our counsel, thereby confessing that they think it evil, or else why should counsel be kept?[145]

A slightly defensive tone is to be found in much of the astrological literature of the period. The almanacs usually carried an introductory discourse justifying the subject and rebutting the aspersions of its clerical enemies.

But such scruples were frequently overcome. The astrologers even had theological arguments to justify their remuneration. When the figure-caster John Vaux was hauled before the High Commission in 1633 he reminded the court that, when Samuel told Saul what had become of his father's asses, Saul had been prepared to pay the fourth part of a shekel of silver for the service rendered. Joseph Blagrave cited the same precedent in an altercation with a Reading minister who wanted to prosecute him for tracing stolen linen. The minister, he happily relates, 'after some pause, said Samuel was to blame'.[146]

No simple formula can summarize the hopeless confusion between astrology and religion in the minds of so many of their adherents. Its complexity is admirably illustrated by the letter which an anonymous client sent to John Booker. He wanted the astrologer to answer a number of typical queries. Would he or his wife die first? Would they have any children? Would his share in a Barbados plantation

143. Above, p. 323. His son took the astrologer's niece as his second wife.
144. Ashm. 225, f. 281; Ashm. 423, f. 178.
145. *Pond. 1609*, sig. C6ᵛ.
146. 1 Samuel, ix, 8; *Durham High Commission*, pp. 34–42; Blagrave, *Blagraves Astrological Practice of Physick*, p. 163. For other instances of the same argument, see Farnworth, *Witchcraft Cast Out*, pp. 6–7; Lilly, *Englands Propheticall Merline* (1644), sig. b2; Butler, *The Most Sacred and Divine Science of Astrology*, i, p. 48.

prosper? But as a postscript he added a further and more unusual question:

> Whether, notwithstanding that the stars show very plainly many cross influences and events upon men (both good men as well as evil men), yet I say whether is it not common that upon both, especially good men who are actually in the state of grace and known themselves to be the adopted sons of God, I say whether doth not these influences commonly fail to take effect upon them either totally or for the most part?[147]

The syntax is confused, but the thought behind the tangled sentence is clear enough: the stars might rule the destinies of unregenerate men, but surely the godly would be immune.

So, instead of remaining two rival systems of belief, pagan astrology and Christian religion proved to have many points of contact. Both astrologers and clients usually found it possible to arrive at a *modus vivendi* which permitted them to reconcile their religion with their practice without too much soul-searching. Yet the preachers feared that the vogue for astrology might lead to the replacement of the Christian God by the planetary divinities of classical antiquity, whose memory was preserved in the names of the months and the days of the week. Astrology, they recalled, had begun as a religion rather than a science, and the Bible contained warnings against star-worship. The celestial bodies were eternal, universal and allegedly omnipotent; might not their contemplation turn into a sort of mystical communion? Had not the heretical Priscillianists of the fourth century worshipped the stars as divine? Philip Stubbes, the Puritan castigator of Elizabethan pastimes, stated the danger which everyone feared.

> Who [he asked], hearing that ... the sun, the moon, the stars, the signs and planets, do give both good things and evil, blessing and cursing, good success and evil success, yea, life and death, at their pleasure ... and that they rule, govern and dispose all things whatsoever, yea, both the bodies and souls of man ... Who, hearing this, ... would not fall from God and worship the creatures that give such blessings unto Man? ... Why should not planets and stars be adored and worshipped as gods, if they could work these effects?[148]

147. Ashm. 225, f. 323.
148. P. Stubbes, *Anatomy of Abuses*, ed. F. J. Furnivall (New Shakspere Soc., 1877–82), ii, pp. 58, 61. For other fears of star-worship, see *The Works*

The danger was, of course, illusory. None of the leading astrologers seems to have been an atheist or star-worshipper. They represented almost every shade of religious opinion, from Roman Catholic to Quaker, but they all claimed that their art was compatible with their religion, and that the heavenly bodies were merely instruments of God's will. At the popular level, however, the balance between astrology and religion may have been occasionally upset. Early Christianity had sometimes been taken for a solar religion, and the Anglo-Saxon kings had to legislate against star-worship.[149] The pagan tradition of planetary deities also survived in medieval iconography. The signs of the zodiac decorated many English churches and may have helped to shape popular religious attitudes. Pictures of the sun and moon were found in several Suffolk churches visited by the Parliamentary iconoclast William Dowsing in 1643–4.[150] Churches themselves were built to face the rising sun. Camden recorded that 'the wild Irish' still knelt before the new moon and recited the Lord's Prayer. In England the moon's supposed influence upon the crops and upon human physiology was readily accepted by the common people, since, as Bacon remarked, 'such thoughts easily find entrance into men's minds by reason of their veneration for the heavenly bodies'.[151] In the seventeenth century it was still common for people to curtsey to the new moon, saying 'Yonder's the Moon, God save her grace.' In Yorkshire, according to John Aubrey, people used to worship the new moon on their bare knees. Country folk, who were taught to rub their hands before the moon as a cure for warts, may well have credited it with a supernatural power, while the psalm used at the ceremony of the churching of women

of Roger Hutchinson, ed. J. Bruce (Cambridge, P.S., 1842), p. 78; J. Swan, Speculum Mundi (Cambridge, 1635), pp. 312–14; and id., Signa Coeli (1652), p. 6; The Works of Mr John Weemse, ii (1636), pp. 70–72; Burgess, CXLV Expository Sermons, p. 396.

149. H. Chadwick, The Early Church (Harmondsworth, 1967), pp. 126–7; G. Storms, Anglo-Saxon Magic (The Hague, 1948), i, pp. 6–7.

150. The Journal of William Dowsing, ed. C. H. Evelyn White (Ipswich, 1885), pp. 16, 25. Most of the examples of stellar iconography cited in J. Seznec, The Survival of the Pagan Gods, trans. B. F. Sessions (New York, 1961), are Italian. For English ones, see, e.g., Archaeol. Journ., ii (1846), p. 89; xxxiv (1877), p. 274; xlv (1888), 112, 421; xlvii (1890), p. 224; J. Fowler in Archaeologia, xliv (1873); Archdeacon Harpsfield's Visitation, 1557, ed. L. E. Whatmore (Catholic Rec. Soc., 1950–51), i, p. 173.

151. Camden's Britannia, ed. E. Gibson (1695), col. 1046; Bacon, Works, v, p. 448.

was a supplication for protection from the influence of the sun and moon alike.[152]

How far such practices affected men's basic beliefs it is difficult to tell. The fifteenth-century author of *Dives and Pauper* was right to complain that 'these days men do worship to the sun, moon and stars', for in 1453 a butcher and a labourer of Standon, Hertfordshire, were formally accused of maintaining that there was no god save the sun and the moon.[153] Sir Thomas More may have had his own country in mind when he wrote that in Utopia 'some worship for God the sun, some the moon, some some other of the planets'. When Richard Baxter arrived at his Kidderminster parish in the mid seventeenth century he found some of his flock so ignorant that they 'thought Christ was the sun ... and the Holy Ghost was the moon'.[154] London sects of 'Saturnians' and 'Junonians' were reported to be worshipping planetary deities in 1641. A group of carousers were reported to have drunk healths 'to the seven planets' in 1648. Three years later an astrological writer admitted that some contemporaries ascribed divine power to the stars, which they 'esteemed as gods, and not as instruments set up by the first cause'.[155] Two other cases throw suggestive light upon what may well have been a more general phenomenon. The first is that of Anne Bodenham, who was executed for witchcraft at Salisbury in 1653. A former servant of the astrologer, John Lambe, she had long practised as a cunning woman, claiming to be able to 'do more than Master Lilly or anyone whatsoever'. It is notable that when dealing with a maid who had convulsive fits she is reported to have proposed a frankly pagan remedy – prayer to Jupiter, 'the best and fortunatest of all the planets'.[156] Even more striking is another Wiltshire case, which came before the

152. Swan, *Signa Coeli*, p. 8; Sir K. Digby, *A Late Discourse ... touching the Cure of Wounds*, trans. R. White (1658), p. 43; Aubrey, *Gentilisme*, pp. 36–7, 83; T. Harley, *Moon Lore* (1885); above, p. 68. An Elizabethan charm based on invocation of the moon is in B.M., Lansdowne MS 96, f. 104.

153. *Dives and Pauper*, f. 29; Thomson, *Later Lollards*, p. 67 (who appears to reject the late K. B. McFarlane's characteristic suggestion that the speaker was drunk at the time (*John Wycliffe and the Beginnings of English Nonconformity* [1952], p. 185)).

154. Sir T. More, *Utopia* (Everyman edn, 1951), p. 117; G. F. Nuttall, *Richard Baxter* (1965), p. 46.

155. *A Discovery of 29. Sects here in London* (1641), p. 7; *Strange Predictions related at Catericke in the North of England* (1648), p. 1; H. Warren, *Magick and Astrology vindicated* (1651), p. 27.

156. E. Bower, *Doctor Lamb revived* (1653), pp. 8, 21.

quarter sessions in 1656. A Lacock weaver, William Bond, was
charged with atheism and blasphemy, and in particular with publicly
affirming that 'there was no God or power ruling above the planets,
no Christ but the sun that shines upon us'; and 'that the twelve
patriarchs were the twelve houses'. This was astrology run wild; and
it is tantalising not to know how many of William Bond's contemporaries may have held similar views.[157]

157. *H.M.C., Various Collections,* i. pp. 132–3. cf. above, p. 203. Some
astrologers certainly believed in planetary angels (e.g., Ashm. 423, f. 218),
while the astrologically-minded first Earl of Shaftesbury 'fancied that after
death our souls lived in stars' (*Bishop Burnet's History of his own Time*
[Oxford, 1823], i, p. 164).

THE APPEAL TO THE PAST

13.

ANCIENT PROPHECIES

> Sometimes he angers me
> With telling me of the moldwarp and the ant,
> Of the dreamer Merlin and his prophecies,
> And of a dragon, and a finless fish,
> A clip-winged griffin, and a moulten raven,
> A couching lion and a ramping cat,
> And such a deal of skimble-skamble stuff
> As puts me from my faith.
>
> Shakespeare, *Henry IV, Part I*

1. *The genre*

As has been seen, contemporaries had many methods by which they thought it possible to gain knowledge of the future. But the ancient prophecy differed from all those yet discussed. It was not a straightforward prediction, but an elusively vague or ambiguous piece of prose or verse, resting on no clearly defined foundation, either magical or religious. Usually, but not invariably, it was attributed to some

BIBLIOGRAPHICAL NOTE: R. Taylor, *The Political Prophecy in England* (New York, 1911) is a pioneering study, though rather general and literary in character. It is not much concerned with the social functions of prophecy, on the grounds that 'particular instances of the direct influence of prophecies are difficult to find'. This is unduly pessimistic. For other useful discussions see Kittredge, *Witchcraft*, chap. 14; J. Webb in *Archaeologia*, xx (1824), pp. 250–71 (on later medieval prophecies); M. H. Dodds, 'Political Prophecies in the Reign of Henry VIII', *Modern Language Rev.*, xi (1916); G. R. Elton, *Policy and Police* (Cambridge, 1972), chap. 2; and C. W. Previté-Orton, 'An Elizabethan Prophecy', *History*, ii (1918). M. E. Griffiths, *Early Vaticination in Welsh with English Parallels*, ed. T. G. Jones (Cardiff, 1937) is concerned with the medieval period. So also for the most part are J. J. I. Döllinger, *Prophecies and the Prophetic Spirit in the Christian Era*, trans. A. Plummer (1873), a valuable introduction to the prophecies of medieval Europe, and N. Cohn, *The Pursuit of the Millennium* (1962 edn), a brilliant analysis of popular messianism. H. Rusche, 'Prophecies and Propaganda, 1641 to 1651', *E.H.R.*, lxxxiv (1969), appeared after this chapter was written.

The prophecies themselves are extant in many manuscript collections. Useful guides to the main *genres* are provided by H. L. D. Ward, *Catalogue of Romances in the Department of Manuscripts in the British Museum*, i (1883), esp. pp. 292–338, and the introduction to Murray, *Erceldoune*.

historical or mythical personage. It was always thought to be old, sometimes very old indeed. This kind of prophecy had been in circulation long before the sixteenth century, but its history is a tangled one, which literary scholars have by no means fully unravelled.

The most common type employed elaborate animal symbolism, much in the style of the Eagles and Dragons of Revelation. In Geoffrey of Monmouth's twelfth-century *History of the Kings of Britain*, the archetypal source for this genre, Merlin's prophecies had related to such figures as the White Dragon and the Red Dragon, the Boar of Cornwall and the Ass of Wickedness. These beasts were subsequently taken to be symbolic allusions to specific countries, families or individuals. This Galfridian type of prophecy was thus both obscure and flexible; it was also particularly well designed to appeal to a feudal society where heraldic emblems were identified with families and individuals in almost totemic fashion. From time to time interpreters compiled full-scale keys to these prophecies indicating which of their contemporaries were to be equated with these mythological beasts.[1] An Elizabethan writer mocked talk of 'eagles and beagles, cats and rats, dogs and hogs, crows and bows, stones and dead men's bones, country hobs and lobs, clouted shoon and midsummer moon',[2] but the Galfridian prophecies were immensely adaptable, and, so long as the monarchy and peerage used such emblems, they could be plausibly applied to fit contemporary events.

Another type was the 'painted prophecy' – an illuminated scroll or picture depicting such subjects as kings, priests and heraldic symbols. This primitive method of telling stories by pictures had a parallel in the emblem books beloved by the Renaissance, and popularized in England by Francis Quarles and George Wither. Painted prophecies, however, were more inscrutable than emblems and carried no accompanying explanatory verses. Like heraldic symbols, pictures were an effective means of communicating with the illiterate, and they gave equal scope for subjective interpretation.

A similar ambiguity characterized the third type of prophecy,

1. A good example is to be found in Bodl., MS Arch. Selden B 8, ff. 266ᵛ–7ᵛ. There are others in Cheshire R.O., DDX 123, f. 23; B.M., Lansdowne MS 122, f. 60ᵛ; *Sundry Strange Prophecies* (1652), pp. 15–16.
2. J. H(arvey), *A Discoursive Probleme concerning Prophesies* (1588), p. 62.

which was based on combinations of letters or numbers. A well-known example was the distich

When Hempe is spun
England's done

Here 'Hempe' was believed to comprise the initial letters of the Tudor monarchs, Henry, Edward, Mary and Philip, Elizabeth. Bacon writes that he first heard this prophecy in childhood, when it was taken to mean that disaster of some kind would follow the death of Elizabeth. After the event, however, it was assumed to have indicated that the realm would change its name from England to Britain.[3]

It would be difficult to draw up a comprehensive list of all the prophecies which are known to have been extant in Tudor and Stuart England, or which still survive in manuscript today. Certainly they run into hundreds, and there seems no limit to the local variations and permutations which they assumed. Very frequently medieval descent was claimed for them by reporting that they had been accidentally discovered in the ruins of some old building, preferably a monastery. Thus there was the *Prophecy found of late in the Abbey of St Benet in Norfolk*;[4] the prophecy discovered by a mason in the wall of a Carthusian house in Somerset;[5] and the others found 'in an old cell at Syon';[6] 'in a manuscript in Pontefract Castle';[7] 'within an altar in Suffolk at the pulling down of the altars in the time of King Edward the 6th';[8] 'in a plate of brass in Folkestone in Kent';[9] 'in the bottom of a mean man's brass pot at St Edmundsbury';[10] 'copied out of a book wherein was Wycliffe's works, lying in a tailor's shop at

3. Bacon, *Works*, vi, p. 464; *Collection of Ancient Scottish Prophecies* (Bannatyne Club, Edinburgh, 1833), p. 63. For other versions and interpretations, see Sir J. Harington, *A Tract on the Succession to the Crown (A.D. 1602)*, ed. C. R. Markham (Roxburghe Club, 1880), p. 17; Ashm. 221, f. 312; T. Heywood, *The Life of Merlin* (1641: 1813 edn), p. 282; W. Lilly, *A Prophecy of the White King* (1644); Harvey, *op. cit.*, p. 60.

4. Printed as *Ignatius his Prophecie* (1642). Other copies in *Mercurius Propheticus* (1643); Ashm. 242, f. 123; Ashm. 47, f. 40; Ashm. 423, f. 265; *C.S.P.D., 1625–49*, p. 662; *H.M.C., 10th Report*, appx, pt iv, p. 23.

5. Lilly, *A Prophecy of the White King*, pp. 29 ff.

6. Bodl., MS Arch. Selden B 8, f. 268.

7. *Merlin Reviv'd* [1681?].

8. Bodl., MS Arch. Selden B 8, f. 272.

9. *C.S.P.D., 1667*, p. 349.

10. Ashm. 423, f. 241.

Harlow in Essex after the Dissolution of the Monasteries';[11] and 'written in an antique scroll lying on a rock at St Michael's Mount, Cornwall'.[12] In 1681 thirty or forty 'old prophecies' were said to have been lately discovered in an old abbey wall near Bridgwater.[13] This conventional pedigree reflected the widely current belief that the monks had been possessed of special occult powers denied to their Protestant successors.[14]

Another popular device was to claim that a prophecy had long been known to one particular family or individual, but was now for the first time being more widely disseminated. Of this type were *A Prophecy which hath been in a manuscript in the Lord Powis's family sixty years; The Prophecy of old Otwell Binns kept by Mr Smith, Vicar of Huddersfield forty years*; and 'An old written paper said to have been brought out of the Tower by Sir William Wade, and stopped in a hole in the wall in his house, where it was taken out after his death'.[15]

Most often, however, the prophecies were attributed to historical individuals who were in no position to deny their authenticity. The many persons upon whom such prophecies were fathered, or out of whose genuine writings 'prophecies' were extracted, included Bede,[16] Gildas,[17] Archbishop Mellitus,[18] Edward the Confessor,[19] Henry II,[20] Becket,[21] Giraldus Cambrensis,[22] Friar Bacon,[23] Chaucer,[24] Savon-

11. B.M., Lansdowne MS 122, f. 31.

12. Ward, *Catalogue of Romances*, i, p. 316.

13. Bodl., Wood MS F 39, f. 354.

14. cf. above, p. 321.

15. Broadside, n.d. (?1685); *Sixe Strange Prophesies* (1642), sig. A4; *Ballads from Manuscripts*, ed. F. J. Furnivall (Ballad Soc., 1868–72), i, p. 319.

16. Murray, *Erceldoune*, appx. ii.

17. *Collection of Ancient Scottish Prophecies*, pp. 42–4; Griffiths, *Early Vaticination in Welsh*, p. 198.

18. *C.S.P.D., 1629–31*, p. 149.

19. For subsequent interpretations of his death-bed dream (*Vita Aedwardi Regis*, ed. F. Barlow [1962], pp. 75–6), see M. Bloch in *Analecta Bollandiana*, xli (1923), pp. 35–8.

20. *The Mirror for Magistrates*, ed. L. B. Campbell (New York, 1960), p. 448.

21. P. A. Brown, *The Development of the Legend of Thomas Becket* (Philadelphia, 1930), pp. 225–37, gives full details.

22. *H.M.C., Pepys*, p. 87; below, p. 472.

23. Who was thought to have prophesied in Welsh; T. Pugh, *British and Out-landish Prophecies* (1658), p. 42.

24. *Doomes-day* (1647), p. 3; below, pp. 466–7.

arola,[25] Ignatius Loyola,[26] James I,[27] Sir Walter Raleigh,[28] and Archbishop Ussher.[29] Others were laid at the door of more shadowy figures: Mr Truswell, 'Recorder of a Town in Lincolnshire';[30] Dickin of Gosner, a Derbyshire tailor;[31] Humphrey Tindall, 'vicar of Wellin two hundred years past';[32] Robert Nixon, supposedly born in the reign of Edward IV, whose Cheshire *Prophecy* enjoyed a steady popularity into the nineteenth century;[33] and, best known of all, Mother Shipton, allegedly a Yorkshire contemporary of Cardinal Wolsey, but not heard of before 1641.[34]

It is a matter for literary detection to determine just how it was that each of these individuals gained their prophetic reputation. Some of them really had been prophets or religious visionaries, like Joachim of Fiore, the twelfth-century abbot,[35] or the medieval saints, Hildegard, Bridget and Vincent, whose apocalyptic predictions relating to the reform of the Church and the fall of Rome were easily acceptable in a Protestant environment; most of the prophecies included in one of the earliest printed collections, James Maxwell's *Admirable and notable prophesies uttered in former times by 24*

25. *A Brief Description of the Future History of Europe* (1650), p. 18.

26. Above, p. 463, n. 4.

27. *King James his Divine Prophecie of the Warres and Distractions of the Present and Future Times* (1645).

28. *All is not Gold that Glisters* (1651). See T. N. Brushfield, *A Bibliography of Sir Walter Ralegh* (2nd edn, Exeter, 1908), p. 166.

29. *Strange and Remarkable Prophesies and Predictions of . . . James Usher* (1678); *The Prophecy of Bishop Usher* (1687); and many reissues.

30. *A True Coppie of a Prophesie* (1642); *Severall Strange Prophecies* (1642); and often reprinted.

31. Josten, *Ashmole*, pp. 624–5.

32. *The Prophecy of Humphrey Tindal* (1642); *Two Prophecies . . . made by Humphrey Tindall* (1644).

33. W. E. A. A(xon), *Nixon's Cheshire Prophecies* (1873). There are two MS collections of prophecies in the Cheshire R.O., both attributed to 'William' Nixon. One (DDX 123) comes from Vale Royal and is a medley largely derived from *The Prophecies of Rymour, Beid and Marlyng* (Murray, *Erceldoune,* appx. ii) and a 1553 prophecy (ibid., appx. iii). The other (DCC 37/1) is a similar work of plagiarism dating from *c.* 1700.

34. *D.N.B.;* W. H. Harrison, *Mother Shipton investigated* (1881). Her prophecies were published in one form or another at least twenty times between 1641 and 1700. A list of some other apocryphal prophets is given in Harvey, *A Discoursive Probleme,* p. 56.

35. On whose influence see M. E. Reeves, *The Influence of Prophecy in the Later Middle Ages* (Oxford, 1969).

famous Romain Catholikes concerning the Church of Rome's defection (1615), were of this kind. The sibylline and neo-sibylline prophecies dating from late antiquity also continued to attract attention.[36] Other so-called 'prophets' had, like Giraldus Cambrensis or Savonarola, been moralists and religious leaders whose warnings of the disasters which would overtake their people if they did not reform had acquired a prophetic character in the eyes of later generations. A good example of this process was provided by the poet George Wither, whose reiterated predictions of the woes in store for unregenerate England seemed, after the coming of the Civil War, to have been based on real fore-knowledge, an illusion their author was happy to encourage.[37]

Yet although many of the prophecies of the sixteenth and seventeenth centuries were rehashed versions of intentionally prophetic utterances of the past, others seem to have arisen almost accidentally. Casual remarks appeared in the light of later events to reveal unusual prescience. Archbishop Ussher, for example, had preached on a text of *Ezekiel* in 1602–3 in such a way that it seemed later that he had been predicting the Irish Rebellion of 1641. Another of his sermons in 1625 subsequently appeared to have been a prediction of the Civil War.[38] A well-known recusant 'prophecy' started life as a hope expressed by a Catholic sympathizer in the course of conversation.[39] Ancient chronicles and histories seem to have been carefully examined for any apparently prophetic implications, and a chance observation could easily gain a prophetic *cachet* for its dead author. In some cases there was not even any real connection between the prophecy and the supposed prophet: 'Chaucer's prophecy', for example, was an anonymous piece of verse, printed in

36. Harvey, *A Discoursive Probleme*, pp. 41–5; S. Batman, *The Doome Warning All Men to the Iudgmente* (1581), pp. 36–8; *Collection of Ancient Scottish Prophecies*, pp. 45–8.

37. His most frequently quoted prophecy was cointained in *Britain's Remembrancer* (1628), canto 8. *Fragmenta Prophetica, or the Remains of George Wither* (1669) collected the predictions scattered through his works. His prophecies also appeared in *Mr Wither His Prophesie of Our Present Calamity* (1643); *Vaticinium Votivum* (Utrecht, 1649); *Mr Geo. Withers Revived* (1683); *A Collection of Many Wonderful Prophesies* (1691).

38. See P. Styles in *Hermathena*, lxxxviii (1956), pp. 20–21; N. Bernard, *The Life ... of ... James Usher* (1656), pp. 89–90.

39. C. A. Newdigate, 'The Tyburn Prophecy of Gregory Gunnes', *The Month*, clxiv (1934).

the 1532 edition of the poet's works, and hence regarded by the Elizabethans as a fourteenth-century prophecy.[40]

The best-known prophet was Merlin, a composite figure to whom were sometimes assigned both the nationalist predictions of the Welsh bard Myrddin, and the prophecies included by Geoffrey of Monmouth in the seventh book of his *History*. Geoffrey's Merlin had been partly created from the prophetic boy, Ambrosius, described in the much earlier work of Nennius; hence the conflation of 'Ambrosius Merlin', as in *The Mystery of Ambros Merlin* (1683). Most of the old Welsh prophecies related to the struggle against the Saxons and Normans and predicted the eventual triumph of the Welsh, led by Arthur, or in other versions, Owain or Cadwalader. Their cloudy language made them adaptable to other contexts, and prophecies ascribed to 'Merlin', whether the Galfridian (Merlin Ambrosius) or the Caledonian (Merlin Silvester), circulated in many different versions. In the Middle Ages, thought one Elizabethan, 'Merlin's prophecies were chained to the desks of many libraries in England with great reverence and estimation'.[41]

Merlin's predictions, though much adapted and distorted in the telling, can usually be referred back to some specific text; and the same is true of the Scottish prophecies attributed to the thirteenth-century Thomas Rymer of Erceldoune, or included in the medley fathered on 'Bridlington' (sometimes the fourteenth-century Austin Canon, John of Bridlington, sometimes his twelfth-century predecessor, Robert of Bridlington).[42] These, as part of *The Whole Prophecies of Scotland, England, France, Ireland and Denmark*, were published at Edinburgh at the beginning of the seventeenth century, and frequently appeared thereafter.[43] The collection was the most important source for the imagery employed by the prophet-mongers of Tudor and Stuart England. Also identifiable are the prophecies based on such Biblical sources as Revelation or the Book of Esdras.

40. G. H. Campbell in *Modern Language Notes*, xxix (1914), pp. 195–6.

41. H. Howard, Earl of Northampton, *A Defensative against the Poyson of Supposed Prophecies* (1620), f. 118ᵛ. On Merlin see E. Anwyl, 'Merlin', in *Encyclopaedia of Religion and Ethics*, ed. J. Hastings (Edinburgh, 1908–26); Introduction by W. E. Mead to *Merlin or the Early History of King Arthur*, ed. M. B. Wheatley (E.E.T.S., 1899); and J. S. P. Tatlock, *The Legendary History of Britain* (1950), chap. xvii.

42. For this work by a partisan of the Black Prince see P. Meyvaert, 'John Erghome and the *Vaticinium Roberti Bridlington*', *Speculum*, xli (1966).

43. The contents of the first two editions (1603 and 1615) are in *Collection of Ancient Scottish Prophecies*.

On rare occasions prophecies were known to have had a definite origin. Thus a copy of the prophecy of Paul Grebner, a German Protestant and Biblical commentator, had been presented to Elizabeth I, and subsequently deposited in the library of Trinity College, Cambridge. It contained predictions relating to the future history of Europe, with pictorial illustrations and a marked anti-Catholic bias. During the following century it was frequently republished, and variously interpreted as heralding the career of Gustavus Adolphus, the execution of Charles I, and the restoration of his son.⁴⁴ So popular was it that like a successful modern film it duly produced its own offspring, in the form of the Royalist pamphlet, *The Visions and Prophecies ... of Ezekiel Grebner, son of Obadiah Grebner, son of Paul Grebner* (1661). Here at least the pedigree was a straight one.

But it was also common for a prophecy to be attributed to different authors by different publishers. *The Prophecy of Thomas Becket*, for example, which concerned the doings of the Lion, the Lily, the Eagle and the Son of Man, was said when published in 1666 to have been discovered only the year previously in an old house at Abingdon, and to have originally been the property of a canon of Glastonbury. Yet William Lilly, who had already published it in 1645, claimed to have found it in an old manuscript collection of prophecies dating from the sixteenth century; while it was said by the editor of *Severall Strange Prophecies* (1642) to have been the work of Mr Truswell, Recorder of Lincoln, and by a later publisher to have been written by Bede. The Quakers, on the other hand, thought it was by Boehme. In 1689 it appeared in print again, this time as *A Prophecy sent by the late Honourable Algernon Sydney*. It had in fact been used in support of Edward III's intervention in France, and also to back up the Yorkist claims of Edward IV.⁴⁵ Equally tangled was the history of another popular prophecy, beginning 'If eighty-eight be past, then thrive'. This was variously said to have been written by

44. The manuscript is briefly described in M. R. James, *The Western Manuscripts in the Library of Trinity College, Cambridge*, ii (Cambridge, 1901), pp. 388–9. The prophecy was summarized in J. Maxwell, *Admirable and Notable Prophecies* (1615), pp. 87–8.

45. Lilly traced it back to a printed version published at Paris in 1530 (Josten, *Ashmole*, pp. 1260–62), and published it in *A Collection of Ancient and Modern Prophesies* (1645). For its medieval history, see Ward, *Catalogue of Romances*, i, pp. 314, 317, 321; Griffiths, *Early Vaticination*, pp. 170–71; Brown, *The Development of the Legend of Thomas Becket*, pp. 229–32. For the attribution to Boehme, see F. E(llington), *Christian Information concerning these Last Times* (1664), pp. 10 ff.

Mother Shipton and by Ignatius Loyola, and to have been 'found in the Abbey of St Benet in Norfolk'.[46]

The textual genealogy of these prophecies thus poses intricate problems. There will be no attempt to tackle them here, for our concern is with the use to which the prophecies were put by contemporaries, not with the circumstances of their original composition. For this purpose it may be reasonably assumed that the majority of prophecies fell into one of two main genres: they were either genuine utterances of an earlier period, reinterpreted to fit new events in flagrant disregard of their original circumstances of composition (much the larger category), or spurious inventions by contemporaries, laying fraudulent claims to a hoary antiquity. Some of the latter convict themselves out of their own mouths; for example, the prophecy issued in 1651 in justification of the new Commonwealth government, purporting to have been uttered by 'a Jesuit in Henry VII's time' (i.e. half a century before the Order of Jesus was founded).[47] Others are revealed as fictitious by internal evidence, for example, *The Prophecy of old Otwell Binns* (1642),[48] which contains a wealth of undisguised allusions to the preoccupations of the Long Parliament. But even in cases of this kind the publishers would make a half-hearted attempt to give their progeny some sort of pedigree by saying it had been 'taken out of a certain library' or 'left at [their] shop by an unknown person'.[49]

The nature of these prophecies may, therefore, be summed up by saying that they were usually of supposedly medieval origin; that they drew their prestige from their antiquity, and that although some contemporaries discussed whether the prophets had got their foreknowledge from God, from conjuration or from astrology, there was on the whole little interest shown in the precise origin and basis of such predictions. For most men it was sufficient that they were there.

2. *Effects*

Most sophisticated writers of the sixteenth and seventeenth centuries affected to despise prophecies, agreeing with Bacon in his essay *Of Prophecies* that they were good for nothing save 'winter talk by

46. C. Syms, *The Swords Apology* (1644), p. 17 ('9'); *Sixe Strange Prophesies* (1643); *Mercurius Propheticus* (1643).

47. *Old Sayings and Predictions* (1651).

48. William Lilly thought it had been forged by 'some prelatical priest'; *A Collection of Ancient and Moderne Prophesies*, p. 44.

49. *The Lord Merlins Prophecy* (1651), p. 7; *Vaticinia Poetica* (1666).

the fire-side'. But like Bacon they also thought they did a great deal of mischief. 'The wiser sort for the most part do utterly scorn them,' commented Sir John Harington, 'yet I find they give a presage and leave an impression in their minds that seem most to scorn them.'[50] This vulnerability was commented upon by many observers, from the Frenchman Commines in the fifteenth century to the astrologer Lilly in the seventeenth. 'Englishmen,' declared a Scottish writer in 1549, 'give firm credit to divers profane prophecies of Merlin and to other old corrupt vaticinators, to whose imagined works they give more faith nor to the prophecy of Isaiah, Ezekiel, Jeremiah or to the Evangel.'[51] Perusal of English history, thought Sir Edward Coke, revealed 'what lamentable and fatal events have fallen out upon vain prophecies carried out of the inventions of wicked men, pretended to be ancient, but newly framed to deceive true men; and withal how credulous and inclinable our countrymen in former times to them have been'.[52] In 1677 the Nonconformist clergyman, Richard Gilpin, complained that 'an old prophecy, pretended to be found in a wall, or taken out of an old manuscript, of I know not what uncertain author, is usually more doted on than the plain and infallible rules of Scripture. This we may observe daily; and foreigners do much blame the English for a facile belief of such things.'[53]

The best testimony to the influence of these predictions was the determination of successive governments to suppress their circulation and punish their disseminators. In the Middle Ages action was taken against the prophecies of Welsh bards and the prophetic utterances of the Lollards. False prophets were periodically apprehended, and seditious glosses on the prophecy of Bridlington brought a friar to the gallows in 1402.[54] Under the Tudors the campaign seems to have been intensified. It is not clear what lay behind the rumour that 'all manner of prophecies' had been made felony by the first ses-

50. Harington, *A Tract on the Succession to the Crown*, p. 17.

51. *The Complaynt of Scotlande*, ed. J. A. H. Murray (E.E.T.S., 1872), p. 82. cf. Taylor, *The Political Prophecy*, p. 85; below, p. 491 (Lilly); F. J. Levy, *Tudor Historical Thought* (San Marino, Calif., 1967), p. 176 (Edward Hall); Kittredge, *Witchcraft*, p. 58 (Jean Creton).

52. E. Coke, *Institutes*, iii, chap. 55.

53. R. Gilpin, *Daemonologia Sacra* (1677), ed. A. B. Grosart (Edinburgh, 1867), p. 174.

54. *Rotuli Parliamentorum*, iii, pp. 508, 583; Meyvaert in *Speculum*, xli (1966), p. 663 n.; *Curia Regis Rolls*, xii, p. 326.

sion of Henry VII's parliament,[55] but Henry VIII and his successors took firm measures against political prophecies of all kinds. An Act of 1541-2 declared that divers and sundry persons had taken it upon themselves to predict the future of those who bore certain animals in their heraldic devices or letters in their names. It made it felony to utter such predictions in future. This statute was repealed in 1547, but in 1549-50 a new Act 'against fond and fantastical prophecies' imposed fines and imprisonment upon those who circulated such predictions with intent to stir up rebellion or civil disturbance. This in turn lapsed on the accession of Mary Tudor but was renewed by a statute of 1563.[56] In addition, the routine machinery of Tudor government – proclamations, orders by the Privy Council, instructions to J.P.s, and inquiries by the bishops – was regularly directed against the prophecies and their authors.[57]

This government concern was provoked by the close link which had always existed between prophecy and action. The prophecies of Merlin had been reissued in the fourteenth century to support the English claim to the throne of France, and in the fifteenth to justify the rival aspirations of York and Lancaster. Many manuscript collections of prophecies were compiled to advance the claims of some participant in the Wars of the Roses.[58] In Wales an enormous output of political prophecy sustained the tradition that the Saxons would one day be expelled. Political prophecies played an important part in the revolts led by Owain Glyndwr against Henry IV, and by Rhys ap Gruffydd against Henry VIII. Tales of Merlin were retold in late sixteenth-century Wales, and volumes of nationalist prophecy continued to worry the English government.[59]

55. C. A. J. Armstrong in *Italian Renaissance Studies,* ed. E. F. Jacob (1960), p. 436.

56. 33 Hen. VIII, c. 14; 3 and 4 Edw. VI, c. 15; 5 Eliz. c. 15 (first debated in 1559).

57. See, e.g., Kittredge, *Witchraft,* p. 227; J. Hawarde, *Les Reportes del Cases in Camera Stellata, 1593 to 1609,* ed. W. P. Baildon (1894), p. 326; L. Hotson, *Shakespeare versus Shallow* (1931), p. 177.

58. Ward, *Catalogue of Romances,* i, pp. 320, 325; Taylor, *The Political Prophecy,* pp. 83, 85; A. E. Parsons, 'The Trojan Legend in England', *Modern Language Rev.,* xxiv (1929), p. 263; C. L. Kingsford, *English Historical Literature in the Fifteenth Century* (Oxford, 1913), pp. 236–7, 262, 358.

59. Griffiths, *Early Vaticination, passim;* Taylor, *The Political Prophecy,* p. 80; W. Garmon Jones, 'Welsh Nationalism and Henry Tudor', *Trans. Hon. Soc. of Cymmrodorion* (1917–18); G. Williams, *The Welsh Church* (Cardiff, 1962), pp. 213–14, 242; *Original Letters Illustrative of English History,* ed. H. Ellis, 2nd ser. (1827), iii, p. 49; *H.M.C., Hatfield,* x, p. 369.

The Irish similarly kept up their hopes of driving out the alien conqueror by disseminating suitable prophecies. Gerald of Wales had seen the fulfilment of ancient prophecies in the conquest of Ireland by Henry II, but in the reign of Elizabeth I the 'prophecy of Giraldus Cambrensis' was used to support the claims of the Irish. In 1593 an inhabitant of County Kildare lost his ears for asserting that a prophecy said an O'Donnell would one day be King of Ireland. Similar prophecies were disseminated during the Ulster Rebellion of 1641; one of them predicted that Sir Phelim O'Neill would drive Charles I and his posterity out of England.[60]

In fact prophecies of one kind or another were employed in virtually every rebellion or popular rising which disturbed the Tudor state. There had been some evidence of this under Henry VII in the conspiracy surrounding Perkin Warbeck, and Edward, Earl of Warwick.[61] In the following reign Cardinal Wolsey had been impressed by the prophecy:

> When this cow rideth the bull
> Then priest beware thy skull.

The dun cow was a royal badge, and the bull was soon taken to be Anne Boleyn.[62] This was but a foretaste of the torrent of prophecies and counter-prophecies unleashed by the breach with Rome in the 1530s, the years which led Chapuys, the Imperial Ambassador, to remark of the English that they were peculiarly credulous, and easily moved to insurrection by prophecies.[63]

During this period prophecies, claiming to be derived from Merlin, Bede, Thomas Rymer, John of Bridlington and similar sources, circulated extensively throughout the country, particularly in the north of England, where the most active resistance to the government was to be found. The clerical opponents of the Reformation systematically invoked Galfridian prophecy to justify their resistance. The Latin verses, dating back to Geoffrey of Monmouth,

60. *H.M.C., Pepys*, p. 87; *H.M.C., Egmont*, i. p. 25; *H.M.C., Ormonde*, ii, p. 245. For other Irish prophecies see *H.M.C., Rawdon Hastings,* iv, p. 185; N. Wallington, *Historical Notices of Events,* ed. R. Webb (1869), ii, p. 34 n.; F. Moryson, *An Itinerary* (Glasgow, 1907–8), iii, pp. 82, 88.

61. *53rd Report of the Deputy Keeper of Public Records,* pp. 32–4 (I owe this reference to Mr C. S. L. Davies); *Memorials of King Henry the Seventh,* ed. J. Gairdner (Rolls Ser., 1858), p. 66.

62. G. Cavendish, *The Life and Death of Thomas Wolsey* (Temple Classics, n.d.), pp. 173–5.

63. *C.S.P. Spanish, 1531–3,* p. 867.

predicting that priests would bear arms, were now taken to imply that the clergy would rise to avenge the depredations upon the Church. In 1535 Alexander Clavell, in Dorset, thought such a rising was imminent. The suggestion proved on investigation to have emanated from an old man called Payne, living near Chideock, who knew that the priests would rise against the King because his master, a learned person dead these fifty years, had told him so. The parish priests, he declared, would rule the realm for three days and three nights, 'and then the white falcon should come out of the North-West and kill almost all the priests'.[64] (The white falcon was the badge of Anne Boleyn.)

The representatives of the old order based many of their hopes upon the favourable interpretation of prophecies of this kind. The monks of Furness believed that Henry VIII would be slain by priests,[65] and the Pilgrims of Grace had their own prophecy testifying to the fitness of Robert Aske to be their leader ('Forth shall come a worm, an Aske with one eye').[66] There were also anti-Cromwellian prophecies:

> Much ill cometh of a small note,
> As Crumb well set in a man's throat,
> That shall put many others to pain,
> God wote; [67]

and sibyllic prophecies concerning 'K. L. M.' (? Katherine and Lady Mary) or 'A. B. C.' (? Anne Boleyn and Cromwell).[68]

Most congenial of all to Papal supporters was the Mouldwarp prophecy, dating from the early fourteenth century, and relating to the evil Mole, the sixth king after John, who would be driven from the land by a dragon, a wolf and a lion, after which England would be divided into three parts. This prophecy had been used by the Percies in their rising against Henry IV in the early fifteenth century,

---

64. *L.P.*, viii, p. 275. The battle of priests also occurred in the predictions made in 1533 by Mistress Amadas, an inveterate enemy of the King and Anne Boleyn, who claimed to have studied prophecies for the previous 20 years, B.M., Cotton MS Cleopatra E IV, ff. 99–100; *L.P.*, vi, pp. 399–400.

65. M. H. and R. Dodds, *The Pilgrimage of Grace* (Cambridge, 1915), i, p. 81; *L.P.*, xii (1), p. 70.

66. A. G. Dickens, *Lollards and Protestants in the Diocese of York* (1959), pp. 128–9.

67. *L.P.* xii(1), no. 318; xii(2), pp. 426–7.

68. *L.P.*, xii(2), pp. 387, 427; Cheshire R.O., DXX 123, f. 8.

and, despite obvious difficulties of chronology, was now brought into action to combat Henry VIII. That the Mouldwarp himself was sitting on the throne of England was an article of faith for some of the rebels engaged in the Pilgrimage of Grace (in which Percy influence was strong),[69] and many Catholic sympathizers disseminated the prediction that Henry would have to fly the realm.[70] John Hale, vicar of Isleworth, was executed in 1535 after declaring that Henry VIII was the Mouldwarp of whom Merlin had prophesied.[71] Richard Bishop of Bungay got into trouble in 1537 for citing a garbled version of the Mouldwarp prophecy to prove that it was a hard world for poor men, but that if only two or three hundred would rise together they would be strong enough to overcome the gentlemen.[72] Another victim of the Mouldwarp legend was the Exeter attorney John Bonnefant, exiled in 1539; he had been denounced by two of his friends with whom he had spent an evening discussing the mouldwarp, the dun cow, the bull and similar fauna.[73]

Among the Catholic clergy such prophecies received wide circulation. In 1537 John Broughton, monk of Furness, spoke of predictions which revealed that if Papal influence could last another four years it would remain for ever. He also forecast that in another three years all would be changed, and the new laws annulled. He based this view on the prophecy that 'a.b.c. and three t.t.t. should sit all in one seat and should work great marvels', and that the 'red rose' (i.e. Henry VIII) should die in his mother's womb (i.e. be slain by Mother Church). This, he told Abbot Roger, 'is a marvellous and a dangerous word'.[74] At Syon the monks studied the prophecies of Merlin.[75] At Malton the Prior talked of a parchment roll on which were painted the moon, the years, and children carrying axes. He showed

69. Dodds in *Modern Language Rev.*, xi (1916), pp. 279–80; Dickens, *Lollards and Protestants*, pp. 126–30. There is a text of the Mouldwarp prophecy in *The Poems of Laurence Minot*, ed. J. Hall (3rd edn, Oxford, 1914), pp. 103–11.

70. *L.P.*, vi, pp. 399–400; ix, p. 267; xii(2), p. 283; xiv(1), p. 379; Dodds, *Pilgrimage of Grace*, ii, p. 169.

71. *L.P.*, viii, pp. 214–15; *Reports of the Deputy Keeper of the Public Records*, iii, pp. 237–8.

72. Sir F. Palgrave, 'The Confessions of Richard Bishop and Robert Seyman', *Norfolk Archaeology*, i (1847), pp. 216–19; *L.P.*, xii(1), pp. 577–8, 585; Elton, *Policy and Police*, pp. 142–3.

73. *Ballads from Manuscripts*, ed. Furnivall, i, p. 476.

74. *L.P.*, vii, appx., p. 642; xii(1), pp. 370–71.

75. *L.P.*, viii, pp. 214–15.

Sir Francis Bigod a prophecy concerning the King's flight from the realm and the recovery of the Church in three years' time.[76] Ancient prophecies were also suspected (though wrongly) to have underlain the predictions of Robert Dalyvell in Hertfordshire in 1537 that Henry VIII would not live beyond Midsummer 1538 unless he reformed, and that 'a ten shilling horse' would carry all the noble blood left in England by that date.[77]

Most of these prophetic traditions came together in the case of John Dobson, vicar of Muston, Yorkshire, who was executed in 1538. He was alleged to have told his parishioners that the King would soon be driven out of the realm and only return to a third part of it; that he who bore the eagle [the Emperor] would rule England; that the dun cow [the Pope] would restore the Church; that Crumb [Cromwell] would fall; that the moon [the Percy family, then in disgrace] would kindle again; that the Cock of the North [Lord Lumley] would do great adventures; and that the scallop shells [the Dacres] would be broken. These utterances were nearly all bits of Galfridian mythology brought up to date. When examined, the priest confessed to having borrowed from the Prior of White Friars, Scarborough, a paper roll made by Merlin, Bede and Thomas of Erceldoune, containing predictions relating to the black fleet of Norway, the eagle, the Cock of the North, the moon, A.B.C., and the various other *dramatis personae*. The Prior of White Friars was then interrogated and explained that he had copied some prophecies from a priest at Beverley and from William Langdale, a Scarborough gentleman. William Langdale was duly apprehended and confessed to lending the Prior a rhymed prophecy about 'A.B.C.' and 'K.L.M.' which he had got from another priest, Thomas Bradley. Bradley pleaded in turn that his prophecies of Merlin and Bede came from William Langley, a parish clerk of Croft.[78]

Prophecies could thus circulate extensively by word of mouth. Sometimes, however, they were disseminated by semi-professional purveyors, like Richard Laynam, who was said in 1546 to have been active in spreading and interpreting prophecies for the previous seventeen years or more. His utterances related to the future battles to be fought in England, the fall of Charing Cross, the Mouldwarp, the Lilly, the Crumb, 'K.L.M.', and the priests who would expel the

76. *L.P.*, xii(1), pp. 248, 499–500.
77. *L.P.*, xii(2), p. 25.
78. *L.P.*, xii(2), pp. 426–8. The charges were later denied (ibid., p. 432), but Dobson was nevertheless executed (ibid., xiii[1], p. 267).

King. In 1535 he had announced that the Pope would be in England before Midsummer. He seems to have first appeared in Wiltshire, but later transferred his operations to London, where he came to the notice of Thomas Cromwell, who thought him a 'mad prophet', but had him lodged in the Tower notwithstanding. In 1546, Laynam was back at large, assuring his clients (who included Lord Bray) that Henry VIII was the last of the six kings predicted by Merlin, and that the monarch would soon be glad to surrender three parts of his realm in order to retain the fourth part in peace.[79]

During his examination in 1546 Laynam testified that 'one, young Hurlok, dwelling about Warminster, Wilts', also carried around books of prophecy. This was presumably a relative of 'old' Harlock, whom a prisoner in Colchester gaol had cited in 1532 as his authority for the dark prediction that 'the White Hare should drive the Fox to the Castle of Care, and that the White Greyhound should run under the root of an oak, and that there should be such a gap in the West that all the thorns of England should have work enough to stop it'. 'Old Harlock' had further added that a peacemaker would come out of the west with 'snow on his helmet'; an agreeable anticipation of the Russian army believed in 1914 to be marching through England 'with snow on their boots'.[80] 'Old Harlock' must have been the William Harlokke who confessed on interrogation in 1530 that his employer at Colchester, a doctor of physic and astronomy, had given him a calendar of prophecies with pictures of the arms of kings and lords. One Byrte of Somerset had told him they indicated a forthcoming battle of priests and much other trouble in the coming three years. An alternative explanation was offered by a Taunton goldsmith, Richard Loweth, who was convinced that the prophecy related to the Dreadful Dragon who was going to land with the Bare-legged Hens. By the Dragon he meant the Irish Earl of Desmond. Loweth, who possessed some prophecies of his own, written in Welsh in a black book, added that a Courteous Knight would land at Sandynford Haven (long foretold as the site of a great battle),[81]

79. *L.P.*, viii, p. 214; xiv(1), p. 382; xxi(1), pp. 513–15. The prophet is variously described as Laynam, Layman and Latham.

80. Invaders with snow on their helmets were expected in 1588 (*C.S.P. Spanish, 1587–1603*, p. 215) and reappear in *Nixon's Cheshire Prophecies*, ed. Axon, p. 41. cf. A Ponsonby, *Falsehood in War-Time* (1928), pp. 63–6 (a reference I owe to Dr B. H. Harrison).

81. Murray, *Erceldoune*, pp. lxxx, 42–3, 57, 62–3. For that matter 'Sandford' was an alternative name for the battle of Bosworth (see *Tudor Royal Proclamations*, ed. P. L. Hughes and J. F. Larkin, i (New Haven, 1964), p. 3).

pitch his banner on a stone, and proceed to do battle with the Blue Boar.

Harlokke indeed moved in a prophecy-minded circle, for his other acquaintances included Thomas Larke of Suffolk, who believed that the White Lion would kill the King; and John Barbour of Norwich, who used to read aloud a book of prophecies to various friends, including a chaplain named William, who declared that the King would not live for more than three years, and that he himself had an even better book of prophecies. For this utterance Harlokke delated the chaplain to the sheriffs of Norwich, but the authorities dismissed the matter as too trifling for their notice.[82]

Traditional prophecies, freely reinterpreted, were thus extensively used as anti-government propaganda. But the King's supporters could also invoke prophecies to justify the breach with Rome. Richard Morison countered the Welsh prophecies by fabricating a Royalist one in which Henry VIII was identified with the Lion in the Book of Esdras.[83] Thomas Gibson gathered prophecies for Cromwell to show that the King would 'win the Holy Cross and also divers realms'. They were derived from the strongly Catholic *Prophecies of Rymer, Bede and Merlin*, but reinterpreted to mean that the King would metaphorically gain the Holy Land by putting the Scriptures in English and overthrowing the Pope.[84] The northern Protestant, Wilfred Holme, devoted his energies to showing it was impossible for Henry VIII to be the Mouldwarp and that he was more accurately identified with Merlin's Lions and Eagles.[85] But most of the government's effort was counter-propaganda designed to offset the prophetic character which so much of the opposition to the Reformation had assumed. Until the end of the reign the authorities were occupied investigating the activities of the Catholic prophets, seizing books of prophecy and imprisoning the more blatant offenders.[86]

82. *L.P.*, iv(3), pp. 2997–8; *Addenda*, i(1), pp. 262–3. The White Lion came out of the *Prophecies of Rymer, Bede and Merlin* (Murray, *Erceldoune*, appx. ii).

83. Dickens, *Lollards and Protestants*, p. 130.   84. *L.P.*, xiii(2), p. 516

85. Dickens, *Lollards and Protestants*, pp. 128–9.

86. See, e.g., *L.P.*, v, p. 694; vi, p. 685; viii, p. 290; ix, p. 133; x, pp. 59, 248, 505; xi, pp. 24, 313; xii(2), p. 223; xiii(2), p. 337; xiv(1), pp. 68, 379; xiv(2), p. 37; xvi, p. 265; xviii(2), pp. 294, 308; xix(1), pp. 284–5; xx(1), p. 125; *Addenda*, i(1), pp. 81–2; *Addenda*, i(2), pp. 549–50, 617; *A.P.C.*, i, pp. 238–9, 449, 509. (I am grateful to Dr Penry Williams for some of these references.)

The association between prophecy and rebellion, however, continued through the reign of Edward VI, and was particularly prominent during the revolts which shook the country in 1549. The risings in the North and East Ridings of Yorkshire were stimulated by what John Foxe called 'a blind and phantastical prophecy', that the King, nobility and gentry would be swept away by a parliament of commoners, who would appoint four regional governors in their place.[87] In London the government rallied opinion against conspirators by dropping handbills in the street citing Merlin's prophecy that the aldermen of Troy (i.e. London) would lose their heads.[88] In Norfolk the peasants who followed Robert Ket were encouraged by a prophecy which they openly proclaimed in public places:

> The country gnooffés [i.e knaves], Hob, Dick, and Hick,
> With clubs and clouted shoon
> Shall fill up Dussindale
> With slaughtered bodies soon.[89]

This was a classic instance of the ambiguous prophecy which bounces back upon its protagonists, for the bodies which filled Dussindale after the battle on 27 August 1549 were those of the rebels themselves. A modern historian has suggested that it was not the prophecy but the breaking of their supply-lines which led Ket's followers to leave their camp on Mousehold Heath;[90] and it may well be that the jingle was 'improved' after the event by government supporters for didactic purposes. But the prophetic element in the revolt was genuine enough. Mousehold Heath had been booked as the venue for some future great event in a prophecy current in the reign of Henry VIII; and talk in Norfolk about a rising of 'clubs and clouted shoon' can be traced back to 1537.[91]

87. A. G. Dickens, 'Some Popular Reactions to the Edwardian Reformation in Yorkshire', *Yorks. Archaeol. Journ.*, xxxiv (1938–9), pp. 163–4.

88. P. F. Tytler, *England under the Reigns of Edward VI and Mary* (1839), i, pp. 208–10.

89. A. Nevil, *Norfolkes Furies, or a View of Ketts Campe*, trans. R. W(ood) (1615), sig. Ki^v. Nicholas Sotherton, 'The Commoyson in Norfolk, 1549' (B.M., Harley MS 1576), f. 258^v, gives a different version ('In Dussens Dale there should the [*sic*] perish both great and small').

90. S. T. Bindoff, *Ket's Rebellion* (Hist. Assoc., 1949), p. 6.

91. Sir F. Palgrave in *Norfolk Archaeology*, i (1847), p. 217; *L.P.*, xii(1), p. 591.

During the aftermath of Ket's rebellion prophecies helped to keep hope alive among the defeated. Between June 1552 and June 1553 at least five persons were arrested by the Privy Council for disseminating prophecies.[92] Norwich, in particular, seethed with prophetic rumours. Each year there was defiant muttering. One dissident predicted three battles for 1554: 'We shall see the King of France in Norwich by mid-summer.' In the same year the Norfolk justices were commanded to search for the disseminators of 'vain prophecies' and 'seditious, false or untrue rumours' – 'the very foundation of all rebellion'.[93]

Mary Tudor's government encountered similar trouble. One of the leading participants in Wyatt's rebellion confessed that it was the influence of a prophecy which finally led him to participate.[94] In London predictions of the Queen's imminent death were circulated, while in Holderness the government ordered a search for persons possessing books of prophecy.[95] The Bishop of Peterborough was ordered to examine one of his canons who had spread prophecies 'out of an old book'. Other Protestant and anti-Spanish prophecies composed during this period still survive in manuscript.[96]

Under Elizabeth the government remained apprehensive about ancient prophecies capable of contemporary application. The leaders of an enclosure riot at Chinley, Derbyshire, in 1569 were closely questioned as to whether they had had any dealings with Mr Bircles of Cheshire concerning prophecies about the nobility, and asked to name the books of prophecy with which they were acquainted: 'Mr Bircles' was doubtless John Birtles, one of those later involved in an alleged conspiracy against the Queen around 1584, when he was found in possession of 'a certain old book of prophecy, wherein

92. *A.P.C.*, iv, pp. 69, 156, 165, 287; *C.S.P.D.*, *1547–80*, p. 46.

93. *Depositions taken before the Mayor and Aldermen of Norwich, 1549–67*, ed. W. Rye (Norfolk and Norwich Archaeol. Soc., 1905), pp. 20, 40, 59; Kittredge, *Witchcraft*, p. 230.

94. Howard, *A Defensative against the Poyson of Supposed Prophecies*, f. 124ᵛ.

95. D. M. Loades, *Two Tudor Conspiracies* (Cambridge, 1965), p. 148; Sheffield Central Lib., Bacon Frank MSS, M4/1 (10 July [1555?]), (calendared in *Sheffield City Libraries. Catalogue of the Arundel Castle Manuscripts* [Sheffield, 1965], p. 220, as 1559; but the Librarian kindly tells me that the document's position in Nathaniel Johnston's MS *Life of Francis Earl of Shrewsbury* shows that the antiquary believed it to belong to the reign of Mary).

96. *A.P.C.*, v, p. 17; Murray, *Erceldoune*, p. 63.

is great pictures, some with beards'.[97] The same link between prophecy and rebellion was demonstrated during the trial of the Duke of Norfolk in 1572 for treasonable involvement in the Ridolfi Plot. Evidence was given that the Duke had been misled by a prophecy about a lion (Norfolk) and a lioness (Mary, Queen of Scots), who would overthrow a lion (Elizabeth I). One of the witnesses, Robert Higford, deposed that the Duke had shown him a prophecy begining *In exaltatione Lunae, Leo succumbat*, saying lightly, 'Higford, thou shalt here see a foolish prophecy.'[98] But it may be that the prognostication preyed on the Duke's mind.

Certainly it was horror at the way in which the ambitions of two successive members of the Howard family, the poet Earl of Surrey, and his son the unlucky Duke of Norfolk, had brought them to the scaffold which led a third member, Henry Howard, Earl of Northampton, to compile his *Defensative against the Poyson of Supposed Prophecies* (1583) in an attempt to expose the wickedness and irrationality of such predictions. 'How many treasons have been set on broach,' he exclaimed. 'How many wicked practices attempted by encouragement of such fond toys.' The fabricators of these prophecies were the architects of sedition: 'certain busy-bodies in the commonwealth, who with limned papers, painted books and figures of wild beasts and birds, carry men from present duties into future hopes'. Lying prophecies of this kind were 'the froth of folly, the scum of pride, the shipwreck of honour and the poison of nobility'. Northampton declared in his book that the bad example of his ancestors had led him to collect samples of such prophecies since he had been sixteen. But his motive for publication may well have been the desire to clear himself from similar imputations.[99]

The struggle with Spain helped to sustain interest in these predictions. Armada year gave retrospective justification to the widely disseminated forecast, attributed to the German astronomer, Johann

97. R. H. Tawney, *The Agrarian Problem in the Sixteenth Century* (1912), p. 329; L. O. Pike, *A History of Crime in England* (1873–6), ii, p. 23.

98. N. Williams, *Thomas Howard, Fourth Duke of Norfolk* (1964), pp. 219–20; W. Murdin, *A Collection of State Papers* (1759), pp. 70–3; S. Haynes, *A Collection of State Papers* (1740), p. 538; *C.S.P.D., Addenda, 1566–79*, p. 421. It seems to have been a version of this prophecy which Bishop Aylmer debunked before Queen Elizabeth, declaring that nothing was to be feared so long as Virgo was in the ascendant. Sir J. Harington, *Nugae Antiquae*, ed. T. Park (1804), ii, p. 37–8.

99. Howard, *A Defensative*, ff. 113, 120ᵛ; *C.S.P.D., 1581–90*, p. 70.

Müller of Königsberg (Regiomontanus), that 1588 would be an *annus mirabilis*.[100] Prophecies had circulated among northern Catholics since the beginning of the reign,[101] and were employed by the supporters of Mary, Queen of Scots; the conspirator Anthony Babington owned a copy of a prophecy attributed to Merlin.[102] The Welshman Morys Clynnog, when proposing a Catholic invasion in 1575-6, thought that good use could be made of the prophetic tradition that Wales would one day be liberated: the people were accustomed to the idea of a fleet coming from Rome, he urged, and could be relied upon to help a Papal army.[103] Catholic priests prophesied that Popery would return and the Mass would last 'for ever and aye'. A 'Golden Day' would see the downfall of Elizabeth and the return of the monasteries.[104] As a Catholic tailor confessed in 1602, 'it is a common speech amongst the principal recusants to hold on the poorer sort by persuading them to hold patience until the good day cometh, and then all will be well; saying still withal that it will not be long before the good day will come'.[105] Mourners at the Queen's funeral in 1603 could not help discussing these predictions.[106] Two years later a gentleman could cite 'twenty-six ancient writers' in support of a prophecy that the religious quarrel would send fire and sword throughout the land between Midsummer and Lammas.[107]

Catholic hopes were often sustained by Galfridian utterances of a

100. W. B. Stone, 'Shakespeare and the Sad Augurs', *Journ. English and Germanic Philology*, lii (1953); G. Mattingly, *The Armada* (Boston, 1959), pp. 175-86.

101. H. Aveling, *Northern Catholics* (1966), pp. 79-80; id., *The Catholic Recusants of the West Riding of Yorkshire, 1558-1790* (Procs. Leeds Philos. and Lit. Soc., 1963), p. 205.

102. *C.S.P.D., 1547-80*, p. 430; Ward, *Catalogue of Romances*, i, p. 302.

103. J. M. Cleary, 'Dr Morys Clynnog's Invasion Projects of 1575-6', *Recusant History*, viii (1966), p. 307.

104. *C.S.P.D., Addenda, 1580-1625*, pp. 105, 108, 110; H. N. Birt, *The Elizabethan Religious Settlement* (1907), p. 441, n. 2; P.R.O., SP 12/151, ff. 112-3v; J. Strype, *The Life and Acts of Matthew Parker* (1711), pp. 360-1; *C.S.P.D., 1603-10*, p. 201; T. Robinson, *The Anatomie of the English Nunnery at Lisbon* (1623), p. 4; R. Bolton, *Some Generall Directions for a Comfortable Walking with God* (5th edn, 1638), p. 14.

105. *H.M.C., Hatfield*, xii, p. 367.

106. J. Clapham, *Elizabeth of England*, ed. E. P. Read and C. Read (Philadelphia, 1951), p. 113.

107. *H.M.C., Hatfield*, xvii, p. 23.

highly Delphic kind, such as the following, attributed to John Tusser, an Essex gentleman, in 1583:

> The Lion ... shall go into Norfolk and there shall be slain of an Elephant. And then the poor commonalty shall take the White Horse for their captain and rejoice because there shall come into England one that was dead, and with him shall come the Royal E, and the dead man shall set the crowns of England on his head. And then the laws shall turn and then the people shall rejoice the dead man's coming, because sorrow and care shall be then almost past. And then ... the royal E, which is the best blood in all the world, shall root out all heresies clean out of this realm restoring the Church and the Catholic Faith. A lion, a horse, a leopard shall crown E. by the help of the great Eagle.[108]

It is difficult to identify the sources of all the imagery employed here. The cross of stone appears in the prophecies of Bridlington; the lion and the leopard may have come from the Book of Daniel (chap. vii) or the prophecy attributed to 'Waldhave'; the eagle was perhaps from *Esdras*. The dead man, however, came from a non-Biblical source: 'There goeth a prophecy that a dead man shall rise that shall make all England rue,' declared an English Catholic émigré in 1575.[109] The Dreadful Dead Man was a stock feature of prophetic literature; and so was 'the royal E'.

Another striking Catholic prophecy was uttered by a Leicester embroiderer, Edward Sawford, in 1586. If harm came to Mary, Queen of Scots, he said, dire consequences would follow: the next Parliament would come to blows; the Queen would be forced to fly to Wales; a foreign invader would land at Chester; and the Crown would several times be lost and won; all those who racked rents, hoarded corn, or otherwise oppressed the poor, would fall before a rising of 'clubs and clouted shoes'. Order would only be restored by the arrival of a dead man, who would install four rulers, and set out for Jerusalem, where he would die and be buried between three 'Kings of Cologne'. When interrogated, Sawford claimed to have been told this elaborate prophecy by an aged Catholic sympathizer named William Byard, but he admitted that the ultimate source was 'the book of King Arthur, which', he said, 'was a[s] pleasant book of fables as ever he read in his life', adding that Merlin 'was a man that

108. Essex R.O., transcript of Essex Assizes records (Assizes 35/25/T; 29 July 1583); sent me by Dr Alan Macfarlane.
109. *H.M.C., Hatfield*, ii, p. 95.

foretold many things to come, yea even to the world's end'.[110] In fact
Sawford's utterances were a curious medley of current myths. The
four rulers who would govern the country were identical with the
four provincial governors expected to take over after the Yorkshire
rising of 1549. The expedition to Jerusalem and the three Kings of
Cologne came from *The Prophecies of Rymer, Bede and Merlin,*
while the 'clubs and clouted shoes' featured in Ket's rebellion. The
'dead man' has already been encountered. The whole episode is a
reminder that popular radicalism could sometimes underlie the
recusant myth of the utopia (what Sawford called 'a pleasant, golden
world') which would come with the restoration of Popery.

The same tendency can be seen in 1586 when Simon Yomans of
Little Dean, Gloucestershire, lamenting the dearth of corn and
victuals, cited a prophecy that there would be three battles during
the next twelve months; the Queen would be slain; four peers would
rule; the Latin law would come in; and thereafter there would be a
merry world.[111] In this case prophetic jargon had fused with the idea
of a lost economic order where food was plentiful and poor men
were looked after. Similarly in nineteenth-century Norfolk it was
believed that Mother Shipton had prophesied that 'the Roman
Catholics shall have this country again, and make England a nice
place once more'.[112]

It is not surprising, therefore, that the recusants, according to Sir
John Harington, were 'generally charged to be more superstitious
and credulous and to attribute more to old prophecies and traditions
of men than either Protestants or Puritans, especially the vulgar
and unlearned sort of them'.[113] Yet the leaders of the Counter-
Reformation gave little encouragement to this sort of prophetic

110. The text, which unfortunately is defective, is in Leicester City
Museum, Archives Dept., B.R. II/18/2, ff. 207–11ᵛ. Various parts are reproduced in J. Thompson. *A History of Leicester* (1849), pp. 297–80;
Records of the Borough of Leicester, ed. M. Bateson, iii (Cambridge, 1905),
pp. 230–31; and *The Cheshire Sheaf,* 3rd ser., xii (1915), pp. 45–6. One section concerns a man and boy ploughing who see a priest and resolve to kill
him; another is a string of verses protesting against current fashions in dress
and popular hypocrisy in general (the latter may be a version of the prophecy said by John Harvey to be by Thomas de Guino; *A Discoursive Probleme,* p. 57. It is almost identical with a passage in the volume of prophecy
in the Cheshire R.O., DDX 123, f. 7ᵛ).
111. P.R.O., SP 12/192, ff. 92, 93.
112. J. Gunn in *Norfolk Archaeology,* ii (1849), p. 304.
113. Harington, *A Tract on the Succession to the Crown,* p. 120.

activity. They were suspicious of all forms of divination, and Merlin was firmly placed upon the *Index*. The prophetic element in Catholic thought was a popular affair, surviving longest among the uneducated. The same was largely true in the Anglican Church, for Bishop Jewel and most of his colleagues regarded 'fond and vain and lying prophecies' as misleading in content and diabolical in origin.[114] Yet although many early Protestants dismissed Merlin as the child of an incubus and the sibyls as 'Satan's prophets', there were others whose attitude was less hostile. The Lollards, for example, had dabbled in Galfridian sources. A London Lollard was spreading the rumour in the 1520s that there would shortly be a battle of priests in which all would be slain; the priests would rule for a time, but then be overthrown; after which it would be a merry world. It was no coincidence that Mole (i.e. mouldwarp) was a favourite Lollard name for worldly clergy.[115]

During the Reformation itself there was occasional recourse to the prophecies of Merlin in justification of the Protestant cause. Bishop Cox cited an ancient Latin prophecy which, he thought, predicted the Dissolution of the Monasteries. The destruction of images was foretold in some of the Cheshire prophecies associated with Robert Nixon. Bishop Bale thought that Merlin had predicted the Reformation; and some Protestants followed medieval authorities in crediting him with divine inspiration. For the authors of *The Mirror for Magistrates* (1559) he was 'learned Merlin whom God gave the spirit to know and utter princes' acts to come'. As the Earl of Northampton remarked in 1583, it was not only ungodly persons who listened to ancient prophecies.[116]

114. P. Zumthor, *Merlin le prophète* (Lausanne, 1943), p. 113; *The Works of John Jewel,* ed. J. Ayre (Cambridge, P.S., 1845–50), ii, p. 880; Foxe, iii, pp. 756–61; *The Sermons of Edwin Sandys,* ed. J. Ayre (Cambridge, P.S., 1841), pp. 67–8; *The Workes of ... William Perkins* (Cambridge, 1616–18), iii, p. 467. The distinction between divine and diabolical prophecy is set out by, e.g., A. Burgess, *CXLV Expository Sermons upon the Whole 17th Chapter of the Gospel according to St John* (1656), pp. 395–6.

115. Foxe, iv, p. 234; G. R. Owst, *The Destructorium Viciorum of Alexander Carpenter* (1952), p. 13, n. 1.

116. J. Strype, *Ecclesiastical Memorials* (Oxford, 1822), i(1), pp. 420–21; Cheshire R.O., DDX 123, f. 9; B.M., Cotton MS, Vespasian E vii, f. 134 (ancient British prophecy relating to fall of Popery); J. Bale, *The First Two Partes of the Actes or Unchast Examples of the Englysh Votaryes* (n.d., 1551?), i, f. 40ᵛ; W. G. Jones in *Trans. Hon. Soc. Cymmrodorion,* 1917–18, p. 12 n.; G. M. Griffiths in *Natl. Lib. Wales Journ.,* vii (1951–2), p. 233; *The Mirror for Magistrates,* ed. Campbell, p. 228; Eloward, *A Defensative,* f. 18ᵛ.

Indeed there were even some Puritans prepared to cast their aspirations in prophetic terms. In the early seventeenth century dislike for episcopacy combined with hopes of James I's eldest son, Prince Henry, to produce a jingle which was said in 1608 to be 'in the mouths of many':

> King Henry the Eight
> Pulled down abbeys and cells.
> The next of that name
> Shall down with bishops and bells.

This piece of doggerel was still in circulation in the last decade of the seventeenth century, when it reflected the Dissenters' hopes, presumably of William Henry, Anne's son and Protestant heir apparent.[117] Strains of more obviously Galfridian prophecy can be detected in radical Protestant thought. A Kentish Brownist was imprisoned around 1626 for writing a book foretelling the destruction of England in three years' time by two kings, one coming from the north and one from the south. A mock-sibyllic prophecy concerning the coming fall of the bishops was in circulation in 1639, and *An old Prophecie of Gostred* [i.e. Grosseteste] *Bishop of Lincoln concerning the Prelates* was published two years later.[118]

The real boost to ancient prophecy, however, came with the Civil War, when Galfridian prophecies joined astrological prognostication and religious revelation to place an unprecedented amount of prophetic advice before the lay public. Although the three genres were distinct, their separate identity was not always preserved; indeed it was the astrologer Lilly who did as much as anyone to bring the ancient prophecies back into circulation. He entitled his almanac *Merlinus Anglicus*, and included an astrological forecast by Kepler in a collection of Galfridian-style predictions.[119] It is doubtful if many readers distinguished astrological forecasts from other predictions based on the interpretation of Scripture (for example,

117. W. Westerman, *The Faithfull Subject* (1608), p. 26; *H.M.C., Hatfield*, xix, p. 242; G. M. Straka, *The Anglican Reaction to the Revolution of 1688* (Madison, 1962), pp. 27–8. The lines were printed in 1653 on the title-page of *A Brief View of the State of the Church of England* by Sir John Harington, who first heard them in August 1606; *Nugae Antiquae*, ed. Park, ii, pp. 3, 8.

118. C. Burrage, *The Early English Dissenters* (Cambridge, 1912), i, p. 202; *C.S.P.D., 1625–49*, p. 613; H.W., *The Prelates Pride* (1641). For Grosseteste's death-bed reflections, see Döllinger, *Prophecies and the Prophetic Spirit*, p. 159.

119. Lilly, *A Prophecy of the White King*.

'Brightman's prophecy'),[120] or delivered oracularly by seers like Merlin. The literature of the Civil War period suggests a disposition to welcome any type of prophetic utterance, regardless of the foundation upon which it purported to rest.

It is also curious that no one seems to have been much worried that Bede, Grosseteste, and the other holy men of the past to whom these predictions were attributed, had been Catholics; in fact Lilly declared that Becket's prophecy was all the more reliable because he had been canonized by the Church.[121] There was a certain irony about the publication during the Puritan Commonwealth of so many utterances attributed to the saints of the Middle Ages, or the leaders of the Counter-Reformation. Yet a prophecy's authority was positively enhanced by a pedigree of this kind. Just as the Catholic past seemed a time when priests enjoyed a magical power denied to their Protestant successors, so was it also regarded as an age when prophecy and foreknowledge were open to holy men.

There was, however, an attempt to give Galfridian prophecy some theological respectability. Thomas Heywood's *Life of Merlin* (1641) reminded readers that God might pick out choice spirits as his prophets. Merlin was now portrayed as not only a Christian but a Protestant. His prophecies, declared one editor in 1658, had been banned by the Council of Trent because 'they thunder out the ruin and subversion of the Pope of Rome'.[122] Lilly also accepted the divine origin of ancient prophecies, though he believed they had been communicated to their authors via the crystal ball.[123]

These two decades thus saw an unprecedented number of traditional prophecies put into print. Before 1640 there had been relatively little publication of prophecies, although they had often been preserved in private manuscript collections. Some had also been published by writers concerned to attack the genre, like John Harvey in his *Discursive probleme concerning prophesies* (1588). But most of them had hitherto been transmitted by oral tradition.[124] From 1641

120. The Apocalyptic commentaries of Thomas Brightman (1562–1607) were said to have been divinely inspired. cf. *A Revelation of Mr Brightman's Revelation* (1641).

121. Ashm. 241, f. 195.

122. Pugh, *British and Out-Landish Prophecies*, p. 71.

123. Lilly, *Autobiography*, pp. 197–8.

124. Apart from the *Whole Prophecies of Scotland* (above, p. 467) and James Maxwell's collection of 1615 (above, pp. 465–6), there had been printed editions of *A Prophesie that hath Lyen hid above these 2000 Yeares* (1610, 1614) (from *Esdras*); *A Nunnes Prophesie* (1615) (Hildegard); *A Prophesie*

onwards this situation rapidly changed. The prophecies of Merlin were made more familiar by the publication of Heywood's *Life of Merlin*, which was a chronological account of English history designed to show the working out of Merlin's predictions, or rather of predictions attributed by Heywood to him. In the same year Mother Shipton made her début[125] and was an instant success. Her murky predictions were also included in *Two strange prophesies* (1642), the first of a genre of prophetic anthologies. So fast did the vogue catch on that *Two strange prophesies* had become *Four several strange prophesies* before the end of 1642, *Seven severall strange prophesies* in 1643, *Nine notable prophesies* in 1644, and no fewer than *Fourteene strange prophesies* by 1649. To the prognostications of Mother Shipton had been added those of Ignatius, Sibylla, Merlin, Thomas Brightman, 'Truswel', 'Otwell Binns', and their like. Many of these prophecies were also issued separately in their own right.

Among other notable anthologies were *Nuncius Propheticus* (1642), a Latin collection from which later selections were sometimes made, and *Mercurius Propheticus, or a collection of some old predictions* (1643), which included Mother Shipton, Ignatius and a string of others, all said to be older than the time of the anonymous editor's great-grandfather, yet speaking 'so directly of the present times as if they had but now been minted'. In 1645 Lilly put out *A Collection of Ancient and Moderne Prophecies*, which included a wide range of current favourites, all interpreted to Charles I's disadvantage. Lilly coyly refused to say whether or not these various predictions were to be regarded as divinely inspired, but pointed out their coincidence with his own astrological findings. In the previous year he had issued *A Prophecy of the White King; and Dreadfull Dead Man explained*. This was a commentary on a version of an old Welsh prophecy in Sir Robert Cotton's library which had already attracted some attention. Lilly's cautious exegesis on its predictions concerning the Lion of Rightfulness and the Chicken of the Eagle clearly implied the King's imminent defeat. Along with the prophecy of the White King were included that of the Dreadful Dead Man; the prophecy of Sibylla Tiburtina, said to have been found carved

of the Iudgment Day, being lately found in Saint Denis Church in France (1620?); and various sixteenth-century editions of Merlin. A more substantial collection was *Prophetia Anglicana et Romana* (Frankfurt, 1608).

125. *The Prophesie of Mother Shipton* (1641).

on a marble stone uncovered by a landslide in Switzerland in 1520; and other texts lifted from John Harvey's attack on prophecies in 1588. The *Prophecy of Ambrose Merlin*, which Lilly had specially translated by Elias Ashmole and published in 1647, came from a book published at Frankfurt in 1608.[126] A rival interpreter was the ex-soldier Christopher Syms, who issued the White King prophecy several times, with a commentary of uncertain but apparently Royalist import. He claimed to have devoted nineteen years to the study of the subject.[127]

The King's defeat led to more scrutiny and re-interpretation of the Galfridian predictions. Paul Grebner's prophecy, presented to Queen Elizabeth I, was now recognized as a forecast of the King's death, but taken by the Presbyterians to indicate the speedy return of Charles II.[128] Lilly countered this in *Monarchy or no Monarchy* (1651), his largest anthology of prophecies to date, including virtually all the previously issued texts, reinforced by an anti-Presbyterian version of Grebner, and a host of old Scottish prophecies by Rymer, Waldhave, *et al.* All pointed in one direction: Charles I was the last King of England, and there was no political future for his son. Lilly concluded with sixteen pages of pictures purporting to 'perfectly represent the future condition of the English nation and commonwealth for many years to come'. Fifteen years later these were to get him into considerable trouble, since one of them, portraying a burning town, seemed to indicate suspicious foreknowledge of the Fire of London.[129]

For Lilly the Interregnum was the culmination and pre-ordained goal of ancient prophecy: 'All or most of our ancient English, Welsh and Saxon prophecies,' he declared, 'had relation to Charles Stuart,

126. *Prophetia Anglicana et Romana;* Lilly's own copy is Ashm. 631. The translation appeared in *The Worlds Catastrophe* (1647), p. 35.

127. Syms, *The Swords Apology*; id., *The White King Raised* (1647; reissued 1649). *The Prophecies of a White King of Brittaine* had originally appeared without any commentary in 1643.

128. *C.S.P.D., 1649–50*, pp. 168–9; *A Prophesie of Paulus Grebnerus* [1649]; MS note in B.M., E 548(27); *The Kingdomes Faithfull and Impartiall Scout*, 16 (11–18 May 1649); *A Brief Description of the Future History of Europe* (1650).

129. Josten, *Ashmole*, pp. 1072–5. Lilly's notes in Ashm. 553(1) show that he had predicted the Fire for 1693 and the Plague for 1667. The original source of his pictures was said by a contemporary to have been 'an old parchment manuscript writ in the time of the monks'; Aubrey, *Miscellanies*, p.121.

late King of England, unto his reign, his actions, life and death, and unto the now present times wherein we live, and unto no other preceding king or times whatsoever'.[130] Contemporaries shared this illusion. In 1651 a prophetic anthology, mostly culled out of *Monarchy or no Monarchy*, claimed to have been

examined by the original papers, sent from the University of Cambridge and other libraries in England and Scotland, licensed and published by authority, and now presented to public view ... to the end that this treatise may be dispersed throughout all the cities and market-towns in England and Wales.[131]

The following year saw the appearance of *Sundry strange prophecies of Merline, Bede, Becket, and others*, a densely packed compendium of the now familiar texts. The genre continued with Thomas Pugh's *British and Outlandish Prophesies* (1658), which used the Welsh and Scottish prophecies to show that Charles I had been the Mould-warp, that Oliver Cromwell was the Welsh hero long awaited, and that Charles II's attempts to secure his restoration were doomed to failure. In March 1659 appeared perhaps the largest collection of all – *Forraign and Domestick Prophesies both antient and modern* – nearly 200 pages of prophetic texts, many of them in Welsh.

The Interregnum was an age of prolific pamphleteering, and it would be wrong to attach significance to every publication of that crowded era. But the prophecies cannot be dismissed as mere ephemera issued for a frivolous or disinterested public. In terms of circulation they were strikingly successful. In his *Autobiography* Lilly claimed that his *Prophecy of the White King* sold 1800 copies in three days. This boast cannot be checked, but the accidental survival of his printer's bill reveals that the *Collection of Ancient and Moderne Prophecies* (1645) went into three impressions, representing a total of 4,500 copies.[132] The actual readership would, of course, have been much greater. Contemporary letters and diaries show how seriously this prophetic literature was taken

130. *Mr William Lilly's True History of King James the First, and King Charles the First* (1715; written 1651), p. 81; pp. 77–105 of this work are meant to demonstrate the prophetic background to Charles I's execution.

131. *The Lord Merlins Prophecy* (1651).

132. Lilly, *Autobiography*, p. 106; H. R. Plomer, 'A Printer's Bill in the Seventeenth Century', *The Library*, new ser., vii (1906).

by clergymen and gentry, as well as by humbler folk.[133] Politicians
were also influenced by it. The Marquis of Montrose came to grief
after allegedly basing his hopes on the prophetic assurance that he
would recover Scotland for the King and lead an army to settle his
other dominions.[134] A pictorial prophecy predicting the Irish mas-
sacres of 1641 was brought over to England by Dean Jones (later
Bishop of Clogher) and solemnly considered by the House of Commons Committee on Irish Affairs. It was said to have been found on
an old scroll hidden in the wall of the fort of Newry.[135] Mother
Shipton's utterances were brought up at every opportunity by one
unidentified 'great statesman'. Among the populace they were
said to be virtually canonical.[136] The people of England, thought
Edward Hyde in 1652, were 'alarmed and even half dead with
prophecies'.[137]

Inevitably the Restoration of Charles II was also discovered to
have been foreshadowed by ancient prophetic utterances. Lilly did
a rapid volte-face, declaring that the King's return had been predicted nearly a thousand years earlier by Ambrose Merlin, and re-
discovering a prophecy in Greek characters, 'exactly deciphering the
long troubles the English nation had from 1641 until 1660'.[138] Some
held the Restoration to have been foretold by Scripture, while
others produced prophecies which, with their references to Monk
and the Rump, had only too obviously been manufactured to fit the
occasion. The Welsh prophet, Arise Evans, however, had predicted
the Restoration as early as 1653, on the basis of the same prophecy
which Lilly had used to announce the end of monarchy in England.[139]

133. *The Diary of the Rev. Ralph Josselin, 1616–83*, ed. E. Hockcliffe
(Camden Ser., 1908), p. 122; *Yorkshire Diaries*, ed. C. Jackson (Surtees Soc.,
1877), p. 63; 'The Diary of John Greene (1635–57)', *E.H.R.*, xliv (1929), p.
111; *H.M.C.*, v, p. 144; *Diary of John Rous*, ed. M. A. E. Green (Camden
Soc., 1856), p. 65; Ashm. 423, ff. 148–9ᵛ; Heywood, *Diaries*, iii, pp. 60–61, 82.
134. L. Echard, *The History of England*, ii (1718), p. 682.
135. Josten, *Ashmole*, p. 1283.
136. Syms, *The Swords Apology*, sig. C4ᵛ; *Nuncius Propheticus* (1642),
sig. A2.
137. *H.M.C., Portland*, ii, p. 139.
138. Lilly, *Autobiography*, pp. 194–8.
139. A. Evans, *A Voice from Heaven* (1653), pp. 7–8. cf. *The Mystery of
Prophesies Revealed* (1660); B.M., Add. MS 34,258, f. 3; and *A Prophecy
lately found amongst the Collections of famous Mr John Selden* (1659).
Other efforts to link the Restoration with ancient prophecies include *The
Strange and Wonderfull Prophesie of David Cardinal of France* (1660);
T. Gadbury, *A Health to the King* (1660), p. 4.

Even some of the educated classes were persuaded that ancient prophecies had foreseen the events of 1660. The virtuoso Elias Ashmole was later told by Sir William Backhouse that in 1659 his tutor had shown him 'an old writing' whose hieroglyphics implied the return of Charles II in the following year.[140] The defeated party also drew consolation from these ancient sources. Prophecies circulated for several years among the Dissenting sects. At Shrewsbury there was talk of the same three imminent battles which had cheered up the monks in the 1530s.[141] In Hertfordshire the Baptists consoled themselves with a prediction that the King would lose his kingdom after three years.[142]

Ancient prophecies thus still retained some prestige. Indeed Mother Shipton gained a new topicality with the Fire of London in 1666. Pepys records that when the news of the conflagration came to Prince Rupert, 'all the Prince said was, that "now Shipton's prophecy was out" '.[143] There was also an attempt to exploit the propaganda value of prophecies during the Anglo-Dutch war. William Lilly was anxious to revive a prophecy attributed to Becket by having it republished in the *London Gazette*. 'I am confident it would put much courage into His Majesty's subjects – now in the nick of time when his Majesty is preparing his forces,' he wrote. 'The English of all nations are most taken with prophecies.' He therefore drafted an explanatory commentary indicating that Becket had foreseen that Charles II would defeat the Dutch and ultimately even recover the Crown of France. There was nothing forced about such an interpretation, he assured his readers. 'It is all deduced from prophets long since deceased and from manuscripts wormeaten with age.'[144] The version ultimately published, however, did not include his exegesis, for Lilly seems to have been beaten to the post by a competitor. The clergyman who put out *The Prophecie of*

140. MS note at end of Ashm. 539(iv).
141. *Diaries and Letters of Philip Henry*, ed. M. H. Lee (1882), p. 128. For the reissue in 1662 of the *Panther Prophecy* predicting the fall of the King and clergy, see C. E. Whiting, *Studies in English Puritanism, 1660–88* (1931), p. 551.
142. P.R.O., SP 29/99, f. 16ᵛ.
143. Pepys, *Diary*, 20 Oct. 1666. cf. W. G. Bell, *The Great Fire of London* (3rd edn, 1923), p. 316.
144. Josten, *Ashmole*, pp. 1048–50; Ashm. 436, f. 49 (in Josten, *Ashmole*, p. 1040, but very probably misplaced); Ashm. 240, f. 120. Lilly's *Paraphrase upon St Thomas à Becket's Prophecy* is in Ashm. 371(3) and 241, ff. 190–200.

Thomas Becket in 1666 asserted that it had been 'lately found in an ancient manuscript at Abingdon', and made no mention of the fact that it had already been published by Lilly in 1645.[145]

During the following decades prophecies were used as propaganda in the Third Dutch War and in the wars against France.[146] They were prominent in the political literature of the Popish Plot and Exclusion Crisis and cited in support of Monmouth.[147] This was the period when Nostradamus resumed his career as a prognosticator of English history. Later his utterances were to be adapted to fit the American War of Independence and the French Revolution.[148] Other prophets were invoked to explain the 1688 Revolution and the triumph of William III.[149] The Jacobites also had their prophecies. As late as 1745 the Duke of Gordon was identified with the Cock of the North mentioned in the fourteenth-century prophecy of Bridlington.[150]

During the eighteenth and nineteenth centuries the prophecies of Nostradamus and Mother Shipton were frequently published for popular consumption, while new 'prophets' arose in the form of Dr Dee, the Elizabethan magician, and Christopher Love, the Presbyterian minister executed during the Commonwealth. Merlin was also periodically brought up to date, as for example in *Merlin's Life and Prophecies . . . His prediction relating to the late contest about*

145. *The Prophecie of Thomas Becket* (1666). On its authorship, see Wood, *Ath. Ox.*, iii, col. 1056; F. Madan, *Oxford Books* (Oxford, 1895–1931), iii, p. 204; T. T(ully), *A Letter written to a Friend in Wilts* (1666).

146. e.g., T. Trigge, *The Fiery Trigon* (1672), p. 1; *The Fortune of France, from the Prophetical Predictions of Mr Truswell, the Recorder of Lincoln, and Michael Nostradamus* (1678); *The Northern Star* (1680), by I. Tongue, according to Wood, *Ath. Ox.*, iii, col. 1263; *A Copy of a Prophecy sent . . . by the late Honourable Algernon Sydney* (1689).

147. *A Prophesie, which hath been in a Manuscript in the Lord Powis's Family sixty years*; J.B., *Good and Joyful News for England: or, the Prophecy of the renowned Michael Nostradamus that Charles the II . . . shall have a son of his own body* (1681); *Merlin Reviv'd* [?1681]; *C.S.P.D., 1685*, p.30.

148. Wing lists five publications of his prophecies between 1672 and 1691. cf. *The Poems and Letters of Andrew Marvell*, ed. H. M. Margoliouth (2nd edn, Oxford, 1952), i, pp. 292–3; E. Leoni, *Nostradamus: Life and Literature* (New York, 1961).

149. *A Strange and Wonderful Prophecy for the Year 1688* (n.d.); *A Collection of Many Wonderful Prophecies . . . plainly foretelling the Late Great Revolution* (1691).

150. Murray, *Erceldoune*, pp. xli–xlii.

the rights of Richmond Park with some other events relating thereto not yet come to pass (1755).[151] Indeed the number of surviving chapbooks of this kind might make one think that there was no difference between the seventeenth century and the nineteenth so far as the cult of ancient prophecy was concerned. Nevertheless, the evidence suggests that after the seventeenth century such prophecies were not usually taken seriously by educated persons. They continued to be issued and read, especially at times of excitement, but their general prestige had substantially diminished. It is hard to demonstrate this conclusion, but few acquainted with this period of history are likely to challenge it.

3. *Sleeping heroes*

It has been seen how political prophecies tended to be invoked at a time of crisis, usually to demonstrate that some drastic change, either desired or already accomplished, had been foreseen by the sages of the past. In this way prophecies were felt to provide a sanction both for resistance to established authority and for the consolidation of a new regime.

A similar stabilizing function was performed by the various prophecies which competing dynasties sometimes found it necessary to invoke in support of their claims to the English throne. Most of these sprang from the mythical account of British history which had been disseminated by Geoffrey of Monmouth in the twelfth century. According to this legend the ancient Britons were the descendants of Brutus, the grandson of Aeneas of Troy, who had conquered the land from Gogmagog and the other giants who had been in possession of it and founded London to celebrate his triumph. Centuries later the invasion of the Saxons had been repelled by King Arthur, who went on to conquer most of Northern Europe, but was wounded in a civil war at home and taken off to recuperate at Avalon. The country was subsequently overrun by the Saxons, but not before the dying Cadwalader, last of the British rulers, had received from an

151. Axon, *Nixon's Cheshire Prophecies*, p. vii, n. The printed catalogue of the B.M. Library gives some indication of the extent of this type of literature. The 1790s seem to have been a particularly active period. On the revival of Nostradamus and Mother Shipton during the First World War, see C. W. C. Oman, 'Presidential Address', *T.R.H.S.*, 4th ser., i (1918), p. 25.

angel the prophetic message that the Britons would one day recover their heritage.[152]

The myth of the eventual return of Arthur or his royal line was cherished in all the Celtic countries; when some French monks visiting Bodmin in 1113 denied that Arthur was still alive their scepticism provoked a riot.[153] Arthur long remained a rallying cause for provincial sentiment in Wales and Brittany, while in England during the Wars of the Roses the British myth was exploited by each of the warring factions. First Edward IV and then Henry VII stressed their affiliations with the British past by having genealogies constructed to prove their descent from the stock of Cadwalader. This connection was heavily emphasized in 1486 when Henry VII had his eldest son named Arthur, after he had been born in Winchester, home of the Round Table.

The triumph of the Tudors was thus hailed by royal apologists as the fulfilment of the prophecies made to the dying Cadwalader, and there was a brief but deliberate cult of Arthur and the *British History*. Henry VIII drew upon the legend of Arthur's Empire to justify his breach with Rome.[154] In the reign of Elizabeth I the expansionist aspects of the myth were further developed by Dee, Hakluyt and similar imperialist writers. In Spenser's *Faery Queene* the monarchy of Elizabeth was celebrated as the apotheosis of the Arthurian tradition.

James I also used the Brutus myth to consolidate his accession to the English throne, by claiming descent from Gruffydd ap Llywelyn, the last Welsh prince, as well as from Henry VII, the reputed des-

152. The story of the Trojan legend, its reception and ultimate rejection, is told by T. D. Kendrick, *British Antiquity* (1950). See also E. A. Greenlaw, *Studies in Spenser's Historical Allegory* (Baltimore, 1932); C. B. Millican, *Spenser and the Table Round* (Cambridge, 1932).

153. Parsons in *Modern Language Rev.*, xxiv (1929), p. 264, n. 2. See in general R. S. Loomis, 'The Legend of Arthur's Survival', in *Arthurian Literature in the Middle Ages*, ed. R. S. Loomis (Oxford, 1959).

154. J. J. Scarisbrick, *Henry VIII* (1968), pp. 272–3. The important article by S. Anglo, 'The *British History* in early Tudor propaganda', *Bull. John Rylands Lib.*, xliv (1961–2), shows, however, that the Tudor cult of Arthur has often been exaggerated. Dr Anglo points out that the genealogical claim to British descent had already been more heavily emphasized by Edward IV and that the stress placed on the British past at the accession of Henry VII was of short duration. To his list of genealogies compiled in support of Edward IV may be added that in Ashm. 27, where heavy weight is laid upon the prophecies of Merlin, Bede, Bridlington, *et al.*

cendant of Cadwalader. The first Stuart thus appeared as the long-lost British King. In addition, the Union of the two kingdoms of England and Scotland could be seen as the fulfilment of the ancient tradition that the lands which Brutus had fatally divided amongst his three sons, and which Arthur had temporarily reunited, would one day be permanently joined under the rule of a single prince. This notion had been used by both sides in justification of the Anglo-Scottish wars. Edward I and Henry IV of England had claimed to be reconstituting Arthur's kingdom, while the Scots argued with equal plausibility that the long-prophesied union was intended to be accomplished by a Scotsman. Both nations made much use of ancient prophecies during the sixteenth century,[155] and in 1640 the Scottish soldiers in Newcastle were once again to give them an aggressive interpretation.[156]

The peaceful union of the two kingdoms in 1603, however, could be plausibly represented as the prophecy's true meaning, and even before James's accession, his English supporters invoked it in justification of his claim.[157] Once he had arrived, it was widely urged that the Brutus legend had been fulfilled. Even the Scots thought the union of the two kingdoms in the ninth degree of the Bruce's blood to have been foreseen by the prophecies of Thomas the Rymer.[158]

In keeping with the myth, the Stuarts assumed their new style as Kings of *Great Britain* ('When Hempe's spun England's done'). Merlin was said to have prophesied that 'the island shall be called by the name of the Brutus, and the name given it by the foreigners abolished'.[159] Against the wishes of the House of Commons, who wanted to preserve the separate names of Scotland and England, the King assumed the new title, declaring 'that the island was Britany,

155. D. Hay in *Procs. Soc. Antiquaries of Scotland*, lxxxix (1955–6), pp. 59–60; *L.P.*, xii(2), p. 28; xiv(1), p. 92. cf. xiv(1), pp. 63, 107; xx(2), p. 246; Murray, *Erceldoune*, pp. xx, xxx; *The Complaynt of Scotland*, ed. Murray, pp. xv, xxxviii.

156. R. Howell, *Newcastle upon Tyne and the Puritan Revolution* (Oxford, 1967), p. 119.

157. Harington, *Tract upon the Succession to the Crown*, pp. 18, 120–23. See R. F. Brinkley, *Arthurian Legend in the Seventeenth Century* (1932), chap. 1, and H. Lhwyd, *The Breviary of Britayne*, trans. T. Twyne (1573), f. 34ᵛ.

158. Murray, *Erceldoune*, pp. xl–xli. cf. *A Brief Description of the Future History of Europe* (1650), p. 11; J. Spottiswoode, *History of the Church of Scotland* (Edinburgh, 1851), i, p. 93.

159. *Six Old English Chronicles*, ed. J. A. Giles (1848), p. 199.

and therefore being King of the whole island he would be King of
Britany, as Brutus and Arthur were, who had the style, and were
kings of the whole island'.[160] Sir William Alexander assured the
monarch that

> The world long'd for thy birth three hundreth years,
> Since first fore-told wrapt in prophetic rimes,

and Drummond of Hawthornden declared that

> This is that king who should make right each wrong,
> Of whom the bards and mysticke Sibilles song,
> The man long promis'd, by whose glorious reign,
> This isle should yet her ancient name regain.[161]

The Stuarts were thus able to exploit the myth of the long-
prophesied deliverer to their own advantage. But this type of belief
was normally associated with popular resistance movements.
Whether the leader was a sleeping hero like Arthur, or Sebastian of
Portugal or the Geraldines and O'Neills in Ireland, not dead, but
merely biding their time, or whether, like the Jewish Messiah, he was
yet to come, his appeal was usually to the defeated and oppressed
awaiting deliverance. This was a universal myth, with counterparts
in the history of virtually every European country, and it rested upon
a prophetic foundation.[162]

In England this type of belief has never inspired mass-movements
comparable in scale to those launched by the pseudo-Fredericks of
medieval Germany. But it has frequently recurred. The two deposed
monarchs, Edward II and Richard II, for example, were both
credited with a posthumous survival; in 1330 Edmund, Earl of Kent,
was executed for activities arising from his belief that his dead

160. J. A. Spedding, *The Letters and the Life of Sir Francis Bacon* (1861–
74), iii, p. 194.
161. Murray, *Erceldoune*, p. xli. This aspect of James's new style is given
only passing mention by S. T. Bindoff, 'The Stuarts and Their Style', *E.H.R.,*
lx (1945) (at pp. 205–6). But Sir William Maurice, whose leading role in
bringing about the change is recognized by Prof. Bindoff (pp. 193, 204), was
said in *Mercurius Propheticus*, pp. 8–9, to have had the prophecy in mind.
162. Examples of such sleeping heroes and would-be Messiahs may be
found in Axon, *Nixon's Cheshire Prophecies*, pp. 64–7; Cohn, *The Pursuit of
the Millennium*, pp. 55, 56–7, 77 ff., 106–12; E. K. Chambers, *Arthur of
Britain* (Cambridge, 1964 edn), pp. 225–7; and C. Hill, *Puritanism and Revolution* (1958), pp. 55–6. For their prophetic basis, see, e.g., M. d'Antas,
Les Faux Don Sébastien. Étude sur l'histoire de Portugal (Paris, 1866), pp.
451–7.

brother Edward II was still alive; and in the early fifteenth century there were rumours that Richard II was living in Scotland, the claim that he was still alive being reiterated as late as 1416.[163]

Similar rumours followed the defeat of popular risings. A year after the slaughter of Ket and his followers, an Earlham woman was overheard to remark that 'there are five hundred of Mousehold men that are gone down to the great Turk and to the Dauphin and will be here again by Midsummer'.[164] In 1570 there was said to be daily talk in the north of the imminent return of the rebels who had been decisively defeated in the rising of the Northern Earls in the previous year.[165] In the 1630s Sir John Coke, Secretary to Charles I, was bombarded with letters from a religious enthusiast assuring him that the Protestant hero, Gustavus Adolphus, had not really been killed at Lützen, but was living in Seleucia and would come again to fight the Whore of Babylon.[166] In the late seventeenth century many west countrymen refused to believe that the Duke of Monmouth had really been executed in 1685. The rumour that he was still alive lasted until the reign of George III. It was reported that another man had been executed in Monmouth's place – Colonel White in one version, 'an old man with a beard' in another – and individuals were periodically apprehended for masquerading as the dead Duke.[167] Yet he was not the last sleeping hero in English history, for the same refusal to accept that a public figure was really dead was to be shown in the cases of General Gordon and Lord Kitchener.[168] In more primitive countries the reluctance to accept the death of a rebel leader can still be found. The decision of the state of Malawi in 1965 to conduct executions in public was taken to demonstrate to the defeated that their leaders were truly dead.[169]

163. Kittredge, *Witchcraft*, p. 53; *V.C.H., City of York*, p. 58; Thomson, *Later Lollards*, p. 16.

164. *Depositions taken before the Mayor and Aldermen of Norwich*, ed. Rye, p. 58.

165. *C.S.P.D., Addenda, 1566–79*, p. 223.

166. *C.S.P.D., 1633–4*, pp. 204–5; *1634–5*, p. 279.

167. N. Luttrell, *A Brief Historical Relation of State Affairs* (Oxford, 1857), i, pp. 356, 386; *York Depositions*, p. 283; Lyme Regis Borough Archives (Town Hall, Lyme Regis), A 3/1, p. 20; *Hereford City Records*, ix, p. 3569; Mrs Arundell Esdaile, 'A Sham Duke of Monmouth in Sussex', *Sussex Notes and Queries*, xi (1946); T. B. Macaulay, *The History of England* (1905), i, pp. 556–7.

168. *The Journal of Beatrix Potter*, ed. L. Linder (1966), p. 146; P. Magnus, *Kitchener* (1958), p. 379.

169. *The Times*, 11 Nov. 1965.

The most curious sleeping hero in our period was the boy-king Edward VI, who died at the age of fifteen in 1553. In his own lifetime it had been necessary for him, as for many other monarchs, to make public appearances so as to refute malicious rumours that he was dead.[170] After his death the situation was paradoxically reversed. In 1588 John Harvey lamented:

> Alas, what fond and vain expectation hath a long time rested in the minds not of one or two or a few, but of great multitudes of the simpler sort in England about King Edward the Sixth, as though they were sure either of his arising from death, or his return from I know not what Jerusalem or other strange land ... And what counterfeit suborned merchants of base parentage have sithence ranged abroad in the country, presuming to term themselves by the rival name of King Edward.[171]

The rumour started very shortly after the accession of Mary Tudor. During the course of her reign several individuals were imprisoned, and a miller's son executed, for impersonating the late King or distributing bills saying that he was alive and living in France.[172] Manuscript versions of prophecies hinting at his return in 1556 are still extant.[173] At this stage Edward was presumably a symbol of Protestantism and anti-Spanish sentiment. Yet the tradition carried on into the reign of Elizabeth, who was herself both Protestant and anti-Spanish.

In 1581 Robert Blosse, alias Mantell, an Essex yeoman and ex-naval gunner, was executed after a series of adventures in which he had begun by disseminating the rumour that Edward VI was alive and ended by impersonating the dead King himself. The original idea that the King was alive had been passed on to him by an Oxford scholar in the reign of Mary, and the notion stuck in his mind. His case caused the Elizabethan government some embarrassment, for in the Attorney-General's opinion there was nothing treasonable about merely saying that Edward VI was alive. Mantell was ultimately convicted for impersonating the King, which *was*, on Marian precedents, an undoubted offence, but promptly escaped from Colchester gaol, where he had been held. The Privy Council, much

170. *The Chronicle and Political Papers of King Edward VI*, ed. W. K. Jordan (1966), p. 13.

171. Harvey, *A Discoursive Probleme*, p. 61.

172. *A.P.C.*, iv, p. 363; v. pp. 122, 221; Loades, *Two Tudor Conspiracies*, p. 148; J. Stow, *The Annales of England* (1592), pp. 1062, 1064–5.

173. In Sloane 2578, ff. 18ᵛ, 20, 32.

flurried, ordered the arrest of the gaoler and of the persons concerned in effecting the escape. In 1581, Mantell, having been recaptured, was sent down to Essex for trial once again, all scruples about the status of his offence having been dissipated by his prisonbreaking. 'The long reserving of him,' declared the Council, 'hath given occasion unto others to cast abroad seditious libels to the disturbance of her Highness's estate.' This time he did not escape the ghastly ritual of a traitor's death.[174]

Six years later another culprit appeared at Essex Assizes on a similar charge. This was William Francis, a smith of Hatfield Peverel, who had denied that King Edward was dead; he further declared that he personally knew the man who had carried King Edward 'in a red mantle into Germany in a ship called the *Harry*', asserting that the so-called tomb of Edward VI contained a hollow piece of lead.[175] In the same year the Leicester embroiderer Sawford also said that the 'dead man' mentioned in Merlin's prophecy was either King Arthur or King Edward VI.[176] In 1589 Edward was reported by a soldier returned from the Low Countries to be alive and living in Spain or France. Twelve years later the rumour cropped up again, in the mouth of a Radnorshire vagrant named Thomas Vaughan, who was examined at Oxford in May 1599. According to him, a substitute child had been put to death in King Edward's place, and he himself had been conveyed to Denmark, where he had become King; in this capacity he had saved the lives of the commons of England, Wales and Ireland by supplying corn and other provisions. This may have been a reference to the contemporary import of Baltic grain in times of scarcity, but it also echoes the mention in several of the prophecies attributed to Bede, Merlin, *et al.* of a King, or Duke, of Denmark who would invade England and seize the throne. Vaughan's interrogators reported to the Lord Treasurer that he was a very simple person, 'little better than a natural'; but it is likely that this Elizabethan beggar's

174. B.M., Lansdowne MS 16, f. 17; *A.P.C.*, xi, pp. 194, 214, 371; xii, pp. 23–4, 29, 353–4; P.R.O., SP 12/186/91–2; SP 12/187/62; Assizes 35/20/5A/7; 35/21/7/3; 35/21/7/24; 35/23/H/48–9 (transcripts in Essex R.O., kindly sent to me by Mr Arthur Searle). I have not been able to resolve all the difficulties of fact and interpretation which the evidence for this case presents. The account in M. E. Cornford, 'A Legend concerning Edward VI', *E.H.R.*, xxiii (1908), is incomplete.

175. P.R.O., Assizes 35/29/Hilary (transcript shown me by Dr Alan Macfarlane).

176. Above, pp. 482–3.

ingenuous words were derived from the hope of a Danish alliance against England which had been preserved in Scottish prophetic verse since the fourteenth century.[177]

An even more elaborate version of the myth of Edward VI was revealed in 1606 to have been propagated by Gervase Smith, parson of Polstead, Suffolk. Smith, who was dissatisfied with King James I because of his failure to persecute the Papists effectively, observed that Merlin's prophecy had stated that E. would be succeeded by I., M., and finally by E. This he interpreted as meaning that King I(ames) would come to ruin at the hands of the Papists, who would set up M(ary) to persecute the Protestants, who would eventually be saved by E(dward), descendant of the house of Cadwalader. The latter, he thought, was probably Edward VI, who was either dead or living 'in Africa' and would be miraculously raised up again. Investigation revealed that Smith had inherited a collection of prophecies from an old man who had died in his house. From these he had learned of M., i.e. Mary, who would restore Catholicism, and E., who would put it down. He assumed that E. was Edward VI, 'who the prophecies say shall rise again'. Smith was a Puritan zealot who felt that the Church of England was not in accordance with the primitive church, and would like to have seen all Catholics put to death. His talk of ancient prophecies had been notorious in the neighbourhood. A few years earlier he had shown a minister a book saying that King Sebastian of Portugal was still alive, a further instance of an apparently obsessive interest in prophecies about lost leaders.[178]

To Gervase Smith Edward VI had appealed as a Puritan hero, yet the earlier impostor, Robert Mantell, had been a suspected Catholic, and the precise attraction of the boy-king clearly varied according to the circumstances. The idea of a deliverer named Edward may have originated with Lambert Simnel, the pretender to Henry VII's throne, who masqueraded as Edward, Earl of Warwick, and was crowned in Dublin as Edward VI. Perkin Warbeck had also exploited the rumour that Edward IV's children were not really dead, but had been secretly conveyed into another country. The notion, however, may have gone back even further;

177. *H.M.C., Hatfield*, ix, pp. 167–8, 173. For the King of Denmark, see Murray, *Erceldoune*, pp. 56, 62; Griffiths, *Early Vaticination*, p. 209; Axon, *Nixon's Cheshire Prophecies*, p. 45.

178. *H.M.C., Hatfield*, xviii, pp. 280–81, 298, 304, 306–7; 316–18, 320–22.

for in 1532 a conjurer declared that Prince Edward, child of Henry VI, had had a son who had been conveyed overseas and whose child was alive in France or Germany; either he or the King of the Scots would reign after Henry VIII.[179] But, basically, the myth of Edward's return was sustained by the many Galfridian and Scottish prophecies promising the return of a dead man or lost leader.[180] One dating from 1552 specifically declared that 'E. shall rise out of his sleep like a live man whom all men thought to be dead'.[181] It was almost certainly a version of this prophecy which came into the hands of John Tusser, Edward Sawford and Gervase Smith. As late as 1652 a published collection of prophecies included a mid-sixteenth-century prediction, attributed to 'Robert Blake', that 'a dead man shall rise'. 'Up Edward the Sixth,' it declared, 'the time is come.'[182]

4. *The roots of prophecy*

How is the appeal of these various prophecies to be accounted for? On one level they may be regarded as simply a propaganda device, based on the eternal truth that nothing is more likely to bring about the success of an enterprise than the conviction of those who undertake it that they are predestined to succeed. From this point of view, the function of ancient prophecies was no different from that of astrological or magical prognostication in general. Selden wrote of prophecies that 'they make a man go on with boldness and courage. . . . If he obtains he attributes much to them; if he miscarries he thinks no more of them, or is no more thought of himself.'[183] Prophecies, as Hobbes put it, were 'many times the principal cause of the event foretold'.[184] Given such obvious political effects, it is not

179. [T. Gainsford], *The True and Wonderfull History of Perkin Warbeck* (1618), pp. 5, 55; *L.P.*, v, p. 695.

180. e.g., Griffiths, *Early Vaticination*, p. 209; Murray, *Erceldoune*, pp. lxxx, 54, 63; Harvey, *A Discoursive Probleme*, pp. 56–7; *The Prophesie of Mother Shipton* (1641); *L.P.*, vi, pp. 399–400.

181. Murray, *Erceldoune*, p. 63. Another version is in Cheshire R.O., DDX 123, f. 13.

182. *Sundry Strange Prophecies* (1652), p. 31. This was one of the 'dead man' prophecies cited by Harvey, *A Discoursive Probleme*, p. 56. There is a version dating from the reign of Mary Tudor in Sloane 2578, ff. 18ᵛ, 20.

183. J. Selden, *Table-Talk* (Temple Classics, n.d.), pp. 123–4.

184. *The English Works of Thomas Hobbes*, ed. Sir W. Molesworth (1839–45), vi, pp. 398–9.

difficult to see why prophecies were often fabricated for the occasion. Such forgeries can be recognised by their tendency to include an exact account of events up to the date of the prophecy's 'discovery', followed by a more shadowy prognostication of what remained in store. The prophecies disseminated at the time of the Popish Plot, for example, usually included a precise outline of the careers of Charles I and Cromwell, before embarking upon hazier utterances concerning the triumph of Protestantism and the fall of Rome.

But the political utility of these prophecies does not explain the disposition to believe them in the first place. Neither does it tell us why men felt the need to manufacture prophecies after the event. For, as often as not, the prophecy was only 'discovered' when the events to which it referred had taken place. As Samuel Butler cynically observed, 'they are never heard of till it is to no purpose'.[185] Most of the predictions based on the ambiguities of surnames, for example, seem likely to have been made up after the event. Henry IV was told that he would die in Jerusalem, but 'Jerusalem' turned out to be the name of a room in a house belonging to the Abbot of Westminster. The Welsh image of Derfel Gadarn would 'set on fire a forest'; it was brought to London by the Henrician reformers and the Franciscan friar John Forest was burned with it. Cardinal Wolsey knew that Kingston would be fatal to him; he was duly arrested by Sir William Kingston.[186] There are many wry stories of this type, but very few can be traced back to a strictly contemporary source. The majority seem to have been invented or 'improved' by persons in search of an edifying tale. Yet although they possess a certain narrative felicity, this does not explain why men should have felt the need to invent them.

The truth seems to be that at the heart of the belief in prophecies there lay an urge to believe that even the most revolutionary doings of contemporaries had been foreseen by the sages of the past. For what these predictions did was to demonstrate that there was a link between contemporary aspirations and those of remote antiquity. Their function was to persuade men that some proposed change was not so radical that it had not been foreseen by their ancestors. This

185. S. Butler, *Characters and Passages from Notebooks*, ed. A. R. Waller (Cambridge, 1908), p. 134.

186. *Notes and Queries*, 2nd, ser., iv (1857), pp. 201–3, 277; v (1858), pp. 37, 174; vii (1859), pp. 395–8; Foxe, iii, p. 319; v, p. 180; A. F. Pollard, *Wolsey* (1929), p. 298.

had the effect of disguising any essentially revolutionary step by concealing it under the sanction of past approval. Prophecies, therefore, were not simple morale-boosters: they provided a 'validating charter' (to adopt the anthropologists' phrase) for new enterprises undertaken in the face of strong contemporary prohibitions. They justified wars or rebellions and they made periods of unprecedented change emotionally acceptable to those who lived in them. As John Harvey put it: they were resurrected 'to serve present turns, and to feed the working humour of busy and tumultuous heads, continually affecting some innovation or other'.[187]

To understand the need for such a validating charter it should be recalled that for sixteenth-century Englishmen the existing political order was not regarded as a matter of mere practical convenience, changeable at will. It was divinely ordained, and God's sanctions would fall upon the rebel wicked enough to challenge it. When a man embarked upon the drastic course of insurrection he was flouting all the moral teaching of the day and cutting himself loose from the whole social and political order in which he had been nurtured. At such times prophecy made its appeal by providing a sanction for such dramatic action. Ideally the prophecy was a divine one, indicating that rebellious activity was in accordance with God's will and therefore not a sin but a positive duty. Hence the theological language in which the successive revolutionary groups of the Civil War period clothed their aspirations. But, as an alternative, recourse could be had to the ancient prophecies, which through their vagueness and ambiguity were easily adaptable to fit new circumstances. Faith in such a prophecy brought authority and conviction to those staking all on a desperate step. It gave a sort of moral justification to those engaged in the gambler's throw of rebellion; and it kept up the spirits of the defeated by assuring them that time was on their side. Sometimes the prophecy was not discovered or invented until the change had already taken place. In those cases its role was to conceal the breach and make it respectable by bringing it into line with the pattern of the past.

The appeal to ancient prophecy was therefore but one aspect of that concern to discover precedents for every radical step which coloured most aspects of English public life in the century before the Civil War. This desire can be seen during the Reformation, when the breach with Rome was presented not as a new departure, but

187. Harvey, *A Discoursive Probleme*, sig. A4.

as a return to the situation which had existed before the Papal
'usurpation'. The Act in Restraint of Appeals to Rome (1533) invoked 'divers old chronicles', which showed England to have originally been an 'empire' independent of Papal jurisdiction. Attempts
were also made to show that Christianity had been established in
Britain by Joseph of Arimathea, centuries before the Papal mission
of St Augustine, or by the fabulous King Lucius of Britain in the
second century A.D. Failing that, the Anglo-Saxon Church was presented by the Elizabethan Archbishop Matthew Parker as the em-
bodiment of perfect Protestant virtue, subsequently corrupted by
medieval Catholicism but now restored to its pristine state.[188] When
even this was reluctantly seen to be unhistorical, theologians fell
back on the primitive Church of the New Testament as their model,
or traced a pedigree of Pre-Reformation Protestants through Wycliffe and the Lollards to the Waldenses and Cathars. The Protestant
religion, thought the great antiquary, Sir Simonds D'Ewes, had
flourished in England 400 years before Augustine; it had been preserved among the Welsh and Scots without interruption until Wycliffe, and had been secretly practised in England from at least the
time of Henry II.[189]

The same anxiety to conceal the fact of unprecedented change was
shown by the early Stuart parliaments. None of the opposition
spokesmen dared to assert that there was no precedent for their
claims. Instead they sought to show that their programme was but
a demand for the restoration of liberties enjoyed by their fourteenth-
century or even Anglo-Saxon predecessors. Political argument took
the form of legal controversy – determining just what the law was –
and all discussion was conducted on the fictitious assumption of an
unchanging constitutional structure. Not until the mid seventeenth
century did the strain of attempting to make all political demands
harmonize with a fictitious model of the past become too much. The
links snapped, and for the first time men were prepared to assert
the inherent merit of a political programme, regardless of whether

188. Many of these efforts are conveniently summarized in G. Williams,
'Some Protestant Views of Early British Church History', *History*, xxxviii
(1953), and Levy, *Tudor Historical Thought*, chap. 3.

189. Sir S. D'Ewes, *The Primitive Practise for Preserving Truth* (1645),
p. 28. cf. Matthew Prideaux's discussion of whether William Rufus, in view
of his quarrel with Anselm, 'in some sort might not be termed a Protestant';
An Easy and Compendious Introduction for Reading all sorts of Histories
(Oxford, 1648), p. 315.

or not it had ever previously been put into effect.[190] Yet, even then, most political thought remained essentially an inquiry into origins; happenings in the state of nature or some other version of the primitive past still determined men's political obligations in the present.

Ancient prophecies, like spurious history, also helped to mitigate the otherwise revolutionary doings of contemporaries. By showing that current political activities were in accordance with the predictions of some long-dead figure, they took the sting out of them. Prophecies disguised the break with the past. Contemporaries were therefore mistaken when they declared that it was the circulation of prophecies which fomented rebellion. Essentially it was the existence of rebellious feeling which led to the circulation of prophecies. The prophecies themselves had been potentially available all the time. Moreover, they were ambiguous and without any necessary reference to contemporary circumstances. It was the rebels who read into them an application to current events and they did so because they wished to do so. At times of stress men scrutinized these ancient myths with a view to extracting from them some sanction for the dangerous courses of action upon which they proposed to embark. Under the pressure of change they most felt the need for reassurance that what was happening had been foreseen by their ancestors and was in some sense part of a larger plan. It was no accident that the periods when prophecies were most prominent in English life were precisely those of rebellion, discontent and violent change – the Reformation and the Civil War, in particular.

All societies seek to establish links with their own past, to display the 'founding charter' which explains and justifies their own existence. In modern times historians rewrite the history of their dead ancestors to show that they too suffered from the problems of sex, class or money which obsess us. In more unsophisticated societies the genealogical history of rulers is endlessly rewritten to maintain the fiction of unbroken continuity with the past, while the first action of the social parvenu is to invent himself a pedigree. The facts of change are rapidly re-interpreted to sustain the illusion of a static society. In such a world all claims must be judged with reference to established norms. A pretender to the throne must demonstrate

190. For this crucial development see Hill, *Puritanism and Revolution*, chap. 3, and ' "Reason" and "Reasonableness" in Seventeenth-century England', *Brit. Journ. Sociology*, xx (1969), pp. 238–9; J. G. A. Pocock, *The Ancient Constitution and the Feudal Law* (Cambridge, 1957), pp. 125–7; W. H. Greenleaf, *Order, Empiricism and Politics* (1964), pp. 269–74.

genealogical continuity. Hence the great cult of prophecies during the fifteenth century: 'When the Civil War was hottest between York and Lancaster,' wrote the Elizabethan Earl of Northampton, 'the books of Beasts and Babies were exceeding rife and current in every quarter and corner of the realm, either side applying and interpreting as they were affected to the title.'[191]

Hence also all the impostors masquerading as the representatives of some branch, real or imaginary, of the royal family. Apart from well-known pretenders like Lambert Simnel, Perkin Warbeck, and all the would-be Sleeping Heroes, there were many less famous eccentrics: Mary Baynton, the Yorkshire woman, who in 1533 gave herself out to be the King's daughter Mary, 'put forth into the broad world to shift for her living';[192] Anne Burnell, who claimed in 1587 to be the child of Philip II;[193] Bartholomew Helson, who in 1607 announced himself the son of Mary Tudor, stolen from Hampton Court;[194] Cornelius Evans, who masqueraded as the Prince of Wales in 1648;[195] and Thomas Tany, who claimed in the 1650s to be the Earl of Essex and the heir to Charles I's throne.[196] There was also the young man named 'Arthur' who entered Spain in 1587, claiming to be the offspring of Elizabeth and Leicester, and the youth who rushed naked into St James's in 1612, pretending to be the ghost of Prince Henry.[197] Absurd though such pretensions may seem to us, they were no more ridiculous than the royal genealogies linking the Yorkists and Tudors to the founding fathers, Adam and Brutus.[198] Ancient prophecies gave ancestry to the actions of contemporaries, as spurious as the Trojan genealogies, but no less effective.

There was, of course, nothing peculiarly English about these attempts to establish a direct link between contemporary society and

191. Howard, *A Defensative*, f. 116ᵛ.

192. *L.P.*, vi, p. 494.

193. M. Eccles, *Christopher Marlowe in London* (Cambridge, Mass., 1934), pp. 145–57.

194. *H.M.C., Hatfield*, xix, p. 177.

195. *C.S.P.D., 1648–9*, pp. 72–3, 349.

196. *D.N.B.*

197. Millican, *Spenser and the Table Round*, p. 40; *The Letters of John Chamberlain*, ed. N. E. McClure (Philadelphia, 1939), i, pp. 391–2. For an Elizabethan named Johnson, who claimed to be the offspring of the mythical heroes, Guy of Warwick and Bevis of Hampton, see *Original Letters illustrative of English History*, ed. Sir H. Ellis, 3rd ser. (1846), iv, pp. 60–61.

198. W. H. Greenleaf, 'Filmer's Patriarchal History', *Hist. Journ.*, ix (1966); Anglo in *Bull. John Rylands Lib.*, xliv (1961–2), pp. 41–8.

the vanished past. The claim to Trojan ancestry had been made by the Romans, the French and others. 'Most of the civilized nations of [the] earth,' wrote Sir Robert Filmer, 'labour to fetch their original from some one of the sons or nephews of Noah.'[199] Ancient prophecies were widely dispersed throughout Europe. The conquests of Gustavus Adolphus were justified by reference to a prediction about the Eagle and the Lion of the North, said to be the prophecy of Paracelsus.[200] In Spanish America prophecies circulating among the Indians prepared the ground for Cromwell's invasion of the West Indies.[201] In Persia there was a prophecy promising success in the wars against the Turk.[202] Prophecies accompanied the outbreak of the revolt of the Catalans in 1640,[203] just as they helped to justify rebellions in England. They were a universal feature of an essentially pre-political world, that is to say, of one where innovation has to be disguised as a return to the past, and where the fact of change is essentially unrecognized.

But by the end of the seventeenth century the Galfridian-style prophecy was in decline. The immediate cause was the growing volume of historical criticism which shattered the legends of Brutus and Arthur and exposed the ancient prophecies for the fictions they were. There had always been a substantial minority of critics who regarded Geoffrey of Monmouth's history with suspicion, and Merlin's prophecies in particular had been handled with caution. 'Divers men hold opinion that there was no such Arthur,' remarked Caxton in 1485. Polydore Vergil's refutation of the Brutus legend in the early sixteenth century was but the culmination of a tradition of scepticism which went back nearly 400 years.[204] Even so, his iconoclasm

199. Quoted in Kendrick, *British Antiquity*, p. 76. On the widespread use of the Trojan myth, see D. Hay, *Europe, the Emergence of an Idea* (Edinburgh, 1957), pp. 48–9.
200. M. Roberts, *Gustavus Adolphus* (1953–8), i, pp. 525–7.
201. *A Collection of the State Papers of John Thurloe*, ed. T. Birch (1742), iii, p. 59.
202. *H.M.C., Hatfield*, xx, p. 54.
203. J. H. Elliott, *The Revolt of the Catalans* (Cambridge, 1963), p. 444. For the European influence of Galfridian prophecy, see Taylor, *The Political Prophecy*, chap. 6.
204. Some medieval critics are listed by R. H. Fletcher in *Studies and Notes in Philosophy and Litre.*, x (1906), pp. 136, 194, 200, 208, 225, 242, 244, 251; Zumthor, *Merlin le prophète*, pp. 95–6; and L. Keeler, *Geoffrey of Monmouth and the late Latin Chroniclers, 1300–1500* (Berkeley and Los Angeles, 1946).

raised a howl of nationalist protest, which encouraged Bale and Leland to resurrect Arthur as a Protestant hero, at a time when the Trojan legend was being discredited by continental scholars. As late as the eighteenth century some stout British nationalists stuck out in Geoffrey of Monmouth's defence. But by this time the tide of informed opinion had permanently turned against him.[205] 'Merlin's drunken prophecies', as William Perkins called them, were generally agreed to be not an ancient British survival but the invention of Geoffrey himself. It also became harder for scholars to take seriously the Stuart claim to descent from the British kings. In 1648 a leading historical textbook dismissed Merlin's prophecies as 'old wives' tales', and by the eighteenth century 'Merlin' was a joke among educated persons.[206]

Historical criticism thus proved incompatible with the retention of primitive founding myths. Under the pressure of Catholic controversy the 'Protestantism' of the Anglo-Saxons wilted away: Thomas Stapleton enumerated no fewer than forty-six differences between sixteenth-century Protestantism and the religion of Bede.[207] The case for the antiquity of Parliament went the same way.[208] Even the ancient Britons were revealed as the counterparts of the half-naked American Indians – 'an idolatrous nation and worshippers of devils', as an M.P. remarked in 1606.[209] On the Continent the

205. G. Huppert, 'The Trojan Franks and Their Critics', *Studies in the Renaissance*, xii (1965); C. A. Patrides, *The Phoenix and the Ladder* (Berkeley, 1964), pp. 53-6; Levy, *Tudor Historical Thought*, p. 184. See also Millican, *Spenser and the Table Round*; Brinkley, *Arthurian Legend in the Seventeenth Century;* D. Bush, *English Literature in the Earlier Seventeenth Century* (Oxford, 1945), pp. 214–15. For an isolated defender, C. A. Ashburton, *A New and Complete History of England* (1798?), Preface.

206. *The Workes ... of William Perkins*, iii, p. 467; Prideaux, *An Easy and Compendious Introduction for Reading all sorts of Histories*, p. 261; E. Jones, *Geoffrey of Monmouth, 1648–1800* (Univ. of Calif. Pubs. in English, 1944), p. 411.

207. M. R. O'Connell, *Thomas Stapleton and the Counter-Reformation* (New Haven, 1964), p. 55. cf. H.B., *Englands Old Religion faithfully gathered out of the History of the Church of England, as it was written by Venerable Bede* (Antwerp, 1658).

208. Pocock, *The Ancient Constitution and the Feudal Law*, pp. 111–12, 152–5, 186, 201–6.

209. *The Parliamentary Diary of Robert Bowyer, 1606–7*, ed. D. H. Willson (Minneapolis, 1931), p. 203, n. 3. See also Kendrick, *British Antiquity*, pp. 121–5; Burton, *Anatomy*, i. p. 86; R. Eburne, *A Plain Pathway to Plantations* (1624), ed. L. B. Wright (Ithaca, New York, 1962), p. 56.

sibylline prophecies were subjected by Isaac Casaubon, G. J. Vossius and David Blondel to rigorous criticism which robbed them of their claim to have anticipated the coming of Christ. The effect was to reduce faith in the possibility of prophecy in general.[210]

Inherent in the idea of ancient prophecy had been the assumption that the sages of the past could have been aware of present-day problems. A growing sensitivity to anachronism made this premise unacceptable. Men's evolving consciousness of the gulf between themselves and their ancestors is not possible to date precisely. Indeed its development seems to have been fitful and uneven. Not until the later eighteenth century did English theatre-audiences expect actors to be dressed in period costume. Yet from the sixteenth century European scholars had begun to apply standards of historical criticism to the study of feudal law, and to appreciate that customs and jurisprudence were bound up with the society of which they formed part, and not to be isolated and appropriated for a different context.[211] It was in the sixteenth century also that an awareness of the difference between present and past styles began to show itself in English art. In the following century John Aubrey pioneered the chronological study of the evolution of English medieval architecture.[212] The period also saw the development of palaeography and allied means of precisely dating historical documents and identifying forgeries. As early as the time of Henry VIII there is evidence of some attempt to purge royal genealogies of their errors; and in the same reign John Rastell was able to discredit an allegedly Arthurian seal in Westminster Abbey.[213] Historians began to split up the past into defined periods of time, evolving the now standard division between ancient, medieval and modern. Terms like 'epoch', 'synchronize', and 'out of date' made their début in

210. Blondel's *A Treatise of the Sibyls* was translated by J. D(avis) in 1661. For examples of the change in English opinion, see, e.g., R. Gell, *Stella Nova* (1649), p. 5; T. Hobbes, *Leviathan* (1651), chap. 12; M. Casaubon, *Of Credulity and Incredulity, in Things Divine* (1670), p. 144; J. Bradley, *An Impartial View of the Truth of Christianity* (1699), chap. 8; W. Whiston, *A Vindication of the Sibylline Oracles* (1715), p. 81.

211. Pocock, *Ancient Constitution and the Feudal Law, passim.*

212. J. G. Mann, 'Instances of Antiquarian Feeling in Medieval and Renaissance Art', *Archaeol, Journ.*, lxxxix (1932), esp. pp. 267–9; H. M. Colvin, 'Aubrey's *Chronologia Architectonica*', in *Concerning Architecture*, ed. J. Summerson (1968).

213. Levy, *Tudor Historical Thought*, p. 74; Anglo in *Bull. John Rylands Lib.*, xliv (1961–2), p. 47.

the language.[214] By the mid seventeenth century the word 'anachronism' itself had appeared.[215]

Of course, the work of the historians and antiquarians did not immediately penetrate the public consciousness. The publication of ancient prophecies reached its peak during the Interregnum, even though the historical work which had undermined their intellectual respectability had been carried out decades before. The paradox was that, like so much other occult medieval learning, ancient prophecies were widely disseminated at the very time when educated men could no longer take them seriously.

But it would be wrong to regard the decline of the belief in ancient prophecy as the mere consequence of new historical techniques. It is true that historical scholarship was the instrument which undermined the founding myths, exposed the fictitious nature of the royal genealogies, and revealed many 'ancient prophecies' to be recent fabrications. A more acute awareness of the difference between present and past had made it harder to pass off a piece of contemporary verse as the work of some Dark Age wizard. But this new historical criticism was itself a symptom of the change as much as a cause. It required a favourable environment in which to emerge. In primitive societies the unfolding of the seasons and the life-cycles of the inhabitants were sufficient to give men a sense of flux and decay but not of structural change. At a more advanced stage of historical development came the cyclical view of history, the view that change did occur, but that in the long run everything came back to where it started. This notion that history waxes and wanes like the moon, so influential in classical times, enjoyed a new vogue during the Renaissance, when it could be maintained that the highest aesthetic and ethical virtue lay in imitation, or rather emulation, of the standards of antiquity.

The reason for the replacement of this cyclical view of history by a linear one is one of the great mysteries of intellectual history. But one may hazard a guess at the answer, by saying that what is most necessary to produce a sense of change is the fact of change. In particular, it takes discernible technological or intellectual move-

214. G. S. Gordon, *Medium Aevum and the Middle Age* (Oxford, 1925); N. Edelman, 'The Early Uses of *Medium Aevum, Moyen Âge*, Middle Ages', *Romanic Rev.*, xxix (1938); O. Barfield, *History in English Words* (new edn, 1962), p. 161.

215. Though only in the sense of a misdating; J. Gregorie, 'De aeris et epochis', in *Gregorii Posthuma* (1650), p. 174.

ment to drive into the minds of contemporaries an awareness of the differences between their world and that of their ancestors. It was notoriously the existence of gunpowder, the printing-press and the mariner's compass which, with the shifting of the world's features under the impact of the geographical discoveries, did most to remind the men of the Renaissance that they could never really recapture the world of the Greeks and Romans. The change may have been assisted by the craft idea of knowledge as cumulative, with each pupil endeavouring to improve upon the technique taught him by his master.[216] Printing certainly did much to emphasise the difference between the present and the past; for every book had a date of publication, and those which survived stood as monuments to past assumptions and ideas. Old books, like old buildings or old genealogies, were relics of the past, but, unlike buildings or genealogies, could not be silently adapted to suit the needs of new generations.

It is true that there had been a great deal of technological progress throughout the Middle Ages. But it is also true, though puzzling, that its psychological effects seem to have been very slight before the fifteenth or sixteenth centuries. It certainly generated no diffused concept of technical progress. On the contrary, an 'inventor' was, as the word indicated, a person who found something which had been lost, not one who devised a new solution unknown to previous generatious. Not until the sixteenth century did it become common to imply that recent events were unprecedented, by describing them as 'news',[217] while the characteristically modern notion that the newest is the best did not establish itself until after a protracted battle between 'ancients' and 'moderns'. Meanwhile, genuine innovators hesitated to believe that they had done any more than restore knowledge which had been in man's possession at some earlier period of history. Just as Renaissance philosophers liked to assume that the Christian religion had been known to Hermes, Orpheus, Plato and the *prisci theologi* who lived long before Christ, so many contemporary scientists represented their contributions as the mere restoration of ancient wisdom, lost since the Fall and surviving only in coterie circles. Thus Copernicanism was said to have been known to the Egyptians; magic went back to Adam; Paracelsian chemistry came *via* Hermes; even Newton's system of the

216. This idea is interestingly discussed by S. Lilley, 'Robert Recorde and the Idea of Progress', *Renaissance and Modern Studies*, ii. (1958). Whether this was the attitude of the average sixteenth-century artisan is another matter.

217. *O.E.D.*

world had been apprehended by the *prisci theologi*, who had passed it down as a 'mystery' for initiates.[218]

The aim of this elaborate mythology, it has been rightly said, was 'to have a past without breaks',[219] and to conceal the fact of innovation. In politics even the Revolution of 1688–9 was presented as a restoration of ancient liberties rather than the foundation of new ones. But by the end of the century it was increasingly apparent that men were doing more than simply treading the paths of their ancestors. For Robert Boyle it was impossible to construct a complete system of truth because at any given moment things were still happening, and new phenomena might refute previous hypotheses. How different was this new notion of progressive revelation from Aristotle's belief that 'almost everything [that is to be known] has been found out'.[220] From the mid seventeenth century 'originality' established itself among literary critics as a quality to be looked for.[221] The acceptance of progress meant replacing faith in the wisdom of our ancestors by the conviction of their ignorance. In such circumstances commentators lost interest in the predictions of Bede or Gildas or in talk of White Kings and Dreadful Dead Men, however authentic the texts. There was now no reason to think that a document from the Dark Ages, no matter how genuine, could reveal foreknowledge of the present age or the outcome of events still to come. Men, in other words, became undisposed to accept the possibility of ancient prophecies as such. Their morale-boosting function declined accordingly.

In all its facets the seventeenth centry testifies to this new emancipation from the past. In political thought the appeal to origins and historic rights was abandoned by many of the radical thinkers of the mid century: even Charles I rejected the argument from precedent before his death.[222] In politics it was appreciated as a time

218. D. P. Walker, 'The *Prisca Theologia* in France', *Journ. Warburg and Courtauld Institutes*, xvii (1954); A. G. Debus, 'An Elizabethan History of Medical Chemistry', *Annals of Science*, xviii (1962); (T. Vaughan), *Magia Adamica: or the Antiquitie of Magic and the Descent thereof from Adam* (1650); R. Ward, *The Life of . . . Dr Henry More*, ed. M. F. Howard (1911), p. 77; J. E. McGuire and P. M. Rattansi, 'Newton and the "Pipes of Pan" ', *Notes and Records of the Royal Soc.*, xxi (1966).

219. Walker, art. cit., p. 258.

220. E. A. Burtt, *The Metaphysical Foundations of Modern Physical Science* (2nd edn, 1932), p. 182; Aristotle, *Politics*, 1264a.

221. L. Pearsall Smith, *Words and Idioms* (1925), pp. 87–9.

222. C. Hill, *Reformation to Industrial Revolution* (1967), p. 160.

of unparalleled upheaval; of 'many new, unusual emergencies, such as our forefathers have not known', as John Wilkins put it in 1649.[223] In medicine the 'new diseases' – scurvy, syphilis, rickets – generated an awareness that even human biology might have different problems at different times. 'In physic indeed,' wrote a commentator in 1670, 'we find that those things which have gone for principles for above a thousand years, none so much as questioning them, within less than thirty years are turned out of doors, very few of the ancient principles standing.'[224] In science the newly perceived infinity of worlds reinforced the belief in the possibility of infinite intellectual progress;[225] while the shift from the timelessness of Aristotelian perfect bodies to the acceptance of movement and change was the essence of the revolution in physics. In technology there was a more encouraging attitude to experiment and innovation.[226] Even in conversation the invocation of traditional wisdom had lessened. An Elizabethan M.P. could make a parliamentary speech consisting almost entirely of proverbs, traditional saws exemplifying the wisdom of his ancestors;[227] a hundred years later this type of discourse was obsolete. As a literary scholar has pointed out, 'trades and mercantile pursuits have coined almost no proverbs'.[228] In commerce past experience was increasingly irrelevant.

In this new mental climate it became increasingly difficult for educated persons to believe that the men of the past could have foreseen modern problems or that their experience could have qualified them to predict their outcome. Ancient prophecies presupposed a continuity between present and past which experience no longer supported. Their decline reflected the growth of a new historical consciousness. The change was slow and difficult, but by

223. J. Wilkins, *A Discourse concerning the Beauty of Providence* (1649), pp. 63–4. cf. Samuel Daniel's totting-up of all the social and political changes which had occurred during the sixteenth century; Levy, *Tudor Historical Thought*, p. 279.

224. L. G. Stevenson, ' "New Diseases" in the Seventeenth Century', *Bull. of the Hist. of Medicine*, xxxix (1965); G. Firmin, *The Real Christian, or a Treatise of Effectual Calling* (1670), p. 52.

225. M. Nicolson, in *Studies in Philology*, xxvi (1927), p. 370.

226. C. Wilson, *England's Apprenticeship* (1965), p. 7.

227. See the remarkable example quoted and discussed by F. P. Wilson in *Procs. Brit. Acad.*, xxvii (1941), pp. 182–3.

228. A. Taylor, *The Proverb* (Cambridge, Mass., 1931), p. 15.

the eighteenth century the point had been reached at which those who wanted a pattern in history had to look for a new formula. They could no longer rest content with a scheme which assumed the greater prescience of earlier generations.

WITCHCRAFT

14.

WITCHCRAFT IN ENGLAND:
THE CRIME AND ITS HISTORY

> The reason of a thing is not to be enquired after, till you are sure
> the thing itself be so. We commonly are at *what's the reason of
> it*? before we are sure of the thing.
>
> John Selden, *Table Talk* (1689), cxxi

1. *The meaning of witchcraft*

THE activities of the cunning men who healed their clients and
traced lost property have already been considered. It is now necessary to turn to that kind of witchcraft which contemporaries thought
harmful or anti-social. It cannot be clearly distinguished from other
sorts, since, as has been seen, many clergy taught that magic, whatever its objective, was reprehensible. At a popular level every kind
of magical activity, including any unacceptable brand of religion,

BIBLIOGRAPHICAL NOTE: Much nonsense has been written on this
subject and the general reader needs to pick his way with caution. For European witchcraft in general there is a large compilation by H. C. Lea:
Materials toward a History of Witchcraft, ed. A. C. Howland (Philadelphia,
1939) (cited as 'Lea, *Materials*'). It is weak on England, but the Preface by
G. L. Burr offers a useful survey of the problems and the literature. Spirited
use is made of this material by H. R. Trevor-Roper in his essay on *The
European Witch-Craze* (Harmondsworth, 1969). A bibliography of other
writing during the last thirty years is provided by H. C. Erik Midelfort,
'Recent Witch Hunting Research', *Papers of the Bibliographical Society of
America*, lxii (1968).
The first scholar to go beyond the printed sources to the actual records
of witchcraft prosecution in England was C. L'Estrange Ewen. In *Witch
Hunting and Witch Trials* (1929) (cited as 'Ewen, i') he calendared the indictments for witchcraft surviving from the Home Circuit, and in *Witchcraft and
Demonianism* (1933) ('Ewen, i') he incorporated the results of a further search
among contemporary pamphlet literature and the records of the other
circuits. He printed additional material in *Witchcraft in the Star Chamber*
(1938) ('Ewen, *Star Chamber*') and *Witchcraft in the Norfolk Circuit* (Paignton, 1939). Ewen's work, which has been undeservedly neglected, was of
very high scholarly quality and is the essential starting-point for any analysis
of English witch-prosecution. There is also much information collected in
Kittredge, *Witchcraft*, although the author's anxiety to show the continuity
of witch-beliefs in England sometimes leads him to blur distinctions between

might be lumped together under the blanket title of 'witchcraft', and there was no special term to indicate maleficent magicians. 'At this day', wrote Reginald Scot in 1584, 'it is indifferent to say in the English tongue, "she is a witch" or "she is a wise woman".'[1] Nevertheless, it is possible to isolate that kind of 'witchcraft' which involved the employment (or presumed employment) of some occult

---

different types of magical activity. Wallace Notestein, *A History of Witchcraft in England from 1558 to 1718* (New York, 1911: 1965 reprint) ('Notestein, *Witchcraft*') is a very able study, pre-Ewen in its chronology of witchtrials, but making excellent use of pamphlet material and providing a valuable preliminary bibliography. K. M. Briggs, *Pale Hecate's Team* (1962) is a sensible account of the literary treatment of witchcraft in the sixteenth and seventeenth centuries. *Witchcraft*, ed. B. Rosen (Stratford - upon - Avon Library, 1969), contains a useful selection of Elizabethan and Jacobean pamphlet literature.

Other writings are more controversial. R. H. Robbins, *The Encyclopedia of Witchcraft and Demonology* (1960) ('Robbins, *Encyclopedia*') is a lavishly illustrated work, designed for a popular market and containing many trivial errors of fact. Its central thesis is disputable (see below, pp. 542–3), but it rests upon a basis of genuine scholarship, contains a valuable bibliography and is a serious contribution to the subject. The much overrated work of Margaret Murray (*The Witch-Cult in Western Europe* (Oxford, 1921); *The God of the Witches* (1931; 2nd edn, 1952)) is devoted to the thesis that witches were adherents of a surviving pagan religion. The inadequacies of this argument are briefly discussed below (pp. 614–15). Miss Murray has had many imitators, of whom perhaps the most interesting is A. Runeberg, *Witches, Demons and Fertility Magic* (Helsingfors, 1947), though he adds no new English material. Some straining of the evidence can also be seen in R. T. Davies, *Four Centuries of Witch-Beliefs* (1947), where Puritanism is made responsible for the persecution of witches and the witch-controversy is seen as the main cause of the English Civil War.

Much the most interesting modern writing on witchcraft has been by social anthropologists, following the path blazed by E. E. Evans-Pritchard in his classic *Witchcraft, Oracles, and Magic among the Azande* (Oxford, 1937). An impressive recent example is M. G. Marwick, *Sorcery in its Social Setting. A Study of the Northern Rhodesian Cewa* (Manchester, 1965). References to others may be found in *Witchcraft Confessions and Accusations*, ed. M. Douglas (A.S.A. Monograph 9, 1970). L. Mair, *Witchcraft* (1969), is an up-to-date summary. Historians will need to take account of these writings if they are to make further progress in this area. They will also need to supplement the evidence collected by Ewen and Kittredge by drawing upon the large quantity of unpublished material still lying buried in the legal and ecclesiastical archives of the period. Meanwhile Alan Macfarlane's *Witchcraft in Tudor and Stuart England* (1970), based on the records for Essex, is the first published work on the subject to combine an anthropological approach with a close study of the original sources.

1. Scot, *Discoverie*, V. ix.

means of doing harm to other people in a way which was generally disapproved of. In this sense the belief in witchcraft can be defined as the attribution of misfortune to occult human agency. A witch was a person of either sex (but more often female) who could mysteriously injure other people. The damage she might do – *maleficium*, as it was technically called – could take various forms. Usually she was suspected of causing physical injury to other persons, or of bringing about their death. She might also kill or injure farm animals or interfere with nature by preventing cows from giving milk, or by frustrating such domestic operations as making butter, cheese or beer. There was a wide range of other possible hostile actions, but in England a witch's alleged activities 'usually came under one of these heads. On the Continent witches were also suspected of interfering with the weather and of frustrating sexual relations between human beings, but in England both these notions were comparatively rare.[2]

The manner in which the witch actually exercised this occult power was also believed to vary. Sometimes her evil influence was conveyed through physical contact: the witch touched her victim or gave out a potent, but invisible, emanation from her eyes. In this case he was said to have been 'fascinated' or 'overlooked'. Alternatively the witch pronounced a curse or malediction which in due course took effect. Here the victim was said to have been 'forspoken'. Rather less common was the witchcraft which involved technical aids – making a wax image of the victim and sticking pins in it, writing his name on a piece of paper and then burning it, burying a piece of his clothing, and so forth.[3] In general, contemporaries seem to have been less interested in the mechanics of the operation than in the fact of the witch's malice.

The belief in the possibility of such happenings was very old by the sixteenth century. On one level it was no more than the logical

2. Provision for marital impotence caused by sorcery was, however, proposed by the authors of the *Reformatio Legum Ecclesiasticarum*, in the reign of Edward VI (ed. E. Cardwell [Oxford, 1850], p. 43). For a few examples of such accusations, see Ewen, ii, p. 93; Kittredge, *Witchcraft*, pp. 113, 441–2; *The Journal of Sir Roger Wilbraham*, ed. H. S. Scott (in *Camden Miscellany*, x (1902), p. 111. cf. below, pp. 541, 642.

3. A comprehensive list of methods may be found in Bernard, *Guide*, pp. 176–82; J. Gaule, *Select Cases of Conscience touching Witches and Witchcrafts* (1646), pp. 128–30; Ewen, ii, pp. 76–82. But, as King James I stressed (*Cobbett's Complete Collection of State Trials*, ii [1809], col. 800), it was always possible that the Devil would invent some new technique.

520   RELIGION AND THE DECLINE OF MAGIC

corollary of the equally widespread possibility in the belief of beneficent magic. The 'good' witch who helped a client to triumph over
an opponent in law or love, or who cured him by transferring his disease to another person, might well be regarded as a 'bad' one by the
injured party. Generally speaking, the cunning folk and the maleficent witches were believed to be two separate species. But they did
sometimes overlap, and there are many examples of village wizards
and charmers who found themselves accused of maleficent witchcraft.[4]

Whether the magic was helpful or harmful, moreover, the belief in
its possibility gained a temporary boost in the sixteenth and seventeenth centuries from the same prevailing intellectual current. The
occult sympathies and vital spirits of the Neoplatonic universe could
be exploited for evil purposes, no less than for good ones. Such
doctrines could explain to the satisfaction of intellectuals why dire
consequences might follow after tampering with the wax image of
a person or with a piece of his clothing. One could harm a man by
manipulating his hair, his fingernail parings, his sweat or his excrement, all of which contained his vital spirits. An excessive belief in
the power of the imagination similarly made it plausible to think
that the object of a witch's imprecations would soon afterwards be
taken ill; and the supposed reality of vital spirits and invisible
emanations justified the idea that certain men could involuntarily
destroy their own cattle, simply by looking at them; a child in his
cradle might also succumb to such 'fascination'. Even Aristotle
taught that the glance of a menstruating woman would tarnish a
mirror.[5] Such theories also magnified the potential efficacy of secret
herbal or chemical preparations; as in any primitive society, poison
still retained magical associations.[6]

4. See below, p. 677.
5. Aquinas, *Summa Contra Gentiles*, iii, 103 (cf. Bacon, *Works*, ii, p. 648);
(C. Irvine), *Medicina Magnetica* (1656); S. Boulton, *Medicina Magica* (1656);
Aubrey, *Gentilisme*, p. 80; id., *Miscellanies*, pp. 172–3; G. F. Still, *The History of Paediatrics* (1931), p. 259. The possibility of ocular fascination was
upheld in an Oxford disputation in 1600; *Register of the University of Oxford*, ii(1), ed· A. Clark (Oxford Hist. Soc., 1887), p. 174.
6. See, e.g., M. Aston, 'A Kent Approver of 1440', *Bull. Inst. Hist. Research*, xxxvi (1963); *C.S.P.D.*, *1595–7*, p. 568; *1598–1601*, p. 400; Peterborough D.R., Correction Book 68 (1636–8), f. 72 (woman accused of witchcraft by poisoning). Joseph Blagrave defined sorcery as the use of poison,
in contra-distinction to witchcraft, which was image-magic; *Blagraves Astrological Practice of Physick* (1671), p. 135. cf. J. Beattie, *Bunyoro. An African
Kingdom* (New York, 1960), p. 73.

But although Renaissance speculations reinforced the belief of intellectuals in the potentialities of maleficent magic, witch-beliefs of this kind were as old as human history, and in no sense peculiarly English, or even European. It was only in the late Middle Ages that a new element was added to the European concept of witchcraft which was to distinguish it from the witch-beliefs of other primitive peoples. This was the notion that the witch owed her powers to having made a deliberate pact with the Devil. In return for her promise of allegiance, she was thought to have been given the means of wreaking supernatural vengeance upon her enemies. Seen from this new point of view, the essence of witchcraft was not the damage it did to other persons, but its heretical character – devil-worship. Witchcraft had become a Christian heresy, the greatest of all sins, because it involved the renunciation of God and deliberate adherence to his greatest enemy. *Maleficium* was a purely secondary activity, a by-product of this false religion. Whether or not the witch injured other people, she deserved to die for her disloyalty to God. Around this conception was built up the notion of ritual devil-worship, involving the sabbath or nocturnal meeting at which the witches gathered to worship their master and to copulate with him.

The main agency responsible for the introduction of this new concept was the Roman Catholic Church, whose intellectuals rapidly built up a large literature of demonology, outlining the manner in which the witches or devil-worshippers were thought to conduct themselves, and laying down the procedure for their prosecution. The new doctrine was developed in a series of edicts culminating in the Papal Bull, *Summis desiderantes affectibus,* of Innocent VIII in 1484, and the compendious treatise by two Dominican Inquisitors, the *Malleus Maleficarum* (1486). Meanwhile the systematic persecution of witches as devil-worshippers, rather than for their acts of malevolence, had been steadily proceeding on the Continent since the early fourteenth century. The origins of this new notion of witchcraft have never been fully uncovered, although they are usually thought to lie in the Church's reaction to the Manichaean (and by implication devil-worshipping) tendencies of the heretical Cathars and their successors.[7]

7. For the emergence of the new attitude, see Lea, *Materials,* and J. Hansen, *Quellen und Untersuchungen zur Geschichte des Hexenwahns und der Hexenverfolgung im Mittelalter* (Bonn, 1901). Much of the relevant literature is discussed by C. E. Hopkin, *The Share of Thomas Aquinas in the Growth of the Witchraft Delusion* (Philadelphia, 1940), and well summarized

The stages by which this new doctrine reached England are extremely difficult to chart, and are not yet clearly established. In itself, the idea of a compact with the Devil was as old as Christianity. Pagans had been regarded as devil-worshippers, and the legend of Theophilus, the monk who transferred his allegiance to Satan, was familiar to the late Anglo-Saxons.[8] It was a commonplace of medieval theology to assert that any magical activity, however beneficent in intention, necessarily involved a tacit compact with the Devil, and should therefore be punished. The church courts often treated crystal-gazing and similar activities as a kind of heresy.[9] But there was a great deal of difference between this idea of a *tacit* compact implicit in an individual's magical dabblings and the myth of *explicit* covenants with Satan made by bands of self-conscious devil-worshippers. It is true that there were plenty of medieval stories about men who made sacrifices to the Devil and of women who succumbed to the embraces of a demon lover. Tales also circulated about mysterious nocturnal revels. In 1303 the moralist Robert of Brunne issued warnings against offering sacrifices to the Devil by witchcraft, while in the early fifteenth century *Dives and Pauper* could assert that witches and other magicians sought out the fiend to 'make him their god'.[10] The demonological treatises by continental writers were only an extension of ideas latent in early medieval Christian theology, and there was, in principle, no reason why England should have offered less fertile soil for their reception than anywhere else in the Christian world. Nevertheless, medieval England does seem to have been largely isolated from the intellectual and judicial trends which encouraged witch persecution on the Continent. For this the substantial independence of the English Church seems to have been largely responsible. England had no Inquisition and no Roman Law; and Papal authority in England was much

by G. L. Burr, 'The Literature of Witchcraft', *Papers of the American Hist. Assoc.,* iv (1890).

8. P. M. Palmer and R. P. More, *The Sources of the Faust Tradition* (New York, 1936), pp. 58–77, for the story. cf. J. T. McNeill and H. M. Gamer, *Medieval Handbooks of Penance* (New York, 1938), pp. 198, 227, 246; Kittredge, *Witchcraft,* p. 239; J. Crawford, 'Evidences for Witchcraft in Anglo-Saxon England', *Medium Aevum,* xxxii (1963).

9. See above, chap. 9, and below, p. 549.

10. Kittredge, *Witchcraft,* p. 51; *Dives and Pauper* (1536), f. 50. cf. C. G. Loomis, *White Magic* (Cambridge, Mass., 1948), pp. 74–5, 77; J. S. P. Tatlock, *The Legendary History of Britain* (Berkeley, 1950), p. 172; Lea, *Materials,* pp. 170–71; Powicke and Cheney, *Councils and Synods,* p. 1062.

reduced. The Bull of 1484 related only to Germany, while the *Malleus Maleficarum* was slow to impinge upon England. It found its way into the libraries of the learned, for English intellectuals were used to buying and reading the publications of foreign presses; but the total absence of an English edition is striking by the side of the thirteen editions on the Continent by 1520. There was no English translation of the *Malleus* until modern times; by contrast it was issued sixteen times in Germany before 1700 and eleven times in France.[11]

Paradoxically, it was left to the strongly Protestant writers of the later Elizabethan period to convey to English readers the contents of this great monument of medieval Catholicism and its numerous imitators and successors. When, in 1584, Reginald Scot refuted the possibility of a diabolical compact in his *Discoverie of Witchcraft*, his adversaries were still all continental writers, though some of them had begun to appear in English translation. But in the following decades continental concepts of witchcraft were widely disseminated, mostly by clergymen, in a series of treatises by such authors as Henry Holland (1590), King James VI (1597), William Perkins (1608), Alexander Roberts (1616), Thomas Cooper (1619) and Richard Bernard (1627).[12] Perkins admirably illustrated the change in intellectual opinion when he said that, as far as he could see, there was no difference whatsoever between the practices of English witches and those of France, Spain, Italy or Germany. In his view the covenant with Satan was the essence of witchcraft, and he urged the execution of all witches without exception, not because of any acts of damage they might have committed but because 'they depend on him as their god'.[13] Sir Edward Coke similarly defined a witch as 'a person that hath conference with the Devil to

---

11. For editions of the *Malleus*, see Lea, *Materials*, p. 306. Two copies were sold at Oxford around 1520; 'Day Book of John Dorne, Bookseller in Oxford, A.D. 1520', ed. F. Madan, in *Collectanea*, i, ed. C. R. L. Fletcher (Oxford Hist. Soc., 1885), p. 132; ibid., ii, ed. M. Burrows (1890), p. 459. Another is known to have been owned by a monk at Durham (*Medieval Libraries of Great Britain*, ed. N. R. Ker (2nd edn, 1964), pp. 72, 256). In the Elizabethan period evidence of ownership becomes more common.

12. (H. Holland), *A Treatise against Witchcraft* (Cambridge, 1590); (James VI), *Daemonologie* (Edinburgh, 1597); Perkins, *Discourse*; Cooper, *Mystery*; Bernard, *Guide*.

13. Perkins, *Discourse*, pp. 192, 170, 257.

consult with him or to do some act'.[14] In Thomas Wilson's *Complete Christian Dictionary* (1612), a 'witch' was said to be 'one that exerciseth devilish and wicked arts, such as be named in *Deut.* 18.10, *Ex.* 22.18'. But in the supplement to the sixth edition (1655) the definition was revised, to become 'anyone that hath any dealings with the Devil by any compact or confederacy whatsoever'. This wording derived from the semi-official commentary on the Scriptures put out by divines from the Westminster Assembly, at the end of the Civil War. In it they explained, 'Some have thought witches should not die unless they had taken away the life of mankind, but they are mistaken ... Though no hurt ensue in this contract at all, the witch deserves present and certain death for the contract itself.' In 1651 Thomas Hobbes said of witches that their trade was 'nearer to a new religion than to a craft or science'.[15]

Many English intellectuals and theologians were thus converted more or less totally to the continental conception of witchcraft. An even wider public was acquainted with the occasional translations of continental demonologists[16] and the frequent published accounts of European witch-trials.[17] These writings undoubtedly influenced English ideas on witchcraft; indeed on several occasions they directly affected the outcome of particular allegations. Robert Boyle confessed that his sceptical inclinations were much checked after he had talked to Perreaud, the Protestant pastor of Macon, author of a tract on *The Devill of Mascon*, while Sir Thomas Browne's citation of a parallel case in Denmark turned the scale against the accused

14. *Institutes*, iii, cap. 6. For similar definitions, see G. Gifford, *A Discourse of the Subtill Practises of Devilles* (1587), sig. Bii; Ewen, i, p. 23 (William West, 1594); A. Willet, *Hexapla in Exodum* (1608), p. 504; T. Tuke, *A Treatise against Painting and Tincturing* (1616), pp. 53–4.

15. *Annotations upon all the Books of the Old and New Testament* (1645), *Ex.* xxii. 18; T. Hobbes, *Leviathan* (1651), chap. 2.

16. L. Daneau, *A Dialogue of Witches*, trans. T. Twyne (1575); L. Lavater, *Of Ghostes and Spirites*, trans. R.H. (1572); S. Michaelis, *A Discourse of Spirits*, attached to his *The Admirable Historie of the Possession and Conversion of a Penitent Woman*, trans. W.B. (1613).

17. *A True Discourse declaring the Damnable Life and Death of one Stubbe Peeter* (1590?); *Newes from Scotland* (1591); *The Historie of ... Doctor Iohn Faustus* (1592) (in Palmer and More, *Sources of the Faust Tradition*, pp. 134–326); *A Strange Report of Sixe Most Notorious Witches* (1601); *The Life and Death of Lewis Gaufredy* (1612); *A Relation of the Devill Balams Departure out of the Body of the Mother-Prioresse of the Ursuline Nuns of Loudun* (1636); *A Certaine Relation of the Hog-Faced Gentlewoman called Mistris Tannakin Skinker* (1640).

in the trial of Rose Cullender and Amy Dury at Bury St Edmunds in 1665.[18]

Yet the influence of these new ideas upon the people at large was only partial. Even on the Continent, the idea of witchcraft as devil-worship, rather than *maleficium*, was slow to triumph. The Papal Bull of 1484 did not mention the sabbath, but stressed the damage which witches could do; in many parts of Germany evidence of *maleficium* was needed to secure a witch's condemnation until the later sixteenth century.[19] In England, where most demonological treatises remained locked up in Latin or some other alien language, witchcraft for most men was still an activity – doing harm to others by supernatural means – not a belief or a heresy. This can be seen in the wording of the Acts of Parliament which first made witchcraft a statutory offence. There were three of these Acts – 1542 (repealed 1547), 1563 (repealed 1604), and 1604 (repealed in 1736).[20] What is striking is that no reference to a diabolical compact was made in either of the first two. In 1542 it was made a felony (and therefore a capital offence) to conjure spirits or to practise witchcraft, enchantment or sorcery, in order to find treasure; to waste or destroy a person's body, limbs, or goods; to provoke to unlawful love; to declare what had happened to stolen goods; or 'for any other unlawful intent or purpose'. Despite some ambiguity of wording (was conjuring an offence in itself or only if performed for an unlawful purpose?), this Act clearly treated the crime of witchcraft as consisting in positive acts of hostility to the community, rather than in relations with the Devil as such. The only possible exception to this

18. Preface to *The Devil of Mascon*, trans. P. du Moulin (2nd edn, Oxford, 1658); Ewen, ii, p. 350. For other instances of reliance upon continental witch-cases see J. Darrell, *A Survey of Certaine Dialogical Discourses* (1602), pp. 54–5; *The Wonderful Discoverie of the Witchcrafts of Margaret and Phillip Flower* (1619), sig. B4ᵛ; F. Moryson, *An Itinerary* (Glasgow, 1907–8), iv, p. 297; J. Hart, *The Diet of the Diseased* (1633), pp. 351–2; B.M., Add. MS 27,402 f. 70, ff. (Thomas Killigrew to Ld Goring [1635], on possession cases in France); H. More, *An Antidote against Atheisme* (1653), iii, *passim*; *The Most True and Wonderful Narration of two women bewitched in Yorkshire* (1658), pp. 5–13; J. Glanvill, *Saducismus Triumphatus* (1681), ii, appx.

19. Lea, *Materials*, p. 305; *George Lincoln Burr. Selections from his Writings*, ed. L. O. Gibbons (Ithaca, New York, 1943), p. 364.

20. Hen. viii, cap. 8 (repealed by 1 Edw. vi, cap. 12); 5 Eliz., cap. 16 (cf. *Commons Journals*, i, p. 59); 1 Jac. 1, c. 12 (repealed by 9 Geo. ii, cap. 5). For 23 Eliz. c. 2, making it a felony to use witchcraft to calculate the Queen's expectation of life, see above, p. 408.

rule was the ban on magic to find lost goods, and for that the explanation may well be that the makers of the Act regarded the practice as fraudulent.

The second witchcraft statute, passed in 1563 after the failure of an earlier bill in 1559, also laid its emphasis upon the maleficent nature of the witch's activities. It was more severe than its predecessor, in that it made it a felony to invoke *evil* spirits for any purpose whatsoever, whether *maleficium* was involved or not. But it was also more lenient, in that witchcraft, enchantment, charming and sorcery were deemed capital felonies only if they actually resulted in the death of a human victim. Should the attempt prove unsuccessful, or if the victim was only maimed, or if only animals were killed, the witch was to incur the milder penalty of a year's imprisonment, with quarterly appearances in the pillory. After a second offence, however, the action became a felony. A reduced penalty was also prescribed for magic designed to find treasure and lost goods, or to provoke to unlawful love; on the second offence, this did not become felony, but was punished by life imprisonment and forfeiture of goods. Here again, therefore, the gravity of the offence depended upon the degree of the injury suffered by the witch's victims, not on any postulated covenant (save in the case of deliberate invocation of *evil* spirits). This leniency contrasted sharply with the attitude of those theologians who would have liked to see all magicians, black or white, consigned to speedy execution.

Only in the third and final witchcraft statute of 1604 did the full continental doctrine take effect. Like its Elizabethan predecessor, it asserted the felonious nature of invocation of evil spirits, and of the witchcraft which resulted in anyone's death. It furthermore declared it to be felony if the victim was only injured; and it replaced life imprisonment by death as the penalty for a second offence in the case of lesser kinds of magic, involving treasure, lost goods, unlawful love, destroying cattle or goods, and attempting unsuccessfully to kill a person. The real novelty, however, came in those sections of the Act which, for the first time in English history, made it a felony to take up a dead body in whole or part for magical purposes, and, even more striking, to 'consult, covenant with, entertain, employ, feed, or reward any evil and wicked spirit to or for any intent or purpose'. In this latter clause the influence of the continental doctrine of the diabolical compact was unambiguous, though, by specifically banning *evil* spirits, the Act still left a loophole for those magicians who believed that the spirits with which they dealt were good ones.

Moreover, the clauses imposing a lighter penalty for less harmful types of magic made it clear that even the legislators of 1604 did not subscribe to the continental notion that a diabolical compact was implicit in every act of witchcraft. Otherwise it would have been pointless for them to draw distinctions between degrees of magic, since all would have been equally reprehensible. As it was, the Act implied that it might be possible, say, to destroy a neighbour's cattle by magical means without necessarily having made any diabolical covenant. This was a position which no educated theologian would have accepted.[21]

The 1604 statute remained law until 1736, when witchcraft ceased to be a statutory offence. It never satisfied the zealots, who would like to have imposed the death penalty for any type of magical activity whatsoever. But it represented the furthest point to which the English law on witchcraft was adapted to fit continental doctrines. For it meant that evidence of relationship with evil spirits or animal familiars was technically sufficient to secure the judicial condemnation of an accused person, regardless of whether or not he or she had harmed anyone.[22] Even so, the evidence of the statute-book, taken as a whole, suggests that in England witchcraft was prosecuted primarily as an anti-social crime, rather than as a heresy.

This impression is confirmed by the records of the trials. In practice, most prosecutions were provoked by alleged acts of damage against other persons and seldom drew on allegations of devil-worship. The relatively few cases of secular prosecution for harmful magic which have survived from the Middle Ages usually sprang directly from acts of malevolence which the witches were thought to have planned or executed. For the most part they were cases of sorcery arising out of political intrigue, in which the accused persons were said to have practised witchcraft to murder their political

21. cf. Bernard, *Guide*, pp. 216–17.
22. It should be added that condemned witches were not burned, but hanged, save for those women convicted of petty treason (i.e. of killing their husbands or masters). But this distinction was not always appreciated by contemporaries any more than it has been by posterity. cf. *Book of Examinations and Depositions, 1570–94*, ed. G. H. Hamilton and E. R. Aubrey (Southampton Rec. Soc., 1914), pp. 158–9; (E. Topsell), *Times Lamentation* (1599), p. 80.

rivals or to gain the favour of the powerful. Suits were also brought in the ecclesiastical courts against humbler folk for using magic to kill or injure others, or to hinder their daily activities. Such practices were certainly thought to have diabolical overtones, and an accused person might well defend himself by protesting his Christian orthodoxy. But charges of deliberate devil-worship are very rare; indeed the only three such allegations which survive, all from the early fourteenth century, were special cases.[23] In the fourteenth and fifteenth centuries various persons were said to have transferred their allegiance to the Devil, but these allegations of heresy were not thought by contemporaries to have anything to do with witchcraft.[24] Conversely, a charge of magic in the church courts hardly ever involved the corollary accusation of devil-worship.[25] In so far as witchcraft was prosecuted in later medieval England it was because it was thought to involve harm to others, not because it was seen as a Christian heresy.

This situation was not changed by the sixteenth-century statutes, for the run-of-the-mill Elizabethan prosecution for witchcraft was still concerned with *maleficium*, not with evil spirits. The idea that witches might renounce God and depend upon the Devil was present from the start, but Elizabethan witches were not usually said to be in direct touch with Satan. No reference in a trial to an oral compact with the Devil is recorded before 1612; and not until the investigations of Matthew Hopkins, the professional witch-finder who was active in the late 1640s, was there sworn evidence testifying to a written covenant. Our knowledge of the evidence presented against the witches depends upon the irregular survival of depositions, either at first-hand or in contemporary pamphlet accounts. This means that we know virtually nothing of what was said at most of the trials. But the evidence which has survived suggests that not until the seventeenth century did the diabolical compact figure very

23. The trial of Dame Alice Kytler in 1324 for ritual witchcraft was in Ireland, not England, and conducted by a French-trained Franciscan. Charges of devil-worship brought against Walter Langton, Bishop of Coventry, in 1301 were not sustained by a Papal commission, while the prosecution of the Templars on similar charges, though organized on a European scale, came unstuck in England; Kittredge, *Witchcraft*, pp. 123, 241–2, 403.

24. e.g., Kittredge, *Witchcraft*, p. 242; C. Jenkins in *Tudor Studies*, ed. R. W. Seton-Watson (1924), p. 71 (a Suffolk man reported dead in 1499 after asserting *quod promisit diabolo talia promissa quod nunquam ero salvatus*).

25. For a possible exception, see Hale, *Precedents*, pp. 36–7 (1493).

WITCHCRAFT: THE CRIME AND ITS HISTORY

prominently in the witch-trials, and even then it was far from being
an indispensable feature.[26]

Even more foreign to the general run of English accusations was
the notion of the witches' sabbath – the nocturnal meeting at which
the Devil was ritually worshipped in a blasphemous manner. There
were a very few scattered allegations in the trials about witches
having met together, but most of these occasions seem to have been
literally picnics by comparison with their continental counterparts.
Nothing approaching a sabbath is to be found in the trial records
before 1612, and the subsequent references to such gatherings are
sporadic and inconclusive.[27] The sexual assaults by incubus and
succubus, so pronounced a theme of the *Malleus* and continental
witch-beliefs, are also much less commonly encountered in England.[28] The notion that witches could fly or change themselves into
animals was even more seldom advanced,[29] and the broomstick,
made famous by subsequent children's fiction, occurs only once in
an English witch-trial.[30]

26. Kittredge, *Witchcraft*, chap. 16; Ewen, ii, pp. 50 ff., 62, 216.
27. Kittredge, *Witchcraft*, chap. 16; Ewen, ii, pp. 57–8, and index, s.v.
'assemblies' (to which p. 317 should be added). To these instances may be
added the meeting alleged in 1667 of three witches on Dunstable Downs to
arrange the bewitching of a child (Bedfordshire R.O., H.S.A., W 1667/51[1]).
The Somerset man accused in 1514 of going annually to 'Mendepe' on the
eve of St John Baptist's day *'ad consulendum demones'* was presumably
engaging in a well-known form of divination (see above, p. 286), but the
Church's implied interpretation of the episode is interesting; A. Watkin,
Dean Cosyn, and Wells Cathedral Miscellanea (Somerset Rec. Soc., 1941),
p. 157.
28. Allegations of carnal union with the Devil are almost exclusively confined to the cases initiated by Matthew Hopkins (Ewen, ii, p. 52). But a few
other sexual cases may be found in Ewen, ii, p. 248; A. C. Carter, *The English
Reformed Church in Amsterdam in the Seventeenth Century* (Amsterdam,
1964), p. 185.
29. For a few cases of alleged flying see Ewen, ii, pp. 83–4, 91–2, and
index, s.v. 'transportation' (to which p. 456 should be added); 'Vic', *Odd
Ways in Olden Days down West* (Birmingham, 1892), p. xii; More, *An Antidote against Atheisme*, p. 129; C. E. Parsons in *Procs. Cambs. Antiqn Soc.*,
xix (1915), p. 36. For metamorphosis into animals: Ewen, ii, p. 86; W. Y.
Tindall, *John Bunyan, Mechanick Preacher* (New York, 1964 reprint), p. 218;
E. Fairfax, *Daemonologia*, ed. W. Grainge (Harrogate, 1882), p. 95; *The
Diary of Abraham de la Pryme*, ed. C. Jackson (Surtees Soc., 1870), pp. 22–3.
Dives and Pauper thought it worth condemning the belief in the possibility
of such a transformation (f. 51).
30. Ewen, ii, p. 337 (1663), though the idea was known from continental
sources, and is occasionally mentioned in contemporary literature, e.g.,

The one common feature of English witch-trials which does indicate some sort of association in the popular mind between maleficent magic and the Devil was the notion that the witch bore on her body the mark of her profession in the form of a spot or excrescence, which could be discovered by searching her for an 'unnatural' mark, usually recognisable because it would not bleed when pricked and was insensible to pain. As early as 1579 this was stated to be 'a common token to know all witches by'. Thereafter it was a relatively common procedure to search the suspect's body for any likely-looking protuberance, which would then be pricked to see whether it hurt.[31] An associated belief was the peculiarly English notion that the witch was likely to possess a familiar imp or devil, who would take the shape of an animal, usually a cat or a dog, but possibly a toad, a rat, or even a wasp or butterfly. This familiar, who performed useful magical services for his mistress, was supposed to have been given by the Devil himself, or purchased or inherited from another witch. The witch's mark was sometimes thought of as a teat from which the familiar could suck the witch's blood as a form of nourishment. It thus became a common procedure in witch-detection to isolate the suspect and wait for some animal or insect to appear as proof of her guilt.

The lore surrounding witch's marks and familiars was considerable, even before it was reinforced by the reference in the Act of 1604 to entertaining and feeding evil spirits. The employment of vampirish familiars for magic purposes had been encountered in medieval legend, while the conjuration of spirits was a stock magical activity. Familiars gained a recognized place in witch-accusations at an early stage. They made their appearance in Essex trials in 1566, 1579 and 1582; indeed a striking instance of the clear association in the popular mind between witchcraft and the presence of a toad in the suspect's house occurred in an ecclesiastical case in Somerset as early as 1530.[32]

Gaule, *Select Cases of Conscience*, p. 111, M. Hopkins, *The Discovery of Witches* (1647), ed. M. Summers (1928), p. 58, and the third Earl of Shaftes-bury's *Sensus Communis* (1709), iv. iii.

31. J. S. Davies, *A History of Southampton* (Southampton, 1883), p. 236; Ewen, ii, index, *s.v.* 'marks'.

32. Ewen, ii, index, *s.v.* 'familiar'; Kittredge, *Witchcraft*, chap. 10. The 1530 case is in Wells D.R., D.1. Medieval instances of traffic in spirits in animal form for magical purposes may be found in Ewen, ii, pp. 33–4, and Kittredge, *Witchcraft*, chap. 10, cf. above, p. 275.

Nevertheless, familiars and devils were very far from being an indispensable feature of English witch-trials, even in the seventeenth century. Neither were they a necessary element in the numerous informal accusations of witchcraft of which we have record because they led, not to a witch-trial, but to a suit for defamation brought, in an ecclesiastical or common law court, by the aggrieved person against whom the charge of witchcraft had been flung. In the formal witch-trials conducted by judges and lawyers, who were educated men, familiar with continental doctrines, it was possible for the theological notion of witchcraft as a devil-worshipping heresy to overlie the simpler popular belief from which the case had originally sprung. The defamation cases by contrast were more spontaneous and less easily manipulated by the lawyers. They provide overwhelming confirmation for the view that for most contemporaries the essence of witchcraft was not its affiliation with the Devil, but its power to inflict damage by occult means, acquired or inherited, upon lives, bodies and property. The numerous suits surviving in diocesan archives, as well as in the records of the civil courts, make frequent reference to such occurrences as fascination by the eyes, image magic, and maledictions followed by evil results. But they hardly ever involve allegations of relations with the Devil, and only very seldom do they refer to witch's marks or familiar spirits. These cases are the best evidence at a popular level, both for the prevalence of witch-beliefs, and for their essentially traditional nature.[33]

The same impression is yielded by the overwhelming majority of the formal trials on the assize circuits. Of the more than 200 persons who are known to have been convicted under the witchcraft statutes on the Home Circuit (Essex, Hertfordshire, Kent,

33. Most of these cases are still unpublished, though a few are discussed in Ewen, i, appx. iii. So far I have encountered only 11 allegations which hint at a concept of witchcraft as anything more than maleficent magic. They are to be found in J. S. Purvis, *Tudor Parish Documents* (Cambridge, 1948), p. 200 (incubus, 1595–6); Ely D.R., B2/14, f. 94ᵛ (devil in a shop, 1597); Ewen, *Star Chamber*, p. 48 (imps and evil spirits, 1615); Carter, *The English Reformed Church in Amsterdam*, p. 185 (devil); *The Reports of . . . Sir Henry Hobart* (4th edn, 1678), p. 129 (devil appears as black man); *H.M.C., Various Collections*, i, p. 122 (evil spirits, 1650); *Quarter Sessions Records*, iii (Somerset Rec. Soc., 1912), p. 362 (conjuring books, 1658); *Hereford City Records*, iv, p. 1683 (animal metamorphosis, 1666); Borthwick, R.VII.H. 4995 (devil's mark, 1682); Bodl., Oxford Archdeaconry Papers, Berks, c. 170, ff. 364, ff. (familiars, 1715). Against this meagre haul should be set over 70 cases in which the type of witchcraft alleged is the power to do *maleficium,* and a further 47 in which it is unspecified.

Surrey and Sussex) between 1558 and 1736, there were, if we except the prosecutions initiated in 1645 by Matthew Hopkins, only seven (or possibly eight) who were not found guilty of having inflicted acts of damage upon their neighbours or their goods. Of these, one was said to have defrauded the Queen's subjects, by claiming that he could find buried treasure by conjuration, while three others were accused of keeping evil spirits with the intention of causing damage to their neighbours. In 1645, under Hopkins's influence, there were sixteen persons convicted for entertaining evil spirits, but seven of them were also accused of killing other people or their animals.[34] Of the 492 indictments for maleficent witchcraft at Essex Assizes only twenty-eight were for invoking or entertaining evil spirits; of these, eighteen were made under the influence of Hopkins and fourteen were combined with accusations of *maleficium*.[35] Indeed, the Hopkins episode apart, there are only twenty-two extant Home Circuit indictments for relations with spirits during the whole period. For other circuits the records are too incomplete to be employed for statistical purposes, but convictions for devil-worship unassociated with *maleficium* appear to have been proportionately as rare.

It seems, therefore, that although the Acts of 1542 and 1563 imposed the death penalty for certain kinds of conjuration, and that of 1604 did so for making a diabolical pact, or for entertaining and feeding evil spirits, it was relatively unusual for such charges to be made, or for them to produce a capital conviction, unless accompanied by positive evidence of *maleficium*. Under the Elizabethan statute, said a commentator, persons were executed 'rather as murderers than as witches', and even after the Jacobean Act, contemporary judges, as Sir Robert Filmer remarked, were unlikely to condemn, unless murder was involved.[36] The only notable exception to this practice was during Hopkins's campaign. Between 1645

34. Ewen, i, *passim*. The actual total of convictions is 205, but an uncertain number (between four and six) of these relate to persons with previous convictions. The seven cases not involving *maleficium* are indictments no. 66 and 88* (which may both relate to the same person), 417, 511*, 524, 594, 727*, 728*; (those marked with an asterisk resulted in the execution of the accused). The Hopkins trials not involving *maleficium* are nos. 628–30, 639–40, 645–8.

35. A. D. J. Macfarlane, *Witchcraft Prosecutions in Essex, 1560–1680: a Sociological Analysis* (Oxford D.Phil. thesis, 1967), p. 44.

36. E. Fairfax, *A Discourse of Witchcraft* (in *Miscellanies of the Philobiblon Soc.*, v) (1858–9), pp. 26–7; (Sir R. Filmer), *An Advertisement to the Jury-Men of England* (1653), p. 2. For three Elizabethan cases of execution

and 1647 some 200 persons may have been convicted in the eastern counties under his influence, many of them for alleged compact. But even during these highly exceptional years, evidence of *maleficium* was frequently invoked, in all probability much more frequently than the mere indictments suggest.[37]

The narrow theological definition of witchcraft, as the power arising from a contract with the Devil, thus never triumphed completely in England, even during the later sixteenth and early seventeenth centuries, when the continental concept was disseminated in many vernacular treatises and reports of leading trials, published with the deliberate intention of stimulating more prosecutions. Continental doctrines however, affected the conduct of many trials and coloured many extracted 'confessions'. This was only to be expected in view of the recommendations in Richard Bernard's *Guide to Grand-jurymen* that a godly divine, 'somewhat well read in the discoveries of witchcraft and impieties thereof', should be assigned 'to be instructing the suspected', so that she might be 'haply prepared for confession'. When an allegation of *maleficium* reached the courts it could easily turn into one of devil-worship, if it fell into the hands of interested lawyers or clergy. Moreover, on technical grounds it was easier to make a convincing case for the prosecution if one could produce a clear confession of compact. *Maleficium* was always harder to prove.[38]

Yet despite the increasing bias of the courts in favour of treating cases along continental lines, the popular concept of witchcraft was never successfully restricted to the notion of devil-worship, and it was not the fear of heresy which animated accusations at the village level. For most men 'witchcraft' remained essentially the power to do harm to others. When in 1588 a group of Essex Puritan ministers discussed the question of witchcraft, they agreed 'that there must be some unusual experience of evil effects to ensue of their displeasure, and some presumption of the death of man or beast'. As a later writer observed, 'In common account none are reputed to

for witchcraft without *maleficium* (one of them against the intention of the court, which failed to realize in advance that invocation was a capital offence), see Ewen, ii, pp. 428, 165–6, 186–7. For some other condemnations, followed by reprieve, see ibid., p. 428; Scot, *Discoverie*, XV.xlii; *Cal. Patent Rolls, Elizabeth*, iv, p. 169; Notestein, *Witchcraft*, p. 383.

37. Ewen, ii, pp. 254–314. cf. Macfarlane, *Witchcraft Prosecutions*, chap. 11.

38. Bernard, *Guide*, pp. 237–8. On the difficulties of getting proof, see below, pp. 686–8.

be witches, but only such who are thought to have both will and skill to hurt man and beast."[39] Such a definition excluded the white witches or cunning men, who attempted to heal the sick or find lost goods; it also omitted those who conjured spirits in an attempt to gain wealth or knowledge. To theologians, such practitioners were all guilty of diabolical compact, but to this consideration the populace at large seems to have been indifferent. In England, as on the Continent, the blurring together of black and white witchcraft was fundamentally alien to popular beliefs. For, as the Essex minister George Gifford stressed in 1587, the people's hatred of witches was not a form of religious intolerance; it sprang from fear of their hostile acts towards their neighbours, not from outrage at their supposed association with the Devil.[40]

2. *The chronology of witch-beliefs*

Sixteenth- and seventeenth-century England thus knew not one concept of witchcraft but two. On top of the popular belief in the power of maleficent magic was imposed the theological notion that the essence of witchcraft was adherence to the Devil. These two ideas were to be found side by side, sometimes apart, sometimes intermingled. But it was the fear of *maleficium* which underlay most of the accusations and trials. How extensive was the belief in the possibility of such occult malevolence? This question is impossible to answer for there is no satisfactory method of quantifying past beliefs. It is not enough to calculate the total number of witch-trials, because many informal allegations failed to produce a formal prosecution and have therefore left no record. The case-books of contemporary doctors reveal how common it could be for patients to convince themselves that they had been bewitched. There are over 120 cases of suspected witchcraft in Richard Napier's case-books (1600–34) and over 50 in those of William Lilly (1644–66).[41] So as far as is known, none of these led to a judicial hearing, and it is only the chance survival of the case-books which enables us to know about them at all. We can only speculate as to why one case was taken up in the courts while another remained a matter of village gossip. No

39. *The Presbyterian Movement in the Reign of Queen Elizabeth*, ed. R. G. Usher (Camden Ser., 1905), p. 70; E. Poeton, 'The Winnowing of White Witchcraft' (Sloane 1954), f. 163.

40. Gifford, *A Discourse of the Subtill Practises of Devilles*, sig. H4ᵛ. cf. R. Mandrou, *Magistrats et sorciers en France au XVIIᵉ siècle* (Paris, 1968), p. 109.   41. Ashm. 1970, f. 109; below, pp. 756–7.

doubt the attitude of the local gentry, clergy and village officials was important. But there is no way of determining the ratio of formal prosecutions to informal allegations. Legal proceedings for witchcraft, in other words, represent the tip of an iceberg of unascertainable dimensions. Even the tip itself is largely concealed from our view, for the survival of legal records has been so patchy as to provide an uncertain basis for generalization. Firm statistics for the extent of witchcraft prosecution are out of the question, and the historian has to content himself with a reasonable guess.

As we have seen, the statutes against witchcraft were in operation between 1542 and 1547, and again between 1563 and 1736. Virtually nothing is known about prosecutions during the first of these periods.[42] For the second, and much longer, phase, it is possible to make a tentative estimate on the basis of the assize and quarter session records which have survived. An analysis of the trials on the Home Assize Circuit, for which seventy-seven per cent of the relevant documents are extant, discloses that between 1559 and 1736 there were 513 persons accused under the witchcraft statutes, of whom just over 200 were convicted and 109 hanged.[43] There were five other assize circuits in the country as well as a large number of independent jurisdictions, so these figures must be multiplied considerably if total figures for the whole country are to be inferred. C. L'Estrange Ewen, to whose pioneering investigations all students are permanently indebted, guessed the total number of executions for witchcraft throughout the period to be something under 1,000.[44] It is difficult to suggest an alternative figure. Other cases can be added to those discovered by Ewen, but, even so, his

42. Ewen found only two prosecutions (i, p. 11, n. 2; ii, p. 408). Virtually no assize records are extant for this period.

43. Ewen, i, *passim*. (Ewen's total of 112 executions (p. 99) is inconsistent with his summary on pp. 102–8.) Account should also be taken of the 13 further accusations known from other sources; ibid., appendix iv, and Ewen, ii, pp. 429–30.

44. Ewen, i, p. 112. The additional evidence which Ewen collected in Ewen, ii, and in his other writings did not lead him to revise his original estimate. Ewen's transcriptions and calculations were not infallible, as Dr Macfarlane has shown in the case of Essex (where the number of known executions was not 82 but 74 and where a total of 36 other persons died in gaol). More important, he gave only cursory attention to some sources and omitted others (notably the records of the King's Bench; the Ely Gaol Delivery Rolls in the C.U.L. [from which extracts concerning witchcraft have been printed by C. E. Parsons in the *Procs. of the Cambs. Antiqn Soc.*, xix (1915) and by E. Porter, *Cambridgeshire Customs and Folklore* (1969), chap.

was probably an outside estimate, though allowance must be made for the many persons who died in prison before or after their trial. In Essex there were twenty-four such deaths between 1560 and 1603. By continental standards, however, the English figure is not high, though the lack of statistical work upon European judicial records means that there is at present no reliable estimate with which to compare it.[45] It is also proportionately lower than the corresponding figure for Scotland, where different legal procedures prevailed.[46] Nevertheless, the volume of prosecution is large enough to call for some explanation. It greatly exceeded the parallel prosecution of Catholic clergy, for the total number of English Catholic martyrs, lay and clerical, executed during the period was only 264.[47] It could also form a substantial part of the total criminal jurisdiction of the day. At the Essex Assizes in the 1580s, a peak period, witchcraft cases formed thirteen per cent of all the criminal business. In the same county over half the villages were involved in prosecutions at one time or another.[48]

The number of witch-trials fluctuated from one decade to another and varied in different parts of the country. For reasons which have never been explained, Essex was particularly subject to such prosecutions, its indictments on the Home Circuit outnumbering those from the four counties of Hertfordshire, Kent, Surrey and Sussex combined. But the uneven survival of records makes it impossible to

---

5]; the Bedfordshire Assize Records, 1662–80 [in the Beds. R.O.], which contain six accusations; and very many Quarter Sessions and municipal records). He also missed some of the references in contemporary literary sources to witch-trials for which the judicial records no longer survive. My incomplete searches have added over 130 witch-trials and 22 executions to those which Ewen discovered, but I cannot improve upon his overall total estimate. Contemporaries had even less idea of the truth. Guesses ranged from John Darrell's assumption in 1600 that 'thousands' had already confessed their witchcraft (*A Detection of that sinnful ... Discours of Samuel Harshnet*, p. 40) to a more sober anonymous estimate of 2,000 executions over the whole period (*The Impossibility of Witchcraft* [1712], sig. A3^v).

45. For some estimates see Ewen, ii, p. 112; E. Brouette in *Satan* (*Etudes carmélitaines*, 1948), pp. 367–7; H. C. Lea, *A History of the Inquisition of Spain* (1906–7), iv, p. 246.

46. G. F. Black, who found over 1,800 accused witches, estimated the total number of Scottish executions at 4,400; 'A Calendar of Cases of Witchcraft in Scotland, 1510–1727', *Bull. New York Public Lib.*, xli–xlii (1937–8).

47. G. F. Nuttall, 'The English Martyrs, 1535–1680: a Statistical Review', *Journal of Ecclesiastical History*, xxii (1971).

48. Macfarlane, *Witchcraft Prosecutions*, pp. 50–51, 299.

draw a satisfactory map indicating the regional distribution of the trials, and no county was free of them. The most acute period was 1645–7, when the campaign led by Matthew Hopkins and his associates resulted in the execution of several hundred witches in Essex, Suffolk, Norfolk and neighbouring counties. There were other notable trials, in Essex in 1582 (involving fourteen persons), and in Lancashire in 1612 (twenty-one persons) and 1633 (twenty). Such *causes célèbres* attracted great attention at the time, for contemporaries, like some modern historians, were dependent for their knowledge of the subject upon the chance appearance of a pamphlet account of a notable trial, and unacquainted with the routine prosecution disclosed by the assize records. It would be wrong to think of witchcraft prosecution as a matter of periodic 'scares'. For the most part the story is of steady and unspectacular annual prosecution. On the Home Circuit the trials were at their zenith during the reign of Elizabeth I, when 455 out of the 790 known indictments were made, the majority during the 1580s and 1590s. It is probable indeed that there were more trials everywhere under Elizabeth than during the whole of the subsequent century. From about 1620 the number of trials on the Home Circuit fell off sharply, to rise spectacularly during the Hopkins period and then to dwindle to a mere trickle for the rest of the century. Elsewhere, for example on the Western Circuit, trials continued at a high rate during the reign of Charles II.

The percentage of trials which ended in the accused's conviction also varied at different periods. It seems to have been particularly high on the Home Circuit at the turn of the sixteenth century (forty-one per cent), and again in the Hopkins period (forty-two per cent). By the reign of Charles II it was low everywhere. On the Western Circuit between 1670 and 1707, for example, there were fifty persons tried for witchcraft (two of them twice), but of these only six were executed, and a seventh condemned but reprieved. In Essex the ratio of acquittals soared as early as 1620, and there were no executions after 1626, save under Hopkins's influence in 1645. Of the 291 persons accused in the county over the whole period, 151 were acquitted. This may be compared with the acquittal rate in France, which was sometimes as low as five per cent.[49] The last person hanged for witchcraft in England was Alice Molland at Exeter in 1685; the last to be condemned, but subsequently reprieved, Jane Wenham at

49. Mandrou, *Magistrats et sorciers en France au XVIIᵉ siècle*, p. 111.

Hertford in 1712. In 1717 at Leicester the last recorded witch-trial in an English civil court took place, when the jury rejected the charge, supported though it was by no fewer than twenty-five witnesses. Finally in 1736 the legislature repealed the 1604 Act, and replaced it by a measure which prohibited accusations of witchcraft or sorcery as such, but imposed a penalty of a year's imprisonment, plus quarterly appearance in the pillory, for those who fraudulently claimed to be able to use magic, tell fortunes, or find lost goods. In the eyes of Parliament witchcraft had thus ceased to be a terrifying reality; it was now deemed to be just another case of vulgar fraud. In fact the old Act had been a virtual dead letter for the previous twenty years, and the statutory charge was well behind the alteration in educated opinion.[50]

As a barometer of the rise and fall of witch-beliefs, however, the record of the witch-trials is inadequate. What it primarily reflects is the attitude of the educated classes: the lawyers who conducted the hearing; the clergyman who interrogated the prisoners; 'the most sufficient freeholders in the county' who constituted the Grand Jury which examined the presentments from the quarter sessions; and the trial jury itself, composed of men of humbler quality, who were nevertheless required by an act of Charles II's reign to be worth at least twenty pounds *per annum* in freehold land and rent.[51] During the seventeenth century such persons grew sceptical, if not of witchcraft, then at least of the possibility of satisfactorily proving that it had occurred. In 1692, for example, the Grand Jury of the Surrey Quarter Sessions was solemnly warned that although witchcraft was a great crime, 'it is so hard a matter to have full proof brought of it, that no jury can be too cautious and tender in a prosecution of this nature'.[52] As a result of this increasingly critical attitude the

<hr/>

50. For all these facts see Ewen, i and ii, and Macfarlane, *Witchcraft Prosecutions, passim*. An accused witch died in gaol at Beccles in 1693 (Ewen, ii, p. 460) and two witches were reported to have been executed at Northampton in 1705, in a pamphlet which Notestein (*Witchcraft*, pp. 375–83) considered to be spurious, but about which Ewen (ii, pp. 381–3) was less certain. The execution of a woman and her six-year-old daughter at Huntingdon in 1716, is reported in a pamphlet of that year which is certainly fictitious (Ewen, ii, p. 461).

51. *The Office of the Clerk of Assize* (1676), p. 48; 16 and 17 Car. II, c. 3 (reduced to £10 by 4 Wm. and Mary, c. 24).

52. *Surrey Archaeol. Collns.*, xii (1895), p. 129. On the role of the Grand Jury in Essex, especially after 1647, see Macfarlane, *Witchcraft Prosecutions in Essex*, pp. 51–2.

number of successful prosecutions declined, even though the laws remained in force.

An examination of the roots of this scepticism must be postponed to a later chapter.[53] Meanwhile it should be remembered that to some extent it had always been there. Nearly everyone agreed that at least some witches were unjustly accused, and that others were victims of their own delusions. Throughout the period damages were awarded for assault, defamation and false arrest in connection with witchcraft accusations, and during the later seventeenth century men were successfully prosecuted for molesting innocent persons.[54]

But the change of opinion among the educated classes was not immediately reflected among the people at large. Once it had become almost impossible to get a conviction in the courts it was only a matter of time before the statute was repealed. But informal accusations continued to be made. Even when the laws were in force there had been cases where a community ignored the normal machinery of prosecution and took the law into its own hand, by maltreating or forcibly 'swimimng' a witch, sometimes bringing about her death in the process. Violence of this kind had occurred, for example, in 1665, 1691, 1694, 1699, 1700, 1701, 1704, 1709, 1717, 1730, and 1735.[55] Despite the readiness of the courts to treat any resulting deaths as cases of murder, these episodes continued after the lapse

53. Below, chap. 18.

54. Ewen, *Star Chamber, passim;* F. A. Inderwick, *Side-Lights on the Stuarts* (1888), p. 166; *Borough Sessions Papers, 1653–1688,* ed. M. J. Hood (Portsmouth Rec. Series, 1971), pp. 142–3; F. Hutchinson, *An Historical Essay concerning Witchcraft* (2nd edn, 1720), pp. 56, 63; Ewen, ii, pp. 381, 458; East Riding Quarter Sessions, 11 Jan. 1648 (E. Riding R.O.) (a labourer bound over to appear at next sessions for assaulting an alleged witch). In 1636 Elizabeth Stile was acquitted of witchcraft at Somerset Assizes and allowed free counsel to bring an action against her prosecutors. This has been hailed as evidence of changing opinion (*Somerset Assize Orders,* ed. T. G. Barnes [Somerset Rec. Soc., 1959], p. 28), but it should be noted that she (or someone of the same name and locality) was accused again in 1665 and died in gaol (Ewen ii, pp. 341–5).

55. See Ewen, ii, pp. 378–80, 390, 445, 458, 460–61; Notestein, *Witchcraft,* pp. 331–2; J. Sutherland, *A Preface to Eighteenth-century Poetry* (Oxford, 1963 edn), pp. 6–7; Kittredge, *Witchcraft,* p. 236; *Records of the County of Wilts.,* ed. B. H. Cunnington (Devizes, 1932), pp. 279–81; *Bedfordshire Notes and Queries,* iii (1890–93), pp. 287–8; F. G. Emmison, *An Introduction to Archives* (1964), plate 8. In 1727 the Justices of Wingham Petty Sessions had to order the officers of the parish of Littlebourne to return a reputed witch to the house from which she had been driven by the community (Kent R.O., PS/W 2, 11 July 1727).

of the Witchcraft Act in 1736, and the lynching of alleged witches remained a sporadic feature of English rural life until the later nineteenth century.[56]

The shift in educated opinion explains why witchcraft accusations were not received sympathetically by the law courts after the later seventeenth century. But how is one to account for the concentration of active witch-prosecution within so short a period? Nearly all the executions for witchcraft in England took place during the second half of the sixteenth century and the first three-quarters of the seventeenth. Yet witch-beliefs as such had existed long before this time. It was accepted in the Middle Ages that there were individuals capable of performing acts of *maleficium* by occult means, just as there were others who used their magic for beneficent purposes. With the exception of the sabbath and the diabolical compact, there was no item of subsequent English witch-beliefs which was not deeply entrenched in the popular imagination long before 1500.[57] Yet until the sixteenth century these occult powers do not seem to have provoked the same concern and indignation. Some medieval lawyers held that sorcerers should be burned alive, a penalty for which the Roman Law provided a respectable ancestry.[58] But, in practice, it seems to have been very rare in England for anything other than a trivial punishment to have been inflicted upon those accused of maleficent magic before 1500. Until the surviving medieval judicial records have been thoroughly sifted it would be wrong to prejudge the issue. But at present, for the whole period between the Norman Conquest and the Reformation, there are not more than half a dozen known cases of supposed witches being executed; and most of these had been involved in plots against the monarch or his friends.[59]

56. Davies, *Four Centuries of Witch-Beliefs*, pp. 188–90; M. Summers, *The Geography of Witchcraft* (1927), pp. 171–83; Kittredge, *Witchcraft*, pp. 236–7; Hutchinson, *An Historical Essay concerning Witchcraft*, pp. 175–6; J. Juxon, *A Sermon upon Witchcraft* (1736). Much evidence about the survival of informal witchcraft accusations in nineteenth-century rural society can be found in the numerous publications of the Folk-Lore Society.

57. As Kittredge, *Witchcraft*, conclusively demonstrates.

58. cf. C. N. L. Brooke in *E.H.R.*, lxxvii (1962), pp. 137–8; and below, pp 549, 554–5.

59. They include the woman incarcerated for life in 1222 (below, p. 549 n.86), Robert le Mareschal, 1326 (Ewen, ii, p. 30; another man died in prison); Margery Jourdemain and Roger Bolingbroke, 1441 (Kittredge, *Witchcraft*, p. 81; a third associate died in the Tower); Mabel Brigge, 1538 (below,

Nor were the allegations made against medieval witches on a par with those levied during the seventeenth century. In the later period it was quite common for multiple acts of damage to be attributed to the machinations of one individual. Thus, to take some random instances, Elizabeth Peacock was accused of killing four persons, laming another, and bringing about the death of eight geldings and seven mares; Philippa Gewen was said to have lamed three persons by her witchcraft and killed a fourth; Martha Rylens was charged with murdering no fewer than five victims. These three cases all come from the records of the Western Assize Circuit between 1670 and 1675.[60] The total number of deaths formally attributed to witchcraft during the sixteenth and seventeenth centuries as a whole must have run into thousands. In Essex alone witches were formally charged with the deaths of 233 people and the illnesses of 108 others.[61] By contrast, the total damage known to have been alleged as the work of witchcraft before 1500 can be summarized as two or three deaths, a broken leg, a withered arm, several destructive tempests and some bewitched genitals.[62] Of course, considerable allowance must be made for the inadequate survival of medieval records, and even more for the fact that most of them have yet to be properly searched. Many cases of medieval sorcery doubtless await discovery. But it is noticeable that in those cases which have so far come to light the usual charge is that witchcraft was *attempted*, not that it was successful.

The literary evidence also suggests that in the sixteenth century contemporaries felt that the witch problem had assumed new proportions. Bishop Jewel asserted in 1559 that during the previous reign 'the number of witches and sorcerers had everywhere become enormous ... This kind of people ... within these few last years are marvellously increased.'[63] 'The land is full of witches,' declared Lord

---

p. 612). See also Kittredge, *Witchcraft*, p. 75, for an Anglo-Saxon case, and Ewen, ii, p. 28, for the semi-condonation of the murder of a witch in 1279. On the dearth of fifteenth century assize records, see Ewen i, p. 71.

60. Ewen, ii, pp. 442–3.   61. Macfarlane, *Witchcraft Prosecutions*, p. 199.

62. To the formal accusations cited in Ewen, ii, p. 39, may be added the cases of murder vaguely alleged in 1490 and 1493 (Hale, *Precedents*, pp. 20, 36–7), the storms frequently said to have been raised by conjurers (Kittredge, *Witchcraft*, pp. 154–5), the withered arm which Richard III tried to blame upon Queen Elizabeth and Jane Shore (ibid., pp. 60–61), and a woman's death popularly attributed to witchcraft around 1500 (C. T. Martin in *Archaeologia*, lx [1907], p. 374).

63. *The Zurich Letters*, ed. H. Robinson (Cambridge, P.S., 1842–5), i.

Chief Justice Anderson in 1602, 'They abound in all places.' Without speedy preventive action, they would 'in short time overrun the whole land'.[64] A witch, thought Bishop Hall in 1650, used to be a rarity. 'Now hundreds are discovered in one shire; and if fame deceive us not, in a village of fourteen houses in the North parts are found so many of this damned breed.' At the time of Matthew Hopkins's activities, a letter-writer thought that more witches had been arraigned in England than at any time since the Creation. Even in 1654 a contemporary assumed it to be obvious that the volume of sorcery was still increasing.[65]

One way of explaining why the possibility of witchcraft seemed particularly menacing during the hundred and twenty or so years after the accession of Elizabeth I is to emphasize that this was the very period when the two separate concepts of witchcraft fused together to produce a new myth. The change can thus be attributed to the superimposition of the theological concept of witchcraft upon the ancient belief in the possibility of *maleficium*. The idea of the witch as a devil-worshipper was a new import from the Continent which it is tempting to make the scapegoat for the unprecedented volume of persecution. In the Middle Ages, it could be argued, the notion that witches were devil-worshippers had not yet taken root; any malicious acts on their part were therefore treated no differently from those committed by any other criminal. It was only when continental ideas poured into sixteenth-century England, after the invention of printing, that witchcraft stood revealed as the greatest crime of all. As soon as witches were seen as heretics and the sworn enemies of God, a campaign was launched to root them out of the land. Hence the subsequent trials and executions.

The most influential exponent of this argument has been Professor Rossell Hope Robbins. His *Encyclopedia of Witchcraft and Demonology* (1959) was devoted to the thesis that the theological concept of witchcraft was 'never of the people', but was imposed from above by the late medieval Papacy. The clerics and lawyers of the Inquisition, he argued, made a trade of their witch-hunting, and by employing torture and leading questions, extracted from their

---

pp. 44–5; *The Works of John Jewel*, ed. J. Ayre (Cambridge, P.S., 1845–50), ii, pp. 1027–8.

64. Ewen, ii, p. 127.

65. *The Works of . . . Joseph Hall*, ed. P. Wynter (Oxford, 1863), viii, p. 35; *Epistolae Ho-Elianae. The Familiar Letters of James Howell*, ed. J. Jacobs (1890), pp. 506, 511; W. Strong, *A Voice from Heaven* (1654), p. 4.

victims the confessions of devil-worship which they themselves had invented. The populace in general only came to accept that witch-craft was heresy 'after decades of pounding in the new doctrine'. In essence the persecution of witches was the product of a cold-blooded campaign launched by self-interested clerics and inquisitors. It had no genuine social roots, but was imposed from above.[66]

Professor Robbins's interpretation is a valuable reminder that the witch-beliefs of our period contained an element for which no earlier precedent is to be found, and he is right to emphasize that this new ingredient had no real popular basis. But as an explanation of the increased witch-prosecution in sixteenth- and seventeenth-century England, his argument will hardly do. It is not just that it does not explain why there should have been such a time-lag be-tween the propagation of continental ideas, in the fourteenth and fifteenth centuries, and the beginning of English persecution, well over a hundred years later. The main difficulty is that, as we have already seen, the great bulk of witchcraft accusations in England did not relate to any alleged heretical activities upon the part of the witch, but to her *maleficium* (or 'sorcery', as Professor Robbins calls it to distinguish it from his narrower conception of 'witchcraft' proper). This was the point at issue in the overwhelming majority of Elizabethan witch-trials. The covenant with the Devil, which Pro-fessor Robbins describes as 'the core of the witchcraft delusion', did not formally become a crime in England until 1604, by which time at least half, and probably more, of the witch-trials had already taken place. On the Home Circuit well over half the executions occurred before the death of Elizabeth. Even after 1604 the diaboli-cal pact was not usually the gravamen of the charge.

On the Continent, moreover, there had been fiscal motives for witch-hunting, since the witch's goods might go to the lord, or the Inquisition, or the officials responsible for the trial.[67] But in England no such incentive existed. The short-lived 1542 Act ordered the forfeiture of the witch's goods and lands, as by felony, but the two subsequent measures of 1563 and 1604 safeguarded the heir's in-heritance and the widow's dower, should the accused person be executed. This did not always work in practice, and if there was no heir the property would go to the manorial lord anyway. The goods

66. Robbins, *Encyclopedia, passim* (quotations on pp. 9, 144).
67. Lea, *Materials*, pp. 417, 699, 701, 702, 810–11, 1231. But cf. ibid., pp. 1124–5; Brouette in *Satan*, p. 379; and Mandrou, *Magistrats et sorciers*. pp. 113–14.

of the three witches of Warboys executed in 1593, for example, were worth forty pounds and fell to Sir Henry Cromwell as lord of the manor. (He gave the money to the corporation of Huntingdon, who used it to finance an annual sermon on witchcraft.)⁶⁸ The law also prescribed forfeiture of goods in those cases where the witch was sentenced to life imprisonment. But in England prosecutions can scarcely ever have had a financial motive. Most of the victims were extremely poor. It is hard to see what their accusers could have gained by the prosecution. Only in a tiny minority of cases can even the glimmer of a financial motive be discerned.⁶⁹ On the Continent, says Professor Robbins, 'witch-hunting was self-sustaining and became a major trade'.⁷⁰ But in England the truth was often the reverse. A witch-trial could sometimes be an expensive affair for the community, as certain Suffolk parishes found in 1645–6, when they had to pay the fees of the witches' gaolers because the accused themselves were too poor to contribute.⁷¹ Executioners and gaolers may have had a financial interest in the proceedings, but no more so than in the prosecution of any other crime.

The only English prosecutions which were obviously stimulated from above, in the continental manner, were the work of the professional witch-finder, Matthew Hopkins, and his associate John Stearne. Hopkins's campaign probably brought him some personal profit, though both he and Stearne denied it.⁷² His two hundred or so victims also constituted a sizeable proportion of the total number

68. Kittredge, *Witchcraft*, p. 306. In Birmingham Reference Library (MS 252, 472) there is a copy of a petition presented to the Council of the Marches at some date between 1619 and 1630 in which the bailiff of the royal manor of King's Norton, Worcs., relates how he successfully established his claim to the property of two executed witches by pleading the custom of the manor, according to which 'felon's goods' were forfeit to the Lord.
69. For example, the inclusion of Alice Nutter, a well-to-do gentlewoman, among the Lancashire witches in 1612, and the willingness of the boy Edmund Robinson to be bought off from his malicious accusations against the Lancashire witches in 1633 (Ewen, ii, pp. 223, 250).
70. Robbins, *Encyclopedia*, p. 111. Professor Robbins cites no English examples when developing his fiscal argument (pp. 111–16), and indeed admits its virtual inapplicability to England (p. 9).
71. Ipswich and East Suffolk R.O., Quarter Sessions Order Book, 1639–57, ff. 79, 80ᵛ, 81, 84. At Ipswich a special rate was levied in 1645 to pay for the prosecution of witches; *Memorials of old Suffolk*, ed. V. B. Redstone (1908), p. 269.
72. Ewen, ii, p. 259, n. 1. cf. the protestations in Hopkins, *The Discovery of Witches*, ed. Summers, pp. 61–2; J. Stearne, *A Confirmation and Discovery of Witch-craft* (1648), p. 60.

of witches executed in England. But professional witch-finders were exceptional. One operated in Berwick and Newcastle in 1649–50 and there may have been one or two others.[73] But at a time when it was customary for professional promoters to initiate prosecutions for every kind of offence their relative absence is notable. Local corporations occasionally financed prosecutions, and local clergy or gentry, influenced by continental ideas, sometimes set out to extract confessions of participation in diabolic witchcraft. But the evidence does not support the view that, the Hopkins affair apart, many English witch-prosecutions were initiated from above.

Moreover, even when they were, they could still have a genuinely popular basis. Witch-finding campaigns have been common in modern Africa and their leaders have not always been free from private fiscal motives. But they are only made possible by people's readiness to believe that witches are the cause of all their troubles and that everything will be well once they are rooted out.[74] In England Hopkins's campaign does not seem to have had so all-embracing a protective purpose, but it nevertheless exploited already existing fears. Although Hopkins ran into some opposition, there is every reason to think that what he did was to turn a higher proportion of informal popular allegations and suspicions into actual prosecutions, twisting them from charges of *maleficium* into allegations of devil-worship in the process. He was helped in this task by the delay in the resumption of normal judicial machinery after the Civil War. The trial of Essex witches at Chelmsford in July 1645 was conducted, not by justices of assize, but by the J.P.s, presided over by the Earl of Warwick, who had no clear judicial status. But it was the readiness of local people to witness against Hopkins's victims which made the episode possible. In Essex alone ninety-two individuals came forward to help.[75]

73. Ewen, ii, p. 454; Ewen, i, pp. 69–70; R. Howell, *Newcastle upon Tyne and the Puritan Revolution* (Oxford, 1967), pp. 232–3. At Crondall, Hants., in 1575 one Robert Dyeres was paid the large sum of £1 'towards his charge about the witch'; W. A. Fearon and J. F. Williams, *The Parish Registers and Parochial Documents in the Archdeaconry of Winchester* (1909), p. 82.

74. See A. I. Richards, 'A Modern Movement of Witch Finders', *Africa*, viii (1935); M. Douglas in *Witchcraft and Sorcery in East Africa*, ed. J. Middleton and E. H. Winter (1963), pp. 135–6; R. G. Willis, 'Kamcape: an Anti-sorcery Movement in South-West Tanzania', ibid., xxxviii (1968); and Mair, *Witchcraft*, pp. 172–7.

75. Notestein, *Witchcraft*, p. 192; Macfarlane, *Witchcraft Prosecutions*, p. 173. cf. Mair, *Witchcraft*, p. 71.

There is no reason, therefore, to think that the persecution of witches in England originated in a campaign led by clerics and lawyers against the instincts of ordinary people. Whatever the role of judges and inquisitors may have been on the Continent, it cannot be said that in England the judiciary ever took much initiative in the prosecution of witches. It is true that some judges displayed a marked desire to obtain a conviction at all costs; for example, Justice Winch and Serjeant Crewe, who incurred James I's displeasure for condemning nine witches at Leicester in 1616 on the most paltry evidence; or Justice Bromley, who in 1612 informed some of the acquitted Lancashire witches that they were undoubtedly as guilty as those who had been condemned.[76] It is also true that the trials were sometimes conducted in what were recognizable, even at the time, as disgraceful conditions. There was so much noise at the arraignment of Mary Spencer in 1634 that she could not hear the evidence brought against her; while the uproar at Anne Bodenham's trial in 1653 was such that judge and prisoner could not hear each other.[77] A few judges also seem to have been eager for maximum publicity to be given to the conviction of accused witches. The influential pamphlet account of the witches of Warboys (1593) was commissioned by Justice Fenner, while Brian Darcy, J.P., was probably himself the author of the account of the witches of St Osyth, Essex (1582).[78]

Nevertheless the judges as a class do not seem to have been any more vindictive towards witches than the rest of their contemporaries. They had no responsibility for initiating prosecutions in the first place; and it was from the bench that the initiative was finally taken to make the Witchcraft Act inoperative, long before it was repealed. As early as 1579, a supposed victim of witchcraft could blame the local magistrates for their slowness in taking action against his persecutors.[79] In 1633 a contemporary remarked that, but for the mercy and discretion of the judges, many more harmless old women would have been condemned. By 1676 it could be said that 'the reverend judges, especially of England now are much wiser, not

76. *C.S.P.D., 1611–18*, p. 398; Potts, sig. X1. For other partisan judges, see Ewen, ii, pp. 126–8.

77. Ewen, ii, p. 125; Aubrey, *Gentilisme*, p. 261.

78. *The Most Strange and Admirable Discoverie of the Three Witches of Warboys* (1593) sig. G2; Notestein, *Witchcraft*, p. 348.

79. Pamphlet by Richard Galis on trial of Elizabeth Stile, 1580 (in Bodl., G. Berks. 1; title-page missing), sigs. B1ᵛ, D1.

only than the proletarian rabble, but than they too who profess themselves to be the great philosophers, ... and give small or no encouragement to such accusations'.[80]

The most notable contribution towards mitigating the rigours of the law was made by Sir John Holt, Lord Chief Justice (1689–1710), who presided over some eleven successive acquittals, and secured the conviction of an impostor for pretending to be afflicted with witchcraft and leading a mob to attack the suspect. 'By his questions and manner of hemming up the evidence,' remarked an observer, '[he] seemed to me to believe nothing of witchery at all.' His example was followed by his colleagues. Mr Justice Powell, presiding over the trial of Jane Wenham in 1712, is said (though not in a contemporary source) to have greeted the more sensational testimony with the cheerful remark that there was no law against flying; he took prompt steps to arrange for her reprieve.[81]

During the last third of the seventeenth century, the witch-trials frequently reflected a struggle by the judiciary to resist pressure from below. When the witch-hunting Somerset J.P., Robert Hunt, personally uncovered a 'hellish knot' of witches, his 'discoveries and endeavours met with great opposition and discouragement from some then in authority'.[82] But there was a limit to what the judges could do in the face of overwhelming popular frenzy. Lord Chief Justice North admitted to having condoned the conviction of three innocent women at Exeter in 1682, for fear that clemency would only spark off a new witch-hunting epidemic by way of reaction. As his brother Roger North recorded,

It is seldom that a poor old wretch is brought to trial upon that account, but there is, at the heels of her, a popular rage that does little less than demand her to be put to death; and if a judge is so clear and open as to declare himself against that impious vulgar opinion, that the devil himself has power to torment and kill innocent children, or that he is pleased to divert himself with the good people's cheese, butter, pigs, and geese, and the like errors of the ignorant and foolish rabble, the countrymen (the triers) cry, this judge hath no religion, for he doth not believe witches.[83]

80. Hart, The Diet of the Diseased, p. 356; The Doctrine of Devils (1676), p. 96. For an attempt by judges in a case of 1658 to stop the jury from convicting on inadequate evidence see The Most True and Wonderfull Narration of Two Women Bewitched in Yorkshire (1658), p. 4.
81. Notestein, Witchcraft, pp. 320–28.
82. Glanvill, Saducismus Triumphatus, ii, pp. 126–7.
83. Ewen, ii, p. 372–3; North, The Lives, i, p. 166 (see also iii, p. 132).

The hatred of witches, therefore, was not obviously inculcated by the judges, and it was certainly not sustained by them. Nor can it be convincingly attributed to the new continental doctrines about devil-worshippers. It was the popular fear of *maleficium* which provided the normal driving-force behind witch prosecution, not any lawyer-led campaign from above. What awoke the indignation of the witch's enemies was the conviction that they were the victims of her acts of malice. Their children fell ill, their cattle died, their butter would not set. The witch was an object of hatred to her neighbours. She was subjected to informal acts of violence, and her conviction at the assizes usually had the full support of the community from which the charge originally emanated.

The basic problem thus remains. Why, if popular witch-beliefs were much the same as they had been in the Middle Ages, was it only during the sixteenth and seventeenth centuries that legal action against witchcraft attained such dimensions? To this question there are only two possible answers. Either the demand for the prosecution of witches suddenly grew, or the facilities for such prosecution had not previously existed. Of these two solutions the second seems much less plausible. It is true that it was only in the sixteenth century that the invocation of spirits became a statutory offence, but it is likely that some sort of machinery had always existed for prosecuting the authors of acts of *maleficium*. The legal situation is by no means clear, but it seems that a woman who killed a man by sorcery was in medieval law as liable to prosecution as if she had used a hatchet. If such cases were seldom encountered before the sixteenth century this was not because of the absence of statutes dealing specifically with witchcraft. The rudimentary state of present knowledge concerning the operation of the criminal law in the later Middle Ages must preclude a definitive judgement, but on the evidence at present available it may reasonably be assumed that the apparent paucity of medieval witch-trials reflects, not the lack of the necessary legal machinery, but the absence of any marked popular desire to take advantage of it.[84]

For in the Middle Ages maleficent sorcerers could generally be hauled before King's Bench or a local court, or made the object of specially appointed commissions or Council inquiries. They could also be denounced along with other magicians before the ecclesiastical courts. But although many wizards were cited before the eccle-

84. See appendix B below, pp. 554–8.

siastical authorities, it is striking that very few of them were charged with having committed acts of *maleficium*. The majority were charmers and crystal-gazers of the traditional kind. They were not maleficent witches at all. And although magical activity was sometimes regarded as heresy,[85] and therefore potentially punishable by burning, there is no clear example of a medieval witch being condemned under the heresy laws.[86] Yet several medieval jurists declared that sorcerers should be burned,[87] and both contemporaries and later authorities assumed they were.[88] The machinery was available, but there seems to have been no desire by either Church or people to take advantage of it. So long as the bulk of medieval judicial records, both lay and ecclesiastical, remains unprinted, it would be foolish to be dogmatic on this point, but all the signs are that a substantial demand for witch-prosecution in medieval England simply did not exist.

For this reason it would be wrong to lay the responsibility for the beginning of systematic persecution upon the passage of the three witch statutes. Much energy has been expended by historians in an attempt to identify the individuals who were responsible for drafting these measures and pushing them through Parliament, although little progress in this matter has yet been made. Nothing is known for certain about the origins of the 1542 Act, while attempts to attribute the statute of 1563 to the influence of the Marian exiles have been demonstrably unsuccessful. Both Acts may have been precipitated by political conspiracies in which magic was employed against the

85. *The Mirror of Justices*, ed. W. J. Whittaker (Selden Soc., 1895), pp. 15–16. Examples are cited in C. L. Ewen, *Séances and Statutes* (Paignton, 1948), p. 3.

86. Apart from the woman sentenced at the Council of Oxford in 1222 to be immured until her death for using sorcery to persuade a young man to masquerade as Christ (F. W. Maitland, *Roman Canon Law in the Church of England* [1898], pp. 167, 175), the only possibility known to me is Margery Jourdemain, who was burned in 1441, but whose offence seems more likely to have been treason than witchcraft (Kittredge, *Witchcraft*, p. 81). No sorcerers appear in the list of heresy trials in the *Report of the Royal Commission on the Ecclesiastical Courts* (*Parliamentary Papers*, 1883 [xxiv]). For maleficent witches in the church courts, see below, p. 554, n. 107.

87. *Britton*, ed. F. M. Nichols (Oxford, 1865), i, pp. 40–42; Sir F. Pollock and F. W. Maitland, *The History of English Law* (2nd edn, Cambridge, 1952), ii, p. 549.

88. T. More, *The Dialogue concerning Tyndale*, ed. W. E. Campbell (1931), p. 234; H. D. Traill in *Social England*, ed. H. D. Traill (1901–4), ii, p. 518; below, pp. 554–5.

reigning monarch. The parliamentary history of the 1604 Bill is better known, and a number of prominent lawyers and ecclesiastics, including some who had been personally involved in previous witch-cases, were on the various committees to which the Bill was sent.[89] It would, however, be quite erroneous to assume that, if only the authors of the various bills could be identified, then the origins of the witch-persecution would be laid bare. For there is no reason to think that any of the legislation was particularly controversial, save the repeal in 1736, which provoked pamphlet protests and some slight parliamentary opposition.[90] However initiated, the Acts could never have been passed without the general support of both Houses of Parliament, who, on such a matter, fairly represented the opinion of educated contemporaries. In any case most of the prosecutions could have been launched without the Acts, for they related to alleged *maleficium*, which seems always to have been indictable. It was only for the less common offences of conjuring, entertaining, pact-making, etc., or for finding lost goods or treasure, that the Acts provided totally new penalties. The most that can be said is that these statutes gave some added publicity to the idea of witchcraft, and that their presence on the statute book helped to sustain the belief, particularly in later years when scepticism was on the increase. It certainly made it difficult for judges to be liberal. As Lord Chief Justice North complained to the Secretary of State in 1682, 'we cannot reprieve them without appearing to deny the very being of witches, which ... is contrary to law'.[91]

Even when the courts ceased to entertain witch-trials, popular feeling against witches continued, as the periodic rural lynchings demonstrated. Such feeling was independent of the legal position, though witch statutes had been necessary before violence directed against suspects could take legal form. Yet before the statutes evidence for popular feeling against maleficent witches is sparse. There was plenty of informal violence in medieval society, but it seems to have been seldom directed against suspected witches.[92] The ecclesi-

89. For the background to the three Acts, see Kittredge, *Witchcraft*, pp. 65–6, 250–64, 307–14.
90. *The Witch of Endor* (1736) and *Antipas, a Solemn Appeal to the Right Reverend the Archbishops and Bishops* (1821), which was directed against the repeal of witchcraft legislation for Ireland; below, p. 694. An isolated critic of the 1604 Act (on unspecified grounds) is mentioned in *H.M.C., Hatfield*, xvi, p. 319.   91. Ewen, ii, p. 373
92. Though cf. the case of 1279 (above, p. 541, n. 59).

astical courts readily dealt with popular magic, but were rarely asked to investigate cases of black witchcraft. The common law provided facilities for the prosecution of most kinds of *maleficium*, but they were seldom invoked. Why was it only in the 1560s that popular feeling against witches became clearly expressed? It is not enough to say that the authorities, under the influence of continental ideas, felt it necessary to intervene against the old crime of witchcraft because it now appeared as a new and deadly heresy.[93] For the prosecutions which ensued were primarily concerned with the traditional, maleficent aspect of witchcraft, not with the imputation of devil-worship. The reason for the new popular demand for witch-prosecution cannot be found in the changing attitude of the legislature and judiciary. It must be traced to a change in the opinion of the people themselves.

Appendix A. The meaning of the term 'witchcraft'

Modern social anthropologists have drawn a distinction between 'witchcraft' and 'sorcery' along the following lines. Witchcraft is an innate quality, an involuntary personal trait, deriving from a physiological peculiarity which can be discovered by autopsy. The witch exercises his malevolent power by occult means, and needs no words, rite, spell or potion. His is a purely psychic act. Sorcery, on the other hand, is the deliberate employment of maleficent magic; it involves the use of a spell or technical aid and it can be performed by anyone who knows the correct formula. Witchcraft, on this definition, is thus an impossible crime and not empirically observable, whereas sorcery really is practised in many primitive societies.[94]

This distinction arose out of the study of Azande witchcraft, but it has been applied to other contexts, even though its relevance to other African societies is nowadays much disputed.[95] Up to a point it can be made to fit English conditions, since there were at least some

93. As is suggested in Robbins, *Encyclopedia*, and Mair, *Witchcraft*, p. 197.

94. The original distinction was made by Evans-Pritchard, *Witchcraft, Oracles and Magic among the Azande*, pp. 21, 387, and has been amplified by M. G. Marwick in *African Systems of Thought*, with preface by M. Fortes and G. Dieterlen (1965), pp. 23–4.

95. See, e.g., *Witchcraft and Sorcery in East Africa*, ed. Middleton and Winter, pp. 2–3, 61, n. 2; V. W. Turner, 'Witchcraft and Sorcery: Taxonomy *vesus* Dynamics', *Africa*, xxxiv (1964), pp. 318–24; M. Douglas, 'Witch Beliefs in Central Africa', *Africa*, xxxvii (1967); J. R. Crawford, *Witchcraft and Sorcery in Rhodesia* (1967), p. 95.

contemporary writers who perceived a difference between 'witch-craft', which was an occult power given by the Devil, requiring no tools or spells, and 'sorcery', which involved the use of images, poisons, etc. Thus, one writer declared in 1653 that sorcery was 'a thing or mischief which is distinct from witchcraft, as thus, witch-craft being performed by the devil's insinuation of himself with witches, ... sorcery being performed by mere sophistication and wicked abuse of nature in things of nature's own production, by sympathy and antipathy'. To exploit nature for a good purpose was legitimate; 'it is the evil of the end which is sorcery'. This comes very close to the modern anthropologist's description of sorcery as 'that division of destructive magic that is socially disapproved or deemed illegitimate'.[96] Francis Bacon anticipated it even more closely when he distinguished witchcraft from sorcery, by noting that a magical technique, like tying knots to prevent the consummation of a marriage, had 'less affinity with witchcraft, because not *peculiar persons only* (*such as witches are*), but anybody may do it'.[97]

The English witch, like her Azande counterpart, was also some-times believed to have physical peculiarities, in addition to the witch's mark. In 1599, for example, a judge, Sir Richard Martin, said that he had heard that the hair of a witch could not be cut off.[98] Others asserted that a witch sitting in bright sunshine would leave no shadow[99] and that witches could shed no tears.[100] The author of a pamphlet account of a trial at Maidstone in 1652 reported that some bystanders wanted the witches burned, 'alleging that it was a received opinion amongst many that, the body of a witch being burnt, her blood is prevented thereby from becoming hereditary to her progeny in the same evil, which by hanging is not'.[101] The idea that witchcraft went in families and might be hereditary was often put forward.[102]

96. W. Freeman, 'Artificiall Alligations and Suspentions shewing the Conjunction of Art and Nature' (1653) (Ashm. 1807), f. 82^v. cf. Marwick in *African Systems of Thought*, p. 22.

97. Bacon, *Works*, ii, p. 660 (my italics).   98. Ewen, ii, p. 190.

99. 'A Touchstone or Triall of Witches discoveringe them by Scripture', (B.M., Royal MS 17 C XXIII), p. 13.

100. Scot, *Discoverie*, II. vi; Bernard, *Guide*, p. 239; Gaule, *Select Cases of Conscience touching Witches and Witchcrafts*, p. 76; Ewen, ii, p. 328; cf. Lea, *Materials*, p. 568.

101. *A Prodigious and Tragicall History of the Arraignment, Tryall, Confession and Condemnation of Six Witches at Maidstone* (1652), p. 5.

102. Ewen, ii, index, *s.v.* 'heredity in witchcraft' (to which p. 264 should be added).

But perhaps the closest approximation to the African conception of completely involuntary witchcraft was the belief in the existence of persons whose eyes had a special power of fascination, like the man who accidentally killed his own cattle by looking at them: one J.P. called such persons 'involuntary witches'.[103] These figures, however, were primarily creations of folklore and seldom made any appearance in the trials. One commentator declared that

the bodies of aged persons are impure, which, when they wax cankered in malice, they use their very breath and their sight, being apt for contagion, and by the Devil whetted for such purposes, to the vexation and destruction of others. For if they which are troubled with the disease of the eyes called *opthalmia* do infect others that look earnestly upon them, is it any marvel that these wicked creatures, having both bodies and minds in a higher degree corrupted, should work both these and greater mischiefs?[104]

But this idea also seems to have hardly ever been invoked in the courts.

In general, therefore, the anthropological distinction between witchcraft and sorcery is of limited utility when applied to England.[105] It can be said that the sorcerer used material objects, whereas the witch did not.[106] But the presence or absence of magical techniques does not seem to have been of great concern to those who took part in the trials. It was the fact of the witch's malignity which interested them. The evidence for this might come from her use of image-magic, animal familiars, curses or other magical techniques, but it could also be inferred from her social situation. She might wreak her malice by using techniques, which were observable, or by ill-wishing, which was not. But the two methods were interchangeable and there was no suggestion that they belonged to different species of offender.

The historian cannot even say, with the anthropologist, that sorcerers existed, whereas witches were imaginary. For some of those accused of being witches really had tried to harm others by mere ill-wishing, unaccompanied by magical techniques. In intention, at

103. Ewen, ii, p. 356; above, p. 520.
104. W. Fulbecke, *A Parallele or Conference of the Civil Law, the Canon Law, and the Common Law* (1618), f. 97.
105. *Pace* M. Gluckman, *Politics, Law and Ritual in Tribal Society* (Oxford, 1965), p. 266, n. 2.   106. Mair, *Witchcraft*, p. 23.

least, witchcraft was not an impossible crime. In execution, it was neither more nor less effective than most of the methods of the sorcerer. It is very probable that a higher proportion of those accused of attempting mental witchcraft were innocent than was the case with those charged with using observable magical techniques. But this is essentially unprovable. What is clear is that the person charged with witchcraft in sixteenth- and seventeenth-century England was never thought to have acted involuntarily. She was the victim of her evil thoughts, but not of any innate physical peculiarity.

Appendix B. The legal status of witchcraft in England before 1563

The practice of any kind of magic had always been an ecclesiastical offence liable to prosecution before the church courts. Cases of *maleficium* were occasionally dealt with in this way, both before and after 1563.[107] Sometimes offenders were handed over by the secular authorities to the bishops or to special ecclesiastical commissions.[108] Indeed as late as 1558 the Privy Council instructed the Bishop of London to proceed against certain conjurers 'according to the order of the ecclesiastical laws'.[109]

The difficult problem is to ascertain whether the secular courts had independent jurisdiction over maleficent sorcery before the passing of the witchcraft statutes. Anglo-Saxon law-makers had certainly prescribed temporal punishments for witchcraft, but subsequent medieval jurists are silent on the subject.[110] Legal writers, from Britton in the thirteenth century to Fitzherbert in the sixteenth, state that sorcery was one of the offences to be inquired into by the

107. For earlier examples, see *Chronicles of the Reigns of Edward I and Edward II*, ed. W. Stubbs (Rolls Ser., 1882–3), i, pp. 236, 275–6; *Durham Depositions*, p. 27; W. M. Palmer in *Procs. Cambs. Antiqn Soc.*, xxxix (1938), p. 74; Hale, *Precedents*, pp. 20, 36, 77; Watkin, *Dean Cosyn and Wells Cathedral Miscellanea*, p. 157; Kittredge, *Witchcraft*, p. 254. There are post-1563 cases in C. M. L. Bouch, *People and Prelates of the Lake Counties* (Kendal, 1948), p. 216; P. Tyler in *Northern History*, iv (1969), p. 95; Wells D.R., A 101(1594); Ewen, ii, p. 162.

108. Kittredge, *Witchcraft*, pp. 241–2; Ewen, ii, pp. 34–5; K. H. Vickers, *Humphrey Duke of Gloucester* (1907), pp. 270–80.

109. *A.P.C.*, vii, p. 22.

110. Pollock and Maitland, *The History of English Law*, ii, p. 553; Coke, *Institutes*, iii, cap. 6; Ewen, i, pp. 3–5.

sheriff (several regarding it as punishable by burning), but there is little other evidence to suggest that the sheriff in fact concerned himself with it.[111] Appeals of sorcery were rare before itinerant justices, and doubt has been expressed as to whether it was a plea of the Crown at all.[112] The early fourteenth-century *Mirror of Justices* suggested that maleficent magic was a form of heresy which could be proceeded against in the King's court, but modern legal historians have dismissed this view as 'nonsense'.[113] In the seventeenth century most legal authorities assumed that witchcraft had been a purely ecclesiastical offence from the Conquest until the Tudor Acts against witchcraft, save that after 1401 burnings had been carried out by the secular authorities under *de haeretico comburendo*.[114]

Modern scholars have found very few cases of sorcery in the medieval records of lay courts. There is, for example, only one instance in the fourteen published volumes of *Curia Regis Rolls* (*temp.* Richard I – 1232).[115] Cases of a political nature frequently came before the special jurisdiction of the Council, which indeed retained some interest in this type of crime, even after the witchcraft statutes had been passed.[116] Of the witch-trials which are known for certain to have occurred in the King's Bench or other temporal courts, several involved issues of fraud or treason and thus did not

111. Pollock and Maitland, op. cit., ii, p. 554; A. Fitzherbert, *The Newe Boke of Justices of the Peas* (1538), f. xxxvi^v; ibid. (1566), f. 143^v. cf. Ewen, ii, p. 27, for an arrest of a sorceress by a sheriff in 1168.

112. *Pleas before the King or his Justices, 1198–1202*, ed. D. M. Stenton (Selden Soc., 1952–3), i. p. 45; ii, p. 24.

113. *The Mirror of Justices*, ed. Whittaker, pp. 59–60; Pollock and Maitland, op. cit., ii, p. 549.

114. Coke, *Institutes*, iii, cap. 6; N. Bacon, *The Continuation of an Historicall Discourse of the Government of England* (1651), p. 257; Sir M. Hale, *Historia Placitum Coronae*, ed. S. Emlyn (1736), i, p. 429; Sir P. Leicester, *Charges to the Grand Jury at Quarter Sessions, 1660–77*, ed. E. M. Halcrow (Chetham Soc., 1953), pp. 16, 73–4.

115. i, p. 108 (1199). There is none mentioned in the summary of the Coram Rege Roll for Easter Term 1470 in *Year Books of Edward IV: 10 Edward IV and 49 Henry VI. AD 1470*, ed. N. Neilson (Selden Soc., 1931), pp. xxv–xxvii, or in the account of King's Bench proceedings in Mich. Term 1488 in M. Blatcher, *The Working of the Court of King's Bench in the Fifteenth Century* (London Ph.D. thesis, 1936), pp. 317–37. (Dr Blatcher kindly tells me that there is none for Mich. Term 1490 either.)

116. See, e.g., *Select Cases before the King's Council, 1243–1482*, ed. I. S. Leadam and J. F. Baldwin (Selden Soc., 1918), pp. xxxiv–xxxv, and for post-1563 cases, Notestein, *Witchcraft*, pp. 385, 387–8.

pose directly the problem of the legal status of maleficent sorcery. The only unambiguous instances, so far discovered, of secular jurisdiction being exercised in cases of *maleficium* are in 1199, 1270 and 1325.[117] Other possible cases occur in 1354 and 1371.[118] There are also examples of sorcerers being punished by local courts,[119] and two instances in the early fifteenth century of special commissions issued to J.P.s to inquire into suspected cases of maleficent sorcery.[120] A few cases also appeared in Chancery.

The clearest statement of the legal situation was made in 1331, when a Southwark jury found that a goldsmith had used image-magic in an unsuccessful attempt to kill two other persons. Since no one had died as a result of his practices, it was decided that the King's Bench had no jurisdiction in the matter; the sorcerer was nevertheless remanded to the Tower, so that the King or the Bishop of Winchester (in whose diocese the offence had been committed) might proceed against him for activities contrary to the Christian faith. In this case it was clearly implied that, if actual death had resulted, the King's Bench could have treated it as a murder case and tried it in the usual way.[121] Similarly in 1371 a necromancer was discharged by the King's Bench, after inquiries had failed to reveal any evidence that he had deceived or harmed the King's people.[122]

Yet many contemporaries continued to find the precise legal situation obscure. A fourteenth-century legal note says that sorcerers are normally triable by the ecclesiastical courts, but that the King can deal with them if he pleases.[123] A Chancery plaintiff in 1432–43 assumed that he had no remedy at common law to restrain a sorcerer who had already broken his leg from practising further black magic against him; and a defendant, accused of hiring a witch to kill the Bishop of St David's around 1500, pleaded that such an offence

117. *Curia Regis Rolls*, i, p. 108; Ewen. ii, pp. 28, 29–30.

118. H. G. Richardson in *T.R.H.S.*, 4th ser., v (1922), pp. 36–7; *Select Cases in the Court of King's Bench under Edward III*, vi, ed. G. O. Sayles (Selden Soc., 1965), pp. 162–3.

119. Ewen, ii, pp. 29, 35; Kittredge, *Witchcraft*, p. 257; *Lathe Court Rolls and Views of Frankpledge in the Rape of Hastings, A.D. 1387 to 1474*, ed. E. J. Courthope and B. E. R. Formay (Sussex Rec. Soc., 1931), p. 153.

120. B. H. Putnam, *Early Treatises on the Practice of the Justices of the Peace* (Oxford, 1924), pp. 91, 241; Ewen, ii, p. 36.

121. *Select Cases in the Court of King's Bench under Edward III*, v, ed. G. O. Sayles (Selden Soc., 1958), pp. 53–7.

122. ibid., vi, pp. 162–3.

123. *Britton*, ed. Nichols, i, p. 42 n.

could only be tried in a spiritual court. Other contemporaries also assumed that sorcery was an ecclesiastical offence.[124] On the other hand, Alice Huntley was accused around 1480 of practising image-magic 'against the law of the Church *and of the King*'.[125]

Right on the eve of the 1563 Act, it seems to have been the opinion of Lord Chief Justice Catlin that the temporal law could not deal with conjurers. His search in 1561 for medieval precedents un-earthed only the doubtful case of 1371; as a result, the offenders with whom he was concerned were sent by the Privy Council to the King's Bench, where they abjured, and were exposed in the pillory.[126] Since no *maleficium* (other than love magic) was involved in this episode, it remains uncertain whether Catlin thought that the com-mon law could have been invoked if no physical damage had occurred. Yet in the same year John Samond was tried at Chelms-ford Assizes on a charge of bewitching two persons to death. He was acquitted, but the indictment spoke of 'felonies and murders'.[127] Two 'witches' executed in Ireland in 1578, before the English Witchcraft Act had been extended there, were condemned, says a seventeenth-century writer, 'by the Law of Nature, for there was no positive law against witchcraft in those days'.[128]

Such cases suggest that legal practice had many vagaries. Not all contemporaries knew what the law was. Even after the passing of the 1563 Act there were irregularities in its actual administration.[129] A reasonable conclusion on the basis of this rather unsatisfactory evidence would be that, until the passing of the Witchcraft Acts, it was not a temporal offence to conjure spirits, or to engage in magical activity as such. But, if fraud was involved, a secular prosecution might well ensue, and if treason, murder or physical injury were

124. Ewen, ii, p. 37; C. T. Martin in *Archaeologia*, lx (1907), p. 375. cf. *Dives and Pauper* (1536), f. 51.

125. Martin in *Archaeologia*, lx (1907), p. 373. For two would-be conjurers who thought in 1531 that the invocation of spirits was illegal without the King's permission, see W. Hone, *The Year Book* (1832), cols. 425–7.

126. Kittredge, *Witchcraft*, pp. 258–9, 556; P.R.O., SP 12/16, f. 136; (Sir E. Coke), *A Booke of Entries* (1614), f. 1. The abjuration itself seems to have been based on the wording of the repealed Act of 1542; Ewen, *Séances and Statutes*, p. 4.

127. Ewen, ii, p. 46 n. A Suffolk Assize case of the same year concerning a magical search for money is cited by Ewen, *Séances and Statutes*, p. 5, and Scot records the punishment of an archer for supposed enchantment in the reign of Mary (*Discoverie*, III, xv).

128. R. Cox, *Hibernia Anglicana* (1689–90), i, p. 354.

129. Ewen, i, pp. 35–9.

alleged, the offence was in practice indictable. This coincides with the view taken by several modern authorities,[130] but it would take a thorough search of the unpublished medieval judicial records to establish it definitely.

130. e.g., Sir W. Scott, *Letters on Demonology and Witchcraft* (4th edn, 1898), p. 183; Traill in *Social England*, ed. Traill, ii, p. 518; H. G. Richardson in *E.H.R.*, li (1936), p. 4, n. 3; *George Lincoln Burr. Selections from his Writings,* ed. Gibbons, p. 360, n. 20.

15.

WITCHCRAFT AND RELIGION

> The Devil, I really believed, was some deformed person out of
> man, and that he could where, when and how, in what shape
> appear he pleased; and therefore the Devil was a great scarecrow,
> in so much that every black thing I saw in the night was the Devil.
>
> Laurence Clarkson,
> *The Lost Sheep Found* (1660), p. 6

> If no devils, no God.
>
> *The Triall of Maist. Dorrell* (1599), p. 8

A SATISFACTORY explanation of English witch-beliefs has to attack
the problem from several different points of view. It has to offer a
psychological explanation of the motives of the participants in the
drama of witchcraft accusation, a *sociological* analysis of the situation in which such accusations tended to occur, and an *intellectual*
explanation of the concepts which made such accusations plausible.
In this chapter the approach will be primarily intellectual. An
attempt will be made to explain the relationship of witch-beliefs to
contemporary religion and to consider how far one was propped up
by the other.

1. *The Devil*

It is obvious that stories about diabolical compacts could never have
gained circulation if contemporary religion had not lent its authority
to buttress the notion of a personal and immanent Devil. Relatively
unimportant in the Old Testament, Satan had been raised by later
Judaism and Christianity to the status of God's grand cosmic antagonist. He was an omnipresent force, ever ready to prey upon man's
weaker instincts and to tempt him away into paths of evil. He was
also an instrument of God's judgement, for the sinners of this world
constituted the members of Satan's kingdom after their death. In
Hell they were subjected to undying torments over which he presided. To help him in his task he had an army of demons and evil
spirits, as numerous and pervasive as the saints and angels of Christ.
He was both one and many, for, as a seventeenth-century writer
explained, 'The Devil is a name for a body politic, in which there

are very different orders and degrees of spirits, and perhaps in as much variety of place and state, as among ourselves." His powers were enormous, for he had himself once been one of God's angels and he knew all the secrets and mysteries of the natural world. To all but the strongest in faith he constituted a ubiquitous and potentially irresistible force.

Generations of medieval theologians had developed an elaborate and sophisticated demonology, which percolated down to ordinary men in a cruder and more immediate form. Demons had no corporeal existence, but it was notorious that they could borrow or counterfeit human shape. Medieval preachers enlivened their sermons with terrifying stories of the Devil's repeated appearances to tempt the weak and to carry away desperate sinners. The horns, tail and brimstone of the medieval stage, and the grotesque creatures of church sculpture and wood-carving, helped to form the popular conception of Satan which has remained iconographically familiar until the present day.[2] The immediacy of this diabolical conception has, however, long disappeared. The Devil who provoked high winds and thunderstorms, or who appeared dramatically to snatch a poor sinner at his cups and fly off with him through the window, is difficult for us today to take seriously. But in the sixteenth century, when all the forces of organized religion had been deployed for centuries in formulating the notion of a personal Satan, he had a reality and immediacy which could not fail to grip the strongest mind.

The Reformation did nothing to weaken this concept; indeed it almost certainly strengthened it. Protestantism was a response to a deep conviction of human sin, a sense of powerlessness in the face

1. J. Glanvill, *Saducismus Triumphatus* (1681), i, p. 35. For the origins of Hebrew and Christian demonology see Lea, *Materials*, pp. 1–105. For English devil-lore in the sixteenth and seventeenth centuries there is T. A. Spalding, *Elizabethan Demonology* (1880), a useful pioneer study, and R. H. West, *The Invisible World. A Study of Pneumatology in Elizabethan Drama* (Athens, Ga, 1939), which makes good use of contemporary treatises. See also Brand, *Antiquities*, ii, pp. 517–22; Ewen, ii, pp. 48–54; K. M. Briggs, *The Anatomy of Puck* (1959), chap. 11.

2. Scot, *Discoverie: A Discourse upon Divels and Spirits*, chap. 11; G. R. Owst, *Literature and Pulpit in Medieval England* (2nd edn, Oxford, 1961), pp. 162–3, 169, 398, 424, 511–15; id., *Preaching in Medieval England* (Cambridge, 1926), pp. 61, 170, 175–7, 181, 201, 248–9, 271, 332, 336; *Mirk's Festival*, ed. T. Erbe (E.E.T.S., 1905), pp. 150–51; T. Wright, *A History of Caricature and Grotesque in Literature and Art* (1865), chap. 4; P. Carus, *The History of the Devil* (1900); A. Graf, *The Story of the Devil*, trans. E. N. Stone (1931).

of evil. Luther often spoke as if the whole world of visible reality and the flesh belonged to the Devil, the Lord of this world.[3] In the long run it may be that the Protestant emphasis on the single sovereignty of God, as against the Catholic concept of a graded hierarchy of spiritual powers, helped to dissolve the world of spirits by referring all supernatural acts to a single source. But if so it was a slow development. For Englishmen of the Reformation period the Devil was a greater reality than ever – the 'prince and God of this world', as John Knox called him.[4] Influential preachers filled the ears of their hearers with tales of diabolic intervention in daily life, recognizable as the cautionary *exempla* of the Middle Ages brought up to date. Hugh Latimer assured his audience that the Devil and his company of evil spirits were invisible in the air all around them. 'I am not able to tell how many thousand be here amongst us.'[5] Men thus became accustomed to Satan's immediacy. In the Elizabethan Communion Service the priest was required to warn any evil livers in his congregation not to come to the table, 'lest after taking of that holy sacrament the Devil enter into you, as he entered unto Judas, and fill you full of all iniquities, and bring you to destruction both of body and soul' – a symbolic warning which many must have taken literally. One Puritan minister was said in 1634 to have assured an old woman that she had been serving the Devil for the past three score years, and said threateningly to another parishioner, 'Sirrah, your black godfather will come for you one of these days.' Around 1597 Thomas Wilkinson, minister of Helmingham, Norfolk, 'in catechising one Estall's boy, told the boy the Devil was upon his shoulders; whereat the boy ran out of the church crying and screeching to the terror of all that were present'.[6] John Rogers, the future Fifth Monarchist, tells us how as a boy he suffered terribly from

3. A theme well developed by N. O. Brown, *Life against Death* (1959), chap. 14.

4. Quoted by M. Walzer, *The Revolution of the Saints* (1966), p. 100. For another Puritan description of the Devil as 'the God of the world', see E. Nyndge, *A True and Fearefull Vexation of one Alexander Nyndge* (1615), sig. A2ᵛ. cf. D. Leigh, *The Mother's Blessing* (1616), p. 177 ('Satan being the prince of this earth').

5. *Sermons by Hugh Latimer*, ed. G. E. Corrie (Cambridge, P.S., 1844), p. 493. On the popularity of the *exempla*, J. W. Blench, *Preaching in England* (Oxford, 1964); A. G. Dickens, *The English Reformation* (1964), pp. 1–3.

6. *C.S.P.D., 1634–5*, pp. 319–20; *Diocese of Norwich: Bishop Redman's Visitation*, ed. J. F. Williams (Norfolk Rec. Soc., 1946), p. 148.

fear of Hell and the devils, whom I thought I saw every foot in several ugly shapes and forms, according to my fancies, and sometimes with great rolling flaming eyes like saucers, having sparkling firebrands in one of their hands, and with the other reaching at me to tear me away to torments. Oh the leaps that I have made, the frights that I have had, the fears that I was in.

For five or six years he went to sleep with his hands clasped in a praying position, so that if the devils came for him they would find him prepared. By day he saw devils in trees and bushes.[7] Nor was the fear of Satan confined to Protestants. A young Elizabethan doctor at Wells kept seeing the Devil, and could only get rid of him by throwing his beads at him. He had been educated by the Jesuits.[8]

The battle with Satan and his hierarchy of demons was thus a literal reality for most devout Englishmen. Such demons, wrote the Calvinist divine, James Calfhill, 'appear to men in divers shapes, disquiet them when they are awake; trouble them in their sleeps, distort their members; take away their health; afflict them with diseases'. The war with Satan was a perpetual combat in which the enemy seemed always to have the advantage. 'An infinite number of wicked angels there are, O Lord Christ,' prayed Thomas Becon, 'which without ceasing seek my destruction. Against this exceeding great multitude of evil spirits send thou me thy blessed and heavenly angels, which may deliver me from their tyranny.'[9] Some Protestant theologians continued to uphold the old Catholic belief in guardian angels, and such angelic intervention was occasionally recorded.[10] But more usually it seemed that God had given Satan a free run. Meteorologists denied that evil spirits were responsible for tempests, but many contemporaries were less certain. 'It is a common opinion,'

7. E. Rogers, *Some Account of the Life and Opinions of a Fifth-Monarchy Man* (1867), pp.13–15.

8. *The Chronicle of the English Augustinian Canonesses Regular of the Lateran, at St Monica's, Louvain*, ed. A. Hamilton (1904), i, pp. 251–2.

9. J. Calfhill, *An Answer to John Martiall's Treatise of the Cross*, ed. R. Gibbings (Cambridge, P.S., 1846), p. 318; (H. Lawrence), *Of our Communion and Warre with Angels* (1646), p. 107; Spalding, *Elizabethan Demonology*, p. 124 n.

10. For some instances see *The Workes of ... Richard Greenham*, ed. H. H(olland) (3rd edn, 1601), p. 37; *The Autobiography of Mrs Alice Thornton*, ed. C. Jackson (Surtees Soc., 1875), p. 4; H. Hallywell, *Melampronoea* (1681), p. 113; R. Baxter, *The Certainty of the World of Spirits* (1691: 1834 edn), p. 91; Turner, *Providences*, i, pp. 9–12. cf. R. H. West, *Milton and the Angels* (Athens, Ga, 1955), p. 50.

wrote an Essex clergyman in 1587, 'when there are any mighty winds and thunders with terrible lightnings that the Devil is abroad.'[11] Diseases might also come this way. The seventeenth-century clergyman, Thomas Hall, knew that his chronic insomnia was the work of Satan, because it was always worse on the night before the sabbath or a religious fast.[12]

The Devil also played a prominent part in the execution of divine judgements. He was 'God's hangman', as James I called him.[13] Stories of Satan's personal appearance in response to the careless talk of a blaspheming layman, or as a means of executing an immediate judgement upon some notorious sinner, were retailed by Philip Stubbes, William Prynne, John Vicars, Edward Burghall, Nehemiah Wallington, Samuel Clarke, Oliver Heywood, Richard Baxter, and a score of anonymous pamphleteers.[14] Most of these anecdotes related to the fate of those who were in the habit of invoking the Devil in daily conversation. In 1631 Mr Pennington, a gentleman of Gray's Inn, whose customary expletive was 'Devil take me!' was visited by a black dog, who left him dead, with his eyes clawed out. 'Devil take him who goes out today', said John Leech of Huntingdonshire in 1662, whereupon he was picked up and carried in the air for twelve miles, dying the following day. There were many such occasions when the Devil appeared in a clap of brimstone to those who impiously drank his health or otherwise invoked his authority.[15]

11. G. Gifford, *A Discourse of the Subtill Practises of Devilles by Witches and Sorcerers* (1587), sig. D3ᵛ. See also Kittredge, *Witchcraft*, pp. 156–8; Kocher, *Science and Religion*, pp. 163–4; Wood, *Life and Times*, ii, p. 184; L. Echard, *The History of England*, ii (1718), pp. 712–13.

12. (H. Holland), *An Exposition of the First and Second Chapter of Iob* (1596), sig. Q4ᵛ; F. J. Powicke in *Bull. John Rylands Lib.*, viii (1924), p. 172.

13. (James VI), *Daemonologie* (Edinburgh, 1597), 'To the Reader'.

14. P. Stubbes, *Anatomy of Abuses* (1583), ed. F. J. Furnivall (New Shakespere Soc., 1877–82), i, pp. 71–3; R. T. Davies, *Four Centuries of Witch-Beliefs* (1947), p. 115, n. 2 (Prynne); J. Vicars, *The Looking-Glasse for Malignants Enlarged* (1645), sig. E1; E. Burghall in *Lancashire and Cheshire Rec. Soc.*, xix (1889), pp. 5–6, 13; Sloane 1457, ff. 23, 26, 29 (Wallington); S. Clarke, *A Mirrour or Looking-Glass both for Saints and Sinners* (1646), pp. 150–51; Heywood, *Diaries*, i, pp. 344–5; Baxter, *The Certainty of the World of Spirits*, pp. 17, 24–5, 26, 53, 66.

15. *H.M.C.*, vii, p. 548; *A Strange and True Relation of one Mr John Leech* (1662); K. M. Briggs, *Pale Hecate's Team* (1962), p. 161; *The Pack of Autolycus*, ed. H. E. Rollins (Cambridge, Mass, 1927), nos. 6, 13, 24, 38; *A Wonderful and Strange Miracle or Gods Just Vengeance against the*

But Satan was not only an agent of divine retribution. He was also a tempter. Once the possibility of his personal appearance in this world had been accepted it was but a short cut to the notion that there were individuals who entered into semi-feudal contracts with him, mortgaging their souls in return for a temporary access of supernatural knowledge or power. Such Faustian legends were in common circulation during the sixteenth and seventeenth centuries. They made excellent cautionary tales, revealing Satan as a trickster and showing how his recruits always came to a bad end. In 1642 a pamphleteer related how Thomas Holt, a Coventry musician burdened with nineteen children, had sold himself to the Devil. When the contract expired, the wretched man was found with his neck broken, and his chest of gold turned to dust. When one Ashbourner, a scholar of St John's College, Cambridge, was depressed by his inability to understand the book he was studying, the Devil appeared to him in the dress of a Master of Arts. He explained the text and offered to make him his scholar, promising a trip to Padua University, and the degree of Doctor of Divinity. Two days later the hapless student's gown was found floating in the river. Less intellectually ambitious was Thomas Browne, a yeoman accused at Middlesex Sessions in 1643 of selling his soul to the Devil for two thousand pounds *per annum*.[16] In 1672 Oliver Heywood recorded the story of the boy who, having read the story of Faustus, decided to invoke the Devil to ask for money; when Satan appeared and offered to make him the best scholar in his school, he panicked and was only saved by prayer. He grew up to be a prominent clergyman near York. More ironical were the cases of the Leicestershire man who sold his soul to the Devil in order to became a famous preacher, and the Huntingdonshire woman who gave herself to Satan, in return for an extraordinary power of prayer which brought ministers from far and wide to admire her virtuosity. She was later executed in New England as a witch.[17]

Cavaliers (1642); *Strange and Terrible News from Ireland* (1673); *A Strange True, and Dreadful Relation of the Devils appearing to Thomas Cox* (1684).

16. L. Southerne, *Fearefull Newes from Coventry* (1642); *A Letter from Cambridge* in *A Strange and True Relation of a Young Woman possessed with the Devill* (1647); *Middlesex County Records*, ed. J. C. Jeaffreson (1886-92), iii, pp. 88-9. Many broadsheet and ballad accounts of similar pacts may be found in J. Ashton, *The Devil in Britain and America* (1896).

17. Heywood, *Diaries*, i, pp. 344-5; Kittredge, *Witchcraft*, p. 579; Heywood, op. cit., ii, p. 269.

Since the Devil was portrayed as 'exquisitely skilful in the knowledge of natural things',[18] the temptation to get in touch with him was great for those seeking worldly success. Others may have succumbed out of self-protection. Matthew Hopkins's associate, John Stearne, remarked that many witches had been drawn to the Devil 'by some sermons they have heard preached; as when ministers will preach of the power of the Devil, and his tormenting the wicked and suchlike'. Ignorant people were seduced by Satan 'coming to them, and asking them, "How do you think to be saved? For your sins are so and so . . . and you heard the minister say that I will torment you. Give me your soul . . . and I will free you of hell-torments" '.[19] The fear of hell-fire was thus paradoxically alleged by some witches as an explanation for their apostasy.

There is some reason for thinking that Satan's overtures were a common form of temptation. The case-books of the Buckinghamshire doctor, Sir Richard Napier, reveal that several of his patients thought they had seen the Devil in human and animal form. In April, 1634, they included Ellen Green, 'troubled in mind, haunted by an ill spirit, whom she saith . . . speaketh to her'; Robert Lucas, 'troubled in his mind, despairing, doubteth whether he be not possessed with an evil spirit'; and Jane Towerton, 'mopish and melancholy . . . and despairing; thought at first she saw as a black dog something appearing to her and forbidding her to serve God and say her prayers, and go to church'.[20] Robert Burton describes how persons who felt themselves damned would 'smell brimstone, talk familiarly with devils, hear and see chimeras, prodigious, uncouth shapes, bears, owls, antics, black dogs, fiends'.[21] In his spiritual struggles John Bunyan thought himself possessed by the Devil and could feel the fiend plucking at his clothes. Many of his godly contemporaries underwent a similar period of religious depression when Satan appeared to them, often in some ugly animal shape, and tempted them to kill themselves or to forsake God.[22] This explicit temptation

18. Cooper, *Mystery*, p. 129.
19. J. Stearne, *A Confirmation and Discovery of Witch-Craft* (1648), p. 59. cf. below, p. 622.
20. Ashm. 412, ff. 119, 121, 115. A list of Napier's patients who had been tempted by spirits is in Ashm. 1790, f. 108.
21. Burton, *Anatomy*, iii, p. 424.
22. J. Bunyan, *Grace Abounding*, ed. R. Sharrock (Oxford, 1962), pp. 32, 34; V. Powell, *Spirituall Experiences of Sundry Beleevers* (2nd edn, 1653), pp. 82–3, 175, 237; W. Allen, *The Captive Taken from the Strong* (1658), p. 3. cf. Lilly, *Autobiography*, p. 33; *The Life and Death of Mr*

was so common and so intense that it is not surprising that those who had undergone it assumed that others must have succumbed.

Of course there were some bold spirits untroubled by these apparitions. Mr Edwards, M.A., of Trinity College, Cambridge, after being reclaimed from his conjurations, declared that the Devil had always appeared to him 'like a man of good fashion', and had never required any compact from him.²³ But normally Satan came to tempt and to seduce. He played upon religious uncertainties, and he provoked men to murder and violence. Until the nineteenth century, juries customarily declared of suicides and criminals that they had been 'led away by the instigation of the devil', and this was not necessarily an empty form of words. Mrs Turner, who was hanged after the murder of Sir Thomas Overbury, said at her execution that she had been in the hands of the Devil, but was now redeemed from him. At York Assizes in 1690 Edward Mangall confessed that he had murdered Elizabeth Johnson because 'the Devil put him upon it; appearing to him in a flash of lightning, and directing him where to find the club wherewith he committed the murder'.²⁴

Religious despair and prohibited desires were thus customarily personified in the crude form of a black man or a strange animal. Such apparitions sprang from an imagination well furnished in childhood with terrors of the kind described by Reginald Scot: 'an ugly devil having horns on his head, fire in his mouth, and a tail in his breech, eyes like a basin, fangs like a dog, claws like a bear, a skin like a Niger and a voice roaring like a lion'.²⁵ Popular conceptions about the appearance of such demons reflected contemporary assumptions as to what was displeasing and perverted, just as visions of the forces of good mirrored the reverse. (One of Vavasor Powell's followers, who had seen Christ, compared him to 'old Rice Williams of Newport', with 'a large grey beard'; and when Jesus appeared in a vision to the future Quakeress, Mary Pennington, he assumed the form of 'a fresh lovely youth, clad in grey cloth, very plain and neat'.)²⁶ Only a minority shared Scot's view that Satan was merely

Vavasor Powell (1671), p. 8; *Satan his Methods and Malice baffled. A Narrative of God's Gracious Dealings with that Choice Christian Mrs Hannah Allen* (1683), p. 15; and p. 199, above.

23. Glanvill, *Saducismus Triumphatus*, i, p. 70.

24. *C.S.P.D., 1611–18*, p. 329; Aubrey, *Miscellanies*, pp. 102–3.

25. Scot, *Discoverie*, VII.xv.

26. A Griffiths, *Strena Vavasoriensis* (1654), p. 6; *Some Account of Circumstances in the Life of Mary Pennington* (1821), p. 24.

a symbol of man's evil temptations, incapable of corporeal existence.[27] For most men the literal reality of demons seemed a fundamental article of faith. As a theologian pointed out, 'The whole scripture and all godly and wise men, as many as have lived from the beginning of the world even unto this day, have confessed that there are evil spirits or devils.'[28]

So essential indeed was the belief in the personification of evil that the dogma was paradoxically elevated into one of the greatest arguments for the existence of God, so that to deny it was to lay oneself open to the charge of atheism. 'If there be a God, as we most steadfastly must believe,' wrote Roger Hutchinson, 'verily there is a Devil also; and if there be a Devil, there is no surer argument, no stronger proof, no plainer evidence, that there is a God.' If men could be persuaded to 'grant that there are devils', thought John Weemes, 'they must grant also that there is a God'.[29] 'Show me a devil,' said a sceptic in 1635, 'and I'll believe there is a God.' The atheist, Richard White, was only converted to a Christian life by the appearance of the Devil one night, in the shape of 'a great ugly man'. Correspondingly, it was after the failure of several attempts to raise the Devil, 'that so I might see what he was', that Laurence Clarkson decided that all religion was 'a lie', and 'that there was no Devil at all, nor indeed no God, but only nature'.[30] The Puritan Richard Greenham maintained that 'it is a policy of the Devil to persuade us that there is no Devil'.[31] For, as another writer pointed out, 'he that can already believe that there is no Devil will ere long believe that there is no God'.[32]

The personification of Good rested upon the same basis as the personification of Evil, and the two concepts were inextricably

27. For the shift to a symbolic view of the Devil, see below, pp. 682–3.
28. *The Decades of Henry Bullinger*, ed. T. Harding (Cambridge, P.S., 1849–52), iv, pp. 348–9.
29. *The Works of Roger Hutchinson*, ed. J. Bruce (Cambridge, P.S., 1842), pp. 140–41; J. Weemse, *A Treatise of the Foure Degenerate Sonnes* (1636), p. 11. The same sentiment is expressed in *The Devill of Mascon* (2nd edn, Oxford, 1658), sig. A3.
30. *Durham High Commission*, pp. 115–16; Baxter, *The Certainty of the World of Spirits*, pp. 24–5; L. Claxton, *The Lost Sheep found* (1660), p. 32,
31. *The Workes of ... Richard Greenham*, ed. H. H(olland) (5th edn, 1612), p. 313.
32. J. Gaule, *Select Cases of Conscience touching Witches and Witchcrafts* (1646), pp. 1–2. cf. H. More, *An Antidote against Atheisme* (1653), p. 164.

interlocked. But there was an almost Manichaean quality to this emphasis upon the Devil's reality. When Agnes Wilson was arraigned as a witch at Northampton in 1612, she was asked how many gods she acknowledged. She answered, 'Two – God the Father, and the Devil.'[33] This was taken as a damning admission, but we may rather see it as an excusable inference from the religious teaching of the day. In the widely influential Great Catechism by the sixteenth-century Jesuit, Peter Canisius, the name of Christ appeared sixty-three times, that of Satan sixty-seven.[34] It is not hard to sympathize with the occasional heretic who proceeded to the conclusion that the Devil was even more powerful than God.[35]

Many social purposes were served by this belief in an immanent devil. Satan was a convenient explanation for strange diseases, motiveless crimes, or unusual success. The stories told about his intervention in daily affairs showed him punishing perjurers and blasphemers, snatching away drunkards, killing the impious. By providing a sanction for conventional morality they discharged the same purpose as the other stories of 'judgements' and 'providences' which the clergy, particularly the Puritan clergy, retailed for the edification of their flock. Satan's interventions could also provide an acceptable explanation for professional failure, a shipwreck, or a fall in a mine.[36] Feelings of guilt evoked by sexual dreams and nocturnal emissions could be assuaged by the reflection that an incubus or succubus must have been at work.

Above all the immanent Devil was an essential complement to the notion of an immanent God. The early Hebrews had no need to personify the principle of evil; they could attribute it to the influence of other rival deities. It was only the triumph of monotheism which made it necessary to explain why there should be evil in the world if God was good. The Devil thus helped to sustain the notion of an all-perfect divinity.

The Devil also operated as a sanction for Christian orthodoxy. Just as the early Christian Church had regarded the pagan gods as demons, so the warring religious sects of the sixteenth and seventeenth centuries claimed that their rivals worshipped Satan himself.

33. Ewen, ii, p. 212.
34. E. Brouette in *Satan* (*Études carmélitaines*, 1948), p. 353, n. 1; P. Canisius, *A Summe of Christian Doctrine* (St. Omer, 1622).
35. An earlier example occurs in Thomson, *Later Lollards*, pp. 36–7.
36. See, e.g., R. Burthogge, *An Essay upon Reason, and the Nature of Spirits* (1694), pp. 216–22.

This was said by Protestants of Catholics, by Catholics of Protestants, and by Christians of Red Indians and other primitive peoples.[37] It was asserted that Luther had been converted to Protestantism by Satan himself,[38] and that the Freemasons dedicated their children to the Devil when taking the mason's word.[39] Men saw the Devil in any manifestation of social wickedness or religious unorthodoxy. A Protestant iconoclast in 1540 could describe the image of Christ in the roodloft as a picture of the Devil, while in 1704 a Yorkshire Nonconformist declared that people who received the sacrament according to Anglican rites were serving not God but the Devil.[40]

Contemporaries were thus fully accustomed to throwing about charges of devil-worship. Diabolical temptation was a reality for many godly persons and the Devil's agency in the world was generally recognized. To this extent the belief that witches might make compacts with Satan is readily intelligible as a consequence of the rhetoric of contemporary religion.

2. Possession and dispossession

The belief in the reality of Satan not only stimulated allegations about diabolical compacts; it also made possible the idea of demoniacal possession. A person into whom an evil spirit had entered could be recognized by the strange physical and moral effects of the intrusion. He would suffer from hysterical fits, wild convulsions and contortions, analgesia, strange vomitings, even total paralysis. From his mouth would come the voices of demons, emitting obscene and blasphemous ravings, or talking fluently in foreign languages previously unknown to the victim.[41] The assault of devils might either be external ('obsession'), or from inside the patient's body ('posses-

37. See, e.g., Spalding, *Elizabethan Demonology*, pp. 28–9; *C.S.P.D., 1601–3*, p. 158; Kittredge, *Witchcraft*, p. 363; *Complete Prose Works of John Milton* (New Haven, 1953–), iv(i), p. 551; A. Hildersham, *CVIII. Lectures upon the Fourth of John* (4th edn, 1656), p. 148.

38. As late as 1821 the Catholic historian John Lingard assisted in the publication of *The Confessed Intimacy of Luther with Satan, at Whose Suggestion He Abolished the Mass.*

39. D. Knoop and G. P. Jones, *A Short History of Freemasonry* (Manchester, 1940), pp. 42–3.

40. A. Gibbons, *Ely Episcopal Records* (1890), p. 419; J. Addy, *Ecclesiastical Discipline in the County of York, 1559–1714* (M.A. thesis, Leeds, 1960), appx. B, p. 67.

41. A typical list of symptoms is given in Bernard, *Guide*, pp. 49–52. See also below, p. 686.

sion'). Strictly speaking, the belief in demonianism was distinct from that in witchcraft. Obsession by the Devil was a well-known stage preceding the conversion of many Puritan saints, and was not necessarily thought to involve the maleficence of some third party. But since it was frequently believed that an evil spirit had entered into a victim because a witch had sent him there, the notions were in practice intertwined. In seventeenth-century England, the epithets 'possessed' and 'bewitched' came very near to being synonymous.

The medieval Church had given theological definition to the doctrines of possession and obsession, but it had also provided a tolerably effective remedy for such complaints. The evil spirit, it said, could be commanded to depart in a formal exorcism conducted by a priest acting in the name of God and the Church, a ceremony which also formed part of the rite of baptism. The saints of the early Church made a reputation for successfully casting out devils and the office of exorcist was by the mid third century established as one of the minor orders. The ritual of exorcism, with the sign of the cross, symbolic breathing (*insufflatio*), holy water, and the command to the Devil to depart in God's name, was further developed by the Catholic Church of the Counter-Reformation in its numerous prescribed manuals of exorcism, not only for possessed persons, but also for poltergeists, haunted houses, and animals or humans suffering from supernaturally inflicted torments.[42]

This ritual was not officially regarded as infallible and might fail because of the victim's sins or the bystanders' lack of faith. Nevertheless, it was believed that demons had a natural horror of the symbolism of Christianity and that the Church had been given a special power with which to cast them out (Mark, xvi, 17). In the Middle Ages the general view seems to have been that, if all conditions were properly observed, the exorcism was much more likely than not to be successful.[43] The application of relics or a visit to a holy shrine might also prove effective means of dispossession.

Protestant opinion, however, viewed the practice of these exor-

42. There is a summary of Counter-Reformation exorcist literature in Lea, *Materials*, pp. 1055–69, and much useful information on Catholic exorcisms in C. Wordsworth, 'Two Yorkshire Charms or Amulets: Exorcisms and Adjurations', *Yorks. Archaeol. Journ.*, xvii (1903).

43. *D.T.C.*, v, *s.v.* 'exorcisme', indicates some lack of theological agreement on this matter. The *Malleus Maleficarum* had given reasons why exorcism could sometimes fail; Lea, *Materials*, pp. 325, 327; cf. Scot, *Discoverie*, XV.xxv and below, p. 594.

cisms with considerable hostility. The Wycliffites had denounced them as sheer necromancy, and their attitude was shared by the Protestant theologians of the Reformation era. The exorcism of the unbaptized child was abandoned in the second Edwardian Prayer Book, and the office of exorcist disappeared with the other minor orders from the Ordinal of 1550. The new theory, as stated, for example, by Bishop Jewel,[44] was that the power to cast out devils had been a special gift, conceded in the heroic age of the early Christian Church, but no longer necessary in a time of established faith. Such miracles were over, and Christians were no longer to believe that the Devil could be frightened by holy water, the sign of the cross or the mere pronunciation of words of Scripture. Would-be exorcists were no better than vulgar wizards. 'If any man amongst us should use such things,' said Jeremy Taylor, 'he would be in danger of being tried at the next assizes for a witch or a conjurer.'[45]

Exorcism was thus generally rejected. Yet cases of possession continued to appear. Indeed evidence has survived of more instances in the later sixteenth and seventeenth centuries than in the era before the Reformation. But what was the pious man to do in face of these diabolical assaults? He still had the protection of his faith, but there was now no automatic procedure for dealing with such cases of possession. A clergyman could no longer *command* a spirit to depart; he could only entreat God to show his mercy by taking the Devil away. Any healing, wrote an Elizabethan preacher, 'is not done by conjuration or divination, as Popish priests profess and practise, but by entreating the Lord humbly in fasting and prayer'. As Bishop Hall put it, 'we that have no power to bid must pray'.[46]

It was difficult to bring men to accept the full implications of this new situation. The idea that a child who cried at his christening was letting out the Devil long survived the formal omission of the exorcism from the baptism service.[47] For a time, moreover, it seemed that the Protestant remedy of fasting and prayer might well be

44. *The Works of John Jewel*, ed. J. Ayre (Cambridge, P.S., 1845–50), iii, p. 273; i, pp. 327–8.
45. *The Whole Works of ... Jeremy Taylor*, ed. R. Heber and C. P. Eden (1847–54), vi, p. 266.
46. (H. Holland), *Spirituall Preservatives against the Pestilence* (1603), pp. 69–70; *The Works of ... Joseph Hall*, ed. P. Wynter (Oxford, 1863), vii, p. 328.
47. For a seventeenth-century example, see Wood, *Life and Times*, iii, p. 279.

developed into a ritual claiming something very near mechanical efficacy. For all their rejection of what they regarded as the 'foul superstition and gross magic'[48] of the Catholic ritual of exorcism, the Puritans laid much stress on the efficacy of this alternative procedure, founded on the words of Mark ix, 29 ('This kind can come forth by nothing, but by prayer and fasting'). The century after the Reformation was to witness many cases of alleged diabolical possession in which Puritan ministers diagnosed the malady, entered into discourse with the devil, and triumphantly ejected it after fasting and prayer.

The true nature of these supposed examples of possession is difficult for us to establish without clinical evidence. The affliction does not seem to have been confined to persons of any particular age, sex or origin, and the concept was almost certainly extended to embrace maladies of widely different kinds. What is noticeable is the way in which the symptoms became stereotyped to conform to popular conceptions of what they should be. One victim's description of Satan as 'an ugly black man with shoulders higher than his head' is typical, and in the account of a case in 1573 the possessed person is revealingly said to have been 'monstrously transformed . . . much like the picture of the Devil in a play'.[49] The influence of Continental cases of possession is also discernible. The two physicians who diagnosed a Hertfordshire girl's possession in 1664 had been to France, where they had seen a whole convent of possessed nuns.[50]

A conspicuous feature of the cases of possession about which details survive is that they frequently originated in a religious environment. Indeed it could be plausibly urged that the victims were engaging in a hysterical reaction against the religious discipline and repression to which they had been subjected.[51] The Devil's presence was particularly likely to be suspected when the patient could not bear the sight or sound of religious objects and language; and exposure to prayer or religious ritual became a litmus-paper test of

48. The words are Joseph Hall's (*Works*, ed. Wynter, vii, p. 327).

49. J. Darrell, *A True Narration of the Strange and Grevous Vexation by the Devil, of 7. Persons in Lancashire* (1600), p. 11; *A Booke Declaringe the Fearfull Vexasion of one Alexander Nyndge* (?1578), sig. B1. For the influence of the published account of the Warboys affair on subsequent cases, see Ewen, ii, p. 183.

50. W. Drage, *Daimonomageia* (1665), p. 38.

51. A theme developed in the stimulating articles by E. Caulfield, 'Pediatric Aspects of the Salem Witchcraft Tragedy', *American Journ. of Diseases of Children*, lxv (1943) (kindly shown me by Mrs R. G. Lewis).

whether or not the patient was possessed. It was reported of James Barrow in 1663 that, 'if any other did take the Bible and mention the word of God or Christ in his hearing, he would roar and cry, making a hideous noise'. The boy Thomas Darling in 1596 only felt his fits come on when he was forced to take part in a prayer-meeting. The ex-bailiff of Dunwich, Thomas Spatchet, found himself unable to take part in religious exercises. The Worcestershire girl Joyce Dovey's fits came on at prayer-time. So did those of the Throckmorton children at Warboys.[52] Such cases recall the preacher Thomas Hall, whose devil-inspired insomnia was at its worst on the eve of the sabbath, or the Puritan, Richard Rothwell, who knew that he was obsessed by Satan because of an overpowering urge to blaspheme and reproach religion.[53]

An intensive régime of religious observance could thus provoke a violent reaction. In France the best-known cases of possession occurred in the nunneries for the same sort of reason. As Freud pointed out, demons were 'bad and reprehensible wishes, derivations of instinctual impulses that have been repudiated and repressed'. He himself regarded diabolical possession as a form of neurosis, associated with unconscious homosexual desires. More recent psychiatrists have considered it to be a severe type of schizophrenia.[54] Whatever its clinical nature, the consequences of possession are unmistakable. It provided both an explanation and a legitimation of the kind of unconventional behaviour which would not otherwise have been tolerated. When a possessed person burst forth with blasphemies and obscenities no one subsequently reproached him for doing so. Nor was the child who rebelled against his religious upbringing by hurling a Bible across the room liable to be punished, so long as

52. J. Barrow, *The Lord's Arm stretched out in an answer of Prayer* (1664), p. 8; Ewen, ii, p. 176; below, n. 73 (for Dovey) and n. 80 (for Spatchet); *The Most Strange and Admirable Discoverie of the three Witches of Warboys* (1593), sigs. C1, C2.

53. Above, p. 563 for Hall; S. Clarke, *The Lives of Two and Twenty Divines*, p. 91 (appended to *A Generall Martyrologie* (2nd edn, 1660)).

54. S. Freud, 'A Seventeenth-century Demonological Neurosis', *Complete Psychological Works*, ed. J. Strachey, *et al.* (1955–), xix; I. Macalpine and R. A. Hunter, *Schizophrenia* (1677) (1956), p. 49. It has been suggested that some may have been cases of ergotism, which produces convulsions and hallucinations (see the account of a recent outbreak in J. G. Fuller, *The Day of St. Anthony's Fire* [1969], kindly pointed out to me by Mrs Menna Prestwich). But it is hard to see how ergotism could have been so selective in its incidence.

it was the Devil who was to blame. On the contrary the child would become the centre of a dramatic ritual of prayer and healing in which he was treated with affectionate concern. To be the victim of possession was a means of expressing forbidden impulses and attracting the attention of otherwise indifferent or repressive superiors.[55]

It is not therefore surprising that so many cases of possession should have been reported among the Puritans and Dissenters. Possession was seldom diagnosed in circles where religion was regarded as a thing indifferent, and it was frequently the godly or ex-godly who were afflicted, their hysterical symptoms returning instantly upon the sight of a preacher or prayer-book. A typical example occurred in the spring of 1574 and was recorded at the time by the Puritan martyrologist, John Foxe. It is worth describing, since Foxe's account seems to have circulated widely in Puritan circles and helped to influence the language and style of many later cases.

The victim was a law student from the north of England named Briggs. He had been to a lecture on the sin against the Holy Ghost, and had misunderstood the lecturer to say that *all* sins came into this category. Searching his conscience and discovering many faults, he persuaded himself that he too had committed the sin and was a reprobate whose prayers were in vain. After several unsuccessful attempts at suicide, he noticed that he was being followed by an ugly dog which would not be driven away. When preparing to jump into the Thames he saw it glaring at him 'with such terrible sparkling eyes' that he realized it was no ordinary dog, but the Devil waiting for his soul. The dog subsequently vanished and a well-meaning physician, diagnosing a case of melancholy, prescribed blood-letting and a purge. But Briggs fell into a trance, and from his lips came forth his part of a dialogue between himself and the Devil which was eagerly recorded by the godly onlookers. The Devil assaulted him with a combination of threats and promises. On the one hand he assured him that there were no pains in Hell, that there was no God, that Christ was not the Son of God, that Christ's parents were unmarried, that the Scripture was false, and that everything happened by mere nature. On the other he urged that he was damned anyway, and that he would do better to settle for his offers of a cupboard of plate, and a seductive 'painted woman' (who temptingly sang and

55. cf. I. M. Lewis, 'Spirit Possession and Deprivation Cults', *Man*, new ser., i (1966), pp. 313–14.

danced before him). This discussion continued at intervals for over a fortnight (the Devil explaining that he took Sundays off to cut purses among the crowd at St Paul's Cross).

In the end Foxe was called in to conduct a special prayer-meeting to reclaim the patient. Addressing the Devil directly ('Thou most wretched serpent . . . O thou foul devil, I command thee to depart'), he engaged the spirit in fluent argument, clearly enjoying the opportunity of a joust of this kind. Satan skilfully counter-attacked by denouncing Foxe as a witch, but ultimately the patient himself was prevailed upon to command the Devil to depart in God's name, and his troubles were over.[56]

There had been a series of such dispossessions since the beginning of Elizabeth's reign involving many clergy, particularly those of vehement Protestant sympathies.[57] The year before the Briggs case, the Puritan Edward Nyndge, who had a university training, had played a leading role in the dispossession of his brother Alexander. It was he who identified the victim's symptoms, and who knew that the right procedure was to conjure the Devil in the name of Jesus to depart.[58] In 1574 there were at least four cases of alleged possession in addition to that of Briggs. In Norwich Bishop Parkhurst ordered fasting and prayer on behalf of a young Dutch girl whom the Devil had assaulted, but elsewhere most of the leaders of the Church were suspicious of these episodes and took action to prevent accounts of dispossession from being circulated. In London and Kent several women were punished for fraudulently simulating the symptoms of possession, and measures were taken against unlicensed printers who disseminated the story of their sufferings.[59]

56. I have used the two accounts in B.M., Harley MS 590, ff. 6–63, and B.M., Lansdowne MS 101, ff. 165–75. Attention was originally drawn to the episode by S. R. Maitland in his pioneering essay, 'Puritan Thaumaturgy', in *Notes on the Contributions of the Rev. George Townsend . . . to the new edition of Fox's Martyrology* (1841–2), i. See also *H.M.C.*, vii, pp. 624–5.

57. I. F(isher), *The Copy of A Letter describing the wonderful Woorke of God in delivering a Mayden within the City of Chester* (1565) (Anne Mylner, involving two Puritan clergy, John Lane and Robert Rogers); B.M., Harley MS 590, f. 69 (wife of Edmond Kingsfield, a London freemason, 1565); Scot, *Discoverie*, VII.iii (a Dutchman at Maidstone, 1572).

58. *A Booke declaringe the Fearfull Vexasion of one Alexander Nyndge* (1578?); E. Nyndge, *A True and Fearefull Vexation of one Alexander Nyndge* (1615) (a slightly different version).

59. *The Zurich Letters*, ed. H. Robinson (Cambridge, P.S., 1842–5), i, p. 303 (two Norwich cases); *The Disclosing of a late Counterfeyted Possesion by the Devyl in Two Maydens within the Citie of London* (1574); *Cor-*

The increasingly political character of these possessions and dispossessions was finally made clear in the later years of Elizabeth's reign by the notorious career of John Darrell, the Puritan exorcist.[60] Darrell, who was a university-educated preacher, conducted by prayer and fasting a series of spectacular cures of allegedly possessed persons, first in Derbyshire in 1586, then in 1596–7 in Nottinghamshire, Lancashire and Staffordshire. In 1589 he was convicted by the High Commission as an impostor who had trained his patients to simulate the now conventional symptoms of disorder in order to demonstrate his curative skill. Some of the most notable Puritan clergy of the day had been assistants at his dispossessions,[61] and the affair produced a head-on collision between the rival factions coexisting in the Anglican Church. A protracted pamphlet controversy not only revealed disagreement about the bona fides of Darrell's patients, but raised the whole question of the possibility of diabolical possession, and the status of the cure by prayer and fasting. In the process the question of the earlier Elizabethan cases was also reopened, Darrell citing them as inspiring precedents, and his opponents making play with what they called 'the cozening of good Master Foxe'.[62]

This debate was coloured by highly partisan considerations. Dar-

respondence of Matthew Parker, ed. J. Bruce and T. T. Perowne (Cambridge, P.S., 1853), pp. 465–6 (Agnes Bridges and Rachel Pinder, London); Scot, Discoverie, VII.i–ii (Mildred Norrington, Westwell, Kent, involving two local clergymen). The later case of Margaret Cooper, a yeoman's wife, involving a number of godly preachers, is described in A True and Most Dreadfull Discourse of a Woman possessed with the Devill ... at Dichet in Somersetshire (1584).

60. For general accounts of his activities, see R. A. Marchant, 'John Darrell – Exorcist', Trans. Thoroton Soc., lxiv (1960) and the same author's The Puritans and the Church Courts in the Diocese of York, 1560–1642 (1960), pp. 300–301; also Notestein, Witchcraft, chap. 4, and Ewen, ii, pp. 116, 181–6. C. H. Rickert, The Case of John Darrell (Gainesville, Florida, 1962) is less reliable.

61. Including Richard Bernard, Arthur Hildersham, John Ireton, John Brinsley, Robert Evington; J. Darrell, A Detection of that Sinnful Shamful Lying and Ridiculous Discours of Samuel Harshnet (1600), p. 170; The Triall of Maist. Dorrell (1599), pp. 44, 66; Marchant, Puritans and the Church Courts, p. 301.

62. J. Deacon and J. Walker, A Summarie Answere to al the Material Points in any of Master Darel his Bookes (1601), p. 238. cf. Darrell, A Breife Narration, sig. C1ᵛ; The Triall of Maist. Dorrell, p. 83; The Replie of John Darrell (1602), p. 18.

rell's well-publicized activities had been used to make propaganda on behalf of the Puritans by suggesting that they had a capacity for miracle-working, perhaps as an alternative tactic after the failure of their attempts to set up a new system of church government in the 1580s. Darrell also took the opportunity to make it clear that the Devil did not share the Puritan distaste for such excesses as long hair. Under Darrell's influence the previously lukewarm inhabitants of Nottingham became zealous hearers of the Word, and it was feared that his activities 'would infect the commonwealth'.[63] The Puritans also saw themselves as striking a blow against Popery. For, as the minister George More, Darrell's closest ally, argued: 'if the Church of England have this power to cast out devils, then the Church of Rome is a false church; for there can be but one true church, the principal mark whereof (as they say) is to work miracles, and of them this is the greatest, namely to cast out devils'.[64]

Fierce repressive action was taken by the bishops. The pamphlet account of Darrell's dispossession of Thomas Darling was called in and the printer imprisoned. Darrell and More were also arrested, and their supporters in Nottingham were threatened with being bound over for good behaviour. In his written justifications Darrell accused the bishops of silencing witnesses and generally conspiring to hush up the true facts. At Cambridge the Vice-Chancellor took action against the sale of Darrell's works. A tailor was arrested and the Puritan William Bradshaw was forced to withdraw temporarily from the University.[65]

The initiative in hounding down Darrell seems to have been taken by the leaders of the Arminian party, newly emerging within the Church of England, and it was they who made the issue of possession a political shibboleth. But there was no doubt in anyone's mind that an emphasis on fasting and prayer was a sign of Puritanism. In practice the issue was associated with other current controversies like the merits of a non-preaching ministry, the propriety of

63. *The Triall of Maist. Dorrell*, pp. 6, 76; *H.M.C., Middleton*, pp. 165–7.
64. G. More, *A True Discourse concerning the Certaine Possession and Dispossessiō of 7 Persons in one familie in Lancashire* (1600), p. 5.
65. Darrell, *A Breife Narration*, sig. Aiij^v; B. Brook, *The Lives of the Divines*, pp. 41 ff. In London in 1603 Thomas Darling, Darrell's former patient, who had matriculated at Oxford in 1600, was sentenced to lose his ears for libelling the Vice-Chancellor; *The Letters of John Chamberlain*, ed. N. E. McClure (Philadelphia, 1939), i, pp. 186–7.

maypoles, and the right of midwives to baptize.[66] Before the Darrell
affair had died down, there erupted several more cases of allegedly
possessed women, around whom Puritan clergy busied themselves
with fasting and prayer.[67] The original Darrell controversy thus fused
with these later outbreaks. Those involved on the Arminian side included Richard Bancroft, Bishop of London, and future Archbishop
of Canterbury; William Neile, Dean of Westminster, and later
Archbishop of York; and William Barlow, Archbishop Whitgift's
chaplain and later Bishop of Lincoln.[68] But the most prominent
figures were the pamphleteers, John Deacon and John Walker, and
the future Archbishop of York, Samuel Harsnet, then Bancroft's
chaplain.

It was Harsnet who exposed Darrell's 'fraudulent practices' in a
powerful tract denouncing the whole affair as a Puritan imposture.
With Deacon and Walker he declared categorically that all exorcisms were in vain, because miracles had ceased. Prayer and fasting
could never expel devils and anyway corporeal possession was a
thing of the past. The Arminians further published an English
translation of the controversial French case of Marthe Brossier, to
show that purely natural causes might underlie supposed cases of
possession. At the Cambridge Commencement William Barlow
publicly maintained that possession was no longer possible.[69]

66. See, e.g., Darrell, *A Detection*, pp. 63, 116; S. Bradwell, 'Marie
Glover's late woefull case' (1603) (Sloane 831), f. 7ᵛ; *The Triall of Maist.
Dorrell*, p. 80.

67. The most notable were those of Mary Glover in 1602, which involved
over half a dozen Puritan clergy (Bradwell, 'Marie Glover's late Woefull
Case' [Sloane 831]; J. Swan, *A True and Breife Report of Mary Glovers
Vexation* [1603]; L. Hewes, *Certaine Grievances* [1641], pp. 12–15), and
Nan Gunter in 1605 (Ewen, *Star Chamber*, pp. 28–36). The religious enthu-
siast, William Hacket, had earlier attempted a dispossession (H. Arthington,
The Seduction of Arthington by Hacket [1592], pp. 10, 14; [R. Cosin], *Con-
spiracie for Pretended Reformation* [1592] p. 5). Other cases are cited by
Darrell in *A Survey of Certaine Dialogical Discourses* (1602), pp. 54 ff.

68. For Neile, *H.M.C.*, *Hatfield*, xvii, p. 471; xviii, p. 423, and for Barlow,
Swan, *A True and Breife Report of Mary Glovers Vexation*, p. 57; and
below, n. 69.

69. S. H(arsnet), *A Discovery of the Fraudulent Practises of John Darrel*
(1599); J. Deacon and J. Walker, *Dialogicall Discourses of Spirits and
Divels* (1601) (p. 329 for Barlow) and *A Summarie Answere* (1601); *A True
Discourse upon the Matter of Martha Brossier* (1599), tr. A. Hartwell (and
dedicated to Bancroft); *The Triall of Maist. Dorrell*, p. 82. Details of the
Brossier affair are given in R. Mandrou, *Magistrats et sorciers en France au
XVIIᵉ siècle* (Paris, 1968), pp. 163–79.

Darrell countered by asserting that fasting and prayer were a recognized means of expulsion. They did not involve any claim to miracle-working, because they did not operate automatically, but only by God's grace. The trouble was that Darrell was not consistent on this point, for in his writings he sometimes said that the method could not fail. On a number of occasions, moreover, both he and other Puritan ministers seem to have directly addressed the Devil, conjuring him to depart, in the old Catholic manner. This happened in several of the cases of 1574, and at Chester ten years previously John Lane had even blown vinegar into the possessed girl's nostrils.[70] This was a different matter from merely supplicating God for his assistance.

The culmination of the controversy was the ruling in Canon 72 of the new Church Canons of 1604 that henceforth no minister, unless he had the special permission of his bishop, was to attempt 'upon any pretence whatsoever whether of possession or obsession, by fasting and prayer, to cast out any devil or devils, under pain of the imputation of imposture or cozenage and deposition from the ministry'. This effectively put an end to the practice, at least as far as conforming members of the Anglican Church were concerned, for in the seventeenth century there seems to have been no subsequent case in which such a licence is known for certain to have been given.[71] During the reign of James I, the King himself and several of the bishops busied themselves in exposing cases of fraudulent possession. When James came to Cambridge in 1615 the University thought it appropriate to stage a play containing an episode mocking the whole procedure of exorcism.[72] Many of the Puritan clergy, however, clung to their belief in the efficacy of fasting and prayer in cases of possession, and continued to hold that any individual minister was entitled to order a local fast when he thought it necessary. The method, wrote Thomas Cooper in 1617, was 'not absolute and necessarily effectual . . . yet profitable and convenient to be

70. For these cases, see above, p. 575.

71. According to R. S. Hawker (*Footprints of Former Men in Far Cornwall* [1870], pp. 103–24), Seth Ward, Bishop of Salisbury, issued a licence to lay a ghost in 1665; but the story is a fabrication; see R. M. Baine, *Defoe and the Supernatural* (Athens, Ga, 1968), chap. vii. For a similar legend, see *Country Folk-Lore, ii*, ed. Mrs Gutch (Folk-Lore Soc. 1901), p. 95.

72. H. N. Paul, *The Royal Play of Macbeth* (New York, 1950), pp. 75–130; Kittredge, *Witchcraft*, pp. 325–7; J. B. Mullinger, *The University of Cambridge from the Royal Injunctions of 1535 to the Accession of Charles the First* (Cambridge, 1884), pp. 537, 545.

used'. There was a long series of dispossessions in the first half of the seventeenth century.[73] The bishops, however, kept a sharp curb on such activities until the Civil War, and were always ready to expose frauds and punish participants. Indeed, as Richard Baxter records, it was to be one of the great Puritan grievances against the bishops that the High Commission showed such hostility to 'fasting and prayer and other exercises which they found much benefit by'.[74] After the Long Parliament met, Darrell's *True Relation* of the dispossession of William Sommers was defiantly republished in September 1641.

With the proliferation of the sects under the Interregnum cases of alleged diabolical possession multiplied. For one of the paradoxes of the condition was that its symptoms were scarcely capable of being differentiated from those of religious ecstasy. Sectaries who engaged in marathon acts of fasting or gave vent to religious prophecy were often said by enemies to have been bewitched, or even to be witches themselves. The Quakers, in particular, were the subject of numerous such charges. George Fox's strong personal magnetism provoked many accusations of witchcraft, while the bodily

73. Cooper, *Mystery*, p. 295. Details of these episodes may be found in W. Hinde, *A Faithful Remonstrance of the Holy Life . . . of Iohn Bruen* (1641), pp. 146-7 ('142-3') (fasting and prayer to cure a bewitched servant); Clarke, *The Lives of Two and Twenty Divines*, pp. 91-4 (John Fox dispossessed, c. 1612, by Richard Rothwell [who on another occasion (p. 91) had had to have the Devil ejected from himself]); (R. Baddeley), *The Boy of Bilson* (1622), p. 50 (unsuccessful Puritan attempt to cure William Perry, 1620); Ewen, *Star Chamber*, pp. 55-6 (prayer for Katherine Malpas, a counterfeit, 1621-2); B.M., Harley MS 6865, ff. 5-8ᵛ (Roger Sterrop of the Somers Is., possessed in 1629, and cured during a public fast); *C.S.P.D., 1634-5*, p. 263 (attempted dispossession of ungodly parishioner by Anthony Lapthorne, Rector of Tretire with Michaelchurch, Herefordshire, 1634); *1637-38*, p. 586 (fraudulent cases of possession); *A Strange and True Relation of a Young Woman Possesst with the Devill* (1647) and 'A True and Briefe Relation of . . . Joies Dovie' (Dr Williams's Lib., Baxter Treatises, vi, no. 211 [ff. 319-22] [dispossession of Joyce Dovie of Bewdley, 1641-46]); Clarke, *The Lives of Two and Twenty Divines*, pp. 216-17 (Robert Balsom ejects a devil from a Scottish steward at Berwick, n.d. [pre-1647]); (M. Moore), *Wonderfull News from the North* (1650) (Balsom and others involved in case of bewitched children of George Muschamp).
74. *Reliquiae Baxterianae*, ed. M. Sylvester (1696), i, p. 33. For episcopal activity see Ewen, ii, pp. 116, 236-7; R. B., *The Life of Dr Thomas Morton* (York, 1669), pp. 72-5; Swan, *A True and Briefe Report of Mary Glovers Vexation*, p. 61; S. B. Babbage, *Puritanism and Richard Bancroft* (1962), p. 333; Davies, *Four Centuries of Witch-Beliefs*, pp. 76-80.

convulsions stimulated by religious excitement at Quaker meetings were hailed as obvious signs of possession.[75] Several ex-Quakers claimed to have been bewitched during their period of conversion,[76] and a few formal charges of this kind were actually brought before the law courts.[77] Other sectaries were suspected of using sorcery to attract followers to their cause.[78] Eccentric behaviour was thus deemed to be divine or satanic, according to the way one looked at it.

In conventional Dissenting circles the reality of diabolical possession and the efficacy of fasting and prayer continued to be upheld until the end of the seventeenth century. Henry Newcome recalled the prayer-meetings held at Cambridge in 1659 to rescue a woman who had promised her soul to the Devil: 'It was a University then, when many Masters of Arts, Fellows of Colleges, could be found to keep a night to such a purpose.'[79] In the fifty years after the Restoration Nonconformist clergymen frequently conducted prayer and fasting to quieten haunted houses, effect physical cures and allay diabolical possession. They also took every opportunity to publish accounts of their activities.[80]

75. *Journal of George Fox*, ed. N. Penney (Cambridge, 1911), i, pp. 3, 38, 104–5, 149, 203, 340, 411; R. Farmer, *The Great Mysteries of Godlinesse and Ungodlinesse* (1655), pp. 79–87; *A Brief Relation of the Irreligion of the Northern Quakers* (1653), pp. 16–20; L. Muggleton, *A Looking-Glass for George Fox* (1756 edn), pp. 44–6; *An Account of the Convincement ... of ... Richard Davies* (3rd edn, 1771), pp. 31, 41; (C. Leslie), *The Snake in the Grass* (1696), pp. xix–xxi; *George Fox's 'Book of Miracles'*, ed. H. J. Cadbury (Cambridge, 1948), pp. 93–5; A. M. Gummere, *Witchcraft and Quakerism* (1908), pp. 18, 31–5.

76. (J. Gilpin), *The Quakers Shaken* (1653); W. Y. Tindall, *John Bunyan, Mechanick Preacher* (1934: reprint, New York, 1964), appx.

77. Tindall, op cit., appx; E. Porter, *Cambridgeshire Customs and Folklore* (1969), pp. 169–72; *A Gagg for the Quakers*, 'To the Reader' (1659) (confession of diabolic witchcraft by five ex-Quakers). It has been suggested that the tall hat associated with witches in modern nursery tales was originally the head-dress of Quaker women preachers; A. M. Gummere, *The Quaker* (Philadelphia, 1901), pp. 194–5.

78. Tindall, op. cit., p. 222; Baxter, *The Certainty of the World of Spirits*, pp. 64–5; *The Harleian Miscellany* (1808–11), vi, p. 393; *The Clarke Papers*, ed. C. H. Firth (Camden Soc., 1891–1901), ii, p. 150 n.; N. Glass, *The Early History of the Independent Church at Rothwell* (Northampton, 1871), pp. 85–7; L. Muggleton, *The Acts of the Witnesses* (1699), p. 63.

79. *The Diary of the Rev. Henry Newcome*, ed. T. Heywood (Chetham Soc., 1849), pp. xxii–xxiii.

80. Accounts of some of these episodes may be found in T. A(ldridge), *The Prevalency of Prayer* (1717), *passim*; *The Records of a Church of Christ, Meeting in Broadmead, Bristol, 1640–87*, ed. E. B. Underhill (Han-

But it was not only the Dissenters who made useful propaganda out of the Anglican abdication from the ancient priestly office of exorcism. Inevitably, the Catholics, who continued to employ the rite on the Continent, invoked it as part of their campaign to reconquer England for the faith in the reign of Elizabeth I, chary though the Counter-Reformation Church normally was about permitting such exorcisms. In 1558, at the last stage of the Marian reaction, a priest from Rome was sent by Bishop Bonner to conjure an evil spirit out of the heretic John Mills, although the supposedly possessed man had laughed in the exorcist's face.[81] In 1585-6 (the time of Darrell's first case), however, a more systematic campaign of exorcising was launched among the members of some leading recusant households, notably those of Sir George Peckham at Denham, Buckinghamshire, and Lord Vaux at Hackney. A number of priests under the leadership of the Jesuit, William Weston, spectacularly ejected devils from maid-servants and others by an elaborate ritual, which involved seating the possessed person in a chair, holding his head over smoking brimstone and forcing him to drink a potion of sack mixed with holy oil and rue, a concoction, according to Harsnet, 'which an honest man would scarce give to an horse'.[82] The main aim was to demonstrate that only the representatives of the true faith had the power to cast out devils. But a number of additional debating points were scored in the process. During his long interrogations, for example, the Devil was prevailed upon to reveal his strongly Protestant sympathies and his terror of the Church of Rome.

The Catholics made such play of these and other exorcisms that the leading participants were eventually seized and examined by the

---

serd Knollys Soc., 1847), pp. 191–5; T. W. W. Smart in *Sussex Archaeol. Collns*, xiii (1861), pp. 67–8; Notestein, *Witchcraft*, pp. 256–7, 315–20; Turner, *Providences*, ii, p. 152; Baxter, *The Certainty of the World of Spirits*, pp. 23, 56; S. Petto, *A Faithful Narrative of the ... Fits which Thomas Spatchet ... was under by Witchcraft* (1693) (Spatchet had been involved in the 1645 Suffolk witch-trials initiated by Matthew Hopkins [Ewen, i, p. 299]. His own fits, which came on in the period 1660–7, were also blamed upon a witch); *H.M.C.*, v, p. 381; R. Bovet, *Pandaemonium* (1684), ed. M. Summers (Aldington, 1951), pp. 101–3; W. Clark, *A True Relation of one Mrs Jane Farrer's of Stebbin in Essex being Possess'd with the Devil* (n.d. [c. 1710]).

81. Foxe, viii, p. 485. For hesitation about permitting exorcism on the Continent, see Lea, *Materials*, pp. 1052, 1054–5.

82. *A Discovery of the Fraudulent Practises of John Darrel*, p. 67.

authorities. In 1603, in the wake of the Darrell controversy, their depositions were published by Samuel Harsnet in his *A Declaration of Egregious Popish Impostures*, a scathing work of polemic.[83] Thereafter it became common to print hostile accounts of Catholic exorcisms on the Continent.[84] The recusants, however, continued their activities. Every year the reports of the Jesuit Mission in England recorded successful exorcisms of bewitched persons and dispossessions of those attacked by evil spirits. In 1626, for example, no fewer than sixty persons were said to have been relieved. Propaganda was also made about the curative efficacy of relics, the agnus dei, holy water and holy wells. In return the bishops did their best to expose frauds, like William Perry, 'the boy of Bilson', whose impostures in 1620 had been encouraged by Popish exorcists.[85]

Many of these cases of supposed possession also involved accusations of witchcraft. Diabolic possession did not necessarily presuppose a human intermediary, but in practice it was common for the victim to see a vision of the witch responsible for his torments, and for preventive action to be taken accordingly. Fits of the type associated with possession were conventionally seen as the result of witchcraft. A number of accusations of witchcraft were made under the

83. This remains the main source for the affair and is the basis of the useful account by T. G. Law, 'Devil-Hunting in Elizabethan England', *The Nineteenth Century*, xxxv (1894). Catholic versions may be found in Diego de Yepes, *Historia Particular de la Persecucion de Inglaterra* (Madrid, 1599), pp. 97–102; *The Troubles of our Catholic Forefathers*, ed. J. Morris (1872–7), ii, pp. 99–103, 174, 282–3, 326–31; *C.S.P.D., 1581–90*, pp. 347–8, 372. For a later episode (diocese of Chester, 1598) see *H.M.C., Hatfield*, viii, pp. 213–14.

84. S. Michaelis, *The Admirable Historie of the Possession and Conversion of a Penitent Woman*, trans. W.B. (1613); *A Relation of the Devill Balams Departure out of the Body of the Mother-Prioresse of the Ursuline Nuns of Loudun* (1636).

85. H. Foley, *Records of the English Province of the Society of Jesus* (1875–83), ii, pp. 6, 17, 20–21, 566, 567, 569–71; iii, pp. 122–3, 446–8; iv, pp. 448, 500; vi, p. 116; vii, pp. xxvi, 1107, 1121, 1122, 1130, 1133–4, 1137–8, 1141, 1145, 1200; *Analecta Bollandiana*, vi (1887), pp. 317–18; and below, pp. 587, 646. See also Ewen, ii, pp. 116–17, 216, 227, 236–7; R. Hunter and I. Macalpine, *Three Hundred Years of Psychiatry, 1535–1860* (1963), p. 151; B. Zimmerman, *Carmel in England* (1899), p. 258; J. Gee, *The Foot out of the Snare* (1624), pp. 54–5 (R. Challoner), *Memoirs of Missionary Priests* (1741–2), i, pp. 187–8; Notestein, *Witchcraft*, p. 315; *The Troubles of our Catholic Forefathers*, ed. Morris, iii, pp. 52–3; Z. Taylor, *The Devil turn'd Casuist* (1696), *passim*; *The Life and Miracles of S. Wenefrede* (1713) p. 116.

influence of the Catholic exorcists, while every one of Darrell's cases resulted in a witch or witches being held responsible for the victim's misfortunes.[86] It may well have been this side of his activities which helped to bring about his downfall. For Harsnet was a disciple of Reginald Scot and bitterly denounced the whole concept of witchcraft. Bancroft also seems to have been sceptical.[87]

For the minority who were sceptical of possession and bewitching it did not matter that the Anglican clergy had renounced one of the most impressive ancient manifestations of clerical power – the ability to cast out devils. In 1603, the year of *A Declaration of Egregious Popish Impostures*, Dr Edward Jorden produced a powerful exposé of the variety of possible natural causes underlying supposed cases of possession.[88] Although his analysis was limited by the contemporary assumption that female hysteria was located in the uterus (or 'mother'), he showed a penetrating awareness of the scope of psychosomatic illness, and a strong reluctance to accept any supernatural explanation where a natural one could be found. He also pointed out that fasting and prayer might be an efficacious cure on purely natural grounds, because they weakened the body and reduced tension. In the last resort, Jorden did not deny that diabolical possession was possible. But his readiness to look for natural causes, if they could be found, recalled the comment of the Protestant divine William Fulke on John Lane's dispossession of the Chester girl in 1564, that it was 'no miracle, but a natural work; the maid perhaps being affected with the mother, or some such-like disease'.[89] This attitude was to become increasingly common during the seventeenth century, when a working doctor like John Symcotts of Huntingdon could deal with many cases of mysterious fits and convulsions without ever feeling the need to invoke the Devil as an explanation.[90]

86. The witches uncovered by Darrell are listed in his *A Detection*, pp. 109–10, and Harsnet, *A Discovery* (1599), pp. 37, 249–50. For others accused in connection with the Protestant dispossessions of 1574, see Ewen, ii, pp. 148–9, and *The Disclosing of a Late Counterfeyted Possession* (1574), sigs. Avj[v], Bj[v]. For accusations arising from Catholic exorcisms, see Ewen, ii, p. 115 n. 2; Baddeley, *The Boy of Bilson*, p. 70; Taylor, *The Devil turn'd Casuist*, p. 2.

87. S. Harsnet, *A Declaration of Egregious Popish Impostures* (1603), pp. 132–8; *The Triall of Maist. Dorrell*, pp. 87–8.

88. E. Jorden, *A Briefe Discourse of a Disease called the Suffocation of the Mother* (1603).

89. W. Fulke, *Stapleton's Fortress Overthrown*, ed. R. Gibbings (Cambridge, P.S., 1848), p. 76.

90. F. N. L. Poynter and W. J. Bishop, *A Seventeenth-century Doctor*

At the end of the century the idea of demonic possession was further weakened by the controversy following the exorcism of a Lancashire gardener, Richard Dugdale, 'the Surey demoniac', a *cause célèbre* which did much to spread scepticism among the educated classes. The claims, first of the Catholics, then of a group of reputable Nonconformist ministers, to have dispossessed this hysterical youth, were exposed in 1697 by Zachary Taylor, an Anglican polemicist. He denounced the boy as an impostor and drew attention to the readiness of those involved to lay a charge of witchcraft against an old woman in the neighbourhood.[91] Meanwhile a growing current of theological opinion was ready to deny the reality of demonic possession even in Biblical times and to reinterpret the possessed in the New Testament as epileptics or sufferers from various hysterical illnesses. This view had been in circulation for some time. In 1555 Bishop Bonner found it necessary to refute heretics who declared that when the Apostles cast out 'devils' they were working like other doctors by medicine and natural means. Sceptics like Scot and Hobbes predictably regarded the New Testament possessions as cases of madness or epilepsy, but even the godly Biblical scholar Joseph Mede held that 'these demoniacs were no other than such as we call madmen and lunatics'. In the Hanoverian period this was to become a characteristic deistical position.[92]

But for most of those living in the immediate aftermath of the Reformation the existence of evil spirits was still a reality. It was also a peril against which the clergy seemed to have abandoned their traditional defence. Apart from those Puritans who put their faith in fasting and prayer, most Protestants seemed content to let the power of exorcism become a Roman Catholic monopoly. They were prepared to seek God's help in cases of supposed possession, but their prayers held no guarantee of success. Faced by such gloomy

(Pubs Beds. Hist. Rec. Soc., 1951); Kocher, *Science and Religion*, pp. 136–42.

91. There is a brief account of the episode in Notestein, *Witchcraft*, pp. 315–19, 371–3. See also *The Diary of Abraham de la Pryme*, ed. C. Jackson (Surtees Soc., 1870), pp. 199–200.

92. E. Bonner, *A Profitable and Necessarye Doctrine* (1555), sig. Dd iv^v; Scot, *Discoverie : A Discourse upon Divels and Spirits*, chap. xiv; T. Hobbes, *Leviathan* (1651), chaps. 34, 45; *The Works of ... Joseph Mede* (1664), i, p. 38; D. Whitby, A *Paraphrase and Commentary on the New Testament* (1703), ii, pp. xxx-xxxi. cf. (A. A. Sykes), *An Enquiry into the Meaning of Demoniacks in the New Testament* (1737); and R. Mead, *Medica Sacra* (1749; Eng. trans. by T. Stack, 1755), chap. ix; below, p. 683.

counsel, the laity reacted differently. Some turned to wizards and charmers, in the hope that they might perform the role from which the clergy had abdicated. Others became their own exorcists; when Margaret Hooper, a yeoman's wife, was possessed in 1641, her husband and brother-in-law summoned their courage and successfully conjured the Devil to depart in the name of the Father, Son and Holy Ghost.[93] Others were driven back upon miscellaneous folk remedies. In 1653 at Oxford the young Anthony Wood, suffering from the ague, was told that the disease was caused by a devil, and that the proper course of action was to jump into the river, and then run quickly out, leaving the evil spirit to drown.[94] A variety of charms and amulets were also used in an effort to gain the protection from demons which religion no longer afforded.

By abandoning so crucial a task as the expulsion of devils, the Protestant clergy were jeopardizing their prestige. It was easy for educated contemporaries like John Selden to scoff at exorcism as 'mere juggling', invented to gain respect for the clergy; but, as Selden himself observed, the clergy enjoyed less respect among ordinary Anglicans than among Puritans or Catholics. In Popish countries the peasants' belief in the priest's magical resources helped to sustain the prestige of organized religion.

If once a priest could bring his parishioners to believe this power of exorcism [declared a writer in 1712], I don't doubt but in time he might graft more pretended miracles upon that stock and set up at last driving away the plague, curing cattle of the murrain, boast of a sovereign remedy against the toothache, recover lost goods, and, in short, be resorted to as a prophet upon all occasions.[95]

In England the medieval stories of sufferers cured by relics and images had not been forgotten. They were still the subject of popular literature and commemorated in the sculpture and carvings of many village churches. Some nostalgia for Catholic times was inevitably generated. 'In Queen Mary's days,' complained an old woman in the seventeenth century, 'churchmen had more cunning and could teach people many a trick that our ministers nowadays know not.'[96]

There can be no doubt that the Anglican Church's confessed im-

93. *Most Fearefull and Strange Newes from the Bishoppricke of Durham* (1641: Newcastle, 1843), p. 16.

94. Wood, *Life and Times*, i, p. 179.

95. J. Selden, *Table-Talk* (Temple Classics, n.d.), pp. 39, 85; *A Full Confutation of Witch-craft* (1712), pp. 44–5.

96. Ady, p. 59.

potence in this sphere was a frequent source of irritation to its defenders. When travelling on the Continent around 1605, Joseph Hall, the future Bishop of Exeter, met a Catholic divine who taunted him with his Church's failure to produce a single miracle. To this Hall, who was to be alone among the bishops in admiring the exploits of John Darrell, was stung into asserting (pace Harsnet) 'that in our Church we had manifest proofs of the ejection of devils by fasting and prayer'. The Catholic answered contemptuously that, if it could be proved that any devil had ever been thus dispossessed in the Church of England, 'he would quit his religion'.[97] At the end of the seventeenth century, a female observer of the attempted dispossession of Susannah Fowles remarked that 'if we of the Church of England did not, and the Popish priests did cast the Devil out of this woman, she did believe that she should be a proselyte to their church'.[98] This was the situation which Darrell had tried to rectify, even taking over some of the patients the Catholics had failed to cure in an effort to beat them at their own game.

It was no wonder that the recusant clergy attracted crowds of admirers when they began their well-publicized campaign of dispossession in 1586. 'In the compass of half a year,' estimated a contemporary, 'no fewer ... were by that means reconciled to the Church of Rome than five hundred persons: some have said three or four thousand.'[99] Fresh tales of exorcism were brought back by Continental travellers: it was after witnessing the exorcism of the Ursuline nuns at Loudun in 1635 that the courtier and diplomat Walter Montagu was converted to Popery. At home the recusant clergy specialized in dealing with cases in which the Protestant ministers had failed. Susannah Fowles was told that 'she would never be cured till the men with hair coats and bare legs came to her from the Portugal Ambassador's'. Even Calvinists were reported to have taken difficult cases to the Papists.[100] The Catholic rite of exorcism, thought Henry Bourne in 1725, 'raised in the vulgar formerly such an opinion of their ignorant priests as to make them be esteemed men of the greatest faith and learning; ... the opinion has reached even our

97. *Works of . . : Joseph Hall*, ed. Wynter, i, p. xxxi. For Hall's favourable view of Darrell, see ibid, viii, pp. 209–10.

98. *The Second Part of the Boy of Bilson: Or, a True and Particular Relation of the Impostor Susanna Fowles* (1698), p. 12.

99. *Troubles of our Catholic Forefathers*, ed. Morris, ii, p. 99.

100. Foley, *Records of the English Province of the Society of Jesus*, ii, pp. 22–3; iii, p. 123; v, p. 993; vii, p. 1098; Zimmerman, *Carmel in England*, pp. 254–7; 'The Tryal of Susannah Fowles' (BM., Add. MS 28,645), ff.3ᵛ–4.

days, and it is common for the present vulgar to say, none can lay
a spirit but a *Popish priest*.'[101]

3. *Witchcraft and religion*

In the Middle Ages the apparatus of organized religion had provided
a substantial measure of protection against the depredations of the
Devil and the maleficence of witchcraft. 'The exorcisms of the
Church are for this very purpose,' declared the authors of the
Malleus Maleficarum, 'and are entirely efficacious remedies for preserving oneself from the injuries of witches.' Holy water, the sign
of the cross, holy candles, church bells, consecrated herbs, sacred
words worn next to the body – such were the means through which
the Christian might secure immunity from the fiend.[102] There were
prayers so potent against the Devil that even wicked men could use
them with certainty of success. Holy bread or water, ran one typical
formula, taken for nine days with the recitation of three Paternosters
and three Aves in honour of the Trinity and St Hubert, would keep
one safe from all disease, witchcraft, mad dogs and the Devil.[103]
Similar remedies could be applied if the witch had already struck,
though the sophisticated admitted that they might conceivably fail.
If this happened, some medieval theologians were even prepared to
allow the use of folk magic, provided it did not involve the invocation
of demons or the transfer of the disease to another person.[104]

The Church may have always been stronger on protection than
cure. But it was a sign of the growing uncertainty of Continental
theologians that later medieval clergymen should have fallen back
on the 'ultimate remedy' and 'last recourse of the Church,'[105] the
extermination of the witch herself. This trend, however, seems to
have had little influence in medieval England, where the Church
continued to offer the faithful a great deal of protection against
supernatural terrors. Growing scepticism affected Catholic intellectuals on the Continent, but in England it was only the Reformation
which disturbed the situation, by drastically reducing the degree of
immunity from witchcraft which could be conveyed by religious

101. J. Brand, *Observations on Popular Antiquities* (1910), p. 113. For
the long survival of this tradition, see, e.g., J. C. Atkinson, *Forty Years in a
Moorland Parish* (1907 edn), p. 59n.
102. *Malleus*, II.i; above, pp. 56, 570.
103. *Dives and Pauper* (1536), ff. 49ᵛ–50; Scot, *Discoverie*, XII.xxi.
104. *Malleus*, II.ii; Scot, *Discoverie*, XII.xix.
105. *Malleus*, II.ii.8.

faith alone. All the old mechanical protections were dismissed as empty symbols, lacking any efficacy in themselves. For how, demanded the Protestant preacher, John Scory, in 1543, could the Devil be afraid of such toys, when the New Testament recorded that he was not even afraid of Christ himself?[106] When Richard Greenham was approached by a woman who believed herself to be bewitched, his advice was essentially negative: she should at all costs refrain from consulting wizards. In addition he recommended prayer, repentance and patience.[107] Like the late medieval canonists,[108] the Protestant clergy also banned recourse to popular counter-magic. They sometimes permitted the removal of magical objects which had been left behind by the witch to further her *maleficium;* one might pull out the pins stuck in a wax doll, for example. But any other form of magical relief was totally prohibited.[109]

The new religion made the situation even bleaker by playing down the importance of guardian angels, and denying the intercessionary power of saints, while at the same time placing an unprecedented stress upon the reality of the Devil and the extent of his earthly dominion. The situation was piquantly symbolized by the change made under Protestant influence in 1558 in the annual procession by St George's Gild, Norwich. The two saints, George and Margaret, were not allowed to appear any more, but it was resolved that 'the Dragon (should) come in and show himself as in other years'.[110]

It is not surprising that many old Catholic formulae retained their value in times of emergency for Protestants who found themselves disarmed in face of the old enemy. As William Perkins complained, 'using the name of Jesus to drive away the Devil or to prevent witchcraft' remained a 'common practice among the ignorant'. When twelve-year-old Agnes Browne was bewitched by Joan Waterhouse in Essex in 1566, she protected herself against the fearful apparition of a black dog with the face of an ape by uttering the holy name.[111] Housewives who baked bread or cakes commonly cut the sign of the

106. J. Strype, *Memorials of ... Thomas Cranmer* (1694), p. 103. For this whole development, see above, chapter 3.

107. *Workes of ... Richard Greenham*, p. 42.

108. Lea, *Materials*, pp. 262, 268, 326, 400, 411, 568.

109. e.g., Perkins, *Discourse*, p. 152; Cooper, *Mystery*, p. 70; Weemse, *A Treatise of the Foure Degenerate Sonnes*, pp. 50–52, 147.

110. D. Rock, *The Church of our Fathers*, ed. G. W. Hart and W. H. Frere (1903–4), ii, p. 343 n.

111. Perkins, *Discourse*, p. 150; Ewen, ii, p. 146 (and other instances on pp. 216, 221).

cross on the top of the dough as a means of protection against evil influences. Men who found themselves in the presence of the bewitched were liable to cross themselves, even in the later seventeenth century.[112] The cunning folk made extensive use of old Catholic formulae: John Dee anointed a possessed maidservant with holy oil in 1590, and a Newcastle midwife, Mistress Pepper, used a bottle of holy water and a silver crucifix in an attempt to cure a bewitched person in 1664.[113] The Laudians were accused in 1641 of teaching that the sign of the cross would drive away demons. Edmund Mayor, rector of Finningham, Suffolk, was even said to have maintained that a Bible in the house would keep out the Devil.[114]

Such doctrines, however, incurred the uncompromising hostility of most contemporary theologians. For Protestantism forced its adherents into the intolerable position of asserting the reality of witchcraft, yet denying the existence of an effective and legitimate form of protection or cure. The Church of England discarded the apparatus of mechanical religious formulae, but it was not prepared to claim that faith alone would protect the godly from witchcraft. Satan, it taught, was an instrument of God's inscrutable judgement, and might well be allowed to try the godly as well to plague the wicked. Certainly it was more unusual for a truly godly man to be bothered by witches, but there was no denying that it could happen. However firm his faith, even the most devout Christian might find himself tried and tested by the *maleficium* of sorcery, no less than by any other misfortune. It was not true that witches had no power against the faithful; they might well be permitted to plague them incessantly.[115]

112. Aubrey, *Gentilisme*, p. 51; *An Account of the Convincement ... of ... Richard Davies*, p. 41; and see above, p. 83.

113. *The Private Diary of Dr John Dee*, ed. J. O. Halliwell (Camden Soc., 1842), p. 35; *York Depositions*, p. 127. For other instances, see W. J. Pressey, 'The Records of the Archdeaconries of Essex and Colchester', *Trans. Essex Archaeol. Soc.*, xix (1927–30), p. 18; Ewen, ii, p. 222; and above, Chapter 7.

114. *A Large Supplement of the Canterburian Self-Conviction* (1641), p. 58; A. G. Matthews, *Walker Revised* (Oxford, 1948), p. 339.

115. For the assumption that the godly were less likely to be attacked, see, e.g., Gifford, *A Discourse of the Subtill Practises of Devilles*, sig. I2; Perkins, *Discourse*, pp. 223–4; Bernard, *Guide*, p. 182; J. Butler, *The Most Sacred and Divine Science of Astrology* (1680), i, p. 43; Lea, *Materials*, p. 268. cf. below, p. 591. Clear statements that faith did not convey immunity may be found in (James VI), *Daemonologie* (Edinburgh, 1597), p. 47; Perkins, op. cit., sig. q5ᵛ; Cooper, *Mystery*, pp. 248–53; Gaule, *Select Cases of Conscience*, p. 136. Some writers suggested that the Devil could not *kill*

What then was the victim to do? He could resort to prayer and supplication; he could search himself with a view to identifying the sins which had thus provoked the Almighty's wrath; he could reform himself and his household; he could fast and pray; and he could continue to place all his trust in God. 'If husbands would say the Lord's Prayer for their wives oftener than they do,' said one writer, 'God would keep their wives from saying their prayers backwards for them so oft as many do.' The astrologer, Joseph Blagrave, declared that 'in all my practice I could never find that ever any man or woman that did daily pray, especially in the morning, were ever taken in the snare of witchcraft that day'.[116] But, in the last resort, all theologians agreed that such steps carried no infallible guarantee of immunity and no certain promise of cure. Even fasting and prayer were said to be less effective against witchcraft than they were in cases of possession.[117]

This view was not as pessimistic as it sounds. The Protestant position was that steadfast faith in God was an infallible protection against the Devil's onslaughts on men's souls, but did not provide a similar immunity for their bodies and goods. But the Devil's real aim in molesting their material goods was to weaken men's faith and seduce them into looking away from God in the hope of relief. *Maleficium* was part of Satan's campaign to capture men's souls. The victim who turned to magic to ward off the Devil's material attacks might gain temporary relief, but the long-term consequences would be infinitely more terrible. On the other hand, the man with Job-like faith might find his goods and his body consumed, but his soul would emerge strengthened by the encounter. As George Gifford put it:

A man [is] tormented sore in his body; he feareth that it is some witch that hath done it. He is advised by his neighbours to send unto some cunning man. Word is sent back, that indeed he hath bad neighbours: let him do such or such a thing, and he shall have ease. Well, he doth it and hath ease. What, shall we think that the Devil is driven out? A woeful driving out. He doth cease from tormenting the body for a time, that he may enter deeper into the soul. He winneth by this driving out.[118]

---

a man unless he had been first persuaded to renounce God (Spalding, *Elizabethan Demonology*, pp. 80–82), but this was not a generally held view.

116. *The Family-Prayers of those Poor Christians* (1675), p. 20; J. Blagrave, *Blagraves Astrological Practice of Physick* (1671), p. 141.

117. Darrell, *A True Narration*, pp. 64–5; Drage, *Daimonomageia*, p. 22.

118. G. Gifford, *Two Sermons upon 1. Peter 5*, vers. 8 and 9 (1597), p. 66.

The proper behaviour in the face of *maleficium* was thus passive endurance, supported by the confident faith that, whatever the Devil might do to a man's body or goods, he could never touch his immortal soul. In the words of John Bunyan:

> Hobgoblin, nor foul fiend
> Can daunt his spirit;
> He knows he at the end
> Shall life inherit.

It is not surprising that these austere counsels were not always acted upon. Evidence from the trials shows that even the witches themselves sometimes thought that religious faith could nullify their spells. Agnes Waterhouse's familiar, the cat Satan, for example, was said in 1566 to have been unable to hurt her neighbour Wardol, because he 'was so strong in faith'. But Agnes was a Catholic, whose familiar would only allow her to pray in Latin, and her assumption may have been derived from the old religion. Joan Cony, hanged in 1589, similarly confessed that her spirits could not hurt those of her neighbours who were distinguished for their faith in God. But she was eighty years old and had presumably been brought up a Catholic. John Walsh, who declared in 1556 that the daily recitation of the Lord's Prayer and Creed would protect a man from harm by witchcraft, is known to have been a servant and pupil of a Marian priest. It was in such cases of obvious Catholic influence that the belief in the protective power of religion was usually to be found.[119]

Those who trod the narrow path, trusting only in God, and renouncing all magical aids, were inevitably subject to some heart-searching. Oliver Heywood, the Yorkshire Dissenting minister, recorded in his diary for May 1683 that a strange illness had fallen upon one of his flock:

He lies in his bed, hath swelling in his throat, hand cannot stir, looks as one affrighted ... One Dr Thornton ... saith it is not a natural dis-

This work contains an excellent exposition of this argument. For similar statements, see, e.g., Calvin, *Institutes*, I.xiv.18; (H. Holland), *A Treatise against Witchcraft* (Cambridge, 1590), sigs. H2^v–3^v; J. Mason, *The Anatomie of Sorcerie* (Cambridge, 1612), pp. 55, 70–71; *The Works of . . . Gervase Babington* (1622), iii, p. 27; Gaule, *Select Cases of Conscience*, p. 138; and above, p. 316, n. 37.

119. Ewen, ii, pp. 145, 167–8, 146–7. For a few similar cases, see ibid., pp. 280, 299; *York Depositions*, pp. 51, 89; Scot, *Discoverie*, III.x; Potts, sig. 13^v; G. Gifford, *A Dialogue Concerning Witches and Witchcraftes* (1593) (Shakespeare Assoc., 1931), sig. I3^v.

temper that he is troubled with, but he hath had some hurt by an evil tongue. He saith he will not prescribe any medicine for him until his water have been tried by fire, i.e., they must take his water, and make a cake or loaf of it, with wheat meal, and put some of his hair into it, and horse-shoe stumps, and then put it in the fire ... Mr D[awson] came up to me the morning after to consult about it. We both concluded it not to be any way of God, having no foundation either in nature or divine revelation in Scripture. I went to Halifax that day ... called o[n] her, told her our thoughts, and then perceived their imagination that, upon their using these means, the witch that had hurt him would come and discover all ... I utterly disliked it ... I told them the right way was to go to God by fasting and prayer, they consented ... and, though [there] were but few, yet we had much of God's presence with us ... I will wait to hear what God will answer. I am sure this is God's way, and it may be God will appear in it for help. If not, his will be done.[120]

Such firmness was commendable in a clergyman, but it was less likely to be encountered in those around him. When Agnes, wife of Richard Harrison, parson of Beaumont, feared in 1582 that she had been bewitched by Agnes Heard, her husband told her: 'Trust in God and put your trust in him only, and he will defend you from her, and from the Devil himself ... Moreover, what will the people say, that I, being a preacher, should have my wife so weak in faith?' When his wife continued to worry, he again exhorted her to prayer, but added significantly that 'he would hang ... the said Annis Heard, if he could prove any such matter'.[121] This revealing conversation shows how little consolation was afforded to those who feared witchcraft by the assurance that if only they had faith they would not so fear. It also shows how such defencelessness led inexorably to the final remedy – the execution of the witch, as the only certain way by which the *maleficium* of the sorcerer could assuredly and legitimately be brought to an end. Religion offered no certain immunity; counter-magic was prohibited. The ultimate onus of checking the damage done by witchcraft thus fell on the courts, and the legal prosecution of the witch became the one sure way out of what was otherwise a total *impasse*. When Hopkins and Stearne came to East Anglia the country folk were said to talk more 'of the infallible and

120. Heywood, *Diaries*, iv, pp. 53–4.
121. *A True and Just Recorde of the Information, Examination and Confession of All the Witches, Taken at S. Oses* (1582), sigs. F2v, F3.

wonderful power of the witch-finders than they do of God, Christ or the Gospel'.[122]

It is now easier to answer the question posed at the end of the previous chapter, and to understand why it was that an unprecedented volume of witch-trials and executions occurred in the century and a half following the Elizabethan religious settlement; and why in England witch-prosecution and the Reformation arrived together. For what the religious changes in the mid sixteenth century did was to eliminate the protective ecclesiastical magic which had kept the threat of sorcery under control. It was because of the popular faith in such remedies that so few instances of positive *maleficium* had been alleged in the Middle Ages, even though the belief in witchcraft was already in existence. In medieval England a man need not be hurt by witches, so long as he observed the prescriptions of the Church. If he did not, he would not be likely to complain. Faith in ecclesiastical magic was thus the obstacle to witch-prosecution. As Lecky remarked, 'if men had been a little less superstitious, the effects of their superstition would have been much more terrible'.[123] But after the Reformation the barrier was withdrawn. Ecclesiastical magic crumbled, and society was forced to take legal action against a peril which for the first time threatened to get dangerously out of hand.

This does not explain why in some other European countries, unlike England and Scotland, witch-prosecution began long before the Reformation. The reason for that is probably to be found in a change of attitude on the part of the leaders of the Church. Later medieval theologians seem to have been steadily working towards that depreciation of the power of ecclesiastical remedies which was consummated by Protestantism. They stressed that exorcism might fail and that God might give permission for the Devil's assaults. Continental intellectuals were thus abandoning their claims for the efficacy of Church magic.[124] They also took a tougher line against the practice of counter-magic than did their predecessors. On the

---

122. Gaule, *Select Cases of Conscience*. p. 93.

123. W. E. H. Lecky, *History of the Rise and Influence of the Spirit of Rationalism in Europe* (1910 edn), i, p, 39.

124. Notable passages in which fifteenth- and sixteenth-century Catholic authorities depreciated the power of ecclesiastical formulae of protection and cure in cases of witchcraft and possession may be found in Lea, *Materials*, pp. 281, 283, 325, 327, 482, 606, 622, 659, 934, 977, 986. cf. Soldan-Heppe, *Geschichte der Hexenprozesse*, ed. M. Bauer (Munich, 1912), i. pp. 167–8.

Continent witch-persecution was initiated early and from above. At first the authorities had to overcome a good deal of popular resistance to the witch-trials.[125] People were afraid to prosecute witches. Hence the emphasis in the *Malleus* and similar works on the powerlessness of sorcerers, once they had been arrested. They also preferred to use folk remedies against the workers of *maleficium*. Hence the stress on the sinfulness of such techniques.

But England seems to have been largely immune from these later medieval theological currents. There was no demand from above for the prosecution of witches and the people remained content to protect themselves by a combination of ecclesiastical and folk magic. The change came only with the great breach effected by the Reformation. It was then that the protective armour of ecclesiastical magic was broken down. When witch-prosecution started in the 1560s it bore an essentially grass-roots character. On the Continent the persecution of witches as a sect of devil-worshippers inevitably started from above. But in England the initial driving force was the fear of *maleficium*. It therefore emanated from below.

Because of this it is misleading to give the history of English witch-prosecution a primarily *political* interpretation by attributing it to the influence of any particular religious group,[126] or even to the clash of different religious groups.[127] Some historians have argued that the Puritans were particularly ready to detect the hand of Satan in daily affairs and it is true that the majority of English authors who wrote at length before the Civil War in favour of witchcraft prosecution had Puritan affiliations. Conversely, a number of prominent sceptics belonged to the Arminian camp.

But a simple equation of strong Protestantism with a strong desire for witch-prosecution will not work. The Henrician Catholic, Sir Thomas More, had favoured capital punishment for the invocation of spirits, and the visitation articles of the Marian bishops showed as much zeal against the practitioners of the magical arts as did those of their successors, the returned Marian exiles. Bishop Bonner's

125. For evidence of popular resistance to the early stages of witch-prosecution, see Lea, *Materials*, pp. 374, 386, 387, 570.

126. As in Davies, *Four Centuries of Witch-Beliefs*.

127. As in H. R. Trevor-Roper, *The European Witch-Craze of the 16th and 17th Centuries* (Harmondsworth, 1969), e.g., at p. 70 ('The persecution in England was sharpest in Essex and in Lancashire – two counties where Catholicism was strong and the Puritan evangelists particularly energetic'). There is no evidence that witchcraft prosecution in either of these two counties was a consequence of religious conflict.

thorough-going views on diabolical pacts are in themselves sufficient
to scotch any notion that such ideas were unknown in England before
the return of the Marian exiles.[128] At the turn of the sixteenth century
the Darrell controversy revealed the existence of a definite division
of opinion between devil-hunting Puritans and sceptical Arminians.
But no Puritan writer on witchcraft ever did more than echo the
opinions of the Catholic demonologists. In the early seventeenth
century there is evidence of occasional intervention by the central
government to prevent the conviction of individual witches, and it
seems clear that accounts of witch-trials were not published during
the period of Laudian censorship.[129] But it is impossible to prove
that the relative drop in the volume of witch-prosecution on the
Home Circuit between 1620 and 1640 was primarily the work of the
central government. Extant visitation articles show that the Laudians
had by no means abandoned the fight against popular magic[130]
(though they do not prove that their authors believed that witches
had any power; the aim might simply have been to root out impos-

128. T. More, *The Dialogue concerning Tyndale*, ed. W. E. Campbell
(1931), p. 27; Bonner, *A Profitable and Necessarye Doctrine*, sig. Hhii. The
earliest inquiries about witchcraft in Frere and Kennedy, *Articles and Injunctions*, are those for 1538 of Shaxton, Bishop of Salisbury, an advanced
Protestant who later recanted (ii, p. 58). For those of the Marian bishops,
see above, p. 307.

129. Davies, *Four Centuries of Witch-Beliefs*, chap. v.

130. Apart from the selection printed in the 2nd Report of the Ritual
Commission (*Parliamentary Papers*, 1867–8, xxviii) there is no modern collection of seventeenth-century visitation articles, and the provisional list
compiled by W. P. M. Kennedy in *E.H.R.*, xl (1925), pp. 586–92, is very incomplete. But a scrutiny of extant articles makes it impossible to accept the
argument (Davies, *Four Centuries of Witch-Beliefs*, chap. v) that the Laudian
bishops abandoned the campaign against sorcery. It is true that inquiries
about magical practices are missing from many visitation articles of the
1630s, but their inclusion had always been irregular. Inquiries were in fact
made by many 'Laudians', e.g. Andrewes (Winchester, 1625); Harsnet (York,
1629); Neile (Winchester, 1628; York, 1633 and 1636); Juxon (London, 1634);
Corbet (Oxford, 1629); and also Laud himself (St David's, 1625; London,
1628, 1631; metropolitical visitation of Lincoln, 1634, Norwich, 1635, and
Winchester, 1635). Similar inquiries were made by the contemporary Archdeacons of Bedford (1629, 1630), Berkshire (1631, 1635), Canterbury (1636),
Norfolk (1634) and Worcester (1638). Davies stresses their omission in Laud's
articles for the Peculiars of Canterbury (1637), but does not mention their
reappearance in his visitation of Lincoln diocese in 1638. The Canons of
1640 proposed to standardize visitation articles, but I cannot discover that
a master copy was ever produced. On the execution of witches in this period,
see below, p. 697, n. 53.

tors and enemies of religion). Laud himself was relatively uninterested in the subject of witchcraft. He told the Duke of Buckingham around 1625 that magical healing was a topic he had 'little looked into'. But of his colleagues, John Cosin regarded popular magic as the invention of the Devil, Jeremy Taylor thought witchcraft an unpardonable sin, and Robert Sanderson wanted magical practitioners to be 'by some severe provisions rooted out of this and every other Christian land'.[131]

Conversely, there is no reason to think that the prosecution of witches owed much to Puritan zeal. In 1646 John Geree, looking back at the early Stuart period, could declare that the toleration of Buckingham's wizard, Dr Lambe, had been 'one of the blackest stains of our corrupt times'.[132] But though, fifty years earlier, John Darrell had declared that with the aid of his confederate William Sommers he would have been able to 'detect all the witches in England',[133] the Civil War was not followed by a Puritan crusade to harry sorcerers out of the land. At this period, as earlier, evidence of sectarian considerations in the trials is singularly lacking. Matthew Hopkins profited by the breakdown of the government, and it is a fair guess that his career would not have been permitted in the Laudian period. But he is not known to have had any positive encouragement from the government or any marked religious predilections of his own. His colleague Stearne was a Puritan, but the sermon preached at the height of the panic by the godly divine Samuel Fairclough seems to have been a relatively temperate affair. The only hint of Puritan fervour was a passing remark, probably by Hopkins himself, to the effect that when the Devil married witches he used the order of service prescribed in the Anglican Prayer Book.[134]

131. (T. Longueville), *The Curious Case of Lady Purbeck* (1909), p. 99; *The Works of ... John Cosin*, ed. J. Sansom (Oxford, 1843–55), ii, p. 113 (and cf. i, pp. 149–50); *Works of ... Jeremy Taylor*, ed. Heber and Eden, iv, p. 546; *The Works of Robert Sanderson*, ed. W. Jacobson (Oxford, 1854), iii, p. 117.

132. J. Geree, *Astrologo-Mastix* (1646), p. 20. cf. the complaint by Elizabethan Puritans that the Church failed to exclude from communion (*int. al.*) 'sorcerers and witches'; *The Seconde Parte of a Register*, ed. A. Peel (Cambridge, 1915), i, p. 152.

133. Harsnet, *A Discovery of the Fraudulent Practises of John Darrel*, pp. 141–2.

134. S. Clarke, *The Lives of Sundry Eminent Persons* (1683), i, p. 172; Gaule, *Select Cases of Conscience*, pp. 63–4. But for an exceptional instance, in which Hopkins's campaign was seen by a Suffolk preacher as part of

After the King's execution there was no orgy of witch-prosecution. When the Sheriff of Cumberland wrote up in 1650 to ask for special directions about dealing with witches the Council of State replied coldly that there were no instructions, other than those contained in the laws of the land.[135] In Scotland the period of Cromwellian rule brought about a significant drop in the volume of witch-persecution.[136] At home the trials of the period stemmed from local circumstances and were unrelated to the triumph of Puritanism at the centre. The key witness against Anne Bodenham, executed at Salisbury in 1653, was typically enough an illiterate maidservant, 'altogether ignorant of the fundamental grounds of religion'.[137]

Witchcraft prosecution in England did not need the stimulus of religious zeal. Essentially it was made possible by the law of the land. Until that law was repealed, or at least until judges and juries tacitly refused to administer it, the formal prosecution of witches in this period needed no impetus from above. Neither could it be prevented from above, save by more systematic government intervention than any for which evidence survives. There is no reason to believe that the trials were ever more than indirectly affected by religious conflict or by the greater or lesser zeal of different religious groups.

But religious beliefs as such were a necessary precondition of the prosecutions. Theologians of all denominations upheld the reality of the Devil's assaults and Protestants denied the possibility of any effective ecclesiastical defence against them. The way was thus left open for the people to take action against the witches from whose *maleficium* they believed themselves to have suffered. To explain the roots of the prosecution, therefore, it is necessary to turn away from happenings at a national level and to direct our gaze at the social environment in which the accusations themselves originated.

---

the fight against superstition announced in the Solemn League and Covenant, see B. Hubbard, *Sermo Secularis* (1648), p. 19.

135. *C.S.P.D., 1650*, p. 159. Parliament intervened to reprieve three witches condemned at Maidstone in 1652, but, in all but one case, the reprieve arrived too late; Ewen, i, pp. 241–2.

136. H. R. Trevor-Roper, *Religion, the Reformation and Social Change* (1967), p. 421; G. F. Black, 'A Calendar of Cases of Witchcraft in Scotland, 1510–1727', *Bulletin of New York Public Lib.*, xlii (1938), pp. 36–8.

137. E. Bower, *Doctor Lamb revived* (1653), p. 38.

16.

THE MAKING OF A WITCH

They themselves, by the strength of fancy, may think they bring
such things to pass which many times unhappily they wish for and
rejoice in when done, out of the malevolent humour which is in
them: which passes with them as if they had really acted it.

Arthur Wilson, 1645
(F. Peck, *Desiderata Curiosa* [1779], p. 476)

Loath they are to confess without torture, which witnesseth their
guiltiness.

King James I
(*Daemonologie* [Edinburgh, 1597], p. 30)

1. *Cursing*

THE belief that it was possible for one person to do physical injury
to another by the mere enunciation of hostile words had a long pre-
history. In the Middle Ages the power to bestow God's curse had
been claimed by the Church and used as a sanction against many
kinds of undesirable behaviour. Papal letters carried an anathema
on those who disregarded their contents; charters and deeds concluded with a curse on their violators; the priest who levied his tithes
had the power to curse recalcitrants; and even monastic librarians
might attach an anathema to each volume as a sanction against
thieves and careless borrowers. Four times a year the general sentence of excommunication by bell, book and candle was pronounced
against all thieves, murderers and enemies of the Church.[1] Laymen
could also avail themselves of this ecclesiastical power of malediction. Thus in the late fifteenth century, when Thomas Perne of Gilden Morden, Cambridgeshire, found that he had been robbed, he
reported the theft to the vicar, who published it in church and
threatened to curse the thieves if the goods were not immediately
restored. It was common for the bishops to issue mandates for the
excommunication of unidentified offenders who had injured private

1. Texts of the general sentence can be found in W. Maskell, *Monumenta
Ritualia Ecclesiae Anglicanae* (2nd edn, Oxford, 1882), iii, pp. 309–30;
York Manual, pp. 86*–94*. The ritual was revived in 1434 after having
apparently been allowed to lapse; J. Johnson, *A Collection of the Laws and
Canons of the Church of England* (Oxford, 1850–51), ii, p. 493.

individuals in this way.[2] The aggrieved party himself might even pronounce the malediction, as in 1521, when the Mayor of Lincoln published a formal curse on those who had improperly removed the records and books of the Common Council.[3]

In Catholic countries such sanctions were maintained by the Roman Church long after the Reformation. In 1628, for example, theft of church silver provoked the Bishop of Barcelona into putting a curse on the land round about, and the subsequent crops were ruined.[4] But for Protestants this human bestowal of God's malediction was a blasphemy, for it implied that the priest or the Church could command God himself. It was a magical manipulation of the Almighty's powers which no human being should attempt. Ordinary men were not even allowed to pray for the defeat of their enemies. This was the view of the Lollards, and it was strongly reiterated by the Protestant Reformers.[5] The medieval procedure of cursing notorious offenders quarterly was given up in 1534.[6] Henceforth no priest could command God in this way; nor was any private individual permitted to call down heavenly wrath upon his enemies. The officers of the Church frequently inquired in the visitations whether any parishioners had been guilty of banning, swearing, or cursing their neighbours or their goods; and the presentment of such cursers was common enough. In 1624 Parliament passed an Act against profane swearing and cursing, and there was a further ordinance issued against offenders under the Commonwealth.[7] But the very

2. C. T. Martin in *Archaeologia*, lx(2) (1907), p. 361; R. Hill, 'The Theory and Practice of Excommunication in Medieval England', *History*, xlii (1957), p. 10. Other examples in *The Cheshire Sheaf*, 3rd ser., xxix (1934), p. 91; *Durham Depositions*, pp. 25–6; *H.M.C., Various Collections*, ii, pp. 48–9; ibid., viii, p. 319; *Medieval Libraries of Great Britain*, ed. N. R. Ker (2nd edn, 1964), p. xvii; W. Tyndale, *Doctrinal Treatises*, ed. H. Walter (Cambridge, P.S., 1848), p. 273; R. Hill, 'Public Penance', *History*, xxxvi (1951), p. 214.

3. *H.M.C., 14th rep.*, appx., pt viii, p. 29.

4. J. H. Elliott, *The Revolt of the Catalans* (Cambridge, 1963), p. 33.

5. *An Apology for Lollard Doctrines*, ed. J. H. Todd (Camden Soc., 1842), pp. xxvi–xxvii; Tyndale, *Doctrinal Treatises*, p. 272; *V.C.H., City of York*, p. 142; J. Marbecke, A *Booke of Notes and Common Places* (1581), p. 268; W. Perkins, *A Golden Chaine* (1591), sig. H1ᵛ; *The Workes of ... Gervase Babington* (1622), iii, p. 28; J. Dod and R. Cleaver, *A Plaine and Familiar Exposition of the Ten Commandments* (18th edn, 1632), p. 97; above, p. 59.

6. *Miscellaneous Writings and Letters of Thomas Cranmer*, ed. J. E. Cox (Cambridge, P.S., 1846), pp. 281–2, 461.

7. 21 Jac. 1, c. 20; *Acts and Ordinances of the Interregnum, 1642–60*, ed. C. H. Firth and R. S. Rait (1911), ii, pp. 393–6.

making of such laws was testimony to the continuance of expletives and maledictions in common speech. 'Even little children will curse [and] damn in a very horrid manner,' wrote a Yorkshire minister in 1682.[8] Profane cursing was common enough for a projector in 1635 to think it worth offering a thousand pounds down and two hundred pounds *per annum* thereafter for the right to collect forfeitures under the Jacobean statute: it was a profitable business so long as there were offenders like Mary Bebb of Shropshire, who was charged a century later with 'profanely uttering sixty-seven curses'.[9]

In practice, moreover, the Anglican Church itself had an ambivalent attitude to formal imprecations. Curses, it was agreed, might still be permitted in circumstances of extreme desperation, for example, in times of persecution.[10] The old general sentence of excommunication had been abandoned, but it was replaced, first by the reading of Chapter 28 of Deuteronomy (devoted to blessings and cursings), and then in 1549 by the Commination service. This ritual, to be followed 'divers times in the year', required the minister to read out general sentences of God's cursings against every type of impenitent sinner – for example, 'Cursed is he that removeth away the mark of his neighbour's land' – to which the congregation made Amen.[11] The service was in keeping with Protestant doctrine, in as much as it was believed to be petitionary rather than automatically effective, but the distinction was not always clear in practice. Under the Laudians, matters went further, and ecclesiastical curses were reintroduced at the consecration of churches or altar plate.[12]

Among radical Protestants there was a further attempt to revive the imprecatory power of the Catholic Church. Edmund Copinger, associate of the Elizabethan fanatic, William Hacket, claimed the power to identify the elect and to denounce vengeance upon the damned.[13] A Puritan minister was said in 1618 to have hurled curses from the pulpit at those who walked out of his lengthy sermons,

8. Heywood, *Diaries*, ii, p. 295.

9. *C.S.P.D., 1635*, p. 287; *Shropshire County Records*, vi, ed. L. J. Lee (1901?), p. 5.

10. H. I(saacson), *Institutiones Piae or Directions to Pray* (1630), pp. 345, 347–9.

11. Frere and Kennedy, *Articles and Injunctions*, ii, p. 55 n.; iii, pp. 254–5, 278, 304.

12. *English Orders for Consecrating Churches*, ed. J. W. Legg (Henry Bradshaw Soc., 1911), p. 310.

13. *C.S.P.D., 1591–4*, pp. 75–6, above, p. 158.

while Thomas Larkham, the unpopular Commonwealth incumbent
of Tavistock, was accused of pronouncing 'the curse of God' upon
a parishioner.[14] During the Civil War the Royalist clergy were quick
to call down God's curse upon those who abolished episcopacy and
proscribed the Anglican Church.[15] Under the Commonwealth
Lodowick Muggleton and John Reeve claimed a divine commission
to bless the godly and to pronounce God's solemn curse upon the
reprobate. Muggleton himself greatly enjoyed issuing curses, whether
in person or by letter; 'It did him more good,' he said, 'than if a man
had given him forty shillings.' His activities led to some spectacular
incidents, in which the power of auto-suggestion seems to have
brought about the rapid demise of several victims. When John
Robins, the Ranter, was damned by Muggleton, he felt a sudden
'burning in his throat'; soon afterwards, however, he began to issue
similar curses himself.[16] Some of the Quakers also pronounced
formal maledictions of this kind upon their enemies and collected
stories about the resulting 'judgements'.[17]

But the real source of the continuing belief in the efficacy of
cursing lay, not in theology but in popular sentiment. For it was
widely assumed that certain types of curse still retained their efficacy.
An unprovoked malediction would only rebound against its author,
but the more justified the curser's anger, the more likely that his
imprecation would take effect. 'Where God bids curse,' declared a
writer in 1659, 'there is cause to fear cursing.'[18] Thus the curse placed
by the monastic founders upon the alienation of their lands was, as
has been seen, still believed by many to be efficacious.[19] Indeed any
malediction following upon some act of great injustice might leave
its mark on later generations. In the Middle Ages one John Tregoss
abused his position as trustee of a Cornish estate by appropriating

14. *C.S.P.D., 1611–18*, p. 609; F. G(lanvile) *et al.*, *The Tavistocke Naboth
proved Nabal* (1658), p. 15.

15. e.g., A. G. Matthews, *Walker Revised* (Oxford, 1948), pp. 264, 295,
336, 337.

16. L. Muggleton, *The Neck of the Quakers Broken* (Amsterdam, 1663),
pp. 18, 20; id., *The Acts of the Witnesses* (1699), pp. 22, 119–20, 49–51, 53–5,
61–3; *A Journal of the Life of ... John Gratton* (1720), pp. 25, 74; *D.N.B.*,
'Robins, J.'.

17. See, e.g., F. Nicholson and E. Axon, *The Older Nonconformity in
Kendal* (Kendal, 1915), p. 48; and above, p. 127.

18. C. B(urges), *No Sacrilege nor Sinne to aliene or purchase the Lands
of the Bishops* (2nd edn, 1659), p. 174; S. Clarke, *A Mirrour or Looking-
Glass, both for Saints and Sinners* (4th edn, 1671), i, p. 134.

19. Above, pp. 112–18.

the land for himself and turning the widow and children out of doors. The injured family made daily supplications on their knees, calling down God's vengeance upon Tregoss and his posterity. As a result there ensued a series of judgements so heavy that, as late as the reign of Charles II, one of the descendants, Thomas Tregoss, a dissenting clergyman, spent many hours praying for the removal of the curse.[20] Similarly, it was the curse called down upon Thomas Arden of Faversham by a mariner's wife, whose land he had unjustly appropriated, which led to his murder in 1551, subsequently commemorated in a famous Elizabethan play.[21] It was very likely, thought a mid-seventeenth-century writer, that curses of the poor might take effect upon enclosing landlords and their families.[22] Some even attributed the misfortunes of the royal house of Stuart to the conduct of their twelfth-century ancestors.[23]

There was also the curse based upon patriarchal authority, reinforced as it was until the mid seventeenth century by the convention that children should kneel to receive the blessing of their parents. This was no sentimental triviality, but a solemn act which Puritans regarded as an obnoxious Popish survival. 'If any child be stiffhearted, stubborn and froward, and will not thus ask blessing,' wrote Richard Whytforde, an early Tudor authority on child-rearing, 'if it be within age, let it surely be whisked with a good rod and be compelled thereunto by force.' In the later seventeenth century Roger North recalled how he had been brought up to reverence his father: 'The constant reward of blessing, which was observed as sacred, was a *petit régale* in his closet.'[24] But if parents had the power to bless, reasoned contemporaries, then why should they not exercise such an authority in reverse? 'The blessing of the parents,' wrote Whytforde,

20. *The Life and Death of Thomas Tregosse* (1671), pp. 3–4.

21. *Holinshed's Chronicles of England, Scotland and Ireland* (1807–8), iii, pp. 1024–31.

22. S. T(aylor), *Common-Good:. or, the Improvement of Commons, Forrests, and Chases by Inclosure* (1652), p. 38.

23. (L. Magalotti), *Travels of Cosmo the Third, Grand Duke of Tuscany through England* (1821), p. 335.

24. R. Whytforde, *A Werke for Housholders* (n.d., copy in Ashm. 1215), sigs. Div^v–Ei; *The Autobiography of the Hon. Roger North*, ed. A. Jessopp (1887), p. 2. Other accounts in R. W(illis), *Mount Tabor* (1639), p. 211; F. Peck, *Desiderata Curiosa* (1779), p. 340; L. Claxton, *The Lost Sheep Found* (1660), p. 5; *The Autobiography of Mrs Alice Thornton*, ed. C. Jackson (Surtees Soc., 1875), p. 64; G. Firmin, *The Real Christian* (1670), p. 268. Puritan disapproval is mentioned in *The Works of Robert Sanderson*, ed. W. Jacobson (Oxford, 1854), ii, p. xxxv.

'doth firm and make stable the possessions and the kindred of the children. And contrary, the curse of the parents doth eradicate and ... utterly destroy both.'

> Dread the curse of parents thine
> It is a heavy thing,

wrote Hugh Rhodes in the reign of Henry VIII.[25] 'A parent ... curses his child, and God says Amen to it. Hereupon the child is obsessed or strangely handled, peradventure perishes.' This, thought John Gaule in 1646, was 'a thing of too common example'.[26] Hence the consternation on such occasions as the fateful wedding day in 1655 when Rachel Dewsall of Hereford 'pulled up her clothes and kneeled down upon her bare knees and cursed her son and her daughter and wished they might never prosper'.[27] Few can have had the presence of mind of the Marian martyr, Julius Palmer, who after his mother refused her blessing and called down Christ's curse upon him for his heresy, gently reminded her that she had no authority to pronounce God's judgements.[28]

But it was above all the poor and the injured whose curses were believed likely to take effect. The legend of the Beggar's curse – the fateful malediction upon those who refused alms – enjoyed a continuous currency from the Dark Ages to the nineteenth century.[29] The idea that God would avenge all injuries, and that moral retribution was to be found in this world no less than the next, was the justification for the curses and maledictions which were such an enduring feature of sixteenth- and seventeenth-century village life. Like other primitive peoples,[30] contemporaries believed that curses worked only if the party who uttered them had been unjustly treated. The Old Testament held out the promise that God would listen to the cry of the widows and the afflicted. The oppressed might be wrong to utter such curses, but that did not mean their imprecations would

25. Whytforde, op. cit., sig. Ei[v]; *Education in Early England*, ed. F. J. Furnivall (E.E.T.S., 1867), p. 73.

26. J. Gaule, *Select Cases of Conscience touching Witches and Witchcrafts* (1646), p. 185. cf. W. Gouge, *Of Domesticall Duties* (3rd edn, 1634), p. 456 ('445') ('God's curse doth oft follow the just curse of a parent').

27. *Hereford City Records*, iii, f. 1404 (the date is approximate).

28. Foxe, viii, p. 209.

29. Kittredge, *Witchcraft*, p. 132; *C.S.P.D., 1634–5*, p. 377. Wordsworth's poem, *Goody Blake and Harry Gill*, is based on this idea.

30. See, e.g., P. Middelkoop, *Curse-Retribution-Enmity as Data in Natural Religion, especially in Timor* (Amsterdam, 1960), pp. 62ff.

not take effect. As a Puritan preacher put it, 'men in anger many times will (though they should not) wreak themselves ... with curses and imprecations [upon those who do not help the poor], and God always will punish their unfaithfulness to him ... with execution of the curses denounced against them'.[31] 'The curses that come from the poor,' agreed Selden, '[do not] hurt me because they come from them, but because I do something ill against them, ... [it] deserves God should hurt me for it.' Or, as William Shenstone put it, in the mid eighteenth century: 'If anyone's curse can effect damnation it is not that of the Pope but that of the poor.'[32]

So, although post-Reformation Protestants usually denied both the propriety and the efficacy of ritual cursing, they frequently believed that, if the injury which provoked the curse were heinous enough, the Almighty would lend it his endorsement. In Shakespeare's plays, the curses pronounced by the characters invariably work.[33] This is not just for dramatic effect; it was a moral necessity that the poor and the injured should be believed to have this power of retaliation when all else had failed.

The religious ideas of the time thus gave plausibility to the maledictions uttered by the submerged sections of Tudor and Stuart society. The court books of the Anglican Church reveal that the line dividing a curse from a prayer was extremely thin, and that imprecations could frequently have a religious flavour about them. Thus, to take some examples from the diocese of Hereford, Margery Bluck cursed Mary Davies in 1630, 'praying to God that an evil end might come of her'; while Catherine Mason in 1614, accusing Robert Davies of having killed her husband, 'prayed to God that his house, children and all that he had, were one wild fire'.[34] Such imprecations were often delivered in ritual form, the woman on her knees in the middle of the street, and a small crowd gathering to watch the event. Joanna Nurden of Much Marcle was presented in 1616 for 'kneeling on her knees' and cursing John Sergeant and his wife. John Smyth cursed William Walton of Yarpole around 1598, 'kneeling on his knees in the churchyard there, and praying unto God that a heavy vengeance and a heavy plague might light on him and all his cattle'.

31. W. Whately, *The Poore Mans Advocate* (1637), pp. 70–71. cf. Exodus, xxii, 22–3; Deuteronomy, x, 18; Proverbs, xxviii, 27.

32. J. Selden, *Table-Talk* (Temple Classics, n.d.), pp. 1–2; *O.E.D., s.v.* 'curse'.

33. cf. E. E. Stoll, in *Pubs. Modern Language Assoc.*, xxii (1907), p. 231.

34. Hereford D.R., C.B. 144; 69 (most of these records are unfoliated).

William Meyrick, the sidesman of Church Stoke, and his cattle, were solemnly cursed by Susanna Meyrick, 'most ungodly upon her knees'. Owen ap Rees was presented in 1605 as 'a common curser of certain of his neighbours, going upon his knees, wishing their houses burnt and other losses unto them and saying that his wife and children should go upon their knees'. Yet more intimidating was Joanna Powell of Westhide who in 1617 'did curse John Smith, one of the churchwardens, upon Thursday last, in Welsh language, kneeling down upon her bare knees and holding up her hands, but otherwise the words he could not understand'.[35]

It may be that such ritual cursing was a particular feature of the Welsh Border country. But this type of behaviour was a characteristic reaction everywhere on the part of those who believed themselves to have been unjustly treated. The records of the church courts contain many examples of men and women who prayed in this ritual way that God would shorten the lives of their enemies, burn their houses, kill their children, destroy their goods, and blast their descendants. Of course such words were often uttered in the heat of temper, and subsequently regretted. But on many occasions they seem to have been pronounced in cold blood and fully intended to take effect. Great ingenuity was deployed in choosing suitable torments for the victim: 'a heavy pox to the ninth generation'; 'pox, piles, and a heavy vengeance'; 'God's curse and all the plagues of Egypt'; these were common curses.[36] So was that of Isabel Leighe of Rickmansworth, who in 1567 'cursed one Baldwyn, when the bell tolled for him, wishing and praying that the Devil might tear him body and soul'.[37] More original were Alice Skilling, who told the minister and churchwardens of Mepal, Cambridgeshire, in 1608 that she hoped 'the meat and drink they ate might go up and down their bellies as men go to harrow', and Jane Smyth, who in 1673 cursed Mrs Rod of Hereford, 'wishing that before she died she might crawl upon the ground like a toad upon all fours'.[38] It was quite usual to invoke 'the plague of God', not uncommon to call on the Devil, and, in Protestant England, by no means unheard of to imitate the example of Elizabeth Weeks, who, in 1617, complained the vicar of Littlebourne, Kent, 'cursed me and my wife, wishing the Pope and

35. Hereford D.R., C.B. 70; 76; 145; 141 f. 86ᵛ; 71.
36. Examples may be found in Hereford D.R., C.B. 71; 75; *Hereford City Records,* iii, f. 1004.
37. Hertfordshire R.O., A.S.A., 7/7, f. 24.
38. Ely D.R., B 2/29, f. 139; *Hereford City Records,* iv, f. 1775.

the Devil take me'.[39] At the end of the Civil War a Londoner, tired of wishing 'a pox of God' on the Parliament, declared that 'she would invent a new curse for them', but the details of her formula do not survive.[40]

Sometimes the curse merged into elaborate ritual magic. There were stones and wells at which imprecations might be uttered with a greater prospect of success. Or the curse could be written on a stone and buried in the ground. A sixteenth-century tablet, found at Lincoln's Inn in modern times, proved to bear magical signs and the inscription, 'That nothing may prosper nor go forward that Ralph Scrope taketh in hand.' Scrope was Treasurer of the Inn in 1564–5. Similar tablets have been found in other parts of the country.[41]

Ritual cursing had been common since the Middle Ages. Thus in 1397 the Bishop of Hereford was informed that whenever Alison Brown of Bromyard uttered a curse God always put it into effect. Similarly, in 1557 Sibyll Dews in Somerset prayed to God and the Virgin Mary that Edward Tyrell should never prosper in body or goods.[42] It is not difficult to see the function such maledictions discharged. They stemmed not just from anger, but from frustration and impotence. When we are in trouble, said Hugh Latimer, some of us go to wizards, 'some again, swear and curse'. 'Poor old people,' wrote John Wagstaffe in 1669, 'when they are abused by the insulting petulancy of others, being unable to right themselves either at law or at combat, for want of money and strength of body, do often times vent the passion of their discontented souls in threats and curses.'[43] It was only if the injured party was too weak to avenge himself in any more obvious way that he had recourse to the substitute of calling down supernatural vengeance. Curses were em-

39. 'P. de Sandwich', 'Some East Kent Parish History', *Home Counties Mag.*, ii (1900), p. 131.

40. *Middlesex County Records*, ed. J. C. Jeaffreson (1886–92), iii, pp. 183–4.

41. W. P. Baildon in *Procs. of the Soc. of Antiquaries of London*, 2nd ser., xviii (1899–1900), pp. 140–47; Kittredge, *Witchcraft*, pp. 132–3; W. Sikes, *British Goblins* (1880), p. 355.

42. A. T. Bannister, 'Visitation Returns of the Diocese of Hereford in 1397', *E.H.R.*, xlv (1930), p. 98; Wells D.R., A 27. On medieval cursing, see W. A. Pantin, *The English Church in the Fourteenth Century* (Cambridge, 1955), p. 197.

43. *Sermons by Hugh Latimer*, ed. G. E. Corrie (Cambridge, P.S., 1844), p. 345; J. W(agstaffe), *The Question of Witchcraft Debated* (1669), p. 64.

ployed by the weak against the strong, never the other way around. It was when children had outgrown normal means of parental control that the dreadful weapon of the father's curse was invoked; and it was when ordinary supplications had failed that the beggar turned upon the rich man who denied him relief. A typical sin of the poor, thought an Elizabethan writer, was 'their banning and cursing when they are not served as themselves desire'.[44] Pure malevolence seldom inspired such maledictions. It took a keen sense of injury, of the kind which induced Anna Hodgson of Easington in the East Riding in 1615 to curse the whole jury of the town when they brought in an unfavourable verdict about her land.[45] Helplessness in the face of their neighbours' hostility and the absence of any alternative means of redress made the ritual curse the resort of the poor and impotent. Like black magic, the curse was what one recent authority has called 'a schizoid type of aggression'.[46] 'They curse us,' wrote a contemporary, 'because they cannot be suffered to kill us.'[47]

Cursing could thus be a substitute for political action. After the failure of enclosure riots in York in 1536, two women were apprehended for cursing the Mayor and his brethren, and wishing the Common Chamber on fire, for enclosing the commons. When the third Duke of Buckingham enclosed land around Thornbury Castle, Gloucestershire, he was cursed by the inhabitants; while two participants in a late Elizabethan enclosure riot were said to have wished 'a plague of God ... upon all gentlemen ... We hope to see a day when we shall have the pulling of them out of their houses by the head and ears.'[48] Class hatred also underlay the outburst of Peter Shaw of North Leverton, Nottinghamshire, who was accused in 1583 of wishing 'that the plague may light in rich men's houses there, that he may have the trailing of some of them to the church, that he may make their black heads and beards knock to the ground'.[49]

44. H. Arth(ington), *Provision for the Poore* (1597), sig. C2.

45. Borthwick, R. VI A 18, f. 221.

46. M. J. Field, *Search for Security* (1960), pp. 202, 316. Dr Field contrasts it with what she calls· 'a healthy quarrelsome type of aggression' (p. 208).

47. R. Younge, *The Cause and Cure of Ignorance* (1648), p. 89.

48. *York Civic Records*, ed. A. Raine (Yorks. Archaeol. Soc. 1939–53), iv, pp. 1–3; R. H. Tawney, *The Agrarian Problem in the Sixteenth Century* (1912), p. 148; E. Skelton, *The Court of Star Chamber in the Reign of Elizabeth* (London M.A. thesis, 1931), i, pp. 174–5.

49. *Southwell Act Books*, xxii, p. 130.

The plotter, John Story, who was executed for treason in 1571, was said to have cursed Queen Elizabeth I daily as part of his grace at meals.[50] In the seventeenth century such curses were directed against the King and the bishops during the period of personal rule, and against the Parliament after the Royalist defeat.[51]

Yet substitute action though it was, the formal imprecation could be a powerful weapon. It exploited the universally held belief in the possibility of divine vengeance upon human evil-doers, and it could strike terror into the hearts of the credulous and the guilty. In 1596 in Essex the wife of Maurice Jones was sent for by one Robgent's wife to treat her with medicine for the colic. But on her arrival she 'fell down upon her knees and after many curses and evil speeches prayed that Robgent's wife might never be cured, but might abide the extremist torments that ever was abidden'. Ever after, 'Robgent's wife hath lain and yet doth lie in great misery and can find no ease'.[52] At Mainstone, in the diocese of Hereford, Thomas Owen's imprecations were so effective that, as was ambiguously reported, 'the minister cannot take rest by night by reason of his cursing', while one of Lodowick Muggleton's victims was struck dumb, fell sick and died ten days after the curse had been pronounced.[53] In 1677 one John Duncalf, in an attempt to evade suspicion of theft, rashly wished that the guilty party's hands might rot off. 'Immediately upon the execration or cursing of himself, he had an inward horror or trembling upon him, a dread and fear of the divine majesty and justice of God, which fear and working of his conscience continued more or less many days after.'[54]

The imagination could thus be as effective a means of destruction as it was of healing. Many observers have noticed how the inhabitants of modern primitive societies can afflict their enemies with aches and pains, vomiting and insomnia, by sheer suggestion; and the dramatic, even fatal, effect of the voodoo curse upon a person who believes in its efficacy is well authenticated. It is also capable of physiological explanation, for shock can decrease blood-pressure

50. W. Camden, *The History of ... Princess Elizabeth* (3rd edn, 1675), p. 168.

51. e.g., *C.S.P.D., 1633–4*, p. 409; *1639*, p. 190; *Middlesex County Records*, ed. Jeaffreson, iii, p. 92; Matthews, *Walker Revised*, p. 223; above, p. 602.

52. Hale, *Precedents*, p. 213.

53. Hereford D.R., C.B. 71 (1616–17); Muggleton; *The Acts of the Witnesses*, pp. 49–51.

54. J. Illingworth, *A Just Narrative* (1678), p. 5 (in S. Ford, *A Discourse Concerning Gods Judgments* [1678]).

and produce dehydration.[55] We should not therefore be surprised that some of the poorer inhabitants of seventeenth-century England found it to their advantage to cultivate a reputation for pronouncing curses which would infallibly take effect. When in 1618 Agnes Howe of Elm, Cambridgeshire, bid 'the plague of God' upon a neighbour's house, it was immediately recalled that she had habitually boasted that 'whom she prayed for, her prayers were heard'. In the previous year Joan Davies was rejected from the Easter Communion at Greete, Shropshire, because the rector had heard her say 'she was bound to curse one of her neighbours, Beatrix Hall . . . and said that the same her neighbour should have her curse so long as she lived, and she doubted not that [she] should [n]ever prosper after her curses'.[56] In 1493 Elena Dalok of St Mary Abchurch had appeared before the Commissary of London's court after bragging that everyone she cursed had subsequently died. In 1634 an inhabitant of Winwick, near Oundle, claimed to know a prayer which would shorten a man's life.[57]

It was at this point that these imprecations could lead on to a charge of witchcraft. 'Cursers are murderers,' wrote a contemporary, 'for if it please God to suffer their curse to take effect, the party cursed is murdered by the Devil.'[58] Diabolical aid was not invariably suspected in these cases. It was not suggested, for example, in 1557, when Robert Bayly and his wife were presented by the Somersetshire parish of Stoke Gifford as notorious scolds and cursers of their neighbours, 'and immediately after the said cursing some mischances follow of it'.[59] But a reputation for successful cursing could easily lead to a formal charge of witchcraft. Thus in 1602 a fourteen-year-old maid, Mary Glover, reported to her mistress that the old charwoman, Elizabeth Jackson, begging at the door, had turned on her and wished 'an evil death to light upon her'. The girl duly languished, and at the ensuing trial for witchcraft much was made of the old woman's 'prophesying threatenings, ever taking effect, which

55. W. B. Cannon, 'Voodoo Death', *American Anthropologist*, new ser. xliv (1942); E. E. Thompson, 'Primitive African Medical Lore and Witchcraft', *Bull. of the Medical Library Assoc.*, liii (1965). The case of a woman who died in Baltimore, U.S.A., after 'severe apprehension and sweating' because of a voodoo curse is reported in *The Times*, 18 Nov. 1966.

56. Ely D.R., B 2/34, f. 12ᵛ; Hereford D.R., C.B. 71.

57. Kittredge, *Witchcraft*, pp. 130–31.

58. R. Kilby, *The Burthen of a Loaden Conscience* (6th edn, Cambridge, 1616), p. 48.

59. Wells D.R., A 27. A similar case of 1611 is in Ewen, ii, p. 394.

Judge Anderson observed as a notable property of a witch'.[60] Another curser was old Cherrie of Thrapston, Northamptonshire, who died in gaol in 1646 while awaiting trial as a witch. He had wished that his neighbour's tongue might rot off, and so it had.[61] This was to be a stock pattern of witchcraft accusation. 'When a bad-tongued woman shall curse a party, and death shall shortly follow,' wrote Thomas Cooper, 'this is a shrewd token that she is a witch.' In the writings of the demonologists, as in the prosecutions before the courts, successful cursing and banning was treated as a strong presumption of witchcraft.[62]

It was ironic that such a presumption should have been so readily made. If the curser was provoked by a genuine injury, it is hard to understand why contemporaries should have been so reluctant to see the outcome as a divine judgement. Yet reluctant they generally were, save in the restricted cases of the curse against sacrilege, and the maledictions of injured parents. The notion that God might avenge the poor by responding to their supplications was one which the Church, like society as a whole, seems to have been unwilling to face directly. Thomas Cooper apparently saw no irony about declaring that, when the witch resorted to 'invocating upon her bare knees (for so the manner is) the vengeance of God' upon her oppressors, the resulting evil was nevertheless the work not of God but of Satan.[63]

But the witch may sometimes have seen herself as the instrument of God. In 1628 one Goody Cross was accused by a London woman of bewitching her child. When directly challenged she broke down and admitted her guilt, though claiming to have been put up to it by someone else. Her way of removing the curse was to say 'God bless thee' to the child, thus indicating the source of the power which she believed her words to possess.[64]

2. The temptation to devil-worship

Cursing, therefore, was a means by which the weak and defenceless tried to avenge themselves upon their enemies. But it was only one of a number of recognized procedures which might achieve the same result. There was ritual fasting, which, particularly before the

60. S. Bradwell, 'Marie Glover's late woefull case' (Sloane 831), ff. 3, 33.
61. Ewen, ii, pp. 306–7.
62. Cooper, *Mystery*, p. 275; Scot, *Discoverie*, I.iii; *The Presbyterian Movement in the Reign of Queen Elizabeth*, ed. R. G. Usher (Camden Ser., 1905), p. 70; Perkins, *Discourse*, p. 202; Bernard, *Guide*, pp. 204–5.
63. Cooper, *Mystery*, pp. 208–9.   64. Ashm. 1730, f. 164ᵛ.

Reformation, was sometimes perverted into a maleficent activity designed to secure the death of some specified victim. In 1519 Elizabeth Robinson of Bowland appeared before the ecclesiastical court of Whalley after publicly declaring her intention of carrying out a 'black fast' against Edmund Parker; and in 1538 Mabel Brigge was executed for practising the same ritual against Henry VIII and the Duke of Norfolk.[65] Thereafter there are few references to the practice, although the Bishop of Durham found it necessary to forbid black-fasting in 1577, and a witch unearthed by Matthew Hopkins in 1645 confessed that one of her imps bore the name 'blackfast'.[66] The remnant of an associated belief came to light in 1607, when a Kentish woman was accused of asking two neighbours to join her in kneeling to worship a snake, and of thanking God that she had overcome her enemies. She denied the charge, explaining that she had merely remarked, after noting a dead snake at her door, that 'they say that if one see[s] a dead snake in the beginning of the year he shall overcome his enemies'.[67] The case reveals how some forms of popular divination could shade off into maleficent magic.

The most common maleficent technique was the use of image-magic, by making a model in wax or clay of the proposed victim and then sticking pins or bristles in the part which was to be afflicted. That this kind of magic was extensively practised there can be no doubt. It had originated in ancient times and was well known both to the Anglo-Saxons and in the Middle Ages.[68] Tudor governments were periodically provoked into carrying out a search for sorcerers, after the discovery of some wax doll with pins stuck in it, feared to be a model of the reigning monarch or one of his family. Such scares occurred throughout the sixteenth century. In the reign of Elizabeth I the lives of both the Queen and her leading counsellors were thought to have been threatened in this way.[69]

65. *Act Book of the Ecclesiastical Court of Whalley*, ed. A. M. Cooke (Chetham Soc., 1901), p. 67; Kittredge, *Witchcraft*, p. 129.

66. *The Injunctions and other Ecclesiastical Proceedings of Richard Barnes*, ed. J. Raine (Surtees Soc., 1850), p. 17; Ewen, ii, p. 292.

67. A. Hussey, 'Visitations of the Archdeacons of Canterbury', *Archaeologia Cantiana*, xxvi (1904), p. 40.

68. The list of instances given in Kittredge, *Witchcraft*, pp. 73–86 and 139, could be easily extended.

69. To the cases listed in Kittredge, *Witchcraft*, pp. 86–90, may be added those in Ewen, ii, p. 449 (presumably 1581; see *A.P.C.*, xiii, p. 80); (R. Cosin), *Conspiracie, for Pretended Reformation* (1592), sig. K1ᵛ. cf. R. C. Strong, *Portraits of Queen Elizabeth I* (Oxford 1963), p. 40.

Wizards who boasted knowledge of the art of making people waste away were employed by Elizabethan malcontents, just as they had been by fifteenth-century conspirators. In 1589 one Mrs Dewse, who felt savagely towards the Lord Chamberlain, the Lord Chancellor, the Recorder of London and others who had been responsible for depriving her husband of his office, was said to have declared that 'she would make all their pictures and prick them with pins, that they might think it was God's doing, because they would suffer thieves to overthrow her husband without any cause'. If this failed, she wanted the conjurer Robert Birche to 'do something by art to destroy all those that are my husband's enemies in a damp, as I heard some were at Oxford Assizes'.[70] (This was a reference to the Black Assize of 1577 when the massive deaths from gaol fever had been attributed by some to the black magic of a Catholic bookseller. A Popish plotter was said in 1587 to have the formula for spreading this particular infection.)[71]

Image-magic made a periodic appearance in the witch-trials. In 1580 some witches at Windsor were said to have made extensive use of pictures in red wax, which they pierced in the head with a 'hawthorn prick'.[72] The eldest son of the Earl of Rutland was thought in 1619 to have died because his glove had been malevolently buried and allowed to rot in the earth. Anne Bodenham in 1653 was also alleged to have needed some of her victim's clothes before her spells could take effect.[73] Sometimes necromancy was practised, with a skull, or a supposedly deadly poison made out of a rotting corpse.[74] Other methods defy classification. In 1662 Philip Benny, a citizen of Hereford, reported that he knew Mary Hodges was plotting mischief against someone, because he had seen her practise witchcraft in her house. At bedtime

she is observed to take the andirons out of the chimney, and put them cross one on other and then she falls down upon her knees and useth some prayers of witchcraft . . . She then makes water in a dish and throws

70. W. H. Hart, 'Observations on Some Documents relating to Magic in the Reign of Queen Elizabeth', *Archaeologia*, xl (1866), pp. 395–6; Kittredge, *Witchcraft*, pp. 89, 419–20.

71. *C.S.P.D., 1581–90*, p. 391. cf. below, p. 667.

72. Ewen, ii, p. 153. cf. ibid., pp. 79–80, and index, *s.v.* 'puppet'.

73. *The Wonderful Discoverie of the Witchcrafts of Margaret and Phillip Flower* (1619), sig. E1ᵛ; E. Bower, *Doctor Lamb revived* (1653), p. 8.

74. For a good example, M. Aston, 'A Kent Approver of 1440', *Bull. of Inst. of Hist. Research*, xxxvi (1963). cf. above, p. 274.

it upon the said andirons and then takes her journey into her garden. This is her usual custom night after night.[75]

The practice of maleficent magic was therefore no mere figment of contemporary imagination. The physical survival of cursing tablets and magical formulae testifies, if proof were needed, to the undoubted existence of techniques by which men tried to do occult harm to their enemies. It is also beyond doubt that a large, though unmeasurable, proportion of those formally accused of witchcraft during the period had manifested some kind of malevolence towards their neighbours, although they had not necessarily practised any actual magic. Often, as we shall see, there would be a grumble, a muttered curse, or a thinly veiled threat to provide evidence for their malignity.

There is, however, very little evidence to suggest that the accused witches were either devil-worshippers or members of a pagan fertility cult. The former view was held by many contemporary theologians and demonologists; the latter derived from Jacob Grimm's suggestion (in his *Deutsche Mythologie* [1835]) that witch beliefs derived from the old Teutonic religion, and was embroidered upon in this century by Dr Margaret Murray in a series of books which have made some influential converts.

The only explanation of the immense numbers of witches who were legally tried and put to death in Western Europe [she wrote] is that we are dealing with a religion which was spread over the whole continent and counted its members in every rank of society, from the highest to the lowest.

She accordingly accepted the literal reality of the sabbath, and the ritual worship of the Devil or 'Horned God', describing the accused witches as members of 'the old religion'. She even considered that as late as the fourteenth century this religion was 'in all probability still the chief worship of the bulk of the people'.[76]

75. *Hereford City Records*, ix, f. 3547.
76. M. A. Murray, *The Witch-Cult in Western Europe* (Oxford, 1921) and *The God of the Witches* (1931) (quotations on pp. 34 and 54); J. Grimm, *Teutonic Mythology* (4th edn, trans. and ed. J. S. Stallybrass, 1883), iii, chap. xxxiv. Miss Murray's views had been outlined earlier in two articles in *Folk-Lore*: 'Organizations of Witches in Great Britain', xxviii (1917), and 'Witches and the Number Thirteen', xxxi (1920). Notable converts to her theory include Sir George Clark (*The Seventeenth Century* [2nd edn, Oxford, 1947], p. 246); Sir Steven Runciman (foreword to reprint of *The Witch-Cult in Western Europe* [Oxford, 1962]); and Dr Christopher Hill (*History*, xxxiv

At the time that she wrote, Dr Murray's interpretation, sub-titled 'a study in anthropology', was the best alternative to the 'rationalist' view that witchcraft was a total delusion, and its persecution the product of bigotry and ignorance. Her effort to penetrate beyond the trials to the reality of popular beliefs reflected a commendable desire to approach European witchcraft in the spirit of detachment normally reserved for the study of primitive tribes. Nevertheless, her conclusions, at least so far as they relate to England, were almost totally groundless. She did not initially have the advantage of being able to study the records of the witch-trials systematically unearthed by C. L. Ewen, and she chose to ignore their implications when they became available. Instead, she depended largely upon the contemporary pamphlet accounts of some of the more famous trials. Most of her evidence, in fact, came from the writings of continental demonologists, and the confessions of accused persons in Scotland and France, where torture was regularly employed to extract desired answers. For England she also drew on confessions, especially those extracted by Matthew Hopkins. Her use of these confessions, moreover, was highly selective, as can be seen, for example, in the extremes of distortion and omission in which she was inevitably involved by her attempt to show that all witches operated in 'covens' of thirteen members. In fact she never succeeded in showing that the word 'coven' ever meant anything in England other than 'association', or that it had any affiliations with the idea of witchcraft."

The truth is that acceptable evidence for the literal reality of ritual devil-worship, whether in England or on the Continent, is

---

[1949], p. 138; *Society and Puritanism in Pre-Revolutionary England* (1964), pp. 187, n. 4, 486; *History and Theory*, vi (1967), p. 121). Dr Hill, however, has now tacitly recanted. cf. the revised edition of his *Reformation to Industrial Revolution* (Harmondsworth, 1969), pp. 115–18, with the first edition (1967), pp. 89–90.

77. cf. M. A. Murray, *The Divine King in England* (1954), pp. 253–4. Talk of 'covens' should have been effectively scotched by Ewen, ii, pp. 59–60. The deficiencies of Miss Murray's historical method were well detailed long ago by G. L. Burr (*American Hist. Rev.*, xxvii [1921–2], pp. 780–3; ibid., xl [1934–5], pp. 491–2; Preface to Lea, *Materials*, pp. xxxviii–xxxix). Kittredge rightly paid little attention to her writings, though indicating his dissent from her main thesis and pointing out some errors of detail (*Witchcraft*, pp. 275, 421, 565). Ewen made a dignified reply to her staggeringly ungenerous notices of his work in his *Some Witchcraft Criticisms* (1938). In her autobiography Miss Murray says that she gave up reading reviews of her own books; *My First Hundred Years* (1963), p. 103.

extremely scanty. The few modern attempts to get behind the assertions of the demonologists and the fictitious 'confessions' extracted
by torture in response to a fixed set of interrogatories, suggest that
even on the Continent ritual devil-worship was probably a myth.[78]
In England there can be little doubt that there never was a
'witch-cult' of the type envisaged by contemporary demonologists
or their modern disciples. Malevolent magic was practised, though
usually by individuals rather than groups. But witches' 'sabbaths'
were almost certainly non-existent. In modern Africa observers
have found it equally difficult to prove the objective existence
of the 'night-witches' whom the inhabitants suppose to be at
work.[79]

English witchcraft, therefore, was neither a religion nor an organization. Of course, there were many pagan survivals – magic
wells, calendar customs, fertility rites – just as there were many types
of magical activity. But these practices did not usually involve any
formal breach with Christianity, and were, as often as not, followed
by men and women who would have indignantly repudiated any aspersions upon their religious faith. In any case, they were quite unconnected with the witch-trials. The prosecution of a witch was not
an inquiry into an heretical religion, but was usually stimulated by
an allegation of *maleficium*. Proof of malevolence, followed by dire
results, could be enough to convince onlookers and juries of the
witch's guilt, even if more sophisticated demonologists preferred to
get evidence of diabolical compact.

On some occasions, however, allegations were made, and confessions obtained, about relations with familiars and evil spirits, even
of compacts with the Devil. Although not the staple constituents of
English witch-trials, they appear often enough in the seventeenth
century to demand some explanation. The veracity of these confessions has been the object of much historical controversy. Modern
anthropologists have found their counterparts in Africa equally
embarrassing, choosing to attribute them to 'malnutrition' or 'de-

78. See in particular the remarks of E. Delcambre, *Le Concept de la
sorcellerie dans le Duché de Lorraine au XVIe et au XVIIe siècles* (Nancy
1948–51), i, pp. 19, 129–31; iii, p. 226. Contrast the literal acceptance of the
accusations and confessions by so otherwise sophisticated an historian as
E. Le Roy Ladurie (*Les Paysans de Languedoc* [Paris, 1966], pp. 407–14)
and, apparently, by H. G. Koenigsberger and G. L. Mosse, *Europe in the
Sixteenth Century* (1968), p. 91.

79. *Witchcraft and Sorcery in East Africa*, ed. J. Middleton and E. H.
Winter (1963), pp. 62–3, 171–2.

pression',[80] just as some seventeenth-century sceptics attributed them to 'melancholy'. Clearly no one formula is sufficient to explain them. When John Palmer confessed at St Albans in 1649 to having turned himself into a toad in order to torment one of his victims, he may have been coaxed or bullied by his persecutors into this admission or he may have been genuinely deluded. At this distance of time there is no way of telling. But what the case shows is that men could confess to actions which were obviously impossible, and that, therefore, the confessions themselves cannot always be taken at their face value. Yet Palmer's patently worthless statement was extensively used by Miss Murray because it contains the nearest approximation in English sources to evidence of organized witchcraft. It enumerates other witches and names Marsh of Dunstable (a well-known contemporary astrologer-magician) as 'the head of the whole college of witches'. On such flimsy foundations has the whole fabric of 'the witch-cult' been reared.[81]

The two elements of fantasy and coercion which made up most of these 'confessions' were fully perceived by Reginald Scot and his followers in England, and by the Jesuit Friedrich Spee after what he had seen in Westphalia.[82] Although the use of torture was theoretically forbidden in English witch-trials, there were many seventeenth-century cases in which victims were kept awake for days, starved, beaten, or otherwise ill-treated. It seems to have been Hopkins's regular practice to deny the accused any sleep until his familiar had appeared. It was no accident that he was more successful than anyone else in extracting confessions of devil-worship. As a contemporary observed, 'witches, long-tortured with watching and fasting, and pinched when but ready to nod, are contented causelessly to accuse themselves, to be eased of present pain'.[83] Account must also be taken of the tendency of most confessions to conform to the preconceived ideas of those who extracted them. Hopkins used a

80. J. R. Crawford, *Witchcraft and Sorcery in Rhodesia* (1967), p. 65; Field, *Search for Security*, pp. 149 ff.

81. Ewen, ii, p. 315; Murray, *The Witch-Cult in Western Europe*, pp. 220–21, 229, 252. For Marsh, see Lilly, *Autobiography*, pp. 121–2; and below, p. 760.

82. Scot, *Discoverie*, II. xii; III. vii–xiii, xvi, xviii; Ady, pp. 124–7; J. Webster, *The Displaying of Supposed Witchcraft* (1677), 66–71. Spee's arguments are summarised in Lea, *Materials*, pp. 697–726.

83. T. Fuller, *The Church History of Britain* (1837), ii, p. 215. For the use of force, see Robbins, *Encyclopedia*, pp. 103–4, 509; Notestein, *Witchcraft*, p. 77; Ewen, ii, pp. 123–4.

standard form of interrogation, which involved questions so leading as to be clearly in the 'have-you-stopped-beating-your-wife?' category. To these, he needed only a monosyllabic answer from the victim; the details of the compact and the familiars could be supplied by the questioner. Such methods had been in vogue even before the days of Matthew Hopkins. When the Reverend Henry Goodcole, Visitor of Newgate, interrogated Elizabeth Sawyer in 1621 his very first question ran: 'By what means came you to have acquaintance with the Devil?' After that had been answered, the rest was relatively plain sailing, although even then the confession was admitted to have been 'with great labour ... extorted from her'.[84] Other striking confessions were also taken down by educated clergy with continental ideas on witchcraft, or extracted by promises of money or tricks of various kinds.[85]

The fact was that, as a contemporary put it in 1624, a witch's 'own free confession ... happeneth very rare and seldom'.[86] (When pondering the implications of this statement, we should recall that by this date the majority of English executions for witchcraft had already occurred.) Most of the extant confessions come from contemporary pamphlets, and therefore relate to only a tiny proportion of the total number of witch-trials and convictions. We do not know how many cases resembled those of Margaret Landish, who in 1645 refused to confess, and made 'a strange howling in the court to the great disturbance of the whole bench'.[87] But it is not surprising that some of the demonologists should have spoken wistfully of the utility of torture,[88] or that the courts had to resolve that the witch's conviction should not be made conditional on her having confessed to the crime.[89] At an early stage in the persecution believers in witchcraft had been forced to explain away this reluctance to confess, by suggesting that the witch might have been silenced by one of her confederates, or even inhibited by the Devil himself.[90]

All these considerations help to weaken the value of those confessions which have survived, especially the particularly schematic ones extracted by Matthew Hopkins, and his like. The closer the

84. H. G(oodcole), *The Wonderful Discoverie of Elizabeth Sawyer a Witch* (1621), sigs. C1, B4.
85. e.g., Ewen, ii, pp. 122, 156, 157, 206, 267.
86. J. Cotta, *The Infallible True and Assured Witch* (1624), p. 102. For a similar observation, see Potts, sig. R4.
87. Ewen, ii, p. 256.
88. e.g., Perkins, *Discourse*, p. 204; Cooper, *Mystery*, p. 276.
89. Ewen, ii, p. 127 (L. C. J. Anderson in 1602).   90. *Malleus*, II.i.2.

confession conforms to the ideas of continental demonologists, the less convincing does it appear when carefully scrutinized. Yet not all the confessions of relations with the Devil can be so easily dismissed. Some were unsolicited, like that of the butcher, Meggs, who voluntarily travelled in from ten or twelve miles away to be searched by Hopkins and duly executed as a witch. Others contained information which seems too unconventional to have been invented by any professional interrogator. Some suspects even insisted on their guilt when not required to do so, like Giles Fenderlyn who claimed in 1652 to be entertaining his familiar in gaol, though no observer could see it.[91] It was these confessions which baffled so intelligent a contemporary as Thomas Hobbes, who admitted that, 'though he could not rationally believe there were witches, yet he could not be fully satisfied to believe there were none, by reason that they would themselves confess it, if strictly examined'.[92]

Today we are perhaps more accustomed to unsolicited confessions, and better equipped to understand the psychology of those who confess to crimes they never committed or obstinately maintain their guilt in face of the evidence. Men may make such confessions in order to attract attention, or to gain peace of mind by publicly acknowledging a long-concealed hostility towards other members of society. Others accuse themselves of every possible sin out of a depressive sense of their own worthlessness.[93] They may even welcome the opportunity of undergoing the ordeal of investigation in the hope of clearing a long-standing slur on their character, or in expectation of being more leniently treated. Thomas Cooper commented in 1617 on how some suspected witches voluntarily came to the victim to be scratched; and it seems clear that some of those informally accused after the lapse of the Witchcraft Act in 1736 were only too anxious to clear themselves by voluntarily submitting to the 'swimming' ordeal. Anthropologists have noticed the same readiness on the part of African suspects to undergo tests for witchcraft in order to get their innocence proved.[94]

91. M. Hopkins, *The Discovery of Witches*, ed. M. Summers (1928), p. 56 (Meggs); Robbins, *Encyclopedia*, p. 104 (Fenderlyn).

92. *The Life of William Cavendish, Duke of Newcastle*, ed. C. H. Firth (1886), p. 198.

93. Field, *Search for Security*, pp. 36–9, cf. J. Caro Baroja, *The World of Witches*, trans. N. Glendinning (1964), pp. 250–51.

94. Cooper, *Mystery*, p. 128; *County Folk-Lore*, I (Folk-Lore Soc., 1895), ii, pp. 186–7; iii, p. 52; M. Douglas, *The Lele of Kasai* (1963), p. 249; id., in *Witchcraft and Sorcery in East Africa*, ed. Middleton and Winter, pp. 133–5.

Such considerations help to explain why suspects might be ready to help a witch-finder with his inquiries, and why they might even volunteer elaborate confessions. But they also suggest that for the historian, confessions unsupported by other evidence can prove little. They do not, however, rule out the possibility that some at least of the suspects really did believe that they had been able to wreak vengeance upon their enemies by the use of curses, magical techniques and even animal familiars. Accustomed by contemporary theological discourse to personify their own evil sentiments and temptations, they may well have thought of themselves as meeting the Devil, the symbol of all that was evil and anti-social, in the way that other contemporaries genuinely believed that they had seen or heard God. They might even have conceived themselves as striking a bargain with him, just as the godly entered into covenant with God. The psychological processes involved are no more obscure (and no less) in the one case than the other; and they are worth some consideration.

3. *The temptation to witchcraft*

Doubtful though the confessions may be as evidence for any actual practice of witchcraft, they are, nevertheless, of incomparable value for the light they throw upon the motives and temptations to which both interrogator and accused assumed that witches were liable to be subject. Before assessing this evidence it is necessary to bear in mind that the judicial records reveal two essential facts about accused witches: they were poor, and they were usually women. Learned authorities never had any doubt that the weaker sex was more vulnerable to the temptations of Satan. James I estimated the ratio of female witches to male at twenty to one. Alexander Roberts put it as high as a hundred to one. In fact, of the one hundred and nine persons whom Ewen showed to have been executed on the Home Circuit only seven were men.[95] Contemporary writers also agreed that witches came from the lowest ranks of society. They

95. (James VI), *Daemonologie* (Edinburgh, 1597), pp. 43–4; A. Roberts, *A Treatise of Witchcraft* (1616), p. 40; Ewen, i, pp. 102–8. Two notable contemporary dissentients on this point were John Chamber, canon of Windsor, who made a digression in his 'A Confutation of Astrologicall Demonologie' (1604) 'to prove that no imputation of witchery or sorcery ought more to lie upon women than upon men' (Bodl., Savile MS 42, f. 131ᵛ), and the sceptic, Thomas Ady, who said that the witches of the Old Testament were usually men (Ady, p. 36).

were usually beggars, thought Scot; 'very miserable poor, the basest sort of people', said Richard Bernard. 'Witches ... for the most part live in extreme beggary,' agreed John Donne. Of nearly six hundred persons accused on the Home Circuit, Ewen calculated that all but four were tradesmen, husbandmen and labourers, or their women-folk. Elsewhere the general pattern appears to be the same. Labourers and their wives or widows always predominate.[96] This was not because witch-beliefs did not circulate in the higher reaches of society. On the contrary, they were familiar at every social level. But in the witch-trials the accused were overwhelmingly drawn from the bottom of the social hierarchy.

It is, therefore, not surprising that the confessions, whether genuine or extorted, agree in suggesting that most accused persons lived in a state of impotence and desperation. Their commonest motive was thought to be the desire to escape from grinding poverty. The Devil promised that they should never want; he offered meat, clothes and money, and was ready to pay their debts. Although he sometimes held out the prospect of great riches, his normal gambit was merely an assurance that his followers would never lack for food or clothes. Elizabeth Pratt was promised in 1667 that 'she should live as well as the best woman in the town of Dunstable'.[97] What is so pathetic about most of these temptations is that the bait was so small. If a specific sum of money was mentioned it was only a few shillings, often less. In 1645 Elizabeth Southern met the Devil on her way to Westleton. He promised her two and sixpence but then failed to let her have it, and 'complained of the hardness of the times'. His advice to Priscilla Collit was that she should make away with her children, for otherwise she would always continue poor.[98] There is no reason why we should doubt the reality of such temptations. The Devil's solutions were only too closely related to the wretched women's plight. On many occasions he tempted them to steal, to commit suicide, or to kill their children so that there would be more food to go round.[99] 'Extremity of affliction', as Thomas Cooper thought, was the primary cause of temptation. The

96. Scot, *Discoverie*, I,iii; Bernard, *Guide*, p. 155; *The Sermons of John Donne*, ed. G. R. Potter and E. M. Simpson (Berkeley and Los Angeles, 1953–62), i, p. 159; Ewen, i, p. 39.

97. Bedfordshire R.O., H.S.A., Winter 1667/54(i). See, in general, Ewen, ii, index, *s.v.* 'Devil; promises of'.

98. Ewen, i, p. 299.

99. e.g., Ewen, ii, pp. 294, 296, 297, 298.

Devil bided his time until a suitable moment arrived, when bereavement or poverty would make his victim ready to welcome his advances. Then he struck, with promises of food, money, and even sexual satisfaction to compensate for spinsterhood or a husband's death.[100]

The confessions of some of Hopkins's victims suggest that not only poverty but also religious despair might provide fertile soil for the Devil's temptations. He appeared to Mary Becket and told her that her sins were so great 'there was no Heaven for her'. He overheard Susan Marchant singing a psalm while milking a cow and 'asked why she sung Psalms, for she was a damned creature; and from that time she received her imps'.[101] Anne Boreham was promised that she should be free from the pains of Hell, while Joan Ruce was told that Satan's imps 'were more able to save her soul than God'. For Elizabeth Richmond the Devil assumed the form of the prophet Daniel.[102]

The hopelessness produced by this combination of religious depression and material poverty may well have bred a desperate willingness to resort to unorthodox methods of salvation. It speaks volumes for the nature of popular religious instruction that Mary Skipper should have confessed to being tempted to become a witch, because the Devil promised 'he would pay her debts and ... carry her to Heaven and ... she should never want'.[103] If ignorant men and women could be persuaded that it was worthwhile to attach themselves to Satan, then the theologians who had created this concept of the Devil had only themselves to blame. But the pull towards Satan could also be felt by the theologically more sophisticated. Devil-worship was one of the temptations experienced by those undergoing the depressive state which usually preceded a Puritan religious conversion. John Rogers, the Fifth Monarchy man, confessed that when he was a young man, too poor to get to Cambridge University, 'the Devil did often tempt me to study necromancy and nigromancy and to make use of magic, and to make a league with him, and that then I should never want'.[104] For persons in a state of

---

100. Cooper, *Mystery*, p. 69; J. Stearne, *A Confirmation and Discovery of Witch-craft* (1648), p. 5. For the Devil as a sex-substitute, Ewen, i, pp. 224, 300.

101. Ewen, i, pp. 306, 297. cf. above, p. 565.

102. Ewen, ii, pp. 284, 296, 295.   103. Ewen, i, p. 313.

104. E. Rogers, *Some Account of the Life and Opinions of a Fifth-Monarchy-Man* (1867), p. 19. cf. above, pp. 565–6.

hopelessness attachment to the Devil symbolized their alienation from a society to which they had little cause to be grateful. In this sense the idea of devil-worship was not a total fantasy. It had what has been called 'subjective reality'. When she saw herself as going over to the Devil, the witch was surrendering to passions with which everyone was familiar and on whose repression society depended.[105]

Witchcraft was thus generally believed to be a method of bettering one's condition when all else had failed. Like most forms of magic, it was a substitute for impotence, a remedy for anxiety and despair. But it differed from the others in that it usually involved acts of malice towards other people. Although the witch might expect to gain some material benefits from her diabolical compact, these were subordinate to her main desire, to avenge herself upon her neighbours. Such a desire was to be found at all levels in society, but it was usually only the poor and helpless who hoped to attain it by witchcraft, because for them the normal channels of legal action or physical force were not available. The desire for revenge, and the inaccessibility of normal agencies for achieving it, were thus the essence of the witch's predicament. 'Lowness of condition,' thought Nathanael Homes, was the first ingredient in the making of a witch:

When men through crosses, wrongs, vexations, wants, etc., are in deep discontent; so that they say in their hearts, what would they not do, that they might be avenged on such and such; at such times as these, the Devil, by voice only, or by some shape also, approacheth near to them, offering them aid ... upon his conditions.[106]

Armed with this new access of supernatural power, the witch could face up to her adversaries. 'The poor old hag,' wrote George Gifford, 'thinketh herself strong that she hath two or three servants as she may seem to plague such as she is offended withal.'[107]

Given such widespread contemporary assumptions about the potentialities of witchcraft, it was hardly surprising that there were persons like Mary Cutford of Rainham, Essex, who, it was reported in 1632, 'did most wickedly wish herself to be a witch for a time that she might be revenged of her adversary'.[108] In Herrick's words:

105. H. R. Trevor-Roper, *The European Witch-Craze of the 16th and 17th Centuries* (Harmondsworth, 1969), p. 52. cf. G. Lienhardt, 'Some Notions of Witchcraft among the Dinka', *Africa* xxi (1951), pp. 317–18.

106. N. Homes, *Daemonologie* (1650), pp. 34–5.

107. G. Gifford, *A Discourse of the Subtill Practises of Devilles* (1587), sig. G1ᵛ.

108. Hale, *Precedents*, p. 254.

>   Old Widow Prouse to do her neighbours evil
>   Wo'd give (some say) her soul unto the Devil.[109]

Ill-treated by their neighbours, many poorer members of society were reduced in their helplessness to threats and imprecations of an indisputably malevolent kind. When such threats were followed by the illness or death of their victim, observers could easily persuade themselves that witchcraft had been employed. And so, of course, could the witch.

> Seeing things sometimes come to pass according to her wishes, curses and incantations [remarked Scot], (the witch), by due examination of the circumstances is driven to see her imprecations and desires, and her neighbours' harms and losses to concur ... and so confesseth that she (as a goddess) hath brought such things to pass.

In 1667 Ursula Clarke of Dunstable was charged with witchcraft after expressing the hope that William Metcalfe would 'waste like dew against the sun', boastfully adding that 'some people had wronged her, but they had as good have let her alone, for she ... had seen the end of Platt, and she had seen the end of Haddon, and she hoped she should see the end of Metcalfe, and that she had never wished nor cursed anything in her life but it came to pass'.[110]

Those modern historians who dismiss the whole notion of witch-craft as groundless are therefore as mistaken as the contemporary demonologists who saw themselves surrounded by a sect of ritual devil-worshippers. For however fanciful the delusions of the accused persons, and however fabricated the confessions extracted from them, some at least of the witches felt genuine hatred for those around them. Although their resort to cursing and banning was a substitute for real action, they may well have genuinely persuaded themselves that an access of supernatural power was helping their curses to take effect. It would be wrong to suggest that all persons accused of witchcraft had had malevolent thoughts about their neighbours. But a substantial proportion of them certainly had, for it was the witch's malignity which gave the charge plausibility in popular eyes, and, though that malignity could be inferred from the witch's social situation, it was often evidenced by her actual be-haviour.

109. *The Poetical Works of Robert Herrick*, ed. L. C. Martin (Oxford, 1956), p. 266.
110. Scot, *Discoverie*, I.ii; Bedfordshire R.O., H.S.A., Winter 1667/52(i). cf. *The Life of William Cavendish, Duke of Newcastle*, ed. Firth, p. 198.

This was why some of the most powerful minds of the seventeenth century believed in punishing so-called witches, even though sceptical as to their actual powers. 'Witches,' declared John Donne, 'think sometimes that they kill when they do not, and are therefore as culpable as if they did.' 'As for witches,' wrote Hobbes, 'I think not that their witchcraft is any real power; but yet that they are justly punished, for the false belief they have that they can do such mischief, joined with their purpose to do it if they can.' Selden said the same:

If one should profess that by turning his hat thrice and crying 'Buz' he could take away a man's life, though in truth he could do no such thing, yet this were a just law made by the state, that whosoever should turn his hat thrice, and cry 'Buz', with an intention to take a man's life, shall be put to death.

The witchcraft statutes could thus be justified as a check on the repression of malevolent feelings, though as Scot pointed out, if mere ill-will was to be punished then men would be driven to the slaughter-house in thousands.[111]

Her curses and imprecations thus symbolized the accused witch's relationship to society. Indeed the Devil conventionally made his first appearance when he heard the woman cursing.[112] He stepped in to resolve her frustrations and make her empty words take effect. Alice Duke confessed in 1665 that she had been persuaded to give her soul to Satan, because he promised that 'if she curse anything with "A pox take it"', she should have her purpose'. Joan Waterhouse likewise confessed in 1566 that, when refused bread and cheese by a neighbour's child, she went home and called up Satan in the form of a great dog, bidding her to go and frighten the girl, which he agreed to do in return for her body and soul.[113] Like everyone else, the witches had been taught to personify their evil thoughts as the intrusion of Satan. By succumbing to temptation they had, symbolically, joined the Devil's army. A few may even have thought that he heard their prayers and granted their wishes.

111. *The Sermons of John Donne*, ed. Potter and Simpson, ix, p. 323; T. Hobbes, *Leviathan* (1651), chap. 2; Selden, *Table-Talk*, p. 150. The same view was expressed by Dryden (*An Essay of Dramatic Poesy* (1668), in *Dramatic Essays* [Everyman edn, n.d.], p. 7). cf. Scot, *Discoverie*, Epistle to Sir Roger Manwood (sig. Aiiij in 1584 edn).
112. e.g., Ewen, ii, pp. 238, 294, 308–9; R. H. West, *The Invisible World. A Study of Pneumatology in Elizabethan Drama* (Athens, Ga, 1939), pp. 95–6.
113. Ewen, ii, p. 345; Ewen, i, p. 320.

Of those who thus mentally allied themselves with Satan, some already had a record of religious indifference or unorthodoxy; a few may even have been real God-haters, like Elena Dalok, who was said in 1493 to have coupled malevolent threats towards others with the unashamed avowal that so long as God remained in Heaven she preferred to be in Hell.[114] Some may have been sinners obsessed by their guilt. Others were self-conscious renegades; like Jane Townsend, who was said in 1670 to have offered to teach girls to become witches by going to church, lying down before the font and forswearing their Christian names seven times.[115] Animal familiars may also have been employed. Fairly convincing evidence that women sometimes equipped themselves with toads in order to hurt other people was supplied by a cunning man in 1566; while a cat called 'Satan' seems to have gone the rounds of a number of poor households in the Essex village of Hatfield Peverel at the same date. The toad-familiar experimentally dissected by William Harvey on a famous occasion clearly had an objective existence.[116]

But whether these domestic pets or uninvited animal companions were seen as magical is another matter. These creatures may have been the only friends these lonely old women possessed, and the names they gave them suggest an affectionate relationship. Matthew Hopkins's victims in Essex included Mary Hockett, who was accused of entertaining 'three evil spirits each in the likeness of a mouse, called "Littleman", "Prettyman" and "Daynty" ', and Bridget Mayers, who entertained 'an evil spirit in the likeness of a mouse called "Prickeares" '. More recently the novelist J. R. Ackerley has written of his mother that

One of her last friends, when she was losing her faculties, was a fly, which I never saw but which she talked about a good deal and also talked to. With large melancholy yellow eyes and long lashes it inhabited the bathroom; she made a little joke of it but was serious enough to take in crumbs of bread every morning to feed it, scattering them along the wooden rim of the bath as she lay in it.[117]

114. Hale, *Precedents*, pp. 36–7 (also quoted above, p. 200). For some other instances of religious scepticism, ignorance or indifference on the part of suspected witches, see Ewen, i, p. 309; Ewen, ii, p. 231; (R. Galis), *The Horrible Acts of Elizabeth Style* (?) (copy in Bodl., G. Berks 1, lacking t.-p.) (1579), sig. Bii[v].

115. Ewen, ii, p. 441.

116. *The Examination of John Walsh* (1566), sig. Avij[v]; Ewen, i, pp. 317–24; Notestein, *Witchcraft*, pp. 160–62.

117. J. R. Ackerley, *My Father and Myself* (1968), p. 174.

THE MAKING OF A WITCH

It is not difficult to imagine what Matthew Hopkins would have made of this relationship.

The absence of any organization, cooperation, continuity or common ritual among witches thus makes it impossible to speak with Miss Murray of a 'witch-cult', leave alone of the 'old religion'. The witch at her most malevolent was an isolated individual, the creature of her own fantasies. She did not hunt in 'covens', and her devil-worship, if any, was a private matter. There may have been a few meetings between like-minded persons bent on doing mischief by magical means,[118] but there is no evidence of ritual sabbaths. The belief in such nocturnal gatherings may, however, have been encouraged by the tendency of wandering beggars to milk other men's cows and sleep in large groups in barns and out-houses, spending the evening piping and dancing.[119] Accused witches had no demonstrable links with a pagan past. If any of them served the Devil, it was only too obviously the same Devil as that portrayed by the conventional religious teaching of the day.

But such possible cases of mental apostasy should not lead us to think that all English witches were devil-worshippers in this symbolic sense. Most accusations of witchcraft related to supposed *maleficium* and did not suggest that the accused person had contemplated even a mental transfer of allegiance to the Devil. If devil-worship was added to the charge, this was usually because of the intervention of an educated would-be demonologist. But since the crime was a mental one only, it becomes impossible for the historian to distinguish the minority of suspects who may have committed it from all the others who were unfairly charged. How can we today separate the allegations which had at least some symbolic truth from those which were in every sense false?

118. For the handful of known possible instances, see above, p. 529, n. 27. There is also the interesting case of Thomas Hope, a cunning man of Aspull, Lancashire, who declared in 1638 that there were half a dozen witches thereabout and that Agnes Hunt 'was chief of the Platt-fold' (Lancashire R.O., QSB 1/202/89). I have not been able to elucidate this expression.
119. In addition to the case of the Berkshire 'rogues' said in 1603 to have danced naked at night in the sheepfolds (Ewen, ii, p. 57), compare the weekly feasts mentioned in *Tudor Economic Documents*, ed. R. H. Tawney and E. Power (1924), ii, p. 345; the various cases cited in C. Bridenbaugh, *Vexed and Troubled Englishmen* (Oxford, 1968), p. 387; and the remarkable nocturnal scene described in M. Prestwich, *Cranfield* (Oxford, 1966), p. 529. For vagrants who milked other men's cows see *Middlesex County Records. Calendar of Session Rolls, Sessions Registers and Gaol Delivery Registers for July to 1 October, 10 James I* (1933), p. 45.

The irony was that the one category could blend into the other. For even the innocent person, under the pressure of interrogation, might come to believe that she was guilty. The supreme paradox was that some of the suspects confessed that they had taken up witchcraft in order to avenge themselves upon neighbours who had falsely called them witches.[120] Society thus forced the role of witch upon its victims.

> Some call me witch,
> And being ignorant of my self, they go
> About to teach me how to be one; urging,
> That my bad tongue (by their bad language made so)
> Forespeaks their cattle, doth bewitch their corn,
> Themselves, their servants, and their babes at nurse.
> This they enforce upon me; and in part
> Make me to credit it.[121]

4. Society and the nonconformist

To appreciate the light in which the witch appeared to her neighbours it is necessary to recall the importance which the inhabitants of sixteenth- and seventeenth-century England attached to social harmony, and the variety of means they employed to check all signs of dispute or nonconformity. This tendency was perhaps particularly marked in the tightly-knit fielden villages, owning common fields and subject to strict regulation by manorial custom. But it was to be found everywhere. Many villages had their occasions for communal feasting and dancing, when miscellaneous grievances were amicably patched up. In some Herefordshire and Shropshire parishes there was even customary eating and drinking at the communion table.[122] It would be easy to exaggerate the efficacy of these 'love feasts', church ales, Easter 'drinkings', and traditional holidays. Bickering and open violence had always been features of village life, and drunken quarrels at times of festivity could trigger off new animosities. But these festivities symbolize the importance attached to harmony and agreement.[123]

120. e.g., Ewen, ii, pp. 312, 343; Bedfordshire R.O., H.S.A., Winter 1667/51(2).
121. *The Witch of Edmonton* (1621), II.i (supposedly by 'William Rowley, Thomas Dekker, John Ford, etc.').
122. *H.M.C., 11th Report*, appx, pt. vii, p. 148.
123. For customary entertainments and their functions, see, e.g., Aubrey, *Gentilisme*, p. 5; *Shropshire Folk-Lore*, ed. C. S. Burne (1883–6), pp. 341–2;

Indeed if the records of Tudor and Stuart village life leave any single impression, it is that of the tyranny of local opinion and the lack of tolerance displayed towards nonconformity or social deviation. Rural society lacked much of the modern concept of privacy and private life. The customs of the countryside required joys and sorrows, weddings and funerals, to be shared with other members of the community; there was no idea of the holiday as 'getting away from it all'. Nor was there any challenge to the view that a man's most personal affairs were the legitimate concern of the whole community. On the contrary, everyone had a right to know what everyone else was doing. This is clearly shown by the presentments and depositions made before the ecclesiastical courts. Eavesdropping may have been technically an offence, but this did not inhibit the witnesses from testifying in adultery cases to what they had seen through a window or hole in the wall. They felt no shame about this, and if in doubt would run to get their friends to look for themselves.[124] These neighbours were observant; they knew if too many members of a family were sleeping in the same bed; or if children were born too quickly after a marriage. They kept an eye on each other's visitors, and were quick to spot any suspicion of scandal. When a new couple moved into the village the inhabitants had no compunction about demanding proof that they were married.[125]

This was quite different from the growing impersonality of London and similar large-scale urban communities.[126] In the villages the

A. C. Chibnall, *Sherington* (Cambridge, 1965), p. 1; Hill, *Society and Puritanism in Pre-revolutionary England*, p. 192; F. D. Price in *Oxoniensia*, xxix–xxx (1964–5), pp. 203–4.

124. Examples may be found in Bodl., Oxford Diocesan Papers, c. 27, f. 239b (adultery, 1637); Leicester City Museum, 1.D. 4/4/590. For the prosecution of eavesdroppers before a court leet, see J. P. Dawson, *A History of Lay Judges* (Cambridge, Mass, 1960), p. 270, n. 212.

125. Typical instances of such neighbourly curiosity may be found in Wells D.R., A 27; Ely D.R., B 2/13, f. 20ᵛ; Bodl., Oxford Archdeaconry Papers, Berks. b 14, f. 122; Borthwick, R. VI. A 18, f. 38ᵛ.

126. cf. William Thomas's remarks upon the privacy enjoyed by sixteenth-century inhabitants of Venice: 'No man there marketh another's doings, or ... meddleth with another man's living ... No man shall ask why thou comest not to church ... To live married or unmarried, no man shall ask thee why. For eating of flesh in thine own house, what day soever it be, maketh no matter. And generally of all other things, so thou offend no man privately, no man shall offend thee, which undoubtedly is one principal cause that draweth so many strangers thither'; *The History of Italy* (1549), ed. G. B. Parks (Ithaca, New York, 1963), p. 83.

texture of life was more like that conveyed by a story told today by the Nyoro, an East African people, about a man who moved into a new village and wanted to find out what his neighbours were like. In the middle of the night he pretended to beat his wife very severely, to see if they would come and remonstrate with him. Yet though he beat a goatskin, while his wife screamed out that he was killing her, nobody came. So the next day the man and his wife packed up and left the village, and went to find some other place to live.[127] This fable would have been entirely intelligible in pre-industrial England. Indeed, when the Duke of Stettin visited the country in 1602 he was informed that 'in England every citizen is bound by oath to keep a sharp eye at his neighbour's house, as to whether the married people live in harmony'.[128] Apart from making presentments in the church courts, villagers had many informal ways of expressing their disapproval of the way a married couple comported themselves: by playing 'rough music' under their window, for example, or 'riding the skimmington', i.e. staging a procession intended to ridicule the cuckolded husbands or wife-beaters.[129]

The importance of neighbourly opinion was recognized by society as a whole. At ecclesiastical law a bad reputation ('ill fame') was sufficient to justify a prosecution,[130] while in the common law courts it was still accepted that the jury might be not impartial assessors, but members of the community from which the offender had sprung, and well-informed about his general standing in the community. When a Yorkshire gentleman had to stand trial for conspiracy in 1680 he demanded, and was granted, a jury composed of gentlemen of quality, from his own county, 'that may be able to know something how I have lived hitherto'.[131]

127. J. Beattie, *Bunyoro, An African Kingdom* (New York, 1960), p. 61.
128. 'Diary of the Journey of Philip Julius, Duke of Stettin-Pomerania, through England in the year 1602', *T.R.H.S.*, new ser., vi (1892), p. 65.
129. For a detailed discussion of this subject, see now E. P. Thompson, 'Le Charivari anglais', *Annales (économies, sociétés, civilisations)*, 27e année (1972).
130. H. Conset, *The Practice of the Spiritual or Ecclesiastical Courts* (2nd edn, 1700), p. 391. An episcopal reminder that men were responsible for their reputation, even if it was undeserved, may be found in (W. Fleetwood), *The Bishop of St. Asaph's Charge to the Clergy of that Diocese in 1710* (1712), p. 42.
131. *The Tryal of Sir Tho. Gascoyne* (1680), p. 5; Sir W. S. Holdsworth, *A History of English Law*, i (3rd edn, 1922), pp. 333, 336.

There were also judicial institutions designed to check those who threatened social harmony. Court leet and quarter sessions provided machinery to deal with cursers, quarrellers, tale-bearers and wranglers of every kind. The cucking stool had been a familiar instrument of punishment since the thirteenth century, but in the Tudor period its use came to be largely confined to the public exhibition or immersion of the scold, that characteristic member of the village community, defined legally as 'a troublesome and angry woman who, by her brawling and wrangling amongst her neighbours, doth break the public peace and beget, cherish and increase public discord'. To control such termagants some communities employed the cucking-stool, while others put the offender in a cage, or led her around the streets by a metal bridle.[132]

The Church was also preoccupied with the need to maintain good relations between its members. The Prayer Book instructed the officiating minister to refuse the Communion to any parishioners between whom there was hatred or malice. When the incumbent visited the sick he was required to interrogate the sufferer to make sure that he was in charity with his neighbours and harboured no grudges. In their visitation articles the bishops and archdeacons inquired into the activities of any scolds or sowers of discord and required offenders to be brought before the church courts for punishment.

The terms in which such offences were described throw much light upon the values of the village communities in the century before the Civil War. A troublemaker might be presented for being 'an ordinary scoffer of his neighbours'; for being 'a busy woman of her tongue'; for being 'a breeder of discord between man and wife, and a breaker of charity'; for being 'a maker of rhymes, thereby to raise slanders'; 'for not being in charity with her neighbours'; 'for scolding and railing of most men, or rather of every man when they do anything in the town's business or affairs contrary to her own mind or not pleasing unto her'; 'for a common scold and a disturber of the whole parish'; for 'libellous and lascivious ballads [on] divers of her neighbours'; for saying there was 'no honest woman in the town'; 'for reporting in our parish that he hath had the use of the bodies of all the women in reach, except seven'; for inventing nick-names;

132. The semantics of this subject are discussed by J. W. Spargo, *Juridical Folklore in England Illustrated by the Cucking-Stool* (Durham, N. Carolina, 1944), and the mechanics (with illustrations) by T. N. Brushfield in *Journ. Architectl, Archaeol., and Hist. Soc. for Chester*, ii (1855–62).

for hanging up horns outside a neighbour's door; 'for terming the parishioners to be a company of jackdaws'.[133]

Once before the ecclesiastical court, such busy-bodies were liable to a form of censure which was designed as much to propitiate the community as to appease the Church. The standard ecclesiastical punishment was the imposition of a penance, by which the offender publicly acknowledged his faults before his neighbours, before being reconciled to the community. Public penance of this kind could be ordered by secular courts as well as by ecclesiastical ones. In medieval towns offenders had sometimes been escorted to gaol by minstrels, drummers and bagpipe players. In the seventeenth century they might be ordered by Star Chamber or quarter sessions to be exposed in pillory or stocks, or paraded in the market-place wearing a paper enumerating their faults. The greatest punishment which the church courts could impose was excommunication, a secular sanction as much as an ecclesiastical one, for in its more serious form it meant that the criminal was cut off, not just from the sacraments of the Church, but from intercourse with the whole community. An excommunicated man was, in theory, not allowed to eat or work with other folk. His testimony was unacceptable in a court of law, and if he died unreconciled his body was 'pitted' in unhallowed ground. The penalty emphasized that the delinquent's essential offence was his rejection of the standards of the society to which he belonged.

Facts like these are necessary if we are to appreciate the high value set on social conformity by this tightly-knit, intolerant world with which the witch had parted company. She was the extreme example of the malignant or non-conforming person against whom the local community had always taken punitive action in the interests of social harmony. Their 'chief fault', wrote Reginald Scot of witches, 'is that they are scolds'. So close was the association between scolding and witchcraft in the popular mind that a foreign visitor, shown the cucking-stool at Honiton in 1760, was actually informed that it had once been used to punish witches.[134]

---

133. These formulae (all from the late sixteenth or early seventeenth century) come from Gloucester D.R., 125, f. 279; Ely D.R., D 2/8, f. 89^v; Gloucester D.R., 40, f. 151^v; Hereford D.R., C.B.64; Borthwick, R. VI A 18, f. 114; Ely D.R., B 2/36, f. 217^v; Gloucester D.R., 20, p. 34; Ely D.R., B 2/24, f. 142^v; ibid., B 2/30, ff. 64^v–65, 70; ibid., B 2/32, f. 70; Hereford D.R., C.B. 145; Ely D.R., B 2/18, f. 67; Hereford D.R., C.B. 71.

134. Scot, *Discoverie*, II.x; Spargo, *Juridical Folklore in England*, p. 100.

The old woman who had recourse to malignant threats in her extremity was therefore liable to pay a high price for the consolation they afforded her. She might be punished as a scold or a curser, as well as running the risk of the more serious charge of witchcraft. Even if she was ultimately acquitted, her family might suffer great hardship during her temporary imprisonment; the Lancashire Quarter Sessions records contain several petitions in which accused persons complain that their dependents have been denied poor relief or that they themselves have had to sell their clothes to pay their gaoler's fees.[135] But quite apart from the risk of formal prosecution, the suspected witch might be ostracized by her neighbours. When the wife of a Devizes weaver was slandered as a witch in 1653 the local bakers refused to allow her to bring her dough to their bakehouses; while it was said of Goodwife Gilnot, who was similarly defamed in Kent in 1641, that 'if she be esteemed such a kind of creature everybody will be afraid of her, and nobody set her a-work, inasmuch as truly she will be utterly undone'.[136] In 1665 a crippled labourer was turned out of his lodging in a Lancashire village because he was suspected of witchcraft; while Sarah Liffen, who died in Great Yarmouth in 1710, 'was so forlorn and wretched a person as she labour'd under the imputation of being a witch, and the youth and other rude folks in the town . . . did often insult and affront her as she walk'd, and at her own house'.[137]

The suspected witch was also liable to informal acts of violence. The ninety-four-year-old Agnes Fenn alleged in 1604 that, after she had been accused of witchcraft, Sir Thomas Grosse and others punched, pricked and struck her, threatened her with firebrands and gunpowder, and finally stabbed her in the face with a knife.[138] Mary Sutton was apprehended in 1612 and beaten with a cudgel 'till she was scarce able to stir';[139] and when Andrew Camp suspected Goodwife Bailey in 1661 of having bewitched his children, he dragged her out of her house into the street, bruising her back and pinching her, and then kneeled upon her breast; 'and when he had her

135. Lancashire R.O., QSB/151/21; 165/12.
136. *H.M.C., Various Collections,* i, p. 127; *The Oxinden Letters, 1607–42,* ed. D. Gardiner (1933), p. 220.
137. Lancashire R.O., QSP/268/6; Norwich D.R., DEP 56 (Bell. c. Norton *et al*).
138. Ewen, *Star Chamber,* pp. 18–19.
139. *Witches Apprehended, Examined and Executed* (1613), sig. C2ᵛ.
140. *Hertford County Records,* i, ed. W. J. Hardy (1905), p. 137.

so under him his wife came and clawed her by the face and said she would claw her eyes out of her head, and her tongue out of her mouth, and called her a damned ... old witch'.[140] Such violence was encouraged by the popular belief that the injured party could recover his health by 'scratching' or drawing blood from the person who had bewitched him. In 1664 George Long, with the aid of two armed soldiers, made a forcible entry into Anne Warberton's house (fatally injuring her child in the process), and then pricked and scratched her until he had drawn a sufficient quantity of blood. There were many similar cases of assault with thorns, needles, bodkins and knives.[141]

Sanctions of this kind inevitably constituted a check upon outbursts of temper, swearing and cursing, or similar expressions of malignity. In sixteenth- and seventeenth-century England, no less than in some modern African societies, witch-beliefs could thus inhibit the expression of vicious feelings,[142] and help to reinforce the prevailing ethic of neighbourliness and communal solidarity. But they increased the sense of isolation experienced by the person who had become estranged from her neighbours, and they enhanced her desire for revenge.

For the helpless old woman who had fallen out with the rest of the community there was only one other available form of retaliation which was as tempting as witchcraft and as difficult of detection. This was arson. In the seventeenth century, as at other times, it was a common means of revenge for those who felt themselves injured by their neighbours. Arson required no great physical strength or financial resources and could be easily concealed. It was an indiscriminate means of vengeance, however, for a fire, once started, was likely to spread. As such, it perhaps appealed especially to those whose hatred for their neighbours was all-embracing.

Some social outcasts were content to pray that their neighbours be consumed by fire, but others resorted to more direct methods. In Hereford, Thomas Williams, arrested in 1616 for affray and assault, swore that on his release he would fire the houses of his accusers. Eleanor Markley, a notorious scold, was charged in 1625 with declaring that, if only John Moore's house were further away from

141. *Records of the County of Wilts.*, ed. B. H. Cunnington (Devizes, 1932), pp. 155–6; Ewen, i, pp. 30–31; Ewen, ii, pp. 190–93; *York Depositions*, p. 96.

142. cf. M. Gluckman, *Politics, Law and Ritual in Tribal Society* (Oxford, 1965), p. 220.

THE MAKING OF A WITCH 635

those of other people, she would have burned it down over his head. Another termagant, Sarah Price, who, it was said in 1613, 'doth commonly kneel down upon her knees and curse her neighbours', coupled her imprecations with the threat to set fire to her house, which immediately adjoined that of several others.[143]

There must be few localities whose records do not reveal similar cases of hostility. Margaret Byx and Ellen Pendleton were executed in 1615 for attempting to burn down Wymondham, Norfolk. The Catholics were suspected of having put them up to it, but Margaret Byx, like some suspected witches, had been persuaded to take part by the promise that she would be carried to another country, where 'she should have ... a good living, better than she had where she was'.[144] Two years later Roger Wright, allegedly a drunkard and blasphemer who refused to work, said that 'he hoped to see the town of Nantwich on as hot a fire as ever it was'. In 1631 three persons were executed at Bury for burning some forty houses at Walberswick, Suffolk. In 1634 Widow Dorothy Walpole 'did take a fire-stick in her hand and swore by God's blood' that she would start a conflagration in Godmanchester; and in 1641 Anna Clerke, a 'lewd woman', was bound over to keep the peace after 'threatening to burn the houses at Soho'.[145]

Similar episodes occurred throughout the seventeenth century. Mary Armstrong was charged in 1667 with firing a house in North Shields and threatening to burn the whole town; while in 1679 Elizabeth Abbott announced that

she would set the town of Newcastle of fire; and that she had viewed the place where she resolved to do it, for she would get pitch and tar, and set fire in the Mayor's shop, or in some other shop where there was lint and tow, and would stand by it that she might be taken, and would own herself to have done it, and would swear before any authority that Mr Riddle and his lady, and Mrs Errington of Denton, and some others were the cause thereof.[146]

143. *Hereford City Records*, ii, ff. 705, 899, 1027.
144. Kittredge, *Witchcraft*, p. 155; *The Official Papers of Sir Nathaniel Bacon*, ed. H. W. Saunders (Camden Ser., 1915), pp. 31–3.
145. *Quarter Sessions Records ... for the County Palatine of Chester, 1559–1760*, ed. J.H.E. Bennett and J. C. Dewhurst (Rec. Soc. of Lancs. and Cheshire, 1940), p. 75; Kittredge, *Witchcraft*, p. 130; *Diary of John Rous*, ed. M. A. E. Green (Camden Soc., 1856), p. 61; *Survey of London*, xxxiii, ed. F. H. W. Sheppard (1966), p. 25.
146. *York Depositions*, pp. 237–8.

Society's reaction to insane cunning of this kind was predictable. Arson had long been a felony, and it was deprived of its benefit of clergy under the Tudors. But without invoking the law the community was fully capable of taking the matter into its own hands. Oliver Heywood noted in his diary for March 1680 how at Wakefield,

sitting in the house we heard a very astonishing noise in the street, multitudes of people shouting – we inquired the cause. They said it was a woman whom they were hurrying to the House of Correction upon a sledge, who (they said) had threatened to burn the town. Some said she was mad, others drunk, but they abused her body in a prodigious manner, whipping her fearfully, carrying her into a dark place like an entry, or dungeon, where they lay their dung. There she lay all night. In the morning her body rose in blebs, miserable sore. Oh, horrid cruelty. It was said she came from Halifax.[147]

The resemblance between this episode and the manifestations of popular hatred against witches in the 'swimmings', or near-lynchings as they became, needs no underlining. Violent action was also taken against scolds. At Calne, Wiltshire, in 1618 a party of three or four hundred men, sounding horns and bells, and led by a drummer, broke into Thomas Wells's house, and seized his wife Agnes, handling her violently, and intending to place her in the cucking-stool.[148] Arson, scolding and witchcraft were all acts of hostility against society to which the poor and rejected might be reduced. They appeared to offer a means of retaliation against a hostile world, and an inarticulate but dramatic form of protest against the hopelessness of their condition. Sometimes the two charges of arson and sorcery overlapped. In Northampton in 1674, for example, Anne Foster was convicted of bewitching the sheep of a rich grazier who had refused to sell her any mutton, and of subsequently setting his house and barns on fire. At Wymondham in 1615 it was said that a wind was raised by conjuration to keep the fire burning.[149]

The ineffectiveness of such protests needs no underlining. The witch, like the arsonist, assumed that the hardships of life were to be attributed to the personal failings of other people rather than to impersonal social causes. Both sought to revenge their hardships by

147. Heywood, *Diaries*, ii, p. 270.
148. Spargo, *Juridical Folklore in England*, pp. 7–8.
149. Ewen, ii, pp. 362–3; above, p. 635. Other examples of alleged arson by witches may be found in Ewen, ii, pp. 194, 302; Ewen, i, pp. 145, 250. cf. below, p. 668.

inflicting personal damage on others, rather than by seeking some form of political or social reorganization. Their attitude, in other words, was incompatible with the political radicalism by which it was ultimately superseded.

In the later seventeenth century witch-prosecutions dwindled; but the proportion of actions for malicious damage against property is said to have multiplied.[150] Burning houses, breaking hedges, treading down corn: such were the means by which the poor retaliated against their betters. Parliament provided fresh legislation against such offences, making it a capital offence to break hedges or burn ricks. But mere repression was an inadequate remedy. 'Burning of houses, and such like effects of unnatural envy,' thought a mid-seventeenth-century writer, would be 'removed when oppression and ignorance of the law of God were removed from the shoulders of the poor'.[151] He might have said the same about witchcraft.

150. By F. A. Inderwick (Side-Lights on the Stuarts [1888], pp. 174–5), who reached this conclusion after working through the Western Circuit assize records for 1670–1712.

151. J. Brayne, The New Earth (1653), p. 73.

17.

WITCHCRAFT AND ITS SOCIAL ENVIRONMENT

He that giveth unto the poor shall not lack: but he that hideth his eyes shall have many a curse.

Proverbs, xxviii, 27

I sold apples, and the child took an apple from me, and the mother took the apple from the child; for the which I was very angry. But the child died of the smallpox.

Statement made by Temperance Lloyd before her execution for witchcraft, 1682 (*A True and Impartial Relation of the Informations against Three Witches* [1682], p. 39)

1. *The utility of witch-beliefs*

So far we have seen that witch-beliefs were encouraged by contemporary religious teaching, with its emphasis on the power of the Devil, and the relative helplessness of those against whom he levied his assaults. We have also seen that a desire for supernatural retaliation was to be found among the weak and helpless members of society, who frequently made no bones about their malevolence. But there is no reason to think that all of those accused of witchcraft had mentally allied themselves with the Devil, or had even uttered threats and curses against their enemies. Our final task, therefore, is to ask why it was that other persons should have thought them guilty of doing so. To answer this we must analyse the circumstances in which accusations of witchcraft came to be made.

In a society technologically more backward than ours the immediate attraction of the belief in witchcraft is not difficult to understand. It served as a means of accounting for the otherwise inexplicable misfortunes of daily life. Unexpected disasters – the sudden death of a child, the loss of a cow, the failure of some routine household task – all could, in default of any more obvious explanation, be attributed to the influence of some malevolent neighbour. There was virtually no type of private misfortune which could not thus be ascribed to witchcraft, and sometimes the list of injuries might be extremely miscellaneous. At Maidstone in 1652, for example, a group of witches was accused of being responsible for the deaths of nine children and two adults, the loss of five hundred pounds' worth of cattle, and the shipwreck of a large quantity of corn.[1]

But a supernatural explanation was particularly seductive in the field of medicine, where human impotence in the face of a variety of hazards was only too obvious. There was, for example, no satisfactory contemporary explanation for the sudden deaths which are today ascribed to cancer or heart disease, while the absence of any germ theory made the onset of many kinds of infection utterly inexplicable. Lacking any natural explanation, men turned to a supernatural one.

> The common people [wrote a doctor in 1735] when incapable of penetrating the reasons of their bodily sufferings, are exceeding prone to charge them on the influence and operation of superior invisible powers; believing, as their phrase is, that they are under an evil tongue, or afflicted by some mischievous eye, [they] impute their maladies to necromancy and witchcraft, [and] are inclined to use spells, charms and anti-magical remedies for their cure.[2]

There was thus a standing disposition to attribute to witchcraft a variety of deaths and diseases, aches and pains, which would cause us no intellectual problem today. Rheumatism, arthritis, creeping paralysis, tuberculosis: all can be recognized in the symptoms of the seventeenth-century witch's supposed victims. Today's doctors, for example, might have no difficulty in diagnosing the case of Roger Boyden, who, when threshing corn, was 'suddenly stricken down to the ground and taken lame, both in his right arm and left leg, and so continued till his death'; or of his daughter, Luce Boyden, who 'after a ravenous manner did devour an extraordinary proportion of sustenance, yet she pined away to skin and bones and so died'. The one clearly had a stroke; the other perhaps cancer, or galloping consumption. Yet in 1605 Margaret Cotton was charged with having brought about both deaths by witchcraft.[3] Such a diagnosis met a genuine emotional need. As Lady Widdrington put it, when told in

---

1. H.F., *A Prodigious and Tragicall History of the Arraignment ... of Six Witches at Maidstone* (1652), p. 6.
2. Sir R. Blackmore, *Discourses on the Gout, Rheumatism, and the King's Evil* (2nd edn, 1735), Preface, p. xl.
3. Ewen, *Star Chamber*, p. 38.

1652 of the fatal illness which had overtaken Alexander Nickle's daughter, 'she could not understand any distemper the child had, ... unless she ... was bewitched'.[4]

It was not only the layman who derived some intellectual satisfaction from this type of explanation. Witch-beliefs also helped to cover up the inadequacies of contemporary medical practitioners.

Seldom goeth any man or woman to a physician for cure of any disease [wrote Thomas Ady], but one question they ask the physician is, 'Sir, do you not think this party is in an ill handling, or under an ill tongue?', or, more plainly, 'Sir, do you not think the party is bewitched?', and to this many an ignorant physician will answer, 'Yes, verily.' The reason is *ignorantiae pallium maleficium et incantatio* – a cloak for a physician's ignorance. When he cannot find the nature of the disease, he saith the party is bewitched.

This picture was undoubtedly only too accurate. There is no shortage of well-documented cases in which a diagnosis of witchcraft was suggested or confirmed by contemporary doctors.[5] Although some authorities suggested that witches could inflict natural diseases,[6] the more usual position was to say that the absence of any identifiable natural cause for an illness was an indication of witchcraft. Even the highest body of the land, the Royal College of Physicians of London, was occasionally prepared to countenance witch-beliefs, if no other explanation for an illness was forthcoming. Thus in the case of John Parker in 1623, the College would not eliminate the possibility of witchcraft, but ruled that 'there may be some, by the strangeness of the sick man's infirmities'.[7] Earlier, in 1602, the College had shown

4. E. Mackenzie, *A Historical, Topographical, and Descriptive View of the County of Northumberland* (2nd edn, Newcastle, 1825), ii, p. 35 (date corrected by Ewen, ii, p. 323).

5. Ady, p. 115. See, e.g., Ewen, ii, pp. 132–6, 169, 176, 250, 256, 272, 350, 369, 403, 457; *A True and Impartial Relation of the Informations against Three Witches* (1682), pp. 2, 3, 5; Heywood, *Diaries*, iv, p. 53; Wells D.R., D 7 (evidence of Robert Andrews, 1555); *Analecta Bollandiana*, vi (1887), p. 319. Cases in which doctors opposed such a diagnosis may be found in Ewen, i, p. 274; Ewen, ii, pp. 134–5; *H.M.C. Hatfield*, xvii, pp. 65, 222–3; E. Jorden, *A Briefe Discourse of a Disease called the Suffocation of the Mother* (1603), sig. F1; (D. Oxenbridge), *General Observations and Prescriptions in the Practice [sic] of Physick ... by an Eminent London Physician* (1715), pp. 46–7.

6. Below, p. 686.

7. C. Goodall, *The Royal College of Physicians of London* (1684), pp. 403–4; Sir G. Clark, *A History of the Royal College of Physicians* (Oxford, 1964–6), i, p. 199.

itself divided over the *cause célèbre* of Elizabeth Jackson, who had been accused of using witchcraft to bring on the fits of fourteen-year-old Mary Glover. The trial was notable for the defence put up by Drs John Argent and Edward Jorden, who contended vainly that the fits had natural causes. But it was the prosecution, assisted by the evidence of at least three other members of the College, including Thomas Moundeford, subsequently seven times President, which ultimately proved successful.[8]

It was thus generally believed that the inability of learned physicians to identify the cause of their patient's sufferings was a strong indication of witchcraft. Justices of the Peace were instructed in Michael Dalton's popular handbook that the first likely sign of witchcraft was 'when a healthful body shall be suddenly taken ... without probable reason or natural cause appearing'.[9] And it was the physician who was the judge of this. Even in the highest reaches of society, where the best medical advice was available, charges of witchcraft could circulate freely. The sudden death of the Earl of Derby in 1594 was at first attributed to image-magic while two supposed witches were executed in 1619 for killing the Earl of Rutland's eldest son, and tormenting other members of the family. Edward Fairfax, the elegant translator of Tasso, charged six women with bewitching his daughters in 1621. Other supposed victims of witchcraft or maleficent magic included the Countess of Bridgwater, Lord Purbeck, Sir John Washington, Lady Jennings and Lord Windsor.[10]

If medical knowledge was often inadequate for diagnosing the illness of men and women, it was even more limited when confronted by the diseases of animals. For, although there were professional farriers, veterinary science was rudimentary. Farmers were not completely ignorant of the subject, of course. In the early seventeenth century the leading handbooks on animal husbandry made no mention of supernatural maladies;[11] and when Nicholas Stockdale was accused in 1600 of bewitching John Richers's sheep, a Norfolk jury

8. R. Hunter and I. Macalpine, *Three Hundred Years of Psychiatry 1535–1860* (1963), pp. 70–75; Ewen, ii, pp. 132–3, 196–9.

9. Quoted in Ewen, i, p. 269. cf. Bernard, *Guide*, p. 25. On the ways of distinguishing between witchcraft and ordinary illness, see below, p. 686.

10. Ewen, ii, pp. 174–5, 202–3, 231–4, 239–44; [T. Longueville], *The Curious Case of Lady Purbeck* (1909), p. 98; Ashm. 1730, f. 251; Notestein, *Witchcraft*, p. 185.

11. e.g., G. Markham, *Markhams Maister-peece, or What doth a Horse-Man Lacke* (1610); L. Mascal, *The Government of Cattell* (1633).

was quite capable of acquitting him by deciding that the animals had burst from over-feeding, after being unwisely put in a field of freshly-cut barley stubble.[12] But the more unusual occurrence might still be attributed to witchcraft – the epidemic which spread through one farmer's herd, but did not affect those of his neighbours, or the disease with perplexing symptoms, like the paroxysms which overtook a Southampton tanner's pigs in 1589, so that they 'danced and leaped in a most strange sort, as if they had been bewitched'.[13]

It is not difficult, therefore, to see that the belief in the possibility of witchcraft served the useful function of providing the victim of misfortune with an explanation when no other was forthcoming. It supplemented the deficiencies of contemporary technique, particularly of medical technique. It did not by any means entirely fill the gap, for witchcraft was conventionally invoked to explain some disasters but not others. It was, for example, only rarely cited as a reason for commercial or industrial failure, and very seldom invoked to explain bad weather or sexual impotence in the way that was so common on the Continent. This may be an optical illusion created by the nature of the evidence which has survived. The allegations made in the law courts were determined by the emphasis of the English statutes upon the specific crimes of killing and injuring men or animals. In Essex, for example, seventy per cent of all accusations related to the death or illness of human beings, and most of the others to injuries to animals. But accompanying pamphlet accounts of the background to the trials reveal that witches could also be blamed for more trivial misfortunes as well, though these were not made the basis of the legal indictment against them.[14] It is hard to know how much allowance to make for the selectivity of the evidence given in the courts, but it certainly yields the impression that there was a stylized character about witchcraft as an explanatory theory. It could not be indefinitely extended to account for any misfortune, but was more plausible when confined to those disasters for which witches were conventionally held responsible.

It must also be recognized that sometimes there were circumstances in which the victim might, either deliberately or unconsciously, set aside an available natural explanation of his misfortune

12. Ewen, *Star Chamber*, p. 20.
13. *Books of Examinations and Depositions, 1570–94*, ed. G. H. Hamilton and E. R. Aubrey (Southampton Rec. Soc., 1914), pp. 158–9.
14. A. D. J. Macfarlane, *Witchcraft Prosecutions in Essex, 1560–1680* (Oxford, D.Phil. thesis, 1967), pp. 199–201. cf. above, p. 532.

for the sake of a supernatural one. Disasters which had come about through a man's negligence or incompetence might be more attractively put down to the malevolence and magical skill of his enemies. When Henry VIII tired of Anne Boleyn he put it about that he had only been attracted to her in the first place because she had practised witchcraft to seduce him.[15] A similar interpretation appealed to lesser men who found themselves in a similar situation. After the fifth Earl of Sussex had abandoned his wife for the sake of a mistress in the reign of James I, the Countess's friends endeavoured to prove that black magic was responsible for her failure to retain her husband's affections. When in 1619 a gentlewoman found that her daughter had eloped with a disreputable ploughboy, whose father had been executed for felony, she attributed the *mésalliance* to 'diabolical sorcery'.[16] This is what has been called the 'face-saving' function of witchcraft.[17]

Such charges of diabolical aid were freely deployed by unsuccessful politicians, baffled by the success of their rivals, from Cardinal Wolsey, who was believed to have bewitched Henry VIII, to Oliver Cromwell, who was well known to have made a contract with the Devil on the eve of the battle of Worcester.[18] Other types of defeat might also be attributed to witchcraft by the unsuccessful, who naturally preferred to believe that their opponents had cheated, rather than to accept that they had been beaten in a fair fight. In a primitive society, witch-beliefs of this kind can act as a severe check to technical progress by discouraging efficiency and innovation. A man who gets ahead in a tribal society is likely to awaken the suspicions of his neighbours. Among the Bemba of Northern Rhodesia, for example, it is said that to find a beehive with honey in the woods is good luck; to find two beehives is very good luck; to find three is witchcraft. In such an environment, witch-beliefs help to sustain a rough egalitarianism. They are a conservative force, acting as a check upon undue individual effort. Similarly, in twelfth-century England the chronicler William Malmesbury could complain that

15. *L.P.,* x, p. 70.
16. C. L. Ewen, 'Robert Radcliffe, 5th Earl of Sussex: Witchcraft Accusations', *Trans. Essex Archaeol. Soc.,* xxii (1936–40); Ewen, *Star Chamber,* p. 12.
17. M. J. Field, *Search for Security* (1960), p. 109.
18. A. F. Pollard, *Wolsey* (1929), p. 101; W. C. Abbott, *The Writings and Speeches of Oliver Cromwell* (Cambridge, Mass., 1937–47), ii, p. 458.

the common people disparaged excellence in any sphere by attributing it to demonic aid.[19]

There is not much evidence, however, to suggest that witch-beliefs had this egalitarian effect in sixteenth- and seventeenth-century England, where commercial life was frankly competitive, and the desire to get ahead increasingly accepted. Mechanical ingenuity was often attributed to sorcery in Tudor times, and there was a case in the reign of Mary of an archer being arrested for witchcraft because he shot too well.[20] But it was rare (though not unknown) for a commercial rival's success to be explained in terms of his magical power.[21] In the sixteenth century, witchcraft, like hidden treasure, was occasionally hinted at as the reason for some particularly blatant example of that social mobility to which contemporaries could never entirely adjust themselves. One James Phillipe of Brignal, Yorkshire, was rumoured to have so enchanted the eighth Lord of Scrope of Bolton (d. 1549), 'that he got such substance of lands and goods which hath brought him from the state of a yeoman, almost to presume with a gentleman, and to be his fellow, yea rather his better'. Such innuendos helped to explain why rewards were not always proportionate to merit, but they seem to have been uncommon. In England witchcraft was an explanation of failure, not of success. 'We think them bewitched that wax suddenly poor,' wrote Reginald Scot, 'not them that grow hastily rich.'[22]

Misfortunes in the military sphere, however, were sometimes put down to a rival's witchcraft. In the fifteenth century English failure in France had been attributed to the sorcery of Joan of Arc, and even in the reign of Charles II a Cornish witch was held responsible

19. *Willelmi Malmesbiriensis monachi de Gestis Regum*, ed. W. Stubbs (Rolls Ser., 1887-9), i, p. 195. This point, probably first made by Sir J. G. Frazer, *Aftermath* (1936), pp. 1-3, has been well developed by M. Gluckman, *Custom and Conflict in Africa* (Oxford, 1955), chap. iv, and id., *Politics, Law and Ritual in Tribal Society* (Oxford, 1965), pp. 59, 221-2.

20. Scot, *Discoverie*, III. xv. cf. below, p. 793.

21. An example involving an Elizabethan raisin-merchant occurs in P.R.O., SP 12/232, f. 122ᵛ (*C.S.P.D.*, *1581-90*, p. 674). For a Jacobean slander case in which the nightly appearance of the Devil was said to be responsible for the plaintiff's wealth, see *The Reports of ... Sir Henry Hobart* (4th edn, 1678), p. 129. John Grigsby, the accountant of the South Sea Company, was 'vulgarly reputed to have studied the black art' (P.G.M. Dickson, *The Financial Revolution in England* [1967], p. 116).

22. *Collectanea Topographica and Genealogica*, v (1838), p. 250; Scot, *Discoverie*, XII.v.

by some for the Duke of York's lack of maritime success again$\int$
the Dutch.[23] When Wardour Castle temporarily managed to hold
out against the Royalists during the Civil War, the besiegers attributed this unexpected resistance to the witchcraft of Robert Balsom, a
Puritan preacher who was one of the beleaguered garrison.[24] James II
was rumoured to have a magical hat, which would reveal the identity
of those who plotted against him, and a Popish necromancer, who
could control the winds and sink William of Orange's fleet.[25]

Many of these accusations were, of course, either disingenuous or
the product of self-deception. The Elizabethan vicar of Brenchley,
Kent, who kept losing his voice when conducting the service, chose
to blame this on the sorceries of one of his parishioners, but the wiser
members of the congregation were unconvinced, for they suspected
he had the French pox.[26] Sea captains might likewise invoke witchcraft to explain why the vessels under their charge had suffered shipwreck or capture at sea.[27] Many accusations emanated from servants
and children seeking to excuse their own negligence – as in the case
of the twenty Lancashire witches of 1634, whose troubles began
when the boy Edmund Robinson invented a fantastic story, to save
himself a whipping for playing truant instead of bringing home his
father's cattle.[28] When in 1582 a cow kicked over Alice Baxter's pail,
thereby losing the morning's milking, she rushed back to her employer to explain that the animal had been petrified by an evil spirit.[29]
'When a country wench cannot get her butter to come,' observed Selden, 'she says the witch is in her churn.' In Africa today witchcraft
may still provide an acceptable excuse for failure, and can be evoked

23. Ewen, ii, pp. 36, 459. For a similar explanation for the defeat of the
Armada, see H. Boguet, *An Examen of Witches*, trans. E. A. Ashwin and
ed. M. Summers (1929), p. 63.

24. S. Clarke, *A Generall Martyrologie* (2nd edn, 1660), ii, p. 213.

25. *Revolution Politicks* (1733), ii, p. 44; B. Magee, 'The Protestant Wind',
The Month, clxxvii (1941), p. 337.

26. Scot, *Discoverie*, I. ii.

27. *C.S.P.D.*, *1667–8*, p. 4; Ewen, ii, p. 458; A. C. Carter, *The English
Reformed Church in Amsterdam in the Seventeenth Century* (Amsterdam,
1964), p. 184; below, p. 668.

28. *C.S.P.D.*, *1634–5*, pp. 141, 152–3. A full account of the case is given
in Ewen, ii, pp. 244–51.

29. W. W., *A True and Just Recorde of the Information, Examination
and Confession of all the Witches, taken at S. Oses* (1582), sig. D4. A very
similar case occurs in J. Strype, *The Life of . . . Sir Thomas Smith* (Oxford,
1820), p. 98.

tȯ account for such divers disappointments as barrenness, impotence, and failure in examinations.[30]

The study of witch accusations is therefore complicated by the existence of many cases in which the witch-beliefs of the day were exploited for selfish purposes, often by downright fraud. Sometimes the main aim was to get the accused person out of the way, for fear she should reveal some guilty secret; as when Joan Peterson was successfully accused and executed in 1652 to prevent her implicating others in a case of conspiracy.[31] Sometimes the charge arose out of some family feud; in the reign of James I, after Thomas Methwold had married Anne Lea against the wishes of her three sisters, the trio conspired to frame him with a witchcraft charge.[32] Fraudulent accusations of this kind were sometimes uncovered in the courts, but others may have escaped detection. Yet such instances must be recognized as essentially parasitic to the witch-beliefs, and in no way their cause. They present some interesting pathological problems, but will be disregarded here.

Disingenuous accusations of witchcraft could never have been made without the prior existence of ingenuous ones. Many men profited by the credulities of their contemporaries, but this is no explanation of how such beliefs came to exist in the first place. Even the fraudulent youth, William Perry, the 'boy of Bilson', coached by recusant priests to simulate possession, admitted to having picked upon Jane Cocks as the one who had bewitched him, because she was already 'a woman ill thought of and suspected for such like things'.[33] Edmund Robinson in 1634 also built his story upon a foundation of local gossip. Many private scores were paid off under the cover of witchcraft accusations, just as they were (to take a parallel instance) during the Marian persecution of Protestant heretics, when victims were often denounced by neighbours and 'friends'.[34] But this does not explain why Protestants (or witches) were being persecuted in the first place.

Why then did a man in all honesty turn to the occult malevolence of his neighbour as an explanation for his misfortunes? So far, it has been suggested that he normally only tended to do so when there

30. J. Selden, *Table-Talk* (Temple Classics, n.d.), p. 98; G. Parrinder, *Witchcraft* (Harmondsworth, 1958), p. 124; *Witchcraft and Sorcery in East Africa*, ed. J. Middleton and E. H. Winter (1963), p. 216.

31. Ewen, i, pp. 272–81.

32. Ewen, *Star Chamber*, p. 12.

33. (R. Baddeley), *The Boy of Bilson* (1622), p. 70.

34. P. Hughes, *The Reformation in England*, ii (1953), p. 274.

was no natural cause immediately apparent. But witchcraft was not the only alternative explanation available. If a man suffered some unexpected reverse he could seek an astrological explanation in the stars; he could blame evil spirits or the fairies; he could ask himself what ritual precaution he had neglected; or he could just shrug his shoulders and blame his bad luck. In many primitive societies virtually all deaths, save those in advanced old age, are attributed to witchcraft or ancestral spirits or some similar phenomenon. But in England at this period men were fully accustomed to the possibility of accident and misadventure.[35] Even if they wanted to blame someone they did not need to invoke witchcraft. They could accuse other enemies of society, like the Catholics, around whom extensive sadistic fantasies had been woven. Catholics, it was said, had started the Civil War by infiltrating themselves in disguise into the Parliamentary party. They had brought about the execution of Charles I, and had disguised themselves as Levellers, Quakers and other revolutionaries. They were behind many of the outbreaks of fire in seventeenth-century towns. They could also attack individuals. The godly layman, William Brettergh, who lived among Papists near Liverpool, was believed to have had his horses and cattle several times killed in the night, 'by seminary priests (no question) and recusants that lurked thereabouts'.[36]

But, of all alternative explanations of misfortune, the most obvious was the theological view that the disaster had been caused by God, either to punish sin, or to try the believer, or for some other unknown but indisputably just purpose. This, however, had never

35. Only four of the forty-seven peoples discussed in L. W. Simmons, *The Role of the Aged in Primitive Society* (New Haven, 1945) regard death as entirely natural (pp. 219–20). cf. J. G. Frazer, *The Belief in Immortality and the Worship of the Dead* (1913; 1968 reprint), i, pp. 33–53; and above, p. 130.
36. *A Briefe Discourse of the Christian Life and Death, of Mistris Katherin Bettergh* (1612), pp. 5–6. Anti-Catholic scares before and during the Civil War have been studied in detail by Dr Robin Clifton in his unpublished D.Phil. thesis, *The Fear of Catholics in England, 1637 to 1645* (Oxford, 1967). There are two useful articles by B. Magee ('Popish Plots in the Seventeenth Century. The Great Panic of 1641', *The Month*, clxxv [1940] and 'The Protestant Wind'; ibid, clxxvii [1941]), and a good summary of the mythology of Popish Plots in W. M. Lamont, *Marginal Prynne* (1963), chap. 6. Catholic responsibility for many outbreaks of fire is luridly alleged in Capt. W. Bedloe, *A Narrative and Impartial Discovery of the Horrid Popish Plot* (1679).

been a comfortable doctrine to swallow. In the first place, it was scarcely consoling to reflect that one's sins had been singled out for divine visitation. According to the Kentish gentleman, Henry Oxinden, it was precisely this refusal to endure the correction of God which led men to blame their adversities upon some neighbour's witchcraft. Certainly it was because he could not believe that God would want to punish *him*, that the vicar of Brenchley had blamed his son's illness upon the witchcraft of old Margaret Simons. Scot sardonically wondered how many witches would have had to be executed if any Elizabethan had been handled by God in the way that Job had been.[37]

But the greatest difficulty about the theological explanation of misfortune was one which it shared with astrological and other explanations, arid that was the diagnosis offered no very promising means of redress. A man could pray to God for relief, but without any certainty of success. The attraction of witch-beliefs, by contrast, was that they held out precisely that prospect of redress which the theologians denied. By personalizing their misfortunes, the victims were able to remedy their situation. To begin with, they could guard themselves against future attacks by using one of the conventional magical preservatives. Of these the most popular were herbs – vervain, dill, rowan – hung above the threshold. But there were other amulets, like horseshoes, which, it was said, were kept in most houses in the West End of London in the seventeenth century.[38] If the witch had already struck, there were plenty of counter-charms designed to force her to reveal herself and call off the spell. A common procedure was to boil, bake, bury, or otherwise deal with, a sample of the victim's urine. When this was done, the witch would suffer great discomfort, usually from being unable to urinate, and thus be forced to reveal herself.[39] Excavations have recently unearthed over twenty examples in London and East Anglia of the 'witch-bottle', a bellar-

37. *The Oxinden Letters, 1607–42*, ed. D. Gardiner (1933), p. 221; Scot, *Discoverie*, I.ii; V.viii.

38. Aubrey, *Miscellanies*, pp. 140–41; id., *Gentilisme*, pp. 27, 82, 104, 191, 204, 231–2; Ewen, ii, pp. 161, 324; Ashm. 219, f. 182; W. Coles, *Adam in Eden* (1657), p. 38; T. Jackson, *A Treatise containing the Originall of Unbeliefe* (1625), p. 177. Other preservatives included 'witch-posts' built into the structure of the house (see M. Nattrass in *Yorks. Archaeol. Journ.*, xxxix [1956–8], pp. 136 ff.).

39. Examples in Ewen, ii, pp. 230, 363, 364, 386, 390; Ewen, i, p. 314; Heywood, *Diaries*, iv, p. 53; Aubrey, *Miscellanies*, p. 140; Sloane 3846, f. 98; Ashm. 1473, p. 658.

mine flask containing the hair, nail-parings, etc., of the victim for whom relief was being sought. Chemical tests confirm that the bottles once contained urine.[40] Their use reflected contemporary assumptions about the power of sympathy. John Locke, for example, advised that the Countess of Shaftesbury's urine should be buried as a cure for her nephritis; while country housewives used to put hot pokers in boys' excrement, believing that this would cause them pain and deter them from ever again defecating outside their front doors.[41] Another practice was to burn a tile or piece of thatch off the roof of the suspect's cottage,[42] or to burn, or bury alive, one of the animals whom she was believed to have bewitched.[43] Other formulae included cutting off and burning the suspect's hair, and making an image of the witch and pricking it with pins. As a contemporary remarked, men 'often become witches, by endeavouring to defend themselves against witchcraft'.[44]

Most of these methods were meant to bring the witch back to the scene of the crime. Once she appeared, the victim, it was believed, could put an end to his illness by scratching her and drawing blood; this was 'the most infallible cure', said the witnesses in the Leicester witch-trial in 1717.[45] Such 'scratching' might involve violence of sundry kinds. Beating the witch was thought by some to be a means of recovery; when old Mother Rogers was suspected in 1593 of

40. R. Merrifield, 'The Use of Bellarmines as Witch-Bottles', *Guildhall Miscellany*, iii (1954); id., in *Folk-Lore*, lxvi (1955), p. 200n.; id. and N. Smedley, 'Two Witch-Bottles from Suffolk', *Procs. Suffolk Inst. of Archaeol.*, xxviii (1958–60); N. Smedley and E. Owles, 'More Suffolk Witch-Bottles', ibid., xxx (1965); Kittredge, *Witchcraft*, p. 103.

41. M. Cranston, *John Locke* (1957), p. 201; Sir K. Digby, *A Late Discourse . . . touching the Cure of Wounds by the Powder of Sympathy*, trans. R. White (1658), pp. 126–8.

42. Kittredge, *Witchcraft*, p. 434; Ewen, ii, pp. 165, 238, 334; *The Municipal Records of the Borough of Dorchester*, ed. C. H. Mayo (Exeter, 1908), pp. 664–5; J. Heydon, *A New Method of Rosie Crucian Physick* (1658), pp. 43–4; Bodl., Oxford Archdeaconry Papers, Berks. c. 170, f. 379.

43. Kittredge, *Witchcraft*, pp. 96, 430–31; Ewen, ii, p. 362; Hale, *Precedents*, pp. 249–50; *Camden Miscellany*, x (1902), p. 69; J. Glanvill, *Saducismus Triumphatus* (1681), ii, p. 193.

44. R. Bovet, *Pandaemonium* (1684), ed. M. Summers (Aldington, 1951), p. 53; Ewen, ii, p. 169; Bodl., MS e Mus. 173, f. 37. Many other such recipes survive. For specialists in counter-witchcraft and their remedies, see above, pp. 219–21.

45. Ewen, i, p. 315. This remedy was practised as early as 1279; Ewen, ii, p. 28. cf. Kittredge, *Witchcraft*, pp. 399–400.

bewitching a child, the cunning man at Hastings, one Zacharias, advised putting a knife in her buttock.[46]

But the best cure of all was to have the witch prosecuted and executed. For the point of such witch-trials was not merely that they afforded the victim the gratification of revenge, but that, according to contemporary belief, they positively relieved the victim. 'The malefice,' wrote John Gaule, 'is prevented or cured in the execution of the witch.' All Robert Throckmorton's children recovered after the execution of the witches of Warboys.[47] The virulence of the prosecutions is thus more intelligible when it is appreciated that the trials were credited with a genuine therapeutic effect upon the victim. The destruction of the witch had become what James I called 'a salutary sacrifice for the patient'.[48] It was, moreover, the only procedure of which the theologians approved, for, of course, they prohibited all counter-magic; even scratching the witch was diabolical, as they saw it.[49]

The great appeal of witch-beliefs, as against other types of explanation for misfortune, was, therefore, that they provided the victim with a definite means of redress. They did not merely offer the intellectual satisfaction of identifying the cause of the mishap; they made it possible to take immediate steps to have things put right, by consulting the cunning man and applying the appropriate magical remedies. Individuals who had endured bad luck for years on end thus came to grasp desperately at the only explanation which could also be a solution. William Godfrey, for example, wrote from the Fleet prison in 1662 a long letter to the astrologer Booker, in which he detailed a catalogue of misfortunes extending over some ten years. First, he had been court-martialled and cashiered; then a surgeon had tried to poison him; after which he had gone to sea, where he endured a series of disasters. Now he had returned home, only to be arrested for debt. As a result, 'the said Godfrey doth think that he is bewitched by some evil body'. He therefore wanted the

46. L. A. Vidler, *A New History of Rye* (Hove, 1934), p. 69. For violence against suspected witches, see above, pp. 633–4.

47. J. Gaule, *The Mag-Astro-Mancer, or the Magicall-Astrologicall Diviner posed, and puzzled* (1652), p. 197; *The Most Strange and Admirable Discoverie of the Three Witches of Warboys* (1593), sig. P4ᵛ.

48. (James VI), *Daemonologie* (Edinburgh, 1597), p. 49.

49. *The Most Strange ... Witches of Warboys*, sigs. B3, C1; W. Gilbert, 'Witchcraft in Essex', *Trans. Essex Archaeol. Soc.*, n.s., xi (1909–10), p. 215; above, pp. 589, 591–2.

astrologer to identify the witch, so that appropriate therapeutic action could be taken.[50] Sometimes, of course, this kind of request sprang from sheer paranoia. Mrs Eleanor Aylett of Magdalen Laver, Essex, complained, first to the two Napiers, then to Lilly, for a period of over ten years, about the torments suffered from witchcraft by her family and herself.[51] In Norfolk Mary Childerhouse petitioned the quarter sessions between 1652 and 1657 because she thought that at least eight persons were practising witchcraft against her.[52] But the main aim of these complaints was always to get something done about the causes of the misfortune. 'Witches,' as a modern anthropologist remarks, 'are potentially controllable by . . . society; the caprices of environment are not.'[53]

Contemporary medicine also suffered by comparison because of its inability to offer a certain cure for every disease, even if it could diagnose it. This came out clearly in 1602, during the trial before Lord Chief Justice Anderson of Elizabeth Jackson for causing Mary Glover's hysterical fits by witchcraft. When Dr Jorden for the defence argued that the girl's illness had a natural cause, Anderson rounded on him: 'What do you call it?', quoth the Judge. '*Passio hysterica*,' said the Doctor. 'Can you cure it?' 'I cannot tell. I will not undertake it, but I think fit trial should be made thereof.'

LORD ANDERSON: Do you think she counterfeiteth?
DR JORDEN: No, in my conscience, I think she doth not counterfeit.
LORD ANDERSON: Then in my conscience, it is not natural. For if you tell me neither a natural cause of it, nor a natural remedy, I will tell you that it is not natural . . . Give me a natural reason and a natural remedy, or a rash for your physic.[54]

Here the judge's assumption seems to have been that the only true diagnosis was one which postulated, not only a cause, but also a remedy. Because Dr Jorden could guarantee no redress by medical means, the judge preferred to accept an explanation in terms of witchcraft.

50. Ashm. 225, ff. 336–7.
51. Ashm. 412, ff. 13ᵛ, 16, 19ᵛ, 117, 125, 141ᵛ, 145ᵛ–6, 153ᵛ, 157, 175ᵛ, 279, 282ᵛ, 292ᵛ; Ashm. 184 (inside back cover); Ashm. 178, f. 31; Ashm. 185, f. 270ᵛ.
52. *Norfolk Quarter Sessions Order Book, 1650–57*, ed. D. E. H. James (Norfolk Rec. Soc., 1955), pp. 39, 64, 93.
53. C. Kluckhohn, *Navaho Witchcraft* (Boston, 1967), p. 107.
54. Hunter and MacAlpine, *Three Hundred Years of Psychiatry*, pp. 74–5.

Witch-beliefs, therefore, served both as an explanation of misfortune, and as an expected means of redress. But why were they invoked by believers at one moment of time and not another? What were the circumstances which brought them into play? How did an individual witch accusation start? The answer to these questions can only be discovered by studying the relationship between the witch and her accuser, and by analysing the common factors underlying the diverse circumstances in which these accusations were made. At this point the historian is indebted to the social anthropologists, who have pioneered this method in their studies of witchcraft elsewhere.

2. *The witch and her accuser*

The first feature which emerges from a scrutiny of witchcraft accusations is an obvious one, but is nevertheless important. This is the fact that it was excessively rare for men to decide that they had been victims of witchcraft without also having a particular suspect in mind. Having hit upon magic as the explanation for their misfortunes, it seldom took them long to identify the probable witch. Usually they knew at once who it must have been. Sometimes they even had the suspect in mind before the witchcraft had been committed: 'I have a suspicion in thee,' said Mary Dingley to Margery Singleton in 1573, 'and if any in my house should miscarry thou shalt answer for it.'[55] But normally the identification of the witch followed hard on the heels of the recognition that witchcraft had been at work.

This feature is admittedly difficult to establish in all cases, since the first extant evidence is usually the formal indictment, in which the offence and the accused person are named simultaneously, and from which it is impossible to reconstruct the thought-processes which had previously gone on in the accuser's mind. In particular, they do not tell us what other suspicions he had entertained. Indeed the indictments even conceal the identity of the persons who first made the accusation. Yet these bald statements tell us a certain amount. They show that the accused witch did not operate from a distance against strangers, but lived in the same neighbourhood, usually in the same village.[56] The witch, in other words, already had

55. Winchester D.R., C.B., 37, 6. 216.
56. Dr Macfarlane has shown that in 410 out of 460 cases in Essex witch and victim came from the same village: *Witchcraft Prosecutions in Essex*, p. 223.

some sort of relationship with her victim before she was believed to have begun to practise her malice.

The depositions, which sometimes survive to accompany the indictments, show that the accuser established the witch's identity in one of a few standard ways. Usually the victim would recall a threat uttered by someone with whom he had recently quarrelled. He might even have nocturnal visions of the witch, or cry out in his fits against his supposed persecutor. In 1653 the six-year-old son of Edward Hodge, labourer, of Benenden, Kent, began to have strange attacks in the night, calling out, 'Father! father! Here comes a black hairy thing will tease and kill me.' When he added, 'Bess Wood ... she will kill me', his parents knew that he had been bewitched by Elizabeth Wood, who already had a reputation for witchcraft, and who had recently quarrelled with the mother.[57] Possessed persons were often called on to name the persons who had afflicted them, and after a little coaxing could usually be prevailed upon to do so. Thus in 1626 Edward Dynham fell into a trance, speaking in three different voices, in one of which, after some encouragement, he revealed the identity of the witches who were tormenting him, and, he said, had already destroyed one victim. The two accused persons, Edward Bull and Joan Creedie, were duly indicted at Taunton Assizes. Any doubt about their guilt was dissipated when a gentlewoman, seized with a mysterious shaking in her side, cried out 'Bull, Bull, Bull'.[58] More rarely, the sight of a toad or some apparent animal familiar in the suspect's house might trigger off an accusation;[59] or the confession of one witch might incriminate another.[60]

But in many cases the victim, or his family, did not identify the witch unaided. Instead they invoked the aid of a white witch – a cunning man, astrologer, or wise woman – who was believed to possess the magical skill necessary to identify the source of misfortune. The client would go to the local wizard, describe his symptoms and invite a diagnosis. After having recourse to one of a variety of magical aids, the wizard would be expected to pronounce as to whether or not the victim was indeed bewitched, and indicate the identity of the evil-doer. This might suggest that the responsibility for identification, and even for the original suspicion of witchcraft, lay not with the victim but with the wizard. In some cases this may

57. Kent R.O., Q/SB/4, ff. 3–5.
58. B.M., Add. MS 36, 674, ff. 189–94ᵛ.
59. Examples in Wells D.R., D1 (1530); Lancashire R.O., QSP., 1/268/6.
60. e.g., Ewen, ii, pp. 152–3, 314–15.

have been true. There certainly were cunning men who planted
suspicions of witchcraft where none had previously grown, and
denounced persons who would not otherwise have been suspected.
Thus, it was said of William Walford of Cold Norton, Essex, in
1619 that 'his order is, when he comes to visit any sick neighbour,
to persuade them that they are bewitched, and tells them withal
[that] except they will be of that belief they can very hardly be
holpen of their disease and sickness'.[61] In the Warboys case the first
mention of witchcraft was by Dr Barrow of Cambridge, who asked,
after the failure of his original prescriptions for the afflicted Throckmorton children, if the possibility of sorcery or witchcraft had been
considered.[62]

There can be little doubt that such persons encouraged accusations of witchcraft which might otherwise never have been made.
The twin beliefs in black witches and cunning men were integrally
connected, the one propping up the other. Contemporaries rightly
called them both 'witches': 'The one twineth; the other untwineth,'
said a Hampshire man in 1532.[63] Ursula Kemp, hanged at Chelmsford for witchcraft in 1582, had protested that 'though she could
unwitch, she could not witch', while John Weemse later wrote that
'there are some witches which the common people call the loosing
witches, who do[es] no hurt at all, but remove[s] only that hurt
which the binding witch lays on the sick person'.[64] Another contemporary considered that the two operated in a sort of doctor-
apothecary relationship: 'the one to torment the bodies both of
man and beasts, that another may be sought unto to remedy the
same; so one ever being a working instrument to another'.[65] It was
in the cunning men's interest to diagnose witchcraft, after all, because they had a near-monopoly of techniques for dealing with it.
In England, no less than in modern Africa, the concept of witchcraft
was dependent upon a parallel acceptance of witch-doctors and

61. Hale, *Precedents*, pp. 244–5.
62. *The Most Strange ... Witches of Warboys*, sigs. B1ᵛ–2. Examples of
the key role played by the cunning men may be found in Ewen, ii, pp. 147,
154, 163, 178, 189, 190, 192, 196, 199, 230, 318, 348, 363, 364.
63. Winchester D.R., C.B. 6, p. 10.
64. *A True and Just Recorde, of ... All the Witches, taken at S. Oses*,
sig. A2; J. Weemse, *A Treatise of the Foure Degenerate Sonnes* (1636),
p. 146.
65. J. Halle, *An Historiall Expostulation*, ed. T. J. Pettigrew (Percy Soc.,
1844), p. 30. cf. E. Lawrence, *Christs Power over Bodily Diseases* (1662),
pp. 116–18.

magic. Thomas Ady unhesitatingly listed the cunning men among the causes of the belief in witchcraft. John Brinley thought that sundry honest persons had been hurried to the gallows on their advice.[66]

Yet the wizard's diagnosis of *maleficium* would not have been acceptable unless the patient himself had found it plausible; and when it came to identifying the witch the evidence suggests that the client was fully capable of rejecting any suggestions he did not welcome. All the wizard did was to confirm the suspicions already present in the client's mind, and strengthen his determination to act upon them. Once again we may cite the anthropological studies which show how the African diviner, despite his imposing apparatus of magical equipment. usually acts as a vehicle for the expression of suspicions which have already been formulated by the client, and normally leaves it to him to put a name to the suspect. 'In most cases,' writes an observer, 'the majority of the inquirers have decided in their own minds who is guilty, and that person is named by the diviner.' Wizards of this kind, remarks another, are usually 'merely the mouthpiece of corporate hostility towards the suspected witch'. The verdicts of the witch-detectors, says a third, must be 'in line with general expectations'.[67] So far as one can tell, this was also the case in England. As when identifying thieves, the wizard would show the client a mirror or a piece of polished stone, and ask if he recognized the face he saw in it. Or he might ask the client for a list of suspects, and carry out a series of tests designed to isolate the guilty one, carefully watching for his customer's reaction as each name was pronounced. A contemporary preacher summarized the procedure: 'A man is taken lame; he suspecteth that he is bewitched; he sendeth to the cunning man; he demandeth whom they suspect, and then sheweth the image of the party in a glass.'[68] But it was usually left to the client to put a name to the guilty party. Around 1630 the wise

66. Ady, p. 169; J. Brinley, *A Discovery of the Impostures of Witches and Astrologers* (1680), pp. 20–21. cf. Bernard, *Guide*, pp. 143–4; E. E. Evans-Pritchard, *Witchcraft, Oracles and Magic among the Azande* (Oxford, 1937), p. 257; above, pp. 219–20, 247.

67. M. Hunter, *Reaction to Conquest* (1936), pp. 308–9; B. Reynolds, *Magic, Divination and Witchcraft among the Barotse of Northern Rhodesia* (1963), pp. 126–7; L. Mair, *Witchcraft* (1969), p. 71; cf. E. K. Gough, 'Cults of the Dead among the Naȳars', in *Traditional India*, ed. M. Singer (Philadelphia, 1959), pp. 261–2; and above, pp. 257–9 and pp. 402–4.

68. G. Gifford, *Two Sermons upon 1. Peter 5, vers. 8 and 9* (1597), pp. 67–8.

woman of Forton, Lancashire, confirmed John Willson's fears that
he was forspoken, but, when asked by whom, said, 'she would not
tell for a thousand pounds'.[69]

This is the point at which the historian can only envy the anthropologist's ability to be present at some of these critical moments, for
full details of these clandestine consultations are inevitably lacking.
But it does seem that the cunning man usually took care to ascertain
who it was that the client himself suspected. Thus in 1579 an ostler
of Windsor developed a back-ache after a quarrel with an old
woman, Mother Stile. When he went to a wise man at Farnham,
the wizard 'told him that he was bewitched, and that there were
many ill women in Windsor, and asked him whom he did mistrust;
and the said ostler answered, ... "Mother Stile". "Well", said the
wise man, "if you can meet her, and ... scratch her, so that you draw
blood of her, you shall presently mend".' In a mid-seventeenth-
century case a worried mother consulted a wizard, John Hutton, as
to who was the cause of her child's illness. Back came the answer,
via a servant: 'Your mistress knows as well who hath wronged her
child as I.'[70] It can be seen in both these cases how the function of the
cunning man was to confirm the suspicions which the victim had
already formed, and thus to create the circumstances which were
necessary to convert a mere suspicion into a positive accusation.
The astrologer Lilly advised his colleagues to diagnose witchcraft,
only 'in places were people are troubled with witches'. The same
was true of witchfinders like John Darrell and Matthew Hopkins.
Darrell's accomplice, William Sommers, confessed that he only
denounced as witches those persons who were already suspected as
such.[71]

The use of counter-magic could also presuppose the existence of
some prior suspicion. One could hardly burn thatch from a suspect's
house without having first decided who the suspect was. Such tests
would seldom lead to the accusation of an unexpected party. Usually

69. Lancashire R.O., QSB/1/64/21.

70. (R. Galis), A Rehearsall both Straung and True of Hainous and Horrible Actions committed by Elizabeth Stile (1579), sigs. Bi^v–ii; (M. Moore),
Wonderfull News from the North (1650), p. 7. Literary testimony to the
key role of the client's prior suspicions may be found in Scot, Discoverie,
V.viii; Xii.xvi; G. Gifford, A Dialogue Concerning Witches (1593) (Shakespeare Assoc. facsimiles, 1931), sigs. B1, C1, D4^v, E4; J. Blagrave, Blagraves
Astrological Practice of Physick (1671), p. 35.

71. Lilly, Christian Astrology, pp. 464–5; S. H(arsnet), A Discovery of
the Fraudulent Practises of John Darrel (1599), p. 102. cf. above, p. 403.

they were self-confirming. It only needed the arrival of the suspected neighbour, curious to find out what was going on, for her guilt to be established. Once the woman had appeared, there was little she could do to help herself. Protestations of innocence were of no avail. It was a bad sign if she inquired too closely about the patient's symptoms; and if, as a gesture of good faith, she agreed to pray for the victim's recovery, this was only taken as the attempt of the witch to lift her spell.[72] If she allowed the patient to scratch her, she ran the risk that his subsequent recovery would establish her guilt; if she refused, then the conclusion to be drawn was obvious. In the Warboys case Lady Cromwell clipped off a lock of Mother Samuel's hair so that it might be burned to relieve the bewitched children: 'Madam, why do you use me thus?' complained the old woman, 'I never did you any harm *as yet*' – a fatal admission.[73]

From the initial accusation to the final judicial hearing, the procedure followed in the witch cases reminds us at every stage that men seldom seek a high degree of proof for what they already believe to be true. The position of the accused in the legal procedure of the day was never comfortable, whatever his offence, but the standard of evidence required to secure a conviction for witchcraft was particularly unexacting. Seventeenth-century demonologists tried to raise it, but their attempts to distinguish definite 'proofs' from mere 'presumptions' of this impossible crime inevitably proved unsuccessful.[74] At a popular level it was easy to become convinced of any suspect's guilt. If she were searched for the Devil's mark, her body was certain to offer some suitable mole or excrescence; if not, then she must have cut it off, or perhaps concealed it by magic; it was known that these marks could mysteriously come and go.[75] As for her familiar, that could be identified the moment a fly buzzed in through the window. If the victim recovered after counter-magic had

72. For two examples of this: Kent R.O., Q/SB2, ff. 14^v, 52, the trap being set in each case by the cunning man, Anthony Harlott. For suspicion aroused by interest in or over-intimate knowledge of the patient's symptoms, see, e.g., J. Cotta, *A Short Discoverie of the Unobserved Dangers of Severall Sorts of Ignorant and Unconsiderate Practisers of Physicke* (1612), pp. 51–3; Cooper, *Mystery*, p. 128; Borthwick, R.VII.H.1327 (1618); Bedfordshire R.O., H.S.A., 1680 Winter/97.

73. *The Most Strange ... Witches of Warboys*, sig. E3.

74. See below, pp. 686–7. On the limitations of the evidence, see Ewen, ii; pp. 119–22; Kittredge, *Witchcraft*, p. 364.

75. J. Stearne, *A Confirmation and Discovery of Witch-craft* (1648), pp. 19, 44–5.

been practised, then the suspect's guilt was demonstrated.[76] If the witch confessed, that settled the issue; if she refused to do so, she was adding perjury to her other sins: like Jennet Device, whose protestations of innocence in 1612 were deemed 'a very fearful thing to all that were present, who knew she was guilty'.[77]

Alone among accused persons, witches could be subjected to a brand of the old judicial ordeal. There was the popular version – 'swimming' her to see if she floated, in which case she was guilty. This device was being used in witch cases in England by 1590. The water, as the instrument of baptism, would reject those who had renounced it.[78] A more sophisticated test, often used in the courts, was to require the suspect to repeat the Lord's Prayer or a passage of Scripture. Any stumblings or omissions were taken as evidence that the passage in question was unsympathetic to the Devil, her master.[79] The judge might even require the witch to command the Devil to cease tormenting his victim; if the patient recovered at that moment, then it went ill with the accused.[80] Everything thus depended upon the prior attitude of those trying the witch. If they were so disposed, it was hard for anyone to escape.[81]

The basic problem, therefore, is that of how the initial suspicion came to be formed. We have seen so far that the witch was a person already known to her victim. If we supplement the laconic indictments with the more detailed depositions and pamphlet narratives, a further fact emerges about her, and that is that she was always believed to bear some previous grudge against him. Obvious though this may be, it does at least rule out the possibility of motiveless

76. For an early-nineteenth-century vicar whose scepticism about witchcraft was broken down by the victim's recovery on the application of a magical phylactery, see above, p. 329.

77. Potts, sig. P2ᵛ.

78. *The Most Strange ... Witches of Warboys*, sig. B3. See Ewen, ii, index, *s.v.* 'swimming test', for subsequent examples of its employment. For the theory underlying it see (James VI), *Daemonologie*, pp. 80–81; J. Cotta, *The Infallible True and Assured Witch* (1624), p. 131. Immersion was sometimes regarded as a means of breaking the witch's contract with the Devil; Bedfordshire R.O., H.S.A. 1667 W54/(i) (confession of Elizabeth Pratt, 1667).

79. Examples in Ewen, ii, pp. 175, 177, 186, 197, 212, 242, 338, 350, 367, 385. cf. L. Hewes, *Certain Grievances* (1641), pp. 9–10. An unusually elaborate version of the procedure is set out in 'A Touchstone or Triall of Witches discoveringe them by Scripture' (B.M., Royal MS 17 C XXIII) (early seventeenth century).

80. *The Most Strange ... Witches of Warboys*, sigs. O4ᵛ–P1.

81. For the way in which acquittals could occur, see below, pp. 687–8.

malignity. Contemporaries may have been horrified by the witch's activities, but they never denied that she had some genuine reason for wishing ill upon her victim. So when the Throckmorton children of Warboys blamed Alice Samuel for their fits, the bystanders at first refused to accept the charge, because they could think of no reason for her malice.[82]

A person who felt he had been bewitched would, therefore, identify the suspect by asking himself who might be likely to bear him a grudge. Usually, the misfortune had already occurred before men started thinking in this way, but sometimes the prior existence of some ill feeling would lead them to look out for the exercise of witchcraft. Thus when Elizabeth Foster, already suspected of witchcraft by the Fairfax family in 1621, touched the younger daughter, her mother exclaimed almost triumphantly, 'Now if Bess Foster be a witch, the child will ail.'[83] Witch accusations required the existence of prior animosities. Even the most fraudulent charge needed to be bolstered up by some suggestion of the accused person's malice if it were to stand.

There now arises the crucial question in the whole analysis. Is it possible to generalize about the sort of grudge which the witch was believed to bear towards her victim? Or was every conceivable type of animosity involved? The answer can only be extracted from those cases where the depositions or pamphlet accounts are sufficiently detailed, and is therefore impossible to represent statistically. But close examination of those cases where the circumstances can be adequately reconstructed reveals that the charge was normally only levied when the accuser felt, not merely that the witch bore a grudge against him, but that the grudge was a *justifiable* one. The witch, in other words, was not thought to be acting out of mere vindictiveness; she was avenging a definite injury. It was not just that victim and witch had quarrelled. The important point is that, paradoxically, it tended to be the witch who was morally in the right and the victim who was in the wrong. This result corresponds with what many anthropologists have found elsewhere.[84]

82. *The Most Strange . . . Witches of Warboys*, sig. B2.

83. E. Fairfax, *A Discourse of Witchcraft* (in *Miscellanies of the Philobiblon Soc.*, v [1858–9]), p. 99. cf. Evans-Pritchard, *Witchcraft, Oracles and Magic among the Azande*, p. 105; R. W. Lieban, *Cebuano Sorcery. Malign Magic in the Philippines* (Berkeley and Los Angeles, 1967), p. 117.

84. Prof. M. G. Marwick found the victim was guilty of some moral fault in 60 per cent of his Cêŵa cases in Zambia; *Sorcery in Its Social Setting* (Manchester, 1965), pp. vii-viii, 8, 241–6, and Table xxv. For the view

There was a wide variety of ways in which the witch might have been caused to take justifiable offence. Sometimes the victim had refused to pay her some legitimate debt which she had called to collect. Thus, in Hertfordshire in 1659, when Frances Rustat was 'strangely handled with great pain, racking and torment', she 'did often say ... that if she died of that distemper ... Goody Free was the cause of her death', adding significantly that she had never been well after buying eggs from the old woman and denying her payment on the excuse that she had no small change.[85] Similarly, when the London cunning woman Joan Peterson had cured Christopher Wilson in 1652, he refused to pay her the fee he had agreed, whereupon she prophesied correctly that he would get ten times worse; and in Yorkshire in 1632 when Mary Atkinson refused to pay Margaret Awcock the money she owed her, the child she was nursing duly fell ill.[86] More direct assaults were also followed by evil consequences. When John Orkton struck Mary Smith's son at King's Lynn in 1616, he found himself growing 'distempered in stomach', and his fingers and toes began to rot. When a servant snatched a pair of gloves from the pocket of Mother Nokes's daughter in Essex, around 1579, he suddenly lost the use of his limbs and was bedridden for eight days. When William Beard of the same county was taken ill in 1651, it was remembered that he had previously cut the tail off Margaret Burgis's cat. After pursuing Margaret Simons's dog with a drawn knife, the fourteen-year-old son of the Elizabethan vicar of Brenchley fell sick, until a white witch was found to cure him.[87] Unprovoked aggression against old women and their dependants was thus thought likely to invite magical retaliation, and many of the extant witch cases follow this same pattern, in which unreasonably injurious behaviour towards the witch is followed by a speedy vengeance.

But the most common situation of all was that in which the victim (or, if he were an infant, the victim's parents) had been guilty of a breach of charity or neighbourliness, by turning away an old

---

that sorcery can only work against a guilty man, see Lieban, *Cebuano Sorcery*, pp. 26, 38–9.

85. Ewen, ii, p. 456.

86. *The Witch of Wapping* (1652), pp. 4–5 (Ewen, ii, p. 320); Borthwick, R.VII.H. 1961.

87. For these cases, see Ewen, ii, pp. 229–30; *A Detection of Damnable Driftes, Practized by Three Witches arraigned at Chelmsford* (1579), sigs. Bi^v–ii; *The Essex Notebook*, viii (1885), p. 88; Scot, *Discoverie*, I, ii.

woman who had come to the door to beg or borrow some food or drink, or the loan of some household utensil. Thomas Ady described the householder's likely reaction when some misfortune followed on the heels of such an encounter:

> Presently he cryeth out of some poor innocent neighbour that he or she hath bewitched him. For, saith he, such an old man or woman came lately to my door and desired some relief, and I denied it, and, God forgive me, my heart did rise against her ... and presently my child, my wife myself, my horse, my cow, my sheep, my sow, my hog, my dog, my cat, or somewhat, was thus and thus handled in such a strange manner, as I dare swear she is a witch, or else how should these things be?[88]

The overwhelmingly majority of fully documented witch cases fall into this simple pattern. The witch is sent away empty-handed, perhaps mumbling a malediction; and in due course something goes wrong with the household, for which she is immediately held responsible. The requests made by the witch varied, but they conformed to the same general pattern.[89] Usually they were for food or drink – butter, cheese, yeast, milk or beer. Sometimes, she would ask to borrow money or a piece of equipment. In all cases denial was quickly followed by retribution, and the punishment often fitted the crime. When Robert Wayts refused Mother Palmer a pot of his beer in Suffolk around 1637, his servants could no longer make beer which would keep fresh. After Mary Ellins, daughter of an Evesham gardener, had thrown stones at Catherine Huxley in 1652, she began to void stones and continued doing so until the witch was executed.[90] At Castle Cary around 1530 Isabel Turner denied Christian Shirston a quart of ale, whereupon 'a stand of ale of twelve gallons began to boil as fast as a crock on the fire'. Joan Vicars would give her no milk, and thereafter her cow yielded nothing but blood and water. Henry Russe also refused her milk, only to find himself unable to make cheese until Michaelmas.[91]

88. Ady, p. 114. cf. Scot, *Discoverie*, prefatory letter to Sir Thomas Scot: 'She was at my house of late; she would have had a pot of milk; she departed in a chafe because she had it not; she railed; she cursed; she mumbled and whispered; and finally she said she would be even with me; and soon after my child, my cow, my sow, or my pullet died, or was strangely taken.'

89. The task of adequately presenting this pattern in statistical form has defeated me. I can only urge the sceptical reader to examine a few witch cases for himself. He should be warned that the relevant details are sometimes omitted in the summaries given in Ewen, ii.

90. Ewen, i, p. 305; Ewen, ii, p. 455.   91. Wells D.R., D 1.

A typical case was that of Margery Stanton of Wimbish, who was tried for witchcraft at Chelmsford in 1579. During the hearing it emerged that her first victim, Thomas Prat, had scratched her face with a needle, and had been subsequently racked with aches and pains; later he snatched a handful of grain from her and gave it to his chickens, most of whom promptly expired. Richard Saunder's wife had refused her yeast, whereupon her child was 'taken vehemently sick, in a marvellous strange manner'. Robert Petie's wife had her turned away from his house, and her child fell ill. William Torner denied her requests, and his child was taken with a fit. Robert Cornell's wife refused her milk, and was taken sick with a great swelling. John Hopwood denied her a leathern thong, and his gelding suddenly died. John Cornell denied her requests, whereupon his cows yielded blood instead of milk. The vicar's wife turned her away, and her little son became sick. Finally, Robert Lathbury refused her request, only to incur the loss of twenty hogs.[92]

These depressing peregrinations from door to door, which were the background to the prosecution of Margery Stanton are typical of a host of similar cases. They are not to be confused with vagrant begging, but illustrate the breakdown of the tradition of mutual help upon which many English village communities had been based. The loan of equipment, or the giving of food or drink, were neighbourly activities, in the common interest. Lending and borrowing had long been standard features of community life: 'The love of thy neighbour shall stand thee in stead,' Thomas Tusser told the Tudor farmer. 'No man of ability is long free from poor coming to his door,' thought Ady in 1655.[93] Margery Stanton's requests were typical enough; what was distinctive about them was that they were consistently refused. The fact that she should be accused of witchcraft, by the very people who had failed to fulfil their accepted social obligations to her, illustrates the essential conflict between neighbourliness and individualism which generated the tensions from which the accusations of witchcraft were most likely to arise. Margery's neighbours were denying her the charity and help which was traditionally required. When shutting the door in her face, however, they were only too well aware of having departed from the accepted ethical code. They knew that they had put their selfish

92. *A Detection of Damnable Driftes*, sigs. Avi[v]–Bi. The vicar was William Harrison, author of the *Description of England* (1577).

93. W. Notestein, *The English People on the Eve of Colonization* (New York, 1954), pp. 81–2; Ady, p. 129.

interests before their social duty. When some minor accident subsequently overtook them or their children or animals, it was their
own guilty conscience which indicated to them where they should
look for the cause of their misfortune.

Refusal of alms was the most characteristic way in which the
witch's supposed victims had failed in their obligations towards her;
many of the accused persons, as Scot pointed out, were women in
the habit of going 'from house to house, and from door to door for
a pot full of milk, yeast, drink, pottage, or some such relief, without
which they could hardly live'.[94] But there were other possible sources
of conflict. Witch cases could arise after disputes over gleaning,
common land, rights of way, or trespass.[95] Witches were accused of
retaliation against such local tyrants as the village constable who
pressed their sons to be soldiers, or the overseer of the poor who put
their children into compulsory service.[96] Joan Pechey, tried at
Chelmsford in 1582, had fallen out with the poor relief collector who
doled her out what she considered to be inferior bread.[97]

The conflict between neighbourliness and a growing sense of
private property is clearly seen in the case of Margaret Harkett, a
sixty-year-old widow of Stanmore, Middlesex, who was executed at
Tyburn in 1585. She had picked a basketful of peas in a neighbour's
field without permission. Asked to return them, she flung them
down in anger; since when, no peas would grow in the field. Later,
William Goodwin's servants denied her yeast, whereupon his
brewing-stand dried up. She was struck by a bailiff who had caught
her taking wood from his master's ground; the bailiff went mad.
A neighbour refused her a horse; all his horses died. Another paid
her less for a pair of shoes than she asked; later he died. A gentleman told his servants to refuse her buttermilk; after which they
were unable to make butter or cheese.[98]

Another cause of offence was a failure to invite the witch to some
common celebration. In the village community a man had a social
duty to invite his neighbours to participate in his christenings,

94. Scot, *Discoverie*, I.iii.

95. Examples in Strype, *The Life of Sir Thomas Smith*, pp. 99–100; *York
Depositions*, p. 74; Wells D.R., D 7 (1555).

96. e.g., Ewen, ii, pp. 290, 347.

97. A *True and Just Recorde, of ... all the Witches, taken at S. Oses*,
sig. A4.

98. *The Several Facts of Witchcraft approved and laid to the charge of
Margaret Harkett* (1585), reprinted in W. H. Dunham and S. Pargellis,
Complaint and Reform in England, 1436–1714 (New York, 1938), pp. 191–4.

funerals, sheep-shearings or harvest homes. Guests attended such occasions as of right, and it was a positive slight to refuse an invitation to anyone who was eligible. When Anne Kerke of Broken Wharf, London, was offered no share of the traditional doles for the poor at the funeral in 1599 of Anne Naylor (for whose mysterious death she was supposed to have been responsible) she was sorely 'vexed that she had none, being a parishioner', and accordingly directed her magical practices against a member of the family.[99] In 1570 an Essex witness deposed against one Malter's wife, that he, 'having a sheep-shearing, about this time, and not inviting her thereto, being his neighbour, she, as he supposed, bewitched two of his sheep; for immediately after they were taken with sickness'.[100] When Jane Milburne pointedly failed to ask Dorothy Strangers to her wedwing supper at Newcastle in 1663, the justly aggrieved Dorothy declared she would make her repent it; Jane was subsequently plagued by several mysterious cats, whom she knew at once to be Dorothy in supernatural disguise.[101] The classic malevolence of the wicked fairy sprang from the failure of the Sleeping Beauty's parents to invite her to the christening.

Witchcraft could also be a justified response to other kinds of uncalled-for behaviour. When Jane Slade, one of Sir Richard Napier's patients, found herself stricken by a mysterious disease in 1634, her first reaction was to suspect Joan Bruce's son, a former suitor, whom she had jilted in favour of another. It is a reasonable guess that she felt herself to have behaved badly towards him.[102] Other typical victims of witchcraft included the gaoler's man who chained old Mother Samuel of Warboys to a bedpost, the Earl of Rutland, who dismissed Margaret Flower from her post in Belvoir Castle, the drunkard in Royston alehouse who persistently abused Mother Stokes, and all those persons who had offensively taunted old women with being witches, only to find themselves struck down as a result.[103] In such cases remorse was an indispensable ingredient, if not in bringing about the misfortune, then at least in providing the victim with an explanation for its occurrence. Even in the

99. *The Triall of Maist. Dorrell* (1599), p. 102.
100. Strype, *The Life of Sir Thomas Smith*, p. 97.
101. *York Depositions*, pp. 112–14.
102. Ashm. 412, f. 126 (and ff. 169, 182^v, 219^v).
103. Ewen, ii, p. 172; *The Wonderful Discoverie of the Witchcrafts of Margaret and Philip Flower* (1619), sigs. E2^v, F3^v–4; Ewen, ii, pp. 200–2; above, p. 628.

accusations stirred up by Matthew Hopkins, the same factors were present; the witches may have been formally accused of devil-worship, but the witnesses against them tended to be victims who had treated them ungenerously in one way or another.[104]

Two essential features thus made up the background to most of the allegations of witchcraft levied in sixteenth- and seventeenth-century England. The first was the occurrence of a personal misfortune for which no natural explanation was immediately forthcoming. The second was an awareness on the victim's part of having given offence to a neighbour, usually by having failed to discharge some hitherto customary social obligation. As often as not, the link between the misfortune incurred and the obligation neglected was furnished by the frank expression of malignity on the part of the suspected witch. Thus when Thomas Harrison and his wife of Ellel, Lancashire, turned the old widow, Jennet Wilkinson, out of her house around 1620, she came and cursed them bitterly, saying, 'Hearest thou, hearest thou (clapping her hands together), . . . this shall be forty pounds loss to thee', and in due course some of their animals were taken sick and died.[105] Of course such threats were sometimes uttered when the witch was technically more in the wrong than her victims, as for example, when she would not pay her debts, or her rent; when she asked for credit; or when she was caught trespassing or stealing.[106] But always there was the clear innuendo that, if only the victim had been kindlier, more charitable, less disposed to stand on his property rights, more understanding of the plight of the weak, the quarrel would not have occurred.

In many cases, moreover, it was not necessary for the suspected witch to have given evidence of her malevolence. The victim's guilty conscience could alone be sufficient to provoke an accusation, since when a misfortune occurred his first reaction was to ask what he had done to deserve it. When William Hoppgood's young pigs behaved peculiarly in 1589, he recalled how, on the previous day, Widow

104. See, e.g., C. E. Parsons, 'Notes on Cambridgeshire Witchcraft', *Procs. Cambs. Antiqn Soc.*, xix (1915), p. 48; [H.F.], *A True and Exact Relation . . . of the late Witches, arraigned . . . at Chelmsford* (1645), p. 35; *The Lawes against Witches and Coniuration* (1645), p. 8; (J. Davenport), *The Witches of Huntingdon* (1646), pp. 5, 7, 8.

105. Lancashire R.O., QSB 1/64/23. cf. above, pp. 605–11.

106. Examples in Strype, *The Life of Sir Thomas Smith*, pp. 99–101; *Diaries and Letters of Philip Henry*, ed. M. H. Lee (1882), p. 152; Ewen, *Star Chamber*, p. 42; *The Case of the Hertfordshire Witchcraft Consider'd* (1712), p. 19.

Wells had come to his door on two occasions, 'there sitting, asking nothing; at length having not anything given unto her [one may note his assumption that something should have been], she departed from thence'. On the basis of this coincidence he warned her that, 'if he took any hurt by her afterwards, he would have her burned for a witch'. It is clear enough from Hoppgood's account of this incident that the source of the witchcraft was his own troubled conscience.[107] A similar case was that of Elizabeth Jackson, convicted of bewitching Mary Glover in 1602. The old woman had passed by the door, where the girl was eating a new wheaten loaf. She 'looked earnestly upon Mary, but, speaking nothing, passed by; and yet instantly returned, and with the like look and silence departed. At which doing the bread which she was chewing fell out of Mary Glover's mouth, and herself fell backwards off the stool where she sat, into a grievous fit'.[108] The Harrison couple who turned Jennet Wilkinson out of her house had been cursed by the widow, but it was their own hard conduct which explained why the wife was unable to rest at night, because of her conviction that 'the said Jennet was at the bed's side disquieting her'.[109]

A similar instance of how the relatively secure might be haunted by their ill-treament of the poor is furnished by Dinah Wiffin's statement, made at Bedford in 1680, that she

several times, upon the sight of John Wright in the street and at her door a-begging, fell a-trembling at the sight of him; and, being forbidden by her husband to give him anything, she did forbear, and hath not given him anything above twice or thrice since about a fortnight after Michaelmas last; and she saith that within three or four months last past she hath in her dreams several times seen the representation of (or imagined she hath seen) the said John Wright stand by her bed-side, and sometimes when she hath been awake. Once she dreamed he was laying his hand upon her; another time she thought he was going to lie on her; ... and on ... Friday last was fortnight, about one o'clock at noon, the said John Wright came to her door a-begging, at which time this deponent was very well, and told him there was nothing for him, upon which he went away, and presently [i.e. immediately] ... this deponent fell a-trembling and so fell into a very violent fit.

107. *Book of Examinations and Depositions, 1570–94*, ed. Hamilton and Aubrey, pp. 158–9.
108. S. Bradwell, 'Marie Glovers late woeful case' (1603) (Sloane 831), f. 6.
109. Lancashire R.O., QSB 1/64/23.

Her fits indeed were so persistent that John Wright found himself in Bedford Gaol on suspicion of witchcraft, though there was no evidence of any malevolence on his part at all.[110] Before a misfortune could be plausibly attributed to witchcraft, therefore, it had to be seen as the outcome of a certain type of social situation. This was why it was very unusual for large-scale disasters, like famine, plague or fire, to be blamed on a witch. For in a witch-case the suspect was usually a person who had been involved in a relationship of real or presumed hostility towards the victim. But the victim of an epidemic or a flood was not an individual or a family, but a whole community. To be plausibly suspected of bringing about such a disaster, it would be necessary to stand in a relationship of hostility, not to this or that individual, but to the community as a whole. The guilty party could only be someone whom everybody was conscious of having ill-treated. An old woman might conceivably be the enemy of a small community, as some of the arson cases show. But she was hardly a suitable adversary for a city or a whole nation. Any scapegoat had to be found elsewhere: sometimes in a fifth-column of Frenchmen, Catholics, or similar national enemies, but usually in the sins of the people, and their misconduct towards, not an individual beggar, but God himself. Those seeking to establish a link between guilt and misfortune had, therefore, to regard such large-scale disasters as acts of God, rather than as the *maleficia* of witches.

The incidence of plague, for example, was too indiscriminate to be plausibly explained in personal terms. It is true that the idea of biological warfare was familiar, and individuals were sometimes accused of spreading infection by natural means.[111] The Scots were said to have poisoned the wells at Newcastle in 1639. Bottles of infected air were rumoured to have been brought in from France in 1665. The Catholics, whose sorcery was thought to have been responsible for the Oxford gaol fever of 1577, were reported in 1641 to have sent a plague-sore in an envelope to John Pym.[112] It was also

110. Bedfordshire R.O., H.S.A., Winter 1680/96–7.
111. Kittredge, *Witchcraft*, chap. 6; *H.M.C., Hatfield*, vii, p. 167; Sir G. Clark in *Medical History*, x (1966), p. 218. The continental idea that plague might be started by the bodies of *dead* witches was known in England (e.g. W. Kemp, *A Brief Treatise of . . . the Pestilence* [1665], p. 8), but does not seem to have had any influence.
112. *C.S.P.D., 1639*, p. 189; C. F. Mullett, *The Bubonic Plague and England* (Lexington, 1956), p. 220; Kittredge, *Witchcraft*, pp. 89, 419–20; S. R. Gardiner, *History of England, 1603–42* (1904–5), x, p. 38. cf. *York Depositions*, p. 154.

possible to identify the Jonah who had brought down such a judgement; when plague struck Barnstaple in 1646 some inhabitants blamed the local Independent congregation and wanted its members turned out of town.[113] But, although epidemics were sometimes thought to have been stimulated by national enemies, they played virtually no part in fostering accusations of witchcraft.

Neither were fires blamed upon witches, save those cases where the outbreak destroyed one individual's property, but not that of the whole community. It was possible for Richard Rosse of Little Clapton, Essex, to blame Henry Celles in 1582 because his barn had mysteriously caught fire,[114] but out of the question for anyone to attribute the wholesale destruction of Tiverton or Northampton to a similar cause. The storm at sea which affected a single ship might sometimes be attributed to witchcraft,[115] but on land the action of a tempest was usually too indiscriminate for such an interpretation to be plausible. Storms which handicapped one of two sides in battle were, of course, a different matter.[116] Witch-beliefs, in other words, did not explain misfortune in general, but only in particular. The fear of witches was not normally interchangeable with the fear of Catholics or Jews. It had an altogether different social function. An accusation of witchcraft originated with someone living in close proximity to the suspect, and was meant to explain some local and personal misfortune. The Popish bogey, by contrast, concerned national dangers, and did not arise out of a personal relationship. Only if witches were conceived of in continental fashion as a devil-worshipping sect, did it become plausible to regard them as enemies of society in general, like the Catholics, and hence to blame them for storms or plagues, in the way that sometimes happened in Europe.[117]

113. *Five Wonders seene in England* (1646), sig. A2.

114. Ewen, ii, p. 162. There are similar cases in ibid., p. 90; Ewen, i, pp. 86, 154–5; J. Spedding, *The Letters and the Life of Francis Bacon* (1861–74), vii, pp. 30–31; S. Clarke, *A Mirrour or Looking-Glass both for Saints and Sinners* (4th edn, 1671), ii, pp. 593–6. cf. above, p. 635.

115. e.g., Ewen, ii, pp. 89–90, 291–2, 448–9, 461; H.F., *A Prodigious and Tragicall History of the Arraignment . . . of Six Witches at Maidstone*, p. 6. Lilly was once asked whether an overdue ship was 'lost or bewitched' (Ashm. 178, f. 41).

116. Kittredge, *Witchcraft*, chap. 8.

117. cf. Lea, *Materials*, pp. 616, 911, 1254; R. T. Davies, *Four Centuries of Witch-Beliefs* (1947), pp. 6–8.

It was, therefore, the prior involvement of the victim in a hostile relationship which made contemporaries invoke witchcraft as the explanation of a misadventure. Without that involvement, no misfortune, however mysterious, could be so explained. With it, even the most natural occurrence might appear sinister. When Thomas and Elizabeth Baxter of Newton-in-Mackerfield, Lancashire, failed to have children who survived, they blamed it in 1636 upon the witchcraft of Joan Elderson; they did not do this because infant mortality was unusual, for it was not, but because they knew that it was her son who stood to inherit their house if they had no direct heirs; and she had already prevented them from trying to buy out his rights.[118]

3. *Witchcraft and society*

Witch-beliefs are therefore of interest to the social historian for the light they throw upon the weak points in the social structure of the time. Essentially the witch and her victim were two persons who ought to have been friendly towards each other, but were not.[119] They existed in a state of concealed hostility for which society provided no legitimate outlet. They could not take each other to law; neither could they have recourse to open violence. In Africa accusations of witchcraft frequently spring from conflicts within the family, for example, between the co-wives of a polygamous husband.[120] But in England the witch and her accuser were very seldom related. The tensions which such accusations usually reflected arose from the position of the poor and dependent members of the community. The charges of witchcraft were a means of expressing deep-felt animosities in acceptable guise. Before a witchcraft accusation could be plausibly made, the suspect had to be in a socially or economically inferior position to her supposed victim. Only then could she be presumed to be likely to have had recourse to magical methods of retaliation, for, had she been the stronger party, more direct methods of revenge would have been at her disposal. This is why there are hardly any cases in which the witch was socially

118. Lancashire R.O., QSB 1/170/55–60.
119. cf. P. Mayer, *Witches* (Grahamstown, 1954), p. 12.
120. cf. M. Fortes, *The Web of Kinship among the Tallensi* (1949), pp. 131–2; E. J. and J. D. Krige, *The Realm of a Rain-Queen* (1943), p. 263; J. Middleton, *Lugbara Religion* (1960), p. 245.

more elevated than the victim;[121] and why witches tended to be poor. It may be that it was easier to pin an accusation on a poor man because he was less able to defend himself.[122] But the essential reason was that the poor man was the one most likely to find himself in the social situation from which witchcraft accusations sprang.

The great bulk of witchcraft accusations thus reflected an unresolved conflict between the neighbourly conduct required by the ethical code of the old village community, and the increasingly individualistic forms of behaviour which accompanied the economic changes of the sixteenth and seventeenth centuries. Of course, there has never been a time when there was no conflict between the needs of the individual and the demands of charity. It would certainly be wrong to think that there were no such difficulties and conflicts in the medieval village. But such tensions as there were then had to find some other outlet, for, as we have seen, it was only the Reformation which, by taking away the protective ritual of Catholicism, made witchcraft appear a serious danger to ordinary people.

Moreover, there is some reason to think that during the Tudor and Stuart period these village conflicts grew particularly acute. The old manorial system had done much to cater for widows and elderly persons by a built-in system of poor relief. The widow enjoyed the right of freebench, that is, of succession to a portion of her late husband's holding, ranging from a quarter to the whole, according to local manorial custom. Should she be incapable of cultivating it herself, she could surrender it to a younger member of the family in return for a guarantee of maintenance. This was a more generous arrangement than the ordinary common law rules for succession to rent-paying land, by which the widow's dower was limited to a

121. The only such cases known to me are the series of accusations made against John Lowes, vicar of Brandeston, Suffolk, by his parishioners, culminating in his execution in 1645 (see C. L. Ewen, *The Trials of John Lowes, Clerk* [1937], and above, p. 330), and against Sir Henry Hunloke by Elizabeth Hole in 1680 (J. C. Cox, *Three Centuries of Derbyshire Annals* [1890], ii, p. 90).

122. cf. F. Hutchinson, *An Historical Essay concerning Witchcraft* (2nd edn, 1720), p. 253. ('Accusations of witches are usually discovered when they come to the better sort'). John Webster commented that if any unusual mark on the human body was to be regarded as a witch-mark 'then few would go free, especially those that are of the poorer sort, that have the worst diet, and are but nastily kept' (*The Displaying of Supposed Witchcraft* [1677], p. 82). Ewen, on the other hand, assumed that witches were drawn from the poorer classes because they were more superstitious (ii, p. 67).

third.[123] There were also various local customary privileges of the poor, varying from the right of three days of gleaning before the stubble was given over to pasture (conceded at some point before the eighteenth century, but taken away in a legal judgement of 1787), to permission to sleep in the church if they had no other accommodation.[124]

The decline of the manorial system has not yet been charted by modern historians, and the working of the laws of inheritance also awaits fuller study. But it seems clear that this period saw the decay of many of these traditional arrangements. Population pressure eroded many of the old customary tenancies, and led to the taking in of the commons and the rise of competitive rents. These changes were disadvantageous to the widow. So were the enclosures and engrossing which broke up many of the old cooperative village communities. This deterioration in the position of the dependent and elderly helps to explain why witches were primarily women, and probably old ones, many of them widowed. 'They are usually such as are destitute of friends, bowed down with years, laden with infirmities,' said a contemporary.[125] Their names appear among the witchcraft indictments, just as they do among the recipients of

123. For these arrangements see F. M. Page, 'The customary poor-law of three Cambridgeshire manors', *Cambridge Hist. Journ.*, iii (1930); id. *The Estates of Crowland Abbey* (Cambridge, 1934), pp. 108–12; G. L. Gomme, 'Widowhood in Manorial Law', *Archaeol. Rev.*, ii (1888–9); J. A. Raftis, *Tenure and Mobility* (Toronto, 1964), pp. 36–40, 42–3; W. G. Hoskins, *The Midland Peasant* (1957), pp. 75, 201–2; R. J. Faith, 'Peasant Families and Inheritance Customs in Medieval England', *Agricultural Hist. Rev.*, xiv (1966), pp. 88, 91; D. Roden, 'Inheritance Customs and Succession to Land in the Chiltern Hills in the Thirteenth and early Fourteenth Centuries', *Journ. Brit. Studies*, vii (1967), p. 5 and n. 18.

124. W. O. Ault, 'By-Laws of Gleaning', *Econ. Hist. Rev.*, 2nd ser., xiv (1961); [Sir G. Gilbert], *The Law of Evidence* (3rd edn, 1769), p. 253; H. Blackstone, *Reports of Cases* (1791–6), i, p. 51; *Depositions taken before the Mayor and Aldermen of Norwich, 1549–67*, ed. W. Rye (Norfolk and Norwich Archaeol. Soc., 1905), p. 18.

125. J. Juxon, *A Sermon upon Witchcraft* (1736), p. 24. The ages of most accused witches are not known, but the assumption of most contemporaries that witches were usually elderly is consistent with what evidence survives. cf. Macfarlane, *Witchcraft Prosecutions in Essex, 1560–1680*, pp. 215–18. The proportion of widows is equally elusive since the indictments often fail to describe them as such even when other evidence shows that they were widowed. Of the 102 women executed on the Home Circuit, only 32 are known to have had husbands alive (Ewen, i, *passim*).

parochial relief.[126] For they were the persons most dependent upon neighbourly support.

At the same time as the position of the poorer members of the community was being exacerbated, the old tradition of mutual charity and help was being eroded by such new economic developments as land hunger, the rise in prices, the development of agricultural specialisation and the growth of towns and commercial values. These trends were accompanied by the disappearance of some of the old mechanisms for resolving village conflicts which had been provided by the manorial courts and by the religious gilds.[127] Many contemporaries believed that theirs was a time of disintegration, by contrast with the vanished harmony of the Middle Ages. Robert Burton, for example, attributed the unprecedented volume of litigation to the decay of the old social bonds: 'no charity, love, friendship, fear of God, alliance, affinity, consanguinity, Christianity, can contain them'.[128]

Much more historical research will be needed before we can see comments of this kind in their proper perspective, and distinguish genuine social analysis from a fuzzy nostalgia for some imaginary merry England. But there was one innovation of the sixteenth century which did undoubtedly sap the old tradition of mutual charity, and that was the national Poor Law, created by a series of Tudor statutes which set up overseers of the poor, charged with levying a rate and making provision for the dependent members of the parish. Nothing did more to make the moral duties of the householder ambiguous. On the one hand the State forbade indiscriminate begging; on the other it continued to uphold the responsibility of the inhabitants of each parish for their own poor, even allowing

126. For the frequent preponderance of elderly women among recognized paupers, see, e.g., J. F. Pound, 'An Elizabethan Census of the Poor', *Univ. of Birmingham Hist. Journ.*, viii (1961–2), pp. 138, 141; F. G. Emmison 'Poor Relief Accounts of Two Rural Parishes in Bedfordshire, 1563–98', *Econ. Hist. Rev.*, iii (1931–2), p. 106; S. and B. Webb, *English Local Government: English Poor Law History: Part I. The Old Poor Law* (1927), p. 160; *Poor Relief in Elizabethan Ipswich*, ed. J. Webb (Suffolk Rec. Soc., 1966), pp. 22, 23, 39, 102–3.

127. On these arbitration-mechanisms, see, e.g., *Cambridge Gild Records*, ed. M. Bateson (Pubs. Cambs. Antiqn. Soc., 1903), pp. 66, 86, 103, 118; C. B. Firth, 'Village Gilds of Norfolk and the Fen Country', *Norfolk Archaeology*, xviii (1911–13), pp. 193–4.

128. Burton, *Anatomy*, i, p. 64. For a characteristic *Balade declaring how Neighbourhood, Love, and True Dealing is Gone* (1561) see *A Collection of Seventy-Nine Black Letter Ballads* (1870), pp. 134–8.

begging within the parish, if permitted by the overseers. The clergy from the pulpit continued to insist on the moral duty of charity, although many local authorities now forbade householders to give alms at the door.[129] In Tudor times the national system was only invoked at times of special emergency, and the loan of food and equipment to neighbours continued in many places to be essential for the routine maintenance of the elderly and infirm. It was probably as important a means of poor relief as the public levies of the poor rate, or the great private benefactions; not for nothing did John Hales describe godly charity as the sinews which held the Commonwealth together.[130]

This uneasy conjunction of public and private charity exacerbated the uncertainty with which contemporaries viewed the poor. They hated them as a burden to the community and a threat to public order. But they also recognised that it was their Christian duty to give them charity when no public relief was forthcoming. The conflict between resentment and a sense of obligation produced the ambivalence which made it possible for men to turn begging women brusquely from the door, and yet suffer torments of conscience after having done so.[131] This ensuing guilt was fertile ground for witchcraft accusations; any subsequent misfortunes could be seen as retaliation on the part of the witch, and class hatred constituted a major stimulus to her prosecution. The tensions which produced witchcraft prosecution at the popular level – and it should be emphasised that these conflicts were not between the very rich and the very poor, but between fairly poor and very poor – were the tensions of a society which no longer held a clear view as to how or by whom its dependent members should be maintained.

129. See, e.g., *York Civic Records*, ed. A. Raine (Yorks. Archaeol. Soc., 1939–53), viii, p. 134; *Norfolk Archaeology*, xxxii (1961), p. 231; E. M. Leonard, *The Early History of English Poor Relief* (Cambridge, 1900), pp. 55, 77, 105, 332; Webb, *English Local Government ... The Old Poor Law*, p. 318. Clerical views on charity are well summarized in W. K. Jordan, *Philanthropy in England, 1480–1660* (1959), pp. 152 ff.

130. Quoted in P. F. Tytler, *England under the Reigns of Edward VI and Mary* (1839), i, p. 115. Jordan (op. cit., p. 42) calculates that only 0.17 per cent of the money disposed of by the charitable foundations went on helping the aged. Lending and giving by neighbours leaves no records and is therefore not discussed in any of the standard histories of poor relief.

131. For a marvellously illuminating example of this ambivalence, too long to be quoted here, see the extract from Abiezer Coppe, *A Fiery Flying Roll* (1649), quoted by J. Crofts in *Procs. Brit. Acad.*, xxvi (1940), pp. 189–91.

In these circumstances, witch-beliefs helped to uphold the traditional obligations of charity and neighbourliness at a time when other social and economic forces were conspiring to weaken them. The fear of retaliation by witchcraft was a powerful deterrent against breaking the old moral code, for to display a lack of generosity to one's neighbours was the quickest way of getting hurt. Witches, it was rightly said, could not harm folk who were liberal to the poor, and the most Christian preservative against witchcraft was to be charitable.[132] When overtaken by a disaster, thought Thomas Ady, we should not ask ourselves, ' "What old man or woman was last at my door, that I may hang him or her for a witch?" . . . We should rather say, "Because I did not relieve such a poor body that was lately at my door, but gave him harsh and bitter words, therefore God hath laid this affliction upon me." '[133] This fitted in well with the clergy's teaching that men who helped the poor would prosper themselves, and that covetousness did not pay.

Conversely, an old woman's reputation for witchcraft might be her last line of defence, ensuring that she was decently treated by her fellow-villagers. An essayist wrote of *A Witch* (1615) that 'a very noble-man's request may be denied more safely than her petitions for buttermilk and small beer'. He was echoing Reginald Scot, who had noticed how 'these miserable wretches are so odious unto all their neighbours, and so feared as few dare offend them, or deny them anything they ask'.[134] One of the characters in George Gifford's *Dialogue concerning Witches* (1593) observes of a suspect: 'I have been as careful to please her as ever I was to please mine own mother, and to give her ever anon one thing or other.' We give them charity 'that they may not hurt us', said Thomas Cooper.[135]

The records confirm the evidence of the pamphleteers on this point. 'I am loathe to displease my neighbour Alldridge,' said an Elizabethan husbandman in 1580, 'for I can never displease him, but I have one mischance or another amongst my cattle.'[136] In Devonshire in 1565 Edward Goodridge advised a neighbour not to pursue a lawsuit against the suspected witch Alse Martyn, 'because he

132. F. Trigge, *A Godly and Fruitfull Sermon* (Oxford, 1594), sig. F4ᵛ.

133. Ady, p. 130.

134. J. Stephens, *Essayes and Characters* (1615), p. 376; Scot, *Discoverie*, I.iii.

135. Gifford, *A Dialogue Concerning Witches*, sig. B1; Cooper, *Mystery*, p. 18.   136. Winchester D.R., C.B. 50, p. 449.

knew what harm she could do'.[137] In the great Lancashire witch-trial of 1612 it was revealed that Jennet Device had been taught a charm by her mother 'to get drink'; that no one could escape the fury of Elizabeth Southernes ('Old Demdike'), if he gave her family 'any occasion of offence, or denied them any thing they stood need of'; and that John Device had been so afraid of being bewitched by the aged crone, Anne Chattox, that he had covenanted to pay her a yearly dole of meal, on condition that she hurt neither him nor his goods; on his death-bed he was convinced that he had been bewitched because the latest instalment had been left unpaid.[138] In Jacobean Yorkshire Elizabeth Fletcher, 'a woman notoriously famed for a witch, ... had so powerful a hand over the wealthiest neighbours about her, that none of them refused to do anything she required; yea, unbesought they provided her with fire and meat from their own tables'.[139] In Flintshire during the Protectorate, Anne Ellis lived by begging and knitting stockings, for which people were prepared to over-pay her, out of fear of her witchcraft.[140] In Hampshire in 1575 Thomas Gooter knew that old Mother Hunt was a witch, because, he said, 'I can no sooner shake a pig of hers or pound her cattle but presently either I or my master have a shrewd turn.'[141] So long as the belief in witchcraft survived, it had a semi-protective character for those who were thought to possess this magical power. As the Chartist, William Lovett, recalled from his Cornish childhood, a reputed witch was treated with respect in the village. 'Anything that Aunt Tammy took a fancy to, few who feared her dared to refuse.'[142]

Witch-beliefs thus discharged a function in early modern England similar to that which they perform in many primitive societies today. They reinforced accepted moral standards by postulating that a breach in the norms of neighbourly behaviour would be followed by repercussions in the natural order. They were a check on the expression of vicious feelings by both the likely witch and her prospective victim. As Professor Evans-Pritchard has written of the

137. 'Vic', *Odd Ways in Olden Days down West* (Birmingham, 1892), p. xii.
138. Potts, sigs. G4, B2, E4.
139. E. Fairfax, *Daemonologia*, ed. W. Grainge (Harrogate, 1882), p. 34.
140. Ewen, ii, p. 333.
141. *Winchester Consistory Court Depositions, 1561–1602*, ed. A. J. Willis (Folkestone, 1960), pp. 25–6.
142. *Life and Struggles of William Lovett* (1920), i, p. 18.

Azande, 'their belief in witchcraft is a valuable corrective to uncharitable impulses, because a show of spleen or meanness or hostility may bring serious consequences in its train'.[143] Witch-beliefs,
like the belief in divine providence, were a manifestation of the
same assumption that the likely cause of material misfortune was
to be found in some breach of moral behaviour.

From this point of view witch-beliefs may be fairly described as
'conservative social forces',[144] upholding the norms of village life.
But they could also have a more radical function. For, although
most contemporaries warned men to be charitable, so as to avoid
supernatural retaliation, there were others who stressed that it was
dangerous to give anything to a suspected witch, and advised that
she be ostracised by the community.[145] A witch who was known to
be such could be subject to violence and harsh treatment. Jane Wenham was described in 1712 as 'a poor woman that has lived for sixteen years under the character of a witch, and by this means ... become so odious to all her neighbours as to be deny'd in all probability
the common necessaries of life ... The more firmly her neighbours
believed her to be a witch, ... the worse they would use her.'[146]

These two different ways of treating a witch were not really inconsistent, for it was only the person suspected of witchcraft who was
to be turned away; and such a suspicion was unlikely to arise so
long as men were neighbourly and charitable. Witch-beliefs, in other
words, upheld the conventions of charity and neighbourliness, but
once these conventions had broken down they justified the breach
and made it possible for the uncharitable to divert attention from
their own guilt by focusing attention on that of the witch. Meanwhile,

143. Evans-Pritchard, *Witchcraft, Oracles and Magic among the Azande*,
p. 117. cf. Marwick, *Sorcery in its Social Setting*, chap. 8; *Witchcraft and
Sorcery in East Africa*, ed. Middleton and Winter, pp. 51–2; V. W. Turner,
Schism and Continuity in an African Society (Manchester, 1957), p. 142;
B. B. Whiting, *Paiute Sorcery* (Viking Fund Pubs. in Anthropology, New
York, 1950), pp. 80–82.

144. Marwick, op. cit., p. 221.

145. See, e.g., Cooper, *Mystery*, pp. 287–8; Stearne, *A Confirmation and
Discovery*, p. 35; *The Hartford-Shire Wonder* (1669), sig. A4. One Lancashire cunning man advised his clients not to give anything to witches without
first putting salt in it; Lancashire R.O., QSB/1/202/89 (1638). For the will
(1603) of an Essex gentleman who specifically exempted suspected witches
from his bequests to the poor, see F. G. Emmison, *Elizabethan Life: Disorder* (Chelmsford, 1970), p. 196.

146. *The Case of the Hertfordshire Witchcraft Consider'd*, p. 69. On
violence and ill-treatment, see above, pp. 633–4.

she would be deterred from knocking at any more unfriendly doors, for fear of swelling the ranks of her accusers. In England, as in Africa, the belief in witches could thus help dissolve 'relations which have become redundant'.[147]

It is not claimed that this interpretation will fit every accusation of witchcraft which occurred during the period. In the majority of prosecutions the surviving evidence is too slight for us to know whether it does not. But where the evidence is reasonably full the kind of relationship between witch and accuser which has been outlined can usually be inferred. The model can also be applied to many Continental accusations, and to some of the witchcraft allegations made in New England.[148] But it does not need to be supported from evidence from these other environments, since there is in principle no reason why the social context of witchcraft accusations should have been the same in different societies.

In England other subsidiary factors were also sometimes involved. A witchcraft accusation was more plausible, for example, when levied against a person who already had a reputation for magical prowess as a white witch or cunning man. Most demonologists taught that white witches could impose spells as well as lift them, and many cunning folk found themselves accused of maleficent witchcraft.[149] Some contemporary sources also suggest that physical abnormalities could be relevant. One popular handbook specifically warned its readers to 'beware of all persons that have default of members naturally, as of foot, hand eye, or other member; one that is crippled; and especially of a man that hath not a beard'.[150] Witchcraft accusations might be levied against the 'old woman with a wrinkled face, a furr'd brow, a hairy lip, a gobbler tooth, a squint eye, a squeaking voice, or a scolding tongue', as John Gaule put it.[151] Men sometimes claimed to recognize witches by their appearance,

147. M. G. Marwick, 'The Social Context of Cewa Witch-Beliefs', *Africa*, xxii (1952), p. 232. cf. Macfarlane, *Witchcraft Prosecutions in Essex*, pp. 280–81.

148. For suggestive indications see Lea, *Materials*, pp. 251–2, 311, 417, 564–5, 612–13, 616–17, 620; *Narratives of the Witchcraft Cases, 1648–1706*, ed. G. L. Burr (Original Narratives of Early American History, New York, 1914), pp. 132, 230, 232, 238, 239, 259–60, 422.

149. I have encountered over forty cases of this kind.

150. *The Compost of Ptolomeus* (n.d. [?1600]; copy in B.M., 718 b 41), sig. H7.

151. J. Gaule, *Select Cases of Conscience touching Witches* (1646), 4–5.

as did Nicholas Widgier, wheelwright of St Dunstan's, Kent, who was convinced in 1651 that the brewer's wife, Dorothy Rawlins, was a witch, because 'she had the eyes of the witches [who] were hanged at Faversham'. 'How often,' thought Thomas Potts in 1613, 'will the common people say, "Her eyes are sunk in her head; God bless us from her." '[152] It was proverbial that bearded women were likely to be witches, and physical ugliness or deformity could thus awaken suspicion.[153]

But when witch accusations permit of close examination they reveal that it was the suspect's conduct and social situation, rather than her physical appearance, which led to her downfall. Even the last item on John Gaule's list of personal characteristics – 'a scolding tongue' – is a social phenomenon, not a physical one. Matthew Hopkins's first victim was one-legged, but it was her consequent dependence upon the support of others, not her physical deformity as such, which lay behind her downfall.[154] The same is true of most of the other ugly old women who were seen as witches. There is no evidence that their physical appearance was relevant to the accusation. Such considerations were very seldom mentioned in the depositions. Moral deviations – illegitimacy, sexual promiscuity – may perhaps have been slightly more relevant, but no more so than in the identification of any other type of criminal.[155] The nature of the surviving evidence makes it quite impossible to assess the role of either factor with any precision. But it is clear that neither was in any way essential.

Nor does it seem necessary to look for a psychological or psychoanalytic explanation of the fact that the majority of accused witches were women. This aspect of the trials is more plausibly explained by economic and social considerations, for it was the women who were the most dependent members of the community, and thus the most vulnerable to accusation. It is true that this aspect of the subject fascinated contemporary demonologists, who readily enlarged upon the deficiencies of the weaker sex and their greater suscepti-

152. Kent R.O., Q/SB/2, f. 27; Potts, sig. M2. cf. chap. 14, appx. A.

153. J. Wodroephe, *The Spared Houres of a Souldier in his Travels* (1623), p. 488; Notestein, *Witchcraft*, p. 215 n.; Potts, sig. G1; *The Wonderful Discoverie of the Witchcrafts of Margaret and Phillip Flower*, sig. C3.

154. Notestein, *Witchcraft*, p. 166; Ewen, ii, p. 266.

155. Examples of accused persons involved in sexual irregularities can be found in Ewen, ii, pp. 168, 204; Notestein, *Witchcraft*, pp. 40, 42–3, 54, 115.

bility to Satan. Undoubtedly there was a strong anti-feminist streak about such monkish fantasies as the *Malleus maleficarum*, where the theme of diabolic copulation and the lore of incubi and succubi were thoroughly explored. But in England the more blatant sexual aspects of witchcraft were a very uncommon feature of the trials, save perhaps in the Hopkins period. The idea that witch-prosecutions reflected a war between the sexes must be discounted, not least because the victims and witnesses were themselves as likely to be women as men.[156]

The most that can be said at present on the sexual aspect of the trials is that the mythology of witchcraft was at its height at a time when women were generally believed to be sexually more voracious than men: 'of women's unnatural, unsatiable lust', wrote the bachelor, Robert Burton, in 1621, 'what country, what village doth not complain'.[157] In the eighteenth century this view was gradually superseded among the middle classes by the notion, exemplarized in Samuel Richardson's *Pamela*, that women were sexually passive and utterly unlascivious.[158] The change neatly coincided with the disappearance of the belief that there were witches who satisfied their sexual appetites by congress with the Devil. Both developments reflected an attempt to curb and repress the open discussion of sexuality. The marked growth of sexual inhibitions reflected in eighteenth-century literature made it harder for moralists and preachers to retail the old stories about sabbaths and succubi. Instead of proclaiming sexuality as a sin they suppressed it as a topic of conversation.[159]

Undoubtedly there is still much about the fantasy side of witchbeliefs which cries out for explanation.[160] The concept of witchcraft provided a way of looking at the world and an imaginative vocabu-

156. cf. Macfarlane, *Witchcraft Prosecutions in Essex*, p. 213.

157. Burton, *Anatomy*, iii, p. 55.

158. cf. M. Schlauch, *Antecedents of the English Novel, 1400–1600* (1963), pp. 122–3, and F. L. Utley, *The Crooked Rib* (Columbus, Ohio, 1944), pp. 49, 50, 163–4, 255–6, with R. P. Utter and G. B. Needham, *Pamela's Daughters* (1937). It is doubtful whether the change had much influence upon the working classes: nineteenth-century editions of the popular sex-handbook, *Aristotle's Masterpiece*, continued to assert that women had more pleasure in sex than men.

159. A point well made by E. Jones, *On the Nightmare* (1931), pp. 229–30.

160. cf. the comments of M. Douglas in *New Society*, no. 358 (7 Aug. 1969).

lary for many individuals who were not themselves directly involved in witchcraft accusations. The image of the witch was made up of different elements, some of which, like the peculiarly English belief in animal familiars, remain largely unaccounted for. All that has been advanced here is a social explanation of the context in which witch accusations were made and an outline of the intellectual assumptions which made them plausible. It is to be hoped that future work will illuminate some of their other aspects.

18.

WITCHCRAFT: DECLINE

*They say miracles are past; and we have our philosophical persons
to make modern and familiar, things supernatural and causeless.*
W. Shakespeare, *All's Well that Ends Well*. II, iii

THE later seventeenth century saw the decline of witch-prosecution
in England and the spread of scepticism about the very possibility of
the offence. Long before the repeal of the Witchcraft Act in 1736 it
had become increasingly difficult to mount and sustain a successful
prosecution in the courts. The explanation for this lies in the changed
attitude of the educated classes who provided the judges, lawyers,
Grand Jurymen and Petty Jurymen, whose collective resistance
effectively brought the trials to an end.

But how is this change of attitude to be accounted for? Here we
encounter the most baffling aspect of this difficult subject. For the
revolution in opinion about witchcraft was almost as silent as the
decay in the intellectual prestige of astrology. The topic inspired a
continuous flow of controversial writing, it is true. But the arguments
employed on either side hardly changed at all. What has to be explained is why it should have taken over a hundred years for the
case urged by the sceptics to become generally acceptable.

The sceptical argument was not necessarily linked to any new
assumptions about the natural world. On the contrary much of the
debate was deliberately conducted within a framework of Protestant fundamentalism. The leading sceptical writers – Reginald Scot,
Samuel Harsnet, Sir Robert Filmer, Thomas Ady, John Wagstaffe,
John Webster, Francis Hutchinson – all urged that the 'continental'
conception of witchcraft as devil-worship was unacceptable because
it had no Biblical justification. This type of witchcraft was not to
be found in the Scriptures, and, as Webster emphasized, 'What the
Scriptures have not revealed of the power of the kingdom of Satan
is to be rejected and not to be believed.'[1] Of course, there was Exodus, xxii, 18, which declared that a witch should not be suffered to
live. This was the text which led John Wesley to assert that 'giving up

---

1. J. Webster, *The Displaying of Supposed Witchcraft* (1677), p. 47.

witchcraft is, in effect, giving up the Bible'. But the sceptics urged that these Old Testament witches had not been devil-worshippers; they were merely wizards and diviners; and the harm they did their enemies was by the use of poisons and similar natural means. Most of them were frauds, who deserved punishment for their impostures, but were incapable of making a corporal pact with Satan. The modern myth of devil-worship, with its night-flying and its sabbaths, was a gross invention of 'friarly authors', an amalgam of Papal fabrication with ancient pagan superstition.[2] In elaborating this theme the sceptics were essentially continuing the traditional Protestant onslaught upon the relics of paganism to be found in the teachings and practice of the Roman Church.

But in arguing that the popular image of Satan lacked scriptural foundation, the sceptics could also draw powerful reinforcement from a new current in contemporary philosophy. Materialists, like Thomas Hobbes and the followers of Descartes, rejected the whole concept of incorporeal substances as a contradiction in terms. By doing so they effectively jettisoned demons from the natural world. Hobbes did not deny that there could be spirits whose bodies were too fine to be perceived by human beings. But he emphatically asserted that they could never be capable of possessing men's bodies or assuming human form. Most demons, he declared, were 'but idols or phantasms of the brain'. Locke did not say that there were no spirits, but he thought it impossible to arrive at any certain knowledge of them.[3] For the opponents of witchcraft prosecution it was a cardinal tenet that the Devil had no temporal power; he could not assume bodily form and his assaults were purely spiritual.[4] Since Satan was a relatively inconspicuous figure in the Old Testament,

2. Scot, *Discoverie*, esp. V.ix; VI.i, ii, v; VII.i; S. Harsnet, *A Declaration of Egregious Popish Impostures* (1603), pp. 132–8; J. Gaule, *Select Cases of Conscience touching Witches and Witchcrafts* (1646), p. 57; (Sir R. Filmer), *An Advertisement to the Jury-Men of England touching Witches* (1653); Ady; J. W(agstaffe), *The Question of Witchcraft Debated* (1669); Webster, op. cit., esp. pp. 57–8; B. B(ekker), *The World Turned Upside Down* (Eng. trans., 1700); F. Hutchinson, *An Historical Essay concerning Witchcraft* (1718: 2nd edn, 1720), chap. xii; *A Discourse on Witchcraft occasioned by a Bill now Depending in Parliament* (1736); J. Juxon, *A Sermon upon Witchcraft* (1736). cf. *Journal of John Wesley*, ed. N. Curnock (1909), v, p. 265.

3. T. Hobbes, *Leviathan* (1651), chaps. 34, 44 and 45; J. Locke, *An Essay Concerning Human Understanding* (1690), ii. 23, 31; iv.3.27.

4. Scot, *Discoverie*, III.iv, vi, xix; VIII.iv; *A Discourse upon Divels and Spirits;* Webster, *The Displaying of Supposed Witchcraft*, pp. 73, 95.

a plausible case for this view could be made on purely Biblical grounds. Several of the religious sects of the Interregnum were to encourage this mode of thinking. Lodowick Muggleton stressed that devils had no bodily existence but were merely evil thoughts in men's minds.[5] The Ranters also interpreted the Devil symbolically; he represented suppressed desires and was not literally a person or creature.[6]

By the end of the seventeenth century this interpretation was becoming more acceptable in orthodox circles. Sir Isaac Newton thought that evil spirits were mere desires of the mind. Devils may have had physical powers before the coming of Christianity, declared Bishop Stillingfleet, but men who accepted the Gospel were no longer capable of receiving any hurt from them in their persons, children or goods.[7] The metaphorical interpretation of the demonic possessions in the New Testament was also gaining ground. 'To have a devil', explained a writer in 1676, 'was a kind of phrase or form of speech.'[8] These trends were emphasized by the decline of Hell – the tendency of many seventeenth-century intellectuals to question the existence of Hell as a localized place of physical torment, and to re-interpret it symbolically as a state of mind, an inner hell.[9] As late as the nineteenth century it was still possible for an ecclesiastical court to rule that a man who denied the personality of the Devil was to be deemed a 'notorious evil liver'. But this opinion was reversed by the Judicial Committee of the Privy Council; and according to the twentieth-century *Encyclopaedia Britannica*, 'it may be confidently affirmed that belief in Satan is not now generally regarded as an essential article of the Christian faith'.[10] But the mere banish-

5. L. Muggleton, *A True Interpretation of the Witch of Endor* (1669), p. 4; id., *The Acts of the Witnesses* (1699), p. 12; id., *A Looking-Glass* (1756 edn), p. 47.

6. H.M.C., *Leybourne-Popham*, p. 57; J. Bauthumley, *The Light and Dark Sides of God* (1650), pp. 28–31. The heterodox Catholic, Thomas White, also took a highly naturalistic view of fantasies about the Devil; *The Middle State of Souls* (1659), p. 190.

7. F. E. Manuel, *Portrait of Isaac Newton* (Cambridge, Mass., 1968), p, 369; *Letters Illustrative of the Reign of William III*, ed. G. P. R. James (1841), ii, pp. 302–3.

8. *The Doctrine of Devils* (1676), p. 36. cf. above, p. 585.

9. See D. P. Walker, *The Decline of Hell* (1964); and C. A. Patrides, 'Renaissance and Modern Views on Hell', *Harvard Theol. Rev.*, lvii (1964); above, pp. 202–3.

10. T. A. Spalding, *Elizabethan Demonology* (1880), p. 83; *Encyclopaedia Britannica* (11th edn, Cambridge, 1911), *s.v.* 'Devil'.

ment of the Devil to his infernal kingdom had in itself been enough
to refute the possibility that witches might make compacts with
him, save in their minds; even if an old woman wanted to give
herself to the Devil, there could be no prospect of her gaining any
influx of supernatural power as a result.

Those influenced by these theological currents of thought thus
came to think it increasingly improbable that God could ever have
allowed witches to exercise any supernatural power, or have intended that they should be persecuted for supposedly doing so. The
standard sceptical position was well defined by Reginald Scot in his
Discoverie of Witchcraft (1584), and did not change much thereafter. All witches, said Scot, came in one of four categories. First
there were the innocent, falsely accused out of malice or ignorance.
Next came the deluded: malevolent, half-crazed persons, who had
convinced themselves that they were in league with the Devil and
made absurd confessions to that effect, but who were actually incapable of harming anyone. Thirdly, there were the genuinely maleficent witches, who injured their neighbours secretly, not by supernatural means, however, but by the use of poison. Finally, there
were the cozeners and impostors, the wizards and charmers who
gulled country folk by falsely pretending to heal diseases, tell fortunes or find lost goods. These last two categories were the witches
who the Bible had said should not be allowed to live. To this extent,
therefore, Scot admitted the existence of 'witches'. But he was certain that none of them could have made a corporal pact with the
Devil or succeeded in harming her neighbours by supernatural
means. He was all for the prosecution of the cunning men and wise
women. But he was implacably opposed to putting old women to
death for being guilty of an impossibility.[11]

At the time Scot's work was said to have made 'a great impression
in the magistracy and also in the clergy'. It was not reprinted in

11. Professor Trevor-Roper, by contrast, argues that Scot and his followers did not shake the foundations of the belief in witchcraft, but merely
questioned its practical interpretation: 'the basis of the myth was beyond
their reach'; *The European Witch-Craze of the 16th and 17th Centuries*
(Harmondsworth, 1969), pp. 75, 88–9, 94, 101. This, however, is to misrepre-
sent Scot's refusal to deny that 'witches' existed. Scot admitted the reality
of impostors, poisoners, scolds and deluded persons, but he made no concessions to the notion that they had any supernatural power ('My question
is not (as many fondly suppose) whether there be witches or nay; but
whether they can do such miraculous works as are imputed unto them';
Discoverie, sig. Aviij^v).

England until 1651, but it nevertheless had a considerable influence. Elizabethan sceptics, like Samuel Harsnet and the physician John Harvey, drew heavily upon it in their published writings, and there is evidence to suggest that its arguments were familiar among the educated laity. The Kentish sceptic, Henry Oxinden, for example, rehearsed them fluently in a private letter of 1641.[12] Even the supporters of the belief accepted much of what Scot had to say on the subject of counterfeits. But most members of the educated classes remained slow to accept the full implications of his thesis. 'Many deny witches at all, or, if there be any, they can do no harm,' wrote Robert Burton in 1621, 'but on the contrary are most lawyers, divines, physicians, philosophers.' Scot's position remained that of a self-conscious minority. Many contemporaries regarded it as tantamount to atheism to deny the reality of spirits or the possibility of supernatural intervention in daily affairs.[13] It was certainly a more rigid position than that actually adopted by the judges and jurymen who brought the witch-trials to an end. So far as can be told, they were not motivated by any coherent ideology of this kind. Their attitude was more modest. What influenced them was not a denial of the possibility of witchcraft as such, but a heightened sense of the logical difficulty of proving it to be at work in any particular case.

This was a difficulty of which everyone had long been aware. Not even the most zealous witch-hunter had ever said that *all* misfortunes were the work of witches. On the contrary the leading authorities always stressed that allegations of witchcraft were not to be made before other possible explanations of the apparent *maleficium* had been considered: it might be an act of God; it might be the direct work of the Devil without the intervention of a witch; it might be the result of imposture; or it might have purely natural causes. All these possibilities were to be carefully investigated before a witchcraft accusation was levied.[14] But this advice posed two perplexing questions. How was one to distinguish witchcraft from all the other possible causes? And how was one to know for certain the identity of the witch?

12. Ady, sig. A3; *The Oxinden Letters, 1607–42*, ed. D. Gardiner (1933), pp. 220–23. On Scot's supporters, see Kocher, *Science and Religion*, chap. 6; Notestein, *Witchcraft*, p. 77, p. 9; The *Discoverie* was reprinted in 1651, 1654 and 1665.
13. Burton, *Anatomy*, i, pp. 202–3. cf. M. Casaubon, *Of Credulity and Incredulity in Things Divine* (1670), p. 171.
14. cf. Bernard, *Guide*, and Gaule, *Select Cases of Conscience, passim*.

In order to distinguish *maleficium* from natural illness the demonologists listed various criteria. These usually boiled down to saying that the disease should have supernatural symptoms incapable of natural explanation; as, for example, when a possessed person displayed superhuman strength or spoke fluently in foreign languages with which he was unacquainted; or when the application of conventional remedies to the patient produced unconventional results.[15] It is obvious that these 'tests' depended entirely upon a consensus of learned physicians as to what was or was not natural. If this consensus broke down, then there was no way of proceeding. Since in any case a minority of intellectuals held that witches could inflict their victims with the symptoms of some ordinary natural disease,[16] the difficulty of recognizing witchcraft when one saw it became even greater.

Contemporaries with open minds on the subject of witchcraft thus became increasingly aware of the logical difficulties involved in making an accusation. Those who saw this problem ranged from the London preacher in 1603 who pointed out that diabolical possession could never be confidently identified, 'because there cannot be assigned any proper token or sign to know that any is essentially possessed; which sign must be apparent in all such as are so possessed and not in any others',[17] to the former Secretary for Scotland who wrote in 1697 that he had no doubt that witches could exist, but that 'the Parlements of France and other judicatories who are persuaded of the being of witches never try them now, because of the experience they have had that it is impossible to distinguish possession from nature in disorder; and they choose rather to let the guilty escape than to punish the innocent'.[18]

Even if the fact of witchcraft could be established, there still remained the problem of identifying the witch. At a popular level this was, as we have seen, no problem. Evidence of *maleficium*, accompanied by express or tacit hostility, was enough to convince the neighbours. In Elizabethan times it also seems to have been enough to secure a conviction in the courts. As William Perkins lamented, 'Ex-

15. J. Cotta, *The Infallible True and Assured Witch* (1624), esp. chap. 10; Bernard, *Guide*, pp. 26–8, 49–52.

16. Sir Thomas Browne declared at the trial of two witches at Bury St Edmunds in 1664 that the Devil could make natural illnesses worse (Ewen, ii, pp. 350–51). cf. Cooper, *Mystery*, pp. 265–8.

17. *Diary of John Manningham*, ed. J. Bruce (Camden Soc., 1868), p. 128.

18. *H.M.C.*, 14th rep., appx., pt. iii, p. 132.

perience shows that ignorant people ... will make strong proofs of such presumptions, whereupon sometimes jurors do give their verdict against parties innocent.'[19] In the early seventeenth century, however, after the passing of the 1604 statute, with its emphasis on the diabolical compact, the commentators set aside the 'presumptions' which had been 'ordinarily used', in favour of stricter standards of proof, based primarily upon evidence of compact. What they now wanted was sworn evidence that the witch kept a familiar or bore the devil's mark on her person; most decisive of all, they hoped for her free confession that she had entered into a pact with Satan.[20] This new emphasis upon evidence of compact can be seen in seventeenth-century legal proceedings, especially during and after the period of the Hopkins campaign. Yet none of these new 'proofs' was infallible. The 'familiar' might be a harmless domestic pet and the 'mark' a natural excrescence.[21] The 'confession' itself could be plausibly discredited by sceptics as the product of fantasy or 'melancholy'. How could one distinguish a true confession from a false one?[22] The more the demonologists insisted on the need for certain proof, the greater the logical difficulties they ran into. The paradox was that their severer view of witchcraft as devil-worship led ultimately to a rise in the acquittal-rate for, without torture of the kind used on the Continent, confessions to such a crime were often unobtainable.

On the Continent the mechanism of prosecution was at times so infallible that, when a contemporary asked some experienced German judges how an innocent person, once arrested for witchcraft, could escape conviction, they were at a loss for an answer.[23] In England the situation was never as bad as this, for even Hopkins, with his modified form of torture, did not achieve a hundred per cent conviction-rate. Unfortunately the evidence is inadequate for us to know how it was that most acquittals during the period were obtained and what reasoning led a Grand Jury to reject any particular indictment or

19. Perkins, *Discourse*, p. 210.

20. Perkins, *Discourse*, pp. 199–219; Ewen, i, p. 61; Cotta, *The Infallible True and Assured Witch, passim*; Cooper, *Mystery*, pp. 276–9; Bernard *Guide*, ii, chaps. 17–18; Gaule, *Select Cases of Conscience*, pp. 80–83.

21. For attempts to distinguish between the appearance of 'natural' and 'unnatural' marks see, e.g., Gaule, *Select Cases of Conscience*, pp. 104–6; M. Hopkins, *The Discovery of Witches*, ed. M. Summers (1928), pp. 52–3.

22. Hopkins, however, claimed to be able to do so (op. cit., pp. 57–9).

23. Lea, *Materials*, p. 707.

persuaded a Petty Jury to refuse to convict. But Richard Bernard in
1627 listed a number of the objections which a Grand Jury might
raise: perhaps the victim was a counterfeit; perhaps he was suffering
from a natural disease, which a better doctor might be able to identify; or perhaps it was a supernatural disease which the Devil had inflicted directly without the intermediate agency of a witch.[24]

Such evidence as there is suggests that acquittals were usually
made along these and similar lines. Demonstrations of the victims'
imposture are particularly well recorded in the pamphlet literature
of the time. But other cases suggest that juries would acquit when
they thought the witch's malice had not been proved; when the witnesses against her were disreputable; when the testimony offered
seemed unduly far-fetched; or when the accused had a record of
regular church-going and godly living. Neither a 'confession' nor a
whole army of hostile witnesses was necessarily enough to secure
a conviction if judge or jury felt unhappy about the case.[25]

What is certain is that the mounting rate of acquittals was the
work of tribunals which did not deny the possibility of witchcraft
as such, but were perplexed by the impossibility of getting certain
proof of it in any particular case. This was partly a tactic adopted by
thoroughly sceptical judges, like L. C. J. North, who advised his
colleagues to display 'a very prudent and moderate carriage' in face
of popular fury against witches, endeavouring 'to convince, rather
by detecting of the fraud, than by denying authoritatively such power
to be given to old women'. This was the attitude of Archbishop
Abbot, when dealing with the alleged bewitching of the impotent
Earl of Essex in the reign of James I. He would not deny that there
was such a thing as witchcraft, but how was he to distinguish it by
its external symptoms from any other physical malady?[26] This was
a real difficulty and not necessarily a mere device employed by the
pusillanimous who did not believe in witchcraft, but were afraid
to say so. But it was a difficulty which had been implicit in the conduct of witch-trials from the beginning. Why did it take so long
for men to grow sensitive to it? This is an impossible question to
answer categorically. All that one can do is to sketch some of the
circumstances by which the change seems to have been precipitated.

24. R. B(ernard), *The Isle of Man* (1627), *Epistle to the Reader*.
25. For examples of such factors at work, see Ewen, i, p. 59–60; Ewen,
ii, pp. 116–18, 149, 190, 229, 236–7, 243, 251, 364–5, 378, 381, 390.
26. R. North, *The Lives of the ... North*, ed. A. Jessopp (1890), i, pp. 166–
7; Notestein, *Witchcraft*, p. 234.

In the first place it must be recognized that the hypothesis of witchcraft, like any other explanatory mechanism, was bound to crack under its own weight, if too frequently invoked. The accusation was easy to make and hard to disprove. It was therefore particularly likely to be animated by malice or imposture. But one had only to be an eye-witness of a patently unjust accusation to be converted to a belief in the need for exercising greater caution in future. The leading sceptical writers seem, almost without exception, to have been provoked into publication by personal acquaintance with incidents of this kind; from Reginald Scot, who had witnessed a number of fraudulent accusations in nearby Kentish villages, to Francis Hutchinson, the future Bishop of Down, whose *Historical Essay concerning Witchcraft* (1718) was precipitated by the condemnation and subsequent reprieve in 1712 of the Hertfordshire woman, Jane Wenham, whom he visited after her release and of whose piety he was convinced.[27] In France it was the series of scandalous cases of hysterical imposture which led the *parlementaires* to discontinue witchcraft prosecution.[28] In England the stimulus seems to have been much the same.

Apart from the influence of individual miscarriages of justice, it is possible to discern the growth of two essentially novel attitudes. The first is the assumption of an orderly, regular universe, unlikely to be upset by the capricious intervention of God or Devil. This view of the world was consolidated by the new mechanical philosophy, but the way to its acceptance had long been prepared by the emphasis of theologians upon the orderly way in which God conducted

27. Scot, *Discoverie*, I.ii; VII.i–ii; XII.xvi; Hutchinson, *An Historical Essay concerning Witchcraft*, p. 165. cf. the cases of Harsnet, provoked by the activities of Darrell and the recusants; Jorden, by the conviction of Elizabeth Jackson (above, pp. 610, 651); Arthur Wilson by the executions at Chelmsford in 1645 (F. Peck, *Desiderata Curiosa* [new edn, 1779], ii, p. 476); Filmer, by executions in Kent in 1652 (*An Advertisement to the Jurymen*, sig. A 2); Ady, by a female impostor at Braintree, and the memory of Matthew Hopkins (pp. 79, 101–2); Webster, by the impostures of Edmund Robinson (*The Displaying of Supposed Witchcraft*, p. 277); the author of *The Doctrine of Devils*, by a case in his parish (pp. 60, 197). Even Bernard's revisionism was prompted by a trial at Taunton Assizes in 1626 (*Guide*, sig. A3; *The Isle of Man*, sigs. A8ᵛ–9), just as John Gaule wrote in response to the activities of Hopkins. Thomas Cooper also had direct experience of witchcraft accusations (*Mystery*, sig. A3, p. 14).

28. R. Mandrou, *Magistrats et sorciers en France au XVIIᵉ Siècle* (Paris, 1968).

his affairs, working through natural causes accessible to human investigation. In the presence of such reasonableness, talk of miraculous happenings came to appear increasingly implausible. It was this conviction, rather than any new psychological insight, which accounts for the scepticism displayed towards the confessions of old women who said that they had seen the Devil, or flown through the air, or killed men by their secret curses. The confessions on which the demonologists laid such weight were unacceptable *a priori*, because as John Webster said, 'it is ... simply impossible for either the Devil or witches to change or alter the course that God hath set in nature'.[29] Accusations of diabolical witchcraft were thus rejected not because they had been closely scrutinized and found defective in some particular respect, but because they implied a conception of nature which now appeared inherently absurd.

The increasing prevalence of this attitude was to vitiate the last-ditch attempts of some later seventeenth-century intellectuals to place the ancient belief in witchcraft upon a genuinely scientific foundation, by sifting through the many inherited tales of the supernatural in order to arrive at those which were authenticated beyond any doubt. This was the motive underlying the psychical researches of Meric Casaubon, Henry More, George Sinclair, Joseph Glanvill and Richard Baxter: even Robert Boyle thought that 'one circumstantial narrative fully verified' was all that was necessary to confound the sceptics.[30] But the task proved impossible. For no one can be persuaded to change his mind by evidence which he regards as implausible. 'Without many witnesses', thought the Deist Charles Blount, 'the testimony of one person alone ought to be suspected in things miraculous.' Many anecdotes were assembled and published, but none was strong enough to pass the test which the sceptics were now in practice applying, and which David Hume was later to elevate into a philosophical principle: namely, that no testimony could establish a miracle unless it were of such a kind that its falsehood would be more astonishing than the fact it was meant to establish.[31]

29. Webster, *The Displaying of Supposed Witchcraft*, p. 68.
30. *The Works of the Honourable Robert Boyle* (1744), v. p. 244. For the others see Robbins, *Encyclopedia*, pp. 44–5, 223–4, 350–51, 470; Notestein, *Witchcraft*, chaps. xii and xiv.
31. C. Blount, *Anima Mundi* (1679), p. 51 (in *The Miscellaneous Works of Charles Blount, Esq.* [1695]); D. Hume, *Essays, Moral, Political, and Literary*, ed. T. H. Green and T. H. Grose (1875), ii, pp. 88–108.

The second assumption underlying the sceptical attitude was the optimistic conviction that it would one day be possible to uncover the natural causes of those events which still remained mysterious. Already it was possible to suggest natural explanations for such phenomena as the insensible witch's 'mark', or the incomprehensible 'confessions'. 'Melancholy' underlay the witches' delusions; the 'incubus' was not a visitation, but a disease; and natural illnesses could account for supposed cases of diabolical possession. Much remained perplexing, but, as John Wagstaffe pointed out,[32] the study of mental illness had barely begun, and there was no telling what future discoveries might be made. The progress made by seventeenth-century scientists was dramatic enough to make most contemporaries aware of the elasticity of natural knowledge, and to imbue some of them with immense confidence in the potentiality of future human achievement. This was a theme which some of the sceptics were to reiterate;[33] and it made it possible for them to discard the explanatory role of witchcraft without leaving too unbearable a void behind.

In the short run, moreover, the sceptical attitude was greatly assisted by the vogue, particularly in the late sixteenth and early seventeenth centuries, of the Neoplatonic conception of the universe as pulsating with many undiscovered occult influences. Many writers were sceptical about witchcraft, precisely because they were so credulous in other matters. They accepted the possibility of sympathetic healing and action at a distance; they believed that stones might have hidden properties, that a corpse might bleed at the approach of its murderer, and that some men could 'fascinate' others by the emanations from their eyes. Scot's scepticism was made possible by his commitment to this tradition, and it was no coincidence that John Webster was sceptical about witchcraft, but believed in the weapon-salve, astral spirits, satyrs, pigmies, mermaids and sea-monsters. It was because these men accepted so wide a range of supposed natural phenomena that they were able to dispense with witchcraft as an explanation of mysterious happenings. It was much easier for them to advance a 'natural' explanation for the witches' *maleficium* than it was for those who had been educated in the

32. Wagstaffe, *The Question of Witchcraft Debated*, p. 67.
33. e.g., Scot, *Discoverie*, sig. Biij; Filmer (quoted below, p. 790); Webster, *The Displaying of Supposed Witchcraft*, p. 17 and chap. 13.

692 RELIGION AND THE DECLINE OF MAGIC

tradition of scholastic Aristotelianism.[34] The sceptics thus explained away apparent mysteries by proffering hypotheses about natural events which we should regard as entirely spurious. In the same way, rationalist physicians like Edward Jorden could reinterpret diabolical possession as hysteria produced by the 'rising of the mother', a natural explanation but a mistaken one.[35]

Renaissance Neoplatonism and its affiliated schools of thought thus provided the vital intellectual scaffolding necessary to prop up the hypothesis that there was a natural cause for every event. When in the later seventeenth century this scaffolding collapsed under the onslaught of the mechanical philosophy it did not need to be replaced. The absurdity of witchcraft could henceforth be justified by reference to the achievements of the Royal Society and the new philosophy.[36] It is true that some of the early converts to the mechanical philosophy had difficulty in making up their minds on the subject of witchcraft, but in the long run theirs was to prove a comprehensive explanation for natural phenomena, and one which needed no external assistance. By an appropriate coincidence, one of the three M.P.s who initiated the repeal of the Witchcraft Act in 1736 was John Conduitt, who married Sir Isaac Newton's niece and was one of his leading admirers and memorialists.

There was, therefore, a continuing stream of scepticism throughout the whole period of witchcraft prosecution in England. Scot's great work was probably no more than an elaborate application of a

34. See, e.g., Scot, *Discoverie*, XIII and XVI.viii–ix; J. H(arvey), *A Discoursive Probleme concerning Prophesies* (1588), p. 79; S. Boulton, *Medicina Magica* (1656), pp. 166–67; Webster, *The Displaying of Supposed Witchcraft*, pp. 290–311; above, p. 520. So far as the belief in spirits was concerned, however, Neoplatonic influence worked in the other direction by upholding faith in all sorts of occult influences. cf. Wagstaffe, *The Question of Witchcraft Debated*, pp. 75–7. There are brief but valuable remarks on this subject in Kocher, *Science and Religion*, pp. 67–70, and Trevor-Roper, *The European Witch-Craze*, pp. 59–60.
35. Above, p. 584.
36. cf. Richard Bentley: 'What then has lessen'd in England your stories of sorceries? Not the growing sect [of free-thinkers], but the growth of Philosophy and Medicine. No thanks to atheists, but to the Royal Society and College of Physicians; to the Boyles and Newtons, the Sydenhams and Ratcliffs.' ('Phileleutherus Lipsiensis', *Remarks upon a late Discourse of Free-Thinking* [2nd edn, 1713], p. 33). cf. Webster, *The Displaying of Supposed Witchcraft*, p. 268, and Hutchinson, *An Historical Essay concerning Witchcraft*, pp. 169–70.

type of rationalist criticism already in vogue. As early as 1578 a Norwich physician, Dr Browne, was accused of 'spreading a misliking of the laws by saying there are no witches'.[37] Scot himself was deeply read in the literature of witchcraft and drew in particular upon the medical findings of the Cleves physician Johan Weyer, whose *De Praestigiis Daemonum* (1563) had urged that many supposed witches were innocent melancholics and that even the guilty ones were mere tools of Satan, incapable of doing harm by their own activities. Scot took this position further by denying even Satan any physical power.

Outside intellectual circles, the movement of opinion is difficult to chart. There is much to support the view that 'doubt was only silenced, not convinced'.[38] The evidence for this does not lie in the isolated utterances of sceptics, like the Elizabethan lawyer, Serjeant Harris, who declared in court in 1593 that the idea that one could do harm by melting wax images was 'a vain and fond conceit'.[39] Rather it is to be found in the many areas of contemporary society where the subject of witchcraft seems to have been seldom or never mentioned: in the world of businessmen and financiers; in the practice of many contemporary doctors; and in most aspects of politics and administration.

In the later seventeenth century the growing volume of scepticism is unmistakable. In 1668 Joseph Glanvill admitted that 'most of the looser gentry and the small pretenders to philosophy and wit are generally deriders of the belief in witches'.[40] In the following year appeared John Wagstaffe's *Question of Witchcraft Debated*, a sweepingly sceptical performance, which was controversial among Cambridge dons, but widely esteemed elsewhere.[41] 'We live in an age and a place,' wrote Robert Boyle to Glanvill in 1677, 'wherein all stories of witchcrafts, or other magical feats are by many, even of the wise, suspected; and by too many that would pass for wits derided and exploded.' There were so many would-be exploders

37. *C.S.P.D., Addenda, 1566–79*, p. 551.
38. *George Lincoln Burr. Selections from his Writings*, ed. L. O. Gibbons (Ithaca, N.Y., 1943) p. 372.
39. P. B. G. Binnall, 'Fortescue *versus* Hext', *Folk-Lore*, liii (1942), pp. 160–61.
40. J. Glanvill, *Saducismus Triumphatus* (1681), Preface (dated 1668), sig. F3.
41. North, *The Lives of the . . . North*, ed. Jessopp, ii, p. 287; Casaubon, *Of Credulity and Incredulity in Things Divine*, p. 177.

of immaterial substances about, thought Henry Hallywell in 1681, that to talk of devils and possession was to invite mockery and contempt. When, around 1694, the Marquis of Halifax compiled his list of 'fundamentals', he had to set against the proposition 'that there were witches', the significant qualification – 'much shaken of late'.[42]

Of course, the belief still retained some vitality in clerical circles; when Francis Hutchinson came to write his book on the subject in 1718 he could cite nearly thirty works published in defence of the notion since 1660. Yet even potential believers were aware of the difficulty of obtaining satisfactory proof in any particular case,[43] while many of the educated laity had come to regard the very notion of witchcraft as an absurdity. Even before the Act was repealed in 1736, the fact that a man feared witches could be cited in the courts as evidence of his insanity. When the Scottish judge Lord Grange opposed the repeal in 1736, Walpole is said to have commented that from that moment he knew he had no more to fear from him politically.[44] By the middle of the century, Conyers Middleton could remark that 'the belief in witches is now utterly extinct'.[45]

At a popular level, of course, this was far from the truth. There had been occasional traces of scepticism, even in the sixteenth century. As early as 1555, one John Tuckie of Banwell, Somerset, said that in his opinion no man or woman could do anything by witchcraft;[46] and he must have had his successors. But few village Scots or mute, inglorious Harsnets have left any trace on the records. If there was a decline in the belief in witchcraft among seventeenth-century cottagers and husbandmen it has yet to be demonstrated. The dwindling number of prosecutions is not evidence that allegations were no longer levied. It only shows that they were no longer seriously entertained by the courts.

But although popular feeling against witches survived the repeal

42. *The Works of the Honourable Robert Boyle*, v, p. 244; H. Hallywell, *Melampronoea* (1681), p. 3; *The Complete Works of George Savile, First Marquess of Halifax*, ed. W. Raleigh (Oxford, 1912), p. 210.
43. Hutchinson, *An Historical Essay concerning Witchcraft*, sigs. a1v–a2v. cf. R. T. Petersson, *Sir Kenelm Digby* (1956), p. 171; Notestein, *Witchcraft*, p. 341; Bentley, *Remarks upon a Late Discourse*, p. 33.
44. N. Walker, *Crime and Insanity in England*, i (Edinburgh, 1968), pp. 55, 58; *D.N.B.*, 'Erskine, James, Lord Grange'.
45. Quoted in L. Stephen, *History of English Thought in the Eighteenth Century* (3rd edn, 1902), i, p. 268.
46. Wells D. R., D 7 (16 May 1555). He was, however, facing a charge of sorcery at the time.

of the Act in 1736, it is possible that the volume of accusations had begun to dwindle. If so, the reasons for this may have been as much social as intellectual. For by the later seventeenth century the conflict between charity and individualism, which had generated so many of the witch accusations in the past, was well on the way to being resolved. The development of the national Poor Law converted the support of the indigent into a legal obligation. In the process, it ceased to be regarded as a moral duty.⁴⁷ '[When] the poor man ... makes known his distress to the parish officers,' William Cobbett was to write, 'they bestow upon him, not alms, but his legal dues.'⁴⁸ The Poor Law had, of course, been established in Tudor times. But its implications were not at first fully appreciated, for it was only invoked intermittently and as a last resort. Private charity remained an important source of maintenance and the authorities often turned a blind eye to begging at the door.⁴⁹ From the early seventeenth century onwards, however, the Poor Law became less of an emergency expedient, more of a regular system of relief. During the century the amount of money raised annually in this way increased more than tenfold. With such organized means of support, the indigent were no longer so dependent upon the voluntary help of their neighbours. 'I am certain,' wrote a late-seventeenth-century commentator, 'that now, care being taken by overseers publicly chosen in every parish, a great many that have compassionate hearts do not much in that kind as they would do otherwise; for what is more natural than to think such care needless ... Many people not only think it needless but foolish to do that which is parish business.'⁵⁰ Private charity continued, but its nature was altering. The merchants and gentry who established the large philanthropic foundations did

47. cf. R. Bernard, *The Ready Way to Good Works* (1635), p. 439.
48. Quoted in M. D. George, *England in Transition* (1935), p. 137.
49. The Act of 39 Eliz. c. 3 (1597–8) allowed begging within the parish when authorized by the authorities, cf. *Poor Relief in Elizabethan Ipswich*, ed. J. Webb (Suffolk Rec. Soc., 1966), pp. 18–19. The intermittent nature of the Poor Law is demonstrated by W. K. Jordan, *Philanthropy in England, 1480–1660* (1959), chap. 5.
50. D. North, 'Some Notes concerning the Laws for the Poor' (B.M., Add. MS 32, 512), f. 31. The annual yield of the poor rate was estimated in 1614 at £30,000–40,000. By 1685 it was put at £665,362 (Jordan, op. cit., p. 141 n; *The Political and Commercial Works of . . . Charles D'Avenant* (1771), i, p. 41). The depressing effect of poor relief upon private charity is discussed by C. Wilson, 'The Other Face of Mercantilism', *T.R.H.S.*, 5th ser., ix (1959), pp. 93–4.

not give away food at the door; neither did old women come to ask them for it.

In such circumstances the tensions and guilt which had produced the old allegations of witchcraft gradually withered away. A man who turned away his neighbour empty-handed could do so with a clearer conscience, for he could tell himself that other ways now existed of dealing with the problem. He need no longer feel the torments of remorse which would once have culminated in an accusation of witchcraft. Witch accusations had reflected a conflict between the communal norms of mutual aid and the individualistic ethic of self-help. But by the end of the seventeenth century, this conflict was on its way to being resolved by the disappearance of the old norms. When this happened the stimulus to witchcraft accusation was to dwindle.

Significantly, witch-beliefs lasted longest in the village communities, where the causes of misfortune could still be seen in personal terms. In country villages the conventions of neighbourliness and mutual help survived into the nineteenth century. Women still came to the door to beg and to borrow, and the man who turned them away empty-handed did so with mixed feeling. It was no accident that Ruth Osborne, who was lynched for witchcraft by a Hertfordshire mob in 1751, had been previously refused buttermilk by the farmer whose subsequent mysterious illness provoked the accusation against her. The majority of other informal witch accusations recorded in the eighteenth, nineteenth and even twentieth centuries conform to the same old special pattern of charity evaded, followed by misfortune incurred.[51]

After 1736 when the possibility of formal prosecution was no longer open, villagers turned to informal violence, counter-magic and the occasional lynching. This procedure was both illegal and a poor substitute for the old witch-trials. For it was not the mere allegation of witchcraft which had had the cathartic effect, but its

51. Robbins, *Encyclopedia*, pp. 368–9 (for Osborne). For others, see, e.g., *Folk-Lore Journ.*, v *(1887)*, p. 158; *Shropshire Folk-Lore*, ed. C. S. Burne (1883–6), pp. 147, 151, 154; *County Folk-Lore*, i (Folk-Lore Soc., 1895), ii, pp. 168–9; *County Folk-Lore*, v (Folk-Lore Soc., 1908), pp. 73, 78; E. J. Begg, 'Cases of Witchcraft in Dorsetshire', *Folk-Lore*, lii (1941), pp. 70–72; R. L. Tongue, *Somerset Folk-Lore*, ed. K. M. Briggs (Folk-Lore Soc., 1965), pp. 69–70; E. J. Rudsdale, 'Witchcraft in Essex', *Essex Rev.*, lv (1946), pp. 187–9; E. W. Martin, *The Shearers and the Shorn* (1965), pp. 72–3.

acceptance and proof;[52] and after 1736 proof had become difficult and means of redress prohibited. In these circumstances witch-beliefs inevitably declined.

The history of witchcraft *prosecutions* in England thus reflects the intellectual assumptions of the educated classes who controlled the machinery of the law courts. The decline in formal prosecution was a consequence of their increasing scepticism about the possibility of the offence, or at least about the possibility of proving it. The history of witchcraft *accusations* on the other hand can only be explained in terms of the immediate social environment of the witch and her accuser. Their highly informal nature makes it impossible to measure fluctuations in its volume with any precision. There seems no way of telling, for example, how far the drop in indictments before the courts in the early eighteenth century was caused by the known hostility of judges and juries to such accusations, how far it reflected a dwindling demand for prosecution on the part of the villagers themselves.

These considerations make it rash to draw too many conclusions from the actual trends in formal prosecution. But it may be stated categorically that no convincing correlation can be established between the chronology of witch-persecution and such general events as the incidence of plague, famine, unemployment or price fluctuations. Neither, in the light of what has been seen about the personal nature of the misfortunes attributed to witches, is there any reason why we should expect such a correlation to exist. It is also wrong to think of 'scares' and 'panics' sweeping the country. Such an impression might be derived from the intermittent survival of pamphlet accounts of the more sensational trials. But the judicial records show that witchcraft prosecution was a regular phenomenon through most of the period. There seems to have been a drop in the number of prosecutions in the twenty years before the Civil War, though this may be partly an optical illusion created by the uneven survival of records.[53] There certainly was an upsurge in the time of Matthew Hopkins, whose activities show to what extent it was possible to stimulate prosecution from above. But even his campaign would have been impossible without the underlying tensions of village

52. cf. J. R. Crawford, *Witchcraft and Sorcery in Rhodesia* (1967), pp. 281–2.
53. At least eight executions are known to have taken place in the 1630s (Ewen, ii, pp. 394, 409–10, 416, 439; Kent R.O., SA/AC 7, f. 198).

society. The animosities which led to the indictment of his victims
were much the same as those which underlay the other trials of the
century. Witchcraft accusation was endemic in English society, but
it was essentially a local phenomenon, and it will be better understood when more is known about the history and structure of the
English village.

ALLIED BELIEFS

19.

GHOSTS AND FAIRIES

Tush, tush. Their walking spirits are mere imaginary fables.
There's no such thing in *rerum natura*.

C. Tourneur, *The Atheist's Tragedy*, iv, iii

The noticing of these supposed supernatural appearances
may seem puerile to some readers. The suppositions in
themselves may be so; but taken in connection with, and
affecting as they did, in a degree, the minds and manners
of the rural population of the period, they are of more consequence than may at the first glance be apparent.

The Autobiography of Samuel Bamford,
ed. W. H. Chaloner (1967), i, pp. 33–4

1. *The theology of ghosts*

IN medieval England it was fully accepted that dead men might
sometimes return to haunt the living. The Catholic Church rationalized the ancient belief in ghosts by teaching that such apparitions
were the souls of those trapped in Purgatory, unable to rest until
they had expiated their sins; and there was no shortage of ghost
stories, or of individuals who personally claimed to have encountered such apparitions.[1] 'Commonly such spirits be fiends,' warned
the fifteenth-century author of *Dives and Pauper*; but he readily admitted that ghosts of the dead might well be sent back by God,
'sometimes for to have help; sometimes to show that the souls live
after the body, to confirm them that be feeble in the faith'.[2]

Most surviving medieval ghost stories are to be found in anec-

1. See, e.g., M. R. James, 'Twelve Medieval Ghost-Stories', *E.H.R.*, xxxvii
(1922); H. E. D. Blakiston, 'Two More Medieval Ghost Stories', ibid., xxxviii
(1923); H. Thurston, 'Broucolaccas; a Study in Mediaeval Ghost Lore', *The
Month*, no. 401 (1897); G. R. Owst, *Literature and Pulpit in Medieval England* (2nd edn, Oxford, 1961), p. 113; *Catalogue of the Romances in the Department of Manuscripts in the British Museum*, iii, ed. J. A. Herbert (1910)
passim; B. Hauréau, 'Mémoire sur les récits d'apparitions dans les sermons
du moyen âge', *Mémoires de l'Institut National de France, Académie des
Inscriptions et Belles-Lettres*, xxviii (1876); (S. Johnson), *Purgatory Prov'd
by Miracles* (1688).

2. *Dives and Pauper* (1536), f. 60. cf. Aquinas, *Summa Theologica*, III,
supp. q.69.iii.

dotal compilations made by the clergy for didactic purposes. But
their details are usually sufficiently precise to suggest that the tales
were not invented, but related to the experiences of real people.
Popular belief in the reality of ghosts is also attested by contemporary moralists and writers. It was a heinous offence for a dying
person to promise to return to the land of the living in order to give
an account of what lay in store; and it was also thought highly improper to try to get in touch with the souls of the departed. Regulations for medieval gilds sometimes included a clause banning any
attempt by the night watch to amuse themselves by summoning up
ghosts during the hours of darkness.[3]

The Church did not allow tales of apparitions to pass uninvesti-
gated. In 1397 an inhabitant of a Hereford parish was charged with
occasioning scandal by publicly declaring that the spirit of his dead
father haunted the area at night; and in 1523 a woman was summoned before the Court of the Archdeacon of Leicester for similarly
reporting that her father had walked after his death.[4] Theologians
taught that it was not in the power of the dead man himself to
choose to return to the earth; and that the living had no means of
forcing him to do so: God alone determined such matters. But the
basic possibility of ghosts, as such, was never disputed.

This situation was dramatically altered by the Reformation. The
reformers denied the existence of Purgatory, asserting that at the
moment of death all men proceeded inexorably to Heaven or Hell,
according to their deserts; from neither world could they ever return. This did not mean that apparitions as such were impossible,
but they could not be the souls of dead men, for those had gone to

> The undiscover'd country from whose bourn
> No traveller returns.

In the first century of the Reformation, Protestant teaching seems
to have been remarkably firm upon this point; certainly it was much
firmer than subsequent generations appreciated. It says a lot for the
shortness of human memory that in the eighteenth century Dr John-

3. *Dives and Pauper*, f. 59; *Catalogue of Romances in the British Museum*,
iii, p. 391; C. J. Holdsworth, 'Visions and Visionaries in the Middle Ages',
History, xlviii (1963), p. 150; *English Gilds*, ed. Toulmin Smith (E.E.T.S.,
1870), p. 194.

4. A. T. Bannister, 'Visitation Returns of the Diocese of Hereford in
1397', *E.H.R.*, xliv (1929), p. 446; A. P. Moore, 'Proceedings of the Ecclesiastical Courts in the Archdeaconry of Leicester, 1516–35', *Assocd Architectl
Socs., Repts and Papers*, xxviii (1905–6), p. 613.

son could describe the existence of ghosts as 'a question which after five thousand years is yet undecided'. Indeed, according to Boswell (who was particularly interested in such matters), Johnson thought the possibility of apparitions a necessary corollary of the doctrine of the immortality of the soul; the only uncertainly, as he saw it, was whether or not such spirits could make themselves perceptible to living men. He himself prayed after his wife's death that he might continue to have the benefit of her ministrations – 'whether exercised by appearance, impulses, dreams, or in any other manner'.[5]

Johnson's views reveal how far the position of the early Protestant reformers had, in this, as in many other respects, been subsequently diluted. For although it may be a relatively frivolous question today to ask whether or not one believes in ghosts, it was in the sixteenth century a shibboleth which distinguished Protestant from Catholic almost as effectively as belief in the Mass or the Papal Supremacy.

In due course, some Catholic theologians also became sceptical of the possibility of ghosts, at least of those in bodily form, but few of the theorists of the Counter-Reformation denied that dead men might revisit their former haunts. All departed souls, they taught, fell into one of three categories. The first two were the damned and the blessed; these everyone agreed could never return. But the third comprised those who were consigned to Purgatory, and these, according to Catholic teaching, might well be sent back for some specific purpose.[6] The Protestants, on the other hand, treated the belief in ghosts as the product of Popish fraud and deception. Even Henry More, who accepted that the soul was an immaterial substance, capable of assuming some aerial vehicle, nevertheless believed that medieval priests used to tie candles to the backs of crabs and set them loose in churchyards to simulate the souls of the dead. As for the apparitions which were still encountered, Protestants agreed that they were not to be mistaken for the souls of the departed, but were to be recognized as spirits; very rarely good ones, more usually evil ones, sent by the Devil in an effort to entrap men's allegiance.

5. *Boswell's Life of Johnson*, ed. G. B. Hill and L. F. Powell (Oxford, 1934–50), iii, p. 298; iv, p. 94; i, p. 235.
6. M. Yardley, 'The Catholic Position in the Ghost Controversy of the Sixteenth Century', in L. Lavater, *Of Ghostes and Spirites Walking by Nyght* (1572), ed. J. D. Wilson and M. Yardley (Oxford, 1929), pp. 221–51. For scepticism by the heterodox Catholic, Thomas White, see below, p. 705.

Their credentials were to be strictly examined, and resolute scepticism was the only defence against their blandishments. The scriptural 'ghost' of Samuel summoned by the Witch of Endor was interpreted as just a diabolical imposture, in which the part of Samuel was probably played by the Devil himself.[7]

To the first generation of reformers, ghosts thus presented no problems. The belief in such spectres, they held, had only arisen in the first place because the Popish clergy had seen it as a means of exploiting popular credulity in order to enhance their own wealth and authority.[8] Some people even thought that there really *had* been more apparitions in the past because the Devil had been attracted to such a promising environment. When Lady Fanshawe saw a ghost in Ireland around 1650, she stayed up for the rest of the night with her husband discussing why such apparitions were so much more common there than in England; they came to the satisfactory conclusion that the cause lay in the greater superstition of the Irish, and their lack of a faith powerful enough to defend them from the attacks of the Devil.[9]

So although men went on seeing ghosts after the Reformation, they were assiduously taught not to take them at their face value. When Sir Thomas Wise saw a walking spirit in the reign of James I, the local archdeacon was inclined to think it might have been an angelic apparition. But the theologian Daniel Featley firmly declared that it must have been an evil spirit, because it was well known that good ones could no longer be expected to appear.[10] The same dilemma is brilliantly shown by Dr Dover Wilson to have been posed by the ghost of Hamlet's father. Much of the drama of the

---

7. For typical statements of the Protestant position see, in addition to Lavater's treatise, which was translated into English in 1572 (above, note 6), G. A(lley), *The Poore Mans Librarie* (1571), ff. 53v–4; J. Northbrooke, *Spiritus est Vicarius Christi in Terra* (n.d. [?1575]), chap. 24; Scot, *Discoverie*, XV. xxxix; *A Discourse of Divels and Spirits*, xxvii, xxviii; (James VI), *Daemonologie* (Edinburgh, 1597), pp. 60–61; Randall Hutchins, *Tractatus de Spectris* (c. 1593), trans. V. B. Heltzel and C. Murley in *Huntington Lib. Qtly*, xi (1947–8); *The Workes of ... Gervase Babington* (1622), ii, pp. 188–9; H. More, *A Modest Enquiry into the Mystery of Iniquity* (1664), p. 134.

8. Scot, *Discoverie*, VII.xv; XV.xxxix; T. Hobbes, *Leviathan* (1651), chap. 2; Ady, p. 147; J. Aubrey, *Brief Lives*, ed. A. Clark (Oxford, 1898), ii, p. 318.

9. *Memoirs of Lady Fanshawe ... by herself* (new edn, 1830), pp. 92–3.

10. Wood, *Ath. Ox.*, iii, cols. 166–8.

play's first act hinges on the uncertainty of the ghost's status. Marcellus regards it as a demon. Horatio begins as an out-and-out sceptic. Even Hamlet himself is uncertain.[11] Despite the truth of the tale the ghost had to tell, every firm Protestant in the audience would have been justified in regarding the apparition as a devil in human form; and, in view of the ultimately catastrophic results of his appearance, we might add that this could have been Shakespeare's own view. The Devil's aim was always to capture men's souls and he was ever ready to exploit any situation to do so. By revealing the truth about his father's death to Hamlet, the ghost sets off a train of consequences which involve Ophelia in the ultimate sin of suicide and Hamlet in a series of murders. If the ghost had never appeared, or if Hamlet had refused to listen to his promptings, these events, and their terrible consequences to soul and body, would never have occurred. There is a whole genre of Elizabethan and Jacobean plays in which ghostly apparitions make their appearance, leaving us to speculate whether they are not really demons in human form rather than the human souls they purport to be.[12]

Protestants did not, of course, assert that God had no power to send human souls back into the world for some special purpose; they merely argued that in practice he never did so. But a minority of advanced sceptics followed Reginald Scot and Thomas Hobbes in dismissing the possibility of any genuine apparition whatsoever. By the end of the seventeenth century there were many educated persons who greeted tales of ghosts and haunted houses with much the same sort of incredulity as that with which they would be received today. 'I am apt to believe,' wrote the Catholic Thomas White in 1659, 'that most of our stories ... if they were examined to the bottom would be found to proceed from the frequent cogitation and passionate affection of the living towards their departed friends.'[13] But most theologians were reluctant to discard visible spirits altogether. Indeed, as atheism became a greater threat to true religion than Popery, they became more sympathetic to the

11. J. Dover Wilson, *What Happens in Hamlet* (3rd edn, Cambridge, 1959), chap. iii.
12. A list of plays with ghosts is given in H. Ankenbrand, *Die Figur des Geistes im Drama der Englischen Renaissance* (Leipzig, 1906). They are discussed by R. H. West, *The Invisible World* (Athens, Ga., 1939), chap. 9, and by Briggs, *The Anatomy of Puck*, chap. 9.
13. T. White, *The Middle State of Souls* (1659), p. 196, and chap. 19, *passim*. cf. *The Diary of Abraham de la Pryme*, ed. C. Jackson (Surtees Soc., 1870), pp. 42, 45.

.dea of ghosts; for, as Ralph Cudworth, the Cambridge Platonist, pointed out, the belief in such apparitions did at least constitute a bulwark against the atheist: 'if there be once any visible ghosts or spirits acknowledged as things permanent, it will not be easy for any to give a reason why there might not be one supreme ghost also, presiding over them all and the whole world'.[14] By the time of Addison's *Spectator* it had become more respectable to believe in ghosts than to be a total sceptic. High Churchmen were not beyond praying for the dead; and the stories collected in Boswell's *Johnson* show that the possibility of ghosts was a reality in the eighteenth century for many educated men, however much the rationalists laughed at them.[15]

So when the Elizabethan bishop, Edwin Sandys, claimed that 'the gospel hath chased away walking spirits',[16] he was over-sanguine. In the early years of Elizabeth I Bishop Pilkington remarked of a ghost recently seen in Blackburn, that such things were 'so common here and none of authority that will gainsay it, but rather believe and confirm it, that every one believes it'. Twenty years later Reginald Scot commented on the paradox that the denial of Purgatory had not put an end to the belief in ghosts: 'we think souls and spirits may come out of heaven or hell and assume bodies'.[17] William Perkins lamented that 'many ignorant persons among us' thought that dead men could reappear. An early-seventeenth-century writer made the same complaint: the conviction that dead men could walk was 'still in the mouth and faith of credulous superstition at this day'.[18] According to Walter Travers, the Elizabethan Puritan, it was 'a question among the learned' as to whether witches could raise the bodies of the deceased. In the reign of Charles I Oxford dons were still debating whether or not ghosts of the dead might not sometimes

14. Quoted by J. Tulloch, *Rational Theology and Christian Philosophy in the Seventeenth Century* (2nd edn, 1874) ii, p. 260.

15. *Spectator*, cx (1711); *Reliquiae Hearnianae*, ed. P. Bliss (2nd edn, 1869), ii, p. 188; *Boswell's Life of Johnson*, ed. Hill and Powell, ii, pp. 178, 182; iii, pp. 297, 349. cf. the scepticism of *Anti-Canidia; or Superstition Detected and Exposed* (?1754), pp. 3–4, and R. Mead, *Medica Sacra*, trans. T. Stack (1755), p. 82.

16. *Sermons*, ed. J. Ayre (Cambridge, P.S., 1841), p. 60.

17. *Correspondence of Matthew Parker*, ed. J. Bruce and T. T. Perowne (Cambridge, P.S., 1853), p. 222; Scot, *Discoverie: A Discourse of Divels and Spirits*, xxvii.

18. Perkins, *Discourse*, p. 115; G. Strode, *The Anatomie of Mortalitie* (2nd edn, 1632), p. 205.

appear. At an abstruse philosophical level the possibility was kept alive by the occult theories of the Neoplatonists, Paracelsians and Behmenists, who believed in astral spirits which lingered on after the body had decayed.[19]

At a popular level many contemporaries encountered an unquestioning belief in ghosts. When the Quaker George Fox was arrested in 1656 he found that his fellow-prisoners in Launceston Castle firmly believed that ghosts walked regularly in the condemned cell.[20] Numerous other writers testified to the popular belief in ghosts, poltergeists, and similar apparitions.[21] Many of these anecdotes related to the clergy, whose Protestant scruples should have taught them otherwise. There was Henry Caesar, the Elizabethan vicar of Lostwithiel, who justified the 'apparition of souls after their departure out of this life', citing the example of Sir Walter Mildmay, who, he alleged, had successfully conjured up the shade of Cardinal Pole. Caesar was allegedly a crypto-Catholic, though he later became a respectable Dean of Ely.[22] But other stories involved clerics of whose firm Protestantism there could be no doubt. The great Puritan divine, William Twisse, owed his spiritual conversion to an experience as a schoolboy at Winchester in the 1590s, when the phantom of a disreputable dead schoolmate appeared to him to report that he was now a damned soul.[23] A group of Jacobean plotters who wanted to frighten away the incumbent of the parish of Radwynter, Essex, thought it worth attempting to do so by faking

19. B. Brook, *The Lives of the Puritans* (1812), ii, p. 318; *The Diary of Thomas Crosfield*, ed. F. S. Boas (1935), p. 17. The doctrine of astral spirits is explained in J. Webster, *The Displaying of Supposed Witchcraft* (1677), pp. 311–20.

20. *The Journal of George Fox*, ed. N. Penney (Cambridge, 1911), i, p. 228.

21. For some ghost-stories, other than those cited below, see Aubrey, *Miscellanies*, pp. 70 ff.; *York Depositions*, pp. 161–2; *Fearfull Apparitions or the Strangest Visions that ever hath been heard of* (1647); *Memoirs of the Life of Mr Ambrose Barnes*, ed. W. H. D. Longstaffe (Surtees Soc., 1867), pp. 228–9; Wood, *Life and Times*, ii, p. 4; B.M., Lansdowne MS 207(c), ff. 413v–4; *Yorkshire Diaries*, ed. C. Jackson (Surtees Soc., 1877), p. 283; J. Glanvill, *Saducismus Triumphatus* (1681), *passim*; R. Baxter, *The Certainty of the World of Spirits* (1691), *passim*; *The Correspondence of Richard Bentley* (1842), i, pp. 105–9; J. B. Burke, *Family Romance; or Episodes in the Domestic Annals of the Aristocracy* (1853), i, pp. 9–14.

22. A. L. Rowse, *Tudor Cornwall* (1941), pp. 335–6; P.R.O., SP 12/173, f. 114; SP 12/176/46 (*C.S.P.D., 1581–90*, p. 205).

23. Aubrey, *Miscellanies*, pp. 86–7.

the apparition of ghosts in the churchyard.[24] The parliamentary Commissioners appointed to survey the palace of Woodstock in 1649 were scared away by a local poltergeist; and the minister of the nearby parish of Wootton busied himself seeking divine aid against the apparition.[25]

John Aubrey thought it was the turmoil of the mid seventeenth century which put an end to old wives' tales about ghosts and spirits: 'When the wars came, and with them liberty of conscience and liberty of inquisition, the phantoms vanish.'[26] But in fact the Civil War sects were sometimes more inclined to accept ghost stories than their Anglican predecessors. When the curate of Minehead claimed to have seen the apparition of a dead parishioner in 1638 the Laudian Bishop of Bath and Wells firmly dismissed it as an imposture;[27] by contrast, a conspicuously high proportion of the ghost stories subsequently collected by Richard Baxter in his *Certainty of the World of Spirits* (1691) were vouched for by men who had been actively associated with the Parliamentary cause. Sectaries were used to seeing ghosts; and the enthusiast, George Foster, declared that devils were 'nothing but the spirits of wicked men deceased'.[28]

But it would be wrong to associate the belief in ghosts with any particular denomination. It was to be found among almost all religious groups, and at virtually every social level. As late as 1684 the New England divine, Increase Mather, found it necessary to reissue the old medieval warning about the spiritual hazards of making covenants to reappear after death.[29] Of the many such bargains struck in the seventeenth century the most famous was that made by John Wilmot, Earl of Rochester, with a gentleman who was later killed at sea by a Dutch cannon-ball; Bishop Burnet, who subsequently effected the rake Earl's death-bed conversion, tells us that the failure of this agreement was one of the reasons for Rochester's long career of infidelity: 'that gentleman's never appearing was a

24. Ewen, *Star Chamber*, p. 15.
25. *The Woodstock Scuffle* (1649); *The Just Devil of Woodstock* (1660); R. Plot, *The Natural History of Oxfordshire* (1677), pp. 206–10.
26. Aubrey, *Brief Lives*, ed. Clark, ii, p. 318.
27. *C.S.P.D., 1637–8*, p. 276.
28. G. Foster, *The Pouring Forth of the Seventh and Last Viall* (1650), p. 51. cf. Turner, *Providences*, i, p. 40.
29. I. Mather, *An Essay for the Recording of Illustrious Providences* (Boston, 1684), pp. 243–5.

great snare to him during the rest of his life'.[30] A more successful outcome attended the compact made by Robert Grebby, chaplain of New College, who died in 1654, after having made a similar promise to reappear and let his acquaintances know whether or not the soul was immortal, a point on which they had all been sceptical. He resolved the question by dramatically reappearing in the room of John Good, tutor of Balliol.[31]

Along with the belief in ghosts went a parallel faith in the possibility of magical action to counteract such spectres. The Roman Catholics of the seventeenth century had their rituals for exorcising haunted houses,[32] but this method was of course shunned by Protestants, who had to rely on prayer alone, accompanied in the case of Puritans and Dissenters by ritual fasting.[33] Formal conjuration was utterly prohibited. Here as elsewhere the village magicians filled the vacuum. To deal with haunted houses, contemporaries often called in the cunning folk;[34] though there were also some renegade ghost-laying clerics, like the late seventeenth-century Fellow of Merton who was said to have quietened several troubled houses.[35]

Ghost-beliefs were also closely linked with the idea of witchcraft, for a person who was troubled by a poltergeist or spectre might well blame a malevolent neighbour for the intrusion. In 1613 a Southwark woman called another 'a hag', asserting 'that her ghost doth continually haunt her and her husband that they cannot thrive'.[36] A similar case, brought to the astrologer Simon Forman in 1600, related to a woman haunted at night by a ghost, which she attributed

30. G. Burnet, *Some Passages in the Life and Death of John, Earl of Rochester* (1787 edn), p. 27.

31. Wood, *Life and Times*, ii, p. 55; id., *Fasti Oxonienses*, ed. P. Bliss (Oxford, 1815–20), i, cols. 387–8. For another such compact, see Turner, *Providences*, i, p. 36.

32. *Notes and Queries*, 3rd ser., viii (1865), pp. 334–5; H. Thurston, *Ghosts and Poltergeists*, ed. J. H. Crehan (1953), appx; above, p. 570.

33. e.g., R. Baxter, *The Certainty of the World of Spirits* (1691: 1834), p. 34; C.U.L., MS Dd. iii.64, f. 151 (poltergeist removed by prayer, 1661).

34. e.g., Aubrey, *Gentilisme*, p. 104; *Sad and Wonderful Newes from the Faulcon at the Bank-Side* (1661), p. 9; *A Full and True Account of a Strange Apparition . . . in Cherrey-tree Alley* (1685), p. 3; *An Exact Narrative of Many Surprizing Matters of Fact uncontestably wrought by an Evil Spirit or Spirits, in the House of Master Jan Smagge, Farmer, in Canvy Island, near Leigh in Essex* (1709), p. 9.

35. Bodl., MS Wood F39, f. 145^v. For others, see M. A. Courtney, 'Cornish Folk-Lore', *Folk-Lore Journ.*, v (1887), pp. 23–6.

36. Ewen, *Star Chamber*, p. 11.

to the witchcraft of her son-in-law."[37] Persons who thought themselves 'hag-ridden' would take their problems to a doctor or wizard: the case-books of Richard Napier contain dozens of examples of patients 'haunted with spirits'.[38] Alternatively, they might employ some traditional prophylactic: a spayed bitch, for example, was said to be able to protect a house against being haunted.[39]

Here, as elsewhere, the wizards spent some time allaying fears which they themselves had created. A good example was Robert Tooley, a 'doctor and conjurer' of Widdicombe-in-the-Moor, whose activities were reported by two Devonshire yeomen in an undated petition of the later seventeenth century. Tooley had managed to persuade a neurotic patient that his troubles emanated from the ghost of a neighbour who had recently hanged himself. He undertook to cure him by conjuration:

> The wife of the said sick man was to get two stout men in the night-time with two swords to go to the grave of the man that hanged himself and the one was to stand at the head of the grave and the other at the foot for an hour's time to flourish their swords whilst the said Tooley with a bottle of brandy stood by to conjure the said spirit; which accordingly was performed and done and a sword run into the middle part of the grave during the which time of conjuration the doctor told the said wife of the sick person that she would hear strange noise in and about the house; and also pretended to cure the sick person by putting of a grey owl cut into [two] parts and newly killed and bound to the head of the said sick person with a new horse shoe, each hole being filled up with nails; and so the sick person was to wear it next to his skin under his armpit; and about 12 o'clock in the night season she was to go to the house of him that hanged himself and fetch 7 motes of straw and he would make a pincase for him to wear under the other arm next his skin and that would be a present cure.

For these various services Tooley charged twenty shillings. But when the sick man, who had got, not better, but worse, during the procedure, understandably refused to pay, the wizard threatened to seize the patient's house by way of satisfaction,

so that they cannot live in quiet but are forced to shut their door when they see him coming, for fear he will turn them out.[40]

37. Ashm. 236, f. 201. The haunting of Spurstow House, Cheshire, was blamed on a suspected witch in 1683; B.M., Add. MS 22,548, f. 99.
38. There is a list in Ashm. 1790, f. 108.
39. Aubrey, *Gentilisme*, p. 53.
40. Royal Institution of Cornwall, Truro, RIC.GAT/8/3 (transcript very kindly sent me by Mr H. L. Douch).

The case reveals both the ingenuity of the rogue Tooley and the survival of the notion that the ghost of a man who had killed himself would not rest quietly until a stake was driven through the corpse's heart. This was indeed the legally required method of burial for suicides until 1823. Similar notions surrounded ordinary corpses. The Devil might possess the body of any person whose sins had not been absolved; and in the early Middle Ages post-mortem absolutions were sometimes given to prevent this happening.[41] Bishop Latimer remarks in one of his sermons that when one of his relatives died, an old cousin gave him a wax candle and told him to make crosses over the body, for she thought the Devil would run away by and by. This would have been at the end of the fifteenth century, but associated notions lingered on. In parts of Lincolnshire it was customary until the First World War to tie the feet of the dead man to prevent him walking.[42]

2. *The purpose of ghosts*

The belief in ghosts, and, even more, the belief of particular individuals that they had actually seen such ghosts, present many interesting psychological problems. But it is no part of our purpose here to consider just how it was that these hallucinations could convince witnesses of undoubted integrity. The social historian should be ready to concede that mental and perceptual processes can be extensively conditioned by the cultural content of the society in which men live: in this period contemporaries were taught that ghosts or similar apparitions existed; they were therefore more likely to see them. But in the present state of knowledge the investigation of these mental and perceptual processes must be left to the psychologist and the psychic researcher. Even so, it may be pointed out that a number of would-be ghost-stories were exposed at the time as the fabrication of interested parties, while others turned out to have been pieces of imposture, engineered by unscrupulous persons in order to achieve some private end. In 1621, for example, one Henry Church sought the hand of the Ipswich widow, Elizabeth Edgar. Finding her reluctant, he engaged several associates to persuade her that it was 'God's secret decree and appointment that he

41. H. Thurston in *The Month*, xc (1897), pp. 502–20.
42. *Sermons by Hugh Latimer*, ed. G. E. Corrie (Cambridge, P.S., 1844), p. 499; E. L. Backman, *Religious Dances*, trans. E. Classen (1952), p. 133.

should be her husband'; and followed up the attack by simulating various apparitions in order to frighten her into yielding her inheritance to him. This plot was ultimately exposed in the Star Chamber,[43] but it is likely that others were not. As late as 1762 the so-called Cock Lane ghost caused a sensation in London; this was a malicious imposture in which the victim was accused by the ghost of poisoning his sister-in-law.[44] Similarly, tales of haunted houses might be put about by the tenants in order to keep down the rent.[45] And, if contemporary Protestant propagandists are to be believed, the Jesuits were not beyond faking the occasional apparition so as to prove the existence of Purgatory and convert impressionable females to the Roman Church.[46]

But frauds of this kind would have been useless had not the possibility of such apparitions been widely accepted. Moreover, they demonstrate the one essential feature of the seventeenth-century ghost-story, which was that the ghost always had some particular reason for his reappearance. His movements were not random or aimless; he was invariably believed to have some end in view and some message to communicate, even if contemporaries sometimes failed to determine just what the message was. Ghosts were no more motiveless than witches; they had an important social role to play. In Shakespeare's plays, for example, there are many ghosts and they always come for a purpose. They are instruments of revenge or protection, they prophesy, or they crave proper burial. Invariably they are taken seriously; ghosts were rare in Elizabethan comedy, and not a subject for frivolity before the eighteenth century. In our period they were active, as a contemporary put it, 'in detecting the murdered, in disposing their estate, in rebuking injurious executors, in visiting and counselling their wives and children, in forewarning them of such and such courses, with other matters of like sort'.[47]

43. Ewen, *Star Chamber*, pp. 15–16.
44. D. Grant, *The Cock Lane Ghost* (1965). For other cases, see, e.g., B. Zimmerman, *Carmel in England* (1899), pp. 258–9; 'Hieronymus Magomastix', *The Strange Witch at Greenwich* (1650), p. 5.
45. Aubrey, *Gentilisme*, p. 104.
46. J. Gee, *New Shreds of the Old Snare* (1624), pp. 1–7, 20–25. An alleged Catholic fraud for a different purpose is reported in *Revolution Politicks* (1733), v. p. 3.
47. H. More, *The Immortality of the Soul* (1659), p. 296. cf. E. E. Stoll, 'The Objectivity of the Ghosts in Shakspere', *Procs. Modern Lang. Assoc.*, xxii (1907), p. 203; West, *The Invisible World*, p. 58.

In the Middle Ages the main purpose of ghosts had been exemplary; they upheld the Church's moral teaching. A ghost returned from Purgatory because of some unrequited crime; it could not rest until it had been confessed and absolved by the priest. In 1343, for example, Bishop Burghesh of Lincoln reappeared in order to seek reparation for misdemeanour committed in his lifetime.[48] Other characteristic medieval ghosts included the canon of Newburgh who returned to confess that he had stolen the Prior's silver spoons; the priest who came to report that he had been damned for dissuading a colleague from becoming a monk; and the concubine who wanted her former lover to arrange masses for her soul in order to ease her pains.[49] Ghosts thus came to confess some unrequited offence, to describe the punishment which lay in wait for some heinous sin, or to testify to the rewards in store for virtuous conduct.

But some medieval ghosts had reappeared so as to rectify some existing social arrangement, to restore ill-gotten goods, or denounce an undetected evil-doer. This was the kind of apparition most commonly reported after the Reformation. The ghost who was unable to rest because of some misdemeanour committed in his lifetime still appeared occasionally; in 1674, for example, a Wiltshire Dissenter met the ghost of his father-in-law, who confessed to having committed a murder; and in 1679 much attention was attracted by the case of a London midwife, whose ghost returned to confess to the murder of two illegitimate children.[50] Such confessions served their social purpose by removing suspicion from living persons. But usually the object of the supposed ghost's visitation was more direct. He came to denounce some specific injustice. He no longer wanted masses said for his soul. Instead, he wished to alter some particular relationship between living people. He would not, however, denounce routine cases of injustice; on the contrary a ghost was a highly exceptional, indeed sensational, affair. He did not compete with ordinary methods of detection or law-enforcement, but reserved

48. *York Depositions*, p. 161 n.

49. M. R. James in *E.H.R.*, xxxvii (1922), p. 419 *Catalogue of Romances in the British Museum*, iii, p. 171; H. E. D. Blakiston in *E.H.R.*, xxxviii (1923).

50. Glanvill, *Saducismus Triumphatus*, ii, pp. 209–15; *Great News from Middle-Row in Holbourn: or a True Relation of a Dreadful Ghost* (1679); *The Pepys Ballads*, ed. H. E. Rollins (Cambridge, Mass., 1929–32), iii, pp. 30–36. Another posthumous confession was recorded in *The Ghost, or a Minute Account of the Appearance of the Ghost of John Croxford Executed at Northampton, August the 4th, 1764*, by 'a Minister of the Gospel' (1764).

his intervention for those cases where an offence would have been undiscoverable by normal means.[51] The supernatural was only invoked at the point where natural remedies proved inadequate.

Sometimes the ghost was seen only by the guilty party. Like the spectre of Banquo, he preyed upon the murderer until the latter was forced into incriminating himself. A case from the North Riding concerned the ghost of one Fletcher, who reappeared around 1624 to haunt his wife's lover, who had been responsible for his murder; under this pressure the criminal broke down and confessed. In Somerset a decade earlier a murderer, who had refused to undergo the ordeal of touching his victim's corpse, finally admitted the crime after being pursued by his victim's ghost.[52] In 1654 one John Baldock confessed that, when serving on a privateer in Guernsey, he had robbed and killed an English soldier; he had been so haunted by the dead man's ghost that he had decided to give himself up.[53] The part played in such dramas by a guilty conscience personifying its own fears is obvious enough. On other occasions the spirit of the murdered person was said to have appeared to a third party, urging him to denounce the crime or revealing the whereabouts of the body. In 1665, for example, a Quaker demanded justice upon the wrongly-acquitted murderer of his son after a vision of the dead boy had appeared to him.[54] In such cases the ghost's role was to provide a justification for the public denunciation of the criminal by a witness when the conventional evidence was not adequate to secure a prosecution.

From the potential criminal's point of view, the role of ghost-beliefs is even more obvious; they served as an extra sanction against

51. This point is stressed by Mather, *An Essay for the Recording of Illustrious Providences*, pp. 219–20.

52. Webster, *The Displaying of Supposed Witchcraft*, pp. 297–8; *The Autobiography and Correspondence of Sir Simonds D'Ewes*, ed. J. O. Halliwell (1845), i, pp. 60–61.

53. *C.S.P.D., 1654*, p. 218. cf. the murderer who believed himself to have been followed continually by two ravens: R. Gough, *Antiquities and Memoirs of the Parish of Myddle* (1875), p. 72.

54. *C.S.P.D., 1664–5*, pp. 206–7. Similar cases in Turner, *Providences*, i, p. 23; R. Surtees, *The History and Antiquities of the County Palatine of Durham* (1816–40), ii, pp. 147–9; Aubrey, *Miscellanies*, pp. 94–105; *The Portledge Papers*, ed. R. J. Kerr and I. C. Duncan (1928), p. 173; M. A. Shaaber, *Some Forerunners of the Newspaper in England, 1476–1622* (Philadelphia, 1929), p. 151, n. 35; T. Heywood, *An Apology for Actors* (1612: 1841 edn), pp. 57–8; *The Diary of Thomas Isham of Lamport (1658–81)*, trans. N. Marlow (Farnborough, 1971).

crime by holding out the prospect of supernatural detection. Even if a man knew that there would be no witnesses to his evil-doing he still had to face the prospect that his victim might return supernaturally to denounce the crime. The title of a pamphlet published in 1679 speaks for itself: *Strange and Wonderful news from Lincolnshire. Or a Dreadful Account of a Most Inhumane and Bloody Murther, committed upon the Body of one Mr Carter by the Contrivance of his elder Brother, who had hired three more villains to commit the Horrid Fact, and how it was soon after found out by the Appearance of a Most Dreadful and Terrible Ghost, sent by Almighty Providence for the Discovery.* The importance of catchpenny tracts of this kind is not to be underrated. They reinforced contemporary moral standards by warning that even the most perfect crime could not pay. One contemporary remarked that ghosts had been so useful in uncovering undetected murders that they could not possibly be evil angels, but must have been sent by God.[55]

Not all the injuries which ghosts returned to avenge involved murder or violent crime. Many stories related to widowers, haunted by their wives for breaking their promise not to marry again, or for neglecting the children of their first marriage.[56] Others were more miscellaneous. The ghost of the astrologer Nicholas Culpepper appeared to his widow Alice bidding her to disown the works which contemporary booksellers were posthumously issuing falsely under his name.[57] The distinguished Oriental scholar Henry Jacob was said to have appeared several times after his death; he failed to speak, but it was generally assumed that he had come to explain that his manuscripts had been pirated under someone else's name.[58]

A similar motive for reappearance was provided by wills which had not been implemented or bequests which had been misappropriated. Here the belief in ghosts was a sanction enforcing respect for the wishes of the dead and guarding against the misappropriation of property. In the Middle Ages, when many ghost-stories emanated from the Church, it was unpaid tithes which frequently provoked such visitations,[59] but by the seventeenth century the in-

55. Webster, *The Displaying of Supposed Witchcraft*, p. 312.
56. *The Works of Thomas Nashe*, ed. R. B. McKerrow (1904–8), i, p. 383.
57. J. Heydon, *The Harmony of the World* (1662), p. 182.
58. Wood, *Ath. Ox.*, iii, cols. 332–3; Aubrey, *Miscellanies*, p. 82; M. Cranston, *John Locke* (1957), p. 188.
59. e.g., Blakiston in *E.H.R.*, xxxviii (1923); Johnson, *Purgatory prov'd by Miracles*, pp. 22–4.

juries to be redressed usually concerned the property of private individuals. A typical case was that of a woman in Beccles, who was haunted by her late husband, because of her failure to carry out his death-bed request to redress the injuries he had done to the poor.[60] Another story concerned the poet Sir William Davenant, who reappeared posthumously to inform the actress Mary Betterton of a legacy which had been only partly paid to the proper recipient.[61] 'Heirs and executors are grown damnable careless, 'specially since the ghosts of testators left walking,' says one of Ben Jonson's characters.[62] Ghosts could also intervene to prevent crimes against the remains of the dead, by scaring away body-snatchers and desecrators of churchyards.[63] Others came to tidy up business matters left unsettled at their death, to prevent false claims upon their estate, and to make sure that their wishes were properly carried out.[64]

Contemporaries also regarded ghosts as potential bearers of warning messages or prophetic utterances. The ghost of a London citizen came back during the Interregnum to tell his married daughter the best way to overcome the entanglements on his estate.[65] Others revealed the location of money and estate documents they had hidden in their lifetime.[66] They brought advance warning of sudden death, as when the ghost of the Duke of Buckingham's father appeared shortly before his assassination in 1628.[67] They appeared to their relatives as a sign that they had that moment quitted this

60. Ashm. 221, f. 223ᵛ. There is a similar case in G. Sinclair, *Satan's Invisible World Discovered* (Edinburgh, 1685: 1871 reprint), pp. 128–31.

61. B.M., Lansdowne MS 207(c), f. 413ᵛ.

62. *Every Man out of His Humour*, II.i.

63. *Games and Gamesters of the Restoration*, ed. C. H. Hartmann (1930), p. 239; W. Sikes, *British Goblins* (1880), pp. 145–6.

64. Glanvill, *Saducismus Triumphatus*, ii, p. 235–7, 238–42, 276–85; *A Narrative of the Demon of Spraiton* (1683); *A Full and True Relation of the Appearing of a Dreadfull Ghost to one John Dyer in Winchester-Yard in Southwark* (1690); Baxter, *The Certainty of the World of Spirits*, pp. 17–18; C. J. Stranks, *The Life and Writings of Jeremy Taylor* (1952), pp. 251–4.

65. C.U.L., MS Dd.iii.64, f. 150.

66. *Strange and Wonderful News from Northamptonshire* (1674); *A Most Strange and Dreadful Apparition of Several Spirits and Visions* (1680); C. R. Beard, *The Romance of Treasure Trove* (1933), pp. 77–80.

67. There are versions of this much-told story in Clarendon, *The History of the Rebellion*, ed. W. D. Macray (Oxford, 1888), i, pp. 51–5; B.M., Lansdowne MS 207(b), ff. 130–1; Aubrey, *Miscellanies*, pp. 79–80; and 'A. Moreton' (D. Defoe), *The Secrets of the Invisible World Disclos'd* (3rd edn, 1738), pp. 280–90. cf. the spectres supposed to appear in churchyards on St Mark's Eve; above, p. 286.

life: Alderman Sir Richard Hart, M.P. and Mayor of Bristol in 1680, saw his daughter's ghost in London on the day she died at home.[68]

Occasionally they brought messages of national importance. In 1587 a ghost appeared to Mary Cocker, the wife of a Hertfordshire labourer, with dramatic instructions concerning the safety of the Queen. From her description it is clear that the iconography of ghosts has not changed much in the intervening centuries. It was, she said, 'a bright thing of long proportion without shape, clothed as it were in white silk, which ... passed by her bedside where she lay'. After it had appeared several times she challenged it in the proper manner: 'In the name of God, what art thou and why troublest thou me?' To which the 'vision or ghost' replied,

'Go to thy Queen and tell her that she receive nothing ... of any stranger, for there is a jewel in making for her which the party, if he could, would deliver to her own hands, or else not deliver it at all; which, if she receive, will be her destruction. And if thou dost not tell her this much (quoth it) thou shalt die the cruellest death that ever died any.' And so presently it vanished away.[69]

Like other spirits, ghosts thus personified men's hopes and fears, making explicit a great deal which could not be said directly. They were also a useful sanction for social norms. In twelfth-century London it was customary to require oaths to be taken on a dead man's tomb, on the principle that the ghost lurking there would avenge any perjury; in the Isle of Man this custom survived until the seventeenth century.[70] The whole conception of Purgatory was particularly important as an incentive to men to be charitable. In parts of Yorkshire it was believed to be prudent to give shoes to the poor, because every man after his death would have to pass along stony country. Those who had donated shoes in their lifetime would be met by an old man who would return to them the identical pair they had once given away for charity.[71] The same tradition was enshrined in the ballad of Whinny-Moor – the gorse terrain through which all dead souls had to pass, and where all those who had not

68. B.M., Lansdowne MS 207(c), f. 413 (story told Gervase Holles by John Dolbye, Recorder of Reading).
69. P.R.O., SP 12/200, f. 65.
70. *Borough Customs*, ed. M. Bateson (Selden Soc., 1904–6), i, p. 48; ii, p. xxxiii; M. Bateson, 'A London Municipal Collection of the Reign of John', *E.H.R.*, xvii (1902), p. 489.
71. 'A Description of Cleveland', *Topographer and Genealogist*, ii (1853), p. 429. For a very close parallel in a thirteenth-century ghost story, see *Catalogue of Romances in the British Museum*, iii, p. 383.

been charitable in their life-time would be pricked and tormented. These legends were debased versions of Catholic teaching about the merit of good works: the needle-pointed bridge over which dead souls had to pass bare-footed was a standard piece of mythology.[72] It is well known that beliefs about Purgatory lingered on in some nominally Protestant circles.[73] But it is notable that at a popular level it was the duties of charity and neighbourliness which they were particularly invoked to reinforce. Witch-beliefs, as we have seen, also buttressed the obligation of charity by teaching that those most likely to suffer were the persons who denied help to their neighbours. Charity indeed possessed a magic value; it reflected the primitive belief in the power of a gift to nullify some potential threat to the donor. This was one of the reasons why doles to poor people were lavishly distributed at gentlemen's funerals until the mid seventeenth century, and in some cases long afterwards. At the funeral of the sixth Earl of Shrewsbury at Sheffield in 1591 doles were distributed to eight thousand poor men, and a throng of beggars drawn from a radius of thirty miles was estimated at twenty thousand.[74] The same propitiatory function underlay the massive charitable requests made on their death-beds by men whose lives had sometimes been devoted to personal aggrandisement and exploitation.[75] But, as the Protestant reformers emphasised, the fear of Purgatory had never proved sufficient to stop men from leaving unpaid debts or failing to restore ill-gotten goods.[76]

72. Aubrey, *Gentilisme*, pp. 31–2. cf. Briggs, *The Anatomy of Puck*, p. 125.

73. See, e.g., W. Maskell, *Monumenta Ritualia* (2nd edn, Oxford, 1882), i, p. 158, n. 12; J. White, *The First Century of Scandalous, Malignant Priests* (1643), pp. 41–2; above, p. 706; below, p. 720.

74. J. C. Cox, *Three Centuries of Derbyshire Annals* (1890), ii, p. 136. cf. L. Stone, *The Crisis of the Aristocracy* (Oxford, 1965), pp. 575–6. Instances from the late seventeenth century and beyond may be found in *Yorkshire Diaries*, ii (Surtees Soc., 1886), p. 105; *The Autobiography of William Stout of Lancaster, 1665–1752*, ed. J. D. Marshall (Manchester, 1967), p. 107; *Surrey Archaeol. Collns*, x (1890–91), pp. 59, 66; *John Lucas's History of Warton Parish*, ed. J. R. Ford and J. A. Fuller-Maitland (Kendal, 1931), pp. 23–4; *County Folk-Lore, Vol. II*, ed. Mrs. Gutch (Folk-Lore Soc., 1901), pp. 307–8, 310–11. But the decline of the practice was lamented by William Allen as early as 1565: *A Defense and Declaration of the Catholike Churchies Doctrine touching Purgatory* (Antwerp, 1565), f. 158.

75. cf. S. L. Thrupp, *The Merchant Class of Medieval London* (Ann Arbor, 1962), pp. 177–8; J. A. F. Thomson, *Clergy and Laity in London, 1376–1531* (Oxford, D.Phil. thesis, 1960), pp. 68–9.

76. *Sermons and Remains of Hugh Latimer*, ed. G. E. Corrie (Cambridge, P.S., 1845), p. 363.

3. *Society and the dead*

As in other societies, therefore, ghosts were a sanction for general moral standards, sustaining good social relations and disturbing the sleep of the guilty." But they were particularly important for the enforcement of obligations towards ancestors. The essential task of ghosts was to ensure reverence for the dead and to deter those who sought to molest their bones or frustrate their dying wishes. This is not a function which would be equally intelligible in every society, for although all societies up to a point require the living to safeguard the wishes of past generations, they differ very much as to the extent to which this obligation is to be observed. Ghost-beliefs are thus more likely to be important in a relatively traditional society, that is to say, one where it is believed that in significant areas of life the behaviour of the living should be governed by the presumed wishes of the dead, and one where the links with the dead are deliberately preserved.

In England, even today, the wishes of the dead are respected. There is a wide freedom of testamentary disposition, and it is not easy to divert the resources of a charitable benefaction from the purpose its founder intended. The basic principle is still that a dying man's wishes, formally expressed, should be legally enforced so far as is socially acceptable. But we recognise that we are free to depart from the social, political, moral or aesthetic preferences of our ancestors; indeed it is generally taken for granted that we will do so. The pace of social and technological change is too fast for it to be possible to stick to ancient ways. To that extent we live in a society which has cut off its roots in the past.

It has already been seen how the function of ancient prophecies was to establish a spurious genealogy for contemporary institutions, and how their decline reflected the emergence of a new attitude to the past, and the rejection of arguments based on custom and precedent. The diminishing importance of ghost-beliefs was linked to the same process. Men grew prepared to accept innovation, unmoved by the prospect of their ancestors turning in their graves. Their relationship to their forefathers ceased to be close enough for the threat of ghostly vengeance to make much sense.

77. cf. E. E. Evans-Pritchard, *The Position of Women in Primitive Societies* (1965), pp. 252–5; J. Beattie, *Bunyoro, an African Kingdom* (New York, 1960), p. 76; G. Lienhardt, *Divinity and Experience* (Oxford, 1961), p. 154; M. Gluckman, *Politics, Law and Ritual in Tribal Society* (Oxford, 1965), pp. 226–9.

This break with the past had been assisted by the events of the Reformation, particularly by the denial of Purgatory, and the accompanying destruction of the many religious foundations devoted to singing prayers for the dead. In the Middle Ages such prayers had been an important aspect of popular religion. Apart from the monasteries, there were the perpetual chantries, traditionally estimated at 2,374 at the Dissolution. These institutions usually existed to celebrate masses for the repose of the soul of the founder or his family, and their liturgy and daily routine often reflected the details of his expressed wishes. Chantries, as Wycliffe pointed out, were a means of perpetuating the founder's name.[78] Medieval wills often contained bequests to pay for the singing of special (non-perpetual) masses on the testator's behalf. These obits, as they were called, combined alms for the poor with masses for the dead. A substantial proportion of the resources of medieval society was thus given over to ensuring the spiritual welfare of its dead members; and the practice of praying for the dead retained its vitality until the sixteenth century.[79] In some areas such rituals lingered on after the Reformation: bell-ringing on All Souls' Eve, 'month-days' and similar celebrations on anniversaries of deaths, offerings of money and food at funerals, 'sin-eating' by scapegoats hired to take on the dead man's sins.[80] So long as it lasted, the doctrine of Purgatory gave impressive reinforcement to the notion of society as a community uniting the dead and the living.

The impulse was not continuous, as can be seen from the significant decision of the abbess and convent of Barking to discontinue all masses for persons who had died more than a hundred years ago.[81] But there was no precedent for the violence of the Reformation, the destruction of the abbeys and chantries, and the violation of the testaments of so many dead persons, in blatant defiance of

78. K. L. Wood-Legh, *Perpetual Chantries in Britain* (Cambridge, 1965), pp. 304–5.

79. W. K. Jordan, *Philanthropy in England* (1959), pp. 306–8; id., *The Charities of London* (1960), p. 278; R. B. Dobson in *Studies in Church History*, iv, ed. G. J. Cuming (Leiden, 1967).

80. e.g., *The Remains of Edmund Grindal*, ed. W. Nicholson (Cambridge, P.S., 1843), pp. 325–6; *County Folk-Lore. Vol. I* (Folk-Lore Soc., 1895), ii, pp. 51, 53; E. Porter, *Cambridgeshire Customs and Folklore* (1969), pp. 26–7; Aubrey, *Gentilisme*, pp. 35–6.

81. G. Baskerville, *English Monks and the Suppression of the Monasteries* (1937), p. 31.

'innumerable wills devoutly made'.[82] Whereas medieval Catholics had believed that God would let souls linger in Purgatory if no masses were said for them, Protestant doctrine meant that each generation could be indifferent to the spiritual fate of its predecessor. Every individual was now to keep his own balance-sheet, and a man could no longer atone for his sins by the prayers of his descendants. This implied an altogether more atomistic conception of the relationship in which members of society stood to each other.[83] No longer would they allocate so much of their resources to the performance of rituals primarily intended for the spiritual welfare of their dead ancestors. 'Now there is no blessing of man's memory at all,' lamented the Catholic William Allen in 1565. As a modern French historian puts it, 'Life ceased to look to death for its perspective.'[84]

The century after the Reformation, however, saw an obsessive concern with the provision of physical memorials to the dead in place of the monasteries and chantries. For the nobility and gentry it was the great age of architectural tombs. These monuments also served as pedigrees and family records, and they were erected to the memory of distant ancestors as well as on behalf of those recently deceased. Noble expenditure on such memorials is thought to have reached a peak in the forty or fifty years preceding the death of James I. Thereafter the style of memorial became more modest.[85] But destruction kept pace with these new erections and the memory of the past was continually being effaced from the popular mind. In any case the common people had no such memorials. Their readiness to break such links with the past was reflected in the iconoclasm which accompanied both the Reformation and the Civil War.

Meanwhile the funeral ceremony was purged of many of its traditional accompaniments. In the sixteenth century aristocratic

82. N. Sander, *Rise and Growth of the Anglican Schism*, trans. D. Lewis (1877), p. 170. cf. J. Gwynneth, *A Declaracion of the State* (1554), f. 45ᵛ; Allen, *A Defense and Declaration of ... Purgatory*, f. 217.

83. cf. C. Hill, *Reformation to Industrial Revolution* (1967), p. 26; Wood-Legh, *Perpetual Chantries in Britain*, p. 313.

84. Allen, *A Defense and Declaration*, f. 169ᵛ; L. Febvre, *Au Coeur religieux du XVIᵉ siècle* (Paris, 1957), p. 58 (*'La vie cessait de chercher dans la mort son point de perspective'*). cf. the demand of the Western rebels in 1549 for the resumption of praying for souls in Purgatory *by name*; F. Rose-Troup, *The Western Rebellion of 1549* (1913), p. 221.

85. Stone, *The Crisis of the Aristocracy*, pp. 579–81; E. Mercer, *English Art, 1553–1625* (Oxford, 1962), chap. vi; J. Weever, *Ancient Funerall Monuments* (1631), 'The Author to the Reader'.

funerals began to move from being a manifestation of the whole feudal community to more modest family affairs. The whole style of contemporary mourning was quite inadequate for the occasion, thought the early Stuart antiquary John Weever.[86] The Puritans objected to ritual mourning, and thought tombs and epitaphs smacked of Popery. They condemned funeral sermons because only the families of the rich could afford to have them. The sectaries even denied that burial need be a religious ceremony at all:[87] once the belief in Purgatory had gone, it no longer seemed necessary to take ritual precautions for the repose of the dead man's soul; and there was no further demand for such Catholic devices as the special holy bell, of which the Irish, according to Jeremy Taylor, believed that

if this bell was rung before the corpse to the grave it would help him out of Purgatory and . . . therefore when anyone died, the friends of the deceased did . . . hire it for the behoof of their dead.[88]

In England funerals became so much simpler that by 1649 a contemporary could describe them as 'in a manner profane, in many places the dead being thrown into the ground like dogs, and not a word said'. Another commentator remarked in 1635 on the contrast between the elaborate funerals of the Papists and 'our silent and dumb obsequies'.[89] At the same time increasing revulsion came to be felt for the practice of embalming or mummifying the dead man's corpse.[90] Such developments paved the way for the hasty and embarrassed funerals of today, when the physical dissolution ot the dead is often symbolically accelerated by the practice of cremation. The lack of a modern ritual adequate to deal with the crisis of death and bereavement has been noted by many contemporary commen-

86. M. E. James, 'Two Tudor Funerals', *Trans. Cumbd and Westmld Antiqn and Archaeol. Soc.*, n.s., lxvi (1966); Weever, *Ancient Funerall Monuments*, p. 17.

87. (R. Bolton), *Mr Boltons Last and Learned Worke of the Foure Last Things* (1632), p. 152; C. Hill, *Economic Problems of the Church* (Oxford, 1956), pp. 182–3; Weever, op. cit., pp. 17–18, 37–8; *C.S.P.D., 1634–5*, p. 319; S. Clarke, *The Lives of Sundry Eminent Persons* (1683), i, p. 129; E. Harris, *A True Relation of a Company of Brownists* (1641); above, p. 75.

88. *The Whole Works of . . . Jeremy Taylor*, ed. R. Heber and C. P. Eden (1847–54), vi, p. 176.

89. N. Strange in Preface to (R. Carier), *A Missive to his Majesty of Great Britain* (1649), p. 12; D. Person, *Varieties* (1635), pp. 164–5.

90. Stone, *The Crisis of the Aristocracy*, p. 579. There is another example (misunderstood by its editor) in *Journ. Hist. Medicine*, xx (1965), p. 217.

tators;[91] and it seems that the beginning of the decline of this traditional *rite de passage* should be traced back to the break effected by the Reformation, though the change also had sociological causes, notably the decline of the tightly-knit community in which an individual death created an immediate void.

Of course, the belief in ghosts did not wither away altogether. Stories of apparitions and haunted houses were very popular in the nineteenth century and are common enough today. Modern investigations reveal that a substantial proportion of people either think they have seen a ghost or accept the possibility that they might see one. Vivid dreams of the dead person are common among those freshly bereaved.[92] But the social function of the belief in ghosts is obviously much diminished, and so is its extent. One of the reasons for this is that it is now more common for people to live out their full life-span, and to die only after they have retired and withdrawn from an active role in society. This reduces the social vacuum they leave behind. The relative absence of ghosts in modern society can thus be seen as the result of a demographic change – 'the disengaged social situation of the majority of the deceased'.[93] The dead, in other words, fade away before they die. In earlier periods, by contrast, it was commoner for men to be carried off at the prime of their life, leaving behind them a certain amount of social disturbance, which ghost-beliefs helped to dispel. The period when the soul wandered loose was that when the survivors were adapting themselves to their new pattern of social relationships.[94] Today that period is often short or even non-existent.

But the main reason for the disappearance of ghosts is that society is no longer responsive to the presumed wishes of past generations. Above a certain social level, this has been only a gradual change, for the landed family has long remained an institution which stretches back into the past and on into the future, providing the context for Burke's famous conception of society as a partnership between the living, the dead, and those not yet born. Land became fully devisable with the abolition of knight-service in

91. See, e.g., G. Gorer, *Death, Grief, and Mourning in Contemporary Britain* (1965), pp. 110–11; A. Macintyre in the *Listener*, 6 June 1968.

92. Gorer, op. cit., p. 54, and id., *Exploring English Character* (1955), pp. 263–4.

93. R. Blauner, 'Death and Social Structure', *Psychiatry*, xxix (1966), a brilliant article to which I am much indebted.

94. Gluckman, *Politics, Law and Ritual in Tribal Society*, pp. 7–8.

1660, but magnates continued to inherit property which was tied up in strict settlements, giving the current representative of the family no more than a life-tenancy. In addition, every kind of property was devised by will. In our period only a few bold spirits looked forward to the time when this power of dead men to determine the property of the living would be abolished.[95] In these circumstances it would be idle to pretend that the hold of the past had been broken or that the wishes of the dead went unrespected. Indeed, the immortality of families, colleges and other corporate bodies was soon to be matched by the continuity of the business firm.

Nevertheless, eighteenth-century England was not a traditional society in the sense that fifteenth-century England had been. Men's actions were less explicitly governed by concern for the wishes of their ancestors or their spiritual welfare. If they stopped seeing ghosts, it was because such apparitions were losing their social relevance, not just because they were regarded as intellectually impossible.

4. *Fairies*

Today's children are brought up to think of fairies as diminutive beings of a benevolent disposition, but the fairies of the Middle Ages were neither small nor particularly kindly. Goblins, elves and fairies were part of that great army of good and bad spirits with which the world was thought to be infested, and they conformed to no single set of characteristics. A modern student of folklore has suggested that most medieval fairies belonged to one of four categories: 'trooping fairies', who passed their time feasting and dancing; hobgoblins or guardian spirits like Puck alias Robin Goodfellow, who performed domestic chores for mortals; mermaids and water spirits; and giants and monsters.[96] But it is doubtful whether such hard and fast divisions can be made. Popular beliefs varied in different parts of the country and were an amalgam of many different traditions. Ancestral spirits, ghosts, sleeping heroes, fertility spirits and pagan gods can all be discerned in the heterogeneous fairy lore of medieval England, and modern inquiries into fairy origins can never be more than speculative.

95. e.g., J. Brayne, *The New Earth* (1653), p. 94.
96. Briggs, *The Anatomy of Puck* (1959), pp. 13–16. This Book, together with M. W. Latham, *The Elizabethan Fairies* (New York, 1930), offers an excellent guide to the fairy-beliefs of the period, but neither is much concerned with their social function.

GHOSTS AND FAIRIES

725

It is clear, however, that elves, goblins and fairies were frequently thought of as highly malevolent. The very word 'fairy' was itself used, as we have already seen, to convey the idea of a malignant disease of spiritual origin which could be cured only by charming or exorcism. The Anglo-Saxons had described persons smitten with a supernatural malady as 'elf-shot', and the term was applied to sick animals in Celtic areas until modern times.[97] In 1677 John Webster wrote that the inhabitants of Yorkshire used 'fairy-taken' as a way of describing someone who has been blasted, haunted or bewitched.[98]

Supernatural maladies of this kind were usually thought to require a supernatural remedy. The fifteenth-century witch of Eye, Margery Jourdemain, was reputed to have been able to charm 'fiends and fairies'; and many cunning folk were prepared to diagnose and treat such cases by charming and incantation.[99] Popular formulae for use against fairies survive in contemporary charmbooks along with recipes against theft, illness and evil spirits.[100] Catholic formulae were also used. One sixteenth-century wizard stated that the fairies had power only over those lacking religious faith. Others commended the use of St John's Gospel or holy water.[101]

For many persons fairies thus remained spirits against which they had to guard themselves by some ritual precaution. It is true that the more sophisticated Elizabethans tended to speak as if fairy-beliefs were a thing of the past; Reginald Scot, for example, wrote in 1584 that Robin Goodfellow was no longer as widely feared as he had been a hundred years previously; as he saw it, the fear of goblins had been replaced by the fear of witches. Yet in the late seventeenth century Sir William Temple could assume that fairy beliefs had only declined in the previous thirty years or so. John Aubrey also put them in the fairly recent past: 'When I was a boy,

97. T. Davidson, 'Elf-Shot Cattle', *Antiquity*, xxx (1956), and id., 'The Cure of Elf-Disease in Animals', *Journ. Hist. of Medicine*, xv (1960).

98. Webster, *The Displaying of Supposed Witchcraft*, pp. 323–4.

99. *The Mirror for Magistrates*, ed. L. B. Campbell (New York, 1960), p. 435; Ewen, ii, p. 447; C. M. L. Bouch, *Prelates and People of the Lake Counties* (Kendal, 1948), p. 216; above, pp. 217–19.

100. Latham, *Elizabethan Fairies*, pp. 37–9, 162–3, 244–5, 247–8; Bodl., Add. MS B 1, f. 20ᵛ; Brand, *Popular Antiquities*, ii, p. 503.

101. *The Examination of John Walsh* (1566), sig. Avjᵛ; Briggs, *The Anatomy of Puck*, p. 80; Latham, op. cit., p. 166.

our country people would talk much of them.'[102] Indeed it seems that commentators have always attributed them to the past. Even Chaucer's Wife of Bath had dated the reign of the elf-queen to 'many hundred years ago', remarking sardonically that the fairies had been driven away by the prayers and charity of the holy friars.[103]

The fact that fairy-beliefs seem to have had childhood associations for most commentators makes it harder to assess their vitality at any particular period. By the Elizabethan age fairy lore was primarily a store of mythology rather than a corpus of living beliefs, but it was sometimes still accepted literally at a popular level. John Penry, for example, writing three years after Scot, remarked that the Welsh peasantry held fairies in an 'astonishing reverence' and dared not 'name them without honour'. A hundred years later the common people of England were still said to believe in them. The fairy tradition is said to have been neglected in the eighteenth century, but abundant evidence of living fairy-beliefs was to be assembled by nineteenth-century collectors of English country folklore.[104] So far as literary references are concerned, the peak age of fairy allusions appears to be the end of the sixteenth century and the beginning of the seventeenth. But as a recent scholar has pointed out, this indicates the growth of a literature with popular roots rather than an increase in fairy-beliefs as such. In France the taste for fairy stories did not reach its peak until the very end of the seventeenth century.[105] But in England it was the Shakespearean period which saw the widespread dissemination of the concept of fairies as a dwarf race of mischievous but fundamentally friendly temperament. It also saw the absorption into the fairy kingdom of the household goblin Robin Goodfellow, who had previously been thought of as quite separate from fairies proper. The older concept of the fairy or goblin as a

102. Scot, *Discoverie*, 'To the Readers'; *The Works of Sir William Temple* (1770), iii, p. 418; Aubrey, *Gentilisme*, pp. 29–30, 102, 125–6, 235. cf. T. Richards, *Religious Developments in Wales (1654–62)* (1923), p. 297; Lucas, *History of Warton Parish*, ed. Ford and Fuller-Maitland, pp. 39–40.
103. *Canterbury Tales*, 'Wife of Bath's Tale', ll. 1–16.
104. J. Penry, *Three Treatises concerning Wales*, ed. D. Williams (Cardiff, 1960), p. 33; F. Knolles, *The Turkish History*, ed. Sir P. Rycaut (6th edn, 1687), ii, p. 180; K. M. Briggs, *The Fairies in Tradition and Literature* (1967), p. 11.
105. Latham, *Elizabethan Fairies*, pp. 14–18, 32–3; Briggs, *The Anatomy of Puck*, p. 6; M. Storer, *Un Episode littéraire de la fin du XVIIe siècle, La Mode des contes de Fées (1685–1700)* (Paris, 1928), p. 15.

malevolent spirit, however, was not entirely lost. Bunyan's Pilgrim, we remember, was not daunted by 'Hobgoblin or foul fiend'.

To contemporary magicians fairies were a valuable source of supernatural power. Many magical compilations of the period contained instructions for conjuring them up in order to learn a variety of occult secrets.[106] Such rituals were much the same as those for conjuring spirits in general. William Lilly took part in several attempts to get in touch with the Queen of the Fairies, believing that she could teach anything one desired to know.[107] Village wizards also claimed to work with fairy aid. We have already encountered the Somerset woman, Joan Tyrry, who knew in 1555 whether or not her neighbours were bewitched because the fairies told her so. Other cunning folk whom the fairies were thought to have helped to cure the sick, tell fortunes, find treasure or otherwise perform their magical role included Mariona Clerk (Suffolk, 1499), one Croxton's wife (London, 1549), John Walsh (Dorset, 1566), Margaret Harper (Yorkshire, 1567), Susan Snapper (Sussex, 1607) and a sixteenth-century vicar of Warlingham, Surrey.[108] In Elizabethan Wales there were said to be swarms of soothsayers and enchanters who claimed to walk with the fairies on Tuesday and Thursday nights.[109] In Cornwall in 1648 Anne Jefferies was believed to live on a diet of sweetmeats brought her by six little people clothed in green. They taught her to prophesy and to carry out miraculous acts of healing.[110]

Spiritual creatures of this kind belong to the same genre as the witch's familiars or the conjurer's demons. In at least one English witch-trial (that of Joan Willimot in 1619) the accused person confessed to having been given a fairy by the Devil.[111] The name 'Oberon' or 'Oberion' was borne by a demon who had been frequently

106. Some are printed in Briggs, op. cit., appx ix. Others may be found in Sloane 3851, f. 129; Bodl., MS e Mus. 173, f. 72ᵛ; Scot, *Discoverie*, XV.x; Latham, *Elizabethan Fairies*, p. 107.

107. Lilly, *Autobiography*, pp. 229–32.

108. *Tudor Studies*, ed. R. W. Seton-Watson (1924), pp. 72–3; *Narratives of the Days of the Reformation*, ed. J. G. Nichols (Camden Soc., 1859), p. 334; *The Examination of John Walsh*; Borthwick, R.VI. A 2, f. 22; G. S. Butler in *Sussex Archaeol. Collns*, xiv (1862), pp. 26–32; *The Gentleman's Magazine Library: Popular Superstitions*, ed. G. L. Gomme (1884), p. 155; above, p. 220. See also Latham, op. cit., pp. 137–41.

109. Penry, *Three Treatises concerning Wales*, p. 33.

110. Turner, *Providences*, ii, pp. 116–20; above, p. 237.

111. *The Wonderful Discoverie of the Witchcrafts of Margaret and Phillip Flower* (1619), sig. E3ᵛ.

conjured by fifteenth- and sixteenth-century wizards, long before the title became associated with the King of the Fairies.[112] John Walsh, the Dorset cunning man, said in 1566 that there were three types of fairies, the white, the green and the black; the last-named were the worst, in his mind indistinguishable from malignant devils.[113]

During the seventeenth century fairy mythology settled down into something approximating to its modern form. The fairies were said to be little people, inhabiting woods or earthen barrows, and organized in a kingdom of their own. Sometimes they came out to dance on grass fairy-rings and allowed themselves to be seen by selected human beings. They were occasionally predatory and might swoop down to snatch an unguarded infant child, leaving a changeling in his place. They might also nip, pinch or otherwise torment a careless housewife or untidy servant-maid. The proper way of propitiating these beings was to sweep the house clean in the evening, leaving out food for them to eat and water and towels with which they might wash; for the fairies depended upon human beings for food, and were fanatics for cleanliness. Thus treated, they might reward their benefactors by leaving money in their shoes, or in the case of Robin Goodfellow, by helping with domestic tasks in return for a bowl of cream. If neglected, they would avenge themselves by washing their children in the beer, stealing milk from the cows and corn from the fields, knocking over buckets, frustrating the manufacture of butter and cheese, and generally making nuisances of themselves.

This practice of setting out food and drink for the fairies had been well known in the Middle Ages and was inevitably condemned by the leaders of the Church, who naturally resented the propitiation of other deities.[114] To ecclesiastics it seemed that people who left out provision for the fairies in the hope of getting rich or gaining good fortune were virtually practising a rival religion. Elves and fairies were either devils or diabolical illusions, declared a number of late medieval writers.[115] This hostility was strengthened by the Reforma-

112. Kittredge, *Witchcraft*, pp. 110, 208, 210; *The Historical Collections of a Citizen of London*, ed. J. Gairdner (Camden Soc., 1876), p. 185; Briggs, *The Anatomy of Puck*, pp. 16, 114–15.

113. *The Examination of John Walsh*, sig. Av.

114. J. T. McNeill and H. M. Gamer, *Medieval Handbooks of Penance* (New York, 1938), p. 335; *Life in the Middle Ages*, ed. G. G. Coulton, i (Cambridge, 1930), p. 33; *Dives, and Pauper* (1536), f. 50.

115. *Malleus*, II.2.viii; A. G. Little, *Studies in English Franciscan History* (Manchester, 1917), p. 230.

tion, whose theologians took away the remaining possibility that fairies might be ghosts of the dead. Fairies could only be good or evil spirits, and of the two possibilities the latter was much more likely. The Puritan Richard Greenham was said to have regarded the fairies as good spirits rather than bad ones. If so, he was exceptional among theologians in so doing. It was pointless trying to distinguish good fairies from bad ones, thought Thomas Jackson; the Devil was behind them all.[116] This was the official doctrine of most Protestant teachers, though like so many other official doctrines its influence upon the people at large was only partial.

On the other hand the Protestant myth that fairy-beliefs were an invention of the Catholic Middle Ages may well have had some effect. Fairies, like ghosts, were said to have been devised by Popish priests to cover up their knaveries. They were 'conceits . . . whereby the Papists kept the ignorant in awe'.[117] This much-echoed view was grossly unfair, not only because fairy-beliefs were older than Roman Catholicism, but because the medieval Church had itself been hostile to fairy mythology. But it was much employed by Protestant polemicists in the century after the Reformation, and found its most attractive poetic expression in Bishop Corbett's *The Faeryes Farewell*. Most of those who remained sympathetic to fairy-beliefs admitted the Roman Catholic character of the fairy kingdom. 'Theirs is a mixt religion,' wrote Robert Herrick, 'part pagan, part papistical.'[118] Goodwin Wharton, who was tricked by Mrs Parish into believing that he had extensive relations with the fairies, or 'lowlanders', as she sometimes called them, was told that they were 'Christians, serving . . . God that way, much in the manner of the Roman Catholics, believing [in] transubstantiation, and having a Pope who resides here in England'.[119]

116. *The Workes of* . . . *Richard Greenham*, ed. H. H(olland) (3rd edn, 1601), p. 42; T. Jackson, *A Treatise containing the Originall of Unbeliefe* (1625), p. 178.

117. Cooper, *Mystery*, p. 123. Similar opinions in E. Fairfax, *A Discourse of Witchcraft*, in *Miscellanies of the Philobiblon Soc.*, v (1858–9), pp. 18–20; *The Workes of* . . . *Joseph Hall*, ed. P. Wynter (Oxford, 1863), viii, p. 202; R. Gough, *Antiquities and Memoirs of the Parish of Myddle* (1875), pp. 37–8; (T.G.), *The Friers Chronicle* (1623), sig. B3ᵛ; Webster, *The Displaying of Supposed Witchcraft*, pp. 175–6; Latham, *Elizabethan Fairies*, pp. 62–3.

118. *The Poetical Works of Robert Herrick*, ed. L. C. Martin (Oxford, 1956), p. 91.

119. B.M., Add. MS 20,006, f. 36ᵛ.

Various theories have been put forward to account for the persistence of these fairy-beliefs. Those seeking a psychological interpretation point to the existence of Lilliputian delusions still familiar to psychiatrists. Fairy hallucinations were associated with mental illness as early as the seventeenth century.[120] Adherents of the so-called 'pygmy theory', on the other hand, prefer to think that the belief in fairies reflected folk memory of a dwarf race of human beings who once inhabited Neolithic barrows.[121] Speculations of this kind are fortunately irrelevant to our purposes. We may accept that fairy-beliefs existed and were passed on by succeeding generations to their children at the nursery stage. Our task is to determine the social consequences of this belief as it was thus inherited.

Modern social anthropologists, studying the survival of fairy-beliefs among the Irish peasantry, have been able to show that such notions can discharge important social functions and help to enforce a certain code of conduct. 'The fairy faith,' it has been said, 'enforces definite behaviour on the countryman.'[122] In early twentieth-century Ireland it was believed that no fairy trouble would come to those who kept their houses clean and tidy. The same was true in seventeenth-century England:

> If ye will with *Mab* find grace,
> Set each platter in his place:
> Rake the fire up, and get
> Water in, ere sun be set.
> Wash your pails, and cleanse your dairies;
> Sluts are loathsome to the fairies:
> Sweep your house; who doth not so,
> *Mab* will pinch her by the toe.

Herrick's lines were both a programme for the careful housemaid and a warning of the sanctions accompanying non-performance. The Queen of the Fairies was, as Ben Jonson put it,

120. cf. R. Hunter and I. Macalpine, *Three Hundred Years of Psychiatry, 1535–1860* (1963), p. 156.

121. Representative statements of these alternative views may be found in M. J. Field, *Search for Security* (1960), pp. 45, 318, and M. A. Murray, *The God of the Witches* (1931), chap. 2. There is a good survey of older theories by J. A. MacCulloch in *Encyclopaedia of Religion and Ethics*, ed. J. Hastings (Edinburgh, 1908–26), *s.v.* 'Fairy'.

122. C. M. Arensberg, *The Irish Countryman* (1937), p. 195, and chap. 6 *passim.*

> She, that pinches country wenches
> If they rub not clean their benches,
> And with sharper nails remembers,
> When they rake not up their embers.

It would be an exaggeration to say that seventeenth-century serving-maids only did their work conscientiously because they were afraid of being tormented by the fairies, but the direction in which fairy-beliefs influenced those who held them is obvious enough. (The same may also have been true of witch-beliefs: stinking utensils and living-quarters were conventionally taken as evidence that animal familiars were present: and men were warned that it was dangerous to leave their excrement where their enemies might find it.)[124]

Nor was domestic untidiness the only vice which the fairies punished. They also tormented servants who neglected their persons or failed to clean their master's horses. They had a great hatred of lust and lechery, and eagerly pinched and nipped those engaged in unchaste activities.[125] They even upheld the virtues of neighbourliness, by lending out household utensils, and insisting upon their prompt return; those who delayed bringing back the spits and pieces of pewter they had borrowed were never helped by the fairies again.[126] The risk of being landed with a fairy changeling similarly reminded men of the need to look after a newborn child very carefully. A moment's neglect might be rewarded by the substitution of a fairy child, who would grow up thin, ugly and retarded. The early weeks of infancy were particularly crucial here, for the fairies were thought most likely to act before the child had been baptized or the mother churched.[127] Contemporaries had obvious religious reasons for believing that this was the period at which the baby was most vulnerable, but the rule that a child should never be left alone at this time could also be justified on more practical grounds of infant care. The fear of baby-snatching was a real one in some country areas, and it can only have had beneficial effects.

In such ways did fairy-beliefs help to reinforce some of the

123. Quoted in Briggs, *The Anatomy of Puck*, pp. 10, 84. cf. Latham, *Elizabethan Fairies*, pp. 129–31; J. Ritson, *Fairy Tales* (1831), p. 92.

124. Ewen, i, pp. 268–9; S. Boulton, *Medicina Magica* (1656), pp. 40, 162.

125. Latham, *Elizabethan Fairies*, pp. 131, 133–4, 249.

126. Aubrey, *Gentilisme*, pp. 123, 235.

127. Latham, *Elizabethan Fairies*, chap. iv; L. Spence, *The Fairy Tradition in Britain* (1948), chap. 13; R. W(illis), *Mount Tabor* (1639), p. 93.

standards upon which the effective working of society depended. They could also operate as a means of accounting for an otherwise unsatisfactory situation. A parent could disown responsibility for a retarded child by declaring that it was a changeling. A quack doctor could cover up his ignorance in the same way. In 1590 it was related at the Hatfield Sessions how Thomas Harding of Ickleford, Hertfordshire, a reputed wizard, had told a woman whose four-year-old child could neither walk nor talk that the brat was a changeling, and that the only hope of redress was to put him on a chair on a dunghill for an hour on a sunny day, in the hope that the fairies would come back and replace him by the child they had stolen.[128] Other types of misfortune or misconduct could also be explained by fairy-beliefs. The man who lost his way on the road might plead that he had been led astray by a will-of-the-wisp; it was well known that fairies specialized in misleading poor travellers.[129] The negligent servant would blame the fairies for interfering with his work: 'when the maids spilt the milkpans, or kept any racket, they would lay it upon Robin'.[130] When Goodwin Wharton found himself sexually too exhausted to sustain his relationship with Mrs. Parish, he was able to surmise that the Fairy Queen had been with him in his sleep, and sucked out the very marrow from his bones in her voraciousness.[131]

Inevitably, moreover, there were the frauds and tricksters, ready to exploit the credulity of their contemporaries. In the mid fifteenth century a band of Kentish poachers stole deer from the Duke of Buckingham's park at Penshurst after blacking their faces and calling themselves the servants of the Queen of the Fairies.[132] The late Elizabethan and Jacobean periods witnessed a series of episodes in which professional tricksters extracted money from their victims under the pretence of investing it with the fairies. Judith Philips, a London cunning woman, was whipped through the City in 1595 after being convicted for extracting large sums of money from gullible

128. Hertfordshire R.O., HAT/SR 2/100 (summarized in *Hertford County Records*, ed. W. J. Hardy, i [Hertford, 1905], p. 3). A later instance of the same formula may be found in Latham, op. cit., pp. 160–61.

129. Latham, op. cit., pp. 135–6; Owst, *Literature and Pulpit in Medieval England*, p. 113.

130. Latham, op. cit., pp. 237–8; Brand, *Popular Antiquities*, ii, p. 484.

131. B.M., Add. MS 20,006, f. 48.

132. *Kent Records. Documents Illustrative of Medieval Kentish Society*, ed. F. R. H. du Boulay (Kent Archaeol. Soc., 1964), pp. 254–5. The editor points out that the same title had been assumed in the previous year by the leader of a political demonstration (p. 217).

clients prepared to pay for the privilege of meeting the Queen of
the Fairies.[133] The nefarious couple, Alice and John West, were
shown in 1614 to have squeezed £40 out of one client on the promise
of forthcoming fairy gold.[134] An even closer approximation to the
fraud portrayed in Ben Jonson's *The Alchemist* occurred a few
years earlier, when Sir Anthony Ashley and his brother were involved in a Chancery suit arising from their efforts to extract money
from a dupe in return for their promise to marry him to the Queen of
the Fairies.[135] At the end of the seventeenth century the ingenuous
Goodwin Wharton was persuaded by Mrs Parish into believing that,
as a result of a political crisis in the fairy commonwealth, she had
managed to get him proclaimed as their King. Every time a meeting
was projected between Wharton and his new subjects it had to be
postponed on some excuse or other, and he was unlucky enough to
be always asleep on the rare occasions when the Fairy Queen did
appear. Yet Wharton's faith survived these transparent mishaps,
and the extraordinary masquerade was sustained for over a decade.[136]

For one striking aspect of fairy-beliefs was their self-confirming
character. The man who believed in fairies could, like the astrologer
or the magician, accept every setback and disappointment without
losing his faith. He knew that he could never count on actually *seeing* the fairies himself, for the little people were notoriously jealous
of their privacy and would never appear to those who were so
curious as to go looking for them. Mrs Parish told Wharton that the
fairies had a way of beckoning to any person they wanted to talk
to which was 'so quick . . . that none but those for whom it was intended could see it'. Nor would they ever reappear to those who betrayed their secrets. Joan Tyrry said in 1555 that she would never
again see the fairies after having been made to confess her dealings
with them before an ecclesiastical court.[137] Everyone knew that a
regular supply of fairy gold would dry up immediately its recipient

133. *The Brideling, Sadling and Ryding, of a Rich Churle in Hampshire,
by the Subtill Practise of one Judeth Philips* (1595); *H.M.C., Hatfield*, v, pp.
81–3; L. B. Wright, *Middle-Class Culture in Elizabethan England* (Chapel
Hill, 1935), p. 443.

134. *The Severall Notorious and Lewd Cousnages of Iohn West, and Alice
West* (1613).

135. C. J. Sisson, 'A Topical Reference in *The Alchemist*', in *Joseph
Quincy Adams Memorial Studies*, ed. J. G. McManaway et al. (Washington,
1948).

136. B.M., Add. MS 20,006, f. 77 and *passim*.

137. Wells, D.R., A 21.

bragged of it to anyone else.[138] It was this elusiveness which made the fairies such admirable vehicles for the confidence trickster. Alice West, for example, impressed upon one of her intended victims that 'there was nothing so necessary as secrecy, for if it were revealed to any, save them three whom it did essentially concern, they should not only hazard their good fortune, but incur the danger of the fairies, and so consequently lie open to great mishaps and fearful disasters'. When the client subsequently fell lame she was quick to remark that the reason must be that he had been telling tales to someone else.[139] There was an impenetrability about fairy-beliefs which protected them from easy exposure. As Sir John Falstaff put it: 'they are fairies; he that speaks to them shall die'.[140]

138. Aubrey, *Gentilisme*, pp. 29, 102.
139. *The Severall Notorious and Lewd Cousnages of Iohn West*, sig. B1.
140. *The Merry Wives of Windsor*, V.5. On the dangers attending traffic with the fairies, see also L. C. Wimberly, *Death and Burial Lore in the English and Scottish Popular Ballads* (Lincoln, Nebraska, 1927), p. 77.

20.

TIMES AND OMENS

> If Swithin wept this year, the Proverb says,
> The weather will be foul for forty days.
> But still exceptions to such rule there are,
> As in this case (except some days be fair).
> Husbandman ply thy work, no time mispending,
> On Providence, not Proverbs, still depending.
> (Adam Martindale), *The Country Almanack* (1675), sig. B2

1. *The observance of times*

THE belief in lucky and unlucky days goes back at least to classical times. The Romans had their *dies nefasti*, and similar concepts were widespread in China and the ancient East. Indeed the idea that certain days are, for some occult reason, propitious for certain actions, and others inappropriate, is to be found among most pre-industrial peoples. It is not to be confused with the development of a seasonal routine by agriculturalists, or even with the semi-astrological idea that certain tasks are best performed at particular phases of the moon; practices of this kind have a self-consciously 'rational' basis, even if the theoretical assumptions on which they rest are in fact mistaken. By contrast, the essential feature of the belief in unlucky days was that no one knew *why* they were unlucky. The rules for their observance were inherited ones, resting on no discernible foundation.

In medieval Europe the best known of these supposedly unfortunate times were the so-called 'Egyptian' or 'dismal' days, a list of dates on which it was thought to be dangerous to embark upon any action of consequence.[1] A man who went for a journey on such a day

---

1. For typical medieval lists, see M. Förster, 'Die altenglischen Verzeichnisse von Glücks – und Unglückstagen', in *Studies in English Philology. A Miscellany in Honor of Frederick Klaeber*, ed. K. Malone and M. B. Ruud (Minneapolis, 1929); Thorndike, *Magic and Science*, i, pp. 685–9; H. Webster, *Rest days* (Lincoln, Nebraska, 1911), p. 155; R. Steele, 'Dies Aegyptiaci', *Procs. Royal Soc. Medicine*, xii (1919); R. H. Robbins in *Philological Qtly*, xviii (1939), p. 321, n. 2; *H.M.C., Montagu of Beaulieu*, pp. 1–2. There is a good discussion in C. F. Bühler, 'Sixteenth-century Prognostications', *Isis*, xxxiii (1941).

might not return; a patient who fell ill would be unlikely to recover. No one seems to have known why these days were called 'Egyptian'; some said it was because it was the ancient Egyptians who had first observed them, others regarded them as the days on which the various plagues had struck Biblical Egypt.[2]

Nor does there seem to have been any clear agreement as to precisely which days of the year they were, for rival sets of dates were in circulation. In England in the sixteenth and seventeenth centuries it was common for lists of such 'evil' days to be printed in almanacs and popular handbooks. But these prognostications seldom agreed with each other, and a diligent reader might have concluded there was virtually no day in the year which was not regarded as unsafe by someone.

Lists of unlucky days were also compiled by many private individuals and can often be found in their personal papers.[3] They were times to be avoided for weddings, journeys, operations, bloodlettings, and any other critical activities. How seriously they were observed is impossible to say, but even Elizabeth I's Treasurer, Lord Burghley, thought it worth mentioning them in his *Advice to his Son*: 'Though I think no day amiss to undertake any good enterprise or business in hand,' he remarks, 'yet have I observed some, and no mean clerks, very cautious to forbear . . . three Mondays in the year.' These were the first Monday in April (supposedly the anniversary of the death of Abel), the second Monday in August (the destruction of Sodom and Gomorrah), and the last Monday in December (the birthday of Judas Iscariot).[4] In Burghley's three taboo Mondays (of which the memory was preserved in popular tradition as late as the nineteenth century) we may recognize a garbled and Biblicised version of the three unsuitable days for blood-letting which had been named by Hippocrates, and disseminated to medieval Europe by

2. Thiers, *Superstitions*, i, pp. 291–2; M. Del Rio, *Disquisitionum Magicarum Libri Sex* (Lyons, 1608), p. 236. The Egyptians had in fact classified all days as good or bad; W. R. Dawson, 'Some Observations on the Egyptian Calendars of Lucky and Unlucky Days', *Journ. Egyptian Archaeol.*, xii (1926).

3. Examples in *Letters and Exercises of . . . John Conybeare*, ed. F. C. Conybeare (1905), p. 68; *The Gentleman's Magazine Library: Popular Superstitions*, ed. G. L. Gomme (1884), p. 154.

4. Cited by Förster in *Studies in English Philology*, p. 277.

5. See, e.g., C. L. S. Linnell, 'The Commonplace Book of Robert Reynys', *Norfolk Archaeology*, xxxii (1958–61), p. 113; and cf. Webster, *Rest Days*, p. 155; Steele, in *Procs. Royal Soc. Medicine*, xii (1919), p. 120.

Isidore of Seville, viz., the Kalends of April and August, and the last day of December.[5]

Closely parallel to the belief in unlucky days was the notion of climacteric years, those periodic dates in a man's life which were potential turning-points in his health and fortune. This idea was based on the doctrine that a man's body changed its character every seven years and that his life was thus made up of 'septenaries'. Every seventh year was a critical time, according to some authorities; only those multiplied by odd numbers (i.e., the seventh, twenty-first, thirty-fifth, forty-ninth, etc.), according to others. The grand climacteric was usually said to be the sixty-third year, being the one arrived at by multiplying seven by nine, two numbers which Pythagorean philosophy had endowed with mystic significance, for reasons which few sevententh-century believers in the doctrine could have explained. But, though scoffed at by some intellectuals and refuted by the clergy, the idea was taken seriously by many contemporaries: 'nowadays', declared a writer in 1603, 'very few exceed the age of sixty-three, because that year is fatal and climacterical'.[6] Very similar was the notion that certain days of the week or dates of the year had a special significance for certain families or individuals. The co-incidence of Oliver Cromwell's death on 3 September 1658 with the anniversary of his victories at Dunbar and Worcester did much to keep the idea alive during the later seventeenth century.[7]

Many of these superstitions about the inherent quality of different times had been vigorously, if unsuccessfully, combated by the medieval Church (although in 1537 Henry VIII appears to have been unwilling to let the bishops denounce the observance of 'dismal days'

6. A. Gethyn in Ashm. 749, f. 11ᵛ. For other contemporary references, see e.g., T. W(right), *A Succinct Philosophicall Declaration of the Nature of Clymactericall Yeeres* (1604); *H.M.C., Hatfield*, vi, p. 139; vii, p. 266; J. Hart, *The Diet of the Diseased* (1633), chap. 3; B.M., Harley MS 6998, f. 250ᵛ; *Diaries and Letters of Philip Henry*, ed. M. H. Lee (1882), pp. 245, 376; Sir T. Browne, *Pseudodoxia Epidemica* (1646), IV.xii; *Original Letters Illustrative of English History*, ed. H. Ellis (2nd ser., 1827), iii, p. 179; A. Macfarlane, *The Family Life of Ralph Josselin* (Cambridge, 1970), p. 99; *O.E.D., s.v.* 'climacteric'.

7. Extensive lore of this kind is collected in J. Gibbon, *Day-Fatality: or Some Observation of Days Lucky and Unlucky* (1679). cf. J. Smyth, *The Berkeley Manuscripts*, ed. Sir J. Maclean (Gloucester, 1883–5), ii, p. 100; *Crosby Records. A Cavalier's Notebook*, ed. T. E. Gibson (1880), pp. 158–9; J. Barnard, *Theologo-Historicus, or the True Life of . . . Peter Heylyn* (1683), p. 185; Aubrey, *Miscellanies*, pp. 1–24.

in their *Institution of a Christian Man*).[8] Theologians cited the Old Testament warnings about the observance of times in their campaign against the belief in Egyptian days. They also attacked seasonal observances, like giving gifts at the New Year to bring luck to the donor and his possessions.[9] The medieval Church had also had to battle against the allied beliefs which surrounded its own rituals, such as the deeply held notion that certain days were unlucky for the performance of baptism.[10]

But the Church itself had endowed every date in the year with some symbolic significance, and nothing did more than the ecclesiastical calendar to reinforce the conviction that time was uneven in quality. Even after the Reformation, the ecclesiastical year was dotted with seasonal taboos and observances. Abstention from meat on Fridays and during Lent gave certain times a dietary peculiarity. The holy days, on which no work was to be done, acquired an additional significance in the lives of country folk, by breaking up the year into memorable units and making it easier to know when each annual task was due to be carried out. In the mid seventeenth century the Yorkshire farmer, Henry Best, drew heavily upon the Church calendar in his review of the year's work. He knew that lambs conceived at Michaelmas would be born before Candlemas; that the ploughing should be over by Andrewmas; that ewes should go to tup at St Luke; that servants were hired at Martinmas; and that hay fields should not be grazed for more than a fortnight after Lady Day.[11] Certain days thus became traditionally appropriate for particular activities. One let blood on St Stephen's Day, weaned lambs on St Philip and St James, and paid the rent on Lady Day. The six-

8. *Miscellaneous Writings and Letters of Thomas Cranmer*, ed. J. E. Cox (Cambridge, P.S., 1846), p. 100. cf. *Corpus Iuris Canonici*, ed. E. Friedberg (Leipzig, 1879–81), i, col. 1046; G. G. Coulton, *Life in the Middle Ages*, i (Cambridge, 1930), p. 33; G. R. Owst, *The Destructorium Viciorum of Alexander Carpenter* (1952), p. 35, and id., in *Studies Presented to Sir Hilary Jenkinson*, ed. J. C. Davies (1957), pp. 291, 302.

9. E. K. Chambers, *The Medieval Stage* (Oxford, 1903), i, p. 269; *Corpus Iuris Canonici*, ed. Friedberg, i, col. 1046; *Mirk's Festial*, ed. T. Erbe (E.E.T.S. 1905), p. 45; Aubrey, *Gentilisme*, p. 89; above p. 82.

10. Powicke and Cheney, *Councils and Synods*, pp. 247, 297–8, 368, 590, 703, 749, 836.

11. *Rural Economy in Yorkshire in 1641, Being the Farming and Account Books of Henry Best*, ed. C. B. Robinson (Surtees Soc., 1857), pp. 3, 27, 76, 134–5. The relationship between the agrarian and Church calendars in the Middle Ages is discussed by G. C. Homans, *English Villagers of the Thirteenth Century* (Cambridge, Mass, 1941), chap. 23.

teenth-century agricultural writer Thomas Tusser offered scores of such maxims to his readers:

> Set garlic and beans at St Edmund the King.
> Pare saffron between the two St Mary's days.
> Have done sowing wheat before Hallowmas Eve.[12]

Almost all annual fairs similarly occurred on specific saints' days, or their eves or morrows. It was the value of such festivals for marking the days for paying rent, or carrying out other secular activities, which explains why the Elizabethan Church Calendar remained so liberally splattered with black-letter saints' days, even though they were not otherwise celebrated as holidays.[13]

These habits were by no means totally irrational, since in England, as elsewhere, the Church year and the agrarian year were intimately related, even though the coincidence was by no means exact. Aristotle remarks that the chief religious festivals of the ancient Greeks occurred after the ingathering of the crops, 'because at such seasons they had most leisure'. Among the Dark Age people of Northern Europe the great feasts were in the winter, because the rigours of the climate had by then brought most kinds of labour to a halt; the Indians of Ecuador today postpone their *fiestas* and weddings until after the harvest.[14] Up to a point the reservation of certain activities to certain times of the year in Tudor England could be justified by reference to the principle that the harvest should take priority over everything else; it was proverbial that

> They that wive
> Between sickle and scythe
> Shall never thrive.[15]

It was also convenient to limit the opportunities for public celebrations which might lead to disorder.[16]

12. T. Tusser, *Five Hundred Pointes of Good Husbandrie*, ed. W. Payne and S. J. Heritage (1878), pp. 57, 128, 223. There is a typical set of such maximus in *Verus Pater* (1622), sig. C1.

13. C. Wheatly, *A Rational Illustration of the Book of Common Prayer* (Oxford, 1839), p. 54.

14. Aristotle, *Nichomachean Ethics*, 1160a; M. P. Nilsson, *Primitive Time-Reckoning*, trans. F. J. Fielden (Lund, 1920), p. 339; B. R. Salz, 'The Human Element in Industrialization', *Econ. Development and Cultural Change*, iv (1955), p. 99.

15. J. Ray, *A Complete Collection of English Proverbs* (5th edn, by J. Belfour, 1813), p. 47; *Norfolk Archaeology*, ii (1849), p. 303.

16. This idea underlay the Roman *dies fasti*; A. K. Michels, *The Calendar of the Roman Republic* (Princeton, N.J., 1967), p. 21.

But the usual attitude to such observances and taboos was notably less rational. Apart from the fact that some of the rules related to movable feasts like Good Friday, which were inherently unsuitable for use in the agricultural calendar, there was a perpetual tendency to justify calendar observances by reference to traditional authority, rather than by arguments of convenience. The medieval clergy had encouraged this notion that saints' days had a supernatural aura, by emphasizing that a sin committed on a holy day was worse than one committed at some other time,[17] and by disseminating anecdotes about the many divine punishments which befell those who were careless in their observance of the ecclesiastical calendar. After the Reformation such notions lingered. Saints' days like St Swithin's remained critical in many popular systems of weather divination. Others kept their taboo associations. Friday, as the day of the Crucifixion, was thought unlucky for any venture, whether marrying, making a journey or even cutting one's nails. There should be no shoeing or ploughing. One could pick stones, but not disturb the soil.[18] St Loy's Day was also a bad one for shoeing horses.[19] Innocents' Day was exceedingly unlucky: 'we dread to do business on Childermas Day', wrote John Aubrey, and many of his contemporaries agreed. Some even thought it inadvisable to begin any new task on the day of the week on which the previous Childermas had fallen.[20] In the reign of Charles I a Puritan preacher got into trouble with the authorities after preaching against the accepted notion that anyone who worked on one of the twelve days of Christmas would become lousy.[21] In Yorkshire at the same period servants thought Monday an unlucky day for moving to a new employer.[22]

The doctrine of the unevenness of time was also upheld in the Church's regulations for the celebration of marriage. In the Middle Ages there had been various seasons when matrimony was not permitted. According to the *Sarum Manual* there were three: Advent

17. J. Myrc, *Instructions for Parish Priests*, ed. E. Peacock (E.E.T.S., 1868), p. 46.

18. Webster, *Rest Days*, pp. 155–6; Brand, *Popular Antiquities*, iii, p. 178; F. G. Lee, *Glimpses of the Supernatural* (1875), i, pp. 281–2.

19. *Homilies*, p. 226.

20. Aubrey, *Gentilisme*, p. 63; T. Jackson, *A Treatise containing the Originall of Unbeliefe* (1625), p. 158; Brand op. cit., ii, p. 167; T. Gataker, *Of the Nature and Use of Lots* (2nd edn, 1627), p. 352; R. H., 'Astrologia Siderata' (Sloane 412), f. 46^v; *O.E.D.*, *s.v.* 'Childermas'.

21. *C.S.P.D., 1634–5*, p. 361.

22. *Rural Economy in Yorkshire in 1641*, ed. Robinson, p. 135.

Sunday to the Octave of (i.e. eight days after) Epiphany; Septuagesima Sunday to the Octave of Easter; and the Sunday before
Ascension Day to the Octave of Pentecost. After the Reformation
the Council of Trent modified this situation by forbidding the celebration of marriage only in Lent and Advent. But the Church of
England preserved the full medieval prohibitions, and, though not
formally included in the Prayer Book or Canons, they were insisted
upon by many of the bishops in their visitation articles. A licence to
marry during the close season could be purchased at a price, but anyone involved in unauthorized weddings at forbidden times was liable
to prosecution in the ecclesiastical courts.[23] The Puritans, like the
Lollards before them, denounced such prohibitions as superstitious;[24]
and both Convocation and Parliament were the scene of Puritan
attempts to make marriage possible at any time of the year. But
they came to nothing, and the prohibitions were still being enforced
at the beginning of the eighteenth century, after an attempt to include them in the Restoration Prayer Book had been foiled.[25]

Rules of this kind were an ecclesiastical version of the various
ancient traditions about appropriate and inappropriate times for
marriage. In fourteenth-century England, after all, there were those
who thought it imprudent to marry under a waning moon.[26] The
adage that those who married in Lent would live to repent reflected
the ecclesiastical taboo upon sexual intercourse at certain holy times.
The Lenten fast may have originally coincided with a shortage of
food at that time of the year, but it acquired other less utilitarian
connotations. It was regarded by many Catholic clergy as an im-

23. For the times and examples of their enforcement: *Sarum Manual*, p. 45
and n. 1; *The Works of . . . John Cosin* (Oxford, 1843–5), ii, p. 109; Frere and
Kennedy, *Articles and Injunctions*, iii, pp. 85, 142; *2nd Report of the Ritual
Commission* (Parlty. Papers, 1867–8, xxxviii), pp. 464, 471, 493; J. C. Cox,
The Parish Registers of England (1910), pp. 81–2; *V.C.H., Oxon.*, ii, p. 43;
R. M. Serjeantson, *A History of the Church of St Giles, Northampton*
(Northampton, 1911), p. 41; Herts. R.O., A.S.A. 7/17/5.
24. Thomson, *Later Lollards*, p. 157; *Puritan Manifestoes*, ed. W. H. Frere
and C. E. Douglas (1907), p. 127; A. Peel, *The Second Parte of a Register*
(Cambridge, 1915), i, p. 259.
25. J. Strype, *Annals of the Reformation* (2nd edn, 1725–31), i, appx. p.
92; id., *The Life and Acts of John Whitgift* (Oxford, 1822), i, pp. 391–2; E.
Gibson, *Codex Juris Ecclesiastici Anglicani* (1713), i, pp.. 517–18; *C.S.P.D.,
1628–9*, p. 129; E. Cardwell, *Synodalia* (Oxford, 1842), i, p. 134, n.; *The
Archdeacon's Court: Liber Actorum, 1584*, ed. E. R. Brinkworth (Oxon. Rec.
Soc., 1942–6), ii, p. ix.
26. Above, p. 352.

proper time for marital intercourse, and the findings of modern demographers suggest that the Lent period in early modern Europe may have been marked by fewer conceptions than at other times of the year. A study of various English parish registers indicates that Lent was the period of fewest conceptions until the seventeenth century, and of fewest marriages until the early nineteenth.[27]

The Puritans strongly opposed most of these notions. Just as they had attacked the prohibited seasons for marriage, so they castigated the observance of Lent,[28] the St Swithin's type of divination,[29] and the celebration of saints' days in general. As one Jacobean satirist makes a Puritan declare,

> it was a passing folly
> To think one day more than another holy.[30]

In the place of the traditional year, dotted irregularly with Church festivals, the Puritans urged a regular routine of six days work followed by a sabbath rest; and they did so with such effect that by the end of the seventeenth century their ideas had been more or less generally accepted by society as a whole.[31] This change in working habits constituted an important step towards the social acceptance of the modern motion of time as even in quality, as opposed to the primitive sense of time's unevenness and irregularity.

But just as the Jewish Sabbath had begun as a taboo day, so the Puritan Sunday was originally regarded by its supporters as a strict rule to be observed to the letter, however inconvenient the practical consequences. Hence the extreme position of some Puritans that it

27. R. Mols, *Introduction à la démographie historique des villes d'Europe* (Louvain, 1954-6), ii, pp. 298–9; *L.P.*, xviii(2), p. 293; R. R. Kucynski, 'British Demographers' Opinions on Fertility, 1660–1760', *Annals of Eugenics*, vi (1935), p. 147; U. M. Cowgill, 'Historical Study of the Seasons of Birth in the City of York, England', *Nature*, ccix (1966), p. 1069; L. Bradley, 'An Enquiry into Seasonality in Baptisms, Marriages and Burials', *Local Population Studies*, 4–6 (1970–71). cf. E. Takahashi, 'Seasonal Variation of Conception and Suicide', *Tokohu Journ. Experimental Medicine*, lxxxiv (1965), p. 219.

28. e.g., J. Hitchcock, 'Religious Conflict at Mapperton, 1597–9', *Procs. Dorset Natl Hist. and Archaeol. Soc.*, lxxxix (1967), p. 228.

29. J. Booker, *Telescopium Uranicum* (1665), sig. C8ᵛ; *Diaries and Letters of Philip Henry*, ed. Lee, p. 142; T. Gataker, *His Vindication of the Annotations* (1653), pp. 125–6.

30. *The Letters and Epigrams of Sir John Harington*, ed. N. E. McClure (Philadelphia, 1930), p. 179.

31. See C. Hill, *Society and Puritanism in Pre-revolutionary England* (1964), chap. 5.

was wrong to travel on Sunday, to cook food, or, according to some sectarians, even to eat it. When the preacher of a funeral sermon for a Surrey gentleman in 1651 commended the dead man for his pious refusal to send for a doctor – because the day on which he had fallen ill happened to be a Sunday[32] – the element of rational calculation in Sunday observance was being patently eclipsed by assumptions of a more primitive kind. Sabbatarianism, as exported by Christian missions in more recent times, rested on supernatural sanctions. When the missionaries explained to the Eskimos that no work should be done on Sundays, the Eskimos thought that they had at last discovered the reason for their misfortunes and observed the new rule strictly.[33] In the seventeenth century, the connection between sabbatarianism and material prosperity was fully accepted by many contemporary preachers, but they usually assumed that it was brought about by divine action, rather than by utilitarian considerations about the most economical way of organizing human labour, of the kind which were to appeal to their Victorian successors. The mystical attributes which Sunday held for some contemporaries are well symbolized by a magical charm which dates from Anglo-Saxon times, but was common in the seventeenth century; it guaranteed the wearer's preservation from all danger, provided he abstained from all labour on the sabbath, right down to washing his face or combing his hair.[34]

So even the Puritans were able to emancipate themselves fully from the assumption that time was uneven in quality and that some occasions were inherently more propitious for performing critical actions than others. The valuable side-effects of such ideas were obvious enough: by confining important ventures to limited periods of the year, they emphasized their critical nature, and concentrated attention upon the need to carry them through carefully. For the belief in lucky and unlucky days usually related to non-routine

32. E. Hinton, *The Vanity of Selfe-Boasters* (Oxford, 1651), p. 51. For the objection to eating on Sunday, C. Burrage, *The Early English Dissenters* (Cambridge, 1912), ii, p. 23. For similar prohibitions, cf. H. T. Buckle, *History of Civilization in England* (1904), iii, p. 275, n. 538.

33. L. Lévy-Bruhl, *Primitives and the Supernatural*, trans. L. A. Clare (1936), p. 50. cf. M. Wilson, *Communal Rituals of the Nyakyusa* (1959), p. 181.

34. C. A. Parker, 'A Seventeenth-century Charm', *Trans. Cumb. and Westmld Antiqn and Archaeol. Soc.*, n.s., xii (1912); *Folk-Lore*, xxviii (1917), pp. 318–19; *County Folk-Lore*, V, ed. Mrs Gutch and M. Peacock (Folk-Lore Soc., 1908), pp. 91–3, 126–7.

activities: getting married, moving house, undergoing surgical operations; the ones in which forethought and close attention were most required. The saints' days and sabbaths, however, put a stop to routine activities as well.. Such communal observances helped to make for social solidarity, by imposing an identical pattern of work and leisure upon individuals whose activities were otherwise differentiated. There were no 'staggered' holidays in the seventeenth century.

The belief in lucky and unlucky days also had an explanatory function. It could account for the success of one venture and the failure of another. All men wish to know the reason for their fortunes, remarked a seventeenth-century sceptic, and, in the absence of any more obvious factors, '*time* and *place* ... are ... reputed lords or disposers of success, good or bad, to which no cause apparent makes evident claim'.[35]

But, essentially, these beliefs about the unevenness of time were the natural product of a society which was fundamentally agrarian in character, and relatively primitive in its technology. They reflected the uneven value which time inevitably possessed for those engaged in agriculture or simple manufacturing operations in which the weather was a crucial factor. The sundry doctrines about unlucky days, saints' days, climacteric years, leap years, etc., were all more easily acceptable in a society dependent upon the seasons for its basic living pattern. The old Church calendar was based on the needs of a people living close to the soil, whereas the Puritan demand for a weekly rhythm in place of a seasonal one emanated from the towns, not the countryside. Even in late medieval England it was notorious that countrymen had a stronger belief in the varying quality of time than did their urban counterparts. 'In cities and towns,' said a fifteenth-century writer, 'men rule them by the clock.'[36] It was the development of more precise methods of mechanical time-reckoning which was to make possible the spread of the mathematical conception of time as a sort of unbroken and uniform tape-measure. By the later seventeenth century the increasing diversity of economic life was breaking up the seasonal routine which had previously governed the lives of most inhabitants; while the invention of the pendulum clock (1657) at last made it possible to keep accurate time. These changes meant that the Newtonian conception of

35. Jackson, *A Treatise containing the Originall of Unbeliefe*, p. 156.
36. *Dives and Pauper* (1536), f. 30ᵛ.

TIMES AND OMENS 745

time as continuously flowing and equable in quality was not just intellectually valid; it had also become socially acceptable. Older attitudes to time duly withered away. John Ray deliberately omitted from his pioneering collection of English proverbs (published in 1703) 'all superstitious and groundless observations of augury, days, hours, and the like', because he wanted them expunged from popular memory. In 1714 a writer declared of the belief in lucky and unlucky days that 'some weak and ignorant persons may perhaps regard such things, but men of understanding despise them'.[37]

2. Omens and prohibitions

The observance of times was but one of the ways in which the inhabitants of sixteenth- and seventeenth-century England thought it possible to avoid bad luck. The same concern lay behind a multitude of other beliefs which we know to have been widely current, even though we have no means of measuring their precise extent and distribution. This last category to be considered comprises a miscellaneous variety of actions and circumstances which were thought to bring unfavourable consequences in their train for some unstated reason. They have their modern counterpart in the notion that bad luck follows the person who spills the salt or walks under a ladder. In earlier times the list of such omens and prohibitions was much longer. 'We have an infinite number ... used amongst us,' wrote a contemporary in 1612.[38]

Up to a point it is possible to rationalize such practices. Some were no more than conservative warnings against the perils of departing from established ways. Even today it is bad to get out of the 'wrong' (i.e. unaccustomed) side of the bed. In the seventeenth century, it was unlucky to disinherit an eldest son, or to lose one of the heirlooms or 'lucks', upon whose safe transmission the welfare of various noble families was thought to depend. The 'luck' was a symbol of

37. Ray, *A Complete Collection of English Proverbs*, p. xv; W. Taswell, *The Church of England not Superstitious* (1714), p. 38.
38. J. Mason, *The Anatomie of Sorcerie* (Cambridge, 1612), p. 90. Typical lists may be found in Scot, *Discoverie*, XI.xiii, xv; G. Gifford, *A Discourse of the Subtill Practises of Devilles* (1587), sigs. C1ᵛ–C2; *The Workes of ... William Perkins* (Cambridge, 1616–18), i, p. 43; J. Melton, *Astrologaster* (1620), pp. 45–7; Bernard, *Guide*, p. 183; *The Works of ... Joseph Hall*, ed. P. Wynter (Oxford, 1863), vi, pp. 109–10; N. Homes, *Daemonologie* (1650), pp. 59–61; Aubrey, *Gentilisme*, p. 26 and *passim*; Brand, *Popular Antiquities*, iii, pp. 160 ff.

continuity and its possession was sometimes even taken as evidence of the holder's title.[39]

Other prohibitions can be seen as prudential injunctions: given the hazards of child-bearing, it is not difficult to guess why it was thought unlucky to choose a pregnant woman as godmother for one's child.[40] Some sprang from a recognizable association of ideas: thirteen was an unlucky number at the table,[41] because of the Last Supper; it was unlucky to make an early will, because many people died after doing so.[42] There were prohibitions reflecting obsolete legal restrictions: the medieval Church had forbidden clerics to go hunting; hence the belief that it was unlucky to be accompanied by a clergyman on a hunting expedition.[43] Other rules clearly helped to sustain the working conventions of daily life: a butcher or horse-dealer who had 'cheapened' (i.e. bargained for) an animal was expected to wish it well if he declined to buy; should the beast die after being spurned, he might be held responsible.[44]

But the limits to such superficial rationalization are easily reached. Why did the men of Cleveland think it wrong to whistle after dark? Why was it lucky to find a four-leaved clover, or old iron, or to have drink spilt on one? Why did significance attach to odd numbers and even numbers, left or right sides? Why did everyone agree that it was bad luck to stumble at the threshold or to wear a diamond wedding-ring? Why was it so fatal to kill swallows that even robbing their nests was thought by 'some old beldames ... a more fearful sacrilege than to steal a chalice out of a church'?[45]

Similar puzzles are posed by the apparently arbitrary selection of actions and objects thought likely to bring supernatural protection.

39. C. R. Beard, *Lucks and Talismans* (n.d.), pp. 34–5, and chap. 5.

40. *Original Letters illustrative of English History*, ed. Ellis (3rd ser., 1846), ii, p. 226.

41. J. Puckle, *The Club* (1711; 1900 edn), p. 157; Brand, *Popular Antiquities*, iii, pp. 264–5.

42. P. S. Clarkson and C. T. Warren, *The Law of Property in Shakespeare and the Elizabethan Drama* (Baltimore, 1942), p. 236.

43. *Dives and Pauper*, f. 68; Scot, *Discoverie*, XI.xv.

44. Scot, *Discoverie*, XVI.viii. There is an accusation arising from an incident of this kind in Gloucester D.R., 50 (1582).

45. 'A Description of Cleveland', *Topographer and Genealogist*, ii (1853), pp. 428–9; Aubrey, *Gentilisme*, pp. 20, 26, 56, 114; Mason, *Anatomie of Sorcerie*, p. 90; Scot, *Discoverie*, XI.xiii, xv; T. Fuller, *The Holy State* (2nd edn, Cambridge, 1648), p. 208; Jackson, *A Treatise containing the Originall of Unbeliefe*, p. 177.

The virtue attributed to certain material entities far exceeded their natural qualities: bay trees offered a protection against thunderstorms; south-running water had magical qualities; vervain and fern seed kept away evil spirits; milk could put out a fire started by lightning; the caul in which a child was born would bring good fortune.[46] It is unlikely that any purely utilitarian theory could ever convincingly explain why these objects were credited with such power, but not others.

The same difficulty is presented by the miscellaneous signs and omens which contemporaries detected in the natural world around them. The behaviour of birds and animals was often given a prognosticatory power: chattering magpies meant that guests were coming; ravens might fortell the plague; a hare crossing one's path augured bad luck.[47] We are familiar enough with such notions today, for we all know that black cats are lucky (or unlucky), and that one magpie is for sorrow but two for joy. But we lack the volume of comparable lore possessed by every seventeenth-century countryman. Neither do we have the same disposition to see portentous significance in trivial events; it would be difficult to imagine the House of Commons reacting in the manner of its Elizabethan predecessor in 1601, when the Lord Treasurer's secretary fainted in the middle of a debate, and 'it was strange to hear the diversity of opinions touching the accident, some saying it was *malum omen*, others that it was *bonum omen*'.[48]

Sophisticated contemporaries often dismissed these various notions as superstitious nonsense. The medieval Church had sternly rejected the belief that birds or animals might be omens of bad luck; and there were many medieval writers who regarded such ideas as the fantasies of ignorant peasants, though admitting that only too often they were also held by 'lewd clerks'.[49] Tudor and Stuart sceptics

46. Browne, *Pseudodoxia Epidemica*, II.vi.6 (bay trees); Jackson, op. cit., pp. 176, 179–80 (vervain and south-running water); *Folk-Lore Journ.*, vi (1888), p. 211 (milk); above, p. 222 (caul).

47. For these and similar beliefs, see *C.S.P.D., 1665–6*, p. 51; R. Bovet, *Pandaemonium*, ed. M. Summers (Aldington, 1951), pp. 130–31; T. C., *Isagoge ad Dei Providentiam* (1672), p. 515.

48. *The Journals of all the Parliaments during the Reign of Queen Elizabeth*, ed. Sir S. D'Ewes (1682), p. 688.

49. Kittredge, *Witchcraft*, p. 45; Owst, *The Destructorium Viciorum of Alexander Carpenter*, p. 34, n. 6; W. A. Pantin, *The English Church in the Fourteenth Century* (Cambridge, 1955), p. 209.

pointed out how such beliefs exploited the power of the imagination. A man who felt that his venture was doomed, because he had stumbled on the threshold when setting out, was usually right, since his heart would no longer be in it. According to his expectations of success or failure, his resolution would be strengthened or weakened, with predictable consequences. 'How certainly will the best cause fall to the ground,' remarked a writer in 1665, 'where the hands which are to support it are weakened by an opinion of some unpromising omen.' This was the line taken by Reginald Scot, Robert Burton, Bishop Sprat and others.[50] Some of these writers pressed the matter further, by trying to uncover the 'rational' foundations on which they assumed some apparently baseless superstitions must have rested. They pointed to the natural causes underlying the behaviour of animals and plants. It was not absurd to use birds as a means of weather prediction, for they might respond more quickly to changes in the air than did humans. It was possible that the rising of a stream near Croydon might indeed presage plague as the local inhabitants believed, for a wet year was often a sickly one. It might well be true that unchaste women were unable to pass through St Wilfrid's needle, the narrow passage in the undercroft of Ripon Minster, for if they were pregnant they would be too large to pass through the crevice.[51] In such ways did seventeenth-century inquirers deal with the popular superstitions of the time. Even when their explanations seem unconvincing, they do at least provide evidence for the change in the intellectual climate. 'Rationalism' of this kind was not new, but it had never been so systematically applied.

Relatively little advance has been made since the seventeenth century in explaining just why it is that men attach superstitious significance to trivial happenings. In modern times three different approaches have been made to the problem, each of them suggestive up to a point, but none of them fully convincing. These may for convenience be termed the utilitarian, the functional and the sym-

---

50. J. Spencer, *A Discourse concerning Vulgar Prophecies* (appended to *A Discourse concerning Prodigies* [1665]), p. 9; Scot, *Discoverie*, XI.xvii; Burton, *Anatomy*, i, pp. 363–4; T. Sprat, *History of the Royal Society*, ed. J. I. Cope and H. W. Jones (St Louis, 1959), pp. 364–5; Brand, *Popular Antiquities*, i, p. 130.

51. Gifford, *A Discourse of the Subtill Practises of Devilles*, sig. C2; J. Childrey, *Britannia Baconica* (1661), pp. 54–5, 163–4, cf. Bacon, *Works*, ii, p. 576; iv, p. 296; W. Charleton, *Physiologia-Epicuro-Gassendo Charltoniana* (1654), pp. 350–51.

bolic. Thus, if we take the example of the bad luck believed to come from spilling the salt, the utilitarian explanation is that salt was a valuable commodity in short supply, which it was important that men should not spill unnecessarily. On this interpretation the objects to which magical importance are attached are those bearing obvious social importance. The limitations of this approach have already been seen. Many of the omens, prohibitions and magically useful commodities seem to have had no utilitarian significance at all, while many of those which were socially useful lacked any magical meaning.

The second approach is the functional one. Here, importance is placed on the socially useful consequences of the belief in question, regardless of its intrinsic merits. Thus a prohibition on salt-spilling standardizes behaviour along useful lines, by preventing waste and encouraging restrained behaviour at table. It also serves as a convenient excuse for any subsequent misfortune, in that it diverts attention from an individual's error or carelessness in execution, by suggesting that the failure of the venture was due to external circumstances beyond his control. Such superstitions, it is argued, are particularly likely to surround critical human activities or states; marriage, pregnancy, travel, difficult technical operations. They are valuable because they focus attention on the meticulous discharge of the particular operation being carried out. Although this interpretation helps to explain the endurance of some of these beliefs, it has nothing to say about their origins as such, and it is positively unilluminating when confronted by rituals and prohibitions lacking functional consequences of any apparent value; for example, the notion that it was unlucky to pass a hare on the road, or that a man should hold his left thumb in his right hand when hiccuping.[52]

The third approach is the symbolic. This starts from the assumption that to understand why it was unlucky to spill salt one must first ask what it was that salt symbolized to contemporaries. This can be done psycho-analytically, as for example in the suggestion that salt is a symbol of semen and that the objection to spilling it reflects an unconscious fear of *ejaculatio praecox*.[53] There are limits to this approach. But the inquiry can also be conducted on the assumption that the idea of salt is only meaningful when it can be fitted back into its place in a system of primitive classification, a private langu-

52. Scot, *Discoverie*, XI.xv.
53. This characteristic explanation is offered by E. Jones, *Essays in Applied Psycho-Analysis* (1923), chap. iv.

age of which it is or was a structural part. This is the method of the structural anthropologists, led by Claude Lévi-Strauss. It is they who have shown that primitive peoples have elaborate systems of classification, linguistic means of ordering their experience. These systems may involve postulating symbolic analogies between human beings and plants, animals or birds and other .parts of natural creation. Around such polarities as left and right, black and white, male and female, are organized elaborate correspondences and analogies. Ritual prohibitions only make sense within this overall framework. The meaning attached to spilling salt, for example, can only be discovered when the idea of 'salt' is fitted back into the system. The symbols themselves are arbitrarily chosen. They have no meaning, save that given by their position within the code. To understand why importance is attached to any particular omen, ritual, prohibition or magical object, one has first to find the 'master-plan'. The symbolic meaning of salt cannot be guessed from its intrinsic qualities. One has to break the 'code'.[54]

Successful though this approach may be when applied to the culturally unified world of primitive peoples, it is doubtful whether much progress can be made with it when dealing with the beliefs of a sophisticated and heterogeneous society, like that of sixteenth- and seventeenth-century England. It is true that thinking by analogy and correspondence had been popular since classical times, and was an essential part of the influential microcosm-macrocosm theory. But the number of 'codes' or 'private languages' which contributed to the cultural inheritance of the period is too great for the constituent elements to be easily disentangled. What we are faced by in this period is not one single code but an amalgam of the cultural debris of many different ways of thinking, Christian and pagan, Teutonic and classical; and it would be absurd to claim that all these elements had been shuffled together to form a new and coherent system. It is possible to investigate the symbolic associations of any individual object, but the results are usually too miscellaneous to be helpful. The hare, for example, was the attendant of the pagan goddess Freya. It was also associated with the harelip, that is, deformity. Who is to say which of these associations gave it its inauspicious character for Tudor countryfolk?[55] How for that matter can one

54. For this approach, see, e.g., C. Lévi-Strauss, *The Savage Mind* (Eng. trans., 1966); and *Totemism*, trans. R. Needham (Harmondsworth, 1969).
55. cf. W. G. Black, 'The Hare in Folk-Lore', *Folk-Lore Journ.*, i (1883);

determine which of salt's many different symbolic roles has ensured its place in popular superstition? In the Old Testament salt symbolizes a bond or covenant. In the medieval Church it was used to drive away evil spirits. In more modern times it has variously been associated with value, bitterness, hospitality, scepticism and social distinction.[56] There is no way of telling which of these roles generated and sustained the belief that it was unlucky to spill it.

There is plenty of scope for future inquiry into the symbolic associations of the various objects which bore portentous significance. Superstition has been defined as 'an unorganised series of survivals of earlier cult practices'.[57] But this is to beg the question. The fact that salt, or black cats, or ladders, may have had some earlier religious significance is not necessarily the reason that they possess superstitious value today. For many elements in ancient religions have disappeared, and those which have apparently survived may have in fact acquired new meanings. By our period the original meaning of such symbols had invariably been lost or distorted. Men observed these rules because they had been brought up to do so, not because they still formed a meaningful part of a language which anyone could speak. It was precisely because such superstitions rested on so obscure a basis that they were to become increasingly unacceptable to the questioning minds of the later seventeenth century.

ii (1884), pp. 25–6; v (1887), pp. 263–5; vii (1889), pp. 23–4; *Folk-Lore*, iii (1892), pp. 441–6.

56. *O.E.D.*, s.v. 'salt'.
57. By E. O. J(ames) in *Chambers Encyclopaedia* (1950 edn), 'superstition'.

CONCLUSION

21.

SOME INTERCONNECTIONS

Whereof I say no more, but that S. Anthony's bliss will help your
pig, whensoever Mother Bungie doth hurt it with her curse.

> Reginald Scot, *Discoverie*, VIII, i

The Fifth-Monarchy ... most resembles Mahomet's coming to
the Turks, and King Arthur's reign over the Britons in Merlin's
prophecies; so near of kin are all fantastic illusions, that you
may discern the same lineaments in them all.

> Samuel Butler, *Characters and Passages
> from Note-Books*, ed. A. R. Waller
> (Cambridge, 1908), p. 46

1. *The unity of magical beliefs*

AFTER so long a survey of so many different aspects of the mental
life of sixteenth- and seventeenth-century England, it is time to pull
together the threads of the argument. First, we must emphasize the
interrelatedness of the main magical beliefs. The links between
magic, astrology and witchcraft were both intellectual and practical.
On the intellectual level, astrology provided a coherent justification
for geomancy, palmistry, physiognomy and similar activities. 'All
these skills of divination are rooted and grounded upon astrology,'
declared Cornelius Agrippa.[1] By postulating correspondences between the heavenly bodies and earthly substances, the palmists and
physiognomists assigned different parts of the face or hand to different signs of the zodiac. Geomancy employed the twelve astrological
houses, and, according to the leading textbook on the subject, was
'none other thing but astrology'.[2] Alchemy also divided up the
metals between the planets, and could be described as mere 'kitchen
magic or chimney astrology'.[3] The astrological choice of times was

1. H. C. Agrippa, *Of the Vanitie and Uncertainty of Artes and Sciences*,
trans. J. San(ford) (1569), f. 54.
2. *The Geomancie of Maister Christopher Cattan* (1591), sig. C2. Ralph
Treswell, who advertised his ability to solve questions by geomancy in 1616,
used almost the same words: *A Publication of Surveying* (1616), sig. B1
(apparently unique copy in History of Science Museum, Oxford).
3. J. Gaule, *The Mag-Astro-Mancer, or the Magicall-Astrologicall-Diviner
Posed, and Puzzled* (1652), p. 192.

important, not only for alchemical operations, but also for the ritual gathering of magical herbs and the conjuration of spirits. According to Robert Fludd, even the choice of ingredients for the weapon-salve had to be determined by astrological investigation;[4] while the witch Ellen Green confessed in 1619 that her spirits came to suck her blood at certain phases of the moon.[5]

The intellectual links between these different beliefs were emphasized by their practical associations with each other. The astrologers themselves were often men of wide-ranging activity. Forman practised astrology, geomancy, medicine, divination by facial moles, alchemy and conjuring. Ashmole's activities were equally diverse. Richard Saunders wrote a series of textbooks on chiromancy and physiognomy. Even Lilly, who did more than anyone to 'purify' astrology, also practised conventional medicine, spirit-raising, treasure hunting and the conjuration of angels and fairies. It is not surprising that a clergyman preaching to the Society of Astrologers in 1649 felt it necessary to warn his hearers to stick to their last: 'Some falling by the ill practice of your lawful art have become, of magi, magicians, and, of wise men, wizards.'[6]

The links between magic and astrology illustrate the way in which the various types of magical or semi-magical belief propped each other up. Like the cunning men, the astrologers dealt with many patients who thought themselves bewitched and hence helped to sustain the belief in witchcraft. Indeed both Richard Saunders and Joseph Blagrave went so far as to declare that astrological diagnosis was the *only* sure way by which witchcraft could be discovered. White witches and cunning men they dismissed as mere cheats, or confederates in league with the black witches.[7] Lilly's case-books contain well over fifty cases of suspected witchcraft altogether, no less than twenty-three of them occurring between Midsummer 1654

---

4. *Doctor Fludds Answer unto M. Foster* (1631), pp. 47–8, 134 ('135').
5. *The Wonderful Discoverie of the Witchcrafts of Margaret and Phillip Flower* (1619), sig. F2v.
6. R. Gell, *Stella Nova* (1649), p. 21.
7. R. Saunders, *The Astrological Judgment and Practice of Physick* (1677), p. 80; J. Blagrave, *Blagraves Astrological Practice of Physick* (1671), p. 124 (misprinted as 140). For astrological rules on witchcraft, see, e.g., Ashm. 1473, p. 63 (Napier); W. Andrews, *The Astrological Physitian* (1656), pp. 74–8; W. W(illiams), *Occult Physick* (1660), p. 158; R. Saunders, *Palmistry* (1663), ii, pp. 143–4, 186–7; W. Salmon, *Synopsis Medicinae* (1671), pp. 50–52; *Thesaurus Astrologiae*, ed. J. Gadbury (1647), p. 238; J. Middleton, *Practical Astrology* (1679), p. 91; R. Ball, *Astrology Improv'd* (2nd edn, 1693), p. 30.

and September 1656.[8] But there are only five in which his verdict survives, and in each one it is negative. One client was told that he was not bewitched, but merely suffering from an occult disease in his private parts, 'occasioned by too much venerian sports'; a noble-woman was assured that she would not die of witchcraft but could count upon a natural death; a gentleman and a silk-weaver's wife at Shoreditch were each told that they were not bewitched; and another case was dismissed as one of 'dropsy stone'.[9]

But there is no doubt that other astrologers did sometimes confirm witchcraft suspicions. John Dee is known to have diagnosed witchcraft by a neighbour.[10] The Norfolk shoemaker, Christopher Hall, was consulted in 1654 on behalf of a woman with cancer of the breast. After erecting an astrological scheme he declared that the cause of her disease was one of the 'three witches' in her own village of Hillington.[11] Such pronouncements were no different in their effects from those made by the cunning men. Astrologers were happy to be regarded as complete authorities on witchcraft, to take all suspicions seriously, and to prescribe measures for the patient's recovery. In this way the belief in witchcraft was constantly reinforced by their activities.

But astrology and witchcraft usually functioned as rival systems of explanation, since to attribute a disaster to the malignity of a neighbour meant ruling out the possibility that it might have an astral cause. Thus in 1635 a patient, 'taken ill with a mopishness', came to Sir Richard Napier because he 'feared he was bewitched or blasted by an ill planet'.[12] It was common to invoke the planets as the direct cause of a mysterious disease. Until well into the eighteenth century the London Bills of Mortality contained frequent instances of deaths attributed simply to 'planet': there were three, for example, in 1662, six in 1665, and four in 1679. To be thus 'planet-struck' or 'blasted' was to be suddenly and inexplicably affected by a paralysing disease, apoplexy, or other kind of sudden death.[13] An animal which lost the

8. Ashm. 427, ff. 5, 38ᵛ, 40ᵛ, 54ᵛ, 60ᵛ, 67ᵛ, 75, 81ᵛ, 87ᵛ, 105, 121ᵛ, 124, 136ᵛ, 173, 191, 216, 219, 220ᵛ, 227, 243ᵛ, 244ᵛ, 255, 273 (of which one relates to a haunted house).

9. Lilly, *Christian Astrology*, pp. 468–9; Ashm. 184, ff. 79, 82ᵛ; W. Lilly, *Merlini Anglici Ephemeris* (1651), sig. F8; Ashm. 427, f. 5.

10. Josten, *Ashmole*, p. 1299.

11. D. E. H. James, 'Rex *versus* Hall – a Case of Witchcraft, 1654', *Norfolk Archaeology*, xxx (1952).

12. Ashm. 412, f. 235ᵛ (my italics).

13. J. Graunt, *Natural and Political Observations* (3rd edn, 1665), p. 26.

use of a limb was similarly said to have been 'planet-struck',[14] just as a person who was mad or distracted might be called 'moon-struck'.[15] The term was also applied to the sudden destruction of growing corn.[16] The cunning folk specialized in dealing with these cases of persons 'taken under an ill planet', in the same way as they dealt with those who had been bewitched. When the Mayor of Rye fell sick at the beginning of the seventeenth century, Susan Snapper was told by a spirit to go to a cunning woman to get some 'planet-water'. Similarly in 1693 the London quack Mary Green claimed to have cured a man who had been 'struck by a planet on his left arm'.[17] In the late nineteenth century white witches were still sometimes known as 'planet-rulers'.[18] Anne Baker, accused of witch-craft in Leicestershire in 1619, elaborated on the mythology of planets, declaring that they came in four colours, 'black, yellow, green and blue, and that black is always death'; she had seen the blue planet strike one Thomas Fairebarne. Here 'planets' seem to have grown into familiars or evil spirits.[19] Her account strongly re-sembles that given by the Dorset cunning man John Walsh in 1566, not of planets, but of 'fairies', which he said came in three types – white, green and black – and the black one always meant death.[20]

This blurring of different magical beliefs was characteristic of the period. The more ambitious astrologers endeavoured to maintain some distinction by subordinating all other activities to the rules of their own art. But the place of astrology at the top of the hierarchy was not so easily preserved. Lilly himself conceded the possibility of knowledge by direct angelic revelation; 'many now living' had

14. e.g. (G. Markham), *Cheape and Good Husbandry for the Well-Order-ing of all Beasts* (1614), p. 13.

15. R. Hunter and I. Macalpine, *Three Hundred Years of Psychiatry, 1535–1860* (1963), p. 131. For 'moon-disease', see J. C. Hodgson, 'The Diary of Timothy Whittingham of Holmside', *Archaeologia Aeliana*, 3rd ser., xxi (1924), p. 208.

16. *Verus Pater* (1622), sig. B6ᵛ (which prescribes bonfires of horn-shavings and animal dung as a remedy [sig. B8]).

17. G. S. Butler, 'Appearance of Spirits in Sussex', *Sussex Archaeol. Collns.*, xiv (1862), p. 31; C. J. S. Thompson, *The Quacks of Old London* (1928), p. 146. For similar claims by another female empiric, see C. Goodall, *The Royal College of Physicians of London* (1684), pp. 354–5.

18. *O.E.D.*, s.v. 'planet'. cf. E. P(oeton), 'The Winnowing of White Witch-craft' (Sloane, 1954), f. 175ᵛ; Bernard, *Guide*, p. 143.

19. *The Wonderful Discoverie of . . . Phillip Flower*, sig. D4.

20. *The Examination of John Walsh* (1566), sig. Av.

been so helped, he thought; alchemy indeed could be learned no other way.[21] According to Reginald Scot some held that even knowledge of astrology could be thus acquired: there was a spirit named *Bifrons* who could make men 'wonderful cunning' in the subject.[22] Some of the lower-grade astrologers had recourse to many traditional kinds of counter-magic.[23] If their practice had an intellectual basis it was a hopelessly confused one.

The one widely practised type of magic which rested on clearly stated astrological foundations was the construction of astrological sigils and talismans, in which appropriate heavenly influences were caught like fruit as they fell and stored up for use when needed. By capturing these astral emanations, the astrologers could divert the power of the heavens to their own ends. So they cast sigils in copper and tin, engraved with astrological symbols and dedicated at astrologically propitious moments; and they used them for all the traditional magical purposes: to procure the favour of great persons and to win the love of women, to keep wives faithful, to guard against diseases and the power of witchcraft, and to give immunity from thunder and lightning. In 1667 Lilly sent a trunkload of them to Ashmole, describing them as 'the greatest arcanas any private person in Europe hath; they were the ten years collection of the Lord Bothwell, given to Sir R. Holborn and by him unto me'.[24] Ashmole frequently employed such remedies at times of personal crisis. He used them against the fleas and mice which infested his house, and for his wife's attacks of vomiting. As a parliamentary candidate for Lichfield in 1678, he cast magic sigils 'for increase of honour and estimation with great men'. Forman, Napier and many of the others had also used magic of this kind.[25] In the 1690s Henry Coley,

21. W. Lilly, *The Starry Messenger* (1645), p. 11; id., *Christian Astrology*, pp. 442–3.

22. Scot, *Discoverie*, XV.ii.

23. For their recommendation of written charms, herbs, and other traditional remedies against witchcraft, see, e.g., Blagrave, *Blagraves Astrological Practice of Physick*, pp. 168–73, 174–5, 183; *Culpeper's School of Physick* (1659), pp. 118, 149.

24. Josten, *Ashmole*, p. 1076. Typical instructions for making sigils may be found in I. Hibner, *Mysterium Sigillorum*, trans. B. Clayton (1698), pp. 158–93.

25. Josten, *Ashmole*, pp. 226, 227, 245, 537, n. 3, 565, 1533, 1539; E. Ashmole, *Theatrum Chemicum Britannicum* (1652), pp. 463–5; Sloane 3822, and Ashm. 431, ff. 122ᵛ, 144–6 (Forman); Ashm. 240, f. 126, and Lilly, *Autobiography*, p. 124 (Napier).

Lilly's adopted 'son', and successor in his astrological practice, was said to be selling astrological sigils at four shillings each, for use as contraceptives by servant-girls.[26] Astrology thus led on to magic, conjuring, alchemy and the limitless horizons of magical investigation. 'Judicial astrology is the key of natural magic,' wrote Ashmole, 'and natural magic the door that leads to this blessed stone.'[27]

Up to a point, of course, astrology was a different type of activity from the magic of the village wizards. It had an elaborate theoretical basis and appealed to educated persons, who could study it for sheer intellectual pleasure. It also offered a more comprehensive service; the wise woman could not provide her clients with such systematic advice about future decisions or so elaborate a character-analysis of themselves or their relatives. Nevertheless, the basic ingredients of astrological practice were much the same as those of the village wizard: lost goods, missing persons, sickness and disease. It is doubtful whether many clients saw any difference between the two types of practitioner. They went to the astrologer, half-expecting him to engage in magic: one of Booker's callers recoiled when he saw the astrologer's clock in its glass case, protesting that 'he would not see things in a glass'.[28] John Gadbury complained that 'some among us, that wear the golden name of astrologers ... very commonly, under pretence thereof, make use of a crystal and other pretended cheats and shifts to gull the sillier sort of people'.[29] There were plenty of would-be astrologers who resorted to sundry kinds of hocus-pocus in order to impress their customers, just as there were conjurers, like William Marsh, the Papist astrologer of Dunstable, who confided to an acquaintance that he used astrology simply as a cover, 'and ... did his business by the help of the blessed spirits'.[30] Both Patrick and Richard Saunders used a crystal ball.[31]

Astrology, however, long retained the capacity to lift itself above most other types of popular magic because of its pretensions to be a genuinely scientific system. Not all its practitioners betrayed their principles by dabbling indiscriminately in other types of magic, or

26. H. G. Dick in *Journ. of Hist. of Medicine*, i (1946), p. 426.
27. Ashmole, *Theatrum Chemicum Britannicum*, p. 443.
28. Ashm. 183, p. 500.
29. Quoted by H. G. Dick in his edition of T. Tomkis, *Albumazar: a Comedy (1615)* (Berkeley and Los Angeles, 1944), p. 37.
30. Aubrey, *Miscellanies*, p. 161.
31. Ashm. 419, ii, f. 1; *William Lilly ... His Past and Present Opinions* (1660), sig. A1ᵛ.

including Galfridian prophecies in their almanacs. John Gadbury, for example, represented the purest kind of astrological rationalism. He opposed the use of astrological sigils, just as he scoffed at the employment of charms in medicine. He was as contemptuous of the way in which Lilly and Culpepper cited the prophecies of the sibyls or Mother Shipton as he was of the delusions of the Fifth Monarchists and the 'judgements' and 'prodigies' collected by the Dissenters. He had never seen a case of witchcraft, he declared, which could not be reduced 'to a natural astral cause'. For him astrology was a purely natural system of divination, based on the meticulous study of cause and effect.[32] It was this aspect of the subject which enabled it to retain prestige among many educated persons who had no respect for charms or other kinds of popular magic.

2. Magic and religion

The unity of the various magical beliefs is easily perceived, but what of their relationship to contemporary religion? Throughout this book the emphasis has been laid upon their essentially parallel functions. Religion, astrology and magic all purported to help men with their daily problems by teaching them how to avoid misfortune and how to account for it when it struck. To stress this point is not to trivialize religion or to reduce it to a mere system of magic. Contemporary Christianity was a many-sided affair. Its elaborate self-fulfilling rituals offered a symbolism of human experience whose social and psychological relevance far transcended the limited and specific contexts in which its more purely magical aspects were invoked. 'Religion,' it has been justly said, 'refers to the fundamental issues of human existence while magic always turns round specific, concrete and detailed problems.'[33] Popular magic in England discharged only a limited number of functions; it provided protection against witchcraft, and various remedies for illness, theft, and unhappy personal relationships. But it never offered a comprehensive view of the world, an explanation of human existence, or the promise of a future life. It was a collection of miscellaneous recipes, not a comprehensive body of doctrine. Whereas the faith of the Christian was a guiding principle, relevant to every aspect of life, magic

32. Gadbury, *Thesaurus Astrologiae*, sig. A8; id., *Nauticum Astrologicum* (1691), p. 77; and references cited above. p. 432, n. 26.

33. B. Malinowski, *A Scientific Theory of Culture and Other Essays* (Chapel Hill, 1944), p. 200.

was simply a means of overcoming various specific difficulties. It is true that magic could sometimes have its expressive aspect. Its rituals for curing the sick or identifying thieves might involve the enactment of satisfying little dramas, not unlike the ceremonies of the Church.[34] The intellectual magician might even have Faustian dreams in which magic became the key to existence. But it remains true that at the popular level magic's role was much more limited than that of religion.

Nevertheless, the contemporary clergy saw the cunning folk and astrologers as their deadly rivals. They did so because they resented a competing pastoral agency, and because they were anxious to replace a magical explanation of misfortune by a theological one. When plague, fire or some other disaster struck, they devoted much energy to refuting the theories of those who attributed the events to the stars, to magic, to fortune or bad luck. In their place they affirmed the sovereignty of God's providence and interpreted his judgements in accordance with the conception they had formed of his intentions. It was the sins of the people which were the cause of the fall of commonwealths, declared a preacher at Paul's Cross in 1609: neither the Fortune of the Epicureans, nor the Destiny of the Stoics, nor the mystical numbers of the Pythagoreans, nor the stars of the astrologers could provide a satisfactory alternative.[35] Plagues did not come from the conjunctions of the planets or the eclipses of the sun, as 'wizards fondly imagine', declared another; they emanated from God's will.[36] At times of great crisis, religious explanations had to compete directly with those offered by astrologers, fortune-tellers and purveyors of ancient prophecies. It was possible to reconcile these other explanations with religious doctrine by arguing that God worked through the stars, or that he was the source of inspiration behind prophets and cunning men, or that he chose to punish sinners by allowing the Devil to torment them with witchcraft. As we have seen, there were many contemporaries who reasoned in this way.[37] But at a popular level it was usual to ignore

34. For this approach to the study of magic in other contexts, see, e.g., J. Beattie, 'Divination in Bunyoro, Uganda', *Sociologus*, xiv (1964), p. 61. It is, however, effectively criticized by J. D. Y. Peel. 'Understanding Alien Belief-Systems', *Brit. Journ. Sociology*, xx (1969), pp. 73–5.

35. L. Dawes, *Sermons* (1653), p. 36. There is a similar passage in A. Dent, *A Sermon of Gods Providence* (4th edn, 1611), sigs. A5–6.

36. R. W(right), *A Receyt to stay the Plague* (1625), p. 15.

37. Above, pp. 316–17, 427, 484, 590.

such rationalizations, and to see witchcraft, prophecies, fairies or ghosts as explanations of misfortune which were essentially different from those offered by the clergy. It was easier to reconcile astrology or natural magic with religion, for these doctrines were seen as purely 'natural' ones by contemporary intellectuals. But the others involved rival conceptions of what the mystical origins of misfortune might be.

What is most notable about the non-religious explanations of misfortune is that they usually shared with theologians the same ethical assumption that suffering was probably due to someone's moral fault, with the most likely culprit the sufferer himself. Although preachers conceded that God might inflict disasters on his people for reasons best known to himself, they constantly returned to the assumption that men were unlikely to suffer undeservedly. Fairies and ghosts were similarly more inclined to torment those who had failed in some aspect of their social duty. Even witch-beliefs, though superficially an attempt to shuffle off the blame on to a third party, were, as we have seen, unlikely to be invoked unless the victim himself was conscious of some moral fault. This implied link between misfortune and guilt was a fundamental feature of the mental environment of this period. By leading the sufferer to review his own moral behaviour, it helped to reinforce existing social norms. Both magic and religion thus became an important means of social control.

In addition to offering rival explanations of misfortune, the magical beliefs competed with religion by claiming to bring supernatural power to bear upon earthly problems. The Reformation took a good deal of the magic out of religion, leaving the astrologers and cunning men to fill much of the vacuum. But the sectarians brought back much of the magic which their early Tudor predecessors had so energetically cast out. During the Interregnum they exploited the possibilities of religion for healing and prophesying in a way unsurpassed in England since the days of the early Christian saints. The practical attractions of enthusiastic religion during these years closely matched those of the magic arts. There was no difference between a sibylline prophecy and a Quaker revelation, thought one contemporary. Another reported of the Fifth Monarchy Men that 'in their lectures and chief conventicles you might have heard such raptures that you would have thought it were a reading on astrology'.[38] When

38. Gadbury, *Natura Prodigiorum*, p. 190; E. Pagitt, *Heresiography* (6th edn, 1662), p. 282.

the transcript of John Dee's conjuring sessions with the spirits was published in 1659, many Puritan divines suspected it as a partisan attempt to discredit religious enthusiasm.[39] To the unsophisticated there was little to choose between a cunning man and a religious leader who healed and prophesied, or between a witch and a godly divine who predicted correctly that divine judgements would fall upon his enemies. It is not surprising that one contemporary, after seeing the cunning woman, Anne Bodenham, at work, should have concluded that she 'was either a witch or a woman of God'.[40]

How far the break with Rome led to an expansion in popular magic is impossible to say. Scot felt that the wise women of his time were taking the place of the healing shrines of the Catholic saints, and they certainly catered for a similar clientele. In times of plague, remarked an Elizabethan theologian, men 'flee for remedy . . . some to certain saints as S. Roch or S. Anthony; and some to the superstitious arts of witchcraft'.[41] 'In Catholic countries,' wrote Robert Southey in 1807, 'the confessor commands the thief to make restitution, – here, the person who has been robbed repairs to a witch or wizard.'[42] Astrology undoubtedly underwent a boom after the Reformation; there was no precedent for the profusion of almanacs and astrological guides which circulated in the seventeenth century. But it is doubtful whether the other divining agencies swelled to fill the gap left by the confessional and the saints. Fifteenth-century visitation records suggest that white witches turned up as frequently then as a hundred years later. Homiletic literature testifies to their prevalence in earlier periods for which the ecclesiastical records are inadequate. It is true that far more is known about Tudor and Stuart wizards than about their medieval predecessors, but it does not follow that the greater survival of evidence reflects any actual increase in their numbers.

The century after the Reformation thus constituted a transitional period, during which a variety of magical agencies continued to offer their services to those for whom the Protestant notion of self-help was too arduous. The hold of any kind of orthodox religion upon the mass of the population was never more than partial. As the author of one of the *Homilies* brutally remarked, if men really

39. *C.S.P.D., 1658–9*, p. 118; Ashm. 1788, f. 65ᵛ; U. Lee, *The Historical Backgrounds of early Methodist Enthusiasm* (New York, 1931), p. 104 n.
40. E. Bower, *Doctor Lamb Revived* (1653), p. 3.
41. (R. Day), *A Booke of Christian Prayers* (1578), sigs. Ggijᵛ–Ggiij.
42. R. Southey, *Letters from England*, ed. J. Simmons (1951), p. 295.

believed that all things came from God, they would not have been so ready to turn elsewhere for help, 'as daily experience declareth ... For if we stand in necessity of corporal health, whither go the common people but to charms, witchcrafts, and other delusions of the Devil?'[43] Even those who stuck to religion sometimes chose to use it for magical purposes upon which the theologians frowned. Yet the Church had all the resources of organized political power on its side, whereas most magical practices were harshly proscribed. The fact that they could still compete so effectively with the recipes of the established Church is testimony to their spontaneous basis in the needs of the people.

Of course, religion ultimately outlived its magical competitors. The wizards and astrologers lost their prestige during the seventeenth century, whereas the Church has continued into modern times to provide a framework for many of society's activities. But this process was not simply a matter of religion driving out its rivals, for the religion which survived the decline of magic was not the religion of Tudor England. When the Devil was banished to Hell, God himself was confined to working through natural causes. 'Special providences' and private revelations gave way to the notion of a Providence which itself obeyed natural laws accessible to human study. Superstition, wrote a leader of the Scottish Enlightenment, 'has yielded only to the light of true religion, or to the study of nature, by which we are led to substitute a wise providence operating by physical causes in the place of phantoms that terrify or amuse the ignorant'.[44] 'The doctrine of a particular providence', wrote John Wesley in 1781, 'is absolutely out of fashion in England – and any but a particular providence is no providence at all.'[45]

So although our period ended with the triumph of religion over magic, it was religion with a difference. Theologians were now more hesitant about explaining individual cases of misfortune, and much readier to accept the frequency of unmerited suffering. Reginald Scot had begun his refutation of those who blamed witches for their misfortunes, by citing the example of Job, an innocent man tormented beyond endurance for God's mysterious purposes. The achievement of natural theology was to effect a final break in the association between guilt and misfortune which had been integral

43. *Homilies*, pp. 480–81.
44. A. Ferguson, *An Essay on the History of Civil Society, 1767*, ed. D. Forbes (Edinburgh 1966), pp. 90–91.
45. *Journal of John Wesley*, ed. N. Curnock (1909), vi, p. 326.

to so many of the primitive beliefs we have considered. The mechanical philosophy of the later seventeenth century could then be comfortably reconciled with orthodox religious teaching. Stoicism had become the basic religious message for those in misfortune, and the prospect of material relief by divine means was only intermittently upheld outside sectarian circles after the seventeenth century. It was the general social importance of religion which enabled it to outlive magic. For magic had no Church, no communion symbolizing the unity of believers. It remains an interesting question as to how religion's social functions made it possible for it to survive when magic had been found redundant. But it would be a *question mal posée* if it were not remembered that the official religion of industrial England was one from which the primitive 'magical' elements had been very largely shorn. At the end of our period we can draw a distinction between religion and magic which would not have been possible at the beginning.

22.

THE DECLINE OF MAGIC

Now my charms are all o'erthrown,
And what strength I have's mine own,
Which is most faint.

W. Shakespeare, *The Tempest*, epilogue

1. *Intellectual changes*

IT is a feature of many systems of thought, and not only primitive ones, that they possess a self-confirming character. Once their initial premises are accepted, no subsequent discovery will shake the believer's faith, for he can explain it away in terms of the existing system. Neither will his convictions be weakened by the failure of some accepted ritual to accomplish its desired end, for this too can be accounted for. Such systems of belief possess a resilience which makes them virtually immune to external argument.

This self-confirming quality appears time and again in all the beliefs which we have examined. A wizard or an astrologer was always able to explain away any apparent failure in his operations by suggesting that there must have been a mistake in his calculations or that he had omitted some vital ritual precaution. If their patients were not cured, recorded a contemporary, 'the wizards blame them that they came not in time, or they applied not the means aright, or that they wanted faith to believe, or at least they acknowledged their power not great enough, and therefore they advised them to go to a more cunning man'.[1] So, even if the practitioner was so incompetent that the client decided to transfer his custom elsewhere, there was no need for his faith in the integrity of the magical art itself to be challenged. Clients might be sceptical of a particular oracle, but never of oracles in general. They seldom pooled their experience with other customers, for their consultations were semi-clandestine

1. Bernard, *Guide*, p. 147. cf. Cooper, *Mystery*, p. 268 ('1. Either they sought too late. 2. Or else they did not apply the medicine well. 3. Or else they did not believe it could do good. 4. Or it hath holpen many others. 5. Or yet it may do good; and therefore seek for more. Go to some other blesser that hath better skill').

and there was no amateur consumer-group waiting to test the result and compare the answers. The reaction against magic could thus never come from the cumulative resentment of disappointed clients. It had to arise from outside the system altogether.[2]

In alchemy the same was true. Time and again the alchemist believed himself on the brink of the discovery of the stone, only for the pot to break and all his labour to be lost. Arthur Dee was convinced that he would have found it, but for an accident at the crucial moment, and his fellow-practitioners shared this optimism:

> ful ofte it happeth so,
> The pot tobreketh, and farewel, al is go!
>   *   *   *
> Although this thyng myshapped have as now,
> Another tyme it may be well ynow.[3]

Alchemy was a difficult spiritual quest, since transmutation could not be accomplished until the adept had purged himself of all vices, particularly of covetousness; that is to say, he could not make gold until he had ceased to want to do so.

Other beliefs had an even more blatant self-confirming character. Contemporaries could laugh with Reginald Scot at the story of the philosopher who believed that if he could keep certain magical pebbles in his mouth while crossing the Channel he would never be sea-sick. But their faith in the efficacy of petitionary prayer was not diminished by the many occasions when the Lord apparently failed to hear the cry of his people, for they knew there were good reasons why he might have chosen to deny their requests. The pilgrims to St Winifred's Well had similarly known that St Beuno would not fail to cure them. If he had not done so by the third time of asking, they would die, but this only meant that he had chosen to grant them extra spiritual rewards instead.[4] Faith in the possibility of divine dreams was not weakened by the certain knowledge that many

2. For modern explanations for the continuing prestige of magic, despite the failures of individual magicians, see E. B. Tylor, *Primitive Culture* (1871), i, pp. 212–3; Sir J. G. Frazer, *The Magic Art* (3rd edn, 1913), i, pp. 242–3; E. E. Evans-Pritchard, *Witchcraft, Oracles and Magic Among the Azande* (Oxford, 1937), pp. 475–8; S. F. Nadel, *Nupe Religion* (1954), p. 151.

3. Chaucer, *Canon Yeoman's Tale*, ll.906–7, 944–5. cf. *The Autobiography and Personal Diary of Dr Simon Forman*, ed. J. O. Halliwell (1849), p. 28; Bacon, *Works*, i, pp. 192–3; iii, p. 497.

4. Scot, *Discoverie*, XIII.xv; (W. Fleetwood), *The Life and Miracles of St Wenefrede* (1713), pp. 103 n.–104 n. cf. above, pp. 136–7.

dreams were lying and devilish.[5] Nor was the belief in the prophetic
character of the Bible overthrown by the mere failure of the Second
Coming to occur on the appointed day; it only meant that there had
been a mistake in the calculation – the millenarians could return to
their Biblical arithmetic with their fundamental convictions un-
shaken. By making assumptions of this kind the adherents of these
various beliefs were able to survive innumerable and inevitable disappointments without losing their basic faith.[6] There was no way in
which these systems of thought could be undermined from inside.

The most difficult problem in the study of magical beliefs is thus
to explain how it was that men were able to break out of them. This
is a topic on which social anthropologists have as yet thrown little
light,[7] and it is one which the historian of Tudor and Stuart England
must also find peculiarly intractable. The period abounded in
sceptics, but it is rarely that one comes upon documented instances
of an individual's loss of faith. Contemporary literature was written
by men who occupied well-defined positions; it throws little light on
how people came to change their minds. Nevertheless, we must try
to determine the circumstances which made traditional modes of
magical thought appear increasingly out-dated.

The first of these was the series of intellectual changes which
constituted the scientific and philosophical revolution of the seventeenth century. These changes had a decisive influence upon the
thinking of the intellectual élite and in due course percolated down
to influence the thought and behaviour of the people at large. The
essence of the revolution was the triumph of the mechanical philosophy. It involved the rejection both of scholastic Aristotelianism and
of the Neoplatonic theory which had temporarily threatened to take
its place. With the collapse of the microcosm theory went the destruction of the whole intellectual basis of astrology, chiromancy,
alchemy, physiognomy, astral magic and their associates. The notion
that the universe was subject to immutable natural laws killed the
concept of miracles, weakened the belief in the physical efficacy of

5. cf. R. Firth, 'The Meaning of Dreams in Tikopia', *Essays presented to
C. G. Seligman*, ed. E. E. Evans-Pritchard, *et al.* (1934), pp. 71–2; above, p.
151.

6. For other instances of this process, see above, pp. 247, 400–401, 656–7,
733–4.

7. cf. I. C. Jarvie and J. Agassi, 'The problem of the rationality of magic',
British Journ. of Sociology, xviii (1967), p. 71 ('The really urgent sociological
problem posed by magic' is 'can people with inefficient magical beliefs come
to be critical of them, under what conditions and to what extent?').

prayer, and diminished faith in the possibility of direct divine inspiration. The Cartesian concept of matter relegated spirits, whether good or bad, to the purely mental world; conjuration ceased to be a meaningful ambition.

At the beginning of the seventeenth century an intelligent contemporary would have found it difficult to predict this outcome. For magic and science had originally advanced side by side. The magical desire for power had created an intellectual environment favourable to experiment and induction; it marked a break with the characteristic medieval attitude of contemplative resignation. Neoplatonic and hermetic ways of thinking had stimulated such crucial discoveries in the history of science as heliocentrism, the infinity of worlds, and the circulation of the blood.[8] The mystical conviction that numbers contained the key to all mysteries had fostered the revival of mathematics. Astrological inquiries had brought new precision to the observation of the heavenly bodies, the calculation of their movements, and the measurement of time.[9]

This union of magic and science was short-lived. Its dissolution was foreshadowed in early-seventeenth-century Europe by a series of intellectual combats: Isaac Casaubon's redating of the hermetic books in 1614; the refutation of Robert Fludd's magical animism by Marin Mersenne and Pierre Gassendi in the decade after 1623.[10] In the later seventeenth century the partnership collapsed. Robert Boyle's chemical investigations destroyed many of the assumptions on which the alchemists had rested their speculations. The Royal Society disproved by experiment the idea that insects could be spontaneously generated. The doctrine of signatures, already denied by some earlier botanists, was rejected from the start by John Ray. Magnetism and electricity, which had previously been seen as occult

8. For an admirable summary of recent work on this subject, see F. A. Yates, 'The Hermetic Tradition in Renaissance Science', in *Art, Science, and History in the Renaissance*, ed. C. S. Singleton (Baltimore, 1967). See also her *Giordano Bruno and the Hermetic Tradition* (1964); T. S. Kuhn, *The Copernican Revolution* (Cambridge, Mass., 1957), pp. 129–30; A. G. Debus, 'Robert Fludd and the Circulation of the Blood', *Journ. Hist. Medicine*, xvi (1961).

9. Taylor, *Mathematical Practitioners*, pp. 79, 181, 195, 230, 235, 320.

10. Yates, *Giordano Bruno and the Hermetic Tradition*, chaps. 21 and 22; L. Cafiero, 'Robert Fludd e la polemica con Gassendi', *Rivista Critica di Storia Della Filosofia*, xix–xx (1964–5). Mersenne's rejection of the animist tradition is thoroughly discussed by R. Lenoble, *Mersenne, ou la naissance du mécanisme* (Paris, 1943).

influences, could now be explained in purely mechanical terms as the movement of particles.[11] The triumph of the mechanical philosophy meant the end of the animistic conception of the universe which had constituted the basic rationale for magical thinking.

Sir Isaac Newton's secret alchemical investigations[12] are a reminder that the change was not accomplished overnight. But the virtuosi who dabbled in magic or alchemy had come to appear increasingly cranky to their scientific colleagues, and the intellectual vitality had departed from the magical guides which continued to be published for the benefit of a lower-class public.

The new science also carried with it an insistence that all truths be demonstrated, an emphasis on the need for direct experience, and a disinclination to accept inherited dogmas without putting them to the test. 'There is no certain knowledge without demonstration,' declared Samuel Butler. The implications of this new attitude can be seen in the stories of how the physician, William Harvey, carefully dissected a toad alleged to be a witch's familiar, and how the mathematician, Henry Briggs, abandoned his interest in astrology, once he discovered that its principles were incapable of demonstration.[13] Indeed this epistemological demand for certain knowledge was eroding the status of every kind of magical belief. It made witchcraft prosecution impossible, discredited astrology, and inculcated scepticism in face of the claims of religious enthusiasts to be directly inspired by God.[14] It also led to a rescrutiny of some hoary old legends. The early scientists, particularly those of Neoplatonic learnings, had tended to accept every story, no matter how bizarre, and then to devote their energies to finding an explanation for it. During the later seventeenth century this attitude changed. As John Webster remarked in 1677, 'there is no greater folly than to be very inquisitive and laborious to find out the causes of such a phenomenon as never had any existence, and therefore men ought to be cautious and to be fully assured of the truth of the effect before they adventure to

11. M. Purver, *The Royal Society: Concept and Creation* (1967), pp. 87, 91; A. Arber, *Herbals* (new edn, Cambridge, 1938), chap. 8; C. E. Raven, *Synthetic Philosophy in the Seventeenth Century* (Oxford, 1945), pp. 20–21; M. Boas, 'The Establishment of the Mechanical Philosophy', *Osiris*, x (1952).

12. F. E. Manuel, *A Portrait of Isaac Newton* (Cambridge, Mass., 1968), chap. 8.

13. S. Butler, *Characters and Passages from Note-Books*, ed. A. R. Waller (Cambridge, 1908), p. 282; above, pp. 626, 437.

14. Above, pp. 685–6, 390, 173. cf. p. 127.

explicate the cause'.[15] Charms, spells and ancient prophecies could offer no resistance to this type of investigation. They derived their authority from antiquity and were revised in the light of experience, for magic, unlike science, never learned from failure but simply explained it away. Characteristically, the Azande of Central Africa, whose magical beliefs form the subject of Evans-Pritchard's classic anthropological study, are said to be 'not experimentally inclined'.[16] The leading English opponents of magical beliefs, by contrast, were conspicuous for their self-conscious insistence on the need to test old opinions and to reject untenable dogmas.[17]

These various developments thus robbed the old magical systems of their capacity to satisfy the educated élite. But it was to be some time before the people at large became fully aware of their implications. The early eighteenth century saw some important efforts to disseminate knowledge to the reading public through manuals and encyclopedias. These works sometimes took an aggressively hostile attitude to the old magical beliefs. In his *Universal Dictionary of Arts and Sciences* (1704) John Harris, F.R.S., dismissed astrology as 'a ridiculous piece of foolery' and alchemy as 'an art which begins with lying, is continued with toil and labour, and at last ends in beggary'.[18] His successor, Ezekiel Chambers, however, was much more cautious in his influential *Cyclopaedia* (1728), preferring to rationalize many of the old beliefs, rather than reject them altogether. Although he dismissed chiromancy as a 'vain and trifling art', and considered sorcery to have been 'at bottom no other than artful poisonings', he took alchemy fairly seriously and allowed the natural part of astrology. He also accepted amulets, occult influences and witchcraft by effluvia from the eye. His work reminds us that the implications of the scientific revolution could take a long time to make themselves fully felt.[19]

15. J. Webster, *The Displaying of Supposed Witchcraft* (1677), p. 251. Selden put the same point more succinctly: above, p. 517.

16. Evans-Pritchard, *Witchcraft, Oracles and Magic among the Azande*, p. 477.

17. Scot, *Discoverie*, 'To the Readers'; (Sir R. Filmer), *An Advertisement to the Jury-Men of England touching Witches* (1653), p. 8; Webster, op. cit., chap. 1.

18. J. Harris, *Lexicon Technicum: or, an Universal English Dictionary* (1704).

19. E. Chambers, *Cyclopaedia: or, an Universal Dictionary of Arts and Sciences* (1728), and the discussion in P. Shorr, *Science and Superstition in the Eighteenth Century* (Columbia Univ. thesis, New York, 1932). See also

For that matter a 'rationalist' attitude had existed long before the work of Galileo or Newton. It was to be found, up to a point, in the writings of the Paduan school of the early sixteenth century. The regularity of the natural world, the impossibility of miracles, and the mortality of the soul were asserted by Pietro Pomponazzi (1462–1525), and reiterated by the 'libertine' thinkers of sixteenth-century Italy and seventeenth-century France. The inspiration for these writers was not the new science so much as the rationalist authors of classical antiquity: Hippocrates, who denied that epilepsy had supernatural causes; Aristotle, who dismissed most 'prophetic' dreams as mere coincidences; Cicero, who repudiated the arts of divination; Epicurus and Lucretius, who showed that the course of the world could be explained without invoking divine intervention; Plutarch, who exposed the superstitions of the Jews.[20] In England too the earliest opponents of magic made more extensive use of these classical authors than they ever did of contemporary science. Reginald Scot had no difficulty in rejecting diabolical influence, before the scientific revolution had scarcely begun.[21] It was as common in Elizabethan England for the social élite to profess contempt for vulgar 'superstitions' as it had been in Augustan Rome.

But Scot and his imitators had, like Pomponazzi, only been able to fill the gap left after the elimination of religious or magical explanations of natural phenomena by invoking spurious 'natural' causes, based on sympathy, antipathy and occult influences. In admitting every kind of prodigy they were blocking the way to a true conception of nature. What the scientific revolution did was to supersede this type of reasoning and to buttress up the old rationalist attitude with a more stable intellectual foundation, based on the mechanical philosophy. It did not matter that the majority of the population of eighteenth-century England had possibly never heard

---

A. Hughes, 'Science in English Encyclopaedias, 1704–1875', *Annals of Science*, vii (1951).

20. A. H. Douglas, *The Philosophy and Psychology of Pietro Pomponazzi*, ed. C. Douglas and R. P. Hardie (Cambridge, 1910), chap. xi; R. Pintard, *Le Libertinage érudit dans la première moitié du XVIIe siècle* (Paris, 1943); H. Busson, *Le Rationalisme dans la littérature française de la Renaissance, 1533–1601* (Paris, 1957); E. Garin, *Italian Humanism*, trans. P. Munz (Oxford, 1965), chap. viii.

21. For Scot's invocation of Cicero and Hippocrates, see *Discoverie*, X.iv; XV.xxx, and for John Wagstaffe's of Lucian, see *The Question of Witchcraft Debated* (1969), appendix. cf. the earlier 'Ciceronian' scepticism of Polydore Vergil; D. Hay, *Polydore Vergil* (Oxford, 1952), pp. 34–45.

of Boyle or Newton and certainly could not have explained the nature of their discoveries. At all times most men accept their basic assumptions on the authority of others. New techniques and attitudes are always more readily diffused than their underlying scientific rationale. 'The average man of today,' wrote the psychoanalyst, Ernest Jones, 'does not hesitate to reject the same evidence of witchcraft that was so convincing to the man of three centuries ago, though he usually knows no more about the true explanation than the latter did.' Most of those millions of persons who today would laugh at the idea of magic or miracles would have difficulty in explaining why. They are victims of society's constant pressure towards intellectual conformity.[22] Under this pressure the magician has ceased to command respect, and intellectual prestige has shifted elsewhere.

2. *New technology*

It is thus possible to argue that these primitive beliefs declined because they had come to be seen as intellectually unsatisfactory. But it must be confessed that the full details of this process of disillusion are by no means clear. One cannot simply attribute the change to the scientific revolution. There were too many 'rationalists' before, too many believers afterwards, for so simple an explanation to be plausible. Let us therefore examine the question from a different point of view. Instead of concentrating on the intellectual status of these beliefs let us consider them in their social context.

At this point it is worth taking account of the argument advanced forty years ago by the anthropologist, Bronislaw Malinowski. Unfashionable though Malinowski's theories now are, they nevertheless constitute one of the few direct assaults on the difficult question of why it is that magical beliefs decline. Magic, he argued, is 'to be expected and generally to be found whenever man comes to an unbridgeable gap, a hiatus in his knowledge or in his powers of practical control, and yet has to continue in his pursuit'. As an alternative to helpless impotence, the savage falls back upon the substitute activity of magical ritual. Sometimes such rites are combined with practical techniques, as, for example, when vegetables are carefully planted and watered, but also encouraged by the recitation of

22. E. Jones, *Papers on Psycho-Analysis* (3rd edn, 1923), p. 122. cf. M. G. Marwick, *Sorcery in its Social Setting* (Manchester, 1965), p. 255; G. Jahoda, *The Psychology of Superstition* (1969), pp. 48–50.

charms. More characteristically, they are employed unaccompanied to deal with unusual difficulties outside the normal routine. The control offered by such magical rites is necessarily illusory, for charms cannot make crops grow or wounds heal. But, though magic in itself is vain, it has valuable side-effects. It lessens anxiety, relieves pent-up frustration, and makes the practitioner feel that he is doing something positive towards the solution of his problem. By its agency he is converted from a helpless bystander into an active agent. Magic gives primitive man confidence; 'it ritualises man's optimism'. Without its power and guidance, Malinowski concluded, 'early man could not have mastered his practical difficulties'.[23]

On this interpretation, therefore, the most important cause of man's recourse to magic is his lack of the necessary empirical or technical knowledge to deal with the problems which confront him. 'Magic is dominant when control of the environment is weak.'[24] When the appropriate techniques become available, magic grows superfluous and withers away. Only in the case of those problems to which men still have no adequate solution does it retain its appeal. It is science and technology which make magic redundant; the stronger man's control of his environment, the less his recourse to magical remedies.

This explanation does not of course make clear why magical rituals should take one form rather than another, for it leaves aside the origin of the mental ingredients which go to make up individual magical fantasies and beliefs. But it does offer an explanation of why magic is invoked at one time rather than another. When applied to the facts of sixteenth- and seventeenth-century society, it makes a good deal of initial sense. The purposes for which most men had recourse to charms or cunning men were precisely those for which an adequate alternative technique was lacking. Thus in agriculture the farmer normally relied upon his own skills; there are no magical charms extant for such automatic tasks as reaping corn or milking cows. But when he was dependent on circumstances outside his

23. Malinowski's thesis is succinctly stated in his 'Magic, Science and Religion', in *Science, Religion and Reality*, ed. J. Needham (1925), and in his essay on 'Culture' in the *Encyclopaedia of Social Sciences* (1930–5), from which two sources my quotations are drawn. For a typical application of it, see R. Firth, *Primitive Economics of the New Zealand Maori* (1929), chap. 7.

24. G. and M. Wilson, *The Analysis of Social Change* (Cambridge, 1945), p. 95. cf. E. E. Evans-Pritchard, *Theories of Primitive Religion* (Oxford, 1965), p. 113 ('the advances of science and technology have rendered magic redundant.').

control – the fertility of the soil, the weather, the health of his animals – he was more likely to accompany his labours with some magical precaution. There were all the traditional fertility rites and seasonal observances: Plough Monday to ensure the growth of the corn; wassailing to bless the apple trees; Rogation processions and Midsummer fires for the crops; corn dollies at harvest time.[25] In Colchester in 1532 a smith's wife was said to practise magic 'to make folks believe they should have a sely [lucky] plough'.[26] In the absence of weed-killers, there were charms to keep weeds out of the corn, and, in place of insecticide and rat-killers, magical formulae to keep away pests.[27] There were also charms to increase the land's fertility.[28]

Similar precautions surrounded other potentially uncertain operations. Care was taken to time such tasks as sowing corn or cutting trees to harmonize with the phases of the moon or some other propitious factor.[29] There were divinatory systems for ascertaining the weather or the future price of corn.[30] There were charms to make horses work harder, to protect cows from witchcraft, to procure healthy stock, and even to influence the sex of future calves.[31] Bee-keeping and chicken-raising had their semi-magical precautions.[32]

25. Above, pp. 54, 71–3. See also N. J. Hone, *The Manor and Manorial Records* (1906), p. 98; Aubrey, *Gentilisme*, pp. 9, 40, 96–7; G. L. Gomme, *The Village Community* (1890), p. 113; H. Bourne, *Antiquitates Vulgares*, ed. J. Brand (1810), pp. 256–7; *Sussex Archaeol. Collns*, i, (1848), p. 110 n.; *County Folk-Lore*, v (Folk-Lore Soc., 1908), pp. 171 ff.; T. M. Owen, *Welsh Folk Customs* (Cardiff, 1959), pp. 48, 115–21; Frazer, *The Magic Art*, ii, 103–4; id., *Spirits of the Corn and of the Wild* (3rd edn, 1912) i, pp. 146–7; ii. pp. 328–3; M. Campbell, *The English Yeoman* (1960), p. 305; A. R. Wright, *British Calendar Customs*, ed. T. E. Lones (Folk-Lore Soc., 1936–40), ii, pp. 85–7, 93–103; iii, pp. 220–21, 287–8.

26. *Essex Rev.*, xlvii (1938), p. 167.

27. Brand, *Popular Antiquities*, iii, pp. 309–10; *Trans. Devon Assoc.*, ix (1877), p. 90; Kittredge, *Witchcraft*, p. 35; M. R. James, *A Descriptive Catalogue of the Manuscripts in the Library of Gonville and Caius College, Cambridge* (Cambridge, 1907–14), ii, p. 444; above, pp. 275, 759.

28. Sloane 3846, f. 45 (seventeenth century).

29. Brand, *Popular Antiquities*, iii, pp. 142 ff.; above, pp. 351–2.

30. G. Markham, *The English Husband-Man* (1613: 1635 edn), pp. 16–18; above, pp. 284, 351.

31. Scot, *Discoverie*, XII.xiv; Kittredge, *Witchcraft*, pp. 35, 41, chap. ix; E. Fairfax, *Daemonologia: A Discourse on Witchcraft*, ed. W. Grainge (Harrogate, 1882), p. 35; Aubrey, *Gentilisme*, p. 89; J. G. Frazer, *Balder the Beautiful* (3rd edn, 1913), ii, pp. 85–6.

32. Brand, op. cit., ii, pp. 300–1; iii, p. 263.

So did the making of bread, beer, yeast and butter – spheres in which witchcraft was particularly feared. Ritual precautions surrounded other household operations: no menstruating woman, for example, could ever pickle beef or salt bacon.[33] Similar prescriptions related to hunting and fishing, both speculative activities; in the fishing trade the fear of witchcraft lingered until the nineteenth century.[34] There was also magic designed to counter human deficiences, moral and physical: charms to prevent the crops being robbed, herbs to allay weariness at the plough, devices like spitting on one's hands to give renewed energy for work.[35]

In many other occupations magical aids were also invoked when problems were too great to be solved by human skill. The dangers of seafaring made sailors notoriously superstitious and generated a large number of ritual precautions designed to secure favourable weather and the safety of the ship.[36] The risks of military adventure encouraged the use of amulets and protective talismans of many kinds. The deficiencies of contemporary medicine drove the sick into the hands of the cunning men and wise women. The slowness of communications and the lack of a police force fostered dependence upon village wizards for the recovery of stolen goods and missing persons. Ignorance of the future encouraged men to grasp at omens or to practise divination as a basis for making decisions. All such devices can be seen as attempts to counter human helplessness in the face of the physical and social environment.

Correspondingly, the decline of magic coincided with a marked improvement in the extent to which this environment became amenable to control. In several important respects the material conditions of life took a turn for the better during the later seventeenth century. The pressure of population, which had caused much

33. Brand, op. cit., iii, pp. 312–33, Aubrey, *Gentilisme*, p. 260; Kittredge, *Witchcraft*, p. 35; Ady, p. 58; Frazer, *Balder the Beautiful*, i. p. 96, n. 2; *County Folk-Lore*, v, pp. 97–8.

34. Brand, op. cit., iii, p. 14; Frazer, *Aftermath* (1936), pp. 28–9; *The Folk-Lore Journ.*, iii (1885), pp. 378–9; 'A Description of Cleveland', *The Topographer and Genealogist*, ii (1853), p. 414; *County Folk-Lore*, ii (Folk-Lore Soc., 1901), pp. 46–53; *Notes and Queries for Somerset and Dorset*, x (1906–7), p. 49. For charms to catch fish, K. M. Briggs, *Pale Hecate's Team* (1962), p. 260; Sloane 3846, f. 54. cf. P. Sébillot, *Le Folk-Lore des pêcheurs* (Paris, 1901).

35. (D. Defoe), *A System of Magick* (1727), pp. 316–7; Brand, op. cit., iii, pp. 259–63, 313.

36. Brand, op. cit., iii, pp. 5, 239–41; Aubrey, *Gentilisme*, p. 67; Ewen, ii, p. 405.

hardship during the previous hundred years, now slackened off. Agricultural improvement brought an increase in food production; in the later seventeenth century the country became virtually self-sufficient in corn, while increased imports were used to keep down prices at times of dearth. The growth of overseas trade and the rise of new industries created a more diversified economic environment. There was no major plague epidemic after 1665 and in the 1670s the disease disappeared from England altogether. By 1700 Englishmen enjoyed a higher level of material welfare than the inhabitants of any other country in the world, save Holland.[37] General circumstances of this kind must have done something to increase human self-confidence. Moreover several further developments may have borne a particular responsibility for the declining appeal of the magical solution.

The first of these was a general improvement in communications. Printed news-sheets began in the early seventeenth century, proliferated during the Interregnum and, though checked until 1695 by the licensing laws, had become an indispensable feature of London life by the end of the century. Thereafter they spread to the provinces. Between 1701 and 1760 a hundred and thirty provincial newspapers had made at least a temporary appearance, and they emanated from no fewer than fifty-five different towns.[38] A penny post was introduced in London in 1680 and the letter-carrying service greatly improved thereafter.[39] These developments were accompanied by an increase in popular literacy, which may have reached a peak in the third quarter of the seventeenth century, when nearly forty per cent of the adult male population may have been able to read.[40] Changes in the mobility of the population are harder to measure, but it is clear that even in Tudor England the village population was never constant. In the later seventeenth century mobility may have increased with the growth of new industries and the constant movement in and out of London.[41] The general effect

37. P. Deane and W. A. Cole, *British Economic Growth, 1688–1959* (2nd edn, Cambridge 1967), p. 38.

38. G. A. Cranfield, *The Development of the Provincial Newspaper, 1700–60* (Oxford, 1962), pp. 22, 27.

39. H. Robinson, *The British Post Office, a History* (Princeton, 1948).

40. L. Stone, 'Literacy and Education in England, 1640–1900', *Past and Present*, xlii (1969), p. 125.

41. For suggestive evidence on this subject, see S. A. Peyton, 'The Village Population in the Tudor Lay Subsidy Rolls', *E.H.R.*, xxx (1915); E. A. Wrigley, 'A Simple Model of London's Importance ... 1650–1750', *Past and*

of all these trends was to keep the provinces more closely in touch with the metropolis, to break down local isolation and to disseminate sophisticated opinion.

Also important were the advertisements which the newspapers had begun to carry. Notices about lost property and missing persons were a feature of the Commonwealth news-sheets and continued thereafter. Lost dogs, stolen horses, runaway apprentices, suspected thieves – all could now be notified to a wider public than the village wizard or town crier had ever been able to command. In 1657 a projector announced the foundation of an Office of Public Advice with eight branches in the London area to deal with inquiries about lost goods and a weekly bulletin of runaway servants and apprentices.[42] From May to September of that year the sixteen-page *Publick Adviser* was devoted to weekly advertisements of this kind; and it had a rival in *The Weekly Information from the Office of Intelligence*, which appeared in July and was also made up of advertisements. There were many later attempts at developing such advertising agencies.[43] For the urban middle classes the coffee-house or newspaper office had become the obvious place to refer problems about lost goods. The need for the cunning man was accordingly reduced.

Meanwhile certain devices were introduced to lessen the incidence of human misfortune. Greater security for men of property was provided by the rise of deposit banking, but nothing yields greater testimony to the new spirit of self-help than the growth of insurance at the end of the seventeenth century. Of course, schemes designed to cushion sufferers from theft, fire, sickness or other disasters were not without precedent. Many of the gilds of medieval England had operated as friendly societies, taking common responsibility for the cost of burying their members or recompensing their losses by fire. Manorial customs of inheritance often provided for the maintenance

Present, xxxvii (1967); and the references assembled by L. Stone in *Past and Present*, xxxiii (1966), p. 30 n.

42. *The Office of Publick Advice newly set up* (1657).

43. *C.S.P.D.*, 1666–7, p. 433; *London Gazette*, lxii (14–18 June 1666); *Publick Advertisements* (1666); *The Cambridge Bibliography of English Literature*, ed. F. W. Bateson (Cambridge, 1940), ii, p. 717; D. Ogg, *England in the Reign of Charles II* (2nd edn, Oxford, 1955), i, p. 97. Most of these schemes were presumably influenced by Hartlib's projected Office of Address (1646); see *Samuel Hartlib and the Advancement of Learning*, ed. C. Webster (Cambridge, 1970), pp. 44 ff.

of the elderly. But the gilds had disappeared and manorial customs were being eroded. For most inhabitants of late Tudor and Stuart England fire, flood, or the sudden death of a close relative could mean total disaster.

Steps to provide artificial security against such hazards were first taken by merchants and shipowners. Marine insurance developed in fourteenth-century Italy and had taken root in England by the mid-sixteenth century. In 1574 indeed the notaries were claiming to have registered policies 'time out of mind'.[44] But for a long time the system remained rudimentary. Underwriting was done by individuals rather than companies and most traders only thought about insuring their goods when the ship was already overdue. The insurance of ships as well as the goods they carried did not become common until the reign of William III. The law relating to the arbitration of insurance disputes also remained unsatisfactory. In such circumstances many merchants preferred to lighten their risks by dividing ownership of the ship and its goods between a number of different individuals. All these uncertainties were reflected in the numerous insurance problems which were brought to astrologers like William Lilly. But in the early eighteenth century the situation changed, with the development of Lloyds coffee-house as a regular meeting-place for underwriters and the foundation in 1720 of two substantial joint-stock companies devoted to marine insurance, the London Assurance and the Royal Exchange.[45]

Other types of insurance were also emerging. The coverage of goods travelling overland by wagon or cart seems to have appeared by the end of Charles II's reign.[46] Fire insurance developed at much the same time. This was primarily as a result of the great Fire of London, though various projectors had come forward with fire schemes during the early seventeenth century,[47] and there had been

44. *Tudor Economic Documents*, ed. R. H. Tawney and E. Power (1924), ii, p. 249.
45. See W. W. Blackstock, *The Historical Literature of Sea and Fire Insurance in Great Britain, 1547–1810* (Manchester, 1910); V. Barbour, 'Marine Risks and Insurance in the Seventeenth Century', *Journ. of Econ. and Business Hist.*, i (1929); R. Davis, *The Rise of the English Shipping Industry* (1962), pp. 87–8, 318, 320, 377; C. Wright and C. E. Fayle, *The History of Lloyds* (1928); W. R. Scott, *The Constitution and Finance of English, Scottish and Irish Joint-Stock Companies to 1720* (Cambridge, 1910–12), iii, pp. 263–6, 396–409.
46. Scott, op. cit., iii, p. 374 n.
47. e.g., *C.S.P.D., 1635–6*, p. 80; *1637–8*, pp. 392–3.

a number of unsuccessful attempts at underwriting before 1680, when Nicholas Barbon announced the foundation of his Fire Office. His was the first of a trio of successful insurance companies: the Fire Office (1681; subsequently the Phoenix), the Friendly Society (1684), and the Hand-in-Hand (1696). The Fire Office levied a premium of 6d. per £1 rental value for brick houses (1/- for wooden ones); the other companies ran on a mutual basis, calling on members to meet losses as they arose. All three did a brisk business which reflected the enormous demand for security of this kind. The Fire Office insured 4,000 houses in its first four years, while the Hand-in-Hand had issued 7,313 policies by 1704, covering houses to the value of £1,284,615 in brick and £125,767 in timber.[48] These early companies confined their activities to London, however, and dealt only with houses. But in the early eighteenth century fire insurance was extended to household goods and trading stock, and to other parts of the country. Of the several substantial companies erected for this purpose the best known was to be Charles Povey's office, which was set up in 1706 and became the Sun in 1710; by 1720 it had issued over 17,000 policies covering goods in many parts of the country to the value of £10,000,000.[49]

Life insurance was slowest to evolve, though it had long been possible to indemnify lives for short periods against defined risks. Tudor shipowners sometimes insured the ship-masters' lives against the perils of the sea. The sale of annuities for lives could be a method of repaying loans at interest and evading the usury laws; and there were many speculative schemes which gambled on the expectation of an individual's life, as in the tontine system, whereby all the group's contributions went to the last survivor.[50] But systematic life insurance for a fixed sum was impossible without accurate actuarial calculation of the current expectation of the insurer's life. The construction of 'life tables' showing an individual's expectation according to his age was first attempted by the London haberdasher, John Graunt, whose *Natural and Political Observations . . . upon the Bills*

48. P. G. M. Dickson, *The Sun Insurance Office, 1710–1960* (1960), pp. 13, 16.

49. Dickson, op. cit., p. 40; Scott, *Joint-Stock Companies*, iii, pp. 372–8.

50. Accounts of these early schemes may be found in C. Walford, 'History of Life Insurance in Great Britain', in *Yale Readings in Insurance. Life Insurance*, ed. L. W. Zartman (New Haven, 1909) and Scott, op. cit., iii, pp. 366–72. A policy on the life of the Countess of Huntingdon (7 May 1601) is in Vol. i of the Herrick Papers (Bodl., MS Eng. hist. c 474).

of Mortality (1662) laid the foundations of the science of demography. Thirty-one years later a more systematic life table, based on figures for Breslau, was compiled by the astronomer, Edmond Halley, and from it was devised a method for calculating the purchase price of annuities.[51] These techniques were to be refined in the eighteenth century.

Between 1699 and 1720 there were over fifty separate projected schemes of life insurance, of which the Amicable Society (1706), based on a modified tontine principle, was the only one to survive the South Sea Bubble. Statistical ignorance was the undoing of most of these early ventures, for, without the appropriate mathematical techniques, they could do no more than create funds by subscription, out of which an unpredictable sum would be paid on a man's death. Only in 1762 did the Society for Equitable Assurances successfully develop a standardized contract, whereby the sum insured and the annual premium could be systematically adjusted to fit the subscriber's age at entry.[52]

But although early insurance of most kinds was a speculative business, its long-term implications were immense. Despite initial hesitations, insurance established itself during the eighteenth century as one of the most basic sources of security for the English middle classes. By 1805 the value of goods insured in England was in the order of £240 million.[53] At a lower social level the eighteenth century saw the launching of pioneer insurance schemes by industrial firms for their employees and the proliferation of working-class friendly societies. Nothing did more to reduce the sphere in which magical remedies were the only form of protection against misfortune. For, as Daniel Defoe remarked in 1697, the principle of mutual insurance made it possible for 'all the contingencies of life [to] be fenced against ... as thieves, floods by land, storms by sea, losses of all sorts, and death itself'.[54]

Another sphere in which a new effort was made to combat mis-

51. Reprinted from *Philos. Trans.*, xvii (1693) in *Journ. of the Inst. of Actuaries*, xviii (1878).

52. M. E. Ogborn, *Equitable Assurances* (1962), chaps. 1–3; Scott, *Joint-Stock Companies*, iii, pp. 389–95. On the inadequacy of earlier data, see J. Smart, *Tables of Interest, Discount, Annuities, etc.* (1726), p. 113.

53. J. H. Clapham, *An Economic History of Modern Britain*, i (Cambridge, 1926), pp. 284–5.

54. Quoted by Dickson, *The Sun Insurance Office*, p. 12.

fortune directly rather than by substitute remedies was that of fire-fighting.[55] The hand-squirt was introduced to England in the last decade of the sixteenth century, and considerable interest was shown in devising mechanical methods for projecting water. The manual fire-engine, with which a gang of men could raise water to a height, was first patented in 1625. It was developed and popularized in the later seventeenth century, a period when many town governments purchased their first fire-engines. The leather hosepipe was a Dutch invention, brought to England in the 1670s. The subsequent invention of the air chamber made possible a steady stream of water instead of a pulsating jet. The early insurance companies ran their own fire brigades, and the beginning of the eighteenth century saw the introduction of the fire-escape. In the reign of Queen Anne an Act of Parliament required every London parish to possess a large fire-engine, a hand-squirt, a leather pipe, and a socket for attachment to the street water supply. After the Fire of London many towns banned or re-banned thatched roofs and wooden buildings, and there was a steady increase in the use of brick. None of these measures eliminated the risk of fire or made it very much easier to control. But they represented an advance on the meagre fire-fighting equipment of most Tudor municipalities, and they reflected faith in the ultimate possibility of a technical solution.

Contemporaries thus gradually grew less vulnerable to certain kinds of disaster. They also developed new kinds of knowledge to supersede mystical explanations of misfortune in terms of witches, ghosts or divine providence. Here the social sciences were as important as the natural ones. Embryonic economics and sociology had developed considerably during the period. By the end of the seventeenth century, it was commonplace for intellectuals to reveal their awareness of the extent to which economic and social hardships could be attributed to impersonal causes, and of the way in which education and social institutions could explain the differences be-

55. G. V. Blackstone, *A History of the British Fire Service* (1957) is the most recent account. C. Walford, *The Insurance Cyclopaedia* (1871–80), iii, and C. F. T. Young, *Fires, Fire Engines and Fire Brigades* (1866), are also useful. The considerable quantity of material available in local records has not yet been fully exploited. But for a beginning to serious work on this subject, see E. L. Jones, 'The Reduction of Fire Damage in Southern England, 1650–1850', *Post-Medieval Archaeology*, ii (1968).

tween different peoples and different social classes.[56] This was to be one of the main themes of the Enlightenment. The explanatory aspirations of astrological inquiry were taken over by these new disciplines. They rejected the notion that social phenomena were purely random; every event, they held, had a cause, even if it was still hidden. This was why Bacon listed Fortune as a non-existent entity. It was to be replaced by new historical laws. 'No government is of so accidental or arbitrary an institution as people are wont to imagine,' thought James Harrington, 'there being in societies natural causes producing their necessary effects as well as in the earth or the air.'[57] The immediacy of the doctrine of divine providence was inevitably much reduced by this assumption that God had bound himself to work through sociological causes as well as physical ones. Witch-beliefs, by contrast, were less affected at first, for they were concerned to explain individual misfortunes, whereas the aim of the social sciences was to account for social developments as a whole. But in the long run psychology and sociology were to supersede the idea of witchcraft by providing a new way in which the victim could blame others for his fate. Instead of accusing witches, he could attribute his misfortunes to the way in which his parents had brought him up, or to the social system into which he had been born.

A further development undermining more primitive explanations of misfortune was the growing awareness, particularly among mathematicians, of the way in which even chance and misfortune were subject to statistical laws and thus capable, up to a point, of being rationally predicted. The formulation of theories of probability was the work of a long series of European mathematicians – Cardan, Fermat, Huygens, Pascal, the Bernouillis and de Moivre. But Englishmen made a distinctive contribution through the empirical study of mortality tables by Graunt, Petty and Halley; and the Royal Society showed considerable interest in the subject. In the last decade of the seventeenth century probability theory was widely

56. For these developments, see, e.g. A. B. Ferguson, *The Articulate Citizen and the English Renaissance* (Durham, N.C., 1965); W. Letwin, *The Origins of Scientific Economics. English Economic Thought, 1660–1776* (1963); M. T. Hodgen, *Early Anthropology in the Sixteenth and Seventeenth Centuries* (Philadelphia, 1964).

57. Bacon, *Works*, iv, p. 61; J. G. A. Pocock, *The Ancient Constitution and the Feudal Law* (Cambridge, 1957), pp. 145–6; J. Toland in *The Oceana of James Harrington, Esq.; and his other Works* (Dublin, 1737), p. xvii.

discussed in English scientific circles.[58] It was also in the later seventeenth century that the word 'coincidence', in the sense of the juxtaposition of causally unrelated events, first appeared. In 1692 John Arbuthnot made the new theories available to a wider public in a translation of Huygens's treatise on gaming odds. A chance event, he declared in the preface, was merely one whose causes were not known; but it was possible to calculate the probability of its taking one form rather than another, even when human beings were involved. For what was politics, but 'a kind of analysis of the quantity of probability in casual events'? There were, thought Arbuthnot, very few topics incapable of being reduced to mathematical reckoning.[59]

It was this nascent statistical sense, or awareness of patterns in apparently random behaviour, which was to supersede much previous speculation about the causes of good or bad fortune. Today it is even possible to predict the likely number of fatal accidents or crimes of violence in the coming year. We take steps to hedge ourselves against misfortunes, but if they happen to us we do not feel the need to seek mystical causes for their occurrence. No doubt few of us today are capable of stoical acceptance of the random caprices of misfortune, but it is the awareness that they are indeed random which distinguishes us from our ancestors.

3. New aspirations

The decline of magic was thus accompanied by the growth of the natural and social sciences, which helped men to understand their environment, and of a variety of technical aids – from insurance to fire-fighting – by which they were able to increase their control of it. Yet the more closely Malinowski's picture of magic giving way before technology is examined, the less convincing does it appear. For the correspondence between magic and social needs had never been more than approximate. It is true that magic was seldom in-

58. See, e.g., *The Correspondence of Isaac Newton*, ed. H. W. Turnbull *et al.* (Cambridge, 1959–), iii, pp. 293–305. This subject is fully treated by I. Todhunter, *A History of the Mathematical Theory of Probability* (Cambridge, 1865), and F. N. David, *Games, Gods and Gambling* (1962). See also E. Coumet, 'La théorie du hasard est-elle née par hasard?', *Annales (économies, sociétés, civilisations)*, 25e année (1970), and above, pp. 143–4.

59. (J. Arbuthnot). *Of the Laws of Chance, or, a Method of Calculation of the Hazards of Game* (1692), Preface; *O.E.D.*, *s.v.* 'coincidence'.

voked when a technical solution was available. But the corollary is not true: the absence of a technical remedy was not of itself sufficient to generate a magical one. For magic was conservative in subject-matter, as well as in its techniques. The village wizards of our period had little in their repertoire to distinguish them from their medieval or, possibly, even their Anglo-Saxon predecessors. Their remedies were traditional and so were the problems for which they catered. The astrologers similarly offered answers to questions which had originally been drawn up by Arabs, living in a different social environment. English magic, in other words, did not automatically expand to fill all new technological gaps, in the way Malinowski suggested. Society's magical resources were the result of its cultural inheritance, as much as of its current problems. Magic has always had to come from somewhere.[60] In Tudor and Stuart England it came from the medieval and classical past, and it was slow to adapt itself to new situations.

This brings us to the essential problem. Why was it that magic did not keep pace with changing social circumstances? Why did its sphere become more limited, even as the English economy was expanding into new domains? For the paradox is that in England magic lost its appeal before the appropriate technical solutions had been devised to take its place. It was the abandonment of magic which made possible the upsurge of technology, not the other way round. Indeed, as Max Weber stressed, magic was potentially 'one of the most serious obstructions to the rationalisation of economic life'. The technological primacy of Western civilization, it can be argued, owes a sizeable debt to the fact that in Europe recourse to magic was to prove less ineradicable than in other parts of the world.[61] For this, intellectual and religious factors have been held primarily responsible. The rationalist tradition of classical antiquity blended with the Christian doctrine of a single all-directing Providence to produce what Weber called 'the disenchantment of the world' – the conception of an orderly and rational universe, in which effect follows cause in predictable manner. A religious belief in order was a necessary prior assumption upon which the subsequent work of the natural scientists was to be founded. It was a favourable

60. See the shrewd comments of A. L. Kroeber, *Anthropology* (new edn, 1948), pp. 308–10.

61. M. Weber, *General Economic History*, trans. F. H. Knight (New York, 1961), p. 265; K. F. Helleiner, 'Moral Conditions of Economic Growth', *Journ. Econ. Hist.* xi (1951), pp. 108–9.

mental environment which made possible the triumph of technology.

There is inevitably a chicken-and-the-egg character to any debate as to whether economic growth produces its appropriate mental character or is produced by it. Most sociologically-minded historians are naturally biased in favour of the view that changes in beliefs are preceded by changes in social and economic structure. But so far as magic and technology are concerned, it seems indisputable that in England the former was on the wane before the latter was ready to take its place. The fourteenth-century Lollards who renounced the Church's supernatural protection against disease and infertility had no effective alternative to put in its place. Their doctrines gave them spiritual security, but no new means of material aid. Neither did the Reformation coincide with any technological revolution: the men of the sixteenth century were more or less as vulnerable in face of epidemics, bad harvests, illness, fire, and all the other environmental hazards as their medieval predecessors. Yet many were able to discard the apparatus of the Church without devising a new magic in its place.

In the later seventeenth century the more general rejection of magic was still unaccompanied by the discovery of new remedies to fill the gap. It is often said that witch-beliefs are a consequence of inadequate medical technique. But in England such beliefs declined before medical therapy had made much of an advance. It is true that the seventeenth century witnessed notable contributions to the study of physiology, anatomy and botany. No history of medicine can omit mention of the work of Harvey on the circulation of the blood, of Glisson on rickets, Willis on the nervous system, and Sydenham on epidemics. The invention of the microscope enabled Robert Hooke to pioneer the study of the cell and paved the way for the eventual discovery of bacteria and the formulation of the germ theory of disease. Robert Boyle's chemical inquiries destroyed the whole basis of the old humoral physiology.

But so far as actual therapy was concerned, progress was negligible. Harvey's great discovery had no immediate practical consequences. 'It seemed to illustrate the theory of medicine,' declared a contemporary, 'yet it made no improvement in the practice thereof.'[62] The sad truth, wrote another, was that although physicians had laboured mightily in chemistry and anatomy, they had added almost

62. A. Broun (1691), quoted in Sir G. Clark, *A History of the Royal College of Physicians* (Oxford, 1964–6), i, p. 301.

nothing to the diagnosis of disease (and, we might add, even less to its cure).[63] 'It was necessary to obtain clear concepts of the action of the body in health,' explains a modern historian of medicine, 'before venturing into discussion of its action in disease.'[64] Indeed it has recently been argued that, with the exception of smallpox inoculation, introduced in the eighteenth century, medical innovations did little to increase the expectation of life until at least the nineteenth century, and made no substantial contribution, sanitary reform apart, until the second quarter of the twentieth.[65] This may be unduly pessimistic.[66] But it seems clear that the expectation of life at birth was *lower* in the late seventeenth century than it had been in the reign of Elizabeth I; it did not regain its mid-Tudor level until the late eighteenth century.[67]

The difference between the eighteenth and sixteenth centuries lies not in achievement but in aspiration. For the intervening period had seen the beginning of positive efforts to improve the level of medical therapy. The Paracelsians introduced new mineral remedies. Bacon wanted a systematic drive to raise the expectation of life and improve therapeutic medicine. Sydenham pioneered epidemiology, looking forward to the time 'when the world, valuing learning for that only therein which is necessary for the good of human life, shall think as well of him that taught to cure disease as those that taught to discourse learnedly about them'.[68] Growing overseas trade with the East made possible a new pharmacology; the volume of drugs imported by the end of the seventeenth century was at least twenty-five

63. J. W(agstaffe), *The Question of Witchcraft Debated* (1669), pp. 66–7.

64. C. Singer and E. A. Underwood, *A Short History of Medicine* (2nd edn. Oxford, 1962), p. 168. But cf. A. B. Davis, 'Some Implications of the Circulation Theory for Disease Theory and Treatment in the Seventeenth Century', *Journ. History of Medicine*, xxvi (1971).

65. T. McKeown and R. G. Brown, 'Medical Evidence related to English Population Changes in the Eighteenth Century', *Population Studies*, ix (1955); T. McKeown and R. G. Record, 'Reasons for the Decline of Mortality in England and Wales during the Nineteenth Century', ibid., xvi (1962).

66. See E. Sigsworth, 'A Provincial Hospital in the Eighteenth and Early Nineteenth Centuries', *Royal Coll. of General Practitioners, Yorks. Faculty Journ.*, June 1966, and M. Drake in *Population Growth and the Brain Drain*, ed. F. Bechhofer (Edinburgh, 1969), p. 228.

67. E. A. Wrigley in *Daedalus* (Spring 1968), pp. 562, 574; T. H. Hollingsworth, *The Demography of the British Peerage* (Supplement to *Population Studies*, xviii [1964]), pp. 56, 70.

68. A. G. Debus, *The English Paracelsians* (1965); Bacon, *Works*, iv, pp. 383, 388; K. Dewhurst, *Dr Thomas Sydenham (1624–89)* (1966), p. 124.

times what it had been at the beginning. Only a few of these, such as quinine for malaria and guiacum for syphilis, were to gain a permanent place in the medical pharmacopoeia, but their introduction reflected a significant urge to experiment.[69] The eighteenth century saw the founding of nearly fifty new hospitals.[70] Whether these institutions did more to spread disease than to cure it is debatable. But, whatever their merits, they helped to displace the amateur, the empiric and the wise woman. They also reflected a new practical, optimistic attitude.

The same spirit of practical self-help can be seen in preventive medicine. Seventeenth-century towns took increasingly strenuous precautions to protect themselves from the plague, by enforcing hygiene, shutting up victims, and imposing restrictions upon the movement of goods and persons from infected areas. There was nothing passive or fatalistic about their attitude,[71] for, as we have seen, the belief in providence was quite compatible with faith in self-help: a combination quaintly expressed by the witness in an Elizabethan lawsuit who said of a man thrown overboard into West Looe harbour that he would have drowned, 'but that God provided a remedy for him by swimming'.[72] Few of the innumerable writers who regarded plague as a punishment for sin took a completely fatalist position. They all began by urging their readers to repent, but most of them ended by advising them to practise better hygiene, to employ suitable medicine, and, failing all else, to run away.

Of course, contemporaries did not succeed in diagnosing the causes of plague. They never learned to associate the disease with the black rat, and the plague's disappearance in the later seventeenth century owed little to human agency, save in so far as it may have been helped by an improvement in living conditions. But it would be wrong to blame the fatalistic element in contemporary theology for this intellectual failure. The fault lay more with the upper classes and intellectuals, who cared less about plague than they might have done, because they knew it was primarily a disease

69. See R. S. Roberts, 'The Early History of the Import of Drugs into Britain', in *The Evolution of Pharmacy in Britain*, ed. F. N. L. Poynter (1965).

70. W. H. McMeneney, 'The Hospital Movement of the Eighteenth Century', in *The Evolution of Hospitals in Britain*, ed. F. N. L. Poynter (1964).

71. As is shown by C. F. Mullett, *The Bubonic Plague and England* (Lexington, 1956).

72. Quoted by A. Everitt in *The Agrarian History of England and Wales* (Cambridge, 1967–), iv, ed. J. Thirsk, p. 631. cf. above, p. 131.

of the poor. This was undoubtedly the reason for the relative indifference displayed by the Royal College of Physicians. The preacher, William Gouge, also revealed the social limits to his sympathies in 1631, when he declared that it was lawful for those who wished to flee from the plague-stricken area, with three exceptions: the magistrates, because they had special responsibilities; the aged, because they were less vulnerable to infection; and 'the poorer and meaner sort', because they 'are not of such use, but may better be spared'.[73]

In medicine, as elsewhere, therefore, supernatural theories went out before effective techniques came in. In the eighteenth century, for example, physicians finally ceased to regard epilepsy as supernatural, although they had not yet learned to understand it in any other way. But they now grasped that the problem was a technical one, open to human investigation, whereas a hundred years earlier, as a contemporary remarked, people were 'apt to make everything a supernatural work which they do not understand'.[74] The change was less a matter of positive technical progress than of an expectation of greater progress in the future. Men became more prepared to combine impotence in the face of current misfortune with the faith that a technical solution would one day be found, much in the spirit in which we regard cancer today. As Sir Robert Filmer expressed it in 1653, 'There be daily many things found out and daily more may be which our fore-fathers never knew to be possible.'[75] Meanwhile contemporaries showed more of that ability to tolerate ignorance which has been defined as an essential characteristic of the scientific attitude.[76]

In other spheres also magic declined without any immediate prospect of a technical substitute. Dwindling reliance on love-potions did not coincide with the invention of some more certain means of gaining the affections of another person, however much faith was placed in the power of cosmetics, deodorants or seductive

73. W. Gouge, *Gods Three Arrows* (1631), p. 25. The same sentiments recur in R. Kephale, *Medela Pestilentiae* (1665), p. 27.

74. O. Temkin, *The Falling Sickness. A History of Epilepsy* (Baltimore, 1945); E. Jorden, *A Briefe Discourse of a Disease called the Suffocation of the Mother* (1603), sig. A3.

75. Filmer, *An Advertisement to the Jury-Men of England* (1653), p. 8. cf. above, p. 691.

76. cf. R. Horton, 'African Traditional Thought and Western Science', *Africa*, xxxvii (1967), pp. 173-4.

manners and clothes. Nor has the place of the village wizard ever
been fully taken by the police force and the advertisement columns
of the newspapers: today's agencies for detecting thieves and recovering missing property are only moderately successful.

Nor can the decline of divination be explained in terms of the
growth of superior methods of prediction. The scientists of the
seventeenth century devoted much effort to improving methods of
weather-forecasting[77] and this type of prognostication is no doubt
now more advanced than it was. So is the prognosis of the outcome
of a disease. But the prediction of future events is more difficult
today than it ever was in the relatively static, custom-bound society
of the past. There is a wider range of choices open to the individual
and a more complex range of circumstances to take into account.
The wonder is not that older systems of divination should have lasted
so long, but that we should now feel it possible to do without them.
The investment programmes of modern industrial firms, for example, require decisions to be taken about future policies at times
when it is often impossible to form a rational view of their outcome.
It is not surprising that industrialists sometimes use barely relevant
statistical projections in order to justify what is essentially a leap in
the dark,[78] or that individuals have recourse to private oracles of
the coin-tossing kind. But no businessman would admit to his share-
holders that this was how he used statistics, and private oracles are
taken to be a symptom of neurosis.[79] The decline of divination has
thus left a gap which society is as yet unable to fill. Perhaps one day
the social sciences will take over the role once discharged by astrology, as they become increasingly orientated towards forecasting
the future.[80] If so, this will be a belated attempt to emulate the prophetic beliefs of the past.

The change which occurred in the seventeenth century was thus
not so much technological as mental. In many different spheres of
life the period saw the emergence of a new faith in the potentialities

77. T. Birch, *The History of the Royal Society* (1756–7), i, pp. 300, 305,
308, 309, 311, 334, 372.
78. E. Devons, 'Statistics as a Basis for Policy', *Lloyds Bank Rev.*, new
ser., xxxiii (1954).
79. O. Fenichel, *The Psychoanalytical Theory of Neurosis* (1946), pp. 300
ff.; R. R. Willoughby in *A Handbook of Social Psychology*, ed. C. Murchison (Worcester, Mass., 1935), p. 481.
80. Their potentialities are surveyed by B. de Jouvenel, *The Art of Conjecture*, trans. N. Lary (1967).

of human initiative. The energetic if unsuccessful Tudor efforts to control poverty and eliminate vagabondage were continued and extended. Agricultural writers campaigned against what they called 'the pattern of ancient ignorance', just as politicians rejected the appeal to precedent. It was a sustained period of innovation, of experiment with ley farming, fen drainage, and new crops: fertilizers in place of fertility rites. 'If one experiment fail,' wrote John Norden in 1607, 'try a second, a third, and many.'[81] In industry there were innovations of many kinds, and the prolonged experiment with ways of using coal in the manufacture of iron reached the eve of successful completion. Equally notable faith in the potentialities of activism and experiment was displayed by the radical groups of the Interregnum, who proposed to remodel the whole of society by legislative action. Their hopes were dashed by the Restoration, but the notion that political remedies could be found for social and economic discontent was less easily checked.

But it was above all the scientists who embodied these new aspirations. Francis Bacon listed as *desiderata* the prolongation of life, the restitution of youth, the curing of incurable diseases, the mitigation of pain, the speeding up of natural processes, the discovery of new sources of food, the control of the weather, and the enhancement of the pleasures of the senses. He wanted divination put on a natural basis so that it would be possible to make rational predictions of the weather, the harvest, and the epidemics of each year. His aspirations were the same as those of the astrologers, the magicians and the alchemists, even if the methods he envisaged were different. He disliked their clandestine habits and dismissed their beliefs as having 'better intelligence and confederacy with the imagination of man than with his reason'. But he conceded that their 'end or pretences' were 'noble'.[82]

Science itself retained some magical overtones, manifested in a preoccupation with the achievement of marvellous effects and a desire to outdo the magicians at their own game. Scientists were often more interested in devising conjuring tricks or secret writing than in catering for contemporary social needs. Yet even at their

81. J. N(orden), *The Surveyors Dialogue* (1607), p. 210. cf. E. Kerridge, *The Agricultural Revolution* (1967), *passim*.
82. Bacon, *Works*, ii, pp. 602–9; iii, pp. 167–8, 289; v, pp. 187–94, 199–200. Bacon's relationship to the magical tradition has been well brought out by P. Rossi, *Francis Bacon. From Magic to Science*, trans. S. Rabinovitch (1968). See also H. Fisch, *Jerusalem and Albion* (1964), pp. 83–6.

most fanciful the scientists and inventors of the seventeenth century reveal a breath-taking faith in the potentialities of human ingenuity. It can be seen in the inventions for which patents were granted during the years before the Civil War. Here are machines for perpetual motion, engines for ploughing without horses or oxen, boats which will sail in all weathers, devices to improve the fertility of the earth, to make houses immune to fire and flood, to control the winds, and to send the insomniac to sleep, 'either with musical sounds or without'.[83] John Wilkins's *Mercury* (1641) contained a variety of formulae whereby 'a man may with privacy and speed communicate his thoughts to a friend at any distance'. This was in the tradition of the Elizabethan Leonard Digges, who, like a wizard, had boasted that his telescope enabled him to declare what was happening seven miles off; or of John Napier, who devised mirrors to catch the sun's rays and burn enemy ships while they were still far away. In *Mathematical Magick* (1648) (so called 'in allusion to vulgar opinion, which doth commonly attribute all such strange operations unto the power of magic'), Wilkins continued these efforts with projects for submarines and 'flying chariots'.[84]

The methods of the scientists were different from those of the magicians. They stood for controlled experiment and innovation. Their flexibility made them ready to consider new problems as they arose. They gradually lost their attitude of reverence for the hermetic wisdom of the past and came to recognize that there was no precedent for their achievements. Above all they relied on unaccompanied human aid. But their ambitions were much like those of the *magi*. 'The end of our foundation,' says Bacon's spokesman in *New Atlantis,* 'is the knowledge of causes and the secret motions of things and the enlarging of the bounds of human empire, to the effecting of all things possible.'[85] In the long run natural science was to change the relationship of man to his environment. By the mid

83. B. Woodcraft, *Titles of Patents of Invention Chronologically arranged* (1854), pp. 2, 9, 12, 13, 15. Similar aspirations were reflected in the projects of Hugh Platte *(The Jewell House of Art and Nature* [1594]), and Cornelis Drebbel (G. Tierie, *Cornelis Drebble [1572–1633]* [Amsterdam, 1932]).

84. J. Wilkins, *Mercury: or the Secret and Swift Messenger* (1641; 2nd edn, 1694); R. T. Gunther, *Early Science in Oxford,* ii (1923), p. 290; E. W. Hobson, *John Napier and the Invention of Logarithms* (Cambridge, 1914), pp. 10–11.

85. Bacon, *Works*, iii, p. 156. This theme is admirably evoked by Sir P. Medawar, 'On the Effecting of All Things Possible', *Listener*, lxxxii (1969).

twentieth century, scientific mastery over nature was such that it seemed to some that men had become gods.[86]

4. Survival

We are, therefore, forced to the conclusion that men emancipated themselves from these magical beliefs without necessarily having devised any effective technology with which to replace them. In the seventeenth century they were able to take this step because magic was ceasing to be intellectually acceptable, and because their religion taught them to try self-help before invoking supernatural aid. But the ultimate origins of this faith in unaided human capacity remain mysterious. We do not know how the Lollards were able to find the self-reliance necessary to make the break with the Church magic of the past. The most plausible explanation seems to be that their spirit of sturdy self-help reflected that of their occupations. Few of these early heretics were simple agriculturalists dependent on the uncontrollable forces of nature. In the fifteenth century most of them were artisans – carpenters, blacksmiths, cobblers, and, above all, textile-workers.[87] They spoke of religion in practical terms, rejecting the miracle of the Mass, because 'God made man and not man God, as the carpenter doth make the house, and not the house the carpenter'; or asserting that 'Ball the carpenter or Pike the mason could make as good images as those which were worshipped'.[88] Their trades made them aware that success or failure depended upon their unaided efforts, and they despised the substitute consolations of magic.

Certainly it is usual to assume that the faith in self-help could not have originated in a purely agrarian environment. 'There is less magic in twentieth- than in sixteenth-century England,' writes Dr Christopher Hill, 'because there is more industry. Magic is agra-

86. E. R. Leach, *A Runaway World?* (1968), p. 1.

87. The link between Lollardy and the clothing industry is demonstrated by J. F. Davis, 'Lollard Survival and the Textile Industry in the South East of England', in *Studies in Church History*, iii, ed. G. J. Cuming (Leiden, 1966). Thomson, *Later Lollards*, unfortunately shows no interest in the sociology of the subject, but mentions individual Lollards of many different occupations, most of them artisans and textile-workers. A similar picture is revealed by J. Fines, 'Heresy Trials in the Diocese of Coventry and Lichfield, 1511–12', *Journ. Eccl. Hist.*, xiv (1963). cf. A. G. Dickens, *The English Reformation* (revd edn, 1967), pp. 51–2.

88. Thomson, *Later Lollards*, pp. 112, 83.

rian."⁸⁹ 'Agriculturists,' declared H. T. Buckle in the mid nineteenth century, 'are naturally, and by the very circumstances of their daily life, more superstitious than manufacturers, because the events with which they deal are more mysterious, that is to say, more difficult to generalize and predict.'⁹⁰ This assumption was held by David Hume, who observed that 'in proportion as any man's course of life is governed by accident, we always find that he increases in superstition'.⁹¹ But it goes back to the seventeenth century itself, for even then the countryman, being more dependent on the forces of nature, was thought to be more aware of the supernatural. 'In this respect,' commented a Jacobean clergyman, 'the frequency of sermons seems most necessary in cities and great towns, that their inhabitants, who ... see for the most part but the works of men, may daily hear God speaking unto them: whereas such as are conversant in the fields and woods continually contemplate the works of God.'⁹² As Thomas Fuller remarked, "Tis not the husbandman, but the good weather, that makes the corn grow.'⁹³

But in fact it is not obvious that magic was essentially agrarian. On the contrary, the evidence of other societies suggests that crafts and simple manufacturing techniques can acquire a good deal of mystery for the uninitiated. Tools can be worshipped as quasi-fetishes; ceremonial rules can be devised to accompany technical procedures; and any specialized occupation can assume a magical charisma: smiths and metal-workers, in particular, have magical associations among many primitive peoples.⁹⁴ In medieval England there were charms and magical observances surrounding the spin-

89. C. Hill, *Society and Puritanism in Pre-revolutionary England* (1964), p. 486.

90. H. T. Buckle, *History of Civilization in England* (1904 edn), iii, pp. 36–7. cf. i, pp. 307–8.

91. *The Natural History of Religion*, sect. iii.

92. T. Jackson, *A Treatise containing the Originall of Unbeliefe* (1625), p. 196.

93. Quoted in *Agriculture and Economic Growth in England, 1650–1815*, ed. E. L. Jones (1967), p. 5.

94. M. Weber, *The Sociology of Religion*, trans. E. Fischoff (1965), pp. 97–8; id., *The Religion of India*, trans. H. H. Gerth and D. Martindale (Glencoe, Ill., 1958), p. 99; H. Webster, *Magic* (Stanford, 1948), pp. 165–7; G. B. Depping and M. Michel, *Wayland Smith, A Dissertation on a Tradition of the Middle Ages*, ed. S. W. Singer (1847); V. G. Childe, *Magic, Craftsmanship and Science* (Liverpool, 1950). For curative powers attributed to an Elizabethan smith, see C. M. L. Bouch, *People and Prelates of the Lake Counties* (Kendal, 1948), pp. 215–16.

ning and weaving of cloth.[95] In the early industrial period the mining industry generated a host of semi-magical practices, ranging from the belief in the existence of subterranean spirits or 'knockers', to a taboo on such actions as whistling underground or working on Good Friday. It also propagated a magical method of finding ore: the divining rod, cut and used in a highly ritual manner, was introduced from Germany in the mid sixteenth century and became popular a hundred years or more later.[96] The building industry similarly gave rise to a mystic fraternity. Because of their mobility, masons devised a secret password in order to identify themselves among strangers. In the seventeenth century English masonic lodges began to attract amateurs in seach of occult wisdom, and non-operative Freemasonry was born.[97] Facts of this kind should make us chary about drawing too facile an equation between agriculture and magic, industry and rationalism. Agriculture, after all, was the first sector of the British economy to become thoroughly capitalized and developed in a 'rational' manner. Magic was rejected by men who had faith in the potentiality of technical innovation but it must be remembered that in the sixteenth and seventeenth centuries much of this innovation was agricultural.

It would also be wrong to presuppose undue 'rationality' on the part of seventeenth-century urban dwellers. It was in London that the sects, with their prophecies and healing miracles, were most successful; and it was there that the busiest astrologers had their prac-

95. Frazer, *Aftermath*, p. 18; G. G. Coulton, *Life in the Middle Ages*, i (Cambridge, 1930), p. 34. Cases of spinning prevented by witchcraft are in A. D. J. Macfarlane, *Witchcraft Prosecutions in Essex, 1560–1680* (Oxford, D.Phil. thesis, 1967), p. 201, and Brand, *Popular Antiquities*, iii, p. 22. Lilly was asked about a bewitched dye-house; Ashm. 427, f. 121^v.

96. P. Sébillot, *Les Travaux publics et les mines dans les traditions et les superstitions de tous les pays* (Paris, 1894), pp. 389–589; C. S. Burne, 'Staffordshire Folk and Their Lore', *Folk-Lore*, vii (1896), pp. 370–71; *Folk-Lore Journ.*, iii (1885), p. 186; Wright, *British Calendar Customs*, i, p. 83; Sir W. Barrett and T. Besterman, *The Divining-Rod* (1926); J. Webster, *Metallographia* (1671), p. 104 ('of which some of our credulous miners have a great opinion'); R. Fludd, *Mosaicall Philosophy* (1659), p. 260; Lord Hylton, *Notes on the History of the Parish of Kilmersdon* (Taunton, 1910), p. 111; J. W. Gough, *The Mines of Mendip* (2nd edn, 1967), pp. 6–7; id., *Sir Hugh Myddelton* (Oxford, 1964), p. 104; A. K. Hamilton Jenkin, *The Cornish Miner* (3rd edn, 1962), p. 43; W. J. Lewis, 'Some Aspects of Lead Mining in Cardiganshire in the Sixteenth and Seventeenth Centuries', *Ceredigion*, i (1950), p. 180.

97. D. Knoop and G. P. Jones, *The Genesis of Freemasonry* (Manchester, 1947).

tices.[98] London was not exempt from witchcraft accusations, and the city seems to have harboured every kind of popular magician. The most that can be said is that in the long run large urban concentrations of population proved themselves inherently unsuitable for the practice of much of the traditional magic of the past. Thief-magic, for example, could function well in a tightly-knit village society, where suspects were personally known to injured party and magician alike; but in the later seventeenth century London had a population of half a million. A man could walk along the streets without recognizing the people he passed, and might not even know his neighbours. There was little room for the magic of the sieve and shears. As relations grew more impersonal there was also less room for the type of conflict which gave rise to witchcraft accusations. Moreover, new ideas circulated more freely in the cities. There was a higher rate of literacy and a more rapid turnover of population. By the nineteenth century traditional magical beliefs were largely restricted to the more intimate communities of the English countryside.

It is therefore possible to connect the decline of the old magical beliefs with the growth of urban living, the rise of science, and the spread of an ideology of self-help. But the connection is only approximate and a more precise sociological genealogy cannot at present be constructed. Too many of the participants in the story remain hidden from view and the representative status of those who are visible is too uncertain. The only identifiable social group which was consistently in the van of the campaign against certain types of magic is the clergy, but their attitude to supernatural claims in general was highly ambivalent. It does not seem possible to say whether the growing 'rationalism' of natural theology was a spontaneous theological development or a mere response to the pressures of natural science. It would make sense, no doubt, if one could prove that it was the urban middle classes, the shopkeepers and artisans, who took the lead in abandoning the old beliefs, but at present there seems no way of doing so. An equally convincing claim could be made for the Arminian clergy of the early seventeenth century or the aristocratic sceptics of the Restoration period.

What can, however, be clearly seen is that by the mid seventeenth century the new intellectual developments had greatly deepened the

98. Above, chap. 10. One contemporary thought Londoners particularly vulnerable to astrologers; F. Wilde, *Prophecy Maintain'd* (1654), p. 67.

gulf between the educated classes and the lower strata of the rural
population. Of course, evidence of the disdain felt by intellectuals
for popular 'superstition' can be found from classical times. But in
the seventeenth century the gulf was emphasized by the appearance
of well-born collectors of popular folklore, like Sir Thomas Browne
in his *Vulgar Errors* or John Aubrey in his *Remaines of Gentilisme
and Judaisme*; for despite their tolerance towards the old ways
such men were acutely conscious of belonging to a different mental
world. Aubrey himself was convinced that it was during the Civil
War period that old beliefs had lost their vitality.[99] But there is plenty
of evidence to suggest that in rural areas there was still much life left
in these ways of thought. 'Notwithstanding the great advances in
learning and knowledge which have been made within the last two
centuries,' declared a preacher in 1795, 'lamentable experience but
too clearly proves how extremely deep these notions are still en-
graven upon the minds of thousands.'[100] Nineteenth-century students
of popular folklore discovered everywhere that the inhabitants of
rural England had not abandoned their faith in healing wells, divination, cunning folk, witchcraft, omens or ghosts. 'Those who are not
in daily intercourse with the peasantry,' it was reported from Lincolnshire in 1856, 'can hardly be made to believe or comprehend the
hold that charms, witchcraft, wise men and other like relics of
heathendom have upon the people.'[101]

Nor had popular religion necessarily changed either. The religion
of the nineteenth century, said Jacob Burckhardt, was 'rationalism
for the few and magic for the many'.[102] The belief in 'judgements'
was frequently upheld by influential clergymen, while many persons
who incurred misfortune continued to ask what they had done to
'deserve' it. The conviction that religion 'worked' and that prayer
got results sustained innumerable people in adversity. Every kind of
religious enthusiasm – mystical healing, millenarian prophecy, messianic preaching – made its periodic return, and not only at a working-class level. Many of the nineteenth-century middle classes were
interested in spiritualism and automatic writing, astrology, haunted

---

99. Aubrey, *Gentilisme*, pp. 22, 24, 26, 33, 34, 36, 41, 43, 59, 81, 103, 120,
138, 171, 202, 205 n.
100. M. J. Naylor, *The Inantity [sic] and Mischief of Vulgar Superstitions*
(Cambridge, 1795), p. iv.
101. E. Peacock in *Notes and Queries*, 2nd ser., i (1856), p. 415.
102. Quoted by E. R. Dodds, *The Greeks and the Irrational* (Berkeley and
Los Angeles, 1963), p. 192.

houses and all the paraphernalia of the occult. Even the fear of witchcraft, that is of occult damage as a result of another's malignity, was revived in Mary Baker Eddy's concept of 'malicious animal magnetism'.[103] Today astrologers and fortune-tellers continue to be patronized by those for whom psychiatrists and psycho-analysts have not provided a satisfactory substitute. The presence of horoscopes in the newspapers and of lucky mascots in cars is consistent with a recent investigator's conclusion that 'about a quarter of the population ... holds a view of the universe which can most properly be designated as magical'.[104] This is a much smaller figure than any which could ever be produced for the seventeenth century, were such analysis possible, but it is not a trivial one.

Indeed the role of magic in modern society may be more extensive than we yet appreciate. There is a tautological character about Malinowski's argument that magic occupies the vacuum left by science, for what is not recognized by any particular observer as a true 'science' is deemed 'magic' and vice versa. If magical acts are ineffective rituals employed as an alternative to sheer helplessness in the face of events, then how are we to classify the status of 'scientific' remedies, in which we place faith, but which are subsequently exposed aᶜ useless? This was the fate of Galenic medicine, which in the sixteenth century was the main rival to folk-healing. But it will also be that of much of the medicine of today. Sociologists have observed that contemporary doctors and surgeons engage in many ritual practices of a non-operative kind. Modern medicine shares an optimistic bias with the charmers and wise women and it has similar means of explaining away any failure.[105] In many other spheres of modern life we also put our trust in activities designed to 'work' (for example, in diplomatic conferences as a means of avoiding war), when all the evidence, if we wished to consider it, suggests that they do not.[106]

103. Described in B. R. Wilson, *Sects and Society* (1961), pp. 126–7, 130, 349.

104. G. Gorer, *Exploring English Character* (1955), p. 269.

105. T. Parsons, *Essays in Sociological Theory* (revd. edn, Glencoe, Ill., 1963), p. 204, n. 10; J. A. Roth, 'Ritual and Magic in the Control of Contagion', *American Sociological Rev.*, xxii (1957).

106. Suggestive remarks on this theme may be found in R. Benedict, 'Magic', in *Encyclopaedia of the Social Sciences* (1933); J. M. Yinger, *Religion, Society and the Individual* (New York, 1957), pp. 47–8; and J. D. Y. Peel, 'Understanding Alien Belief-Systems', *British Journ. Sociology*, xx (1969).

Anthropologists today are unsympathetic to the view that magic is simply bad science. They stress its symbolic and expressive role rather than its practical one. They would therefore maintain that the wizard's conjurations or the wise woman's charms were not really comparable with pseudo-science. In so far as the two activities had a different pedigree and a different intellectual status this is obviously true. But all the evidence of the sixteenth and seventeenth centuries suggests that the common people never formulated a distinction between magic and medicine. 'We go to the physician for counsel,' argued contemporaries, 'we take his recipe, but we know not what it meaneth; yet we use it, and find benefit. If this be lawful, why may we not as well take benefit by the wise man, whose courses we be ignorant of?'[107] The modern working-class woman who remarks that she doesn't 'believe' in doctors[108] is acknowledging the fact that the patient still brings with him an essentially uninformed allegiance. Usually he knows no more of the underlying rationale for his treatment than did the client of the cunning man. In such circumstances it is hard to say where 'science' stops and 'magic' begins.

What is certain about the various beliefs discussed in this book is that today they have either disappeared or at least greatly decayed in prestige. This is why they are easier to isolate and to analyse. But it does not mean that they are intrinsically less worthy of respect than some of those which we ourselves continue to hold. If magic is to be defined as the employment of ineffective techniques to allay anxiety when effective ones are not available, then we must recognize that no society will ever be free from it.

107. Perkins, *Discourse*, p. 155. cf. above, pp. 226–7.
108. cf. R. Hoggart, *The Uses of Literacy* (Harmondsworth, 1958), p. 17.

INDEX

Places in England and Wales are indexed under their respective counties. Books of the Bible and Biblical texts appear under *Bible*. Saints' days, church feasts, and other festivals are under *calendar*. Individual saints are under *saints* and peers under their titles.

calendar: agrarian, 81–2, 735, 738; church, 438, 738–45

dates, fixed: 1 Jan. (New Year's day; Circumcision), 54, 80, 82, 350; 12 Jan. (Twelfth Day; Epiphany), 71, 743; 25 Jan. (St Paul), 284; 2 Feb. (P.V.M.), 738; 25 Mar. (Annunciation V.M.), 49, 738; 24 April (Eve of St Mark), 286, 716n; 25 April (St Mark), 35, 71; 1 May (May Day; SS Philip & James), 54, 738; 3 May (Invention of Cross), 70; 23 June (Midsummer Eve; Eve of St John Baptist), 54, 82, 286, 529n; 24 June (Midsummer Day; St John Baptist), 54, 776; 25 June (St Loy), 740; 28 June (St Peter's Eve), 82; 15 July (St Swithin), 284, 740, 742; 15 Aug. (Assumption V.M.), 738; 29 Sep. (Michaelmas), 82, 738; 18 Oct. (St Luke), 738; 31 Oct. (Hallowmas Eve), 739; 1 Nov. (All Souls Eve), 720; 11 Nov. (Martinmas), 738; 20 Nov. (Edmund, king and martyr), 739; 30 Nov. (St Andrew), 738; 25 Dec. (Christmas), 54, 82, 284, 303, 351, 740; 26 Dec. (St Stephen), 738; 28 Dec. (Childermas), 740

dates, movable: Advent Sunday, 740–41; Ascension Day, 71, 72; Easter, 82, 189, 190, 433n; octave of, 741; Good Friday, 82; Lent, 738, 741; Palm Sunday, 71; Pentecost (Whitsunday), 433; octave of, 741; Plough Monday, 54, 75, 81, 776; Rock Monday, 82; Rogation week, 71, 74, 75; Septuagesima Sunday, 741; Shrove Tuesday, 75, 82

calendar customs, 54, 75, 81–2, 616, 776

Calfhill, James, 60, 562

Calvin, John: on Catholic sacraments, 60; on God's power, 92, 94, 99; on predestination, 439–40; on Moses, 323; on astrology, 396, 425, 436; Lilly's view of, 445n

Calvinism: and alchemy, 321; and astrology, 435–40

Cambridge Platonists, 240, 706

Cambridge University: magic and magicians at, 269n, 297, 446; astronomy and astrology at, 354, 358, 362, 363, 369, 419, 420; prophecies at, 489; opinion on Greatrakes at, 241; Behmenism at, 448; views on witchcraft at, 693; views on exorcism at, 579; prayer meeting at, 581; mentioned, 39, 92n, 139, 172, 283, 291, 373, 392, 438; colleges: Caius, 269n, 403, 419n; Catharine Hall, 419n; King's, 269n; Queens', 420n; St John's, 564; Trinity, 468, 566

Cambridgeshire, 192, 216, 217; Brinkley, 239; Cambridge, 191, 372, 373, 654; Comberton, 82n; Dry Drayton, 15; Dullingham, 218; Elm, 610; Ely: Archdeacon of, 329; cathedral, 168; diocese (of Ely), 197, 200, 204, 311; gaol delivery rolls, 535n; Gilden Morden, 329, 599; Mepal, 606; Stapleford, 226; Stourbridge Fair, 346; Sutton, 278; Willingham, 82n; Wisbech, 192

Camden, William: and astrology, 385; on the Irish, 456

Camisard prophets, 150, 171

Camp, Andrew, 633

Campion, Edmund, 419

candles, holy, *see* holy candles

Canisius, Peter, 568

Canne, John, 65, 322n

Canons, Anglican Church: of 1604, 135, 186, 579; of 1640, 596n

Captain Pouch, 165, 276

Cardan, Jerome (Cardano, Girolamo), 343, 386, 400, 784

Cardiganshire: Cardigan priory, 49

Carier, Benjamin, 184

Carleton, George, Bp of Chichester, 107, 430, 436, 440

Carmarthenshire, 221

Carpenter, Richard, 452

Carr, Widow, 219

Carthusians, 154

Cartwright, Thomas, 134, 187

Cary: Grace, 163; Mary, 162

Case, John, astrologer, 342, 381, 393, 448n

Casaubon, Isaac, 267, 509, 770; Meric, 172, 322, 417, 690

Casson, John, 254

Castlehaven, George Touchet, 1st Earl, 162

casuistry, 124, 188

Catalans, and prophecies, 507

catechizing, 64, 180, 561

Elizabeth, wife of Edward IV, 541n
Elizabeth, wife of Henry VII, 31
Elizabeth, queen of Bohemia, 163
Elkes, Dr, 275
Ellins, Mary, 661
Ellis, Anne, 317, 675
Ellwood, Thomas, 127
Elmet, Mother, 211
elves, see fairies
embryology, 125
empirics, 14, 16
enclosures: riots against, 165, 479, 608;
  judgements on, 113–14, 602–3; check
  perambulations, 74; cursed, 602, 608;
  effects, 671
England: economy and social structure,
  3–5, 778; as elect nation, 106–7,
  170; illegitimacy in, 184; intellectual
  isolation of, 267, 341, 522–3; becomes
  Britain, 463, 495
English: their vulnerability to prodigies,
  103–4; and to prophecies, 469–70,
  472–3
Enlightenment, 784
Enoch, 157, 323; Book of, 324n
enthusiasm, religious, 156–71, 176–8;
  despised, 172–3, 771
ephemerides, 347, 358, 375
Epicureans, 764
Epicurus, 773
epidemics, 7, 8; as judgements, 129;
  explained astrologically, 388–9;
  blamed on Jonahs, 668; and witchcraft, 668, 697. See also diseases;
  plague; sickness
Erasmianism, 72, 73n
Erbury, Dorcas, 150
Erceldoune, see Rymer
Erra Pater, 350
Errington, Mrs, 635
Ersfield, Lady, 376
eschatology, 166–71
Esdras, prognostication of, 350
Eskimos, 743
Essex, 381, 563; religion in, 67, 73, 80,
  138, 194–5, 196, 609; astrology in,
  357n; prophecy in, 160, 482, 499;
  wizards in, 226, 253n, 294, 299, 318,
  324; witchcraft in, 145, 531–40 passim,
  545, 589, 595n, 626, 642, 652n, 660,
  664; Barking, 720; Beaumont, 593;
  Birden, 362; Bradwell-near-the-Sea,
  202; Braintree, 689n; Chelmsford,

324, 545, 557, 654, 662, 663, 689n;
  Colchester, 37, 141, 190, 406, 442,
  476, 498, 776; Coggeshall, 369; Cold
  Norton, 654; Earl's Colne, 96;
  Goldhanger, 448n; Great Totham, 43;
  Hatfield Peverel, 499, 626; Harlow,
  464; Holland Magna, 191; Horn-
  church, 219; Little Clapton, 668; Little
  Wigborough, 453; Magdalen Laver,
  651; Quendon, 410; Radwynter, 707;
  Rainham, 623; Rayleigh, 157; Saffron
  Walden, 349; St Osyth, 546; Wimbish,
  662
Essex (see also Cromwell, Thomas):
  Frances, Countess of, 222, 278, 363,
  380; Robert Devereux, 2nd Earl, 276,
  343, 370; Robert Devereux, 3rd Earl,
  168, 688
Estall, —, 561
Ettrick, William, 329
Eure, Mary, 230
Europe: astrology in, 341, 357; charms
  in, 214–15; prophecies in, 506–7;
  witches in, 519, 522–3, 677; witch-
  beliefs in, 521–5 passim, 529, 534, 542,
  668; witch-prosecution in, 522, 524,
  536, 543, 544, 594, 615, 687; ideas of
  possession in, 572, 587; study of
  magic in, 266–7; its emancipation
  from magic, 786–7
Evan, Enoch ap, 176
Evangelicals, 129
Evans: Mr, Essex minister, 191; Arise,
  165n, 433, 490; Cornelius, 506; John,
  403, 450; Mathias, 297, 413n
Evans-Pritchard, Prof. E. E., 402, 551n,
  675, 772
Evelyn, John, 355
Everard: Comfort, 448; John, 268, 322;
  Robert (?), 448; William, 176, 448 (?)
evil spirits, 241; numbers and powers,
  56, 561–2, 727–8; lords of this world,
  320n; protection against, 32, 34, 47,
  48, 56, 60–61, 71–2, 81, 328–9; explain
  illness and misfortune, 130–31, 219,
  586, 647; conjuration of, 272, 319,
  320n (see also conjuration); as ghosts,
  703, 704, 708; as fairies, 728; compact
  with, see witchcraft; haunting by, 565;
  existence affirmed, 566–7; denied,
  682–3, 693; symbolic view of, 683, 770.
  See also Devil; familiars; possession
Evington, Robert, 576n

Wilson: Agnes, 568; Arthur, 250, 689n; Christopher, 660; John, 422; J. Dover, 704; Thomas, theologian, 524; Thomas, astrologer's client, 370

Wiltshire, 31, 196, 246, 281, 362, 457, 476, 713; Calne, 636; Chippenham, 197; Clyffe Pypard, 297; Devizes, 633; Fordedown, 31; Lacock, 203, 458; Marlborough, 20, 98; Melksham, 203; St Oswaldsdown, 31; Salisbury, 23, 113, 118, 457, 598; Cathedral, 47, 330; Wardour castle, 645; Warminster, 476; Wilton, 281; Winterbourne Bassett, 81

Winch, Sir Humphrey, 546

Winchester, William Paulet, 1st Marquis of, 343

Windsor, Thomas, 6th Lord, 641

wine, 22; communion, 180

Wing, Vincent, 399

Wingate, Edmund, *Arithmetic*, 359

Winstanley, Elizabeth, 277

Winstanley, Gerrard: on clergy, 80; on judgements, 123; on heaven, 203; and astrology, 445

Winter, Dr Samuel 136

Winthrop: John, 124, 409n; John, junr, 322n

Wise, Sir Thomas, 704

wise men, women, *see* wizards

Wiseman: Jane, 33; Richard, 10, 242

witch-beliefs: before 1500, 520–21, 540; ingredients of, 521–34, 542–3; and religion, 534, 559–98 *passim*, 681–3, 762; fraudulently exploited, 546–7, 642–3, 645–6, 688–9; offer hope of redress, 648–52; explanatory role, 638–45, 691–2, 762, 763, 784; social effects, 634, 643–4, 673–7, 731; and astrology, 755; decline, 538–9, 681–98, 787; after 1736, 539, 696–7, 777, 798, 799. *See also* devil-worship; *maleficium*; witchcraft; witchcraft, maleficent; witches; witch-trials

witch-bottles, 648

witchcraft: loose contemporary use of the term, 517–18, 523–4; seen in Catholicism by Lollards and Protestants, 33, 58–65, 69–71, 78–9, 84–8; and in Anglicanism by Puritans and sectaries, 79–80; sectaries accused of, 158, 580–1; divided into helpful (white) and harmful (black), 316, 534; this distinction rejected by clergy, 305,

316, 517–18, 519, 533–4; as devil-worship, 521–34, *and see* devil-worship; as infliction of *maleficium*, *see* witchcraft, maleficent. *See also* witch-beliefs; witches; witch-trials

witchcraft, maleficent: defined, 518–19, 533, 551–4; supposed sources and techniques, 220, 519–20, 521, 533, 551–4, 611 (*see also* Devil; devil-worship); damage attributed to, 540–42 (*see also maleficium*); legal status, 525–7, 531–3, 539–42, 548–9, 554–8; new laws proposed for, 306, 519n, 523, 524; difficulty of proving, 533, 538–9, 686–7, 694, 697; attempts to prove scientifically, 690; scepticism concerning, 524, 538–9, 546–7, 550, 584, 616–17, 625, 681–98, 761–6
accusations: frequency, 534–5; by possessed persons, 570, 583–4, 585, 646; damages for wrongful, 539; social context of, 659–78, 694–8; *diagnosis:* by astrologers, 377, 756–7; by doctors, 592–3, 640–42, 654, 685, 686; by fortune-tellers, 359; by wizards, 219–20, 247, 315, 654–6; *protection against:* magical, 219–20, 296–7, 315, 588, 593, 634, 649, 653–4, 656, 660 (*see also* counter-witchcraft); religious, 221, 315–16, 588–91, 592, 594 (*see also* exorcism); and ghost beliefs, 709–10; sexual aspects, 678–9; as excuse for failure, 247, 643–5; as explanation of misfortune, 519, 638–52, 665, 685–6; prosecution of, *see* witch-trials. *See also* witches; witch-beliefs

witchcraft, ritual, *see* devil-worship

'witch-cult', non-existence of, 616, 627

witches, maleficent: supposed activities and techniques, 518–19, 540, 551–4, 613–14, 625–6, 656, 665, 668; numbers, 541–2; sex, 519, 620–22, 671, 678–9; ages, 671; dress, 581n; physical attributes, 530, 552–3, 677–8 (*see also* witch's mark); social and economic situation, 200, 544, 620–21, 632–3, 662, 669–70, 671, 674–5, 678; temptations, 564–5, 620–26, 627–8, 636–7, 659–69, 674–5; intentions, 276, 553–4, 611, 614, 619, 621–2, 634, 636, 674–6; prior relationship with victims, 652–3, 658–70, 673, 696–8; confessions,

852 INDEX

witches – *cont.*
533, 615–22, 653, 658, 687, 690, 691,
727, 756, 758; religion, 568, 592,
611, 614, 622–6; hardships during
prosecution, 633; charitable treatment of, 674–6; informal violence
against, 539–40, 546, 548, 550, 632–4,
636, 649, 676, 696; ostracism of, 633,
676–7; punishment of, justified, 624–5.
See also witchcraft, maleficent; witch-
trials
witch-finders, witch-hunters: activities,
544–5, 547; fiscal motives, 543–5;
popular appeal, 545, 593–4, 619–20,
656, 664–5. *See also* Hopkins, Matthew
witch-posts, 648n
witch's mark, 530, 531, 657, 687, 691
witch-trials, 530, 531; evidence for,
528–9, 615, 618–19; geographical
distribution, 536–7; in Middle Ages,
527–8, 540–1, 548–9, 555–7; numbers,
292–4, 534–8; chronology, 537–8,
540–41, 548–9, 595–6, 636, 637, 670,
696–7; chronology explained, 540–3,
547–51, 594–98 *passim*, 670–4,
694–8; therapeutic purpose, 649–51;
how initiated, 542–7, 595–8; nature of
charges in, 526–33, 611–12, 613–14,
641–3; role of judges, 531–3, 545,
546–8, 681, 685, 697; role of jury, 533,
538 & n, 547n, 681, 685, 687–8, 697;
procedure, 546; evidence and proof,
261, 262, 528, 530–1, 533, 552, 610–11,
616, 618–19, 624, 652–3, 656–9,
686–8, 771; witnesses, 545; torture in,
615, 617, 618, 687; interrogations, 533,
615, 616, 617–19, 628; confessions,
see witches; convictions and acquittals,
531–2, 535–8, 539, 681, 687–9;
executions, 23, 532n, 535–7, 540,
544–5, 592, 646, 697n; deaths in gaol,
536, 538n, 611; cost, 544; pamphlet
accounts, 528, 538n, 546, 596, 618,
688, 697. *See also* Europe; witchcraft,
maleficent; witches
Wither, George, 462, 466
wizards (cunning/wise men/women,
sorcerers, good/white witches,
conjurers, sorcerers, etc.), 14, 16, 138,
143, 209–10, 252–64, 517, 520, 613,
684, 764, 791;,numbers, 291–6, 326;
occupations, 295–6; scale of business,
called 'witches', 518; fees, 210,

238, 244–5, 278–9, 295–8, 710;
supposed sources of their power, 215,
219–20, 237, 242, 316–18, 323–4, 762;
how techniques learned, 221, 271–2,
786; equipment, 217–20, 252–6, 272–3,
275–6, 280–81, 285, 323, 351; use of
books, 271–2, 284–5, 323, 350–51; use
of non-magical remedies, 215, 226–7,
246–7; use of charms and prayers,
209–22, 225–7 (*see also* charms);
religious attitudes, 316–17, 319–20,
321, 323–4, 592; legal status, 292,
298–9, 306, 525–7; frauds?, 289–90,
298
services: *see* divination; dreams,
interpretation of; fortune-telling;
healing, magical; love-magic; missing
persons; theft, magical detection of;
treasure; other services, 275–7; as
advisers, 314; take place of saints,
316, 764; rivals of clergy, 313–17,
762–3; diagnose and treat witchcraft,
218–21, 247, 296–7, 315–16, 648–9,
650, 653–6, 600; deal with ghosts,
710; and fairies, 725, 727, 732; and
the planet-struck, 757–8; popularity,
291, 292, 298, 299, 311–12; un-
popularity, 291; prosecution of, 237,
292–5, 302–13, 548–9; accused of black
witchcraft, 311, 520, 677, 756; attitude
of Church to, 301–32 *passim*; their
clients prosecuted, 293, 308–9, 315–16;
excuses, 767; reasons for their prestige,
244–51, 289–91, 767–8; survival of,
294–5, 798; declining prestige, 765
Wolsey, Thomas, Cardinal-Abp of York,
78, 115, 465; and astrology, 342; and
magic, 277, 643; and prophecies, 472,
502
women: as astrologers, 356, 380, 448;
as clients of astrologers, 369, 373, 376,
379n; sectaries, 159; inferior position
of, 163; and prophecy, 163, 164; as
witches, 519, 620–21, 678–80; the
more lustful sex, 679–80
Wood: Anthony, 381n, 431, 586;
Elizabeth, 653; Mr, preacher, 315
Woodcock, B. L., 294n
Woodhouse, John, 356
Woods, Mary, 222, 287
Woodward, William, 161
Woolston, Thomas, 126
Worcestershire, 276, 291, 573; Bewdley,

FOR THE BEST IN PAPERBACKS, LOOK FOR THE 🐧

In every corner of the world, on every subject under the sun, Penguin represents quality and variety – the very best in publishing today.

For complete information about books available from Penguin – including Pelicans, Puffins, Peregrines and Penguin Classics – and how to order them, write to us at the appropriate address below. Please note that for copyright reasons the selection of books varies from country to country.

In the United Kingdom: Please write to *Dept E.P., Penguin Books Ltd, Harmondsworth, Middlesex, UB7 0DA*

If you have any difficulty in obtaining a title, please send your order with the correct money, plus ten per cent for postage and packaging, to *PO Box No 11, West Drayton, Middlesex*

In the United States: Please write to *Dept BA, Penguin, 299 Murray Hill Parkway, East Rutherford, New Jersey 07073*

In Canada: Please write to *Penguin Books Canada Ltd, 2801 John Street, Markham, Ontario L3R 1B4*

In Australia: Please write to the *Marketing Department, Penguin Books Australia Ltd, P.O. Box 257, Ringwood, Victoria 3134*

In New Zealand: Please write to the *Marketing Department, Penguin Books (NZ) Ltd, Private Bag, Takapuna, Auckland 9*

In India: Please write to *Penguin Overseas Ltd, 706 Eros Apartments, 56 Nehru Place, New Delhi, 110019*

In Holland: Please write to *Penguin Books Nederland B.V., Postbus 195, NL-1380AD Weesp, Netherlands*

In Germany: Please write to *Penguin Books Ltd, Friedrichstrasse 10–12, D–6000 Frankfurt Main 1, Federal Republic of Germany*

In Spain: Please write to *Longman Penguin España, Calle San Nicolas 15, E–28013 Madrid, Spain*

In France: Please write to *Penguin Books Ltd, 39 Rue de Montmorency, F-75003, Paris, France*

In Japan: Please write to *Longman Penguin Japan Co Ltd, Yamaguchi Building, 2–12–9 Kanda Jimbocho, Chiyoda-Ku, Tokyo 101, Japan*

The Second World War (6 volumes)   Winston S. Churchill

The definitive history of the cataclysm which swept the world for the second time in thirty years.

1917: The Russian Revolutions and the Origins of Present-Day Communism
Leonard Schapiro

A superb narrative history of one of the greatest episodes in modern history by one of our greatest historians.

Imperial Spain 1496–1716   J. H. Elliot

A brilliant modern study of the sudden rise of a barren and isolated country to be the greatest power on earth, and of its equally sudden decline. 'Outstandingly good' – *Daily Telegraph*

Joan of Arc: The Image of Female Heroism   Marina Warner

'A profound book, about human history in general and the place of women in it' – Christopher Hill

Man and the Natural World: Changing Attitudes in England 1500–1800
Keith Thomas

'A delight to read and a pleasure to own' – Auberon Waugh in the *Sunday Telegraph*

The Making of the English Working Class   E. P. Thompson

Probably the most imaginative – and the most famous – post-war work of English social history.

FOR THE BEST IN PAPERBACKS, LOOK FOR THE

A CHOICE OF PENGUINS AND PELICANS

The French Revolution Christopher Hibbert

'One of the best accounts of the Revolution that I know . . . Mr Hibbert is outstanding' – J. H. Plumb in the *Sunday Telegraph*

The Germans Gordon A. Craig

An intimate study of a complex and fascinating nation by 'one of the ablest and most distinguished American historians of modern Germany' – Hugh Trevor-Roper

Ireland: A Positive Proposal Kevin Boyle and Tom Hadden

A timely and realistic book on Northern Ireland which explains the historical context – and offers a practical and coherent set of proposals which could actually work.

A History of Venice John Julius Norwich

'Lord Norwich has loved and understood Venice as well as any other Englishman has ever done' – Peter Levi in the *Sunday Times*

Montaillou: Cathars and Catholics in a French Village 1294–1324
Emmanuel Le Roy Ladurie

'A classic adventure in eavesdropping across time' – Michael Ratcliffe in *The Times*

Star Wars E. P. Thompson and others

Is Star Wars a serious defence strategy or just a science fiction fantasy? This major book sets out all the arguments and makes an unanswerable case *against* Star Wars.

FOR THE BEST IN PAPERBACKS, LOOK FOR THE

A SELECTION OF PEREGRINES

The Uses of Enchantment Bruno Bettelheim

Dr Bettelheim has written this book to help adults become aware of the irreplaceable importance of fairy tales. Taking the best-known stories in turn, he demonstrates how they work, consciously or unconsciously, to support and free the child.

The Rise of the Novel Ian Watt

Studies in Defoe, Richardson and Fielding. 'This book is altogether satisfying within the wide framework of its scheme . . . Every page of Dr Watt's admirably written book repays study, as enlivening and enriching the works the purport of which we are too often inclined to take for granted' – *The Times*

Orientalism Edward W. Said

In *Orientalism*, his acclaimed and now famous challenge to established Western attitudes towards the East, Edward Said has given us one of the most brilliant cultural studies of the decade. 'A stimulating, elegant yet pugnacious essay which is going to set the cat among the pigeons' – *Observer*

The Selected Melanie Klein

This major collection of Melanie Klein's writings, brilliantly edited by Juliet Mitchell, shows how much Melanie Klein has to offer in understanding and treating psychotics, in revising Freud's ideas about female sexuality, and in showing how phantasy operates in everyday life.

The Raw and the Cooked Claude Levi-Strauss

Deliberately, brilliantly and inimitably challenging, *The Raw and the Cooked* is a seminal work of structural anthropology that cuts wide and deep into the mind of mankind. Examining the myths of the South American Indians it demonstrates, with dazzling insight, how these can be reduced to a comprehensible psychological pattern.